Federal Telecommunications Law

Federal Telecommunications Law

Second Edition

Peter W. Huber
Partner, Kellogg, Huber, Hansen, Todd & Evans

Michael K. Kellogg
Partner, Kellogg, Huber, Hansen, Todd & Evans

John Thorne
Lecturer on Law, Columbia Law School
Senior Vice President and Deputy General Counsel,
Bell Atlantic

ASPEN LAW & BUSINESS
A Division of Aspen Publishers, Inc.
Gaithersburg   New York

This publication is designed to provide accurate and authoritative information in regard to the subject matter covered. It is sold with the understanding that the publisher is not engaged in rendering legal, accounting, or other professional services. If legal advice or other professional advice is required, the services of a competent professional person should be sought.

—From a *Declaration of Principles* jointly adopted by a Committee of the American Bar Association and a Committee of Publishers and Associations.

Copyright © 1999 by Aspen Law & Business
A Division of Aspen Publishers, Inc.
A Wolters Kluwer Company

Permissions
Aspen Law & Business
1185 Avenue of the Americas
New York, NY 10036

Library of Congress Cataloging-in-Publication Data

Huber, Peter W., 1952–
    Federal telecommunications law / Peter W. Huber,
Michael K. Kellogg, John Thorne. — 2nd ed.
      p.   cm.
    Includes index.
    ISBN 0-7355-0647-7
    1. Telecommunication—Law and legislation—United States.
I. Kellogg, Michael K., 1954– . II. Thorne, John, 1956– .
III. Title.
KF2765.K45 1999   99-27267
343.7309'94—DC21   CIP

Printed in the United States of America

2 3 4 5 6 7 8 9 0

About Aspen Law & Business

Aspen Law & Business — comprising the former Prentice Hall Law & Business, Little, Brown and Company's Professional Division, and Wiley Law Publications — is a leading publisher of authoritative treatises, practice manuals, services, and journals for attorneys, financial and tax advisors, corporate and bank directors, and other business professionals. Our mission is to provide practical, solution-based how-to information keyed to the latest legislative, judicial, and regulatory developments.

We offer publications in the areas of banking and finance; bankruptcy; business and commercial law; construction law; corporate law; pensions, benefits, and labor; insurance law; securities; taxation; intellectual property; government and administrative law; real estate law; matrimonial and family law; environmental and health law; international law; legal practice and litigation; and criminal law.

Other Aspen products treating regulatory and technology issues include:

Administrative Law Treatise
Antitrust Law
Copyright
Corporate Partnering
Drafting License Agreements
Epstein on Intellectual Property
Internet and Technology Law Desk Reference: Key Terms and Cases
Law and the Information Superhighway
Law of Electronic Commerce
Law of the Internet
Scott on Computer Law
Scott on Multimedia Law
Venture Capital & Public Offering Negotiation

ASPEN LAW & BUSINESS
A Division of Aspen Publishers, Inc.
A Wolters Kluwer Company
www.aspenpublishers.com

SUBSCRIPTION NOTICE

This Aspen Law & Business product is updated on a periodic basis with supplements to reflect important changes in the subject matter. If you purchased this product directly from Aspen Law & Business, we have already recorded your subscription for the update service.

If, however, you purchased this product from a bookstore and wish to receive future updates and revised or related volumes billed separately with a 30-day examination review, please contact our Customer Service Department at 1-800-234-1660, or send your name, company name (if applicable), address, and the title of the product to:

ASPEN LAW & BUSINESS
A Division of Aspen Publishers, Inc.
7201 McKinney Circle
Frederick, MD 21704

For Sophie, Mike, and Steve—P.W.H.

For Lucy—M.K.K.

For Sara—J.T.

Summary Table of Contents

Table of Contents

2

Telephone Economics and Price Regulation   79

Table of Contents

3

The Powers of the FCC   209

4
Antitrust
323

5
Equal Access, Unbundling, and Interconnection   405

8

Telecommunications Equipment   **651**

Table of Contents

9

Long-Distance Services

10

Wireless Services   861

11

Data Services and the Internet   981

12

Information Services   1075

13

Video Services   1159

Table of Contents

14

Privacy, Intellectual Property, and Free Speech   1209

Table of Contents

Preface

Telecommunications is a dynamic and important industry. Not surprisingly, therefore, a large body of law has developed around it. The first edition of this treatise, published in 1991, supplied the first comprehensive treatment of the federal law that shapes this industry.

The industry has changed profoundly since that time. With the passage of the 1996 Telecommunications Act, the law has changed even more. This second edition is a complete rewrite of the first. We have restructured and rearranged, and added. The first edition's lengthy treatment of the Bell Divestiture Decree has been sharply compressed. The 1996 Act and its regulatory aftermath have supplied a surfeit of material to fill the void. Much of the material in the first edition may remain of interest, however, to both legal historians and those seeking a deeper understanding of the origins, logic, and meaning of current law.

The book is now roughly divided into two main parts. Chapters 2 to 7 address material logically approached under legal and regulatory headings: economics, jurisdiction, antitrust, interconnection, universal service, and mergers and acquisitions. Chapters 8 to 13 are organized by category of product or service: equipment, long-distance services, wireless services, data and Internet services, information services, and video services. The final chapter covers telecom-related aspects of privacy, intellectual property, and free speech. There is some inevitable overlap, and there is extensive cross-referencing throughout.

No one can doubt the central role telecommunications has assumed in our economic and social lives; the existence of a legal treatise addressing this subject requires no further explanation. The identity of its authors may. One of the three principal authors works directly for a Bell Company; the two others regularly represent Bell companies, among many other clients in the industry. This is not, however, a Bell Company book. The opinions expressed herein are those of the authors and should not be attributed to any company.

We have throughout tried to present an objective picture of the legal and regulatory landscape. As is inevitable in a treatise, our own views on the numerous issues we discuss are not hidden. To the extent that we have a brief, it is in favor of the genius of competition. To the extent that we have a beef, it is with those who would twist the regulatory and judicial process to protect their own narrow interests (and with the legislators, regulators, and judges that permit them to do so). To the extent that we have a passionate conviction, it is that the technologies of freedom cannot be suppressed.

An additional 13 lawyers have played such major roles in the rewriting and editing of parts of the book that they must rank as co-authors of various chapters. Their names appear in their respective chapters. All of them are partners or associates at the Washington, D.C., law firm of Kellogg, Huber, Hansen, Todd & Evans. One of them—Evan Leo—not only co-authored Chapter 3, but also took primary responsibility for coordinating the entire project. We have received further, invaluable research and editorial assistance from three other staff attorneys: Georgia Deoudes, Greg James, and Brad Jones.

There are numerous other people to thank, and without their assistance, completion of the book would not have been possible. One of us (PWH) has received patient support and encouragement from Larry Mone and the Manhattan Institute for Policy Research. All three of us benefited from our talented and dedicated group of telecom researchers—Elizabeth Anderson, Tom Anderson, Jed Birmingham, Adam Coates, Mary Ann Endo, Jeremy Friedman, Shad Gohn, Adam Guglielmo, Chelsea Haga, David Hults, Alexander Moulton, Todd Ricketts, and Brian Walsh—who carefully checked on the citations and indefatigably (and cheerfully) ran down source materials.

Preface

This book is a collaborative work. The three principal authors contributed equally to its writing, and each of us worked on all of its chapters.

We invite readers to contact us regarding errors, new developments, or other matters via e-mail: Peter Huber at <pwhuber@bellatlantic.net>, Michael Kellogg at <mkellogg@khhte. com>, and John Thorne at <74577.2026@compuserve.com>. We also accept paper responses addressed to Peter Huber or Michael Kellogg at Kellogg, Huber, Hansen, Todd & Evans, 1301 K Street, NW, Suite 1000 West, Washington, DC 20005, fax (202) 326-7999, or to John Thorne at Bell Atlantic, 1320 N. Courthouse Road, 8th Floor, Arlington, VA 22201, fax (703) 974-0775.

July 1999
P.W.H
M.K.K.
J.T.

About the Authors

Peter Huber is a Senior Fellow of the Manhattan Institute for Policy Research and is partner in the law firm of Kellogg, Huber, Hansen, Todd & Evans in Washington, D.C. He earned his J.D. from Harvard University summa cum laude, then clerked for Judge Ruth Bader Ginsburg on the D.C. Circuit of Appeals, and later for Justice Sandra Day O'Connor on the U.S. Supreme Court. He taught at MIT for six years and writes a regular column for Forbes.

Michael Kellogg is managing partner in the law firm of Kellogg, Huber, Hansen, Todd & Evans in Washington, D.C. After graduating from Stanford and Oxford, Mr. Kellogg earned his J.D. from Harvard magna cum laude, clerked for Judge Malcolm Wilkey of the U.S. Court of Appeals, D.C. Circuit, and then for U.S. Supreme Court Justice William H. Rehnquist. He went on to serve as Assistant U.S. Attorney for the Southern District of New York, Criminal Division. From 1987–1989 he served as Assistant to the Solicitor General of the United States Department of Justice.

John Thorne teaches telecommunications law at Columbia Law School and is Senior Vice President and Deputy General Counsel of Bell Atlantic, where he heads Bell Atlantic's antitrust, merger, intellectual property, and constitutional litigation. He was a summa cum laude mathematics major at Kenyon College, was Order of the Coif at Northwestern University Law School, and clerked for Chief Judge Walter J. Cummings of the United States Court of Appeals, Seventh Circuit.

Federal Telecommunications Law

1

An Industry in Transition

§1.1 Introduction

The first edition of this book was published in 1992. On page 3, we wrote:

> A new paradigm of unfettered competition—without entry barriers, quarantines, or tariff regulation—is beginning to emerge. The transition is by no means complete. Indeed, regulation today is at its apogee, because a smooth transition to competition requires that new rules be erected before the old can be dismantled.

Four years later Congress passed the Telecommunications Act of 1996. What was "beginning to emerge" in 1992 is now well under way; this second edition marks the beginning of the middle. Regulatory means and ends have shifted fundamentally. Now, the unqualified regulatory objective for all levels of this industry is competition. If anything, however, the sheer volume of regulation has increased dramatically, as regulators have sought to manage all the particulars of the transition. Our third edition will describe, we hope, the beginning of the end, when competition will flourish in a truly deregulated environment.[1] The road, however, has been a long and winding one.

For most of this century, telephony was viewed as a natural monopoly.[2] The high cost of fixed plant, the steadily declining average cost of service, and the need for all customers to interconnect with one another made it seem both sensible and inevitable to have a single, monopoly provider. The Bell System was born on that premise, and with it an elaborate body of regulation designed to reconcile private monopoly with the public good.

The old regulatory paradigm had three basic pillars. First, the *protected franchise:* would-be competitors were barred from competing or even interconnecting with the enfranchised carrier; natural monopoly thus became a self-fulfilling prophecy. Second, the *quarantine:* the monopolist was restricted to its regulated sphere and barred from exporting its expertise (and the corrosive influence of its monopoly) into adjacent competitive markets. Third, *cradle-to-grave regulation:* prices, terms, and conditions of the monopolist's services had to be sold to regulators before they could be sold to customers.

The old regulatory paradigm served the country adequately for over half a century, permitting the Bell System to deploy the best, most technologically sophisticated telephone system in the world. Bell also deployed Bell Labs and funded it with the enormous profits of the Bell System. And Bell Labs, apparently unfamiliar with regulatory paradigms, developed new technologies that made competition in telephony inevitable.

Today, the two overarching technological trends in the industry are fragmentation and convergence. There are, on the one

---

[1] Although the industry has changed dramatically since the 1996 Act was passed, much of the material contained in our first edition, and the two supplements to it, is still of more than just historical interest. We have necessarily abridged the treatment of much pre-1996 Act information in this edition—particularly material concerning the AT&T consent decree—that is still legally relevant in many contexts today. Information about the prior edition and our two supplements can be found at <http://www.phuber.com>. You may also order these books online from our publisher at <http://www.aspenpub.com> or <http://www.amazon.com>.

[2] *See* §2.1.2.

hand, more switches, more lines, more networks, and many more levels of interconnection—the old integrated, centralized media are being fragmented into many smaller, more autonomous parts. On the other hand, interconnections are proliferating as never before: direct interconnections between competing wireline phone companies and interconnections between different media that never used to compete at all.[3] Television is leaving the air in favor of the wires; the telephone is leaving the wires in favor of the air. Copper and coax, wired and wireless, terrestrial and satellite: digital data networks are rapidly emerging as the new, universal, universally interconnected standard for the transmission of everything—voice, data, video, the lot.

These industry-transforming developments are not, of course, unconditionally welcome on all sides of all the industries involved; "every invention," as Joel Mokyr has noted, "is born into an uncongenial society, has few friends and many enemies."[4] Precisely the same technological developments support new competition *by* the phone company and *against* it, and incumbents on opposite sides of traditional regulatory fences have quite different views about which kind of competition should come first. Thus, television broadcasters want to contain phone and cable companies, just as radio broadcasters once hoped to contain television and just as newspapers once hoped to contain radio. Cable companies want to contain phone companies and vice versa. Providers of Internet services would prefer to contain both. Landline phone companies see a real threat in wireless services, which provide far more convenience; wireless carriers see a real threat in the landline system, which still provides the dominant hub for ubiquitous interconnection. Much of the time, for many of the protagonists, the paramount regulatory objective is to preserve the status quo, and so to fend off the instability of untrammeled new competition.

The dynamics of the new technology have forced regulatory change regardless. The protected franchise has disappeared. The quarantine was eliminated in its entirety by the 1996 Act. Pervasive regulation of prices and terms of service is now rapidly

[3] Chapter 5 discusses the rules governing these interconnections.
[4] J. Mokyr, The Lever of Riches 183 (1990).

3

giving way to prices and terms set by competition. These changes have in turn wrought fundamental changes in the nature, purpose, and complexity of regulation.

Under the old regulatory model, for example, there was no need for interconnection or equal access standards—the only interconnection was between customers and their monopoly carrier.[5] We may likewise anticipate a day when interconnection regulations will once again become unnecessary: competitive forces will balance out, and interface standards will be set through market forces, voluntary agreements, and evolutionary consensus as they are in other industries, most notably the computer industry. Today, however, while dominant carriers still mingle with fledgling competitors, interfaces are regulated more pervasively than ever before. And day by day the interfaces multiply as equipment providers, long-distance carriers, Internet providers, wireless providers, and—more recently and importantly—competitive providers of local exchange service all clamor for new forms of access, steadily blurring the lines between customers and providers.

Price regulation, too, has become vastly more complicated.[6] With a single monopoly provider, the regulator's task was relatively simple: ensure that the monopolist enjoyed no more than a "fair" rate of return.[7] Within that overall stricture, regulators were free to shuffle costs and prices—which they did with enthusiasm, mostly in pursuit of universal service.[8] Through the "separations" process—the division of costs between interstate and intrastate jurisdictions—the Federal Communications Commission (FCC) and state regulators heavily subsidized local connections by loading costs onto interstate services.[9] This helped attract long-distance competition. And with competition came today's dismaying spectacle of regulators vowing to embrace competition, maintain subsidy, and protect fledgling competitors all at the same time.

---

[5] See §5.1.2.
[6] Chapter 2 discusses various forms of price regulation.
[7] See §2.2.3.
[8] See §§2.5, 6.2.
[9] See §6.2.1.2.

Most complicated of all have been relations among regulators themselves.[10] Telecommunications began as a local industry heavily regulated by local authorities. For most of this century, local exchange revenues dwarfed those from long-distance service; regulation was accordingly centered in local commissions, and the FCC's role was correspondingly modest. Hewing to tradition, the Bell divestiture decree divided markets along strictly geographic lines. But the whole point of telephony is to erase geography—so the better service gets, the more difficult it is to regulate through a hodgepodge of independent, uncoordinated, geographically defined authorities. In the final analysis, local, introverted regulation is irreconcilable with a network that must function outward, nationally and beyond. Thus, the major trend today—pushed by the FCC, though resisted by many states—is toward a steady contraction of local power.[11]

For now, we are at the high-water mark of regulation, with major components of both the old and the new regulatory regimes still in place. The shift from managing monopoly to managing competition was accelerating rapidly in 1992, when our first edition appeared, though we described it then as "one of the great if unheralded regulatory initiatives of our day." The heralds finally made it to Congress, and what emerged was the 1996 Act. Our ability to compete in the new global markets will turn in significant part on how—and how quickly—critical disputes are resolved and its objectives are attained.

§1.2 The Rise of Monopoly: Technology

§1.2.1 Telephones and Wires

The history of telephony begins, as it ends, with the working ends, the parts on customer premises that are actually seen and used. Most of the modern telephone network—a gigantic spider-

---

[10] Chapter 3 discusses the relationship between federal and state regulators.
[11] *See* §§3.8–3.9.

web of wires and switches, satellites, radio towers, and trans-oceanic cables circling the globe—is completely invisible to end users. But it was the telephone itself that spawned all the rest. And as we shall see, a later generation of customer premises equipment impelled the revolutionary changes in marketplace and law that we see all around us today.

The idea of "telephony" (from the Greek, "far speaking") tantalized inventors since time immemorial, but nineteenth-century inventors were the first seriously to explore the possibility. In 1831, Michael Faraday demonstrated that a piece of iron vibrating in a magnetic field produces electrical pulses. Soon thereafter, in 1835, Samuel Morse invented the essential elements of a telegraph.[12] A quarter century later, a German researcher, Philipp Reis, developed a device that used a membrane, electrodes, and an electric current to transmit pitch.[13]

Alexander Graham Bell produced his first rough plans for a "harmonic telegraph" in 1872. Within a few years, he had developed the "phonautograph," which translated sounds into visible markings.[14] By 1875, he was in a neck-and-neck race with Elisha Gray,[15] co-founder of the Western Electric Company, to create a workable telephone. In June of that year, Bell discovered the basic principles of the electromagnetic microphone and speaker, the key elements of a telephone. And on February 14, 1876, Bell filed his historic patent application at the U.S. Patent

[12] More primitive systems, using a deflecting magnetic needle, had already been developed and installed in England. Morse introduced the electromagnet and the pencil-marked strip recorder.

[13] The Reis telephone was later considered a threat to the Bell patents, but Judge Lowell of the U.S. Circuit Court of Massachusetts ruled that "[t]he deficiency was inherent in the principle of the machine. . . . [A] century of Reis would never have produced a speaking telephone." The Telephone Cases, 126 U.S. 1, 193 (1888). Subsequently, however, others (including one curator of the division of electricity of the Smithsonian Institution) have maintained that small changes to the Reis telephone would have enabled it to transmit speech. See J. Brooks, Telephone: The First Hundred Years (1975).

[14] The phonautograph used a human ear, which vibrated when words were spoken. The vibrations moved a lever that created a wave pattern on a piece of smoked glass.

[15] In 1888, Gray invented the telautograph, an electrical device for reproducing and transmitting handwriting and line drawing—the forerunner, in effect, of the facsimile machine.

Office. Just a few hours later, in the same office, Gray filed a notice of a pending application for a patent on a similar device. The U.S. Supreme Court ultimately ruled, however, that the invention belonged to Bell.[16] Bell did undoubtedly win the race to build an actual working telephone. The famous words—"Mr. Watson, come here, I want you"—were transmitted from Bell to his assistant in a nearby room on March 10, 1876.

First there was the box telephone—an iron diaphragm encased in a wooden block. Bell's assistant, Thomas Watson, then developed the "Thumper," the first telephone signaling device, subsequently superseded by electric "call bells" and, still later, by "magneto call bells." By 1878, Bell was installing two "telephones" at each station—one for talking, the other for listening—so that the user would not constantly have to shift the unit between mouth and ear.[17] "French" handset telephones (in which the handset contains both transmitter and receiver) arrived in the United States in 1927.

From the beginning, Bell confidently predicted that some day "a telephone in every house would be considered indispensable. . . ."[18] Others were much more skeptical. Western Union, the (then) giant telegraph company, flatly rejected an early offer to purchase Bell's patents.[19] Smaller competitors knew better; imitations of Bell's invention soon inundated the market. The Bell Company brought over 600 patent infringement suits in the two decades after the telephone's invention.[20]

§1.2.2 The Telephone Exchange

Telephones created an immediate need for telephone wires to connect them. Before long, telephone poles and wires prolif-

---

[16] *See* The Telephone Cases, 126 U.S. at 2.

[17] *See* G. Smith, The Anatomy of a Business Strategy: Bell, Western Electric, and the Origins of the American Telephone Industry 17–21 (1985).

[18] R. Garnet, The Telephone Enterprise: The Evolution of the Bell System's Horizontal Structure, 1876–1909, at 12 (1985).

[19] *See id.* at 11.

[20] *See* G. Faulhaber, Telecommunications in Turmoil: Technology and Public Policy 1 (1987); Garnet, The Telephone Enterprise at 15.

erated in city streets, so much so that the New York state legislature required all telephone wires in major cities to be routed underground.[21]

Initially, telephones were linked one to one.[22] It took until 1878, two years after the invention of the telephone itself, for the budding new telephone companies to grasp the necessity of a telephone "exchange." The telephone exchange—a simple switchboard at first—radically increased a telephone's utility by enabling each phone to reach any other phone connected to the same exchange. Demand for service increased dramatically. By the mid-1880s, multiple unit switching systems allowed operators to work in banks, each serving the same array of telephones. The first automatic switching system was patented in 1889; a series of pulses was used to raise and then rotate a shaft to make the appropriate contact.[23] A patent for dialing devices was granted in 1898. Newark, New Jersey, boasted the first semiautomatic switching system in 1914. Omaha, in 1921, housed the first fully automated system.

The advent of the telephone exchange gave rise to the first rumblings about the need for—or inevitability of—monopoly provision of telephone service.[24] A central switchboard and the wires leading to it represented a large, fixed capital investment; the costs of an exchange seemed to decline rapidly as more subscribers were added. By fragmenting the market, competition appeared to drive up costs and nullify the key advantage of a central exchange, which was to connect everyone to everyone else.

§1.2.3   Interexchange Connections

Local exchanges also raised the possibility of "interexchange" connections over longer distances. While few individual owners

[21] *See* Brooks, Telephone: The First Hundred Years at 87. *See also* N. Wasserman, From Invention to Innovation: Long-Distance Telephone Transmission at the Turn of the Century 37–38 (1985).

[22] *See* Garnet, The Telephone Enterprise at 15.

[23] *See* Telecommunications Systems, Macropaedia: Knowledge in Depth 498 *in* 28 New Encyclopaedia Britannica (1986) (hereinafter *Macropaedia Britannica*).

[24] *See* Garnet, The Telephone Enterprise at 23.

of telephones could afford to run lines over great distances, the owners of exchanges clearly could.

Initially, however, there was no technology to support such service. Even short telephone connections were of very poor quality. Thunderstorms filled lines with static; switchboards caused all manner of cross-talk. Signal quality deteriorated rapidly over "long" distances—distances that, in Watson's view, spanned more than about two miles.[25] Until the turn of the century, most long-distance service was expensive and almost unusable.

In the late 1890s, Bell engineer George Campbell discovered that "loading the lines"—concentrating inductance in coils along the lines—could greatly improve transmission quality.[26] The first long-distance cable using Campbell's invention was demonstrated successfully in September 1899.[27] The subsequent struggle to acquire and control the loading patent would be "the most hotly contested and economically significant . . . since the original Bell patents of 1876."[28]

Then in 1906, Lee DeForest developed the audion—the first vacuum tube electronic amplifier.[29] Audions could be used to make a "repeater" with the capacity to amplify an electric signal. Placed at suitable intervals along a telephone wire, repeaters could sustain the strength of a signal over almost any distance. For the next four decades, the vacuum tube amplifier would be the key component of all telecommunications, broadcast, and (eventually) the first-generation electronic computers. The Bell System purchased DeForest's patent in 1913.[30]

Thus, the key technologies needed for telephone service of the kind we know were developed in the four decades between

[25] *See* T. Watson, Exploring Life: The Autobiography of Thomas A. Watson 89–96 (1926).

[26] Wasserman, From Invention to Innovation at 76.

[27] *Id.* at 78.

[28] *Id.* at 91.

[29] *Macropaedia Britannica* at 498.

[30] Gerald Brock has argued that DeForest's audion posed a threat to Bell because it would efficiently and accurately amplify not only telephone signals, but also radio signals. *See* G. Brock, The Telecommunications Industry: The Dynamics of Market Structure 162 (1981).

1876 and 1913. The invention of the telephone led to the invention of the local exchange; the invention of the local exchange
led to the development of the technology needed for interexchange service. Each major restructuring of the network in the
eight decades since has been triggered by breakthrough developments in one or another of these three principal tiers of the
industry.

§1.2.4   The Development of Radio

By 1895, when Bell's major patents on the telephone had just
expired, the new wonder of the technological world was not communication with wire, but communication without it. That year
Guglielmo (G.M.) Marconi produced the first practical radio.
The following year Britain granted Marconi his first patent on a
radio—still known, at the time, for precisely what it did not
require—wires. It was the "wireless telegraph," or just the "wireless."[31]

Radio looked, at first, like a major new competitive threat to
telephone service. Marconi himself had conceived of it as a messaging system, principally for ships.[32] In short order, the wireless
telegraph became a wireless telephone—radio communication
of human speech first occurred on Christmas Eve in 1906 between Brant Rock, Massachusetts, and ships in the Atlantic
Ocean. And Lee DeForest's vacuum tube amplifier, the audion,
improved radio transmission as dramatically as it improved telephony. By all logic, the development of radio and the electronic
amplifier[33] should have ushered in an era of fierce competition
between the two infant industries of radio and telephone. Bell
itself recognized the threat: in 1909, the company's chief engineer sought research funds to put the company "in a position of

[31] See §10.1.
[32] E. Doering, Federal Control of Broadcasting Versus Freedom of the Air
4 (1939).
[33] See De Forest Radio Tel. & Tel. Co. v. Radio Corp. of Am., 20 F.2d 598
(3d Cir. 1927).

control with regard to the art of wireless telephony, should it turn out to be a factor of importance."[34]

Competition did indeed start out on a reasonably promising track. Fearing that Britain would become the world hub for radio, just as it had already become for the undersea cable network, the U.S. government backed the formation of a strong radio manufacturing company, the Radio Corporation of America (RCA).

With the early technologies, however, radio's great advantage was not in point-to-point messaging, but in point-to-everywhere broadcast. David Sarnoff, who started as a telegraph operator for the Marconi Wireless Telegraph Company of America, was perhaps the first to recognize this. In 1916, he submitted his idea for a "radio music box" to the management of Marconi. Westinghouse inaugurated the nation's first true radio station, KDKA in Pittsburgh, in 1920. Bell put its own station, WEAF, on the air in New York City in 1922.

RCA and Westinghouse, the two early leaders in radio, planned to operate radio stations at a loss to promote the profitable sale of radios. The idea of giving away the broadcast to sell the radios worked for a short while, but was doomed to fail in the long run: once patents expired, anyone could build a radio. Bell understood this from the beginning and adopted quite a different approach. The only sustainable revenues in broadcast, the company recognized, would come from the sale of airtime. So Bell developed a plan to build transmitters and sell airtime to all comers—entire chunks of airtime, which buyers could fill with a mix of program and advertisement as they saw fit. Bell decided, in short, to run radio just like its phone business, as a common carrier. The company earned solid profits in the first few years of its operations, while RCA was losing money.

§1.3 The Rise of Monopoly: Regulation

When commercial telephone service began in the United States in 1877, Bell held all the essential patents. The company

---

[34] *Quoted in* I. de Sola Pool, Technologies of Freedom 31 (1983).

thus enjoyed a complete and legal monopoly. By 1894, however, the essential patents had either expired or been narrowly construed by the courts. Thousands of independent telephone companies took advantage of the opportunities offered by the newly available technology. By 1902, 451 of the 1,002 cities with phone service had two or more companies providing it. By 1907, when a phone census was taken, the "independents" owned nearly as many phone stations as Bell.[35] Average rates were cut in half, and Bell's average return on investment had fallen over 80 percent.

At about this time, Theodore Vail, a brilliant administrator, took charge of the declining Bell empire. The Bell System had lost its original patents on the telephone, but it had acquired new ones, through which it now enjoyed a critical edge at the opposite end of the network, in providing quality long-distance connections. Vail believed passionately in universal service, to be supplied by one company—his own. Bell therefore offered its superior long-distance service to its own local affiliates, but not to others. The company likewise refused to sell equipment or to provide interconnection even to those independents that did not directly compete with it. As a result, phone companies not affiliated with the Bell System either folded or were acquired.[36] In 1910, Vail bought Western Union, which 35 years earlier had declined to purchase Bell's patent.

By 1915, when Bell had established transcontinental service, Vail could describe the Bell System as "an ever-living organism" that possessed "one of the largest laboratories of the application of science to industrial development in the world." In 1908, Vail announced the company's new slogan, "One Policy, One System, Universal Service."

[35] *See* A. S. Lavey, The Public Policies That Changed the Telephone Industries into Regulated Monopolies: Lessons from 1915, 39 Fed. Comm. L.J. 171, 179 (1987).

[36] *See* G. O. Robinson, The Federal Communications Act: An Essay on Origins and Regulatory Purpose, *reprinted in* A Legislative History of the Communications Act of 1934, at 7 (M. D. Paglin ed., 1989); D. Burch, Common Carrier Communications by Wire and Radio: A Retrospective, 37 Fed. Comm. L.J. 85, 87 (1985). *See* §6.1.1.1.

§1.3.1   Common Carriage

It is at this point in the history of telecommunications that regulation could have forcefully intervened to prevent the rise of monopoly service by forbidding boycotts and requiring carriers to interconnect with one another. Multiple carriers might well have coexisted and competed under such a regime without a balkanized network in which telephone owners could talk only with other customers of the same carrier. The fundamental question arose early on: *Must carriers carry other carriers?* At first, the answer was no; the direct result was the creation of the largest, most powerful telecommunications monopoly the world has ever known.[37] From the 1960s until 1996, the answer was a tentative yes, and the results were the breakup of that same monopoly and a fundamental, irreversible shift toward competition.[38] With the passage of the 1996 Telecom Act, the answer is no longer tentative at all. The Act's core provisions direct incumbent local phone companies to "unbundle" their networks and offer competitors interconnection at low costs.[39]

The earliest common carriers were created when the Crown awarded an exclusive monopoly to a company operating such things as a ferryboat, a wharf, or, for a time, a printing press. The English common law gradually developed rules that both contained monopolists' excesses and defended their monopolies.[40] Crown monopolies were required to charge only "reasonable and nondiscriminatory" rates, provide adequate service, and accept all customers on the same terms, without discrimination. In time, these principles came to extend to any firm "affected with

---

[37] *See* §3.11.1.

[38] *See* §§5.1.2.1–5.1.2.2.

[39] *See* §§5.1.2.3, 5.5.

[40] "If a ferry is erected on a river, so near another ancient ferry as to draw away its custom, it is a nuisance to the owner of the old one. For where there is a ferry by prescription, the owner is bound to keep it always in repair and readiness for the ease of all the king's subjects; otherwise he may be grievously amerced: it would be therefore extremely hard if a new ferry were suffered to share his profits, which does not also share his burden." 3 W. Blackstone, Commentaries 219 (1768).

a public interest" that held itself open to the general public and purported to serve all comers. In return, common carriers enjoyed important legal privileges, most particularly limits on their liabilities—limits appropriate to a business that could not legally discriminate among those it chose to serve. America inherited these core principles from England.

Telegraph and telephone companies are quite clearly "common carriers."[41] They have long been expected to serve all comers and charge similar rates for similar services. They could not generally be sued for the content transmitted over their systems, or for the damage caused by garbled or lost transmissions. They soon came to be viewed as paradigm "common carriers," so common, so ubiquitous, so routinized that one could scarcely imagine them operating in any other way—except, as it turned out, when a would-be "customer" happened to be another carrier.

The problem had been faced—and resolved correctly—half a century before the birth of telephony, in legislation for telegraphy. The Post Roads Act of 1866 required telegraph companies to interconnect and accept each other's traffic.[42] If similar obligations had been imposed on telephone companies, local exchanges might have remained competitive as companies could have differentiated their prices and services. They all might have offered interconnection with other companies, including long-distance connections. But legislators, regulators, and the courts missed the opportunity and adopted instead a narrow understanding of a common carrier's obligations to carry its competitors' traffic.

The problems first appeared in the *Express Packages Cases,* decided by the Supreme Court in 1885. Four major express companies, the grandparents of today's overnight courier services,

---

[41] *See* §3.11; *see also* J. Thorne, P. Huber, & M. Kellogg, Federal Broadband Law §5.3 (1995) (hereinafter *FBL*).

[42] "A telegraph company represents the public when applying to another telegraph company for service," a New York court would later declare, "and no discrimination can be made by either against the other, but each must render to the other the same services it renders to the rest of the community under the same conditions." People *ex rel.* Western Union Tel. Co. v. Public Serv. Commn. of New York, 230 N.Y. 95, 129 N.E. 220, 12 A.L.R. 960 (1920).

had worked out a cozy territorial division of the business. They didn't do much hauling themselves. Instead, they reserved an entire railway car, or perhaps half a car; paid wholesale rates for the space; and used their own agents to load, unload, and supervise packages consigned to their care. In 1880, one of the major railroads abruptly announced it would no longer sell space on those terms; express companies would be treated like ordinary retail customers. Faced with immediate financial ruin, the express companies rushed to court. Their arrangements with the railroads (they argued), though originally simple matters of contract, had become matters of common "law and usage." The U.S. Supreme Court disagreed.[43]

Perhaps the express companies got what they deserved. For 30 years, they had systematically monopolized their end of the business by agreeing not to infiltrate each other's territories. For that reason, no very strong common carriage tradition had evolved between express companies and railways. And yet the principle announced by the Supreme Court would have decades of unfortunate consequences. Common carrier obligations, it seemed, extended from the aristocracy of the business world to the serfs and peasants of "the public." But a railroad baron owed nothing to an express package baron. The duty of a common carrier not to discriminate did not extend to other carriers asking for service.

The same principle was adopted in telephony. In 1903, a company that would soon be acquired by the Interstate Telephone Company won permission to install a telephone system in Newport, Washington.[44] The owner of the system agreed not to compete against Pacific Telephone and to connect all long-distance calls to Pacific's network. When Interstate bought the system in 1911, it ceased both practices. When Pacific demanded to be reconnected, Interstate claimed that the original agreement illegally excluded other carriers. A federal judge disagreed, ruling that "Each telephone company is independent of all other telephone companies"; common carrier law did not require telcos

---

[43] The Express Packages Cases, 117 U.S. 1 (1885).
[44] Pacific Tel. & Tel. Co. v. Anderson, 196 F. 699 (E.D. Wash. 1912).

"to accord to any such outside organization or its patrons connection with its switchboard on an equality with its own patrons."[45] Other cases around this time reached the same result, despite the existence of state statutes requiring universal carriage. For example, the Supreme Court of Tennessee conceded that although "Telephone and telegraph companies are common carriers, this does not mean that a telephone company is bound to permit another telephone company to make a physical connection with its lines."[46]

In 1910, Congress had its first major chance to correct this imbalance.[47] The Act brought interstate telecommunications within the regulatory jurisdiction of the Interstate Commerce Commission (ICC) and included telecommunications companies within the definition of "common carrier," thereby obligating them "to provide service on request at just and reasonable rates, without unjust discrimination or undue preference."[48] But the Act did not require a common carrier to carry other carriers. The ICC might have taken steps to remedy this, but was fixated at the time on railroads and insecure with respect to exercising its powers. As a result, the Bell System continued its march toward monopoly unchecked.

§1.3.2 Antitrust

In 1912, fresh on the heels of its victory against Rockefeller,[49] the U.S. Justice Department threatened to take on Vail. There followed a great deal of sound and fury, no doubt reflecting America's traditional populist mistrust of monopoly. In the end,

---

[45] *Id.* at 703 (citing State v. Cadwallader, 172 Ind. 619, 87 N.E. 644, 89 N.E. 319 (1909)).

[46] Home Tel. Co. v. People's Tel. & Tel. Co., 141 S.W. 845, 848 (1911). *See also* Home Tel. Co. v. Sarcoxie Light & Tel. Co., 236 Mo. 114, 139 S.W. 108, 113 (1911).

[47] Commerce Court (Mann-Elkins) Act, ch. 309, §7, 36 Stat. 539 (1910). The Mann-Elkins Act is discussed in §3.2.2.

[48] Essential Communications v. AT&T, 610 F.2d 1114, 1118 (3d Cir. 1979) (citing Mann-Elkins Act §§7, 12).

[49] Standard Oil Co. of N.J. v. United States, 221 U.S. 1 (1911).

however, government officials would conclude that monopoly in communications was much more tolerable than monopoly in oil.

In a 1913 agreement between the U.S. Attorney General and a Bell vice-president, N. C. Kingsbury, the company agreed to stop acquiring independent phone companies and to connect the remaining independents to Bell's long-distance network.[50] Bell also agreed to divest itself of Western Union. It appeared to be at least a partial victory for the trustbusters at the Justice Department—an honorable armistice signed by vigilant public servants to contain all-too-acquisitive private interests. But the Kingsbury Commitment was really nothing of the sort.

It did indeed stop the growth of Bell's financial empire—for a few short years, in any event—but it did nothing to promote competition in either telephony or telegraphy. Local exchange monopolies were left intact, utterly free to continue to refuse interconnection to other local exchange companies. Bell's monopoly long-distance service was reinforced: Bell would be required to interconnect with all local exchanges, but there was no provision for any competition—or interconnection—among long-distance carriers. Western Union was indeed spun off—but only to provide telegraphy, not telephony.

The government solution, in short, was not the steamy, unsettling cohabitation that marks competition, but rather a sort of competitive apartheid, characterized by segregation and quarantine. Markets were carefully carved up: one for the monopoly telegraph company, one for each of the established monopoly local telephone exchanges, one for Bell's monopoly long-distance operations. Bell might not own everything, but some monopolist or other would dominate each discrete market. The Kingsbury Commitment could be viewed as a solution only by a government bookkeeper who counted several separate monopolies as an advance over a single monopoly, even absent any trace of competition among them.

To judge by actions, then, rather than words, government officials had no strong objection to monopoly telephone service. It was just that the Bell empire had been getting too big and

---

[50] *See* §4.1.

wealthy. For reasons of bureaucratic convenience, government officials preferred single-serving monopolies to the large economy-size monopolies. This was especially true for state regulators. For them, a local telephone monopoly was both welcome and convenient. The problem with the burgeoning Bell System was that it had been growing larger than local politics.

Kingsbury was the first—though, as we shall see, by no means the last—antitrust quarantine placed on the Bell System.[51] The Bell System remained a colossal corporate empire; although it had agreed not to grow by acquisition, nothing prevented it from building up businesses it already owned. It continued to enjoy almost blanket state and federal government protection against competition within its own businesses. The outward expansion of the monopoly had perhaps been stopped, but there was certainly no promise in the Kingsbury Commitment for any new competition within the confines of the Bell Empire.

§1.3.3   The Separation of Radio and Telephony

Radio, originally conceived as an alternative to the telephone, was born within a decade of the signing of the Kingsbury Commitment. Bell took an immediate interest in the new technology. But competition was the last thing that the new radio companies wanted, and there quickly developed a united opposition to Bell's presence in the new market. The code word was "monopoly," and monopoly was resoundingly condemned. In the 1920s, however, that did not mean government-licensed broadcasters or dominant national networks. It meant Bell, and its common carrier notions for marketing the new medium. In Congress and elsewhere, the alarm was sounded: no monopoly in radio. This really meant: no competition—at least not from Bell.

Bell got the message. Ever since the Kingsbury Commitment, the company had adopted a philosophy of accommodating politics rather than fighting it. Bell managed its exit from the broadcast business with characteristic brilliance.

[51] *See* §§4.2–4.4.3.

By 1926, it was already clear that much of the future of radio broadcast lay in networking. Indeed, the first radio networks were established that year. And the links between radio stations needed by the national radio networks were not going to be over the air—they were going to be by wire. Wire could provide much higher transmission fidelity over long distances. And, in any event, it was uneconomic to use powerful transmitters and to crowd the airwaves with signals that were being transmitted point to point, from an originating station out to its network affiliates. This meant that much of the flow of information ultimately delivered over the air would in fact occur by wire. The wire networks would move the programs out to the cities and towns. The radio stations would provide local distribution. Or, viewed another way, the phone system would be used for the long-distance transmission of radio signals and radio transmitters primarily for the last-mile connections.

Here, then, were the perfect elements of a market-dividing deal. Bell already had a wire network. The new radio companies wanted to dominate local over-the-air broadcast. The markets would be simply and cleanly carved up to reduce competition in both sectors. That was exactly what happened.

In 1926, Bell sold its flagship radio station, WEAF, to RCA, for $1 million, to serve as the nucleus of RCA's broadcasting network. RCA committed to use Bell's lines, rather than Western Union's, for its networking. Patents on the single critical piece of technology common to both telephony and broadcast—the audion, the electronic amplifier—had previously been pooled by Bell and the leading radio companies.[52] The patent-pool contract was renegotiated to exclude Bell entirely from the over-the-air end of radio broadcasting, while Bell's exclusive hold over the wire network, and all point-to-point messaging systems, was strengthened. It was really the Kingsbury Commitment all over again, this time negotiated privately. Bell stopped expanding its local radio operations and indeed agreed to get out of the local distribution end of the business altogether. In return, the remaining local radio stations agreed to interconnect only through

---

[52] *See* Radio Corp. of Am. v. Lord, 28 F.2d 257 (3d Cir. 1928).

§1.3.3 An Industry in Transition

Bell's long-distance network. A gentlemanly agreement, reached under political pressure, had once again replaced competition with complementary monopolies. RCA then used WEAF as the centerpiece of its wholly owned broadcasting subsidiary, the National Broadcasting Corporation (NBC). NBC quickly acquired a position of complete dominance in radio,[53] almost as overwhelming (for a time) as Bell's in telephony.[54]

The Radio Act of 1927 sealed the deal.[55] It reaffirmed the general prohibition on "monopoly" of the airwaves—meaning that *competition* over the airwaves was prohibited, at least if it came from Bell. The Act forbade cross-ownership of telephone companies and broadcasting stations[56] and flatly rejected the operation of radio stations as "common carriers."[57] None of this could have concerned top officials at RCA or Bell very much. Congress merely cemented and strengthened a division of markets and territories that the parties had already voluntarily embraced.[58]

---

[53] Fifteen years later NBC was finally forced to divest one of its two national networks into what became the American Broadcasting Company. *See* National Broad. Co. v. United States, 319 U.S. 190 (1943).

[54] The American Newspaper Publishers Association then launched a vehement attack against radio in Congress and before the Federal Radio Commission. Radio and press representatives negotiated a cease-fire in 1933. The agreement called for dissolution of network radio news-gathering operations, restrictions limiting newscasters to covering "background matter," and restrictions on news broadcasting. The radio would carry no more than two five-minute news broadcasts (after 9:30 A.M. and 9:00 P.M. so they wouldn't interfere with reading the newspaper). Each news item was limited to 30 words, and the broadcast was to conclude with the language "See your daily newspaper for further details." *See* D. Doeden, The Press-Radio War: A Historical Analysis of Press-Radio Competition 1920–1940, at 130–131 (1975) (Ph.D. dissertation, Northwestern University); The Week, New Republic, Jan. 3, 1934, at 209.

[55] *See* Radio Act of 1927, 44 Stat. 1162 (1927).

[56] *See id.* §17. *See also FBL* §4.6.2.

[57] *See* de Sola Pool, Technologies of Freedom at 136–138.

[58] The hostility against any taint of common carrier operations of radio has survived to this day. The FCC's rules against "time brokering" of radio airtime were invoked not long ago against the Cosmopolitan Broadcasting Corporation, which operated an FM radio station, WHBI, licensed to serve Newark, New Jersey, but effectively in competition with the many radio stations in New

§1.3.4   Regulation After 1934

The Kingsbury Commitment and the 1927 Radio Act defined the regulatory landscape until the Federal Communications Act of 1934 was signed into law on June 18.[59] By this point, monopoly provision of telephone service had become so familiar it seemed inevitable. Several ponderous studies officially confirmed that it was, a conclusion perfectly consonant with the New Deal political winds then blowing. Monopoly was, in any event, the clear premise of the 1934 Act. The monopoly telephone company was to provide service to all customers at "just and reasonable" prices.[60] New firms would be permitted to compete only if they demonstrated that the "public convenience and necessity" so required.[61] And the monopoly was required to provide connection to newcomers only if a commission found such connection "necessary or desirable in the public interest."[62]

For some economists, these arrangements seemed to make perfect sense.[63] If telephony was indeed a natural monopoly, competition would be futile and inefficient and so should be forbidden. Without competition, however, prices would have to be regulated, or they would be set too high. The regulator—advised by a large staff of economists, of course—would intervene

---

York City. WHBI failed to make a profit with "black-oriented" broadcast, so in 1969 it began selling most of its airtime in large units to "time brokers." These brokers resold the time in smaller units, mostly to foreign language and ethnic specialty programmers, but also to individuals in five-minute segments between 3:00 and 6:00 A.M. As a result, WHBI ended up broadcasting material in Spanish, Italian, Greek, Hungarian, Arabic, Polish, Brazilian, Portuguese, Lithuanian, Slovakian, Croatian, Albanian, Ukrainian, Romanian, Armenian, Yugoslavian, Bulgarian, and Norwegian; by 1972, Korean, Macedonian, Urdu, Hindi, Bengali, Japanese, and Russian had been added to the list. Everyone seemed happy about the arrangement except the FCC, which promptly terminated Cosmopolitan's broadcasting license. *See* Cosmopolitan Broad. Corp. v. FCC, 581 F.2d 917 (D.C. Cir. 1978), *cert. denied,* 454 U.S. 1143 (1982).

[59] *See* §3.2.5.
[60] 47 U.S.C. §201(a), (b).
[61] *Id.* §214(a).
[62] *Id.* §201(a).
[63] *See* §2.1.2.

as a visible surrogate for the invisible hand of the market, the invisible hand being altogether too invisible when it came to guiding the business practices of a monopoly.

But regulators, it turned out, much preferred to emulate governments than to mimic markets—they preferred transferring wealth to promoting efficiency.[64] For many years, the paramount regulatory objective in all of telephony, at both state and federal levels, was to promote universal service: a telephone within arm's reach of the chicken in every pot.[65] The 1934 Communications Act itself established this as one of the FCC's several missions.[66] So the dominant objective was to push local telephone rates down. As for universal service to other telephone companies, equipment providers, and sellers of long-distance service and such, well, the Communications Act hadn't meant *that* kind of universality. Universal service was something for consumers, not providers.[67]

The pricing arrangements that developed in this regulatory climate violated the most elementary principle of economic efficiency.[68] The cost of connecting subscribers to the interstate network is largely "non-traffic-sensitive," but was recovered through per-minute markups on long-distance calls. Common costs were not merely distributed between local and long-distance service, but triply overdistributed to the long-distance side.[69] Interconnections between the public phone network and all other devices and services were the most expensive of all—they were illegal. Thus, in the fullness of time, the Bell System would seek (and receive) from the FCC a solemn order forbidding the attachment of an alien device to its network—to wit, a plastic cup called a Hush-a-Phone that slipped over the mouthpiece to provide some small measure of quiet and privacy in otherwise crowded

[64] *See* §2.2.1.
[65] *See* §6.2.
[66] *See* 47 U.S.C. §151.
[67] *See* §§8.4, 9.4.
[68] *See* §2.3.
[69] *See* §2.3.3.3.

offices.[70] Telephone service remained largely local, and therefore regulated primarily by state public utility commissions (PUCs). And the PUCs were the most zealous of the zealous when it came to subsidizing local operations and promoting universal service.[71]

In retrospect, at least, it is remarkable to see how many opportunities there were to set the industry on a competitive path and how persistently these opportunities were neglected or deliberately turned aside. What would finally become the core interconnection and unbundling provisions of federal law in 1996 could have been put in place on any number of occasions, decades earlier. The courts might have done the job in the beginning by simply building on ancient principles of common carriage. A one-sentence decision in the *Express Packages Cases* might have made all the difference—a sentence to the effect that common carriers really were *common* carriers, even for business brought to them by other carriers. State legislatures and public utility commissions had the next opportunity to set things on the right track; faced with unduly narrow interpretations from the courts, they, too, could have insisted that carriers really had to be carriers, for each other as well as for the general public. The federal government, first through the ICC and later the FCC, could have demanded the same, at least for interstate traffic. The market itself would have taken care of things, given time, for there was more profit to be made in interconnection and growth than in boycotts and stasis. Every opportunity was missed, however, and when government intervened, it did so not to promote market forces, but to outlaw them once and for all. Indeed, at almost every stage, the government systematically approved and upheld the boycotts, the exclusive dealing, and the inevitable attrition and fratricide that rapidly transformed telephony from an industry of flourishing competition to one of entrenched monopoly.

[70] *See* §8.4.1.
[71] The rule of thumb among many state regulators, it has been said, is the Pizza Test: the monthly fee for basic residential phone service must not under any circumstances be permitted to exceed the price of a pizza—medium size, with two ingredients.

Guessing at motives, especially a century later, is not a very useful exercise. But by all appearances, government authorities—in the courts, in the state agencies and legislatures, and in the federal government—were quite content to let the telephone industry slip from the unruliness of competition to the quiet order of monopoly. Perhaps government officials saw and welcomed what lay ahead. They would arrive at the scene of the great competitive battles late in the day. They would shoot the wounded, congratulate the victors, and then claim the new empire of monopoly as their own. It was an empire worth controlling. At its apogee, the Bell System had annual revenues of $58 billion, had total assets of $138 billion, and employed over 1 million people. No other company in the world was as large. Indeed, most other nations owned and produced little by comparison.

§1.3.5 Zoning Media

The government did not just maintain a Bell System monopoly within telephony. It also carefully maintained divisions between telephony and other media and among those other media themselves.[72] It was tidy arrangement, in which each medium of communication performed a particular function, pursuant to its own particularized set of regulations.

Certainly, considerations of engineering efficiency historically favored different architectures for different types of communications. The telephone network was optimized for point-to-point voice communications between individuals. Broadcasting infrastructure was designed for point-to-all transmissions. Cable plant began life as a "community antenna," distributing video from a local headend without two-way or switching capabilities. All of these architectures and capabilities originated in the day of analog technology and narrowband transmission. Only data networks, which arrived much later, were designed from the outset

---

[72] See FBL ch. 7.

around a digital, broadband model that supported both point-to-point and point-to-multipoint transmission.

These basic engineering differences made it easy for regulators to maintain different regulatory regimes for different media and the communications companies that operated them. Drawing legal distinctions between a "common carrier" "phone company" and a "broadcaster" was straightforward. Until the advent of digital computers and modems, there was too little in the way of "data communications" to merit much regulatory attention at all.

Thus, a company or network zoned as a carrier is required to convey the content of others; one zoned as a broadcaster must carry content of its own. The 1934 Communications Act defines telephony, the common carrier paradigm, as two-way intercommunicating voice service.[73] It defines broadcasting, by contrast, as one-way dissemination of radio communications.[74] With varying degrees of conviction, regulations promulgated under the 1934 Act have curtailed video on phone lines,[75] voice on cable,[76] and point-to-point messaging on broadcast media.[77] Phone companies have also been required to separate any enhanced services they may provide from basic carriage.[78] Similarly, carrier services offered on the subcarrier and VBI bands of broadcast spectrum are regulated separately from the broadcasting.[79]

Much zoning has traditionally occurred during licensing.[80] Section 214 of the 1934 Act requires phone companies to obtain

---

[73] *See* 47 U.S.C. §153(47). *See also* Domestic Public Radio Service, 76 F.C.C.2d 273, 281 ¶13 (1980).

[74] *See* 47 U.S.C. §153(6). *See also* 47 U.S.C. §525(5)(A) (defining cable services as "one-way transmission" of video or other like services).

[75] *See* §13.7.1; *FBL* §§7.4.4, 8.4.6.

[76] Local telephone companies have long held exclusive franchises for the provision of local telephone service. *See* §§3.2.1, 6.1.2.

[77] *See* Subscription Video, Report and Order, 2 F.C.C. Rec. 1001, 1003–1004 ¶¶23–28 (1986).

[78] *See* §12.7.

[79] *See* FM Licensees: Amendment of the Commission's Rules Concerning Use of Subsidiary Communications Authorizations, 48 Fed. Reg. 28,445, 28,446–28,448 (1983); §11.8.2.

[80] *See* §3.13.5.

advance FCC permission before constructing new interstate facilities.[81] Section 201 empowers the Commission to regulate devices connected to the telephone network and thus, in principle, to regulate every service offered over a telephone line by a phone company or anyone else.[82] The FCC has used this authority to restrict phone companies to providing basic voice services, and little else.[83] The FCC is likewise granted plenary authority over use of the radio waves and has used it over the years to prescribe in great detail how spectrum may be used.[84] Radio licenses are generally issued for a specific use, such as public broadcasting.[85] A licensee may not convert its spectrum to any other use without first obtaining FCC approval.[86]

For the most part, existing regulatory codes for telephone, cable, and broadcast treat "data" services as largely beneath or outside official attention.[87] "Enhanced services" have been excluded from the ambit of "basic," regulated telephony. They are exempt from access charges and almost completely free of most other forms of common carrier regulation.[88] Data services provided over mobile radio, cable, terrestrial broadcast, and DBS have been largely excused from most forms of rate, content, and carriage regulation. Data has long been the "incidental" service tagged onto something else older and more important. As such, data has been the fortunate beneficiary of regulatory accident, inattention, neglect, and indifference. Wires and radios

---

[81] *See* 47 U.S.C. §214(a).

[82] *See id.* §201.

[83] *See* §3.11.1.

[84] Under section 307(b), the Commission is simply required to oversee the distribution of broadcast "licenses, frequencies, hours of operation, and power among the several states and communities as to provide a fair, efficient and equitable distribution of radio service to each of the same." 47 U.S.C. §307(b).

[85] *See FBL* §§4.6.2–4.6.3.

[86] The Commission may revoke a station license for any reason that would have warranted refusing a license in the first place. 47 U.S.C. §312(a). Licenses may not be transferred without Commission approval. *Id.* §310(d). *See* §10.3.1.

[87] We discuss the regulation of data in detail in Chapter 11.

[88] *See* §12.6.2.

alike will all soon be digital, and bandwidth is increasing rapidly in every medium. "Data" traffic is growing far faster than analog voice or video. And on broadband, digital channels, "data" encompasses everything. But as we discuss below, a digital world transforms everything into "data." The data inmates are taking over the regulatory asylum.

§1.4   The Fall of Monopoly: Technology

The genius of capitalism, as Lenin might have pointed out, is that it develops its own rope, for hanging as much as for other purposes. Even in the shelter of its government-embraced monopoly, the monstrous Bell System remained a for-profit enterprise with some residual instinct to provide better, faster, and cheaper service. The company had been founded on technology, and technology would remain its strength. In time, Bell would establish the greatest peacetime research program the world has ever known, at Bell Laboratories in Murray Hill, New Jersey. The company set its scientists in pursuit of better telephones, better networks, and better switches. The pursuit would span radio, then broadband communications, and then telephone exchanges and would end finally where the industry had begun—with the telephone box, now called a computer.

§1.4.1   Broadband Communications

Since 1927, Bell had been barred from broadcast radio. But not all radio waves spread out like ripples on a pond; at sufficiently short wavelengths, radio waves can be made to move in straight lines, like beams of light and at the same speed. And these electromagnetic waves, especially at higher frequencies, have enormous capacity to carry information accurately over long distances. Realizing this, the broadcasters would push their way up the radio spectrum and by the 1950s would be transmitting the considerable volumes of information required for television. Telephone companies, especially Bell's long-distance arm, needed equally high-capacity—"broadband"—transmission systems, but systems that could operate over much larger distances, more securely, and more reliably.

Bell Labs researchers began to investigate wave-guide transmission in 1931. The idea was to use the high transmission capacities of high-frequency airwaves, but with signals confined in ducts to maintain quality and assure secure, point-to-point transmissions. By 1934, other researchers had developed a variation on the same idea—the coaxial cable, a copper sheath with a wire running down its center. "Coax," it turned out, could carry huge amounts of information with low attenuation. Within two years, Bell had installed its first coaxial cables in New York. Coax would eventually supply many of the high-capacity "trunks" of the telephone network until the end of World War II.

Meanwhile, research at Bell Labs was laying the foundation for another broadband alternative, microwave communications. Harold T. Friis and his colleagues developed the horn-reflector antenna, now a standard fixture on microwave towers. Unlike their longer-wavelength cousins listed on the dial of any car radio, microwaves—short-wavelength radio waves—travel in straight lines and can be accurately focused. Because of their comparatively high frequency, microwaves can also carry far more information; even early systems were designed to carry up to 1,000 voice circuits. Their final advantage for long-distance transmission, especially in rural areas, was also the most obvious: microwave towers could be placed 20 or 30 miles apart, and a single license from the FCC could substitute for the cumbersome process of obtaining rights-of-way over the entire span. By 1959, microwave systems comprised 25 percent of Bell's long-distance network.[89]

Coax and microwaves would transform more than the telephone industry.[90] John Walson, Sr., of Mahanoy City, Pennsylvania, recognized that coaxial cable was the perfect medium for

[89] See Vietor, AT&T and the Public Good: Regulation and Competition in Telecommunications, 1910–1987, in Future Competition in Telecommunications 27, 52 (S. Bradley & J. Hausman eds., 1989).

[90] See §§11.8, 13.1.

connecting homes in rural areas with poor television reception to a large, community, "master antenna." He began work on his first "community antenna television" system in 1948.[91] Others took up the idea. Antennas were placed on hilltops, on tall buildings, on masts. Distant signals were picked up and piped to viewers over coaxial cable. Before long, antenna operators began using microwave systems to beam in television signals to the master antennas from still farther afield. Hence the origins of cable television. By 1955, there were 400 such systems in operation, serving 150,000 subscribers.

Not long after, in 1963, a small start-up firm, Microwave Communications Inc. (MCI), underfunded and understaffed, would apply to the FCC to construct a microwave line between St. Louis and Chicago.[92] MCI told the FCC it would offer business customers "interplant and interoffice communications with unique and special characteristics";[93] in fact, what MCI had in mind was direct competition with Bell's long-distance operations.[94]

§1.4.2 The New Switch

MCI could consider offering private, dedicated, high-capacity connections to large business customers only because by the 1960s those customers had begun to acquire on their own premises the equipment that would make such connections useful. It had taken the telephone to create the original demand for a telephone network almost a century before. Now, a new generation of sophisticated electronic equipment in private hands—a new generation of "local exchanges," so to speak—was beginning to create demand for the kinds of competing long-distance services that MCI proposed to offer.

[91] See M. Hamburg, All About Cable §1.02, at 1–6 (rev. ed. 1985).
[92] See §9.3.2; P. Temin, The Fall of the Bell System: A Study in Pricing and Politics 47–54 (1987). See generally L. Kahaner, On the Line: The Men of MCI—Who Took On AT&T, Risked Everything, and Won! (1986).
[93] Quoted in Temin, The Fall of the Bell System at 50.
[94] For the FCC's (and the Bell System's) reaction to this competitive challenge, see §§9.3.5–9.4.3.1.

Appropriately enough, Bell Labs had once again been at the forefront in creating the new technology. The technology of telephone exchanges had languished for some years after the first electromechanical switches began to be used. It had not been until 1938 that the first "crossbar" central switching office was installed in Brooklyn. As late as 1951, operators were still being used to dial almost 40 percent of domestic long-distance calls.[95]

In 1936, Bell Labs' Director of Research had first discussed with physicist William Shockley the possibility of creating electronic telephone exchanges. Electronic switching, however, required a better amplifier than the vacuum tube technology pioneered by Lee DeForest. While each triode vacuum tube was capable of operating as a switch in a telephone exchange, an exchange needed thousands of such switches; tubes used too much power, and generated too much heat, to be packed together in the numbers required. Shockley and his Bell Labs colleagues Walter Brattain and John Bardeen set off in search of something better. They found it in 1947: the transistor. A Nobel Prize followed in 1956; in late 1963, Bell installed its first electronic switching system.[96]

The transistor, like the vacuum tube it displaced, was a switch, only much more compact and energy-efficient. Switches are the heart of a telephone exchange, for it is by opening and closing an appropriate set of switches that a single continuous line is created between Romeo in San Francisco and his Juliet in New York. Switches are also the heart of a computer: by shifting on and off like beads moving on an abacus, switches can keep track of numbers, and numbers can keep track of everything.

Before the advent of the transistor, both computers and telephone exchanges had required large, cumbersome, costly, custom-configured, labor-intensive centers. With the new electronics, much more powerful telephone switches and computers could be built into much more compact and reliable units—minicomputers and private branch exchanges (PBXs). Larger institutions—hospitals, universities, corporate headquarters, and so

[95] Brooks, Telephone: The First Hundred Years at 244.
[96] *Id.* at 279.

on—had once relied on a few centralized mainframes to do their computing and on Centrex services to handle their telephone requirements, even for internal telephone calls within a single office building. Now, these same functions could be—and rapidly were—located in stand-alone units on private premises. Competing manufacturers of PBXs and minicomputers proliferated. By the late 1970s, even Bell was systematically downgrading Centrex service and migrating its larger customers to PBXs.

This dispersion of electronic intelligence created a host of new centers, held in private hands, capable of communicating by wire and in need of the connections to support the same. As had happened almost a century earlier with the rise of the telephone itself, the new talking boxes created new demand. What was critically different about the new-generation local exchanges, whether PBXs or communicating computers, was that they were owned and controlled not by a small number of quasi-governmental, monopoly phone companies, but by a larger number of private, competitive institutions. For the most part, these private owners welcomed competitive bidding for their telecommunications needs. MCI, as we have seen, was one of the first to target the new demand.

At the same time, the transistor was also fulfilling its original mission, which was to transform the public telephone exchange: a new generation of electronic switches was deployed in the 1960s and 1970s. These switches were far more efficient, powerful, and flexible than the old switches they replaced. They could support levels of interconnection—and thus offer customers a variety of choices—that would have been prohibitively slow, complex, and unreliable in the days when switching was accomplished by human operators or electromechanical devices. As MCI built up its business in the 1970s, the company resolved to carry competition back up the network—to compete not just in connecting private computers and switches, but also in connecting the public exchanges operated by Bell and other public telephone companies. The capabilities of the new electronic switches made that aspiration quite realistic; as every telephone user knows today, such switches can be programmed with databases to route traffic automatically, Hatfields to Bell, McCoys to MCI, effortlessly and invisibly whenever either places a long-distance call.

§1.5 The Fall of Monopoly: Regulation

Shockley and his colleagues discovered the transistor in 1947, but neglected to inform lawyers in the antitrust division of the Department of Justice. Two years later those lawyers filed suit to break up the Bell System.[97] In 1956, Shockley, Brattain, and Bardeen traveled to Stockholm to collect their Nobel Prizes. The government's antitrust lawyers traveled less far that same year: to a district court in these scientists' home state of New Jersey, where on January 4 the government lawyers threw in the towel on their case. It mattered very little. The important antitrust work was being done by the monopolist itself, at Bell Labs. The first scent of competition was already in the air, discernible even in the torpid air of the nation's capital.

Although the basic premise of the Communications Act was that telephone service, both local and long distance, was a natural monopoly, the FCC's statutory mandate was broad enough to permit competition where the Commission, in its wisdom, thought competition might serve the public interest. When microwaves, satellites, and developments in customer premises equipment, computers, and radio communications began to make competition feasible in the 1950s and thereafter, the Commission came under intense pressure from would-be competitors to do just that. The FCC slowly warmed to the idea that competition might not be so bad after all.

For a period, it even moved out ahead of the courts. In 1951, for example, the Commission authorized a radiotelegraph company to open new circuits to Portugal and the Netherlands, in direct competition with another company that already provided

---

[97] See §4.4.3. This suit is discussed in greater detail in the first edition of this treatise, M. Kellogg, J. Thorne, & P. Huber, Federal Telecommunications Law §4.3 (1992) (hereinafter *FTL1*).

similar service.[98] Suddenly discovering a "national policy in favor of competition," the FCC authorized duplicate facilities; competition is in the public interest, the Commission declared, wherever it is "reasonably feasible." In a 1953 ruling, however, the Supreme Court could not discern the "national policy" on which the FCC had relied. The "encouragement of competition as such has not been considered the single or controlling reliance for safeguarding the public interest," the Court stated.[99] "To say that national policy without more suffices for authorization of a competing carrier wherever competition is reasonably feasible," the Court continued, "would authorize the Commission to abdicate what would seem to us one of the primary duties imposed on it by Congress."[100] The Commission would have to do a better job at articulating just how competition would serve the public interest.[101]

If authorizing competition had been the only thing required, a new national policy might have evolved with little protest. But the old national policy came with an old set of franchises, quarantines, and cross-subsidies that were fundamentally irreconcilable with competition. The government, as in an M. C. Escher drawing, soon found itself fighting an antimarket monstrosity that was largely of its own creation.

Under the paradigm of regulated monopoly, the FCC sought to promote universal service at a reasonable cost. Regulators accordingly set rates based on carriers' overall costs, making an attempt to align prices of individual services with their attendant costs. Long-distance rates were used to subsidize local rates. Business rates subsidized residential rates. Urban rates subsidized rural rates. So long as telephone service remained an end-to-end monopoly, gaps between price and cost did not really matter.

When competition arrived in some segments of the industry, so, too, did the significant problem of "cream skimming." New

---

[98] MacKay Radio and Tel. Co., 15 F.C.C. 690 (1951) (*Three Circuits*), rev'd, RCA Communications, Inc. v. FCC, 201 F.2d 694 (D.C. Cir. 1952), *vacated and remanded*, FCC v. RCA, 346 U.S. 86 (1953).

[99] FCC v. RCA, 346 U.S. at 93.

[100] *Id.* at 95.

[101] *Id.* at 93.

competitors would naturally target low-cost, high-price services, such as high-density routes between major cities. If the Bell System lowered its long-distance prices in response, other subsidies would have to be eliminated, over the vehement protest of state regulators and those receiving the subsidies. If the Bell System did not lower its prices, it would lose the business, and with it the subsidy, too. At the same time, regulators felt compelled to protect fledgling competitors from the potentially overwhelming might of the Bell System, out of the fear that the company that could arbitrarily set price above cost could also arbitrarily set it below, and so ruin the competition.

Schooled in the ethic of end-to-end service, the Bell System made it quite plain from the outset that it viewed competition as a direct threat to the higher objective of seamless, universal public service. And Bell had at its disposal a potentially decisive weapon to use against that competition: its control over the local exchange. The local exchange would in fact prove to be the most durable component of the old monopoly—either because (as some maintain) local exchange service is a "natural" monopoly or because (as others have suggested) monopoly is most fiercely protected here by reactionary state regulators. In any event, competitors in all segments of the telephone industry depended on access to (or interconnection with) the local exchange to reach their customers.

In managing a transition to competition, a large part of the FCC's responsibility was thus to ensure that the Bell System did not refuse competitors fair access to the local exchange or shift costs from competitive ventures to local exchange operations.[102] The twin dangers of discrimination and cross-subsidization occupied the attention of the FCC for decades before the Justice Department and the courts—dissatisfied with the FCC's efforts—engineered the Bell System's dismemberment. The Commission's alleged failure to deal adequately with the coexistence of monopoly and competitive markets served as a major impetus in the breakup.

---

[102] See §2.3.

Nonetheless, the Commission's record had been (and would be) better than generally acknowledged. Indeed, most of the transition to a competitive marketplace—complete with safeguards to protect that competition from any bottleneck abuses—was in place prior to divestiture. The Commission's efforts were sometimes clumsy, and often too slow. But by and large, things were moving in the right direction when the Department, spurred on by MCI, filed the suit that altered the face of the industry forever.

The FCC's reforms were directed at four different markets. With customer premises equipment and long-distance service, previously monopolistic markets were opened to competition. Protected franchises were eroded, quarantines were lifted, and rate-of-return regulation was replaced by price caps and even by prices set by competitive forces. With enhanced and wireless services, brand new markets were opened to competition from the beginning. Rules governing interconnection were changed in parallel: telephone companies were required to provide service to all comers, including competing carriers. Across the board, exclusive franchise gradually gave way to open competition.

§1.5.1 Customer Premises Equipment (CPE)

The Bell System had long sought to provide "end-to-end" service to its customers. This included not only the wires and switches that made up the phone network, but also the CPE that customers wanted to connect to the network. Bell tariffs forbade all "foreign attachments"—meaning equipment not provided by Bell itself.

Regulators endorsed this practice for almost 70 years.[103] It was not until the 1970s that the foreign attachment provisions were finally and decisively eliminated and standard CPE interfaces with the network were established. The landmark decision came

---

[103] For a discussion of the FCC's evolving CPE policies, see §8.4.

in 1968, in *Carterfone*.[104] At issue was a device permitting direct communication between a wireless radio and the landline network. The Bell System objected to the device, but failed to demonstrate that it would harm the network in any way. The Commission held that any form of CPE could be attached to the network "so long as the interconnection does not adversely affect the telephone company's operations or the telephone system's utility for others."[105]

With this ruling, the Commission seemingly opened the way for a complete line of competitive products that would interconnect with the network on customer premises. Yet almost immediately, the Commission began to waver.[106] And the Bell System, in filing replacement tariffs, narrowly construed the Commission's directive and tried to interpose expensive "protective connecting arrangements" (PCAs) between non-Bell CPE and the network. By 1975, however, the Commission had screwed up its courage to throw out PCAs and replace them with its own much simpler standards.[107] Finally, in 1980, CPE sales by Bell and other carriers were "detariffed" so that carriers themselves would be free to compete on equal terms in the open market.[108] The provision of CPE, the Commission held, was simply no longer a part of "communications common carriage." Even now, the Commission hesitated again: Bell (and later the divested Regional Companies) would be permitted to provide CPE only through separate subsidiaries—the quarantine still held sway. That last wall would fall, however, in 1985.[109]

---

[104] *See* §8.4.1.2.

[105] Use of the Carterfone Device in Message Toll Telephone Service, Decision, 13 F.C.C.2d 420, 424, *recons. denied,* 14 F.C.C.2d 571 (1968) (hereinafter *Carterfone*).

[106] On reconsideration, for example, it insisted that it was not "open[ing] the door to customer ownership of telephone handsets." *Carterfone,* 14 F.C.C.2d at 572.

[107] *See* §8.4.1.2.

[108] *See* §8.6.1.

[109] *See* §8.3.

§1.5.2 Enhanced Services

From a technological perspective, the issues raised by enhanced services were identical to those in the CPE proceedings.[110] Online information services, after all, are provided by telephone-compatible equipment located on some telephone customer's premises. But from a market perspective, CPE and enhanced services started worlds apart. Online electronic information services evolved only after the winds of competition had begun to blow. The FCC accordingly chose not to regulate the new services at all—except as they might be provided by telephone companies. In the spirit of the old quarantine, the Commission resolved that "enhanced services" would not under any circumstances become entangled with plain old telephone service.[111]

The definitional problems soon became overwhelming. A first set of lines was drawn among pure "data processing," "hybrid data processing," "hybrid communications," and pure "communications." A few years later the Commission tried a simpler pair of definitions—"basic" and "enhanced" services—the former to be regulated strictly, the latter to be deregulated and quarantined from "basic" telephony.[112] Then for a while the Commission flirted with three categories: "basic services," "services ancillary to communications," and "non-communications services." All of this definitional hot air was needed, it was thought, to contain a single company—Bell. The divisions survived divestiture, but only by a few years. It became increasingly apparent to the Commission that in a post-divestiture world the costs of structural separation outweighed any conceivable benefits. In 1986, the FCC finally decided to end structural separation for the enhanced services of AT&T and the divested Bell companies.

---

[110] For a discussion of computer-based enhanced services, see Chapter 12.
[111] *See* §12.3.
[112] *See* §12.4.

§1.5.3   Long Distance

In the 1940s, long-distance service was provided exclusively over wires, and the same basic economics that seemed to preclude competition in local service applied equally to long-distance service.[113] The development of microwave and satellite technologies radically changed that picture, making competition both practical and inevitable. Competition was spurred, in addition, by the Bell System's policy of nationwide price-averaging and the heavy subsidies from long-distance to local service.

Initially, the pressure for competition came from large businesses, which sought to build microwave links solely to satisfy their own private communications needs. As time wore on, however, various "specialized" common carriers sought to provide service on traffic-intensive routes to smaller businesses that could not afford their own private facilities. Eventually, these specialized common carriers sought and gained permission to serve the public at large, though this still meant, largely, the urban public. Only the Bell System had the obligation of universal service.

The first few, faltering steps in the direction of a competitive marketplace were taken by the Commission in 1959, when the Commission allowed private users to construct point-to-point microwave facilities.[114] A decade later a deeply divided Commission granted MCI's long-pending application to provide private microwave service for businesses as a "specialized common carrier" and then extended its decision to others by establishing general conditions for entry. The Commission also forbade any tariff restrictions on the resale and sharing of long-distance private line services and sought to regulate the terms, conditions, and charges for the interconnection of the private lines of the specialized common carriers with the local distribution facilities of existing common carriers. With a strong shove from the D.C. Circuit Court of Appeals, the Commission eventually opened a

---

[113] For a discussion of the FCC's evolving long-distance policies, see §§9.2.–9.5.
[114] See §9.3.2.

new rulemaking proceeding and in 1980 formally adopted an open-entry policy for all interstate services.[115]

Thwarted in its efforts to prevent competition through regulation, however, the Bell System tried to make competition unprofitable by dramatic price reductions on competitive routes. The system of nationwide price-averaging—and the subsidies embedded in that system in an effort to promote universal service—was the first casualty of competition.[116] Few disputed the Bell System's right to bring prices in line with costs to meet competition. But many disputed whether the new tariffs reflected costs or a below-cost attempt to drive out competition. Charges of cross-subsidization and cream-skimming were freely traded. The specialized common carriers (using a fully distributed costing methodology) accused the Bell System of below-cost, predatory pricing and sought to have its tariffs declared unlawful. The Bell System (using a marginal cost method) claimed its tariffs were cost-based and justified by competition. The Commission was unable to tell the difference and sank into a state of almost complete paralysis. These disputes lasted for decades and contributed to the sense that the Bell System was simply too large and too unwieldy for the Commission adequately to regulate.[117] That in turn helped spur the Justice Department's calls for breaking up the Bell System.[118]

§1.5.4 Wireless Services

To create interconnection rules for CPE and long-distance competitors, the FCC had to dismantle decades-old practices based on Bell's hegemony. With enhanced services, the Commission began at the other extreme, with a policy of complete telco exclusion. Only with wireless services did it get things right from the start.[119]

[115] See §9.4.2.
[116] See §§2.5, 6.1.1.2.
[117] See §2.2.
[118] See *FTL1* §4.4.
[119] For a discussion of the FCC's wireless policies, see §10.8.1.

What it did, from the start, was to embrace competition—but reject quarantine. Wires are dedicated facilities that (in the last mile, at least) may lie idle most of the time; radio spectrum, by contrast, is a shared resource. Thus, the economics of providing wireless services—and the costs of embedded plant—are completely different from those for landline local exchange service.[120] Whether or not the local landline exchange is characterized by the steadily declining average cost of a natural monopoly, the Commission recognized that the market for wireless services plainly is not.

Thus, when it first allocated frequencies for "land mobile services" in 1949, the FCC granted separate blocks to telephone companies and to "miscellaneous" or "limited" common carriers.[121] The Commission consistently maintained that procompetitive policy thereafter. In the paging market, the FCC likewise licensed sufficient frequency to permit multiple providers in every service area. And it continued to encourage competition by allocating additional channels as needed and by allowing radio broadcasters to use FM subcarrier frequencies for paging. When it began to issue cellular telephone licenses in the early 1980s, the FCC allocated two licenses for every service area, prohibited any licensee from owning a significant interest in both licenses, and thereafter encouraged the development of other radio technologies capable of providing directly competitive services. The Commission complemented its procompetitive licensing policies with active industry oversight. Most important, it required all landline telephone companies to provide unaffiliated wireless concerns with interconnection equal in type, quality, and price to that enjoyed by affiliates.[122] Both competition and service have flourished under these arrangements.

[120] *See* G. Calhoun, *Digital Cellular Radio* 68–86 (1988).
[121] General Mobile Radio Serv. Allocation of Frequencies Between 25 & 30 Megacycles, Report and Order, 13 F.C.C. 1190, 1228 (1949).
[122] *See* §§5.3.1, 10.5.1.

§1.6 The Fall of Monopoly: Antitrust

By the early 1980s, with some prodding from the courts, the FCC was thus moving firmly toward competition in CPE, enhanced services, long distance, and wireless. The Commission could not easily dismantle Bell's corporate structure, but it could unpack the network itself. It could require Bell to interconnect with other long-distance carriers, wireless carriers, paging companies, information service providers, and, in time, other local exchange carriers, too. Equal access principles were evolving incrementally, product by product, service by service. The pace of change was too slow to satisfy newcomers, who were often still thwarted in their attempt to interconnect. But it also seemed too quick for Bell and state regulators, who saw traditional franchises and subsidies evaporating under the radiant heat of competition. Matters went to court. And the courts . . . the courts at one time or another, in one place or another, sided with every side on every issue.[123]

§1.6.1 Customer Premises Equipment

The first private antitrust case involving CPE was decided summarily in favor of Bell in 1940.[124] An inventor had obtained a patent on an automatic dialer, which allowed "certain preselected call stations [to] be signaled by a single manipulation, pressing a button."[125] The inventor was out of luck. Subsequent CPE cases ended in much the same way.[126] *Carterfone* itself began as an antitrust suit; a federal district court ruled that the FCC had primary jurisdiction, and the Fifth Circuit affirmed in 1966, in an opinion replete with language strikingly deferential

---

[123] *See* Chapter 4.

[124] Pastor v. AT&T, 76 F. Supp. 781 (S.D.N.Y. 1940).

[125] *Id.* at 782. An amusing irony is that had Bell permitted that technology to advance, both MCI and the federal government would have had much less to complain about three decades later, when both made the absence of "1+ dialing" the centerpiece of their attacks on the Bell System.

[126] *See* §8.4.1.2.

to the FCC.[127] For the next decade or so, Bell and other telephone companies continued to win easy dismissals of foreign attachment antitrust cases.

The FCC's decisive shift in favor of CPE competition in 1975, however, changed the atmospherics completely. An avalanche of antitrust suits followed, attacking Bell PCA tariffs as a sham designed to delay the advent of competition.[128] Cases that only a few years earlier would have been decided summarily by reference to extant tariffs were now litigated. A 1979 ruling of the Third Circuit reversed a trial judge's dismissal of a suit by a distributor of an answering device called the Code-a-Phone.[129] A small Connecticut terminal equipment vendor won $16.5 million on various charges of discriminatory interconnection and Bell's abuse of its "utility function."[130] Another case in the same circuit involved a five-month trial directly attacking Bell's PCA tariffs; a jury awarded Litton $276.8 million.[131]

Predictably, that verdict triggered a raft of me-too suits, with many plaintiffs hoping to invoke offensive collateral estoppel. But the easy victories did not materialize. The D.C. Circuit declined to apply offensive collateral estoppel in a 1984 ruling. Most other courts reached similar decisions. Ironically, the last PCA case reembraced the logic of the early cases and vindicated Bell completely.[132]

§1.6.2 Enhanced Services

None of the antitrust suits against the Bell System in the 1960s and 1970s focused on Bell provision of information services.

---

[127] See Carter v. AT&T, 365 F.2d 486, 492 (5th Cir. 1966).

[128] See §8.4.2.

[129] See Essential Communications v. AT&T, 610 F.2d 1114 (3d Cir. 1979).

[130] Northeastern Tel. Co. v. AT&T, 651 F.2d 76 (2d Cir. 1981), *cert. denied,* 455 U.S. 943 (1982). The Second Circuit reversed all but one aspect of the verdict, and the case was subsequently settled.

[131] See Litton Sys., Inc. v. AT&T, 700 F.2d 785 (2d Cir. 1983), *cert. denied,* 464 U.S. 1073 (1984). This verdict was affirmed.

[132] See Phonetele, Inc. v. AT&T, 889 F.2d 224 (9th Cir. 1989), *cert. denied,* 60 U.S.L.W. 3599 (Mar. 3, 1992).

Indeed, most of the antitrust litigation relating to information services has occurred outside the telephone industry and has focused on the content—software, news wire services, movies, airline reservation systems, and so on—rather than the conduit.[133]

§1.6.3 Long Distance

The private antitrust suits attacking Bell's dominance of the long-distance market matured in the 1970s, smack in the middle of the turnaround in policy under the joint (if often uncoordinated) impetus of the FCC and the D.C. Circuit Court of Appeals.[134] Three of these cases supply a record of a judiciary at war with itself—mirroring, in other words, the schizophrenic policies emanating at that time from the FCC.

In March 1974, MCI sued Bell for monopolizing long-distance communications.[135] Six years later a Chicago jury awarded MCI $600 million, trebled to $1.8 billion. On appeal, the Seventh Circuit accepted some aspects of the verdict, but rejected others. Bell ultimately paid some $113 million. A second private suit was filed in 1980 by an independent telephone company that had sought to provide local telephone service in a new real estate development.[136] Bell had refused interconnection with its long-distance facilities and refused to assign the company a block of telephone numbers. A federal district court awarded $55 million in treble damages; however, the Fifth Circuit reversed on an error in jury instructions.[137]

Sprint (at that time Southern Pacific Communications) was the really unlucky one. It filed suit in 1978. After a 33-day bench trial, federal Judge Richey accepted Bell's defense chapter and

---

[133] See *FTL1* §3.8.
[134] See §4.3.
[135] See MCI v. AT&T, 708 F.2d 1081 (7th Cir.), *cert. denied,* 464 U.S. 891 (1983).
[136] See Mid-Texas Communications Sys., Inc. v. AT&T, 615 F.2d 1372 (5th Cir.), *cert. denied,* 449 U.S. 912 (1980).
[137] See *id.* at 1391.

verse. The D.C. Circuit Court of Appeals affirmed.[138] The most interesting part of this last case, however, is the one least remembered. The case had originally been assigned not to Judge Richey, but to Judge Joseph C. Waddy. Judge Waddy had also been assigned the federal government's 1974 case against Bell. Judge Waddy, however, died in 1978. Sprint's case was reassigned to Judge Richey; the federal government's was reassigned to Judge Harold Greene. Had the docket assignments been reversed, the Bell System would still be intact today.

§1.7   The Fall of Monopoly: The Bell System Divestiture

Judge Greene quickly took control of the case he had inherited.[139] The action was ultimately settled, so he never had a direct opportunity to rule on whether Bell had violated the antitrust laws. In ruling on Bell's motion to dismiss at the close of the government's case in chief, however, he telegraphed where he was headed. The gargantuan Bell System was too large; something had to be done. Bell, a company with some understanding of telegraphs, took the hint and soon thereafter acceded to the government's terms.

The essence of the settlement was that telephony could be split into two pieces. The larger of the two—the local exchange—was deemed to be a necessary and desirable monopoly that might quite properly be granted an exclusive franchise, but that should be regulated and quarantined in return. The smaller, comprising long-distance service and equipment markets, were thought to be competitive—at least potentially, though not yet in actuality. This piece should not be regulated, should not be

---

[138] See Southern Pacific Communications Co. v. AT&T, 556 F. Supp. 825 (D.D.C. 1983), aff'd, 740 F.2d 980 (D.C. Cir. 1984), cert. denied, 470 U.S. 1005 (1985).

[139] The circumstances leading up to the entry of the decree, and the decree itself, are discussed in greater detail in FTL1 §4.5.

quarantined, and should not escape competition by way of any exclusive franchise or any equivalently cozy relationship with the divested local franchisees. Competitors dependent on the monopoly services should therefore enjoy "equal access" to Bell local exchanges.[140]

The proposal was thus, at one and the same time, enormously liberating for the one-third of Bell that would become AT&T and more confining than anything that had come before for the two-thirds of Bell that would become the seven Regional Bell Operating Companies (or RBOCs or BOCs, as they came to be known). The seven RBOCs would be forbidden, with minor exceptions, to provide any service other than local exchange service. In particular, they would be forbidden to provide long-distance service or "information services" or to manufacture telecommunications equipment and CPE.[141] It was all based on a tidy economic model—tidier on paper than in reality. And tidier before Judge Greene addressed it than it would become thereafter.

The proposed settlement was duly presented to Judge Greene. He immediately took charge of the settlement process and revised the terms of the decree. Almost single-handedly, Judge Greene crafted an intricate common law of decree jurisprudence. His courtroom became a shadow FCC, an independent authority that scrutinized, cajoled, modified, hectored, and enforced indefatigably, in pursuit of Judge Greene's own understanding of where antitrust law intersected with the public interest, convenience, and necessity.[142]

Our first edition dealt with these battles at considerable length. This edition still cites many of them for two reasons. First, it is not possible fully to understand the changes wrought by the 1996 Act without understanding the 12 years of decree jurisprudence that preceded it. Second, the Act itself adopts,

---

[140] *See FTL1* ch. 5.
[141] *See FTL1* ch. 6.
[142] *See FTL1* ch. 7.

expressly and wholesale, very significant segments of decree jurisprudence.

We must also take note of the divestiture that wasn't. Certainly, no account of the antitrust epic that reshaped telephony in the 1980s would be quite complete without mention of the other great battle between the federal government and private enterprise, fought in parallel during the same years. In 1969, government lawyers begin contemplating the future of the computer business. The future, to them, is plain enough: an IBM monopoly as far as the eye can see. What is to be done?

Release Bell to provide competition? Certainly not. To be sure, half or so of all federal and state regulators embrace the Bell monopoly and work vigorously to protect it. The other half, however, wish to punish Bell for the sin of monopoly and, short of that, to make sure that it does not fall prey to the sin of gluttony. Bell, in other words, is to be utterly excluded from any role in the computer industry. Almost no one in government recalls that it was Bell's research labs—not IBM's—that discovered the transistor, the key to all modern computers.

So instead of letting another established firm compete against IBM, the government resolves to have IBM compete against itself—the objective: break up IBM; the means: a mammoth antitrust suit. In the following 13 years of litigation, this will prove to be one of the slowest and most expensive, paper-clogged, and useless antitrust lawsuits ever undertaken; it comes to be known as the Antitrust Division's "Vietnam." The suit is ultimately abandoned on the same day that the Bell divestiture is announced.

In the interim, three engineers will found a new company that will do the job the litigators never complete. The engineers plan to manufacture an altogether novel device called a microprocessor. They will take a familiar device, the transistor, and make it smaller—a hundred million times smaller, in fact, and still growing smaller year by year. The power of the microprocessor grows apace. It is a power destined to shatter not only the computer monopoly, but the telephone monopoly, too, and thus to make nonsense of much of the FCC and decree jurisprudence that has come before. The new microprocessor company is called Intel.

§1.8 The Fall of Monopoly: Fragmentation and Convergence

The Intels of the world were underestimated by regulators and antitrust authorities time and time again from the 1960s until the 1980s. This is somewhat surprising. After all, the regulatory convulsions of the 1960s and 1970s, which culminated in the Bell divestiture of 1984, all flowed directly from discoveries at Bell Labs, most notably the discovery of the transistor in 1947.

The first-generation computers in 1956 were monstrous devices built around huge racks of vacuum tubes. But the new transistor soon came to the notice of Jack Kilby, an engineer who had been designing compact systems for hearing-aid companies. In 1958, Kilby moved to the Dallas headquarters of Texas Instruments and had a brainstorm. By then, transistors were already being made on silicon. Why not make resistors and capacitors, too, on the same medium, and thus manufacture entire circuits all at once, in one process, on one substrate?[143] Why not, in other words, manufacture an "integrated circuit"? Robert Noyce, another alumnus of Bell Labs then working at Fairchild Semiconductor, soon radically improved on Kilby's design. In 1968, Noyce and a colleague set up their own new company— Intel. And Intel would eventually become master of the microprocessor, the computer on chip, that would transform all of telephony, computing, and broadcast.

The integrated circuit continued the transistor's restructuring of telephony, but accelerated the pace of change a thousandfold. Transistors were shrunk from the size of a fingernail to the size of a hair, to the size of a microbe and smaller. The economics of producing electronic equipment shifted dramatically. Designing a single advanced microprocessor may require a billion-dollar investment. Thereafter, any number of copies can be stamped out at very little cost. The technology thus triggered an efflorescence of new desktop and office systems, as well as consumer

---

[143] *See* T. R. Reid, The Chip: How Two Americans Invented the Microchip and Launched a Revolution 133 (1984).

electronics. All depended on the same fundamental component—the transistor. All operated digitally. All could be mass-
produced at little cost once the electronics for the first unit had
been designed.

The result has been a radical technological transformation,
characterized by two seemingly contradictory trends: *fragmentation* and *convergence*.

The first major technological trend today continues to be one
of fragmentation. The once centralized network is becoming
decentralized. "Terminals"—dumb end points to the network—
are giving way to "seminals"—nodes that can process, switch,
store, and retrieve information with a power that was once
lodged exclusively in a few fortified centers, massive switches, and
mainframe computers. This is the fragmentation.

The second transcendent reality is convergence. Wires and
wireless media, for example, remained separate for most of the
first century of telecommunications. But it is clear today that
wire and wireless define the two halves of a boundless telecosm.
From a physicist's perspective, they are not very different. Radio
waves come in an infinite range of frequencies. AM radio is low
on the dial. Ruby-red laser light is high. Fiber-optic transmission
is just radio on speed: the oscillating crystal of an old-fashioned
radio is replaced by an oscillating cavity of gas called a laser. The
only real difference between wireless and wire is the "wave
guide"—the wire itself. An ordinary radio transmitter shines
outward in all directions—it "broadcasts." An electronic or photonic transmitter points its signal into a shielded tunnel of metal
or glass—it "drills."

The tunnel solves the problem of interference. Any number of
"radios" can transmit side by side on wires; when one strand is
filled, another can be unrolled next to it. The wire also excludes
dust and rain, so the signal is more dependable. A wire can turn
corners, dodge buildings, or track the curvature of the earth.
And a wire can be more private. The National Security Agency
much prefers glass to air.

Does wire, and particularly glass, therefore have a decisive
edge over wireless? Not always. Wireless is often more efficient
for one-to-many communication and is essential for mobility. It

is less private—but the whole point of "broadcast" is to reach lots of people. Overall, wired networks offer more capacity and privacy, but are most efficient only for stationary, "narrowcast" connections.

One vivid illustration of this convergence is cellular telephony, made possible by the synthesis of radio, telephone, and computers. The key problem with the early radio telephones, which persisted until the 1980s, was that there just didn't seem to be enough spectrum available to allow simultaneous use of very many of them. A few dozen stations pretty much fill up the dial of a radio—and radio telephone requires radio stations in pairs to sustain two-way conversation.

In the 1940s, researchers at Bell Labs proposed an ingenious solution. Radio telephones should be low-power, short-range devices. The same frequencies could then be used again and again (just as they are with cordless home telephones); a radio conversation on East 42d Street would not interfere with another one on the same frequency on West 51st. A city would be divided into many separate "cells," each one served by its own low-power transmitter. The capacity of a cellular system could then be increased almost indefinitely by shrinking cells and increasing their number. But cellular telephony required, in exchange, highly sophisticated transmitters and receivers and massive coordination among cells to "hand off" calls and coordinate frequencies as the car phone on 42d Street moved toward 51st. No one had the technology to perform this—until the advent of microelectronics.

After the FCC finally approved commercial cellular telephone systems in 1982, the market grew explosively. The new exchanges —"mobile telephone switching offices"—secured the right to interconnect with the established landline exchanges.[144] By 1990, entrepreneurs and regulators were considering a second generation of over-the-air telephone systems—"personal communications services" (PCS)—based on "microcells," with base stations linked to either private or public exchanges.[145] Each new

[144] *See* §§5.3.1, 10.5.
[145] *See* §10.4.3.

cluster of exchanges that appeared on the scene opened up new possibilities for service from competing networks. Cellular companies have quickly recognized the advantages of "clustered" service and have established dedicated links between their own exchanges and those of the long-distance carriers. PCS operators have turned to cable companies to provide transport among the transceivers that will be used to support their service.

A less visible, but equally revolutionary merger of radio and telephone technologies has occurred below ground, during almost exactly the same years as cellular systems were being deployed above. This, too, evolved directly from technological developments set in motion at Bell Labs several decades earlier.

The development of coaxial cable and microwave transmission marked major advances in the continuing quest for ever more capacious, reliable, secure transmission systems. For telephonic purposes, microwaves represented an important advance over ordinary radio because they operated at much higher frequencies, capable of carrying much more information over focused paths. Push the frequencies higher still, and you get ultrahigh-frequency radio waves, better known as light. A light beam can be shaped and modulated to carry information just like Marconi's radio waves, but in vastly larger amounts. Light is best transmitted in a wave guide, similar (in principle) to those developed by Bell Labs in the 1930s. Extremely pure, hair-thin strands of glass serve admirably.

Fiber-optic systems represent today's pinnacle of telecommunications technology, the finest merger (so far) of radio, telephone lines, and electronics. Integrated circuits provide the highly sophisticated transmitters and receivers at each end of the line. A single strand of glass can today transmit thousands of simultaneous telephone conversations[146] or hundreds of color television signals. With such capacities, demand for fiber has come primarily from the higher levels of the network, where

---

[146] Although the present capacity is 24,000 simultaneous conversations, "[e]xperts suggest a theoretical carrying capacity of about 600 million [simultaneous] conversations." M. Yates, The Promise of Fiber Optics, Pub. Util. Fort., Aug. 15, 1990, at 14.

traffic from many callers is consolidated into interexchange trunks. Fiber is now rapidly replacing copper, coaxial cable, and microwave everywhere in the telephone network except (so far) in the short last stretch to the user's home.

Wireline telephony, wireless telephony, broadcast television, and cable television now share a single, integrated future—a future of one (or more) switched, digital, broadband networks, networks that combine the broadband carrying capacity of cable television, the digital power and flexibility of computers, and the switched addressability of telephones. In digital systems, a bit is a bit, whether it represents a hiccup in a voice conversation, or the price at which AT&T stock is selling at this particular instant, or a strand of hair in a rerun of *I Love Lucy*. The lines among media formerly segregated by mode of transmission (radio versus landline) and function (telephone, cable, broadcast, computer) are disappearing. We are moving toward a myriad of mixed media (radio/landline), integrated (digital), broadband networks, all interconnecting seamlessly to one another.[147]

We are not there yet. Despite the torrents of electronic information cascading into our offices and homes, the telecosm is still young and, in critical respects, unformed.

Along one dimension, television is broad and telephone narrow. Broadcast television delivers high bandwidth—it transmits an enormous amount of data very fast. Telephone lines are a thousand times narrower. Along a second dimension, however, telephone is broad and television narrow. There are about 150 million telephone lines in the country, but only about 1,500 TV broadcast stations. From this perspective, television is a hundred thousand times narrower than the telephone network. Television

---

[147] Ithiel de Sola Pool anticipated this trend as early as 1983, in his landmark Technologies of Freedom. "For the first three-quarters of the twentieth century the major means of communications were neatly partitioned from each other, both by technology and by use," Pool wrote. "Now the picture is changing. Many of the neat separations between different media no longer hold. . . . The explanation for the current convergence between historically separated modes of communication lies in the habitability of digital electronics." de Sola Poole, Technologies of Freedom at 26–27.

is a one-way technology, connecting the few to the many. Telephone gives everyone both a transmitter and a receiver.

The missing parts of the network create a remarkable financial paradox. The narrow connections, which are consumed too sparingly, are far more lucrative than the broadband ones, which are consumed in profligate excess. In round numbers, the Super Bowl attracts 100 million viewers and $100 million in sponsors' cash. The game lasts four hours. That's about 25 cents per viewer-hour. While sports enthusiast Jane Doe watches the big game, John prefers to chat with his college roommate on the phone. The connection is still very narrow. Yet for entertainment that good, John is willing to pay about $12 an hour to his long-distance phone company.

Multiply these numbers across 150 million households and offices, and you arrive at a comparatively small TV entertainment industry and a much larger telephone industry. Providing a broadband signal—sound and full-motion color video—and occupying the average American many hours every day, broadcast and cable combined generate revenues of $80 billion a year. Though each telephone line is used only about 25 minutes a day, local telephony alone generates about $120 billion a year. Long-distance calling generates another $100 billion. In total, then, telephony generates nearly three times the revenues of video.

Broadcast delivers a great deal, but the network behind it is steeply hierarchical. Telephone is narrow, but egalitarian. That simple difference accounts for the two-way telephone's two-for-one revenue edge over one-way television. If we have to choose, thin, two-way connectivity is worth far more than a fat, but one-way channel. But we don't have to choose anymore. Modern digital transmission technology offers both.

It will surely come; the only question is how quickly. The technology to supply almost limitless bandwidth is now at hand. Broadband networks already occupy the top tiers of the telephone network, operated by regional and national telephone companies, and the top tiers of the broadcast networks, operated by video carriers. Only the last mile remains to be conquered. And Congress itself undertook that task with the Telecommunications Act of 1996.

§1.9   The End of Monopoly: The 1996 Telecommunications Act

As noted, the AT&T consent decree assumed that the local exchange was a natural monopoly and therefore left that monopoly intact. Many state regulators, however, concluded otherwise and began to embrace local competition. By 1996, Congress was ready to finish the job. In February of that year, Congress passed, and President Clinton signed into law, a sweeping reform of U.S. telecommunications regulation. For better or worse, the Telecommunications Act of 1996 will likely be remembered as the most important piece of economic legislation of the twentieth century. It runs some 100 pages of impenetrably dense and convoluted prose. Its overarching objective is to transition the entire industry from regulated monopoly to unregulated competition. Completing the process will take a decade or more, but the transition is already well under way.[148]

The 1996 Act broadly preempts most state laws to the extent that those laws explicitly bar competitive entry.[149] It specifically affirms the right of cable operators to compete head to head against local telephone companies.[150] The legal path has been cleared to allow electric utilities and gas companies to build communications networks, too.[151]

But the 1996 Act does not stop there, by clearing away the obstacles to new entry. It also requires incumbent carriers affirmatively to assist the new entrants in three distinct ways. First, the 1996 Act allows a competitor to construct its own network and "interconnect" with the incumbent telephone company "for the transmission and routing" of traffic between the two net-

---

[148] *See generally* J. Kearney & T. Merrill, The Great Transformation of Regulated Industries Law, 98 Colum. L. Rev. 1323 (Oct. 1998).

[149] 47 U.S.C. §253(d); *see* §3.8.

[150] Telecommunications Act of 1996 §302(b)(1) (repealing 47 U.S.C. §533(b)). *See* §13.7.2.6; *see also FTL1* §14.8 (and 1995 Supp.); *FBL* §7.4.4.

[151] The 1996 Act authorizes the Commission to permit registered holding companies to offer telecommunications services through a separate, single-purpose telecommunications subsidiary. *See* Telecommunications Act of 1996 §402(b)(2)(A) (to be codified at 15 U.S.C. §§79 et seq., amending Public Utilities Holding Company Act §34(a)(1)).

works.[152] Such interconnection is crucial to competitive entry because it allows customers on the new network to place calls to, and to receive calls from, customers on the incumbent's network.

Second, Congress required incumbent telcos to offer competitors "access to network elements on an unbundled basis at any technically feasible point" and "in a manner that allows requesting carriers to combine such elements."[153] Congress added this provision because it recognized that some key parts of the incumbents' network would be difficult to reproduce immediately. For instance, Congress understood that cable television companies planned to use their existing door-to-door networks to carry telephone calls as well as TV signals, but lacked the switches needed to direct calls from one customer to another. Conversely, some interexchange companies might have the necessary switches, but lack the loops to the customers' premises. By requiring access to parts of the incumbents' network, Congress allowed such companies to enter local markets as facilities-based carriers without reproducing the incumbent's complete network.

Third, the 1996 Act requires incumbent local exchange carriers (LECs) "to offer for resale at wholesale rates any telecommunication service that the carrier provides at retail to subscribers who are not telecommunications carriers."[154] Resale permits entry by potential competitors who have no facilities of their own.

The flip side of these obligations placed on incumbent LECs is supposed to be a new freedom to compete. The two remaining pillars of traditional regulation—the quarantine and end-to-end price regulation—are not long for this world. The 1996 Act sets in place an express mechanism for eliminating the long-distance restrictions on BOCs. A number of those restrictions— on wireless and out-of-region services—have already been removed. Others are due to sunset. The main ones will be eliminated when state and federal regulators conclude that incumbent local phone companies have opened their networks sufficiently to put competition on a robust trajectory.

[152] 47 U.S.C. §251(c)(2); *see* §5.5.3.4(i).
[153] 47 U.S.C. §251(c)(3); *see* §5.5.3.4(ii).
[154] 47 U.S.C. §251(c)(4)(A); *see* §5.5.3.6.

As for pricing regulation, the new statute calls for the elimination of all implicit subsidies and their replacement by a new explicit universal system funded in an equitable and non-discriminatory way by all providers of telecommunications services.[155] And Congress called on the FCC to forbear from regulating, consistent with the public interest, wherever such regulation is not necessary to ensure that charges are just and reasonable or to protect consumers.[156] As competition spreads at all levels of the network, traditional price regulation should be its first victim.[157]

In August 1996, the FCC promulgated rules purporting to implement these requirements; many of those rules were challenged in the courts and have yet to be fully resolved.

§1.9.1   *The Transitional Regulatory Paradigm: Regulating Interconnection in the Unexclusive Franchise*

Open entry is now the norm in local exchange markets, as it is elsewhere in the industry. The old and simple regulatory principle of exclusive franchise has given way to a new and complex set of rules governing interconnection among horizontal local competitors. The principle underlying the 1996 Act, however, is still a simple one: carriers sell carriage, and their obligation to do so does not depend on whether the customer is itself a competing carrier. That principle is over a century old, dating back to (though not affirmed in) the *Express Packages Cases*.

This shift from the exclusive franchise to unbundled interconnection fundamentally changes both the process and the objectives of federal regulation. In the past, when local exchange carriers were legal monopolies, all the interconnection issues were vertical, not horizontal.[158] Customer premises equipment,

---

[155] 47 U.S.C. §254; *see* Chapter 6.
[156] 47 U.S.C. §160.
[157] *See* Chapter 2.
[158] *See* §5.2.

long-distance services, enhanced services, and wireless services were *complements of,* not *substitutes for,* local exchange service. The principal terms and conditions of interconnection overseen by the Commission—such things as access charges—were not those between direct horizontal competitors. Without such horizontal competition, the Commission had little information on which to ground its regulatory rulings. Despite pious pronouncements about benchmarks, all the monopolies looked pretty much alike.

The principal regulatory issues before the Commission today are of a fundamentally different character: they concern *horizontal* interconnection, not *vertical;* direct competitive substitutes, not complements.[159] Competing local carriers now interconnect with incumbents and compete directly against them. Several thousands of interconnection agreements have been signed, and hundreds more are being negotiated. The most important "consumers" of local exchange service now include such "customers" as AT&T, Sprint, Frontier, and MCI/WorldCom. The members of this new class of customer-competitor know a great deal about the local exchange business—they are currently local exchange carriers themselves. And these customers are being joined by incumbent local carriers, too, as those incumbents venture to compete outside their traditional service areas.

With horizontal interconnection taking center stage, the FCC's primary mission is no longer to set terms, conditions, or rates in an informational vacuum. It is to play its role, along with the states, as arbitrator of interconnection among actual horizontal competitors. Most significant, the regulation of horizontal interconnection can rely on direct, quantitative measures of performance and success. The Commission has access to quantitative counts of interconnection agreements signed, minutes exchanged, local numbers ported, and customers switched. No comparable measures of regulatory efficacy were available with regard to vertical interconnection.

[159] *See* §5.3.

The 1996 Act also institutes a variety of procedural mechanisms that provide competitive LECs (CLECs) and the Commission alike with relevant data.[160] Both CLECs and the Commission have access to the terms of every interconnection agreement that has been negotiated and may use those terms as a basis for comparison. Indeed, requesting telecommunications carriers can do more than that: the 1996 Act requires LECs to "make available any interconnection, service, or network element provided under an agreement approved under [§251] to which it is a party to any other requesting telecommunications carrier upon the same terms and conditions as those provided in the agreement."[161] Thus, the Commission and consumers have at their disposal an abundance of new, publicly filed information on which to base their assessment of what types of interconnections are fair and reasonable.

As horizontal competition increases—and it is increasing rapidly—the importance of many traditional types of Commission regulations will diminish apace. For example, the Commission has previously used benchmarks to help determine access charges and productivity factors.[162] As the number of horizontal competitors multiplies, the importance of access charges will decline simply because long-distance carriers will increasingly reach their customers through CLECs rather than incumbent LECs (ILECs). As Internet and enhanced-service traffic continues to rise—and it is rising very fast—the importance of access charge rates will decline further because those services do not pay access charges at all.[163] And regulation will be entirely irrelevant to a fast-growing number of competitive services, including high-speed access services offered by incumbent local

---

[160] For example, each interconnection agreement negotiated under section 252 must include "a detailed schedule of itemized charges for interconnection and each service or network element included in the agreement." 47 U.S.C. §252(a)(1).

[161] *Id.* §252(i).

[162] *See, e.g.,* Price Cap Performance Review for Local Exchange Carriers, Fourth Report and Order, CC Docket No. 94-1, and Second Report and Order, CC Docket No. 96-262, 12 F.C.C. Rec. 16,642 (1997).

[163] *See* Regulatory and Policy Problems Presented by the Interdependence of Computer and Communications Services and Facilities, Final Decision and

carriers through separate subsidiaries, because they will not be regulated at all.

§1.9.2 The Rise of Competition

Since divestiture, there has been a steady, inexorable rise in competition in all levels of the industry. MCI and Sprint developed into full-fledged national carriers to compete with AT&T; other, smaller carriers built regional networks, and hundreds of resellers entered the market, too. Unexpected though it was by the framers of the decree, competition began to emerge in local markets, too, particularly in the business of providing "exchange access service," i.e., the local transport of calls to the nearest "point of presence" of a long-distance carrier. In 1984, Teleport Communications Group (TCG) was formed; the company began as a partnership among Western Union, Merrill Lynch, and the Port Authority of New York and New Jersey and was later acquired by cable companies Cox, TCI, Continental, and Comcast. (TCG was purchased by AT&T in 1998.) Teleport and other competitive access providers (CAPs) began building fiber-optic networks designed to provide exchange access for high-volume customers. These networks were typically built as rings that snake through metropolitan areas, passing the major office buildings where large businesses typically locate.

This process has accelerated rapidly since 1996—wherever competition makes strategic and economic sense for the new entrants. That competitive sphere includes business services of all kinds: short-haul toll services, wireless services, many data services, and other enhanced services. As of late 1998, nearly 300 companies were providing competitive local exchange carrier

---

Order, 28 F.C.C.2d 267 (1971), *aff'd in pertinent part sub nom.* GTE Serv. Corp. v. FCC, 474 F.2d 724 (2d Cir. 1973); Amendment of §64.702 of the Commission's Rules & Regulations (Second Computer Inquiry), Final Decision, 77 F.C.C.2d 384, *modified on recons.*, 84 F.C.C.2d 50 (1980), *modified on further recons.*, 88 F.C.C.2d 512 (1981), *aff'd sub nom.* Computer and Communications Indus. Assn. v. FCC, 693 F.2d 198 (D.C. Cir. 1982), *cert. denied,* 461 U.S. 938 (1983), *aff'd on second further recons.*, 56 Rad. Reg. 2d (P & F) 301 (1984).

service of some description—companies like MCI/WorldCom and AT&T/TCG, cable companies, interexchange carriers, providers of personal communications services, providers of shared tenant services (e.g., service to apartment buildings), and others. Well over 2,000 interconnection agreements had been reached. New capital investments by competitors had surpassed new capital investment by the incumbents. Competitive local carriers had installed over 700 switches and were deploying new switches much faster than the incumbents.

Since passage of the 1996 Act, cable operators have begun offering data services to a rapidly growing number of customers in this high-growth segment of the market. Once customers get used to relying on cable for high-speed data services, they may migrate more readily to cable voice services.

Wireless markets are likewise growing very rapidly. By late 1998, providers of wireless PCS had concluded negotiations and signed close to 200 interconnection agreements with incumbent wireline carriers. PCS providers have launched commercial service in markets that serve most of the U.S. population. Wireless prices are falling, and the time is fast approaching when wireless will be seen as a genuine substitute for wireline service.

§1.10 The Network of the Future: Going Digital

Today, all networks are going digital, and they are getting there fast—not just wireline telephone networks, but wireless networks, cable, and broadcast, too. Some carriers are upgrading or replacing existing facilities with new, digital components. Others are entering markets with digital technology from the ground up. All are adding bandwidth (to support voice and video), two-way capabilities (to support real-time voice), and error correction (to support data).

Telephony. The digitization of the telephone network has been under way for over 20 years. Almost all long-distance transmissions are already digital. The local network is now catching up. Local digital switching has become ubiquitous in the last decade. Even existing copper plant is being upgraded to provide digital circuits. The integrated services digital network (ISDN) is already widely available, and prices have dropped significantly.[164] More recently, phone companies have begun deploying digital subscriber line (xDSL) technologies, which support simultaneous digital transmission of voice and video over existing copper plant.[165]

Cable. Fiber optics, signal compression technology, and other digital technologies are rapidly transforming cable television into cable telecommunications. Many cable operators are past the halfway point in upgrading their networks to a digital hybrid fiber coax (HFC) architecture that is capable of delivering telephone and other advanced information and two-way services. Cable operators have already begun to offer cable modems to exploit their bandwidth and new interactive capabilities. According to some estimates, one-third of all Internet users will be accessing the Internet over cable networks by 2002. Providers of "wireless cable"—like multipoint multichannel distribution service (MMDS)[166] and local multipoint distribution service (LMDS)[167]—will use recently obtained regulatory freedoms to upgrade to two-way digital services.

Wireless. Wireless media are going digital from the top down and the bottom up. Multiple-digital PCS networks are now being built in virtually every major metropolitan area in the United States.[168] Existing cellular systems, which have traditionally used analog technology, are simultaneously being converted to digital radio. Nextel has also converted much of its specialized

---

[164] *See FBL* §2.7.3.

[165] DSLs have advanced electronics—DSL modems—installed on either end of the line that provide advanced signal processing, digital multiplexing, and compression algorithms to transmit a tremendous amount of information. *See FBL* §2.7.4.

[166] *See FBL* §2.5.1(vi).

[167] *See FBL* §2.5.1(vii).

[168] Unlike conventional cellular, PCS networks were designed from the start as digital networks, transmitting information in bits instead of analog waves.

mobile radio (SMR) spectrum into an all-digital, nationwide wireless network.

Broadcast. Over the next decade, terrestrial analog television will give way to digital advanced television. The affiliates of the big four networks went digital in the top 10 markets on November 1, 1998.[169] Broadcasters have already announced aggressive budgets for digital conversion. Digital satellite television has been available since 1994. Direct broadcast satellite (DBS) is now making the transition from wholesale to retail markets, not only for broadcast services, but for Internet/data services, too. Hughes Electronics offers high-speed Internet access via DBS nationwide.

Satellites. Beyond DBS, several companies are now making enormous investments to deploy global digital satellite networks. Iridium has launched a 66-satellite network and began providing worldwide commercial service in late 1998. Teledesic, the $9 billion joint venture between Craig McCaw and Bill Gates, expects to be up and running by 2002. Numerous other satellite ventures have also been formed. This is the "Orbiting Internet" or "Fiber in the Sky."

Digital networks are very much more flexible and powerful than the analog networks they are replacing. They offer more bandwidth. They more readily support two-way capabilities. And with encryption, they support addressing and narrowcasting, which can erase traditional distinctions between "broadcast" and "telecom" services.

Bandwidth. Digitization alone will sharply increase the effective bandwidth of existing networks. Digital signals can be much more efficiently multiplexed than analog signals. ISDN boosts the capacity of copper wire by a factor of 4. Digital signals can

---

[169] These top 10 markets serve 30 percent of U.S. television households. By November 1999, the top 30 markets—covering 53 percent of U.S. TV households—will convert to digital. *See* Advanced Television Systems and Their Impact upon the Existing Television Broadcast Service, Fifth Report and Order, 12 F.C.C. Rec. 12,809, 12,841 ¶76 (1997).

also be compressed. Advanced compression, multiplexing, and modulation can condition analog copper wire to carry multiple megabits of data per second, or full-motion video, or multiple voice calls. Assymetrical digital subscriber line (ADSL), for example, increases the effective capacity of copper wire by a factor of 350. DBS operators already use 6 MHz bands (what analog broadcasters use to transmit one channel) to deliver six or more video channels. Terrestrial broadcasters will deliver high-definition digital television within the same 6 MHz bands, with space left over for data services. Digital cable plant can support the equivalent of 750 MHz (or even 1 GHz) of bandwidth, transmitting over 100 video channels and high-speed two-way cable modem services. Digital video compression can increase the bandwidth of existing coaxial or copper networks by a factor of between 10 and 24. Digital cellular technologies increase the capacity of existing cells and spectrum between three and ten times current levels.

Two-Way Capabilities. As the bandwidth increases, addressing and filtering become essential. Addressability alone is often a close substitute for two-way capability when the return path is used only to lodge a request for information. A credit card can be verified in response to a request initiated over a two-way phone line; alternatively, it can be verified by continuously transmitting an encoded, suitably addressed list of invalid cards to a storage device at the point of sale.

Digital technology also makes it easy to plug together two-way services by interconnecting hybrid networks. That is often the best way to proceed when upstream and downstream bandwidth requirements are highly asymmetric. Cable or satellite, for example, can provide a downlink, with telephone lines or narrowband terrestrial wireless closing the loop. The abundance of cheap digital processing makes it easy to combine different media in this way.

Two-way capabilities, or at least addressability, can also be added with encryption and scrambling devices. Sophisticated coding algorithms that scramble what is sent can be readily combined with terminal equipment smart enough to decode it.

The descramblers installed at the end of the cable television lines perform such functions today. So do numerous types of communications software located in personal computers. With enough encoding of this type, it is possible to add two-way capabilities to any type of digital bandwidth and convert it for any use. For example, television and cellular telephony both use broadcast technology: a pocket cellular phone, like a TV station, transmits outward in all directions. A television station uses 6 MHz; a cellular telephone network uses 25 MHz. Combine four TV licenses and encode the signals, and you have the makings of a cellular network.

In sum, digital technology and high bandwidth obliterate engineering and economic distinctions among different types of electronic communications. And not simply because "a bit is a bit." The key point is that high-bandwidth digital networks, both wired and wireless, are extremely flexible. They can readily be configured and interconnected to mimic any of the capabilities of any of the old, analog systems.

And it is on digital data networks that all traffic, of every description, is going to move. If fax is included as "data," as it should be, data traffic probably already equals or exceeds voice traffic on phone networks. And the volume of data traffic is growing much faster than voice, even on wireless phone networks. Much of this increase can be explained by the increase in the number of people using the Internet and the related rise in second residential telephone lines and computer modems. Digital video traveling over phone lines will tilt the balance toward data further still. With this new universe of data telecom, services will compete in ways that are unexpected and largely unfamiliar today.

§1.11   The Network of the Future: The Internet

The Internet (together with the World Wide Web, which operates as a set of software protocols on it) is probably the best model at hand today for the broadband architecture of the future. It is already the world's largest communications system, the data archipelago of the planet. It spans the national, regional, and local communications networks used by commercial, government, and educational organizations worldwide. It is also, at the same time, an array of independently owned and managed networks, separately funded, separately developed, and separately maintained, with no single entity or agency in charge of managing everything.

The Internet has no defined structure—it is best described as a network of networks. At the physical level, it is a network of millions of computers, joined together by wires and radios of varying bandwidth.[170] At the virtual level, it is a common set of protocols: the "Transmission Control Program/Internetworking Protocol" (TCP/IP) and HTTP—the code of the World Wide Web. Computers, modems, and set-top boxes surround the Internet at its periphery. At the far end is the "host"—another computer that processes requests from its clients, whenever they come a-calling. Providing the links in between are several thousand "Internet service providers" and a handful of major backbone providers. For a variety of technical reasons, Internet-based voice telephony is not yet convenient, or of very good quality, but that is changing, and rapidly. A number of carriers are already offering phone-to-phone service domestically, including AT&T, MCI, Sprint, and a number of start-ups (including Qwest and Level 3). AT&T has announced plans to deploy Internet protocol telephony for local calling on TCI and TCI-affiliated cable systems.

A broadband Internet will offer decentralized and bandwidth and nonhierarchical connectivity, but not simplicity or uniformity. It will be an inelegant mix of glass, coax, and copper, of terrestrial transmitters and satellites. No one technology will prevail. Bandwidth and two-way capabilities will constantly improve. The technological mix will constantly change. Bandwidth and connectivity will proliferate, but so will complexity and unpredictability. It has been suggested that the airwaves and the landline network are trading places—that everything that now goes by wire will go by air and vice versa. But what is really going on is a hybridization of technology, not a simple exchange

[170] *See* §11.2.2.

of chairs. Both wireless and landline technologies can provide broadband links; the choice will therefore depend on such factors as the need for mobility, population densities (which sharply affect the relative costs of wire and wireless), and overall network economics. The market will use broadband media in unexpected ways if regulators will let it. Unforeseen synergies between different broadband media—satellite and cable, for example—will create entirely new markets and wholly new categories of services. They will also utterly destroy traditional regulatory boundaries among the various media.[171]

§1.12 The Market of the Future: Customer Segmentation

Under the traditional regulatory paradigm, all customers were treated equally. Universal service required that all be served, and nondiscrimination principles precluded favoritism. In the new marketplace, however, customers are sharply segmented. They fall into four basic groups: multinationals, small and mid-size businesses, boomers, and Aunt Tillie.

Multinationals. Approximately one-third of incumbent phone company revenues comes from 1 percent of the biggest customers—multinational business customers. They demand one-stop suppliers of state-of-the-art service. They buy more data traffic than voice. Within 10 years, 90 percent of their traffic will be data and only 10 percent voice. Local competitors like WorldCom are going after this market almost exclusively. And they are winning a big share of it. In the first quarter of 1998, for the first time, local competitors added more new business lines than did Regional Bells.

Small and Mid-size Businesses. These customers are not anchor tenants. No one will build a network out to them. But they will be picked up in increasing numbers by competitors who have

---

[171] *See generally* E. Leo & P. Huber, The Incidental, Accidental Deregulation of Data . . . and Everything Else, 6 Indus. & Corp. Change 807 (1997).

built their networks to serve large businesses and who have capacity to spare. The fiber rings through downtown areas can serve the flower shop on the ground floor along with the multinational in the penthouse and the various law and accounting firms in between.

Boomers.   One residential customer in six spends over $100 a month on telecom services. These are affluent customers. They travel a lot. They use the Internet a lot. They want to buy bundled service. They want one-stop shopping. For this group of customers, data traffic will soon exceed voice. Ten years from now these customers will be using five to ten times as much service—mostly data service—as they do today. These customers are heavy users of wireless, too. Wireless carriers are adding new subscribers twice as fast as wireline carriers are adding new lines. (Wireless carriers added 14 million new subscribers in 1998, for a total of 70 million.)

Aunt Tillie.   Aunt Tillie represents about five out of every six residential subscribers. These subscribers live in suburbs, or smaller towns, or rural areas. They are still using phone service pretty much the same way they did 20 years ago. They spend $10 to $30 a month on phone service. They want Wal-Mart and McDonald's phone service. Most still look to AT&T for their long-distance service—and to a Bell Company for their local service. They will buy data and wireless services, too—but only when prices drop, services get easier to use, and familiar, brand-name companies offer plug-and-play packages. WorldCom won't touch them. MCI is transitioning away from serving them. Sprint won't target them. AT&T doesn't want them, at least not their local business. They are still served almost exclusively by traditional phone companies. Only the lowest cost provider, the one that successfully captures economies of scope and scale, can afford to serve them. They will buy only from a very trusted brand name; they view telecommunications as too important to entrust to unknown upstarts. They want reliable, familiar service. That's why most of them never switched from AT&T in their long-distance service.

§1.13 The Market of the Future: Bundled Services

To serve the most desirable of these customers, companies will increasingly offer packages of bundled services. The breakup of Bell in 1984 separated telephone equipment from local service and local service from long distance. The post-1996 competitors will bring them all back together.

Equipment is already routinely recombined with service in many markets. Cellular companies give away phones; cable companies supply converters; modem and PC manufacturers bundle in start-up subscriptions to online services. Phone companies will be fully back in the same game soon enough.

The companies are reuniting geographically as well. Long-distance carriers like AT&T and MCI are already free to build their networks down to the consumer. They are doing so as fast as they can. Soon local phone companies will win permission to build long-distance facilities, or affiliate with existing long-distance carriers, or resell their services. They will do so at once.

The divisions between local and long-distance services have already all but disappeared in data communications. Internet connections cost the same whether they are used to move data across the street or around the globe. Indeed, on the Internet, it is almost impossible even to track where calls originate, what communications paths are traveled, or where information is ultimately delivered or consumed. Content is readily hybridized; a display on a single computer can be synthesized out of data residing on, and delivered from, any number of others, located anywhere on the globe. Divisions between local and long-distance wireless services are fading, too. GTE and Sprint have been bundling local cellular service with long-distance service for some years. By the turn of the century, all wireless carriers will sell one-brand, one-bill, one-stop, integrated wireless service.

With voice and data, wire and wireless, the new, reintegrated phone companies won't offer their customers "equal access" to other vendors. No principle of common carriage requires that they should so long as they sell what they sell to anyone who wants to buy it, other vendors included. The whole marketing pitch will center on just the opposite: the simplicity and reliability of shopping from a single name-brand provider, with nothing to pick but the name.

AT&T will exploit its strong brand identity as aggressively as anyone and will prosper by doing so. A significant fraction of consumers will buy their phone service—all of it, end to end—from AT&T—just as they did in 1980. But many others won't. That will be the difference.

Year by year we can expect to see further erosion of the boundaries that traditionally segmented the industry. It is no longer useful to think of broadband pipes as ordinary wires. They are bundles of virtual channels, carrying clusters of constantly evolving services. With the triumph of digital technology, the old divisions among voice, video, and data services disappear once and for all. A full-bore digital, broadband network will empower everyone to cast broadly or narrowly at will. The online world already does so: anyone can create a bulletin board, and anyone can post musings on it, whether wise, foolish, tasteful, crass, or crude, to be read by the world. With digital, broadband technology, the text-based bulletin boards will support voice and video. Broadband carriers will have room to carry anything anywhere: on their networks, anyone who chooses will be an instant broadcaster. Tomorrow's broadcasters will have the power to narrow and address their signals at will: on their networks, anyone who chooses will be an instant carrier.

Pure carriage can certainly survive as a business in a digital, broadband world, and undoubtedly will. But who will provide pure carriage, on which assemblies of wires and radios, is much less clear. The owner of a UHF station licensed to broadcast sitcom reruns 24 hours a day might do far better using the same spectrum to transmit digital, wireless e-mail, a common carrier service.[172] In rural areas, wireless telephony may be both cheaper and much more valuable than wired; the best use of existing phone wires may be for a next generation of digital video-on-demand.

---

[172] *See generally* H. Shelanski & P. Huber, Administrative Creation of Property Rights to Radio Spectrum, 41 J.L. & Econ. 581 (1998).

A few die-hard providers may decide to keep their businesses strictly on one side of the old definitional line or the other, or be forced to do so by reactionary regulators. For the most part, however, the clean, familiar legal divisions between carriers and broadcasters will be impossible to maintain. In the broadband telecosm, "carriers" and "casters" will compete head to head in a single unbounded arena.

§1.14   The Market of the Future: Industry Structure

With bundling and an increasing focus on the needs of large customers, mergers are inevitable. After two decades of fragmentation, the center of the industry is now entering a period of rapid consolidation. In both U.S. and international markets, the telecom industry is consolidating, both horizontally and vertically, through mergers and alliances. Measured by revenues earned, approximately half of the U.S. telecom industry was involved in a merger or acquisition in 1997 and 1998, including Bell Atlantic/NYNEX/GTE, WorldCom/MFS/Brooks Fiber/MCI, AT&T/TCG/TCI, and SBC/PacTel/Ameritech. Almost half (8 million) of the 20 million phone lines served by independent phone companies have been transferred by merger or acquisition in the past decade.

These trends reflect a fundamental economic fact—so fundamental indeed that it used to be considered immutable and was often codified as the law of exclusive franchise. Network industries are characterized by powerful economies of scale and scope. Scale and scope are critical factors in purchasing and deploying new technologies and services. Large buyers of equipment are able to negotiate large discounts with hardware and software vendors, such as Nortel and Lucent. Purchases of bulk services, like wholesale interexchange traffic or Internet backbone access, also become much cheaper with scale. Large providers of service can distribute the costs of funding or soliciting bids for the development of new technology over an extended base of operations. Size likewise diminishes the costs and risks of developing new services. Scale eliminates many duplicative general and administrative costs, providing selling and maintenance efficiencies. Geographic scale and scope are equally important to national and multinational customers. Large companies like AT&T and MCI/WorldCom can plausibly bid to serve a large customer's telecom needs around the world.

Small wonder, then, that the major players in the industry are very large. Collectively, Bell Companies represent 44 percent of the nation's telecom revenues and a still larger percentage of the nation's telecom workers. The larger Regional Bells (like Bell Atlantic and SBC) own about $60 billion in capital plant and invest $6 billion a year in new capital plant. AT&T already serves 100 million phone lines. Only MCI/WorldCom (28 million lines) and Sprint (12 million lines) can currently lay similar claim to national identities, with established customer bases in every major market and state.

This is not to say that niche players will not still thrive. Indeed, niche players were the first to prosper in the emerging competitive environment. They offered differentiated, specialty services to only a select, high-profit segment of the market. The 1996 Act's resale and unbundling requirements have significantly reduced entry barriers, and newcomers have no responsibility (at least none comparable to that of incumbents) to offer universal service. These competitors are quite rationally focusing all their competitive energies on the very largest business customers, while ignoring less profitable residential customers. Their competitive strategy is defined by how selectively they choose their customers and how few customers they actually serve. They leave the mass market, particularly the low-margin residential market, to others.

But while many companies can and will be effective regional or niche competitors, only a small number of companies can realistically hope to be full-service companies, offering a local, long-distance, and international service bundle nationwide and beyond. The financial challenge is daunting. The capital costs for facilities-based local competition in the United States generally range from several hundred to several thousand dollars per customer, depending on demographics, services provided, and facilities deployed. Customer acquisition costs run several hundred dollars more. Incumbent local phone companies serve 150 million customers and have already sunk capital investments in excess of $200 billion in the United States.

Thus, even as the niche players multiply and prosper, the center of the industry is restructuring, and the big are indeed getting bigger. But the competitive implications of mergers, acquisitions, and sheer size must be assessed in the context of the equally profound transformation of geographic and product markets. In the old order, each provider was confined to its own geographic territory and shielded from competition by an exclusive franchise. There are no exclusive geographic territories in the new: every player may compete everywhere. In the old order, each provider was confined to a particular category of service: local, long-distance, wireless, or data service. Those lines are all collapsing in the new: every player may provide complete bundles of service. AT&T, MCI/WorldCom, Sprint, and a host of foreign carriers are all quite clearly on a similar competitive trajectory, transforming themselves into national and global providers of integrated telecom services.

Consolidation trends notwithstanding, competition is still increasing. The new industry order now emerging is one of four to six well-financed, full-service, national (eventually global) companies, competing head to head to provide a full bundle of services in every major market. Numerous smaller regional players and providers of specialized services will continue to compete against the big nameplates by offering specialized and differentiated services. The upshot will be fewer national or global nameplates and more niche competitors, but—at the same time—far more competition all around.

§1.15 The Market of the Future: Global Trends

The global market for all telecommunications services was approximately $700 billion in 1996 and has been growing an estimated 20 percent per year. Traditional local and long-distance voice services account for 60 percent of the total.

International services account for 10 percent of the total. North America accounts for 28 percent of all worldwide access lines and 33 percent of worldwide revenue. Europe accounts for 38 percent of access lines and 33 percent of revenue. Asia accounts for 26 percent of access lines and 26 percent of revenue.

Global markets are characterized by three major trends: privatization, open entry, and interconnection. But most of the world (with a few exceptions, e.g., Great Britain, New Zealand) is one to two decades behind the U.S. in implementing these initiatives. Most countries have separated wireline from wireless services and permit wireless competition. But no other country has followed the U.S. model of divesting the local from the domestic long-distance operations of their incumbent wireline carrier. And in many countries, the incumbent telephone service provider also provides cable service.

Most major foreign carriers have expanded their operations globally through alliances with, investments in, or acquisitions of foreign carriers. All major U.S. long-distance carriers are pursuing comparable global strategies: forging multinational alliances with major foreign incumbents and investing in wireless and data providers in foreign countries. Virtually all major wireline incumbents have acquired foreign interests. As of this writing, there are three major global alliances, too.[173]

§1.16 Conclusion

The competitive struggles discussed in this book are not abstract lessons in economics. They have a very real effect on American competitiveness and the quality of American life. The "information" sector of the economy makes up a large percentage of GNP and of the workforce. Even companies outside the

---

[173] Global One (Sprint, France Telecom, Deutsche Telekom), WorldPartners (AT&T, KDD, Unisource, Singapore Telecom, Telstra, and several non-equity partners), and Unisource (Dutch, Swedish, Swiss, and Italian post, telephone, and telegraph companies (PTTs)). AT&T and British Telecom have announced plans to merge their international operations into a jointly owned company that would have $10 billion in revenues.

information arena are allocating a steadily increasing fraction of their budgets to telecommunications. Since most unit costs of telecommunications are dropping rapidly, even a slowly growing telecommunications budget represents a much more rapid growth in telecommunications usage. By all indications, these numbers will continue to grow rapidly.

And by all indications, the supply of bandwidth will grow to meet this demand. As it does, free markets will become increasingly difficult to repress. The genius of a market is that it elicits information about what people have and what they want. That information, however, becomes powerful only when it is communicated to others. The invisible hand has no power unless guided by visible eyes and ears. The expanding universe of high-bandwidth telecommunications will allow communication as never before.

What, after all, are the essential ingredients of a market? Communication, to connect together the willing buyer and the willing seller. Promises, so that trades begun today can be consummated tomorrow. Memory, so that promises will be kept. Memory, to record what belongs to whom. Promises again, to create all other rights beyond property rights because all social norms depend on a shared commitment to enforce them. Promises again, by which honest traders agree to ostracize cheats, deadbeats, and thieves. Promises and memories, trust and loyalty: these are the essentials on which all else in the marketplace is constructed. And broadband is communication at its most capacious and powerful, with the wires and the ether terminating at electronic scribes, records, and memories, a laser-light weaver of trust and loyalty.

The giant trusts and corporations that evolved in the early days of capitalism will not reappear. The old corporation operated in the image of Big Brother, as a homogeneous, collectivist autocracy, dominated by a single, all-powerful leader. Such structures cannot survive. Independent yet tightly interconnected business groups, linked by network yet disciplined in all their relationships by market forces, will replace them. In this world, people will be paid because they work, not because they show up daily on the factory floor or in some glass-walled office. Services delivered over the new network will be metered with absolute precision. Specialists will specialize as never before.

Items supplied over the network—most of all labor—will be valued with scrupulous accuracy. People who really produce will be in high demand, and no one will care at all about their race or religion, their sex, their social graces, their physical appearance, or how they smell. Quality services will be purchased wherever they can be found, across the street or across the ocean. Inferior services will be priced accordingly, and incompetence will not be purchased at all, however much employment commissions may protest. No government agencies will even be able to keep track of what is being supplied where, still less to dictate who should be employed or on what terms.

The factory will be irrevocably changed. A car manufacturer will become a truly efficient assembler of parts provided by hundreds of independent suppliers. Secretaries, accountants, designers—most of the enterprise's support services—will be replaced by independent outsiders, knitted together into an efficient whole by the network. Suppliers, assemblers, distributors, and customers will be coordinated with meticulous precision. Even the largest factory will operate with no inventory, no warehouses, no fitful starts and stops caused by shortage of supply or excess of output. A customer's order will be conveyed instantly up the chain of production to the assembly line, and back further still to the factory's suppliers of paint, tires, and radios, and hence back to their suppliers of rubber and steel. Industrialism no longer requires collectivism. Cooperation will be by consent.

Marketing will be transformed beyond recognition. In primitive societies, the market operates with tiny stalls and without reliable currency; trading extends only as far as goods can be carried. In a barter economy, the seller exchanges the pig directly for a dozen chickens. Payment is assured, but the process is terribly cumbersome. In societies that are stable enough to issue currency and imbue it with value, money marks a great advance. It records value in a standardized form that is widely understood; it conveys value without any need to transport pigs or chickens. The paper itself is worthless except for the information it conveys. Money, then, is just another network—a system of communication, a record of past effort, and a promise of future return. With money, the record is on paper, a primitive, inefficient, and vulnerable medium of communication. And a single, master record keeper, the government treasury, with a single, centralized printing press, has absolute power to determine value.

But there is ultimately only one valuable currency: the currency of reputation, of stable, honest, reliable loyalty. Once it is established of a man, or a leader, or a nation's central banker that his word is his bond, he can issue currency at will. Once it is established that he is a chiseler, a deadbeat, or a thief, no amount of currency will do him much good, for his paper will be shunned wherever he tries to peddle it. The value of money thus depends on trust and promises among the people who control the records. If the network is powerful enough, nobody controls the records, or at least no central authority does. Trust begins between individuals; then it coalesces among larger groups; then it coalesces in larger groups still. Today, we put our trust in a thousand different private currencies in varying degrees: personal checks, stock certificates, bonds, credit card slips, futures contracts, green stamps, and patronage accounts of every kind. The network enables us to confirm that an account has assets, that a business is functioning, or that an individual faithfully pays his bills. Private enterprises issue countless private currencies by verifying credit, clearing checks, evaluating investments, dealing in futures, and insuring risks.

As the power of the network increases, so, too, will the power and reliability of private currency. With perfect communication, the government bank is no longer needed—currencies of every imaginable description can be created by the market itself, like all other goods. Virtually every kind of good can become the equivalent of a banknote, available for inspection, conveyance, and storage at any distance.

For better or for worse—mostly for better—telecommunications will transform the face of democracy. Opinion polls, call-in shows, and electronic town meetings usurp the "mediating function" of people like Sam Donaldson and George Will. The middleman in the dialogue of democratic government is cut out of the process, in much the same way as Sears is now cut out by mail-order catalogues and 800 numbers. Governments, it has been noted, derive their just powers from the consent of the governed. Now, we have at hand technologies for securing consent in ways never before imagined. Consent can now be sought directly, quickly, and efficiently on issues both large and small. The man on the couch can have precisely the same chance as Dan Rather to raise his hand and say something rude when the President steps into the room. The machines behind the network can tally national opinion not only instantaneously, but also with a level of delicate precision that would have left Jefferson breathless. Power will move into constantly shifting communities of shopkeepers, housewives, Yale bulldogs, fruit-juice thinkers, nudists, sandal wearers, sex maniacs, Quakers, nature-cure quacks, pacifists, and phesbian leminists. The networked society will be shaped by the accumulation of individual decisions to meet or stay apart, to buy or sell, to speak or remain silent.

Until recently, freedom of the press still belonged only to the few who owned one. But the Internet and other broadband technologies give a voice to the average citizen, the one who has never before owned a printing press or a broadcast station. By giving people the power to speak freely, such technologies also give them the right. No law will be able to repeal the technologies of freedom.

Ignorance—or at least rigid class ignorance, which endures generation after generation—cannot survive this technological transformation. People will be able to educate themselves and their children if they wish to do so. The state may continue to own the public schools—the buildings themselves—but broadband can create a school out of any pair of desks. The great universities, the great libraries, will no longer be in places; they will reside in cyberspace, securely out of reach of torches and bonfires. Heresy can no longer be eradicated by fire. Heresy is now fire itself, pulses of light in a network of glass.

In today's world, the entertainment industries still pitch their programs at what the great mass of people share in common— their prurience, their neurotic fears—and still rely on crude polling to estimate how many people were sufficiently attracted by sex and violence to endure advertisements for sugared cereal and laundry soap. Much of this will disappear. Every hobby and pastime — cage-birds, fretwork, carpentry, bees, carrier pigeons, home conjuring, philately, chess — will have at least one channel devoted to it, and often several. Gardening and livestock-keeping will have at least a score between them. Then there will be the sporting channels, the radio channels, the children's cartoons, the large range of channels devoted to the movies and all more or less exploiting women's legs, the various trade channels, the soap-opera channels, the needlework channels, and countless others. Ours will become, once again, a nation of flower lovers and stamp collectors, pigeon fanciers, amateur carpenters, coupon snippers, darts players, and crossword-puzzle fans. The days of mindless broadcast to the mindless masses are at an end.

Amid all this freedom there will still be prurience, violence, necrophilic reveries, and the repulsive art of Salvador Dali. Yet in the broadband telecosm, speech in public spaces no longer needs to be regulated. Public spaces — or at least the ones of any importance — are no longer surrounded by walls or gates. Bulletin boards, auditoriums, theaters, schools, stadia, squares, subway walls — electronic replacements for all the traditional public fora — can be created on demand. The network gives the pamphleteer and soap-box orator not just a place in Speaker's Corner, but the whole of Hyde Park. There is room for pacifists, Communists, anarchists, Jehovah's Witnesses, temperance reformers, Trotskyists, Freethinkers, vegetarians, and any number of plain lunatics: all will be able to speak out over the network, and all will receive a good-humored hearing from anyone who chooses to listen. The network will be Alsatia, where no opinions are outlawed. There has never been any place like it before in the physical world.

The network will supply room enough for every sight and sound, every thought and expression that any human mind will ever wish to communicate. It will make possible a wildness of spirit, where young minds can wander in adventurous, irresponsible, ungenteel ways. It will contain not innocence, but a sort of naive gaiety, a buoyant, carefree feeling, filled with confidence in the future and an unquenchable sense of freedom and opportunity. It will be capitalist civilization at its best. It will be the new frontier, and also the last frontier, for it extends as far as any human mind may wish to range.

The regulatory debates will not disappear in this new world, but they can be expected to shift to a higher plane. Close government regulation of the electronic media has historically been justified on the theory that over-the-air channels were scarce[174] and that landline media were monopolies. The differences between the two media were also thought to justify fundamentally different approaches to the twin problems of privacy and free speech. But the media are rapidly converging, and scarcity has been abolished. The old regulatory preoccupation with segregation and scarcity will soon be history; the debate will have turned to more important matters. For beyond the quarantine, beyond the exclusive franchise, beyond pricing regulation, beyond even the endless quarrels about state and federal regulatory jurisdiction lie the two great issues of the information age: free speech and its mirror image, privacy—the right to telecommunicate, one might say, and the right not to.

[174] Red Lion Broad. Co., Inc. v. FCC, 395 U.S. 367, 376 (1969).

2

Telephone Economics and Price Regulation*

§2.1 Introduction

§2.1.1 Basic Economics of Local Telephony

The local exchange, which generates over half of the industry's gross revenues, is also its last great citadel of economic regulation. The regulatory picture is extraordinarily complex. Every phone call has two or more ends, and many calls involve two or more carriers. Every phone call consists of a bundle of different

*This chapter was co-authored by Henk Brands: Partner, Kellogg, Huber, Hansen, Todd & Evans; University of Amsterdam (LL.B., 1987); Columbia University School of Law (J.D., 1990); Law Clerk, Honorable Stephen Breyer, U.S. Court of Appeals, First Circuit, 1990–1991; Law Clerk, Honorable David H. Souter, U.S. Supreme Court, 1991–1992; Law Clerk, Honorable Stephen Breyer, U.S. Supreme Court, 1994–1995.

services: transport, switching, access to databases, billing services, and so forth. Every component of the network, every interface between carrier and customer, and every interface between carriers may involve assessment of a regulated fee.

Local phone companies spend an average of between $27 and $37 per month[1] to provide a local phone line and dial tone for normal levels of local calling.[2] The average business subscriber pays a monthly fee for a basic line, dial tone, and subscriber line charge (SLC) that aligns fairly closely to that average cost—about $27 per month—plus an average of about 1.7 cents per minute for local calls.[3] The average residential subscriber, by

[1] The figures in this section are from 1996.

[2] These figures are national averages for all lines, urban and rural, residential and business. They include the average non-traffic-sensitive (NTS) costs of providing "interexchange access," here assumed to be $6 per line per month. See MTS and WATS Market Structure, Phase I, Third Report and Order, 93 F.C.C.2d 241 (1983) (hereinafter Access Order). The $27 and $37 figures were derived from two different cost studies, one by Federal Trade Commission (FTC) staff and one by Hatfield Associates.

The FTC staff has calculated that between 1983 and 1987 the average cost per line of providing basic local service (excluding interexchange access) fell from $35.51 to $33.15 per month. See Comments of the Staff of the Bureau of Economics of the Federal Trade Commission at tbl. 2, Expanded Interconnection with Local Telephone Company Facilities, CC Docket No. 91-141 (FCC Mar. 5, 1993) (hereinafter FTC Comments). Assuming costs have continued to decline at that rate and adjusting for inflation, local service would cost around $31 per month per line; adding $6 for interexchange access yields the $37 figure.

Hatfield Associates, a telecommunications consulting firm, has estimated that costs are substantially lower: the so-called Hatfield Model version 3.1 estimates the cost of providing local service by state and by carrier within each state; weighting these costs by the number of lines for each carrier in each state yields a national average cost of around $21 per line per month. See Hatfield Associates, Hatfield Model Release 3.1 Model Description, CC Docket No. 96-45 (FCC Feb. 28, 1997) (hereinafter Hatfield Model Release 3.1). Adding $6 for interexchange access yields the $27 figure. Aspects of the Hatfield Model, which was endorsed by AT&T and MCI, have been criticized by FCC staff as overly aggressive. See, e.g., J. Atkinson et al., FCC, The Use of Computer Models for Estimating Forward-Looking Economic Costs: A Staff Analysis ¶26 (Jan. 9, 1997).

[3] See FCC, Reference Book of Rates, Price Indices, and Household Expenditures for Telephone Service 24 (Mar. 1997) (hereinafter FCC Reference Book). The $27 per month rate includes measured service, SLC, and touch-tone service. Until 1997, the business SLC was roughly $6 per month per line, closely aligning with actual costs of NTS access.

contrast, pays a basic fee of only about $17.[4] In addition, every major incumbent local carrier offers "lifeline" service of some kind, at rates averaging about half the regular basic rate, to subscribers who cannot afford more.[5]

Incumbent local phone companies on average make up a net of $4 to $5 of the residential revenue shortfall on fees charged to provide interexchange access.[6] For subscribers that make few, if any, interexchange calls, the cost of providing a basic loop and dial tone remains well above the price charged. Only the very heaviest interexchange callers pay off the whole subsidy through interexchange access charges alone.

The average residential customer generates, in addition, about $6 per month in local toll (intraLATA) charges.[7] On average,

[4] *See id.* at 17. This rate is for unlimited local calls, touch-tone service, and a $3.50 SLC. Although the FCC has noted that the $3.50 SLC is not sufficient to cover the NTS costs of interexchange access, it has refrained from raising it, under pressure from consumer-advocacy groups, state regulators, Congress, and Judge Harold Greene to keep local telephone service affordable. *See, e.g.,* Access Charge Reform, Price Cap Performance Review for Local Exchange Carriers, Transport Rate Structure and Pricing, and End User Common Line Charges, First Report and Order, 12 F.C.C. Rec. 15,982, 15,992–15,993 ¶24 (1997) (hereinafter *Access Charge Reform Order*).

[5] *Access Charge Reform Order,* 12 F.C.C. Rec. at 15,994 ¶27.

[6] This figure is derived by multiplying the average number of minutes of calling between local access and transport areas (interLATA calling) generated by a residential line by the average amount per minute that local exchange carriers (LECs) charge interexchange carriers (IXCs) for interstate access and subtracting the cost of that access. According to Federal Communications Commission (FCC) phone-bill surveys, the average residential line made and received 249 minutes per month of interLATA calling. *See* Industry Analysis Division, FCC, Long Distance Market Shares, First Quarter 1997 at tbl. 11 (July 1997) (hereinafter *FCC Long Distance Market Shares*) (reporting 1996 surveys of 6,700 residential lines, which generated 835,000 interLATA minutes of use). LECs charge IXCs an average of 3.5 cents a minute to deliver those calls. *See* Industry Analysis Division, FCC, Statistics of Communications Common Carriers at tbls. 2.6, 6.2 (1995/1996 ed. 1996) (hereinafter *FCC Statistics of Common Carriers*) (in 1995, total access revenues, excluding SLCs and private line access were $19.5 billion; total originating and terminating interLATA minutes were 548 billion). The average residential line therefore generates nearly $9 per month in access revenue. Assuming that access costs are half the rate charged, interLATA access generates $4 to $5 profit per residential line per month. *See FTC Comments* at tbl. 2.

[7] This figure was calculated by multiplying the quotient of total LEC intraLATA toll revenue divided by the total number of intraLATA toll minutes

intraLATA service is priced at about twice the incremental cost of the service.[8] Here, the revenue earned by the incumbent local phone company on the average residential line begins to catch up with cost. Finally, local phone companies make up another part of the shortfall from basic services—another $4 per average residential line per month—on vertical services like call waiting and Caller ID.[9]

---

by the average number of intraLATA toll minutes per month generated by each residential line; this yielded a result of $5.80 per month in local toll revenue. *See FCC Long Distance Market Shares* (LECs generated $14 billion in local toll revenue in 1996); *FCC Statistics of Common Carriers* at tbl. 2.6 (22.8 billion total local toll calls in 1995). To derive the total average number of intraLATA toll minutes per month generated by each residential line, we assumed (1) that the average intraLATA toll call is the same length (3.5 minutes) as the average intrastate interLATA toll call, *see id.* (20.1 billion intrastate interLATA calls made in 1995; 77 billion originating minutes—assuming that originating minutes are half of total); and (2) that 52 percent of intraLATA toll minutes generated per month are from residential lines, *see id.* (52 percent of all interLATA minutes per month are generated by residential lines), which means that there were 43 billion residential interLATA toll minutes in 1995, or 400 minutes per year (34 per month) per line.

[8] This is a conservative estimate: MCI has estimated its own local toll margins at 66 percent. *See* K. M. Leon, Lehman Brothers, Inc., Investext Rpt. No. 1567651, MCI Communications—Company Report at *6 (Mar. 7, 1995); *see also* R. Klugman, PaineWebber Inc., Investext Rpt. No. 1537197, RBOCs and GTE—Industry Report at *33 (Dec. 13, 1994) (hereinafter *RBOCs and GTE Industry Report*) (margins for local toll calls are "typically an astronomical 80–90 percent").

[9] This figure was calculated by weighting the prices of various vertical services with the penetration of such services and adjusting for costs. Adjusted for penetration, call waiting generates an average of $2.55 per residential line per month; voice mail, $0.83 per month; Caller ID, $1.17; additional lines, $1.50; and all other services combined, $0.50 per month. The following assumptions were made: (1) call-waiting penetration nationwide is 51 percent at a cost of $5 per month; voice-mail penetration is 11 percent at a cost of $7.50 per month; Caller ID penetration is 18 percent at a cost of $6.50 per month; and second residential lines penetration is 15 percent at a cost of $10 per month, *see* D. Reingold et al., Merrill Lynch Capital Markets, Investext Rpt. No. 1864842, Telecom Services: RBOCs & GTE—Industry Report at tbl. 10a (Feb. 19, 1997) (penetration rates); SWBT Tariffed Rates in Houston, Texas (proxy for service prices); (2) all other vertical services—including speed dialing, three-way calling, and many others—have a combined penetration of around 10 percent and a total cost of $5 per month; and (3) vertical services are provided at 60 percent margins above cost, *see, e.g., RBOCs & GTE Industry Report* at tbl. 7.

In the aggregate, local phone service is, of course, a solvent business. But this is so only because some components are profitable enough to make up for others that are not. Overall, local phone companies lose a net of about $19 billion a year—about $15 per month per line—providing basic local service to residential subscribers.[10] The losses are offset by above-cost prices charged for local business service, interLATA access charges, local toll charges, and vertical services.

These numbers did not arise by accident; they reflect an intricate mix of underlying cost and overlying regulatory policy. The costs alone are economically complex, mainly because telephone networks are capital-intensive resources, involving huge fixed costs that are common to many different services. Regulation adds layer on layer of additional complication. The FCC and state utility commissions have long interpreted their charters as directing them to maintain "affordable rates" for all subscribers.[11] To that end, regulators require incumbent phone companies to offer service at uniform rates to all residential subscribers in their service areas, however much it may actually cost to serve the most distant, difficult-to-reach customers and however few additional, more profitable services beyond basic dial tone customers may use.[12] As the FCC has noted, low rates for basic residential service are maintained "through, among other things, a combination of: geographic rate averaging, high rates for business customers, high interstate access rates, high rates for intrastate toll

---

[10] This assumes the median local service cost figure of $27 per line per month. Using the FTC's cost estimate of $31 per line per month yields a deficit of more than $24 billion per year; using the Hatfield data yields a deficit of more than $12 billion per year.

[11] According to the FCC, they have accomplished that goal. In 1996, the Commission determined that rates then in effect were indeed "affordable." *See* Federal-State Joint Board on Universal Service, Report and Order, 12 F.C.C. Rec. 8776, 8780–8781 ¶2 (1997) (hereinafter *Universal Service Order*).

[12] As the California Public Utilities Commission (PUC) has noted, this requires each local phone company "to set a rate which reflect[s] an average of the higher cost exchanges with the more profitable exchanges." California Decision No. 96-10-066 at 24, Rulemaking on the Commission's Own Motion on Universal Service and to Comply with the Mandates of Assembly Bill 3643, Rulemaking No. 95-01-20 (Cal. PUC Oct. 25, 1996).

service, and high rates for vertical features and services such as call waiting and call forwarding."[13]

Urban users subsidize rural ones, business subscribers subsidize residential, and long-distance service subsidizes local. Costs can be, and often are, loaded on (or off) terminal equipment, voice service, data lines, high-capacity trunks, lines used by alarm companies, and so on and so forth.

In most markets, subsidies of any kind are inefficient. Whether and to what extent this is so in local telephony, however, is more complicated. The value of the telephone network is enhanced each time a customer is added to the network: every new connection creates what economists call a positive "network externality."[14] Because consumers base their decision to subscribe on only the benefit they themselves receive, telephone penetration may be lower than is economically efficient, and subsidized telephone access may promote efficiency.[15] And whether or not an access subsidy promotes efficiency, it may promote social equity by benefiting low-income consumers.

For most of this century, both federal and state regulators assumed telephone service (including local service, long-distance service, etc.) was a natural monopoly. If that was a problem, it was also an opportunity. With only one provider on the scene,

---

[13] *Access Charge Reform Order,* 12 F.C.C. Rec. at 15,988 ¶11; *see also* California Decision No. 96-10-066 at 24, Rulemaking on the Commission's Own Motion on Universal Service and to Comply with the Mandates of Assembly Bill 3643, Rulemaking No. 95-01-20 (Cal. PUC Oct. 25, 1996) ("The LECs were *also* able to price certain services above costs so as to subsidize basic local exchange service, which was generally priced below cost.").

[14] *See, e.g., Universal Service Order,* 12 F.C.C. Rec. at 8783 ¶8 ("[a]t the simplest level, increasing the number of people connected to the telecommunications network makes the network more valuable to all of its users by increasing its usefulness to them."); *id.* ("Increasing subscribership also benefits society in ways unrelated to the value of the network per se. For example, all of us benefit from the widespread availability of basic public safety services, such as 911."); *see also* Reed Hundt, Chairman, FCC, Remarks Before the Institute for International Economics, Washington, D.C. (Oct. 23, 1996) ("Economists teach us that the more people who use the network, the more valuable it becomes to each user. Within countries this provides a strong reason for promoting universal service.").

[15] *See, e.g.,* A. Kahn & W. Shew, Current Issues in Telecommunications: Pricing, 4 Yale J. on Reg. 191, 241–243 (1987).

regulators enjoyed a politically painless opportunity to pursue social policy objectives "off-budget": by adjusting rates paid for particular services or by particular categories of users, they could "tax and spend" without depleting the public fisc and thus without the pressures and publicity usually accompanying taxes and wealth transfers. So long as the phone company earned acceptable returns overall, prices for particular services or groups of customers could be pushed up or down with impunity. And they were.

The heyday of that regulatory paradigm lies behind us now. The FCC and the states began to abandon it in the 1970s and 1980s. At least psychologically, Congress finished the job in 1996. The new regulatory objective is to promote competition and to reduce rates toward cost.

§2.1.2 Yesterday's Regulatory Paradigm: "Natural Monopoly"

In competitive markets, each individual producer becomes less efficient after reaching a certain size, so that there are many producers vying to meet consumers' demands. In a "natural monopoly," by contrast, a single producer can supply consumers at a lower per-unit cost than could two or more producers.[16] A natural monopoly is "characterized by economies of scale over the entire range of output that the market will take."[17] In a natural monopoly, therefore, stable competition is impossible in the

[16] *See generally* W. Bolter, Telecommunications Policy for the 1990s and Beyond 32–45 (1990); S. Breyer, Regulation and Its Reform 15–17 (1982); G. Faulhaber, Telecommunications in Turmoil: Technology and Public Policy 106 (1987); A. Kahn, 1 The Economics of Regulation 11–12 (1970); W. Sharkey, The Theory of Natural Monopoly 12–20, 54 (1982); J. Wenders, The Economics of Telecommunications—Theory and Policy 11–41 (1987); L. Johnson, Boundaries to Monopoly and Regulation in Modern Telecommunications, *in* Communications for Tomorrow: Policy Perspectives for the 1980s, at 127, 136 (G. Robinson ed., 1980); R. Posner, Natural Monopoly and Its Regulation, 21 Stan. L. Rev. 548 (1969).

[17] *See* W. Baumol, O. Eckstein, & A. Kahn, Competition and Monopoly in Telecommunications Services 5, Bell System Exhibit No. 46, FCC Docket No. 19129, Phase II.

long run and wasteful in the short.[18] In a natural-monopoly industry, competition is therefore both unattainable and imprudent as a policy objective.

Is the telephone industry (or any part of it) a natural monopoly?[19] Until the 1960s, the answer was generally presumed to be yes, from end to end. Until 1996, the answer was still presumed to be yes, at least in part. The 1996 Act reversed the presumption. But the question still does not admit of any short or easy answer.[20] In the last decade, new technology has rapidly and radically changed the cost structure of the telephone industry. Perceptions about the market have changed even faster, and that is important in itself: a monopolist ceases to behave like one if it becomes convinced (correctly or not) that its market is "contestable."[21] Policy makers have also come to recognize that even if markets are less than perfectly competitive, regulation is often ineffectual or worse because of inadequate information about the true costs of efficient production. Economic objectives may prove irreconcilable with noneconomic ones, and the schismatic regulation that results may be worse than no regulation at all.

[18] *Cf.* R. Ely, Outlines of Economics 621–650 (1937).

[19] For a survey of conflicting viewpoints on the natural-monopoly question, see J. Haring, Office of Plans and Policy, FCC, Implications of Asymmetric Regulation for Competition Policy Analysis, (OPP Working Paper No. 14, 1984); *see also* D. Kaserman & J. Mayo, Long-Distance Telecommunications Policy—Rationality of Hold, Pub. Util. Fort., Dec. 22, 1988, at 24; D. Evans & J. Heckman, A Test for Subadditivity of the Cost Function with an Application to the Bell System, 74 Am. Econ. Rev. 615 (1984) (concluding that the Bell System was not a natural monopoly).

[20] For a sample of the range of possible answers, see D. Evans & J. Heckman, Natural Monopoly, *in* Breaking Up Bell: Essays on Industrial Organization and Regulation 127 (D. Evans ed., 1983); A. Phillips, The Impossibility of Competition in Telecommunications: Public Policy Gone Awry, *in* Regulation Reform and Public Utilities 7 (M. Crew ed., 1982); Kahn & Shew, Current Issues in Telecommunications at 191–192. *See also* Domestic Telecommunications Common Carrier Policies, Part 1: Hearings on the Communications Act of 1934, Revisited Before the Senate Comm. on Com., Sci. and Transp., 95th Cong., 1st Sess. (1977) (statement of Alfred E. Kahn); J. Meyer, The Economics of Competition in the Telecommunications Industry 146–147 (1980); W. Baumol, Contestable Markets: An Uprising in the Theory of Industry Structure, 72 Am. Econ. Rev. 1, 6 (1982).

[21] *See* Sharkey, The Theory of Natural Monopoly at 54–58; Baumol, Contestable Markets at 3; M. Schwartz, The Nature and Scope of Contestability Theory, 38 Supp. Oxford Econ. Papers 37 (1986).

What is clear, in retrospect at least, is that economic regulation of telephony long outlasted monopoly itself. For many years, it simply propped up *un*natural monopolies created by comfortable collaboration between government regulators and entrenched incumbents in a conspiracy against upstarts eager to compete.[22] At the very least, passage of the 1996 Telecommunications Act reversed the attitudes and presumptions of U.S. regulators profoundly, and probably irrevocably.

§2.1.3 Today's Regulatory Paradigm: Interconnection, Unbundling, and the Transition to Competition

The 1934 Communications Act presumed that end-to-end monopoly would be shadowed by end-to-end regulation. Every service and every carrier would be tariffed. In that world, regulators did not have to worry about the efficiency of different options for recovering costs: if a particular pricing option was inefficient, there were no competitors to profit from (and thereby correct) the inefficiency. It was economically inefficient, for example, for a phone company to charge more than actual cost for the monthly rental of a phone, but it was politically convenient. Businesses with multiple lines and affluent homeowners renting two or more phones would subsidize the great mass of residential subscribers who rented only one; that was intended. Under regulatory oversight, the phone company taxed some services and subsidized others. So long as the books balanced, shareholders remained reasonably content.

When the network itself began to unravel, so, too, did these regulatory schemes. Once competitors are allowed to sell telephone sets, or long-distance service, or anything else previously supplied by the monopoly phone company, the rate charged for that part of the network will inevitably be driven toward cost. This has four fundamental regulatory implications.

---

[22] *See* R. Poole, Unnatural Monopolies: The Case for Deregulating Public Utilities (1985).

First, so long as the prices of some services remain regulated, there has to be some regulatory mechanism (a) to keep track of costs incurred in providing those services and (b) to regulate the prices charged. Under rate-of-return regulation, regulators must at least monitor what is being spent to provide the regulated service alone. (Not so under a pure price-cap regulatory regime, but purity has yet to be attained.) This requires a formal process of "cost separations." We discuss these issues in section 2.2.2 below.

Second, prices charged for services on the other side of the divide—the competitive side—must be formally deregulated. We address that process briefly in sections 2.1.4, 2.3.1.1, 2.3.3.3(x), and 2.4.2.1 below and more fully in subsequent chapters that discuss the evolution of these competitive markets.[23]

Third, new tariffs must be put in place at each new interface to determine how much the regulated side of the network may charge the unregulated.[24] Section 2.3 covers "vertical" connections between local exchange carriers, on the one hand, and providers of equipment, "enhanced services," long-distance services, and Internet services, on the other. Section 2.4 covers the more "horizontal" connections between incumbent local exchange carriers and their emerging competitors: wireless carriers, "competitive access providers," resellers, and "unbundlers."

Finally, as price regulation evolves, regulators must rethink their policies to promote universal service. Taxing one service to subsidize another is easy in a monopoly environment. But subsidies are doubly poisonous to competition: they suppress competition wherever the money gets spent (i.e., they render impossible competition on services that are subsidy recipients, even if competition would otherwise be sustainable), and they promote uneconomic competition wherever the money gets collected (i.e., they encourage competitive entry on services that are

---

[23] *See* sections [detariffing subsections and longer treatments in the full chapters that deal with other services long-distance, wireless, internet, etc.].

[24] The local exchange remains at the center of this kind of regulation, but similar issues have arisen, and will arise again, in other segments of the network. Can AT&T (say) charge MCI or Sprint whatever AT&T likes to carry their traffic to points where they do not have facilities? How much may a dominant operator of an Internet backbone network charge smaller Internet access providers for connection? *See* §2.3.3.3.ii.

subsidy sources, even if competition would not otherwise be sustainable). Section 2.5 discusses federal price-regulation policies as they relate to universal service; Chapter 6 addresses universal service more fully.

§2.1.4 Tomorrow's Regulatory Paradigm: Regulatory Forbearance

As competition takes root in the network, the weeds of regulation can and plainly should be extracted. The FCC recognized this as soon as it began planting competitive flowers in the 1970s. But the 1934 Act made no allowance for accompanying deregulation. It presumed end-to-end monopoly, so it required end-to-end regulation.

As discussed below in connection with the detariffing of long-distance services in section 2.3.3.3(x), the FCC fought a ten-year battle for the power to instruct carriers not to file tariffs at all. But the Commission's good intentions were repeatedly thwarted in court. The 1934 Act, the courts concluded, gave the Commission no freedom not to regulate. Any authority to forbear, the Supreme Court ruled, would have to come from Congress.[25] Congress supplied it in the 1996 Act. It empowered the FCC to forbear from enforcing virtually all requirements in the Communications Act and its regulations.[26]

Congress delivered, but not without certain conditions. Prior to forbearing, the Commission must make certain findings, including that forbearance is in the public interest.[27] And two key provisions are ineligible for forbearance:[28] the interconnection

---

[25] *See* MCI v. AT&T, 512 U.S. 218, 233–234 (1994); *see also* Southwestern Bell Corp. v. FCC, 43 F.3d 1515 (D.C. Cir. 1995); AT&T v. FCC, 978 F.2d 727 (D.C. Cir. 1992); MCI v. FCC, 765 F.2d 1186 (D.C. Cir. 1985).

[26] *See* 47 U.S.C. §160(a).

[27] A request for forbearance is deemed granted unless the Commission denies it within 15 months after it was filed. *See* 47 U.S.C. §160(c). The public-interest finding may also be based on the Commission's determination that "forbearance will enhance competition among providers of telecommunications services." *Id.* §160(b).

[28] *Id.* §160(d).

rules applicable to incumbent LECs (ILECs)[29] and the rules governing BOC entry into the interLATA market.[30] But this ineligibility is not permanent. The Act permits the Commission to forbear once "it determines that those requirements have been fully implemented."[31] What "full implementation" entails in this context, the statute does not say.

The Commission has already begun using its new power to forbear. At the first available opportunity, the Commission on its own motion did what courts had prevented it from doing in the preceding decade: it ordered long-distance carriers to cease filing tariffs.[32] And in response to a request by two competitive access providers (CAPs), the FCC decided to forbear from requiring nonincumbent LECs to file tariffs for interstate access.[33]

§2.1.4.1   Section 706 and the New Power to Forbear

Whereas section 160 merely *permits* the Commission to forbear, section 706(a) *requires* forbearance in certain circumstances. Section 706(a)[34] provides that "[t]he Commission . . . shall encourage

---

[29] *See id.* §251(c).

[30] *See id.* §271.

[31] *Id.* §160(d).

[32] *See* Policy and Rules Concerning the Interstate, Interexchange Marketplace, Second Report and Order, 11 F.C.C. Rec. 20,730 (1996). MCI quickly appealed the order, arguing that the Commission overstepped the bounds of its authority by embracing mandatory (as distinguished from permissive) detariffing. The D.C. Circuit Court of Appeals stayed the FCC's order pending MCI's appeal. *See* MCI Telecomms. Corp. v. FCC, No. 96-1459 (D.C. Cir. Feb. 13, 1997). Although the case was argued in 1997, the court has yet to issue a decision on the merits. Meanwhile, the FCC's order remains stayed.

[33] *See* Hyperion Telecommunications, Inc. Petition for Forbearance, Time Warner Communications Petition for Forbearance, Complete Detariffing for Competitive Access Providers and Competitive Local Exchange Carriers, Memorandum and Opinion and Order and Notice of Proposed Rulemaking, 12 F.C.C. Rec. 8596, 8597, ¶1 (1997) (hereinafter *Hyperion*). In the ruling, the Commission adopted a *permissive* detariffing regime. Thus, non-ILECs are permitted, but not required, to file FCC tariffs for interstate access service. The Commission simultaneously began a rulemaking to determine whether it should implement *mandatory* detariffing. *See id.*

[34] *See* 47 U.S.C. §157 note (a).

the deployment on a reasonable and timely basis of advanced telecommunications capability to all Americans . . . by utilizing, in a manner consistent with the public interest, convenience, and necessity, price cap regulation, regulatory forbearance, measures that promote competition in the local telecommunications market, or other regulating methods that remove barriers to infrastructure investment."[35] The section defines "advanced telecommunications capability" to mean "high-speed, switched, broadband telecommunications capability that enables users to originate and receive high-quality voice, data, graphics, and video communications." To reinforce this mandate, Congress also directed the Commission to undertake an inquiry, starting within 30 months of the 1996 Act's enactment and regularly afterwards, to determine "the availability of advanced telecommunications capability to all Americans."[36] If that capability is not "being deployed to all Americans in a reasonable and timely fashion," the Commission *"shall take immediate action* to accelerate deployment of such capability by removing barriers to infrastructure investment and by promoting competition in the telecommunications market."[37]

Section 706 by its terms requires the Commission to grant regulatory relief if it accelerates deployment of infrastructure for advanced telecommunications services. The breadth of the mandate is indicated by its catch-all authorization to use any "regulating methods"—even ones "other" than those specifically listed. That authority is reinforced by the general grant of implementing authority contained in section 4(i) of the Communications Act.[38] The Commission itself has stressed its responsibilities and authority to promote development of Internet and related services: "[s]ection 706 does not require that the FCC wait two and

---

[35] The same provision directs "each State commission with regulatory jurisdiction over telecommunications services" to do the same. *See id.* (§706(a)).

[36] *See id.* (§706(b)).

[37] *Id.* (emphasis added).

[38] Section 4(i) of the Communications Act, 47 U.S.C. §154(i), authorizes the Commission to "perform any and all acts, make such rules and regulations, and issue such orders, not inconsistent with this Act, as may be necessary in the execution of its functions." One of the Commission's "functions" is specified in section 706.

a half years before trying to explore ways to deliver advanced telecommunications services to all America, especially including rural America. . . . [W]e are very mindful of the urgency of this matter.[39]

§2.2 Monopoly: Cost Separation and Regulation

§2.2.1 Common Costs

A "joint" or "common" cost is a cost that needs to be incurred only once to produce two services.[40] Telephone and gas services are supplied over mostly separate facilities, and they therefore have few joint or common costs. But a single set of lines and switches can supply many different kinds of telephone service: local and long distance; retail and wholesale; residential and business; voice, facsimile, data, and video.[41] This is particularly true of *subscriber plant*—the line dedicated to connecting an end user's home or business to the telephone company's local switching office.[42]

Joint and common costs are often viewed as a source of possible market abuse.[43] In particular, when a monopoly service and potentially competitive services have common costs, the provider of the monopoly service may be able to extend some of its

[39] Testimony of Reed E. Hundt, Chairman, FCC, Before the Senate Comm. on Com., Sci. and Transp. (June 18, 1996).

[40] See Sharkey, The Theory of Natural Monopoly at 38. Economists commonly distinguish between joint costs and common costs. If output proportions can be varied, then separate marginal production costs can be identified, and costs are said to be common; if outputs are produced only in fixed proportions, then there are no separate incremental costs, and costs are said to be joint. See Kahn, 1 The Economics of Regulation at 79. In the long run, few costs are truly joint: even sheep can be bred to produce proportionally more wool or mutton.

[41] See Kahn & Shew, Current Issues in Telecommunications at 194; MCI Telecomms. Corp. v. FCC, 675 F.2d 408, 410 (D.C. Cir. 1982).

[42] See, e.g., National Assn. of Regulatory Util. Commrs. v. FCC, 737 F.2d 1095, 1103 (D.C. Cir. 1984) (NARUC v. FCC), cert. denied, 469 U.S. 1227 (1985); MCI Telecomms. Corp. v. FCC, 750 F.2d 135, 137 (D.C. Cir. 1984).

[43] See, e.g., M. Meitzen, Shared Costs and the Cash Cow Debate: Who Gets Milked?, Pub. Util. Fort., Apr. 1, 1991, at 32, 34.

monopoly power to the potentially competitive services. In particular, it may try to have the monopoly service's captive ratepayers foot the bill for the common costs, thereby bestowing on itself a cost advantage over rivals in potentially competitive markets — possibly to the point of bankrupting them. But joint and common costs are also a source of efficiency: they give rise to economies of scope.[44] By definition, where different products have joint or common costs, a single firm can produce them together more cheaply than multiple firms can produce them separately.

Thus, the incidence of joint and common costs poses a persistent regulatory dilemma: to what extent should monopolists be permitted to venture outside their monopoly domain? A permissive policy risks proliferating monopoly, thereby reducing efficiency.[45] A restrictive policy may deny consumers the benefit of economies of scope, just as surely reducing efficiency. Depending on numerous factors (including the extent to which adjacent markets are amenable to competition and the size of scope economies involved), regulators have reached different answers in different markets and at different times.

If a monopolist *is* permitted to venture into adjacent markets, the incidence of joint and common costs continues to give rise to tricky economic issues. If the monopolist's rates are regulated (as they usually are), regulators mindful of economic efficiency must determine the "right" price for different services whose costs are joint and common. Which service should bear what portion of joint and common costs? The difficulty here is that in telecommunications it is extraordinarily difficult to determine which service "causes" which costs to be incurred. And without that information, allocation between services is essentially arbitrary.[46]

---

[44] *See, e.g.,* E. Bailey & A. Friedlander, Market Structures and Multiproduct Industries, 20 J. Econ. Lit. 1024, 1031 (1982); D. Spulber, Regulation and Markets 114–120 (1989).

[45] Monopoly itself is, of course, usually wasteful because monopolists tend to charge too much and produce too little. (This is not necessarily true if a monopolist is able to engage in effective price discrimination, but effective price discrimination is often impossible. *See, e.g.,* A. C. Harberger, Monopoly and Resource Allocation, 44 Am. Econ. Rev. 77 (1954).)

[46] *See* Kahn, 1 The Economics of Regulation at 77–86.

Matters are even more complicated if a portion of common costs consists of "sunk" costs—which in the telecommunications industry is the rule rather than the exception. Once an investment has been made (that is, the cost has been "sunk"), it should in theory immediately be forgotten: ideally, price is tied to the *incremental* costs of operation.[47] Thus, if a single bridge crossing causes only 50 cents in incremental costs (say, wear and tear), then ideally the bridge owner should charge 50 cents—regardless of what the bridge cost when he built it a decade ago.[48] But if sunk costs were immediately forgotten, the bridge would never be built: river crossers, not costs, would sink.[49]

The obvious alternative is to charge enough to cover not only wear and tear, but also depreciation and interest to cover the sunk investment (say, 50 cents for wear and tear and $1.00 for depreciation and interest). But that alternative just as surely fosters inefficiency.[50] Motorists who would have been willing to pay 50 cents (the cost directly attributable to their crossing) might not be willing to pay $1.50: they might drive an additional ten miles to avoid the toll, spending, say, $1.00 in gasoline. Or a ferryboat might set up shop right next to the bridge upon determining that the marginal cost of ferrying a motorist across the river is only $1.00. These alternate river crossings involve

---

[47] *See id.* at 70.

[48] The example was originated by J. Dupuit, On the Measurement of the Utility of Public Works, Annales des Ponts et Chaussees (2d ser., vol. 8, 1844), *reprinted in* 2 International Economic Papers 83 (1952). Hotelling and Kahn have expanded on the example. *See* H. Hotelling, The General Welfare in Relation to Problems of Taxation and of Railway and Utility Rates, 6 Econometrica 242 (1938); Kahn, 1 Economics of Regulation at 87-88; *see also* S. Breyer, Economists and Economic Regulation, 47 U. Pitt. L. Rev. 205 (1985).

[49] Thus, "marginal cost is (only) the place to *begin*." Kahn, 1 Economics of Regulation at 67 (footnote omitted). Where sunk costs exist, pricing all services at marginal cost would result in losses because marginal costs are below average costs. *See id.* at 70–75; Spulber, Regulation and Markets at 115; R. Braeutigam, Optimal Policies for Natural Monopolies, *in* 2 Handbook of Industrial Organization 1289 (R. Schmalensee & R. Willig eds., 1989); J. Laffont & J. Tirole, The Regulation of Multiproduct Firms Part II: Applications to Competitive Environments and Policy Analysis, 43 J. Pub. Econ. 37 (1990).

[50] *See* Breyer, Regulation and Its Reform at 18; Kahn, 1 Economics of Regulation at 66–67.

expenditures of greater societal resources than bridge crossings and are therefore inefficient.[51]

Economists usually prescribe so-called *Ramsey pricing*[52] as the most efficient scheme for recovering the sunk costs in the bridge example. The basic idea of Ramsey pricing is to recover a disproportional share of sunk costs from consumers whose demand is the least elastic (that is, who most need the service and are least able to switch to alternatives). Allocating costs this way will least affect consumers' behavior, thus preventing inefficient consumption choices.[53] Applied to telephony, Ramsey pricing principles would have regulators load fixed costs common to providing local and long-distance services disproportionally onto *local* rates, which subscribers view as more of a necessity and for which fewer alternatives are available.[54]

At least until 1996, telecom regulators have typically followed precisely the opposite course. For example, in the face of political pressure to keep rates for basic residential service low, they have heaped fixed common costs disproportionally on long-distance users.[55] (As for telecom "ferryboats," regulators simply refused to give them an operating license.) And even among users of the same service, regulators have consistently allowed social policies to triumph over economic efficiency: they have required telephone companies to charge different users the same rates, even if different users are quite dissimilar insofar as the cost of providing service is concerned. For example, suburban homeowners pay the same rate as urban apartment dwellers, even if a homeowner requires a much longer and therefore more expensive line to connect to the downtown central office.[56]

---

[51] *See* Breyer, Economists and Economic Regulation at 212.

[52] *See* F. Ramsey, A Contribution to the Theory of Taxation, 37 Econ. J. 47 (1927); *see also* Kahn & Shew, Current Issues in Telecommunications at 247.

[53] *See* Sharkey, The Theory of Natural Monopoly at 50–51; W. Baumol & D. Bradford, Optimal Departures from Marginal Cost Pricing, 60 Am. Econ. Rev. 265 (1970).

[54] *See* J. Panzar & R. Willig, Free Entry and the Sustainability of Natural Monopoly, 8 Bell J. Econ. 1 (1977); A. Kahn, The Next Steps in Telecommunications Regulation and Research, Pub. Util. Fort., July 19, 1984, at 13.

[55] *See generally* J. Bonbright, Principles of Public Utility Rates (1961).

[56] *See* A. Kahn, The Road to More Intelligent Telephone Pricing, 1 Yale J. on Reg. 139, 141 (1984).

The regulation of common costs in telephony has thus raised all the familiar problems of government tax-and-spend programs. The regulator is responsible, at least indirectly, for investment in a publicly shared resource: the telephone network. The revenues to support that investment must be raised from users of the service—but that burden can be shared in an infinite variety of ways, as it can be in any tax program. The monopolist serves as the regulator's agent on both ends—taxing low-cost consumers and spending to subsidize high-cost ones.[57] Inevitably, there will be quarrels about who must pay, who will benefit, and which government authorities will supervise the collection of revenues and allocation of benefits.

§2.2.2   Separations and Cost Accounting

Traditional rate regulation built an accounting bridge from the producer's side of telephony—rife with joint and common costs—to the consumer's—rife with rate averaging and bundling. Somehow or other, joint and common costs must be divided and then reassembled.

§2.2.2.1   Federal and State Spheres of Authority[58]

A long-distance trunk connecting an exchange in New York to one in Washington is obviously interstate in nature. But a call from Wall Street to Capitol Hill uses more than that trunk—it also uses local lines and switches in both New York and Washington.

---

[57] See E. Zajac, Fairness or Efficiency: An Introduction to Public Utility Pricing 59, 72 (1978); Kahn & Shew, Current Issues in Telecommunications at 192–193; Meitzen, Shared Costs and the Cash Cow Debate at 32; R. Posner, Taxation by Regulation, 2 Bell J. Econ. & Mgmt. Sci. 22 (1971); G. Brock, Office of Plans and Policy, FCC, Telephone Pricing to Promote Universal Service and Economic Freedom (OPP Working Paper No. 18, 1986).

[58] See generally P. Temin, The Fall of the Bell System: A Study in Pricing and Politics 19-27 (1987); R. Gabel, Development of Separations Principles in the Telephone Industry (1967); Kahn & Shew, Current Issues in Telecommunications at 194–199; Meitzen, Shared Costs and the Cash Cow Debate at 32, 35.

Should the price of the long-distance call cover some portion of those "local" costs? Who should decide: state or federal regulators?

To an important extent, a 1930 Supreme Court ruling, *Smith v. Illinois Bell Telephone Co.*, has provided the answer.[59] In *Smith*, a local telephone company had filed suit in federal district court arguing that the Illinois PUC had fixed its payphone rates at a level so low as to result in a confiscatorily low return on its investment (thereby unconstitutionally taking its property). In determining its return, the company had followed the Bell System's established method of "board-to-board" accounting: it had allocated to its state rate base 100 percent of the costs of facilities between the handset and the long-distance switchboard. The defendants attacked this separations method in the district court, but the district court sided with the telephone company, saying that, quite apart from the issue's slight significance, the company's separation method was reasonable.[60] Though the district court agreed that interstate facilities must be separated from the state rate base, it held that "including exchange property as interstate property" was not required.[61]

Starting from the uncontested premise that some kind of separation was required,[62] the Supreme Court reversed. The company's board-to-board separations method, the Court held, failed to reflect "the indisputable fact that the subscriber's station, and the other facilities of the Illinois Company which are used in connecting with the long-distance toll board, are employed in the interstate transmission and reception of messages," thereby "ignor[ing] altogether the actual uses to which the property is

[59] 282 U.S. 133 (1930). For further discussion of *Smith*, see M. Kellogg, J. Thorne, & P. Huber, Federal Telecommunications Law §2.5 (1992) (hereinafter *FTL1*).

[60] Illinois Bell Tel. Co. v. Moynihan, 38 F.2d 77, 83 (N.D. Ill.) (Moynihan), *rev'd*, 282 U.S. 133 (1930). The court observed that because only one-half percent of all calls were interstate, the separations issue "cannot affect the result in this case." *Id.*

[61] *Id.*

[62] *See* Illinois Bell Tel. Co. v. Moynihan, 282 U.S. 133, 148 (1930) ("separation of the intrastate and interstate property . . . is essential to the appropriate recognition of the competent governmental authority in each field of regulation").

put."[63] Thus, there would have to be some kind of "apportionment" to ensure that "the intrastate service to which the exchange property is allocated will [not] bear an undue burden."[64] Until that apportionment was made, the Court could not adequately evaluate the telephone company's takings claim: "the validity of the order of the state commission can be suitably tested only by an appropriate determination of the value of the property employed in the intrastate business."[65]

§2.2.2.2   Dual Authority Under the Communications Act of 1934

Strictly speaking, the Supreme Court in *Smith* held no more than that in a takings suit a telephone-company plaintiff must deduct some portion of the value of "exchange property" (attributable to interstate usage) from its intrastate rate base before a court can properly evaluate the claim. But *Smith*'s approach to jurisdictional separation has proved to be of much broader and more lasting importance because Congress took it as its conceptual model in the Communications Act of 1934.[66]

Sections 1 and 2(a) of the 1934 Act gave the FCC rate-making authority over interstate service,[67] but section 2(b) of the Act emphatically denied it jurisdiction with respect to "charges, classifications, practices, services, facilities, or regulations for or in connection with intrastate communication service."[68] Thus, by

[63] *Id.* at 150–151.

[64] *Id.* at 151.

[65] *Id.* at 149.

[66] For a full discussion of the allocation of regulatory authority between the FCC and state regulators, see Chapter 3.

[67] *See* 47 U.S.C. §§151, 152(a).

[68] *Id.* §152(b). Section 2(b) was intended to ensure that the holding of Houston, E. & W. Tex. Ry. Co. v. United States, 234 U.S. 342 (1914) (*The Shreveport Rate Case*) would not apply to telephone service. In that case, the Supreme Court had interpreted the Interstate Commerce Act to empower the Interstate Commerce Commission (ICC) to prevent discrimination by requiring interstate railroads to alter rates on intrastate routes where those rates differed from ICC-regulated rates on comparable interstate routes. In effect, the Shreveport Rate Case provided the ICC broad rate-making power with respect to intrastate service.

and large, the FCC would regulate only rates for interstate long-distance service; the states would regulate rates for local service. Because, at the time, both interstate service and local service were provided by monopolist carriers subject to rate-of-return regulation, the Act's basic jurisdictional outline raised the same separations question as that addressed in *Smith* (though in a different context): what costs should be allocated to which rate base?

The 1934 Act's answer was to empower the FCC to promulgate separation rules apportioning telephone companies' assets between state and federal rate bases. Section 221(c) authorizes the Commission to "classify the property" of any carrier and to "determine what property of [a] carrier shall be considered as used in interstate or foreign telephone toll service."[69] Section 221(d) adds that the Commission may "value only that part of the property . . . determined to be used in interstate or foreign telephone toll service."[70] Before exercising its powers under section 221, the FCC must consult "the State commission . . . of any State in which the property of [the relevant] carrier is located."[71] Moreover, Congress in 1971 amended the statute to require the FCC to "refer any proceeding regarding the jurisdictional separation of common carrier property and expenses between interstate and intrastate operations, which it institutes pursuant to a notice of proposed rulemaking . . . to a Federal-State Joint Board."[72]

Section 221 does not by its terms say that the FCC's separation rules preempt inconsistent state measures. And one could readily imagine a logically coherent system under which federal and state regulators would each independently determine the

[69] 47 U.S.C. §221(c).

[70] *Id.* §221(d).

[71] *Id.* §221(c).

[72] *Id.* §410(c). Joint boards are composed of four state and three federal commissioners. *See id.* The "recommended decision" of a joint board is not binding on the FCC. *See id.* Section 410(c) was introduced at the urging of the National Association of Regulatory Utilities Commissioners; NARUC complained that the FCC was allocating too many costs to the intrastate jurisdiction, to be recovered through local charges, and not enough to the interstate jurisdiction, to be recovered through long-distance charges. *See* 117 Cong. Rec. 15,979–15,981 (1971).

size of their own rate-of-return rate base[73]—no less than one could imagine a system under which federal and state regulators each independently determine their own depreciation practices.[74] But the Supreme Court in dictum,[75] and courts of appeals with varying levels of authoritativeness,[76] have rejected such a dual system. This conclusion does, of course, find support in the consultation requirements of sections 221(c) and 410(c): why consult the states if the FCC's rules would not bind them?[77]

In any event, with some exceptions,[78] the FCC's separations issues have given rise to little tension with state regulators: for the most part, the FCC has voluntarily pursued state-friendly policies by loading a disproportional share of joint and common costs into the federal rate base, thereby depressing state-regulated rates for local service (and making state regulators' jobs easier). Indeed, the FCC allowed NARUC to participate in drafting its first set of separations rules (known as the Separations Manual), which was adopted in 1947.[79]

Although all carriers continue to be required to separate their costs on their books, the practical significance of jurisdictional

---

[73] See Hawaiian Tel. Co. v. Hawaii Pub. Util. Commn., 827 F.2d 1264, 1278–1281 (9th Cir. 1987) (Ferguson, J., dissenting), *cert. denied,* 487 U.S. 1218 (1988).

[74] The Supreme Court in Louisiana Public Service Commission v. FCC, 476 U.S. 355 (1986) (*Louisiana PSC*), held that despite section 220(b), which expressly empowers the FCC to promulgate depreciation rules, the FCC lacks authority to preempt states' depreciation rules different from its own.

[75] *Id.* at 375.

[76] See Hawaiian Tel. Co. v. Hawaii Pub. Util. Commn., 827 F.2d at 1275 (so stating where appellants had conceded the point); State Corp. Commn. of Kan. v. FCC, 787 F.2d 1421, 1426–1427 (10th Cir. 1986) (*SCC of Kansas*) (basing its conclusion on pre-*Louisiana PSC* preemption cases).

[77] See *SCC of Kansas,* 787 F.2d at 1425–1426; *but cf. Louisiana PSC,* 476 U.S. at 367, 377–380.

[78] See 47 U.S.C. §221(c).

[79] See *generally* American Tel. & Tel. Co. and the Associated Bell System Companies, Charges for Interstate and Foreign Communication Service, Memorandum Opinion and Order, 3 F.C.C.2d 307, 309–311, ¶¶11–16 (1966). In 1969, the FCC replaced the Separations Manual with a set of rules found in 47 C.F.R. Part 36. See Prescription of Procedure for Separating and Allocating Plant Investment, Operating Expenses, Taxes, and Reserves Between the Intrastate and Interstate Operations of Telephone Companies, Report and Order, 16 F.C.C.2d 317 (1969).

separation has diminished in recent years. Separation rules determine the size of carriers' rate bases (and therefore their rates) under rate-of-return regulation. But under price-cap regulation—which, since the late 1980s, federal and state regulators have increasingly embraced—rates are independent of costs. For that reason, the FCC recently inquired whether the time has come to abolish the separations process altogether.[80] As the Commission noted, however, separation of costs remains relevant to some extent even under price-cap regulation, and some carriers continue to be subject to rate-of-return regulation on either the state or the federal side (or both).[81]

§2.2.2.3 Divisions of Authority Under the Telecommunications Act of 1996

Despite all the complications attending the 1934 Act's division of regulatory authority, that division at least reflected the Act's allocation of responsibilities for substantive regulation. Long-distance service (or, more precisely, interstate long-distance service) would be regulated by the FCC; Title II of the Act contains numerous detailed rules and guidelines governing that task. Local service (or, more precisely, intrastate service) would be regulated by the states; the Act included essentially no rules as to how the states should acquit themselves of that task.

The 1996 Act abandons this modicum of tidiness: jurisdictional lines no longer follow the distinction between intra- and interstate service. The Act, intended to allow competition to penetrate into the heart of the local exchange, contains detailed rules—all involving intrastate matter—governing resale, interconnection, and unbundling.[82] Although the Act leaves the implementation of some of these new rules to the states,[83] it

---

[80] *See* Jurisdictional Separations Reform and Referral to the Federal-State Joint Board, Notice of Proposed Rulemaking, 12 F.C.C. Rec. 22,120, 22,136 ¶32 (1997).

[81] *See id.* at 22,138–22,140 ¶¶38–42.

[82] *See* 47 U.S.C. §§251, 252.

[83] *See, e.g., id.* §251(c)(4)(B) (resale); *id.* §251(f) (exemption and modification authority); *id.* §252(b) (arbitration); *id.* §252(e) (approval of interconnection agreements); *id.* §252(f) (review of SGAT).

expressly entrusts others to the FCC.[84] The implementation of still other matters is not specifically entrusted to either side of the jurisdictional divide; whether federal or state regulators should be responsible for implementation there has proved very contentious indeed.[85] Chapter 3 discusses these jurisdictional issues in more detail.

§2.2.2.4   Separations by Cost Category

Quite apart from jurisdictional separation, federal regulators (and their state counterparts) have traditionally gone through countless additional stages of cost slicing, chopping, and dicing. Costs and revenues of regulated businesses are divided from unregulated ones. Different rates of return are applied to debt, preferred stock, and common equity.[86] In theory, though much less so in practice, it has been important to distinguish between *traffic-sensitive* (TS) and *non-traffic-sensitive* (NTS) costs.[87] (Some costs (like the cost of carriage between central office switches) depend quite closely on the volume of traffic handled;[88] others (like the cost of the dedicated line to a subscriber's home) do not.[89]) Costs are then finally divided among dozens of different categories—switched and nonswitched, intrastate and interstate, intraLATA and interLATA.[90]

---

[84] *See, e.g., id.* §251(b)(2) (number portability); *id.* §251(c)(4)(B) (resale); *id.* §251(d)(2) (identification of network elements that must be unbundled); *id.* §251(e)(1) (number administration); *id.* §251(g)(1) (access discrimination); *id.* §251(h)(2) (definition of incumbent local exchange carrier (ILEC)); *id.* §252(e)(5) (failure to act by state commission).

[85] *See generally* AT&T Corp. v. Iowa Utils. Bd., 119 S. Ct. 721 (1999).

[86] *See* El Paso Natural Gas Co. v. Federal Power Commn., 449 F.2d 1245, 1250 (5th Cir. 1971).

[87] *See* Kahn, The Road to More Intelligent Telephone Pricing at 140–141.

[88] *See* NARUC v. FCC, 737 F.2d at 1104.

[89] *See id.* ("The basic cost of installing and maintaining a local loop remains the same whether the subscriber or 'end user,' uses the loop to make one call or a hundred, and whether those calls are local or long-distance.")

[90] *See* P. Huber, The Geodesic Network: 1987 Report on Competition in the Telephone Industry 3.53 (1987).

§2.2.2.5 Allocating Costs to Services

The ostensible purpose of this process is to charge the right price for each individual service. Each service should bear its own costs (the reasoning runs); costs must thus be subdivided finely enough to permit appropriate allocation.

Traffic-sensitive costs can indeed often be attributed reasonably accurately to the various services that cause them. Common costs, many of which are non-traffic-sensitive, are another matter. Absent causation data that is usually unavailable, there is no "correct" allocation here—every allocation is arbitrary to some degree. When a new service is supported by—or grafted onto— an existing, productively used facility, should it be priced to reflect *incremental* or *fully* distributed cost?[91] As the bridge example in section 2.2.1 illustrates, incremental costing takes the existing base of operations—management, physical plant, and such—as a given and considers only additional costs attributable to the new service. All non-traffic-sensitive common costs are then borne by the existing (often monopoly) services. Fully distributed costing allocates common costs among all services on "some basis indicating each service's contributing share of that cost."[92] The distribution is usually made on the basis of "relative use," with usage measured in some common unit—minutes of telephone traffic, for example. The FCC's general policy has been to require fully distributed costs, which allow ratepayers for monopoly service to "participate in the economies of scale and scope which we believe can be achieved through integration of non-regulated" and regulated services.[93]

---

[91] *See generally* MCI v. FCC, 675 F.2d 408, 410 (D.C. Cir. 1982) (upholding FCC's decision to prescribe fully distributed costing (FDC) with respect to AT&T).

[92] MCI v. FCC, 675 F.2d at 410–411.

[93] Separation of Costs of Regulated Telephone Service from Costs of Non-regulated Activities, Report and Order, 2 F.C.C. Rec. 1298, 1312 ¶109 (1987) (hereinafter *Joint Cost Order*). The FCC has noted that "in theory" fully distributed costs are not necessary to avoid cross-subsidy; cross-subsidy is "avoided when all of the long run incremental costs of an activity are borne by that activity." *Id.* Nevertheless, the FCC has determined that fully distributed costing minimizes the risk that monopoly services cross-subsidize

Properly speaking, joint and common costs have nothing to do with cross-subsidy; they involve real (if administratively inconvenient) efficiencies of production. On the other hand, joint and common costs do create opportunity for accounting hanky-panky. A regulated utility that is also involved in an unregulated competitive business may have both the incentive and the opportunity to shift the costs of competitive operations to the regulated side of the line. The incentive comes from rate of return (though not from true price-cap) regulation. If regulators fail to catch the cost misallocation, the cross-subsidizer may exceed its permitted rate of return by shuffling costs (and thus profits) between regulated and competitive operations. Thus, maintaining the cleanest possible line between the costs of *regulated* and *nonregulated* services is an important objective.

§2.2.2.6 The Joint Cost Order

At the federal level, the FCC's 1987 Joint Cost Order is the principal regulatory vehicle for accomplishing this goal.[94] The Order established two separate, but complementary sets of rules[95] applicable to all local exchange and dominant interexchange carriers.[96] The first set establishes a cost-allocation

---

competitive ones. *See, e.g.,* AT&T Long Lines Department, Memorandum Opinion and Order, 61 F.C.C.2d 587, 589, ¶4 (1976), *on recons.,* 64 F.C.C.2d 971 (1977), *on further recons.,* 67 F.C.C.2d 1441 (1978), *aff'd sub nom.* Aeronautical Radio, Inc. v. FCC, 642 F.2d 1221 (D.C. Cir. 1980), *cert. denied,* 451 U.S. 920 (1981).

[94] *See Joint Cost Order,* 2 F.C.C. Rec. at 1298, *on recons.,* 2 F.C.C. Rec. 6283 (1987) (hereinafter *Joint Cost Order on Reconsideration*), *on further recons.,* 3 F.C.C. Rec. 6701 (1988) (hereinafter *Joint Cost Order on Further Reconsideration*). In promulgating these rules, the FCC explained that "protecting ratepayers from unjust and unreasonable interstate rates is the primary purpose behind the accounting separation of regulated from nonregulated activities, just as it is the purpose behind all of our accounting and cost allocation rules. Our commitment to cost-based rates demands close attention to the manner in which the costs a company uses to support its interstate and access tariff filings are separated from the other costs of the company." *Joint Cost Order,* 2 F.C.C. Rec. at 1303 ¶37.

[95] The rules governing the allocation of costs were placed in Part 64 of the Commission's rules. *See* 47 C.F.R. §§64.901 et seq. The rules governing transactions with affiliates were placed in Part 32. *See id.* §32.27.

process to separate the costs of regulated and nonregulated activities offered by a carrier. The second governs transactions between a carrier and its affiliates.[97] Any doubt regarding the proper allocation of costs among regulated and unregulated services is resolved against the latter.[98]

§2.2.2.7   Common Costs

Under the FCC's fully distributed costing principles, each activity must bear its full share not only of the costs directly attributable to it, but also of general overhead costs.[99] The Commission has acknowledged that this method necessarily entails some economic distortion. Ordinarily, a producer decides whether to offer a new product or service by comparing anticipated revenues with long-run incremental costs. But incremental costs always depend on what is already being produced or, put

[96] The FCC's accounting safeguards are not binding on the states, but almost every state commission uses the FCC's rules at least as the starting point for its own processes. Moreover, as a result of the joint cost allocation rules and the jurisdictional separations rules, the intrastate costs assigned to the states are stripped of all costs associated with activities defined as nonregulated by the FCC. Thus, the "default" position is the setting of intrastate rates based on intrastate costs that reflect the FCC's determination of what are regulated services.

[97] "[I]nsuring just and reasonable rates for services that remain subject to regulation requires guarding against cross-subsidy of nonregulated ventures by regulated services," the Commission explained, "and that cross-subsidy can result either from the misallocation of common costs or from improper intracorporate transfer pricing." *Joint Cost Order,* 2 F.C.C. Rec. at 1303 ¶33. A monopoly carrier LEC might be able to inflate its costs (and thus its rate base and thus its rates), for example, by purchasing equipment from an unregulated affiliate at unrealistically high prices. The rules aim to prevent this.

[98] All investments, revenues, and expenses associated with products and services subject to federal or state tariff regulation are classified for accounting purposes as "regulated" except as otherwise expressly provided by the Commission. *See* 47 C.F.R. §32.14(a)–(b). Preemptively deregulated activities and activities (other than incidental activities) never subject to regulation are classified as "nonregulated." Activities that qualify for incidental treatment under the policies of the FCC and activities that have been deregulated by a state are classified as regulated activities. Services that the FCC has deregulated, but whose regulation by the states the FCC has not preempted are classified as regulated activities until the FCC decides otherwise. *See id.* §32.23.

[99] *See id.* §64.901(b)(2).

differently, what activities are already carrying the freight of common overhead. This, however, was precisely what the FCC declined to accept. Even if regulated activities came first and unregulated activities second, the FCC would not permit all the efficiencies of joint production to accrue to the later arrivals. Some efficiency would be sacrificed to ensure a "fair" sharing with ratepayers.

Common costs are, once again, the heart of the problem. They are grouped into homogeneous cost categories and allocated between regulated and nonregulated activities based, whenever possible, on direct analysis of their origin or, failing that, into some cost category that seems more or less right. When all else fails, a general allocation factor is used based on the ratio of all expenses directly assigned or attributed to regulated and non-regulated activities.[100]

With central office equipment and cable and wire facilities (network plant), however, the Commission concluded that allocation based on relative use would consistently allocate too few costs to new services.[101] So it focused on projected *peak* usage by the new service, on the logic that peak usage would dictate the costs of deploying extra capacity.[102] Once allocated to nonregulated use, investments may not be reallocated to regulated use even if the nonregulated use of network plant decreases or indeed never materializes.[103] This ensures that investment risk

---

[100] The general allocation factor is computed by calculating the ratios of the amounts of expenses, wages, and assets directly assigned or attributed to regulated and nonregulated services. *See Joint Cost Order,* 2 F.C.C. Rec. at 1313 ¶¶122–123.

[101] The Commission cited two reasons: "the lag between investment and demand, and the likelihood that new nonregulated network services will experience higher growth rates than established regulated services. Investment must be placed in anticipation of future demand, while actual use measurements are of necessity measurements of historical use." Thus, a focus on actual use entails allocating all current costs, including the cost of excess capacity installed in anticipation of nonregulated use based on usage of network plant in the current period. Excess capacity cost caused by nonregulated activity may thus be borne in large measure by regulated activities. *Joint Cost Order on Reconsideration,* 2 F.C.C. Rec. at 6287–6288 ¶¶37–39.

[102] *See id.* at 6287–6288 ¶39.

[103] *See Joint Cost Order on Further Reconsideration,* 3 F.C.C. Rec. at 6705 ¶29. The FCC considered these rules "essential to the integrity of a cost allocation

incurred in nonregulated ventures is not shifted to the regulated side. By contrast, if demand for a nonregulated service exceeds original forecasts, both undepreciated baseline cost and interest must be reallocated.[104]

§2.2.2.8 Affiliate Transactions

The FCC's rules also address the transfer of assets between regulated and nonregulated affiliates.[105] Such transactions must be recorded on the carrier's books at market or tariff price if such a price can be determined. If not, transactions must be recorded at the higher of net book cost or fair market value (for transfers from the regulated to the unregulated side) or at the lower of the two (for transfers the other way).[106] The regulated

---

system which requires cost allocations, like their associated investment decisions, to be made in anticipation of network usage, and which seeks to prevent regulated activities from absorbing nonregulated costs, either at the start of a forecast period or subsequently." *Joint Cost Order on Reconsideration*, 2 F.C.C. Rec. at 6290–6291 ¶64.

[104] This reallocation causes the nonregulated activity to assume the costs that would have been allocated to it had the forecast been accurate and thus protects ratepayers from underwriting the costs of unused capacity, which is eventually used to meet unforeseen nonregulated demand. Reallocations will be retroactive to the year in which an underforecast was made. Moreover, reallocations are to be made each year for each previous three-year period for which actual usage data or a new forecast establishes a need for reallocation. *See Joint Cost Order on Further Reconsideration*, 3 F.C.C. Rec. at 6705 ¶33.

[105] The affiliate transaction rules, like the cost allocation rules, apply to all dominant carriers. *See Joint Cost Order*, 2 F.C.C. Rec. at 1304 ¶¶42–49; *see also* 47 C.F.R. §32.27(f). They also apply to transfers between regulated and nonregulated accounts, as well as regulated and nonregulated affiliates, to ensure "that carriers do not seek to avoid [the] rules by reincarnating a nonregulated affiliate as an operating division." *Joint Cost Order on Reconsideration*, 2 F.C.C. Rec. at 6296 ¶121. Transactions between two regulated affiliates, however, do not present the same potential for cost shifting and need not adhere to the rules. *See id.* at 6296 ¶122.

[106] *See Joint Cost Order*, 2 F.C.C. Rec. at 1300 ¶5. When a carrier provides to an affiliate a service that is neither tariffed nor provided to third parties or when a carrier receives from an affiliate a service that is not provided to third parties, the Commission requires the carrier to record that service at a cost determined in accordance with the cost allocation standards discussed in the text: "If we were to allow a holding company or its affiliate to provide services to both carrier and noncarrier affiliates without fully allocating the costs of

side always gets the benefit of the doubt.[107] The FCC acknowledged that this might discourage some transactions, but thought that this was, on balance, better than risking the cost shifting that might otherwise occur.[108] The D.C. Circuit rejected a challenge to the rules by Southwestern Bell and GTE, concluding that "the FCC had adopted measures reasonably designed to prevent systematic abuse of ratepayers."[109]

§2.2.2.9 The Uniform System of Accounts

One of the Commission's very first acts was to prescribe a Uniform System of Accounts (USOA) for telephone companies.[110] The USOA was designed to facilitate rate-base determinations in

---

those services," the FCC explained, "we would create the incentive for carriers to escape the cost allocation rules by moving their service departments into nonregulated affiliates." *Joint Cost Order on Reconsideration,* 2 F.C.C. Rec. at 6297 1304 ¶130.

[107] *See Joint Cost Order on Reconsideration,* 2 F.C.C. at 6293 ¶92. The FCC justified this asymmetry on two grounds. First, ratepayers generally bear the economic burden of most utility assets and hence are entitled to the gain when the market value of the assets exceeds net book cost. *See id.* at 6295 ¶¶114–115. Second, requiring an asset transferred to the regulated entity to be recorded on the regulated books at the lower of fair market value or book value protects ratepayers from potential dangers of rate base inflation that could arise if an asset is transferred at an artificially high price. *See id.* at 6295–6296 ¶116.

[108] *See id.* at 6296 ¶117.

[109] Southwestern Bell Corp. v. FCC, 896 F.2d 1378 (D.C. Cir. 1990). According to the court, diversified telephone companies possess "a natural incentive" to shift costs to their regulated telephone service and thereby guarantee the recovery of those costs from ratepayers. *Id.* at 1379. "Based on its past experience in regulating intracompany asset transfers and the complexity of these transactions," the court explained, "the FCC could reasonably conclude that [its affiliated transaction rules] were necessary to brake the carriers' potential for abuse." *Id.* at 1381. Although the court recognized that the FCC's rules might sometimes injure ratepayers by discouraging advantageous intracompany transactions, the court held that "the FCC was entitled to conclude that 'on balance prevention of cost shifting is the more important goal.'" *Id.* The FCC, the court explained, has an obligation "to discourage inflation of the regulated company's rate base by less than arms-length transactions," and it "may seek to avoid the threat of cost misallocation with disincentives built into the accounting rules." *Id.* at 1382.

[110] *See* 47 C.F.R. Part 32.

the traditional top-to-bottom monopoly model. It aggregated expenses and classified them according to the organization that incurred them rather than by the particular activities or services. It relied on a three-digit numbering of accounts that was inflexible, perpetuated archaic presentations, and constrained future expansion along technological or functional lines.

In July 1978, the Commission therefore initiated a drastic revision that would span almost a decade.[111] It adopted its new accounting system on January 1, 1988.[112] The new USOA disaggregates and realigns balance sheet and income statement accounts to track technical distinctions, products, and services[113]

---

[111] *See* Revision of the Uniform System of Accounts and Financial Reporting Requirements for Telephone Companies (Parts 31, 33, 42, and 43 of the FCC's Rules), Notice of Proposed Rulemaking, 70 F.C.C.2d 719 (1978). The Commission later established the Telecommunications Industry Advisory Group (TIAG) and charged it with developing a revised USOA. In 1984, the TIAG filed its report, which the Commission adopted with some modifications. *See* Revision of the Uniform System of Accounts for Telephone Companies to Accommodate Generally Accepted Accounting Principles (Parts 31, 33, 42, and 43 of the FCC's Rules), Report and Order, 102 F.C.C.2d 964, 965 ¶¶3–5 (1985) (hereinafter *Revised Uniform System of Accounts*).

[112] *See* Revision of the Uniform System of Accounts and Financial Reporting Requirements for Class A and Class B Telephone Companies (Parts 31, 33, 42, and 43 of the FCC's Rules), Report and Order, 60 Rad. Reg. 2d (P & F) 1111 ¶108 (1986) (hereinafter *Financial Reporting Requirements*). The new USOA provides different requirements for two classes of carriers: Class A companies (or Tier 1 LECs, as they are usually called), with annual gross operating revenues of $100 million or more, and Class B companies, with annual gross operating revenues of less than $100 million. Carriers in Class B are subject to fewer accounting rules than Class A carriers. The Commission noted, however, that "many small companies maintain more detailed systems (at a Class A level) because of state imposed requirements or because they see it themselves as being more advantageous for settlements purposes. We will not in this order supersede the requirements of the states as the states perceive them. However, both the states and the small companies should be aware that this new USOA will prompt a new separations review, which is likely to result in a two-tiered separations process—one for the larger companies and one for the smaller companies. If equitable treatment can be achieved for the smaller companies, we expect their perceptions to change, and their burdens will not be as great as they anticipate." *Id.* ¶109.

[113] A two-dimensional matrix is used to classify expenses (a) according to their specific function (advertising, for example) and (b) according to their type (salaries and wages, benefits, rents, and other). A new four-digit numbering scheme is used, which is logically ordered and flexible enough to

and creates a fistful of new accounts.[114] All this facilitates assigning costs to particular activities or services. It is now easier to identify functions used to provide nonregulated services. The new accounts provide significantly more detail about revenues, expenses, and assets. The new USOA also incorporated, to an extent, generally accepted accounting principles (GAAP).[115]

§2.2.2.10 Enforcement Mechanisms

The FCC's *Joint Cost Order* required the major LECs (so-called Tier I LECs) and AT&T to file cost allocation manuals setting out in detail how they will implement the prescribed standards.[116] The manuals describe a company's nonregulated activities, list and justify all activities accounted for as "incidentals," show all corporate affiliates, identify affiliates that engage in

---

permit further expansion. These accounts are listed in Part 32 of the Commission's rules. Each account begins with 32 followed by a four-digit number. Accounts are broken down into general categories, such as balance sheet accounts, revenue accounts, and expense accounts.

[114] For nonregulated activities, clearing accounts for certain costs, subsidiary record category requirements for certain accounts, separate accounts for capitalized leases, and separate and distinct expense accounts for depreciation and amortization. *See Financial Reporting Requirements* ¶3 & app. A.

[115] *See* Revision of the Uniform System of Accounts and Financial Reporting Requirements for Class A and Class B Telephone Companies (Parts 31, 33, 42, and 43 of the FCC's Rules), Memorandum Opinion and Order, 2 F.C.C. Rec. 1086 (1987). GAAP is a set of accounting standards recognized in the accounting profession that most nonregulated enterprises use as the basis for their external financial statements and reports. It directs the recording of financial events and transactions and relates how assets, liabilities, revenues, and expenses are to be identified, measured, and reported. In very broad terms, GAAP requires that assets and liabilities be recorded at historical cost, that revenue be realized when the earning process is complete, that costs be matched with the revenues they helped to generate, that disclosure be full and adequate, that accounting principles be applied consistently between accounting periods, and that accounting data be objectively determined and verifiable. *See Revised Uniform System of Accounts*, 102 F.C.C.2d at 964–965, 964 n.1.

[116] Although the Commission's cost allocation standards apply to all local exchange carriers and dominant interexchange carriers, only companies with more than $100 million in operating revenues were initially required to file and obtain approval of their cost allocation manuals. *See Joint Cost Order*, 2 F.C.C. Rec. at 1300 ¶4.

transactions with the telco and describe those transactions, and specify the cost categories and apportionment methods to be used in connection with each account.[117] They are to be updated regularly and reviewed by the Commission.[118]

These same carriers are also required to submit to annual independent audits,[119] with the FCC, in effect, auditing the auditors.[120] The independent auditor's annual report must attest that the telco is complying with its cost manual and that cost allocations are the product of accurate methods.[121] The audit must also confirm that a carrier's joint cost allocation reports to the FCC comply in all material respects with the company's cost

---

[117] *See id.* at 1328 ¶240. The original manuals were due on or by September 1, 1987. *See id.* at 1327–1328 ¶¶232–235. The Commission required some significant revisions; they were refiled in early 1988. *See* Computer III Remand Proceedings: Bell Operating Company Safeguards, and Tier 1 Local Exchange Company Safeguards, Notice of Proposed Rulemaking and Order, 6 F.C.C. Rec. 174, 177 ¶¶17–22 (1990) (hereinafter *Computer III Proceedings*). After further modifications, the Commission approved them.

[118] *See Computer III Proceedings,* 6 F.C.C. Rec. at 177 ¶18.

[119] *See Joint Cost Order,* 2 F.C.C. Rec. at 1330–1331 ¶¶243–259.

[120] The independent audit program is considered an adjunct to, not a replacement for, the Commission's own audit program. *See id.* at 1330–1333 ¶¶250–274 ("We view the independent audits as an important aid in fulfilling our responsibilities, not a delegation of such responsibilities."). The Commission requires all contracts for the provision of attestation services to contain an express provision that, in the event of an FCC staff audit, the carrier to be audited and the auditor hereby expressly agree to provide FCC staff access to auditor workpapers. *See id.* at 1333–1334 ¶¶275–283.

[121] In accounting jargon, the attestation must take the form of a "positive opinion" of compliance. *See id.* at 1330–1331 ¶¶254–257. As part of its "Statement on Standards for Attestation Engagement," the American Institute of Certified Public Accountants (AICPA) states that an attest report should be limited to one or two standards of assurance—an examination leading to a "positive opinion" or a review leading to an expression of "negative assurance." When expressing a positive opinion, the practitioner should clearly state whether in his or her opinion the presentation of assertions is presented in conformity with established or stated criteria. In providing a negative assurance, the petitioner's conclusion need state only whether any information came to the practitioner's attention on the basis of the work performed that indicates that the assertions are not presented in all material respects in conformity with established or stated criteria. *See Joint Cost Order on Reconsideration,* 2 F.C.C. Rec. at 6304 ¶¶183–186; *see also Computer III Proceedings,* 6 F.C.C. Rec. at 178–179 ¶¶28–32 (strengthening standard used by independent auditors).

allocation manual and applicable rules.[122] Auditors must verify compliance with all accounting, affiliate transaction, and joint cost allocation rules.[123]

Finally, telcos are subject to permanent reporting and data retention rules.[124] Carriers are expected to maintain a complete audit trail of all cost allocations and affiliate transactions;[125] the FCC has committed to monitor cost allocation results and to establish a database for comparing forecasts with actual results.[126] Details are set forth in the Commission's so-called *Armis Order.*[127] The Order established an automated system of reports for collecting the financial and operating data needed to monitor carrier compliance with accounting, joint cost, jurisdictional separations, rate-base disallowance, rate-of-return, and access charge rules.[128] The Order also established a series of additional—and elaborate—reporting requirements. The Commission is empowered to seek stiff penalties for accounting violations.[129]

§2.2.2.11 Foxes and Chickens

The accounting rules promulgated in 1988 plainly represented a serious attempt to ensure that costs are allocated fairly to the ·activities that cause them. Of course, the rules were directed at telcos. The real challenge remains one of persuading regulators themselves. It may well be that cross-subsidy is an important problem that is of legitimate concern.[130] But it is also

---

[122] *See* Responsible Accounting Officer (RAO) Letter 12, DA 90-1491 (rev. Oct. 19, 1990). The FCC has proposed to adopt similar independent audit requirements on an ongoing basis in its *Computer III Proceedings,* 6 F.C.C. Rec. at 178–179 ¶¶28–32.

[123] *See Joint Cost Order,* 2 F.C.C. Rec. at 1330–1331 ¶256.

[124] *See id.* at 1328–1329 ¶¶241–242.

[125] *See id.* at 1328–1329 ¶242.

[126] *See id.*

[127] *See* Automated Reporting Requirements for Certain Class A and Tier 1 Telephone Companies (Parts 31, 43, 69, and 60 of the FCC's Rules), Report and Order, 2 F.C.C. Rec. 5770 (1987) (hereinafter *Armis Order*), *on recons.,* 3 F.C.C. Rec. 6375 (1988).

[128] *See Armis Order,* 2 F.C.C. Rec. at 5770.

[129] *See* 47 U.S.C. §§220(d), (e), 501, 502, 503(b)(2)(B). *See also FTL1* §2.15.2.

[130] *See* Meitzen, Shared Costs and the Cash Cow Debate at 32; N. Cornell, M. Pelcovits, & S. Brenner, A Legacy of Regulatory Failure, 7 Reg. 37, 39

a highly convenient excuse for more regulation rather than less. Besides, the most extensive and inefficient cross-subsidies in telephony have been deliberate creations of the regulatory establishment itself.

§2.2.3 Rate-of-Return Regulation and Price Caps[131]

Telephone companies traditionally were subject to rate-of-return or "cost-plus" regulation.[132] A telco spends money on plant and operations. If those costs are prudently incurred, the telco has a right to charge enough to recover them. A reasonable return on investment is also part of the telco's aggregate *revenue requirement.* If a telco is found to have earned more than a reasonable rate of return, it may under certain circumstances be required to reduce its rates.[133]

A telco's investment *rate base* is its undepreciated investment.[134] The original cost of a given item of equipment enters the rate base when that item enters service. As it depreciates over

---

(July/Aug. 1983) (discussing pre-divestiture cross-subsidization opportunities); *see also* MCI v. FCC, 675 F.2d at 410 ("The FCC has long been concerned that AT&T might 'cross-subsidize' its more competitive services by allocating excessive costs to the monopoly services and thereby increasing monopoly rates.").

[131] *See also FTL1* §2.13.2 (FCC procedures for reviewing rates); *id.* §2.13.3 (FCC prescription of rates); *id.* §12.9 (price-cap regulation of long-distance services).

[132] *See generally* Distrigas of Mass. Corp. v. Federal Energy Reg. Commn., 737 F.2d 1208, 1211 (1st Cir. 1984); National Telecommunications and Information Agency, Comprehensive Review of Rate of Return Regulation of the U.S. Telecommunications Industry, 51 Fed. Reg. 36,837, 36,839 (1986). There are some differences between rate-of-return and cost-plus regulation. For example, rate-of-return regulation is usually based on costs in a "test year," *see* Kahn, 1 Economics of Regulation at 26, whereas true cost-plus regulation would make more frequent adjustments, *see FTL1* §2.12.3.

[133] *See, e.g.,* AT&T v. FCC, 836 F.2d 1386 (D.C. Cir. 1988) (overturning FCC rule that required telephone companies to refund earnings in excess of their expected rate of return); *id.* at 1394 (Starr, J., concurring); *see generally* 47 U.S.C. §204(a) (FCC may require refunds).

[134] The rate base typically consists of total historical investment minus total prior depreciation. *See, e.g., Distrigas,* 737 F.2d at 1211.

time—as a function of wear and tear or technological obsolescence—the asset's contribution to the rate base is reduced accordingly.[135] Because much of the cost of providing service
involves depreciating assets, the rate base and its depreciation
are the focus of "most of the litigation in the American regulatory experience."[136] A telco's allowed *rate of return* is supposed to
reflect a blend of its cost of debt and its cost of attracting equity
capital. Some have suggested that, particularly when regulators
allow a rate of return that is too high, rate-of-return regulation
may induce telephone companies to make unnecessary investments (a phenomenon known as "goldplating").[137]

Price-cap (or "price-minus") regulation is the most widely
practiced alternative to rate-of-return regulation. In the 1980s
and 1990s, this approach found favor in many regulatory circles,
including the FCC and most states.[138] The idea is to select some

[135] *See generally* W. Bolter & D. Irwin, Depreciation Reform (1980). *See also*
Southern Bell Tel. & Tel. Co. v. FCC, 781 F.2d 209, 212 (D.C. Cir. 1986); New
England Tel. & Tel. Co. v. Public Utils. Commn. of Me., 742 F.2d 1, 3 (1st Cir.
1984); 47 C.F.R. §31.01-3(n) (1985); Amendment of Part 31 (Uniform System
of Accounts for Class A and Class B Telephone Companies), Report and
Order, 83 F.C.C.2d 267 (1980) (hereinafter *Property Depreciation*), *on recons.*, 87
F.C.C.2d 916 (1981); Prescription of Revised Percentages of Depreciation,
Order, 92 F.C.C.2d 920 (1982); Cornell, Pelcovits, & Brenner, A Legacy of
Regulatory Failure, 7 Reg. 37; J. R. Fogarty, Capital Recovery: A Crisis for
Telephone Companies, A Dilemma for Regulators, Pub. Util. Fort., Dec. 8,
1983, at 13.

[136] Kahn, 1 Economics of Regulation at 36. Exactly which costs may be
included in the rate base has also been the subject of much controversy. *See,
e.g.*, Illinois Bell Tel. Co. v. FCC, 911 F.2d 776 (D.C. Cir. 1990).

[137] *See* H. Averch & L. Johnson, Behavior of the Firm Under Regulatory
Constraint, 52 Am. Econ. Rev. 1052 (1962); *see also* W. Baumol & A. K.
Klevorick, Input Choices and Rate-of-Return Regulation: An Overview of the
Discussion, 1 Bell J. Econ. & Mgmt. Sci. 162 (1970); Cornell, Pelcovits, &
Brenner, A Legacy of Regulatory Failure at 39. Whether or not rate-of-return
regulation has this effect is a controversial subject among economists. *See*
Kahn, 2 Economics of Regulation at 106–108; Breyer, Regulation and Its
Reform at 49–50; W. Boyes, An Empirical Examination of the Averch-John-
son Effect, 14 Econ. Inquiry 25 (1976); R. Braeutigam & J. Panzar, Diversifi-
cation Incentives Under "Price-Based" and "Cost-Based" Regulation, 20 Rand
J. Econ. 373 (1989); P. L. Joskow & R. G. Noll, Regulation in Theory and Practice: An Overview, *in* Studies in Regulation 10–14 (G. Fromm ed., 1981).

[138] For an overview of price-cap regulation, see Palmer, Rate-of-Return Versus Price Caps: The Long Distance Regulation Battle, 14 Colum.-VLA J. L. &

price today, usually the price currently set by cost-plus regulation, and then deflate it at a fixed annual rate on the assumption that the telco's costs will diminish over time as its productivity increases. Under rate-of-return regulation, the regulator attempts to police costs, but has no real discretion over price. In practice, rate-of-return regulation usually culminates in poor regulation of cost,[139] with prices floating upward. Under price-cap regulation, the regulator sets the price, but then abandons any attempt to control costs, hoping they will float downward naturally.

§2.2.3.1 Depreciation in Monopoly and Competitive Environments

In a monopoly environment, it was comparatively easy for regulator and regulatee to come to terms with regard to depreciation principles. Regulatory errors could simply be incorporated into the company's business practices. If regulators declared, for example, that the technology of copper wire would have a useful life of 30 years (say), a phone company could see to it that the copper in question was indeed used for 30 years, regardless of what new technology might come along in the interim. Accounting considerations influenced—indeed dictated—the way operations were conducted. The demands of accountants substituted for the demands of a market—just as they were intended to under rate-of-return regulation.

Beginning in the 1970s, however, a real long-distance market began to function, creating its own independent set of demands.

Arts 571 (1990); *see also* Policy and Rules Concerning Rates for Dominant Carriers, Report and Order and Second Further Notice of Proposed Rulemaking, 4 F.C.C. Rec. 2873, 2889–2883, ¶¶29–35 (1989) (hereinafter *AT&T Price Cap Order*).

[139] In the three decades after the passage of the Communications Act, the FCC rarely concerned itself with AT&T's cost of service or its rate structure. Claims of questionable carrier practices were resolved by informal measures. *See* R. Wiley, The End of Monopoly: Regulatory Change and the Promotion of Competition, *in* Telecommunications and the Law 147, 148–149 (W. Sapronov ed., 1988).

The accountants might insist that microwave relays in the long-distance network had a remaining book life of 20 years. But the advertisements of a newly arrived competitor would feature the sound of a dropping pin, transmitted with crystalline fidelity over an all-new fiber-optic network. By the early 1980s, the Bell System had accumulated a vast library of accounting books that belonged alongside dime-store novels and other works of fiction. The books grossly overvalued assets. Shortly after divestiture was announced, AT&T took $7.3 billion of write-offs on various assets, mostly customer premises equipment.[140] By 1987, it was widely estimated that the book value of telephone company investments exceeded market value by $25 billion dollars.[141]

The overvaluation of the Bell System's assets resulted from a convergence of several factors. First, some economists maintained that rate-of-return regulation had encouraged goldplated investments.[142] And because goldplated assets are not necessarily useful assets, their book value exceeded their market value. Second, competition spurs innovation—which is to say, it shortens the useful life of existing technology. A user of a product or service recognizes obsolescence much faster than a regulatory accountant.[143] Finally, the 1970s saw the beginning of significant technological progress in telecommunications-related equipment, which had originated in Bell's own laboratories 20 years earlier with the discovery of the transistor. Even if nothing else had changed, the microprocessor revolution and the advent of fiber optics would have forced significant write-offs of older equipment. For these reasons, the "question of how to ensure adequate and timely capital recovery [became] perhaps the most critical issue confronting the telephone industry."[144]

---

[140] *See* Wrong Number: AT&T's Earning Shocker and What It Means, Barrons, Oct. 24, 1983, at 15.

[141] *See* Kahn & Shew, Current Issues in Telecommunications at 222. For a dissenting opinion, see Telecommunications Reports, Oct. 27, 1986, at 9.

[142] *See supra* note 98.

[143] *Cf.* Bolter & Irwin, Depreciation Reform at 29–78.

[144] Fogarty, Capital Recovery at 13.

The FCC began to respond seriously in 1980, when it announced changes in two major depreciation practices.[145] First, the FCC changed the way in which carriers were required to group property subject to depreciation—a change from the "vintage year" to the "equal life" approach. Second, it replaced "whole life" depreciation with the "remaining life" method to permit midcourse corrections in remaining-life estimates as soon as the need for correction becomes evident. In 1981, the FCC further announced that all costs of "inside wiring" could be "expensed" in the year incurred.[146]

Through NARUC, their national association, state regulators immediately sought a declaration from the FCC that state commissions were still permitted to follow different depreciation practices for intrastate rate-making purposes. In April 1982, the FCC agreed, over the dissent of two commissioners who argued that an important federal policy—nothing short of the "brave new world" of competition—was at stake. Shortly thereafter the Commission reversed itself, ruling that section 220 of the Communications Act empowered it to preempt inconsistent state depreciation rates and that, quite apart from the specific preemptive power granted in section 220, federal preemption was permitted when necessary "to avoid frustration of validly adopted federal policies." As discussed in section 2.2.2.2, the Supreme Court, in a 1986 ruling, disagreed. Section 152(b), the Court concluded, constitutes "a congressional denial of power to the FCC to require state commissions to follow FCC depreciation practices for intrastate ratemaking purposes."[147]

---

[145] *See Property Depreciation,* 87 F.C.C.2d at 916 ¶¶49–62; Proceedings to Allocate Depreciation Reserve as Required by the Final Order in Docket No. 20188, Supplemental Opinion and Order, 87 F.C.C.2d 1112 (1981). Summaries of these developments with full citations to the administrative record appear in Virginia State Corporation Commission v. FCC, 737 F.2d 388 (4th Cir. 1984), *rev'd sub. nom.* Louisiana Public Service Commission v. FCC, 476 U.S. 355 (1986).

[146] *See* Amendment of Part 31, Uniform System of Accounts for Class A and Class B Telephone Companies, First Report and Order, 85 F.C.C.2d 818, 828 ¶34 (1981) (hereinafter *Uniform System of Accounts*).

[147] *Louisiana PSC,* 476 U.S. at 374.

Regulatory divisions were thus reaffirmed once again. Indeed, with divestiture, those lines now almost tracked corporate boundaries. The FCC retained full authority over AT&T, the so-called Other Common Carriers (OCCs) like MCI and Sprint, and the unarguably national markets for telecommunications equipment. Meanwhile, the states regulated the local services offered by the Bell Operating Companies (BOCs), GTE, and other independents. The areas of greatest regulatory instability were at the fracture lines, where the long-distance network merged into the local one: the access charges the long-distance companies had to pay to LECs in connection with interstate long-distance calls. Here, the ghost of *Smith* still required separation of the inseparable.

§2.2.3.2 Price Caps for Local Exchange Carriers

Within its own sphere of authority, however, the FCC still had much to do. The adoption of "remaining life" and "equal life" depreciation practices would, in time, help correct the "substantial deficiency" in telco depreciation reserves, but much of the correction would come late in the life of an asset.[148] More fundamentally, the FCC was becoming convinced that no amount of changes in rules would ever transform FCC accountants into accurate, flexible, responsive controllers of telco costs generally. A consensus developed that regulation would perform better if it did not attempt such detailed cost accounting at all. This consensus eventually led the FCC to adopt price-cap regulation for LECs' access charges on interstate calls.[149]

---

[148] *See* Fogarty, Capital Recovery at 14.

[149] *See* Policy and Rules Concerning Rates for Dominant Carriers, Notice of Proposed Rulemaking, 2 F.C.C. Rec. 5208 (1987); Further Notice of Proposed Rulemaking, 3 F.C.C. Rec. 3195 (1988). The Report and Order adopting price-cap regulation for AT&T and the Second Further Notice proposing price-cap regulation for LECs were published as one document. *See* Policy and Rules Concerning Rates for Dominant Carriers, Supplemental Notice of Proposed Rulemaking, 5 F.C.C. Rec. 2176 (1990) (hereinafter *LEC Supplemental Notice*); Second Report and Order, 5 F.C.C. Rec. 6786 (1990) (hereinafter *LEC Price Cap Order*); Erratum, 5 F.C.C. Rec. 7664 (1990), *modified on recons.*, 6 F.C.C. Rec. 2637 (1991); *see also FTL1* §2.12.3.

On January 1, 1991, the FCC shifted the largest LECs[150] from a "cost-plus" system to an incentive-based system similar to the price-cap regulation that already governed AT&T.[151] The system placed a cap on LEC interstate charges subject to an annual adjustment that would ensure that prices fall in real, inflation-adjusted terms.[152] The interstate access price-cap index consisted of a measure of inflation,[153] a productivity offset,[154] and exogenous costs.[155] Under the plan, LECs were given a choice between an annual productivity offset of 3.3 or 4.3 percent; LECs choosing the former, less challenging, offset would be subject to more onerous "sharing" obligations (which are further explained below). The 3.3 and 4.3 percent offsets included a so-called consumer productivity dividend (CPD) of half a percent,

---

[150] Mandatory application of the price-cap system was limited to the seven Regional Bell Operating Companies (RBOCs) and GTE. Price-cap regulation became optional for mid-sized and smaller LECs. National Exchange Carrier Association (NECA) pool members continued to be subject to rate-of-return regulation; they were not permitted to opt for price-cap regulation. *See LEC Price Cap Order*, 5 F.C.C. Rec. at 6819 ¶¶266–270. LECs that were still subject to rate-of-return regulation collectively accounted for less than 10 percent of industry revenues. *See Access Charge Reform Order*, 12 F.C.C. Rec. at 15,993 ¶25.

[151] *See LEC Price Cap Order*, 5 F.C.C. Rec. at 6819 ¶¶266–270. At the time, the FCC believed that because AT&T was exposed to more competition than the LECs, price-cap regulation of AT&T presented fewer regulatory risks than price-cap regulation of the LECs and that therefore a "more cautious and careful approach" was appropriate with respect to the LECs. *Id.* at 6787 ¶4. Thus, the LEC price-cap regime contained safeguards (e.g., "sharing") that the FCC deemed unnecessary for AT&T.

[152] *See id.* at 6792–6827 ¶¶47–331.

[153] As it had with respect to the AT&T price-cap regime, the Commission found the Gross National Product Price Index (GNP-PI) to be the best inflation adjuster, reflecting changes in costs without being susceptible to LEC manipulation. *See id.* at 6792–6793 ¶¶50–54.

[154] Because "the productivity growth embedded in the [GNP=PI] data has not fully reflected changes in the costs of factors of production for LECs or the changes in their prices . . . the higher than average growth in LEC productivity has resulted in lower than average telephone prices, relative to inflation." *Id.* at 6796 ¶75. The productivity offset factor reflects this fact and allows rates to decline relative to inflation. *See id.*

[155] Exogenous costs are costs that lie outside the carrier's control; such costs are created by events like changes in separations policies, tax law changes, USOA amendments, transitional and long-term support changes, and the reallocation of regulated and nonregulated costs. *See id.* at 6807–6810 ¶¶166–189.

intended to reflect future productivity growth (above and beyond historical growth), which the FCC hoped would result from price-cap regulation's efficiency-enhancing incentives.[156]

The price cap limits only total revenue; without more, the FCC's price-cap regime would allow carriers to make drastic changes in their rate structure. For example, carriers might (heaven forbid!) seize the opportunity to move closer to the Ramsey pricing ideal. Or carriers might act on more sinister incentives to decrease rates for relatively competitive services, while increasing rates for relatively noncompetitive services.[157] To prevent this, the Commission divided LECs' services into four "baskets," each subject to its own price cap, so that a rate cut in one basket would not buy a carrier the right to increase rates in another.[158] In two baskets, the FCC limited price flexibility even further by creating sub-baskets (so-called service categories)[159] and "price bands": rate changes greater than 5 percent would require special cost justification.[160]

As the starting point for price-capped rates, the Commission used July 1, 1990, rates.[161] Carriers eligible for optional price-cap regulation would have to make an "all or nothing" choice so

---

[156] *Id.* at 6787–6788 ¶¶5–8, 6796–6799 ¶¶74–102.

[157] *See id.* at 6788 ¶11.

[158] The four baskets are common line services, traffic-sensitive services, special-access services, and interexchange services. *See id.* at 6788 ¶13, 6812 ¶¶209–215.

[159] The service categories in the TS basket are local switching, local transport, and information. The four categories in the special-access basket are voice grade/WATS/metallic/telegraph, audio/video, high capacity/Digital Data Service, and wideband data/wideband analog. *See id.* at 6788 ¶14, 6812–6813 ¶¶216–223.

[160] Price bands limit rate changes to plus or minus 5 percent per year. A carrier may make a change within the band on 14 days' notice, and the new tariff has a presumption of legitimacy. *See id.* at 6788 ¶¶11–12, 6813–6814 ¶¶224–226.

[161] *See id.* at 6789 ¶17, 6814–6816 ¶¶230–244. The Commission found July 1, 1990, rates to be reasonable (although not perfect) and to reflect the best that rate-of-return regulation could produce. *See also* Annual 1990 Access Tariff Filings, Order, 5 F.C.C. Rec. 4142 (1990); Annual 1990 Access Tariff Filings, Memorandum Opinion and Order, 5 F.C.C. Rec. 4177 (1990); Represcribing the Authorized Rate of Return for Interstate Services of Local Exchange Carriers, Order, 5 F.C.C. Rec. 7507 (1990); Local Exchange Carrier Access

as to prevent the shifting of costs to rate-of-return regulated affiliates.[162] As was the case in AT&T's price-cap regime, tariff filings complying with the price-cap structure would be permitted on short (14-day) notice and would have a presumption of lawfulness.[163] Below-band changes would require cost showings and 45 days' notice,[164] whereas above-band rate changes would require a detailed cost showing and 90 days' advance notice.[165]

The FCC's initial price-cap plan contemplated extensive "sharing"—a feature that added a distinct rate-of-return flavor to the new plan. If a carrier was too efficient, it had to share part or all of its excess earnings with ratepayers in the form of future rate decreases. The extent of a carrier's sharing obligations depended on the productivity offset it had elected. If the carrier chose the smaller offset of 3.3 percent, the sharing obligation began at 1 percent above the prescribed industry rate of return; above that point, the carrier shared half its profits with customers. The carrier shared all its profits beginning at 5 percent above the prescribed rate of return. For carriers that opted for the higher offset of 4.3 percent, sharing began at 2 percent above the prescribed rate of return and became complete at 6 percent.[166]

In March 1993, the D.C. Circuit upheld the FCC's price-cap regime for LECs in the face of minor challenges by small local telephone companies to the so-called all-or-nothing and permanent-choice rules.[167] Under the all-or-nothing rule, a LEC

Tariff Rate Levels, Order to Show Cause, 4 F.C.C. Rec. 762 (1988); Local Exchange Carrier Access Tariff Rate and Earning Levels, Order to Show Cause, 5 F.C.C. Rec. 482 (1990); Local Exchange Carrier Access Tariff Rate and Earnings Levels, Memorandum Opinion and Order and Supplemental Order to Show Cause, 5 F.C.C. Rec. 1070 (1990).

[162] See LEC Price Cap Order, 5 F.C.C. Rec. at 6789 ¶18, 6819–6820 ¶¶271–279; see also AT&T Price Cap Order, 4 F.C.C. Rec. at 3178 ¶628.

[163] LEC Price Cap Order, 5 F.C.C. Rec. at 6822 ¶289.

[164] See id. at 6824 ¶¶305–311.

[165] See id. at 6789 ¶19, 6821–6822 ¶¶287–289, 6823 ¶¶296–299. These adjustment mechanisms replaced more liberal mechanisms existing under rate-of-return regulation. See generally Southwestern Bell Tel. Co. v. FCC, 10 F.3d 892 (D.C. Cir. 1993).

[166] See LEC Price Cap Order, 5 F.C.C. Rec. at 6801–6807 ¶¶120–165.

[167] See National Rural Telecom Assn. v. FCC, 988 F.2d 174 (D.C. Cir. 1993).

choosing price-cap regulation would be required to shift all its affiliates to price caps as well. This rule was designed to prevent LECs from trying to benefit by shifting costs from a price-cap affiliate to a rate-of-return affiliate. The permanent-choice rule makes the choice for price-cap regulation irrevocable: once a LEC opts for price-cap regulation, it can never go back to rate-of-return regulation. This rule was designed to prevent a LEC from opting for price caps while plant improvements pay off (slimming down) and converting back to rate of return when new investments must be made (fattening up). The D.C. Circuit rejected arguments that the FCC's refusal to adopt less draconian safeguards was arbitrary and capricious.

§2.2.3.3   The 1997 Price-Cap Order

The 1990 price-cap order called for further review in 1994. As promised, the Commission initiated its review at that time.[168] The Commission tentatively concluded that price caps had successfully held down prices[169] and improved service,[170] while boosting carriers' profits.[171] The FCC completed the review in 1995, making only minor changes to the existing regime.[172] Much more radical changes followed in May 1997, when the FCC adopted new price-cap rules designed "to further the new procompetitive,

---

[168] *See* Price Cap Performance Review for Local Exchange Carriers, Notice of Proposed Rulemaking, 9 F.C.C. Rec. 1687 (1994) (hereinafter *LEC Price Cap Review Notice*).

[169] Interexchange access prices were "$1.5 billion lower than at the start of price caps, despite overall inflation in the economy of over 11.6 percent. . . . During the first three years of price caps, all of the LECs have kept their rates at or below the applicable PCIs; none has requested above-cap rates." *Id.* at 1691 ¶25.

[170] The FCC explained that although "[s]ervice quality monitoring data indicate that service quality under price caps has been similar to levels under rate of return regulation," price-cap regulation did not prevent LECs from "extend[ing] their service in non-urban areas from 11.5 million lines to 17.4 million lines." *Id.* at 1691 ¶¶27, 29.

[171] LECs' average rates of return on interstate services surpassed the 11.25 percent target and reached 12.25 percent. *See id.* at 1691 ¶26.

[172] Price Cap Performance Review for Local Exchange Carriers, First Report and Order, 10 F.C.C. Rec. 8961, 8970–8973, ¶¶19–26 (hereinafter *LEC Price Cap Performance Review*).

deregulatory paradigm set out in the Telecommunications Act of 1996."[173]

The most important change was to increase the productivity offset to 6.5 percent.[174] Where did that number come from? The Commission's accountants and economists derived it from a "total factor productivity" (TFP) increase,[175] an "input price differential,"[176] and a "consumer product dividend" (CPD) of 0.5 percent.[177] In 1990, the FCC had added a CPD to the productivity factor indicated by historical productivity growth because it expected the new price-cap regime to spur even greater future productivity growth. In 1997, the FCC did not explain why a CPD continued to be necessary—except to say that it would help "[t]o ensure that consumers share in all increases in LEC efficiency, and to provide efficiency enhancing incentives to those LECs whose past performance has exceeded the industry average."[178]

The increased productivity offset thus reached a level that the FCC itself admitted to be in excess of what is "reasonable."[179] The increased offset has particularly troubling implications for investment in advanced services: it may transform any well-engineered, efficiently priced, new broadband service into a source of steadily growing loss in subsequent years. The more advanced the technology deployed, the greater the threat: where advanced technology is concerned, further technological

[173] *See* Price Cap Performance Review for Local Exchange Carriers, Access Charge Reform, Fourth Report and Order, CC Docket No. 94-1, and Second Report and Order, CC Docket No. 96-262, 12 F.C.C. Rec. 16,642, 16,645 ¶1 (1997) (hereinafter *Fourth and Second Reports and Orders*).

[174] *Id.* LECs can no longer choose between one of several productivity factors—the 6.5 percent factor applies to all relevant LECs. *Id.* at 16,704 ¶¶158–159.

[175] Total factor productivity is the ratio of an industry's total output to its total input. *See id.* at 16,648–16,649 ¶9.

[176] The input price differential accounts for differences between changes in LEC input prices and input prices for the entire U.S. economy. *See id.* at 16,648–16,649 ¶¶8–9.

[177] *See id.* at 16,648 ¶8.

[178] *See id.* at 16,699 ¶145.

[179] Although the FCC set the offset at 6.5 percent, historical productivity gains (the measure the Commission admittedly considers most reliable) have never approached that level. *See id.* at 16,695–16,697 ¶¶137–141.

advance is less likely to deliver the additional improvements in performance and declines in price that the Commission presumes into existence indefinitely into the future.

A more sensible change brought by the 1997 Order was the elimination of "sharing."[180] LECs are no longer required to share any part of their profits with ratepayers, however great their profits may be.[181] Low profits are another matter. The new price-cap rules retain a "low end adjustment mechanism" that guarantees carriers a certain minimum rate of return—now the last holdover from rate-of-return regulation.[182] Under this mechanism, a LEC whose rate of return falls below 10.25 percent may raise its price-cap index to push returns back up to 10.25 percent.[183]

In *United States Telephone Ass'n v. FCC*, No. 97-1469 (D.C. Cir. 1999), the D.C. Circuit rejected the FCC's increase of the productivity offset as arbitrary and capricious. The court upheld the FCC's decision to eliminate sharing.

§2.3 Vertical Links to the Local Exchange

Regulated local exchange carriers must be permitted to recover their costs, somehow or other. But from whom? End users were the obvious candidates in the days of end-to-end monopoly, though even then not quite the only ones.[184] Today, the money may also come from other carriers; from voice traffic; from data; from traffic that originates or terminates on the ILEC's own network; or from traffic that flows to or from wireless networks, long-distance networks, and the Internet. Charges can be assessed on a flat-rate or per-minute basis or as a percentage of the interconnecting carrier's total revenues.

---

[180] *See id.* at 16,649 ¶¶10–11.

[181] *See id.*

[182] *See id.* at 16,649 ¶11.

[183] *See id.* at 16,691 ¶127.

[184] Even when there was no competition, phone companies had to connect to each other, both domestically and internationally. As discussed below, this created a number of opportunities for regulators to establish intercarrier billing principles.

Viewed in terms of the traditional market, the local exchange network connects "vertically" to four main adjacent markets: (1) customer premises equipment, (2) "enhanced services," (3) long-distance networks, and (4) the Internet. To designate these as "vertical" markets is to track regulatory history—not the economic present or future. With today's technology, and in today's economic environment, both equipment and data networks can substitute for standard wireline voice service, and they increasingly do.

§2.3.1 Connecting Customer Premises Equipment and Inside Wiring to the Local Exchange

As discussed in section 1.2, Bell's original patents were on the telephone itself; the wires in between just supplied a suitable incentive to lease one. But the patents eventually expired. And while competition prevailed, as it did for some years in the early telephone industry, costs had to be loaded where they were incurred—largely in the network.[185]

When the phone industry settled back into monopoly, Bell and its regulators gradually began loading more and more charges on to the nominal "rental" charge for the terminal equipment. Of course, it didn't matter what things were called; if the monthly rental fee for the inferior black telephone was too high, the price of the wire to which it attached was correspondingly low. The subscriber had little reason to care; he cared only about the price of the system—not its components.

But the subscriber and the phone company began to care a lot when the FCC opened up the interface between line and telephone to competition. As discussed in section 8.4, it did so in the 1970s.

---

[185] *See generally* J. Thorne, P. Huber, & M. Kellogg, Federal Broadband Law §6.7 (1995) (hereinafter *FBL*).

§2.3.1.1   Detariffing CPE and Inside Wiring

The consequences were inevitable. The equipment itself had to be detariffed. And costs previously loaded disproportionately onto monopoly phones had to be shifted upstream, onto what were still, at that time, the monopoly local phone lines. As discussed more fully in section 8.3, CPE was duly moved, step by step, out of the ambit of both federal and state rate regulation. In 1980, the Commission detariffed and unbundled CPE, removing CPE prices from the tariffs detailing transmission pricing.[186] In the end, there would be no CPE costs left to separate between state and federal jurisdictions. A five-year timetable to eliminate "embedded" CPE from the rate base was established; the phase-out was completed by 1986.[187] All CPE acquired after January 1, 1983, was to be excluded at once.[188] In 1990, the Commission extended the deregulation of equipment connecting to

[186] *See* Amendment of Section 64.702 of the Commission's Rules and Regulations (Second Computer Inquiry), Final Decision, 77 F.C.C.2d 384 (1980) (hereinafter *Computer II*). The Fourth Circuit had already upheld the FCC's assertion of general jurisdiction over CPE, even though such equipment is commonly used more for intrastate than for interstate calls. *See* North Carolina Utils. Commn. v. FCC, 552 F.2d 1036 (4th Cir. 1997) (NCUC v. FCC); *FTL1* ch. 10. The Fourth Circuit had noted that it did not have before it an FCC attempt "to control the *rates* for exclusively local service." NCUC v. FCC, 552 F.2d at 1047. But when the FCC's jurisdiction over rates came before the D.C. Circuit in 1982, that court "saw no reason to distinguish between 'preemption principles applicable to state ratemaking authority and those applicable to other state powers.'" NARUC v. FCC, 737 F.2d at 1114 (quoting Computer & Communications Indus. Assn. v. FCC, 693 F.2d 198, 215, 216 (D.C. Cir. 1982), *cert. denied*, 461 U.S. 938 (1983)). A subsequent decision by the D.C. Circuit likewise affirmed the decision gradually to eliminate CPE from the rate base. *See* MCI v. FCC, 750 F.2d at 141–142.

[187] *See* Procedures for Implementing the Detariffing of Customer Premises Equipment and Enhanced Services (Second Computer Inquiry), Memorandum Opinion and Order, 104 F.C.C.2d 509 (1986).

[188] *See Computer II*, 77 F.C.C.2d at 438–447 ¶¶140–161. Because embedded CPE was more difficult to deregulate, the Commission devised a policy under which a base amount of CPE would be reduced at a rate of $1/_{60}$ per month over a five-year period, at which point all embedded CPE should be removed from the rate base. *See* Amendment of Section 64.702 of the Commission's Rules & Regulations (Second Computer Inquiry), Memorandum Opinion and Order on Further Reconsideration, 88 F.C.C.2d 512, 518-528 ¶¶18–45 (1981); Memorandum Opinion and Order, 84 F.C.C.2d 50, 65-69 ¶¶46–55;

the telephone network by unbundling and detariffing inside wiring.[189] The Commission simultaneously preempted any inconsistent state regulation of CPE. The D.C. Circuit affirmed.[190]

§2.3.2 Connecting "Enhanced Services" to the Local Exchange

As far back as the Exchange Network Facilities for Interstate Access (ENFIA) negotiations of the 1970s, discussed below in section 2.3.3.2, MCI worried about price discrimination in favor of data carriers. Indeed, the ENFIA talks almost foundered on this issue. All new carriers wanted cheaper connections than AT&T, but none wanted to face a competitor that received cheaper connections still. Nonetheless, the ENFIA tariffs went into effect without requiring what were then called "enhanced service providers" (ESPs) to pay the same (discounted) access tariffs; this was grudgingly accepted by voice carriers like MCI.

When digital computers first began to multiply, the FCC resolved to leave "enhanced services" outside the ambit of telephone regulation.[191] The FCC ruled that all providers of "computer enhanced services" (as well as computers themselves and other forms of "customer premises equipment") would be left

---

Amendment of Part 67 of the Commission's Rules and Establishment of a Joint Board, 89 F.C.C.2d 1, 19–20 ¶32 (1982) (hereinafter *Joint Board*); *see also* MCI v. FCC, 750 F.2d at 139–140. The policy encouraged state commissions to adopt policies favoring the sale of embedded CPE, thereby eliminating it from the rate base. *See Joint Board,* 89 F.C.C.2d at 18–20 ¶¶30–33, 24–25 ¶42.

[189] *See* Review of Sections 68.104 and 68.213 of the Commission's Rules Concerning Connection of Simple Inside Wiring to the Telephone Network and Petition for Modification of Section 68.213 of the Commission's Rules, Filed by the Electronic Industries Association, Report and Order and Further Notice of Proposed Rulemaking, 5 F.C.C. Rec. 4686 (1990).

[190] *See* Computer & Communications Indus. Assn. v. FCC, 693 F.2d at 210. For a detailed discussion of the court's ruling, see *FTL1* §2.8.

[191] *See* Regulatory and Policy Problems Presented by the Interdependence of Computer and Communication Services and Facilities, Final Decision and Order, 28 F.C.C.2d 267 (1971), *aff'd in relevant part sub nom.* GTE Serv. Corp. v. FCC, 474 F.2d 724 (2d Cir. 1973).

completely unregulated.[192] No franchise. No tariffs. No oversight of any kind. To make sure that no state regulator did otherwise, the FCC ruled all state regulation of "enhanced services" pre-empted,[193] even as it declared that it would "forbear" from regulating them itself.[194]

As discussed in section 12.4, the FCC would thereafter generally view providers of "enhanced services" in the same light as the computers they used—as operators of "equipment" rather than as providers of carrier services. The Commission recognized, however, that this was an arbitrary call. It has repeatedly revisited the issue, most recently in the access-charge proceeding of 1997 (discussed in section 2.3.4.2 below). But it has never changed course.

The Commission preserved the access-charge exemption in its 1983 access-charge proceeding, concluding that the exemption was necessary to preserve the financial viability of the new online industry.[195] This blatant discrimination was accepted calmly by the court of appeals that reviewed the 1983 access-charge initiative.[196] Under the exemption, ESPs were treated as end users, paying the same local rates as any business user, including interstate subscriber line charges and special-access surcharges.[197] Given the ESPs' high volumes of usage, ESPs paid much less than they would if they were subject to the access-charge regime applicable to long-distance carriers.[198]

[192] *Computer II,* 77 F.C.C.2d at 428 ¶113 (enhanced services); *id.* at 447 ¶¶160–161 (CPE).

[193] *See id.* at 428–429 ¶¶114–117. The Commission determined that enhanced services fell within its "ancillary" jurisdiction as incidental transmissions over the interstate telecommunications network.

[194] *Id.* at 428 ¶113.

[195] *See* MTS and WATS Market Structure, Memorandum Opinion and Order, 97 F.C.C.2d 682, 715 ¶83 (1983). The Commission held that imposing access charges on ESPs would cause "rate shock": "these entities would experience huge increases in their costs of operation which could affect their viability." *Id.*

[196] *See* NARUC v. FCC, 737 F.2d 1095.

[197] *See* Amendments of Part 69 of the Commission's Rules Relating to Enhanced Service Providers Order, Order, 3 F.C.C. Rec. 2631, 2635 nn.8, 53 (1988) (hereinafter *Part 69 Order*).

[198] *See Access Charge Reform Order,* 12 F.C.C. Rec. at 16,132 ¶342.

In 1987, the Commission considered requiring ESPs to pay the same usage-sensitive access charges as voice long-distance carriers. The FCC acknowledged that its earlier distinction made no sense — ESPs use precisely the same local lines that are used for voice calls, and indeed use them (on a per-customer basis) a lot more.[199] ESPs had had "ample notice of our ultimate intent to apply interstate access charges to their operations and ample opportunity to adjust their planning accordingly."[200] As such, the "rate shock" problem the Commission had noted in 1983 should not have been a problem. Moreover, the Commission was concerned that ESPs were not paying their fair share of the costs associated with universal service.[201]

But the Commission's proposal was met by vocal opposition, including opposition from members of Congress who otherwise worship at the altar of universal service.[202] In the face of this criticism, the Commission in the end concluded that enhanced-services markets (jumbled at the time by the FCC's approval of the BOCs' Open Network Architecture (ONA) plans and Judge Greene's approval of BOC provision of transport for enhanced services) were in a "volatile period" and that further shocks to the industry caused by the imposition of access charges on ESPs would be harmful to the public interest.[203] The FCC again revisited the idea of levying access charges on ESPs in early 1997, but the idea again went nowhere.[204] The FCC did no more than raise monthly fees for second residential phone lines, the lines most often used for data access.[205]

[199] *See* Amendments of Part 69 of the Commission's Rules Relating to Enhanced Service Providers, Notice of Proposed Rulemaking, 2 F.C.C. Rec. 4305 (1987) (hereinafter *Amendments of Part 69*).

[200] *Id.* at 4306 ¶8.

[201] *See id.*

[202] *See* Immediate Hill Backlash, FCC Considers Linking ESP Access Charges to ONA, Comm. Daily, Nov. 17, 1988, at 1 ("cyclone of protest from Congress, NTIA and hundreds of computer-service users").

[203] *See Part 69 Order*, 3 F.C.C. Rec. at 2633 ¶14.

[204] *See Access Charge Reform Order*, 12 F.C.C. Rec. at 16,133 ¶344.

[205] *See id.* at 16,014 ¶78.

§2.3.3   Connecting Long-Distance to Local Carriers

§2.3.3.1   Connecting Long-Distance to Local Carriers: The Rise of a Subsidy

In the wake of the Supreme Court's 1930 ruling in *Smith v. Illinois Bell Telephone Co.*,[206] it was commonly thought that some fraction of each local telco's costs had to be allocated to interstate accounts under federal jurisdiction.[207] In effect, one-quarter (say) of each telephone handset, local line, and central office switch would be regulated by the FCC; the other three-quarters would be regulated by the appropriate state regulator. There might be only a single physical asset and (in pre-divestiture days) only a single phone company. But there would still be two sets of books, two depreciation rates, two armies of accountants, and two schedules of rates. At first, all of this was merely inconvenient. In time, it would become disastrous.

The problem at first was mainly psychological. Consumers were accustomed to paying flat-rate lease or purchase charges for tangible things like equipment and variable charges for intangible things like services. A flat monthly charge seemed reasonable for a telephone handset and the jack in the wall (that is, the local line) to which it connects. A long-distance call, by contrast, seemed like it should be sold on a metered basis: you pay only if and when you make the call. Local regulators, being close to the tangible end of things, drifted toward buffet-style pricing for everything: a single monthly fee covered your phone and your local wire; you could use them (locally) as much as you liked. By contrast, federal regulators adopted by-the-drink pricing for everything: you paid for everything by the call, by the minute. The upshot of these disparate approaches was subsidy, mispricing, and inefficiency across the board.

From an economic perspective, flat-rate pricing is appropriate (i.e., efficiency enhancing) for flat-rate costs: costs that don't

---

[206] *See FTL1* §2.5.
[207] This interstate allocation, however, was not put into practice until the advent of the Separations Manual in 1947, 17 years after the *Smith* decision.

vary with usage. This is true of a telephone handset or the local line connecting it to the nearest exchange: their costs are, for the most part, not traffic sensitive; the phone and line cost what they cost, whether used once an hour or once a year. Costs that do vary with usage require by-the-drink pricing. Switches, interexchange trunks, and so on typically represent costs of that kind. They are traffic sensitive: the higher the usage, the greater the costs. But the lines drawn first by *Smith,* and subsequently by the Communications Act, did not divide the universe in this way. *Both* local and long-distance services entail *both* kinds of costs. Ideally, then, both kinds of service should incorporate both kinds of pricing—a flat-rate fee to cover NTS costs and a variable usage fee to cover TS costs. In practice, however, the feds imposed usage fees, whereas the locals (for the most part) favored flat rates. The result was a subsidy flowing from heavy users of long-distance service to heavy users of local service.

The original Separations Manual provided for the allocation of subscriber plant equipment between the state and federal jurisdictions according to relative use.[208] Even this was inconsistent with Ramsey pricing, which would have loaded NTS costs on local rates. But at least it incorporated the intuitive logic of pricing based on fully distributed costs, with costs distributed according to relative use.

These nice economic problems were soon dwarfed, however, by purely political ones. It became politically attractive to accept high long-distance rates and low local rates—to dump costs onto interstate users and siphon revenues back in the other direction. The benefits for local regulators were obvious. The FCC, too, could gain political credit by emphasizing the most populist of its statutory mandates, universal service, above all others.[209]

---

[208] *See* MCI v. FCC, 750 F.2d at 137.

[209] Section 1 of the Communications Act directs the FCC to "regulat[e] interstate . . . commerce in communication by wire and radio so as to make available, so far as possible, to all people of the United States a rapid, efficient, Nation-wide and world-wide wire and radio communication service with adequate facilities at reasonable charges." 47 U.S.C. §151; *see* NARUC v. FCC, 737 F.2d at 1108 n.6 (rejecting contention that FCC has no responsibility to promote universal service).

Thus, for two-and-a-half decades, the FCC, state commissions, and AT&T allocated more and more of the costs of local plant to the interstate jurisdiction.[210] Gradually, it came to be accepted that facilities (like handsets and local lines) used in common for both local and long-distance calling were used for long-distance calling more than the untrained eye might suppose.

In 1970, the trained eyes focused on the joint FCC-state utility board and revised the Separations Manual. This revision, which came to be known as the Ozark Plan, assigned 3.3 percent of NTS costs to federal accounts for every additional one percent of interstate calling.[211] Astonishingly, the common costs of local and long-distance service were going to be distributed, not just "fully," but at triple the rate indicated by relative usage. Why? Because it wouldn't be fair (the logic ran) to allocate costs in simple proportion to actual minutes of local and long-distance calling. People make more local calls because they're "free," but this shouldn't count against anyone (least of all local regulators) in deciding how much of the equipment's cost is properly attributable to interstate calling.[212]

Astonishing though it was, the Ozark Plan went wholly unchallenged in the courts. One would have expected long-distance interests to scream bloody murder. But AT&T was the only long-distance carrier on the scene, and because it controlled the local Bell Operating Companies,[213] most of the inflated Ozark

---

[210] *See, e.g.,* Temin, The Fall of the Bell System at 26–27.

[211] *See* Prescription of Procedures for Separating and Allocating Plant Investment, Operating Expenses, Taxes and Reserves Between the Intrastate and Interstate Operations of Telephone Companies, Report and Order, 26 F.C.C.2d 247 (1970) (*hereinafter Procedures for Separating and Allocating Plant Investment*); *see also* Amendment of Part 67 of the Commission's Rules and Establishment of a Joint Board, Notice of Proposed Rulemaking and Order Establishing a Joint Board, 78 F.C.C.2d 837, 841 ¶13 (1980) (*hereinafter Establishment of a Joint Board*).

[212] *See* MCI v. FCC, 750 F.2d at 137–138 & n.3; *Procedures for Separating and Allocating Plant Investment*, 26 F.C.C.2d at 250–252 ¶¶9–11; American Telephone and Telegraph Co. and the Associated Bell System Companies Charges for Interstate and Foreign Communication Service, Interim Decision and Order, 9 F.C.C.2d 30, 102 (1967).

[213] *See* United States v. AT&T, 552 F. Supp. 131, 162 (D.D.C. 1982). Since 1960, the Bell Operating Companies have been responsible for over 80 percent

payments were going to occur within its own corporate family.[214] It didn't have much reason to care: it made money regardless.

Despite the disproportionate costs it bore, long-distance traffic nevertheless grew steadily over the years—faster than local traffic. As it did, Ozark steadily shifted more and more costs onto the federal side of the ledger.[215] Interstate usage increased from 5.5 percent of telephone usage to 8.3 percent between 1972 and 1983; NTS costs allocated to the interstate jurisdiction increased from approximately $1.9 billion to $11.2 billion.[216] By 1980, roughly one-quarter of the cost of access lines was being provided by long-distance tolls, even though long-distance calls accounted for only 8 percent of access line usage.[217] Four years later fully 26 percent of costs associated with local exchange plant were being assigned to the interstate jurisdiction.[218] AT&T, the nation's main long-distance carrier, was sending about half of the revenues it collected straight back to local exchange companies.[219] Transfer payments amounted to some $11 billion a year.[220] Where did the money come from? From inflated per-minute charges on every interstate long-distance call, which, in time, amounted to as much as 10 cents per minute.

---

of all telephones in the United States and have collected 85 percent of all local service revenues. *See, e.g.,* United States v. AT&T, 524 F. Supp. 1336, 1348 n.33 (D.D.C. 1981).

[214] AT&T made similar payments, called "settlements," to the independent telephone companies, which kept them from complaining.

[215] *See* Kahn & Shew, Current Issues in Telecommunications at 194–195.

[216] *See* MCI v. FCC, 750 F.2d at 138; *Establishment of a Joint Board,* 78 F.C.C.2d at 842.

[217] *See* Faulhaber, Telecommunications in Turmoil at 73.

[218] *See Joint Board,* 89 F.C.C.2d at 4–5 ¶7, *modified,* 90 F.C.C.2d 52 (1982), *recons. denied,* 91 F.C.C.2d 558 (1982), *aff'd sub nom.* MCI v. FCC, 750 F.2d at 135; MCI Telecomms. Corp. v. FCC, 712 F.2d 517, 523 n.4 (D.C. Cir. 1983). In 1986, the FCC capped the interstate allocation factor at 25 percent. *See* MCI v. FCC, 750 F.2d at 140 n.28, 141 n.33; Jurisdictional Separations Procedures, Amendment of the Commission's Rules and Establishment of a Joint Board, 49 Fed. Reg. 7934 (1984) (hereinafter *Jurisdictional Separations Procedures*).

[219] *See* Faulhaber, Telecommunications in Turmoil at 73.

[220] The $11 billion estimate includes both interstate and intrastate contributions. *See* Kahn & Shew, Current Issues in Telecommunications at 197; *see also* N. Cornell & R. Noll, Local Telephone Prices and the Subsidy Question (1985).

Without a doubt, these transfers contributed to universal service. Between 1940 and 1980, the real price of local service declined 55 percent;[221] subscribership increased from 37 percent of households in 1940[222] to well over 90 percent.[223] Frequent users of long-distance service (primarily business users) ended up paying for the nation's telephone plant at rates wholly out of proportion to the actual costs of providing their service. Subscribers who didn't use toll service at all received phone service below cost.[224] Not surprisingly, would-be competitors recognized that there were lucrative opportunities to undercut the inflated rates AT&T was forced to charge for its long-distance service.[225]

§2.3.3.2 Connecting Long-Distance to Local Carriers: Muddling into Unbundling and Interconnection Tariffs

Meanwhile, as discussed in section 9.3, the FCC decided that competition in long-distance service was both feasible and desirable. Between 1959 and the late 1970s, the Commission would pursue a profoundly schizophrenic policy, inflating Bell's long-distance-to-local subsidy on the one hand, while slouching toward long-distance competition on the other. AT&T spent the same two decades attempting to stave off the new competition, while simultaneously fighting for permission to adjust its prices to meet its rivals' rates.

The FCC's Above 890 decision in 1959 triggered the first round of adjustments.[226] Fearing that its largest customers might decide

---

[221] Despite the FCC's cost shifting, the price of long-distance service decreased even more as rapid advances in technology steadily diminished costs. Long-distance rates in 1978 were only 8.6 percent higher than they had been in 1950 even though the Consumer Price Index had increased by 171 percent. *See* Economic Report of the President (1980); AT&T, Bell System Statistical Manual 807 (1982).

[222] *See* Bureau of the Census, U.S. Dept. of Commerce, Statistical Abstract of the U.S. 495 (90th ed. 1969).

[223] *See* Telecommunications Reports, June 2, 1986, at 6.

[224] *See* Faulhaber, Telecommunications in Turmoil at 73.

[225] *See id.* at 18.

[226] *See* Allocation of Frequencies in the Bands Above 890 Mc, Report and Order, 27 F.C.C. 359 (1959), *recons. denied,* 29 F.C.C. 825 (1960).

to build their own private communications networks, AT&T filed its first so-called Telpak tariff.[227] Under Telpak, AT&T would provide bulk quantities of private-line circuits at significant volume discounts off the rates for individual private-line circuits. Telpak thus lowered AT&T's rates for precisely those customers most likely to be tempted to defect to the competition, self-provision.

Questions immediately arose whether Telpak rates were discriminatory or below cost; lengthy administrative and legal proceedings followed. Theretofore, AT&T had never had to break down the costs of each individual interstate service. But the Telpak investigation made this necessary, and a final determination on Telpak's lawfulness was postponed pending the outcome of an investigation of AT&T's cost-allocation practices.[228] In its first Final Decision, the Commission ruled that the multiple channel rates were unreasonably discriminatory in that "like" services were being offered at different rates.[229] The FCC directed AT&T to demonstrate that the rates in its tariffs were both justified by competitive necessity and high enough to cover actual costs.[230] The proceedings dragged on until 1981, when AT&T finally withdrew the Telpak tariff entirely.[231]

[227] See AT&T Tariff FCC No. 250, Telpak Services and Channels, Memorandum Opinion and Order, 30 F.C.C. 625 (1961); Memorandum Opinion and Order, 37 F.C.C. 1111 (1964) (hereinafter *Telpak*); Memorandum Opinion and Order, 38 F.C.C. 761 (1965), *aff'd sub. nom.* American Trucking Assns., Inc. v. FCC, 377 F.2d 121, 126 (D.C. Cir. 1966), *cert. denied*, 386 U.S. 943 (1967); *see also* AT&T v. FCC, 449 F.2d 439, 442–443 (2d Cir. 1971).

[228] See Wiley, Telecommunications and the Law at 156; *see also American Trucking Assns.* 377 F.2d at 121; AT&T v. FCC, 449 F.2d at 442.

[229] See AT&T Tariff FCC No. 250, Telpak Services and Channels, Memorandum Opinion and Order, 30 F.C.C. 625 (1961).

[230] The two showings, the Commission explained, were interrelated. Meeting a competitive threat or obtaining new business that would not otherwise be obtained may be necessary to contribute to the overall economy of the business. "Unless such retained or obtained business does contribute to the overall economy of the operation, however, there is no valid justification for the volume rates. If the volume rates are not high enough to cover the costs attributable to the business retained or obtained, they do not contribute to the overall economy of the operation, but on the contrary, impose a burden on other classes of users." *Telpak*, 37 F.C.C. at 1115–1116 ¶12.

[231] For a capsule discussion of a proceeding that (as of 1980) "appear[ed] destined to provide lifetime careers for its antagonists," see G. Brock, The

The next major regulatory mortar was launched in 1969 with the FCC's 4-3 approval of MCI's application for a new point-to-point microwave service.[232] Within two years, the Commission's Specialized Common Carrier decision had established a new general policy favoring competitive provision of "intercity" private lines.[233] "Established carriers" were directed to interconnect with the new entrants to provide local distribution at either end of entrants' private lines.[234]

The negotiations between Bell and MCI went nowhere and finally collapsed in the late summer of 1973. Bell then unilaterally submitted tariffs to public utility commissions in the states in which MCI sought interconnection. It declined even to file these tariffs with the FCC, relenting (under protest) only when the FCC ordered it to do so.[235] In *Bell System Tariff Offerings*, the Commission declared that local-to-long-distance interconnections were matters for federal, not state, tariffing.[236] Bell filed private-line tariffs with the FCC in November 1973.

Telecommunications Industry: The Dynamics of Market Structure 207–210 (1981).

[232] *See* Microwave Communications, Inc., Application for Construction Permits to Establish New Facilities in the Domestic Public Point-to-Point Microwave Radio Service at Chicago, Ill., St. Louis, Mo., and Intermediate Points, Decision, 18 F.C.C.2d 953 (1969), *recons. denied,* Memorandum Opinion and Order, 21 F.C.C.2d 190 (1970).

[233] *See* Establishment of Policies and Procedures for Consideration of Application to Provide Specialized Common Carrier Services in the Domestic Public Point-to-Point Microwave Radio Service and Proposed Amendments to Parts 21, 43, and 61 of the Commission's Rules, First Report and Order, 29 F.C.C.2d 870 (1971) (hereinafter *Specialized Common Carriers*), *aff'd sub nom.* Washington Util. & Transp. Commn. v. FCC, 513 F.2d 1142 (9th Cir.), *cert. denied,* 423 U.S. 836 (1975).

[234] *See Specialized Common Carriers,* 29 F.C.C.2d at 940 ¶157.

[235] Bell contended that "the interconnection facilities are entirely intrastate, that the offerings are strictly of a local nature, and that consequently, the activities involved . . . are local and subject to state and local regulation exclusively." Bell System Tariff Offerings of Local Distribution Facilities for Use by Other Common Carriers, Decision, 46 F.C.C.2d 413, 416 ¶4 (hereinafter *Bell System Tariff Offerings*); Memorandum Opinion and Order, 48 F.C.C.2d 676, *aff'd sub nom.* Bell Tel. Co. of Pa. v. FCC, 503 F.2d 1250 (3d Cir. 1974), *cert. denied,* 422 U.S. 1026 (1975).

[236] *See Bell System Tariff Offerings,* 46 F.C.C.2d at 413 ¶6. On review, the Ninth Circuit upheld this ruling; the court rejected protests of Bell and state

Entrants immediately challenged the tariffs. MCI and others protested that Bell was overcharging them, that they were buying the same "line-side" connections as ordinary business customers and should therefore not be expected to contribute to the interstate subsidy of local plant—or at least not as much as AT&T, which obtained superior "trunk-side" connections.[237] The FCC initiated a new investigation.[238] Before it held any hearings, however, the parties entered into an interim settlement.[239] Although the newcomers received reductions from the rates appearing in the August 1974 tariffs—30 percent discounts on intraexchange voice grade wire-pair facilities and 21 percent discounts on interexchange voice-grade facilities within a single state[240]—both sides remained unhappy.[241]

Meanwhile, as described in section 9.4, MCI rushed to move far beyond private lines to a full-fledged, switched-access long-distance service available to all. This was not what the FCC had in mind when it licensed MCI in 1969 or when it issued its *Specialized Common Carriers* decision in 1971, but it was what the Court of Appeals for the D.C. Circuit desired in 1977, as it indicated in its imaginative *Execunet I* ruling.[242] AT&T and the Commission

---

commissions, who insisted (correctly) that private-line competition "would serve to increase the burden to intrastate telephone users by reason of the diversion of interstate usage of telephone network facilities to the detriment of telephone users whose rates are regulated by state authorities." Washington Utils. & Transp. Commn. v. FCC, 513 F.2d at 1146.

[237] *See* NARUC v. FCC, 737 F.2d at 1107.

[238] *See* AT&T, Offer of Facilities for Use by Other Common Carriers, Memorandum Opinion and Order, 47 F.C.C.2d 660 (1974).

[239] *See* AT&T, Offer of Facilities for Use by Other Common Carriers, Memorandum Opinion and Order, 52 F.C.C.2d 727 (1975) (hereinafter *Settlement Agreement*).

[240] *See* Investigation of Access and Divestiture Related Tariffs, Memorandum Opinion and Order, 57 Rad. Reg. 2d (P & F) 188 ¶85 (1984). The agreement contemplated that these rates would be superseded by tariffed rates after a one-year moratorium. *See Settlement Agreement*, 52 F.C.C.2d at 738 n.2. The Commission accepted the settlement agreement and terminated its investigation, *see id.*, at 732-733 ¶13, but did "not necessarily approv[e]" its terms, *id.*

[241] *See* MCI v. FCC, 712 F.2d at 524.

[242] MCI Telecommunications Corp., Decision, 60 F.C.C.2d 25, app. B at 62–64 (1976) (letter order of July 2, 1975 (F.C.C. 75-799)); *rev'd*, MCI

immediately petitioned for certiorari, arguing that the D.C. Circuit's decision would result in a "massive diversion of MTS traffic from the switched network." "Cream-skimming" new entrants would compete only for the profits to be won on high-density long-distance routes, thereby undermining the entire scheme of price-averaging and long-distance-to-local subsidies that had been built up over the years.[243] But the Supreme Court declined to get involved.

The FCC initiated a new inquiry into the MTS and WATS market structure,[244] declaring that it would investigate "whether and how [charges paid by interexchange carriers for interconnecting with local plant] can be equitably imposed on all interstate services."[245] But there wasn't much need for investigation. The FCC now faced a completely insoluble set of problems, largely of its own creation. Competition in the long-distance market had begun when companies like MCI offered separate links—"facilities bypass"—around local telcos' switches. But the newcomers had quickly recognized they could bypass the charges without building any facilities at all; they would simply use a local telco's own private lines. A private line could be used to route calls from (say) Washington to a so-called leaky PBX in New York and hence into the New York local network.[246] Or an FX (foreign exchange) line could be leased to terminate the calls directly in the New York public exchange. The beauty of it was that all the lines—indeed everything one might possibly need, other than a corporate logo—could be leased from Bell itself, mostly at flat, non-traffic-sensitive rates. The interstate subsidy

---

Telecomms. Corp. v. FCC, 561 F.2d 365 (D.C. Cir. 1977) (*Execunet I*), cert. denied, 434 U.S. 1040 (1978).

[243] See MCI v. FCC, 580 F.2d 590, 594 (D.C. Cir.) (*Execunet II*), cert. denied, 434 U.S. 790 (1978).

[244] See MTS and WATS Market Structure, Notice of Inquiry and Proposed Rulemaking, 67 F.C.C.2d 757 (1978) (hereinafter *MTS and WATS Market Structure*).

[245] *Id.* at 759 ¶8.

[246] In this scenario, a business user would have MCI connect its PBXs in both cities. On the New York end, the business user (subscribing to Bell's local service) would route its long-distance calls onto Bell's local switched network. To Bell's local switch in New York, such calls appeared no different than calls that originated on the New York PBX.

of local NTS costs was recovered almost entirely from traffic-sensitive charges on switched long-distance services. So the newcomers relied on unswitched private lines. Put simply, the OCCs were arbitrageurs, exploiting price dislocations created by a rotten system of regulatory taxes and subsidies.

The impasse that followed was not amenable to principled resolution. The OCCs vehemently maintained that they were ordinary private *buyers* (no different from any large business user) and should be billed accordingly. AT&T, of course, saw them as competing sellers and demanded that they pay their share of the local subsidies on the same terms as AT&T's own long-distance affiliate. Both were right. What was wrong was Bell's regulatorily imposed rate structure, which had permitted sharp discrepancies between costs and prices to build up over the years under the Ozark Plan of cost separations. Nonetheless, with vague hope more than realistic expectation, the FCC opened an MTS/WATS market structure docket to determine "what reimbursement interstate services should make to local operating companies for the use of local plant" and "whether and how these charges can be equitably imposed on all interstate services."[247] In the meantime, the FCC encouraged negotiations among the parties to arrive at interim "rough justice" tariffs.[248]

Several months of public meetings culminated in the execution, in December 1978, of an Interim Settlement Agreement (known as the *Exchange Network Facilities for Interstate Access* or *ENFIA Agreement*) among AT&T, MCI, and a number of other OCCs and telcos.[249] The OCCs would pay substantially more

---

[247] *MTS and WATS Market Structure,* 67 F.C.C.2d at 759 ¶8.

[248] *See* Exchange Network Facilities for Interstate Access (ENFIA), Memorandum Opinion and Order, 91 F.C.C.2d 1079, 1080-1081 ¶4 (1982) (hereinafter *Investigation Order*); *see generally* Brotman, Communications Policy-Making at the FCC: Past Practices, Future Direction, 7 Cardozo Arts & Ent. L.J. 55, 99 (1988).

[249] *See* Exchange Network Facilities for Interstate Access (ENFIA), Memorandum Opinion and Order, 71 F.C.C.2d 440 (1979) (hereinafter *ENFIA Agreement*); Memorandum Opinion and Order, 90 F.C.C.2d 6 (1982) (hereinafter *Extension Order*); Memorandum Opinion and Order, 90 F.C.C.2d 202 (1982) (hereinafter *Suspension Order*); *Investigation Order,* 91 F.C.C.2d at 1079; Order on Reconsideration, 93 F.C.C.2d 739 (1983) (hereinafter *Reconsideration Order*), *aff'd sub nom.* MCI v. FCC, 712 F.2d at 524; AT&T, Applicability of the

(roughly three times more[250]) than they had been paying for interconnection, but still substantially less (35 to 45 percent less) than AT&T was paying for local distribution.[251] And other interstate carriers using the local exchange—data carriers, for example, operating so-called value-added networks—would pay nothing.[252] The *ENFIA Agreement* was to expire when the FCC got around to making its own decision or after five years, whichever came first.[253]

The discount ostensibly reflected the inferior forms of interconnection that Bell provided the OCCs. In fact, what it reflected was a political deal, a stop-gap private resolution of two irreconcilable public policies. On the one hand, the FCC had embraced the Ozark Plan, under which Bell's long-distance operations would continue to supply a massive subsidy to local operations. On the other, the FCC (propelled by the D.C. Circuit Court of Appeals) had signed up new competition in the long-distance market without first ensuring that all newcomers would be full-fledged subsidizers just like AT&T. The former policy reflected a long legacy of misregulated monopoly; the latter, a short legacy of misregulated competition. The situation clearly could not last. The stage was set for another round of "separations" involving a good bit more than costs.

ENFIA Tariff to Certain OCC Services, Order, 91 F.C.C.2d 568 (1982) (hereinafter *Applicability To Resellers Order*); *see also Access Order*, 93 F.C.C.2d 241; *see generally FTL1* §12.7.1.

[250] *See* Brock, The Telecommunications Industry at 226–228.

[251] The *ENFIA Agreement* provided that OCCs would pay progressively higher access rates. In part, this was intended to reflect the increasing quality of interconnection OCCs would receive. It also reflected a simple compromise, under which OCCs were protected from rate shock. *See ENFIA Agreement*, 71 F.C.C.2d at 446–447 ¶18, 455 ¶40; *Extension Order*, 90 F.C.C.2d at 18–19 ¶¶31-35.

[252] The correction of disparities in exchange access rates charged to the various classes of interexchange carriers was a primary goal in the MTS and WATS market structure investigation. *See* MCI v. FCC, 712 F.2d at 529, 531–532.

[253] *See ENFIA Agreement*, 71 F.C.C.2d at 444 ¶11; *Investigation Order*, 91 F.C.C.2d at 1080-1085 ¶¶3–18. In fact, the discounted ENFIA rates remained in effect until May 1985, when the switched-access tariffs implementing the Commission's access-charge regime became effective.

§2.3.3.3   Connecting Long-Distance to Local Carriers: Access Charges[254]

The FCC blessed the ENFIA deal[255] and then slogged forward with its original docket, aimed at reviewing the separations procedures in their entirety.[256] The next stage resulted in the first fundamental reexamination of separations and price structure in the half a century since *Smith*.[257]

(i) Freezing Interstate Contributions to Non-Traffic-Sensitive Costs. The 1980 review raised critical questions about the treatment of NTS plant. The FCC had finally recognized that the federal share of local NTS costs was grossly inflated.[258] So the FCC decided to freeze the total interstate contribution to NTS plant at the 1981 percentage[259] until more comprehensive revisions could be completed.[260] This marked the end of the three-for-one Ozark Plan. In 1983, the FCC extended the freeze until 1986, after which it would be replaced by a 25 percent allocation.[261]

MCI and the Louisiana Public Service Commission both challenged the interim freeze of the NTS separations formula, though

---

[254] Current regulations governing access charges are set forth in Part 69 of the Commission's rules. *See* 47 C.F.R. Part 69.

[255] *See ENFIA Agreement,* 71 F.C.C.2d at 456 ¶42. The FCC issued an *Extension Order,* 90 F.C.C.2d at 6, which extended the *ENFIA Agreement,* on April 14, 1982. After this order was challenged and upheld, AT&T immediately filed tariff revisions. On April 30, 1982, the FCC issued an order suspending the tariff revisions and scheduling an investigation. The chronology and relevant orders are summarized in MCI v. FCC, 712 F.2d at 524.

[256] *Establishment of a Joint Board,* 78 F.C.C.2d at 837.

[257] *See* Federal-State Joint Board, Order Inviting Comments and Suggested Information Requests, 46 Fed. Reg. 32,281 (1981); Further Notice of Proposed Rulemaking, 46 Fed. Reg. 63,357 (1981).

[258] *See Joint Board,* 89 F.C.C.2d at 4–5 ¶7.

[259] "[W]hile the freeze imposed a cap on the percentage of non-traffic sensitive costs allocated to the interstate jurisdiction, it allowed a growth in the absolute dollar allocation." MCI v. FCC, 750 F.2d at 139. NTS cost increases would remain in proportion to the interstate share of the total costs. *See Joint Board,* 89 F.C.C.2d at 13–14 ¶¶22–23.

[260] *See Joint Board,* 89 F.C.C.2d at 6 ¶9.

[261] *See Jurisdictional Separations Procedures,* 49 Fed. Reg. at 7934.

on opposite grounds.[262] MCI argued that the NTS burden had been frozen when it should have been slashed; the Louisiana PSC insisted that the NTS burden should continue growing. *Smith*, MCI pointed out, required cost separation to be based on relative usage, whereas the subsidy had been frozen (after years of Ozark inflation) at a level almost three times above what relative usage would dictate. The D.C. Circuit easily rejected both challenges; whatever the lawfulness of the Ozark Plan, which MCI had neglected to challenge in 1970, the FCC was now making a reasonable attempt to clean up the existing mess.[263]

(ii) The Genesis of Access Charges.   The D.C. Circuit issued its decision upholding the freeze on the allocation of NTS costs in 1984. By then, however, "separations" had taken on an altogether new significance. While the appeal was pending, the Bell System had been dismantled. The battle—centered in the federal government itself—between monopoly, with its attendant subsidies and price averages, and competition, with its attendant pressure toward cost-based pricing, had finally been won by the forces favoring competition. In the federal government's sphere of influence—which included interstate communications and, by and large, equipment—the new policy would unequivocally tilt toward competition. Readjusting federal pricing schemes now became a matter of considerable urgency.

The divestiture decree ostensibly required BOC tariffs for exchange access to be both equal for all carriers and based on cost (or at least "cost justified").[264] No one really believed that this was immediately possible; AT&T, the BOCs, all decree intervenors,

---

[262] MCI v. FCC, 750 F.2d at 141 & n.34.

[263] *See id.* at 141–142.

[264] *See* Modification of Final Judgment app. B, §B(2), *reprinted in* United States v. AT&T, 552 F. Supp. 131, 233 (D.D.C. 1982) (hereinafter *Decree*) ("Each tariff for exchange access shall be filed on an unbundled basis specifying each type of service, element by element, and no tariff shall require an interexchange carrier to pay for types of exchange access that it does not utilize. The charges for each type of exchange access shall be cost justified and any differences in charges to carriers shall be cost justified on the basis of differences in services provided.").

and Judge Greene himself assiduously ignored or wished away this requirement ever since.[265] The "cost justified" requirement meant nothing in practice; access charges could and did subsidize local telephone service then, as they still do now.[266] The decree's solemn demands for nondiscriminatory pricing proved equally empty. Access charges could be averaged, Judge Greene

---

[265] The decree's mandate of nondiscriminatory pricing was wheeled out on only one significant occasion, when AT&T accused U S WEST of discriminatory pricing in a bid to win a federal government contract in 1985. Both Judge Greene and the D.C. Circuit sided with AT&T. *See* United States v. Western Elec. Co., 846 F.2d 1422, 1425 (D.C. Cir.), *cert. denied,* 488 U.S. 924 (1988). At that time, Judge Greene confidently declared that the decree's mandate against discriminatory pricing was "crystal clear" and "not fact-specific." United States v. Western Elec. Co., Memorandum and Order, No. 82-0192, at 2–3 (D.D.C. Mar. 31, 1987). For its part, a divided panel of the court of appeals acknowledged that the "relevant sections of the [Modification of Final Judgment] are not entirely free from ambiguity." United States v. Western Elec. Co., 846 F.2d at 1427. (The ambiguity acknowledged by the court of appeals stems from the anomaly that provisions originally intended to prevent discrimination *in favor of* AT&T were now being invoked to prevent discrimination *against* AT&T.) The appellate court concluded, nonetheless, that prohibiting the discrimination involved "comports better with the purposes of the MFJ, as evidenced by its text and by contemporaneous statements of its objectives." *Id.*

[266] In approving the decree, Judge Greene expressly declared that "[t]he decree would leave state and federal regulators with a mechanism—access charges—by which to require a subsidy from intercity service to local service." United States v. AT&T, 552 F. Supp. at 169 & n.161; United States v. Western Elec. Co., 569 F. Supp. at 990, 999; Competitive Impact Statement at 48, United States v. Western Elec. Co., No. 74-1698 (D.D.C. Feb. 10, 1982) (hereinafter *Competitive Impact Statement*). According to Judge Greene, "The proposed decree requires the Operating Companies to file tariffs which are cost-justified, but it does not limit the authority of the regulators to allocate costs pursuant to their regulatory policies. Thus, these tariffs may be set at a level which continues the current allocation of interexchange revenues." United States v. AT&T, 552 F. Supp. at 196 n.271; *see also* United States v. Western Elec. Co., 569 F. Supp. at 1007 ("it is these regulators, rather than the Court, which have jurisdiction to resolve the policy issues involved in the calculation of access charges"). Judge Greene went so far as to suggest that regulators were free to include "ghost costs" in the rate base or otherwise engage in creative valuation of the RBOCs' assets to maintain universal-service subsidies. *See* United States v. AT&T, 552 F. Supp. at 192 n.248, 203 n.303. The "cost justified" requirement could not in any event be construed to require pricing at marginal costs. Pricing all services at marginal cost would bankrupt the RBOCs: where there are fixed costs, marginal costs are below average costs. *See FTL1* §9.1.

held.[267] Regulators, he further declared, could engage in "value pricing" of access services and require AT&T to pay a premium for superior access regardless of underlying costs.[268] The decree itself contained a "notwithstanding" clause, which preserved the OCCs' right to receive traffic at the same unit cost as AT&T in any exchange area, even if delivered to facilities more distant than AT&T's.[269] Without such an exemption, all OCCs would have gone bankrupt in short order.

---

[267] *See* United States v. Western Elec. Co., 569 F. Supp. at 1007 n.79 (approving geographically averaged access rates and declining to require "that higher-than-average-cost areas [not be] combined with lower-than-average-cost areas"). At the time of divestiture, Judge Greene permitted NYNEX and Bell Atlantic to continue providing interexchange service in two high-density corridors on the eastern seaboard. *See FTL1* §4.8. The RBOCs were not, however, required to impute to their corridor services the same access charges that they would assess competing carriers. *See* United States v. Western Elec. Co., 569 F. Supp. at 1018 n.144. Some inequality in access charges was "reasonable," Judge Greene held, because the RBOCs' services in the corridors "were sanctioned specifically to preserve for interstate callers in these areas the advantages of the existing local networks." *Id.* at 1107. The Justice Department noted that "both the access charges and the rates charged to customers for corridor service are within the jurisdiction of the FCC" and suggested that the district court leave this issue to the FCC. *See* Memorandum of the United States in Response to the Court's Opinion of April 20, 1983, at 11 n.*, United States v. Western Elec. Co., No. 82-0192 (D.D.C. May 5, 1983).

[268] *See* United States v. AT&T, 552 F. Supp. at 199 n.287. Judge Greene declined to impose the premium charges himself, however, reasoning that a court "lacks the expertise and flexibility to determine the amount of such a premium." The decree itself incorporated a clause (which expired by its own terms in September 1991) that equalized access rates notwithstanding the lower cost of providing access service to AT&T. *See Decree* app. B, §B(3), *reprinted in* 552 F. Supp. at 233–234. The rule applied only "to charges for the transmission of calls above end offices and does not apply to other services provided as part of exchange access." *Competitive Impact Statement* at 33. This clause was intended to neutralize the cost advantage AT&T would otherwise have enjoyed as a result of its legacy of sharing arrangements and co-location with the RBOCs. *See* United States v. AT&T, 552 F. Supp. at 197 n.278; Response of the United States to Public Comments on Proposed MFJ at 101 (May 20, 1982).

[269] *Decree* app. B, §B(3), *reprinted in* 552 F. Supp. at 233–234 ("Notwithstanding the requirements of paragraph (2), from the date of reorganization specified in section I until September 1, 1991, the charges for delivery or receipt of traffic of the same type between end offices and facilities of interexchange carriers within an exchange area, or within reasonable subzones of an exchange area, shall be equal, per unit of traffic delivered or received, for all

Following divestiture, the decree court and the Department of Justice wisely deferred to the FCC and state regulators on all tariff issues.[270] According to Judge Greene, the Modification of Final Judgment (MFJ) required as much: its intent had been to avoid "a re-creation of the FCC's Common Carrier Bureau in the guise of an arm of the Judiciary."

In the early 1980s, the FCC moved forward, initiating its access-charge proceeding.[271] The 1981 freeze on interstate contributions to NTS costs was still in place, still slated to fall to a fixed 25 percent in 1986. But the sums in question—about $11 billion a year—were still being recovered entirely as per-minute charges on long-distance calls, a highly inefficient arrangement. The FCC now prepared to implement sweeping reforms.

---

interexchange carriers; provided, that the facilities of any interexchange carrier within five miles of an AT&T class 4 switch shall, with respect to end offices served by such class 4 switch, be considered to be in the same subzone as such class 4 switch.").

[270] *See, e.g.,* United States v. Western Elec. Co., 578 F. Supp. 653, 654 (D.D.C. 1983) (when the FCC did not approve access tariffs prior to divestiture, decree court granted temporary waiver allowing BOCs to provide access to AT&T on a contractual basis); Memorandum Order, United States v. Western Elec. Co., No. 82-0192 (D.D.C. Dec. 14, 1984) (extending waiver for BOCs to provide special access to AT&T on a contractual basis); Reply of the United States to AT&T's Motion to Compel Compliance with the Decree at 10, United States v. Western Elec. Co., No. 82-0192 (D.D.C. June 21, 1984) (recommending that decree court not consider AT&T's complaint regarding non-cost-justified tariffs "until the full procedures provided by Florida law, including review by the Florida Supreme Court of a final order of the Florida PSC, have been completed"); Memorandum Order at 5, United States v. Western Elec. Co., No. 82-0192 (D.D.C. June 28, 1985) (exchange access rates, which favored the state of Oregon over AT&T, did not "constitute unlawful discrimination under the decree because of the differing public policy considerations affecting both sets of rates").

[271] *See Access Order,* 93 F.C.C.2d at 241, *modified on recons.,* 97 F.C.C.2d 682 (1983), *modified on further on recons.,* 97 F.C.C.2d 834 (1984), *aff'd in part sub nom.* NARUC v. FCC, 737 F.2d at 1095, *modified on further recons.,* Memorandum Opinion and Order, 49 Fed. Reg. 46,383 (1984); Memorandum Opinion and Order, 50 Fed. Reg. 18,249 (1985), *aff'd on further recons.,* Memorandum Opinion and Order, 50 Fed. Reg. 43,707 (1985). *See also* A. Kahn, Concluding Comments: The Future of Access, *in* Telecommunications Access and Public Policy 249 (M. A. Baughcum & G. Faulhaber eds., 1984); Wiley, Telecommunications and the Law at 166–167.

The single overarching philosophy of the reforms was to price *lines,* not *minutes,* at least insofar as money was being spent on lines, not minutes. Truly traffic-sensitive costs—switching costs, for example—would continue to be charged according to usage. Non-traffic-sensitive costs—the costs of lines, in particular—would be charged without reference to usage. The FCC accordingly assembled a quiver of new "line charges" to recover non-traffic-sensitive costs that had previously been recovered through per-minute rates.

(iii) The Subscriber Line Charge.   The FCC's first and most controversial proposal was to require LECs to collect a flat, $6-a-month "subscriber line charge" (SLC) directly from each subscriber.[272] On roughly 100 million lines, this charge would have generated about $7 billion a year; long-distance carriers would have been able to slash their access-charge payments to LECs by that same amount. Telephone users would have seen an immediate $6 increase in the flat-rate component of their monthly phone bill; long-distance phone rates would immediately have dropped sharply—between 5 and 10 cents a minute. In a single, clean step, a large part of the Ozarkian inefficiencies accumulated over the years would have been swept away.

Competing carriers—both local and long distance—would have seen sharp changes, too. A booming "local bypass" business had developed, selling large customers and long-distance carriers the ability to circumvent the inflated access charges they otherwise had to pay to local exchange companies.[273] If all NTS

[272] The D.C. Circuit later affirmed the FCC's decision "in all major respects," NARUC v. FCC, 737 F.2d at 1103, remanding only for further consideration of certain minor issues, *see id.* at 1125–1127.

[273] At the time of divestiture, AT&T had explained to the court: "Because their current rates recover the non-traffic sensitive costs of access through usage sensitive prices, the BOCs are extremely vulnerable to bypass competition. . . . Bypass is not a distant threat awaiting future technology. The technology is here today in the form of rooftop antennae, coaxial cable, lightguide, microwave, satellite, digital termination service, and cellular radio systems. These technologies are in use now, allowing high volume telephone users to bypass the BOCs' local networks." AT&T Response to the Court's April 20, 1983 Opinion Concerning LATAs at 16–17, United States v. Western Elec. Co., No. 82-0192 (D.D.C. May 5, 1983) (footnotes omitted). Although

costs would be recovered through SLCs, the bypassers would suddenly lose the price umbrella that had allowed them to enter the industry.[274] MCI and other long-distance carriers would be affected, too. The good news for them was that their access charges would not over time rise to the inflated levels AT&T paid. The bad news was that AT&T's charges would fall quickly toward the low levels that they now paid. The substantial cost advantage the OCCs had enjoyed under the ENFIA regime would evaporate.

The FCC's SLC proposal elicited violent opposition from consumer-advocacy groups, state regulators, Congress, and (surprisingly) Judge Greene,[275] forcing the FCC to compromise. The Commission held to its commitment to impose the $6 SLC on multiline businesses, but backed off from its intent to impose a charge of this size immediately for residential and single-line business lines. On reconsideration, the Commission chose to

---

the court disagreed with AT&T's assessment, the court praised bypass technology as "more advanced and less expensive than the present method of transmission which depends upon a cumbersome system of poles and wires. Bypass would provide telecommunications service directly to the subscriber by means of satellites, microwave towers, or other advanced technological innovations at a lower cost than such service is available now. . . . If and when bypass technology becomes technically and economically feasible for widespread use, it should have the effect of reducing telephone costs and charges across the board, to the benefit of consumers, the economy, and the nation." United States v. AT&T, 552 F. Supp. at 175.

[274] A local exchange facility can be bypassed through "facilities bypass" by using private communications facilities to connect with a long-distance carrier or through "service bypass" by using private lines leased from the local company at flat rates. *See* Kahn & Shew, Current Issues *in* Telecommunications at 196–197, n.16; *Access Order,* 93 F.C.C.2d at 241 app. F; FCC Common Carrier Bureau, Bypass of the Public Switched Network (Dec. 19, 1984); *See* G. Gill, F. McFarlan, & J. O'Neill, Bypass of Local Operating Companies: Opportunities and Policy Issues, *in* Future Competition in Telecommunications 253–274 (S. Bradley & J. Hausman eds., 1989).

[275] *See* United States v. Western Elec. Co., 569 F. Supp. at 998–1000; *see also* United States v. Western Elec. Co., 627 F. Supp. 1090, 1096 n.18 (D.D.C. 1986) ("[t]he assumption that high-quality, low-cost telephone service would be provided by the local companies was an essential ingredient in the Court's determination that the consent decree was in the public interest"); United States v. Western Elec. Co., 592 F. Supp. 846, 861–867 (D.D.C. 1984) (in considering waiver requests, effects on local ratepayers must be taken into account).

institute further proceedings on the magnitude of the end-user charge after the transition, on the categories of low-income subscribers who should be exempted from end-user charges, on the shape of the transition, and on mechanisms sensitive to the particular needs of small telephone companies in high-cost areas.[276] The Commission ended up preserving the freeze on the percentage of NTS costs to be recovered from interstate usage and settled on a $3.50 SLC cap for residential users.[277] The FCC also promised to monitor closely the SLC's effect on the goal of preserving universal telephone service.[278] The SLC was challenged in court; the D.C. Circuit upheld it.[279]

(iv) The Centrex Line Charge.   The FCC gave special consideration to the impact of the SLC on Centrex services. Centrex service provides the equivalent of a private branch exchange (PBX)—with features like four-digit dialing, intercom, and conference calling—but does so using central telco facilities. Because it hauls all traffic, including "internal" calls, to a central office, Centrex typically requires about six times as many local loops as a PBX.[280] Logically, the new SLC would have applied to each and every Centrex line, with the (economically sensible) result that PBXs would have become much more attractive relative to Centrex service.

---

[276] MTS and WATS Market Structure, Memorandum Opinion and Order, 49 Fed. Reg. 7810, 7812–7813 (1984) (hereinafter *MTS and WATS Further Reconsideration Order*).

[277] *See* Kahn & Shew, Current Issues in Telecommunications at 196–197. In the *MTS and WATS Further Reconsideration Order,* the FCC decided that residential and single-line business end-user charges should not exceed $4 per line per month through 1990. *See MTS and WATS Further Reconsideration Order,* 49 Fed. Reg. at 7810–7813; *see also LEC Price Cap Order* 5 F.C.C. Rec. at 6793 ¶57.

[278] *See MTS and WATS Further Reconsideration Order,* 49 Fed. Reg. at 7812–7813.

[279] By the time the SLC came up for review in the D.C. Circuit, the FCC had backed off considerably, and the size of the SLC for residential users was still under review. As the court noted, the FCC had "not decided the size of the charge, the shape of the transition, or the class of persons affected." The court limited its approval of the plan accordingly. *See* NARUC v. FCC, 737 F.2d at 1120.

[280] *See id.* at 1122.

The FCC, however, accepted the argument of various state commissions that Centrex rates were *already* priced above cost to help subsidize local rates and that telcos should therefore be allowed to adjust Centrex rates downward to compensate for the rising SLC. The full multiline business access rate (of $6 per line) would therefore be applied only prospectively to newly installed Centrex lines. Existing Centrex plant would be subject to transitional access charges, not to exceed $2.00 in 1984 and rising to $3.00 during 1985 and 1986.[281] The charges would be reexamined in supplemental proceedings, with the help of the joint board and with special attention to the problem of "stranded investment."[282] The Commission decided that there should be a monthly single-line rate for Centrex subscribers for each line between the end user's premises and the carrier's Class 5 Office; this charge would be computed by "dividing one-twelfth of the projected annual revenue requirement for the End User Common Line element by the projected average number of local exchange service subscriber lines in use during such annual period."[283] The D.C. Circuit upheld this aspect of the SLC ruling, too, in the face of arguments that Centrex was being treated either too harshly or too leniently.[284]

(v) The Private-Line Charge. The FCC's third line charge was a flat $25-a-month "special access" surcharge on private lines supplied by local telcos to originate or terminate interstate connections.[285] The logic here was roughly as follows. Private lines are used to funnel interstate traffic into or out of the public local exchange. Even with the SLC, regular users of the public local exchange don't fully cover the interstate share of local exchange costs. Therefore, everyone else, private-line users included,

---

[281] *See* MTS and WATS Market Structure, Memorandum Opinion and Order, 48 Fed. Reg. 42,984, 42,991–42,992 (1983) (hereinafter *MTS and WATS Reconsideration Order*).

[282] *See id.* at 42,992.

[283] *See* 47 C.F.R. §69.104(a), (c), (d).

[284] *See* NARUC v. FCC, 737 F.2d at 1122–1124.

[285] *See* MTS and WATS Reconsideration Order, 48 Fed. Reg. at 42,997, 43,019 app. A.; 47 C.F.R. §69.115(b)–(c).

must pitch in. The Commission took a stab at estimating how much interstate traffic is carried over private lines and then plucked the $25 figure out of thin air.[286] The court of appeals upheld this as a reasonable attempt to deal with a real problem in the complete absence of hard data and took some comfort in the FCC's promise to reassess the level of the surcharge later in a separate proceeding.[287] Despite these promises, however, the $25 charge was still in place at the end of 1990. [288]

(vi) The Carrier Common Line Charge.   The FCC's plan provided that traffic-sensitive costs would continue to be recovered from interexchange carriers according to actual usage.[289] Under the original plan, all other costs—all NTS costs—were to be shifted directly to end users by way of the subscriber line charge; there would then have been no further debate about how to allocate any of those costs to interexchange carriers. But the $6-a-month SLC had not survived, at least not for all users.

There thus came into existence a carrier common line charge (CCLC) to be paid by long-distance carriers, including OCCs, resellers, and other carriers previously subject to the ENFIA tariffs.[290] OCCs and resellers were to pay a rate based on the projected relative use attributable to the average OCC line.[291] FX

---

[286] *See MTS and WATS Reconsideration Order,* 48 Fed. Reg. at 43,019 app. A.; 47 C.F.R. §69.115. As the Commission frankly conceded to the court of appeals, "No data are presently available on the percentage of private lines that are connected to PBXs or other switching machines. . . . Because private lines are not routinely metered, the FCC also had no data on the extent of 'leakage' from such private lines or on the percentage of leakage that is jurisdictionally interstate. . . . Rather than abandon entirely the possibility of recovering a fair part of interstate local exchange costs from private line users, the FCC undertook to develop a reasonable surrogate for the carrier charges." NARUC v. FCC, 737 F.2d at 1139–1140 (quoting FCC's Brief at 97–98).

[287] *See* NARUC v. FCC, 737 F.2d at 1138–1142.

[288] *LEC Price Cap Order,* 5 F.C.C. Rec. at 6793 ¶57.

[289] *See Access Order,* 93 F.C.C.2d at 297–315 ¶¶197–249.

[290] *See MTS and WATS Reconsideration Order,* 48 Fed. Reg. at 42,997, 43,018 app. A; 47 C.F.R. §69.105(a).

[291] *MTS and WATS Reconsideration Order,* 48 Fed. Reg. at 43,018 app. A.; 47 C.F.R. §69.105, *as amended by MTS and WATS Further Reconsideration Order,* 49 Fed. Reg. at 7829.

users would likewise pay a nonaveraged per-minute/per-line charge according to the actual use of each FX line.[292] Together with the private-line surcharge, this would address the problems caused by "leaky PBXs" and other "service bypass" arrangements.

Predictably, the OCCs objected vehemently. MCI estimated that it would pay approximately $355 for each access line, whereas users of comparable private-line facilities would pay only $25.[293] MCI was right: the FCC still had not succeeded in bringing prices into line with costs. Its continuing attempts to cover NTS costs with usage-based charges had inevitably led to new pricing dislocations and inequalities. The novel part of it all was that MCI found itself on the losing end of pricing inequities—after years of building a business on the exploitation of even more outrageous price discrepancies to the detriment of AT&T.[294]

The court of appeals rejected this attack, too. The FCC had done the best it could to set access charges in line with how much traffic would really flow into or out of the public local exchange; OCCs would pay more for identical lines, but would be using those lines more heavily. The FCC and the court of appeals had muddle-through pragmatism on their side; MCI, with nothing more than logic and principle to back it, was bound to lose. "Recovery of the balance of NTS costs through the usage-based carrier common line charge and special access surcharge," the court of appeals declared, "is not inconsistent with the decision to impose flat-rate end user charges."[295] Not inconsistent, one must suppose, only in the ethereal world of telephone pricing, where inconsistency is so rampant it is the norm.

---

[292] *See MTS and WATS Further Reconsideration Order,* 49 Fed. Reg. at 7922.

[293] *See* NARUC v. FCC, 737 F.2d at 1133.

[294] As the appellate court pointed out, "MCI has itself benefitted from transitional rate structures implemented to avoid potentially fatal rate increases both under the ENFIA Agreement and under the Commission's access-charge scheme, in which OCCs pay a lesser rate for their access connections than does AT&T although the equivalent costs of providing that OCC and AT&T access may not be fully reflected in the rate differential." *Id.* at 1135 (footnote omitted).

[295] *Id.* at 1134. The court continued: "The portion of costs which temporarily or permanently will not be borne by the end users, which forms the

(vii) The AT&T Premium.   The 1983 access-charge proceeding had as its objective to create equal access charges for equal connections—at least as among interexchange voice carriers connecting through the public switched network. Even here, however, the FCC could not finish the job at once. The divestiture decree had established an objective of fully "equal access" for all interexchange carriers, but allowed the conversion to be phased in through September 1, 1986.[296] In the interim, AT&T's "carrier's carrier" charge was to be maintained at a "premium" above the charge paid by the OCCs.[297] By 1987, equal access had in fact been widely implemented, and access charges were moving quickly toward uniformity.

But the rules creating the premium have been repeatedly extended. The 1982 divestiture decree included a "short-wire" provision, entitling an OCC whose point of presence was within a certain range from a BOC central office to receive traffic at the same rate as AT&T—even if AT&T's point of presence was nearer to the central office than the OCC's so that the BOC's costs in carrying traffic there were lower.[298] The MFJ clause to that effect expired on September 1, 1991.[299] But in 1991, the FCC again intervened to protect competitors (though not competition) and kept the discriminatory arrangement in place.[300]

---

basis for carriers' access charges, is essentially a subsidy. This subsidy is not logically attributable to a particular class of carriers. The Commission's decision to recover NTS costs from end users on a flat-rate basis therefore does not require it also to assess the subsidized balance of those costs on a flat-rate basis from the interexchange carriers." *Id.*

[296] *See Decree* app. B, §A(1), *reprinted in* 552 F. Supp. at 232–233.

[297] *Access Order,* 93 F.C.C.2d at 244 ¶5.

[298] *See FTL1* §9.6.3.

[299] The MFJ required that "until September 1, 1991, the charges for delivery or receipt of traffic of the same type between end offices and facilities of interexchange carriers within an exchange area . . . shall be equal, per unit of traffic delivered or received, for all interexchange carriers." *Decree* app. B, §B(3), *reprinted in* 552 F. Supp. at 233–234.

[300] *See* MTS and WATS Market Structure, Transport Rate Structure and Pricing, Order and Further Notice of Proposed Rulemaking, 6 F.C.C. Rec. 5341, 5344 ¶¶12–14 (1991); *see* M. Lewyn, The Little Guys of Long-Distance Are Mighty Nervous, Bus. Wk., June 3, 1991, at 29.

The Commission extended the rule again in 1992 with an interim rate structure that had essentially the same effect.[301]

In May 1997, the FCC finally laid out permanent rules that will eventually do away with the equal-charge rule and its interim-rate-structure variant. The FCC itself admitted it has been dragging its feet: "Because we have not announced a definite and detailed end state[,] . . . we have afforded carriers little opportunity to plan, adjust, and develop their networks in preparation for such a rate structure, despite our lengthy period of 'transition.'"[302] The permanent rules are being phased in over a two-year period ending January 2000 and are designed to make transport pricing completely cost-based.[303] The FCC explained that "to the extent that we designed the interim rate structure to facilitate the growth of small IXCs in competition with AT&T, we find that such protective rules are no longer necessary."[304]

(viii) The Unbundling of Access Charges. As discussed in more detail in section 5.3.2, the Commission in 1992 adopted rules that permitted expanded interconnection to CAPs and other bypass providers.[305] These rules, which unbundled LEC services, required a corresponding unbundling of access charges.

Under prior LEC tariffs, interstate special-access customers generally had to pay two so-called channel-termination charges: (1) a charge covering transmission from the customer's premises to the LEC's central office and (2) a charge covering transmission from the central office to an interexchange carrier's point

---

[301] *See* Transport Rate Structure and Pricing, Petition for Waiver of the Transport Rules Filed by GTE Service Corporation, Report and Order and Further Notice of Proposed Rulemaking, 7 F.C.C. Rec. 7006, 7010–7023, ¶¶7–32 (1992).

[302] *Access Charge Reform Order,* 12 F.C.C. Rec. at 16,054 ¶166.

[303] *See id.* at 16,055 ¶169, 16,067 ¶198.

[304] *Id.* at 16,059–16,060 ¶180.

[305] *See* Expanded Interconnection with Local Telephone Company Facilities, Amendment of the Part 69 Allocation of General Support Facility Costs, Report and Order and Notice of Proposed Rulemaking, 7 F.C.C. Rec. 7369, 7380–7381, ¶¶14–18 (1992) (hereinafter *Expanded Interconnection Order*).

of presence (POP).[306] Because LECs would not allow the two kinds of channel termination to be purchased separately, this rate structure prevented CAPs from offering partial bypass (e.g., telco carriage from a customer's premises to an end office followed by bypass from the end office to the interexchange carrier's POP). That in turn preserved price-averaged, distance-insensitive, universal-service subsidies built into the pricing of local service. As access is unbundled and competitive carriers begin providing the more concentrated legs of local access, price-averaging and distance-insensitive rates will be increasingly difficult to maintain.

The FCC, however, decided that the competitive benefits of more special-access competition outweighed the potential harm done to the universal-service subsidy.[307] Under the "worst-case separations effects" hypothesized by one local telco—which the Commission found to be overblown in any event—special-access interconnection would add less than $1 per line per month to the cost of local access service. This, the FCC concluded, was not "of a magnitude to threaten subscribership."[308]

---

[306] In addition, special-access customers had to pay for any necessary interoffice transmission when the POP and the customer's premises were not served by the same LEC central office.

[307] The FCC based that conclusion in part on the experience of states that had already implemented similar initiatives for intrastate toll calls. For example, the New York PSC had ordered LECs in its jurisdiction to allow CAPs and others to interconnect with both unswitched and switched intrastate services at LEC central offices, using either physical collocation or a form of virtual collocation as an alternative. *See* Regulatory Response to Competition at 21–32, Op. No. 89-12, Case 29469 (N.Y. PSC May 16, 1989) (ordering private-line interconnection); Order Regarding OTIS II Compliance Filing, Cases 29469 and 88-C-004 (N.Y. PSC May 8, 1991) (approving physical collocation tariff for private-line interconnection); Comparably Efficient Interconnection Arrangements, Op. No. 91-24, Cases 88-C-004, 88-C-063, and 91-C-1174 (N.Y. PSC Nov. 25, 1991) (ordering LECs to unbundle portions of local loops); Pooling, Collocation and Access Rate Design at 23-70, Op. No. 92-13, Case 28425 (N.Y. PSC May 29, 1992) (ordering interconnection to switched services).

[308] *Expanded Interconnection Order,* 7 F.C.C. Rec. at 7381 ¶17. The Commission nevertheless imposed its expanded-interconnection requirements only on Tier 1 telcos. Requiring smaller LECs to offer expanded interconnection, the Commission concluded, might "tax their resources and harm universal service and infrastructure development in rural areas," particularly because

But rather than formally unbundle the special-access rate structure into separate transmission and connection charges, the Commission required local telcos to create new connection charge elements for services they provide to interconnectors.[309] Telcos and interconnectors would be allowed to negotiate the rates, terms, and conditions of these connection charge subelements, but local telcos would be required to file those agreements and then make them available to all similarly situated interconnectors under tariff.[310]

At the same time, the FCC afforded the LECs a measure of pricing flexibility to respond to competition.[311] The Commission determined that to bring special-access rates more in line with costs, LECs providing expanded interconnection would be permitted to implement a pricing system dividing study areas (within which prices must be averaged) into different traffic-density-related rate zones.[312] Failing to change the existing system of rate averaging, the Commission stated, would "seriously constrain access competition and potentially deprive customers of the attendant benefits."[313]

(ix) The 1997 Access Charge Reform Order. The FCC's 1997 *Access Charge Reform Order* brought two important changes in the previously existing access-charge scheme. First, the Commission expressly recognized that the overall sum LECs currently earn in connection with interstate access exceeds the cost of providing that service.[314] To that extent, the Commission determined, access charges reflect an implicit subsidy, the result of almost half a century of separations manipulation.[315] The

---

demand for expanded interconnection in rural areas would usually come from a single large user. *Id.* at 7398 ¶56.

[309] *Id.* at 7424–7425 ¶120.

[310] *See id.* at 7442–7443 ¶159. Telcos would be allowed to recover a reasonable share of overhead through connection charges, but may not impose a charge to recover for lost subsidies. *See id.* at 7422 ¶115.

[311] *Id.* at 7422 ¶115.

[312] *See id.* at 7454–7455 ¶179.

[313] *Id.* at 7457 ¶184.

[314] *See, e.g., Access Charge Reform Order,* 12 F.C.C. Rec. at 15,994 ¶28.

[315] *See id.* at 15,995 ¶29.

Commission interpreted section 254 of the 1996 Act and its leg-islative history[316] to require the elimination of any such implicit subsidies.[317] On this reasoning, extensive rate cuts might be required.

But this aspect of the order turned out to be of primarily pro-grammatic significance: the Commission interpreted section 254 as requiring only *eventual* (not immediate) elimination of im-plicit subsidies.[318] And the Commission saw reasons not to act immediately: it lacked the tools to identify just what portion of access charges represents subsidy and what portion represents costs,[319] and immediate cuts might cause "rate shock" for some end users.[320] Thus, the Commission declined to adopt what it called a "prescriptive approach": a policy aimed at reducing rates to costs forcibly. Instead, it would adopt a "market-based ap-proach": for now, it would hope that emerging competition would bring rates in line with costs.[321] On appeal, the Eighth Circuit held that by taking this approach the Commission did not act arbitrarily.[322]

Closely related to the Commission's "market-based approach" was its reaffirmation of its earlier conclusion that incumbent

---

[316] *See* 47 U.S.C. §254(e) ("[a]ny [universal service] support should be explicit"); *Joint Explanatory Statement of the Committee of Conference* at 131 ("[A]ny support mechanism continued or created under the new section 254 should be explicit, rather than implicit as many support mechanisms are today.").

[317] *See Access Charge Reform Order,* 12 F.C.C. Rec. at 15,997 ¶33. The idea is, of course, that if there are going to be any subsidies at all, they should be explicit. *See id.*

[318] *See id.* at 15,987 ¶9, 16,002 ¶47. On appeal, the Eighth Circuit deferred to this reading. *See* Southwestern Bell Tel. Co. v. FCC, 153 F.3d 523, 537, 549 (8th Cir. 1998).

[319] *See, e.g., Access Charge Reform Order,* 12 F.C.C. Rec. at 15,988–15,989 ¶13, 16,002 ¶45.

[320] *See id.* at 16,002 ¶46.

[321] *See id.* at 15,986 ¶7. On the same day, the Commission issued a price-cap order that increased the productivity offset to 6.5 percent, thereby dras-tically reducing access charges. *See Fourth and Second Reports and Orders,* 12 F.C.C. Rec. at 16,642. Ostensibly, this price-cap cut was based on the merits— i.e., reflected an honest attempt to estimate future productivity—and did not represent a watered-down version of the "prescriptive approach."

[322] *See* Southwestern Bell Tel. Co. v. FCC, 153 F.3d 523, 546–549 (8th Cir. 1998).

LECs may not collect access charges in connection with lines that competitive LECs (CLECs) (including long-distance carriers turned CLEC) lease on an unbundled basis.[323] Although the determination was important, it did not allow long-distance carriers to replace all conventional access arrangements with unbundled access. If long-distance carriers buy exchange access on an unbundled basis, they, in effect, become the end user's LEC and therefore must provide whatever other services the end user may desire — including local exchange service.[324] Thus, depending on how unprofitable local service is, long-distance carriers will in all likelihood often stay with the conventional arrangement.

Second, and of greater immediate importance, the Commission implemented far-reaching modifications to LECs' access-charge *rate structure*. As early as 1983, the FCC articulated the goal of having LECs recover non-traffic-sensitive costs of exchange access service through flat fees and traffic-sensitive costs through usage-based (usually per-minute) fees.[325] Fourteen years later, however, the Commission had come no closer to realizing that goal.[326] A significant share of NTS cost was still loaded onto the per-minute access fees that local phone companies charged long-distance carriers.[327] And that, the Commission concluded, amounted to an implicit (and thus unlawful) subsidy from heavy to light users of interstate long-distance service.[328]

Instead, the Commission determined, it would finally require LECs to recover all NTS costs through flat fees.[329] Flat fees, of

---

[323] See *Access Charge Reform Order*, 12 F.C.C. Rec. at 16,129–16,131 ¶¶337–340. On appeal, the Eighth Circuit sustained this aspect of the FCC's decision, too. See Southwestern Bell Tel. Co. v. FCC, 153 F.3d 523, 540–541 (8th Cir. 1998).

[324] See Implementation of the Local Competition Provisions in the Telecommunications Act of 1996, First Report and Order, 11 F.C.C. Rec. 15,499, 15,679 ¶357 (1996) (hereinafter *Local Competition Order*).

[325] *Access Order*, 93 F.C.C.2d at 322 ¶¶281–282.

[326] As it admitted in 1997, the Commission "has not always adopted rules that are consistent with this goal." *Access Charge Reform Order*, 12 F.C.C. Rec. at 15,992–15,993 ¶24.

[327] See *id.* at 15,998–15,999 ¶37.

[328] See *id.* at 15,986 ¶6.

[329] See *id.* at 15,999–16,000 ¶38.

course, already existed: the Commission could simply have raised the SLC. And the Commission did just that for nonprimary residential and multiline business lines. But having learned from events in 1983, it did not do this for primary residential and single-line business lines.[330] Instead, the Commission created a new fixed fee (the "presubscribed interexchange carrier charge" (or PICC)) that LECs would collect from end users' presubscribed long-distance carrier.[331] The PICC starts at $0.53 per month for the first year[332] and will gradually increase until the sum of the SLC and the PICC covers non-traffic-sensitive common line costs.[333]

For other lines (nonprimary residential lines, multiline business lines), LECs will now generally recover the entirety of common line costs through increased SLCs,[334] which they will ultimately be permitted to raise to $9.00.[335] Price hikes on the SLC for nonprimary residential lines must be phased in gradually,[336] but those on multiline business lines may be implemented immediately.[337] The Commission expects that LECs will be able to use the higher SLC to recover common line costs from almost all nonprimary residential and multiline business access lines.[338] To the extent LECs cannot fully recover common line

---

[330] See id. at 16,010–16,011 ¶73. On appeal, the Eighth Circuit permitted this, holding that the FCC's refusal to raise the residential SLC did not amount to an implicit subsidy. See Southwestern Bell Tel. Co. v. FCC, 153 F.3d 523, 538 (8th Cir. 1998).

[331] See Access Charge Reform Order, 12 F.C.C. Rec. at 16,004 ¶55.

[332] See id. at 16,020–16,021 ¶94.

[333] See id. at 16,005 ¶56, 16,020–16,021 ¶94. Although creating the PICC may have been politically more attractive than raising the SLC, one may legitimately ask whether its practical effect was much different: most long-distance carriers, of course, passed the PICC on to their customers. See, e.g., S. Rosenbush, New Long-Distance Fees Draw Fire from FCC, USA Today, Feb. 26, 1998.

[334] See Access Charge Reform Order, 12 F.C.C. Rec. at 16,000 ¶39.

[335] Id. at 16,014 ¶78.

[336] See id. at 16,005–16,006 ¶60. LECs will be permitted to charge a per-minute CCLC on originating minutes until SLC and PICC ceilings increase enough to recover common line revenues. See id.

[337] See id. at 16,000 ¶39.

[338] See id.

costs through increased SLCs, LECs may charge PICCs on these lines, too.[339]

(x) Detariffing Long-Distance Services. After the FCC's 1983 regime of access charges had been established with its own set of subsidies, it became possible for the FCC to consider detariffing long-distance services, just as it recently had done for CPE and just as it had done from the outset for enhanced and wireless services.[340] If the market was competitive and each carrier bore a proportional share of access charges, comprehensive regulation of long-distance carriers was no longer necessary.

As discussed in detail in Section 9.5, the FCC began by first permitting and later requiring "nondominant" long-distance carriers (carriers other than AT&T) not to file tariffs—a policy known as "forbearance."[341] To make it easier for AT&T to respond to other carriers' competitive initiatives, the Commission then replaced the rate-of-return regulation applicable to AT&T with price-caps regulation.[342] In 1995, the FCC eliminated even this modest residue of regulation; at that time, it determined that AT&T no longer had substantial market power and should therefore be declared nondominant.[343]

---

[339] *See id.* at 16,005 ¶59. The PICC ceilings for these lines for the first year are $1.50 for nonprimary residential lines and $2.75 for multiline business lines, with gradual increases after the first year. *See id.*

[340] The detariffing of these services is discussed in sections 2.3.1.1 and 2.4.3.1 and in Chapters 8 and 9.

[341] *See* Policy and Rules Concerning Rates for Competitive Common Carrier Services and Facilities Authorizations Therefor, Notice of Inquiry and Proposed Rulemaking, 77 F.C.C.2d 308 (1979); First Report and Order, 85 F.C.C.2d 1 (1980); Further Notice of Proposed Rulemaking, 84 F.C.C.2d 445 (1981); Second Report and Order, 91 F.C.C.2d 59 (1982); Order on Reconsideration, 93 F.C.C.2d 54 (1983); Second Further Notice of Proposed Rulemaking, 47 Fed. Reg. 17,308 (1982); Third Further Notice of Proposed Rulemaking, 48 Fed. Reg. 22,292 (1983); Third Report and Order, 48 Fed. Reg. 46,791 (1983); Fourth Report and Order, 95 F.C.C.2d 554 (1983); Fourth Further Notice of Proposed Rulemaking, 96 F.C.C.2d 922 (1984); Fifth Report and Order, 98 F.C.C.2d 1191 (1984); Sixth Report and Order, 99 F.C.C.2d 1020 (1985).

[342] *See AT&T Price Cap Order,* 4 F.C.C. Rec. at 2873.

[343] *See* Motion of AT&T Corp. to Be Reclassified as a Non-dominant Carrier, Order, 11 F.C.C. Rec. 3271 (1995).

For ten years, the Commission's authority to forbear from regulating the services of common carriers was the subject of heated court battles. The Commission steadfastly claimed that the 1934 Act permitted it to forbear, but the Supreme Court ultimately concluded that section 203(a) of the Act *required* the FCC to enforce the tariff-filing obligations against all common carriers.[344] The authority to forbear, the Supreme Court ruled, would have to come from Congress.[345]

In 1996, it finally did. With exceptions not here relevant, the new Act authorized the Commission to forbear from enforcing *any* provision of the Communications Act and regulations.[346] Exercising its newfound authority, the FCC on October 31, 1996, adopted a mandatory detariffing regime for nondominant (that is, all) interexchange carriers.[347] But the long-distance forbearance saga still did not end. MCI (perhaps wishing to preserve the benefits of the "filed tariff" doctrine, under which it is for all practical purposes immune from customers' contract suits) went to court, arguing that section 160 did not empower the Commission to prohibit carriers to file tariffs — only to permit carriers not to file tariffs. The D.C. Circuit granted a stay pending appeal;[348] the case is still under consideration as of this writing.

§2.3.3.4 Connecting Long-Distance Carriers to Local Carriers in Other Countries

International rates and payments are typically established through bilateral operating agreements between U.S. carriers and their foreign counterparts. These agreements specify methods of interconnection, rates of payment for completion of outgoing

[344] *See* MCI v. AT&T, 512 U.S. 218 (1994); *see also* Southwestern Bell Corp. v. FCC, 43 F.3d 1515 (D.C. Cir. 1995); AT&T v. FCC, 978 F.2d 727 (D.C. Cir. 1992); MCI v. FCC, 765 F.2d 1186 (D.C. 1985).

[345] *See* MCI v. AT&T, 512 U.S. at 233–234.

[346] *See* 47 U.S.C. §160.

[347] *See* Policy and Rules Concerning the Interstate, Interexchange Marketplace, Implementation of Section 254(g) of the Communications Act of 1934, as amended, Second Report and Order, 11 F.C.C. Rec. 20,730 (1996).

[348] *See* MCI Telecomms. Corp. v. FCC, No. 96-1459 (D.C. Cir. Feb. 13, 1997).

calls, and routing of incoming calls. A U.S. carrier's income is determined by the agreed rate of payment (called the "accounting rate") and the routing of incoming calls.[349] The accounting rate is a fixed sum (usually charged per minute), which in theory is divided equally between the two carriers. In fact, however, the accounting rate is simply twice the amount the originating carrier must pay the terminating carrier to have a call completed. What the originating carrier really earns is the difference between the rate it charges customers and the rate it pays foreign carriers.

Because the U.S. long-distance industry is competitive, U.S. international rates are significantly lower than those in most other countries.[350] As a result, far more international calls originate in the United States and terminate abroad than the other way around: in 1990, the ratio (in calling minutes) was about 1.7 to 1.[351] Foreign post, telephone, and telegraph companies (PTTs) therefore disproportionally profit from any increase in the rates carriers pay to have their calls terminated.[352] The upshot is a significant trade deficit in international settlements:[353] a net outflow of some $2.8 billion in 1990, a figure that has grown 25 percent a year since 1975.[354]

---

[349] *See* L. Johnson, International Telecommunications in 1 New Directions in Telecommunications Policy 92 (P. Newberg ed., 1989); *see also* Regulation of International Accounting Rates, Notice of Proposed Rulemaking, 5 F.C.C. Rec. 4948 (1990) (hereinafter *International Accounting Rates*); U.S. Dept. of Commerce, U.S. Telecommunications in a Global Economy 62 (1990) (report from the Secretary of Commerce to Congress and the President); S. Chiron & L. Rehberg, Fostering Competition in International Communications 38 Fed. Comm. L.J. 1, 42–44 (Mar. 1986).

[350] *See* Telephone Services: A Growing Form of "Foreign Aid," N.Y. Times, Oct. 21, 1990, at F5.

[351] *See id.*; *see also* Johnson, 1 New Directions in Telecommunications Policy at 96–98.

[352] *See* Stanley, Balance of Payments, Deficits, and Subsidies in International Communications Services, 43 Admin. L. Rev. 411 (1991).

[353] *See* Telephone Services: A Growing Form of "Foreign Aid," N.Y. Times, Oct. 21, 1990, at F5 ("Americans who make international telephone calls are paying extra to subsidize foreign countries' postal rates, local phone service, even schools and armies.").

[354] *See* FCC, Trends in the International Communications Industry at 8.

The FCC has intervened to prevent even greater unfairness, which would result if competing U.S. carriers bargained individually with monopolists abroad. Foreign PTTs are in a position to "whipsaw" U.S. carriers, playing them off against each other to extract the most favorable (and unequal) possible settlement terms. The FCC has therefore established an "International Settlement Policy" (or ISP), which requires uniform accounting rates between foreign and domestic carriers.[355] All incoming international traffic must be allocated to U.S. carriers in proportion to the outgoing traffic they deliver. The Commission also insists that U.S. carriers pay identical "landing" fees to foreign telcos.[356] To enforce these requirements, the Commission reviews the operating agreements U.S. carriers execute with foreign counterparts; departures from uniformity are permitted only in limited circumstances.[357]

In 1991, the FCC authorized carriers to reduce their accounting rates without undergoing full-blown review under the ISP;[358] a carrier must still, however, certify that any reduced rate it may negotiate is available to other carriers and that it will receive only a proportionate share of return traffic.[359] The FCC has also attempted to assist U.S. carriers in reducing the levels of international accounting rates generally.[360]

In November 1996, the FCC further eased settlement rate regulation by allowing U.S. carriers negotiating terminating rates to ignore the pricing aspects of previous bilateral accounting rate regulations in the FCC's ISP so long as the originating country allows U.S. carriers to enter and compete in the country's domestic market (or, alternatively, so long as the U.S. carrier can

[355] *See International Accounting Rates,* 5 F.C.C. Rec. at 4948.
[356] *See* Implementation and Scope of the International Settlements Policy for Parallel International Communications Routes, Report and Order, 51 Fed. Reg. 4736 ¶¶3, 36, 48–49 (1986) (hereinafter *Parallel International Communications Routes*), *on recons.,* 2 F.C.C. Rec. 1118, 1122–1123 (1987).
[357] *See id.* ¶51.
[358] *See* Regulation of International Accounting Rates, Report and Order, 6 F.C.C. Rec. 3552, 3553 ¶¶3, 7–10 (1991) (hereinafter *Phase I*).
[359] *Id.* at 3554 ¶¶13–14, 3555 ¶20.
[360] *See id.* at 3552; Regulation of International Accounting Rates, Fourth Report and Order, 11 F.C.C. Rec. 20,063 (1996) (hereinafter *Phase II*).

prove that ignoring the ISP price will promote domestic competition and will not allow the foreign telco to abuse its market power).[361] Carriers are required to file with the Commission all non-ISP arrangements that affect more than 25 percent of traffic to or from one country and all non-ISP arrangements between a foreign telco and any U.S. carrier affiliate (or partner, whenever the partnership involves providing basic services).[362]

In August 1997, the FCC further tried to lower international rates by requiring U.S. carriers to negotiate rates with foreign telcos no higher than an FCC-set benchmark.[363] Before the order, the average settlement rate paid by U.S. carriers was $0.35 per minute;[364] the order set a new maximum of $0.15 to $0.23 per minute, depending on the level of economic development of the foreign telco's home country.[365] The order went into effect in August 1998 for settlement rates with the most developed foreign countries; it will be phased in gradually through 2003 with respect to other countries.[366] Further steps will no doubt follow: the FCC acknowledged that even these reduced rates are still significantly above cost.[367]

§2.3.4 Connecting the Internet to the Local Exchange

The last chapter of the access-charge story, and probably the most important, has nothing to do with Ozark or PICCs. It centers on the Internet.

As discussed above in section 2.3.2, the FCC decided in the 1970s and early 1980s to treat "enhanced services" like the computers that provided them (CPE)—and not like the lines over

---

[361] *See Phase II*, 11 F.C.C. Rec. at 20,064 ¶2.

[362] *See id.* at 20,064 ¶3, 20,082–20,083 ¶48.

[363] *See* International Settlement Rates, Report and Order, 12 F.C.C. Rec. 19,806 (1997) (hereinafter *International Settlement Rates*).

[364] *See id.* at 19,823–19,824 ¶37.

[365] *See id.* at 19,815–19,816 ¶19.

[366] *See id.* at 19,816 ¶22.

[367] *See id.* at 19,815–19,816 ¶19.

which these services moved (long distance). Providers of enhanced services were accordingly treated as local business customers rather than as long-distance carriers. That simple, if arbitrary, decision meant that thereafter Internet providers would, in large part, be on the receiving end of subsidies, and not on the paying end.

Because local rates for most LECs are an all-you-can-eat flat monthly fee and because most Internet service providers (ISPs) themselves charge a flat fee,[368] residential users can cause significant costs on LECs' voice networks by using the network for hour upon hour of "free" dial-up Internet access. Whereas voice calls typically last only 3 to 5 minutes, the average Internet "call" lasts 17 to 20 minutes.[369] Long calls put a significant strain on local networks,[370] requiring LECs to invest heavily to upgrade their networks.[371] And so long as ISPs receive below-cost access through the conventional voice network, they have little economic

---

[368] See K. Werbach, Office of Plans and Policy, FCC, Digital Tornado: The Internet and Telecommunications Policy 48 (OPP Working Paper No. 29, Mar. 1997).

[369] See id. at 58–59. In one study, Pacific Bell found that 30 percent of all Internet calls on its network last more than a half-hour and over 7 percent last more than 24 hours. See Pacific Telesis Group, Executive Summary of Surfing the Second Wave: Sustainable Internet Growth and Public Policy (Mar. 24, 1997).

[370] A local switch is engineered to carry calls from only a small fraction (typically one-eighth) of the lines that connect to it. Voice calls follow a predictable pattern that makes it extremely unlikely that all circuits will be busy. Longer Internet calls disrupt this logic. In 1996, Bell Atlantic estimated that if only 15 percent of all households were on the Internet at any one time, switch capacity would have to be doubled to accommodate the new traffic. See Bell Atlantic, Report of Bell Atlantic on Internet Traffic (visited Dec. 9, 1998) <http://www.ba.com/ea/fcc/report.htm>; see also Superhighway Traffic Taxes Current LEC Network, Telephony, July 29, 1996.

[371] See Pacific Telesis Group, Executive Summary of Surfing the Second Wave. PacTel has estimated that it will receive $150 million in incremental ISP-related revenue through the year 2001, but will have to spend over $300 million to keep up with ISP demand. See id. at §5.0. Bell Atlantic has estimated that in 1996 it would receive $8.2 million in ISP-related revenues, but would need to spend $22 million to keep up with ISP demand. See Bell Atlantic, Report of Bell Atlantic on Internet Traffic; see also Superhighway Traffic Taxes Current LEC Network, Telephony, July 29, 1996.

incentive to migrate traffic to separate packet-switched data networks.[372]

The Commission revisited the issue of access charges for ISPs in its access-charge reform proceeding in the wake of the 1996 Act. The FCC again decided not to impose access charges on ISPs, once more invoking the "rate shock" rationale it embraced in 1983.[373] Access charges for voice traffic were inefficiently high in any event, the FCC determined.[374] The Commission did, however, raise the ceiling on the monthly subscriber-line charge local phone companies may collect on *second* (and additional) residential phone lines.[375] Thus, LECs would "receive incremental revenue from Internet usage through higher demand for second lines by consumers."[376]

The FCC's refusal to impose access charges upon ISPs has protected the enhanced-services industry from the telephone industry, but not the other way around. Nothing in the FCC's regulations prevents a provider of enhanced services from building a phone company out of the back of its computers. So take the deregulated tail of the telephone (the "enhanced service"), build it out to make a complete dog, and you have a deregulated phone company. To be sure, the new beast must continue supplying enough "enhancements" to its transport to keep it on the deregulated side of the "basic"/"enhanced" line, but that may not take much. Free voice mail alone might not do the trick,[377] but free dial-up services for morning weather or traffic reports (say) might. Nobody knows the full answer.

---

[372] *See* Pacific Telesis Group, Executive Summary of Surfing the Second Wave.

[373] *See Access Charge Reform Order,* 12 F.C.C. Rec. at 16,133 ¶¶344–345 ("We think it is possible that had access rates applied to ISPs over the last 14 years, the pace of development of the Internet and other services may not have been so rapid. Maintaining the existing pricing structure for these services avoids disrupting the still-evolving information services industry."). On appeal, the Eighth Circuit held this to be a reasonable exercise of agency discretion. *See* Southwestern Bell Tel. Co. v. FCC, 153 F.3d 523, 541 (8th Cir. 1998).

[374] *See Access Charge Reform Order,* 12 F.C.C. Rec. at 16,133 ¶345.

[375] *See id.* at 16,014 ¶78.

[376] *See id.* at 16,133–16,134 ¶346.

[377] *See* Federal-State Joint Board on Universal Service, Report to Congress, 13 F.C.C. Rec. 11,501, 11,530 ¶60 (1998).

We do know the answer for e-mail. E-mail substitutes, in some measure, for fax connections and telephone talk time. And the same packet-switched data networks that carry e-mail can carry live voice conversations, too, though not yet as well as one might like. In other words, the outlines of the fully deregulated phone company are rapidly taking shape, all under the legally pregnant, but technologically and economically meaningless, label of "enhanced service."

Just how much is it worth to wrap a little "enhancement" around your telephone company? If your lines are long, almost 7 cents a minute. Unenhanced long-distance phone companies like AT&T and MCI pay local phone companies about that much to originate and terminate ordinary voice calls. But any provider offering a service that can be labeled "enhanced" pays nothing.

§2.3.4.1 Detariffing the Internet and Advanced Services

As discussed more fully in section 11.7, section 706 of the 1996 Telecommunications Act[378] empowers the FCC to forbear from regulating advanced telecommunication services. Section 706 might be seen as something of a "super forbearance" provision. As explained above, section 10 of the Communications Act, as amended,[379] already generally requires the FCC to forbear where regulation is no longer necessary to keep rates at competitive levels. With respect to "high-speed, switched, broadband telecommunications" services, section 706 provides that the need for forbearance is even greater.

Section 706 makes the rapid development of the relatively new telecom infrastructure a national priority. It directs both the FCC and state regulators to "encourage the deployment" of a "high-speed, switched, broadband telecommunications capability" to "all Americans," including, "in particular, elementary and secondary school and classrooms," "on a reasonable and timely

---

[378] *See* 47 U.S.C. §157 note.
[379] *Id.* §160.

basis."[380] The "advanced telecommunications capability" called for in the Act must "enable[] users to originate and receive high-quality voice, data, graphics, and video telecommunications."[381]

The statute further directs the Commission to conduct an inquiry "within 30 months after the date of enactment of this Act, and regularly thereafter," into "the availability of advanced telecommunications capability to all Americans."[382] If, as a result of the inquiry, the Commission finds that advanced telecommunications capability is not being "deployed to all Americans in a reasonable and timely fashion," the Commission must "take immediate action to accelerate deployment of such capability by removing barriers to infrastructure investment and by promoting competition in the telecommunications market." [383]

Thus far, the Commission has been unwilling to make significant use of section 706. In particular, the Commission determined in its first "inquiry" that matters were coming along just fine, so that it did not have to do anything immediately.[384] Business subscribers, the Commission found, have long had ready access to broadband facilities.[385] Residential subscribers, too, the Commission determined, were (or would be) adequately served by LECs' digital subscriber line (DSL) offerings and by cable operators' modem services[386]—even in rural areas.[387] Indeed, the Commission's upbeat report predicted that broadband access will be more competitive than voice access, saying that "[t]he preconditions for monopoly appear absent."[388]

---

[380] *Id.* §157 note (§706(a)).

[381] *Id.*

[382] *Id.* §157 note (§706(b)).

[383] *Id.*

[384] *See* Inquiry Concerning the Deployment of Advanced Telecommunications Capability to All Americans, Report, CC Docket No. 98-146 (Feb. 2, 1999).

[385] *See id.* ¶¶11, 26.

[386] *See id.* ¶¶12, 91. The Commission pointed out that at the end of only the second year of deployment 350,000 consumers were already receiving cable-modem service and another 25,000 were receiving DSL service. *See id.* ¶91.

[387] *See id.* ¶69.

[388] *See id.* ¶48; *see also id.* ¶52.

§2.3.4.2   The (Marketplace) Genesis of New Access Charges

While the FCC focused on the access charges that Internet service providers would (or, as it turned out, would not) pay to local phone companies, an elite group of these providers was quietly hatching plans to begin imposing access charges on the rest.

The Internet divides roughly into five layers.[389] At the bottom are some 80 million users (as of mid-1999). Then comes local access, supplied mostly by local phone companies. Then about 5,000 Internet service providers connect high-speed business lines and individual dial-up connections to Internet terminal equipment.[390] Then some 39 national firms operate national Internet backbone networks,[391] which interconnect at 11 major network access points (NAPs).[392] And, finally, there are 140 million servers, the computers on which content is stored and transactions are executed.

Until 1997, the major backbones and ISPs operated under "peering" arrangements, under which they exchanged traffic at no charge. In May 1997, WorldCom/UUNet broke ranks and began charging smaller ISPs and backbone operators for interconnection. Only ISPs that could "route traffic on a bilateral and equitable basis" to and from WorldCom/UUNet would be given free interconnection.[393] Several of the smaller backbones complained,[394] but quickly capitulated. MCI, BBN, and Sprint

---

[389] See generally J. Rickard, Internet Architecture, Boardwatch Magazine Directory of Internet Service Providers 6 (July/Aug. 1997).

[390] See J. Rickard, Backbone Performance Measurements, ISP Directory (Winter '98-Spring '99).

[391] See id.

[392] See Rickard, Internet Architecture at 8–13.

[393] See R. Barrett, UUNet Sets Official Peering Requirements, Interactive Week Online, May 13, 1997 <http://www.zdnet.com/zdnn/content/inwo/0513/inwo0001.html>.

[394] For example, NetRail, a backbone headquartered in Atlanta, called WorldCom's decision to stop peering "a restriction of free trade." J. Poole, Midrange ISP Prices Climb; UUNet, Sprint End Free Traffic Services, InfoWorld, May 5, 1997, at 10. Similarly, GeoNet Communications, a backbone headquartered in Redwood City, California, suggested that "ISPs might band together to maintain peering." T. Abate & J. Swartz, Internet Fee Feud

then followed suit: they, too, began charging smaller operators.[395]

The upshot: from within the community of backbones there emerged an elite, self-selected group of nine true "peers,"[396] several of which were formulating plans for further consolidation as of this writing. The nonpeers were forced to pay up to several hundred thousand dollars per month in charges for interconnection with one of the nine peers and were generally required to discontinue peering with the other backbones.[397] The group of nine, the self-defined peers, had become the dominant suppliers of the true Internet backbone; the rest were now, in varying degrees and ways, their customers.

To date, the Internet peering rates have been wholly unregulated. Suppliers of backbone services do not even file tariffs. It remains to be seen whether, or for how long, regulators and disgruntled competitors will allow this to continue.

§2.3.4.3 The Divided House

Digital networks of every kind are adding bandwidth (to support voice and video), two-way capabilities (to support real-time voice), and error correction (to support data). Voice, video,

---

Heats Up over a Firing, S.F. Chron., May 6, 1997, at C1. And CAIS Internet stated, "[W]e disagree with UUNet's new peering position and believe it may be anti-competitive." CAIS Press Release, CAIS Internet Responds to New UUNet Peering Policy, PR Newswire, May 1, 1997; *see also* UUNet Technologies to Cut Off Free Connections to Its Internet Backbone, Business Wire, Apr. 25, 1997 ("The move is seen as a power play designed to force smaller providers to pay for access—or possibly go out of business.").

[395] *See* B. Riggs, Free Ride Is Over for Small ISPs, LAN Times, May 26, 1997, at 19.

[396] *See* AOL, WorldCom Asset Swap Sends Chill Down Backbone (Workgroup Computing Report, Sept. 23, 1997) (citing Nathan Stratton, CEO of NetRail). The nine include WorldCom/UUNet, MCI, Sprint, AT&T, PSINet, America Online, Cable & Wireless, IBM, and BBN. According to WorldCom/UUNet, the amount of traffic passing between it and the nonpeering backbones is insignificant. *See* P. Lambert, UUNet Fees Threaten to Break Up Internet, Interactive Week, Apr. 30, 1997 <http://www.zdnet.com/zdnn/content/inwk/0413/inwk0024.html> (citing Alan Taffel, UUNet Marketing Vice-President).

[397] *See* P. Lambert, UUNet Fees Threaten to Break Up Internet, Interactive Week, Apr. 30, 1997.

and data are converging on the same wireless and wireline networks.[398] All media are moving toward a common currency of digital transmission. The demand for and supply of bandwidth is increasing in every medium, and scrambling, addressing, and two-way capabilities are being added across the board. Digital technology and high bandwidth obliterate engineering and economic distinctions between different type of electronic communication. And not simply because "a bit is a bit." The key point is that high-bandwidth digital networks, both wired and wireless, are extremely flexible. They can readily be configured and interconnected to mimic any of the capabilities of any of the old analog systems.

Within a few years, if it does not already, "data" traffic will exceed all other kinds on all communications networks.[399] If fax is included as "data," as it should be,[400] data traffic probably already equals or exceeds voice traffic on phone networks.[401] And

[398]The FCC has long recognized that, with "technological developments and the digitization of the network, it will be increasingly impractical to distinguish between voice, data, graphics or video transmissions." Telephone Company-Cable Television Cross-Ownership Rules, Sections 63.54–63.58, Second Report and Order, Recommendation to Congress, and Second Further Notice of Proposed Rulemaking, 7 F.C.C. Rec. 5781, 5828 n.232 (1992).

[399]As long ago as 1961, AT&T predicted that the amount of data traffic would eventually exceed the amount of voice traffic on the public telephone network. See R. Hough, Future Data Traffic Volume, Computer (Sept./Oct. 1970) (quoting Frederick R. Kappel, President, AT&T, speech to the North Carolina Citizens' Association, Mar. 22, 1961). This prediction long met with considerable resistance. See, e.g., id. (prophecies regarding need for additional capacity due to increase in data traffic "have little basis in fact"); A. M. Noll, Voice vs. Data: An Estimate of Future Broadband Traffic, IEEE Communications Magazine, June 1991, at 22 ("Today's prediction that data traffic will outstrip voice traffic again seems to be more wishful thinking than the result of any realistic analyses.").

[400]For example, faxes can be sent over the Internet using off-the-shelf software programs, such as WinFax Pro 8.0 by Symantec. See B. Emmerson, Internet Gives You the Fax of Life, The European, Apr. 17, 1997. The volume of fax transmissions has exploded in the last decade, from 10 billion pages in 1987 to about 95 billion pages in 1994. See MultiMedia Telecommunications Association, 1996 MultiMedia Telecommunications Market Review and Forecast 132 (1996). Fax traffic is forecasted to grow from a 1996 total of 863 trillion bits per day to 1.06 quadrillion bits per day in 2001. See More Traffic on the I'way, Industries in Transition (Jan. 1997).

[401]See More Traffic on the I'Way ("Data traffic . . . constituted approximately one half of all user traffic in 1996 and will account for about 60 percent

the volume of data traffic is growing much faster,[402] even on wireless phone networks.[403] Much of this increase can be explained by the exploding popularity of the Internet[404] and the related increase in second residential telephone lines[405] and computer modems.[406] Digital video traveling over phone lines

---

in 2001."); N. Flaherty, Shine Stays on Copper, Electronics Times, Feb. 27, 1997 ("last year the overall market for data traffic was larger than the market for voice traffic") (citing Dave Romero, Manager of Transmission IC Marketing, Lucent Technologies); M. Rockwell, Data Titans Raise Voice on Telecom, Comm. Week, Dec. 9, 1996 ("'At some point in the next few years, data traffic on the public net could equal or surpass voice traffic.'") (quoting Mike Smith, Analyst, Datapro Inc.). Data traffic has already exceeded voice traffic in certain corporate markets. See D. J. Edmonds et al., Bear, Stearns & Co., Investext Rpt. No. 2510862, Intermedia Communications Inc.—Company Report at *3 (Sept. 13, 1996).

[402] In North America, the growth of data traffic was 30 percent in 1996, compared to only 3 percent for voice. See Northern Telecom Aims for U.S. $2B Sales in Asia in 3-4 Years, Bus. Times, Mar. 11, 1997. One analyst has estimated that over the next five years voice traffic will grow 4 percent per year, while data traffic will grow by more than 40 percent annually. See J. L. Barlage et al., Smith Barney, Ind. Rpt. No. 1761069, Technology Topics at 6 (July 9, 1996); see also D. J. Edmonds et al., Bear, Stearns & Co., Investext Rpt. No. 2510862, Intermedia Communications Inc.—Company Report at *3 (Sept. 13, 1996) ("packet-based services are forecasted to grow at 43%").

[403] According to a one study, data traffic—currently almost nonexistent on most mobile networks—will be the dominant form of mobile traffic by 2005, generating as much as 75 percent of total traffic. See EU Mobile Multimedia Market to Boom, Digital Cellular Report, Mar. 12, 1997.

[404] Vinton Cerf, a pioneer of the Internet and Senior Vice-President for Internet Architecture at MCI, predicts that the number of computers connected to the Internet will grow from about 16 million in 1997 to 200 million by 2000. See R. Mikkelsen, *Internet Pioneer Says Growth Explosive, But Slows*, Reuter Bus. Rpt., Feb. 28, 1997.

[405] According to one study, the demand for some 6 million "second" residential subscriber lines in 1995— almost half of all "second" residential lines—can be attributed principally to online access. See L. Selwyn & J. Laszlo, Economics and Technology, Inc., The Effect of Internet Use on the Nation's Telephone Network (Jan. 22, 1997) (prepared for the Internet Access Coalition). According to Bell Atlantic, between one-third and two-thirds of second lines are purchased solely for data services, such as Internet access and fax machines. See Joint Comments of Bell Atlantic and NYNEX on Notice of Inquiry at 11, Usage of the Public Switched Network by Information Service and Internet Access Providers, CC Docket No. 96-263 (FCC Mar. 24, 1997).

[406] Domestic modem sales increased from 3.3 million units in 1990 to 19 million in 1995. See Forecast Revenue and Shipments of Modems (Dial-Up,

will tilt the balance toward "data" further still. One recent study predicts that by 2001 voice will make up only 4 percent of total traffic on public and private telecommunications networks,[407] while "data" will account for 95 percent and video and fax for the remaining 1 percent.[408]

With this new universe of "data telecom," services will compete in ways that are unexpected and largely unfamiliar today. For example, Caller ID, a rudimentary "data" service, can significantly shorten phone calls: many businesses already combine it with "pop-screen" computer software for precisely that purpose. E-mail and fax can have a similar effect: more is said in writing, so there is less to talk about over the phone.[409] A great deal of "voice" traffic is already asymmetric and one-way. Voice mail, standard menu-driven recordings, 900/976 dial-it services, and most fax traffic can easily migrate onto a broadband, digital Internet. Commercial services already convey fax transmissions over the Internet, particularly to overseas destinations, to avoid long-distance charges.

As networks go digital and services converge, neither phone companies nor regulators will be able to maintain price structures built on the assumption that voice and data are fundamentally different.

§2.3.5 Lessons in Price Misregulation

For many decades, common costs of telephone service were allocated in violent conflict with the prescription of Ramsey pric-

---

Leased-Line and Private Line), US, Computer Industry Forecasts, July 15, 1993 (citing Market Intelligence, The Numbers Sheet, Computer Reseller News, May 17, 1993, at 15).

[407] This estimate does not include "traffic" on cable or broadcasting networks. It does include wireless networks, such as cellular and PCS.

[408] More Traffic on the I'way, Industries in Transition (Jan. 1997).

[409] The Internet already delivers more "mail" than the U.S. Postal Service, and the number of e-mail users is expected to triple in the next five years. The Electronic Messaging Association predicts that the number of employees using e-mail will grow from approximately 23 million in 1994 to 72 million by the year 2000. See Sulloway & Hollis, E-Mail Communications: Employers' Friend or Foe?, New Hampshire Employment Law Letter, Apr. 1996.

ing.[410] Telephony was transformed when regulators finally began considering the pricing inefficiencies that they had originally demanded and endorsed. The 1984 Bell System divestiture could be viewed as the logical (though long-delayed) culmination of *Smith v. Illinois Bell.* The battle all along was between monopoly, with its attendant subsidies and price averages, and competition, with its attendant demands for cost-based pricing. The forces favoring competition finally prevailed.

Prices were then readjusted sharply. The decade of the 1980s witnessed a rapid, unprecedented decline in the cost of long-distance telephone calls. The subscriber line charge, together with the FCC's other "line charge" reforms, transferred roughly $4 billion in charges away from long-distance carriers to the monthly phone bills of consumers.[411] Partly as a result of this, interstate calling volumes grew dramatically. In absolute terms, however, the size of the transfer payments from long-distance carriers to local companies did not decline. The *percentage* allocation had been frozen, but that percentage was applied to a steadily rising base of investment. As of 1991, access charges still accounted for 25 percent of local telco revenues, but almost half of the cost of a long-distance call.[412] Fortunately, the number of minutes of interstate calling has grown faster than anything else, so the markup per minute has steadily declined.

A second lesson from the pricing adjustments that did occur after divestiture is that subsidies may not be quite so essential as had long been thought. The decades of price misregulation that culminated in the Bell divestiture were justified all along as necessary to promote universal service. What in fact happened to universal service when a $4 billion correction was finally made in the 1980s? Despite sharp increases in flat monthly fees, universal service was not harmed in the least. According to gloomy predictions made before the new line charges were introduced, the

---

[410] *See* J. Griffin, The Welfare Implications of Externalities and Price Elasticities for Telecommunications Pricing, 64 Rev. Econ. Stat. 59, 66 (1982).

[411] The figure is derived by multiplying $40 per year per line by 100 million lines.

[412] *See* 1991 U.S. Industrial Outlook at 29-2, 29-3 (1991).

subscriber line charge would cause a nationwide decline in telephone penetration of as much as eight percentage points.[413] No such decline ever occurred; to the contrary, telephone penetration is about as high today as ever before.[414]

§2.4 Horizontal Connections to Local Exchange Carriers

§2.4.1 Reciprocal Compensation: Local-to-Local Traffic Hand-Offs in the Old Days

So long as local service remained a monopoly, a traffic hand-off between LECs did not require much regulation. Such hand-offs did occur. GTE and PacBell provide service to adjacent neighborhoods in Los Angeles, for example, and small independent phone companies operate side by side with the Bell Operating Companies in thousands of little islands of coverage across the country. "Free" calling areas often cross such boundaries; when they do, the two interconnecting phone companies could, in principle, charge each other.

They almost never did, historically. Each company simply terminated the other's traffic at no charge: the basic economic model for such arrangements was "bill and keep."[415] The simplicity and stability of these arrangements can be attributed largely to the circumstances in which they arose. The independents served fewer then 20 percent of customers nationwide, and far fewer than that in contiguous communities where direct, local-company-to-local-company traffic hand-offs were necessary. The old Bell System was too large to worry about them much, and in any event, the independents served mostly rural

[413] *See* NARUC v. FCC, 737 F.2d at 1108.

[414] As of March 1998, 94.1 percent of the nation's households subscribed to telephone service. *See* Industry Analysis Division, FCC, Trends in Telephone Service 85 (July 1998). Immediately before divestiture (in November 1983), penetration stood at 91.4 percent. *See id.*

[415] *See, e.g.,* Implementation of the Local Competition Provisions in the Telecommunications Act of 1996, Notice of Proposed Rulemaking, 11 F.C.C. Rec. 14,171, 14,253–14,254 ¶243 (1996).

customers, who were being subsidized (indirectly) by Bell's long-distance arm in any event.

§2.4.2 Competitive Access Providers

When the FCC first began to foster "bypass" service by competitive access providers,[416] CAP service was expected to link large businesses directly to interexchange carriers.[417] Beginning in 1992, however, the Commission released a series of orders giving CAPs not only a right to bypass, but also a right to interconnect with any LEC, and to do so on the LEC's own premises (through so-called collocation).[418] The courts eventually rejected the FCC's requirement for "physical" collocation (leaving in place only the requirement for "virtual" collocation),[419] but the 1996 Telecom Act has since reinstated the requirement that a LEC offer physical collocation if an interconnector requests it.[420]

The Commission initially declined to establish "a detailed rate structure" for physical and virtual CAP collocation, explaining that "such a structure could be overly inflexible."[421] Instead, it simply directed that LECs' prices be based on "direct costs" and only a "reasonable amount of overhead costs"[422] and that charges

---

[416] *See* Cox Cable Communications, Inc., Memorandum Opinion, 102 F.C.C.2d 110 (1985), *vacated as moot,* 61 Rad. Reg. (P & F) 967 (1986).

[417] *See* §5._.

[418] *See Expanded Interconnection Order,* 7 F.C.C. Rec. at 7369; Expanded Interconnection with Local Telephone Company Facilities, Second Report and Order and Third Notice of Proposed Rulemaking, 8 F.C.C. Rec. 7374 (1993); Expanded Interconnection with Local Telephone Company Facilities, Memorandum Opinion and Order, 9 F.C.C. Rec. 5154 (1994) (hereinafter *Virtual Collocation Order*).

[419] *See* Bell Atlantic v. FCC, 24 F.3d 1441 (D.C. Cir. 1994); *see generally* §5.3.2.

[420] *See* 47 U.S.C. §251(c)(6). The FCC has expanded CLEC collocation rights further still. *See* Deployment of Wireline Services offering Advanced Telecommunications Capability, First Report and Order and Further Notice of Proposed Rulemaking, CC Docket No. 98-147 (rel. Mar. 31, 1999).

[421] *See* Virtual Collocation Order, 9 F.C.C. Rec. at 5186 ¶114; Local Exchange Carriers' Rates, Terms, and Conditions for Expanded Interconnection Through Physical Collocation for Special Access and Switched Transport, Second Report and Order, 12 F.C.C. Rec. 18,730, 18,745 ¶23 (1997).

[422] *Virtual Collocation Order,* 9 F.C.C. Rec. at 5187 ¶121.

for collocation and interconnection be assessed separately.[423] The FCC did declare, however, that rates would "receive careful scrutiny by Commission staff."[424] LECs were directed to submit data proving that their prices were in fact cost-based.[425] When the LECs did so, the Commission did not like what it saw: in 1995, it rejected most LECs' virtual-collocation tariffs.[426] The Commission completed its review of most physical-collocation tariffs in 1997, again rejected them all, and ordered refunds for physical-collocation payments received after December 1994.[427]

§2.4.2.1　Detariffing Competitive Access Providers

From the outset, the Commission treated competitive access providers as nondominant and therefore not subject to formalized rate regulation. Before 1996, however, the Communications Act required competitive access providers to file tariffs just like MCI, Sprint, and other competitive long-distance carriers.[428] No more. In 1997, the FCC used its newfound forbearance authority to permit CAPs not to file tariffs.[429] The FCC simultaneously issued a notice of proposed rulemaking asking whether it should prohibit CAPs to file tariffs.[430] As of mid-1999, the FCC has not yet acted on the proposal.

---

[423] See id. at 5186 ¶115.

[424] Id. at 5187 ¶121.

[425] See id. at 5186 ¶117.

[426] See Local Exchange Carriers' Rates, Terms, and Conditions for Expanded Interconnection Through Virtual Collocation for Special Access and Switched Transport, Report and Order, 10 F.C.C. Rec. 6375 ¶2 (1995).

[427] See Local Exchange Carriers' Rates, Terms, and Conditions for Expanded Interconnection Through Physical Collocation for Special Access and Switched Transport, Second Report and Order, 12 F.C.C. Rec. at 18,730, 18,735 ¶4 (1997). Despite all this back-and-forth at the FCC, CAPs and ILECs have signed interconnection agreements at a rapid pace. As of July 1997, CAPs had entered into 971 interconnection agreements with ILECs. See USTA, Interconnection Agreements by State (July 1, 1997).

[428] See MCI v. AT&T, 512 U.S. 218 (1994).

[429] See Hyperion, 12 F.C.C. Rec. at 8596 ¶1.

[430] Id.

§2.4.3 Wireless Carriers

The Commission has long required LECs to provide unaffiliated wireless carriers interconnection at the same rate offered to LEC wireless affiliates.[431] In 1993, Congress added a blanket access requirement: "Upon reasonable request of any person providing commercial mobile service, the Commission shall order a common carrier to establish physical connections with such service pursuant to the provisions of section 201 of this Act."[432] LECs accordingly must provide "reasonable and fair interconnection" to all commercial mobile radio service (CMRS) providers, including personal communication service (PCS) providers[433] and private mobile radio service (PMRS) providers.[434] Moreover, in the wake of the 1996 Act, the FCC has determined that CMRS providers are "telecommunications carriers" for purposes of section 251 and are therefore entitled to the interconnection privileges that section affords CLECs.[435]

The question of how much telcos may charge cellular companies for the right to interconnect with the landline network has been more troublesome than establishing interconnection rights themselves. Interconnection tariffs have generally been fixed to the satisfaction of both the carriers and the state regulators, though sometimes only after protracted and heated negotiations. At issue was usually whether wireless carriers should be treated as co-carriers (i.e., be treated the same as independent LECs) or as end users.[436]

---

[431] See, e.g., An Inquiry into the Use of the Bands 825–845 MHZ and 870–890 MHZ for Cellular Communications Systems, 86 F.C.C.2d 469, 495–496 ¶¶53–57 (requiring interconnection for cellular systems). Many of the FCC's interconnection requirements were duplicated in waiver orders issued by the district court overseeing the MFJ. In virtually every MFJ waiver involving radio operations by BOC affiliates, Judge Greene required them to provide equal interconnection to the landline switch. See §§5.6, 10.5.2.

[432] 47 U.S.C. §332(c)(1)(B).

[433] See Implementation of Sections 3(n) and 332 of the Communications Act, Regulatory Treatment of Mobile Services, Second Report and Order, 9 F.C.C. Rec. 1411, 1497–1498 ¶230 (1994) (hereinafter Second CMRS Order).

[434] See id. at 1511 ¶273.

[435] See Local Competition Order, 11 F.C.C. Rec. at 15,998–15,999 ¶1012.

[436] See §10.5.

In 1996, the FCC released detailed interconnection pricing rules implementing section 251 of the 1996 Telecommunications Act. The Court of Appeals for the Eighth Circuit vacated these interconnection pricing rules *except* insofar as they apply to interconnection with CMRS providers. In sections 152(b) and 332(c), the court explained, Congress specifically precluded the states from regulating CMRS-related prices, empowering the FCC to do so instead.[437] Thus, the court allowed the FCC's pricing rules to remain in effect with respect to CMRS providers, even though it struck down the same rules so far as they concerned CLECs.[438]

The new rules require reciprocal-compensation rates for all CMRS-ILEC interconnection.[439] These rates must be symmetrical: the CMRS provider may charge the ILEC the same amount the ILEC charges the CMRS provider for transport and termination of calls.[440] CMRS providers that had entered into interconnection agreements with ILECs before the new rules took effect are "entitled to renegotiate these arrangements with no termination liability or other contract penalties" if the agreement "provides for non-reciprocal compensation."[441] While the parties negotiate a new agreement, the CMRS provider may charge the ILEC the same rates the ILEC is charging it.[442]

---

[437] *See* Iowa Utils. Bd. v. FCC, 120 F.3d 753, 800 n.21 (8th Cir. 1997), *rev'd in other part sub nom.* AT&T v. Iowa Utils. Bd., 119 S. Ct. 721 (1999).

[438] *See id.* at 800 n.21. The rules that remained in effect for CMRS are set forth in 47 C.F.R. §§51.701, .703, .709(b), .711(a)(1), .715(d), and .717. *See* Summary of Currently Effective Commission Rules for Interconnection Requests by Providers of Commercial Mobile Radio Services, Public Notice, 12 F.C.C. Rec. 15,591 (1997).

[439] *See Local Competition Order,* 11 F.C.C. Rec. at 15,997 ¶1008; *see also* Summary of Currently Effective Commission Rules for Interconnection Requests by Providers of Commercial Mobile Radio Services, Public Notice, 12 F.C.C. Rec. 15,591 (1997) (citing 47 C.F.R. §51.703).

[440] *See* 47 C.F.R. §51.711(a). This rule applies even to providers of paging services, even though such providers usually only terminate (and do not originate) traffic. *See Local Competition Order,* 11 F.C.C. Rec. at 15,997 ¶1008. Indeed, the FCC's Common Carrier Bureau has said that a LEC may not charge a paging provider even for establishing interconnection *facilities. See* A. R. Metzger, Jr., Chief, FCC Common Carrier Bureau, Letter to K. Davis et al., DA 97-2726 (Dec. 30, 1997).

[441] *See* 47 C.F.R. §51.717.

[442] *See id.* §51.717(b).

§2.4.3.1   Detariffing Wireless Services

Under legislation passed in 1993,[443] the Commission has express statutory authority to eliminate Title II's tariffing requirement for certain classes of mobile carriers, provided the Commission determines that enforcement of the tariffing requirement is not necessary to ensure that charges are "just," "reasonable," and nondiscriminatory.[444]

§2.4.4   Competitive Local Exchange Carriers

§2.4.4.1   Competitive Local Exchange Carriers: Pure Resellers

As discussed in Chapter 5, the 1996 Act requires all local exchange carriers to permit resale of their services[445] and further obligates incumbent LECs to offer their retail services to other carriers at wholesale rates.[446] But what are reasonable wholesale rates for a service that is already being provided to residential customers below cost? The carrier buying the service will claim that "wholesale" implies a sufficient discount off "retail" to permit the reseller to make a profit. The carrier selling the service will claim that it should not be required to sell to another carrier below cost, so that the proper "wholesale" rate is actually above the artificially low retail rate.

Congress appears to have sided mostly with the resellers on this point. The Act provides that wholesale rates must be set not on the basis of the wholesaler's costs, but rather "on the basis of retail rates charged to subscribers for the telecommunications service[s] requested, excluding the portion thereof attributable to any marketing, billing, collection, and other costs that will be avoided by the local exchange carrier."[447] Though not without

---

[443] *See FTL1* §13.3.19.
[444] *See* 47 U.S.C. §332(c)(1)(A).
[445] *See id.* §251(b)(1).
[446] *See id.* §251(c)(4).
[447] *Id.* §252(d)(3).

ambiguity, this language seems to imply that one starts with the retail rate as a benchmark (regardless of underlying costs) and then subtracts certain specific costs listed in the Act.[448]

In its August 1996 *Local Competition Order,* the FCC promulgated detailed rules governing resale pricing.[449] The Commission ostensibly left the precise wholesale rates of resold services up to the states, but promulgated detailed rules just short of the ultimate determination of prices.

The 1996 Act provides that wholesale prices must be based on a LEC's existing "retail rates" minus costs that "will be avoided" by the LEC in selling the service at wholesale rather than retail.[450] (Avoided costs include items like marketing, billing, and collection.)[451] The FCC, however, directed that wholesale discounts be based on retail rates less any costs that hypothetically "can be avoided," whether or not those costs actually are avoided by the LEC.[452] In other words, the FCC read the statutory term "avoided costs" to mean "costs reasonably avoidable by a hypothetical, ideally efficient company." And if states lacked sufficient information to establish rates this way, they were directed to set interim wholesale rates between 17 and 25 percent lower than the retail rate.[453]

When incumbent LECs provide services for resale, they *are* entitled to continue to collect access charges.[454] The FCC determined that section 251(c)(4) gives entrants a right to resell only

---

[448] Alternatively, this language could be read (more sensibly, but perhaps less plausibly) to require a wholesale price below the retail rate only if the subtraction of avoidable costs brings actual costs below the retail rate. This reading would turn on the phrase "a portion thereof": if retail rates are below cost, there is no "portion thereof" that is "attributable to . . . costs that will be avoided." The FCC decided otherwise, rejecting this argument. *See Local Competition Order,* 11 F.C.C. Rec. at 15,971–15,973 ¶¶954–957.

[449] *See id.* at 15,930–15,984 ¶¶863–984; 47 C.F.R. §§51.607–.611.

[450] 47 U.S.C. §252(d)(3).

[451] *See id. Local Competition Order,* 11 F.C.C. Rec. at 15,955 ¶908.

[452] *See Local Competition Order,* 11 F.C.C. Rec. at 15,956 ¶911.

[453] *See id.* at 15,963 ¶932.

[454] *See id.* at 15,982–15,983 ¶980 ("IXCs must still pay access charges to incumbent LECs for originating or terminating interstate traffic, even when their end user is served by a telecommunications carrier that resells incumbent LEC retail services.").

local exchange service—not exchange access service.[455] When they resell local service, "IXCs must therefore still purchase access services from incumbent LECs outside of the resale framework of 251(c)(4), through existing access tariffs."[456]

The resale phenomenon required the Commission to modify the way in which the subscriber line charge is collected from end users who obtain their local service from a reseller.[457] The difficulty was that the ILEC would no longer have a "direct commercial relationship" with the end user, so that the ILEC "could not bill [the] SLC directly to the end user."[458] For its solution, the Commission looked to its March *1995 Rochester Waiver Order:*[459] the ILEC would bill the reseller—not the end user—for the SLC.

As more fully discussed in Chapters 3 and 5, the Eighth Circuit stayed most of the Commission's resale pricing rules in October 1996[460] and vacated them in July 1997.[461] Section 252 (c)(2) and (d), the court held, explicitly assigns authority over pricing to the states—not the FCC.[462] The court rejected the FCC's argument that section 251(d)(1) and the general rulemaking provisions of the 1934 Act empower the Commission to regulate rates.[463] If there was any remaining doubt, the court held, section 2(b) resolved it: under that provision, federal jurisdiction over intrastate pricing exists only if the Act unambiguously provides it.[464] Section 2(b), the court said, "remains a *Louisiana*-built fence that is hog tight, horse high, and bull strong,

---

[455] *See id.*

[456] *Id.*

[457] *See id.* at 15,983–15,984 ¶¶981–984.

[458] *See id.* at 15,983 ¶981.

[459] *See* Rochester Tel. Corp., Petition for Waivers to Implement Its Open Market Plan, Order, 10 F.C.C. Rec. 6776 (1995).

[460] *See* Iowa Utils. Bd. v. FCC, 109 F.3d 418 (8th Cir. 1996).

[461] *See* Iowa Utils. Bd. v. FCC, 120 F.3d 753 (8th Cir. 1997), *rev'd sub nom.* AT&T v. Iowa Utils. Bd., 119 S. Ct. 721 (1999).

[462] *See id.* at 793–800.

[463] *See id.*

[464] *See id.* at 796. The "impossibility exception" of Louisiana Public Service Commission v. FCC, 476 U.S. 355 (1986), was simply inapplicable, the court held. *See Iowa Utils. Bd.,* 120 F.3d at 798–800.

preventing the FCC from intruding on the states' intrastate turf."[465]

The response of the FCC (and particularly then FCC Chairman Reed Hundt) was outrage.[466] Uniform national prices were essential, the Chairman declared: "We need an immediate national definition of 'cost' set forth by the FCC, so this key term won't vary confusingly and uncertainly from state to state."[467] The Eighth Circuit had ignored *Chevron v. Natural Resources Defense Council*,[468] the Chairman charged; "the FCC should be given deference, as Supreme Court authority requires, for any reasonable interpretation of congressional intent and its application of policy."[469] The Chairman promised an immediate trip to the Supreme Court.[470]

And the FCC succeeded in persuading the Court to grant review.[471] Meanwhile, not wanting to leave anything to chance,

---

[465] *Iowa Utils. Bd.,* 120 F.3d at 800.

[466] Chairman Hundt complained that "judicial intervention in the interconnection case hurt competition badly"; asserted that, "[u]ntil the Eighth Circuit interconnection decision, no court in 60 years has issued a decision constraining this agency from defining terms in a congressional statute"; accused the Eighth Circuit of "substitut[ing] its judgment for ours"; and urged Congress to amend the Act "until courts finally submit to its direction." Reed Hundt, Chairman, FCC, The Light at the End of the Tunnel vs. the Fog: Deregulation vs. the Legal Culture, Remarks Before the American Enterprise Institute, 1997 FCC LEXIS 4330, at *9, *10, *12 (Aug. 14, 1997). His criticism of the stay decision had been even harsher. *See, e.g.,* Reed Hundt, Chairman, FCC, Remarks Before the International Radio & Television Society, 1996 FCC LEXIS 5840, at *15–*16 (Oct. 18, 1996) ("a grievous error" and "an astounding piece of judicial activism"); Hundt Calls Court Stay of FCC Rules Example of Extreme Judicial Activism, Daily Report for Executives, Oct. 17, 1996, at C-1 ("[t]he kind of awesome supremacy that the Chinese emperors would exercise over every rice-picking effort in the country").

[467] Reed Hundt, Chairman, FCC, The Light at the End of the Tunnel vs. the Fog: Deregulation vs. the Legal Culture, Remarks Before the American Enterprise Institute, 1997 FCC LEXIS 4330 (Aug. 14, 1997).

[468] 467 U.S. 837, 843 (1984).

[469] Reed Hundt, Chairman, FCC, The Light at the End of the Tunnel vs. the Fog: Deregulation vs. the Legal Culture, Remarks Before the American Enterprise Institute, 1997 FCC LEXIS 4330 (Aug. 14, 1997).

[470] *See* FCC News Release, Statement of FCC Chairman Reed Hundt on 8th Circuit Court of Appeals Decision on Telephone Interconnection Case (July 18, 1997) ("The antidote to the 8th Circuit decision can be found in the United States Supreme Court. That is where we should now go for relief.").

[471] *See* AT&T v. Iowa Utils. Bd., 118 S. Ct. 879 (1998).

the FCC sought to enforce its pricing rules indirectly. As more fully discussed in Chapters 3 and 9, the Commission in August 1997 rejected Ameritech's application for permission to provide long-distance service in Michigan.[472] In doing so, it explained (in dictum) that section 271(c)(2)(B)'s competitive checklist empowers the FCC to impose national pricing standards on BOCs seeking interLATA relief.[473] The FCC then proceeded to reimpose the very pricing principles that the Eighth Circuit had struck down.[474] The Eighth Circuit was not amused: in unusually critical language,[475] it ordered the FCC to refrain from any further attempts to avoid the court's mandate.[476]

But, ultimately, the FCC triumphed in the Supreme Court. In *AT&T Corp. v. Iowa Utilities Board*,[477] the Court (in a 5-3 decision, with Justice O'Connor recused) rejected all jurisdictional challenges to the FCC's pricing rules. Writing for the Court, Justice Scalia relied heavily on section 201(b),[478] which was added to the Communications Act in 1938 and provides that "[t]he Commission may prescribe such rules and regulations as may be necessary in the public interest to carry out the provisions of this Act." According to the Court, this provision gave the FCC general authority to make rules interpreting any part of the Communications Act, including section 251.[479] Thus, the Court found it

---

[472] *See* Application of Ameritech Michigan Pursuant to Section 271 to Provide In-Region, InterLATA Services in Michigan, Memorandum Opinion and Order, 12 F.C.C. Rec. 20,543 (1997).

[473] *See id.* at 20,696–20,697 ¶¶285–286.

[474] Carefully avoiding explicit reference to its vacated rules, the Commission noted: "We have previously set forth our view that the requirement for the use of forward-looking economic costs is to be implemented through a method based on total element long-run incremental cost or TELRIC." *Id.* at 20,698–20,699 ¶290. Therefore, the agency stated, "for purposes of checklist compliance, prices for interconnection and unbundled network elements must be based on TELRIC principles." *Id.*

[475] *See* Iowa Utils. Bd. v. FCC, 135 F.3d 535, 538 (8th Cir. 1997) ("A more clear violation of our mandate could hardly be imagined."), *petition for cert. filed,* No. 97-1519 (Mar. 13, 1998); *id.* at 539 ("The FCC's justification for its reassertion of local pricing authority lacks even the scent of merit.").

[476] *See id.* at 543.

[477] 119 S. Ct. 721 (1999).

[478] 47 U.S.C. §201(b).

[479] AT&T v. Iowa Utils. Bd., 119 S. Ct. at 721,729.

unnecessary to determine whether section 251 itself might provide an independent basis for federal regulatory jurisdiction.[480]

Section 2(b) presented no obstacle, the Court held, because section 201(b) "*explicitly* gives the FCC jurisdiction to make rules governing matters to which the 1996 Act applies."[481] This does not render section 2(b)'s "give the Commission jurisdiction" language superfluous: those words might apply to the FCC's so-called ancillary jurisdiction (jurisdiction to make rules in areas not expressly addressed in the statute).[482] The Court recognized that in its reading section 2(b) would have little "practical effect" insofar as the 250 series was concerned.[483] But that was simply "because Congress, by extending the Communications Act into local competition, has removed a significant area from the States' exclusive control."[484]

Nor did the Court see any counterindication in section 252 (c)(2), which provides that the states, in the course of arbitrating interconnection disputes, "shall . . . establish any rates for interconnection, services, or network elements."[485] The FCC's rate-related standards and methodology, the Court held, simply do not infringe on the states' "establish any rates" turf: "It is the States that will apply those standards and implement that methodology, determining the concrete result in particular circumstances. That is enough to constitute the establishment of rates."[486]

It is probably fair to say that the Court's conclusion was driven by its view of the alternative: the Court deemed "a federal program administered by 50 independent state agencies" to be "surpassing strange."[487] In the end, it appears, the "novel" nature of

---

[480] *Id.* at 732.

[481] *Id.* at 730 (emphasis in original).

[482] *Id.* at 730–736.

[483] *Id.* at 731 n.8.

[484] *Id.*

[485] 47 U.S.C. §252(c)(2).

[486] AT&T v. Iowa Utils. Bd., 119 S. Ct. at 721, 732.

[487] *Id.* at 730 n.6. In addition, the Court noted that certain subsections of section 251 expressly contemplate FCC rulemaking; the Court found it "most unlikely that Congress created such a . . . hodgepodge" of dovetailing state and federal regulation. *Id.* at 731 n.8.

a regime under which extensive "federal policymaking has been turned over to state administrative agencies" seems to have been more than the Court could bear.[488] Despite the Court's recognition that the statute was "in many important respects a model of ambiguity or indeed even self-contradiction,"[489] that novelty sufficed to place the default rule of section 2(b) offside.

Though the Commission's victory was no doubt important as a matter of principle, its practical significance by now may be limited. While the *Iowa Utilities Board* case was being litigated, most states used their price-setting authority in ways closely following the FCC models.[490] It remains to be seen whether, in the wake of the *Iowa Utilities Board* decision, the FCC will nevertheless reassert plenary authority over pricing—something that, in light of its limited practical significance, some states will no doubt perceive as a heavy-handed exercise of central authority.

§2.4.4.2   Competitive Local Exchange Carriers: Unbundlers

As discussed in Chapter 5, the 1996 Act requires LECs to allow competitors to lease network equipment—so-called unbundled network elements. LECs have a "duty to provide, to any requesting telecommunications carrier for the provision of a telecommunications service, nondiscriminatory access to network elements on an unbundled basis at any technically feasible point on rates, terms, and conditions that are just, reasonable, and nondiscriminatory."[491]

---

[488] *Id.* at 733 n.10.

[489] *Id.* at 738.

[490] *See, e.g.,* J. I. Klein, Assistant Attorney General, Antitrust Division, U.S. Department of Justice, The 1996 Telecommunications Act: An Antitrust Perspective, Written Statement Before the Subcommittee on Antitrust, Business Rights and Competition, Committee on the Judiciary, U.S. Senate, Washington, D.C., at 6 (Sept. 17, 1997); Application of Ameritech Michigan Pursuant to Section 271 of the Communications Act of 1934, as amended, to Provide In-Region, InterLATA Services in Michigan, Memorandum Opinion and Order, 12 F.C.C. Rec. 20,543, 20,697 ¶288 (1997) (hereinafter *Michigan Order*).

[491] 47 U.S.C. §251(c)(3).

But not all network elements are automatically subject to un-bundling. Section 251(d)(2) provides that, "[i]n determining what network elements should be made available . . . , the Commission shall consider, at a minimum, whether . . . failure to provide access . . . would impair the ability of the telecommunications carrier seeking access to provide the services that it seeks to offer."[492] The test for elements that are "proprietary in nature" is even more stringent: access to such network elements must be "necessary."[493]

As interpreted by the FCC, however, the "necessary" and "impair" standards had little significance. The Commission viewed section 251(c)(3), which requires ILECs to provide "access to network elements on an unbundled basis at any technically feasible point," as empowering it to require access to any element "for which it is technically feasible to provide access on an unbundled basis."[494] The "necessary" and "impair" standards of section 252(d)(2), the Commission held, merely empowered it to decline to exercise the full measure of the authority granted in section 251(c)(3).[495] For the moment, the Commission required access to seven kinds of network elements.[496]

In addition, the FCC determined that the states would be permitted to require access to additional elements in the course of arbitration.[497] States *would* be subject to the "necessary" and "impair" standards,[498] but these standards posed a low hurdle indeed. As for the "necessary" test, access would be required unless it would be possible for a CLEC to provide the service it

---

[492] *Id.* §251(d)(2)(B).

[493] *Id.* §251(d)(2)(A). By way of examples, the *Local Competition Order* mentioned "elements with proprietary protocols or elements containing proprietary information." *Local Competition Order,* 11 F.C.C. Rec. at 15,641 ¶282.

[494] *Id.* at 15,640–15,641 ¶278.

[495] *See id.* at 15,641 ¶279, 15,643 ¶286.

[496] *See* 47 C.F.R. §51.319. These were (1) the local loop, (2) the network interface device, (3) switching capability, (4) interoffice transmission facilities, (5) signaling networks and call-related databases, (6) operations support systems functions, and (7) operator services and directory assistance. *See id.*

[497] *See Local Competition Order,* 11 F.C.C. Rec. at 15,640 ¶277, 15,641 ¶281; 47 C.F.R. §51.317.

[498] *See Local Competition Order,* 11 F.C.C. Rec. at 15,641 ¶281; 47 C.F.R. §51.317.

proposed to offer by using other, nonproprietary elements *within the ILEC's network.*[499] As for the "impair" standard, access would be required if the ILEC's failure to provide access to the desired network element would increase (however slightly) the CLEC's cost, again as compared with providing service over other unbundled elements of the ILEC's network.[500]

What rates would ILECs be permitted to charge CLECs for these unbundled elements? The Act requires that prices for unbundled elements be set "based upon the [incumbent's] cost."[501] Interpreting that standard, the FCC "coin[ed]" a new method for measuring costs known as "total element long run incremental cost" or TELRIC.[502] Under TELRIC, prices are determined on the basis of only the incremental, forward-looking cost of a hypothetical, ideally efficient, state-of-the-art network.[503] TELRIC does not permit the consideration of costs that incumbent LECs incurred in constructing their networks, but have not yet recovered through their regulated rates.[504] It prohibits consideration of even the actual incremental or "forward-looking" costs that an ILEC may incur; only the costs of a hypothetical, perfectly efficient network count.[505]

Just as the Commission established a default range for resale rates, it promulgated "proxy" prices for unbundled network elements. If a state commission concludes that it does not have enough cost information to determine TELRIC rates, it must follow the proxies.[506] In the near term, these proxy prices were for all practical purposes mandatory: as the FCC acknowledged, it was a virtual impossibility for most states to determine TELRIC rates within statutory timetables.[507] In the longer term, the

---

[499] *See Local Competition Order,* 11 F.C.C. Rec. at 15,642 ¶283; 47 C.F.R. §51.317(b)(1).

[500] *See Local Competition Order,* 11 F.C.C. Rec. at 15,643 ¶285; 47 C.F.R. §51.317(b)(2).

[501] 47 U.S.C. §252(d)(1).

[502] *Local Competition Order,* 11 F.C.C. Rec. at 15,845–15,846 ¶678.

[503] *See id.* at 15,848 ¶685, 15,850 ¶690.

[504] *See id.* at 15,857–15,858 ¶705.

[505] *See id.* at 15,848–15,849 ¶¶684–685.

[506] *See* 47 C.F.R. §51.513(a).

[507] *See Local Competition Order,* 11 F.C.C. Rec. at 15,812 ¶619.

proxies would continue to constrain the states: a state that would depart from the proxies must justify itself on the basis of a detailed factual record, which would be subject to review before the FCC itself.[508]

The FCC arrived at specific proxy rates not on the basis of any individualized review of costs, but using theoretical, national cost "models"—models that the FCC recognized may lead to inaccurate cost estimates[509]—and data plucked from a small sample of previous state rate orders that used standards substantially different from the FCC's own.[510] To say that the proxies descended into detail would be an understatement. For instance, the proxy rate for an unbundled local loop in Missouri is $18.32; the ceiling in California is $11.10.[511] For tandem switching, the proxy is $0.0015 per minute of use.[512] The proxy rate for terminating local traffic is $0.004 per minute.[513] And so on.

As already discussed in section 2.4.4.1 above, a group of states and LECs immediately sought a court stay of the pricing rules on jurisdictional grounds. The Eighth Circuit granted a stay, finding that the petitioners had shown a likelihood that the FCC had invaded the regulatory authority of the states.[514] In its later decision on the merits, the court reaffirmed the views expressed in its stay opinion: the Commission had "exceeded its jurisdiction in promulgating the pricing rules regarding local telephone service."[515] According to the court, authority to make these pricing calls had been assigned to the states, not the Commission.[516] The court's merits decision rejected, however, the argument that the FCC had misinterpreted the "necessary" and "impair" standards.[517]

---

[508] *See id.*

[509] *See id.* at 15,857–15,858 ¶705.

[510] *See id.* at 15,894–15,895 ¶¶792–794, 15,960–15,963 ¶¶925–932.

[511] *See* 47 C.F.R. §51.513(c)(1).

[512] *See id.* §51.513(c)(5).

[513] *See id.* §51.707(b)(1).

[514] *See* Iowa Utils. Bd. v. FCC, 109 F.3d 418, 423–425 (1996).

[515] Iowa Utils. Bd. v. FCC, 120 F.3d 753, 792 (1997), *rev'd sub nom.* AT&T v. Iowa Utils. Bd., 119 S. Ct. 721 (1999).

[516] *Id.* at 793–800. Because the court found that the FCC lacked jurisdiction, the court saw no need to pass on the rules' merits. *See id.* at 800.

[517] *Id.* at 810–812.

The Supreme Court came out the other way on both counts.[518] As discussed in section 2.4.4.1 above, the Court held that section 201(b) provided the FCC with sufficient authority to promulgate pricing rules and that section 152(b) posed no obstacle.[519] On the "necessary" and "impair" standards, however, the Court (over the dissent of Justice Souter) sided with the ILECs.[520] According to the Court, "[T]he Act requires the FCC to apply *some* limiting standard, rationally related to the goals of the Act, which it has simply failed to do."[521] If Congress would have wanted limitless availability of network elements, "[i]t would simply have said (as the Commission in effect has) that whatever requested element can be provided must be provided."[522]

In particular, the Court faulted the Commission for limiting the relevant comparisons to the ILECs' *own* network elements: because "any entrant will request the most efficient network element that the incumbent has to offer," the FCC's test, in effect, rendered the "necessary" and "impair" standards nugatory.[523] Moreover, the Court held that the Commission's determination that "*any* increase in cost (or decrease in quality) imposed by denial of a network element renders access to that element 'necessary,' and causes the failure to provide that element to 'impair' the entrant's ability to furnish its desired services is simply not in accord with the ordinary meaning of those terms."[524]

Accordingly, the Court vacated the FCC's rule setting forth the list of seven required elements[525] and remanded the case so that the Commission could promulgate a new, lawful rule.[526] As of mid-1999, the remand rulemaking was underway. In that context, the proper interpretation of the Court's decision — requiring the FCC to "giv[e] some substance to the 'necessary' and

---

[518] AT&T v. Iowa Utils. Bd., 119 S. Ct. 721 (1999).
[519] *See id.* at 729–732.
[520] *See id.* at 734–735.
[521] *Id.* (emphasis in original).
[522] *Id.* at 735.
[523] *Id.*
[524] *Id.* (emphasis in original).
[525] *Id.* at 736.
[526] *Id.*

'impair' requirements"[527] without saying just how much substance—will no doubt be the subject of vigorous debate. At least in the view of Justice Breyer, who concurred in this aspect of the Court's decision, section 251(d)(2) contemplates a standard not very different from the "essential facilities" doctrine familiar in antitrust law.[528] It seems fairly clear that at least some of the elements on the Commission's list of seven would not pass muster under that standard.

§2.4.4.3   Resellers Under Another Name: Rebundlers

As more fully discussed in Chapter 3, the FCC's August 1996 Order permitted CLECs to provide service to end users simply by reassembling unbundled network elements leased from an ILEC—even if they did not add a single element of their own.[529] Because the FCC's list of network elements required to be made available on an unbundled basis included *all* portions of the ILEC's network,[530] a CLEC could simply reconstitute the ILEC's entire prix fixe menu by ordering the constituent elements à la carte.

What is more, the FCC required the ILEC to do the reconstituting for the CLEC.[531] ILECs, in other words, were required to supply a so-called unbundled network element (UNE) platform. In effect, this gave CLECs a second way to offer services without using any of their own facilities: they could either buy a finished service for resale or purchase rebundled UNEs. It was as if GM had been directed to sell not only Chevies, but also rebundled Chevies—all the constituent parts of the car not as parts, but preassembled, same as any other Chevy, but under the new, "rebundled Chevy" nameplate.

---

[527] *Id.*
[528] *Id.* at 753.
[529] *See Local Competition Order,* 11 F.C.C. Rec. at 15,666–15,671 ¶¶328–341.
[530] *See* 47 C.F.R. §51.319; *see generally* §2.4.4.2.
[531] *See Local Competition Order,* 11 F.C.C. Rec. at 15,647–15,648 ¶¶293–295; *see* 47 C.F.R. §51.315(c)–(f).

This created an obvious pricing problem. The Act called for different prices for the (otherwise identical) "resale" and "rebundled" Chevies.[532] At least if the retail rate was above cost (as, for example, in the case of business service), the "RUNE" price would be much lower than the "reseller" price. Nobody would buy service as a "reseller" under such a regime—all would buy "rebundled UNEs" instead. Worse: CLECs would buy RUNEs where they were selling to businesses and finished services where they were selling to residential customers.

In its July 1997 merits decision, the Eighth Circuit as a practical matter put a stop to the platform phenomenon. The Act *does* permit CLECs to order up a full platform of UNEs, the court held: it rejected the ILECs' challenges to the "all elements" rule, under which CLECs were entitled to lease UNEs even if they did not add a single piece of equipment of their own.[533] But, the court held, ILECs cannot be required to *reassemble* the leased elements.[534] The Act provides that ILECs must provide UNEs "in a manner that allows requesting carriers to combine such elements."[535] This language, the court concluded, means that CLECs must do their own rebundling.[536] Thus, the court set aside rules making ILECs responsible for reassemblage.[537] More important, the court (on rehearing) set aside a rule prohibiting ILECs to separate requested network elements that were already combined.[538]

This latter ruling did not survive Supreme Court review unscathed.[539] The Supreme Court had no difficulty agreeing with

---

[532] *Compare* 47 U.S.C. §252(d)(1) (cost plus a reasonable profit for UNEs) *with id.* §252(d)(3) (retail rate minus "costs that will be avoided" for resold service).

[533] *See* Iowa Utils. Bd. v. FCC, 120 F.3d at 814–815.

[534] *See id.* at 813.

[535] 47 U.S.C. §251(c)(3).

[536] *See* Iowa Utils. Bd. v. FCC, 120 F.3d at 813.

[537] *See id.* (setting aside 47 C.F.R. §51.315(c)–(f)).

[538] *See* Iowa Utils. Bd. v. FCC, 1997 U.S. App. LEXIS 28652 (8th Cir. Oct. 14, 1997) (incorporated at 120 F.3d at 813) (setting aside 47 C.F.R. §51.315 (b)).

[539] The Supreme Court did not address the reassemblage rules of 47 C.F.R. §51.315(c)–(f). The aspect of the Eighth Circuit decision setting aside those rules was not appealed to the Supreme Court.

the Eighth Circuit that the "all elements" rule was consistent with the statute, saying simply that the Act imposes no requirement that CLECs bring in some of their own facilities before they become entitled to lease UNEs.[540] But the Court could not agree with the aspect of the Eighth Circuit's decision striking down the UNE-separation rule. According to the Court, section 251(c)(3) simply "does not say, or even remotely imply, that elements *must* be provided only in [separated] fashion and never in combined form."[541] The Court found that it was "well within the bounds of the reasonable" for the FCC to prohibit ILECs to disconnect already assembled UNEs simply to raise rivals' costs.[542]

Whether this is the end of the platform battle remains to be seen. As the Supreme Court made clear, the FCC promulgated its list of seven required elements (together comprising the entire network) under an insufficiently exacting reading of the "necessary" and "impair" standards of section 251(d)(2).[543] It may well be that, on remand from the Supreme Court's decision, the FCC will decide that some of the seven elements previously required cannot pass muster under the proper reading of the statute. If so, the platform issue diminishes in practical significance because CLECs will be required to add some of their own facilities. Thus, the Supreme Court was careful to point out that the remand proceeding may make the entire platform issue "academic."[544]

§2.4.4.4 Reciprocal Compensation

The 1996 Act requires all LECs to "establish reciprocal compensation arrangements for the transport and termination of telecommunications."[545] Such arrangements must "provide for the mutual and reciprocal recovery by each carrier of costs associated with the transport and termination on each carrier's net-

---

[540] *See* AT&T v. Iowa Utils. Bd., 119 S. Ct. 721, 737 (1999).
[541] *See id.* (emphasis in original).
[542] *Id.*
[543] *See* §2.4.4.2.
[544] AT&T v. Iowa Utils. Bd., 119 S. Ct. at 736.
[545] 47 U.S.C. §251(b)(5).

work facilities of calls that originate on the network facilities of the other carrier."[546] Those "costs" must be determined "on the basis of a reasonable approximation of the additional costs of terminating such calls."[547] Put differently, the Act requires an originating carrier to pay the terminating carrier the marginal cost (not the fully distributed cost) of terminating a call on the terminating carrier's network.[548]

For purposes of regulatory debate, it may be well to observe that this focus on traffic direction and marginal cost has little to do with restraining market power or mimicking competitive market conditions and everything to do with policy (i.e., a policy aiming at helping competitors). The "originator pays marginal cost" rule takes no account of the true value of interconnection. The value of interconnecting with a competing network depends on the size and attractiveness of its subscriber base.[549] Thus, in a competitive environment, compensation would presumably be a function of those factors; marginal costs would be of secondary concern. As backbone providers and ISPs know well, small networks would pay, and large ones would collect. No one would bother much about costs.

Nor would anyone bother much about the direction of traffic: in an unregulated environment, compensation would flow simply to the more valuable network, regardless of traffic direction. One might think that traffic direction ultimately does not matter much under an "originator pays" rule either: traffic volumes

---

[546] *Id.* §252(d)(2)(i). The Act provides that carriers may waive their right to mutual recovery by offsetting reciprocal obligations, including "bill and keep" arrangements, whereby carriers bill only end users, not other carriers, on the assumption that each carrier receives equal value from interconnection. *See id.* §252(d)(2)(B)(i).

[547] *Id.* §252(d)(2)(A)(ii).

[548] Oddly, section 252(d)(2)(B)(ii) then proceeds to prohibit state commissions "to engage in any rate regulation proceeding to establish with particularity the additional costs of transporting or terminating calls, or to require carriers to maintain records with respect to the additional costs of such calls." This provision would seem to forbid regulators to gather precisely the information they need to determine marginal costs. The FCC has determined that this provision does not preclude TELRIC-based cost studies, reading section 252(d)(2)(B)(ii) to refer only to traditional rate-of-return proceedings. *See Local Competition Order,* 11 F.C.C. Rec. at 16,024 ¶1056.

[549] *See generally* M. Mueller, Universal Service 25–27 (1997).

will usually be in rough balance, so that no money changes hands. But the "originator pays" rule itself skews traffic direction. For example, because Internet service providers only receive (not originate) calls, they have become valuable magnets for terminating traffic, which is more fully explained in Chapters 3 and 11. CLECs compete to become ISPs' local service providers, and (at least if this traffic is ultimately deemed "local") ILECs may end up paying hundreds of millions of dollars for the "privilege" of routing their subscribers' ISP-bound calls onto CLECs' networks.[550]

However this may be, the 1996 Act says "originator pays marginal cost," and that is the rule the FCC adopted in its *Local Competition Order*.[551] The Commission equated marginal costs with its TELRIC approach[552] and accordingly directed states to conduct TELRIC-based studies of the cost of termination.[553] For purposes of such a study, it will usually be the *ILEC*'s costs that count: the FCC directed that rates generally should be the same in both directions, at the level of the ILEC's costs.[554] The FCC left state commissions two other options: commissions were permitted either to adopt a proxy range set by the FCC (at 0.2 and 0.4 cents per minute for termination)[555] or to impose a "bill and keep" arrangement (under which no money changes hands) where traffic flows both ways are roughly equal.[556] Given the expense and difficulty of conducting cost studies, these two options would presumably appear attractive to most states.

On appeal, all these rules met the same fate as the other interconnection-pricing rules. The Eighth Circuit vacated them in

---

[550] *See, e.g.,* Bell Atlantic Says FCC Is Giving Little Help on Sec. 271 Application, Comm. Daily, Mar. 2, 1998, at 1.

[551] *See Local Competition Order,* 11 F.C.C. Rec. at 16,008–16,058 ¶¶1027–1118; 47 C.F.R. §§51.701–.717.

[552] *See Local Competition Order,* 11 F.C.C. Rec. at 16,023 ¶1054.

[553] *See id.* at 16,024–16,026 ¶¶1055–1059.

[554] *See id.* at 16,040–16,044 ¶¶1085–1093. Departure from this rule is permitted only if a CLEC submits a cost study showing that its costs are higher than the ILEC's. *See id.* at 16,042 ¶1089.

[555] *See id.* at 16,024 ¶1055, 16,026–16,028 ¶¶1060–1062.

[556] *See id.* at 16,024 ¶1055, 16,054–16,058 ¶¶1111–1118.

whole,[557] holding that the FCC lacked jurisdiction to interfere in these intrastate matters.[558] In light of its jurisdictional holding, the court saw no need to pass on the rules' merits.[559] But the Supreme Court reversed the Eighth Circuit's jurisdictional holding and remanded to the Eighth Circuit.[560] On remand, the Eighth Circuit will have to confront the ILECs' many arguments that the FCC's substantive pricing rules conflict with the statute. As of this writing, the Eighth Circuit has yet to commence its remand proceedings.

§2.4.4.5 Wholesale Versus Retail Price Regulation

As discussed in sections 2.4.4.1 and 2.4.4.2 above, the 1996 Act directs either federal regulators or their state counterparts (the jurisdictional battles are still in progress) to regulate the *wholesale* rates that CLECs pay ILECs for either full-service packages or unbundled network elements. Meanwhile, ILECs' retail rates are also subject to exacting regulation: state regulators set rates for local exchange and intrastate exchange-access service, and the FCC regulates rates for interstate exchange-access service. Should retail rates continue to be regulated? Is it even practical to do so? As discussed in section 2.4.4.3 above, trying to regulate the same basic services under several different names almost inevitably leads to contradiction and arbitrage. The problems are likely to be especially acute if federal regulators regulate wholesale rates and state regulators regulate retail rates.

According to former FCC Chief Economist Joseph Farrell, "Smoothly functioning wholesale regulation . . . permits and indeed almost demands retail deregulation. If multiple providers can compete for a customer's business and promptly supply it at a reasonable overall cost, even if they do so by leasing the incumbent's facilities, then it would seem that prompt

[557] *See* Iowa Utils. Bd. v. FCC, 120 F.3d at 819 n.39.
[558] *See id.* at 793–800.
[559] *See id.* at 800.
[560] *See* AT&T v. Iowa Utils. Bd., 119 S. Ct. at 733.

deregulation of all charges to the provider's end-user will be appropriate. . . . There should be no need for regulators to resolve the difficult issue of 'how' end-users want to pay the cost of service—how much in flat charges, how much in usage charges, how much for special features, etc. . . . Indeed, if regulators continue to regulate the incumbent's retail prices, and don't happen to replicate the solution that the incumbent and the customer jointly find most beneficial, it puts the incumbent at an artificial competitive disadvantage. Thus, *while there are obvious risks in premature deregulation of incumbents, there are also risks in waiting too long.*"[561]

§2.5   Universal Service

Perhaps the most daunting task assigned to the Commission by the 1996 Act was a thorough review and restructuring of the existing federal universal-service guarantees, a task to be conducted in collaboration with a new Federal-State Joint Board.[562] The review was long overdue: the universal-service guarantee had evolved into a rat's nest of implicit subsidies and accounting sleight of hands utterly unsuited to a competitive marketplace. Section 254 of the 1996 Act arguably directed that this structure be ripped apart and rebuilt afresh.

Though section 254 runs on for almost 2,000 words, the outline of its ambitious plan is found in just a few terse sentences. Implicit subsidies are out; explicit ones are in.[563] Only carriers that have been certified by a state commission as "eligible carriers"—presumably including all or most of the ILECs—may receive support.[564] Who funds the new communal pot? All "tele-

---

[561] Joseph Farrell, Chief Economist, FCC, Prospects for Deregulation in Telecommunications (rev. version May 30, 1997) (emphasis in original). For similar views, see Alfred Kahn, Letting Go: Deregulating the Process of Deregulation 54–60 (1998).

[562] *See* 47 U.S.C. §254(a). Universal service issues are more fully discussed in Chapter 6.

[563] *See* 47 U.S.C. §254(e) (universal-service support "should be explicit").

[564] *See id.; see also id.* §214(e)(2).

communications carriers" providing interstate telecommunications service.[565] How much should go into the pot? Contributions should be "sufficient to achieve the purposes of this section."[566] How is the burden allocated among contributors? Each must contribute "on an equitable and nondiscriminatory basis."[567] Congress left it to the FCC to elaborate on these generalities.[568]

Congress left unclear what, if any, role the states are to play. Section 254 provides that the states "may adopt regulations not inconsistent with the Commission's rules to preserve and advance universal service."[569] It is unclear whether, like the FCC, states are under an obligation to replace implicit subsidies with explicit ones. If section 254 should be read to impose such an obligation, the provision works an intrusion on states' core authority to regulate intrastate retail rates that goes well beyond that effected in sections 251 and 252. There is little legislative history on point, and it is difficult to believe that Congress would discard decades of state autonomy over the regulation of retail rates in such terse and vague terms. Yet there are hints in the statute to this effect,[570] and loose language in the Supreme Court's *Iowa Utilities Board* decision assumes it to be so.[571]

---

[565] *See id.* §254(b)(4), (d). In addition, "[a]ny other provider of telecommunications" not qualifying as a telecommunications carrier "*may* be required to contribute." *Id.* §254(d) (emphasis added).

[566] *Id.* §254(e).

[567] *Id.* §254(d).

[568] *See id.* §254(a)(2).

[569] *Id.* §254(f); *see also id.* §253(b).

[570] *See id.* §254(b)(5) ("There should be specific, predictable and sufficient Federal *and State* mechanisms to preserve and advance universal service.") (emphasis added); *id.* §254(f) (state may advance universal service only by adopting "specific, predictable, and sufficient mechanisms"). *But see id.* §251(c)(4)(B) (expressly protecting states' residual pricing schemes).

[571] *See* AT&T v. Iowa Utils. Bd., 119 S. Ct. 721, 737 (1999). In the *Iowa Utilities Board* case, ILECs attacked FCC rules about UNE "platforms" by arguing that they would foster "Government-sanctioned regulatory arbitrage." *Id.* at 737. "Currently, state laws require local phone rates to include a 'universal service subsidy,'" *id.*, the ILECs argued, in that residential customers' below-cost rates are offset by business customers' above-cost rates. Requiring platforms to be made available, the ILECs urged, would eliminate ILECs' subsidy sources, causing the entire state-sponsored cross-subsidization scheme to

Rather than address any of these fundamental issues in depth, Congress devoted the detailed balance of section 254 to other matters. For example, Congress in great detail addressed the definition of the "universal service" ideal: what services should be included in the minimum package that carriers receiving federal support must offer their subscribers? Thus, the statute charges the FCC with defining (and from time to time redefining) the contents of this bundle.[572] In doing so, the Commission is to take account of technological advances; maybe assymetrical digital subscriber lines (ADSL) will someday be part of the required universal-service bundle.[573]

Separately, section 254 calls for an entirely new subsidy initiative, under which newly favored parties (schools, libraries, and rural healthcare providers) are entitled to purchase telecommunications and related services at discounts to be determined by the FCC.[574] The firms providing service at discounted rates are entitled to reimbursement through the same subsidy mechanisms the FCC is to establish in connection with high-cost support.[575] This new subsidy scheme will be funded by the same contributors as the subsidy for high-cost areas.[576]

Finally, section 254(g) requires the Commission to ensure that long-distance rates for rural and high-cost users are no higher than long-distance rates for urban and low-cost users and that long-distance carriers maintain nationally averaged rates.[577] Section 254(g) requires an implicit subsidy, plain and simple: low-cost subscribers shall pay more so that high-cost subscribers may pay less.[578] Section 254(g) perhaps merely codified a policy the FCC traditionally pursued on an informal basis through the

---

collapse. The Court was unimpressed, saying that section 254 "requires that universal-service subsidies be phased out, so whatever possibility of arbitrage remains will be only temporary." *Id.* at 737.

[572] *See* 47 U.S.C. §§214(e)(1)(A), 254(a)(2), (c), (e).
[573] *See id.* §254(c)(1).
[574] *See id.* §254(h)(1)(A), (B).
[575] *See id.*
[576] *See id.* §254(d).
[577] *See id.* §254(g).
[578] *See Universal Service Order,* 12 F.C.C. Rec. at 8784 n.15.

tariff-review process, [579] but that codification is decidedly at odds with section 254's overall thrust to replace implicit with explicit subsidies.

In May 1997, the FCC took its first stab at effectuating section 254's new mandate; the resulting *Universal Service Order* is more fully discussed in Chapter 6.[580] In the Order, the Commission took steps to try to make subsidies "explicit." Although some subsidies were already explicit before 1997, most were not.[581] Most simply took the form of uneconomically high prices charged to some users or for some services and uneconomically low prices charged to or for others.[582] Inflated rates for urban lines, business lines, intra- and interstate long-distance service, and vertical services have been the principal sources of implicit universal-service subsidies.[583]

As the Commission observed, Congress did not intend subsidies to be made explicit as an end in themselves.[584] Instead, the FCC read the Act as intending that subsidies be made "measurable" and "portable"[585] so that competing carriers can assess the profitability of serving subsidized end users and pocket the subsidy upon persuading an end user to switch carriers. Portability may also one day enable the Commission "to set subsidy levels through competitive bidding rather than through regulation."[586] The FCC has taken no concrete steps in that direction, however, and it is hard to imagine that it will do so anytime soon.

On the issue of federal and state jurisdiction, the FCC took the view that section 254 addresses subsidies not only at the federal level, but also at the state level. Something would therefore

---

[579] *See* MTS and WATS Market Structure, Report and Third Supplemental Notice of Inquiry and Proposed Rulemaking, 81 F.C.C.2d 177, 194 ¶73 (1980).

[580] *See Universal Service Order,* 12 F.C.C. Rec. at 8776.

[581] *See generally id.* at 8784 ¶10; *Access Charge Reform Order,* 12 F.C.C. Rec. at 15,994–15,996 ¶¶28–31.

[582] *See Universal Service Order,* 12 F.C.C. Rec. at 8784 ¶10.

[583] *See id.* at 8784–8785 ¶12, 8785–8786 ¶14.

[584] *See Access Charge Reform Order,* 12 F.C.C. Rec. at 15,997 ¶33.

[585] *See id.* at 15,997 ¶33; *Universal Service Order,* 12 F.C.C. Rec. at 8786 ¶15.

[586] *See Access Charge Reform Order,* 12 F.C.C. Rec. at 15,997 ¶33; Universal Service Order, 12 F.C.C. Rec. at 8890 ¶207.

have to be done about implicit subsidies at the state level,[587] but *it* would not do it: the Commission stated that, at least initially, this would be a task for the states,[588] and it strongly encouraged them to clean house.[589] Does the FCC have authority to intervene if a state does not meet its obligation? To date, no court has addressed the question, and even the FCC seems torn on the issue.[590]

It is probably fair to say that in light of its limited reach the Commission's *Universal Service Order*'s immediate impact does not match its ambition. For one thing, implicit subsidies under state control (which, in dollar terms, likely dwarf those under federal control) are left untouched. For another thing, the Commission declined to reorder even long-distance access charges, by far the most important implicit subsidy under federal control. The few federal programs that *are* affected (such as Long Term Support and the previously existing Universal Service Fund) were relatively small in size to begin with and affect only the most rural LECs. None of this is to say the Universal Service Order is unimportant. It may well provide the blueprint for things to come—just not in the near term.

§2.6   Constitutional Limits

How much of everything that precedes in this chapter is consistent with the Constitution? Equal-protection principles are

---

[587] *See Universal Service Order* at 8785–8786 ¶14; *see also Access Charge Reform Order,* 12 F.C.C. Rec. at 15,985 ¶3, 15,988 ¶¶10–12.

[588] *See Universal Service Order,* 12 F.C.C. Rec. at 8785–8786 ¶14; *Access Charge Reform Order,* 12 F.C.C. Rec. at 15,988 ¶10.

[589] *See Access Charge Reform Order,* 12 F.C.C. at 15,988 ¶11.

[590] *Compare Universal Service Order,* 12 F.C.C. Rec. at 8785–8786 ¶14 ("[t]he Commission, in light of section 2(b) of the Communications Act, does not have control over the local rate-setting process") (footnote omitted) *with id.* ("States . . . must *in the first instance* be responsible for identifying intrastate implicit universal service support") (emphasis added); *Access Charge Reform Order,* 12 F.C.C. Rec. at 15,988 ¶10 ("states are *initially* responsible for identifying implicit intrastate subsidies") (emphasis added); *id.* ("the Act does not *require,* nor did Congress intend, that we *immediately* institute a vast set of wide-ranging pricing rules applicable to interstate *and intrastate* services") (emphasis

becoming increasingly important as the formerly separate businesses of broadcast, cable, and carriage converge into a single marketplace. A second strand of constitutional principle—the traditional due process and takings limits on rate setting for common carriers—is still relevant, perhaps more than ever now that competitors are at hand to do the "taking" if regulators will not step aside.

§2.6.1 Equal Protection

In the communications industry today, unequal regulation is the rule. The 1934 Communications Act, the two subsequent Cable Acts, the 1996 Telecommunications Act, and the FCC's various implementations of these laws for broadcasters and carriers, landline and wireless, probably could not be made uniform even if the FCC tried.[591] The real differences that still separate various media and categories of service probably still justify manifestly unequal regulation.

But markets are converging faster than regulation. As various communications markets converge, the intricate regulatory structure now in place may well sink below the horizon of rationality. Identical services offered by evenly matched providers to the same consumers will end up being regulated in wildly different ways. Internet telephony is a fledgling example. At some point, equal protection limits should kick in.

---

added); *id.* ¶11 ("Congress intended that states . . . must *in the first instance* be responsible for identifying intrastate implicit universal service support") (emphasis added).

[591] The FCC, of course, has not tried. *See, e.g.,* Implementation of Sections of the Cable Television Consumer Protection and Competition Act of 1992: Rate Regulation, Notice of Proposed Rulemaking, 74 Rad. Reg. 2d (P & F) 1247 ¶15 n.16 (1993) ("it was Congress' expectation that cable rates should not be regulated in the same manner as common carriers"); Implementation of Section 25 of the Cable Television Consumer Protection and Competition Act of 1992, Report and Order, MM Docket No. 93-25, ¶59 (Nov. 25, 1998) ("DBS and cable are separate and distinct services, warranting separate and distinct obligations.").

The Supreme Court's 1993 ruling in *FCC v. Beach Communications*[592] indicates that the Court still reviews only the rationality of differing regulatory approaches. Whether other aspects of regulation might engage stricter equal-protection review is unclear. Equal protection concerns may be defused, moreover, by timely FCC approval of flexible tariffs or a decision to forbear entirely from regulating as competition unfolds. Cable rate regulation automatically disengages when cable is "subject to effective competition."[593] So, too, may price regulation of carriers. As regulation itself recedes, so will complaints about unequal regulatory burdens.

§2.6.2 *Due Process and Takings*

Due process and the takings clause limit government's power to price-regulate private enterprise into giving away assets to customers. Telephone companies have litigated these issues for decades in connection with rate-of-return regulation, pole attachments, and so on.[594]

It remains possible that the FCC's unbundling rules, even those not vacated by the Eighth Circuit, constitute an unconstitutional taking of LEC property. The Eighth Circuit found that the issue was not ripe for review: interconnection agreements were not far enough along for the court to determine whether ILECs were receiving just compensation for access to their networks.[595] It is not enough, the court explained, to show that a government procedure for compensation by itself is unjust; the complaining party must actually go through the process and then demonstrate that it emerged unjustly compensated.[596] For ILECs, that means completing state arbitrations first.[597] The

---

[592] 508 U.S. 307, 313–320 (1993).

[593] *See* 47 U.S.C. §543(a)(2).

[594] *See* §§3.11.3 (cases addressing constitutional limitations on rate-of-return regulation), 13.4.1 (history of the 1978 Pole Attachments Act).

[595] *See* Iowa Utils. Bd. v. FCC, 120 F.3d at 818.

[596] *See id.*

[597] *See id.* The court further noted that any such takings challenge could be presented to a federal district court under the review provisions of section 252(e)(6). *See id.*

court did, however, note that it was "skeptical that the remaining FCC unbundling rules will effect an actual taking."[598] No takings issues were appealed to the Supreme Court.

Even disregarding the ripeness obstacle, the line of authority usually associated with *FPC v. Hope Natural Gas Co.*, 320 U.S. 591 (1944), no doubt poses a hurdle. Under this line of authority, "it is not theory but the impact of the rate order which counts. If the total effect of the rate order cannot be said to be unreasonable, judicial inquiry . . . is at an end. The fact that the method employed to reach that result may contain infirmities is not then important."[599] Thus, for example, the exclusion of a particular investment from a utility's rate base cannot effect a taking if regulators could constitutionally have reached the same result by including the investment in the rate base, but setting a lower rate of return.[600] The FCC has argued that a refusal to allow recovery of costs is therefore without constitutional significance so long as a carrier still achieves an overall return that is above a confiscatory level.[601]

Applying the "end result" principle in this way seems somewhat to stretch the holding of *Hope* and similar authorities. The

[598] *See id.* Several parties brought a second takings claim to the Eighth Circuit, arguing that the FCC's unbundling rules would constitute an unconstitutional taking of intellectual property—from third-party vendors who supply network hardware and software to ILECs. *See id.* at 817. The court ruled that the parties lacked standing to raise such claims, *see id.* at 817–818, and again noted that it was "skeptical of the merits of such claims," *id.* at 817.

[599] FPC v. Hope Natural Gas Co., 320 U.S. at 602.

[600] *See* Duquesne Light Co. v. Barasch, 488 U.S. 312 (1989); *see also id.* at 315 ("it has not been shown that the rate orders . . . fail to give a reasonable rate of return on equity"); Jersey Central Power & Light Co. v. FERC, 810 F.2d 1168, 1181 (D.C. Cir. 1987) (en banc) ("absent the sort of deep financial hardship described in *Hope* there is no taking").

[601] This is the argument the FCC made in its *Local Competition Order:* "*Hope Natural Gas* requires only that the end result of our overall regulatory framework provides LECs a reasonable opportunity to recover a return on their investment. In other words, incumbent LECs' overall rates must be considered, including the revenues for other services under our jurisdiction. . . . However, we may not consider incumbent LECs' revenue derived from services not under our jurisdiction. Smith v. Ill. Bell, 282 U.S. 133 (1930)." *See Local Competition Order,* 11 F.C.C. Rec. at 15,871 ¶737 & n.1756; *see also* Illinois Bell Tel. Co. v. FCC, 988 F.2d 1254, 1263–1264 (D.C. Cir. 1993); J. Gregory & D. F. Spulber, Deregulatory Takings and the Regulatory Contract (1997).

basic idea behind *Hope* and *Duquesne* was that courts should not pass on individual components of a rate-setting order so long as the overall impact of the order is nonconfiscatory.[602] That idea should not imply that rate regulators are permitted to set a rate for an individual service at a level that is admittedly confiscatory so long as revenue from *other* services within the agency's jurisdiction allows the utility to achieve an overall return on investment that is not unfair.[603]

§2.7 Conclusion

We conclude where this chapter began, with the basic economics of local phone service. The basic loop and dial tone are provided, to residential subscribers at least, at a rate well below cost. Incumbent local phone companies make up the difference on service to business users, local toll, access charges, and vertical services.

The immediate effect of this regulation is to channel close to 100 percent of new competition and new investment into only about 30 percent of the total market. Competitors naturally direct all their competitive efforts toward the high end of the market. Any company with money to invest in new networks will build out to business customers who currently pay $30 a month for metered service before it builds out to residential customers who currently pay a flat-rate $17 for unmetered service. If they enter residential markets at all, reselling Bell service is by far the cheapest way to enter. No economically rational entrant will build anything that it can buy from others more cheaply, or indeed below cost. Facilities-based competition by new entrants, and new investment by incumbents, will occur only when interconnection prices are properly aligned with underlying costs.

[602] *See Duquesne,* 488 U.S. at 314 ("Errors to the detriment of one party may well be canceled out by countervailing errors or allowances in another part of the rate proceeding. The Constitution protects the utility from the net effect of the rate order on its property.").

[603] *See* Brooks-Scanlon Co. v. Railroad Commn., 251 U.S. 396, 399 (1920) ("a carrier cannot be compelled to carry on even a branch of business at a loss, much less the whole business of carriage").

And what incentives are there to deploy new technology? Even when provided by the incumbent itself, new high-bandwidth technology puts traditional sources of profit in jeopardy. High-speed digital lines will be used mostly for Internet traffic, which generates no access charges, even when used for fax or Internet telephony.[604] And almost every increase in bandwidth will reengage a snake's nest of old regulatory pricing debates. An integrated services digital network (ISDN), for example, involves one line that, depending on the particular flavor, contains 3 or 24 digital channels. It took the FCC more than two years to decide whether ISDN lines should therefore be subject to 1, not 3 or 24, subscriber line charges.[605]

That was in 1995. In 1997, the Commission changed course: it ordered one, newly calculated, ISDN-only SLC to be charged per ISDN line, but changed the amount.[606] The SLC helps to pay for interstate uses of local networks. Meanwhile, many of those who use local phone networks most heavily to reach the Internet pay no access charges at all.[607] The FCC recognized in 1987 that this distinction makes no sense—interstate data callers use precisely the same local access lines as interstate voice callers, and indeed, on a per-customer basis, use them much

---

[604] *See Access Charge Reform Order,* 12 F.C.C. Rec. at 16,131–16,132 ¶341.

[605] The Common Carrier Bureau (CCB) and the Commission reached opposite conclusions. *See* Common Carrier Bureau Will Not Enforce Current Rules on Application of Subscriber Line Charges to ISDN Service, Action, 10 F.C.C. Rec. 13,473 (1995), *rev'g* NYNEX Telephone Companies, Revisions to Tariff FCC No. 1, Transmittal No. 116, Memorandum Opinion and Order, 7 F.C.C. Rec. 7938 (CCB 1992), *aff'd on recons.,* 10 F.C.C. Rec. 2247 (1995).

[606] *See Access Charge Reform Order,* 12 F.C.C. Rec. at 16,032 ¶116. The FCC reserved judgment on the application of SLCs to non-ISDN high-bandwidth technologies that, like ISDN, create more than one communications channel per wire. ADSL, for example, contains three major channels: a high-speed (6 Mbps) downstream channel, a medium-speed (640 kbps) upstream channel, and a voice channel. But the upstream and downstream channels can each be divided into as many slower channels as the user desires. *See* ADSL Forum, ADSL Tutorial: Twisted Pair Access to the Information Superhighway <http://www.adsl.com/adsl_tutorial.html>. Judging from the FCC's treatment of ISDN, ADSL lines will likely be assessed a unique SLC, adjusted to reflect any additional costs to the LEC. *See Access Charge Reform Order,* 12 F.C.C. Rec. at 16,032 ¶116, 16,035–16,036 ¶126.

[607] *See Access Charge Reform Order,* 12 F.C.C. Rec. at 16,131–16,132 ¶341; *Part 69 Order,* 3 F.C.C. Rec. at 2631.

more heavily.[608] But the disparate treatment remains in place because, in the ten years since, nobody has been able to muster the political consensus needed to correct it.[609]

Interconnection and unbundling mandates complicate the investment incentives further still. The general formula for competition in the 1996 Act will probably force incumbents to unbundle (at prices based on incremental cost) the equipment used to provide these new lines and to offer the complete service for resale at sharp discounts to all comers. If local phone companies introduce these services successfully, competitors will be able to buy them piece by piece, at sharp discounts, and capture the profits. For just the same reason, competitors have little incentive to deploy the technology themselves. Why would they, when the FCC has directed that they may buy the existing network below cost and successful new technologies at cost[610]—with no need to face the risk of losing unsuccessful investments? With rules like that, it is, of course, doubtful that in the long run there will be many successful new technologies to unbundle.[611]

Over the long term, mandatory unbundling, like mandatory bundling, will be economically arbitrary, no less so when conducted for ostensibly procompetitive purposes. Much of it will be economically wasteful. Market forces ordinarily decide just how many outlets a supermarket sets up; regulators trying to prescribe the equivalent for a phone company are almost certain to

---

[608] *See Amendments of Part 69,* 2 F.C.C. Rec. at 4305.

[609] *See* Immediate Hill Backlash, FCC Considers Linking ESP Access Charges to ONA, Comm. Daily, Nov. 17, 1988, at 1 ("[a] cyclone of protest from Congress, NTIA and hundreds of computer-service users" killed FCC initiative). In its *Access Charge Reform Order,* the FCC succeeded in raising only the SLC on second residential phone lines, the lines most often used for data access. *See Access Charge Reform Order,* 12 F.C.C. Rec. at 16,014 ¶78, 16,133 ¶344.

[610] *See Local Competition Order,* 11 F.C.C. Rec. at 15,642 ¶282 (1996).

[611] The CEO of AT&T—which, though usually clamoring for more extensive unbundling, recently found itself on the receiving end of possible unbundling obligations in connection with its newly purchased cable operations—put it this way: "No company will invest billions of dollars to become a facilities-based broadband services provider if competitors who have not invested a penny of capital, nor taken an ounce of risk, can come along and get a free ride on the investments and risks of others." AT&T Scoffs at Possible Common Carrier Status, Telecommunications Reports, Nov. 9, 1998, at 23.

settle on too few or too many. Traditional antitrust law requires unbundling only to the extent that the provider can control price and output of two plainly discrete products. But in their new rush to promote the competition they not long ago suppressed, regulators have a more ambitious agenda. The unbundling of local phone company networks has become an article of regulatory faith. How much gets unbundled, and at what pace, will depend relatively little on economic logic. It will depend largely on effective advocacy and lobbying in regulatory and political circles. It will, in short, be as bad as Commission prescription ever is.

The one saving grace is that today's regulatory initiatives, inept though they inevitably must be, may accelerate the correction of yesterday's. Sometimes two wrongs do make a right, or at the very least a lesser wrong, and that may well be the case here. Local networks would never have been sewn up so tightly, with so few points of interconnection, had not regulatory policies of the past demanded one-stop shopping, one-size-for-all service, and even averaged prices for all. The business arrangements that were created as a result disserved consumers yesterday, and impede the rapid transition to competition today. What Hush-a-Phone commissions helped cement together yesterday, Bust-a-Monopoly commissions must now help take apart.

In sum, the new unbundling and price regulation are turning out to be quite as arbitrary as the old bundling and price regulation. It is far from clear that the new price-regulating mandates, ostensibly intended to promote competition, are much more efficient, overall, than the old price-regulating mandates intended to promote universal service. Comparing the FCC of the 1990s to the FCC of the 1950s brings to mind Mae West's approach to hard choices: "Between two evils, I always pick the one I never tried before."

3

The Powers
of the FCC*

§3.1 Introduction

Federal regulation of the telecommunications industry is
entrusted primarily to the Federal Communications Commission
(FCC), an entity created by the Federal Communications Act of
1934.[1] The 1934 Act reflected the New Deal, proregulatory ori-
entation of the period in which it was passed. It also, however,
attempted to impose a strict separation between interstate and
intrastate matters, restricting the new FCC to the former and
leaving the latter to the discretion of state regulatory authorities.
Since interstate services were extremely limited in 1934, the
influence and authority of the FCC were likewise limited. Most
of telephony was local telephony, regulated by the states pursuant to a grant of exclusive franchises. Many of the most interesting developments in telecommunications law this century

*This chapter was co-authored by Evan T. Leo: Associate, Kellogg, Huber,
Hansen, Todd & Evans; University of California at Los Angeles (B.A., 1990);
The George Washington University Law Center (J.D., with honors, 1993).
 [1] 47 U.S.C. §151 (1998).

have focused on the efforts of the FCC to increase its own importance, in keeping with and even outstripping the increasing importance of interstate markets.

In the Telecommunications Act of 1996, Congress wrought a fundamental change in the existing regulatory paradigm. The 1996 Act, unlike its New Deal counterpart, is decidedly deregulatory in tone. But it is strikingly regulatory in effect. For example, the 1996 Act eliminates exclusive state franchises and sweeps away most other existing barriers to competition. At the same time, however, the Act actively encourages and assists such competition by imposing, in sections 251 and 252, an unprecedented array of obligations on local exchange carriers to interconnect with new entrants, to provide retail services for sale at wholesale rates, and to provide access to "unbundled network elements," piece-parts of the incumbents' network that new entrants can use to provide service. The 1996 Act has thus significantly increased the sheer amount of regulation as a means of managing the transition from a regime of franchised monopoly to one of open competition.

The full extent of these new obligations is described in Chapter 5. For purposes of this chapter, two points are of interest. First, the 1996 Act supplements, rather than supplants, the 1934 Act. Thus, the basic regulatory structures of the 1934 Act remain in place, and superimposed on those are the additional regulatory requirements of the new Act. All the pre-1996 law remains largely intact and is still important.

Second, in order to implement these new regulatory requirements, the 1996 Act has substantially increased regulatory authority—but whose regulatory authority? The FCC's or the states'? The FCC believes that the 1996 Act has fundamentally changed the balance of power between state and federal regulators. According to the Commission, the "1996 Act moves beyond the distinction between interstate and intrastate matters that was established in the 1934 Act"[2] and grants the FCC authority

---

[2] Implementation of the Local Competition Provisions in the Telecommunications Act of 1996, First Report and Order, 11 F.C.C. Rec. 15,499, 15,513 ¶24 (1996) (hereinafter *Local Competition Order*), *modified on recons.* 11 F.C.C.

"without limitation" to regulate local telephone service.[3] As the FCC's then Chairman declared in plainer terms, the 1996 Act threw the states' traditional intrastate authority into "the trash can of history."[4]

Not surprisingly, the states have taken a different view, finding in the 1996 Act a large area of still exclusive state regulatory authority and a much more limited role for the FCC in opening local markets to competition. After winning some initial battles in the courts, however, the states have lost the war. According to the Supreme Court, not only has the Maginot line between intrastate and interstate matters been bypassed; it has been obliterated by the 1996 Act. The state commissions, on matters covered by the 1996 Act, are now a subject people, bound to do the bidding of the FCC and left only with whatever discretion the FCC decides to afford them.

This chapter begins by summarizing the regulatory environment until 1934, including the period from 1910 through 1934, during which the industry was under the oversight of the Interstate Commerce Commission. We then discuss the jurisdiction of the FCC, starting with the 1934 Act, and the critical series of preemption cases decided under that Act, as well as the new preemption authority expressly granted to the FCC by the 1996 Act. Next, we describe the basic features of common carrier regulation under the 1934 Act, as amended by the 1996 Act, including the obligations of common carriers, FCC control over ratemaking, industry oversight, and the review and enforcement of FCC decisions. We close by discussing the 1996 Act's express grant of forbearance authority to the FCC: herein lies the true deregulatory potential of the 1996 Act. As markets become truly competitive, the FCC has the power to forbear from regulating and even to suspend the operation of statutory provisions currently governing those markets. The most important regulatory

---

Rec. 13,042 (1996), *vacated in part,* Iowa Utils. Bd. v. FCC, 120 F.3d 753 (8th Cir. 1997), *rev'd sub nom.* AT&T v. Iowa Utils. Bd., 119 S. Ct. 721 (1999).

[3] *Local Competition Order,* 11 F.C.C. Rec. at 15,559–15,560 ¶115.

[4] Hundt Looks Toward "Radical" Overhaul of Regulatory Regimes, Major Business Moves, Telecommunications Report, July 15, 1996, at 6.

authority granted to the FCC by the 1996 Act is the authority not to regulate.

§3.2 Regulation Prior to 1934

§3.2.1   1877–1910

Commercial telephone service in the United States began in 1877. At first, the Bell Telephone Company[5] held the essential patents and hence enjoyed a complete monopoly.[6] Yet during this period, Bell did not extend service to many rural or residential areas; after 15 years of Bell monopoly, only 300,000 telephones—or 1 telephone for every 240 people—had been installed.[7]

By 1894, however, the essential Bell patents had either expired or been narrowly construed by the courts. These changed circumstances encouraged thousands of independent telephone companies to rush into the market. A phone census in 1907 found over six million telephones in use, nearly as many of them owned by the "independents" as by Bell. Average rates for telephone service had been halved, and Bell's average return on investment had fallen by over 80 percent.[8]

---

[5] The Bell Telephone Company was renamed the American Bell Telephone Company in 1880 and was incorporated as the American Telephone & Telegraph Company (AT&T) in 1900. We will, however, use "the Bell System" or simply "Bell" to refer to the company prior to divestiture in 1984. "AT&T" will refer to the post-divestiture company.

[6] The validity of these patents was upheld by the Supreme Court in the Telephone Cases, 126 U.S. 1 (1888).

[7] See, e.g., Hearings on H.R. 8301 Before the House Committee on Interstate and Foreign Commerce, 73d Cong., 2d Sess. 259 (1934) (hereinafter House Hearings) (statement of Dr. David Friday), reprinted in A Legislative History of the Communications Act of 1934, at 259 (M. D. Paglin ed., 1989); W. G. Lavey, The Public Policies that Changed the Telephone Industries into Regulated Monopolies: Lessons from Around 1915, 39 Fed. Comm. L.J. 171, 177 (1987) (historical background on telephone industry and AT&T).

[8] See House Hearings at 260 (statement of Dr. David Friday); Lavey, The Public Policies that Changed the Telephone Industries into Regulated Monopolies at 177–178.

Many remote (and unprofitable) areas remained unserved, however, and the quality of service was generally low. In places where phone companies competed head to head, there seemed to be unnecessary duplication and confusion.[9] Moreover, Bell aggressively sought to restore its monopoly position. It refused to sell equipment or to provide interconnection to independents even in areas it did not serve, and it acquired many of the independents that provided competing long-distance service.[10]

For quite different reasons, many players in the industry came to favor federal regulation. The independents wanted the federal government to stop Bell's expansion and require Bell to provide interconnection. State and local governments hoped to end "inefficient competition" and expand service. Bell itself wanted to consolidate its dominant position and legitimize a monopoly—its own.[11] Bell's Chairman, Theodore Vail, spoke publicly in favor of regulation, sounding a theme ("cream skimming") that would become a Bell System rallying cry for the next half century. Despite its own record of having sought out the most profitable routes, Bell now resolved "to serve the whole community" and embraced regulation to avoid "aggressive competition covering only that part that was profitable. If there is to

[9]*See* L. Pressler & K. V. Schieffer, A Proposal for Universal Telecommunications Service, 40 Fed. Comm. L.J. 351, 356 (1988); Lavey, The Public Policies that Changed the Telephone Industries into Regulated Monopolies at 177–178. For an alternative perspective, see R. Gabel, The Early Competitive Era in Telephone Communication, 1893–1920, 34 Law & Contemp. Probs. 340 (1969).

[10]*See* G. O. Robinson, The Federal Communications Act: An Essay on Origins and Regulatory Purpose, *reprinted in* A Legislative History of the Communications Act of 1934, at 7 (M. D. Paglin ed., 1989). *See also* D. Burch, Common Carrier Communications by Wire and Radio: A Retrospective, 37 Fed. Comm. L.J. 85, 87 (1985); Lavey, The Public Policies that Changed the Telephone Industries into Regulated Monopolies at 179. Bell was not alone in its refusal to provide interconnection to other carriers. In fact, most telephone companies refused to connect to other systems; a much noted feature of telephone service was how many of the people who owned telephones could not talk to each other.

[11]*See* R. McKenna, Preemption Under the Communications Act, 37 Fed. Comm. L.J. 1, 8 (1985); Pressler & Schieffer, A Proposal for Universal Telecommunications Services at 356; Robinson, The Federal Communications Act at 6–7.

be state control and regulation," Vail argued, "there should also be state protection."[12]

§3.2.2   1910–1934

Congress responded with the Mann-Elkins Act of 1910, which brought interstate telecommunications within the regulatory jurisdiction of the Interstate Commerce Commission (ICC).[13] The Act defined telcos as "common carriers" and so obligated them "to provide service on request at just and reasonable rates, without unjust discrimination or undue preference."[14] The ICC could set aside "unjust or unreasonable" carrier rates. But the tariff filing provisions of the Interstate Commerce Act were never extended to communications carriers, and this curious omission crippled the ICC's ability to regulate.[15] And though the Interstate Commerce Act empowered the ICC to direct railroads to interconnect with each other, the Commission was granted no express authority of that type with regard to telcos.

[12] As a contemporary commentator has noted, "[R]egulation is a two-sided coin; on one side lies the aspect of public protection—profit limitations, the obligation to provide service at nondiscriminatory rates, and so forth. The other side of the coin bears the aspect of utility protection—including bars to competitive entry, exclusive franchise, and the right of eminent domain. With an insight that was to serve Bell corporate interests well, Vail anticipated the limited inroads that public regulation would make in obtaining the first series of objectives and the extensive benefits conferred by the second." Gabel, The Early Competitive Era in Telephone Communication at 356 (statement of Theodore Vail, Bell Chairman, *quoted in* G. W. Brock, The Telecommunications Industry: The Dynamics of Market Structure 158–159 (1981)).

[13] Mann-Elkins Act of 1910, ch. 309, 36 Stat. 539 (1910).

[14] Essential Communications v. AT&T, 610 F.2d 1114, 1118 (3d Cir. 1979) (citing Mann-Elkins Act of 1910, ch. 309, §§7, 12, 36 Stat. 539).

[15] *See* K. A. Cox & W. J. Byrnes, The Common Carrier Provisions—A Product of Evolutionary Development, *reprinted in* A Legislative History of the Communications Act of 1934, at 28 n.26 (M. D. Paglin ed., 1989). The ICC recommended in its 1911 annual report to Congress that a filing requirement be added, but legislative action was not taken on this proposal until the 1934 Act.

The ICC aggressively oversaw telephony nonetheless. It investigated Bell's monopolistic practices and, together with the Justice Department, extracted from Bell the Kingsbury Commitment—a commitment through which Bell agreed to provide interconnection to the independents and to refrain from further acquisitions.[16] The ICC also established a uniform system of accounting for the industry.[17]

In the 24 years of its regulatory oversight, however, the ICC presided over only four telco rate proceedings.[18] It left rates entirely to the carriers, intervening only when a carrier discriminated among customers.[19] And the Commission never prescribed uniform depreciation rates, though directed by statute in 1920 to do so "as soon as practicable."[20] In 1921, the Commission was authorized to approve telco consolidations;[21] thereafter it approved almost all of them.[22] For the most part, the Commission was preoccupied with railroad regulation;[23] in addition to lacking

---

[16] *See* §4.4.1; *see also* Robinson, The Federal Communications Act at 8.

[17] *See* Northwestern Bell Tel. Co. v. Railway Commn., 297 U.S. 471, 477 (1936).

[18] *See* Robinson, The Federal Communications Act at 7; Cox & Byrnes, The Common Carrier Provisions at 29 n.34.

[19] *See Essential Communications,* 610 F.2d at 1119.

[20] *See Northwestern Bell Tel.,* 297 U.S. at 477 (quoting Transportation Act of 1920).

[21] Willis-Graham Act of 1921, ch. 20, 42 Stat. 27 (1921). This Act overturned the Kingsbury Commitment and permitted consolidations subject to ICC approval, conferring antitrust immunity on those approved.

[22] *See* Robinson, The Federal Communications Act at 8 ("[a]part from presiding over consolidation of the telephone industry (and the growth of AT&T as the centerpiece of the industry) . . . the ICC contributed very little to the development of regulatory policy in this field"); *see also* 77 Cong. Rec. 8822 (1934) (remarks of Sen. Dill) ("the Interstate Commerce Commission has given what might be called cursory attention to the regulation of telephone and telegraph matters, but in practical operation the regulation of the telephone and telegraph companies has been really nothing effective").

[23] *See* Cox & Byrnes, The Common Carrier Provisions at 25–26; 77 Cong. Rec. 4139 (1934) (remarks of Sen. Dill); Study of Communications by an Interdepartmental Committee, *reprinted in* A Legislative History of the Communications Act of 1934, at 101–119 (M. D. Paglin ed., 1989) (*Interdepartmental Committee Report*); 77 Cong. Rec. 10,315 (1934) (remarks of Rep. Rayburn).

broad statutory authority over communications,[24] the ICC never formulated any national plan for the industry.[25]

§3.2.3 The Shreveport Rate Case

Though in many respects it lacked either the will or the authority to regulate telephony effectively, the ICC had, in one critical respect, far more power than the FCC that would succeed it. What the ICC had was sweeping power to preempt inconvenient state regulation. That power had been affirmed by the Supreme Court in 1914, in *The Shreveport Rate Case*.[26]

The case involved railroads, but the principle it established was one of broad federal preeminence. Certain railroads had charged higher rates for shipments from Louisiana to Texas than for shipments of comparable distance wholly within Texas. The *intra*state rate was the highest permitted by Texas regulation; the ICC found, however, that the *inter*state rate was reasonable. The ICC concluded that this differential was discriminatory; the railroads would therefore have to raise their intrastate rates.[27] In the name of nondiscrimination, the ICC claimed the right to set intrastate rates whenever it set interstate rates.[28]

---

[24] *See, e.g.,* H.R. Rep. No. 1850, 73d Cong., 2d Sess. 4 (1934) ("the act never has been perfected to encompass adequate regulation of communications, but has really been an adaptation of railroad regulation to the communications field").

[25] *See Interdepartmental Committee Report* at 101–119.

[26] Houston & Tex. Ry. v. United States, 234 U.S. 342 (1914) (*The Shreveport Rate Case*).

[27] *See id.* at 346–350.

[28] The ICC quickly did just that and thereby all but eliminated the states' regulatory role. *See, e.g.,* Cox & Byrnes, The Common Carrier Provisions at 55; *House Hearings* at 136 (statement of John E. Benton) ("It is common knowledge that under the Interstate Commerce Act the power of the Interstate Commerce Commission has been so extended that State regulation of intrastate railroad rates has become little more than nominal."); Regulation of Interstate and Foreign Communications by Wire or Radio, and for Other Purposes, Hearings on S. 2910 Before the Senate Committee on Interstate Commerce, 73d Cong., 2d Sess. 156 (1934) (hereinafter *Senate Hearings*) (statement of Andrew R. McDonald, First Vice-President of the Executive Committee of the National Association of Railroad and Utilities Commissioners)

The Supreme Court agreed that Congress had the power to prevent discrimination in favor of intrastate shipments: interstate and intrastate rates "are so related that the government of the one involves the control of the other."[29] And Congress, the Court ruled, had indeed delegated its authority to the ICC to do just that by outlawing "any undue or unreasonable preference or advantage" in carrier tariffs.[30]

§3.2.4   Smith v. Illinois Bell Telephone Co.

A second fateful Supreme Court regulatory decision was handed down in 1930. *The Shreveport Rate Case* had affirmed federal power to regulate even intrastate rates. *Smith v. Illinois Bell Telephone Co.*[31] considered quite similar issues from the opposite end and required local regulators and their regulatees to limit their attention to intrastate costs and facilities.

Smith involved a challenge to an order of the Illinois Commerce Commission prescribing rates for telephone service in the city of Chicago. Illinois Bell charged that the rates were confiscatory. As proof, it submitted an accounting study that allocated all of the telco's local plant costs to intrastate service. The lower court accepted this study, after finding that only one-half of 1 percent of calls were interstate and only a tiny fraction of property in Chicago was used in furnishing interstate service. The Supreme Court reversed. According to the Court, the costs of "interstate" plant had to be separated from the costs of "intrastate" plant before state-approved rates could be lined up against the telco's costs. "While the difficulty in making an exact apportionment of the property is apparent, and extreme nicety

---

("In railroad cases, State regulation has become practically a dead letter, due to the Shreveport doctrine. . . .").

[29] *The Shreveport Rate Case*, 234 U.S. at 351. The Court refused to limit Congress's remedial options to lowering the interstate rates: "[o]therwise, it could prevent the injury to interstate commerce only by the sacrifice of its judgment as to interstate rates." *Id.* at 355.

[30] *See id.* at 355–356, 358–359 (citing §3, 24 Stat. 379, 380 (1887)).

[31] 282 U.S. 133 (1930). This case is discussed further in §2.2.1.

is not required . . . it is quite another matter to ignore altogether the actual uses to which the property is put. . . . [U]nless an apportionment is made, the intrastate service to which the exchange property is allocated will bear an undue burden."[32]

It can be argued that *Smith* was consistent with *The Shreveport Rate Case:* the earlier case had broadened the horizons of federal regulation, while the later narrowed the state regulatory inquiry. However, while the earlier ruling rested on the impossibility of separating *intra*state activities from their *inter*state consequences, the later ruling demanded that just such a separation be performed. The two decisions might nonetheless have coexisted comfortably, with federal authority broadening by way of *Shreveport* and state authority shrinking by way of *Smith,* as telephony evolved from primarily an intrastate to primarily an interstate industry. Politics, however, intervened.

§3.2.5   Genesis of the 1934 Act

By the late 1920s, support began to emerge for sweeping regulatory revision, although this time Bell was not among the supporters.[33] Instead, Bell found itself the principal target of the new legislation. State authorities wanted an effective federal counterweight to the Bell System.[34] They also wanted clear limits on that federal authority—specifically a repudiation of *The Shreveport Rate Case*—to solidify their own claims to jurisdiction.[35]

---

[32] *Smith,* 282 U.S. at 150–151.

[33] *See Senate Hearings* at 76 (statement of Walter S. Gifford, President of Bell).

[34] *See id.* at 69 (statement of Paul Walker, Chairman of the Corporation Commission of the state of Oklahoma) ("[t]he telephone problem is so vast that a State or a State commission . . . is practically helpless"); *see also House Hearings* at 71 (statement of Kit F. Clardy, Chairman of the Legislative Committee of the National Association of Railroad and Utilities Commissioners); *Senate Hearings* at 179 (statement of John E. Benton, General Solicitor for the National Association of Railroad and Utilities Commissioners); *House Hearings* at 134–135 (statement of John E. Benton).

[35] *See, e.g.,* Cox & Byrnes, The Common Carrier Provisions at 29–30; McKenna, Preemption Under the Communications Act at 8–9. The ICC had

By 1934, 45 states had established their own regulatory commissions,[36] and 98 percent of telephone calls still did not cross state lines.[37]

The convergence of interests favoring new regulation proved overwhelming. On February 26, 1934, President Roosevelt asked Congress to create a separate federal communications commission.[38] By June 9 of that year, both Houses had passed legislation.[39] The President signed the Federal Communications Act of 1934 into law on June 18.[40]

The Act's objective, as stated in its opening section, was to "make available, so far as possible, to all the people of the United States a rapid, efficient, Nation-wide, and world-wide wire and radio communication service with adequate facilities at reasonable charges."[41] Most of the Act's provisions dealing with telecommunications were drawn directly from the Interstate Commerce Act, though the new Commission was given some new powers to regulate tariffs and services. The Act also contained several clauses expressly limiting federal authority to interstate service.

---

never sought to exercise preemptive power over intrastate telephone rates, but state authorities feared that it someday might. *See, e.g., House Hearings* at 136 (statement of John E. Benton). After the Mann-Elkins Act, section 3 of the Interstate Commerce Act applied fully to telecommunications carriers. *See House Hearings* at 135–136 (statement of John E. Benton) ("The Interstate Commerce Commission has the same power now to override State regulation in the telephone field as it has in the railroad field. . . .").

[36] *See, e.g., Senate Hearings* at 138–139 (statement of F. B. MacKinnon, President of United States Independent Telephone Association). Most of the state commissioners pursued a policy of "universal service," whereby the telecommunications industry was required or encouraged to extend service to unprofitable areas and permitted to make up the loss by increasing rates in other areas. *See* Pressler & Schieffer, A Proposal for Universal Telecommunications Services at 357.

[37] *See, e.g., Senate Hearings* at 96 (statement of Sen. Dill); E. Noam, Federal and State Roles in Telecommunications: The Effects of Deregulation, 36 Vand. L. Rev. 949, 955 (1983).

[38] S. Doc. No. 244, 73d Cong., 2d Sess. (1934).

[39] *See* 78 Cong. Rec. 10,968 (1934) (House); 78 Cong. Rec. 10,912 (1934) (Senate).

[40] *See* 77 Cong. Rec. 12,452 (1934).

[41] Federal Communications Act of 1934, ch. 652, §1, 48 Stat. 1064 (1934) (codified as amended at 47 U.S.C. §151 (1988)). The new Commission was to

The Act is divided into six subchapters.[42] Subchapter I creates and defines the structure and jurisdiction of the FCC.[43] Telephony is covered primarily in subchapters II and IV.[44] This Act would govern telephony for over 60 years, and when Congress passed the Telecommunications Act of 1996, it did so largely as a series of additions to, not replacements of, the 1934 Act.

§3.3   The Jurisdiction of the FCC

The Communications Act of 1934 purports to restrict the FCC to the regulation of "interstate and foreign communication by wire and radio," while denying it any "jurisdiction with respect to . . . intrastate communication service."[45] This has created "a persistent jurisdictional tension,"[46] which has grown rapidly more acute in recent years. Indeed, there exists a fundamental paradox in the belief that a service whose entire purpose is to transcend distance and geographic boundaries can be regulated by dual authority divided along strictly geographic lines.

§3.3.1   FCC Authority

At the outset, the Communications Act describes the FCC's authority in sweeping terms, extending to "all interstate and foreign communication by wire or radio."[47] "Communications" is defined equally broadly, to include "the transmission of writing,

---

regulate radio as well as wire communications and hence replace the Federal Radio Commission established by the Radio Act of 1927, 44 Stat. 1162 (1927).

[42] A seventh subchapter dealing with cable television was added in 1984. 47 U.S.C. §§521 et seq.

[43] 47 U.S.C. §§51–158.

[44] Subchapter III contains special provisions governing radio (*id.* §§301 et seq.), and subchapters V and VI contain other miscellaneous provisions (*id.* §§501–510, 601–613).

[45] 47 U.S.C. §152(a), (b).

[46] Public Util. Commn. of Tex. v. FCC, 886 F.2d 1325, 1329 (D.C. Cir. 1989).

[47] 47 U.S.C. §152(a).

signs, signals, pictures, and sounds of all kinds . . . , *including all instrumentalities, facilities, apparatus, and services* (among other things, the receipt, forwarding, and delivery of communications) *incidental to such transmission.*[48] The Act goes on to cover telephony and radio broadcast in detail, but the Commission's jurisdiction is not limited to any particular technology.[49] The Supreme Court has concluded that new communications technologies fall within the FCC's "ancillary jurisdiction."[50] This reading is supported by what is now codified as section 154(i) of Title 47,[51] which provides that "[t]he Commission may perform any and all acts, make such rules and regulations, and issue such orders, not inconsistent with this chapter, as may be necessary in the execution of its functions."[52] Section 154(i) is a "necessary and proper clause" empowering the Commission to "deal with the unforeseen . . . to the extent necessary to regulate effectively those matters already within the boundaries."[53]

§3.3.2 State Authority

While it grants the FCC expansive powers over interstate communications, the Act also affirms the regulatory prerogatives of the states. Nullifying *The Shreveport Rate Case,*[54] section 152

[48] *Id.* §153(b), (c) (emphasis added).

[49] *See* United States v. Southwestern Cable Co., 392 U.S. 157, 172 (1968) (upholding FCC jurisdiction over cable TV on the ground that the regulatory authority of the FCC is not restricted to "those activities and forms of communication that are specifically described by the Act's other provisions").

[50] *See id.* at 178. *See also* FCC v. Pottsville Broad., 309 U.S. 134, 138 (1940) ("Underlying the whole [Communications Act] is recognition of the rapidly fluctuating factors characteristic of the evolution of broadcasting and of the corresponding requirement that the administrative process possess sufficient flexibility to adjust itself to these factors.").

[51] For clarity, all sections are referred to as they have been codified in Title 47.

[52] 47 U.S.C. §154(i).

[53] North Am. Telecomms. Assn. v. FCC, 772 F.2d 1282, 1292 (7th Cir. 1985).

[54] *See, e.g., House Hearings* at 136 (statement of John E. Benton); *Senate Hearings* at 156 (statement of Andrew R. McDonald). *See* Cox & Byrnes, The Common Carrier Provisions at 57. *See also Senate Hearings* at 179 (colloquy

expressly denies the FCC any jurisdiction over "charges, classifications, practices, services, facilities, or regulations for or in connection with intrastate communication service by wire or radio."[55] As the Supreme Court has concluded, the 1934 Act sought "to divide the world of domestic telephone service neatly into two hemispheres — one comprised of interstate service, over which the FCC would have plenary authority, and the other made up of intrastate service, over which the states would retain exclusive jurisdiction."[56] Leaving aside certain express and relatively recent exceptions concerning obscene or harassing phone calls,[57] radio licensing,[58] and cable,[59] section 152 creates a "rule of statutory construction" limiting the powers granted to the FCC elsewhere in the Act.[60] The sweeping mandate of this section cannot be ignored; the vast majority of calls in 1934 were intrastate, and the 73d Congress undoubtedly believed it was reserving to the states a considerable amount of authority. State regulation of all purely intrastate telephone activity was clearly expected to be exclusive.[61]

---

between Senators Dill and Long to the effect that the Act provided "[p]rotection against the *Shreveport* decision").

[55] 47 U.S.C. §152(b).

[56] Louisiana Pub. Serv. Commn. v. FCC, 476 U.S. 355, 360 (1986) (*Louisiana PSC*). Section 152 also denies the FCC jurisdiction over carriers engaged in interstate communications solely through physical connection with the facilities of a separate carrier except with respect to sections 201–205. *See* 47 U.S.C. §152(b)(2). This provision was intended to ease the regulatory burden on small independent telephone companies. *See* 77 Cong. Rec. 8846 (1934) (remarks of Sen. Clark).

[57] 47 U.S.C. §223.

[58] *Id.* §301.

[59] *Id.* §§521 et seq.

[60] *Louisiana PSC*, 476 U.S. at 376–377 n.5.

[61] Section 221(b) expands this reservation of authority to the states to include regulation of exchange service where "a portion of such exchange service constitutes interstate or foreign communication." 47 U.S.C. §221(b). "Although the language of the section is sweeping," its legislative history indicates that it "was merely intended to preserve state regulation of local exchanges that happened to overlap state lines." NARUC v. FCC, 746 F.2d 1492, 1500 (D.C. Cir. 1984) (citation and internal quotations omitted); NCUC v. FCC, 552 F.2d 1036, 1045 (4th Cir. 1977) (*NCUC II*), cert. denied, 434 U.S. 874 (1977); NCUC v. FCC, 537 F.2d 787, 795 (4th Cir. 1976) (*NCUC I*), cert. denied,

§3.3.3 Dividing the Indivisible

The fundamental problem with this verbally neat division of the regulatory turf is that nothing in telephony is purely intrastate, nor would many telephone users wish it to be. The same telephones and most of the same wires and switches are used for both intrastate and interstate activity. "[V]irtually all telephone plant that is used to provide intrastate service," the Supreme Court has recognized, "is also used to provide interstate service, and thus is conceivably within the jurisdiction of both state and federal authorities."[62] All interstate calls begin in one state and end in another state; virtually all intrastate "services" are therefore "incidental" to interstate communications.

Normally, a federal agency may preempt state regulation that obstructs accomplishment of its congressionally prescribed mission.[63] That was the rationale of *The Shreveport Rate Case*, which effectively permitted the ICC to set intrastate railroad rates. But in direct reaction to *Shreveport* and in brazen defiance of the realities of telephony, Congress purported to preserve an area of exclusive state jurisdiction in the Communications Act.

Congress anticipated this difficulty up to a point by authorizing the FCC to devise a procedure for separating a carrier's property into intrastate and interstate uses.[64] Pursuant to section

---

429 U.S. 1027 (1976); Puerto Rico Tel. Co. v. FCC, 553 F.2d 694, 698–699 (1st Cir. 1977); New York Tel. Co. v. FCC, 631 F.2d 1059, 1064–1065 (2d Cir. 1980); Computer and Communications Indus. Assn. v. FCC, 693 F.2d 198, 217 (D.C. Cir. 1982) (CCIA) (rejecting earlier dicta providing a more expansive interpretation in Kitchen v. FCC, 464 F.2d 801 (D.C. Cir. 1972)). *See also* S. Rep. No. 781, at 5 ("Paragraph (b) [of Section 221] . . . will enable [State] commissions, where authorized to do so, to regulate services in metropolitan areas overlapping State lines."); H.R. Rep. No. 1850, at 7 (same); Cox & Byrnes, The Common Carrier Provisions at 52–53.

[62] *Louisiana PSC,* 476 U.S. at 360.

[63] *See, e.g.,* City of New York v. FCC, 486 U.S. 57, 63 (1988); Capital Cities Cable, Inc. v. Crisp, 467 U.S. 691, 694 (1984); Fidelity Fed. Sav. & Loan Assn. v. de la Cuesta, 458 U.S. 141, 152 (1982); Hines v. Davidowitz, 312 U.S. 52, 70 (1941).

[64] 47 U.S.C. §221(c). The "separations" process derives from the Supreme Court's Smith decision, which was decided four years before the passage of the Act. Smith, 282 U.S. at 146–148. *See* §2.2.2.

221(c), the FCC has promulgated a complex set of rules governing jurisdictional separations.[65] The "separations" process nevertheless remains essentially arbitrary. Although books of account can be carved up in some way between state and federal authorities, many other subjects of regulation cannot be divided at all. If a phone company provides a telephone, it is possible, after some suitably solemn procedure, to declare that one-quarter of the cost and price of the telephone belongs under federal authority and three-quarters under the state's authority. But either customers have the right to buy their telephones from independent suppliers or they do not; a regulation granting the right to buy one-quarter of a telephone from an independent supplier would be worthless.

The Act sheds no useful light on regulatory jurisdiction over such matters. Sections 220 and 410 do appear to acknowledge the problem, but offer at best precatory measures for federal-state consultation, seemingly in the hope that the FCC and state regulators will find ways to agree on regulatory policy, thereby mooting any jurisdictional dilemma. Section 220, for example, governs regulation of depreciation and accounting.[66] The first seven subsections—which permit the FCC to classify property and prescribe depreciation charges—were based on the Interstate Commerce Act.[67] The next three subsections were inserted

---

[65] These are codified at 47 C.F.R. §36 (1997). In 1971, section 410(c) was added to require submission of any additional proposed separations rules to a Joint Federal-State Board.

[66] In 1934, some states argued that depreciation rates should be left entirely to state authority. *See Senate Hearings* at 181–182 (statement of John E. Benton, General Solicitor for the National Association of Railroad and Utilities Commissioners). The House responded by reserving to the states the power to set depreciation rates on property devoted to intrastate service. *See* 78 Cong. Rec. 10,987 (1934). Bell, however, objected to this proposal on the ground that multiple rates of depreciation would require it to maintain multiple sets of books. *See House Hearings* at 190–192 (statement of Walter S. Gifford, President of Bell). In the end, the drafters of the legislation simply fudged the issue without resolving it.

[67] *See* Cox & Byrnes, The Common Carrier Provisions at 51. As noted above, the ICC had prescribed a system of accounting for the telecommunications industry and had been instructed, but failed, to do the same with respect to depreciation.

at the behest of the states, ostensibly to safeguard their own authority over depreciation rates.[68] According to subsection (h), the FCC *may* defer to state-prescribed depreciation rates and accounting practices; nothing, however, compels it to do so, and there is no guidance at all as to whose depreciation rates and accounting methods should be used for property that cannot be separated jurisdictionally.[69] Other subsections provide no more guidance. Subsection (i) merely requires the FCC to notify and consult with state commissions before promulgating accounting and depreciation regulations. Subsection (j) requires the FCC to report to Congress its views about how further to harmonize federal-state jurisdiction over accounting and depreciation.[70]

Section 410 is likewise all procedure and no substance. It provides for joint state-federal boards to resolve regulatory issues of joint concern. But although the Act mandates that "any proceeding regarding the jurisdictional separation of common carrier property and expenses between interstate and intrastate operations" be referred to such a board, the state members of

---

[68] *See, e.g., Senate Hearings* at 180–182 (statement of John E. Benton); *see also* Louisiana PSC, 476 U.S. at 378–379 n.6.

[69] Subsection (h) provides, in pertinent part, that the "Commission may classify carriers . . . and may, if it deems such action consistent with the public interest, except the carriers of any particular class or classes in any State from any of the requirements under this section in cases where such carriers are subject to State commission regulation with respect to matters to which this section relates." 47 U.S.C. §220(h). It has been argued that section 220 gives the FCC the power to regulate depreciation and accounting with respect to *all* property, including that devoted to intrastate use, but that subsection (h) permits the FCC to defer to state regulation. The Supreme Court, however, rejected this contention, pointing to the background rule of construction in section 152 that the FCC has no power to regulate in any way property devoted to intrastate use. *See Louisiana PSC*, 476 U.S. at 376–378.

[70] At one point in the legislative process, the states persuaded the House to include in subsection (j) an express guarantee of each state's authority to prescribe depreciation rates for intrastate plant. *See Louisiana PSC*, 476 U.S. at 378 n.6. The Conference Committee, however, rejected this provision after Bell opposed it. *See also Senate Hearings* at 95–97 (statement of Walter S. Gifford, President of Bell). The Supreme Court has rejected the proposition that the failure to adopt the states' version evidences an intent to preempt all state regulation of depreciation, reasoning that it at best displays a desire not to resolve the jurisdictional issue. *See* Louisiana PSC, 476 U.S. at 378–379 n.6.

the Joint Board have no voting power.[71] Thus, the ultimate decision is entirely within the discretion of the FCC. Furthermore,
with respect to other regulatory issues of joint concern, the FCC
has complete discretion whether to submit them to a board and
is not bound in any way by the board's decision.[72] Like section
220, section 410 relies entirely upon the FCC's forbearance to
settle the jurisdictional division.

§3.3.4 Jurisdiction Under the 1996 Act

The 1996 Act has greatly complicated the issue of where federal jurisdiction ends and state jurisdiction begins. In sections
251 and 252 of the Act—which require incumbent local telephone companies to interconnect with and assist new entrants—
the Act directly controls intrastate issues that were once the
exclusive province of the states. To that extent, the Act federal-
izes these local interconnection issues. But the respective roles of
the state and federal agencies in implementing these market-
opening provisions have been a matter of considerable dispute.

As an initial matter, it is clear that the members of the 104th
Congress did not want either state or federal regulators in the
picture. To introduce competition while at the same time preserving the Act's stated goal of "reduc[ing] regulation,"[73] the
104th Congress crafted a system that relied primarily on private
negotiations between incumbent LECs and new competitors.
Thus, section 251 imposes on incumbent LECs and new entrants
"[t]he duty to negotiate in good faith in accordance with section
252 . . . the particular terms and conditions of agreements to fulfill the duties" described above.[74] Section 252 in turn provides
that an incumbent LEC "may negotiate and enter into a binding
agreement" with a new entrant "without regard" to any of the
pricing, technical, and quality standards set out in the Act.[75]

---

[71] *See* 47 U.S.C. §410(c).
[72] *Id.* §410(a).
[73] Telecommunications Act of 1996, 110 Stat. 56 (1996).
[74] 47 U.S.C. §251(c)(1).
[75] *Id.* §252(a)(1).

As a backstop to its primary reliance on privately negotiated agreements, however, Congress enlisted the aid of state public utility commissions to ensure that local competition was implemented fairly and with due regard to the local conditions and the particular historical circumstances of local regulation under the prior regime. Under section 252, either party to a negotiation may ask the state commission to mediate.[76] And if the parties are unable to agree on all issues within 135 days after the competitor's initial request for negotiation, either party may petition the state commission to arbitrate any "open issues."[77] In particular, in the absence of a negotiated agreement, the Act provides that "a State commission shall . . . establish any rates for interconnection, services, or network elements" in accordance with pricing standards spelled out in the statute.[78] In addition to providing a mechanism to resolve disputes, this backstop ensures that incumbents have an incentive to negotiate reasonable agreements to avoid the risk of an adverse result before state arbitrators.

Once a state commission has finally approved an arbitrated agreement, any aggrieved party may bring an action in federal district court to determine whether the decision "meets the requirements of section 251 . . . and [section 252]."[79]

According to the states, in contrast to the broad reliance placed on private negotiations backed up by state-supervised arbitrations, Congress gave the FCC only a limited, narrowly circumscribed role in implementing the Act's local competition provisions. For example, Congress gave the FCC "exclusive jurisdiction" over the administration of "telecommunications numbering," including the responsibility to make numbers available "on an equitable basis."[80] It also gave the FCC a role in defining an LEC's duty to provide "number portability,"[81] in determining what network elements should be unbundled,[82] in prescribing

---

[76] *Id.* §252(a)(2).
[77] *Id.* §252(b)(1).
[78] *Id.* §252(c)(2), (d).
[79] *Id.* §252(e)(6).
[80] *Id.* §251(e)(1).
[81] *Id.* §251(b)(2).
[82] *Id.* §251(d)(2).

permissible resale restrictions,[83] and in providing for the treatment of comparable carriers as "incumbents."[84] The states contend that aside from these discrete, enumerated tasks—and others described below—Congress scrupulously avoided authorizing the FCC to intrude on the states' traditional exclusive jurisdiction to oversee intrastate telephone service.

Not surprisingly, the FCC saw a quite different picture. It has interpreted sections 251 and 252 of the 1996 Act as a major shift in the balance of state and federal jurisdiction, asserting that with the 1996 Act "Congress created a regulatory system that differs significantly from the dual regulatory system it established in the 1934 Act. That Act generally gave jurisdiction over interstate matters to the FCC and over intrastate matters to the states. The 1996 Act alters this framework, and expands the applicability of both national rules to historically intrastate issues, and state rules to historically interstate issues."[85] The Commission took section 251(d)(1)'s directive to "establish regulations to implement the requirements of this section" as a charge of authority from Congress to establish national regulations for all aspects of interconnection.

The Commission's decision to exercise its authority in this fashion was based on a number of different concerns. The Commission feared that some state commissions would not deregulate sufficiently and instead would continue to protect incumbent carriers. Even if state commissions did deregulate, this process would surely produce different standards from state to state, creating an inefficient patchwork of regulations that would delay local competition and raise costs for both incumbents and new entrants. The Commission therefore believed that detailed, nationally applicable rules were the best method to implement the provisions of the 1996 Act and thereby encourage local com-

[83] *Id.* §251(c)(4)(B).
[84] *Id.* §251(h)(2).
[85] Implementation of the Local Competition Provisions in the Telecommunications Act of 1996, First Report and Order, 11 F.C.C. Rec. 15,499, 15,544 ¶83 (1996) (hereinafter *Local Competition Order*), *modified on recons.*, 11 F.C.C. Rec. 13,042 (1996), *vacated in part,* Iowa Utils. Bd. v. FCC, 120 F.3d 753 (8th Cir. 1997), *rev'd. sub nom.* AT&T v. Iowa Utils. Bd., 119 S. Ct. 721 (1999).

petition. These rules would form minimal standards that states would be required to apply when reviewing and arbitrating interconnection agreements under section 252.

In pursuit of this goal, the Commission established extensive, detailed regulations governing the various aspects of interconnection.[86] In a 700-page, 3,200-footnote opus, the Commission undertook to promulgate "uniform, national rules" addressing every conceivable local interconnection issue and declared those rules "binding on the states, even with respect to intrastate issues."[87] Although the FCC conceded that the 1996 Act "do[es] not contain explicit grant of intrastate authority to the Commission,"[88] it nevertheless proclaimed that it had authority "without limitation"[89] to issue such binding rules because in its view the "1996 Act moves beyond the distinction between interstate and intrastate matters that was established in the 1934 Act."[90]

Numerous parties, including state commissions (which did not like the intrusion on their authority) and incumbent LECs (which did not like the substance of some of the FCC's rules, particularly those governing pricing[91]), petitioned for review of the FCC's Order. Those petitions were consolidated in the Eighth Circuit pursuant to 28 U.S.C. §2112(a)(3). A number of the states, as well as some incumbent LECS, sought an interim stay of the FCC's pricing rules pending judicial review. The Eighth Circuit granted the requested stay in October 1996 because of "what appear[ed] to be the rather clear and direct indication [in the statutory text] that the state commissions"—not the FCC—"should establish prices."[92]

After further briefing and oral argument, the court of appeals confirmed its earlier tentative holding that the plain language of section 252 "directly and straightforwardly assigns to the states" the authority to set prices.[93] As to the other terms and conditions

---

[86] *Id.* at 15,544–15,552 ¶¶84–103.
[87] *Id.* at 15,512 ¶22, 15,551 ¶101.
[88] *Id.* at 15,544 ¶84.
[89] *Id.* at 15,559–15,560 ¶115.
[90] *Id.* at 15,513 ¶24.
[91] *See* §3.10.3.
[92] Iowa Utils. Bd. v. FCC, 109 F.3d 418, 424 (8th Cir. 1996).
[93] Iowa Utils. Bd. v. FCC, 120 F.3d at 797.

of interconnection, the court of appeals held that, absent an express grant of authority to the FCC, section 2(b)'s retention of intrastate jurisdiction to the states precluded the FCC from exercising any jurisdiction. "[S]ection 2(b)," the court held, "remains a *Louisiana* built fence that is hog tight, horse high, and bull strong, preventing the FCC from intruding on the states' intrastate turf."[94]

The Supreme Court, however, granted certiorari to review the Eighth Circuit's decision and pretty much dismantled the *Louisiana*-built fence. In a decision in *Iowa Utilities Board* issued on January 25, 1999, a 5-3 majority of the Court[95] concluded that the FCC has untrammeled authority to implement all the provisions of the 1996 Act.[96] The Court, in a decision written by Justice Scalia, relied on section 201(b), a 1938 amendment to the Communications Act of 1934, which provides that "[t]he Commission may prescribe such rules and regulations as may be necessary in the public interest to carry out the provisions of this Act."[97] Since Congress expressly directed that the 1996 Act be inserted into the 1934 Act, the Court concluded that the Commission's rulemaking authority extends to the local competition provisions of the 1996 Act.

The Court found section 2(b)—which states that "nothing in this chapter shall be construed to apply to give the Commission jurisdiction with respect to" intrastate matters—inapplicable because the 1996 Act clearly and expressly "applies" to intrastate matters. The states had argued that the words "to give the Commission jurisdiction" in section 2(b) meant that even if the statute applied to intrastate matters, the FCC had no jurisdiction to implement those provisions. The majority found the argument "imaginative," but unpersuasive. "Commision jurisdiction," the Court stated, "always follows where the Act 'applies.'"[98] In

---

[94] *Id.* at 800.

[95] Justice O'Conner was recused, as she has been from most telecommunications cases, apparently because she owns AT&T stock.

[96] AT&T Corp. v. Iowa Utils. Bd., 119 S. Ct. 721 (1999) (*Iowa Utilities Board*).

[97] 47 U.S.C. §201(b).

[98] AT&T v. Iowa Utils. Bd., 119 S. Ct. at 731.

other words, the FCC's reach extends as far as Congress's grasp. As for the phrase "to give the Commission jurisdiction," the Court said that was intended to cover only cases of so-called ancillary jurisdiction, whereby the FCC asserts jurisdiction over an area not directly addressed in the Act.[99] The Court proceeded to limit *Louisiana PSC* to that context, in which the Commission attempts to regulate services over which is has "not explicitly been given rulemaking authority."[100]

The Court then addressed whether "certain individual provisions in the 1996 Act negate particular aspects of the Commission's implementing authority." Specifically, the Court looked to whether the FCC's detailed pricing rules ran afoul of section 252(c)(2), which "entrusts the task of establishing rates to the state commissions." The Court found no inconsistency because the states still get to "apply [the FCC's] standards and implement [the FCC's] methodology, determining the concrete result in particular circumstances. That is enough to constitute the establishment of rates."[101] The Court went on to reverse a number of other jurisdictional holdings of the Eighth Circuit—governing state review of preexisting interconnection agreements between incumbent LECs and other carriers, regarding rule exemptions, and regarding dialing parity—finding in each case that the FCC had plenary authority to dictate rules to "guide" the state commission judgments.[102]

In a rather remarkable concluding paragraph, the Court criticized Congress for passing "a piece of legislation that profoundly affects a crucial segment of the economy worth tens of billions of dollars" and yet "is in many important respects a model of ambiguity or indeed even of self-contradiction." The Court noted that the FCC had taken some of these ambiguities and run with them in ways that Congress might well not have intended. "But Congress is well aware that the ambiguities it chooses to produce in a statute will be resolved by the implementing agency,"

---

[99] *Id.*
[100] *Id.* at 731 & n.7.
[101] *Id.* at 732.
[102] *Id.* at 733.

and absent "clear limits" in the statute, it is not the Court's job to rein in the agency.[103]

Justice Thomas, joined by the Chief Justice and Justice Breyer, dissented. In Justice Thomas's view, "Congress consciously designed a system that respected the States' historical role as the dominant authority with respect to intrastate communications." Thus, although Congress chose specifically to address intrastate issues in the 1996 Act, it still left it primarily to the states, not the FCC, to implement those provisions. "I simply do not think that Congress intended to limit states' authority to mechanically apply whatever methodologies, formulas, and rules that the FCC mandated."[104] Justice Breyer elaborated on the last point in a separate dissent, noting that the FCC's rules leave the states "little or no freedom to choose among reasonable rate-determining methods according to the State's policy-related judgments, assessing local economic circumstances or community need."[105] After canvassing various ways in which the Act's pricing requirements might be implemented to a better effect than the FCC's own rules, Justice Breyer concluded: "The FCC's regulations do not set forth an outer envelope surrounding a set of reasonable choices; instead, they constitute the kind of detailed policy-related rate-setting that the statute in respect to local matters leaves to the States."[106]

§3.4 Preemption in the Era of Uncontested Monopoly

The 1934 Act left entirely open the question of regulatory jurisdiction for any matters that did not divide neatly and obviously into intrastate and interstate spheres—which is to say, virtually every important matter in any aspect of telephony.

For many years, state and federal regulators generally agreed on regulatory policy, and jurisdictional conflicts were therefore

[103] *Id.* at 738.
[104] *Id.* at 745 (Thomas, J., dissenting).
[105] *Id.* at 751 (Breyer, J., dissenting).
[106] *Id.* at 753.

avoided. In the wake of *Smith,* the FCC asserted final responsibility for allocating property between interstate and intrastate service, relegating the states to an advisory role.[107] Accordingly, although the states could choose the rate of return applicable to intrastate services, the division of the rate base was left entirely to the FCC.[108] Both the FCC and state regulators, however, placed their highest priority on providing universal service, which meant pushing down rates for residential local service and boosting charges to business and long-distance users,[109] so there was little controversy even on this issue.[110]

Both federal and state levels shared quite similar goals as to other matters as well. Both embraced the paradigm of regulated monopoly offering end-to-end service: customer premises equipment (CPE), inside wiring, and local service were all bundled

---

[107] 47 U.S.C. §410(c). Congress eventually validated this practice in 1971 by formalizing the state's advisory role while granting the FCC full authority to make final decisions. Under section 410(c), the FCC is required to refer any rulemaking proceeding regarding the jurisdictional separation of common carrier property and expenses between interstate and intrastate operations to a Federal-State Joint Board for a recommended decision. But the states have no vote in the FCC's final determination. *See* S. Rep. No. 362, 92d Cong., 1st Sess. 6 (1971) (statute achieves "joint participation without abandoning Federal superintendence in the field").

[108] In State Corp. Commission of Kansas v. FCC, 787 F.2d 1421, 1425–1427 (10th Cir. 1986), the Tenth Circuit reaffirmed the FCC's plenary authority over the allocation of equipment costs between intrastate and interstate services. In that case, the states sought to increase the sample periods employed by local telephone companies to separate the costs of equipment used in both interstate and intrastate service and to divide interstate revenues among themselves. The result of such an increase would have been a larger allocation of costs to the interstate rate base. The FCC decided to preempt any state attempts to alter the sample period, and the court of appeals affirmed, noting that such state action would "encroach upon core federal authority over interstate communications, as well as frustrate the established policy that [the sample period] remain constant." *Id.* at 1428. The Tenth Circuit explained that even "[s]tate regulation which formally restricts only intrastate communications may not stand when it encroaches upon federal authority over interstate matters." *Id.* at 1427.

[109] *See* J. R. Haring & K. B. Levitz, The Law and Economics of Federalism in Telecommunications, 41 Fed. Comm. L.J. 294–296 (1989); McKenna, Preemption Under the Communications Act at 18–19; Noam, Federal and State Roles in Telecommunications at 956 n.48.

[110] *See* §§2.5, 6.1.

into a single tariffed package; usage of long-distance service was measured, but access to the service itself was likewise part of the same monopoly package. Both favored excluding competition so that subsidies could be maintained.

Competition arrived anyway. New telecommunications technologies — such as microwave, satellites, and computers — made competition and new services both possible and inevitable. The FCC adjusted faster than state regulators. Beginning in the mid-1950s, and reaching full force in the 1970s, the Commission dramatically realigned its regulatory priorities to promote competition and deregulation.[111] CPE, enhanced services, inside wiring, and long-distance service were each in turn opened to competition and then detariffed in varying degrees. Many state regulators, however, continued to face intense political pressure to maintain subsidies that had become established under the old monopoly.[112] They preferred to exclude competition, which in turn allowed them to keep the incumbent's products and services under tariffs that bore no necessary relationship to costs, but that allowed for subsidies. The FCC responded by preempting the states in such areas as CPE and interconnection, and with near unanimity, the courts upheld the FCC's power to do so.[113]

§3.5   The Rise of FCC Preemption Power

A 1976 decision by the Fourth Circuit, *North Carolina Utility Commission v. FCC (NCUC I)*,[114] established federal preemption power through the adoption of a pro-preemption standard that

[111] McKenna, Preemption Under the Communications Act at 32–33; Haring & Levitz, The Law and Economics of Federalism in Telecommunications at 296–297; Noam, Federal and State Roles in Telecommunications at 956 n.48. The principal FCC and judicial decisions in this process are discussed in §§10.4, 11.6–11.8, and 12.3–12.5.

[112] *See, e.g.,* Note, An Assessment of State and Federal Jurisdiction to Regulate Access Charges After the AT&T Divestiture, B.Y.U. L. Rev. 376, 405–406 (1983).

[113] Issues connected with preemption in the context of cable television are dealt with in Chapter 13.

[114] 537 F.2d 787 (4th Cir. 1976).

would prevail until 1986. Several states had sought to forbid the connection of privately supplied terminal equipment to the public network unless the equipment was used exclusively for interstate communications. The FCC had preempted such orders as contrary to an evolving federal policy of open competition in markets for customer premises equipment.[115] The Fourth Circuit acknowledged that CPE was then used 97 percent of the time for intrastate calls, but nevertheless sustained preemption.[116]

A year later, in *North Carolina Utilities Commission v. FCC* (*NCUC II*),[117] the Fourth Circuit reiterated this test. This time it upheld an FCC order permitting the interconnection of all registered CPE. The court noted simply that "separation of terminal equipment used exclusively for local communication is a practical and economic impossibility."[118] The court of appeals brushed aside as irrelevant state commission fears "that increased substitution of independently provided terminal equipment for

---

[115] Telerent Leasing Corp. et al., Petition for Declaratory Rulings on Questions of Federal Preemption on Regulation of Interconnection of Subscriber-Furnished Equipment to the Nationwide Switched Public Telephone Network, Memorandum Opinion and Order, 45 F.C.C.2d 204 (1974). *See* §10.7.5.

[116] The court of appeals explained: "We have no doubt that the provisions of Section [152(b)] deprive the Commission of regulatory power over local services, facilities and disputes that in their nature and effect are *separable from and do not substantially affect the conduct or development of interstate communications*. But beyond that, we are not persuaded that Section [152(b)] sanctions any state regulation, formally restrictive only of intrastate communication, that in effect encroaches substantially upon the Commission's authority under Sections 201 through 205." *NCUC I,* 537 F.2d at 793 (emphasis added). Judge Widener in dissent argued that section 152(b) "should be read literally and to deny the FCC jurisdiction over intrastate facilities even though incidentally used in interstate commerce." *Id.* at 797. The majority acknowledged that the FCC's assertion of jurisdiction "unavoidably affects intrastate as well as interstate communication. And, by the same token, both would be restricted by any state action that prevented such interconnection." *Id.* at 792. Since CPE normally handles both intrastate and interstate calls, a state decision to forbid the interconnection of non-telco-supplied CPE would "frustrate" the federal decision to permit it. *Id.* at 791. The majority therefore concluded that "[t]he Commission must remain free to determine what terminal equipment can safely and advantageously be interconnected with the interstate Communications network and how this shall be done." *Id.* at 793.

[117] 552 F.2d 1036 (4th Cir. 1977).

[118] *Id.* at 1043.

carrier-supplied equipment will reduce revenues and the corresponding amount of money available to subsidize other services and facilities."[119] "In the end," the court of appeals explained, "the problem of subsidy reduces to the tactical problem of obtaining sufficient revenues to cover the difference between the cost of providing subsidized service and the regulated price of subsidized service. Whether that amount is obtained by overcharging on PBXs, by overcharging on business phone exchange service, or even by direct legislative appropriation, is largely academic as far as statutory jurisdiction is concerned."[120]

NCUC I and *NCUC II* together affirmed the FCC's power to preempt state regulation if the matter in question *either* was inseparable from an interstate service *or* affected an interstate service significantly. In 1977, the D.C. Circuit endorsed this same test in *California v. FCC*.[121] The FCC had directed local Bell companies to provide interconnection to independent suppliers of foreign exchange (FX) and common control switching arrangements (CCSA) services.[122] But when the Southern Pacific Communications Company (later to become Sprint) sought permission to operate such services intrastate as well, the California Commission objected. Southern Pacific obtained a declaratory ruling from the FCC requiring interconnection on the grounds that preventing connection for intrastate calls while permitting it for

---

[119] *Id.* at 1048.

[120] *Id.* at 1048. *See also* Fort Mill Tel. Co. v. FCC, 719 F.2d 89 (4th Cir. 1983) (upholding FCC's preemption of South Carolina State Commission's order requiring entity to connect its PBX with South Carolina carrier rather than carrier in North Carolina).

[121] 567 F.2d 84, 87 (D.C. Cir. 1977) (per curiam), *cert. denied,* 434 U.S. 1010 (1978).

[122] Foreign exchange service permits a customer in one city to obtain local business line service in a distant city or exchange area without incurring a toll charge. Service is obtained by leasing a full-time, point-to-point private line channel. CCSA service permits a large customer through his own network of private lines to dial all stations in the network or to dial off-network telephone subscribers through interconnection with local exchange service, FX, or WATS lines. *See* Bell System Tariff Offerings of Local Distribution Facilities for Use by Other Common Carriers, Decision, 46 F.C.C.2d 413 (1974), *aff'd sub nom.* Bell Tel. Co. v. FCC, 503 F.2d 1250 (3d Cir. 1974), *cert. denied,* 422 U.S. 1026 (1975). *See* §9.4.

interstate calls would be "technically and practically difficult."[123]
The D.C. Circuit affirmed in a brief per curiam, citing *NCUC I*.[124]

In 1980, the Second Circuit adopted the test in *New York Telephone Co. v. FCC*.[125] "The key to jurisdiction is the nature of the communication itself rather than the physical location of the technology," the court reasoned.[126] "The calls for which the [New York] surcharge is imposed clearly go from one state to another. . . . Even if the local exchange service is separable technologically and in terms of cost assessment from the dedicated private line in FX and CCSA service . . . there is no doubt that the [New York] surcharge on interstate FX/CCSA users, ranging up to 1600% higher than the charge for comparable service to intrastate users, substantially affects the conduct or development of interstate communication and encroaches upon FCC authority."[127] In a quite similar case decided the same year, the D.C. Circuit affirmed the FCC's broad discretion *not* to take preemptive action if so inclined.[128]

---

[123] American Telephone & Telegraph Co. and the Associated Bell System Cos. Interconnection with Specialized Carriers in Furnishing Interstate Foreign Exchange (FX) Service and Common Control Switching Arrangements (CCSA), Memorandum Opinion and Order, 56 F.C.C.2d 14, 19 ¶18 (1975).

[124] Judge Robinson dissented on the grounds that the Commission "did not . . . undertake to explain why such a difficulty would arise, nor how close that difficulty is to impossibility." California v. FCC, 567 F.2d at 90 (footnotes omitted).

[125] New York Tel. Co. v. FCC, 631 F.2d 1059, 1065–1066 (2d Cir. 1980). At the insistence of the New York Public Service Commission, New York Telephone filed a tariff with the FCC imposing substantial access charges on interstate FX/CCSA customers. The FCC disallowed the tariff, and the Second Circuit affirmed.

[126] *Id.* at 1066.

[127] *Id.*

[128] Diamond Intl. Corp. v. FCC, 627 F.2d 489 (D.C. Cir. 1980). Diamond had installed an interstate private line network that connected with New York Telephone's public network. Diamond paid Bell's interstate tariff for the line (which included a component for interconnection with the local network). New York Telephone also charged an intrastate tariff for the interconnection. Diamond complained to the FCC that it was being double-billed, but the FCC declined to take action. The D.C. Circuit affirmed on the ground that "[n]othing in the record suggests that the Commission's decision to refrain from exercising jurisdiction over the additional . . . charges billed to Diamond will substantially affect the conduct or development of interstate Communications." *Id.* at 493. The court stressed, however, that it was not saying that the

Shortly thereafter the D.C. Circuit permitted the FCC to pre-empt state rate-making authority altogether.[129] In its *Computer II* inquiry, the FCC decided to separate CPE from basic telephone service.[130] The cost of providing CPE had historically been apportioned between interstate and intrastate use and then bundled into the appropriate transmission rates. The FCC was determined to have CPE deregulated entirely. If local exchange companies continued to provide CPE under state tariffs, however, the equipment in question might be either subsidized or overpriced, inhibiting competition all around. The FCC therefore concluded that state regulation of CPE had to be eliminated. The D.C. Circuit Court of Appeals upheld this decision: "[w]hen state regulation of intrastate equipment or facilities would interfere with the achievement of a federal regulatory goal, the Commission's jurisdiction is paramount and conflicting state regulations must necessarily yield to the federal regulatory scheme."[131] The court of appeals accepted the Commission's explanation that "[o]nly if charges for CPE are entirely separate from charges for transmission service will consumers be free to select the CPE that best suits their individual needs and preferences."[132]

Most significantly, the court of appeals dismissed as irrelevant "any distinction in this case between preemption principles applicable to state rate-making authority and those applicable to other state powers."[133] Even though section 152(b) was specifically passed to preclude FCC preemption of state rate-making as

---

FCC could not intervene if it found it appropriate to do so. Furthermore, the D.C. Circuit suggested that if there were evidence that the surcharge of which Diamond complained would "substantially affect the conduct or development of interstate communications," then the FCC would possess not merely the discretion, but also the duty to assert its "primary jurisdiction" over state tariffed rates. *Id.*

[129] *CCIA*, 693 F.2d at 214–216.

[130] Amendment of Section 64.702 of the Commission's Rules and Regulations (Second Computer Inquiry), 77 F.C.C.2d 384 (1980) (hereinafter *Computer II*). *See* §12.4.2.

[131] *CCIA*, 693 F.2d at 214.

[132] *Id.* at 215.

[133] *Id.* at 216.

had occurred in *The Shreveport Rate Case,* "the Act itself does not distinguish between authority over rates and authority over other aspects of Communications."[134] Thus, "preemption of state tariffs on CPE is justified because state tariffs would interfere with the consumer's right to purchase CPE separately from transmission service and would thus frustrate the validly adopted federal policy."[135] The court of appeals also rejected the suggestion that the FCC could preempt the states only by means of affirmative regulations, not through deregulation. By deregulating CPE, the states argued, the FCC was taking CPE out of the FCC's Title II jurisdiction and hence was outside of its authority to preempt state regulation. The court of appeals explained that the FCC was creating not a "vacuum of deregulation," but "a different, *affirmative* regulatory scheme through its ancillary jurisdiction."[136]

With that decision, the balance of power between the FCC and the states shifted decisively—and irrevocably, it seemed—into the federal arena. Two years later, in 1984, the same court upheld the FCC's power to impose a federal "line charge" on every telephone customer nationwide.[137] In a second 1984 decision, the D.C. Circuit approved an FCC rule prohibiting state restrictions on the resale and sharing of all intrastate wide area telecommunications services (WATS).[138] Federal preemption was given its broadest conceivable expression by Judge Harold Greene when he entered the consent decree that broke up the Bell System. Almost offhandedly, Judge Greene observed that the services affected by the breakup order—services that included every

---

[134] *Id.*

[135] *Id.*

[136] *Id.* at 217 (emphasis added).

[137] The charge covered "that portion of *their necessarily-incurred local telephone plant costs* assigned under *Smith* to the interstate jurisdiction." National Assn. of Reg. Util. Commissioners v. FCC, 737 F.2d 1095, 1115 (D.C. Cir. 1984) (NARUC v. FCC) (emphasis in original).

[138] NARUC v. FCC, 746 F.2d 1492 (D.C. Cir. 1989). Charges for ordinary long-distance service are based on use, with a toll being assessed for each call. In contrast, AT&T's WATS subscribers are usually entitled to unlimited use of the WATS service in exchange for a fixed fee.

conceivable type of phone service—were "of course" neither separable from interstate services nor without effect on those services.[139]

§3.6 *Louisiana Public Service Commission*

The rise of FCC power at the expense of the states was sharply reversed by the Supreme Court's 1986 decision in *Louisiana Public Service Commission v. FCC* (*Louisiana PSC*).[140] The FCC had promulgated new depreciation rules for telecommunications

---

Satellite Business Systems (SBS), using its own earth stations and satellites, offered voice services in competition with AT&T's WATS and message toll service (MTS) offerings. It was not, however, economically feasible for SBS to obtain enough earth stations to gain access to each of the approximately 17,000 local exchanges in the country. Accordingly, for SBS customers who placed calls to areas where SBS did not have earth stations, SBS leased services from the local telephone companies and then resold them to its customers. State prohibitions on resale and sharing in the state tariffs of most local telcos prevented SBS from using intrastate WATS for this purpose. As a result, SBS was often required to route a call to an earth station far outside the state to which the call was going. SBS then used an interstate WATS system to deliver the call, since the Commission had already permitted the resale of interstate WATS.

In response to a petition from SBS, the FCC extended its order to permit the resale of intrastate WATS. NARUC claimed that the Commission had exceeded its authority, "since here the use of intrastate facilities was not absolutely required to complete an interstate communication." *Id.* at 1498. The court was unimpressed: "The dividing line between the regulatory jurisdictions of the FCC and states depends on 'the nature of the communications which pass through the facilities [and not on] the physical location of the line'" (quoting California v. FCC, 567 F.2d at 86). "If the Act's goal of providing uniform, efficient service is ever to be realized, the Commission must be free to strike down the costly and inefficient burdens on interstate communications which are sometimes imposed by state regulation." *Id.* at 1501.

[139] United States v. AT&T, 552 F. Supp. 131, 156 (D.D.C. 1982), *aff'd sub nom.* Maryland v. United States, 460 U.S. 1001 (1983).

[140] 476 U.S. 355 (1986).

equipment.[141] A related order[142] provided that the cost of labor and material associated with the installation of wire on customer premises would henceforth be "expensed" in the year incurred. These new rules were designed to permit carriers to upgrade their equipment in response to rapid technological changes and thus to remain viable in the new competitive environment the FCC had endorsed.

Upon a motion for clarification filed by NARUC, the FCC (by a 3-2 vote) stated that this did not prevent state commissions from adopting different depreciation rates.[143] While state regulatory agencies had, as a general matter, in the past gone along with the FCC's rates, in this instance it was quickly apparent that most state commissions would not follow the FCC. Upon reconsideration, the FCC reversed itself and unanimously held that section 220 of the Act automatically preempts inconsistent state depreciation rates.[144] "[A]dequate capital recovery" was essential,

---

[141] Amendment of Part 31 (Uniform System of Accounts for Class A and Class B Telephone Companies) so as to Permit Depreciable Property to Be Placed in Groups Comprised of Units with Expected Equal Life for Depreciation Under the Straight-Line Method, Report and Order, 83 F.C.C.2d 267 (1980) (hereinafter *Property Depreciation*), *recons. denied,* 87 F.C.C.2d 916 (1981). The Order permitted companies to group plant for depreciation purposes based on its estimated service life (rather than, as had previously been done, according to its year of installation) in order to match capital recovery more accurately with capital consumption. The Order also sought to promote improved accounting accuracy by replacing "whole life" depreciation with the "remaining life" method so that if estimates on which depreciation schedules were premised prove erroneous, they could be corrected in midcourse in a way that would assure that the full cost of the asset would ultimately be recovered.

[142] Amendment of Part 31, Uniform System of Accounts for Class A and Class B Telephone Companies, of the Commission's Rules and Regulations with Respect to Accounting for Station Connections, Optional Payment Plan Revenues and Related Capital Costs, Customer Provided Equipment and Sale of Terminal Equipment, First Report and Order, 85 F.C.C.2d 818 (1980).

[143] Amendment of Part 31, Uniform System of Accounts for Class A and Class B Telephone Companies, of the Commission's Rules and Regulations with Respect to Accounting for Station Connections, Optional Payment Plan Revenues and Related Capital Costs, Customer Provided Equipment and Sale of Terminal Equipment, Memorandum Opinion and Order, 89 F.C.C.2d 1094, 1097 ¶¶7–8 (1982).

[144] Amendment of Part 31, Uniform System of Accounts for Class A and Class B Telephone Companies, of the Commission's Rules and Regulations

the Commission reasoned, to its broad mission of promoting communications services. State depreciation rates that did not permit adequate capital recovery in the competitive environment that the Commission was promoting would frustrate federal objectives.[145]

The Fourth Circuit affirmed, but relied on its general *NCUC* preemption test rather than on the specific force of section 220.[146] The court acknowledged that "the instant appeal raises no question of actual physical impossibility of complying with dual federal and state regulation."[147] Nonetheless, separate state

---

with Respect to Accounting for Station Connections, Optional Payment Plan Revenues and Customer Provided Equipment and Sale of Terminal Equipment, Memorandum Opinion and Order, 92 F.C.C.2d 864 (1983) (hereinafter *Amendment of Part 31*). At the time that the FCC made the amendment, 47 U.S.C. §220 provided in pertinent part:

> (b) The Commission shall, as soon as practicable, prescribe for [the carriers subject to this Act] the classes of property for which depreciation charges may be properly included under operating expenses, and the percentages of depreciation which shall be charged with respect to each of such classes of property, classifying the carriers as it may deem proper for this purpose. The Commission may, when it deems necessary, modify the classes and percentages so prescribed. Such carriers shall not, after the Commission has prescribed the classes of property for which depreciation charges may be included, charge to operating expenses any depreciation charges on classes of property other than those prescribed by the Commission, or after the Commission has prescribed percentages of depreciation, charge with respect to any class of property a percentage of depreciation other than that prescribed therefor by the Commission.

Section 220 has since been amended by the Telecommunications Act of 1996. *See* 47 U.S.C. §220.

[145] Amendment of Part 31, 92 F.C.C.2d at 876 ¶33.

[146] Virginia State Corp. Commn. v. FCC, 737 F.2d 388 (4th Cir. 1984), rev'd, 476 U.S. 355 (1986). The court noted that "[a]lthough flexibility in depreciation practice presented little threat to the efficient operation of a monopolistic telecommunications industry, improper capital recovery does pose a true threat in today's competitive market. Thus, the FCC reasonably decided to preempt by issuing orders intended to speed capital recovery and improve accuracy of depreciation calculations, thereby enhancing competition." *Id.* at 394.

[147] *Id.* at 396.

depreciation schedules would pose "an impediment to rapid development of interstate facilities."[148]

By a 5-2 margin, the Supreme Court reversed.[149] The Court acknowledged the tension between the broad jurisdictional grant to the FCC in section 151 and the express reservation of state authority in section 152(b). The "separations process" of section 410(c), however, "naturally reconciled" the conflict and created a "*dual* regulatory system."[150] "Because the separations process literally separates costs . . . between interstate and intrastate service, it facilitates the creation or recognition of distinct spheres of regulation."[151] Within their sphere, the states are sovereign.[152] Once costs have been separated, it is "possible" to apply different rates and methods of depreciation; there is thus no jurisdiction for FCC preemption of state authority.[153] Though section 220 might arguably be read to preempt state depreciation practices, the section was too ambiguous[154] to override the express command of section 152(b).[155] The Court simply declined to "define fully" the scope of section 220.[156]

---

[148] *Id.* Judge Widener, who had dissented in *NCUC I* and *NCUC II*, did so here as well. He argued that the FCC was plainly and improperly involving itself in setting intrastate rates, just as the ICC had done in *Shreveport*. He explained, "The upshot of the case is that the FCC decided that the carriers needed more revenues than the state regulatory agencies were willing to provide, so it decided to impose different depreciation rates on intrastate equipment for the very purpose of, and thus effectively, raising the intrastate rates to the subscribers just as surely as if it had done so directly." *Id.* at 399.

[149] Chief Justice Burger and Justice Blackmun dissented without opinion. Justices Powell and O'Connor did not take part in the case. *Louisiana PSC*, 476 U.S. at 379.

[150] *Id.* at 370 (emphasis in original).

[151] *Id.* at 375.

[152] *Id.* at 364, 371.

[153] *Id.*

[154] It is "at least possible," the Court noted, "that the section was intended to do no more than spell out the authority of the FCC over depreciation in the context of interstate regulation." *Id.* at 377. And "[i]t is similarly plausible" that the section "was addressed to the plenary authority of the FCC to dictate how the carriers' books would be kept for the purposes of financial reporting." *Id.* at 377–78.

[155] *Id.* at 377.

[156] *Id.* at 378.

It is difficult to comprehend how the Court could have found this reasoning satisfying. However ambiguous it may be, a more convincing reading of section 220 is that it does indeed empower the FCC to set depreciation charges and classifications for all of a carrier's property. Section 220(b) states that once the FCC prescribes depreciation rates for carriers subject to the Act, carriers shall not "charge to operating expenses any depreciation charges on classes of property other than those prescribed by the Commission" or "charge with respect to *any class of property* a percentage of depreciation other than that prescribed therefor by the Commission."[157] No complementary authority is reserved to state commissions. To the contrary, section 220(h) specifically states that the FCC "*may* . . . except the carriers of any particular class or classes in any State from any of the requirements under this section *in cases where such carriers are subject to State commission regulation with respect to matters to which this section relates.*"[158] The clear implication is that FCC depreciation schedules are preemptive *unless* the FCC expressly declares otherwise.[159]

In defense of the Supreme Court, the Fourth Circuit had relied exclusively on the general authority of the FCC set out in section 151 rather than on its specific authority under section 220. That general argument was far too broad, for it wholly eviscerated the jurisdiction reserved to the states in section 152(b). This portion of the Court's opinion, which tries to articulate a sphere of state regulatory authority protected by the statute as a whole, is far more important than its narrow, and probably incorrect, holding regarding section 220.

The Court properly recognized that the first half of the *NCUC* test—that state regulation may be preempted whenever it "sub-

---

[157] 47 U.S.C. §220(b) (emphasis added).

[158] *Id.* §220(h) (emphasis added).

[159] This reading of the statute is supported by its legislative history. In 1934, Congress specifically rejected a proposal to add a section 220(j) to the statute that stated that nothing in the statute would "limit the power of a State commission to prescribe, for the purposes of the exercise of its jurisdiction with respect to any carrier, the percentage rate of depreciation to be charged to any class of property." *See* S. 2910, 73d Cong., 2d Sess. (1934); H.R. 8301, 73d Cong., 2d Sess. (1934).

stantially affects" interstate telecommunications—nullifies section 152(b) entirely because of the pervasive interdependence of interstate and intrastate plant.[160] That some state practices may "imped[e]" or "frustrate" federal regulatory goals[161] is simply a natural consequence of Congress's decision to establish a dual regulatory regime in an area that is inherently unified. If it were otherwise, *Shreveport* would still be good law. In rate-making, which includes both choosing the rate of return to apply to the rate base and determining the size of the rate base through depreciation practices, the separations process carves out distinct spheres in which the FCC and the state commissions can operate independently. But for the language of section 220, it would be easy to conclude that this was the intent of Congress.

In *Louisiana PSC,* the Supreme Court did recognize, however, that where such "separation" of spheres is not possible, the FCC's authority must remain supreme. This critical aspect of the *NCUC* test was thus preserved by the Court. Indeed, the Court specifically distinguished and cited with approval both *NCUC I* and *NCUC II* as cases upholding preemption "where it was *not* possible to separate the interstate and the intrastate components of the asserted FCC regulation"[162] or where a state rule "would negate" a federal one.[163] Thus, its reasoning about section 220 aside, the Court may have struck about the right balance between sections 151 and 152.

As noted,[164] much of the impact of *Louisiana PSC* has been blunted by the Court's recent decision in *Iowa Utilities Board.* Its holding has been limited to areas of "ancillary jurisdiction" not

---

[160] It may well be, for example, that state depreciation rates will not allow sufficient modernization and hence will impede the development of the nation's telecommunications infrastructure. But if section 152(b) is to mean anything, that sort of justification cannot be sufficient to support a preemption order. Under the scheme of dual regulatory responsibility Congress chose to establish, there is nothing the FCC can do to ensure that the states grant a higher return.

[161] These are the tests for preemption proposed by the Fourth Circuit, Virginia v. FCC, 737 F.2d at 396.

[162] *Louisiana PSC,* 476 U.S. at 375–376 n.4 (emphasis in original).

[163] *Id.*

[164] *See* §3.3.

directly addressed by the Communications Act. In those areas, however, the so-called impossibility exception, and the post-*Louisiana PSC* cases implementing it, may still prove important.

§3.7 Preemption After *Louisiana PSC*

The first two cases decided after *Louisiana PSC* were relatively straightforward. In *California v. FCC,* California challenged an FCC order preempting state regulation of intrastate radio common carriers. The FCC was concerned that state regulators were impeding entry in order to protect existing common carriers; the FCC justified its order, however, not on the basis of its Title II authority to regulate interstate common carriers, but rather under its Title III authority over radio transmissions. The FCC believed that restrictive state regulations were "frustrating the FCC's efforts to encourage competition," which was the best means to make the best use of the radio spectrum.[165]

The D.C. Circuit had little difficulty reversing. While conceding that the FCC has exclusive jurisdiction "over all the channels of radio transmission" (47 U.S.C. §301), the court explained that "[t]he Act commits regulation of the common carrier aspects of intrastate radio transmission to the states."[166] Since the services in question were concededly both intrastate and common carriage, the court held that section 152(b) precluded preemption. "That such regulation impedes entry may well be an unfortunate consequence of Congress's division of regulatory jurisdiction between federal and state authorities, but only Congress may change that division of authority."[167]

Another equally straightforward case, with the opposite result, was *Hawaiian Telephone Co. v. Public Utility Commission of Hawaii,*[168] in which the Ninth Circuit upheld an injunction against a state regulatory commission that mandated a decrease in rates

---

[165] 798 F.2d 1515, 1518 (D.C. Cir. 1986).
[166] *Id.* at 1520.
[167] *Id.* at 1518.
[168] 827 F.2d 1264 (9th Cir. 1987), *cert. denied,* 487 U.S. 1217 (1988).

based on the state's own separations procedure. The FCC, the court held, has exclusive authority to divide the rate base between intra- and interstate services.[169] In reaching this conclusion, the Ninth Circuit explained that the Act provided this express authority[170] and that a single rate base cannot be separated in two different ways[171] without jeopardizing a telco's right to earn revenues on 100 percent of its assets.[172] Thus, FCC control plainly meets the "not possible to separate" test of *Louisiana PSC*.[173]

The D.C. Circuit had more trouble applying *Louisiana PSC* in three cases it decided in quick succession in 1989. *NARUC v. FCC*[174] dealt with an FCC order preempting state regulation of inside wiring installation.[175] The FCC had sought to encourage competition by requiring telcos to unbundle installation charges from regulated services and then by detariffing inside wiring. The D.C. Circuit concluded that the FCC had the authority to require the unbundling of installation charges, but that its attempt to preclude states from setting tariffs for inside wiring was inappropriate.[176]

After *Louisiana PSC*, the court explained, "the Commission may only preempt state regulation over intrastate wire communication

---

[169] *Id.* at 1274–1276.

[170] 47 U.S.C. §§221(c), 410(c).

[171] *Hawaiian Tel. Co.*, 827 F.2d at 1275. Separations for interstate rate-making and separations for intrastate rate-making are "two sides of the same coin." *Id.* at 1264.

[172] *Id.* at 1275.

[173] Indeed, as the court of appeals explained, the Supreme Court in Louisiana PSC relied on the existence of a uniform, FCC-controlled separations procedure to show that depreciation could be separated into distinct intra- and interstate components. "[I]t is only after a uniform separations formula has been applied that a state's independent depreciation rule for intrastate rate-making can be protected from federal preemption." *Id.* at 1276 (emphasis in original).

[174] 880 F.2d 422 (D.C. Cir. 1989).

[175] "Inside wiring" refers to "the telephone wires within a customer's home or place of business that are on the customer's side of the point of intersection between the telephone company's communications facilities and the customer's facilities." *Id.* at 425. *See* §8.2.2.

[176] NARUC v. FCC, 880 F.2d at 428–431.

to the degree *necessary to keep such regulation from negating the Commission's exercise of its lawful authority*" over interstate communication.[177] The FCC was within its rights in deciding to encourage competition in the provision of inside wiring because the same wiring is used for both intrastate and interstate calls and cannot be unbundled for interstate purposes alone. Once unbundled, however, the *costs* of wiring could be separated and regulated (or deregulated) in different ways by state and federal authorities.[178] In any event, the FCC had failed to demonstrate that state tariffing "would negate the federal policy of establishing a competitive inside wiring market."[179] The court accordingly remanded the matter to the FCC.

The general preemption test stated by the court was correct, but its remand order made little sense. A customer will buy one set of inside wiring from one provider—either a telco or some independent supplier—for one price. It is simply not possible to regulate one-half of that price and deregulate the other half. Either the entire price will, in effect, be deregulated, or the separate state/federal allocation of costs and revenues will give way. In other words, either state regulation will be displaced, or the FCC will lose control of the separation process.[180] The former

---

[177] *Id.* at 425 (emphasis added).

[178] "The circularity of the FCC's argument is readily apparent: state authority over inside wiring must be preempted as the costs of the wiring are not severable; they are not severable because they are no longer subject to the jurisdictional separations process; but the costs are not subject to the separations process because inside wiring has been preemptively deregulated. Were we to accept this argument, the Commission would have unchecked authority to force state deregulation of any activity it chose to deregulate at the interstate level." *Id.* at 429.

[179] *Id.* at 430.

[180] The court of appeals appeared to recognize this point, though in a rather vague way. The court acknowledged that "the Commission may properly proscribe state tariffs that would result in the subsidization of the installation and maintenance of inside wiring by the general ratepayers because it would allow telephone companies to undercut alternative providers of inside wiring services." *Id.* at 430. Presumably, then, the FCC could also properly proscribe state tariffs that would result in the subsidization of ratepayers by charges for inside wiring because that would render telephone companies unable to compete against alternative providers. It follows that only state tariffs that were neither too high nor too low, but just right, would be permissible.

possibility was the one the D.C. Circuit rejected in this ruling; the latter had been rejected shortly before by the Ninth Circuit in *Hawaiian Telephone Co.* The D.C. Circuit had itself set forth the correct analysis in its 1982 opinion upholding the FCC's order unbundling and detariffing CPE. The court argued that the cases were different—with CPE, the FCC had met its burden of showing that state tariffs would "necessarily thwart achievement of a free and competitive" market, but it failed to do so with inside wiring.[181] But in reality, all the FCC had done was treat inside wiring exactly like CPE.

In the following case, *Illinois Bell Telephone Co. v. FCC,*[182] the D.C. Circuit swung to the opposite extreme. In 1987, the FCC had decided to permit the Bell Operating Companies (BOCs) to market CPE without establishing separate subsidiaries. The new freedom was conditioned, however, on the BOCs' agreement to permit independent CPE vendors to operate as sales agents for BOC services like Centrex so that all players in the market could offer "one-stop shopping."[183] Several BOCs claimed that this condition would entail additional costs and hence affect their intrastate rates. The D.C. Circuit rejected the challenge in a very broad statement of the FCC's authority. Centrex supports both interstate and intrastate communications, and Centrex users pay interstate access charges.[184] According to the D.C. Circuit, the way in which Centrex is marketed "does not appear capable of severance into discrete interstate and intrastate components."[185] "Even if Centrex were a purely intrastate service, the FCC might well have authority to preemptively regulate its marketing if—

But to be "just right," such tariffs would have to match competitive levels, which is just another way of saying that the charges would have to be set by the market, not by the state regulators.

[181] *Id.* at 431.

[182] Illinois Bell Tel. Co. v. FCC, 883 F.2d 104 (D.C. Cir. 1989).

[183] Furnishing of Customer Premises Equipment by the Bell Operating Companies and the Independent Telephone Companies, Report and Order, 2 F.C.C. Rec. 143, 156 ¶90 (1986) (hereinafter *BOC Structural Relief Order*). *See* §8.3.

[184] *Illinois Bell Tel. Co.*, 883 F.2d at 114.

[185] *Id.* at 115.

as would appear here—it was typically sold in a package with interstate services. Marketing realities might themselves create inseparability."[186]

The result may well have been correct, but the reasoning was far too expansive. Most intrastate telecommunications services connect to the interstate network and incur access charges for that privilege. But that is surely not sufficient, after *Louisiana PSC*, to vest control over the marketing of all intrastate services in the FCC. Centrex, in particular, seems an unlikely candidate for such control, as the Ninth Circuit pointed out in the earlier case of *McDonnell Douglas Corp. v. General Telephone Co. of California*[187] There, the Ninth Circuit found no federal cause of action in a suit brought by a customer over the rates charged for Centrex service. The court of appeals explained that Centrex was inherently an intrastate service, a fact that was not changed by "the capacity it possesses to be patched into interstate telecommunications nets. . . . If CENTREX service of the type described here becomes interstate merely because it can be connected with other wire systems that are interstate, then it is difficult to imagine what type of telephone service would not qualify as interstate in a similar manner."[188]

On its third try, *Public Utilities Commissions of Texas v. FCC*,[189] the D.C. Circuit seemed to have struck the proper balance. The Atlantic Richfield Company (ARCO) had a private microwave system between its facilities in Plano and Dallas. Dissatisfied with the service it was getting from GTE, its local carrier in Plano, ARCO decided to access the public network in Dallas, where its carrier was Southwestern Bell Company (SBC), even for calls originating from (or terminating in) Plano. ARCO ordered more trunk lines from SBC in Dallas and dropped those of GTE in

---

[186] *Id.* at 113 n.7. *See also* Southwestern Bell Tel. Co. v. Public Util. Commn. of Tex., 812 F. Supp. 706 (W.D. Tex. 1993) (preempting Texas Public Utilities Commission rule requiring Southwestern Bell Telephone to obtain affirmative permission from its Texas customers to use customer-specific "customer proprietary network information" (CPNI) to market supplemental services or release customer-specific CPNI to third parties).

[187] 594 F.2d 720 (9th Cir. 1979).

[188] *Id.* at 724 n.3.

[189] 886 F.2d 1325 (1989) (*PUC of Texas*).

Plano. GTE complained to the Texas Public Utilities Commission (PUC), which ordered SBC not to provide the extra trunk lines on the grounds that such action would be inconsistent with state regulations setting carrier franchise boundaries. The FCC then issued an order preempting the state's order.[190]

The D.C. Circuit affirmed, noting that the trunks in question were to be used to handle both interstate and intrastate calls. The court cautioned that "even when the equipment that the FCC wishes to regulate is used inseparably and interchangeably for intrastate and interstate calling, the FCC must limit its regulation to the interstate aspects if it can do so."[191] But the FCC concluded that it was not possible for SBC to block intrastate calls originating from (or heading to) Plano, while permitting all interstate calls over its trunk lines. Nor did the Texas PUC or GTE suggest that the FCC could have fashioned a narrower preemption order.

The following year, in *Public Service Commission of Maryland v. FCC*,[192] the D.C. Circuit upheld FCC preemption of the rates local telephone companies may charge interstate carriers to disconnect a customer for nonpayment. The court noted that the disconnect service has both intrastate and interstate aspects, since a disconnection prevents a customer from making both types of calls.[193] The court acknowledged that the FCC found that it was technically impossible to disconnect for in-state calls without at the same time disconnecting for out-of-state calls and that the state "has not introduced any evidence . . . to cast doubt on this finding."[194] The court explained that preemption promoted the valid federal goals of preventing the states from subsidizing local service with interstate revenues and of promoting competition in a service to interstate carriers.[195]

---

[190] The case presented a situation similar to the case found in Fort Mill Telephone Co. v. FCC, 719 F.2d 89 (4th Cir. 1983). Both cases addressed the question of where a company would be allowed to locate its private branch exchange (PBX).

[191] *PUC of Texas,* 886 F.2d at 1333.

[192] 909 F.2d 1510 (D.C. Cir. 1990).

[193] *Id.* at 1511.

[194] *Id.* at 1516.

[195] *Id.*

A series of Ninth Circuit cases explore further the boundaries of the post-*Louisiana PSC* preemption jurisprudence. In *California v. FCC*,[196] the Ninth Circuit reviewed several FCC orders, known as *Computer III*,[197] that released the BOCs from a requirement that they offer "enhanced services"[198] through separate subsidiaries and preempted states from regulating or tariffing those services.

The FCC offered two arguments in support of its preemption order. First, the phrase "of any carrier" in section 152(b) is, by definition of the Act, limited to telecommunications services offered on a common carrier basis. Pursuant to its Title I "ancillary jurisdiction," the Commission had concluded that "enhanced services" should not be offered on a common carrier basis—that is, should not be covered by Title II at all. The FCC therefore reasoned that section 152's reservation of authority to the states did not apply. The Ninth Circuit properly rejected this wholly circular argument. Section 152 applies to all intrastate communication services offered *by* carriers and is not confined to services offered in a common carrier capacity.[199] At a minimum, therefore, it covers services offered "in connection with" common carrier services, which necessarily include enhanced services.[200]

The FCC also sought to bring enhanced services within the "impossibility exception" found in section 152(b).[201] The court of appeals acknowledged that footnote 4 of *Louisiana PSC* and the cases following it provide such an exception, but declared that the exception is narrow and that the FCC did not meet its burden of showing that *all* state regulation of enhanced services

[196] 905 F.2d 1217 (9th Cir. 1990).

[197] For a detailed discussion of *Computer III* and related proceedings, see §§5.4 and 12.5.1–12.5.3.

[198] "Enhanced services" are services that combine the transmission and processing of data. California v. FCC, 905 F.2d at 1223 n.3.

[199] *Id.* at 1240–1242.

[200] "The FCC's position," the court of appeals noted, "reduces to the anomalous proposition that §[152(b)(1)] strictly limits the Commission's explicitly granted Title II powers, but imposes no restriction at all on the implied authority derived from those powers. We cannot agree." *Id.* at 1240.

[201] *Id.* at 1242.

would make federal (de)regulation impossible.[202] As an example of state regulation that could coexist with valid federal regulation, the court of appeals pointed to state structural separation requirements affecting companies that operate *only* intrastate, such as "voice mail services that are offered to discrete locales within a state," alarm services, and database services for schools.[203] The court of appeals acknowledged that if the states imposed structural separation requirements, the BOCs might be unable to offer such services, but concluded that, under the statute, that was a matter of concern for the states, not the FCC. "The Commission has failed to explain why requiring communications carriers to offer *intra*state enhanced services through a separate corporation would frustrate the Commission's goal of giving communications carriers the freedom to choose whether to integrate or separate their *inter*state operations."[204] Because some state regulation could coexist with federal regulation, the FCC's blanket preemption order was invalid.

There are some flaws in the Ninth Circuit's decision. For example, the court of appeals fails to appreciate that even "voice mail services that are offered to discrete locales within a state" can receive calls from out of state. Thus, the FCC could properly be concerned with whether those services are regulated by the states in a way that is incompatible with federal regulation. The same is likely to be true of almost all enhanced services. Very few will be wholly intrastate; therefore, very few will be susceptible to state regulation and tariffing. But the court of appeals correctly put the burden on the FCC to make its case with respect to specific services. The Commission's preemption order was perfunctory and wholly undiscriminating. In effect, the FCC decided (as it did for inside wiring) to treat all enhanced services as a type of sophisticated CPE. But whereas CPE is obviously used inseparably for interstate and intrastate communications—so that it cannot be deregulated for one purpose and regulated for the other—that is not necessarily (or at least not obviously) the case

---

[202] *Id.* at 1242–1244.
[203] *Id.* at 1244.
[204] *Id.*

for enhanced services.[205] Accordingly, the court properly remanded to the FCC for a more careful determination of the
scope of its order.[206]

On remand, the FCC explained that each of the enhanced services in question had both an interstate and an intrastate component and that while a BOC technically could comply with state
structural separation requirements on just the intrastate portion
of these jurisdictionally mixed services, it would not be economically or operationally feasible for them to do so. Several
state commissions again appealed, but the Ninth Circuit had
little trouble disposing of their contentions.[207] The court of
appeals upheld the FCC preemptions under the impossibility
exception developed by the Fourth Circuit in the CPE cases. The
court also rejected the novel contention that the FCC may preempt state action only when it is acting pursuant to specified regulatory duties under Title II of the Act, not when it is acting to
implement the more general goals of Title I.[208]

---

[205] Presumably, a carrier that wanted to escape state regulation could simply configure its service offering to involve an interstate component. For
example, an alarm services provider could place its remote monitoring station
across state lines. Special restrictions applicable to the Bell Companies, however, may restrict their ability to make such adjustments. See §12.7.5.

[206] For a detailed discussion of the apparent conflict between the Ninth
Circuit and the Supreme Court as to the standard of proof governing Commission preemption of state regulations, see Note, California v. Federal Communications Commission: Continuing the Struggle Between Sections 151 and
152 of the Communications Act, 40 Cath. U. L. Rev. 893 (1991).

[207] California v. FCC, 39 F.3d 919 (9th Cir. 1994), cert. denied, 514 U.S. 1050
(1995).

[208] In California v. FCC, 4 F.3d 1505 (9th Cir. 1993), the Ninth Circuit
addressed another aspect of the FCC's treatment of enhanced services, its
Open Network Architecture Order. See Chapter 12; see also §5.4.1. In that
order, the FCC required all basic service elements (BSEs) to be offered in federal tariffs. The FCC set rates for those BSEs that potentially could be used
for interstate service, but did not require that these rates be used. In other
words, an enhanced service provider could buy the same service out of state
tariffs. The court found that the FCC tariff requirement did not preempt
states from regulating intrastate services, but rather established a dual federal
and state tariffing structure for BSEs, with states retaining the authority to set
rates for those BSEs that are used for intrastate service. The court held that
this dual system complied with the Supreme Court's decision in Louisiana
PSC.

In a case raising a similar issue, the Ninth Circuit upheld an FCC rule limiting state restrictions on per-line (as opposed to per-call) blocking of Caller ID.[209] In formulating the rule, the FCC had found that per-line blocking was contrary to its goal of promoting widespread interstate Caller ID services. The court held that the FCC's preemption of the state regulations fit within the impossibility exception and was a "reasonable exercise of its discretion, based on consideration of relevant factors, and supported by the record."[210]

---

[209] California v. FCC, 75 F.3d 1350 (9th Cir. 1996), *cert. denied,* 517 U.S. 1216 (1996).

[210] *Id.* at 1360, citing California v. FCC, 905 F.2d at 1230. Two cases have dealt, in at least facially conflicting ways, with preemption of state common law claims. AT&T Corp. v. Fleming and Berkley, No. 96-55212, 1997 U.S. App. LEXIS 33674, 1997 WL 737661 (9th Cir. 1997) (opinion unpublished), involved an appeal from a grant of summary judgment in favor of AT&T in an action under 47 U.S.C. §203 to recover an unpaid telephone bill. Appellants argued that the charges in question were due to calls place by a criminal "hacker" and that it was therefore unjust and unreasonable for AT&T to charge them for those calls. Appellants also argued that triable issues of fact remained with respect to various state and common law defenses asserted by appellants.

The Ninth Circuit affirmed, noting that "[a]s a result of the broad provisions of the Communications Act, courts generally have held that state causes of action on regulated activities are preempted." *Id.* at *20. Appellants argued that the savings clause of the Communications Act, 47 U.S.C. §414 ("[n]othing in this chapter contained shall in any way abridge or alter the remedies now existing at common law or by statute, but the provisions of this chapter are in addition to such remedies"), preserved their common law claims. The court of appeals, however, found that the FCC had ruled that long-distance providers may bill customers for fraudulent telephone calls and that appellants' state law claims, if allowed, would conflict with this ruling and interfere with the Commissions' authority.

In Vermont v. Oncor Communications, Inc., 166 F.R.D. 313 (D. Vt. 1996), by contrast, a district court held that a Vermont state law consumer protection suit for alleged "slamming" of pay phones was not preempted because 47 U.S.C. §207 specifically provides the FCC and federal district courts concurrent jurisdiction over damage claims against common carriers and because section 414 explicitly preserves existing common law or statutory remedies in addition to the remedies provided for under Title 47. "A common-law right, even absent a savings clause," the court explained, "is not to be abrogated unless it be found that the preexisting right is so repugnant to the statute that the survival of such right would in effect deprive the subsequent statute of its efficacy. . . ." 166 F.R.D. at 320.

In summary, following *Louisiana PSC,* it appears that an FCC preemption order must satisfy the following three requirements: (1) the order must serve valid goals brought under FCC jurisdiction by the Communications Act, (2) the preemption of intrastate telecommunications regulation must be necessary to avoid frustrating these goals, and (3) the preemption order must be narrowly tailored to take away from the states only those aspects of the regulation that cannot be separated into intra- and interstate components. In applying this test, appellate courts have clearly taken to heart the Supreme Court's admonition that Congress intended a *"dual* regulatory system" for telecommunications, with both state and federal regulators playing a significant role in shaping the industry.[211] These basic principles should still be valid following *Iowa Utilities Board* for cases involving the Commission's ancillary jurisdiction (i.e., issues not directly addressed under the Act). Where the Act does directly address an issue, however, even in general terms, the FCC now has a clear mandate to press ahead, regardless of how many intrastate toes it steps on.

§3.8   Preemption of State Barriers to Entry

The 1996 Act gave the FCC a new and very important weapon in its battle with the states. In keeping with the 1996 Act's goal of encouraging competition through the opening of local markets, section 253 of the 1996 Act preempts in sweeping terms state and local barriers to entry:

> No State or local statute or regulation, or other State or local legal requirement, may prohibit or have the effect of prohibiting the ability of any entity to provide any interstate or intrastate telecommunications service.[212]

---

[211] *Louisiana PSC,* 476 U.S. at 370 (emphasis in original).
[212] 47 U.S.C. §253(a).

Section 253(d) empowers the FCC to implement this broad mandate.[213]

Under the 1996 Act, however, states still retain the regulatory authority to impose competitively neutral regulations necessary to preserve and advance universal service, public safety, and consumer protection.[214] States and local regulators are also permitted to manage the public rights-of-way and charge "fair and reasonable compensation" from those who want to run their wires above or beneath the city streets, provided such management is performed on a competitively neutral, nondiscriminatory basis.[215]

Before the Commission can preempt a state legal requirement under section 253(d), therefore, it must engage in the following analysis. First, it must determine under subsection (a) whether a particular state law will "prohibit or have the effect of prohibiting the ability of any entity to provide any . . . telecommunications service."[216] Second, if it concludes that the local law has such an effect, the Commission must then determine whether the law is nevertheless permissible either because it imposes, on a competitively neutral basis, requirements necessary to preserve and advance universal service, protect the public safety and welfare, or otherwise serve the consumer goals of subsection (b) or because it qualifies as a nondiscriminatory, competitively neutral management of public rights-of-way under subsection (c). Only

---

[213] *Id.* §253(d).

[214] *Id.* §253(b). Any state universal service regulations must also be consistent with universal service provisions of 47 U.S.C. §254. 47 U.S.C. §253(b). For further discussion of section 254, see §6.3.

[215] 47 U.S.C. §253(c). The states are also permitted to require any telecommunication carrier seeking to provide service in a rural telephone company's service area to meet the requirements set forth in section 214(e)(1) for designation as an eligible telecommunications carrier before allowing it to provide service unless the rural telephone company serving the area has been awarded an exemption under section 251(c)(4) that would prevent any competitor from meeting the requirements of section 214(e)(1). 47 U.S.C. §253(f). These various "savings" clauses, which limit FCC preemption under section 253, do not apply to commercial mobile service, for which state regulation is separately preempted under section 332(c)(3). 47 U.S.C. §253(f)(2); *see* §10.2.

[216] 47 U.S.C. §253(a).

after the Commission finds that a state law actually or effectively prohibits the ability of any entity to provide a telecommunications service, and that such a law is not "saved" by subsection (b) or (c), may the FCC conclude the state provision is preempted under federal law. And, even then, the Commission may preempt the enforcement of that state provision only "to the extent necessary to correct such violation or inconsistency."[217]

The Commission has already had several opportunities to explore the scope of its preemption power under section 253. The Commission first applied section 253 in *Classic Telephone*.[218] Classic Telephone, Inc. (Classic) petitioned the Commission to preempt the decisions of two Kansas cities that denied telecommunications franchises to Classic. The two cities claimed that the scope of the Commission's section 253 preemption authority did not extend to local franchising and that under section 2(b) and the holding of *Louisiana PSC*, the Commission lacked the authority to preempt the cities' decisions. The cities also asserted that even if the Commission had preemption power over such matters in general, the cities' refusals to grant the franchises to Classic were protected under section 253(b) and (c).

The Commission agreed with Classic and preempted the cities' decisions. The Commission initially noted that section 253 is an express statutory grant of preemption power from Congress and that the limitations of section 2(b) and *Louisiana PSC* were therefore not applicable.[219] Furthermore, the "plain language of section 253 does not exempt from the scope of federal preemption purely local matters of franchising authority."[220] The Commission also considered whether the cities' decisions were saved under subsection (b). Unlike subsection (c), which specifically preserves the regulatory authority of state *and* local governments in specific areas, subsection (b) refers only to the authority of states. However, the Commission found that while subsection (b)

---

[217] *Id.* §253(d).

[218] Classic Telephone, Inc. Petition for Preemption, Declaratory Ruling and Injunctive Relief, Memorandum Opinion and Order, 11 F.C.C. Rec. 13,082 (1996) (hereinafter *Classic Telephone*).

[219] *Id.* at 13,094–13,095 ¶¶23–24.

[220] *Id.* at 13,094 ¶23.

grants authority only to states, it is within the absolute discretion of states to delegate their government powers as they see fit. Therefore, the Commission concluded that subsection (b) applies to any locality to which the state has specifically delegated regulatory authority.[221]

Turning to the substantive claims, the Commission found that the cities' denials of Classic's franchise requests were not a permissible exercise of regulatory authority under subsection (b), but indicated rather "that the Cities simply did not want to authorize the entry of a competitive telecommunications provider."[222] In support of this conclusion, the Commission first noted that the cities had not applied their franchise authority in a "competitively neutral" manner, but allegedly disqualified Classic based on service quality concerns, while granting the applications of similarly situated incumbent local exchange carriers (LECs).[223] Furthermore, the cities had adopted the most restrictive regulatory scheme possible—an absolute prohibition on entry—rather than less restrictive measures, such as clearly defined service quality requirements or legitimate enforcement actions.[224] In addition, the cities failed to demonstrate that these restrictive methods were necessary to achieve the stated public interest goals—a requirement of section 253(b). Accordingly, the Commission concluded that the decisions rejecting the franchise applications were not entitled to protection under subsection (b).[225]

[221] *Id.* at 13,100–13,101 ¶34. In reaching this conclusion, the Commission relied on the Supreme Court's reasoning in Wisconsin Public Intervenor v. Mortier, 501 U.S. 597 (1991), which held that "a federal statute that plainly authorizes States to regulate, and is also plainly silent with reference to local governments, should not be construed as leaving localities with no regulatory authority, but only that the localities could not claim the regulatory authority explicitly conferred upon the States that might otherwise have been preempted by federal law. . . . [A]n unwillingness by Congress to grant political subdivisions regulatory authority . . . does not demonstrate an intent to prevent the States from delegating such authority to its subdivisions. . . ." *Id.* at 609 (internal quotation marks omitted).

[222] *Classic Telephone,* 11 F.C.C. Rec. at 13,101 ¶36.

[223] *Id.* at 13,101 ¶37.

[224] *Id.* at 13,102 ¶38.

[225] *Id.* The Commission also rejected the cities' attempt to justify their denials under subsection (c)'s public rights-of-way management exception,

The Commission next considered the scope of section 253 in *New England PCC,* a case in which the Connecticut Department of Public Utility Control (CDPUC) had issued a regulation permitting only incumbent LECs and certified LECs to provide pay phone service; the regulation explicitly prohibited an entire class of carriers—non-LECs—from lawfully providing such service anywhere in the state.[226] The Commission found that the CDPUC's regulation was not neutral on its face, barring independent (non-LEC) pay phone providers from providing a telecommunications service.[227] The regulation also substantially raised the costs of providing pay phone service by requiring all new entrants also to offer local exchange service, thus creating a significant barrier to entry into the pay phone-services market.[228] As an initial defense, the CDPUC asserted that the prohibition was a reasonable exercise of the authority explicitly reserved for the state by section 253(b) and therefore not subject to preemption.[229] The Commission rejected this claim, noting that it would "require us to employ a relaxed interpretation of the term 'necessary' that is inconsistent with Congress's purpose of removing regulatory barriers to entry in the provision of telecommunications services."[230] The Commission emphasized that a state's action must be not only reasonable, but also necessary to the preservation of universal service and the other public-interest goals in subsection (b). As in *Classic Telephone,* the Commission preempted the Connecticut regulation, finding that the CDPUC had impermissibly chosen the most restrictive means available without demonstrating the necessity of a flat prohibition.[231]

---

noting that neither city had considered issues relating to public right-of-way management or related compensation and that it was now too late for them to assert this justification to avoid preemption. *Id.* at 13,103–13,104 ¶¶40–41.

[226] New England Public Communications Council Petition for Preemption Pursuant to Section 253, Memorandum Opinion and Order, 11 F.C.C. Rec. 19,713 ¶1 (1996) (hereinafter *New England PCC*).

[227] *Id.* at 19,721–19,722 ¶20.

[228] *Id.*

[229] *Id.* at 19,722 ¶21.

[230] *Id.*

[231] *Id.* at 19,722–19,723 ¶22. The Commission further held that even if the CDPUC regulation had been permissible under section 253, it was, "on its

The Commission further defined its standards for preemption in *Huntington Park*.[232] The Commission was asked to preempt an ordinance enacted by the city of Huntington Park, California, that limited the number and regulated the placement of pay phones in the city's central business district, ostensibly for the purpose of reducing criminal activity.[233] In its petition for preemption, the California Payphone Association (CPA) asserted that this ordinance erected a barrier to entry by limiting the placement of pay phones to locations that would not be commercially viable and by leaving Pacific Bell as the only viable provider of pay phone service in the central business district. Therefore, according to the CPA, the ordinance was not competitively neutral.[234] The Commission rejected the CPA's assertions and refused to preempt the ordinance, finding that the ordinance did not violate the prohibitions of section 253(a).

In reaching its conclusion, the Commission first noted that on its face the ordinance did not prohibit the ability of any entity to provide pay phone service. Unlike the absolute prohibitions in *Classic Telephone* and *New England PCC*, the Huntington Park ordinance applied only to a small area of the city; the ordinance only limited, but did not prohibit, the opportunities to provide service.[235] The ordinance's limitations also applied to all parties equally and were therefore competitively neutral on their face.[236] The Commission addressed whether the ordinance nevertheless had the effect of prohibiting the ability of any entity from providing pay phone service in the central business district.[237] To

---

face, inconsistent with the terms, tenor and purpose of section 276 and our implementing rules" and was therefore equally subject to preemption by the Commission pursuant to section 276(c), which provides safeguards and regulations for provision of pay phone service. *Id.* at 19,726 ¶27.

[232] California Payphone Association Petition for Preemption of Ordinance No. 576 NS of the City of Huntington Park, Ca. Pursuant to Section 253(d) of the Communications Act of 1934, Memorandum Opinion and Order, 12 F.C.C. Rec. 14,191 (1997) (hereinafter *Huntington Park*).

[233] *Id.* at 14,196 ¶10.

[234] *Id.* at 14,198–14,200 ¶¶15–16.

[235] *Id.* at 14,205–14,206 ¶30.

[236] *Id.* at 14,211–14,212 ¶45.

[237] *Id.* at 14,206–12,208 ¶¶31–37.

make its determination, the Commission considered "whether the Ordinance materially inhibits or limits the ability of any competitor or potential competitor to compete in a fair and balanced legal and regulatory environment."[238] The Commission found that nothing in the ordinance or in the city's prior conduct demonstrated a preference for any particular service provider,[239] and the CPA had failed to show how the requirement that pay phones be placed indoors was either "impractical and uneconomic."

The CPA also alleged that the ordinance violated the objectives of section 276 and its implementing regulations. However, the Commission had already concluded in its *Pay Telephone Reconsideration Order*[240] that "'a state can identify, for public safety reasons, areas where no competitor can place a pay phone' as long as the state does not 'draw distinctions that allow some class of competitors to enter the pay phone market and not others.'"[241] The Commission thus refused to preempt the ordinance under section 276, following the same reasoning applied under section 253.

---

[238] *Id.* at 14,206 ¶31.

[239] *Id.* at 14,208 ¶37. To support its claim that the ordinance was not competitively neutral, the CPA pointed to Pacific Bell's contract with the city to provide service in otherwise restricted areas, which it alleged amounted to an arbitrary and potentially absolute barrier to entry. The Commission, noting that Pacific Bell's contract specifically allowed the city to contract with other parties, rejected this characterization, noting that "[w]e cannot agree that the City's exercise of its contract authority as a location provider constitutes, per se, a situation proscribed by Section 253(a). The City's contracting conduct would implicate Section 253(a) only if it materially inhibited or limited the ability of any competitor or potential competitor to compete in a fair and balanced legal and regulatory environment in the market for pay phone services in the Central Business District. In other words, the City's contracting conduct would have to actually prohibit or effectively prohibit the ability of a pay phone service provider to provide service outdoors on the public rights-of-way. . . ." *Id.* at 14,209 ¶38.

[240] Implementation of the Pay Telephone Reclassification and Compensation Provisions of the Telecommunications Act of 1996, et al., Order on Reconsideration, CC Docket Nos. 96-128, 91-35 (Nov. 8, 1996) (hereinafter *Pay Telephone Reconsideration Order*).

[241] Huntington Park, 12 F.C.C. Rec. at 14,211 ¶44 (citing *Pay Telephone Reconsideration Order* ¶140).

Whereas *Classic Telephone, New England PCC,* and *Huntington Park* all addressed state or local administrative regulations, the Commission's first occasion to consider the preemption of a state statute was in its *Texas Preemption Order.*[242] The Public Utility Regulatory Act of 1995 (PURA95) was enacted by the Texas legislature for the stated purpose of fostering competition in the local exchange marketplace. For the first time in the state's history, Texas law allowed telecommunications service providers other than the incumbent LEC to enter the local exchange market as either resellers (for which a Service Provider Certificate of Operating Authority (SPCOA) was necessary) or as facilities-based providers (for which they needed to obtain a Certificate of Operating Authority (COA)). As part of its comprehensive scheme, PURA95:

- required that COA competitors "build-out" their own networks over a minimum geographic area and provide at least 60 percent of their service on facilities not owned by the incumbent LEC;[243]

- prohibited the largest interexchange carriers from obtaining SPCOAs, thereby requiring them to be (at least in part) facilities-based providers of local service;[244]

- mandated a minimum wholesale discount of 5 percent to permit holders of SPCOAs to purchase the local exchange services of an incumbent LEC for resale;[245] and

- forbade municipalities from providing telecommunications services in a competition with private entities.[246]

---

[242] The Public Utility Commn. of Tex.; The Competition Policy Institute, IntelCom Group (USA), Inc., et al., Petitions for Declaratory Ruling and/or Preemption of Certain Provisions of the Tex. Public Utilities Regulatory Act of 1995, Memorandum Opinion and Order, 13 F.C.C. Rec. 3460 (1997) (hereinafter *Texas Preemption Order*).

[243] *Id.* at 3472–3473 ¶26.

[244] *Id.* at 3466–3467 ¶14. This limit "effectively prohibit[ed] the three largest . . . IXCs from providing local exchange services through resale without some facilities build-out." *Id.*

[245] *Id.* at 3467 ¶15.

[246] *Id.* at 3467 ¶16.

Eight separate petitions challenging these provisions of PURA95 were filed in the spring of 1996, and the Commission consolidated them into a single proceeding.[247]

After almost 18 months of comments and ex parte proceedings, the Commission issued its decision on October 1, 1997. Before turning to the merits of these individual challenges, the Commission discussed its preemption authority under the 1996 Act. The Commission declared section 253 to be a broad mandate to strike down state and local regulations that inhibited competition. Section 253, the Commission explained,

> expressly empowers—indeed, obligates—the Commission to remove any state or local legal mandate that "prohibits or has the effect of prohibiting" a firm from providing any interstate or intrastate telecommunications service. We believe that this provision commands us to sweep away not only those state or local requirements that explicitly and directly bar an entity from providing any telecommunications service, but also those state and local requirements that have the practical effect of prohibiting any entity from providing service. As to this latter category of indirect, effective prohibitions, we consider whether they materially inhibit or limit the ability of any competitor or potential competitor to compete in a fair and balanced legal and regulatory environment.[248]

Significantly, the Commission noted that its review of a challenged regulation would be informed by the ways in which the state or local regulatory authority interprets or applies the state provision under review.[249]

The Commission also asserted a more generalized preemption power based simply on the fact that it is the agency charged with implementing the Act. The Commission acknowledged that section 601(c)(1) of the 1996 Act states that the Act is not to be construed as an implied preemption of state or local laws.[250]

---

[247] *Id.* at 3468–3469 ¶19.
[248] *Id.* at 3470 ¶22.
[249] *Id.* at 3464–3465 ¶7.
[250] *Id.* at 3485–3486 ¶51.

Similarly, section 251(d)(3) directs the Commission not to preclude enforcement of any state commission regulation establishing the access and interconnection obligations of local exchange carriers that is consistent with the requirements of section 251 and that does not substantially prevent implementation of the requirements of section 251 and the 1996 Act's local competition provisions.[251] But these preservations of state authority must be balanced against the 1996 Act's preemption provisions. For example, section 261(c) allows a state to impose requirements on telecommunication carriers for intrastate service that are necessary to further competition for local service, but only to the extent that such regulations are not inconsistent with the 1996 Act's local competition provisions or with the Commission's implementing regulations.[252]

From these multiple provisions of the 1996 Act, the Commission concluded that, although Congress did not intend to oust altogether the states from playing a role in the development of competitive telecommunications markets,[253] Congress also did not intend to permit state regulations to conflict with or impede implementation of the 1996 Act.[254] Thus, states cannot "impose any requirement that is contrary to the terms of sections 251 through 261 or that stands as an obstacle to the accomplishment and execution of the full objectives of Congress."[255]

Turning to the merits of the case, the Commission preempted the enforcement of PURA95's "build out" requirement for facilities-based providers, holding "that section 253(a) bars state or local requirements that restrict the means or facilities

---

[251] *Id.*

[252] *Id.* Although the Eighth Circuit had determined that section 261(c) applied only to those additional state requirements that are not promulgated pursuant to section 251 or any other section of Part II of the 1996 Act, the Commission believed that it was applicable here because PURA95 had been enacted prior to the 1996 Act. *Id.* (citing *Iowa Utils. Bd.*, 120 F.3d 753, 807 (8th Cir. 1997), *rev'd sub nom.* AT&T v. FCC, 119 S. Ct. 721 (1999)).

[253] *Id.* at 3486 ¶52.

[254] *Id.*

[255] *Id.* (internal quotation marks omitted) (citing *Louisiana PSC*, 476 U.S. at 369).

through which a party is permitted to provide service."[256] Rejecting the argument that a law "prohibits" an entity from providing
a service only when it absolutely bars it from providing any services, the Commission instead interpreted this term to include
any regulation that would foreclose any particular method of providing telecommunications services.[257] Therefore, to the extent
that PURA95 foreclosed the ability of the largest interexchange
carriers from entering the market exclusively as resellers, it
prohibited these entities from providing telecommunications
service.[258] Furthermore, the Commission also found that the
build-out requirement had the effect of prohibiting parties from
providing service insofar as it imposed the burden of having to
make a substantial financial investment in facilities.[259]

The Commission also rejected arguments that the COA build-
out requirement was justified under section 253(b). The Commission found that the build-out provision was not competitively
neutral on its face, for it singled out COA holders and required
them to construct their own facilities. Moreover, according to the
Commission, the Texas PUC had not demonstrated that the regulation was necessary to advance its public goals.[260] The Commission further found that even if the COA build-out provision
did not violate section 253(a), it would still be preempted on the

---

[256] *Id.* at 3496 ¶74. The Commission also preempted a PURA95 prohibition on granting a COA in rural markets.

[257] *Id.* To support this conclusion, the Commission noted that section 253
applied to "telecommunications service," which was defined as "the offering
of telecommunications for a fee directly to the public . . . *regardless of the facilities used.*" *Id.* (citing 47 U.S.C. §153(46)) (emphasis in original). When read
conjunctively, these two provisions "provide that no state or local requirements may prohibit or have the effect of prohibiting any entity from providing any offering of telecommunications directly to the public for a fee
regardless of the facilities used."

[258] *Id.* at 3497 ¶77.

[259] *Id.* at 3498 ¶78.

[260] *Id.* at 3500 ¶82. In support of its conclusion that such a requirement was
not "necessary" to advance the public goals of subsection (b), the Commission
noted that Congress had reached a different conclusion by establishing a
national framework for competitive entry into the local exchange marketplace
that did not impose a build-out requirement. *Id.* at 3501 ¶83.

independent ground that as a limitation on resale it conflicted with section 251(c)(4)(B) of the Act.[261]

Turning to the question of whether PURA95 could lawfully prohibit the largest interexchange carriers from obtaining SPCOAs, the Commission concluded that it was not necessary to preempt this provision because holders of a COA (the only certificate for which AT&T, MCI, and Sprint were eligible) no longer were prohibited from being pure resellers.[262] The Commission acknowledged that while PURA95 did impose on COA holders some quality-of-service obligations that are not imposed on SPCOA holders, "this differing state regulatory treatment had not been shown on this record to prohibit or have the effect of prohibiting a COA holder from providing any telecommunications service."[263]

The Commission also refused to preempt PURA95's provisions allowing SPCOA holders to obtain tariffed, flat-rated local exchange service for resale at a discount from the LEC's state tariff rate. The Commission found that this 5 percent discount was merely the minimum discount allowed and that nothing in PURA95 prevents an SPCOA holder from obtaining a greater discount through negotiations and arbitrations under sections 251 and 252 of the federal Act.[264]

The final significant issue considered by the Commission was whether PURA95 could lawfully prohibit a municipality from offering telecommunications services. Again, the Commission did not preempt this provision, finding that a political subdivision of a state is not an "entity" separate from the state, and

---

[261] *Id.* at 3504 ¶91. Section 251(c)(4)(B) imposes a duty on LECs to offer telecommunications services for resale on terms that are reasonable and nondiscriminatory. The Commission found that by requiring COA holders to serve a certain portion of their build-out area using facilities other than those of the incumbent LEC, PURA95 significantly limits a COA holder's right to resell the services of an incumbent LEC, thus interfering with the operation of section 251(c)(4)(B). *Id.* at 3504–3505 ¶¶91–92. This last argument seems a bit of a stretch, since section 251(c)(4)(B) by its terms applies to incumbent LECs, not to the states.

[262] *Id.* at 3516 ¶¶118–119.

[263] *Id.* at 3517 ¶120 (internal quotations omitted).

[264] *Id.* at 3526 ¶138.

therefore not subject to section 253(a).[265] Noting that "the scope of authority delegated by a state to its political subdivisions is an area that traditionally has been within the purview of the states," the Commission held that preempting this provision "would insert the Commission into the relationship between the state . . . and its political subdivisions in a manner that was not intended by Section 253."[266] This was the only aspect of the Commission's order that was appealed. The D.C. Circuit affirmed in a short opinion, noting that federal law "may not be interpreted to reach into areas of State sovereignty unless the language of the federal law compels the intrusion."[267] The Court found no compelling indication in section 253(a)'s reference to "any entity" that "Congress deliberated over the effect this would have on State-local government relationships or that it meant to authorize municipalities, otherwise barred by State law, to enter the telecommunications business."[268]

The Commission's preemption analysis under section 253 is thus relatively straightforward. First, the Commission considers whether the challenged regulation violates section 253(a) because it (1) erects an absolute bar that prevents a particular entity from providing a telecommunications service, (2) forecloses any entity from engaging in any particular method of providing a telecommunications service, or (3) materially inhibits or limits the ability of any competitor or potential competitor to compete in a fair and balanced legal and regulatory environment. If the regulation violates section 253(a), the Commission

---

[265] *Id.* at 3544 ¶179.

[266] *Id.* at 3545 ¶181, 3544 ¶179. The Commission explained that "[i]f we were to construe 'entity' in this context to include municipalities, which . . . are merely, 'instrumentalities' of the state, Section 253 would prevent the states from prohibiting their political subdivisions from providing telecommunications services, despite the fact that states could limit the authority of their political subdivisions in all other respects." *Id.* at 3546–3547 ¶184. This issue is the only one decided in the Texas Preemption Order that has been appealed. *See* City of Abilene v. FCC et al., Nos. 97-1633, 97-1634 (D.C. Cir. filed Oct. 11, 1997).

[267] City of Abiline v. FCC, No. 97-1633, slip op. at 5–6 (Jan. 5, 1999).

[268] The court did note, however, that the issue of "whether public utilities are entities within §253(a)'s meaning" was not before it. *Id.* at 8 n.7.

then considers whether it is nevertheless saved from preemption by section 253(b). If the challenged regulation has been promulgated by a locality, the Commission must first determine whether the state has properly delegated its authority to the locality so that it may act for the state under the circumstances. The state or locality must then demonstrate that the otherwise impermissible regulation is both "competitively neutral" and "necessary" to advance one of the public goals set forth in subsection (b) and that a less restrictive means of accomplishing these goals was unavailable. If the state or locality is unable to satisfy this burden, the Commission will preempt the legal requirement, but "only to the extent necessary" to avoid the conflict with federal law.

§3.9 Other Forms of Preemption Authority Under the 1996 Act

In addition to section 253, the Communications Act, as amended by the 1996 Act, contains other express preemptions of state authority over such services as mobile radio services,[269] pay phone services,[270] cable telephony services,[271] telco-supplied video programming services,[272] intraLATA toll services,[273] Internet and data services,[274] and direct-to-home satellite services.[275] Together with section 601(c) of the 1996 Act—which states that the "Act and the amendments made by this Act shall not be construed to modify, impair, or supersede Federal, state, or local law unless expressly so provided in such Act or amendments"[276]—these express grants of federal preemption power provide specific, bright-line guidance for certain issues, unlike

---

[269] 47 U.S.C. §332(c)(3). *See* §10.2.
[270] *Id.* §276(c). *See* §8.4.4.
[271] *Id.* §541(b). *See* §11.8.1.
[272] *Id.* §571. *See* §13.2.
[273] *Id.* §271(e)(2)(b). *See* §9.7.
[274] *Id.* §157 note. *See* §11.7.
[275] *Id.* §152 note. *See* §11.8.2.
[276] *Id.* *See* §3.8.

the more nebulous, multifactor test of section 253. Furthermore, whereas section 253 permits federal preemption only in those instances where state and local governments have erected barriers to entry, the service-specific grants limit FCC preemption to situations in which states have failed to perform their assigned duties.

§3.10 Regulating Through the Back Door?

In addition to preemption power, the 1996 Act bestows on the Commission additional sources of authority to ensure that state commissions and carriers are complying with their obligations under the 1996 Act. First, section 252(e)(5) allows the FCC to substitute itself for a state commission that has failed to carry out its responsibilities under section 252. Second, section 208 sets out a complaint process that allows the FCC to entertain complaints against any carrier for violations of the Act. Third, section 271 requires the Commission to determine, as part of its review of a BOC application for in-region, interLATA (local access and transport area) relief, whether the BOC has complied with a "competitive checklist" that mirrors most of the obligations of sections 251 and 252.

§3.10.1   Section 252(e)(5)

Section 252(e)(5) of the 1996 Act directs the Commission to assume responsibility for any proceeding or matter in which the state commission "fails to act to carry out its responsibility" under this section.[277] In order to "provide for an efficient and

[277] Section 252(e)(5) states:

COMMISSION TO ACT IF STATE WILL NOT ACT.—If a State commission fails to act to carry out its responsibility under this section in any proceeding or other matter under this section, then the Commission shall issue an order preempting the State commission's jurisdiction of that proceeding or matter within 90 days after being notified (or taking notice) of such failure, and shall assume the responsibility of

fair transition from state jurisdiction should [the Commission] have to assume the responsibility of the state commission" under section 252, the Commission has established interim procedures for exercising this preemption authority as part of its *Local Competition Order.*[278] The Commission determined that it would narrowly construe what constituted a failure "to act to carry out [the state commission's] responsibilities" under section 252.[279] The Commission chose to interpret a failure to act to mean a state's failure to complete its duties in a timely manner, which in turn limited the Commission to acting only "where a state commission fails to respond, within a reasonable time, to a request for mediation or arbitration, or fails to complete arbitration within the time limits of Section 252(b)(4)(C)."[280] Conversely, the Commission determined that section 252(e)(5)'s preemption authority is not triggered when an interconnection agreement is "deemed approved" under section 252(e)(4) due to state commission inaction.[281] The Commission further placed the burden of proof on the party alleging that a state commission has failed

---

the State commission under this section with respect to the proceeding or matter and act for the State commission.

47 U.S.C. §252(e)(5).

[278] Implementation of the Local Competition Provisions in the Telecommunications Act of 1996, First Report and Order, 11 F.C.C. Rec. 15,499, 16,127 ¶1283 (1996) (hereinafter *Local Competition Order*), *modified on recons.* 11 F.C.C. Rec. 13,042 (1996), *vacated in part,* Iowa Utils. Bd. v. FCC, 120 F.3d 753 (8th Cir. 1997), *rev'd sub nom.* AT&T v. Iowa Utils. Bd., 119 S. Ct. 721 (1999). The Commission elected to adopt only minimal interim procedures, allowing "the Commission to learn from the initial experiences and gain a better understanding of what types of situations may arise that require Commission action." *Id.* at 16,128 ¶1284.

[279] *Id.* at 16,128 ¶1285.

[280] *Id.*

[281] *Id.* at 16,128 ¶1286; *see also* Petition of MCI for Preemption Pursuant to Section 252(e)(5) of the Telecommunications Act of 1996, Memorandum Opinion and Order, 12 F.C.C. Rec. 15,594, 15,611 ¶25 n.97 (1997) ("We emphasize . . . that the Act does not authorize us to find that a state commission has failed to act within the meaning of Section 252(e)(5) merely because the state commission allows an agreement submitted for approval under Section 252(e)(1) to go into effect automatically by declining to reject the agreement within the 30-day time frame established in Section 252 (e)(4).").

to act.[282] The Commission also has held that it retains jurisdiction over any matter and proceeding for which it assumes responsibility under section 252(e)(5).[283] The Commission's interim rules were subsequently upheld by the Eighth Circuit.[284]

In July 1997, MCI petitioned the Commission to preempt the Missouri Public Service Commission (Missouri PSC) with respect to the interconnection arbitration proceedings with Southwestern Bell Telephone Company (SWBT).[285] MCI's initial petition for arbitration sought "arbitration of virtually every detail" of interconnection.[286] At the direction of the Missouri PSC, MCI narrowed this request to 41 specific unresolved issues, to which MCI added Item 42—a catch-all category for any and all other unresolved issues.[287] The Missouri PSC promptly commenced formal hearings and issued its arbitration order within section 252's nine-month deadline.[288] It resolved the first 41 issues presented by MCI, but held that Item 42 failed to present a clear issue for arbitration and therefore required no resolution by the PSC.[289] MCI then petitioned the FCC, claiming that the state commission's failure to arbitrate Item 42 constituted a "failure to act" and required the Commission to take over the Missouri PSC's role under section 252(e)(5).[290]

The FCC denied MCI's petition.[291] It held that section 252 (e)(5)'s preemption authority must be determined in light of the responsibilities that Congress charged the states to perform under section 252. The Commission found that section 252(b) (4)(A) requires a state commission conducting an arbitration to

---

[282] *Local Competition Order*, 11 F.C.C. Rec. at 16,128 ¶1285.

[283] *Id.* at 16,129 ¶1289.

[284] *Iowa Utils. Bd.*, 120 F.3d 753 (8th Cir. 1997).

[285] Petition of MCI for Preemption Pursuant to Section 252(e)(5) of the Telecommunications Act of 1996, Memorandum Opinion and Order, 12 F.C.C. Rec. 15,594 ¶1 (1997).

[286] *Id.* at 15,604 ¶15.

[287] *Id.* at 15,600 ¶10. Specifically, MCI's Item 42 posed this question: "What should be the other terms of interconnection?" *Id.* at 15,601 n.36.

[288] *Id.* at 15,597 ¶5.

[289] *Id.* at 15,601–15,602 ¶11.

[290] *Id.* at 15,604 ¶15.

[291] *Id.* at 15,617 ¶40.

"limit its consideration . . . to the issues set forth in the petition and in the response."[292] Based on this limitation, the Commission held that "a state commission may not be found to have 'failed to act' within the meaning of Section 252(e)(5) if the issue or issues that are the subject of the preemption petition were never clearly and specifically presented to the state commission in accordance with any procedures set forth by the state commission."[293] MCI had fallen short of satisfying its own duty under section 252(b)(2), as well as the relevant Missouri PSC rules to present any open issues clearly and specifically so that the issue could be arbitrated.[294]

§3.10.2 The Section 208 Complaint Process

In its *Local Competition Order*, the Commission asserted general authority over complaints alleging violations of sections 251 and 252. The FCC grounded this assertion in section 208, which allows it to entertain a complaint for any violation of the Act or its regulations.[295] The Commission stated in the *Local Competition*

---

[292] *Id.* at 15,611 ¶27 (citing 47 U.S.C. §252(b)(4)(A)).

[293] *Id.* The Commission found that "it would be inconsistent with the Act's grant of authority to the state commissions to arbitrate disputes if we interpreted the statute to authorize us to preempt the state commissions for 'failing' to arbitrate disputes that were not clearly and specifically presented to the state commission in the first instance for arbitration." *Id.*

[294] MCI has also asked the Commission to preempt several provisions of the Arkansas Telecommunications Regulatory Reform Act of 1997. *See* MCI's Petition for Expedited Declaratory Ruling Preempting Arkansas Telecommunications Regulatory Reform Act of 1997 (filed June 3, 1997). As in Missouri, MCI has asked the Commission to assume the responsibilities of the Arkansas Public Service Commission (Arkansas PSC) with respect to any arbitration or similar proceeding under section 252 of the 1996 Act. MCI has alleged that the provisions of the Arkansas Act so severely curtail the powers of the Arkansas PSC that it has become impossible for the Arkansas PSC to fulfill its duties under the 1996 Act. In support of this claim, MCI has pointed to section 9(d) of the Arkansas Act, which prohibits the Arkansas PSC from establishing any unbundling of network elements or interconnection requirements beyond those expressly required by the 1996 Act. The issue is currently pending before the FCC.

[295] *See Local Competition Order*, 11 F.C.C. Rec. at 15,561–15,565 ¶¶121–128. Section 208(a) allows any person to file a complaint with the Commission

Order that, as an alternative to an action in federal district court under section 252(e)(6), an aggrieved party could file a section 208 complaint with the Commission, alleging that the incumbent LEC or requesting carrier has failed to comply with the requirements of sections 251 and 252 of the Act or the pertinent Commission rules. According to the FCC, such a complaint could be filed "even if the carrier is in compliance with an agreement approved by the state commission."[296] Alternatively, a complaint could allege that the incumbent local exchange carrier was in violation of the terms of a negotiated or arbitrated agreement. The Commission justified its assertion of authority by explaining that, "in acting on a Section 208 complaint, we would not be directly reviewing the state commission's decision, but rather, our review would be strictly limited to determining whether the common carrier's actions or omissions were in contravention of the Communications Act."[297]

The Commission's claims of authority were rejected by the Eighth Circuit in the *Iowa Utilities Board* case. The Eighth Circuit held that any claim by the Commission of authority under section 208 to review state commission determinations or to enforce the terms of interconnection agreements was contrary to "[t]he language and design of the Act."[298] Specifically, the Eighth Circuit held that although the terms of subsection 252(e)(6) do not explicitly state that federal district court review is the exclusive remedy available to an aggrieved party, "courts traditionally presume that such special statutory review procedures are intended to be the exclusive means of review."[299]

The Eighth Circuit further noted that allowing the Commission to have review or enforcement authority over matters under these sections "would provide the FCC with jurisdiction over intrastate communication services in contravention of Section

---

regarding "anything done or omitted to be done by any common carrier subject to this Act, in contravention of the provisions thereof." 47 U.S.C. §208(a).

[296] *Local Competition Order,* 11 F.C.C. Rec. at 15,564 ¶127.

[297] *Id.* at 15,564–15,565 ¶128.

[298] Iowa Utils. Bd., 120 F.3d at 803.

[299] *Id.* at 803–804.

2(b)."[300] Specifically, if the Commission were given the authority to review and enforce matters under sections 251 and 252, it would essentially have the power to reopen state commission determinations of just and reasonable rates for interconnection, unbundled access, and resale, all of which the Eighth Circuit determined were the sole province of the state commissions under the 1996 Act.[301]

The court of appeals further noted that "the state commission's plenary authority to accept or reject these agreements necessarily carries with it the authority to enforce the provisions of agreements that the state commissions have approved."[302] By contrast, "nothing in the Act even suggests that the FCC has the authority to enforce the terms of negotiated or arbitrated agreements or the general provisions of sections 251 and 252."[303] Indeed, as the court pointed out, "[t]he only grant of any review or enforcement authority to the FCC is contained in subsection 252(e)(5), and this provision authorizes the FCC to act only if a state commission fails to fulfill its duties under the Act."[304] The Eighth Circuit concluded that "[t]he FCC's expansive view of its authority under Section 208 is thus contradicted by the language, structure, and design of the Act."[305]

The Supreme Court, however, concluded that the Eighth Circuit "erred in reaching this claim because it is not ripe."[306] Accordingly, the scope of the FCC's authority under section 208 is still an open question.

§3.10.3 The Section 271 Process

Under section 271 of the 1996 Act, Bell Operating Companies remain prohibited from providing long-distance services origi-

---

[300] *Id.* at 804.
[301] *Id.*
[302] *Id.*
[303] *Id.*
[304] *Id.*
[305] *Id.*
[306] AT&T Corp. v. Iowa Utils. Bd., 119 S. Ct. 721, 733 (1999).

nating from their local service regions until they receive approval from the Commission.[307] One of the requirements for approval is that a BOC satisfy the "competitive checklist" of section 271(c)(2) (B).[308] The checklist in turn requires that the BOC make available interconnection, unbundled network elements, resale, and transport and termination "in accordance with the requirements of Sections 251(c)(2) and 252(d)(1)."[309] As discussed above, the Eighth Circuit determined that the 1996 Act requires state commissions, and not the FCC, to determine the rates involved in implementing the local competition provisions of the Act.[310]

The Eighth Circuit's holding on pricing was called into question by the Commission in its review of Ameritech's section 271 application to provide long-distance service in Michigan.[311] After rejecting Ameritech's application on other grounds, the FCC went on to assert that it had an independent obligation to determine BOC compliance with the checklist and therefore an independent obligation to evaluate whether a BOC had complied with the Act's pricing requirements.[312] From this premise,

---

[307] See 47 U.S.C. §271(a).

[308] See id. §271(d)(3)(A).

[309] See id. §271(c)(2)(B)(i). For a further discussion of section 271, see §9.6.2.

[310] Iowa Utils. Bd., 120 F.3d at 796 ("the Act plainly grants the state commissions, not the FCC, the authority to determine the rates involved in the implementation of the local competition provisions of the Act"); see also Iowa Utils. Bd. v. FCC, 135 F.3d 535, 540 (8th Cir. 1998) ("The FCC's role is, in fact, quite simple: It must ascertain whether each individual applicant BOC has complied with the individual state commission's pricing scheme applicable to it and in effect at the time of the application. This can be done in part simply by asking the state commission whether the applicant BOC has complied with the state commission's pricing rules, as contemplated by section 271(d)(2)(B).").

[311] Application of Ameritech Michigan Pursuant to Section 271 of the Communications Act of 1934, as amended, to Provide In-Region, InterLATA Services in Michigan, Memorandum Opinion and Order, 12 F.C.C. Rec. 20,543 (1997) (hereinafter Michigan Order).

[312] Id. at 20,694–20,700 ¶¶281–297. "We conclude that Congress must have intended the Commission, in addressing section 271 applications, to construe the statute and apply a uniform approach to the phrase 'based on cost' when assessing BOC compliance with the competitive checklist." Id. at 20,697 ¶288.

the FCC concluded that it also had independent authority to determine exactly what those pricing requirements might be. The Commission stated that because the pricing rules are contained in a federal statute, those rules are presumed to have a uniform meaning nationwide and expediency dictated the Commission must establish such a standard.[313] Thus, although the Commission did not contest that section 271(c)(2)(B) requires compliance with section 251(c) and (d) of the Act and conceded that (under the Eighth Circuit's decision) it lacked the authority to prescribe a national pricing methodology to implement section 252(d), it nonetheless concluded that it could prescribe such a national pricing methodology for purposes of BOC interLATA entry under section 271.[314] Accordingly, the Commission announced that it would not grant a BOC's section 271 application unless the rates were based on the pricing principles established by the Commission in its First Report and Order—the very same principles that the Eighth Circuit had previously concluded the Commission lacked the jurisdiction to impose.[315]

In response to a joint petition filed by the BOCs and a number of state commissions, the Eighth Circuit issued a writ of mandamus, in which it directed the FCC to cease and desist attempting to apply its pricing principles in the section 271 context.[316] The court concluded that section 271 merely incorporates by reference the pricing principles of sections 251 and 252.

---

[313] *Id.* at 20,696–20,697 ¶286 ("The Commission, pursuant to its responsibility under section 271, therefore must apply uniform principles to give content to the cost-based standard in the competitive checklist for each state-by-state section 271 application.").

[314] *Id.* at 20,695–20,699 ¶¶284–293.

[315] *Id.* at 20,699 ¶¶292–293; Iowa Utils. Bd., 120 F.3d at 798–799 ("[T]he terms of the Act clearly indicate that Congress did not intend for the FCC to issue any pricing rules, let alone preempt state pricing rules regarding the local competition provisions of the Act.").

[316] *Iowa Utils. Bd.,* 135 F.3d at 543 ("The Federal Communications Commission is ordered to confine its pricing role under section 271(d)(3)(A) to determining whether applicant BOCs have complied with the pricing methodology and rules adopted by the state commissions and in effect in the respective states in which such BOCs seek to provide in-region, interLATA relief.").

It is not a separate grant of authority to interpret those principles. Thus, although the FCC has authority to determine compliance with those principles by the BOCs, this compliance is limited to "ascertain[ing] whether each individual applicant BOC has complied with the individual state commission's pricing scheme applicable to it and in effect at the time of the application."[317] Indeed, "state commissions—not the FCC—have the exclusive authority to determine the pricing requirements of section 252(d)."[318]

In rejecting the Commission's attempt to exercise pricing authority, the Eighth Circuit castigated the Commission in unusually strong terms, stating that the Commission was guilty of doing precisely what it was "expressly forbidden . . . from doing"[319] and that the Commission's actions were an attempt to "coerce" state commissions.[320] The court of appeals pointedly noted that "a policy argument bottomed on an agency's view of expediency can never justify the agency's disregard of the existing mandate of a federal court in a case in which the agency was a party litigant."[321]

The FCC sought certiorari on this issue, and the matter was held pending the outcome of the *Iowa Utilities Board* decision. The Court has since granted the petition, vacated the Eighth Circuit's decision, and remanded the matter for reconsideration in light of that decision.[322]

[317] *Id.* at 540.

[318] *Id.* at 539.

[319] *Id.* at 538. The Eighth Circuit also concluded that the Commission had "flout[ed]" the court's decision and that the Commission's decision to "promulgate its policy decision . . . in an advisory opinion appended to a section 271 order" was "clearly calculated" to "evade ordinary appellate review." *Id.* at 542. The court of appeals further accused the Commission of attempting to "forum-shop" and concluded that the Commission's use of its advisory opinion was an "intimidation tactic" designed to force state commissions to adopt the pricing regime favored by the Commission. *Id.*

[320] *Id.* at 538.

[321] *Id.* at 540.

[322] AT&T Corp. v. Iowa Utils. Bd., 119 S. Ct. 721 (1999).

§3.11   The Obligations of Common Carriers

The core of the 1934 Act's regulation of telephony is found in Title II, which deals with common carriers. Sections 201 through 230 provide the basic structure of common carrier obligations, as well as the basic framework for FCC oversight of the terms and conditions of service by common carriers. These provisions constitute what is now Part I of Title II, entitled Common Carrier Regulations. Parts II and III—Development of Competitive Markets and Special Provisions Concerning Bell Operating Companies—were added as part of the Telecommunications Act of 1996. These latter provisions are designed to promote competition by expanding the obligations of common carriers to include interconnection and other services provided to other common carriers.

The Communications Act defines "common carrier" tautologically, as "any person engaged as a common carrier for hire, in interstate or foreign communication by wire or radio."[323] The meaning of the term was already well established at common law in 1934; it referred simply to any carrier that holds itself out to the public for hire on general terms.[324] Thus, the FCC's regulations define "communications common carrier" simply as "[a]ny person engaged in rendering communications service for hire to the public."[325] The definition is given specific content by sections 201 through 203, which require carriers to provide service on demand, at tariffed rates that are just and reasonable, and without any unreasonable discrimination or undue preference. The

---

[323] 47 U.S.C. §153(h).

[324] See, e.g., United States v. California, 297 U.S. 175, 182 (1936); Washington ex rel. Stimson Lumber Co. v. Kuykendall, 275 U.S. 207, 211 (1927); New Jersey Steam Navigation Co. v. Merchants' Bank, 47 U.S. 343, 381–383 (1848). See generally Note, Redefining "Common Carrier": The FCC's Attempt at Deregulation by Redefinition, 1987 Duke L.J. 501, 506–511.

[325] 47 C.F.R. §21.2. Starting in 1980, the Commission began to manipulate the definition of "common carrier" as part of its effort to deregulate and introduce competition into the telecommunications industry. Carriers defined as "non-dominant" (i.e., without market power) were required to satisfy only minimal Title II requirements, while "dominant" carriers remained subject to stricter rules. See §9.5.1.

general substantive requirements of sections 201–205 extend to any "connecting carriers" as well.

§3.11.1 Service on Demand

A common carrier serves all comers within the scope of its service area.[326] Thus, one of the cornerstones of the 1934 Act is section 201(a)'s requirement that every carrier "furnish . . . communication service upon reasonable request therefor" to any member of the general public. The Act also addresses a carrier's relations with other carriers. Section 201 requires a carrier to interconnect with other carriers "in cases where the Commission, after opportunity for hearing, finds such action necessary or desirable in the public interest."[327]

Must a carrier interconnect with other carriers upon request? It has been argued that such an obligation is created by the "upon reasonable request" clause of section 201(a),[328] but the plain language of the subsection suggests that interconnection is required only when the FCC so directs. Indeed, the Commissioner of the ICC testified during the House hearings that this section conditioned the duty to interconnect on affirmative action by the FCC and urged that the clause be rewritten to make interconnection an absolute requirement.[329] The change was never made, however. Courts have accordingly agreed that section 201(a) does not require interconnection absent an FCC directive.[330]

---

[326] As the Supreme Court has explained, "A common-carrier service in the communications context is one that 'makes a public offering to provide [communications facilities] whereby all members of the public who choose to employ such facilities may communicate or transmit intelligence of their own design and choosing. . . .'" FCC v. Midwest Video Corp., 440 U.S. 689, 701 (1979) (footnote omitted).

[327] 47 U.S.C. §201(a).

[328] See, e.g., Cox & Byrnes, The Common Carrier Provisions at 42–43.

[329] See House Hearings at 91 (statement of Frank McManany).

[330] See, e.g., Southern Pac. Comm. Co. v. AT&T, 556 F. Supp. 825, 975 (D.D.C. 1983), aff'd, 740 F.2d 980 (D.C. Cir. 1984), cert. denied, 470 U.S. 1005

The critical innovation of the 1996 Act was to create just such a new requirement. New section 251 places a host of interconnection obligations on all carriers, and the burdens on the incumbent are especially onerous. These obligations, and the regulations that implement them, are described in detail in Chapter 5. The key point for our purposes is that the notion of serving all comers—limited, in the age of monopoly, to the general public—has been expanded, in the age of competition, to include other carriers.

§3.11.2 At Tariffed Rates

A second cornerstone of the 1934 Act is section 203's requirement that carriers file a schedule "showing all charges for itself and its connecting carriers. . . ."[331] Filed rates are binding on both the carrier and the public.[332] A carrier may not provide service unless it has filed with the FCC and kept open for public inspection schedules showing all of its charges for interstate services.

The tariff filed with the FCC must contain a summary of basic rates, terms, and conditions, as well as cost justifications, and must note the class of service, the effective and expiration dates, and the names of all participating or connecting carriers.[333] Under well-established principles of common carriage, the relationship between customer and carrier may not be altered in any way by private agreement.[334] The Act specifically reaffirms that

---

(1985); Woodlands Telecomms. Corp. v. AT&T, 447 F. Supp. 1261, 1265 (S.D. Tex. 1978).

[331] Section 203 thus filled a glaring gap in ICC regulation, see §3.2.2, by adapting the filing and suspension provisions of the Interstate Commerce Act to the telecommunications industry.

[332] See, e.g., Marco Supply Co. v. AT&T, 875 F.2d 434, 436 (4th Cir. 1989).

[333] 47 C.F.R. §§61.33, .38, .54.

[334] See, e.g., Louisville & Nashville Railroad v. Maxwell, 237 U.S. 94 (1915) (establishing filed-rate doctrine in railroad cases). The Supreme Court recently confirmed the continuing validity of the "filed rate doctrine" in American Tel. & Tel. Co. v. Central Office Tel., Inc., 118 S. Ct. 1956 (1998); Maislin Indus. v. Primary Steel, Inc., 110 S. Ct. 2759, 2765 (1990).

prohibition[335] and provides for forfeiture of treble the amount of any untariffed rebate actually received.[336]

The Commission attempted to relax the requirements of section 203 in order to promote competition in the long-distance industry. Relying on modification authority granted the Commission by section 203(b),[337] the Commission began by adopting a policy of "permissive detariffing" for so-called nondominant carriers,[338] making tariff filing for these carriers optional.[339] The Commission's efforts at regulatory forbearance prior to the 1996 Act peaked in 1985, when the Commission made detariffing mandatory by affirmatively prohibiting nondominant carriers from filing tariffs.[340]

---

[335] 47 U.S.C. §203(c).

[336] *Id.* §503(a).

[337] Section 203(b) states: "The Commission may, in its discretion and for good cause shown, modify any requirement made by or under the authority of this section either in particular instances or by general order applicable to special circumstances or conditions except that the Commission may not require the notice period . . . to be more than one hundred and twenty days." *Id.* §203(b)(2).

[338] Dominant carriers are those with market power; nondominant carriers are all the others. Basically, all carriers were considered nondominant except AT&T and the BOCs. The Commission has subsequently concluded, however, that the BOCs will be nondominant once they are granted section 271 relief, provided they comply with the separate subsidiary requirements of section 272. Policy and Rules Concerning the Interstate, Interexchange Marketplace, Further Notice of Proposed Rulemaking, 13 F.C.C. Rec. 21,531, 21,544–21,545 ¶24 (1998). The Commission has now declared even AT&T to be nondominant in long-distance. Motion of AT&T Corp. to Be Reclassified as a Non-dominant Carrier, Report and Order, 11 F.C.C. Rec. 3271, 3273 ¶1 (1995) (hereinafter *AT&T Reclassification Order*).

[339] The process of deregulation was a gradual one. In its Policy and Rules Concerning Rates for Competitive Common Carrier Services and Facilities Authorizations Therefor, First Report and Order, 85 F.C.C.2d 1 (1980), the Commission merely relaxed the filing procedures for nondominant carriers. The Policy and Rules Concerning Rates for Competitive Common Carrier Services and Facilities Authorizations Therefor, Second Report and Order, 91 F.C.C.2d 59 (1982), adopted permissive detariffing for some nondominant carriers, which was then extended to most other nondominant carriers by the Policy and Rules Concerning Rates for Competitive Common Carrier Services and Facilities Authorizations Therefor, Fourth Report and Order, 95 F.C.C.2d 554 (1983).

[340] Policy and Rules Concerning Rates for Competitive Common Carrier Services and Facilities Authorizations Therefor, Sixth Report and Order, 99 F.C.C.2d 1020 (1985).

MCI challenged the Commission's detariffing requirement, which required MCI not only to stop filing tariffs, but also to cancel all tariffs then on file. The D.C. Circuit struck down the Commission's obligatory detariffing policy, holding that section 203(a)'s command that "[e]very common carrier . . . shall . . . file" tariffs is mandatory and that the Commission's modification authority under section 203(b) "suggest[ed] circumscribed alterations — not . . . wholesale abandonment or elimination of a requirement."[341]

The D.C. Circuit likewise struck down permissive detariffing in a belated challenge brought by AT&T in 1992.[342] Two weeks after that decision, however, the Commission released yet another report and order that again affirmed its permissive detariffing policy as a valid use of its modification authority under section 203(b).[343] The Supreme Court affirmed the D.C. Circuit's summary reversal, holding that the Commission's permissive detariffing was not a minor modification as envisioned by section 203(b), but rather "a fundamental revision of the statute, changing it from a scheme of rate regulation in long-distance common-carrier communications to a scheme of rate regulations only where effective competition does not exist."[344]

The Supreme Court concluded that the clear language of section 203(b) gives the Commission authority to make only minor, incremental, nonfundamental changes.[345] Since the tariff-filing requirement is "the heart of the common-carrier section of the Communications Act," on which much of the rest of the Communications Act is premised, any change eliminating this requirement can be viewed only as fundamental.[346] The Court

---

[341] MCI v. FCC, 765 F.2d 1186, 1191, 1192 (D.C. Cir. 1985).

[342] AT&T v. FCC, 978 F.2d 727 (D.C. Cir. 1992), *cert. denied,* 509 U.S. 913 (1993). The D.C. Circuit held that "[w]hether detariffing is made mandatory, as in the Sixth Report, or simply permissive, as in the Fourth Report, carriers are, in either event, relieved of the obligation to file tariffs under section 203(a). That step exceeds the limited authority granted the Commission in section 203(b) to 'modify' requirements of the Act." *Id.* at 736.

[343] Tariff Filing Requirements for Interstate Common Carriers, 7 F.C.C. Rec. 8072 (1992), *stayed pending further notice,* 7 F.C.C. Rec. 7989 (1992).

[344] MCI v. AT&T, 512 U.S. 218, 231–232 (1994).

[345] *Id.* at 225–229.

[346] *Id.* at 229.

§3.11.2   The Powers of the FCC

further noted that section 203(b) was intended to apply "to special circumstances or conditions," a limitation the Commission had surely exceeded by deregulating 40 percent of all long-distance customers and all long-distance carriers except one.[347] Finally, the Court rejected the Commission's claim that its interpretation of section 203(b) "furthers the Communications Act's broad purpose of promoting efficient telephone service," observing that

> estimations . . . of desirable policy cannot alter the meaning of the Federal Communications Act of 1934. For better or worse, the Act establishes a rate-regulation, filed-tariff system for common-carrier communications, and the Commission's desire "to 'increase competition' cannot provide [it] authority to alter the well-established filed rate requirements." . . . "[S]uch considerations address themselves to Congress, not to the courts. . . ."[348]

The FCC again attempted to relax the filing requirements for nondominant common carriers in its *Range Tariff Order*.[349] The Commission proposed to adopt a policy permitting nondominant common carriers to file a range of rates, as opposed to tariffs specifying actual charges. Relying on the Supreme Court's decision in *MCI v. AT&T*, the D.C. Circuit again vacated the FCC's order, finding that the "clear and definite language" of section 203 "does not encompass the concept of ranges" and therefore the Commission's order exceeded the limited modification authority granted by section 203(b).[350] With section 160 of the 1996 Act, however, the FCC has been granted a new power to forbear from applying existing regulatory requirements.[351] As competition increases, we can anticipate

---

[347] *Id.* at 232.

[348] *Id.* at 233–234. Congress in fact took these considerations to heart in passing the 1996 Act, which adds substantial new forbearance authority to the Commission's regulatory arsenal. *See* §3.15.

[349] Tariff Filing Requirements for Nondominant Common Carriers, Memorandum Opinion and Order, 8 F.C.C. Rec. 6752 (1993) (hereinafter *Range Tariff Order*).

[350] Southwestern Bell Corp. v. FCC, 43 F.3d 1515, 1520 (1995).

[351] *See* §3.15.

increasing numbers of carriers being excused from the obligation to file tariffs.

§3.11.3 Just and Reasonable Rates

The traditional economic justification for regulation is that without it monopolists will price their goods above efficient levels.[352] More colloquially, there is much talk in this context of "fairness" and of the need to prevent unseemly profit or price gouging. "Fairness," along with the takings clause of the Fifth Amendment, however, dictates that a private carrier be allowed to realize a reasonable return on investment.[353] Rate regulation must therefore steer between the extremes of private monopoly and public confiscation. It generally does so in an ad hoc, pragmatic manner.[354]

---

[352] See §2.2; see generally G. Stigler, The Theory of Economic Regulation, 2 Bell J. Econ. & Mgmt. Sci. 3 (1971); R. Posner, Natural Monopoly and Its Regulation, 21 Stan. L. Rev. 548 (1969); H. Demsetz, Why Regulate Utilities?, 11 J.L. & Econ. 55 (1968).

[353] "[A] regulated carrier is entitled to recover its reasonable expenses and a fair return on its investment through the rates it charges its customers." *Louisiana PSC*, 476 U.S. at 364–365. The Supreme Court has in fact changed dramatically its interpretation of the requirements of the "just compensation" clause as applied to public utilities. The Court moved from no oversight at all to a highly rigid test that left commissions with little or no flexibility and from there to a highly pragmatic test that appears to have left utilities with little or no protection. *Compare* Munn v. Illinois, 94 U.S. 113, 133–134 (1877) ("[I]t has been customary from time immemorial for the legislature to declare what shall be a reasonable compensation. . . . We know that this is a power which may be abused; but that is no argument against its existence. For protection against abuses by legislatures the people must resort to the polls, not to the courts.") *with* Smyth v. Ames, 169 U.S. 466, 546–547 (1898) ("the basis of all calculations as to the reasonableness of rates to be charged . . . must be the fair value of the property being used . . . for the convenience of the public") *and* Federal Power Comm'n v. Hope Natural Gas Co., 320 U.S. 591 (1944) ("Rates which enable [the company] to operate successfully, to maintain its financial integrity, to attract capital, and to compensate its investors for the risks assumed certainly cannot be condemned as unjust and unreasonable . . . even though they might produce only a meager return on a rate base computed on the 'present fair value' method.").

[354] See, e.g., Cedar Rapids Gas Light Co. v. Cedar Rapids, 223 U.S. 655, 669 (1912) (Holmes, J.); United States v. FCC, 707 F.2d 610, 612, 618 (D.C. Cir. 1983) ("ratemaking is not an exact science").

Section 201(b) declares unlawful any tariffs, rates, charges, or other practices that are "unjust or unreasonable."[355] This same phrase had been included in the Interstate Commerce Act. It has been generally accepted that a carrier is entitled to recoup the actual expense of the service plus a "proportionally fair" contribution toward fixed cost. But the words conceal a quagmire of uncertainty. All calculations depend on predictions of costs and service demands during the period the rates will be in effect. A carrier must link any proposed rate increase to the cost of service or capital.[356] It must submit a cost of service study covering the past 12 months,[357] a projection of costs study,[358] and any additional relevant cost or marketing data,[359] as well as complete explanations of the bases for the studies and data.[360] The FCC has developed a variety of pragmatic tools to deal with the many inescapable uncertainties.[361]

The principle that rates set by the Commission should be cost-based was examined by the D.C. Circuit in *Competitive Telecommunications Assn. v. FCC*.[362] AT&T and the Competitive Telecommunications Association (CompTel), a trade association representing over 150 interexchange carriers, challenged the Commission's interim rate structure governing access charges paid by interexchange carriers to local exchange carriers. To protect newer and smaller interexchange carriers, whose service made use of tandem switches, the Commission set tandem switch rates at 20 percent of cost. However, to ensure full cost recovery for the LECs, the Commission implemented the "Residual Interconnection Charge (RIC), a per-minute charge levied

---

[355] 47 U.S.C. §201(b). The FCC has primary jurisdiction over claims that rates are not just or reasonable. *See* Ambassador, Inc. v. United States, 325 U.S. 317, 324 (1945).
[356] 47 C.F.R. §§61.38(b), .40(a).
[357] *Id.* §61.38(b)(1)(i).
[358] *Id.* §61.38(b)(1)(ii).
[359] *Id.* §61.38(d).
[360] *Id.* §61.38 (b)(1).
[361] *See* §2.2.
[362] Competitive Telecomms. Assn. v. FCC, 87 F.3d 522 (D.C. Cir. 1996).

upon both dedicated and common line users of local transport services."[363]

AT&T alleged that this rate structure was not cost-based and that it compelled large interexchange carriers with dedicated access lines to subsidize smaller interexchange carriers that used common access lines. The D.C. Circuit held that while the Commission is not required to establish purely cost-based rates, the Commission must "specially justify any rate differential that does not reflect cost."[364] The court remanded the case to the FCC for review, with directions to either develop a cost-based alternative to the RIC or "provide a reasoned explanation of why a departure from cost-based rate-making is necessary and desirable in this context."[365]

The Commission's access rates were again challenged in *Competitive Telecommunications Assn. v. FCC.*[366] In that case, CompTel challenged the FCC's finding that the cost-based interconnection requirement imposed by the 1996 Act did not include the transport and termination of interexchange traffic.[367] The court held that even if CompTel was correct and access rates were not cost-based, such rates did not necessarily violate the 1996 Act. Relying on section 251(g) of the 1996 Act,[368] the court stated, "[I]t is clear from the [1996] Act that Congress did not intend all access charges to move to cost-based pricing."[369]

---

[363] *Id.* at 525.

[364] *Id.* at 529 (citing Alltel Corp. v. FCC, 838 F.2d 551, 556–558 (D.C. Cir. 1988)).

[365] *Id.* at 532.

[366] Competitive Telecomms. Assn. v. FCC, 117 F.3d 1068 (8th Cir. 1997).

[367] The Commission has concluded that such a definition subverted the 1996 Act's goal of assuring that rates for telecommunications services are cost-based.

[368] Section 251(g) requires that after the 1996 Act is enacted, a LEC must provide exchange access, information access, and exchange services for such access to interexchange carriers (IXCs) in accordance with the same equal access and nondiscriminatory interconnection restrictions and obligations (including receipt of compensation) that applied to the carrier prior to enactment until such restrictions or obligations are explicitly superseded by regulations prescribed by the Commission.

[369] Competitive Telecomms. Assn. v. FCC, 117 F.3d 1068, 1072 (8th Cir. 1997).

The Commission's authority to set rates (albeit under a differently worded provision) was also examined in *Illinois Public Telecommunications Assn. v. FCC.*[370] In response to the 1996 Act's directive in section 276 that the Commission "establish a per call compensation plan to ensure that all payphone service providers are fairly compensated for each and every completed intrastate and interstate call using their payphone,"[371] the Commission, inter alia, deregulated the local pay phone coin rate. The National Association of the State Utility Consumer Advocates (NASUCA) challenged this action, arguing that by relying on market forces to determine prices, the Commission was failing to set rates as required by section 276. The court held that the Commission's approach satisfied the requirements of section 276, stating that "[a] market-based approach is as much a compensation scheme as a rate-setting approach."[372] It should be stressed, however, that unlike sections 201 and 202, which require that rates be just and reasonable, the pay phone rates in question are governed by section 276(b)(1)(A), which requires that pay phone service providers be "fairly compensated."[373]

§3.11.4 *Without Unreasonable Discrimination*

An otherwise "reasonable" rate may nevertheless run afoul of section 202's proscription of "unreasonable discrimination" or "undue preference."[374] "The prohibition against different charges to different customers for like services under like circumstances," one court has noted, "is flat and unqualified. The pertinent section of the statute bristles with 'any.' It is made unlawful for 'any' carrier to make 'any' unjust discrimination by 'any' means, or to make 'any' undue preference to 'any' particular person, or to

---

[370] Illinois Pub. Telecomms. Assn. v. FCC, 117 F.3d 555 (D.C. Cir. 1997).
[371] 47 U.S.C. §276(b)(1)(A). For a detailed discussion of the Commission's implementation of section 276, see §8.6.3.
[372] Illinois Pub. Telecomms. Assn. v. FCC, 117 F.3d at 563.
[373] 47 U.S.C. §276(b)(1)(A).
[374] This section was taken directly from the Interstate Commerce Act.

subject 'any' person to 'any' undue prejudice."[375] Other courts have likewise concluded that section 202 imposes an absolute obligation on carriers to avoid discrimination in charges with respect to "like" communication services, regardless of particular customer needs or public objectives.[376]

In practice, however, no rigid equal treatment obligation is really enforced. Whether one service (to a residential consumer, say) is "like" another (to a small business, say) is itself a determination filled with considerations of public policy and private need. Moreover, as the D.C. Circuit pointed out in 1984, the Act forbids only *"unreasonable* discrimination. . . . The reasonableness of the price disparity must be judged by the circumstances in which it is assessed."[377] "Competitive necessity"—a carrier's desire to meet a competitor's offer—has, for example, been considered a legitimate ground for discrimination.[378] The D.C. Circuit likewise upheld the FCC's determination that favorable prices for enhanced service providers were "necessary to preserve their financial viability, and hence avoid adverse customer impacts."[379] In another ruling, the D.C. Circuit attempted to set forth a formal, three-part analysis for assessing charges of discrimination, but the formula in fact remains highly elastic.[380] As discussed in sections 2.3.3 and 9.5, price discrimination remains the norm rather than the exception across the telephone industry.

§3.11.5 Private Contracts

Interconnection between carriers can be governed by tariffed rates, but it need not be. Private contracts are permitted under

---

[375] American Trucking Assn. v. FCC, 377 F.2d 121, 130 (D.C. Cir. 1996), *cert. denied,* 386 U.S. 943 (1967).

[376] *See, e.g.,* Western Union v. FCC, 568 F.2d 1012, 1018 (2d Cir. 1977), *cert. denied,* 436 U.S. 944 (1978); American Trucking Assn. v. FCC, 377 F.2d at 130.

[377] NARUC v. FCC, 737 F.2d at 1136 (emphasis added).

[378] *See, e.g.,* AT&T v. FCC, 449 F.2d 439, 448 (2d Cir. 1971).

[379] NARUC v. FCC, 737 F.2d at 1136.

[380] First, the FCC must determine whether "like" facilities are used to provide both services. This test, the D.C. Circuit has explained, turns on "functional

the 1934 Act[381] and are expressly encouraged under the 1996 Act, in which privately negotiated/state-arbitrated agreements take the place of tariffed rates. Section 211(a) of the 1934 Act requires intercarrier contracts to be filed with the Commission.[382] And section 201(b) gives the FCC the power to set aside such contracts if the FCC is of the opinion that the contract is "contrary to the public interest." Except as limited by other, more specific provisions of the Communications Act, this term means no more (or less) than the FCC (or a reviewing court) wants it

---

equivalency." Ad Hoc Telecommunications Users Comm. v. FCC, 680 F.2d 790, 795 (D.C. Cir. 1982). That is, in applying this test, the FCC must "look[] to the nature of the services offered" and determine if customers perceive them as performing the same functions. American Broad. Co. v. FCC, 663 F.2d 133, 139 (D.C. Cir. 1980) (ABC v. FCC). "Considerations of cost differentials and competitive necessity are properly excluded" from this determination and may be introduced "only when determining whether the discrimination is unreasonable or unjust." Id. at 139. See also MCI v. FCC, 917 F.2d 30, 39 (D.C. Cir. 1990); Western Union v. FCC, 568 F.2d at 1019 n.15.

Second, the FCC must assess whether the amounts paid under the two pricing schemes for demonstrably "like" services are different. Finally, if there is such a disparity, the FCC must decide whether it is "just and reasonable." MCI v. FCC, 842 F.2d 1296, 1307 (D.C. Cir. 1988). "Perfect parity of charges is not necessary to meet the test of Section 202(a), but the FCC must articulate with precision its reasons for tolerating any discrepancies it uncovers." Id. at 1307. This requires a case-by-case determination of differences and justifications. The burden is always on the discriminating carrier to justify the difference between services. See, e.g., ABC v. FCC, 663 F.2d at 133; Western Union v. FCC, 568 F.2d at 1018. Section 210 creates a narrow exception to the antidiscrimination imperative of section 202 for officers, agents, and employees (and their families) of common carriers, who may be given "franks"—free or reduced price passes—by any carrier.

[381] Indeed, up to a point they take precedence over filed rates. Under the so-called Sierra-Mobile doctrine, federal agencies are precluded from permitting regulated carriers unilaterally to abrogate their private contracts by filing tariffs altering the terms of those contracts. FPC v. Sierra Pacific Power Co., 350 U.S. 348 (1956); United Gas Pipe Line Co. v. Mobile Gas Service Corp., 350 U.S. 332 (1956). The Court in Sierra recognized the authority of a regulatory agency to modify contracts that might "cast upon other consumers an excessive burden," but required that contract modification follow investigation and a determination that the contract was unjust, unreasonable, unduly discriminatory, or preferential. The Sierra-Mobile doctrine has been applied to the FCC. See, e.g., Bell Tel. Co. of Pa. v. FCC, 503 F.2d 1250, 1275–1282 (3d Cir. 1974).

[382] The FCC may exempt any carrier from filing "minor" contracts.

to mean.[383] In the verbal hand-waving that accompanies any application of this standard, it is considered good form to write something sincere about both the Communications Act's broader purposes and the specific prescriptions of sections 201 and 202.[384]

The FCC does not, however, have unilateral power to transform private contracts into public tariffs. For a time, several local telephone companies, with FCC permission, offered "dark" fiber to some select customers.[385] The fiber was supplied on an "individual case basis"; each service contract was negotiated separately and specifically tailored to particular customer needs.[386] Several years later, after various rounds of review,[387] the Commission decided that carriers should offer dark fiber to all comers at standard rates. It directed the carriers to terminate existing contracts and file tariffs. The telephone companies complied. The Commission rejected the rates they proposed and prescribed new ones.[388] Rather than offer dark fiber at those prices, the telephone companies sought to withdraw from the market entirely. The Commission denied that request, too; under

---

[383] Vague though the term "public interest" may be, the Supreme Court has rejected the contention that it amounts to an unconstitutional delegation of legislative power, reasoning that the remainder of the Act provides sufficient context and reference points to guide the FCC's discretion. *See* National Broad. Co. v. United States, 319 U.S. 190, 225–226 (1943).

[384] *See* MCI v. FCC, 712 F.2d 517, 534 (D.C. Cir. 1983).

[385] "Dark" fiber is access to a fiber-optic line with no associated electronics; it is the line itself that is leased, rather than a certain amount of bandwidth.

[386] *See* Investigation of Access and Divestiture Related Tariffs, Memorandum Opinion and Order, 97 F.C.C.2d 1082, 1143 (1984).

[387] *See* Local Exchange Carriers' Individual Case Basis DS3 Service Offerings, Memorandum Opinion and Order, 4 F.C.C. Rec. 8634 (1989); Memorandum Opinion and Order of Reconsideration, 5 F.C.C. Rec. 4842 (1990); Order, 5 F.C.C. Rec. 6772 (1990); Suspension Order, 6 F.C.C. Rec. 1436 (1991); Suspension Review Order, 6 F.C.C. Rec. 4776 (1991); Prescription Order, 6 F.C.C. Rec. 4891 (1991).

[388] Local Exchange Carriers' Individual Case Basis DS3 Service Offerings, Suspension Order, 6 F.C.C. Rec. 1436 (1991); Suspension Review Order, 6 F.C.C. Rec. 4776 (1991); Prescription Order, 6 F.C.C. Rec. 4891 (1991).

section 214, it has the power to license exit just as it licenses entry.[389]

The D.C. Circuit ruled that the Commission's section 214 power extends only to common carrier services and that dark fiber offerings had never risen to that level.[390] The Commission possibly could assert "ancillary jurisdiction" over private offerings of common carriers (under section 152 of the Communications Act),[391] but only common carrier activity falls within the Commission's Title II authority.[392] The Commission had never purported to employ its ancillary jurisdiction to craft an equivalent of section 214 for private carriers; the court specifically declined to decide whether it could.[393]

This ruling seems to create an opening for telephone companies, perhaps broader than the appellate court anticipated. Many services can be offered in ways that place them squarely outside the definition of "common carriage." Traditional cable

[389] Southwestern Bell Telephone Co., US WEST Communications, Bell Atlantic Telephone Co., BellSouth Telephone Co., Applications for Authority Pursuant to Section 214 of the Communications Act of 1934 To Cease Providing Dark Fiber Service, Memorandum Opinion and Order, 8 F.C.C. Rec. 2589 (1993). Section 214 provides that "no carrier shall discontinue, reduce, or impair service . . . unless and until there shall first have been obtained from the Commission a certificate that neither the present nor future public convenience and necessity will be adversely affected thereby." 47 U.S.C. §214(a).

[390] Southwestern Bell Tel. Co. v. FCC, 19 F.3d 1475, 1484 (D.C. Cir. 1994) ("In this instance, the Commission short-circuited any analysis of whether petitioners held themselves out indifferently to all potential users of dark fiber, by pronouncing an insupportable per se rule that a filing of a piece of paper with the FCC constitutes an offer of common carriage.").

[391] Id. The Commission has general regulatory jurisdiction over "all interstate and foreign communications by wire or radio . . . and . . . all persons engaged within the United States in such communication [except for communication in the Canal Zone]." 47 U.S.C. §152(a). This jurisdiction "is restricted to that reasonably ancillary to the effective performance of [its] various responsibilities" under Titles II and III of the Act. United States v. Southwestern Cable Co., 392 U.S. 157, 178 (1968); see also FCC v. Midwest Video Corp., 440 U.S. 689 (1979); United States v. Midwest Video Corp., 406 U.S. 649 (1972).

[392] The Commission may also, however, require common carriers to supply information regarding their private carriage offerings pursuant to section 211, which permits the Commission "to require the filing of any . . . contract[ ] of any carrier." 47 U.S.C. §211(b).

[393] Southwestern Bell, 19 F.3d at 1484.

television, for example, is plainly *not* a "carrier" service within the meaning of the Communications Act.

The 1996 Act has largely obliterated the traditional regulatory lines between "carriers" and "customers." Carriers buy service from each other in large quantities; customers are often value-added resellers. The 1934 Act's attempt to divide the world between section 201–203 "customers" and section 211 "carriers" is irreconcilable with modern network realities and with the 1996 Act. These provisions, however, still survive, and the law developed thereunder is still important.

§3.12 FCC Control over Rate-Making

The FCC has broad authority to screen both prices and terms of proposed rates, investigate existing rates, and, if necessary, prescribe alternatives. Section 201 gives the FCC supervisory power over a carrier's "charges, practices, classifications, and regulations."[394] It may control which carriers compete, where they compete, and under what kinds of corporate structures they complete. Section 214 requires advance FCC blessing for the construction of new facilities[395] or the discontinuation of service.[396] The FCC may regulate which types of devices may or may

---

[394] 47 U.S.C. §201(b).

[395] *Id.* §214(a). A carrier seeking to construct new lines or to extend existing lines must submit an application to the FCC describing the proposed construction or extension, the service to be provided, cost estimates, proposed tariff changes, and the factors showing public need. *See* 47 C.F.R. §63.01.

Section 214 was ostensibly added for reasons of efficiency so that the FCC might prevent inefficient duplication of facilities and equipment. *See* Mid-Texas Communication v. AT&T, 615 F.2d 1372, 1379 (5th Cir.), *cert. denied,* 449 U.S. 912 (1980). Although competition is a relevant factor in this determination, the FCC must also take into account safety, efficiency, public need, and financial integrity. *See, e.g.,* Phonetele, Inc. v. AT&T, 664 F.2d 716, 722 (9th Cir. 1981) (Kennedy, J.), *cert. denied,* 459 U.S. 1145 (1983); United States v. FCC, 652 F.2d 72, 104 (D.C. Cir. 1980) (en banc); Hawaiian Tel. Co. v. FCC, 498 F.2d 771 (D.C. Cir. 1974); Mid-Texas, 615 F.2d at 1379; Northeastern Tel. Co. v. AT&T, 477 F. Supp. 251 (D. Conn. 1978).

[396] 47 U.S.C. §214(a). A carrier seeking to discontinue or reduce service must submit an application describing the nature of the proposed change, any

not be connected to the network and how they may or may not be used. Section 201, for example, has been interpreted to empower the FCC to forbid hotels with their own private exchanges to charge guests more for long-distance phone calls than standard telco rates.[397]

§3.12.1 FCC Control Over Competition

These powers have given the FCC virtually unlimited power to suppress competition if it so chooses. Indeed, as discussed in section 1.5, the emergence of competition in the industry prior to the 1996 Act depended critically on FCC initiative or, more precisely, on FCC retreat from its own prior anticompetitive policies.

Section 201 provided the authority, for example, to reintroduce competition into CPE markets after a six-decade lapse.[398] Section 214 authorizations allowed microwave carriers to deploy competitive long-distance facilities, and section 201 mandates that permitted both interconnection and resale were likewise critical in introducing competition to long-distance markets.[399] For years, the choice for or against competition was left almost entirely to the FCC's unguided discretion. Finally, in 1983, Congress amended the Act to make clear that "[i]t shall be the policy of the United States to encourage the provision of new technologies and services to the public" and to require any person who opposes a new technology or service to "demonstrate that such proposal is inconsistent with the public interest."[400] By 1983, however, the shift toward competition was already irre-

---

tariff changes, the reasons for the discontinuation or reduction, and the factors showing that the public would not be adversely affected. *See* 47 C.F.R. §63.505.

[397] Ambassador, Inc. v. United States, 325 U.S. 317 (1945).

[398] Use of the Carterphone Service in Message Toll Telephone Services, Decision, 13 F.C.C.2d 420 (1968), *recons. denied*, 14 F.C.C.2d 571 (1968). *See* §8.4.1.2.

[399] *See* §9.4.

[400] 47 U.S.C. §157(a) (as added Dec. 8, 1983).

vocable.[401] In the 1996 Act, Congress decided to put a heavy thumb on the scales in favor of new entry by affirmatively requiring the incumbents to assist their would-be competitors.

§3.12.2   FCC Procedures for Reviewing Rates

Carriers need not obtain FCC approval before changing their filed rates. They must, however, give 90 days' advance notice. Under section 204(a), the FCC—acting on either a complaint or its own initiative—may suspend the tariff for up to five more months while it holds a hearing.[402] If the Commission's investigation is not completed within that period, the tariff goes into effect. The FCC may, however, order the carrier to keep an accurate record of amounts received under a new tariff and may subsequently order a refund.[403] Under the original 1934 Act, the FCC could only suspend a tariff in its entirety. In 1976, Congress added section 204(b), which permits the FCC to allow tariffs to take effect in part or temporarily.[404] Procedures under section 204(b) are less rigorous; the FCC need not engage in hearings or make a formal "just and reasonable" determination.

The Act did not originally impose any deadline on a final FCC ruling as to a tariff's lawfulness. As competition increased in the

---

[401] *See* §1.4.

[402] 47 U.S.C. §204(a)(1). The FCC must give the carrier written reasons for the suspension. *Id.*

[403] *Id.*

[404] The FCC may make effective all or part of a tariff change proposal "on a temporary basis pending further order of the Commission . . . based upon a written showing by the carrier or carriers affected, and an opportunity for written comment thereon by affected persons, that such partial authorization is just, fair, and reasonable." Section 204(b) does not, of course, mandate that no tariff may go into effect absent such a written finding. Section 204(a) permits any tariff to go into effect absent FCC action to the contrary, and section 204(b) does not override section 204(a) in that respect. It simply adds extra flexibility, "[n]otwithstanding the provisions of Subsection (a)," to permit the FCC to conduct an investigation of the lawfulness of a tariff without suspending it pending the outcome. *See* MCI v. FCC, 627 F.2d 322, 334–335 (D.C. Cir. 1980).

1980s, FCC review became slower and slower.[405] The D.C. Circuit eventually imposed a "rule of reason" deadline. According to the court, the Act "assumes" that "rates will be finally decided within a reasonable time encompassing months, occasionally a year or two, but not several years or a decade."[406] In 1989, Congress amended the Act to require that an investigation conclude within 12 months after a tariff takes effect—three additional months are allowed for factual questions of "extraordinary complexity."[407] Thus, the 1989 amendment provided that at the outer limit an FCC investigation had to be completed within 23 months after the tariff is first filed.[408] But under section 205, a carrier's rates remain subject to challenge and investigation at any time, either on the Commission's own initiative or upon complaint.

In 1992, the D.C. Circuit was asked to determine the limits of FCC rate-making authority over the setting of access charges. The Commission was concerned that Illinois Bell, among others, had set its access charges unreasonably high. The Commission ordered an investigation of these charges, but refused to suspend the tariff or to issue an accounting order pending the outcome. It eventually ordered lower rates and refunds of excess collections received during the investigation.[409]

Illinois Bell appealed that decision, arguing that the Commission could not mandate the return of any excess charges collected by the carrier unless it followed the procedures of section 204(a)(1) and either suspended the tariff or issued an accounting order. The D.C. Circuit agreed. Section 204(a)(1) both creates and limits the power to order refunds. When a complaint is filed, the Commission may suspend it, hold a hearing, and

---

[405] See §9.5.

[406] MCI v. FCC, 627 F.2d at 340 (finding delay of four years unreasonable and remanding to Commission to recommend within 30 days a feasible schedule for final determination of a just and reasonable WATS tariff).

[407] 47 U.S.C. §204(a)(2)(A), prior to amendment by 1996 Act.

[408] Ninety days' advance notice, followed by five months' suspension, twelve months for a hearing, and three months for factual questions of extraordinary complexity. The 1996 Act amended these provisions, changing the maximum time allowed for a hearing to 5 months, thereby reducing the outer limit for an investigation's completion to 16 months. See 47 U.S.C. §502.

[409] Annual 1988 Access Tariff Filings, Memorandum Opinion and Order on Reconsideration, 4 F.C.C. Rec. 3965 (1989).

then issue a rate order. For as long as a hearing is pending on a tariff, the Commission may require an accounting of amounts collected under it. When the hearing is completed, the Commission may order a refund. But if it fails to follow these procedures, it may not thereafter order a refund.[410]

§3.12.3   FCC Prescription of Rates

Section 205 also delineates the FCC's remedial powers upon finding that a tariff is unlawful.[411] The FCC itself may announce what the tariffed rate for the service will be.[412]

Alternatively, it may simply order a carrier to eliminate an unacceptable rate disparity[413] or specify which rate is to be raised or lowered.[414] In prescribing a new rate, however, the FCC must specifically find it to be "just, fair, and reasonable," not merely "the best of the alternatives discussed herein."[415] In short, the FCC must do what a carrier normally does: anticipate both costs and demand, allocate common costs, and calculate a fair rate of return.

As a general rule, retroactive rate adjustment is forbidden[416] except when the Commission has invoked section 204 beforehand and has required a carrier to keep special account of a tariff under ongoing review. Thus, customers may not recoup

[410] Illinois Bell Tel. Co. v. FCC, 966 F.2d 1478, 1482 (D.C. Cir. 1992).

[411] 47 U.S.C. §205(a).

[412] See Chapter 2 for more detail on the substance of price regulation. See also M. Crew & P. Kleindorfer, The Economics of Public Utility Regulation 210–234 (1986); S. Breyer, Regulation and Its Reform 299–314 (1982); F. Scherer, Industrial Market Structure and Economic Performance 481–486 (2d ed., 1980); A. Kahn, The Economics of Regulation: Principles and Institutions 25–54 (1970); A. Kahn, The Road to More Intelligent Telephone Pricing, 1 Yale J. on Reg. 139 (1984).

[413] See, e.g., Western Union v. FCC, 568 F.2d at 1020.

[414] See, e.g., Western Union Tel. Co. v. FCC, 815 F.2d 1495 (D.C. Cir. 1987).

[415] AT&T v. FCC, 449 F.2d at 450 (internal quotations omitted) (reversing prescription where FCC expressly disclaimed former finding).

[416] TRT Telecomms. Corp. v. FCC, 857 F.2d 1535, 1547 (D.C. Cir. 1988). See generally Arkansas La. Gas Co. v. Hall, 453 U.S. 571, 578 n.8 (1981); Arizona Grocery Co. v. Atchinson, Topeka & Santa Fe Ry. Co., 284 U.S. 370, 390 (1932).

amounts overpaid under a tariff later found to be unreasonable.[417] Nor may a carrier recoup any shortfall if filed rates prove to be too low. Indeed, it has traditionally been "a cardinal principal of rate-making that a utility may not set rates to recoup past losses, nor may the Commission prescribe rates on that principle."[418] Current rates must be based on current conditions and should not be set either to refund excess profits from the past or to make up for lost profits.[419] Both the carrier and its customers may thus plan securely in reliance on filed rates.

The Communications Act plainly contemplates the prescription of *rates,* not rates of return. By the 1960s, however, it was becoming apparent that the FCC could not feasibly police telephony rate by rate, service by service.[420] In 1967, the FCC announced that it would prescribe a rate of return instead.[421] The Commission would fix the target rate of return, and the carrier would set tariffs designed to earn this rate of return overall. In *Nader v. FCC,*[422] the D.C. Circuit approved this approach. "On

---

[417] *Arizona Grocery Co.,* 284 U.S. at 390.

[418] Nader v. FCC, 520 F.2d 182, 202 (D.C. Cir. 1975).

[419] Board of Commrs. v. New York Tel. Co., 271 U.S. 23, 31–32 (1926) (holding that excess past depreciation cannot be applied to overcome deficits in future earnings caused by otherwise confiscatory rates). This principle was originally based on the "just compensation" clause, applicable to the states through the Fourteenth Amendment. "The just compensation safeguarded to the utility by the Fourteenth Amendment," the Court explained in justifying its holding, "is a reasonable return on the value of the property used *at the time that it is being used for the public service." Id.* (emphasis added). Its continued validity as a constitutional requirement was called into question by the Court's decision in Federal Power Comm'n v. Hope Natural Gas Co., 320 U.S. 591 (1944), which concluded that the Constitution is satisfied provided that the utility obtains sufficient funds to attract capital and maintain its financial integrity. *See id.* at 605. It may still be valid, however, as a general principal of rate-making embodied in the Communications Act. *See* TRT Telecomms. Corp. v. FCC, 857 F.2d at 1546; Nader v. FCC, 520 F.2d at 202.

[420] *See* §2.2.3.

[421] AT&T, Charges for Interstate and Foreign Communications Service, Interim Decision and Order, 9 F.C.C.2d 30 (1967). *See also* American Telephone & Telegraph Company, and the Associated Bell System Companies, Charges for Interstate Telephone Service, Transmittal Nos. 10989 and 11027, Decision and Order, 38 F.C.C.2d 213 (1972).

[422] Nader v. FCC, 520 F.2d at 201.

its face," the court of appeals acknowledged, "Section 205 only authorizes the Commission to prescribe charges, classifications, regulations and practices, not rates of return. . . . [I]mplicit in this literal reading of the statute is the proposition that the Commission must determine each cost component of a rate or charge before it may make a prescription."[423] But "any literal interpretation" of section 205, the court of appeals concluded, would be "overly simplistic."[424] "The Commission's inability to determine the lawfulness *vel non* of [particular rate] increases within a reasonable time suggests that it verges on losing its ability to effectively regulate at all."[425] Accordingly, since "there is no explicit statutory prohibition against prescribing a rate of return,"[426] the D.C. Circuit yielded to pragmatic necessity.

By prescribing a rate of return, the FCC needed to determine only one (and that the most general) of the variables relevant to setting rates, and even with respect to this one variable, the Commission was given "broad discretion in selecting the appropriate methodology for calculating the rate of return."[427] The

---

[423] *Id.* at 203.

[424] *Id.*

[425] *Id.* at 207.

[426] *Id.*

[427] United States v. FCC, 707 F.2d 610, 612 (D.C. Cir. 1983) (upholding "weighted cost of capital approach," whereby the rate is calculated based on the cost of debt, the cost of equity, and the proportion of each in the company's capital structure). Since "rate-making is not an exact science . . . rate of return decisions are appropriately treated as policy determinations in which the agency is acknowledged to have expertise." *Id.* at 618. *See also* MCI v. FCC, 675 F.2d 408, 415–416 (D.C. Cir. 1982) (noting the inherently "political" nature of the FCC's allocation of common costs in the Separations Manual; "elements of fairness and other noneconomic values inevitably enter the analysis of the choice to be made."). Thus, even if "[e]ach step in the FCC's calculation is to some extent guesswork," as long as it is *"reasoned* guesswork," as long as it "is plausible [and] tethered to the Commission's general experience," it will be approved by the courts. NARUC v. FCC, 737 F.2d at 1141 (emphasis added). The courts have declined to "divorce the difficulty of the regulatory dilemma from the reasonableness of its resolution." *Id.* (approving surcharge applied to PBX users as not "unreasonable or unsound").

It is, however, arbitrary and capricious for the FCC not to consider a "significant" alternative approach proposed by a party. City of Brookings Mun.

FCC was also able to fulfill its constitutional obligation to ensure, in the abstract, that a carrier could cover its capital costs, while leaving to the carrier the messy and uncertain process of translating a rate of return into specific charges for specific services.[428] Carriers, however, were now left with an open opportunity to tilt all critical assumptions concerning projected costs and demand in their own favor. Carriers that exceeded their prescribed rate of return even by a large amount could plead miscalculation with impunity; no retroactive rate adjustment was permitted.

The groundwork was thus laid for the courts also to abandon the well-established rule against retroactive rate adjustments. In *New England Telephone & Telegraph Co. v. FCC,*[429] the D.C. Circuit did just that. The Commission's refund order, the court reasoned in a deliberate bit of verbal obfuscation, was "more precisely considered a prospective rate adjustment to compensate for past surpluses" than a "refund."[430] While acknowledging that such a refund order is not provided for by section 205, the court determined that the order was a reasonably necessary enforcement mechanism and therefore authorized by the FCC's power to issue orders "as may be necessary in the execution of its functions."[431]

A year later, however, in *AT&T v. FCC,*[432] the D.C. Circuit appears to have had some second thoughts. This time it struck

---

Tel. Co. v. FCC, 822 F.2d 1153, 1169 (D.C. Cir. 1987). For a detailed discussion of pricing issues, see Chapter 2.

[428] *See* AT&T v. FCC, 836 F.2d 1386, 1390 (D.C. Cir. 1988).

[429] New England Tel. & Tel. Co. v. FCC, 826 F.2d 1101 (D.C. Cir. 1987).

[430] *Id.* at 1107.

[431] *Id.* (construing 47 U.S.C. §154(i)). "This case," the D.C. Circuit claimed, is "no different from one in which the Commission prescribed actual rates and the carrier, either intentionally or inadvertently, collected higher charges. Although no carrier has yet been so brazen, there can be little doubt under such circumstances but that the Commission would be well within its authority in forcing the carrier to disgorge the unlawful excess." *Id.* at 1108. The Court cited in support of this proposition United States v. Corrick, 298 U.S. 435 (1936). But in that case, the Supreme Court held only that the Commission can reject *filings* in excess of prescribed rates, not that the Commission can collect refunds based on filed rates in excess of prescribed rates. *Id.* at 439–440.

[432] AT&T v. FCC, 836 F.2d 1386.

down a general FCC rule that would have required each carrier to refund all revenues exceeding a target rate of return by more than a specified amount. The Commission had purported to set a rate of return that was "at the same time a minimum and a maximum" allowable return. The FCC claimed, in other words, to have located a rate perfectly calculated to ensure both a fair return on capital and a fair price to the consumer.[433] But the rule provided only for refunds, not for recoupment of any shortfall, thus endangering the carriers' constitutionally guaranteed fair return on investment.[434] The court purported to distinguish *New England Telephone & Telegraph Co.* on the grounds that that case involved a specific refund order on specific facts without any internal contradiction of the Commission's own theory of rate-of-return regulation.[435]

In concurrence, Judge Starr strongly criticized any authorization for a refund rule as outside the specific statutory mechanism.[436] "Once the schedule is filed and allowed to go into effect," he noted, "carriers (and consumers) are entitled to rely on it, except for the one special situation addressed (and procedurally safeguarded) in Section 204."[437] Judge Starr contended that "[a]lthough *Nader* added a new wrinkle to the rate regulatory system by allowing the Commission to prescribe the rate of

---

[433] "If the rate were higher, the balance would tip in favor of the investor; if lower, it would tip in favor of the consumer. According to the Commission, therefore, its selected rate of return is the proper balance between these interests and hence the minimum return the carrier requires." *Id.* at 1390.

[434] *See id.* at 1392.

[435] In fact, the court in New England said that "[t]he Commission has concluded that a guaranteed minimum annual return is not essential to protect [a carrier's right to earn an overall reasonable return]. That conclusion is a reasonable one." New England Tel. & Tel. Co. v. FCC, 826 F.2d at 1109.

[436] AT&T v. FCC, 836 F.2d at 1393–1396.

[437] *Id.* at 1394. Under the "filed rate doctrine" articulated in the area of energy regulation, which "has its origins in . . . cases interpreting the Interstate Commerce Act" and "has been extended across the spectrum of regulated utilities," the Commission "may not impose a retroactive rate regulation and, in particular, may not order reparations." Arkansas La. Gas. Co. v. Hall, 453 U.S. 571, 577–578 n.8 (1981). *See, e.g., Arizona Grocery Co.,* 284 U.S. at 390 ("Where the Commission has . . . declared what is the maximum reasonable rate to be charged by a carrier, it may not at a later time . . . subject a carrier

return (*a mere component of a rate*), I am at a loss to understand why *Nader* brings with it an *enforcement mechanism* that contravenes the terms, structure, and goals of the Act itself."[438] In short, "[t]he Commission, inspired by its own victory in *Nader*, has turned the regulatory world upside down."[439]

The D.C. Circuit denied suggestions to take both *New England Telephone & Telegraph* and *AT&T v. FCC* en banc. Thus, the tension between the two cases is unresolved, as is the current status of the rule against retroactive rate adjustments, although *AT&T v. FCC* has been subsequently affirmed in broad terms by the Sixth Circuit.[440] Furthermore, the D.C. Circuit subsequently reaffirmed its *AT&T* holding in setting aside yet another FCC effort to inflict refunds for overearnings.[441] In *Virgin Islands Telephone Corp. v. FCC*, the D.C. Circuit noted that the Commission's action "leads to the same systematic bias against carriers—forcing carriers to disgorge excess profits, but absorb shortfalls—that we held unlawful in *AT&T*."[442] Within a single monitoring period, the Commission could not shave a carrier's earnings peak without taking into account the earnings valleys.[443]

---

which conformed thereto to the payment of reparation measured by what the Commission now holds it should have decided in the earlier proceeding to be a reasonable rate."); *see* Robin Pipeline Co. v. FERC, 795 F.2d 182, 189 n.7 (D.C. Cir. 1986) (the Commission "may not order a retroactive refund based on a post hoc determination of the illegality of a filed rate's prescription").

[438] AT&T v. FCC, 836 F.2d at 1395 (emphasis in original).

[439] *Id*. at 1394.

[440] Ohio Bell Tel. Co. v. FCC, 949 F.2d 864 (1991) (striking down FCC order that required carriers to refund overearnings of access charges, while precluding those carriers from setting off underearnings against overearnings).

[441] Virgin Islands Tel. Corp. v. FCC, 989 F.2d 1231 (D.C. Cir. 1993). Vitelco filed short-term rate increases in anticipation of lower demand after Hurricane Hugo. As it turned out, demand increased, Vitelco's operating expenses fell below normal, and its annualized earnings while the rates were in effect consequently soared to triple its authorized rate of return. Although Vitelco's earnings were supposed to be monitored over a two-year period, the FCC ordered refunds on the ground that the carrier had overearned during a six-month period when the higher rates were in effect. *Id*. at 1235–1236.

[442] *Id*. at 1239.

[443] The court also held that the FCC had improperly "ignored the factors that should be considered in determining whether remedial action is necessary." *Id*. "[T]he prospective selection of a tariff that will generate the

The implication of this line of cases appears to be that if the FCC simply articulates its rate of return as falling within a zone of reasonableness (so that the rate of return can be adjusted within that zone to recoup past losses or refund past excesses), then the rule against setting prospective rates to recoup past losses (or refund excess charges) will fall.

In any event, the question may be somewhat mooted by the FCC's shift from rate-of-return regulation to price caps. Price caps, as the term implies, set limits on prices, not profits. This incentive-based regulatory scheme allows carriers to "earn greater profits through increased efficiency and market innovations and, ideally, to pass some of the cost savings on to consumers."[444] Price caps rely less on controversial cost allocations; therefore, they avoid the problems of retroactive rate adjustments caused by rate-of-return-generated inflated rate bases. The FCC implemented price caps for AT&T in 1989 and for all Tier 1 LECs the following year.[445]

---

prescribed rate of return is necessarily an imprecise endeavor." *Id.* Consequently, "once the Commission finds that a carrier has exceeded (as a pure mathematical matter) its prescribed rate of return, it should then consider other relevant factors in determining whether a rate is unreasonable and a refund warranted." *Id.* Among the relevant considerations are "whether the carrier's projections were reasonable at the time they were made," whether ratepayers suffered actual harm, whether "changes in the market environment" affected a carrier's return, and whether "overriding equitable considerations" favor or disfavor remedial action. *Id.* at 1240.

[444] Palmer, Rate-of-Return Versus Price-Caps: The Long-Distance Regulation Battle, 14 Colum.-VLA J. L. & Arts 571 (1990). But requiring carriers to reduce rates in excess of their cost savings was ruled impermissible in United States Tel Assn. v. FCC, No. 97-1469, slip op. (D.C. Cir. May 21, 1999).

[445] *See* Policy and Rules Concerning Rates for Dominant Carriers, Notice of Proposed Rulemaking, 2 F.C.C. Rec. 5208 (1987); Further Notice of Proposed Rulemaking, 3 F.C.C. Rec. 3195 (1988); Second Further Notice of Proposed Rulemaking, Report and Order, 4 F.C.C. Rec. 2873 (1989) (hereinafter *AT&T Price Cap Order*). Adopting Price Cap Regulation for AT&T, Report and Order, and Price Cap Regulation for LECs, Second Further Notice of Proposed Rulemaking, were published as one document. *See Policy and Rules Concernign Rates for Dominant Carriers,* Supplemental Notice of Proposed Rulemaking, 5 F.C.C. Rec. 2176 (1990); Second Report and Order, 5 F.C.C. Rec. 6786 (1990) (hereinafter *LEC Price Cap Order*); Erratum, 5 F.C.C. Rec. 7664 (1990), *modified on recons.,* 6 F.C.C. Rec. 2637 (1991), *aff'd sub nom.* National Rural Telecom Assn. v. FCC, 988 F.2d 174 (D.C. Cir. 1993). *See* §2.2.3.2.

But the advent of price caps has raised other retroactive rate-making issues. One element of the Commission's price-cap regulations was a sharing mechanism that entailed a one-time adjustment to a local exchange carrier's price-cap index when its rate of return for the previous year has exceeded a prescribed threshold. This correction in the price-cap index for future rates was designed to ensure that customers "shared" in the additional, unexpected productivity gain of the LEC. This structure allowed the Commission to pursue a kind of rate-of-return result under a price-cap regime by adjusting the price-cap index if an LEC's profits exceed a predetermined rate of return. The Commission originally believed that sharing would rarely occur. In practice, however, sharing became routine, with the price caps of most LECs in the sharing zone.

As part of a performance review of the price-cap regulation system,[446] the Commission determined that its calculation of the original productivity offset had been erroneous, resulting in an improperly low productivity offset. Accordingly, it recalculated and increased the productivity offset. To prevent its initial error from being imbedded in future rates, the Commission ordered carriers to adjust their price-cap indices retrospectively so that the indices were at the levels they would have been had the Commission initially set the productivity offset at the correct level.[447] The Commission also instituted an "add-back" rule, which required carriers to include sharing adjustments as part of revenues when determining productivity gains and the following year's sharing adjustment.[448] Carriers were required to adjust their 1994 revenues to determine their 1995 sharing requirement.

LECs challenged both of these changes as impermissible retroactive rate-makings, contending that they improperly required carriers retrospectively to adjust their price-cap indices in

---

[446] *See* Price Cap Performance Review for Local Exchange Carriers, First Report and Order, 10 F.C.C. Rec. 8961 (1995).

[447] *Id.* at 9069–9070 ¶¶245–256.

[448] Price Cap Regulation of Local Exchange Carriers: Rate-of-Return Sharing and Lower Formula Adjustment, Report and Order, 10 F.C.C. Rec. 5656, 5659–5666 ¶¶16–50 (1995).

order to reclaim prior revenues.[449] The D.C. Circuit rejected this claim, finding that both changes had only future effects.[450] As stated by the court,

> The sharing rules, including the add-back rule, are purely prospective. They determine how much a carrier can charge for services that it will provide in the future. . . . [T]hey do not require carriers to refund money they have already earned. Rather, the sharing rules draw upon the "antecedent facts" of a [LEC's] prior earnings and sharing obligations—and what those earnings indicate about the [LEC's] productivity—in establishing the [LEC's] sharing obligation for the next period. A regulation is not made retroactive "merely because it draws upon antecedent facts for its operation."[451]

In 1997, the Commission made further, more significant revisions to its price caps.[452] As part of its "plan to construct a dynamic regulatory framework to further the new pro-competitive, deregulatory paradigm" set out in the 1996 Act, the Commission eliminated its sharing requirements, concluding that they "substantially undercut the efficiency incentives of price cap regulation and retained some of the cost-misallocation incentives inherent in rate-of-return regulation."[453] Instead, the Commission adopted what is characterized as a "reasonable, challenging price cap plan that effectively requires price cap LECs to reduce inflation-adjusted prices for interstate access services by approximately 6.5 percent annually."[454] According to the Commission, "This new price cap reflects a more reliable productivity estimate . . . one that is based on a careful analysis of the rate of growth of incumbent LEC total factor productivity (TFP) and the rate of

---

[449] Bell Atlantic v. FCC, 79 F.3d 1195 (1996).

[450] *Id.* at 1208.

[451] *Id.* at 1206–1207.

[452] Price Cap Performance Review for Local Exchange Carriers, Fourth Report and Order, CC Docket No. 94-1, and Second Report and Order, CC Docket No. 96-262, 12 F.C.C. Rec. 16,642 (1997).

[453] *Id.* at 16,645 ¶1.

[454] *Id.*

change of LEC input prices."[455] In *United States Telephone Assoc. v. FCC*, No. 97-1469 (May 21, 1999), the D.C. Circuit struck down the FCC's choice of a 6.5 percent annual reduction and affirmed its elimination of sharing.

§3.12.4   Rate-Making Under the 1996 Act

The 1996 Act has added the difficult question of what rates an incumbent should charge to its competitors for interconnection, for services available for resale, and for unbundled network elements. Section 252(d) of the 1996 Act expressly assigns to "State commission[s]" the authority to determine "just and reasonable" rates.[456] The FCC nevertheless declared that Congress intended the *federal* agency to take the lead role in implementing the statutory pricing provisions. The Commission accordingly asserted jurisdiction to adopt "national pricing rules" and to relegate the states to the subordinate and largely ministerial role of applying those rules.[457]

In particular, the Commission mandated a new pricing methodology known as "total element long run incremental cost" (TELRIC), which required states to set prices based solely on the incremental, forward-looking cost of an ideally efficient network.[458] The FCC then defined in elaborate detail the steps that state commissions must take to adhere to the TELRIC standard.[459] The Commission further specified the result that states must reach as to every other pricing issue of consequence, from the extent of geographical rate "deaveraging" (at least three different rate zones in each state) to the appropriate divisions

---

[455] *Id.*

[456] 47 U.S.C. §252(d).

[457] Implementation of the Local Competition Provisions in the Telecommunications Act of 1996, First Report and Order, 11 F.C.C. Rec. 15,499, 15,544 ¶85, 15,557–15,558 ¶111 (1996) (hereinafter *Local Competition Order*), *modified on recons.* 11 F.C.C. Rec. 13,042 (1996), *vacated in part,* Iowa Utils. Bd. v. FCC, 120 F.3d 753 (8th Cir. 1997), *rev'd sub nom.* AT&T v. Iowa Utils. Bd., 119 S. Ct. 721 (1999).

[458] *Local Competition Order,* 11 F.C.C. Rec. at 15,515 ¶29.

[459] *See, e.g., id.* at 15,844–15,862 ¶¶672–715.

between recurring and nonrecurring charges.[460] The FCC even ordered each state to apply specific FCC-prescribed rates (known as "proxy" prices) until the state could conduct a detailed cost study in compliance with the FCC's newly minted TELRIC methodology.[461]

As already noted,[462] the FCC's order was challenged in the Eighth Circuit by a number of state commissions and incumbent LECs. The Eighth Circuit granted a stay of the pricing rules because of "what appear[ed] to be the rather clear and direct indication [in the statutory text] that the state commissions"—not the FCC—"should establish prices."[463]

After full briefing and argument, the court of appeals confirmed its earlier tentative holding that the plain language of section 252 "directly and straightforwardly assigns to the states" the authority to set prices.[464] Those specific congressional directives were entirely sufficient to resolve the issue of pricing jurisdiction. The court made plain, however, that, even if there were "[a]ny ambiguity," it would be resolved against the FCC because of the jurisdictional proscription of section 2(b), as interpreted in *Louisiana PSC*.[465] As the court of appeals explained, "[T]he prices that incumbent local exchange carriers may charge their new competitors for interconnection, unbundled access, and resale . . . qualify as 'charges . . . for or in connection with intrastate communications service.'"[466]

---

[460] *See* 47 C.F.R. §51.507(d)–(f).

[461] *Local Competition Order*, 11 F.C.C. Rec. at 15,515 ¶29, 15,883–15,884 ¶¶767–771.

[462] *See* §3.3.4.

[463] Iowa Utils. Bd. v. FCC, 109 F.3d 418, 424 (8th Cir. 1996).

[464] Iowa Utils. Bd. v. FCC, 120 F.3d at 797.

[465] *Id.* at 796.

[466] *Id.* (quoting 47 U.S.C. §152(b)). In a separate appeal that was briefed and argued independently of the main appeal and that the court decided in a separate opinion, the Eighth Circuit concluded that the FCC lacked jurisdiction to issue mandatory rules governing the states' implementation of "intraLATA toll [i.e., short-haul long-distance] dialing parity." California v. FCC, 124 F.3d 934, 942–943 (8th Cir. 1997). The court of appeals relied on the express terms of section 271(e)(2)(B)—which "indicates that state commissions, not the FCC, have the authority to issue intraLATA dialing parity

The Supreme Court granted certiorari and reversed the Eighth Circuit, concluding that "[t]he Commission may prescribe such rules and regulations as may be necessary in the public interest to carry out the provisions of this Act."[467] Since Congress expressly directed that the 1996 Act be inserted into the 1934 Act, the Court concluded that the Commission's rulemaking authority extends to the local competition provisions of the 1996 Act. More specifically, the Court found no inconsistency between the FCC's detailed pricing rules and section 252(c)(2), which "entrusts the task of establishing rates to the state commissions." The states, the court noted, still get to "apply [the FCC's] standards and implement [the FCC's] methodology, determining the concrete result in particular circumstances. That is enough to constitute the establishment of rates."[468]

Justice Thomas, in a dissent joined by the Chief Justice and Justice Breyer, found cold comfort in this limited role for the states. In Justice Thomas's view, Congress did not intend "to limit States' authority to mechanically apply whatever methodologies, formulas, and rules that the FCC mandated."[469] Justice Breyer elaborated on the last point in a separate dissent, noting that the FCC's rules leave the states "little or no freedom to choose among reasonable rate-determining methods according to the State's policy-related judgments, assessing local economic circumstances or community need."[470] After canvassing various ways in which the Act's pricing requirements might be implemented to better effect than the FCC's own rules, Justice Breyer concluded: "The FCC's regulations do not set forth an outer envelope surrounding a set of reasonable choices; instead, they constitute the kind of detailed policy-related rate-setting that the statute in respect to local matters leaves to the states."[471]

---

rules"—as well as on the court's analysis of section 2(b) in *Louisiana PSC*. *Id.* at 942.

[467] AT&T v. Iowa Utils. Bd., 19 S. Ct. 743; *see* 47 U.S.C. §201(b).
[468] *Id.* at 732.
[469] *Id.* at 745 (Thomas, J., dissenting).
[470] *Id.* at 751 (Breyer, J., dissenting).
[471] *Id.* at 753.

§3.13   Industry Oversight Provisions

§3.13.1   *Transactions*

As noted in section 3.11.5, section 211 of the 1934 Act requires carriers to file with the FCC all contracts they enter into with other carriers. The FCC may also require carriers to file contracts made with noncarriers.[472] Section 215 directs the FCC to "examine" the transactions entered into by carriers and to report to Congress whether any of these transactions have adversely affected service or rates. The Senate originally considered empowering the FCC to void or modify carrier transactions, to condition transactions between a carrier and its corporate affiliates on Commission approval, and to require carriers to make purchases only through competitive bids.[473] Bell, however, vehemently objected to this "usurpation of the functions of management by public authority" and declared that "[b]usiness would just stop" while awaiting FCC approval.[474] The bill was therefore amended simply to instruct the FCC to report later on the need for such powers.[475] In the end, no legislation creating such powers was ever enacted.[476]

§3.13.2   *Internal Management*

Section 212 prohibits all interlocking directorates between common carriers absent FCC approval.[477] An exception covers a parent carrier and subsidiaries in which it holds at least a 50

---

[472] 47 U.S.C. §211(b).

[473] S. 2910, 73d Cong., 2d Sess. §215 (1934).

[474] *Senate Hearings* at 78, 80 (statement of Walter S. Gifford). Much of the testimony of Bell's president at the Senate hearings was devoted to this section of the proposed bill. *See id.* at 78–84.

[475] 47 U.S.C. §215(a). *See* 77 Cong. Rec. 8824 (May 15, 1934) (remarks of Sen. Dill).

[476] *See* Cox & Byrnes, The Common Carrier Provisions at 44.

[477] A person seeking to become an officer in two or more carriers must apply to the FCC and provide "a full explanation of the reasons why grant of the authority sought will not adversely affect either public or private interests

percent interest. Section 218 authorizes the FCC to inquire into the management of carriers.

That same section also empowers the FCC to obtain any information it may need from carriers, their parents, and their subsidiaries. The following section allows the FCC to demand annual reports from carriers and their affiliates, detailing such things as capital stock issued, dividends paid, the identities of the largest shareholders, other debts, the number of employees and their salaries, the names of officers and directors and their compensation, a complete annual balance sheet, and anything else.[478] Section 213 permits the FCC to make its own valuation of any property owned or used by a carrier. Upon request, a carrier must file an inventory of its property,[479] the original cost of its property,[480] and any other information or records that may be needed.[481]

§3.13.3 Depreciation

As discussed in Chapter 2, an important part of the cost of telephone service is the cost of capital investment in fixed physical plant. That cost depends in turn on depreciation rates and accounting rules. Section 220 authorizes the FCC to prescribe both. It has done so through rulemaking for accounting rules[482] and adjudication for depreciation.[483] As discussed earlier, the Act is deliberately vague as to the division of federal and state authority in this regard.[484]

. . . [and] address whether grant of the permission requested could result in anticompetitive conduct." 47 C.F.R. §62.11.

[478] 47 U.S.C. §219(a). The FCC does require such reports. 47 C.F.R. §43.21(a). Reports must be filed for each calendar year by April 1 of the succeeding year.

[479] 47 U.S.C. §213(b).

[480] *Id.* §213(c).

[481] *Id.* §13(f).

[482] *See* 47 C.F.R. §§32 et seq.

[483] *See Louisiana PSC,* 476 U.S. at 360–363.

[484] *See* §3.3.3.

§3.13.4   Mergers and Consolidations

Section 221(a) of the 1934 Act empowered the Commission to regulate mergers and consolidations.[485] Any merger or acquisition involving a common carrier has to be approved in advance. Once the FCC approved a transaction as "in the public interest," however, it was exempt from the federal antitrust laws.

The 1996 Act repealed section 221(a). Thus, the FCC no longer has authority to exempt transactions from the ordinary application of the federal antitrust laws. All major telecom mergers now go through standard Hart-Scott-Rodino review.[486] "[O]ne of the underlying themes of the bill," the conference statement declared, is "to get both [the FCC and the Department of Justice] back to their proper roles."[487] The new law stops short, however, of directing the FCC to leave competitive considerations out of its own reviews of mergers conducted in connection with its responsibilities under the Communications Act.[488] As discussed in Chapter 7, the extent to which the FCC should duplicate the competitive review conducted by the Department of Justice has become an important issue in the light of increasing consolidation in the industry.

§3.13.5   Transfer of Licenses

The Commission retains significant "public interest" review authority over mergers whenever (as is always the case) they involve a transfer of licenses. Section 310(d) of the Communications Act provides in part:

---

[485] Section 221(a) derives from the Willis-Graham Act of 1921, ch. 20, 42 Stat. 27 (1921). That statute authorized the ICC to approve the consolidation of properties of telephone companies into single companies if such consolidation is "of advantage to the persons to whom service is to be rendered and in the public interest. . . ." The statute granted express immunity from the antitrust laws for such consolidations.

[486] 15 U.S.C. §8a.

[487] S. Conf. Rep. No. 104-230, at 201 (1996).

[488] Id.

> No construction permit or station license, or any rights there-under, shall be transferred, assigned, or disposed of in any manner, voluntarily or involuntarily, directly or indirectly, or by transfer of control of any corporation holding such permit or license, to any person except upon application to the Commission and upon finding by the Commission that the public interest, convenience and necessity will be served thereby.

A transfer of control can be de jure (50 percent or more voting power passes into the hands of a new party) or de facto (control actually resides in a party that does not possess nominal voting control). The Commission has thus stated that an evaluation of corporate control must look beyond ownership percentages to the particular facts of any given situation. Because section 310 of the Act does not prescribe any particular formula for what constitutes transfer of control, the Commission has long held that a case-by-case analysis of the totality of the circumstances is appropriate.[489]

When assessing de facto transfer questions, the Commission has looked at a number of factors beyond stock ownership.[490] For example, the Commission in the past has examined the specific terms of agreements between the licensee and the minority shareholder.[491] In order to conclude that a transfer of control has taken place, the Commission must find that a minority shareholder exercises influence "to the degree that [it] is able to 'determine' the licensee's policies and operation, or 'dominate' corporation affairs."[492]

The Commission's standards and procedures for evaluating license transfers are discussed in detail in Chapter 7.

---

[489] McCaw Cellular Communications, Memorandum Opinion and Order, 66 Rad. Reg. 2d (P & F) 667, 673–674 (1989); Petroleum Communications, Inc., Order on Reconsideration, 61 Rad. Reg. 2d (P & F) 711, 719 (1986).

[490] News International PLC, Memorandum Opinion and Order, 55 Rad. Reg. 2d (P & F) 945, 950 (1984); Stereo Broadcasters, Inc., Memorandum Opinion and Order, 55 F.C.C.2d 819, 821 ¶7 (1975); WHDH, Inc., Memorandum Opinion and Order, 16 Rad. Reg. 2d (P & F) 185, 194 (1969).

[491] See News International PLC, 55 Rad. Reg. 2d at 951.

[492] Id. at 950.

§3.14 Procedural and Administrative Provisions

§3.14.1 Review of FCC Decisions

Challenges to FCC orders must be brought in a federal court of appeals pursuant to 28 U.S.C. §2342.[493] Challenges to FCC orders may initially take the form of a request for reconsideration by the FCC itself,[494] but a petition for reconsideration to the Commission is required only if the party seeking judicial review was not a party to the original proceeding or relies on questions of fact or law on which the FCC had no opportunity to pass.[495]

---

[493] 47 U.S.C. §402 (a). Venue is anywhere the petitioner resides or has its principal office or in the D.C. Circuit. 28 U.S.C. §2343. Orders concerning construction permits and certain other specific matters, however, may be appealed only to the D.C. Circuit. 47 U.S.C. §402(b). Section 402(b), unlike section 402(a), does not expressly provide for the possibility of a stay, but the Supreme Court has held that, absent express congressional statement to the contrary, it is within the general equitable powers of a court reviewing administrative action to stay the enforcement of the judgment pending the outcome of the appeal. Scripps-Howard Radio v. FCC, 316 U.S. 4, 11 (1942).

[494] 47 U.S.C. §405(a).

[495] Id. Section 405 has been construed to "codify the judicially created doctrine of exhaustion of administrative remedies." Washington Assn. for Television & Children v. FCC, 712 F.2d 677, 681-682 (D.C. Cir. 1983). Thus, review of any issues not raised before the Commission is barred. MCI v. FCC, 842 F.2d at 1302. Review of issues that are not timely raised before the Commission is also barred. Northwestern Ind. Tel. Co. v. FCC, 872 F.2d 465 (D.C. Cir. 1989), cert. denied, 493 U.S. 1035 (1990).

The denial or grant of a petition for reconsideration is in turn appealable as provided by section 402(a). 47 U.S.C. §405(b)(2). Thus, as the Seventh Circuit noted in North American Telecommunications Assn. v. FCC, 772 F.2d 1286, "we could be faced with a case where, the Commission having issued an order and we having upheld it, a party to the review proceeding could come back to us on a petition to review an order denying a petition for reconsideration filed within 30 days of the original order." This statutory defect "would be tolerable," the court explained, "if the Commission had stringent criteria for reconsideration, since on the second judicial review the only issue open is whether the Commission erred in denying the petition to reconsider, not whether it erred in its original order. The Commission's rules of procedure, however, contain a catch-all provision that allows the Commission to reconsider its decision de novo even if no new material is presented and the Commission not infrequently proceeds on that basis." Id. 47 C.F.R. §1.429(b)(3).

Judicial review of FCC orders is based on the standards specified in the Administrative Procedure Act.[496]

§3.14.2   Enforcement

The Commission has broad discretion to decide where and how to enforce the Act.[497] It can either institute its own internal enforcement proceedings or go directly to district court. Under section 401(a), a federal district court has jurisdiction over FCC enforcement actions that allege that "any person" has failed to comply with "any" provision of the Act.[498] The Commission has broad subpoena power to obtain testimony, documents, and other material from anyone, including entities not subject to FCC regulation.[499]

The proper procedure for a private party who claims injury from a carrier's violation of FCC rules or regulations is to file a complaint with the FCC for initial resolution. The complainant can then, if necessary, seek appellate review of the FCC's disposition of the complaint or enforcement in district court of any resultant FCC order. Section 401(b) provides for enforcement in district court of "any order of the Commission" by either the United States or "any party injured thereby."[500] This provision ensures that private parties (and district judges) do not bypass the FCC's authority to provide the first interpretation of its own

---

[496] 5 U.S.C. §706.

[497] *See* Long-Distance Telecomms. Litig. v. ITT, 831 F.2d 627 (6th Cir. 1987) (claims based on provisions prohibiting unjust or unreasonable discrimination are within primary jurisdiction of FCC).

[498] 47 U.S.C. §401(a).

[499] *Id.* at §409(e); Authority to Issue Subpoenas, Order, 10 F.C.C. Rec. 707 (1994) ("[t]he agency's power of subpoena is not confined to those over whom it exercises regulatory jurisdiction, but extends to private individuals and entities over whom it does not").

[500] 47 U.S.C. §401(b). The enforcement action may be brought against "any person [who] fails or neglects to obey any order of the Commission other than the payment of money, while the same is in effect." *Id.* A state PUC is considered a "person" within the meaning of this provision and hence is subject to the jurisdiction of federal courts in actions to compel obedience to FCC orders. Hawaiian Tel. Co. v. Public Util. Commn. of Haw., 827 F.2d at 1264.

rules and regulations.[501] Thus, private parties may seek injunctions only to enforce specific orders of the Commission, and "orders" do not include FCC rulemaking decisions.[502]

The defendant in an enforcement action may not challenge the general validity of the FCC order at issue, but may only raise such a challenge in the D.C. Circuit.[503] A district court issuing an enforcement injunction need only determine "that the order was regularly made and duly served" on the party. The court even lacks jurisdiction over a defense that the FCC acted beyond the scope of its powers if the agency has previously addressed that challenge in an order directly reviewable by a court of appeals.[504]

---

[501] This statutory limitation dovetails with the more general doctrine of primary jurisdiction, discussed more fully in Chapter 4. For example, in All-net Communications Serv., Inc. v. National Exchange Carrier Assn., Inc., 965 F.2d 1118 (D.C. Cir. 1992), the issue was whether a district court should entertain a suit for a declaratory judgment concerning certain payment obligations. The D.C. Circuit found that although the district court had "subject matter jurisdiction in the conventional sense," the Commission had primary jurisdiction over the matters in dispute. The court explained that "[t]he primary jurisdiction doctrine rests both on a concern for uniform outcomes (which may be defeated if disparate courts resolve regulatory issues inconsistently), and on the advantages of allowing an agency to apply its expert judgment. Expertise, of course, is not merely technical but extends to the policy judgments needed to implement an agency's mandate." Id. at 1120.

[502] New England Tel. & Tel. v. Public Utils. Commn. of Maine, 742 F.2d 1 (1st Cir. 1984) (holding district court lacked authority to issue injunction enforcing FCC rule requiring state PUCs to follow a certain method for calculating depreciation of telephone company equipment). Several other courts have granted or upheld injunctions in this context, but without directly addressing the question of whether the FCC's decision constituted an "order" within the meaning of section 401(b). See, e.g., Southwestern Bell Tel. Co. v. Arkansas Pub. Serv. Commn., 738 F.2d 901 (8th Cir. 1984); South Central Bell Tel. Co. v. Louisiana Pub. Serv. Commn., 570 F. Supp. 227 (M.D. La. 1983); Pacific Northwest Bell Tel. Co. v. Washington Util. & Transp. Commn., 565 F. Supp. 17 (W.D. Wash. 1983); Chesapeake & Potomac Tel. Co. v. Public Serv. Commn. of Maryland, 560 F. Supp. 844 (D. Md. 1983).

[503] 47 U.S.C. §402(b).

[504] See FCC v. ITT World Communications, Inc., 466 U.S. 463, 468 (1984) ("Exclusive jurisdiction for review of final FCC orders, such as the FCC's denial of respondent's rulemaking petition, lies in the Court of Appeals. . . . Litigants may not evade these provisions by requesting the District Court to enjoin action that is the outcome of the agency's order."). See also Telecommunications Research and Action Ctr. v. FCC, 750 F.2d 70 (D.C. Cir. 1984)

Some provisions of the Act contain their own specific penalty provisions.[505] Discrimination, for example, is punishable by a $6,000 fine plus $300 a day.[506] Similar penalties apply for failure to file a schedule of tariffs,[507] failure to obey a prescription order,[508] refusal to provide service ordered by the Commission,[509] and failure to comply with accounting requirements.[510] Section 501 makes willful violations of the Act punishable by a fine of not more than $10,000 and imprisonment up to one year.[511] Violations of FCC rules are punishable by a fine of $500 a day.[512] These criminal provisions apply to "any person," customers as well as carriers. Other provisions address customers specifically.[513] A carrier's officers, agents, or employees may be vicariously liable under section 217.[514]

§3.14.3   Private Rights of Action

Sections 206 through 209 create private rights of action to remedy substantive violations of the Act. Under section 207, any person harmed by such a violation may file an action for damages before the Commission pursuant to section 208 or in United States district court pursuant to section 206.[515]

(petition alleging unreasonable delay and seeking writ of mandamus to compel action by FCC was subject to exclusive jurisdiction of court of appeals).

[505] The penalties were recently increased significantly, in many cases more than tenfold. *See* Pub. L. No. 101-239, tit. III, §3002, 103 Stat. 2131. The numbers in the text reflect those in the 1996 Act.

[506] 47 U.S.C. §202(c).

[507] *Id.* §203(e).

[508] *Id.* §205.

[509] *Id.* §214(d).

[510] *Id.* §220(d).

[511] *Id.* §501.

[512] *Id.* §502.

[513] *See, e.g., id.* §223.

[514] Section 216 declares that the Act applies equally to receivers and trustees of common carriers. 47 U.S.C. §216.

[515] *Id.* §207. However, the plaintiff cannot do both—he or she must elect to remedy the grievance through either an administrative proceeding or a lawsuit. *Id.*

The section 206 right of action encompasses only claims that a carrier has violated the *Act*, not for example, violations of FCC regulations[516] or general tort or contract claims.[517] There is likewise no private right of action under the Act against a carrier solely because of its physical connection with the facilities of another carrier.[518] And while "connecting carriers" are subject to the substantive requirements of the Act, they cannot be sued in private actions for damages under the Act.[519] Congress viewed the connecting carriers as "weak, rural exchanges" and apparently

---

[516] The section provides:

> In case any common carrier . . . shall omit to do any act, matter, or thing in this chapter required to be done, such common carrier shall be liable to the person or persons injured thereby for the full amount of damages sustained in consequence of any such violation of the provisions of this chapter, together with a reasonable counsel or attorneys fee, to be fixed by the court in every case of recovery, which attorney's fee shall be taxed and collected as part of the costs in the case.

Id. §206.

[517] *See* Nordlicht v. New York Tel. Co., 799 F.2d 859, 861–862 (2d Cir. 1986), *cert. denied,* 479 U.S. 1055 (1987). Some cases indicate, however, that there may still be federal question jurisdiction over such claims. For example, in Ivy Broadcasting Co. v. AT&T, 391 F.2d 486, 489 (2d Cir. 1968), the court held that a complaint for grossly negligent and unreasonably delayed installation and testing of special telephone lines does not fall within the jurisdiction of sections 206–207, but that the claim was nevertheless governed by federal common law. "[Q]uestions concerning the duties, charges and liabilities of telegraph or telephone companies with respect to interstate communications service," the Court explained, "are to be governed solely by federal law. . . . Where neither the Communications Act itself nor the tariffs filed pursuant to the Act deals with a particular question, the courts are to apply a uniform rule of federal common law." *Id.* at 491. *Accord* Kaufman v. Western Union, 224 F.2d 723 (5th Cir. 1955), *cert. denied,* 350 U.S. 947 (1956); O'Brien v. Western Union, 113 F.2d 539 (1st Cir. 1940). *Cf. McDonnell Douglas Corp.,* 594 F.2d at 724–725 (claim concerning discrimination in intrastate rates for Centrex service does not present a federal question because section 152(b) exempts such rates from the coverage of the Act).

[518] There is actually a split in the circuits on this issue, but the matter is not open to serious dispute. *Compare* Comtronics, Inc. v. Puerto Rico Tel. Co., 553 F.2d 701, 704 (1st Cir. 1977) (no private right of action against connecting carriers) *with* Ward v. Northern Ohio Tel. Co., 300 F.2d 816 (6th Cir. 1962) (a private right of action does lie against connecting carriers).

[519] Their liability is expressly limited by section 152(b). *See Comtronics,* 553 F.2d at 705.

considered the civil penalties of sections 201–205 "sufficient to insure compliance with federal law."[520] In a section 206 complaint, carriers may be assessed attorney's fees on top of actual damages.[521]

The section 208 process, unlike that under section 206, also allows consideration of violations of FCC regulations. Attorney's fees, however, are not available in section 208 complaint proceedings.

A private party has no right to seek injunctive relief to enforce "provisions" of the Communications Act. Section 401(a) reserves that authority to the Commission.[522] A private party may, however, seek injunctive relief to enforce "orders" of the Commission under 47 U.S.C. §401(b).[523] The courts have respected this distinction, rejecting parties' efforts to obtain injunctive relief with respect to provisions of the Act itself.[524]

§3.15 Forbearance: The Authority Not to Regulate

In light of the extensive regulations that are so much a part of the 1996 Act, the assertion that the Act is "deregulatory" seems

---

[520] *Id.* at 706.

[521] 47 U.S.C. §206.

[522] "The district courts of the United States shall have jurisdiction, upon application of the Attorney General of the United States at the request of the Commission, alleging a failure to comply with or a violation of any of the provisions of this chapter by any person, to issue a writ or writs of mandamus commanding such person to comply with the provisions of this chapter." 47 U.S.C. §401(a). There is one exception, however. *See id.* §274(e)(2) (creating private right to injunctive relief for violation of electronic publishing restrictions in section 274).

[523] "If any person fails . . . to obey any order of the Commission . . . the Commission or any party injured thereby, or the United States . . . may apply to the appropriate district court . . . for the enforcement of such order." *Id.* §401(b).

[524] *See, e.g.,* Pacific Northwest Bell Tel. Co. v. Washington Utils. & Transp. Commn., 565 F. Supp. 17, 21 (W.D. Wash. 1983) ("401(a) . . . [is] directed to the prosecution of violations of provisions of the chapter by the FCC and 401(b) is directed to enforcement of FCC orders"), *remanded on other grounds,* 827 F.2d 1242 (9th Cir. 1986); New England Tel. & Tel. Co. v. Public

more rhetoric than reality. However, amid the 1996 Act's numerous requirements and demands, section 160 holds the potential to bring about this promised deregulation by providing the Commission with the authority to forbear from enforcing provisions of the Communications Act, as well as any of its regulations.[525] Section 160 gives to the Commission what the courts had taken away, just as the Commission lost the final round of a decade-long battle over whether it could forbear from requiring nondominant interexchange carriers to file tariffs.[526] While the Commission steadfastly claimed that it had the power to forbear, the Supreme Court and the D.C. Circuit (on three separate occasions) concluded that section 203(a) of the 1934 Communications Act gave the Commission no such authority.[527]

Congress has now provided the Commission with this power, although only if certain conditions are satisfied. Prior to forbearing, the Commission must make several general findings, including an express finding that forbearance is in the public interest.[528] Moreover, the Act protects from section 160 forbearance two key provisions:[529] the interconnection obligations specific to incumbent LECs[530] and the guidelines for BOC entry into the interLATA market.[531] But Congress's reservation of these two provisions is not permanent. The Act permits the Commission

---

Utils. Commn. of Maine, 742 F.2d at 5 ("subsection (a) . . . allows the Commission to ask a federal court to enjoin 'a failure to comply with or a violation of any of the provisions' of the Act; . . . subsection (b) . . . allows a private litigant to require compliance with a Commission 'order'").

[525] See 47 U.S.C. §160.

[526] For a more complete discussion of the FCC's prior attempts at forbearance, see §9.5.

[527] MCI v. AT&T, 512 U.S. 218 (1994); Southwestern Bell Corp. v. FCC, 43 F.3d 1515 (D.C. Cir. 1995); AT&T v. FCC, 978 F.2d 727 (D.C. Cir. 1992); MCI v. FCC, 765 F.2d 1186 (D.C. Cir. 1985).

[528] A request for forbearance will be deemed admitted unless the Commission denies it no later than 15 months from the time it is submitted. 47 U.S.C. §160(c). The public interest finding may also be based on the Commission's determination that "forbearance will promote competition among providers of telecommunications services." Id. §160(b).

[529] Id. §160(d).

[530] Id. §251(c).

[531] Id. §271.

to forbear from them once "it determines that those requirements have been fully implemented."[532] Presumably, "full implementation" arrives when a BOC secures interLATA relief on a
regionwide basis, or perhaps even a statewide basis.

The Act makes several additional legitimate deregulatory ges-
tures. The FCC now must rule within 5 (as opposed to 12)
months on the lawfulness of any LEC's charges or practices,[533]
and LEC tariffs will become effective within 7 days (in the case
of a reduction in rates) or 15 days (in the case of an increase in
rates).[534] The Act also requires the Commission to waive section
214 requirements for the extension of any line.[535]

Finally, Congress has directed the Commission to hold a proceeding every two years to review all regulations issued under
the Act and determine whether they remain in the public interest.[536] The Commission must then repeal or modify any
regulation that fails this test.[537] The Commission, however, has
interpreted this requirement rather loosely, claiming that it need
not conduct a single, overarching proceeding to review all regulations, but can simply do so in the context of other, pending
rulemaking proceedings.[538]

---

[532] *Id.* §160(d).

[533] Telecommunications Act of 1996 §402(b)(1) (amending 47 U.S.C.
§§204(a), 208(b)).

[534] *Id.* §402(b)(1) (amending 47 U.S.C. §204(a)).

[535] *Id.* §402(b)(2)(A).

[536] *Id.* §402(a) (amending 47 U.S.C. §161(a)).

[537] 47 U.S.C. §161(b).

[538] *See* General Action, Report No. GN 98-1 (Feb. 5, 1998) (noting that the
FCC initiated 31 proceedings as part of the 1998 biennial regulatory review);
see also Separate Statement of Commissioner Harold W. Furchtgott-Roth,
Computer III Further Remand Proceedings: Bell Operating Company Provision of Enhanced Services and 1998 Biennial Regulatory Review—Review
of Computer III and ONA Safeguards and Requirements, Further Notice of
Proposed Rulemaking, 13 F.C.C. Rec. 6040, 6120 (1998) (expressing concern
that the FCC will not fulfill its mandate under section 11 to review *all* regulations).

SBC Communications Inc. has challenged this assertion in a petition requesting the Commission to conduct the full proceeding required in 47
U.S.C. §161(a). SBC Communications, Inc. Petition for Section 11 Biennial
Review (FCC filed May 8, 1998). The Commission has not acted on SBC's
petition and apparently plans simply to ignore it.

The Act specifically eliminates or modifies certain regulations of undeniable absurdity: the Commission may now employ independent auditors,[539] authorize the use of private organizations for certifying home electronic equipment,[540] and designate independent entities to conduct inspections of amateur radio stations.[541] In addition, the Commission need no longer prescribe depreciation rates for all common carriers; instead, it need only prescribe rates when appropriate.[542]

It is forbearance, or the possibility of it, that represents the best hope for a truly deregulated telecommunications marketplace. The Commission on many occasions (such as the original, ill-fated forbearance policy) has shown a willingness to push hard for deregulation. As local competition advances and the scope of the BOCs' interLATA relief broadens, the Commission will have every reason to forbear from more and more of its regulations. While only time will tell, it may be that the 1996 Act will live up to its billing and gradually create a procompetitive and deregulated telecommunications market.

---

[539] Telecommunications Act of 1996, §403(e) (amending 47 U.S.C. §220(c)).
[540] *Id.* §403(f) (amending 47 U.S.C. §302).
[541] *Id.* §403(a) (amending 47 U.S.C. §154(f)(4)).
[542] *Id.* §403(d) (amending 47 U.S.C. §220(b)).

4
Antitrust*

§4.1 Introduction

The U.S. telecommunications industry has been shaped more by antitrust law than by any federal or state regulation. From the beginning of this century to the present day, antitrust suits have been pressed against telephone companies by both the federal government and private parties. In 1977, for example, about 40 private suits were pending against the Bell System, together with the federal suit that would lead to the Bell breakup seven years later.[1] Although the three most important antitrust initiatives against the Bell System—federal government suits filed in 1913, 1949, and 1974—provide no body of authority on the antitrust merits because all three suits were settled, these cases live on in various legislative and regulatory commands that imitate the consent settlement decrees. As discussed below and in other

---

*This chapter was co-authored by Silvija A. Strikis, Associate, Kellogg, Huber, Hansen, Todd & Evans; University of Maryland (B.S., *summa cum laude*, 1985); Georgetown University Law Center (J.D., *summa cum laude*, 1995); Law Clerk, Honorable Harry T. Edwards, U.S. Court of Appeals, D.C. Circuit, 1995–1996; Law Clerk, Honorable Sandra Day O'Connor, U.S. Supreme Court, 1997–1998.

[1] AT&T, 1977 Annual Report 17 (1978).

chapters,[2] the Antitrust Division of the Department of Justice has used settlements to achieve results it likely would not have obtained through litigated cases. Other federal government antitrust cases filed in connection with mergers—GTE's 1983 purchase of Sprint, AT&T's 1994 purchase of McCaw, British Telecom's 1994 partial acquisition of MCI, TCI's 1994 reacquisition of Liberty, and Sprint's 1995 alliance with the French and German national telephone companies—were settled as well.[3] The Telecommunications Act of 1996 supersedes several of these decrees, but simultaneously adopts and incorporates much of their structure and economic logic.[4]

Almost all of the private cases filed against the Bell System concluded by the early 1980s. The 1984 Bell System breakup apparently sated the appetites of antitrust plaintiffs for a time. But a new wave of private antitrust cases began in the mid-1990s.[5] Even

[2] *See, e.g.,* §§5.1.2, §9.4. *See generally* A. Douglas Melamed, 10 A.B.A. Antitrust J. (1995) (criticizing overuse of antitrust consent decrees).

[3] United States v. GTE Corp., 603 F. Supp. 730 (D.D.C. 1984) (GTE/Sprint Decree); Complaint, United States v. AT&T Corp., Civ. Act. No. 94-01555 (HHG) (D.D.C. July 15, 1994) (AT&T/McCaw merger) (Judge Harold Greene somehow never got around to entering the government's proposed consent decree involving the AT&T/McCaw merger); United States v. MCI Communications Corp., 1994-2 Trade Cas. (CCH) ¶70,730 (D.D.C. 1994) (MCI/BT Decree); United States v. Tele-Communications Inc., 1996-2 Trade Cas. (CCH) ¶71,496 (D.D.C. 1994) (TCI/Liberty Decree); United States v. Sprint Corp., 1996-1 Trade Cas. (CCH) ¶71,300 (D.D.C. 1995) (Sprint/FT/DT Decree). The MCI/BT merger is discussed in more detail in Chapter 7.

[4] Section 601 of the 1996 Telecommunications Act vacated antitrust consent decrees involving AT&T, GTE, and the AT&T/McCaw merger. *See* 47 U.S.C. §152 note. Portions of these decrees requiring "equal access" and "nondiscrimination" were continued temporarily pending FCC rulemaking. *See* 47 U.S.C. §251(g).

[5] *E.g.,* Bell Atlantic Corp. v. AT&T Corp., Civ. Act. No. 94-3682 (ERK) (E.D.N.Y. 1994) (Clayton Act case against merger that impeded competition in cellular infrastructure equipment); Bell Atlantic Corp. v. AT&T Corp., A-5013-92-T2, A-5090 92T2 (D.N.J., Feb. 7, 1995) (counterclaim against local exchange carrier for monopolization of intraLATA toll service); Bell Atlantic Corp. v. AT&T Corp., No. 5-96-CV-45 (E.D. Tex., Feb. 14, 1996) (claim against long distance carrier for monopolization of long distance Caller ID service and counterclaim against local exchange carrier for monopolization of local Caller ID service); CalTech International Telcom v. Pacific Bell, CV-97-2105 CAL (N.D. Cal. June 5, 1997) (complaint by "competitive" local exchange carrier against incumbent local exchange carrier); GTE New Media Servs. Inc.

the government has begun to shake off its consent decree torpor in favor of litigating cases.[6]

This chapter summarizes basic antitrust principles and discusses their application to various segments of the telecommunications industry.[7] We also review here the major telecommunications antitrust suits brought by the federal government,

---

v. Ameritech Corp., Civ. Act. No. 97-2314 (D.D.C. Oct. 6, 1997) (complaint of territorial allocation and group boycott of Internet Yellow Pages services); Electric Lightwave Inc. v. U S WEST, Inc., 97-CV-1073 (D. Wa. June 30, 1997) (complaint by competitive local exchange carrier against incumbent); Online Yellow Pages, Inc. v. Bell Atlantic Corp., 98-CV-1073 (W.D. Pa. Jan. 12, 1998) (complaint of leveraging by local exchange carrier of market power from the print Yellow Pages business into Internet Yellow Pages); Appell v. NYNEX Corp., 97-CV-270 (D. Vt. Aug. 15, 1997) (complaint of monopolization by local exchange carrier of Caller ID equipment), *dismissed,* No. 98-7583 (2d Cir. June 23, 1998); CTC Communications, Inc. v. Bell Atlantic Corp., Civ. Act. No. 97-CIV-395-P-C (D. Me. Jan. 29, 1997) and Bell Atlantic v. CTC Communications, Inc., 98-CIV-0048 (S.D.N.Y. 1998) (dispute involving agent of local exchange carrier's attempts to market resold incumbent services to agency customers); Independent Payphone Service Providers for Consumer Choice (IPSPCC) v. Bell Atlantic Corp., Civ. Act. No. 98-0127 (TFH) (D.D.C. filed Jan. 16, 1998) (complaint of interference with contracts to provide long-distance service to pay phones); Discon, Inc. v. NYNEX Corp., 93 F.3d 1055 (2d Cir. 1996) (complaint against "boycott" by local exchange carrier and supplier of central office removal services), *judgment vacated by* 119 S. Ct. 493 (1998); Stephenson v. Bell Atlantic N.J., No Civ. A. 96-1217 (JBS) (D.N.J. filed Mar. 13, 1996) (claim of monopolization by local exchange carrier of inside wire maintenance).

[6] *See* Complaint, United States v. Microsoft Corp., Civ. Act. No. 98-1232 (D.D.C. filed May 18, 1998) (complaint against anticompetitive acts in operating systems market); Complaint, United States v. Primestar, Inc., Civ. Act. 98-CV-01193 (D.D.C. May 12, 1998) (complaint against acquisition of orbital satellite video programming provider by cable company).

[7] Many antitrust cases in this industry are really typical business disputes couched in antitrust terms having no structural significance to the industry. We do not address them further in this chapter.

In 1972, for example, a California district court declined to dismiss a suit brought by a local independent telephone company challenging the division of revenues between it and the local Bell company. The case was never prosecuted and was ultimately dismissed in 1979. Citizens Utils. Co. v. AT&T, 1973-2 Trade Cas. (CCH) ¶74,756 (N.D. Cal. 1972); Citizens Utils. Co. v. AT&T, 595 F.2d 1171 (9th Cir.), *cert. denied,* 444 U.S. 931 (1979).

Another suit was brought by employees of Western Electric charging that Western Electric and the local Bell Operating Company violated antitrust laws by agreeing not to hire each other's employees without a six-month waiting period. Thomsen v. Western Elec. Co., 680 F.2d 1263 (9th Cir.), *cert. denied,* 459

focusing on their contribution to the larger body of antitrust jurisprudence. Chapter 7 addresses government review of mergers and acquisitions. We leave the discussion of *private* antitrust suits to the substantive chapters to which they relate—telecommunications equipment (Chapter 8), long-distance services (Chapter 9), wireless services (Chapter 10), and information services (Chapter 12).

§4.2 Principles

Congress enacted the Sherman Antitrust Act in 1890 (Sherman Act),[8] barely a decade after Alexander Graham Bell had invented the telephone. The immediate targets of the legislation were the great railroads and industrial trusts of the nineteenth century. The telephone industry was still very much in its infancy; computers would not be born for another half century. For its broad scope, the Sherman Act itself is remarkably brief. United States antitrust law has thus been shaped, like the common law, by the accumulation of judicial rulings. This section discusses the principles of antitrust law of most relevance to the telecommunications industry.

U.S. 991 (1982). The court of appeals held that Bell's common ownership of both Western Electric and the operating company precluded the suit because there can be no conspiracy within a single enterprise. *Id.* at 1266. The court also ruled that the employees lacked standing because they did not compete in the markets that the companies allegedly monopolized (the telecommunications equipment and services markets) and the employment restrictions arguably aided competitors in those markets by forcing skilled personnel to go to non-Bell companies. *Id.* at 1267.

　See also Ottensmeyer v. Chesapeake & Potomac Tel. Co., 756 F.2d 986 (4th Cir. 1985) (telephone company did not violate antitrust laws by giving police information that led to a search of plaintiffs' premises to find evidence that plaintiffs were violating Maryland law and defrauding telephone company); Gordon v. Illinois Bell Tel. Co., 330 F.2d 103 (7th Cir.), *cert. denied*, 379 U.S. 909 (1964) (answering service terminated for nonpayment of bills).

　[8] Sherman Antitrust Act, ch. 647, 26 Stat. 209 (1890) (codified as amended at 15 U.S.C. §§1–7).

§4.2.1 Essential Facilities Doctrine

The essential facilities doctrine requires a firm with monopoly power in one market to deal equitably with competing firms operating in adjacent markets that depend on it for essential inputs. The doctrine originated in a 1912 Supreme Court decision, *United States v. Terminal Railroad Assn. of St. Louis,*[9] in which the Court required joint owners of a railroad switching junction to afford competing railways access to the junction "upon such just and reasonable terms and regulations as will . . . place every such company upon as nearly an equal plane as may be with respect to expenses and charges as that occupied by the proprietary companies."[10] The four elements required to establish liability under the essential facilities doctrine are (1) control of the essential facility by a monopolist, (2) a competitor's inability practically or reasonably to duplicate the essential facility, (3) the denial of the use of the facility to a competitor, and (4) the feasibility of providing the facility.[11]

[9] 224 U.S. 383 (1912).

[10] *Id.* at 411. As the Court of Appeals for the D.C. Circuit put it 65 years later, "[W]here facilities cannot practicably be duplicated by would-be competitors, those in possession of them must allow them to be shared on fair terms." Hecht v. Pro-Football, Inc., 570 F.2d 982, 992 (D.C. Cir. 1977) (quoting A. Neale, The Antitrust Laws of the United States 67 (2d ed. 1970)), *cert. denied,* 436 U.S. 956 (1978). *See also* Aspen Skiing Co. v. Aspen Highlands Skiing Corp., 472 U.S. 585, 600–601 (1985).

The essential facilities doctrine has recently been applied to microprocessor technology in a district court case that found that Intel Corporation, as a monopolist in the market for high-performance microprocessors, had a duty to supply a computer products manufacturer, Intergraph Corporation, with CPUs and essential technical information. *See* Intergraph Corp. v. Intel Corp., 3 F. Supp. 2d 1255 (N.D. Ala. 1998). Intel's alleged failure to deal with Intergraph sprouted from a dispute between the companies regarding Intel's demands for access to chip technology owned by Intergraph. Intel appealed the district court's decision, and at the December 9, 1998, oral argument before the Federal Circuit, judges on the panel seemed to express reservations about Intergraph's argument. As Judge S. Jay Player commented to Intergraph's counsel, "[y]ou started playing hard ball with a 600-pound gorilla, and when the gorilla swung back, you didn't like it." *See* Wintel's Other Half in Hotseat, Law News Network (Dec. 10, 1998) <http://www.lawnewsnetwork.com/stories/dec/e121098d.html>.

[11] *See, e.g.,* Caribbean Broad. Sys., Ltd. v. Cable & Wireless PLC, 148 F.3d 1080, 1088 (D.C. Cir. 1998); MCI v. AT&T, 708 F.2d 1081, 1132 (7th Cir.) *cert. denied,* 464 U.S. 891 (1983).

The landmark application of the essential facilities doctrine to a wire-based utility was the 1973 Supreme Court decision *Otter Tail Power Co. v. United States.*[12] Otter Tail, with an electric power monopoly, had refused to sell power at wholesale rates to local municipal retailers and had also refused to allow those retailers to use its power lines to "wheel" in power from distant suppliers. The Court held that Otter Tail's electric lines were an essential facility and that Otter Tail's refusal to allow access to them violated section 2 of the Sherman Act.[13]

The essential facilities doctrine has limits. The plaintiff must demonstrate the infeasibility of duplicating the facilities in question; the doctrine does not, for example, require "a firm that has engaged in the risks and expenses of research and development . . . in all circumstances to share with its rivals the benefits of those endeavors. . . ."[14] The facility owner is also not required to sacrifice its own use of a facility for the advantage of competitors or to permit a mere middleman to insert itself between the facility owner and the ultimate customer. The operators of a shopping mall, for example, do not have a right simply to displace the local electrical utility by buying power wholesale and reselling it at retail rates to their shopping mall tenants.[15] For liability to be imposed under the essential facilities doctrine,

---

[12] 410 U.S. 366 (1973).

[13] *Id.* at 380–381.

[14] Berkey Photo, Inc. v. Eastman Kodak Co., 603 F.2d 263, 281 (2d Cir. 1979), *cert. denied*, 444 U.S. 1093 (1980). *See* MCI v. AT&T, 708 F.2d at 1153 n.113 (distinguishing *Berkey Photo:* "MCI did not ask AT&T for advance knowledge of its new products, unlike the plaintiffs in *Berkey Photo;* nor did MCI suggest that AT&T abandon a technical innovation in favor of an already existing alternative as in Memorex Corp. v. IBM Corp., 636 F.2d 1188 (9th Cir. 1980), *cert. denied*, 452 U.S. 972 (1981)."); United States v. AT&T, 604 F. Supp. 316, 324 (D.D.C. 1985) (denying government's motion to make AT&T's 800 database available to all interexchange carriers; the "purpose" of an antitrust decree is limited "to remov[ing] barriers to entry" and is "not the artificial creation of competition by enabling [competitors] to share AT&T's interexchange capabilities and facilities to which they are not otherwise entitled").

[15] Almeda Mall, Inc. v. Houston Lighting & Power Co., 615 F.2d 343 (5th Cir.), *cert. denied*, 449 U.S. 870 (1980). As the court explained, "[T]he activity sought by the appellants is more akin to mere 'substitution' than to competition. By achieving the goal to resell electricity on the retail level, appellants will be merely plugging themselves into the flow of electricity and reaping

there must be two markets at issue: the essential facility must be a facility or service that the plaintiff needs from one market in order to compete with the defendant in a second market.[16]

The ordinary remedy for violation of the essential facilities doctrine is to order the holder of the facility to provide access. "Absolute equality" is not mandated;[17] the scope of the remedy is usually pragmatic, based on what is reasonable and feasible

§4.2.2 Tying

A closely related antitrust principle prohibits "tying."[19] As explained by Justice O'Connor in 1984, "Tying is a form of mar-

---

profits as a non-competitive middleman." *Id.* at 353. *See also* HyPoint Tech., Inc. v. Hewlett-Packard Co., 949 F.2d 874, 878 (6th Cir.) (finding no antitrust violation in defendant's change in computer service policies; although the change led to plaintiff's loss of service contract business, there was no harm to competition because plaintiff functioned as a "non-competitive middleman"), *cert. denied,* 503 U.S. 938 (1992).

[16] *See* MCI v. AT&T, 708 F.2d at 1132 (the essential facilities doctrine applies only when defendant is extending "monopoly power from one stage of production to *another,* and from one market into *another*") (emphasis added). The essential facilities doctrine thus does not compel a monopolist to allow pure resale of its products. Section 2's aim of prodding cost reduction through competition would not be significantly advanced by compelling competition limited to the typically small marketing slice of a service; indeed, there often will be significant added costs in setting up means for resale competition. And any such duty would necessarily embroil federal courts in the de novo determination of proper "wholesale rates," a process that could not be avoided, as in the typical essential facilities case, by simply ordering access to an already existing upstream input.

[17] United States v. AT&T, 524 F. Supp. 1336, 1360 (D.D.C. 1981); *see also* Southern Pacific Communications Co. v. AT&T, 740 F.2d 980, 1009 (D.C. Cir. 1984) (same), *cert. denied,* 470 U.S. 1005 (1985).

[18] Thus, for example, in the 1974 government case against AT&T, the district court stated: "[P]roblems of feasibility and practicability may be taken into account by the Court in determining the sufficiency under the law of the access to essential facilities granted by defendants to non-Bell carriers." United States v. AT&T, 524 F. Supp. at 1361. *See also* MCI v. AT&T, 708 F.2d at 1133 (upholding jury determination that interconnections for foreign exchange (FX) and common carrier switching arrangement (CCSA) service "could have been feasibly provided. No legitimate business or technical reason was shown for AT&T's denial of the requested interconnections.").

[19] *See* International Salt Co. v. United States, 332 U.S. 392 (1947). Tying and essential facilities abuses are similar in that market power in one market

keting in which a seller insists on selling two distinct products or
services as a package."[20] Justice O'Connor set out three threshold criteria to be met in any tying case:

> First, the seller must have power in the tying-product market. . . .
> Second, there must be a substantial threat that the tying seller
> will acquire market power in the tied-product market. No such
> threat exists if the tied-product market is occupied by many sta-
> ble sellers who are not likely to be driven out by the tying, or if
> entry barriers in the tied-product market are low. . . . Third,
> there must be a coherent economic basis for treating the tying
> and tied products as distinct. . . . For products to be treated as
> distinct, the tied product must, at a minimum, be one that some
> consumers might wish to purchase separately without also pur-
> chasing the tying product.[21]

Tying is also usually thought to present anticompetitive risks
when used by a regulated industry to circumvent regulation by
extending monopoly power into adjacent unregulated markets.[22] It is never an antitrust violation, however, to tie or bundle together the components of what is properly viewed as a
single product or service.[23] This point, though often overlooked,
is of some importance in telephony, where market boundaries
are often far from clear.[24]

---

is used to gain power in another. A firm violating the essential facilities doctrine, however, engages in an outright refusal to deal, whereas a tying firm
simply inflates the price of access (to the grinder, say) by requiring customers
to buy something else (salt) that they could buy competitively elsewhere.

[20] Jefferson Parish Hospital District No. 2 v. Hyde, 466 U.S. 2, 33 (1984)
(O'Connor, J., concurring in the judgment).

[21] *Id.* at 37–39 (footnotes, citations, and emphasis omitted). *See also* Eastman Kodak Co. v. Image Technical Servs., Inc., 504 U.S. 451, 461 (1992).

[22] *See* Fortner Enters., Inc. v. United States Steel Corp., 394 U.S. 495, 513
(1969) (White, J., dissenting) *see also Jefferson Parish*, 466 U.S. at 36 n.4 (O'Connor, J., concurring in the judgment); Roy B. Taylor Sales, Inc. v. Hollymatic
Corp., 28 F.3d 1379, 1383 (5th Cir. 1994), *cert. denied*, 513 U.S. 1103 (1995).

[23] *See Fortner Enters.*, 394 U.S. at 507; Multistate Legal Studies, Inc. v. Har-
court Brace Jovanovich Legal & Prof. Publications, Inc., 63 F.3d 1540,
1546–1547 (10th Cir. 1995), *cert. denied*, 516 U.S. 1044 (1996); Souza v. Estate
of Bishop, 821 F.2d 1332 (9th Cir. 1987); Foster v. Maryland State Sav. & Loan
Assn., 590 F.2d 928, 931 (D.C. Cir. 1978), *cert. denied*, 439 U.S. 1071 (1979).

[24] P. Huber, M. Kellogg, & J. Thorne, The Geodesic Network II: 1993
Report on Competition in the Telephone Industry ch. 1 (1993) (hereinafter

§4.2.3 "Leveraging" and Refusals to Deal

Complaints of leveraging and refusals to deal are variations on the essential facilities and tying doctrines that frequently appear in telecom antitrust cases. These alternative theories, though often poorly articulated, are generally presented in order to avoid one or another of the requirements of the more accepted causes of action.

Both the essential facilities and the tying doctrines, for example, focus on the likelihood of market power being acquired in an adjacent competitive market. Some cases have suggested that it is unnecessary to inquire into the effects of a monopolist's conduct on a second market under a theory of "monopoly leveraging."[25] As one (skeptical) court explained, the leveraging theory "holds that it is an act of monopolization for a firm having monopoly power in one market to exploit that power as a 'lever' to secure competitive advantages in a second market, irrespective of the degree of market power actually achieved by the defendant within the second market."[26]

Geodesic Network II). *See also* United States v. Microsoft Corp., 147 F.3d 935, 949–950 (D.C. Cir. 1998) (describing courts' "narrow and deferential" evaluation of assertions that products have been combined to provide technical benefits; seeking to avoid "'technical inquiry into the justifiability of product innovations'" (quoting Response of Carolina, Inc. v. Leasco Response, Inc., 537 F.2d 1307, 1330 (5th Cir. 1976)).

[25] The case most often cited as recognizing the monopoly leveraging theory is *Berkey Photo*, 603 F.2d 263, in which the Second Circuit stated in dictum that "the use of monopoly power attained in one market to gain a competitive advantage in another is a violation of section 2, even if there has not been an attempt to monopolize the second market." *Id.* at 276. More recently, however, the Second Circuit has called into question the applicability of this dictum to non-"tying" cases and has reaffirmed that there remains in any case the requirement of "tangible harm to competition." *See* Twin Laboratories, Inc. v. Weider Health & Fitness, 900 F.2d 566, 570–571 (2d Cir. 1990); *see also* AD/SAT v. Associated Press, 920 F. Supp. 1287, 1304–1305 (S.D.N.Y. 1996).

[26] Air Passenger Computer Reservations Sys. Antitrust Litig., 694 F. Supp. 1443, 1472 (C.D. Cal. 1988) (rejecting monopoly leveraging as distinct section 2 claim), *aff'd sub nom.* Alaska Airlines, Inc. v. United Airlines, Inc., 948 F.2d 536, 546 (9th Cir. 1991) (rejecting monopoly leveraging as distinct section 2 claim; "[u]nless the monopolist uses its power in the first market to acquire and maintain a monopoly in the second market, there is no section 2 violation"), *cert. denied*, 503 U.S. 977 (1992); *see also* Fineman v. Armstrong World

There is also a substantial body of antitrust law dealing with boycotts, market foreclosure, and refusals to deal. In each case, the monopolist is able to place competitors at a disadvantage because of its dominance of the market.[27] Boycotts involve the cooperation of several firms in one market so that the group's concerted actions and refusal to deal with other firms outside of the group impede or even eliminate competition.[28] Market foreclosure is similar to "leveraging" in that a monopolist uses its own power to obtain control over a second market—one that

---

Indus., Inc., 980 F.2d 171, 206 (3d Cir. 1992) (rejecting *Berkey Photo;* holding that monopoly leveraging claim requires proof of "threatened or actual monopoly in the leveraged market"), *cert. denied,* 507 U.S. 921 (1993); Association for Intercollegiate Athletics for Women v. NCAA, 735 F.2d 577, 586 & n.14 (D.C. Cir. 1984) (noting "substantial academic criticism cast upon the leveraging concept" in *Berkey Photo*); United States v. Microsoft Corp., 1998-2 Trade Cas. (CCH) ¶72,261 (D.D.C. 1998) (rejecting monopoly leveraging claim); *cf.* Spectrum Sports, Inc. v. McQuillan, 506 U.S. 447, 457 (1993) (explaining that liability for attempted monopolization under section 2 requires "proof of a dangerous probability that [defendants] would monopolize a particular market and specific intent to monopolize"). *But see Berkey Photo,* 603 F.2d 263; Kerasotes Michigan Theatres, Inc. v. National Amusements, Inc., 854 F.2d 135, 137 (6th Cir. 1988) (adopting *Berkey Photo*'s leverage theory in reversing dismissal of section 2 claim), *cert. dismissed,* 490 U.S. 1087 (1989); Sargent-Welch Scientific Co. v. Ventron Corp., 567 F.2d 701, 711 (7th Cir. 1977) ("A specific intent to monopolize need not be shown to establish the offense of monopolization when the monopolist undertakes anticompetitive actions.").

[27] *See, e.g., Aspen Skiing Co.,* 472 U.S. at 601–603 (explaining grounds for antitrust liability for refusals to deal); Lorain Journal Co. v. United States, 342 U.S. 143, 154 (1951) (refusal to deal part of a scheme to use monopoly power to destroy threatened competition in violation of the "attempt to monopolize" clause of section 2); Image Technical Servs., Inc. v. Eastman Kodak Co., 125 F.3d 1195, 1210–1212 & n.6 (9th Cir. 1997) (affirming validity of jury instructions regarding refusal to deal that defined exclusionary conduct as "practices that unreasonably or unnecessarily impede fair competition"), *cert. denied,* 118 S. Ct. 1560 (1998).

[28] It is generally agreed that boycotts by organizations made up of several entities acting together are anticompetitive and illegal under antitrust law. *See, e.g.,* Klor's, Inc. v. Broadway-Hale Stores, Inc., 359 U.S. 207, 212 (1959); United States v. Realty Multi-List, Inc., 629 F.2d 1351 (5th Cir. 1980). *See generally* C. Havighurst, Doctors and Hospitals: An Antitrust Perspective on Traditional Relationships, 1984 Duke L.J. 1071. The Supreme Court recently ruled that a single firm cannot be said to have engaged in a boycott that is a per se violation of the antitrust laws. *See* NYNEX Corp. v. Discon, Inc., 119 S. Ct. 493 (1998), discussed further at §4.2.5.

supplies the market the monopolist dominates—thereby withholding necessary supplies from competitors.[29] Despite considerable litigation, questions concerning the circumstances under which a single-firm monopolist has a duty to deal with other firms remain the "most unsettled and vexatious in the antitrust field."[30]

§4.2.4 Predatory Pricing and Cross-Subsidies

Another common allegation in telecom antitrust cases is "predatory pricing"—pricing below cost to drive competitors out of the market in the hope of monopoly profits thereafter.[31] Predatory pricing is much simpler in theory than in practice. The evolving consensus among both economists[32] and courts[33] is that

---

[29] An example of market foreclosure was presented in United States v. Aluminum Co. of America, 148 F.2d 416 (2d Cir. 1945), in which several electric utilities agreed to supply no aluminum manufacturer other than Alcoa, thus creating a scarcity of electricity and impeding the efforts of competing companies. *See generally* T. Krattenmaker & S. Salop, Anticompetitive Exclusion: Raising Rivals' Costs To Achieve Power over Price, 96 Yale L.J. 209 (1986).

[30] Byars v. Bluff City News Co., Inc., 609 F.2d 843, 846 (6th Cir. 1979). *See Twin Laboratories*, 900 F.2d at 571.

[31] "Predatory pricing is essentially a three-phase process. . . . First, a seller temporarily cuts his price with the intent of eliminating his competitors or deterring potential competitors from entering the market. Second, the damage to or discouragement of competitors enables the predator to create or maintain a monopoly. Third, the predator recoups revenues lost through the temporary price cut by charging higher, monopoly prices." Irvin Indus., Inc. v. Goodyear Aerospace Corp., 974 F.2d 241, 244 (2d Cir. 1992). *See generally* P. Areeda & D. Turner, Predatory Pricing and Related Practices Under Section 2 of the Sherman Act, 88 Harv. L. Rev. 697 (1975); W. Baumol, Quasi-Permanence of Price Reductions: A Policy for Prevention of Predatory Pricing, 89 Yale L.J. 1 (1979); S. Benz, Below-Cost Sales and the Buying of Market Share, 42 Stan. L. Rev. 695 (1990); T. Campbell, Predation and Competition in Antitrust: The Case of Nonfungible Goods, 87 Colum. L. Rev. 1625 (1987); M. Denger & J. Herfort, Predatory Price Claims After *Brooke Group*, 62 Antitrust L.J. 541 (1998).

[32] M. Coate & A. Kleit, Exclusion, Collusion and Confusion: The Limits of Raising Rivals' Costs (FTC Bureau of Economics Working Paper No. 179, 1990).

[33] *See* Matsushita Elec. Indus. Co. v. Zenith Radio Corp., 475 U.S. 574, 595–598 (1986).

aggressive (but entirely legitimate) competition is too often confused with "predation." Because new entry is likely to be attracted by the monopolist's eventual attempt to raise prices above costs, predation is "rarely tried, and even more rarely successful."[34]

A more plausible variation of this theory is directed against defendants having a base of regulated operations in monopoly markets. The charge here is that some costs of unregulated operations have been (or will be) shifted to the regulated operations, from which they are passed on to ratepayers. The incentive to engage in such shifting can be created by rate-of-return regulation, which limits monopoly revenues to costs plus a fixed return on capital. Shortcomings in such regulation can create an opportunity for such cost shifting if the accounting of the regulated operations can be manipulated. The allocation of costs between closely related and interdependent businesses is often an essentially arbitrary exercise; many economists therefore take cross-subsidy concerns very seriously, particularly when regulated and unregulated businesses incur significant common or joint costs that cannot be clearly attributed to one business or the other.[35]

Charges of predatory pricing and cross-subsidy often go hand in hand. If the costs of one line of business are misallocated to others, then there is the opportunity to price services below true cost as part of a systematic campaign to bankrupt the competition. Even if only partially successful, cross-subsidy may undermine competition or efficiency on both sides of the regulatory line. Prices of the regulated service may rise above costs, while production of the unregulated good or service may shift into the hands of an inefficient provider.

[34] *Id.* at 589. *See also* Brooke Group Ltd. v. Brown & Williamson Tobacco Corp., 509 U.S. 209, 226 (1993).

[35] *See, e.g.,* M. Meyerson, Ideas of the Marketplace: A Guide to the 1996 Telecommunications Act, 49 Fed. Comm. L.J. 251, 287 & n.228 (1997); L. Sullivan, Elusive Goals Under the Telecommunications Act, 25 Sw. U. L. Rev. 487, 522 (1996).

§4.2.5 Transfer Pricing and Self-Dealing

A variety of cross-subsidy may arise when one unregulated arm of a company deals directly with a regulated affiliate, such as when the unregulated manufacturing subsidiary of the old Bell System (Western Electric) sells equipment to the regulated Bell Operating Companies (BOCs). In these circumstances, prices may once again be distorted to circumvent rate-of-return regulation. By inflating the price of the goods sold, the unregulated arm can realize supercompetitive profits at the expense of the regulated business and ratepayers.[36] Again, the theory assumes that regulation is strict enough to keep the prices of regulated operations in line with costs, but not strict enough to monitor the costs themselves.

In another variation of the scheme, the regulated business might set up an unaffiliated supplier to sell unregulated products to the regulated firm at above-market prices; the goal would be to evade regulation by forcing ratepayers to bear the higher costs, while arranging a secret kickback to the regulated firm. In *Discon, Inc. v. NYNEX Corporation*,[37] the Second Circuit held that an agreement between a regulated firm and its supplier to overcharge ratepayers (followed by secret kickbacks) could be a section 1 (possibly per se unlawful) boycott of other would-be suppliers and a section 2 conspiracy to monopolize the supplied product. The Supreme Court vacated the Second Circuit's judgment and held that a buyer's decision to purchase from a particular seller is not a group boycott that is a per se violation of

---

[36] Transfer pricing is defined as the price of goods and services exchanged between a parent company and its affiliates. *See generally* I. Ayres & F. Miller, "I'll Sell It to You at Cost": Legal Methods to Promote Retail Markup Disclosure, 84 Nw. U. L. Rev. 1047 (1990); J. Huddleston, Comment, Can Subsidiaries Be "Purchasers" from Their Parents Under the Robinson-Patman Act? A Plea for a Consistent Approach, 63 Wash. L. Rev. 957 (1988); K. Kelly, Note, Using Market Bidding To Regulate the Transfer Price of Utility-Affiliate Cost, 36 Stan. L. Rev. 1215 (1984); J. Knapp, Comment, Effective State Regulation of Energy Utility Diversification, 136 U. Pa. L. Rev. 1677 (1988); D. Pierce, Reconsidering the Roles of Regulation and Competition in the Natural Gas Industry, 97 Harv. L. Rev. 345, 365–366 (1983).

[37] Discon, Inc. v. NYNEX Corp., 93 F.3d 1055 (2d Cir. 1996), *judgment vacated,* 119 S. Ct. 493 (1998).

section 1 of the Sherman Act.[38] The Supreme Court remanded the case to the Second Circuit to consider whether NYNEX's conduct could violate the antitrust laws under the most stringent rule of reason, while noting that "on the basis of the facts alleged," Discon was unlikely to succeed on that claim.[39] Commentators had criticized the Second Circuit for confusing antitrust violations with regulatory fraud.[40] To the extent that it relied on regulatory evasion as the sole basis for antitrust liability, the Second Circuit's now-vacated decision conflicted with decisions of other circuits that have held that overcharging consumers is not an antitrust problem absent impairment of rivals' opportunities to compete.[41]

---

[38] NYNEX Corp. v. Discon, Inc., 119 S. Ct. 493 (1998).

[39] See id. at 500.

[40] See P. Areeda & H. Hovenkamp, Antitrust Law ¶1644(c), at 726–728 (Supp. 1997) (The Second Circuit "effectively turns a claim of fraud into an antitrust claim. For example, any seller under a cost-plus contract might secretly conspire with a supplier to provide goods at inflated costs, paying a secret rebate to the seller, and with the effect of excluding alternative suppliers. As in any case of fraud or misrepresentation, the result will be that the contracted-for good is more costly and consumers are injured. But no antitrust violation is apparent unless this activity threatens monopoly in a properly defined market."). The government told the D.C. Circuit in the Bell System litigation that regulatory evasion through cost-shifting from a competitive market to a regulated one is not a *competitive* concern unless it also results in the threat of market power in the unregulated market. U.S. Brief at 29, United States v. Western Elec. Co., No. 87-5388 (D.C. Cir. Apr. 17, 1989).

[41] See, e.g., Blue Cross & Blue Shield United of Wisconsin v. Marshfield Clinic, 65 F.3d 1406, 1412–1413 (7th Cir. 1995) (Posner, C.J.) ("[T]he antitrust laws do not regulate the prices of natural monopolists. A natural monopolist that acquired and maintained its monopoly without excluding competitors by improper means . . . can therefore charge any price it wants, for the antitrust laws are not a price-control statute or a public-utility or common-carrier rate-regulation statute.") (citations omitted), cert. denied, 516 U.S. 1184 (1996); Alaska Airlines, 948 F.2d at 548 ("Government regulation, as opposed to treble damages and criminal liability under the Sherman Act, is generally thought to be the appropriate remedy for the difficulties posed by natural monopolies."); United States Football League v. National Football League, 842 F.2d 1355, 1361 (2d Cir. 1988) ("Setting a high price may be a use of monopoly power, but it is not in itself anticompetitive."); Williamsburg Wax Museum, Inc. v. Historic Figures, Inc., 810 F.2d 243, 252 (D.C. Cir. 1987) ("imposition of a high price is not, in and of itself, an anticompetitive act");

§4.3   The Implications of Regulation

Most of the antitrust theories discussed above concern pairs of markets in which monopoly power in one is extended into the other. Frequently, the incentive for such conduct is the fact that returns in the monopoly market are limited by regulation. But regulation invariably also covers the terms and conditions of service, including obligations to interconnect, to deal, and to sell service without discrimination. Can the regulatory process itself be exploited as an integral part of an antitrust abuse? Does the existence of comprehensive regulation immunize a firm from antitrust liability? Or can regulation that raises the antitrust concern in the first place also allay it?

§4.3.1   Abuse of the Regulatory Process

As discussed in Chapter 8, a key allegation in one series of antitrust cases was that AT&T had used tariff filings with the FCC and other regulatory agencies for purposes of delay and complication. A principal defense against such charges is the *Noerr-Pennington* doctrine, which provides antitrust immunity to companies that are "petitioning the government."[42] An exception to the *Noerr-Pennington* defense is the "mere sham" rule.[43]

Kartell v. Blue Shield of Mass., Inc., 749 F.2d 922, 927 (1st Cir. 1984) (Breyer, J.) ("Ordinarily, however, even a monopolist is free to exploit whatever market power it may possess when that exploitation takes the form of charging uncompetitive prices."), *cert. denied*, 471 U.S. 1029 (1985); Trace X Chem., Inc. v. Canadian Indus., Ltd., 738 F.2d 261, 267–268 (8th Cir. 1984) ("a monopolist . . . set[ting] profit maximizing prices . . . is 'the normal, rational response of a business . . . seeking to maximize profits, sales, or revenues.'") (citations omitted), *cert. denied*, 469 U.S. 1160 (1985).

[42] The *Noerr-Pennington* doctrine developed from the Supreme Court's decisions in Eastern Railroad Presidents Conference v. Noerr Motor Freight, Inc., 365 U.S. 127 (1961), and United Mine Workers of America v. Pennington, 381 U.S. 657 (1965). *See* Allied Tube & Conduit Corp. v. Indian Head, Inc., 486 U.S. 492, 499 (1988) (citing *Noerr, Pennington*, and California Motor Transport Co. v. Trucking Unlimited, 404 U.S. 508 (1972)).

[43] *See Noerr*, 365 U.S. at 144; *see also* Professional Real Estate Investors, Inc. v. Columbia Pictures Indus., Inc., 508 U.S. 49, 55, 60–61 (1993) (decrying

The defense and the mere sham doctrine have been tested repeatedly in litigation involving telcos. While the results have been mixed, *Noerr-Pennington* immunity has fared reasonably well overall. *Noerr-Pennington* does not provide immunity, however, against antitrust claims directed at price or other terms contained in tariffs.[44]

§4.3.2 *General Immunity*

If *Noerr-Pennington* limits plaintiffs' use of the regulatory record as a sword against obstructionist defendants, can defendants in-

---

courts of appeals for "defin[ing] 'sham' in inconsistent and contradictory ways"; explaining that "sham" litigation requires an "objectively baseless" lawsuit motivated by "use of the government process . . . as an anticompetitive weapon") (internal quotation marks and alteration omitted); Classic Communications, Inc. v. Rural Tel. Serv. Co., Inc., 956 F. Supp. 910, 917–918 (D. Kan. 1997) (applying *Professional Real Estate* standard in finding petitioning of government was not a sham). In *Noerr,* the Supreme Court also noted that "[t]here may be situations in which a publicity campaign, ostensibly directed toward influencing governmental action, is a mere sham to cover what is actually nothing more than an attempt to interfere directly with the business relationships of a competitor." 365 U.S. at 144.

[44] In Cantor v. Detroit Edison Co., 428 U.S. 579 (1976) four Justices rejected AT&T's argument as amicus curiae and held that a tariff filed by an electric utility could not evade scrutiny under the antitrust laws simply because it was filed in accordance with state law and approved by a state agency. The plurality stated:

> [N]othing in the *Noerr* opinion implies that the mere fact that a state regulatory agency may approve a proposal included in a tariff, and thereby require that the proposal be implemented until a revised tariff is filed and approved, is a sufficient reason for conferring antitrust immunity on the proposed conduct.

428 U.S. at 601–602. Chief Justice Burger did not concur in that portion of the plurality's opinion, but his objection went to the plurality's construction of the "state action" exemption doctrine under Parker v. Brown, 317 U.S. 341 (1943), and he said nothing in disagreement with the plurality's interpretation of *Noerr. Cantor,* 428 U.S. at 604–605. Justice Blackmun's concurrence also did not address *Noerr,* but rather suggested reliance on "a rule of reason, taking it as a general proposition that state-sanctioned anticompetitive activity must fall like any other if its potential harms outweigh its benefits." *Id.* at 610.

voke it as a shield? In *Otter Tail,* the Supreme Court's first significant opinion addressing this question, the defendant pointed out that the Federal Power Act grants the Federal Power Commission (FPC) authority to compel interconnection as "necessary or appropriate in the public interest."[45] But the Court concluded that by enacting the legislation, Congress had "rejected a pervasive regulatory scheme . . . in favor of voluntary commercial relationships."[46] According to the Court, "When these relationships are governed in the first instance by business judgment and not regulatory coercion, courts must be hesitant to conclude that Congress intended to override the fundamental national policies embodied in the antitrust laws."[47] Other courts have repeatedly voiced similarly skeptical views toward claims of implied antitrust immunity.[48] The general rule is that antitrust immunity will be implied only where required to make a regulatory scheme work, and even then, only to the minimum extent necessary.[49]

How much immunity does the Communications Act deliver under these rules of construction? The answer has varied over time. The success of claims of immunity has generally depended on how clearly they have been supported by pronouncements and findings of regulatory officials.[50]

---

[45] Otter Tail Power Co. v. United States, 410 U.S. at 373. Indeed, when Otter Tail refused to connect competing wholesalers to its transmission lines, municipalities had sought FPC relief, one of them successfully.

[46] *Id.* at 374.

[47] *Id.*

[48] *See, e.g.,* Georgia v. Pennsylvania R.R. Co., 324 U.S. 439, 456 (1945). "Repeal of the antitrust laws by implication is not favored and not casually to be allowed. Only where there is a 'plain repugnancy between the antitrust and regulatory provisions' will repeal be implied." Gordon v. New York Stock Exchange, 422 U.S. 659, 682 (1975) (quoting United States v. Philadelphia Natl. Bank, 374 U.S. 321, 350–351 (1963)). *See also* United States v. National Assn. of Sec. Dealers, 422 U.S. 694, 719–720 (1975).

[49] Silver v. New York Stock Exch., 373 U.S. 341, 357 (1963); *see also* National Gerimedical Hosp. & Gerontology Ctr. v. Blue Cross of Kansas City, 452 U.S. 378, 389 (1981); *MCI,* 708 F.2d at 1102.

[50] *See* United States v. AT&T, 552 F. Supp. 131, 157 (D.D.C. 1982), *aff'd mem. sub nom.* Maryland v. United States, 460 U.S. 1001 (1983); United States v. AT&T, 524 F. Supp. at 1345; United States v. AT&T, 461 F. Supp. 1314,

The earliest federal regulation of telecommunications occurred under section 7 of the Mann-Elkins Act of 1910,[51] which simply required telephone and telegraph companies to provide service upon request at just and reasonable rates without unjust discrimination or undue preference.[52] Later the Willis-Graham Act of 1921 authorized the Interstate Commerce Commission (ICC) to approve the consolidation of telephone company properties into single companies if such consolidation was "of advantage to the persons to whom service is to be rendered and in the public interest"[53] and granted antitrust immunity for such consolidations.[54] In other respects, however, the industry remained subject to the antitrust laws.[55] The Federal Communications Act of 1934[56] carried forward, almost verbatim, many provisions of

---

1320–1330 (D.D.C. 1978); *see also Southern Pacific,* 740 F.2d at 999–1000; MCI v. AT&T, 708 F.2d at 1101–1105; Northeastern Tel. Co. v. AT&T, 651 F.2d 76, 82–84 (2d Cir. 1981), *cert. denied,* 455 U.S. 943 (1982); Phonetele, Inc. v. AT&T, 664 F.2d 7 16, 726–737 (9th Cir. 1981) *cert. denied,* 459 U.S. 1145 (1983); Sound, Inc. v. AT&T, 631 F.2d 1324, 1327–1331 (8th Cir. 1980); Mid-Texas Communications Sys., Inc. v. AT&T, 615 F.2d 1372, 1377–1382 (5th Cir.), *cert. denied sub. nom.* Woodlands Telecomms. Corp. v. Southwestern Bell Tel. Co., 449 U.S. 912 (1980); Essential Communications Sys., Inc. v. AT&T, 610 F.2d 1114, 1116–1125 (3d Cir. 1979). *See generally* R. Haar, AT&T and the Antitrust Laws: A Strict Test for Implied Immunity, 85 Yale L.J. 254, 269 (1975); G. Hillebrand, The Application of Antitrust Law to Telecommunications, 69 Cal. L. Rev. 497, 509–511 (1981).

[51] Mann-Elkins Act of 1910, ch. 309, §7, 36 Stat. 539, 544–547. *See* §2.3.

[52] *See* Mann-Elkins Act of 1910, ch. 309, §7, 36 Stat. 544–547, §12, 36 Stat. 551–554. The Mann-Elkins Act did not subject the telecommunications industry to the broad tariff and regulatory jurisdiction exercised by the ICC over railroads. *See Essential Communications,* 610 F.2d at 1117–1120 (detailing early regulation of telecommunications and railroad industries).

[53] Willis-Graham Act of 1921, 42 Stat. 27 (codified as amended at 47 U.S.C. §221(a)), *repealed by* Telecommunications Act of 1996, §601(b)(2), Pub. L. 104–104, 110 Stat. 143.

[54] *Id.*

[55] MCI v. AT&T, 708 F.2d at 1100–1101. *See Mid-Texas,* 615 F.2d at 1378 n.3 ("The existence of an explicit exemption in one part of the [Communications] Act does not provide authority for the proposition that other actions not directly covered are impliedly exempt."); Industrial Communications Sys., Inc. v. Pacific Tel. & Tel. Co., 505 F.2d 152, 156 (9th Cir. 1974).

[56] Federal Communications Act of 1934, ch. 652, 48 Stat. 1064 (codified as amended at 47 U.S.C. §§151–614).

the earlier statutes, including the Willis-Graham antitrust exemption for consolidations of competing local telephone systems.[57]

The unstated, but clear premise of the 1934 Act and parallel state statutes was that telephone service is best provided by way of a monopoly. The monopoly telco was obliged to provide telephone service to all customers at "just and reasonable" (usually averaged) prices.[58] New firms were allowed to provide competing services only if they proved that the "public convenience and necessity" so required.[59] The monopoly carrier was required to connect to the new firms only if a commission found such connection "necessary or desirable in the public interest."[60]

From the 1930s until the 1960s, both federal and state regulators generally approved of—and indeed actively supported—the monopoly provision of telephone services and equipment. Perhaps for that reason, the issue of antitrust immunity was not often tested by private litigants. But thereafter regulatory attitudes began to shift quickly.

From the 1960s on, telcos were sued with increasing frequency, and their attempts to invoke broad antitrust immunity met with declining success. The courts that considered the Bell System's claims of antitrust immunity generally held that such immunity would be appropriate only where (1) there is an "actual or potential" conflict between Federal Communications Commission (FCC) regulation and antitrust laws;[61] (2) the actions complained of are "required or approved by the Federal Communications Commission, pursuant to its statutory authority, in a way that is incompatible with antitrust enforcement;"[62] or (3) regulatory

[57] *Compare* Mann-Elkins Act §7, 36 Stat. 544–547, §12, 36 Stat. 551–554 *with* Federal Communications Act of 1934, 47 U.S.C. §§201(b), 202(a). *See also* 47 U.S.C. §221(a) (now repealed).
[58] 47 U.S.C. §201(a), (b).
[59] *Id.* §214(a).
[60] *Id.* §201(a).
[61] *E.g., Essential Communications,* 610 F.2d at 1121 ("the determination of a possible antitrust exemption turns, in our view, on conflict, actual or potential, between an obligation imposed by the 1934 Act and an antitrust remedy").
[62] MCI v. AT&T, 708 F.2d at 1102. For example, in Hughes Tool Co. v. Trans World Airlines, Inc., 409 U.S. 363, 388–389 (1973), the Court held that

controls on entry and price preclude the defendant's exercise of monopoly power as a matter of fact.[63]

For example, the Seventh Circuit held in 1982 that the FCC's discretionary power to require interconnection did not conflict with the duty to interconnect established in *Otter Tail*.[64] In a 1980 case involving terminal equipment, the Third Circuit rejected the Bell System's assertion of general immunity under the public interest standard of the Communications Act, noting that the FCC itself had been pushing for competition in that market for many years.[65] Bell was likewise denied general immunity from antitrust attacks that pivoted on its tariffed rates. For example, the Seventh Circuit ruled that immunity against charges of predatory pricing presented a "closer question" than immunity respecting interconnection practices, but denied the immunity.[66]

---

where the Civil Aeronautics Board had specifically authorized certain transactions between a parent and its subsidiary, those transactions were immunized from antitrust liability by section 414 of the Federal Aviation Act, 49 U.S.C. §1378.

[63] *See* §4.3.4.

[64] "Although the FCC has authority to compel interconnection under section 201(a) of the [Federal Communications Act of 1934], the initial decision whether to interconnect rests with the utility, and the record shows that the FCC did not control or approve of AT&T's actions here. Nor has the FCC supervised AT&T's interconnection practices so closely that the FCC's approval could be inferred." MCI v. AT&T, 708 F.2d at 1103 (citing *Gordon*, 422 U.S. 659).

[65] *Sound, Inc.*, 631 F.2d at 1330. In light of the FCC's policy, the court concluded that "the maintenance of an antitrust suit will not conflict with the operation of the regulatory scheme authorized by Congress but will supplement that scheme." *Id. See also* MCI v. AT&T, 708 F.2d at 1104 ("[T]he interconnection policies adopted by the FCC during the time period relevant to this litigation appear designed to promote rather than inhibit competition in the specialized telecommunications field. Thus, the allowance of antitrust liability is likely to complement rather than undermine the applicable statutory scheme.").

[66] MCI v. AT&T, 708 F.2d at 1104. Courts have generally cited three reasons for rejecting immunity in cases relating to tariffed rates. First, under the Communications Act, the carrier, not the Commission, sets the rates, and the carrier may file a new or revised tariff at any time. *See id.* (citing 47 U.S.C. §204); *Sound, Inc.*, 631 F.2d at 1330. Second, tariffs go into effect automatically, most of them without receiving review by the Commission. MCI v. AT&T, 708 F.2d at 1104–1105; *Phonetele*, 664 F.2d at 733; *Essential Communications*, 610 F.2d at 1124; MCI v. FCC, 561 F.2d 365, 374 (D.C. Cir. 1977) (*Execunet*),

But the Seventh Circuit, subsequently joined by several other circuits, did accept a limited immunity for good-faith denials of interconnection required by a carrier's "concrete, articulable concerns for the public interest."[67] Courts have also acknowledged that, in case of direct conflict between a regulatory mandate and the antitrust laws, a regulated entity enjoys immunity for "action taken under compulsion of law."[68] They have likewise accepted that a tariff approved after an FCC hearing should be much less vulnerable to antitrust attack than one merely filed, but never reviewed.[69] Overall, as summarized by the Third Circuit, "the determination of a possible antitrust exemption turns . . . on conflict, actual or potential, between an obligation imposed by the 1934 Act and an antitrust remedy. . . ."[70]

The 1996 Telecommunications Act, by mandating a detailed regime of activities for opening telephone and video markets to competition, creates many additional possibilities for conflict and incompatibility between regulatory and antitrust enforcement. Yet the 1996 Act provides that nothing added or amended by it "shall be construed to modify, impair, or supersede the applicability of any of the antitrust laws."[71] This savings clause

---

cert. denied, 434 U.S. 1040 (1978). Third, the tariff provisions of the Communications Act provide remedies for customers, not competitors. *See Essential Communications,* 610 F.2d at 1120. *But see* 47 U.S.C. §207 ("[a]ny person claiming to be damaged" may bring a complaint).

Immunity for tariffed rates, however, might be appropriate if the rates are due to "regulatory coercion" or if the Commission "dictated" or "approved" the carrier's tariff filings. MCI v. AT&T, 708 F.2d at 1105. During the 1974 government antitrust case against AT&T, the FCC maintained that when it has prescribed or specifically approved a tariff, its judgment must control. *See* United States v. AT&T, 461 F. Supp. at 1327 n.39; *cf.* Jeffrey v. Southwestern Bell, 518 F.2d 1129 (5th Cir. 1975) (state action immunity from antitrust laws granted where challenged rate had been approved by municipality after thorough hearings).

[67] *See* MCI v. AT&T, 708 F.2d at 1138. The D.C. Circuit explicitly adopted this same formulation some years later. *Southern Pacific,* 740 F.2d at 1010. The Ninth and Fifth Circuits describe the standard in similar terms. *See Phonetele,* 664 F.2d at 737–738; *Mid-Texas,* 615 F.2d at 1390.

[68] *Essential Communications,* 610 F.2d at 1124 (citing Parker v. Brown, 317 U.S. 341); *id.* at 1120–1121.

[69] *Id.* at 1124.

[70] *Id.* at 1121.

[71] Telecommunications Act of 1996, §601(b)(1).

appears primarily intended to allow ordinary antitrust scrutiny of mergers between firms that, due to the Act, had become potential competitors.[72] Nothing in the legislative history indicates that this savings clause was meant to eliminate the usual (limited) forms of regulatory immunity.

§4.3.3   *Primary Jurisdiction*

The doctrine of primary jurisdiction is relevant in cases where direct conflict between antitrust and regulatory mandates seems likely.[73] When presented with such a situation, courts will generally suspend antitrust proceedings in order to allow the regulatory agency the first chance at resolving the apparent conflict.[74]

---

[72] *E.g.*, Conference Rep. on S. 652, Telecommunications Act of 1996, Cong. Rec. H1171 (Feb. 1, 1996) (Representative Conyers: "[T]he bill contains an all-important antitrust savings clause which ensures that any and all telecommunications merger and anticompetitive activities are fully subject to the antitrust laws. Telco-cable mergers and all other broadcast, media, or telecommunications transactions will be fully subject to antitrust review. . . . "); Cong. Rec. S692 (Feb. 1, 1996) (Senator Leahy: "There are so many things I like about this bill. . . . The conference agreement also includes a very strong savings clause to make clear that mergers between companies in the media and communications markets are subject to a thorough antitrust review."); Cong. Rec. S8472 (June 7, 1995) (Senator Thurmond: "I am particularly pleased that the amendment adopted to restrict telephone-cable mergers contains a savings clause which makes absolutely clear that the antitrust laws are maintained. . . . [T]he Department of Justice and the Federal Trade Commission still have the authority and the obligation under the law to consider whether any telephone-cable merger, acquisition, or joint venture violates the antitrust laws.").

[73] "The doctrine of primary jurisdiction represents a version of the administrative exhaustion requirement under circumstances in which a judicially cognizable claim is presented but "'enforcement of the claim requires the resolution of issues which, under a regulatory scheme, have been placed within the special competence of an administrative body. . . .'" Goya Foods, Inc. v. Tropicana Prods., Inc., 846 F.2d 848, 851 (2d Cir. 1988) (quoting United States v. Western Pac. R.R. Co., 352 U.S. 59, 64 (1956)).

[74] *See, e.g.*, Pan Am. World Airways v. United States, 371 U.S. 296 (1963); Ricci v. Chicago Mercantile Exch., 447 F.2d 713 (7th Cir. 1971); Carter v. AT&T, 250 F. Supp. 188 (N.D. Tex.), *aff'd*, 356 F.2d 486 (5th Cir. 1966), *cert. denied*, 385 U.S. 1008 (1967).

For example, Judge Greene stated in 1978 that "if and when conflicts [between regulatory and antitrust standards] should become apparent after the issues have been crystallized, matters relating to them will be referred to the Commission under the doctrine of primary jurisdiction."[75] The doctrine does not, however, give the FCC or other regulators general authority to moot antitrust claims or to provide primary or final interpretation of antitrust decrees.[76]

§4.3.4   Regulation as a "Fact of Market Life"

Even if regulation does not provide antitrust immunity as a matter of law, "an industry's regulated status is an important 'fact of market life,' the impact of which on pricing and other competitive decisions 'is too obvious to be ignored.'"[77] Thus, the regulatory environment must be an integral part of any factual inquiry.

For example, as the Bell System cogently argued in the 1974 government case, high market shares do not in themselves establish market power within a regulated industry. Until changes in FCC regulatory philosophy in the late 1960s and 1970s, Bell operated under a legally protected monopoly. As a result, Bell correctly pointed out, high market shares "are almost totally irrelevant"; in any analysis that pivots on market shares, the "alleged markets [are treated] not as products of regulation, but as though they had come into being through a long history of open competition."[78] The Bell System aptly analogized its position to

[75] United States v. AT&T, 461 F. Supp. at 1349–1350 (citation and emphasis omitted).

[76] See United States v. Western Elec. Co., Inc., 846 F.2d 1422, 1432–1433 (D.C. Cir.) (rejecting the argument that the FCC, by ruling on certain tariff matters, could moot an issue of pricing discrimination properly raised under an antitrust decree), cert. denied, 488 U.S. 924 (1988).

[77] MCI v. AT&T, 708 F.2d at 1105 (quoting ITT v. GTE Corp., 518 F.2d 913, 935–936 (9th Cir. 1975) (footnote omitted) (ITT v. GTE II)). See also United States v. AT&T, 524 F. Supp. at 1347; Mid-Texas, 615 F.2d at 1385.

[78] Memorandum in Support of Defendants' Motion for Involuntary Dismissal Under Rule 41(b) at 26, United States v. Western Elec. Co., No. 74-1698 (D.D.C. July 10, 1981).

that of the holder of a patent one day after the patent has expired.[79]

Two appellate courts have agreed that this line of argument, and the underlying facts, presents a valid issue for the jury.[80] But in the 1974 government case, Judge Greene dismissed this argument as "but a variation of defendants' broader claim that compliance with the communications laws satisfies all obligations under the antitrust laws. . . ."[81]

The fact of regulation likewise rebuts the so-called *Alcoa* presumption that the possession of monopoly power necessarily implies monopolistic intent and conduct.[82] Common carriers are expressly required to anticipate and meet all demands for service; a firm's compliance with the common carrier provisions of the Communications Act cannot therefore establish its willful violation of the Sherman Act.[83]

Similarly, a regulated telephone company may present "established regulatory policies" as part of its factual defense to refusals to interconnect. A carrier may deny interconnections without antitrust consequences if it has "a reasonable basis in regulatory

---

[79] Economists make the same analogy respecting the opening up of local telephone business to competition under the 1996 Act. *See* FCC Chief Economist Joseph Farrell, Creating Local Competition (May 15, 1996) (transcript available at <http://www.fcc.gov/Bureaus/OPP/econspch.txt>).

[80] MCI v. AT&T, 708 F.2d at 1107 (citations omitted). The D.C. Circuit agreed with the Seventh Circuit that in a regulated industry market share is a "questionable" indicator of market power. *Southern Pacific*, 740 F.2d at 1000 (citations omitted). *See also* Metro Mobile CTS, Inc. v. NewVector Communications, Inc., 892 F.2d 62, 63 & n.1 (9th Cir. 1989).

[81] United States v. AT&T, 524 F. Supp. at 1347. In addition, the court found that AT&T's market power was not solely an artifact of regulation. *Id.* at 1347–1348 (footnotes omitted).

[82] United States v. Aluminum Co. of Am., 148 F.2d 416, 432 (2d Cir. 1945); *see also* American Tobacco Co. v. United States, 328 U.S. 781, 813–814 (1946).

[83] *See* MCI v. AT&T, 708 F.2d at 1108. The Seventh Circuit has held instead that the plaintiff must "prove that each allegedly anticompetitive act or practice attributed to AT&T was done with the intent to maintain a monopoly in the relevant market." *Id.* (footnote omitted). *See also* City of Mishawaka v. American Elec. Power Co., 616 F.2d 976, 985 (7th Cir. 1980), *cert. denied*, 449 U.S. 1096 (1981); K. Watson & T. Brunner, Monopolization by Regulated "Monopolies": The Search for Substantive Standards, 22 Antitrust Bull. 559, 574–579 (1977).

policy to conclude, and in good faith conclude[s], that denial of interconnections is required by concrete, articulable concerns for the public interest."[84] And a firm may also point to the fact of regulation as evidence that it lacks power over price. But in each case, the role of regulation is simply part of the factual inquiry; regulation raises no absolute defense as a matter of law.[85]

§4.3.5 The Filed Rate Doctrine

This doctrine provides quite broad immunity against *customers* who claim antitrust damages from having been required to pay tariffed rates. The doctrine originated in a 1922 opinion of Justice Brandeis.[86] The rule was considered essential to protect the "paramount purpose" of tariffing—the "prevention of unjust discrimination."[87] But as Justice Brandeis also noted, "[A] combination of carriers to fix reasonable and non-discriminatory rates may be illegal. . . . The fact that these rates had been approved by the Commission would not, it seems, bar proceedings by the Government"[88] or by competitors. The courts of appeals have more recently reaffirmed this view.[89]

---

[84] MCI v. AT&T, 708 F.2d at 1138. The Fifth Circuit reached the same result in *Mid-Texas*, 615 F.2d 1372.

[85] In the 1974 case, for example, Judge Greene ruled that the government had met its initial burden of showing that in fact regulation had not effectively controlled the Bell System's exercise of monopoly power. United States v. AT&T, 524 F. Supp. at 1346 n.24. The Seventh Circuit likewise treated power over price as a factual issue, noting that regulation could constrain such power. MCI v. AT&T, 708 F.2d at 1107.

[86] Keogh v. Chicago & Northwestern Ry. Co., 260 U.S. 156 (1922).

[87] *Id.* at 163.

[88] *Id.* at 161–162 (citations omitted).

[89] *See, e.g.,* Cost Management Servs., Inc. v. Washington Natural Gas Co., 99 F.3d 937, 946 (9th Cir. 1996); Litton Sys., Inc. v. AT&T, 700 F.2d 785, 807 (2d Cir. 1983), *cert. denied,* 464 U.S. 1073 (1984); *Essential Communications,* 610 F.2d at 1121–1124. However, when a competitor seeks damages for a monopolist's failure to extend the competitor preferential rates in disregard of governing tariffs, the filed rate doctrine would govern. *See* AT&T v. Central Office Tel., Inc., 118 S. Ct. 1956, 1962–1963 (1998); Square D Co. v. Niagara Frontier Tariff Bureau, Inc., 476 U.S. 409 (1986); Taffet v. Southern Co., 967 F.2d 1483, 1492 (11th Cir.), *cert. denied,* 506 U.S. 1021 (1992); Pinney Dock & Transp.

§4.3.6 State Action

In the 1943 holding of *Parker v. Brown*,[90] the Supreme Court recognized that the Sherman Act was not intended to prohibit state governments from imposing restraints on competition. As the Court reiterated in 1985, the conduct of a private firm following state policy is immune from antitrust attack if the policy is "clearly articulated and affirmatively expressed."[91] Most courts have held that the anticompetitive conduct need not be specifically compelled by the state.[92] Moreover, the state may embrace competition in some respects while simultaneously seeking to

---

Co. v. Penn Cent. Corp., 838 F.2d 1445, 1457 (6th Cir.), *cert. denied sub nom.* Pinney Dock & Transp. Co. v. Norfolk & Western Ry. Co., 488 U.S. 880 (1988). Courts have also not recognized an exception to the filed rate doctrine when there are allegations of fraud upon the regulatory agency. *See* Wegoland Ltd. v. NYNEX Corp., 27 F.3d 17, 20–21 (2d Cir. 1994); H.J. Inc. v. Northwestern Bell Tel. Co., 954 F.2d 485, 489–490 (8th Cir.), *cert. denied,* 504 U.S. 957 (1992).

[90] Parker v. Brown, 317 U.S. 341 (1943). *See also* California Retail Liquor Dealers Assn. v. Midcal Aluminum, Inc., 445 U.S. 97 (1980) (*Midcal*); New Motor Vehicle Bd. v. Orrin W. Fox Co., 439 U.S. 96 (1978); City of Lafayette v. Louisiana Power & Light Co., 435 U.S. 389 (1978) (*Lafayette*); *Cantor,* 428 U.S. 579. This doctrine "reflects Congress' intention to embody in the Sherman Act the federalism principle that the States possess a significant measure of sovereignty under our Constitution." Community Communications Co., Inc. v. City of Boulder, 455 U.S. 40, 53 (1982). Some tension exists in application of the doctrine, for, as the Ninth Circuit recently explained, "a broad interpretation of the doctrine may inadvertently extend immunity to anticompetitive activity which the states did not intend to sanction." *Cost Management Servs.,* 99 F.3d at 941.

[91] Southern Motor Carriers Rate Conference, Inc. v. United States, 471 U.S. 48, 57 (1985) (citing *Midcal,* 445 U.S. at 105 (quoting *Lafayette,* 435 U.S. at 410)). The state must also "provide[ ] active supervision of anticompetitive conduct undertaken by private actors." Federal Trade Commn. v. Ticor Title Ins. Co., 504 U.S. 621, 631 (1992). The purpose of this requirement is to "determine whether the State has exercised sufficient independent judgment so that the details of the rates or prices have been established as a product of deliberate state intervention, not simply by agreement among the parties." *Id.* at 634–635.

[92] In explaining its holding in *Southern Motor Carriers,* the Supreme Court in *Ticor* described "the Government's contention [in *Southern Motor Carriers* as] being that a pricing policy is not an articulated one unless the practice is compelled"; the *Ticor* Court then stated, "We rejected that assertion. . . ." 504 U.S. at 639. In *Southern Motor Carriers,* indeed, the Supreme Court expressly

promote noncompetition policies. "[A] state regulatory scheme need not be antithetical to competition to be exempt from federal antitrust scrutiny."[93] But the routine filing of tariffs by a utility typically is not sufficient to engage immunity.[94]

Most courts have reached similar conclusions for tariffs filed by telcos.[95] One court ruled that a telco "clearly me[t]" the test for state action immunity when state regulators approved access charges that it imposed on another local company.[96] Another court ruled that the Bell System qualified for state action and *Noerr-Pennington* immunity against charges that it manipulated private-line rates so as to drive small remote alarm system operators out of business.[97] But in approving the 1982 AT&T Decree, Judge Greene rejected all *Parker v. Brown* arguments presented by state regulators. He reasoned that the subjects of the lawsuit—long distance and equipment—were provided in national markets. From that assumption, he leapt quickly to the conclusion that he had general authority to fashion an appropriate remedy, even one that reached deeply into the domain of state regulation.[98]

---

held that "a state policy that expressly *permits,* but does not compel, anticompetitive conduct may be 'clearly articulated' within the meaning of [the state action immunity test]." 471 U.S. at 61 (emphasis in original; footnote omitted). *See also* Sandy River Nursing Care v. Aetna Cas., 985 F.2d 1138, 1147 (1st Cir.), *cert. denied,* 510 U.S. 818 (1993); Lease Lights, Inc. v. Public Serv. Co. of Okla., 849 F.2d 1330, 1332–1333 (10th Cir. 1988), *cert. denied,* 488 U.S. 1019 (1989).

[93] Metro Mobile CTS, Inc. v. NewVector Communications, Inc., 661 F. Supp. 1504, 1514 (D. Ariz. 1987), *aff'd,* 892 F.2d 62 (9th Cir. 1989).

[94] *Cantor,* 428 U.S. 579. Though Detroit Edison had filed a tariff reflecting its light-bulb exchange program, nothing indicated that Michigan actually regulated it. *See id.* at 584–585, 595. Indeed, Michigan law did not even require the tariff to mention the program. However, the validity of *Cantor* has been in doubt since *Southern Motor Carriers,* 471 U.S. at 60, made immunity available without state compulsion. *See, e.g.,* Davis v. Southern Bell Tel. & Tel. Co., 755 F. Supp. 1532, 1538 (S.D. Fla. 1991); *Metro Mobile,* 661 F. Supp. at 1513.

[95] *See, e.g., Essential Communications,* 610 F.2d at 1125.

[96] DFW Metro Line Servs. v. Southwestern Bell Tel. Co., 901 F.2d 1267, 1269 n.6 (5th Cir.), *cert. denied,* 498 U.S. 985 (1990).

[97] Sonitrol of Fresno, Inc. v. AT&T, 629 F. Supp. 1089 (D.D.C. 1986).

[98] United States v. AT&T, 552 F. Supp. at 158. Judge Greene likewise brushed aside arguments by the states that, in enacting the Communications Act, Congress intended to prevent federal preemption of the state regulation

§4.3.7 Tenth Amendment

It has also been argued, though for the most part unsuccessfully,[99] that the Tenth Amendment limits a federal court's power to invade the regulatory domain reserved to the states.[100] In a strongly antifederalist decision, the Ninth Circuit recently held that federal courts may second-guess whether states have correctly interpreted their own mandates as authorizing anticompetitive conduct; thus, even when a state public utility commission directly requires the conduct, obedience to the commission is not protected by state action immunity if a federal court later decides the commission was acting ultra vires.[101] Federalism issues have been addressed in several recent Supreme Court decisions, and the scope of state authority is far from settled in many contexts.[102] The interrelationship between federal and state regulation in enforcement of the antitrust laws may also evolve over time.

---

of telecommunications permitted by that statute. *Id.* at 156. Subsequent decisions of the Supreme Court and various courts of appeals, however, have clarified that the Communications Act was intended to preserve a substantial role for state regulation. *See* §§3.5–3.7. In dissenting from the summary affirmance of the divestiture decree, Justice Rehnquist wrote that he was "troubled by the notion that a district court, by entering what is in essence a private agreement between parties to a lawsuit, invokes the Supremacy Clause powers of the Federal Government to pre-empt state regulatory laws." Maryland v. United States, 460 U.S. 1001, 1002 (1983) (Rehnquist, J., dissenting).

[99] *See, e.g.,* United States v. AT&T, 552 F. Supp. at 155–156.

[100] *See* National League of Cities v. Usery, 426 U.S. 833 (1976), *overruled by* Garcia v. San Antonio Metro. Transit Auth., 469 U.S. 528 (1985).

[101] Columbia Steel Casting Co. v. Portland General Elec. Co., 111 F.3d 1427 (9th Cir. 1996), *cert. denied,* 118 S. Ct. 1688 (1998). The United States filed an amicus brief urging the Ninth Circuit to deny state action immunity, and the Supreme Court asked for the Solicitor General's views on whether the case warranted review. The Solicitor General recommended that certiorari not be granted, arguing that the court of appeals had applied the correct test for state action immunity, even if there was some question about its interpretation of the relevant facts. *See* Brief for the United States as Amicus Curiae, Portland General Elec. Co. v. Columbia Steel Casting Co., No. 97-49 (U.S. filed Apr. 14, 1998). The Supreme Court declined to hear the case.

[102] *See, e.g.,* California v. Deep Sea Research, Inc., 118 S. Ct. 1464 (1998); Idaho v. Coeur d'Alene Tribe of Idaho, 521 U.S. 261 (1997); Seminole Tribe of Fla. v. Florida, 517 U.S. 44 (1996).

§4.4   A Brief History of Government Cases

Federal government antitrust suits aimed at restructuring the Bell System are almost as old as the Bell System itself. Three major consent decrees between the government and Bell were entered between 1914 and 1982. The government obtained similar decrees governing GTE in 1984 and AT&T/McCaw's cellular business in 1994.

The upshot: Between 1984 and 1996, the industry was regulated at least as much by federal decree as by federal commission; the most critical aspects of industry structure were regulated by decree entirely. The description of Judge Greene's superintendence of the AT&T, GTE, and McCaw decrees from 1982 to 1996 consumed six chapters of the prior edition and supplement of this book. Although the 1996 Act eliminated the prospective effect of all these decrees[103] and although the decrees themselves were settlements without findings of antitrust liability,[104] much of

---

[103] Section 601(a)(1)–(3) of the 1996 Act, 47 U.S.C. §152 note.

[104] Even the 1982 AT&T Decree, often cited as a definitive antitrust ruling, provided that none "of its terms or provisions shall constitute any evidence against, an admission by, or an estoppel against any party or BOC." United States v. AT&T, 552 F. Supp. at 228. Judge Greene's approval of that decree pursuant to the Tunney Act did not adjudicate antitrust liability, but ensured that the settlement was within the broad reaches of the public interest. Later, in approving the similar GTE Decree, Judge Greene reaffirmed that none of the government's claims of wrongdoing by the Bell System had been established:

> [Counsel for GTE]: When it came to assessing whether the AT&T decree was in the public interest, its provisions were accordingly viewed against an evidentiary background of misconduct by the Bell system which had impeded . . . competition in the long distance business.

> THE COURT: That is just not correct. There never was a judgment in that case, so you can't say there was an evidentiary background of misconduct when the Court never found misconduct. The settlement occurred before the trial was over.

United States v. GTE Corp., No. 83-1298, Tr. at 22–23 (D.D.C. Nov. 22, 1983); *see also* United States v. GTE Corp., 603 F. Supp. 730, 736 n.26 (D.D.C. 1984) ("[The] AT&T case was settled before the Court could draw any definitive conclusions concerning either the sufficiency of the government's evidence to sustain a finding of liability or the validity of AT&T's various legal and factual defenses."); Southern Pacific Communications Co. v. AT&T, 740

the decree lore remains relevant to future antitrust cases and, to a limited extent, relevant to interpreting and applying the 1996 Act.[105]

§4.4.1 The 1914 Bell Decree

At the turn of the century, telephone service in many areas was offered by competing local companies. Bell had established a superior long-distance network, and it was using that advantage to gain control of local companies by interconnecting its long-distance lines only with its own local affiliates.[106] The long-distance monopoly thus provided "leverage" over local exchange competition.

In 1913, the federal government challenged this strategy in an antitrust suit to block Bell's acquisition of a small long-distance company in Oregon. The suit alleged that Bell had monopolized telephone service between Oregon and Washington and between Washington and Idaho. AT&T Vice-President Nathan Kingsbury responded with a letter to the Attorney General[107] that paved the way for a consent decree entered by a federal court in 1914.[108] In its Kingsbury Commitment, Bell agreed to refrain from acquiring competing independent telephone companies, to submit

---

F.2d 1011, 1022 (D.C. Cir. 1984) ("The [1982 AT&T Decree] contains no liability findings. The only mention of liability is the nonliability clause."); *cf.* Maryland v. United States, 460 U.S. 1001, 1004 (1983) (Rehnquist, J., dissenting) (explaining that parties' settlement of the case avoided findings as to liability).

[105] For example, section 251(g) of the 1996 Act, 47 U.S.C. §251(g), continues the equal access and nondiscrimination provisions of the decrees until superseded by the FCC.

[106] P. Temin & L. Galambos, The Fall of the Bell System 9 (1987).

[107] Letter from Nathan C. Kingsbury, AT&T, to James C. McReynolds, Attorney General (Dec. 19, 1913) (hereinafter Kingsbury Commitment).

[108] United States v. AT&T, 1 Decrees & Judgments in Civil Federal Antitrust Cases 554 (D. Or. 1914) (No. 6082), *modified,* 1 Decrees & Judgments in Civil Federal Antitrust Cases 569 (D. Or. 1914), *modified,* 1 Decrees & Judgments in Civil Federal Antitrust Cases 572 (D. Or. 1918), *modified,* 1 Decrees & Judgments in Civil Federal Antitrust Cases 574 (D. Or. 1922) (hereinafter 1914 Decree).

then-pending acquisitions for approval by the Department of Justice and the Interstate Commerce Commission, and to make "[a]rrangements . . . promptly under which all other telephone companies may secure for their subscribers toll service over the lines of the companies of the Bell System."[109] The consent decree contained several additional remedies designed to restore competition in Oregon, Washington, Montana, and Idaho, including a provision similar to modern day "equal access" to facilitate choice between competing long-distance carriers.[110] The decree also explicitly provided for its own modification "as may from time to time be necessary in order to conform to the development of telephony and to maintain the efficiency of the service. . . ."[111]

Under the Kingsbury Commitment, Bell also agreed to divest itself of Western Union. The Commitment appeared to be at least a partial victory for the trustbusters at the Justice Department—an honorable armistice signed by vigilant public servants to contain all-too-acquisitive private interests. But the Kingsbury Commitment was really nothing of the sort.

It did indeed stop the growth of Bell's financial empire—for a few short years, in any event—but it did nothing to promote competition in either telephony or telegraphy. Local exchange monopolies were left intact, utterly free to continue to refuse interconnection to other local exchange companies. Bell's monopoly long-distance service was reinforced: Bell would be required to interconnect with all local exchanges, but there was no provision for any competition—or interconnection—among long-distance carriers. Western Union was indeed spun off, but only to provide telegraphy, not telephony.

---

[109] Kingsbury Commitment at 3–4.

[110] Paragraphs Eighth and Ninth of the 1914 Decree provided that a caller in Seattle, Tacoma, or Bellingham "desiring to use long-distance lines shall be connected by [the] 'A' operator with the station of the recording operator of the company whose lines he specifies, or if he expresses no choice he shall be connected with the recording operator of the Pacific Company, who shall ascertain the company of his choice and the call shall be completed over the lines of that company."

The decree also "perpetually" enjoined AT&T "from continuing to monopolize or attempting to monopolize said commerce or any part thereof. . . ." 1914 Decree, Third Paragraph.

[111] 1914 Decree, Fourteenth Paragraph.

The government solution, in short, was not the steamy, unsettling cohabitation that marks competition, but rather a sort of competitive apartheid, characterized by segregation and quarantine. Markets were carefully carved up: one for the monopoly telegraph company, one for each of the established monopoly local telephone exchanges, and one for Bell's monopoly long-distance operations. Bell might not own everything, but some monopolist or other would dominate each discrete market. The Kingsbury Commitment could thus be viewed as a solution by a government bookkeeper who counted several separate monopolies as an advance over a single monopoly, even absent any trace of competition among them.

In any event, the Kingsbury Commitment was quickly gutted. Even during the years the Commitment remained in effect, the Department of Justice considered over 100 Bell-independent consolidations or exchanges of property and permitted almost all of them to be consummated. During World War I, from 1918 to 1919, the Postmaster General took over operation of the telephone industry and, like post, telephone, and telegraph companies (PTTs) throughout the world, directed the competing local systems to consolidate into a single national network.[112] In 1921, Congress passed the Willis-Graham Act, which overrode the Kingsbury Commitment and gave the Interstate Commerce Commission authority to exempt telephone company mergers from the antitrust laws.[113]

[112] Act of Congress Covering Taking Over of Wires, 40 Stat. 904 (1918); President's Proclamation Taking Over Telephone and Telegraph Systems, 40 Stat. 1807 (1918); Postmaster General, Bulletin No. 2, Order No. 1783, Order Assuming Possession and Control (Aug. 1, 1918); Postmaster General, Bulletin No. 3, Consolidation of Competing Telephone Systems (Aug. 7, 1918); *cited in* Government Control and Operation of Telegraph, Telephone and Marine Cable Systems, August 1, 1918 to July 31, 1919, at 45–46, 62–63 (1921).

[113] Willis-Graham Act, ch. 20, 42 Stat. 27 (1921) (codified as amended at 47 U.S.C. §221(a)), *repealed by* Telecommunications Act of 1996 §601(b)(2) , Pub. L. 104–104, 110 Stat. 143. Between 1921 and the enactment of the Communications Act in 1934, 275 telephone company acquisitions were presented to the ICC, and 272 were approved.

Public sentiment was against competition. Newspaper editorials of the time described the situation as "chaotic," "a hindrance," "a nuisance," and "wasteful duplication." The Beaumont Enterprise opined that "[t]wo telephones

§4.4.2   The 1956 Bell Decree

In 1949, the government filed a second antitrust action,[114] this time alleging that Bell had attempted to monopolize telecommunications equipment and services through its practices of acquiring and licensing patents.[115] (Much of the government's evidence concerned Bell's vigorous technological innovation;[116] AT&T would make these same facts the center of its *defense* in the 1974 case that was to follow.[117]) The government demanded that

---

are as useless as two bulky horses." An editorial in the Burlington, Iowa, Evening Gazette (Apr. 9, 1897) expressed this view: "If there is anything in the world that would reconcile any business community to have no telephone at all, it is a few months experience with two systems."

[114] In New Jersey, AT&T's headquarters.

[115] Complaint, United States v. Western Elec. Co., No. 17-49 (D.N.J. Jan. 14, 1949) (*1949 Complaint*). The complaint's key allegation was as follows: "The basis for the success of AT&T in occupying and controlling almost the entire telephone operating and manufacturing fields and for its extensive activities outside the telephone industry has been due largely to its development and exploitation of patents." *Id.* at 14. The government alleged engaging in predatory accumulation and exploitation of patents, self-dealing, eliminating competing manufacturers through acquisitions and termination of purchasing contracts, eliminating competition by foreign manufacturers, using patent licensing power to block competition in long-distance radio and television circuits, coordinating the operations of the various branches of the Bell System with the result of fixing equipment prices and refusing to deploy more efficient equipment, charging higher prices to nonaffiliated purchasers, and charging patent royalties to nonaffiliated manufacturers.

[116] For example, the 1949 Complaint charged that Bell engaged in predation through the innovations of AT&T's Bell Labs research arm:

> [Bell Labs] is charged with assuming and making effective the policies of AT&T in the field of scientific research and patents. Its research activities have included exploration of the fields of physics, chemistry, applied mathematics, characteristics of materials, optics, acoustics, electronics, the physiology of speech and hearing. It has developed and designed apparatus, circuits and transmission lines for wire and radio telephony and telegraphy, broadcasting, sound recording and reproduction, telephoto service, generation and modulation, transmission and radiation of high frequency electric currents and ultra short waves.

Id. at 15.

[117] *See* Defendants' Third Statement of Contentions and Proof at 309–319, 1406–1416, United States v. Western Elec. Co., No. 74-1698 (D.D.C. Mar. 10, 1980) (noting Bell Labs' creation of the transistor, sound motion pictures,

Western Electric, Bell's manufacturing arm, be divested and broken into three separate entities. Bell was to cancel its exclusive dealing contracts with Western Electric; the BOCs would thereafter procure equipment by competitive bidding.[118] The company would retain Bell Labs, but would be required to license its patents and related technical information to all comers "on a nondiscriminatory and reasonable royalty basis."[119]

The case was settled in 1956 by a consent decree referred to (ambitiously) as the "Final Judgment."[120] The company agreed to grant nonexclusive licenses to all comers for all existing and future Bell System patents.[121] For a reasonable fee, Bell would also furnish licensees with the technical information needed to manufacture the equipment in question.[122] Western Electric would thereafter manufacture only equipment used in providing telephone service.[123] Bell would also stay out of any business "other

---

radio astronomy, magnetic bubbles, superconducting junctions, charge-coupled devices, long-haul microwave, satellite TV transmission, solid-state lasers, and many similar innovations). Scientists at Bell Labs discovered the wave nature of matter (which confirmed the theory of quantum mechanics), the pervasive background microwave radiation (which confirmed the Big Bang theory), information theory (key to entropy theory and black holes), and systems engineering techniques that sent the Apollo astronauts to the moon.

Today, courts generally recognize vigorous innovation as an incident of healthy competition. *See, e.g.,* J. Sidak, Debunking Predatory Innovation, 83 Colum. L. Rev. 1121 (1983).

[118] To that end, they would publish their requirements "in such a manner as to enable any qualified manufacturer, seller, distributor, supplier, or installer of telephones, telephone equipment or apparatus to compete on a fair, nondiscriminatory and competitive basis for the manufacture, sale, distribution, or installation of the requirements of the Bell System." *1949 Complaint* at 71.

[119] *Id.* at 72.

[120] United States v. Western Elec. Co., 1956 Trade Cas. (CCH) ¶68,246 (D.N.J. 1956) (hereinafter 1956 Decree). The settlement acknowledged no patent or other abuses; its terms were accepted "without . . . constituting any evidence or admission by any party in respect of any such issues." *Id.* (preamble).

[121] *Id.* §X.

[122] *Id.* §XIV.

[123] *Id.* §IV(A). This effectively barred Bell from participating in the infant computer industry that a Bell invention (the transistor) had created and thus set the stage for what would eventually become a massive antitrust suit against IBM.

than the furnishing of common carrier communications services,"[124] though it would be allowed to supply services of any kind to the federal government.[125]

In the 28 years it remained in effect, there were only two major disputes about the scope and enforcement of the 1956 Decree. In the late 1960s, a private carrier challenged New Jersey Bell's offering of a private communications system to hospitals. The carrier argued that this was not a "common carrier" service.[126] District Judge Shaw agreed on the merits, but nonetheless denied relief. "[I]f every party who could allege that it was the beneficiary of an antitrust decree could enter the picture to enforce the decree," Judge Shaw reasoned, "[w]e would have a volume of litigation that would be almost impossible for the Court to handle."[127]

In 1980, Bell questioned whether the 1956 Decree allowed it to provide "enhanced" services. The FCC had previously ruled that data processing services were not common carrier services[128] and had thus (indirectly) engaged the 1956 Decree to bar Bell from offering such services. In its 1980 inquiry,[129] however,

---

[124] *Id.* §V. "Common carrier communications services" were defined as "communications services and facilities . . . the charges for which are subject to public regulation under the Communications Act of 1934 [or state laws]." *Id.* §II(i).

[125] *Id.* §§IV(B)(3), V(a); *see also id.* §II(g) (exclusion for patents invented by "employees of subsidiaries exclusively engaged in the performance of contracts with the plaintiff"); *id.* §IV(A) (exclusion for "equipment manufactured for the plaintiff"), *id.* §VI ("this Section shall not prevent the defendants or their subsidiaries from buying any equipment for sale or lease to, or supplying any equipment to . . . the plaintiff"); *id.* §X(G)(2)(a) (exempting "any transfer of patents or rights thereunder to the plaintiff or any agency thereof"); *id.* §XV(C)(2) (allowing certain patent restrictions involving the plaintiff).

[126] United States v. Western Elec. Co., 1968 Trade Cas. (CCH) ¶72,415 (D.N.J.), *aff'd mem. sub nom.* Clark Walter & Sons, Inc. v. United States, 392 U.S. 659 (1968).

[127] *Id.*

[128] *See* §12.4.

[129] Amendment of Section 64.702 of the Commission's Rules and Regulations (Second Computer Inquiry), Final Decision, 77 F.C.C.2d 384 (1980) (hereinafter *Computer II*), *modified,* 84 F.C.C.2d 50 (1980) (hereinafter *Reconsideration Order*), *further modified,* 88 F.C.C.2d 512 (1981) (hereinafter *Further Reconsideration Order*), *aff'd sub nom.* Computer and Communications Indus.

the FCC had concluded that Bell should be permitted to provide enhanced services, subject to certain safeguards.[130] Bell immediately sought a declaration that the 1956 Decree permitted it to offer enhanced services. Despite opposition from the Department of Justice, which was by then embroiled in the 1974 lawsuit, the New Jersey district court agreed.[131]

The 1956 Decree has since been attacked by some observers, most notably Judge Greene, as "patently inadequate,"[132] "ineffectual,"[133] and a backdoor political deal.[134] Others, however,

---

Assn. v. FCC, 693 F.2d 198 (D.C. Cir. 1982), *cert. denied sub nom.* Louisiana Pub. Serv. Commn. v. FCC, 461 U.S. 938 (1983).

[130] *See* §12.4.2. The FCC stated its view that Bell could offer untariffed enhanced services without running afoul of the 1956 Decree's prohibition. The Commission also stated that if this opinion ultimately proved erroneous, it would "feel compelled to reassess" and revise its structure so that Bell could provide enhanced services. *Computer II,* 77 F.C.C.2d at 495 ¶281.

[131] United States v. Western Elec. Co., 531 F. Supp. 894 (D.N.J. 1981). The government appealed to the Third Circuit; while the appeal was pending, the 1982 consent decree replaced the 1956 Decree, the appeal was dismissed, and the district court's decision was vacated as moot. Order, United States v. Western Elec. Co., No. 17-49 (D.N.J. Mar. 25, 1982).

Judge Greene would later offer his view (in dictum) that Bell was not in fact permitted to offer untariffed enhanced services under the 1956 Decree. *See* United States v. AT&T, 552 F. Supp. at 138–139 n.17, 178 n.198, 180 n.204. Judge Greene also offered his view that the FCC had no power to "relieve AT&T of its obligations under the antitrust laws, and more specifically under the 1956 decree." *Id.* at 178 n.198 (emphasis omitted).

[132] 552 F. Supp. at 170.

[133] *Id.* at 223.

[134] *Id.* at 136–138. The scandals surrounding the entry of the 1956 Decree are rather dry by modern standards. Among other things, Judge Greene criticized Bell's attempt to have prosecution of the 1949 antitrust case postponed until the conclusion of the Korean War. Bell had "contend[ed] that the antitrust litigation was forcing key Bell Laboratories and Western Electric executives involved in important national defense projects to divert their attention from that work to preparations for trial." *Id.* at 136 & n.8. In response to Bell's contention, "Secretary of Defense Lovett requested the postponement in a letter to the Attorney General dated March 20, 1952." *Id.* at 136 n.9. While Judge Greene deplored this political maneuver, he also noted that it didn't work, since the Justice Department refused to suspend prosecution of the action. *Id.* at 136.

After the war, Bell continued to lobby the Justice Department, the Defense Department, and the FCC in order to settle the case on some basis other than the divestiture of Western Electric. *Id.* at 136, 137–138 n.14. Bell had done

have praised the decree, noting that the Bell System thereafter achieved new heights in providing service, lowering price, and developing new technology.[135]

§4.4.3 The 1982 Bell Decree

On November 20, 1974, the government filed its third antitrust action against the Bell System.[136] The complaint alleged an unlawful combination among various Bell entities resulting in the monopolization of both long-distance sevice and the manufacture of telecommunications equipment.[137] The government initially sought the divestiture of Western Electric and Bell Laboratories from AT&T.[138] Although very similar relief had been unsuccessfully sought 20 years earlier, the district court ruled that the 1956 Decree was no bar to the new action.[139]

The core of the Bell System's defense was that its actions had been sanctioned by the Federal Communications Act and state

---

significant service for the Defense Department during World War II and the Korean War, and that agency supported Bell's attempt to settle. Judge Greene was especially critical of an incident in which the Defense Department requested Bell's help to prepare a memorandum explaining the benefits of an integrated Bell System. As Judge Greene retells the event:

> AT&T obliged, and in early July, it provided the Defense Department with a memorandum which urged settlement of the suit without the divestiture of Western Electric. The memorandum was drafted in such a way as to make it appear that the Defense Department rather than AT&T had prepared it and, with two relatively minor exceptions, a letter identical to the memorandum was sent out the next week to the Attorney General over the signature of Secretary of Defense Wilson.

Id. at 137 n.12.

[135] Temin & Galambos, The Fall of the Bell System at 15–19.

[136] United States v. AT&T, 552 F. Supp. 131. For general histories of the Bell System and its breakup, see S. Coll, The Deal of the Century (1986); A. Stone, Wrong Number (1989); Temin & Galambos, The Fall of the Bell System (1987).

[137] United States v. AT&T, 524 F. Supp. 1336, 1342 & n.2 (D.D.C. 1981); Competitive Impact Statement at 5, United States v. Western Elec. Co., No. 74-1698 (D.D.C. Feb. 10, 1982).

[138] The government would subsequently amend its demands several times.

[139] United States v. AT&T, 524 F. Supp. at 1374.

laws. Neither side presented any significant argument that Bell had engaged in any surreptitious or well-concealed schemes; to the contrary, both sides conceded that Bell had pursued its policies quite openly with the approval of federal and state regulators.[140]

§4.4.3.1   Litigation and Settlement

The case was initially assigned to U.S. District Judge Joseph C. Waddy. He, however, became terminally ill in 1978, having done nothing to advance the case in its four years under his oversight. On June 22, 1978, the case was reassigned to Judge Harold H. Greene,[141] on his first day on the federal bench.[142] Within a matter of weeks, Judge Greene had appointed two special masters to deal with claims of privilege in the discovery process[143] and had directed the parties to file status memoranda on all outstanding issues. On August 21, 1978, all pending motions were reargued.[144] Judge Greene ruled on them on October 18, 1978.[145] He then directed the parties to negotiate and stipulate to the facts prior to trial.[146]

---

[140] *See* Defendants' Third Statement of Contentions and Proof, United States v. Western Elec. Co., No. 74-1698 (D.D.C. Mar. 10, 1980); Plaintiff's Third Statement of Contentions and Proof, United States v. Western Elec. Co., No. 74-1698 (D.D.C. Jan. 10, 1980).

[141] United States v. AT&T, 461 F. Supp. 1314, 1320 n.16 (D.D.C. 1978).

[142] The chief judge of a district court has discretion to reassign pending cases. *See* 28 U.S.C. §137. Judge Greene was a logical choice for a difficult case. As chief judge of the local District of Columbia court, Judge Greene had developed a reputation as an undauntable judicial administrator. In 1968, for example, antiwar protesters in Washington, D.C., attempted a strategy of being arrested in such large numbers as to clog the local court system. Judge Greene arranged three shifts of judges and gave each arrested protester an individual hearing.

[143] United States v. AT&T, 461 F. Supp. at 1320 n.15.

[144] *Id.* at 1320.

[145] *Id.* at 1314. As Judge Greene explained, "[T]he Court has been committed ever since it assumed judicial control over this case to bring it to trial in the minimum possible period of time consistent with fairness to the parties." United States v. AT&T, 88 F.R.D. 47, 50 (D.D.C. 1980) (footnotes and citation omitted).

[146] To make the stipulation process, and ultimately the trial of the case, more manageable, the parties subdivided the case into 82 "episodes" involving

In the stipulation process, the government identified various markets or submarkets that Bell had allegedly monopolized: local telecommunications service, intercity telecommunications service, terminal equipment (telephone sets, private branch exchanges (PBXs), key systems, and the like), and network switching and transport equipment used by the BOCs and Long Lines.[147] While the government did not contend that the BOCs' monopolies of local telephone service were unlawful, it did allege unlawful monopolization of the intercity and equipment markets.

Trial began on January 15, 1981. After a six-week hiatus during which the parties tried unsuccessfully to settle the case, the government called its first witness on March 4, 1981. The government completed the presentation of its case-in-chief four months later, after examining close to 100 witnesses and introducing thousands of documents and thousands more stipulations. At that point, Bell moved to dismiss. On September 11, 1981, Judge Greene denied the motion and wrote a lengthy explanatory opinion.[148] That ruling has since been cited, by Judge Greene himself among others, for the proposition that the district court actually issued a final judgment on the merits of the government's case.[149] The ruling, however, made at the midpoint

---

particular competitors or types of telecommunications equipment. United States v. AT&T, 88 F.R.D. at 49, 51. By the time of trial, there were only sixty-some contested episodes. United States v. AT&T, 524 F. Supp. at 1343. "Many of these episodes constitute[d] major antitrust disputes in their own right." United States v. AT&T, 88 F.R.D. at 51 n.21. The court, however, refused to compartmentalize its rulings on liability on an episode-by-episode basis. The court stated that "there is but a single claim of violation of the Sherman Act before the Court"; Bell's behavior in one episode "may thus be relied upon to sustain other evidence so as to form a pattern of conduct made unlawful by that statute." United States v. AT&T, 524 F. Supp. at 1344.

[147] During the lengthy identification and winnowing of the contested facts, the government dropped several of its claims, United States v. AT&T, 88 F.R.D. at 52, including claims relating to mobile radio services and transport of cable TV signals. *Compare* Plaintiff's First Statement of Contentions and Proof at 206–223 (Mar. 10, 1978) *with* Plaintiff's Third Statement of Contentions and Proof at 1010–1067 (Jan. 10, 1980).

[148] United States v. AT&T, 524 F. Supp. 1336.

[149] *See, e.g.*, United States v. Western Elec. Co., 673 F. Supp. 525, 531–532 (D.D.C. 1987) (citing decision on AT&T's motion to dismiss for the proposition

of the trial, was based only on the proof adduced during the government's case-in-chief[150] and was only "a tentative and inconclusive ruling" subject to change after hearing the defendants' evidence.[151]

In ruling on Bell's motion to dismiss, Judge Greene found that the government's proof regarding the long-distance market "tend[ed] to show that defendants have sought in a variety of ways to exclude the competition by restricting interconnection to the local facilities."[152] Judge Greene held that Bell had no valid regulatory defenses to the interconnection claims and refused to dismiss this aspect of the government's case.[153] Judge Greene also refused to dismiss the government's "novel" theory that Bell had priced long-distance services without regard to cost.[154] Subsequently, Judge Greene suggested that Bell unlawfully "subsidiz[ed]" its intercity services using "revenues from the monopoly local exchange services,"[155] although admittedly "no final decision was reached" on this question.[156]

---

that "AT&T had been able to violate the antitrust laws in a number of ways over a long period of time"), *aff'd in part,* 900 F.2d 283 (D.C. Cir.), *cert. denied sub nom.* MCI v. United States, 498 U.S. 911 (1990).

[150] United States v. AT&T, 524 F. Supp. at 1342 n.5.

[151] *Id.* at 1343 (internal quotation and citation omitted).

[152] *Id.* at 1353. Judge Greene held that "the local facilities controlled by Bell are 'essential facilities'" to which Bell was obliged to provide "non-discriminatory access." *Id.*

[153] *Id.* at 1357–1361.

[154] *Id.* at 1370. "The government does not allege an intertemporal shift in profits—a sacrifice of profits in the short-run in return for more than their recoupment in the long-run—but an inter-service shift. Specifically, it is claimed that the Bell System has engaged in pricing practices which allow it to sacrifice profits from one service and to recoup the lost profits during the same period in another service. In such circumstances, a pricing-without-regard-to-cost approach is not necessarily inappropriate. . . ." *Id.* at 1360 (citation omitted).

[155] United States v. AT&T, 552 F. Supp. at 165. *See also id.* at 188 ("If the Operating Companies were free to provide interexchange service . . . [they] would also have the ability to subsidize their interexchange prices with profits earned from their monopoly services.").

[156] *Id.* at 169 n.160. Subsequently, Judge Greene appeared to recognize that the subsidy in fact flowed in the opposite direction, from long distance to local services. United States v. AT&T, 552 F. Supp. at 169 & n.161. *See also* United States v. Western Elec. Co., 569 F. Supp. at 1072 (acknowledging that

Judge Greene likewise declined to dismiss the government's claims that Bell had made it difficult for customers to attach their own customer premises equipment (CPE) to the telephone network.[157] But he criticized the government's allegations concerning the Bell System's provision of its own network equipment[158] and dismissed the part of the government's case involving claims of cross-subsidy and predatory pricing in the equipment market.[159]

None of the government's allegations was in fact ever finally adjudicated in Judge Greene's courtroom or elsewhere: shortly after the 1981 ruling, Bell and the government agreed to their second settlement of the lawsuit.[160] The proposed decree had four basic provisions.[161] First, it required AT&T to divest its local

---

"the Operating Companies received a substantial portion of revenues from interexchange services through the division of revenues process").

[157] United States v. AT&T, 524 F. Supp. at 1349–1351. Judge Greene noted, however, that "Defendants will, of course, have the opportunity, as part of their own case, to introduce evidence both to contradict the government's proof and to show affirmatively that the facts are not what the government's witnesses described them to be." *Id.* at 1351.

[158] Judge Greene observed that much of the government's evidence was "not particularly convincing" and was discredited by "vigorous cross examination which tended to introduce a significant number of facts of affirmative value to defendants." *Id.* at 1372 n.154.

When he entered the 1982 Decree, Judge Greene again noted the "relative paucity of evidence" that the Bell System had impeded competition in procurement of telecommunications equipment. United States v. AT&T, 552 F. Supp. at 163 n.137. He explained that the government had presented evidence of only 16 "questionable episodes" of "arguably anticompetitive activity." *Id.* Even as to those 16 episodes, Judge Greene was skeptical of any linkage between the alleged anticompetitive conduct and market power. *Id.*

[159] United States v. AT&T, 524 F. Supp. at 1380–1381. Judge Greene also rejected the government's proposed definition of the relevant market for equipment that the Bell System purchased for its own use. *Id.* at 1377–1379.

[160] The decree itself (*reprinted in* United States v. AT&T, 552 F. Supp. 131 at 226–234 (D.D.C. 1982) (hereinafter 1982 Decree)) provided that it was not a final adjudication of the government's claims. Section III provides: "Neither this [decree] nor any of its terms or provisions shall constitute any evidence against, an admission by, or an estoppel against any party or BOC." *Id.* at 228.

[161] Much of the language of the 1982 Decree was drawn from a Senate bill, S. 898, 97th Cong. 1st Sess. (Oct. 20, 1981), that was pending at the time the decree was drafted. *E.g., compare* 1982 Decree §IV(A) (definition of affiliate) *with* S. 898 §103(1) (nearly identical); *compare* 1982 Decree §IV(K) (definition

Bell telephone operating companies (BOCs).[162] Second, it required the BOCs to provide equal interconnections to long-distance carriers and information providers and barred certain acts defined as discriminatory.[163] Third, it prohibited the BOCs from engaging in competitive long-distance, information services, or equipment businesses,[164] or indeed any other competitive businesses at all.[165] Fourth, it freed AT&T from the restrictions of the 1956 Decree.[166] Ultimately, Judge Greene's only adjudicated finding was that the decree, as modified by Judge Greene himself, was "within the reaches of the public interest."[167]

---

of interexchange telecommunications) *with* S. 898 §103(18)) (identical); *compare* 1982 Decree §IV(O) (definition of telecommunications) *with* S. 898 §103(36) (identical); *compare* 1982 Decree §IV(P) (definition of telecommunications service) *with* S. 898 §103(39). The decree even gives a definition of "transmission facilities," *see* 1982 Decree §IV(Q), that is nearly identical to S. 898 §103(41), even though the term is nowhere used in the decree.

According to Richard Levine, the Justice Department lawyer who drafted the decree as it was finally proposed to the district court, William Baxter had instructed him to draft the decree in terms that were to the extent possible consistent with the terms of the pending Senate bill. *See* Coll, The Deal of the Century at 304–305; Temin & Galambos, The Fall of the Bell System at 268–269.

[162] United States v. AT&T, 552 F. Supp. at 141; *see also* 1982 Decree §I(A)(2), (4), 552 F. Supp. at 227. The portions of the BOCs' businesses not needed to provide local telephone service were to be separated out and transferred to AT&T.

[163] United States v. AT&T, 552 F. Supp. at 142. In the decree as approved, the contracts through which the Bell System had integrated its different entities were to be canceled. 1982 Decree §I(A)(3), 552 F. Supp. at 227. Post-divestiture relations were to be conducted on a nondiscriminatory, primarily tariffed basis. *Id.* §§II(A), II(B), 552 F. Supp. at 227.

[164] United States v. AT&T, 552 F. Supp. at 143; *see also* 1982 Decree §II(D) (1), (2), 552 F. Supp. at 227.

[165] The proposed decree barred the BOCs from providing any other "product or service," besides local telephone service "that is not a 'natural monopoly service actually regulated by tariff.'" United States v. AT&T, 552 F. Supp. at 143; *see also* 1982 Decree §II(D)(3), 552 F. Supp. at 227.

[166] United States v. AT&T, 552 F. Supp. at 143; *see also* 1982 Decree (preamble), 552 F. Supp. at 226 ("the Final Judgment entered on January 24, 1956, is hereby vacated in its entirety"). The proposed decree also contained various enforcement-related provisions.

[167] United States v. AT&T, 552 F. Supp. at 151 (quoting United States v. Gillette Co., 406 F. Supp. 713, 716 (D. Mass. 1975)). In approving the decree, Judge Greene stated that "[i]t would be inappropriate for the Court at this

§4.4.3.2 The Approval Process

In approving the proposed decree, subject to certain modifications, Judge Greene wrote at some length about the need to break up the Bell System simply because of Bell's "substantial domination of the telecommunications industry in general."[168] The antitrust laws "embody 'a desire to put an end to great aggregations of capital because of the helplessness of the individual before them.'"[169] "'If we will not endure a king as a political power we should not endure a king over the production, transportation, and sale of any of the necessaries of life.'"[170] Judge Greene went on to quote at some length a dissenting opinion of Justice Douglas, to the effect that power over the economy should not be in the hands of "an industrial oligarchy," subject to the "whim or caprice, the political prejudices, the emotional stability of a few self-appointed men."[171] Judge Greene's views in this regard differ sharply from those expressed by the Seventh Circuit in an opinion dealing with MCI's private antitrust suit against Bell.[172]

---

juncture to draw definitive conclusions with regard either to the sufficiency of the evidence to sustain a finding of liability or to the validity of AT&T's various legal and factual defenses. The Court is not called upon, in this public interest proceeding, to render a final judgment on this case; indeed, not all the evidence that may bear on the issues has yet been adduced." *Id.* at 161. *See also* United States v. Western Elec. Co., 900 F.2d 283, 289 (D.C. Cir.) ("the district court made no explicit findings of liability in the course of the Tunney Act proceedings"), *cert. denied sub nom.* MCI v. United States, 498 U.S. 911 (1990).

[168] United States v. AT&T, 552 F. Supp. at 163.

[169] *Id.* at 163–164 (quoting United States v. Aluminum Co. of Am., 148 F.2d 416, 428 (2d Cir. 1945) (footnote omitted), and citing Standard Oil Co. v. United States, 221 U.S. 1, 50 (1911); United States v. Trans-Missouri Freight Assn., 166 U.S. 290, 323–324 (1897)).

[170] *Id.* at 164 (quoting 21 Cong. Rec. 2457 (1890) (remarks of Sen. Sherman)).

[171] *Id.* (quoting United States v. Columbia Steel, 334 U.S. 495, 536 (1948) (Douglas, J., dissenting)).

[172] "We acknowledge with approval the populist origins of the antitrust laws as well as the preeminent role of the Sherman Act as a charter of economic freedom. But we also believe that . . . larger concerns about broad pro-competitive policy, economic concentration and political power have been,

Judge Greene concluded that the proposed divestiture would be in the public interest, but directed that the decree be modified in five major respects.[173] The parties (somewhat reluctantly) consented to the changes, and on August 24, 1982, Judge Greene gave first-round approval to the modified decree. This was by no means the end of the matter: no detailed divestiture plan had yet been formulated. But the divestiture process was now formally under way. Two days later, on August 26, 1982, Judge Greene authorized approximately 110 public and private entities and organizations to intervene in any aspects of subsequent hearings and appeals.

Seventeen of the intervenors immediately appealed Judge Greene's entry of the settlement decree, arguing that the decree was inconsistent with state laws aimed at ensuring economical and universal intrastate telephone service.[174] Two other intervenors also appealed, arguing that Judge Greene gave the BOCs

---

and are being at this very moment, effectively addressed by the regulators, and possibly by the Congress." MCI v. AT&T, 708 F.2d at 1110 (footnote omitted).

[173] Under section VIII of the 1982 Decree, the BOCs would be permitted (1) to market customer telephone equipment and (2) to publish printed advertising directories. 1982 Decree §§VIII(A), VIII(B), 552 F. Supp. at 231. In addition, (3) the BOCs could enter other businesses, even over the Justice Department's objection, upon a showing of no substantial possibility they could use their monopoly power to impede competition in the new market, 1982 Decree §VIII(C), 552 F. Supp. at 231, and (4) AT&T was barred for seven years from electronic publishing, 1982 Decree §VIII(D), 552 F. Supp. at 231. Finally, (5) Judge Greene reserved the power to construe and enforce the decree on his own motion. 1982 Decree §VIII(I), 552 F. Supp. at 232. Judge Greene also specified numerous lesser modifications of the proposed decree, regarding such matters as the terms of access the BOCs must provide non-AT&T interexchange carriers (1982 Decree §VIII(F), 552 F. Supp. at 232), the assignment of facilities to the BOCs (1982 Decree §VIII(G), 552 F. Supp. at 232), and the amount of the Bell System's debt to be borne by the divested BOCs (1982 Decree §VIII(H), 552 F. Supp. at 232). For further discussion of the decree's provisions, see M. Kellogg, J. Thorne & P. Huber, Federal Telecommunications Law (1992) (hereinafter *FTL1*) chs. 6 & 7 (line of business restrictions), ch. 5 (equal access and nondiscrimination), ch. 13 (mobile services).

[174] *See* Joint Jurisdictional Statement of the States of Maryland, et al., No. 82-952 (joint statement of nine states and seven utility regulatory commissions); Jurisdictional Statement of the People of the State of Illinois, No. 82-1001.

either too few or too many rights in the former Bell System's CPE business.[175] With three Justices dissenting, the Supreme Court summarily affirmed Judge Greene on February 28, 1983.[176] Justice Rehnquist wrote that he was "troubled by the notion that a district court, by entering what is in essence a private agreement between parties to a lawsuit, invokes the Supremacy Clause powers of the Federal Government to pre-empt state regulatory laws."[177] In addition, Justice Rehnquist questioned whether the discretionary policy judgments made by Judge Greene under the guise of the public interest inquiry were within the judicial power.[178]

The breakup of the Bell System was to be the largest judicially supervised divestiture in history. In order to effect the "radical separation of the Operating Companies from AT&T"[179] without

---

[175] Tandy Corporation argued that the decree should have required AT&T to divest its "Phone Center" retail stores to the BOCs and should not have eliminated AT&T's compulsory patent licensing obligations under the 1956 Decree. *See* Jurisdictional Statement of Tandy Corp., No. 82-953. The North American Telephone Association (NATA) argued that the decree should not have permitted the BOCs to market CPE at all. *See* Jurisdictional Statement of NATA, No. 82-992. (Yet, in its Opposition to the Motions to Affirm at 6, NATA stated: "We freely concede that the consent agreement entered by the District Court was in the 'public interest' as that term is used in the statute.")

The Solicitor General agreed with NATA's criticism that the additional decree modifications Judge Greene imposed made the decree less desirable. "[T]he public interest would have been served better by the initial decree than by the decree subsequently agreed to by the parties and approved by the court." Motion to Affirm at 29 n.35 (Dec. 22, 1982). The Solicitor General argued that the modified decree should be upheld nonetheless because "the latter decree also — on the whole — serves the public interest, and this is the standard by which the decree, as finally agreed to by the parties and entered by the court, must be judged." *Id.* According to the Solicitor General, the only question before the Court was "[w]hether the district court erred in concluding that the consent decree entered in this case was in the public interest" (*id.* at i) — an issue going to the decree "as a whole" rather than "its piece parts." *Id.* at 26.

[176] Maryland v. United States, 460 U.S. 1001 (1983). On November 10, 1982, the district court had certified the appeals directly to the Supreme Court under the Expediting Act, 15 U.S.C. §29(b).

[177] Maryland v. United States, 460 U.S. at 1002 (Rehnquist, J., dissenting).
[178] *Id.* at 1006.

[179] United States v. Western Elec. Co., 569 F. Supp. 1057, 1076 (D.D.C.), *aff'd mem. sub nom.* California v. United States, 464 U.S. 1013 (1983).

crippling telephone service, the decree as drafted by the parties had delegated the details of divestiture to AT&T. AT&T was to have six months from the entry of the decree to devise a Plan of Reorganization to be approved by the Department of Justice.[180] Divestiture would occur within 12 months thereafter. Judge Greene had refused, however, to approve the decree unless the parties agreed to submit the reorganization plan to the court for its approval.[181]

The parties proceeded to obtain the court's approval in two steps. First, they divided all Bell territory into geographically based "exchange" areas, or "LATAs."[182] Second, they divided the Bell System's assets, liabilities, employees, and customer accounts corresponding to the LATAs. On December 16, 1982, AT&T submitted to the Justice Department a 471-page Plan of Reorganization for dividing assets and implementing divestiture. As required under section I(A)(1) of the decree,[183] the Department of Justice conducted an independent examination of the plan. The Department demanded over 20 amendments. AT&T responded with a revised plan on March 14, 1983.[184] Ten days later

[180] 1982 Decree §I(A), 552 F. Supp. at 226.

[181] United States v. AT&T, 552 F. Supp. at 214–217. The court explained that "the ever present possibility of collusion between the Department of Justice" and Bell required it to oversee the implementation of the decree. *Id.* at 215. Otherwise, "the parties could simply enter into a consent decree which easily passed muster in the public interest proceeding, and then proceed with its implementation, or non-implementation, without fear of judicial interference." *Id.* The court accordingly required the parties to add a section to the decree providing that "the plan of reorganization shall not be implemented until approved by the Court as being consistent with the provisions and principles of the decree." 1982 Decree §VIII(J), 552 F. Supp. at 232.

[182] *See* 1982 Decree §IV(G), 552 F. Supp. at 229. *See also* Joint Mem. of the United States and AT&T Concerning Procedures for Review of the Reorganization Plan at 1–2, United States v. Western Elec. Co., No. 82-0192 (D.D.C. Aug. 31, 1982) ("As a practical matter, approval of the LATA exceptions should be secured, to the extent possible, before final formulation of the reorganization plan. . . . The definition of exchange areas . . . will govern the division of assets and corresponding allocation of liabilities."); United States v. Western Elec. Co., 569 F. Supp. at 1062 n.6 ("the drawing of geographic boundaries naturally preceded any division of assets between AT&T and the Operating Companies").

[183] 552 F. Supp. at 142, 226.

[184] AT&T Response to Objections to Its Proposed Plan of Reorganization, United States v. Western Elec. Co., No. 82-0192 (D.D.C. Mar. 14, 1983).

the Department released another response to AT&T's revisions and public comments that had been filed,[185] demanding 12 more amendments. AT&T acquiesced.

Judge Greene then invited additional memoranda from the parties, the seven to-be-divested regional companies, and intervenors addressing six separate issues.[186] Some 50 intervenors filed comments, raising hundreds of issues involving virtually every provision of the plan. Judge Greene then conducted a hearing on June 2 and heard live testimony from three of the designated regional chief executive officers.

On July 8, 1983, Judge Greene issued a 159-page opinion that concluded that the amended plan would not be approved unless it were further modified in six major respects.[187] AT&T amended the plan to adopt Judge Greene's modifications, and the court entered an order approving the amended plan on August 5, 1983. The State of California, the California Public Utilities Commission, and the New York State Department of Public Service

---

[185] Response of the United States to Public Comments and Action on AT&T's Proposed Plan of Reorganization, United States v. Western Elec. Co., No. 82-0192 (D.C.C. Mar. 24, 1983).

[186] These issues were (1) who would bear the costs of reconfiguring the local networks and of providing equal access, (2) apportionment of contingent liabilities for pre-divestiture events, (3) assignment of the Bell name and logo, (4) the BOCs' rights after divestiture to Bell patents, (5) assignment of No. 4ESS switches, and (6) the size and functions to be performed by the BOCs' jointly owned Central Services Organization (Bellcore). *See* Memorandum, United States v. Western Elec. Co., No. 82-0192 (D.D.C. May 10, 1983); Memorandum, United States v. Western Elec. Co., No. 82-0192 (D.D.C. May 17, 1983).

[187] United States v. Western Elec. Co., 569 F. Supp. at 1123–1124. The district court required AT&T (1) to guarantee the BOCs' recovery of equal access and network reconfiguration costs, (2) to assign the Bell name and logo to the BOCs, and (3) to grant the BOCs royalty-free licenses to all existing patents owned or controlled by AT&T and all other patents issued to AT&T on or before five years after the date of divestiture. The court further held (4) that the BOCs would be permitted to keep or construct their own interexchange facilities used for internal functions or communicating with customers; (5) that the BOCs may not perform interexchange order writing, order typing, or other provisioning exclusively for AT&T; and (6) that the decree does not relieve AT&T or the BOCs from bargaining in good faith with the labor unions with the exception of certain structural matters related to dividing the Bell System into eight independent companies. *See id.*

immediately appealed; the Supreme Court again summarily affirmed.[188]

At this point, Judge Greene thought he was done.[189] Just in case his "expectations with respect to the good faith and fidelity of the parties to the letter and the spirit of the decree be disappointed,"[190] Judge Greene retained sua sponte enforcement authority.[191] But absent a showing of bad faith, enforcement was to be in the hands of the Department of Justice.[192] Judge Greene did not expect to hear again from the parties except for the Department's triennial reviews of the line of business restrictions.[193]

At the stroke of midnight on December 31, 1983, the transfer of assets was completed, and the BOCs were reorganized into seven regional companies, the stock in which was spun off to AT&T shareholders.[194]

Nowhere was it written that the BOCs would be organized into seven regional holding companies.[195] To the contrary, the decree

---

[188] California v. United States, 464 U.S. 1013 (1983). The California and New York appellants argued that three provisions of the Plan of Reorganization—assignment to the BOCs of "complex" inside wiring, accounting for capitalized labor costs of connecting inside wire to telephone handsets, and the average cost of Pacific Telephone's long-term debt—were inconsistent with the decree.

[189] "There comes a time, once the basic documents have been approved, when the Court, rather than to superintend on an intensive basis the actual implementations of the reorganization, should, in the interest of keeping judicial involvement to a necessary minimum, leave compliance to the managers of the business interests directly involved, with such oversight as is vested in the Department of Justice by the decree." United States v. Western Elec. Co., 569 F. Supp. at 1120 (citation and footnote omitted).

[190] Id.

[191] 1982 Decree §VIII(I), 552 F. Supp. at 232.

[192] United States v. Western Elec. Co., 569 F. Supp. at 1119 n.279. Enforcement of the decree is discussed further in Chapter 5.

[193] The triennial reviews and decree modifications are discussed in greater detail in the first edition of this treatise. See FTL1 chs. 6 & 7.

[194] Overlooked throughout this process, however, were AT&T's minority interests in Cincinnati Bell and Southern New England Telephone. The decree did not require divestiture of these companies, nor did it subject them to any line of business restrictions. Shortly after divestiture, however, AT&T sold its stake in these concerns, which now operate as independent entities completely free of any decree restrictions.

[195] Section I(B) of the decree indeed provided for the creation of a central organization jointly funded and utilized by the seven BOCs for the purpose

states that "nothing in this decree shall require or prohibit the consolidation of the ownership of the BOCs into any particular number of entities."[196] Both the Assistant Attorney General and AT&T's general counsel testified before Congress that the consent decree would have allowed AT&T to combine all of the BOCs into a single holding company.[197] But AT&T ultimately settled on seven holding companies on its own without subsequent objection from the Justice Department or Judge Greene.[198]

---

of (1) meeting national security and emergency preparedness requirements and (2) administering such functions and services as can most efficiently be performed on a centralized basis. This organization would later be renamed Bell Communications Research (Bellcore). Bellcore was expected to provide primarily technical support in the "construction, operation, and maintenance of [BOC] local exchange networks." *See* United States v. Western Elec. Co., 569 F. Supp. at 1114 (citing AT&T Response to Objections to Its Proposed Plan of Reorganization at 505–512 (Mar. 14, 1983)). It was also to provide procurement support services, legal services, regulatory support services, marketing (including billing and sales support) services, financial services, human resources development, and employee relations. In November 1997, the BOCs completed the sale of Bellcore to Science Applications International Corp.

[196] 1982 Decree §I(A)(4), 552 F. Supp. at 227. Several BOCs recently combined their cellular operations. In June 1994, Bell Atlantic and NYNEX announced that they would combine their wireless properties in a joint venture valued at $17.5 billion. L. Cauley, Bell Atlantic and NYNEX Are Planning to Combine Cellular Phone Businesses, Wall St. J., June 30, 1994, at A3. Following closely behind, AirTouch and U S WEST announced a $13 billion joint venture of their own, in which AirTouch would control 70 percent. R. Ringer, Big Merger in Cellular by U S WEST, N.Y. Times, July 26, 1994, at D1.

[197] *See* United States v. Western Elec. Co., 797 F.2d 1082, 1091 (D.C. Cir. 1986) (citing AT&T Proposed Settlement: Hearings Before the Senate Committee on Commerce, Science and Transportation, 97th Cong., 2d Sess. 73 (1982) (testimony of William F. Baxter); Department of Justice Oversight of the United States v. American Telephone and Telegraph Lawsuit: Hearings Before the Senate Committee on the Judiciary, 97th Cong., 2d Sess. 112, 141–142 (1982) (prepared statement of William F. Baxter; testimony of Howard J. Trienens)). *See also* United States v. AT&T, 552 F. Supp. at 142 n.41 ("The number of new Operating Companies is not specified in the settlement proposal. AT&T has indicated that its reorganization plan will provide for the amalgamation of the twenty-two Operating Companies into seven regional Operating Companies."); 1982 Decree §I(A)(4), 552 F. Supp. at 227.

[198] The executives believed that the seven regional companies would be granted relief from the decree's line-of-business restrictions sooner than a smaller number of larger companies. On the other hand, some consolidation

§4.4.3.3 Overview of the 1982 Decree as Approved

The proposed decree separated what were thought to be "local monopolies" from what were thought to be "competitive" markets. This tracked the Department of Justice's theory that "the anticompetitive problems inherent in the joint provision of regulated monopoly and competitive services are otherwise insoluble."[199] AT&T was to retain all competitive markets—and to be allowed to enter any new markets that it chose. The BOCs were to retain all monopoly operations—and to be barred from diversifying into any competitive businesses. And the BOCs were to provide "equal access" to AT&T and its competitors in the use of their local exchange facilities. The remaining BOC monopolies would be tightly limited to small geographic areas.[200]

But Judge Greene had different views. He acknowledged the "conceptual neatness" of the government's theory, but declared that it "fail[ed] to take account of circumstances far more complex than these undifferentiated rules acknowledge." He pointed to major differences between a "vast, vertically integrated" Bell System providing local service, long-distance service, and equipment and the divested BOCs, which would "have a monopoly in only one geographic portion of one of these markets—local telecommunications." The old Bell System had "few powerful competitors"; the BOCs, by contrast, would "be faced with the most potent conceivable competitor: AT&T itself." The BOCs thus presented much less of a threat to competition. "[T]he only similarity between the divested Operating Companies and the present Bell System is that both possess a monopoly in local telecommunications. That single circumstance—important though it

---

of the individual BOCs was needed to reduce earnings fluctuations due to decisions of individual state regulators.

[199] Response of the United States to Public Comments on Proposed Modification of Final Judgment at 57, United States v. Western Elec. Co., No. 82-0192 (D.D.C. May 20, 1982).

[200] 1982 Decree §IV(G), 552 F. Supp. at 229.

may be—is not a sufficient basis upon which to restrict competition generally in the name of the antitrust laws."[201]

Accordingly, Judge Greene refused to approve the decree unless the parties modified it to allow the BOCs to publish printed Yellow Pages[202] and to market, though not manufacture, customer premises equipment.[203] He also insisted that the parties add to the decree an explicit provision allowing for removal of other line-of-business restrictions upon a showing "that there is no substantial possibility that [a BOC] could use its monopoly power to impede competition in the market it seeks to enter."[204] At the time, the Department of Justice strongly opposed these changes;[205] within a few years, however, it was the Department that was urging further liberalization and Judge Greene who was often strongly opposed.[206]

---

[201] United States v. AT&T, 552 F. Supp. at 187. AT&T accepted the line-of-business restrictions in the form proposed by the Justice Department, but repeatedly stated that the restrictions were not its "idea." Defendants' Reply Memorandum at 1, United States v. Western Elec. Co., No. 82-0192 (Aug. 19, 1982). Howard Trienens, AT&T's principal lawyer, told Judge Greene:

> I'm against restrictions. I'll be happy if nobody is restricted on anything. After their divestiture occurs, let [the BOCS] do what they want.

> The Court: I'm not sure I follow you entirely. Are you saying that you agree to the restrictions on the BOCs because you think they are a good thing, or are you saying you agree to them because Justice required it as a part of the bargain?

> Mr. Trienens: The fact is it's the latter.

Argument Tr. at 25,211, United States v. Western Elec. Co., No. 82-0192 (D.D.C. June 29, 1982). See also United States v. AT&T, 552 F. Supp. at 186 n.227 ("It appears that the Department is the principal proponent of the restrictions on the Operating Companies. AT&T has generally taken the stance that it agreed to these restrictions as part of the overall settlement.").

[202] 1982 Decree §VIII(B), 552 F. Supp. at 231.

[203] Id. §VIII(A), 552 F. Supp. at 231.

[204] Id. §VIII(C), 552 F. Supp. at 231.

[205] The United States specifically sought reconsideration of the court's ruling regarding customer premises equipment sold to multiline business customers, so-called complex CPE. The court denied reconsideration. United States v. AT&T, 1982-2 Trade Cas. (CCH) ¶64,980 (D.D.C. 1982).

[206] Although the decree contained no provision calling for continued interstitial lawmaking by the district court, Judge Greene retained a relatively free

§4.4.3.4 The Transfer of Assets from AT&T to the BOCs

The assets of the Bell System were divided principally according to whether they were used for intraLATA or interLATA services. The basic point of division between the two networks was the Class Four switch.[207] The Department of Justice estimated that about 80 percent of the assets fell cleanly on one side of a LATA line or the other.[208] The rest were allocated according to "predominant use."[209]

At the request of the BOC chief executive officers, Judge Greene assigned to the BOCs all facilities used for equipment or communications between BOC personnel and for communications between the BOCs and their customers, even if these facilities crossed LATA boundaries.[210] Although Judge Greene personally drafted the two decree provisions permitting BOCs to provide CPE and to publish Yellow Pages, he treated the assets of these businesses quite differently. The existing CPE business was assigned to AT&T, the existing Yellow Pages business to the BOCs. Curiously, however, inside wiring—telephone wiring on customer premises—was assigned to the BOCs, Judge Greene

---

hand to mold the restrictions to promote the decree's purposes. He uniformly favored broad readings of the decree restrictions and then granted waivers to mitigate their impact. The effect inevitably was to lodge greater control over BOC activities in the district court itself. *See FTL1* §6.7.

[207] *See* United States v. Western Elec. Co., 569 F. Supp. at 1003–1004 n.60.

[208] Ever mistrustful of collusion between the Bell System and the Department of Justice, Judge Greene required the parties to insert a specific standard in the decree for the allocation of these facilities. 1982 Decree §VIII(G), 552 F. Supp. at 232.

[209] *See* United States v. Western Elec. Co., 569 F. Supp. at 1064 n.20. Waivers of the predominant use test were granted for equipment needed by the BOCs to provide equal access. *See id.* at 1015 n.125. Section I(A)(1) of the decree required AT&T to supply the BOCs with "sufficient facilities [and] systems . . . to permit the BOCs to perform, independently of AT&T, exchange telecommunications and exchange access functions . . . and [that are] sufficient to enable the BOCs to meet the equal exchange access requirements. . . ." 552 F. Supp. at 226.

[210] United States v. Western Elec. Co., 569 F. Supp. at 1097, 1101. For additional discussion, see *FTL1* §4.9.2.

declaring that this wire "is as much a 'bottleneck' as are the subscriber access lines."[211] Soon thereafter the FCC declared precisely the opposite;[212] inside wire has been separated from the regulated rate base and is now provided competitively, like all other forms of CPE. After some initial confusion, it was agreed that mobile services would go to the BOCs on the theory that they fell within the definition of "local exchange" functions.[213]

Post-divestiture liabilities attributable to pre-divestiture events (including, of course, private antitrust suits) were apportioned among AT&T and the BOCs on the basis of their relative net investments as of the date of divestiture.[214] The decree required AT&T to assign to the BOCs rights in the technical information that AT&T's competitors would need for interconnection,[215] including all patents.[216] AT&T's original plan of reorganization provided that after the divestiture both AT&T and the BOCs could continue to use the "Bell" name in any way. Judge Greene,

---

[211] United States v. Western Elec. Co., 569 F. Supp. at 1129.

[212] Detariffing the Installation and Maintenance of Inside Wiring, 51 Fed. Reg. 8498 (1986), *on recons.*, 1 F.C.C. Rec. 1190 (1986), *on further recons.*, 3 F.C.C. Rec. 1719 (1988), *remanded sub nom.* National Assn. of Regulatory Util. Commrs. v. FCC, 880 F.2d 422 (D.C. Cir. 1989).

[213] For further discussion see *FTL1* §§1.7.4, 4.9.5, 13.2. In April 1994, however, Pacific Telesis spun off its wireless operations into a separate new company, renamed AirTouch Communications. *See* AirTouch Communications Is Spun Off from Pacific Telesis Group—Two-Year Plan Comes to Fruition, Bus. Wire, Apr. 4, 1994.

[214] *See* United States v. Western Elec. Co., 569 F. Supp. at 1069. For further discussion, see *FTL1* §4.9.6.

[215] *See* United States v. AT&T, 552 F. Supp. at 177. Section I(A)(1) directed AT&T to transfer to the BOCs sufficient "rights to technical information" for the BOCs to operate independently of AT&T. In addition, under section I(C) of the decree, up to September 1, 1987, the BOCs were permitted to call on AT&T, Western Electric, and Bell Laboratories to provide additional necessary information. For further discussion, see *FTL1* §4.9.7.

[216] When it submitted its Plan of Reorganization, AT&T proposed to give the BOCs only patents relating to exchange, exchange access, and printed directory advertising services. United States v. Western Elec. Co., 569 F. Supp. at 1082. But Judge Greene ruled that the original commitment to license "all" patents meant just that, including even "patents for services which the decree currently prohibits [the BOCs] from offering." *Id.* at 1086. The court explained that it "may, in the future, allow the Operating Companies to enter lines of business presently prohibited to them." *Id.* at 1090 (footnote omitted).

however, insisted that the continued sharing of the name would confuse consumers thereby favoring AT&T[217] and so assigned to the BOCs the sole right to the Bell name and logo to be used only with an appropriate geographic modifier (e.g., "Southwestern Bell").[218] AT&T was allowed to continue to use the "Bell" name only with respect to Bell Laboratories and its foreign operations.[219]

§4.4.3.5   AT&T Unbound

Under the agreement reached between the Bell System and the Department of Justice, AT&T was to be completely freed of the 1956 Decree restrictions and obligations upon divestiture.[220] AT&T would be prohibited only from reacquiring any of the BOCs.[221]

Judge Greene demanded one major change to this agreement. While AT&T was permitted to provide data processing services (barred under the 1956 Decree), Judge Greene decided that AT&T should be barred for an additional seven years (until 1989) from providing "electronic publishing over its own transmission facilities."[222] Judge Greene was more willing to free AT&T

---

[217] *Id.* at 1075.

[218] *Id.* at 1081. Part of the court's stated reason was specifically to make the BOCs strong competitors in the provision of CPE. "To deprive the Operating Companies of the use of the Bell logo and the Bell name in the CPE area would effectively cripple their efforts to become viable competitors in this market." *Id.* at 1079.

[219] *Id.* at 1081 n.96, 1123. For further discussion, see *FTL1* §4.9.9.

[220] *See* 1982 Decree (preamble), 552 F. Supp. at 226.

[221] *Id.* §I(D), 552 F. Supp. at 227; 552 F. Supp. at 170 n.166.

[222] 1982 Decree §VIII(D), 552 F. Supp. at 231. Judge Greene defined electronic publishing as "the provision of any information which a provider or publisher has, or has caused to be originated, authored, compiled, collected, or edited, or in which he has a direct or indirect financial or proprietary interest, and which is disseminated to an unaffiliated person through some electronic means." United States v. AT&T, 552 F. Supp. at 181. This moratorium was not limited to transmissions over telephone lines (although it did not apply to transmissions over facilities in which AT&T had no interest): it embraced television, radio, and "electronic publications which appear either by audio means, on video screens, or in printed form," and it applied both to "the one-way dissemination of information that is the norm in print publishing" and

immediately from the 1956 Decree's mandate that Bell license its patents and associated technical information to all comers.[223] Finally, Judge Greene rejected suggestions that he bar AT&T from building local facilities in competition with the BOCs[224] on the ground that such a prohibition would only put AT&T at a competitive disadvantage against other firms[225] and that state regulators would protect the BOCs' interests.[226]

§4.4.3.6 Interpretation, Enforcement, and Modification

"The Court has no wish to be engaged on a long-range basis in oversight of the telecommunications industry," Judge Greene wrote the year before divestiture, or even "to superintend on an intensive basis the actual implementation of the reorganization."[227] According to Judge Greene, undue delay in resolving the dispute would hold "the most serious consequences for the operation of the network and can only multiply the costs of uncertainty that have plagued the industry far too long."[228]

---

to "interactive transaction services," such as "shop-at-home" services. The prohibition covered all types of information, including "news, business and financial reports, editorials, columns, sports, features, and electronic advertising." *See id.* at 180–181 & nn.205–208. For further discussion, see *FTL1* §4.10.1.

[223] For further discussion, see *FTL1* §4.10.2.

[224] United States v. AT&T, 552 F. Supp. at 175.

[225] *Id.*

[226] *Id.* For a summary of the bypass that then occurred, see *Geodesic Network II* ch. 2.

[227] United States v. Western Elec. Co., 569 F. Supp. at 1119, 1120 (citation and footnote omitted). Judge Greene continued:

> [S]uch an oversight role would not be consistent with the principle of proper judicial restraint; and the kind of interference which it implies would not be fair to those who will manage AT & T and the Operating Companies. . . . There comes a time, once the basic documents have been approved, when the Court . . . should, in the interest of keeping judicial involvement to a necessary minimum, leave compliance to the managers of the business interests directly involved, with such oversight as is vested in the Department of Justice by the decree.

Id. at 1119–1120.

[228] United States v. AT&T, 552 F. Supp. at 213 (quoting AT&T Reply Comments at 3). *See also* United States v. AT&T, 88 F.R.D. at 50.

Intensive superintending materialized, however, Judge Greene's original plans notwithstanding. Discerning the meaning of the decree's restrictions proved to be one of the most complex aspects of federal regulation of telephony in the post-divestiture world. As we discussed in depth in the first edition of this treatise,[229] the jurisprudence of decree restrictions had a life of its own. Some of these complications were due to irreconcilable tensions in the decree itself. The decree's definitions of prohibited and permitted activities and services overlapped time and again in fundamental aspects, not just trivial detail.[230] The various decree permissions and prohibitions were incessantly contradictory because they did not reflect any external market verities. The decree assumed neat divisions among telephone equipment, local transport and switching, long-distance transport and switching, and services that provide information via telecommunications. But telecommunications markets never aligned with this theoretical model; they aligned instead with customers' needs for generating, processing, storing, and conveying information—needs that cut indiscriminately across the decree's divisions.[231]

---

[229] See, in particular, *FTL1* chs. 6 & 7.

[230] In construing the decree, Judge Greene "consistently regarded as paramount the decree's purposes whenever the language itself permitted more than one interpretation." United States v. Western Elec. Co., 578 F. Supp. at 655 (footnotes omitted). The D.C. Circuit generally took a much narrower view, stating that "construction of a consent decree is essentially a matter of contract law." United States v. Western Elec. Co., 846 F.2d 1422, 1427 (D.C. Cir. 1988) (citations and internal quotations omitted), *cert. denied sub nom.* Bell Atlantic v. United States, 488 U.S. 924 (1988). *See also* United States v. Western Elec. Co., 900 F.2d at 293; United States v. Western Elec. Co., 894 F.2d at 1390; United States v. Western Elec. Co., 894 F.2d 430, 434 (D.C. Cir. 1990); United States v. Western Elec. Co., 797 F.2d 1082, 1089 (D.C. Cir. 1986), *cert. denied sub nom.* U S West, Inc. v. United States, 480 U.S. 922 (1987). On the other hand, the D.C. Circuit on several occasions relied on "fundamental purposes" of the decree to justify expansive interpretations of its language. *See* United States v. Western Elec. Co., 894 F.2d at 1392, 1394; United States v. Western Elec. Co., 797 F.2d at 1088.

[231] Providers of telecommunications products and services not subject to the decree's restrictions typically engage in all these activities. *See Geodesic Network II* ch. 1; *see also* P. Huber, The Geodesic Network: 1987 Report on Competition in the Telephone Industry ch. 1 (1987) (hereinafter *Huber Report*).

In practice, the Department of Justice's interpretation of the decree ultimately mattered most. The Department had a constant, ongoing process for responding to inquiries and investigating complaints. Its views were endorsed by the D.C. Circuit $11\frac{1}{2}$ times in the first 13 post-divestiture appeals.[232] The FCC sometimes offered its views,[233] but had "no original or primary jurisdiction to construe or apply the terms of the MFJ."[234] However interpreted, the decree's meaning was a matter of law, not fact; the district court's readings were subject to de novo review.[235]

The decree placed initial responsibility for compliance on the parties themselves.[236] Judge Greene made it a point of decree litigation to accept comments from anyone who cared to file them. But he required third parties to seek enforcement through the Department of Justice. Willful violations of the decree were viewed as criminal matters.[237]

---

[232] The court of appeals has acknowledged reason to carefully consider, if not defer to, the Department's interpretations. United States v. Western Elec. Co., 846 F.2d at 1429 n.5.

[233] See, e.g., §12.___ (discussing the FCC's opinion that AT&T was permitted under the 1956 decree to provide data processing services).

[234] United States v. Western Elec. Co., 846 F.2d at 1433.

[235] United States v. Western Elec. Co., 907 F.2d at 1209; United States v. Western Elec. Co., 907 F.2d at 164; United States v. Western Elec. Co., 900 F.2d at 293; United States v. Western Elec. Co., 894 F.2d at 434; United States v. Western Elec. Co., 846 F.2d at 1427; United States v. Western Elec. Co., 797 F.2d at 1089.
Judge Greene had urged deference for his interpretations of several amendments to the decree that he drafted and imposed on the parties. See United States v. Western Elec. Co., 673 F. Supp. at 533 n.24; United States v. Western Elec. Co., 569 F. Supp. at 1079 n.88. The court of appeals firmly rejected this claim to deference. United States v. Western Elec. Co., 900 F.2d at 294. But see United States v. Western Elec. Co., 846 F.2d at 1429 (a decree interpretation "is bolstered" by the district court's "rejection of the appellants' argument, because the judge who rejected their argument was the very same judge who authored the footnote to which they [now] appeal[ ]").

[236] Section V directed AT&T, the BOCs, and their affiliates to advise their "officers and other management personnel with significant responsibility for matters addressed in this Modification of Final Judgment [MFJ] of their obligations hereunder." BOCs (though not AT&T) were specifically required to notify officers and managers of MFJ obligations and to obtain a solemnly signed certification in return. See 1982 Decree §V(2), 552 F. Supp. at 230.

[237] On February 16, 1993, Judge Greene found NYNEX guilty of criminal contempt for its operation of a prohibited information service and fined the

The 1982 Decree contained two independent tracks for the review of decree modifications.[238] Uncontested modifications (i.e., those not opposed by the other parties to the decree, the Department and AT&T) were reviewed under section VII,[239] to which a lenient "public interest" standard of review applied. Section VIII(C) of the decree applied to contested modifications. It provided that line-of-business restrictions "shall be removed upon a showing by the petitioning BOC that there is no substantial possibility that it could use its monopoly power to impede competition in the market it seeks to enter."[240] The first seven years of post-divestiture decree litigation were conducted in most instances under the section VIII(C) standard.[241]

§4.4.4   The GTE Decree[242]

GTE, the largest of the non-Bell telcos, was incorporated as the General Telephone Company in 1935.[243] It was formed in a bankruptcy reorganization of the Associated Telephone Utilities

---

company $1 million. United States v. NYNEX Corp., 814 F. Supp. 133 (D.D.C. 1993). The D.C. Circuit reversed. United States v. NYNEX Corp., 8 F.3d 52 (D.C. Cir. 1993). According to the appellate court, the decree's line between providing customer premises equipment (which was allowed) and providing information services (which at the time of the alleged contempt was prohibited) was ambiguous; NYNEX's conduct could fairly have been characterized as either. An essential element of criminal contempt is a violation of a "clear and reasonably specific order of the court," *id.* at 54, an element that was not present, *id.* at 57.

[238] Memorandum and Opinion at 6–8, United States v. Western Elec. Co., No. 82-0192 (D.D.C. May 25, 1982).

[239] *See* 1982 Decree, 552 F. Supp. at 231.

[240] *Id.*

[241] Early on Judge Greene announced that he would consider section VIII(C) motions only after review by the Department of Justice. United States v. Western Elec. Co., 592 F. Supp. at 873. Multiyear delays in waiver reviews by the Department became the norm.

[242] A full discussion of the GTE litigation and decree can be found in *FTL1* ch. 8.

[243] The name was changed to General Telephone & Electronics Corporation following the company's merger with Sylvania Electronic Products, Inc., in 1959. The present name, GTE Corporation, was adopted in 1982.

Company, a holding company for a number of small independents. GTE grew rapidly through the acquisition of numerous small telephone companies and gradually branched out into other lines of business.[244] At one time or another, it has provided interexchange services, manufactured telecommunications hardware, and offered various information services, including a value-added network, an electronic funds transfer network, video programming, data processing, and educational services.

Until 1983, GTE, like other independent telcos, relied on AT&T to provide most interexchange services to its customers. In 1983, however, GTE sought to acquire Sprint from Southern Pacific. Sprint was (and remains) the third largest interexchange carrier after AT&T and MCI WorldCom.[245] GTE also sought to acquire the Southern Pacific Satellite Company from the Southern Pacific (Railroad) Company.[246]

One might have expected the Justice Department to have welcomed the rise of a third viable competitor in the long-distance market, particularly because the Department had just finished persuading Judge Greene that the long-distance market had been monopolized by AT&T. But flush with its victory over the Bell System, Justice decided to sue GTE instead. Justice filed an antitrust suit against GTE based on the same theories as its case against Bell. The parties filed a proposed consent decree to settle the case on the same day.[247] They asked Judge Greene to accept the case as "related" to *United States v. AT&T;* Judge Greene "reluctant[ly]" agreed.[248]

The decree that concluded the GTE suit was, however, significantly different than the Modification of Final Judgment acceded to by the Bell System. GTE was allowed to acquire Sprint and GTE Spacenet, subject to a number of conditions designed to limit any

---

[244] *See* 1 Moody's Public Utility Manual 1834–1835 (1989).

[245] *See* United States v. GTE Corp., 603 F. Supp. 730, 733 n.15 (D.D.C. 1984); Surprise Plunge at Utd Telecom, Fin. Times, July 18, 1990, at 24.

[246] United States v. GTE Corp., 603 F. Supp. at 731.

[247] *Id.* at 730.

[248] Memorandum, United States v. GTE Corp., No. 83-1298 (D.D.C. May 6, 1983).

incentive or ability of the General Telephone Operating Companies (GTOCs) to discriminate against other interexchange carriers or to cross-subsidize GTE's competitive operations.

The decree required GTE to "maintain total separation within the corporation between the local Operating Companies and the newly-acquired Southern Pacific companies."[249] The GTOCs were further required to provide equal access to competing interexchange carriers[250] and were prohibited from providing interexchange services or owning related facilities.[251] The decree also barred GTE from acquiring any other interexchange telecommunications provider for a period of ten years.[252] The GTOCs, unlike the Bell Operating Companies (BOCs), were allowed to continue providing information services.[253]

Much of the history and substance of the GTE Decree became out of date shortly after it was entered. The government's suit was triggered by GTE's acquisition of Sprint. It was based on the theory that the combination of local exchange operations and Sprint's long-distance service would prove too potent for the market. Information services raised similar concerns. But in fact the market quickly proved too potent for GTE. The drafters of the GTE Decree very carefully specified that GTE was not to acquire another company like Sprint for the next ten years. Within five years, however, GTE was struggling to sell the money-losing Sprint it owned rather than to buy another company like it. With the sale of Sprint, GTE also unloaded a large

---

[249] United States v. GTE Corp., 603 F. Supp. at 737.

[250] *See* United States v. GTE Corp., No. 83-1298, §V(A) & app. B (D.D.C. Dec. 21, 1984) (hereinafter GTE Decree).

[251] *Id.* §V(C). It did, however, allow them to phase out their interexchange operations so as to recover their original investment.

[252] *Id.* §VI. This provision ensured that any further GTE growth in the interexchange market would come from internal expansion rather than through the elimination of a competitor by merger or acquisition. United States v. GTE Corp., 603 F. Supp. at 739–740.

[253] The decree relied on formal structural separation to expose any discrimination or cross-subsidy. No separate subsidiary was required here; separate "divisions" were deemed acceptable. This was in contrast to the FCC's program in effect at that time for enhanced services, which required a separate corporate subsidiary. *See* §11.3.

portion of its online information services business. Here again, the theory that animated the GTE Decree was resoundingly repudiated in the market. Cross-subsidy, discriminatory interconnection, and supercompetitive profits never materialized. Perhaps all this is simply a tribute to the perfectly crafted protections contained in the GTE Decree, but one cannot forget that the big debate in 1984 was whether these protections were simply too weak to guard against the anticompetitive stratagems that GTE would inevitably devise.

On April 13, 1995, GTE moved to terminate its decree.[254] GTE asserted that the sale of its Sprint and Spacenet affiliates (the Sprint assets) to United Telecommunication between 1986 and 1992 removed the underlying need for the decree. Before Judge Greene ruled on GTE's request, Congress eliminated the GTE Decree entirely in the 1996 Telecommunications Act.[255]

§4.4.5 The AT&T/McCaw Decree[256]

AT&T acquired McCaw Cellular Communications (McCaw) on September 19, 1994. The closing came nearly two years after the two companies first disclosed plans for an alliance.[257] At the time, the $17.5 billion transaction was the second largest merger in U.S. history.[258] The acquisition combined two major players in cellular telephony. AT&T was both the major supplier of cellular network equipment and the dominant interexchange cel-

---

[254] Motion of GTE Corporation To Terminate the Decree, United States v. GTE Corp., No. 83-1298 (D.D.C. filed Apr. 13, 1995).

[255] Section 601 of the 1996 Telecommunications Act vacated the GTE Decree. *See* 47 U.S.C. §152 note.

[256] *See FTL1* ch. 7A for a full discussion of the AT&T/McCaw litigation and decree. See §10.5.2 for a discussion of the private antitrust action brought against AT&T/McCaw.

[257] In November 1992, AT&T announced plans to buy 33 percent of McCaw Cellular Communications for $3.75 billion, with an option to purchase control for an additional $700 million. J. Keller & R. Smith, AT&T, Seeking To Enter the Cellular Era, in Talks for 33% of McCaw for $3.73 Billion, Wall St. J., Nov. 5, 1992, at A3. In August 1993, AT&T proposed to buy McCaw outright.

[258] Gambling on Thin Air, Economist, Aug. 21, 1993, at 49. On top of the $12.6 billion purchase price, AT&T assumed McCaw's $4.9 billion of debt. *Id.*

lular carrier. McCaw was the nation's largest provider of local cellular service.

AT&T's purchase of McCaw was subject to scrutiny by the Department of Justice,[259] which, after examining voluminous merger-related documents submitted by the two companies, concluded that the merger would violate the federal antitrust laws.[260] The Department did not assert (as it had in the original suit against Bell[261]) that any particular segment of the market was likely to be monopolized in violation of the Sherman Act. It alleged instead violations of the Clayton Act—reduced competition in three markets because of the merger.[262] The Department concluded that the merger would eliminate McCaw as a competitor of AT&T in the cellular interexchange market.[263] In addition, it found that the merger would give AT&T an incentive to abuse its position as a locked-in equipment supplier to McCaw's competitors. The Department stated that by withholding equipment and services or raising its prices, AT&T had the power to increase the costs and decrease the capabilities of its equipment customers.[264] Cellular subscribers would likely bear the brunt of AT&T's market power in the form of lower-quality and higher-cost cellular services.[265]

---

[259] *See* Complaint, United States v. AT&T Corp. and McCaw Cellular Communications, No. 94-01555 (D.D.C. July 15, 1994) (*McCaw Complaint*). Concurrent proceedings by the Federal Communications Commission and the California Public Utilities Commission were also held. *See* Opinion and Order, Joint Application of American Telephone and Telegraph Company, Ridge Merger Corporation and McCaw Cellular Communications, Inc. for Authorization To Transfer Indirect Control of Airsignal of California, et al., from McCaw Cellular Communications, Inc. to American Telephone and Telegraph Company, Dec. 94-04-0402 (Cal. P.U.C. Apr. 6, 1994) (approving transfer of licenses subject to conditions).

[260] Competitive Impact Statement at 4–5, United States v. Western Elec. Co., No. 74-1698 (D.D.C. Feb. 10, 1982) (*Competitive Impact Statement*).

[261] *See* §§1._, 4.4. *See also* United States v. AT&T, 524 F. Supp. at 1342 n.2; *Competitive Impact Statement* at 5; United States v. Western Elec. Co., 552 F. Supp. at 135–136.

[262] *McCaw Complaint* at 1–2.

[263] *Competitive Impact Statement* at 13.

[264] *Id.* at 10.

[265] *Id.*

After negotiations with AT&T and McCaw, the Department entered into a proposed consent decree that would have placed substantial restrictions on the operations of AT&T/McCaw.[266] That settlement was submitted to Judge Greene for approval under the Tunney Act on July 25, 1994, and was still pending before the court in February 1996, when Congress mooted it with the passage of the 1996 Act.[267]

The proposed decree was designed to (1) prevent discrimination by AT&T against McCaw's cellular competitors, (2) prevent AT&T/McCaw from exercising market power in the provision of interexchange services to McCaw's cellular customers, and (3) prevent misuse of confidential information that McCaw obtains about AT&T's equipment customers.[268] The provisions included limitations on the degree of structural integration that can occur between AT&T and McCaw,[269] equal access and nondiscrimination requirements,[270] and restrictions on the distribution of proprietary customer information.[271]

---

[266] Proposed Final Judgment, United States v. AT&T Corp. and McCaw Cellular Communications, Inc., No. 94-01555 (D.D.C. July 15, 1994) (*Proposed Final Judgment*).

[267] *See* 47 U.S.C. §152 note.

[268] *Competitive Impact Statement* at 4–5.

[269] Section III of the proposed decree required McCaw and McCaw's wireless services affiliates to "be maintained as corporations or partnerships . . . separate from AT&T." *Proposed Final Judgment* §III(A).

[270] The proposed decree adopted equal access obligations for McCaw that largely paralleled those imposed on the BOCs in the divestiture decree. Like the BOCs, McCaw would have been required to "provide to all [i]nterexchange [c]arriers [e]xchange [a]ccess on an unbundled basis that is equal in type, quality, and price to that provided to AT&T." *Compare Proposed Final Judgment* §IV(D)(1) *with* 1982 Decree §II(A), 552 F. Supp. at 227 (requiring that BOCs provide tariffed access equal "to that provided to AT&T and its affiliates") *and* Proposed Order, §VIII(L)(3) *attached to* Memorandum of the United States in Response to the Bell Companies' Motion for Generic Wireless Waivers, United States v. Western Elec. Co., No. 82-0192 (D.D.C. July 25, 1994) (requiring that BOC wireless companies provide access equal "to that provided to any interexchange service provided by that BOC or any affiliates thereof").

[271] The proposed decree prohibited AT&T from disclosing the confidential information of its equipment customers directly to McCaw. *Proposed Final*

§4.5   Common Law Standards and Procedures
         for Decree Modification

Most antitrust decrees are entered by consent.[272] Modifications of antitrust decrees often occur according to a predetermined sunset or by consent.[273] The standard of review for unopposed modifications is lenient: "the relevant inquiry for the court is whether the resulting array of rights and liabilities comports with the 'public interest.'"[274] Approval is usually "perfunctory."[275]

Judgment §V(A)(1)(a); *cf.* GTE Decree §IV(A)(3) (prohibiting the transfer of proprietary information between the GTOCs and their interexchange affiliates); *see also* §8.__.

[272] M. DeBow, Judicial Regulation of Industry: An Analysis of Antitrust Consent Decrees, 1987 U. Chi. Legal F. 353, 353 (1987) W. Donovan & B. McAlister, Consent Decrees in the Enforcement of Federal Anti-trust Laws, 46 Harv. L. Rev. 885, 886 (1933); R. Posner, A Statistical Study of Antitrust Enforcement, 13 J.L. & Econ. 365, 385–388 (1970).

[273] In 1979, the Justice Department adopted a policy generally limiting the life of antitrust decrees it negotiates to no more than ten years. *See* DeBow, Judicial Regulation of Industry at 358 (citing ABA Antitrust Section, Antitrust L. Dev. 362 (2d ed. 1984)). In 1981, Assistant Attorney General William F. Baxter initiated the "Judgment Review Project" to review the 1,200 extant decrees in the Department's civil cases. By mid-1987, some 90 judgments had been modified or terminated. *Id.* at 358–359.

[274] *See* United States v. Western Elec. Co., 900 F.2d at 305 (citing United States v. American Cyanamid Co., 719 F.2d 558, 565 (2d Cir. 1983), *cert. denied*, 465 U.S. 1101 (1984); United States v. National Finance Adjusters, Inc., 1985-2 Trade Cas. (CCH) ¶66,856 (E.D. Mich. 1985)). *See also* Sam Fox Publishing Co. v. United States, 366 U.S. 683, 689 (1961); Donaldson v. Read Magazine, 333 U.S. 178, 184 (1948); United States v. Bechtel Corp., 648 F.2d 660, 666 (9th Cir.), *cert. denied*, 454 U.S. 1083 (1981); United States v. Columbia Artists Management, Inc., 1987-1 Trade Cas. (CCH) ¶67,600, (S.D.N.Y. 1987); United States v. G. Heileman Brewing Co., 563 F. Supp. 642, 647 (D. Del. 1983); United States v. National Broad. Co., 449 F. Supp. 1127 (C.D. Cal. 1978); United States v. Mid-America Dairymen, Inc., 1977-1 Trade Cas. (CCH) ¶61,508 (W.D. Mo. 1977); United States v. General Elec. Co., 1977-2 Trade Cas. (CCH) ¶61,659 (E.D. Pa. 1977); United States v. Gillette Co., 406 F. Supp. 713, 716 (D. Mass. 1975); United States v. Swift & Co., 1975 Trade Cas. (CCH) ¶60,201 (N.D. Ill. 1975); J. Anderson, Modifications of Antitrust Consent Decrees: Over a Double Barrel, 84 Mich. L. Rev. 134, 135 (1985).

[275] 2 P. Areeda & D. Turner, Antitrust Law ¶330g (1978). The 1956 decree was modified in just this way in Judge Vincent Biunno's courtroom a few days before Judge Greene reasserted control. *See* §4.4.2.

Decree modifications opposed by the government are more difficult to obtain. Under Justice Cardozo's rule in *United States v. Swift & Co.*,[276] "unless the parties have expressly agreed otherwise, an antitrust defendant can prevail on a contested motion to reduce or eliminate its obligations only if it can make 'a clear showing of grievous wrong evoked by new and unforeseen conditions.'"[277] There has, however, been some trend toward loosening *Swift*, especially when it appears that a federal court is slipping into the role of full-time administrator of a public institution.

The Supreme Court's 1991 decision in *Board of Education v. Dowell*[278] and its 1992 decision in *Rufo v. Inmates of the Suffolk County Jail*[279] articulate the modern standard for decree modification.[280] *Dowell* involved a decree issued against the Oklahoma City Board of Education upon a finding that residential segregation had resulted in one-race schools. The Tenth Circuit overturned the district court's vacating of the five-year-old decree on the ground that the "grievous wrong" standard of *Swift* had not been met. The Supreme Court reversed. Unlike the decree at issue in *Swift*, the desegregation decree was not "intended to operate in perpetuity."[281] Thus, vacating the decree did not require an "additional showing of grievous wrong."[282]

---

[276] United States v. Swift & Co., 286 U.S. 106 (1932).

[277] United States v. Western Elec. Co., 900 F.2d at 305 (quoting *Swift*, 286 U.S. at 119).

[278] Board of Educ. of Okla. City v. Dowell, 498 U.S. 237 (1991) (*Dowell*).

[279] Rufo v. Inmates of Suffolk Cty. Jail, 502 U.S. 367 (1992).

[280] In *Dowell*, the Supreme Court held that *Swift* was not the standard for termination of an injunction entered in a school desegregation case. In *Rufo*, the Court held that *Swift* does not apply in other "institutional reform" litigation. *See also* Money Store, Inc. v. Harriscorp Finance, Inc., 885 F.2d 369, 374 (7th Cir. 1989) (Posner, J., concurring) ("[I]nstitutional reform litigation directed against a private rather than a public entity" is an "intermediate case" between public institutional reform litigation and "litigation over property rights" in which the *Swift* "hard line against modification . . . is sensible.").

[281] *Dowell*, 498 U.S. at 248.

[282] *Id.* at 247 (internal quotations omitted). As the Court explained, "[A] finding by the District Court that the Oklahoma City School District was being

387

Rufo involved the appeal of a county sheriff to modify a consent decree requiring construction of a new jail. The Court's opinion significantly relaxed the "grievous wrong" standard of *Swift*. Under *Rufo*, a decree may be modified if "a significant change either in factual conditions or in law" has been shown.[283] Changed facts support modification when the changes "make compliance with the decree substantially more onerous," when "a decree proves to be unworkable because of unforeseen obstacles," or when "enforcement of the decree without modification would be detrimental to the public interest."[284] Changed law supports modification when "one or more of the obligations placed upon the parties has become impermissible under federal law," when "the statutory or decisional law has changed to make legal what the decree was designed to prevent," or when the parties "had based their agreement on a misunderstanding of the governing law."[285]

While both *Dowell* and *Rufo* involved institutional reform litigation, the Supreme Court did not limit its holdings to that context. Rather, the Court indicated that application of the relaxed standard turns on two key factors: (1) whether the decree involves the supervision of changing conduct or conditions, thus being tentative and provisional (as in *Rufo* and *Dowell*), or whether the conditions are fixed and the decree is intended to operate in perpetuity (as in *Swift*); and (2) whether the impact of the decree affects the public interest (as in *Rufo* and *Dowell*).[286]

The Second Circuit applied the flexible *Dowell/Rufo* standard in *Patterson v. Newspaper & Mail Deliverers' Union*.[287] The Equal

---

operated in compliance with the commands of the Equal Protection Clause . . . , and that it was unlikely that the school board would return to its former ways, would be a finding that the purposes of the desegregation litigation had been fully achieved." *Id.*

[283] *Rufo,* 502 U.S. at 384.

[284] *Id.* (citations omitted).

[285] *Id.* at 388–390. *See also* Agostini v. Felton, 117 S. Ct. 1997, 2006 (1997) (explaining that "a court errs when it refuses to modify an injunction or consent decree in light of" significant changes in facts or "in either statutory or decisional law").

[286] *See Rufo,* 502 U.S. at 378–382; *Dowell,* 498 U.S. at 246–249.

[287] Patterson v. Newspaper & Mail Deliverers' Union of N.Y., 13 F.3d 33 (2d Cir. 1993), *cert. denied,* 513 U.S. 809 (1994); *see also* Building & Constr. Trades

Employment Opportunity Commission and a class of minority employees sued newspaper distributors for discrimination, and a consent decree was entered. Reviewing an order of the district court that later vacated the decree, the court held that *Dowell/Rufo* was the appropriate standard: "If a decree seeks pervasive change in long-established practices affecting a large number of people, and the changes are sought to vindicate significant rights of a public nature, it is appropriate to apply a flexible standard in determining when modification or termination should be ordered in light of either changed circumstances or substantial attainment of the decree's objective."[288] More recently, in a case involving the dissolution of a consent decree in an antitrust action, the Second Circuit explained that the flexible *Dowell/Rufo* standard would apply, but that in most cases the antitrust defendant "should be prepared to demonstrate that the basic purposes of the consent decrees—the elimination of monopoly and unduly restrictive practices—have been achieved" consistent with the Supreme Court's pre-*Dowell* jurisprudence.[289]

Judge Greene's first occasion to apply the *Dowell/Rufo* standard to the divestiture decree came in his April 5, 1994, ruling

---

Council, AFL-CIO v. National Labor Relations Bd., 64 F.3d 880 (3d Cir. 1995) (applying *Rufo* in assessing whether consent judgments enforcing NLRB orders should be modified); Proctectoseal Co. v. Barancik, 23 F.3d 1184 (7th Cir. 1994) (affirming dissolution of decree prohibiting defendant from serving on corporate board based on changes in relevant law).

[288] *Patterson,* 13 F.3d at 38; *see* Hendrix v. Page & Page, 986 F.2d 195, 198 (7th Cir. 1993) (although *Rufo* involved institutional reform litigation, its "'flexible standard' . . . is no less suitable to other types of equitable case").

[289] United States v. Eastman Kodak Co., 63 F.3d 95, 101 (2d Cir. 1995) (citing United States v. United Shoe Mach. Corp., 391 U.S. 244 (1968)).

At issue in the *Kodak* case were a 1921 decree that barred Kodak from marketing private-label film (film manufactured by Kodak, but marketed under the brand of a retail outlet, such as Wal-Mart) and from negotiating exclusive dealing contracts and other nonprice vertical restraints and a 1954 decree limiting Kodak's freedom to connect film sales with film processing. *Id.* at 98. The *Kodak* trial court held a nine-day evidentiary hearing and found that market conditions had changed dramatically in the decades since the two decrees had been entered. Kodak no longer had market power in the world market, or even in the United States, for color film manufacturing and sales. *Id.* at 99–100. The appellate court concluded that the district court had not abused its discretion in making those findings. *Id.* at 108–109.

on AT&T's section I(D) waiver motion.[290] The D.C. Circuit subsequently agreed with the application of the *Dowell/Rufo* standard to the consent decree.[291] IBM likewise relied on *Rufo* in its motion to vacate the consent decree under which it operated until 1997.[292]

Imposition of new burdens on an unwilling defendant plainly requires new proceedings. The government must prove that further relief is indispensable to prevent or remedy a violation of federal law.[293] Modifications that impose new burdens may be somewhat easier to obtain if the decree was entered after an initial finding of liability.[294]

Finally, decree modifications are mandatory when applicable law has changed. A consent decree is not a marriage contract; the parties cannot purchase the court's power by exchanging mutual vows.[295] When the statute underlying a decree is amended,

[290] United States v. Western Elec. Co., 154 F.R.D. 1 (D.D.C. 1994). Despite the "factual similarities between the decree in this case and that in *Swift*," Judge Greene held that "requests for modifications of the decree governed by a common law standard should be considered in light of the standard set forth in *Rufo*." *Id.* at 9.

[291] *See* United States v. Western Elec. Co., 46 F.3d 1198, 1203 (D.C. Cir. 1995) (explaining that "*Rufo* gave the coup de grace to *Swift* and that the Supreme Court's summary of what might render a modification equitable relates to all types of injunctive relief") (internal quotations omitted).

[292] Memorandum of Law in Support of IBM's Motion To Terminate the 1956 Consent Decree, No. 72-344 (S.D.N.Y. 1994).

[293] Hughes v. United States, 342 U.S. 353, 357–358 (1952); Ford Motor Co. v. United States, 335 U.S. 303 (1948); Chrysler Corp. v. United States, 316 U.S. 556 (1942); United States v. International Harvester Co., 274 U.S. 693, 702 (1927).

[294] *See* United States v. United Shoe Mach. Corp., 391 U.S. 244, 249 (1968). *But see* United States v. AT&T, 552 F. Supp. at 155 n.102 ("The fact that the decree would be issued pursuant to the parties' consent is irrelevant to its status, for a consent decree has the same effect as a decree issued after a finding of liability on the merits.") (citing *Swift*, 286 U.S. at 115).

[295] *See* Firefighters v. Stotts, 467 U.S. 561, 576 n.9 (1983); System Fedn. No. 91 v. Wright, 364 U.S. 642, 651 (1961). *But see Rufo*, 502 U.S. at 389 (parties could settle dispute over constitutional violations "by undertaking to do more than the Constitution itself requires" or "more than what a court would have ordered absent the settlement"); Local No. 93 v. Cleveland, 478 U.S. 501, 521– 522 (1986) (parties could voluntarily agree to a consent decree provision that provides for racial preference in promotions, even though such a provision could not have been included in a litigated judgment).

therefore, the parties "have no power to require of the court continuing enforcement of rights the statute no longer gives."[296]

§4.6 Access, Interconnection, and Essential Facilities

From the earliest days of the industry, it came to be accepted that telephone companies had no obligation to interconnect with each other's facilities. A few early rulings did recognize a general obligation for telcos to serve as "carriers' carriers,"[297] but most did not.[298] As late as 1930, a federal court of appeals would find no obligation to interconnect after a Bell company notified a local independent that its interconnection would be terminated.[299]

---

[296] System Fedn. No. 91 v. Wright, 364 U.S. at 652. *See also* Pennsylvania v. Wheeling & Belmont Bridge Co., 59 U.S. 421, 431–432 (1855) (if, after entry of "a continuing decree," the statute underlying the decree has been modified, "it is quite plain the decree of the court cannot be enforced" with respect to provisions that are no longer supported by the statute).

[297] In 1910, for example, the St. Louis Court of Appeals ruled that an exclusive contract between Home Telephone and Granby Telephone was unenforceable when Home sought to enjoin Granby from interconnecting with the Bell System. Home Tel. Co. v. Granby & Neosho Tel. Co., 147 Mo. App. 216, 126 S.W. 773 (1910). This decision, however, was overruled by the Supreme Court of Missouri. *See* Home Tel. Co. v. Sarcoxie Light & Tel. Co., 236 Mo. 114, 139 S.W. 108 (1911) (*Sarcoxie*) (upholding the legality of such an exclusive contract). *See also* Campbellsville Tel. Co. v. Lebanon L. & L. Tel. Co., 118 Ky. 277, 80 S.W. 1114, 84 S.W. 518 (1905) (public interest obligated the two telephone companies to continue an agreement to interconnect as long as either company maintained an exchange in those communities); State v. Skagit River Tel. & Tel. Co., 85 Wash. 29, 147 P. 885, 151 P. 1122 (1915) (upholding a public service commission order that two telephone systems make a physical connection), *modified,* 89 Wash. 625, 155 P. 144 (1916).

[298] *E.g.,* Pacific Tel. & Tel. Co. v. Anderson, 196 F. 699, 703 (E.D. Wash. 1912) ("the authorities agree that at common law each telephone company is independent of all other telephone companies . . . [and] is not bound to accord to any such outside organization or its patrons connection with its switchboard on an equality with its own patrons."). *See also* State v. Cadwallader, 172 Ind. 619, 87 N.E. 644, 89 N.E. 319 (1909); *Sarcoxie,* 139 S.W. 108; Home Tel. Co. v. People's Tel. Co., 125 Tenn. 270, 141 S.W. 845 (1911).

[299] Oklahoma-Arkansas Tel. Co. v. Southwestern Bell Tel. Co., 45 F.2d 995 (8th Cir. 1930), *cert. denied,* 283 U.S. 822 (1931). The Eighth Circuit declared

Indeed, the court held that a state law mandating interconnection would constitute a "taking" and so require compensation.[300] Similarly, the 1934 Communications Act required interconnection only to the extent the FCC found it "necessary or desirable in the public interest."[301] The 1914 consent decree between Bell and the federal government[302] had indeed provided for interconnection between Bell's long-distance network and independent local exchanges in the Pacific Northwest, but this mandate, directed exclusively at the Bell System, remained the exception, not the rule. This was not a legal environment in which any part of the telephone network was likely to be labeled an "essential facility," to which would-be competitors enjoyed broad antitrust rights of interconnection.

§4.6.1   Evolution of the Essential Facilities Doctrine in the Telecommunications Industry

For many years, until well into the 1960s, prevailing regulatory and common carrier norms lent no support to the notion that wire-based carriers were obliged to interconnect with their competitors. Then, rapidly evolving technology, the Supreme Court's decision in *Otter Tail,* and a shift in the regulatory climate at the FCC created new expectations and business norms.

As discussed in detail in Chapter 5, however, the FCC began permitting and requiring more liberal interconnection in the 1970s. In 1969, the FCC approved a six-year-old application from Microwave Communications, Inc., which later became MCI Communications Corporation (MCI), to operate a long-distance telephone system between Chicago and St. Louis.[303] The service

---

that the Bell company had no contractual, common law, or statutory duty to interconnect. *Id.* at 997–999.

[300] *Id.* at 999. *Cf.* Loretto v. Teleprompter Manhattan CATV Corp., 458 U.S. 419 (1982).

[301] Communications Act of 1934, 47 U.S.C. §201(a).

[302] *See* §4.4.1.

[303] Applications of Microwave Communications, Inc., Decision, 18 F.C.C.2d 953, 966 ¶37 (1969); Applications of Microwave Communications, Inc., Memorandum Opinion and Order, 21 F.C.C.2d 190 (1970). *See* §9.3.2.

in question was point to point and required no interconnection with the public network.[304] But pressure for interconnection mounted rapidly. MCI complained that Bell was misusing its power over local telephone service to gain a competitive advantage over long-distance competitors, and the Commission held that "established carriers with exchange facilities should, upon request, permit interconnection or leased channel arrangements on reasonable terms and conditions to be negotiated with the new carriers."[305] At one point, amid much confusion over the various parties' rights and obligations, Bell briefly disconnected some of MCI's circuits.[306] In 1978, the D.C. Circuit, giving a remarkably broad reading to existing FCC precedents, ruled that

---

[304] Applications of Microwave Communications, Inc., Decision, 18 F.C.C.2d at 953–954 ¶1.

[305] Establishment of Policies and Procedures for Consideration of Application To Provide Specialized Common Carrier Services, First Report and Order, 29 F.C.C.2d 870, 940 (1971) (footnote and citation omitted) (hereinafter *Specialized Common Carriers*).

[306] Based on a letter from the Chief of the FCC's Common Carrier Bureau interpreting the *Specialized Common Carriers* decision, on November 2, 1973, MCI sought an injunction requiring Bell to provide interconnections for MCI services known as FX and CCSA, which were a hybrid of private line and switched services.

On December 31, 1973, the United States District Court for the Eastern District of Pennsylvania issued a preliminary injunction ordering Bell to provide the interconnections sought by MCI on the theory that such interconnections were contemplated and required by the FCC's *Specialized Common Carriers* decision. MCI Communications Corp. v. AT&T, 369 F. Supp. 1004 (E.D. Pa. 1973). Bell provided the required interconnections, but immediately appealed the injunction. Meanwhile, the FCC, on December 13, 1973, issued its own order requiring Bell to show cause why it should not be held to have violated the *Specialized Common Carriers* decision by refusing to provide the interconnections requested by MCI.

On April 15, 1974, the Third Circuit reversed the preliminary injunction issued against Bell. MCI Communications Corp. v. AT&T, 496 F.2d 214 (3d Cir. 1974). The next day, despite assurances that the FCC's "show cause" decision was expected "any day now" and despite FCC warnings that disconnection of MCI's customers would violate the Communications Act, Bell disconnected some of MCI's customers on 24 hours' notice. On April 23, 1974—eight days after the Third Circuit had vacated the injunction obtained by MCI—the FCC issued a decision ordering Bell to provide the disputed interconnections. Bell System Tariff Offerings of Local Distribution Facilities for Use by Other Common Carriers, Decision, 46 F.C.C.2d 413 (1974) (hereinafter *Bell System Tariff Offerings*), aff'd sub nom. Bell Tel. Co. v. FCC, 503 F.2d 1250 (3d Cir. 1974),

MCI was entitled to interconnection for the full array of services that it might choose to offer over its facilities.[307]

The Bell System did not welcome these changes and resisted them with some persistence. Meanwhile, companies like MCI pushed interconnection demands to their limits. The FCC, predictably enough, split the difference, as did courts reviewing the FCC's actions.

The results of the ensuing antitrust suits were mixed. For the most part, plaintiffs won clear-cut victories when FCC policies and regulations most clearly supported their right to interconnect and compete, but otherwise lost. Similar issues arose—and were decided in much the same way—in litigation concerning the interconnection of customer premises equipment. While Judge Greene made his inclinations fairly clear in ruling on AT&T's motion to dismiss, it is much less clear whether his extensive dictum on essential facilities and interconnection obligations would have been upheld had the case been litigated to a conclusion.

Chapter 9 discusses in more detail the private antitrust actions against the Bell System, such as MCI's[308] and Southern Pacific's actions[309] against AT&T for monopolization of long-distance services. Other chapters summarize the private antitrust actions involving wireless services, equipment, and information services.[310] It is worth noting here, however, the profound impact that a single administrative decision had on antitrust litigation against the Bell System. The federal government's 1974 case and Southern Pacific's private suit were both originally assigned to federal District Judge Joseph C. Waddy. Judge Waddy died in 1978. The Southern Pacific suit was then reassigned to Judge

---

cert. denied sub nom. AT&T v. FCC, 422 U.S. 1026 (1975). Bell provided the requested interconnections within ten days of the FCC's order.

[307] See §9.4.1.

[308] MCI v. AT&T, 708 F.2d 1081.

[309] Southern Pacific Communications Co. v. AT&T, 556 F. Supp. 825 (D.D.C. 1983), aff'd, 740 F.2d 980 (D.C. Cir. 1984), cert. denied, 470 U.S. 1005 (1985).

[310] See Chapter 10 (wireless services); Chapter 8 (equipment); Chapter 12 (information services).

Richey, who soon thereafter ruled flatly in Bell's favor and was upheld on appeal. The federal government's case was reassigned to Judge Greene, who took quite a different view of the industry and actively propelled the litigation toward its final, dramatic conclusion. Had the docket assignments been reversed, the Bell System would still be intact today.

§4.6.2 Essential Facilities Aspects of the 1974 Government Case

While the private antitrust suits by MCI, Southern Pacific, and others were unfolding toward resolution, the federal government's 1974 action that culminated in the breakup of the Bell System was pending.[311]

In ruling on the Bell System's motion to dismiss at the close of the government's case-in-chief, Judge Greene ruled that the Bell System enjoyed no regulatory immunity.[312] He accepted that "[t]he local monopoly is a lawful one,"[313] but that "the local facilities controlled by Bell are 'essential facilities'" for long-distance carriers. On this basis, Judge Greene found that "AT&T was under an obligation to furnish equal or substantially equal access to its intercity competitors."[314] But the government's evidence "tend[ed] to show that defendants [had] sought in a variety of ways to exclude the competition by restricting interconnection to the local facilities."[315] Bell had refused to provide FX and CCSA services to specialized common carriers and had "attempted to prevent competitors from offering metered long-distance service that would compete with AT&T's own reg-

---

[311] The parallel cases had several points of connection. For example, MCI shared its discovery materials with the federal government. AT&T v. Grady, 594 F.2d 594 (7th Cir. 1978), *cert. denied sub nom.* AT&T v. MCI Communications Corp., 440 U.S. 971 (1979); *see also* MCI v. AT&T, 708 F.2d 1081.

[312] United States v. AT&T, 524 F. Supp. at 1347–1348.

[313] *Id.* at 1352 n.65.

[314] *Id.* at 1353; *see also* United States v. Western Elec. Co., 569 F. Supp. at 1067 n.32 (citing United States v. AT&T, 524 F. Supp. at 1356, 1360).

[315] United States v. AT&T, 524 F. Supp. at 1353.

ular long-distance service."[316] Bell had also included a "customer premises" provision in its interconnection tariff that prevented competitors from "piecing out" Bell's network by offering competitive carriage over low-cost routes, while reselling Bell's services elsewhere to provide what the end user would perceive as universal service. The government claimed this was "illegal not under the essential facilities doctrine, but as the equivalent of unlawful tying arrangements—that is, that AT&T 'tied' provision of the services for which it held a monopoly (i.e., service on routes for which competition had not developed) to purchase of AT&T service along routes which competitors did indeed serve."[317]

While Judge Greene's opinions in connection with divestiture are widely cited, it bears repeating that this action was ultimately settled; the interlocutory rulings were never appealed, and the legal doctrines established by the case (as distinguished from much of the dictum) concern only the entry and modification of consent decrees, not substantive standards of antitrust liability.

§4.7   Cross-Subsidy and Predatory Pricing

Major network services cases have all involved parallel charges of cross-subsidy, predatory pricing, and variations on these theories to the effect that services have been mispriced and costs misallocated. Equipment cases have raised similar claims. Private antitrust actions relating to cross-subsidy and predatory pricing in the provision of long-distance, wireless, and information services and equipment are discussed in other portions of this treatise.[318] This section discusses pricing aspects of the federal government's suit against the Bell System.

---

[316] United States v. AT&T, 552 F. Supp. at 161 (footnotes omitted); *see also* *id.* at 195.

[317] United States v. AT&T, 524 F. Supp. at 1354 n.76 (citation omitted).

[318] *See* Chapter 9 (long-distance services); Chapter 10 (wireless services); Chapter 12 (information services); Chapter 8 (equipment).

§4.7.1 Pricing Aspects of the 1974 Federal Case: Services

The government's principal pricing claim at trial was that the Bell System had priced its services without regard to costs. So far as it went, this charge was certainly accurate. As discussed in section 9.4, Bell's prices had long been shaped by regulatory policies aimed at promoting universal service by keeping basic local subscription rates artificially low at the expense of artificially high prices elsewhere.[319] When competition materialized, Bell sought to adjust, although it contended (and the government did not attempt to prove otherwise[320]) that even with the adjustments, all of its long-distance prices remained well above marginal costs. The government claimed anticompetitive manipulation by Bell through "price-based costing" rather than the "cost-based pricing" expected from a regulated utility.[321]

Judge Greene refused to dismiss the government's admittedly "novel" pricing theory.[322] In contrast to the appellate decisions discussed above, he took the view that pricing below marginal cost was not the only standard for identifying predatory pricing and emphasized the possible interrelationship between cross-subsidy and predatory pricing.[323] He also identified as a possible antitrust issue the fact that Bell had priced identical connections differently depending on whether they were to be used to provide private line or ordinary switched services.[324] In a later opinion, Judge Greene went so far as to suggest that Bell had unlawfully "subsidiz[ed]" its intercity services using "revenues from the monopoly local exchange services,"[325] although "no final decision was reached" on this question.[326]

---

[319] For example, in 1980, 25 percent of the cost of exchange plant was allocated to interstate service even though the relative usage of the exchange plant for such services was only 10 percent. Temin & Galambos, The Fall of the Bell System at 26, fig. 4.

[320] United States v. AT&T, 524 F. Supp. at 1367 n.127.

[321] Id. at 1366.

[322] Id. at 1370.

[323] Id. at 1369 (citation omitted).

[324] Id. at 1356–1357.

[325] United States v. AT&T, 552 F. Supp. at 165; see also id. at 188.

[326] Id. at 169 n.160.

According to almost all other analyses, this last finding was incorrect. There is very little doubt that subsidies in fact flowed from long-distance operations to the local exchange.[327] The government has abandoned the claim made at trial that local telephone revenues subsidized Bell's intercity rates;[328] it has since recognized that the subsidy flowed the other way.[329] And one must note, once again, that Judge Greene's views on predatory pricing and cross-subsidy remain pure dictum; these issues were never finally adjudicated.[330]

§4.7.2   Pricing Aspects of the 1974 Federal Case: Equipment

The federal government attempted to make central-office equipment a centerpiece of its 1974 case against the Bell System. As summarized by Judge Greene, the government alleged "that AT&T used its control over the local Operating Companies to force them to buy products from Western Electric even though other equipment manufacturers produced better products or products of identical quality at lower prices."[331]

On Bell's motion to dismiss, Judge Greene dismissed the part of the government's case involving the pricing of equipment,[332] lambasting the government's evidence as "sparse" and its expert testimony as "weak," "incredible," and grounded in "cursory knowledge of telecommunications equipment pricing practices."[333] On charges of self-dealing and market foreclosure, Judge Greene

---

[327] See §9.4.

[328] See Testimony of William H. Melody, United States v. Western Elec. Co., No. 74-1698 (D.D.C. June 8, 1981); Testimony of Nina Cornell, United States v. Western Elec. Co., No. 74-1698 (D.D.C. June 19, 1981); Testimony of Bruce Owen, United States v. Western Elec. Co., No. 74-1698 (D.D.C. June 22, 1981).

[329] United States v. AT&T, 552 F. Supp. at 169 n.161. See §9.4.

[330] See also United States v. AT&T, 552 F. Supp. at 169 & n.161; United States v. Western Elec. Co., 569 F. Supp. at 1072.

[331] United States v. AT&T, 552 F. Supp. at 163.

[332] United States v. AT&T, 524 F. Supp. at 1380–1381.

[333] Id. at 1380.

would state that "the government's procurement case was not extremely strong,"[334] "not particularly convincing,"[335] and discredited by "vigorous cross examination which tended to introduce a significant number of facts of affirmative value to defendants."[336]

As to other equipment-related claims, Judge Greene stated his views on CPE markets in ruling against the Bell System's motion to dismiss the government's case. The government's evidence, he concluded, had "tended to show" that Bell's protective connecting arrangements (PCAs) were unnecessary, overengineered, overpriced, hard to obtain, and of dubious value in protecting the telephone network and had suppressed competition from independent CPE providers.[337] Bell had considered the less restrictive alternative of a certification program and had concluded it was feasible, but had rejected it to protect its revenues and market position.[338] Subsequent experience had proved PCAs to be unnecessary.[339] Judge Greene acknowledged, however, "some merit" in Bell's claim that the FCC had been responsible for the delay in the development of interconnection standards.[340]

Judge Greene would subsequently claim credit for the rise of competition in CPE markets.[341] In fact, however, the FCC's certification program had been fully implemented well before the

---

[334] United States v. AT&T, 552 F. Supp. at 163 n.137.

[335] United States v. AT&T, 524 F. Supp. at 1372 n.154.

[336] *Id. See also* United States v. AT&T, 552 F. Supp. at 174.

[337] United States v. AT&T, 524 F. Supp. at 1349–1350. *See also* United States v. AT&T, 552 F. Supp. at 162–163.

[338] United States v. AT&T, 524 F. Supp. at 1350. In addition, Judge Greene found that Bell was "aware of (and . . . encouraged) the barrier to competition created by the unavailability and inadequate maintenance of the PCAs as well as of the additional economic barrier [they] created because of their added cost." *Id.* Judge Greene did not rely on the government's proof that Bell's opposition to the certification program was a sham. The court held that Bell's regulatory posturing was protected under the *Noerr-Pennington* doctrine. *Id.* at 1350 n.54, 1352, 1363 & n.110, 1364.

[339] United States v. AT&T, 552 F. Supp. at 162–163.

[340] *Id.* at 163 n.136.

[341] *See* United States v. Western Elec. Co., 569 F. Supp. 990, 996 n.28 (D.D.C. 1983); United States v. Western Elec. Co., 569 F. Supp. at 1122.

decree was entered, and Bell's market share in all types of CPE was already declining rapidly.[342]

§4.7.3 Discussion

The outcomes of cases charging telcos with predatory pricing and cross-subsidy are mixed, but generally favorable to telco defendants. Such charges are raised frequently and are taken seriously by both economists and jurists. But in the two major Bell System cases litigated to a conclusion,[343] the charges were almost completely rejected. The cross-subsidy theory that Judge Greene would later emphasize in various interlocutory and post-divestiture opinions was flatly rejected by the Seventh Circuit in the MCI private antitrust action.[344] Other equipment cases discussed in Chapter 8 similarly rejected charges of price and cost manipulation as farfetched or unsubstantiated.

There is no dispute that large business concerns offering a wide variety of services have an abundant opportunity to allocate many of their costs in varied ways, particularly fixed costs, overhead costs, and other similar expenses. But it takes considerably more than such flexibility to establish an antitrust violation. Indeed, joint and fixed costs remain an unsolved puzzle in economic theory; neither theory nor common practice supplies any single "correct" methodology for allocating expenses of this kind, in competitive markets or elsewhere.[345]

Finally, one should note that many of the concerns about cross-subsidy are abating now, as regulators abandon rate-of-return regulation in favor of price-cap regulation[346] and abandon

---

[342] For example, AT&T's share of the large PBX market dropped from roughly 70 percent in 1979 to approximately 25 percent in 1982. *See* Huber Report at 16.5 & n.15.

[343] *See* MCI Communications v. AT&T, 708 F.2d 1081 (7th Cir. 1983); Southern Pacific Communications Co. v. AT&T, 740 F.2d 980 (D.C. Cir. 1984). See §9.4.3.1–9.4.3.2.

[344] For further discussion of this case, see §9.4.3.1.

[345] *See* §2.2.1.

[346] *See* §2.2.3.

monopoly and regulation itself in favor of competition. The incentives for cross-subsidy by regulated utilities originate in rate-of-return regulation, which favors cost-loading on the regulated side of the business. Price-cap regulation, to the extent implemented, eliminates such incentives. Competition eliminates not only the incentive to cross-subsidize, but the ability, too.

With regard to equipment, charges of market foreclosure, transfer pricing, and other antitrust abuses by telcos have often focused on relations between telcos and affiliated equipment manufacturers. Economic theory suggests that there may be many incentives for anticompetitive conduct built into affiliations of this kind. But the theory has rarely been tested or vindicated in the crucible of an antitrust trial litigated to conclusion.

Though courts have consistently denied claims of absolute antitrust immunity by virtue of regulation, the CPE cases illustrate that regulation has nonetheless shaped the antitrust environment. So long as the FCC backed telco monopolies, independent CPE providers met with no success in antitrust litigation. Antitrust victories materialized only when telcos resisted or simply lagged behind in changing regulatory policies. If Bell and other telcos had quickly accepted and accommodated the FCC's *Carterfone* ruling,[347] it seems unlikely that they would have suffered any subsequent defeats in equipment-related antitrust litigation.

§4.8 Conclusion

Antitrust law remains by far the best instrument for policing economic behavior. It has been said that a screwdriver is not very good for driving a nail, but the question must be, Compared to what? Compared to a banana it is pretty good. Much the same

---

[347] Use of the Carterphone Device in Message Toll Telephone Service, Decision, 13 F.C.C.2d 430 (1968) (hereinafter *Carterfone*). *Carterfone* is discussed further in §§5.1.2.1 and 8.4.1.2.

holds for antitrust law. It is not a perfect instrument for promoting competition, but it is vastly better than a regulatory commission.

The FCC tries to work out most things in advance—and while it frets, the market waits. Antitrust lawyers attack specific problems retrospectively, after they have been presented as concrete facts. And when problems are fixed, or fix themselves, the antitrust lawyers leave. Most antitrust suits are prosecuted outside the shadow of commissions, and most reach compact conclusions. The defendant is vindicated, or the jury returns a verdict commensurate with the plaintiff's economic injury. Any money verdict is automatically trebled; this acts as a powerful deterrent for the defendant and anyone else engaged in similar business practices. If the subject of the suit is a proposed merger, either the merger is blocked, or it goes through. If the suit involves charges of attempted monopolization, specific anticompetitive practices may be proscribed. If the suit involves charges of actual monopolization, the monopolist may be broken up into two or more pieces.

These verdicts are usually clean. The ones with the fewest words—pure monetary verdicts—often speak the loudest. MCI's first suit against AT&T culminated in a treble-damage verdict of $1.8 billion, serious money even by AT&T's standards, still serious even after it was cut to $113 million on appeal.[348] The AT&T divestiture decree, which took effect a year after a federal appellate court affirmed the MCI award, merely built on what private suits were already accomplishing. Even if AT&T had never been broken apart, the MCI verdict, and the threat of an indefinite chain of others like it, would have forced Bell to open up its networks quickly enough.

The antitrust verdicts with the most potential for mischief are those that order an end to anticompetitive practices. Prospective orders require ongoing enforcement. But even these can be comparatively simple to administer, and their enforcement can remain largely in private hands. There is no commission on the scene, no permanent bureaucracy, no army of federal employees

[348] See §9.4.3.1.

hanging around indefinitely to meddle and mess up. Or at least there need not be if decrees are carefully drafted and intelligently enforced.

Commission-free decrees have successfully addressed virtually every issue discussed in this treatise. They have required interconnection and have thus enforced principles of common carriage. They have required unbundling of content and conduit or the dissolution of patent pools. They can force copyright owners to give access to their copyrights. Anything that an economic commission can order, an antitrust court can order, too. The difference is that the antitrust court acts on a specific complaint against specific parties. It bases its judgment on a solid record of things that have already happened, not things that might (or might not) someday come to pass.

Even the most ambitious antitrust decrees don't try to solve everything. Commission-centered laws carve up and segregate the entire telecommunications universe into fixed settlements and townships. Antitrust law is applied case by case, to a specific enterprise in a specific market, to Oshkosh Telephone, but not Okefenokee Cable. This creates more uncertainty than rules codified by a commission. But it allows for much more flexibility and a much more precise focus on concrete problems. Consent decrees normally sunset automatically after ten years. They can be vacated sooner.

When the FCC gets paralyzed by an excess of lawyers or simply grows senile or indolent, entire industries grind to a halt because permissions to get on with life are no longer forthcoming. Under the antitrust laws, economic life goes on, albeit not always perfectly, until the constable arrives. Economic life organized under functioning antitrust laws allows the law-abiders to grow and build while the pursuit of wrongdoers is under way. The social costs of paralysis-by-analysis in the FCC far outweigh the costs of possible paralysis among antitrust prosecutors.

Understandably enough, the FCC does not yet see things quite this way. Indeed, as we discuss in Chapter 7, the Commission still insists on conducting a highly duplicative "public interest" review of all major telecom mergers, after they have been cleared by the Department of Justice. But the 1997 remarks of Joel Klein, the Department's Assistant Attorney General for Antitrust, seem to strike the right note for a deregulatory future. We are moving into "a deregulated environment." But "exclusive dealing, control over essential facilities, and the use of market power" continue to raise significant antitrust concerns," Mr. Klein observes, "[e]specially in network industries." "[T]he Telecom Act explicitly keeps the antitrust laws in force. This serves not only to guard against any anticompetitive consolidation, but also against any other practices that violate the antitrust laws. Once regulation begins moving off center stage, we are prepared for the possibility that antitrust enforcement may be necessary to ensure full and fair competition in these markets."[349]

---

[349] Joel I. Klein, Acting Assistant Attorney General, Antitrust Division, U.S. Department of Justice, Preparing for Competition in a Deregulated Telecommunications Market, Remarks Presented at Willard Inter-Continental Hotel, Washington, D.C. (Mar. 11, 1997).

5

Equal Access, Unbundling, and Interconnection*

§5.1 Introduction

The name itself implies uniform treatment for all comers: *common* carrier. But the principle is as complex, delphic, and evolutionary as "equal protection," its conceptual cousin in the Bill of Rights. Nondiscrimination obligations have long been imposed by common law and antitrust courts and by state and federal regulators. In 1996, these principles were expounded on at some length by Congress itself. At some point, these principles may also implicate the takings clause, and possibly even the free speech clause of the Constitution.[1]

---

*This chapter was co-authored by Sean A. Lev, Partner, Kellogg, Huber, Hansen, Todd & Evans; Williams College (B.A., *magna cum laude*, 1988); Harvard Law School (J.D., *magna cum laude*, 1992); Phi Beta Kappa; Law Clerk, Honorable Patricia M. Wald, U.S. Court of Appeals, D.C. Circuit, 1992–1993, Attorney, U.S. Dept. of Justice, Civil Division, Appellate Staff, 1993–96.
[1] *See* §§5.3.2, 14.6.

This chapter explores the evolution of unbundling and inter-connection mandates from a unified perspective, with particular emphasis on the latest chapter of this story, the post-1996 un-bundling of the local exchange. The remainder of this section outlines the common carriage principles of the 1934 Commu-nications Act. Sections 5.2 through 5.4 discuss interconnection rules developed by the Federal Communications Commission (FCC) for customer premises equipment,[2] pay phones,[3] cable TV providers (at least insofar as access to telephone poles is con-cerned),[4] enhanced services,[5] and long-distance companies.[6] Section 5.5 discusses the rules established under the 1996 Tele-communications Act and the FCC rules for interconnections between competitors for local exchange service.

§5.1.1 Interconnection Law: Historical Antecedents

A right to interconnect on more or less equal terms can be traced back to the telegraph statutes of the 1800s. The Post Roads Act of 1866, which allowed telegraph companies to run their lines freely along post roads and to fell publicly owned trees for telegraph poles, required the telegraph companies in turn to interconnect and accept each other's traffic.[7] If telephone companies at the turn of the century had been held to similar obligations early on, local exchanges might have remained com-petitive by differentiating their price and services. All might have offered complete service through interconnection with other companies, including—during the lifetime of the Bell patents

---

[2] See §5.2.1.
[3] See §5.2.2.
[4] See §5.2.3.
[5] See §5.2.4.
[6] See §5.2.5.
[7] A New York court would later declare, "A telegraph company represents the public when applying to another telegraph company for service, and no discrimination can be made by either against the other, but each must render to the other the same services it renders to the rest of the community under the same conditions." People ex rel. Western Union Tel. Co. v. Public Serv. Commn., 230 N.Y. 95, 129 N.E. 220, 12 A.L.R. 960 (1920).

on superior long-distance technology—the best available long-distance connections. But somehow legislators, regulators, and the courts drifted toward a narrow understanding of a common carrier's obligations to carry its competitors' traffic.[8]

Telegraph and telephone companies plainly fit the "common carrier" model. Almost from the beginning, they were expected to serve all comers and charge similar rates for similar services. They could not easily be sued for libelous utterances transmitted over their systems or for many other expensive or hurtful consequences that might ensue when transmissions were garbled or lost. They soon came to be viewed as paradigm "common carriers," so common, so ubiquitous, so routinized that one could scarcely imagine them operating in any other way—except, as it turned out, when a would-be "customer" happened to be another carrier.

A common carrier's duty not to discriminate ceased when another carrier came asking for service. The same principle would come to be applied in telephony. In 1903, for example, what would become the Interstate Telephone Company won permission to install a telephone system in Newport, Washington.[9] An early owner of the system agreed he would not extend the system outward to compete against Pacific Telephone and would connect all long-distance calls to Pacific's network. When Interstate bought the system in 1911, it immediately cut off Pacific and connected the Newport exchange to its own long-distance lines.

---

[8] Disputes over interconnection first appeared in the Express Packages Cases, decided by the Supreme Court in 1886. Four major express companies, the grandparents of today's overnight courier services, had worked out a cozy territorial division of the business. They didn't do much hauling themselves. Instead, they reserved an entire railway car, or perhaps half a car; paid wholesale rates for the space; and used their own agents to load, unload, and supervise packages consigned to their care. In 1880, one of the major railroads abruptly announced that it was entering the overnight business itself and would no longer sell space to the express companies on the prior terms; express companies would be treated like ordinary retail customers. Faced with immediate financial ruin, the express companies rushed to court. Their arrangements with the railroads (they argued), though originally simple matters of contract, had become matters of common "law and usage." The U.S. Supreme Court disagreed. Express Packages Cases, 117 U.S. 1 (1886).

[9] Pacific Tel. & Tel. Co. v. Anderson, 196 F. 699 (E.D. Wash. 1912).

Pacific demanded reconnection; Interstate answered that the original contract was illegal in that it froze out other carriers. Not at all, ruled a federal judge. "[E]ach telephone company is independent of all other telephone companies"; common carrier law did not require telcos "to accord to any such outside organization or its patrons connection with its switchboard on an equality with its own patrons."[10] Other cases of the era were to the same effect, even in the teeth of state statutes requiring universal carriage. "Telephone and telegraph companies are common carriers," the Supreme Court of Tennessee conceded, "[b]ut this does not mean that a telephone company is bound to permit another telephone company to make a physical connection with its lines."[11]

Congress had its first important chance to correct this balkanized environment when it passed the Mann-Elkins Act of 1910.[12] The Act brought interstate telecommunications within the regulatory jurisdiction of the Interstate Commerce Commission (ICC) and included telecommunications companies within the definition of "common carrier," thereby obligating them "to provide service on request at just and reasonable rates, without unjust discrimination or undue preference."[13] But the Act failed to specify a common carrier's obligations to other carriers. The ICC might have taken steps to correct this failure, but was preoccupied by railroads and uncertain of its powers. The Bell System's march toward monopoly thus continued, unchecked.

§5.1.2 Interconnection Under Monopoly

Interconnection disputes were tiresome and messy. Impatient policymakers decided they could be resolved more quickly by

[10] *Id.* at 703 (citing State v. Cadwallader, 172 Ind. 619, 87 N.E. 644, 89 N.E. 319 (1909)).

[11] Home Tel. Co. v. People's Tel. & Tel. Co., 141 S.W. 845, 848 (Tenn. 1911). *See also* Home Tel. Co. v. Sarcoxie Light & Tel. Co., 139 S.W. 108, 113, 236 Mo. 114 (1911).

[12] 36 Stat. 539 (1910).

[13] Essential Communications v. AT&T, 610 F.2d 1114, 1118 (3d Cir. 1979) (citing Mann-Elkins Act §§7, 12).

ignoring them entirely. Monopolists would not need to interconnect, at least not with other competing carriers. Duly franchised by regulators, the monopolies arrived, and interconnection disputes largely disappeared.

The process began with a 1913 agreement between the U.S. Attorney General and a Bell vice-president, N. C. Kingsbury. Under that agreement, the company agreed to stop acquiring independent phone companies and to connect the remaining independents to Bell's long-distance network.[14] But the local exchange monopolies themselves were not disturbed; local carriers remained free to continue refusing interconnection to other *local exchange* competitors.

So long as local service remained a monopoly, regulators did not have to concern themselves much with regulatory traffic hand-offs between competing LECs. Hand-offs did occur, but not between direct competitors. For instance, GTE and PacBell provide service to adjacent neighborhoods in Los Angeles, and small independent phone companies operate side by side with the Bell companies in thousands of small islands of coverage across the country. "Free" calling areas often cross such boundaries, and when they do, the two phone companies could, in principle, be charging each other. As discussed in section 2.__, however, payments of this sort have never been made historically. Comparable bilateral operating agreements between U.S. carriers and their foreign counterparts evolved to specify methods of interconnection, rates of payment for completion of outgoing calls, and routing of incoming calls.[15]

§5.1.2.1 Transitional Years at the FCC: 1968–1984

The FCC's first serious attempt at requiring interconnection to the telephone network involved equipment, not other carriers. In the 1968 *Carterfone* decision, the Commission held that

[14] *See* §§1.3.2, 4.4.1.
[15] *See* §2.3.3.4.

any form of customer premises equipment (CPE) could be attached to the network "so long as the interconnection does not adversely affect the telephone company's operations or the telephone system's utility for others."[16] At issue was a device permitting direct communication between a mobile radio and the landline network. The Bell System objected to the device, but failed to demonstrate that it would harm the network in any way. With this ruling, the Commission seemingly opened the way for a complete line of competitive products that would interconnect with the network on customer premises.

The Commission gradually turned away from protecting monopoly and toward promoting competition. It lacked the power simply to dismantle Bell's corporate structure, but it could unpack the network itself. It could require Bell to interconnect with other long-distance carriers, mobile carriers, paging companies, information service providers, and, in time, other local exchange carriers, too.

In its 1970 *Specialized Common Carrier* proposal, the FCC declared for the first time: "[W]here a carrier has monopoly control over essential facilities we will not condone any policy or practice whereby such carrier would discriminate in favor of an affiliated carrier or show favoritism among competitors."[17] Since 1970, the Commission has steadily elaborated on that single core principle. By 1980, with some prodding from the courts, the

[16] Use of the Carterfone Device in Message Toll Telephone Service, 13 F.C.C.2d 420, 424, *recons. denied*, 14 F.C.C.2d 571 (1968) (hereinafter *Carterfone*).

[17] Establishment of Policies and Procedures for Consideration of Applications To Provide Specialized Common Carrier Services in the Domestic Public Point-to-Point Microwave Radio Service and Proposed Amendments to Parts 21, 43 and 61 of the Commission's Rules, Notice of Inquiry To Formulate Policy, Notice of Proposed Rulemaking and Order, 24 F.C.C.2d 318, 347 ¶67 (1970) (hereinafter *Specialized Common Carrier*). Now that equal access for carriers is a widely accepted and admired principle, there has been some inevitable jockeying to claim credit for inventing the idea. *See, e.g.*, United States v. AT&T, 552 F. Supp. 131, 195–200 (D.D.C. 1982); United States v. GTE Corp., 603 F. Supp. 730, 743–746 (D.D.C. 1984) (requiring the Bell Operating Companies and GTE, respectively, to provide all interexchange carriers with access that is "equal in type, quality and price" to that provided to AT&T and its affiliates). Modification of Final Judgment §II(A), *reprinted in* United States v. AT&T, 552 F. Supp. at 227 (hereinafter *Decree*).

FCC had implemented, or was steadily implementing, interconnection regulation for CPE,[18] enhanced services,[19] long distance,[20] and wireless.[21]

Interconnection regulation thus evolved incrementally, product by product, service by service. The pace of change was too slow to satisfy newcomers, who were often still thwarted in their attempt to interconnect. But it also seemed too quick for Bell and state regulators, who saw traditional franchises and subsidies evaporating under the radiant heat of competition. Matters went to court. And the courts . . . the courts at one time or another, in one place or another, sided with every side on every issue.[22]

§5.1.2.2 Equal Access and the Bell Divestiture Decree: 1984–1996

The lawsuit that culminated in the Bell System divestiture in 1984 revolved around the issue of nondiscriminatory interconnection. The core of the government's case was "that the [Bell] Operating Companies provided interconnections to AT&T's intercity competitors which were inferior in many respects to those granted to AT&T's own Long Lines Department."[23] The divestiture Decree accordingly contained equal access and nondiscrimination provisions specifically addressing competition in the long-distance market.[24] Equal access was designed with the

---

[18] *See* §8.4.

[19] *See* §12.2.1.

[20] *See* §9.4.

[21] *See* §10.5.

[22] *See* Chapter 3.

[23] United States v. AT&T, 552 F. Supp. at 195; *see also* United States v. AT&T, 524 F. Supp. 1336, 1352 (D.D.C. 1981).

[24] These provisions, unlike the line-of-business restrictions, were the subject of painstaking negotiation between the parties. *See* §9.4. Drafts of the various decrees from the extended "quagmire" negotiations show repeated changes, counterproposals, and discussion regarding the equal access requirements. One of the key issues was whether the Decree would specify the precise physical facilities at which the interexchange carriers would interconnect with the Regional Bell Operating Company (RBOC) networks. Ultimately, the Department agreed with AT&T that equal access could be defined in terms of service rather than facilities.

specific purpose of preventing favoritism between AT&T and competing providers of long-distance and information services.[25]

But the framers of the Decree, despite grand language in the document itself, clearly did not fully grasp what equal access implied. They—Judge Harold Greene most emphatically of all—still accepted a top-down vision of telephony, a world with small consumers at one end of the network and gargantuan carriers at the other. They still embraced the core notion of a monopoly franchise—of a single, anointed local carrier dominating the bottom two-thirds of the network with the government's blessing. The trouble with this vision was that it missed all the important activity in the middle—the large customers who might become providers, the resellers who would combine services and equipment in new packages of services, the upstart mobile carriers. The Decree was strong on equal access for the few companies like MCI that had complained long and loud about unfair treatment. But the Decree ranged from weak to wrong on equal access for everyone else.

Most obvious, as the Decree itself fully recognized, competition was possible in the most local of all local telephone operations, on a customer's own premises. The Decree handed most of *that* part of the business over to AT&T, though the RBOCs retained control of pay phones[26] and were also permitted to market customer premises equipment.[27] In due course, Judge Greene would allow RBOCs into "information gateways"; the Court of Appeals for the D.C. Circuit would then allow them into information services generally.[28] All of these businesses were at least partially competitive, and all could be served by BOCs operating within the confines of individual local access and transport areas (LATAs). So, in a process more reminiscent of

[25] *See* United States v. AT&T, 552 F. Supp. at 142–143, 195–197, 209 n.327; *see also* Competitive Impact Statement at 26–27, United States v. Western Elec. Co., No. 82-0192 (D.D.C. Feb. 10, 1982).

[26] *See* §8.4.4.

[27] United States v. AT&T, 552 F. Supp. at 191–193.

[28] United States v. Western Elec. Co., 767 F. Supp. 308, 332 (D.D.C. 1991) (Judge Greene felt constrained by an earlier D.C. Circuit decision to remove the restriction on information services, *see* United States v. Western Elec. Co., 900 F.2d 283, 307–309 (D.C. Cir. 1990)).

common law than consent decrees, Judge Greene gradually set about reinventing the equal access requirement from scratch.[29]

The 1982 Bell Decree's equal access mandate was only one of four that the Department of Justice drafted before 1996. The others appear in the GTE/Sprint Decree,[30] the AT&T/McCaw Decree, and a generic waiver for Bell Company wireless affiliates. As discussed more fully below, however, the AT&T/McCaw Decree was overtaken by the 1996 Act before it came into legal effect,[31] and the generic wireless waiver was mooted by a provision of the 1996 Act expressly addressing wireless service.[32]

§5.1.2.3 Overview of the Interconnection and Unbundling Mandates of the 1996 Act

The 1996 Act granted the FCC six months to establish regulations implementing the interconnection/unbundling requirements of the Act.[33] On August 8, 1996, the last day of the six-month period, the FCC issued its 700-page, 3,200-footnote *Local Competition Order*,[34] which sets out rules dictating the rates

[29] *E.g.*, United States v. Western Elec. Co., 890 F. Supp. 1 (D.D.C. 1995) (wireless services); United States v. Western Elec. Co., 1986-1 Trade Cas. (CCH) ¶67,148 (paging services); United States v. Western Elec. Co., No. 82-0192 (D.D.C. Feb. 26, 1986) (paging services); United States v. Western Elec. Co., 1987-1 Trade Cas. (CCH) ¶67,452 (D.D.C. Jan. 28, 1987) (cellular services); United States v. Western Elec. Co., No. 82-0192 (D.D.C. Feb. 18, 1993) (cellular services); United States v. Western Elec. Co., No. 82-0192 (D.D.C. Sept. 20, 1994) (video and audio programming by satellite and other means); United States v. Western Elec. Co., No. 82-0192 (D.D.C. Sept. 21, 1993) (cable service); United States v. Western Elec. Co., No. 82-0192 (D.D.C. Oct. 24, 1994) (same); *see also* United States v. Western Elec. Co., No. 82-0192 (D.D.C. Nov. 14, 1988); United States v. Western Elec. Co., No. 82-0192 (Feb. 15, 1991); United States v. Western Elec. Co., No. 82-0192 (May 11, 1994); United States v. Western Elec. Co., 604 F. Supp. 256, 261–262 (D.D.C. 1984).

[30] The GTE Decree was imposed as a condition of GTE's 1983 acquisition of Sprint. *See* M. Kellogg, J. Thorne & P. Huber, Federal Telecommunications Law §§8.2, 8.4.4, 8.6 (1992) (hereinafter *FTL1*) (and Supp.); *see also* United States v. GTE Corp., 603 F. Supp. 730, 731, 744 (D.D.C. 1984).

[31] *See* §9.5.2.

[32] *See* §10.5.2.

[33] 47 U.S.C. §251(d)(1).

[34] Implementation of the Local Competition Provisions in the Telecommunications Act of 1996, First Report and Order, 11 F.C.C. Rec. 15,499 (1996) (hereinafter *Local Competition Order*).

and other terms and conditions of certain intrastate telecommunications services. In setting these rules, the FCC "coin[ed]"
a new standard for measuring cost known as "total element long
run incremental cost" or "TELRIC."[35] TELRIC generally requires prices to be set based solely on the incremental, forward-
looking cost of a hypothetical, ideally efficient, state-of-the-art
network.[36] The FCC also prescribed a comprehensive set of uniform national rules, binding on state arbitrators, that purported
to implement the Act's requirement that incumbent LECs interconnect and provide access to network elements on an unbundled basis.[37] Likewise, the rules purported to require incumbents
to upgrade their networks in order to provide interconnection
and network elements of a quality superior to that provided by
the existing network and superior to what the incumbent provides itself.[38]

The Regional Bell Operating Companies and GTE filed petitions to challenge the FCC order, contending that the FCC
lacked jurisdiction to issue regulations governing the prices and
other terms and conditions of intrastate services and that a
number of particular regulations adopted by the FCC violated
the 1996 Act, were arbitrary and capricious, and raised serious
constitutional questions.[39] The RBOCs argued that Congress
assigned exclusively to the states, not the FCC, jurisdiction to
determine rates under 47 U.S.C. §§251 and 252. In October
1997, the Eighth Circuit issued a stay on the operation and effect
of the pricing provisions (as well as the so-called pick-and-
choose rule) found in the *Local Competition Order* pending its consideration of the petitions for review.[40] The Supreme Court
denied the applications filed by the FCC and multiple private
parties to vacate that stay.[41] Then, in a decision issued in July

[35] *Id.* at 15,846 ¶678.
[36] *Id.* at 15,848 ¶685.
[37] *Id.* at 15,624–15,627 ¶¶241–248.
[38] *Id.* at 15,615 ¶225, 15,692 ¶382.
[39] Brief for Petitioners Regional Bell Companies and GTE, Iowa Utils. Bd.
v. FCC, No. 96-3321 (8th Cir. Nov. 18, 1996).
[40] Iowa Utils. Bd. v. FCC, 109 F.3d 418 (8th Cir. 1996) Opinion.
[41] FCC v. Iowa Utils. Bd., 117 S. Ct. 378 (1996).

1997 and amended on rehearing in October 1997, the Eighth Circuit confirmed its earlier tentative conclusion that the FCC lacked authority to issue pricing rules and further determined that some, but by no means all, of the FCC's unbundling rules were substantively inconsistent with the 1996 Act.[42] The FCC, joined by AT&T, MCI, and other private parties, filed petitions for certiorari seeking review of some of the Eighth Circuit's jurisdictional and nonjurisdictional rulings; the RBOCs and other incumbents filed cross-petitions seeking review of other determinations made by the court of appeals.

The Supreme Court granted those petitions and, in January 1999, issued its decision. The Court's ruling was a mixed bag for all involved.[43] The FCC won the jurisdictional battle. The Court concluded that 47 U.S.C. §201(b) gave the FCC authority to implement all the provisions of the Communications Act, including those added by the 1996 Act. On the merits, however, the Supreme Court determined that the FCC's method of determining which network elements must be provided was fundamentally flawed because, among other things, the FCC did not satisfactorily consider whether particular network elements could be obtained from sources other than the incumbent. The Court thus vacated all the FCC's rules requiring access to particular elements and required the Commission to reconsider each of those determinations.

§5.2   Vertical Links to the Local Exchange

§5.2.1   Customer Premises Equipment and Inside Wiring

§5.2.1.1   Interconnection and Unbundling

Under the old Bell System, CPE was bundled in with service and sold as a single, end-to-end integrated package. The Bell

---

[42] Iowa Utils. Bd. v. FCC, 120 F.3d 753 (8th Cir. 1997), *aff'd in part, rev'd in part sub nom.* AT&T v. Iowa Utils. Bd., 119 S. Ct. 721 (1999).

[43] AT&T v. Iowa Utils. Bd., 119 S. Ct. 721 (1999).

tariffs contained various "foreign attachment" provisions that prohibited any non-Bell System product from being interconnected with Bell's network.[44] For a while, the FCC upheld these provisions against competitors seeking to connect their CPE to the ends of Bell's lines. In 1956, the D.C. Circuit reversed the Commission's policy with regard to the Hush-A-Phone device and set the Commission on a course to permitting greater interconnection of competitive CPE.[45] On remand, the Commission set forth its basic policy that a CPE device could be attached to the network so long as it did not cause any harm.[46] Over a decade later, in the 1968 *Carterfone* decision,[47] the Commission reaffirmed this principle, but made it clear (on reconsideration) that it did not apply to devices that actually interact electronically with the telephone network itself.[48]

Bell exploited the Commission's narrow ruling by filing new tariffs that permitted attachment only of various "mechanical" devices (such as the Hush-A-Phone and Carterfone) that involve no electrical connection to the network. Bell also permitted cus-

---

[44] A typical provision reads as follows: "No equipment, apparatus, circuit, or device not furnished by the Telephone Company shall be attached to or connected with the facilities furnished by the Telephone Company, whether physically, by induction or otherwise, except as provided in this tariff. In case any such unauthorized attachment or connection is made, the Telephone Company shall have the right to remove or disconnect the same; or to suspend the service during the continuance of said attachment or connection; or to terminate the service." Jordaphone Corporation of America v. AT&T, 18 F.C.C. 644, 647 (1954).

[45] Hush-A-Phone Corp. v. United States, 238 F.2d 266 (D.C. Cir. 1956).

[46] Hush-A-Phone v. AT&T, Decision and Order on Remand, 22 F.C.C. 112 (1957).

[47] 13 F.C.C.2d 420, *recons. denied,* 14 F.C.C.2d 571 (1968).

[48] AT&T "Foreign Attachment" Tariff Revisions in AT&T Tariff FCC Nos. 263, 260, and 259, Memorandum Opinion and Order, 15 F.C.C.2d 605 (1968), *on recons.,* 18 F.C.C.2d 871 (1969). In order to route calls, it is necessary to send signals to the appropriate switches. When a caller picks up a telephone, the very act of going "off-hook" sends a signal to the caller's end office and establishes a circuit connection with the end office that is heard as a dial tone. When the caller punches in a number, the digits are signaling information necessary to route the call. And when the caller hangs up, that action signals the network to disconnect the circuits it has established. These signals are known as network control signals because they control the operation of the switches and circuits that make up the telephone network.

tomers to connect various types of terminal equipment (including private branch exchanges (PBXs), key systems, computers, and private microwave systems), but only indirectly through interconnecting devices known as protective connecting arrangements (PCAs). Instead of rejecting these tariffs immediately, the Commission initiated what became lengthy and complex proceedings designed to erase the boundaries between the telephone system and the competitive world.[49]

In 1975, the Commission finally issued its new Part 68 rules, which embodied the idea that adequate network protection could be provided without telco-supplied PCAs.[50] The rules established a registration program through which users were permitted to connect any type of CPE to the telephone network, provided either that the equipment was connected through protective circuitry registered with the Commission or that the equipment was itself registered with the Commission.[51] The Commission later extended these rules to include PBXs, key telephone systems, regular handsets, and coin telephones.[52] Finally, the Commission preempted any state regulation that would interfere with its registration program, thus ensuring a uniform national policy in favor of competition in CPE.[53] The Fourth Circuit

---

[49] *See e.g.,* AT&T Co.'s Proposed Tariff Revisions in Tariff FCC No. 263 Exempting Mebane Home Telephone Co. of North Carolina from the Obligation To Afford Customers the Option of Interconnecting Customer-Provided Equipment to Mebane's Facilities; AT&T Transmittal No. 12321, Memorandum Opinion and Order, 53 F.C.C.2d 473 (1975).

[50] Proposals for New or Revised Classes of Interstate and Foreign Message Toll Telephone Service (MTS) and Wide Area Telephone Service (WATS), First Report and Order, 56 F.C.C.2d 593 (1975) (hereinafter *Proposals for New or Revised MTS and WATS I*).

[51] *Id.* at 599 ¶17. The option of registering only discrete protective circuitry, rather than all the terminal equipment, eliminated unnecessary documentation relating to total system design and performance criteria and thus removed the need for filing proprietary information with the Commission.

[52] Proposal for New or Revised Classes of Interstate and Foreign Message Toll Telephone Service (MTS) and Wide Area Telephone Service (WATS), Second Report and Order, 58 F.C.C.2d 736 (1976). *See also* Registration of Coin Operated Telephones Under Part 68 of the Commission's Rules and Regulations, Memorandum Opinion and Order, 57 Rad. Reg. 2d (P & F) 133 (1984).

[53] *See Proposals for New or Revised MTS and WATS I,* 56 F.C.C.2d 593 (purpose of new Part 68 "is to provide for uniform standards"). With the Commission firm in its resolve to introduce competition into the CPE market, Bell

upheld the Commission's new rules against protests by various telcos and state utility commissions.[54]

§5.2.1.2   Equal Access Under the Bell Divestiture Decree

The Bell Divestiture Decree made no mention of interconnection rights for providers or owners of CPE.[55] Judge Greene assumed that the Part 68 rules would take care of the ability of

---

sought protection from Congress. It convinced friendly legislators to introduce the Consumer Communications Reform Act of 1976. The purpose of the Act was to "'reaffirm'" congressional intent to afford the states complete authority over terminal equipment, including authority over devices used partly in interstate service. Note, Competition in the Telephone Equipment Industry: Beyond Telerent, 86 Yale L. J. 538, 539 n.5 (1977). Since the states were eager to use CPE sales to subsidize local rates, passage of the Act would in all likelihood have continued the Bell monopoly. But the Act never passed.

[54] North Carolina Utils. Commn. v. FCC, 552 F.2d 1036 (4th Cir.), *cert denied*, 434 U.S. 874 (1977).

[55] The omission is curious. As discussed in Chapter 8, CPE presented the oldest, best understood, indeed prototypical "equal access" concern. Moreover, the equal access rights needed by "information service providers" (which the Decree *does* address) are in fact identical to those required by users of telecommunications-related CPE. Information services are just PBXs, modems, computers, and related equipment operating from some information service provider's premises. The BOCs have the same ability and incentive to use their "bottleneck" position to injure competition in the CPE industry that they are said to have in the information services industry. *See e.g.*, Report and Recommendations of the United States Concerning the Line of Business Restrictions Imposed on the Bell Operating Companies by the Modification of Final Judgment at 131–132, United States v. Western Elec. Co., No. 82-0192 (D.D.C. Feb. 2, 1987) ("because non-integrated information services connect to the local BOC's network in a manner similar to CPE (indeed, they often are provided through CPE), the competitive risks involved in BOC provision of such services would be comparable to those presented by BOC provision of CPE"). *See also* Motion of the United States for Removal of the Information Services Restriction of the Modification of Final Judgment at 23 n.30, United States v. Western Elec. Co., No. 82-0192 (D.D.C. Aug. 22, 1990). It is also significant that the FCC has historically treated CPE and enhanced services alike, applying similar regulatory safeguards to each. *See* §§8.4, 12.4. The competitive long-distance business itself—as to which the Decree evinced a great deal of concern—had sprung into existence around privately owned switches—first those located on end-user premises and then ostensibly private switches operated by MCI.

rival providers to interconnect their CPE to the Bell companies' local networks.[56]

Judge Greene was in fact so confident about competition in CPE that he resolved to permit the RBOCs themselves to compete in the market in question; they could provide (though not manufacture) customer premises equipment.[57] Soon thereafter, however, in various rulings interpreting the Decree, Judge Greene began concocting an extensive new cluster of interconnection requirements for CPE. These decisions effectively extended the Decree's equal access mandates to all conventional forms of CPE.[58]

§5.2.1.3 Pricing

A description of the detariffing of CPE can be found at section 8.3. The pricing issue we are concerned with here is the amount a local exchange carrier (LEC) can charge for interconnecting a customer's own CPE to the LEC's lines. For ordinary residential handsets, this is a fairly simple matter. There is no charge. The

---

[56] *See* United States v. AT&T, 552 F. Supp. at 191–192, nn.244, 246.

[57] Order, United States v. Western Elec. Co., No. 82-0192 (D.D.C. Aug. 24, 1982). Judge Greene proceeded over the objection of the Department of Justice. Memorandum of the United States in Response to Court's Opinion of August 11, 1982, at 7 n.*, United States v. Western Elec. Co., No. 82-0192 (D.D.C. Aug. 19, 1982) ("The consent Decree, as written, only prohibits discrimination by the BOCs between AT&T and other enterprises, [not between RBOCs themselves and their direct competitors in the business of providing CPE.]"). This "drafting error," which barred the RBOCs only from discrimination between AT&T and AT&T's competitors, was corrected when the Department negotiated the subsequent GTE Decree, which prohibited GTE from discriminating "between the interexchange telecommunications services, information services, or customer premises equipment *of GTE* (including any information services of a GTOC) and the interexchange telecommunications services, information services, or customer premises equipment *of other persons.*" GTE Decree §V(B), United States v. GTE Corp., No. 83-1298 (D.D.C. Dec. 21, 1984) (emphasis added). Similarly, Judge Greene used the leverage of the waiver process to extract various additional equal access and nondiscrimination requirements from the RBOCs in intraLATA toll service (*see* §9.6.1), information services, mobile services, and foreign ventures.

[58] *See generally FTL1* §5.3.2 (detailing Judge Greene's subsequent interpretation of the Decree with regard to CPE).

customer simply pays for the line and can then hang all he likes on the back of it.[59]

With more complicated forms of CPE, pricing issues become more involved. PBX "DID" trunks, for example, have numbers associated with them, so charges can be loaded on the number in proportion to the amount of customer premises equipment hanging on the line. The FCC has also imposed special access surcharges on "leaky PBXs," private lines used to funnel interstate traffic into or out of the public local exchange.[60]

§5.2.2 Pay Phones

Since 1984, the FCC has treated pay phones like any other piece of customer premises equipment.[61] The Divestiture Decree assigned both coin-operated and credit card public telephones to the RBOCs.[62] The ink was scarcely dry on the Decree when, in February 1984, Pacific Bell declined to provide interconnection to coinless telephones that AT&T wanted to install at the Los Angeles airport during the 1984 Summer Olympics. Judge Greene found this contrary to Pacific Bell's responsibilities under the Decree because it interfered with a central premise of the Decree, that interexchange carriers should be allowed to interconnect to local exchanges without discrimination.[63] With this decision, Judge Greene began to cobble together a Decree-based set of interconnection rules for pay phones and other forms of CPE.

The 1996 Act completes the process of moving pay phones into the fully deregulated ambit of "customer premises equipment."

---

[59] In earlier times, "equipment located on customer premises—everything from handsets to mainframe computers—was provided only under lease, and then only grudgingly, with strict instructions that nothing was to be tampered with in any way." P. Huber, The Technological Imperative for Competition, in Future Competition in Telecommunications 105, 105–106 (Stephen P. Bradley & Jerry A. Hausman eds., 1989).

[60] 47 C.F.R. §§69.115(a), (b).

[61] See §8.4.4.

[62] See id.

[63] United States v. Western Elec. Co., 583 F. Supp. 1257 (D.D.C. 1984).

The 1996 Act gave the Commission nine months to establish comprehensive regulations to govern the provision of pay phone service,[64] and the Commission has done so. Not only did the Act permit Bell Companies to continue competing in the provision of pay phones, but also it authorized them, for the first time since divestiture, to act as agents for location providers in the selection of an interexchange carrier.[65] All pay phone providers, Bell companies included, are now permitted to bundle long-distance services with the pay phone itself and now pay the premises owners a fee (or collect one from them) based on the cost of the equipment and the levels of both local and long-distance usage. LEC pay phone operations are not required to be in a separate subsidiary, but certain nonstructural safeguards apply.[66]

§5.2.3   Pole Attachments

As we discuss in greater detail in Chapter 13, in the early days of cable there were numerous disputes between local telephone companies and cable operators over cable operators' ability to string their wires on the telephone companies' existing poles. The FCC took the first steps toward regulating this interconnection in 1970.[67] The FCC essentially required a telco to surrender control over its poles and conduits as a precondition to requesting permission to offer cable channel services.

In 1978, Congress enacted the Pole Attachment Act.[68] This legislation gave the FCC authority to regulate rates and terms of cable television pole attachments wherever states failed to impose such regulation themselves.[69] On this basis, the Commission established a mathematical formula for determining "just

[64] *See* 47 U.S.C. §276(b)(1).

[65] *See* 47 U.S.C. §276(b)(1)(D).

[66] *See* §8.6.3.

[67] *See generally* A. Siegel, The History of Cable Television Pole Attachment Regulation, 6 Comm. & the Law 9 (1984).

[68] 47 U.S.C. §224.

[69] *Id.* §224(c)(1) ("Nothing in this section shall . . . give the Commission jurisdiction with respect to rates, terms, and conditions for . . . pole attachments in any case where such matters are regulated by a State.") In the 1984

and reasonable" attachment rates[70] and set up a detailed complaint procedure to encourage private resolution of most disputes.[71] The Act did not provide an absolute right of pole access—access remained, in principle, a matter of contract negotiation.[72] In practice, however, cable companies have since been able to run wire to the doorsteps of over 90 percent of the nation's residences.[73]

As we discuss below (section 5.5.2.4), the 1996 Act expands even further the cable operator's ability to obtain access to the local exchange carrier's poles.

§5.2.4　Enhanced Services: Interconnection, Open Network Architecture, Comparably Efficient Interconnection, and Unbundling

The FCC's initial approach to information services was to lump them together with CPE in relation to interconnection obligations. Interconnection rules and tariffs for providers of information services evolved in lockstep with those applicable to providers of CPE.[74]

Cable Act, Congress also amended the Pole Attachment Act to provide that a state would not be considered to be regulating pole attachments unless it had issued rules and was acting promptly on complaints. *See id.* §224(c)(3).

[70] 47 C.F.R. §1.1409(c).

[71] *Id.* §1.1404.

[72] *See* FCC v. Florida Power Corp., 480 U.S. 245, 251 n.6 (1987) ("The language of the Act provides no explicit authority to the FCC to require pole access for cable operators, and the legislative history strongly suggests that Congress intended no such authorization.") (citations to legislative history omitted).

[73] National Cable Television Association, Cable Television Developments 1-A (Sept. 1991). In upholding the FCC's rural exemption, the D.C. Circuit explained that the opportunities for telcos to use control over pole attachments to gain a monopolist's premium from providers of cable services decreased with passage of the Pole Attachment Act. *See* National Cable Television Assn., Inc. v. FCC, 747 F.2d 1503, 1505 n.1 (D.C. Cir. 1984); *see also* Telephone Company-Cable Television Cross-Ownership Rules, Notice of Inquiry, 2 F.C.C. Rec. 5092, 5093–5094 ¶13 (1987) (discussing ameliorating effect of the Pole Attachment Act).

[74] *See* §12.5.1.

But as we discuss at greater length in section 5.4.2 below, the regulation went much further than that. Once computers and switches began to connect, it became clear that they could connect in a wide range of different ways. The CPE and information service rules metamorphosed into more general rules for "comparably efficient interconnection," then into rules for "open network architecture."

All the early interconnection orders were market specific. The very first ones were indeed device specific and are remembered by the name of the device itself—the Hush-A-Phone, for example. From the device, the Commission then generalized to a specific market—CPE, information service, competitive access providers, wireless operators, long-distance carriers. The 1996 Act completes the process—its unbundling mandates are stated in general terms and apply to any interconnector that seeks to provide a telecommunications service, a broad category indeed. Whether all interconnectors are entitled to the same rights under those statutory provisions and whether the statute imposes the same obligations in all geographical areas are still open questions facing the FCC.

§5.2.5 Interconnecting Long Distance to Local Wireline Carriers

The right of competitive long-distance carriers to interconnect their facilities with those of local exchange carriers first emerged through the hard-fought battles of the 1970s, which pitted individual long-distance carriers, most often MCI, against local exchange companies, most often AT&T's Bell Companies.[75]

When divestiture separated AT&T from local exchange operations, the Commission directed all local exchange carriers (not just the former Bell affiliates) to undertake equal access conversions.[76] From 1984 until 1996, equal access and interconnection

---

[75] See §9.3.2.

[76] MTS and WATS Market Structure Phase III, Report and Order, 100 F.C.C.2d 860 (1985); Investigation into the Quality of Equal Access Services, Memorandum Opinion and Order, 60 Rad. Reg. 2d (P & F) 417, 419 (1986).

rules evolved in parallel, and not always consistently, before the Commission and the Decree court. A third body of equal access regulation developed under the GTE Decree. Although the AT&T Divestiture Decree has been superseded by the 1996 Act on a going-forward basis, the Decree's equal access requirements and the law interpreting these requirements remain important today as the backdrop against which those rules were passed. Moreover, section 251(g) of the 1996 Act requires each local exchange carrier to continue to provide exchange access, information access, and exchange services for such access in accordance with whatever equal access and nondiscrimination requirements applied to that carrier on the date immediately preceding the statute's enactment until such time as those obligations are expressly superseded by Commission regulations.

Many of the unbundling and equal access mandates of the 1996 Act—discussed in section 5.5 below—will remain of principal interest to those concerned with the local-long-distance interface. These include provisions that address dialing parity, operator services, directory assistance, directory listings, signaling, and call routing and completion.

Tariffs for long-distance carrier interconnection to local networks have evolved in step with the interconnection rules. We survey those rules in section 2.3.3.2 and address them in more detail in section 9.4.

§5.2.6 Interconnecting Local Toll Networks to the Local Exchange

As recently as 1997, most states still allowed LECs to route all "1+" intraLATA toll traffic to themselves. To use another carrier, a customer had to dial an additional four digits (0 plus a three- or four-digit access code). LECs had the overwhelming share of the profitable intraLATA toll market in each of these states, and these revenues provided a substantial part of the surplus needed to provide subsidized local service to high-cost customers.

This was still true in some states in early 1999. But as discussed in section 5.5.2.3 below, section 251(b)(3) of the 1996 Act sets up a framework for migrating intraLATA toll markets into the same presubscribed-carrier regulatory framework set up for the rest of the long-distance market (the interLATA toll market) in the 1980s.[77] Moreover, the Supreme Court's 1999 decision affirming the FCC's jurisdiction to implement the 1996 Act has resulted in reinstatement by the Eighth Circuit of an FCC rule, 47 C.F.R. §51.211(a), requiring implementation of intraLATA dialing parity in all states in 1999. By the time the Eighth Circuit reinstated the rule, however, the FCC had issued an order extending implementation schedules by several months.

§5.3 Horizontal Connections to Local Exchange Services

The AT&T Divestiture Decree was written on the assumption that local competition was not feasible because local telephone operations were a natural monopoly. Equal access obligations within the monopoly would have been useless or worse. The old approach was to bar competitors from entering the local exchange market, forbid the "natural monopolist" from extending operations into adjacent markets, and regulate the price and terms of franchised services. "The local monopoly is a lawful one," Judge Greene declared in 1981.[78]

This clean, bifurcated economic model of competition natural and desirable above the local exchange and monopoly natural and desirable within it was quite elegant. It suffered from only a single defect: the model was wrong. All sorts of competition *were* possible within the local exchange. In the 1996 Act, Congress finally recognized this. But both state and federal regulators had been moving steadily in that direction much earlier.

---

[77] *See* §9.4.4.3.
[78] United States v. AT&T, 524 F. Supp. at 1352 n.65.

§5.3.1   Wireless-Wireline Interconnection

The FCC has over the years developed an elaborate set of rules to govern interconnection between wireline and wireless carriers.[79] These have required equal treatment of affiliated and unaffiliated wireless carriers; they have also extended to specific technical guidelines that must be offered whether or not used by the wireline LEC's wireless affiliate.[80] To facilitate enforcement of the equal interconnection requirements, the Commission has also imposed various separate subsidiary mandates.[81] Interconnection tariffs and contracts have evolved apace.[82] Many of the FCC's interconnection requirements were duplicated in waiver orders issued by the district court in its continuing oversight of the Decree, though those are now largely of historical interest.[83]

§5.3.2   Competitive Access Providers

In the 1980s, competitive access providers (CAPs) began providing access service to customers large enough to justify their own private connections. CAPs, which operate primarily in metropolitan business centers, have set up their own fiber-optic or

---

[79] See §10.5.

[80] See, e.g., The Need To Promote Competition and Efficient Use of Spectrum for Radio Common Carrier Services, Memorandum Opinion and Order, 59 Rad. Reg. 2d (P & F) 1275 (1986); The Need To Promote Competition and Efficient Use of Spectrum for Radio Common Carrier Services, Declaratory Ruling, 2 F.C.C. Rec. 2910 (1987); Amendment of the Commission's Rules To Establish New Personal Communications Services, Notice of Proposed Rule Making and Tentative Decision, 7 F.C.C. Rec. 5676 (1992). See §10.5.1.

[81] See §10.8.2. See also FTL1 §13.3.2 (describing Judge Greene's separate subsidiary requirements for BOC wireless operations). See, e.g., United States v. Western Elec. Co., 578 F. Supp. at 643 (waivers for interLATA BOC cellular services made contingent on the use of separate subsidiaries); Opinion and Order, United States v. Western Elec. Co., No. 82-0192 (D.D.C. May 14, 1986); Memorandum Opinion and Orders, United States v. Western Elec. Co., No. 82-0192 (D.D.C. June 20, 1986) (separate subsidiary requirements for out-of-region paging operations by BOC affiliates).

[82] See §10.5.1.

[83] See §10.8.2.

microwave systems to connect users to interexchange carriers' points of presence. It was not until the early 1990s, however, that the FCC took steps to guarantee interconnection to these new competitors.

In 1992, the Commission announced the adoption of rules permitting "expanded interconnection" for special-access (e.g., private line) customers of the CAPs and other bypass providers.[84] The Commission concluded that expanded interconnection should be made available to all parties who wish to terminate their own special-access transmission facilities at LEC central offices, including competitive access providers, interexchange carriers, and end users.[85]

In 1993, the Commission adopted expanded interconnection requirements for switched access services. This ruling, which again applied to all the largest (Tier 1) LECs,[86] mirrored the previously promulgated rules for special access. It required carriers to provide physical collocation upon request, although they were free to negotiate virtual collocation agreements. In return, local carriers were granted some limited pricing flexibility. Additionally, the terms under which a specific collocation arrangement was provided need not be made generally available except at the end office where it was offered.[87]

Several local exchange carriers challenged the physical collocation aspects of these expanded interconnection issues as exceeding the Commission's statutory authority. In *Bell Atlantic v. FCC,* the Court of Appeals for the D.C. Circuit struck down parts of the Commission's order.[88] Specifically at issue was whether the

---

[84] Expanded Interconnection with Local Telephone Company Facilities, Report and Order and Notice of Proposed Rulemaking, 7 F.C.C. Rec. 7369, 7381 ¶18 (1992).

[85] *Id.* at 7403 ¶65.

[86] A Tier 1 carrier is a LEC with sustained interstate revenues of at least $100 million. *See* Policy and Rules Concerning Rates for Dominant Carriers, Second Report and Order, 5 F.C.C. Rec. 6786, 6819 ¶260 (1990).

[87] Expanded Interconnection with Local Telephone Company Facilities, Second Memorandum Opinion and Order on Reconsideration, 8 F.C.C. Rec. 7341 (1993).

[88] *See* Bell Atlantic Tel. Cos. v. FCC, 24 F.3d 1441 (D.C. Cir. 1994). While not an express constitutional challenge to the order, the LECs' petition relied

Commission could properly order carriers "to establish physical connections with other carriers" under the authority of section 201(a) of the Communications Act.[89] The appellate court concluded it could not. Because the Commission's order appeared to constitute a taking under the Fifth Amendment,[90] the court strictly reviewed the claimed statutory basis for the action.[91] After undertaking that review, the appellate court concluded that the Commission's statutory authority to order "physical connections" did not empower the Commission to "grant third parties a license to exclusive physical occupation of a section of the LECs' central offices."[92] The court thus vacated the physical collocation aspects of the order and remanded the virtual collocation issues to the Commission.[93]

On remand, the Commission expanded its "virtual collocation" requirements, with physical collocation left as an option for local carriers if they preferred it.[94] Under the FCC's virtual collocation regime, interconnectors were permitted to specify the kind of equipment they wanted; LECs were then required to buy or lease that equipment and file a tariff to cover it.[95] The

---

heavily on the "takings" implications, under the Fifth Amendment, of physical collocation. *See id.* at 1444, n.1 ("[p]etitioners' brief, in places, appears to argue that even if the Commission had authority to impose physical co-location we must nonetheless decide whether that imposition inflicted a 'taking'"). This proved decisive to the court: the constitutional dimension of the case tilted the court toward a stricter review of the statutory issues. *See id.* at 1445–1447.

[89] 47 U.S.C. §201(a). The court did not reach the issue whether, even if the Commission had statutory authority to impose physical collocation, such collocation inflicted an uncompensated taking. "The Tucker Act, 28 U.S.C.A. §1491(a)(1), vests exclusive jurisdiction over takings claims that exceed $10,000 in controversy . . . in the United States Claims Court." Bell Atlantic v. FCC, 24 F.3d at 1444–1445 n.1.

[90] Bell Atlantic v. FCC, 24 F.3d at 1446–1447.

[91] *Id.* at 1445 ("statutes will be construed to defeat administrative orders that raise substantial constitutional questions").

[92] *Id.* at 1446.

[93] *Id.* at 1447. The court found that virtual collocation, which was permitted instead of physical collocation "in only two narrow circumstances," could not "survive our abrogation" of physical collocation itself.

[94] Expanded Interconnection with Local Telephone Company Facilities, Memorandum Opinion and Order, 9 F.C.C. Rec. 5154 (1994).

[95] *Id.* at 5170–5171 ¶¶49–50.

Commission reaffirmed that only physical collocation of circuit-terminating equipment in LEC end offices would meet all technical objectives.[96] Customers that had signed on for term discounts with LECs were to be offered a reasonable chance to take advantage of the new offerings.[97]

Several Bell companies again challenged the Commission's order in the D.C. Circuit.[98] In March 1996, a month after the 1996 Act was signed into law, the D.C. Circuit disposed of these petitions for review, noting that once the Commission issued regulations pursuant to the new Act, "any questions about the future effect of the [Expanded Interconnection Order] under review will be moot."[99] Because the Commission's order would be in effect until the new rules were promulgated,[100] the court remanded the Expanded Interconnection Order to the Commission in light of the 1996 Act.[101]

§5.4 Unbundling the Local Exchange: Developments, 1984–1996

Even as it continued to prescribe market-specific interconnection rules for competitive access providers, the FCC, soon followed by some leading states, began to develop a more general strategy of unbundling and interconnection. Much (but not all) of what follows in this section has been superseded by the (federally preemptive) unbundling and interconnection mandates

---

[96] *Id.* at 5159–5160 ¶12 ("If physical collocation is unavailable, however, we conclude that virtual collocation is the best alternative.").

[97] *Id.* at 5208 ¶204.

[98] Petition for Review by Pacific Bell and Nevada Bell, Pacific Bell and Nevada Bell v. FCC, No. 94-1547 (D.C. Cir. Aug. 10, 1994); Petition for Review, U S WEST Communications, Inc. v. FCC and United States, No. 94-1612 (D.C. Cir. Sept. 2, 1994).

[99] Pacific Bell v. FCC, No. 94-1547 (D.C. Cir. 1996).

[100] As the Commission noted at the time, section 251(g) of the new Act preserves equal access and interconnection obligations in place when the Act was passed until such time as the Commission alters such obligations.

[101] Pacific Bell v. FCC, No. 94-1547 (D.C. Cir. 1996).

of the 1996 Act. As we note at the end of this section, the Commission has also suggested repealing its open network architecture and comparably efficient interconnection rules on the ground that they have been superseded by the 1996 Act.

§5.4.1 *Open Network Architecture*

The FCC's first attempt at unbundling the core of the local exchange network was the open network architecture (ONA) proceeding of the late 1980s.[102] The objective here was to ensure that independent providers of online information services had access to key components of basic local phone service. Thus, although the unbundled elements under ONA plans were available to any type of competitor, the elements themselves were specifically designed for information service providers.

The FCC's *Computer I* order was that if phone companies were simply excluded from information service markets, interconnection would take care of itself under the normal tariffing process. A phone company excluded from this market would presumably have no incentive to make life difficult for "customers" in it. As discussed in the next sections, however, the FCC's *Computer II* and *Computer III* began the process of relaxing this policy of "maximum separation." In *Computer III,* the Commission directed LECs to unbundle their local networks and to interconnect with unaffiliated providers on the same ("comparably efficient") terms as they connected with their own information service affiliates. In exchange, the Commission eliminated structural separation for AT&T and the BOCs and permitted them to engage in the joint marketing of enhanced and basic services.[103] The Commission's ONA mandate was the

---

[102] Amendment of Section 64.702 of the Commission's Rules and Regulations (Third Computer Inquiry), Report and Order, 104 F.C.C.2d 958, 1086 (1986) (hereinafter *Computer III*), *vacated,* California v. FCC, 905 F.2d 1217 (9th Cir. 1990).

[103] *Id.* at 1012 ¶99.

genesis of what would eventually be transformed into the unbundling mandate (section 251(c)(3)) of the 1996 Act.

The Commission sketched the outlines of its program and left it to the BOCs to develop, in the first instance, detailed ONA plans in line with these general requirements. The plans themselves were then opened to public comment. In reviewing them, the FCC refined its requirements, but the general outlines of the program remained intact. BOCs were directed to offer unbundled "building blocks," known as basic service elements (BSEs), to outsiders under tariff.[104] All ONA services were to be available to any buyer.

Each set of basic services that a BOC incorporated into an enhanced service offering of its own was also to be made available to outsiders under tariff.[105] All basic network capabilities used by the carrier's enhanced service offerings, including signaling, switching, billing, and network management, were to be unbundled, and a BOC was to buy BSEs for its own enhanced service offerings on precisely the same tariffed terms as outsiders.[106]

The initial set of BSEs was to be based on expected market demand and the likely costs of unbundling them from existing services. BOCs were urged to consult with enhanced services competitors before filing their ONA plans.[107] Each ONA plan had to describe all of the "key" BSEs requested by outsiders and explain why they were or were not being provided.[108] BOCs would also have to lay out procedures for outsiders to follow in requesting new BSEs on their own initiative.[109] Within 120 days after receiving any complete written request for a new ONA capability, a BOC would have to indicate whether it would provide

[104] *Id.* at 1064 ¶214. The Commission concluded that such unbundling was essential to give outsiders an opportunity to use network services flexibly and economically and to deter possible discrimination. *Id.*

[105] *Id.* at 1064–1065 ¶215.

[106] *Id.* at 1040 ¶¶158, 159.

[107] *Id.* at 1065–1066, ¶217.

[108] Amendment of Sections 64.702 of the Commission's Rules and Regulations (Third Computer Inquiry), Memorandum Opinion and Order on Reconsideration, 2 F.C.C. Rec. 3035, 3056 ¶150 (1987) (hereinafter *Phase I Reconsidered*).

[109] *Computer III,* 104 F.C.C.2d at 1066 ¶217.

the capability and, if so, when and at what price.[110] Any party making the request would then be entitled to pursue the matter with the Commission. BSEs were to be offered under tariff. Some elements would be subject to dual state and federal jurisdiction, but to promote uniformity of structure and nomenclature among state and federal tariffs, the Commission established a joint state/federal conference to address the issue.

The Commission stressed that ONA was to be a long-term, developmental process, not a one-time alteration of the network.[111] The initial set of key BSEs was to be implemented within one year of approval of an ONA plan. But ONA plans would also include a schedule for the phased introduction of further capabilities.[112]

The BOCs duly filed initial ONA plans. The Commission approved some and disapproved others.[113] The BOCs then filed amended plans, which the Commission approved subject to certain further modifications.[114] The BOCs' "common model" (devised in collaboration with Bellcore) required all providers of enhanced services to obtain access to BSEs through tariffed switching and transport services described as basic serving arrangements (BSAs). Examples of BSAs include line-side and trunk-side circuit-switched service, line-side and trunk-side

---

[110] Filing and Review of Open Network Architecture Plans, Memorandum Opinion and Order, 4 F.C.C. Rec. 1, 208 ¶397 (1988) (hereinafter *BOC ONA Order*).

[111] *BOC ONA Order*, 4 F.C.C. Rec. at 200 ¶378. Thus, the FCC repeatedly emphasized that ONA "is a public policy, not a prescription of a particular network architecture. ONA should be 'technology-neutral'—its principles do not depend on the particular details of network technology. *Id.*

[112] BOCs would file three-year deployment schedules for their initial ONA services and include in these schedules, as feasible, other (i.e., noninitial) ONA services that they would introduce prior to July 1992. *Phase I Reconsidered,* 2 F.C.C. Rec. at 3055 ¶143.

[113] *BOC ONA Order*, 4 F.C.C. Rec. 1. AT&T also filed its own, streamlined ONA plan, as required in the *Computer II* Reconsideration Order. Amendment of §64.702 of the Commission's Rules and Regulations (Second Computer Inquiry), Memorandum Opinion and Order, 84 F.C.C.2d 50 (1980). That plan was approved with only minor adjustments on the same day.

[114] Filing and Review of Open Network Architecture Plans, Memorandum Opinion and Order, 5 F.C.C. Rec. 3103 (1990) (hereinafter *BOC ONA Amendments Order*).

packet-switched service, and various grades of local private line service. A provider was to order one or another of these services to access additional BSEs. Complementary network services (CNSs) were optional, unbundled BSEs, such as calling number identification or stutter dial tone. Ancillary network services (ANSs) included enhanced services offered by a carrier, such as protocol conversion, or other deregulated, non-common-carrier services, such as billing and collection. These were not technically BSEs at all.

In the *BOC ONA Order*, the Commission rejected these arguments and generally approved the BOCs' model. The Commission noted that while even more fundamental unbundling might ultimately be a socially desirable goal, it was premature at that time. "To require the BOCs to provide ONA based on a more disaggregated, and as yet unspecified, architecture," the Commission explained, "would be extremely costly and disruptive of the schedule that we have established for ONA implementation."[115] And in any event, any higher level of unbundling at that time would have raised the possibility of full-scale competition in providing basic local service, an issue that the Commission was not yet eager to address.

In the end, the open network architecture was so much sound and fury signifying nothing. With few exceptions, the BOCs sold no BSAs or BSEs to the enhanced service providers. The enhanced service providers did not want or need them after all.

§5.4.2 Comparably Efficient Interconnection

In addition to unbundling its basic services, carriers subject to the ONA obligations were required to provide competing providers with "comparably efficient interconnection" (CEI).[116] The BOCs and AT&T both had to provide competitors with

---

[115] *BOC ONA Order*, 4 F.C.C. Rec. at 42 ¶70.
[116] Amendment to Sections 64.702 of the Commission's Rules and Regulations (Third Computer Inquiry), Report and Order, 2 F.C.C. Rec. 3072, 3073 ¶2 (1987) (hereinafter *Phase II Order*).

access to basic services "comparable in efficiency" to the access they used themselves in supplying enhanced services of their own.[117] Competitors were either to be permitted to collocate their equipment on BOC premises or to be offered means of concentrating traffic to interconnect efficiently from a distance.[118]

The *Computer III* order required each BOC to make available to outsiders standardized hardware and software interfaces "able to support transmission, switching, and signaling functions identical to those utilized in the enhanced service provided by the [BOC]."[119] The technical characteristics of BSEs—including transmission speed, error rates, delays, reliability, abbreviated dialing options, and derived channel capabilities (such as Data-Over-Voice)[120]—were likewise to be offered on equal terms to all users, affiliated or otherwise. The Commission stated it would favor ONA plans in which carrier-affiliated providers used the same interconnection facilities as competitors. A carrier proposing to integrate its own enhanced services in basic service software or hardware, while requiring outsiders to interconnect in a different manner, would "bear a somewhat heavier burden" of demonstrating that its design satisfied the CEI requirements.[121]

But the Commission declined to impose any requirement of absolute equality. The "equal access" standard, the Commission explained, must be interpreted "in a reasonable and efficiency-promoting manner"; it does not demand "impossible or grossly inefficient over-engineering of the network so that absolute equality is always achieved."[122] In evaluating whether CEI had in fact been achieved, the Commission looked for any systematic differences in service access, end-user perceptions of inequality, or technical differences affecting the competitive position of outside providers.[123]

---

[117] *Computer III*, 104 F.C.C.2d at 1027 ¶131.
[118] *Id.* at 1036 ¶147.
[119] *Id.* at 1039 ¶157.
[120] *Id.* at 1041 ¶162.
[121] *Id.* at 1066 ¶218.
[122] *Phase I Reconsidered*, 2 F.C.C. Rec. at 3048 ¶92.
[123] *Id.*

The Commission anticipated that most enhanced services provided by the BOCs would be collocated with their basic network facilities. In light of problems relating to security, maintenance, and the availability of space, however, the Commission expressly declined to require BOCs to offer collocation to outsiders.[124] BOCs were required to minimize transmission costs for those providers instead.

The Commission likewise rejected requests that all outsiders be charged the same for interconnection, regardless of their networks' distance from a BOC's central office.[125] The Commission did not want to "destroy true efficiencies that may be available because of collocation or integration. . . . An averaging requirement would deprive consumers of opportunities to use highly efficient services at prices that directly reflect those efficiencies."[126]

None of the BOCs' ONA plans offered collocation to unaffiliated ESPs. Instead, the carriers agreed to charge themselves the same rates for access that they charged others. In evaluating these plans, however, the Commission recognized that precise price parity was impossible as long as noncollocated ESPs paid different amounts for access depending on their distance from the central office. The Commission therefore retreated from its strong stance against averaging and announced instead a "two-mile rule." Any provider, affiliated or unaffiliated, collocated or otherwise, was to be charged the same price for transmission if located within two miles of the central office to which it is connected. Beyond two miles, providers could charge distance-sensitive rates.[127]

Finally, the Commission addressed the costs of "common interconnection facilities" used by multiple providers of enhanced

---

[124] The Commission "found the space-availability issue particularly troubling, since in a competitive enhanced services market the demand for space in which to collocate may well outstrip the supply. This could be particularly true in urban areas, where available office space may be scarce and the enhanced services market may be quite active." *Computer III*, 104 F.C.C.2d at 1038 ¶152.

[125] *Phase I Reconsidered*, 2 F.C.C. Rec. at 3052 ¶121.

[126] *Id.* at 3053 ¶125.

[127] *See BOC ONA Order*, 4 F.C.C. Rec. at 86–88 ¶¶168–169, 171.

services. All providers were to be charged the same "Basic Inter-connection Charge."[128] A BOC providing enhanced services would pay this charge like all others, even if it used a quite different (and more efficient) form of direct, on-premises connection. By mandating averaged pricing here, the FCC aimed to encourage BOCs to deploy the most economic forms of interface facilities.[129]

§5.4.3 *Nonstructural Safeguards*

In addition to the ONA/CEI requirements, the Commission imposed several nonstructural safeguards in these proceedings.[130]

Both AT&T and the BOCs were required to file quarterly reports comparing service provided to their enhanced service affiliates with service provided to competitors.[131] The reports addressed the timing of installation and maintenance of basic services, as well as various quality and reliability parameters prescribed by the Commission.[132] The reports also described any complaints received from CEI users testing new CEI offerings.[133]

In its *Computer III* order and supplemental notice, the FCC tentatively concluded that the BOCs should also expand the role of "central operating groups" (COGs) to perform the same functions in the enhanced services market that they performed in the CPE market.[134] Subsequently, however, the Commission concluded that this was unnecessary.[135] It elected instead to require the BOCs, like AT&T, simply to "describe in their CEI plans the procedures they will utilize to ensure the nondiscriminatory pro-

---

[128] *Phase I Reconsidered*, 2 F.C.C. Rec. at 3051 ¶113.

[129] *Computer III*, 104 F.C.C.2d at 1051 ¶181.

[130] *See* §12.5.1.

[131] *Computer III*, 104 F.C.C.2d at 1055–1056 ¶192.

[132] *Id.*

[133] *Id.*

[134] *Id.* at 1056–1057 ¶193. *See* §8.4.3.2 for a description of the COGs process.

[135] *Phase II Order*, 2 F.C.C. Rec. at 3084 ¶87.

vision of basic services."[136] In subsequent proceedings, the Commission streamlined these procedures even further: BOCs could dispense with reports on service quality by demonstrating that they could not discriminate in the quality of service they provided to affiliated and unaffiliated vendors. In an amendment to its ONA plan, each BOC was required to describe how its provisioning procedures precluded discrimination. Thereafter, the BOC simply filed an annual affidavit, signed by the officer principally responsible for installation procedures, attesting that the company had not in fact discriminated with respect to the quality of the services it provides.[137]

In evaluating the BOCs' ONA plans, the Commission found that all but one of the BOCs had shown that their provisioning procedures precluded quality-based discrimination.[138] All used mechanized systems to assign equipment and facilities; the systems were programmed to assign automatically the next available facility in inventory. The systems were blind to the identity of the customer ordering service and contained no information about the relative quality of facilities in inventory except to classify them in accordance with standard descriptions and codings. Quality-based discrimination would thus be highly unlikely.

Each of the BOCs had likewise demonstrated that it assigned repair dates to customers using standardized procedures, which turned on such nondiscriminatory criteria as available work force and the exigency of a service problem. BOC personnel generally handled trouble reports on a first-come, first-serve basis. In this context, however, the Commission elected to retain the maintenance reporting requirement as a nonstructural safeguard and required each BOC to show total orders, due dates missed, and average intervals for each category within its installation and maintenance reports.[139]

---

[136] *Id.* at 3082 ¶73.

[137] Amendment to Sections 64.702 of the Commission's Rules and Regulations (Third Computer Inquiry), Memorandum Opinion and Order on Reconsideration, 3 F.C.C. Rec. 1150, 1160 ¶76 (1988) (hereinafter *Phase II Reconsidered*).

[138] The exception was Bell Atlantic, which was required to make a further showing in its amended plan. *BOC ONA Order,* 4 F.C.C. Rec. at 248–249 ¶481.

[139] *BOC ONA Order,* 4 F.C.C. Rec. at 249 ¶482.

§5.4.3.1   CPNI

Customer proprietary network information (CPNI) includes, with some exceptions, virtually all information about a customer's use of network services that a BOC may acquire in providing those services. (As we discuss in Chapter 14, section 222 of the 1996 Act defines CPNI and imposes various obligations on all telecommunications carriers to protect the confidentiality of such information.)

In the *Computer III*/ONA proceedings, the Commission adopted an asymmetrical set of rules governing BOC use of CPNI. The BOCs were not required to make CPNI available to outsiders absent a specific request from the customer that they do so. But the FCC specifically declined to adopt a "prior authorization" requirement for use of CPNI by the BOCs. The BOCs could make such CPNI available to their own enhanced service providers absent a specific request for confidentiality by the customer. Thus, either way, the customer had to take action to eliminate the asymmetry. And the customer, of course, generally does nothing. The Commission did, however, require BOCs to notify their multiline business customers—but not residential or single-line business customers—of these rights on an annual basis.[140]

The reason for this asymmetry was clearly stated. The FCC found that there was no easy way to provide equality of access to CPNI without either imposing broad restrictions on joint marketing, which would be inconsistent with the removal of structural separation, or, in effect, making CPNI generally available to all CPE vendors, which would be inconsistent with legitimate customer expectations about confidentiality. But the Commission concluded that the absence of a "prior authorization" rule would not give the BOCs any significant advantages over competitors. The Commission reasoned that "the most valuable information in marketing enhanced services is not CPNI, but comes directly from the customer, relates to its information pro-

---

[140] *Phase II Order*, 2 F.C.C. Rec. at 3096 ¶¶162–164.

cessing needs, and is equally available to both BOCs and ESPs."[141] Indeed, many ESPs already possess marketing information more valuable than CPNI, and the BOCs would be entering any enhanced service market with zero market share. "[A] customer's knowledge that the enhanced services market is competitive will result in the customer contacting competing ESPs, even if a BOC makes an initial enhanced service solicitation."[142]

The Commission concluded, however, that aggregated CPNI should be treated differently. It might prove valuable for targeting potential customers and for marketing enhanced services,[143] and it implicates no individual's expectation of privacy. BOCs were therefore required to disseminate this information to outsiders on the same terms and conditions, and at the same price, as to the BOCs' own providers of enhanced services.

§5.4.3.2 Network Disclosure

The FCC's network disclosure rules prevented BOCs from designing new network services or changing network technical specifications to the advantage of their own enhanced service providers.[144] BOCs were required to disclose information about changes in their networks or new network services at two different points in time. First, they were required to do so at the "make/buy" point[145]—that is, when a BOC decides to make itself, or procure from an unaffiliated entity, any product whose design affects or relies on the network interface.[146] Second, a BOC was required publicly to disclose technical information

---

[141] Amendment of Sections 64.702 of the Commission's Rules and Regulations (Third Computer Inquiry), Memorandum Opinion and Order on Further Reconsideration and Second Further Reconsideration, 4 F.C.C. Rec. 5927, 5929 ¶20 (1989) (hereinafter *Phase II Further Reconsidered*).

[142] *Id.*

[143] *Phase II Order,* 2 F.C.C. Rec. at 3097 ¶166.

[144] *Id.* at 3087 ¶107.

[145] *Id.*

[146] The network information subject to disclosure includes only network changes or new basic services that affect the interconnection of enhanced services with the network. *Id.* at 3087 ¶111. These network disclosure rules parallel those for CPE.

about a new service 12 months before its introduction. If the BOC could introduce the service within 12 months of the make/buy point, it was required to make a public disclosure at the make/buy point. In no event, however, could the public disclosure occur less than six months before the introduction of the service.[147]

§5.4.4   *Carriers to Whom the ONA Proceedings Applied*

In its *Computer III* order, the Commission concluded that the full panoply of ONA/CEI requirements should apply equally to AT&T. The Commission reasoned that AT&T was still sufficiently dominant in interexchange markets that it might otherwise engage in various forms of discrimination against competitors. On reconsideration, the Commission reaffirmed this conclusion, but decided AT&T would be allowed to rely on service-specific CEI plans.[148] Market restraints on AT&T's ability to act anti-competitively, the Commission now concluded, were sufficient to make complete ONA/CEI requirements unnecessary.[149]

AT&T's modified ONA plan would still have to describe capabilities available to transport basic service functions, how transport would be provided in a nondiscriminatory manner, what procedures would be used in responding to requests by local exchange carriers for new forms of transport, and how AT&T would implement CEI and other nonstructural safeguards.[150] Like the BOCs, however, AT&T would be allowed to avoid reports on the quality of basic services by demonstrating instead that its internal procedures precluded any quality-based discrimination and submitting an annual affidavit attesting to that fact.[151]

---

[147] *Phase II Reconsidered,* 3 F.C.C. Rec. at 1164–1165 ¶116.
[148] *Phase I Reconsidered,* 2 F.C.C. Rec. at 3042 ¶49.
[149] *Id.* at 3042 ¶¶46–47.
[150] *Id.* at 3043 ¶52.
[151] *Phase II Reconsidered,* 3 F.C.C. Rec. at 1151–1152 ¶6.

In its *Computer III* order, the Commission did not decide whether to apply *Computer III* requirements to independent LECs.[152] On reconsideration, it decided not to do so.[153] The independents, the Commission reasoned, lacked the BOCs' potential to engage in anticompetitive conduct. Though the independents had not been subject to *Computer II* separate subsidiary rules, no competitors had ever complained of any discriminatory conduct.[154] For all of these companies, even nonstructural safeguards might prove too burdensome and costly.[155] The Commission reserved the right, however, to revisit the question after implementation of ONA by the BOCs.[156]

In a December 1992 Notice of Proposed Rulemaking, the Commission proposed to apply the *Computer III* requirements to GTE.[157] Noting that its merger with Contel had made GTE the largest local exchange carrier by many measures, the FCC tentatively concluded that GTE should be subject to the same ONA requirements as the BOCs. The Commission also noted that the experience gained through implementation of BOC ONA plans made the imposition of nonstructural safeguards much less burdensome than would have been the case had these requirements been instituted initially.[158] The FCC made that conclusion final in 1994.[159]

§5.4.5 Judicial Response to the ONA Proceedings

The FCC's ONA decisions were repeatedly subject to judicial review in the Ninth Circuit.

---

[152] *Computer III,* 104 F.C.C.2d at 1027 ¶132.

[153] *Phase II Order,* 2 F.C.C. Rec. at 3099 ¶188.

[154] *Id.* at 3101 ¶202.

[155] *Id.* at 3101 ¶204.

[156] *Id.* at 3099 ¶188.

[157] Application of Open Network Architecture and Nondiscrimination Safeguards to GTE Corporation, Notice of Proposed Rulemaking, 7 F.C.C. Rec. 8664, 8664 ¶1 (1992).

[158] *Id. See also id.* at 8668 ¶16.

[159] Application of Open Network Architecture and Nondiscrimination Safeguards to GTE Corporation, Report and Order, 9 F.C.C. Rec. 4922 (1994).

The Ninth Circuit was first called on to review the FCC's *Computer III* decision.[160] Two arguments were placed before the court: (1) that the FCC acted arbitrarily and capriciously in relying on nonstructural, as opposed to structural, safeguards for the provision of enhanced services; and (2) that the FCC's preemption of state regulation of enhanced services violated section 2(b) of the Communications Act, which denies the FCC jurisdiction over "charges, classifications, practices, services, facilities, or regulations for or in connection with intrastate communication service by wire or radio of any carrier."[161]

In *California I,* the Ninth Circuit found that the FCC had not satisfactorily addressed either of these issues. The Commission had not adequately demonstrated that its new policy of relying on nonstructural safeguards instead of structural protections was a legitimate response to changed circumstances that allegedly diminished potential cross-subsidization issues.[162] While other justifications might exist for the FCC's new policy, the Commission had yet to articulate such reasons; accordingly, the matter had to be remanded.[163]

Turning to the preemption question, the Ninth Circuit focused its analysis on the Commission's assertion that dual regulation of enhanced services falls within the "impossibility" exception to section 2(b)(1) recognized by the Supreme Court's decision in *Louisiana Public Service Commission v. FCC.*[164] That exception, the Court noted, may be invoked only when state and federal regulation cannot feasibly coexist. The relevant question was thus "whether the FCC's regulation of interstate enhanced services would necessarily be frustrated by all possible forms of state-imposed structural separation requirements and by all state-imposed nonstructural safeguards that are inconsistent with *Computer III* requirements."[165] Enhanced services might be

---

[160] *California v. FCC,* 905 F.2d 1217 (9th Cir. 1990) (*California I*).
[161] 47 U.S.C. §152(b)(1).
[162] *California I,* 905 F.2d at 1237.
[163] *Id.* at 1238–1239.
[164] 476 U.S. 355 (1986) (*Louisiana PSC*). For further, more detailed discussion of *Louisiana PSC,* see §3.6.
[165] *California I,* 905 F.2d at 1243.

offered on a purely intrastate basis; the FCC had not explained how structural separation of such purely *intra*state enhanced services would interfere with a carrier's provision of *inter*state enhanced services.[166] Since the FCC had yet to carry its burden on that point, that issue, too, was remanded to the Commission.

The FCC's ONA proceedings returned to the Ninth Circuit in 1993 (*California II*).[167] That case did not involve review of the FCC's remand proceedings in the first case, but rather several post-*Computer III* orders in which the Commission, among other things, approved some specific ONA schemes.[168] MCI argued that in those orders the FCC "significantly altered, without reasoned justification, the scope and purpose of ONA as articulated in *Computer III*."[169] This change allegedly "dilute[d] the technical and regulatory standards that justified the FCC's decision to lift structural separation" in *Computer III*.[170] The FCC responded that it had not changed its policies: *Computer III* "did not impose any strict technological standards as a precondition to the lifting of structural separation," but rather "provide[d] the groundwork for what was to be a developing and evolutionary technological process."[171]

The Ninth Circuit found that the FCC had not implemented any significant, unexplained departure from prior ONA policy.[172] The appellate court did, however, reject the Commission's claim that ONA had always been intended as an evolving standard.[173] It agreed with MCI that the ONA plans as approved did not accomplish fundamental unbundling and that the FCC's approval

[166] *Id.* at 1244.
[167] California v. FCC, 4 F.3d 1505 (9th Cir. 1993) (*California II*).
[168] *See id.* at 1506 n.1 (the orders under review were *BOC ONA Order,* 4 F.C.C. Rec. 1; Filing and Review of Open Network Architecture Plans, Memorandum Opinion and Order on Reconsideration, 5 F.C.C. Rec. 3084 (1990) (hereinafter *ONA Reconsideration Order*); *BOC ONA Amendments Order,* 5 F.C.C. Rec. 3103; and Computer III Remand Proceedings, Report and Order, 5 F.C.C. Rec. 7719 (1990) (hereinafter *ONA Remand Order*)).
[169] *California II,* 4 F.3d at 1510–1511.
[170] *Id.* at 1511.
[171] *Id.*
[172] *Id.* at 1506.
[173] *Id.* at 1511.

of these plans constituted a change from its prior position that complete ONA was a prerequisite to the elimination of structural separation.[174] The appellate court did not, however, set aside the orders implementing ONA.[175] Those orders "did not themselves lift structural separation [or] explain the conditions under which [structural] separation [could] be lifted." The court was "aware that the FCC has since ordered the lifting of structural separation" again on remand from the court's *California I* decision, but noted that that issue was not currently before it.[176]

That issue was put before the Ninth Circuit in 1994 in *California III*.[177] On remand from the first Ninth Circuit case, the FCC had reinstated structural integration for the BOCs, but at the same time had revised in some respects the nonstructural safeguards it had originally proposed. On review this time, the Ninth Circuit concluded that the Commission had "adequately responded to the concerns we expressed in *California I* by increasing the nonstructural safeguards designed to prevent the BOCs from passing on the costs of their enhanced services to their telephone customers paying regulated rates."[178] But the Commission had retreated, without adequate explanation, from its prior position that only full ONA would prevent discrimination.[179] The FCC had argued that other regulatory safeguards (CEI, nondiscrimination reporting requirements, and network disclosure rules) would prevent access discrimination even without full ONA,[180] but had not satisfactorily explained why it had taken a different position in *Computer III*.[181]

---

[174] *Id.* at 1513.

[175] *Id.* at 1516.

[176] *Id.* at 1513.

[177] California v. FCC, 39 F.3d 919 (9th Cir. 1994) (*California III*).

[178] *Id.* at 923. Moreover, the implementation of price-cap regulation had also "reduce[d] any BOC's ability to shift costs from unregulated to regulated activities, because the increase in costs for the regulated activity does not automatically cause an increase in the legal rate ceiling." *Id.* at 926–927 (citing United States v. Western Elec. Co., 993 F.2d 1572, 1580 (D.C. Cir. 1993), *cert. denied,* 510 U.S. 984 (1993)).

[179] *California III,* 39 F.3d at 923.

[180] *Id.* at 929.

[181] *Id.*

The *California III* court did, however, conclude that the FCC adequately addressed the preemption issues raised in *California I*. On remand from that earlier decision, the Commission had proposed to preempt only state regulation of intrastate communications that would necessarily thwart or impede federal regulation. "The enhanced services market generally is national or regional in scope," the Commission cautioned, "and a degree of certainty and uniformity may be necessary to enable the enhanced services market to develop in the way that both state commissions and this Commission desire."[182] Thus, the Commission proposed to preempt state structural regulation that as a practical matter would prevent carriers from integrating their interstate operations.[183] The final order preempted any

> state requirements for structural separation of facilities and personnel used to provide the intrastate portion of jurisdictionally mixed enhanced services, state CPNI rules requiring prior authorization that is not required by our rules, and state network disclosure rules that require initial disclosure at a time different than the federal rule.[184]

The Commission declined to preempt any other state safeguards, but said it would review them, if necessary, on a case-by-case basis.[185] Since all enhanced services are likely to be "jurisdictionally mixed," the upshot of the Commission's decision was almost as broad as its initial preemption order. But by simply leaving to the states the onus of showing that any services for which they want to require separate subsidiaries are wholly intrastate, the Commission made its order impervious to attack on appeal. In approving the Commission's response on remand, the Ninth Circuit emphasized that the new FCC order was "narrower

---

[182] Computer III Remand Proceedings, Notice of Proposed Rulemaking and Order, 6 F.C.C. Rec. 174, 181 ¶47 (1990).

[183] *Id.* at 182 ¶50.

[184] Computer III Remand Proceedings, Report and Order, 6 F.C.C. Rec. 7571, 7630–7631 ¶121 (1991).

[185] *Id.* The Commission noted, for example, that states might require a separate corporate entity with separate books of account without thwarting federal objectives. *Id.* at 7632 ¶122.

than the order it issued in *Computer III*"[186] and that the Commission had thus "met its burden of showing that its regulatory goals of authorizing integration of services would be negated by the state regulations."[187]

After the Ninth Circuit struck down the Commission's revised *Computer III*/ONA rules, the Common Carrier Bureau issued an *Interim Waiver Order,* granting the Bell companies a waiver of the *Computer II* rules to enable them to continue providing enhanced services on an integrated basis under existing CEI plans.[188] In February 1995, the Commission opened a *Computer III* further remand proceeding to evaluate the nonstructural safeguards that were imposed on the Bell companies in the *Computer III*/ONA framework.[189] This proceeding sat idle for over two years. As discussed in the following section, the Commission has initiated a reevalution of its *Computer III* rules in light of the 1996 Act.

§5.4.6   *ONA and CEI After the 1996 Act*

The 1996 Act leaves undisturbed the Commission's ONA requirements, which will "continue to govern" the provision of data services by the Bell companies and other entities.[190] According to the Commission, these requirements remain "the only regulatory means by which certain independent [information service

---

[186] *California III,* 39 F.3d at 932.

[187] *Id.* at 933.

[188] *See* Bell Operating Companies' Joint Petition for Waiver of Computer II Rules, Memorandum Opinion and Order, 10 F.C.C. Rec. 1724 (1995) (hereinafter *Interim Waiver Order*). In October 1995, the Common Carrier Bureau denied petitions to reconsider its *Interim Waiver Order* and approved 12 CEI plans and 13 CEI plan amendments. *See* Bell Operating Companies Joint Petition for Waiver of Computer II Rules, Order, 10 F.C.C. Rec. 13,758 (1995).

[189] *See* Computer III Further Remand Proceedings, Notice of Proposed Rulemaking, 10 F.C.C. Rec. 8360 (1995).

[190] *See* Computer III Further Remand Proceedings: Bell Operating Company Provision of Enhanced Services, Further Notice of Proposed Rulemaking, 13 F.C.C. Rec. 6040, 6054 ¶20 (1998) (hereinafter *Computer III Remand Further Notice*).

providers] are guaranteed nondiscriminatory access to BOC local exchange services used in the provision of intraLATA information services."[191]

The ONA unbundling requirements have been almost wholly unused. Are they even legally necessary in light of the 1996 Act's unbundling requirements? Under section 251(c)(3) of the 1996 Act, LECs are required to offer unbundled network elements only to "telecommunications carriers." The Act defines a telecommunication carrier as a provider of "telecommunications services," which in turn is defined as the "offering of telecommunications for a fee directly to the public, or to such classes of users as to be effectively available directly to the public, regardless of the facilities used."[192] The FCC has concluded that Internet service providers (ISPs) are not providing telecommunications services.[193]

The Commission has, however, proposed to eliminate certain parts of the Commission's *Computer III* and ONA rules, including its ONA and nondiscrimination reporting requirements, network information disclosure rules, and rules governing the use of CPNI.[194] The Commission also sought comment on whether section 251 and the Commission's implementing regulations issued thereunder eliminate the need for ONA:

> For example, is ONA unbundling still necessary for ISPs that are also telecommunications carriers for whom Section 251 unbundling is available? As for pure ISPs, does the fact that they can obtain the benefits of Section 251 by becoming telecommunications carriers, or by partnering with or obtaining basic services

---

[191] Implementation of the Non-Accounting Safeguards of Sections 271 and 272 of the Communications Act of 1934, as Amended, First Report and Order and Further Notice of Proposed Rulemaking, 11 F.C.C. Rec. 21,905, 21,970–21,971 ¶134 (1996).

[192] 47 U.S.C. §§153(44), (46).

[193] Federal-State Joint Board on Universal Service, Report and Order, 12 F.C.C. Rec. 8776, 9180–9181 ¶789 (1997). This view was confirmed in the Universal Service Report to Congress. Federal-State Joint Board on Universal Service, Report to Congress, 13 F.C.C. Rec. 11,501, 11,522–11,523 ¶43 (1998).

[194] *Computer III Remand Further Notice,* 13 F.C.C. Rec. at 6085–6112 ¶¶78–124.

from competitive telecommunications providers, render ONA unnecessary?[195]

The Commission has yet to resolve these questions.

§5.4.7   State Unbundling Initiatives: 1984–1996

State regulators have traditionally controlled the core issues of local wireline competition. The traditional practice of such regulators was to protect the exclusive franchise and the universal service it engendered. But in recent years, states, one by one, began turning decisively against maintenance of local exchange monopolies. By 1996, leading states across the country were drafting aggressive unbundling mandates.[196] Six months before the 1996 Act was signed into law, 30 states had already allowed full competition for the provision of switched local exchange service or had in place some statutory mandate to open the local market to competition.[197] Another 12, along with the District of

---

[195] *Id.* at 6091 ¶95.

[196] Opinion and Order Concerning Comparably Efficient Interconnection Arrangements, and Instituting Proceeding, Opinion No. 91-24, Proceeding on Motion of the Commission To Review Telecommunications Industry Interconnection Arrangements, Open Network Architecture, and Comparably Efficient Interconnection, Case 88-C-004 (N.Y.P.S.C. Nov. 25, 1991); Order, Illinois Bell Telephone Company: Proposed Introduction of a Trial of Ameritech's Customers First Plan in Illinois, No. 94-0096 (Ill. C.C. Apr. 7, 1995); Michigan Telecommunications Act of 1995, S.B. 722 (Oct. 26, 1995); Entry, Commission Investigation Relative to Establishment of Local Exchange Competition and Other Competitive Issues, Case No. 95-845-TP-COI (Ohio P.U.C. Sept. 27, 1995); Order Instituting Rulemaking on the Commission's Own Motion into Competition for Local Exchange Service; Order Instituting Investigation on the Commission's Own Motion in Competition for Local Exchange Service, R.95-04-043 (Cal. P.U.C. Apr. 26, 1995); Order Instituting Investigation; Rulemaking on the Commission's Own Motion To Govern Open Access to Bottleneck Services, R.93-04-003, I.93-04-002 (Cal. P.U.C. Apr. 7, 1993).

[197] As of September 1, 1995, the 23 states that had authorized switched local exchange competition were Arizona, Connecticut, Georgia, Illinois, Iowa, Maine, Maryland, Massachusetts, Michigan, Minnesota, Montana, Nebraska, Nevada, New Mexico, New York, Ohio, Oregon, Tennessee, Texas,

Columbia, were investigating the possibility of competitive entry.[198] Two others did not forbid competition, but did not embrace it by statute either.[199] At most, five states (Alaska, Arkansas, Idaho, Mississippi, and South Dakota) remained committed to local monopoly.

New York was one of the first states to inject competition into local markets. In 1991, the New York Public Service Commission (NYPSC) ordered New York LECs to unbundle their loops and ports for all business and residential services.[200] This broke the local network into two basic, tangible components: transmission (the loop) and switching (the port). The 1991 order ultimately eschewed the elements or functions-based approach of the FCC's ONA proceeding in favor of a tangible, services-based approach. "[T]he LECs' networks," the NYPSC initially observed in 1989, "neither can nor should be immediately disaggregated to the last screw or wire."[201]

In November 1994, the NYPSC agreed to an Open Market Plan proposed by Rochester Telephone.[202] The plan created a

---

Utah, Washington, Wisconsin, and Wyoming. The seven states that had a legislative mandate to open the local exchange to competition were Alabama, California, Colorado, Florida, New Hampshire, North Carolina, and Virginia. *See* National Association of Regulatory Utility Commissioners, Report on the Status of Competition in Intrastate Telecommunications at tbl. 8 (updated and republished Oct. 4, 1995).

[198] These states were Hawaii, Indiana, Kansas, Kentucky, Missouri, New Jersey, Oklahoma, Pennsylvania, Rhode Island, South Carolina, Vermont, and West Virginia. *Id.*

[199] These states were Delaware and North Dakota. *Id.*

[200] Opinion and Order Concerning Comparably Efficient Interconnection Arrangements, and Instituting Proceeding, Opinion No. 91-24, Proceeding on Motion of the Commission To Review Telecommunications Industry Interconnection Arrangements, Open Network Architecture, and Comparably Efficient Interconnection, Case 88-C-004 (N.Y.P.S.C. Nov. 25, 1991).

[201] Opinion and Order Resolving ONA Issues on Adopting a Statement of ONA Principles, Opinion No. 89-28 at 8, Proceeding on Motion of the Commission To Review Telecommunications Industry Interconnection Arrangements, Open Network Architecture, and Comparably Efficient Interconnection, Case 88-C-004 (N.Y.P.S.C. Sept. 11, 1989).

[202] Opinion and Order Approving Joint Stipulation and Agreement, Petition of Rochester Telephone Corporation for Approval of Proposed Restructuring Plan, Case 93-C-0103 (N.Y.P.S.C. Nov. 10, 1994). Rochester Telephone

new holding company, Frontier Corporation, and two primary
subsidiaries, Rochester Telephone, a traditional LEC, and Frontier Communications, a lightly regulated reseller. Rochester Telephone retained all of the assets necessary to provide universal
local dialtone, including all network infrastructure. Rochester
was required to afford competing providers the "right to interconnect with the network facilities of [Rochester] at particular
central offices or tandems of their choice provided that
[Rochester] is accorded reciprocal interconnection rights to the
network of the requesting party."[203] These carriers were also
granted "non-discriminatory access to [Rochester's] bottleneck
network functionalities, services, and databases (including, but
not limited to, intercept, directory assistance, 911, E-911 and
SS7-related databases and services)."[204] The Rochester Plan unbundled not only loops and ports, but also various "functionalities" and "databases." But Rochester was to provide only local
services deemed noncompetitive by the NYPSC.[205] Those services would be provided on a retail basis to end users and could
be sold in bulk to independent retailers, including Frontier
Communications.[206] Rochester and its competitors were permitted to petition the NYPSC at any time to reclassify any service
as competitive.[207] If the petition was granted, Rochester could

---

has 513,000 local access lines. Frontier Corporation, Frontier at a Glance
(1995).

[203] Appendix at 44, Opinion and Order Approving Joint Stipulation and
Agreement, Petition of Rochester Telephone Corporation for Approval of
Proposed Restructuring Plan, Case 93-C-0103 (N.Y.P.S.C. Nov. 10, 1994). Ro-
chester was also required to form a Committee on Standards and Cooperative
Practices with carriers currently offering or planning to offer telephone ser-
vice in the Rochester region. See id. at 40–41.

[204] Id. at 45.

[205] The NYPSC initially categorized the majority of Rochester's existing
operations as noncompetitive. Id. at 29–30.

[206] Id. at 31; Frontier Reviews New Rochester Plan, Responds to AT&T
Complaints, Comm. Daily, Apr. 28, 1995, at 3.

[207] Appendix at 14–15, Opinion and Order Approving Joint Stipulation
and Agreement, Petition of Rochester Telephone Corporation for Approval of
Proposed Restructuring Plan, Case 93-C-0103 (N.Y.P.S.C. Nov. 10, 1994). The
plan clearly contemplated services migrating from monopoly to competitive,
but not the reverse.

transfer the facilities that provide the service to Frontier.[208] Following approval of the plan, Rochester began providing services to resellers, including Frontier, at a 5 percent discount from retail rates.

California took an even more aggressive approach. In 1993, the California Public Utilities Commission (CPUC) proposed a tentative list of "functions," "capabilities," and "resources" to be unbundled and listed "[a]ll transport, switching, call processing and call management capabilities" that a LEC might supply.[209] The Commission further identified "designated resources" used "to support the operations, management, service initiation, maintenance, repair, or marketing of the preceding network capabilities"[210] and "electronic service order entry and status systems," "diagnostic, monitoring, testing and network reconfiguration systems," and "traffic data collection systems."[211] In 1995, the California Commission issued an interim order detailing its first steps in the unbundling process. It described six network elements that "at a minimum" were to be unbundled by January 1, 1996: subscriber loops, line-side ports, signaling links, signal transfer points, service control points, and special-access connections.[212]

---

[208] *Id.* The NYPSC, for example, has deemed Centrex, high-speed data, and voice mail as competitive. *Id.* at 29–30. The NYPSC further broke down competitive services into either regulated or nonregulated services. The former included telephone answering services, voice mail services, and advanced communications services for Centrex, *id.* at 33–34, whereas the latter included terminal equipment sales, services, and leases; packet switching; and fiber-optic wiring services, *id.* at 32–33.

[209] Order Instituting Rulemaking and Order Instituting Investigation at 24–27, Rulemaking on the Commission's Own Motion To Govern Open Access to Bottleneck Services, R.93-04-003, I.93-04-002 (Cal. P.U.C. Apr. 7, 1993).

[210] *Id.*

[211] The CPUC suggested it was just following the FCC's ONA model. *Id.* at 17 (quoting *Computer III*, 104 F.C.C.2d at 1019–1020 ¶113). The Commission acknowledged that "some differences" would exist "because of a different weighing of concerns and local conditions." Order Instituting Rulemaking and Order Instituting Investigation at 44, Rulemaking on the Commission's Own Motion To Govern Open Access to Bottleneck Services, R-93-04-003, I.93-04-002 (Cal. P.U.C. Apr. 7, 1993).

[212] Order Instituting Rulemaking on the Commission's Own Motion into Competition for Local Exchange Service; Order Instituting Investigation on

The Illinois Commerce Commission (ICC) similarly issued an unbundling order requiring "incumbent LECs to unbundle their networks and to offer interconnection at all 'logical interconnection points,' including the interface between the feeder and distribution plant."[213]

In Michigan, the legislature passed a telecommunications bill with some modest unbundling provisions. Michigan LECs were required by July 1996 to unbundle loops and ports.[214] The Michigan Public Service Commission was also authorized to order additional unbundling.[215] By the year 2000, Ameritech and other Michigan LECs would be required to adjust their individual service prices "to ensure that the rates are not less than" the cost of providing the service.[216] LECs were required to align their rates "to reflect the existing variations in costs to provide basic local exchange services based upon differences in geographic areas, classes of customers, calling patterns and volumes, technology, and other factors."[217]

In September 1995, the staff of the Public Utilities Commission of Ohio released recommendations for the establishment of local exchange competition in the state.[218] Competing local providers would be free to define their own service areas, using established LEC exchanges as the basic geographical unit. Each incumbent LEC, *as well as any new facilities-based provider,* would be required to unbundle its "network and associated functionalities into the most reasonably disaggregated components capable of being offered for resale"[219] and make all tariffed services

---

the Commission's Own Motion into Competition for Local Exchange Service, R.95-04-043 (Cal. P.U.C. Apr. 26, 1995).

[213] Order at 99–100, Illinois Bell Telephone Company: Proposed Introduction of a Trial of Ameritech's Customers First Plan in Illinois, No. 94-0096 (Ill. C.C. Apr. 7, 1995).

[214] Michigan Telecommunications Act of 1995, S.B. 722 §355(b) (Oct. 26, 1995).

[215] *Id.* (loop and port unbundling is the "minimum" required).

[216] *Id.* §304A(1)–(2).

[217] *Id.* §304A(3)(C). The LECs were required to develop a variety of calling plans "that reflect customer calling patterns." *Id.* §304B.

[218] *See* Entry, Commission Investigation Relative to the Establishment of Local Exchange Competition and Other Competitive Issues, Case No. 95-845-TP-COI (Ohio P.U.C. Sept. 27, 1995).

[219] *Id.,* App. A at 11.

available for resale. The staff "recommend[ed] unbundling only upon a bona fide request."[220]

§5.4.8 The Department of Justice's Unbundling Initiative

While the Divestiture Decree was still in effect, the Department of Justice formulated its own prototypical unbundling model in negotiations with Ameritech.[221] In return for Department support of limited interexchange relief, Ameritech committed to unbundle its local network.[222] Shortly afterward Ameritech appeared to recognize that it had struck a bad deal and began to back away in anticipation of the 1996 Act.

The Ameritech model built on existing FCC orders, pursuant to which Ameritech had already unbundled local switching, trunking links, and tandem switching for interstate competitive access providers and had unbundled vertical services for enhanced services providers.[223] The new deal required Ameritech to make these unbundled services available to local competitors as well. Furthermore, SS7 "call set up" services were required to be offered on an unbundled basis to local exchange and access competitors using an interface at the signal transfer point (STP), under a separate, unbundled tariff.[224] Ameritech would allow exchange carriers "switch-to-switch integration" with Ameritech's

---

[220] Id.

[221] See FTL1 §6.3.4 (Supp. 1995).

[222] Proposed Order, attached to Motion of United States for a Modification of the Decree, United States v. Western Elec. Co., No. 82-0192 (D.D.C. Apr. 3, 1995) (hereinafter Proposed Order). The essential difference between the Rochester and Ameritech plans, according to EDS consultant Richard Levine, is that "[i]n one case [Rochester] it's unbundling the company, the other [Ameritech] is unbundling the network." V. Vittore, Rochester Telephone: Blueprint for Change, America's Network, Jan. 15, 1995, at 24.

[223] Petition for Declaratory Ruling and Related Waivers To Establish a New Regulatory Model for the Ameritech Region at A-9, Petition for a Declaratory Ruling and Related Waivers to Establish a New Regulatory Model for the Ameritech Region, DA 95-854 (FCC Mar. 1, 1993).

[224] Id. at A-3.

network,[225] and the switches would provide equal access for local as well as interexchange calls.[226]

The proposed deal also committed Ameritech to "loop and port unbundling."[227] A loop was defined as "the transmission facility between the network interface on a subscriber's premises and the main distribution frame in the serving central office";[228] a port "include[d] dial tone, a telephone number, local switching, local calling, . . . directory assistance, a white pages listing, operator services, and access to interexchange and intraLATA toll carriers."[229] The Proposed Order required Ameritech to offer access to unbundled and separately priced support functions, such as call completion, 611, 911, operator services, directory listings, and directory assistance.[230] Ameritech planned to offer those services "under reasonable, nondiscriminatory terms."[231] Other provisions of the Ameritech plan required a plan for implementing full number portability[232] and the provision (under reasonable terms) of access to telephone poles and other conduits.[233]

[225] *Id.* at A-4.
[226] *Id.* at A-5.
[227] Proposed Order ¶9(a), *attached to* Motion of United States for a Modification of the Decree, United States v. Western Elec. Co., No. 82-0192 (D.D.C. Apr. 3, 1995).
[228] *Id.* ¶1(m) (definition).
[229] *Id.* ¶1(n) (definition).
[230] *Id.* ¶9(e)–(f).
[231] *Id.* ¶9(f). The FCC said that the sum of the prices of the unbundled parts was required to be equal to or less than the price of a bundled network access line and that each was required to be individually priced above cost. This is, of course, impossible for any bundled service that is currently sold below cost. S. McCarthy, Ameritech Feels Heat on Open Network Plan, Telephony, July 3, 1995, at 8.
[232] Customers were to be given the ability to switch carriers and retain phone numbers without sacrificing functionality. Proposed Order ¶¶1(q) (definition), 9(g), 28, *attached to* Motion of United States for a Modification of the Decree, United States v. Western Elec. Co., No. 82-0192 (D.D.C. Apr. 3, 1995). Until full number portability was achieved, the interim solution would have permitted customers to retain their numbers when switching local exchange carriers. *Id.* ¶9(g).
[233] *Id.* ¶9(d).

§5.5 Unbundling the Local Exchange Under the 1996 Act

§5.5.1 General Duties of Telecommunications Carriers

Section 251(a) of the 1996 Act (1) imposes on every "telecommunications carrier" an affirmative duty to interconnect with other carriers and (2) enjoins all carriers from installing network features, functions, or capabilities that prevent telecommunications network interconnectivity. To the extent that a carrier is engaged in providing for a fee either domestic or international telecommunications, directly to the public or to such classes of users as to be effectively available to the public, the carrier falls within the definition of "telecommunications carrier."[234] We discuss these two requirements of section 251(a) in turn.

§5.5.1.1 Duty to Interconnect

Under section 251(a)(1), each telecommunications carrier has the duty to interconnect directly or indirectly with the facilities and equipment of other telecommunications carriers. In its *Local Competition Order,* the FCC found this meant that telecommunications carriers "should be permitted to provide interconnection pursuant to section 251(a) either directly or indirectly, based upon their most efficient technical and economic choices."[235] The duties of section 251(a) apply to all telecommunications carriers, although incumbent LECs may have interconnection obligations beyond part (a). The understanding that all carriers must permit some form of interconnection reflects the FCC view that "even for telecommunications carriers with no market power, the duty to interconnect directly or indirectly is central to the 1996 Act and achieves important policy objectives."[236]

---

[234] *Local Competition Order,* 11 F.C.C. Rec. at 15,989 ¶992. *See also* 47 U.S.C §153(49) (statutory definition of "telecommunications carrier").
[235] *Local Competition Order,* 11 F.C.C. Rec. at 15,991 ¶997.
[236] *Id.*

§5.5.1.2   Duty Not to Impede Network Interconnectivity

Section 251(a)(2) requires each telecommunications carrier not to install network features, functions, or capabilities that do not comply with the guidelines and standards established pursuant to section 255 or 256—the statutory provisions relating to access for persons with disabilities and coordination of technology standards. When the *Local Competition Order* was issued, the Commission had not developed standards or guidelines for section 255 or 256. Accordingly, the FCC found "that it would be premature at this point to attempt to delineate specific requirements or definitions of terms to implement Section 251(a)(2)."[237]

A proceeding to implement section 255 was, however, subsequently undertaken jointly by the Commission and the Architectural and Transportation Barriers Compliance Board as directed by the 1996 Act.[238] In its proposed rulemaking, the FCC stated that "Section 251(a)(2) [is] a straightforward extension of the notion that a telecommunications transmission should be virtually 'transparent' in terms of its interaction with customer supplied information. In the context of Section 255, that is, the telecommunications network should facilitate—not thwart—the employment of accessibility features by end users."[239] The goal of "transparency" in the network may not be unqualified, however. The Commission noted, "for example, [that] the bandwidth of any given service offering is limited, and accessibility enhancements that depend on information that requires more bandwidth than the selected telecommunications channel provides will likely be unreliable."[240] The FCC thus reached the tentative conclusion that "Section 251(a)(2) governs carriers' configuration of their network capabilities. It does not make them

---

[237] *Id.* at 15,991–15,992 ¶998.

[238] *See* Implementation of Section 255 of the Telecommunications Act of 1996; Access to Telecommunications Services, Telecommunications Equipment, and Customer Premises Equipment by Persons with Disabilities, Notice of Proposed Rulemaking, 13 F.C.C. Rec. 20,391 (1998).

[239] *Id.* at 20,422–20,423 ¶63.

[240] *Id.*

guarantors of service providers' decisions regarding how to assemble services from network capabilities, and it does not impose requirements regarding accessibility characteristics of the underlying components."[241] Finally, the FCC noted that "[i]t may be that the rules and policies for this complex area will have to be developed on an ad hoc basis as we gain experience resolving actual problems that arise under Section 255."[242]

Section 256 directs the FCC to implement procedures for oversight of coordinated network planning by telecommunications carriers and other providers of telecommunications service. It also allows for the development "by appropriate industry standards-setting organizations" of network interconnectivity standards for "A) public telecommunications networks used to provide telecommunications service; B) network capabilities and services for individuals with disabilities and; C) information services for subscribers of rural telephone companies."[243] In the *Local Competition Order,* the FCC said that it had asked the Network Reliability and Interoperability Council (NRIC) for recommendations on how to implement section 256.[244]

---

[241] *Id.* at 20,423–20,424 ¶65.

[242] *Id.* at 20,424 ¶66.

[243] 47 U.S.C. §256(b)(2)

[244] *Local Competition Order,* 11 F.C.C. Rec. at 15,992 ¶998. The Network Reliability and Interoperability Council is the successor to the Network Reliability Council that was first organized by the FCC in January 1992 following a massive 557 network failure. Then, as now, the Council was composed of CEO-level representatives of about 35 carriers, equipment manufacturers, state regulators, and large and small consumers. The Council's Charter was revised, and its title changed to the present Network Reliability and Interoperability Council, by the FCC in April 1996 to advise the FCC on how section 256 of the Telecommunications Act—"Coordination for Interconnectivity"—should be implemented. The NRIC's amended Charter asked the Council to provide recommendations both for the FCC and for the telecommunications industry that, when implemented, would assure optimal reliability and interoperability of, and accessibility and interconnectivity to, public telecommunications networks. The objective of the recommendations was to ensure the ability of users and information providers to transmit and receive information between and across telecommunications networks. A full history of the NRIC is available from the Office of Engineering and Technology, FCC, Network Reliability and Interoperability Council Page <http://www.nric.org>.

The NRIC's report was presented to the FCC in July 1997.[245] The key message of the report was that the Commission should let marketplace forces resolve most network interoperability issues as the nation tries to bring additional competition to the telecommunications industry. The Council made clear, however, that the FCC could not leave interoperability issues entirely to private activities. It called on the FCC to establish a list of national services for which there is a compelling need for interoperability. The Council also developed a set of tools to address specific interoperability issues. To address concerns about the potential of Internet usage to cause congestion on the public switched network, it developed an Internet Interconnection Specification Template to guide network planning between Internet services providers and common carriers who interconnect with them to deliver Internet services to end users. To improve access to telecommunications standard-setting processes by individuals with disabilities and consumers in rural areas, the Council developed recommendations for the standards organizations, the FCC, and those communities.

Although the FCC has not implemented formal rulemaking procedures based on the NRIC report, it has established a Network Reliability and Interoperability Home Page to promote coordination for interconnectivity. The page provides links to standards-related organizations and information to assist in accomplishing access and interoperability objectives.[246]

§5.5.2   General Duties of All Local Exchange Carriers

Under section 251(b), every "local exchange carrier" has a duty (1) to permit resale of its services without unreasonable or

---

[245] NRIC Network Interoperability: The Key to Competition (July 15, 1997). This report is available at the Office of Engineering and Technology, FCC, Network Reliability and Interoperability Home Page <http://www.nric. org>.
[246] See Office of Engineering and Technology, FCC, Network Reliability and Interoperability Home Page <http://www.fcc.gov/oet/network/>.

discriminatory conditions; (2) to provide number portability; (3) to provide dialing parity and nondiscriminatory access to telephone numbers, operator services, directory assistance, and directory listings; (4) to afford access to poles, ducts, conduits, and rights-of-way; and (5) to establish reciprocal compensation arrangements for the transport or termination of telecommunications. The term "local exchange carrier" is defined to include those who provide both exchange services and exchange access. It does not, however, include providers of commercial mobile services unless the FCC specifically concludes that such service providers should be included.[247]

§5.5.2.1 Resale

Section 251(b)(1) imposes a duty on all LECs to offer certain services for resale. It requires LECs "not to prohibit, and not to impose unreasonable or discriminatory conditions or limitations on, the resale of its telecommunications services."[248]

As the Commission has noted, the resale obligations of all LECs are different from the obligation of incumbent LECs under section 251(c)(4), which we discuss in detail below at section 5.5.3.6. The obligations that apply to all LECs under section 251(b)(1) apply to more services. They require the resale of *all* telecommunications services offered by the carrier.[249] In contrast, section 251(c)(4), by its terms, applies exclusively to telecommunications services that a carrier provides at retail to subscribers who are not telecommunications carriers.[250]

On the other hand, unlike section 251(c)(4), section 251(b)(1) does not contain a pricing requirement—it does not specify that services must be made available for resale at any particular rate or pursuant to any particular methodology. As the Commission concluded, "[T]he 1996 Act does not impose wholesale pricing requirements on nonincumbent LECs."[251]

---

[247] 47 U.S.C. §153(44).
[248] *See also* 47 C.F.R. §51.603(a).
[249] *See also id.*
[250] *See also* 47 C.F.R. §51.605(a).
[251] *Local Competition Order,* 11 F.C.C. Rec. at 15,981 ¶976.

The limitation on "unreasonable or discriminatory conditions or limitations" does, however, apply in both instances, and it is discussed below in section 5.5.3.6.

§5.5.2.2 Number Portability

Section 251(b)(2) requires all LECs to provide "to the extent technically feasible, number portability in accordance with requirements" that the Commission shall prescribe. The 1996 Act defines "number portability" as "the ability of users of telecommunications services to retain, at the same location, existing telecommunications numbers without impairment of quality, reliability, or convenience when switching from one telecommunications carrier to another."[252]

In June 1996, the Commission issued its *First Number Portability Order*.[253] Under that order, all LECs were to begin the phased deployment of a long-term service provider portability method in the 100 largest Metropolitan Statistical Areas (MSAs) no later than October 1, 1997, and to complete deployment in those MSAs by December 31, 1998.[254] Number portability was to be provided in these areas by all LECs to all requesting telecommunications carriers, including commercial mobile radio services (CMRS) providers.[255]

After December 31, 1998, each LEC must make number portability available within six months after receiving a specific request by another telecommunications carrier in areas outside

---

[252] *See* 47 U.S.C. §153(30). In its Notice of Proposed Rulemaking, the FCC defined three types of number portability: (1) service provider—the ability to retain one's number when changing service providers, (2) service—the ability to retain one's number when changing services, and (3) location—the ability to retain one's number when changing physical locations. Telephone Number Portability, Notice of Proposed Rulemaking, 10 F.C.C. Rec. 12,350, 12,355–12,356 ¶13 (1995).

[253] Telephone Number Portability, First Report and Order and Further Notice of Proposed Rulemaking, 11 F.C.C. Rec. 8352 (1996) (hereinafter *First Number Portability Order*).

[254] 47 C.F.R. §52.23(b).

[255] *First Number Portability Order*, 11 F.C.C. Rec. at 8357 ¶6.

the 100 largest areas MSAs in which the requesting carrier is operating or plans to operate.[256]

Rather than mandating a particular technology for the provision of long-term number portability, the Commission adopted a flexible, technology-neutral approach. The Commission determined that it was unnecessary to mandate a particular technology because there was sufficient momentum in the industry toward the deployment of compatible methods nationwide.[257] In addition, the Commission found that there was insufficient information on the record to select one of the proposed long-term methods and that referring the issue to an industry body for a recommendation would likely delay implementation of number portability that was already under way in several states.[258] The Commission also noted that dictating a particular method of number portability might stifle innovation by foreclosing the ability of carriers to improve on methods already being deployed or to implement compatible hybrid methods.[259] The Commission did however, adopt nine criteria that any long-term number portability method must satisfy.[260]

---

[256] *Id.* at 8394 ¶80; 47 C.F.R. §52.23(c).

[257] *First Number Portability Order,* 11 F.C.C. Rec. at 8377 ¶46.

[258] *Id.*

[259] *Id.*

[260] Those criteria were that any method must (1) support existing network services, features, and capabilities; (2) efficiently use numbering resources; (3) not require end users to change their telecommunications numbers; (4) not require telecommunications carriers to rely on databases, other network facilities, or services provided by other telecommunications carriers in order to route calls to the proper termination point; (5) not result in unreasonable degradation in service quality or network reliability when implemented; (6) not result in any degradation of service quality or network reliability when customers switch carriers; (7) not result in any carrier having a proprietary interest; (8) be able to accommodate location and service portability in the future; and (9) have no significant adverse impact outside the areas where portability is deployed. *Id.* at 8373–8374 ¶41. The Commission removed the fourth criterion in its reconsideration order. Telephone Number Portability, First Memorandum Opinion and Order on Reconsideration, 12 F.C.C. Rec. 7236, 7247 ¶19 (1997) (hereinafter *First Number Portability Reconsideration Order*).

The Commission further concluded that until long-term service portability is available, all LECs must provide currently available interim number portability measures—methods such as remote call forwarding and direct inward dialing—as soon as reasonably possible after a specific request from another carrier. CMRS providers did not need to provide such measures because of technical considerations specific to that industry.[261]

In the same order, the Commission enunciated cost recovery principles designed to ensure that costs of currently available interim number portability measures were borne by all telecommunications carriers on a competitively neutral basis. States could employ various cost recovery mechanisms so long as they were consistent with these overarching principles.[262] The Commission determined that a "competitively neutral" cost recovery mechanism must satisfy two criteria. First, such a cost recovery mechanism should not give one service provider an appreciable incremental cost advantage over another service provider when competing for a specific subscriber. In other words, the incremental payment made by a new entrant for winning a customer cannot put the new entrant at an appreciable cost disadvantage relative to any other carrier that could serve that customer.[263] Second, such a cost recovery mechanism should not have a disparate effect on the ability of competing service providers to earn normal returns on their investment. If, for example, the total costs of currently available number portability were to be divided equally among four competing local exchange carriers, including both the incumbent LEC and three new entrants, the new entrant's share of the cost may have been so large, relative to its expected profits, that the entrant would decide not to enter the market. In contrast, recovering the costs of currently available number portability from all carriers based on each local exchange carrier's relative number of active telephone numbers would not violate this criterion, since the amount to be recovered

---

[261] *First Number Portability Order,* 11 F.C.C. Rec. at 8356 ¶6.

[262] *Id.* These initial cost-recovery criteria applied only to the interim portability measures. Once long-term number portability standards were in place, a different cost-recovery regime would also be installed. *Id.* at 8415 ¶121.

[263] *Id.* at 8420 ¶132.

from each carrier would increase with the carrier's size, measured in terms of active telephone numbers or some other measure of carrier size.[264] While the FCC's initial order mandated number portability, the Commission declined to require provision of either service or location portability.[265]

In its subsequent *First Number Portability Reconsideration Order*,[266] the FCC addressed two major issues. The Commission concluded that query on release (QOR)[267] was not an acceptable long-term number portability method.[268] The Commission also adjusted certain implementation schedules for number portability.[269]

In its *Second Number Portability Order*,[270] the Commission adopted, with certain modifications, the recommendations that were made by the North American Numbering Council (NANC) pursuant to the FCC's request in its *First Number Portability Order.* Specifically, the FCC (1) adopted the NANC's recommendation that seven regional number portability databases be established, coinciding with the boundaries of the seven original BOC regions; (2) adopted the NANC's recommendation that Lockheed Martin IMS and Perot Systems, Inc., serve as the administrators for the regional number portability databases; (3) adopted the technical and operational standards proposed by the NANC for the provision of number portability by wireline carriers; (4) required that the carrier immediately preceding the terminating

---

[264] *Id.* at 8421 ¶135.

[265] For a description of service or location portability, see 47 U.S.C. §153(30).

[266] 12 F.C.C. Rec. 7236.

[267] QOR determines under what circumstances a database query is performed. Under QOR, the signaling used to set up a telephone call is routed to the end office switch to which the dialed telephone number was originally assigned (the release switch), i.e., according to the NPA-NXX (access code) of the dialed number. If the dialed number has been transferred to another carrier's switch, the previous switch in the call path queries the database to obtain the routing information. The call is then completed to the new carrier's switch. *First Number Portability Order,* 11 F.C.C. Rec. at 8361 ¶17.

[268] *Number Portability Reconsideration Order,* 12 F.C.C. Rec. at 7265–7266 ¶47.

[269] *Id.* at 7283 ¶78 (extending deadlines for wireline number portability); *but see id.* at 7312 ¶134 (affirming deadlines for wireless portability).

[270] Telephone Number Portability, Second Report and Order, 12 F.C.C. Rec. 12,281 (1997) (hereinafter *Second Number Portability Order*).

local exchange carrier be responsible for ensuring that number portability databases are queried; (5) permitted LECs to block calls that have not been queried when failure to do so is likely to impair network reliability; (6) directed the NANC to complete and submit to the Commission recommendations on the sharing of numbering information between the regional number portability database administrators and the North American Numbering Plan Administrator; (7) directed the NANC to develop standards and procedures regarding the provision of number portability by CMRS providers; (8) adopted, on an interim basis only, the NANC's recommendation that the regional limited liability companies (LLCs), already established by carriers in each of the original BOC regions, manage and oversee the local number portability administrators, subject to review by the NANC; (9) directed the NANC to provide national-level oversight of local number portability administration; and (10) adopted the NANC's recommendation that the Commission create a committee to oversee number portability deployment in the top 100 MSAs.[271]

The *Third Number Portability Order* again addressed how telecommunications carriers could recover the costs of implementing long-term number portability.[272] As with interim portability,[273] the Commission adopted requirements to ensure that the costs of establishing number portability were borne by all telecommunications carriers in a way that put no carrier at a competitive disadvantage.[274] The Commission also decided that the shared industry costs of number portability, such as the costs associated with building and operating regional number portability databases, would be generally allocated to all common carriers based on the companies' intrastate, interstate, and international end-user telecommunications revenues for each region.[275] Incumbent

---

[271] *Id.* at 12,283 ¶3.

[272] Telephone Number Portability, Third Report and Order, 13 F.C.C. Rec. 11,701 (1998) (hereinafter *Third Number Portability Order*).

[273] 47 C.F.R. §52.9

[274] *Third Number Portability Order,* 13 F.C.C. Rec. at 11,719–11,720 ¶28.

[275] *Id.* at 11,745–11,746 ¶¶87–92, 11,754–11,757 ¶¶105–110, 11,761 ¶¶116–117.

local telephone companies were permitted, but not required, to recover costs directly related to providing long-term number portability through a monthly end-user charge that would be subject to review by the Commission, but such a charge could start no earlier than February 1, 1999, and could last no longer than five years.[276] Only consumers in areas where number portability is available could be assessed such a charge.[277] Finally, the Commission found that carriers other than incumbent local telephone companies, including wireless carriers and competitive local telephone companies, could recover costs directly related to providing long-term number portability in any lawful manner.[278]

In October 1998, the Commission adopted a *Second Number Portability Reconsideration Order.*[279] That order clarified that all LECs must discontinue using interim number portability methods in areas where a long-term number portability method had been implemented.[280] It also rejected a Nextel request that the Commission establish an industry committee to develop a single, nationwide number portability methodology[281] and declined to adopt an SBC Communications proposal that the Commission decide not to consider location portability until service provider number portability is deployed in the 100 largest MSAs.[282] Finally, the FCC directed further NANC investigation of the technical feasibility for all carriers to implement 500/900 portability,[283] redefined "covered SMR" to apply more specifically to those services that compete with wireless and wireline providers in the two-way, real-time voice market,[284] and rejected a request for preemption of state number portability requirements for CMRS carriers.[285]

---

[276] *Id.* at 11,776 ¶142.

[277] *Id.* at 11,776–11,777 ¶143.

[278] *Id.* 11,774 ¶136.

[279] Telephone Number Portability, Second Memorandum Opinion and Order on Reconsideration, 13 F.C.C. Rec. 21,204 (1998) (hereinafter *Second Number Portability Reconsideration Order*).

[280] *Id.* at 21,211–21,212 ¶16.

[281] *Id.* at 21,218 ¶25.

[282] *Id.* at 21,219–21,220 ¶29.

[283] *Id.* at 21,224–21,225 ¶41.

[284] *Id.* at 21,228 ¶51.

[285] *Id.* at 21,233–21,234 ¶63.

In December 1998, the Common Carrier Bureau issued the *Number Portability Cost Classification Order.*[286] In that order, the Bureau provided guidance to LECs regarding the tariffs they may file for recovery of long-term number portability costs.[287] The Bureau adopted a two-part test for identification of the implementation provision of telephone number portability, that is, eligible local number portability costs. "[T]o demonstrate that costs are eligible for recovery through the federal charges recovery mechanism, a carrier must show that these costs: (1) would not have been incurred by the carrier 'but for' the implementation of number portability; *and* (2) were incurred 'for the provision of' number portability service."[288] Additionally, the Bureau addressed the portion of joint costs that LECs can treat as carrier-specific costs directly related to providing number portability and prescribed a method for apportioning these costs among number portability and non-number-portability services.[289] Third, the Bureau provided guidance on the allocation of eligible costs among various local number portability charges, that is, end-user charges and prearranged and default query charges.[290] Finally, the Bureau adopted guidelines for LECs and other interested parties on the cost support that must be provided in the LEC tariff filings.[291]

---

[286] Telephone Number Portability Cost Classification Proceeding, Memorandum Opinion and Order, CC Docket No. 95-116 (Dec. 14, 1998) (hereinafter *Number Portability Cost Classification Order*). The Common Carrier Bureau set out the policies and procedures in the *Number Portability Cost Classification Order* pursuant to authority delegated by the Commission in the *Third Number Portability Order. See Third Number Portability Order,* 13 F.C.C. Rec. at 11,740 ¶75.

[287] *Third Number Portability Order,* 13 F.C.C. Rec. at 11,740 ¶72.

[288] *Number Portability Cost Classification Order* ¶10.

[289] *See id.* ¶¶23–24 ("We interpret the Commission's language regarding incremental costs as requiring that incumbent LECs subtract the costs of an item without the telephone number portability functionality from the total costs of that item with the telephone number portability functionality. Only the difference, the incremental cost incurred for the provision of portability, is an eligible long-term number portability cost.").

[290] *See id.* ¶¶40–42.

[291] *See id.* ¶¶48–54.

§5.5.2.3 Local Dialing Parity

Section 251(b)(3) requires all local exchange carriers to "provide dialing parity to competing providers of telephone exchange service and telephone toll service." Congress has defined dialing parity as meaning "that a person that is not an affiliate of a local exchange carrier is able to provide telecommunications services in such a manner that customers have the ability to route automatically, without the use of any access code, their telecommunications to the telecommunications service provider of the customer's designation from among 2 or more telecommunications service providers."[292] The statutory dialing parity requirements apply not only to telephone toll services (discussed above in section 5.2.5), but also to "telephone exchange services."[293] The Commission has required LECs to permit telephone exchange service customers within a defined local calling area to dial the same number of digits to make a local telephone call, notwithstanding the identity of a customer's or the called party's local telephone service provider.[294] This mandate ensures that "customers of competitive service providers are not required to dial additional access codes or personal identification numbers in order to make local telephone calls."[295] In reaching that conclusion, the Commission rejected the position, advocated by Ameritech, that Congress intended only to preclude the use of access codes and did not intend to preclude the dialing of extra digits. The Commission interpreted Congress's prohibition against "the use of any access code" as encompassing the dialing of any extra digits, since "consumers would not perceive a functional difference between having to dial extra digits and having to dial an access code when using a competing provider's services."[296]

---

[292] 47 U.S.C. §153(15).
[293] 47 U.S.C. §251(b)(3).
[294] *See also* 47 C.F.R. §51.207.
[295] Implementation of the Local Competition Provisions of the Telecommunications Act of 1996, Second Report and Order and Memorandum Opinion and Order, 11 F.C.C. Rec. 19,392, 19,428 ¶64 (1996) (hereinafter *Second Local Competition Order*).
[296] *Id.*

The Commission refused to implement a specific timetable for LECs to implement the local dialing parity requirements, noting its "expectation that local dialing parity will be achieved through LECs' compliance with other section 251 requirements."[297] The Commission also declined to prescribe guidelines addressing the precise methods, such as presubscription, that LECs must use to accomplish local dialing parity. It stated instead that it "anticipate[d] that local dialing parity will be achieved upon implementation of the number portability and interconnection requirements of section 251."[298]

The Commission further declined to adopt rules that ensure that local calling areas are consistently defined for LEC wholesale and retail services. It did, however, make clear that the number of digits that had to be dialed did not necessarily define whether a call was local or toll. A competing local exchange carrier would therefore not be required to "define its local calling area to match the local calling area of an incumbent LEC."[299]

The Commission did adopt "national rules" for LECs to recover the costs of implementing dialing parity "in order to ensure that dialing parity is implemented in a pro-competitive manner."[300] The Commission determined that these rules should mirror those adopted for number portability, since "[m]any of the network upgrades necessary to achieve dialing parity, such as switch software upgrades, are similar to those required for number portability."[301] The Commission accordingly ruled that the rates for dialing parity should be recovered on a competitively neutral basis.[302] Moreover, the Commission stated that LECs could recover only the incremental costs of implementing number portability, which could include "dialing parity-specific

---

[297] *Id.* at 19,429 ¶68.
[298] *Id.* at 19,430 ¶71.
[299] *Id.* at 19,432 ¶75.
[300] *Id.* at 19,440 ¶92.
[301] *Id.* at 19,440 ¶93.
[302] *Id.* Section 251(e)(2) of the 1996 Act states that "the cost of establishing . . . number portability shall be born by all telecommunications carriers on a competitively neutral basis, as determined by the Commission." This statutory provision does not apply to the dialing parity requirement. *Id.* at 19,441 n.225.

switch software, any necessary hardware and signaling system upgrades, and consumer education costs that are strictly necessary to implement dialing parity."[303] These costs must be recovered from all providers of telephone exchange service and telephone toll service[304] in the area served by a LEC, including that LEC, using a competitively neutral allocator established by the state.[305]

In August 1997, the Eighth Circuit, acting in a companion case to *Iowa Utilities*,[306] vacated the FCC's dialing parity rules[307] insofar as those rules applied to intrastate intraLATA services.[308] In reasoning that echoed its *Iowa Utilities* decision, the court relied chiefly on section 2(b)'s proscription on FCC regulation of intrastate services—a proscription that, in the court's view, was not overturned as to dialing parity by any language in new section 251 of the Act. Accordingly, the court held that the Commission did not have the jurisdiction to regulate this matter[309] and concluded that section 2(b) applied here even though the 1996 Act dialing parity rules apply to intraLATA calls, not intrastate calls. Because "approximately 98% of intraLATA calls (local or toll) are intrastate," the court held that "Section 2(b) remains an obstacle" to FCC authority in this area, to the extent the calls at issue are intrastate.[310]

---

[303] *Id.* at 19,441–19,442 ¶95.

[304] By contrast, under section 251(e)(2), number portability costs must be recovered from all telecommunications carriers, a broader class. *Id.* at 19,442 ¶95. *See also* 47 C.F.R. §51.215(a).

[305] "States may use any of the allocators described in the Number Portability Order, or any other allocator that meets the criteria we have established. States should apply the principles we adopt today, and the other guidelines for recovering costs of currently available number portability measures, in establishing more specific cost recovery requirements for dialing parity." *Id.* at 19,442 ¶95. *See also* 47 C.F.R. §§51.215(a)–(b).

[306] Iowa Utils. Bd. v. FCC, 120 F.3d 753 (holding that the FCC lacked authority to set prices for interconnection, access to an incumbent's network elements, and resale under the 1996 Act), *rev'd in relevant part*, AT&T v. Iowa Utils. Bd., 119 S. Ct. 721 (1999).

[307] 47 C.F.R. §§51.205–51.215.

[308] California v. FCC, 124 F.3d 934 (8th Cir. 1997), *rev'd in relevant part*, AT&T v. Iowa Utils. Bd., 119 S. Ct. 721 (1999).

[309] *Id.* at 941.

[310] *Id.* at 940.

The Supreme Court reversed that decision for the same reason it invalidated the Eighth Circuit's other jurisdictional determinations. The Court concluded that section 201(b) generally provided the FCC with authority to implement all of the Communications Act, regardless of whether the telecommunications traffic at issue was intrastate or interstate. As Justice Scalia explained, "We think that the grant [of authority] in §201(b) means what it says: The FCC has rulemaking authority to carry out the 'provisions of this Act,' which include §§251 and 252, added by the Telecommunications Act of 1996."[311]

Even before the Supreme Court reversed the Eighth Circuit's ruling, the Eighth Circuit's decision did not apply to the Commission's authority over *inter*state dialing parity. The rules adopted by the FCC were thus unaffected insofar as they applied to those interstate matters. This caused SBC Communications to seek declaratory relief from the Commission to the effect that there is no current obligation to implement interstate intraLATA dialing parity for interstate toll calls on February 8, 1999. SBC argued that "the effect of the Eighth Circuit's California decision undercuts the bases for the intraLATA toll dialing parity rules promulgated in the *Second* [*Local Competition*] *Order*, would result in a structure the FCC expressly rejected, and would cause consumer confusion and additional opportunities for abusive practices such as slamming."[312] In the alternative, SBC sought a waiver or suspension to avoid these consumer issues, as well as to avoid confusion raised by other ongoing events. Within days of the Supreme Court's decision, MCI filed an emergency motion to dismiss SBC's petition, arguing that SBC's obligation to provide intraLATA toll dialing parity by February 8, 1999, was now fully in effect.[313] SBC opposed the motion, arguing that the Commission must still determine whether it has the statutory

---

[311] AT&T v. Iowa Utils. Bd., 119 S. Ct. at 730.

[312] Petition of Southwestern Bell Telephone Company, et al. for Expedited Declaratory Ruling on Interstate IntraLATA Toll Dialing Parity or, in the Alternative, Various Other Relief, NSD File L-98-121 (Sept. 18, 1998).

[313] MCI's Emergency Motion to Dismiss, NSD File No. L-98-121 (Jan. 27, 1999).

authority to require Bell companies to comply with a national deadline in the face of state statutes and regulations that have established different dates for implementing intraLATA toll dialing parity.[314] On March 25, 1999, the Commission denied SBC's petition and established a revised implementation schedule for interLATA toll dialing parity.[315]

§5.5.2.4   Access to Rights-of-Way

Section 251(b)(4) imposes on each LEC the "duty to afford access to the poles, ducts, conduits, and rights-of-way of such carrier to competing providers of telecommunications services on rates, terms, and conditions that are consistent with Section 224" of the Communications Act. Section 224 is the Pole Attachment Act. Its most relevant provision is section 224(f)(1), which requires a utility to grant telecommunications carriers and cable operators nondiscriminatory access to all poles, ducts, conduits, and rights-of-way owned or controlled by the utility—an obligation, however, that does not extend so far as to require that access to incumbent LECs, which are excluded from the definition of "telecommunications carriers" for purposes of section 224. States can preempt all federal regulation of pole attachments by certifying that they have issued and made effective rules and regulations implementing their regulatory authority over pole attachments.[316] Otherwise, utilities may deny access only "where there is insufficient capacity and for reasons of

[314] *See also* AT&T Communications of Va. v. Bell Atlantic-Va., Inc., 35 F. Supp. 2d 463 (E.D. Va. 1999) (holding that while the 1996 Act establishes a duty on behalf of all LECs to implement intrastate intraLATA dialing parity, Congress left this implementation to the FCC and the states).

[315] *See* Implementation of the Local Competition Provisions of the Telecommunications Act of 1996, Order CC Docket No. 96-98, ¶7 (FCC rel. Mar. 23, 1999) (establishing September 6, 1999 as the latest possible date by which a LEC must implement its plan).

[316] *See* 47 C.F.R. §§1.1401–1.1416. These sections contain the Commission's rules on pole attachments. They have been amended in part by the Commission in accordance with the 1996 Act. *See* Implementation of Section 703(e) of the Telecommunications Act of 1996, Report and Order, 13 F.C.C. Rec. 6777 (1998) (hereinafter *Pole Attachment Order*).

safety, reliability and generally applicable engineering purposes."[317] Only utilities that use their facilities and rights-of-way
"in whole or in part, for wire communications" are subject to this
requirement.[318]

In the *Local Competition Order,* the Commission declined to
prescribe specific rules to govern access to rights-of-way, stating
that because of the numerous types of utilities involved in very
different parts of the country, "no single set of rules can take into
account all of the issues that can arise in the context of a single
installation or attachment."[319] The Commission instead adopted
five rules of general applicability to "require utilities to justify
any conditions they place on access."[320]

First, in evaluating a request for access, a utility may continue
to rely on national industry standards and codes to prescribe
rules with respect to capacity, safety, reliability, and general engineering principles.[321] Second, federal requirements, such as
those imposed by the Federal Energy Regulatory Commission
(FERC) and the Occupational Safety and Health Administration
(OSHA), will continue to apply to utilities to the extent such requirements affect requests for attachments to utility facilities
under section 224(f)(1).[322] Third, state and local requirements
affecting pole attachments must be considered.[323] Fourth, where
access is mandated, the rates, terms, and conditions of access
must be uniformly applied to all telecommunications carriers
and cable operators that have or seek access.[324] Fifth, a utility
may not favor itself over other parties with respect to the provision of telecommunications or video programming services.[325]

---

[317] 47 U.S.C. §224(f)(2).

[318] *Id.* §224(a)(1).

[319] *Local Competition Order,* 11 F.C.C. Rec. at 16,068 ¶1145. "The record
makes clear that there are simply too many variables to permit any other
approach with respect to access to the millions of utility poles and untold
miles of conduit in the nation." *Id.* at 16,067–16,068 ¶1143.

[320] *Id.* at 16,071 ¶1150.

[321] *Id.* at 16,071 ¶1151; 47 C.F.R. §1.1403(a).

[322] *Local Competition Order,* 11 F.C.C. Rec. at 16,072 ¶1152.

[323] *Id.* at 16,072 ¶1153 (citing 47 U.S.C. §224(c)(1)).

[324] *Id.* at 16,073 ¶1156 (citing 47 U.S.C. §224(f)(1)); 47 C.F.R. §1.1416(b).

[325] *Local Competition Order,* 11 F.C.C. Rec. at 16,073 ¶1157 (citing 47 U.S.C.
§224(f)(1)); 47 C.F.R. §1.1403(a) ("[a] utility shall provide . . . nondiscriminatory access").

The Commission held that under section 224(f)(1) a utility must take the steps necessary to expand capacity for telecommunications carriers and cable operators only if the utility's own needs require such expansion.[326] The Commission refrained from crafting a specific rule "that prescribes the circumstances in which, on the one hand, a utility must replace or expand an existing facility in response to a request for access and, on the other hand, it is reasonable for the utility to deny the request due to the difficulties involved in honoring the request."[327] It stated instead that utilities must "take all reasonable steps to accommodate requests for access in these situations" and that "[b]efore denying access based on a lack of capacity, a utility must explore potential accommodations in good faith with the party seeking access."[328]

With respect to a utility reserving space for its own use, the Commission created separate rules for electric and telecommunications or video services utilities. Electric utilities are permitted to reserve space "if such reservation is consistent with a bona fide development plan that reasonably and specifically projects a need for that space in the provision of its core utility service."[329] Electric utilities must, however, permit use of their reserved space by cable operators and telecommunication carriers until such time as the utility has an actual need for that space.[330] Then electric utilities must give the displaced cable operator or telecommunications carrier the opportunity to pay for the cost of any modifications needed to expand capacity and to continue to maintain their attachments.[331] On the other hand, a utility providing telecommunications or video services may not reserve space.[332] The Commission found that "Section 224(f)(1) requires nondiscriminatory treatment of all providers of such services and does not contain an exception for the benefit of such a provider

---

[326] *Local Competition Order,* 11 F.C.C. Rec. at 16,075 ¶1162.
[327] *Id.* at 16,076 ¶1163.
[328] *Id.*
[329] *Id.* at 16,078 ¶1169.
[330] *Id.*
[331] *Id.*
[332] *Id.* at 16,079 ¶1170.

on account of its ownership or control of the facility or right-of-way. Congress seemed to perceive such ownership and control as a threat to the development of competition in these areas, thus leading to the enactment of the provision in question."[333]

Prior to the 1996 Act, section 224(b)(1) gave the Commission power to "regulate the rates, terms, and conditions for pole attachments."[334] But former section 224(c)(1) preempted such authority where a state regulated such matters. This "reverse preemption" was conditioned on the state following certification procedures and meeting certain compliance requirements laid out in section 224(c)(2) and (3). Under section 224(f)(1), the 1996 Act expanded the jurisdiction of the FCC "to include not just rates, terms and conditions, but also the authority to regulate *non-discriminatory access* to poles, conduits and rights of way."[335] Yet in section 224(c)(1), the Act expanded the preemptive authority of the states to match the expanded authority of the Commission.[336]

Although some have argued before the Commission that new section 251(b)(4) suggests Congress sought federal access regulations of universal applicability,[337] the Commission has interpreted section 224(c)(1) to be a clear grant of authority to the

---

[333] *Id.*

[334] 47 U.S.C. §224(b)(1).

[335] *Local Competition Order,* 11 F.C.C. Rec. at 16,104 ¶1232 (emphasis added).

[336] 47 U.S.C. §224(c)(1) now provides: "Nothing in this section shall be construed to apply to, or give the Commission jurisdiction with respect to rates, terms and conditions, or access to poles, ducts, conduits and rights-of-way as provided in subsection (f) of this section, for pole attachments in any case where such matters are regulated by a state."

[337] In relevant part, section 251(b)(4) imposes on LECs "[t]he duty to afford access to the poles, ducts, conduits, and rights-of-way of such carrier to competing providers of telecommunications services on rates, terms and conditions that are consistent with Section 224." Several parties argued that since this provision contained no specific reference to the possibility of state regulation (and neither did the competitive checklist of section 271), a LEC would not be relieved of the access requirements of section 224(f) by state regulation in the same area. *See Local Competition Order,* 11 F.C.C. Rec. at 16,105 ¶¶1233–1234.

states to preempt federal regulation in these cases.[338] "Thus, when a state has exercised its preemptive authority under Section 224(c)(1), a LEC satisfies its duty under Section 251(b)(4) to afford access by complying with the state's regulations."[339] When a state has not exercised its authority, a LEC meets its obligations by following federal rules. Finally, the Commission took notice of the fact that Congress did not amend the certification process at section 224(c)(2). As a result, it held that "upon the filing of an access complaint with the Commission, the defending party or the state itself should come forward to apprise [them] whether the state is regulating such matters."[340] When this is done, the complaint will be dismissed without prejudice.[341]

In addition to the rules implementing new local access provisions established in the *Local Competition Order,* the FCC issued a separate order to implement the amended section 224(e)(1).[342] This section governs rates for pole attachments used in the provision of telecommunications services, including single attachments used jointly to provide both cable and telecommunication service. The Commission encourages parties to negotiate the rates, terms, and conditions of pole attachment agreements themselves,[343] but consistent with section 224(e)(1), regulatory formulas were adopted for when parties fail to resolve their disputes.[344]

§5.5.2.5 Reciprocal Compensation

Section 251(b)(5) provides that all LECs, including incumbent LECs, have the duty to "establish reciprocal compensation arrangements for the transport and termination of telecommunications."[345] In basic terms, reciprocal compensation works as

[338] *Local Competition Order,* 11 F.C.C. Rec. at 16,106 ¶1238.
[339] *Id.* at 16,106 ¶1239.
[340] *Id.* at 16,107 ¶1240.
[341] *Id.*
[342] *Pole Attachment Order,* 13 F.C.C. Rec. 6777.
[343] *Id.* at 6787 ¶16.
[344] *See* 47 C.F.R. §§1.1409(e)(1)–(3), 1.1417, 1.1418.
[345] 47 U.S.C. §251(b)(5).

follows. When a customer of Carrier A places a local call to a customer of Carrier B, Carrier A must pay Carrier B for terminating the call. Conversely, when a customer of Carrier B places a local call to a customer of Carrier A, Carrier B must pay. The Act provides that state commissions shall not consider reciprocal compensation arrangements to be just and reasonable unless they provide for the mutual and reciprocal recovery by each carrier of the costs associated with the transport and termination on each carrier's network of calls that originate on the other's network; such costs are to be determined on the basis of the reasonable approximation of the additional costs of terminating such calls.[346] In other words, the Act looks to the marginal cost of carrying the additional traffic, not the fully distributed costs of the network.[347]

A key threshold question that the Commission addressed in its *Local Competition Order* requirement was whether "transport and termination of telecommunications" under section 251(b)(5) are limited to traffic within a local exchange. The Commission concluded that section 251(b)(5)'s reciprocal compensation obligations "should apply only to traffic that originates and terminates within a local area."[348] State commissions could determine what geographic areas should be considered "local areas" for the purpose of applying reciprocal compensation obligations.[349]

In the years since the FCC issued that Order, the question of what traffic qualifies as "local"—and thus is subject to reciprocal compensation obligations—has proven to be one of the most financially significant issues that has arisen in the wake of the 1996 Act. In particular, as we discuss in detail in Chapter 11, an enormous amount of litigation before state commissions, federal courts, and the FCC has involved the question of whether calls to Internet service providers are "local" and thus provide the

---

[346] *Id.* §252(d)(2).
[347] *See* §2.4.4.4.
[348] *Local Competition Order,* 11 F.C.C. Rec. at 16,013 ¶1034.
[349] *Id.* at 16,013 ¶1035. The Commission retained the authority to define the local service area for calls to or from a CMRS network in light of the Commission's exclusive authority to define the authorized license areas of wireless carriers. *Id.* at 16,014 ¶1036.

basis for reciprocal compensation liability. Not surprisingly, the rulings on this issue have been driven largely by the jurisdictional interests of the bodies issuing them.

In the teeth of decades of precedent establishing that communications are to be analyzed on an end-to-end basis, state commissions have repeatedly held that the part of an Internet communication that travels from the end user to an Internet service provider is a severable local call (and hence subject to state jurisdiction). Under that reasoning, incumbents have been required to pay tens of millions of dollars in reciprocal compensation fees to competitive LECs (CLECs) under those parties' interconnection agreements. As the CEO of one company positioned to benefit from such rulings has frankly acknowledged, obtaining reciprocal compensation for Internet traffic is a "boondoggle" that provides some telecommunications companies with vast profits for doing almost no work.[350] To date, however, the federal courts have affirmed the states' conclusion on this issue, but those decisions are now on appeal.[351]

The FCC, however, ruled in late 1998 that Internet traffic is interstate, *not* local.[352] The FCC reiterated in February 1996 that ISP communications involve a single, nonlocal call.[353] The FCC recognized that, in light of that result, State commissions might have to "re-examine" their conclusions that incumbents agreed to absorb massive reciprocal compensation liabilities where those conclusions were based on a contrary, two-call understanding. In the FCC's view, however, in some cases such decisions might be

[350] *See* Comm. Daily, Sept. 17, 1998, at 4 (remarks of Chuck McMinn, Chairman of Covad Communications).

[351] Southwestern Bell Tel. Co. v. Public Util. Commn. of Tex., MO-98-CA-43 (W.D. Tex. Jun. 16, 1998), *appeal pending*, No. 98-50787 (5th Cir.); Illinois Bell Tel. Co. v. WorldCom Techs., Inc., No. 98 C 1925 (N.D. Ill. Jul. 23, 1998), *stay denied*, 157 F.3d 500 (7th Cir. 1998).

[352] GTE Tel. Operating Cos., GTOC Tariff No. 1, GTOC Transmittal No. 1148, Memorandum Opinion and Order, CC Docket No. 98-79, ¶19 (Oct. 30, 1998).

[353] Implementation of the Local Competition Provisions in the Telecommunications Act of 1996, Inter-Carrier Compensation for ISP-Bound Traffic, Declaratory Ruling in CC Docket No. 96-98 and Notice of Proposed Rulemaking in CC Docket No. 99-68 (rel. Feb. 26, 1999).

defensible if based on other grounds. The FCC further concluded that, while reciprocal compensation could not be required under section 251(b)(5) for Internet traffic, state commissions might nonetheless require incumbents to pay such compensation in arbitrations—where, by definition, incumbents did *not* agree to such a rule—at least until the FCC completes a pending rule-making on compensation for that traffic. The FCC stated that "[a]lthough reciprocal compensation is mandated under section 251(b)(5) only for the transport and termination of local traffic, neither the statute nor our rules prohibit a state commission from concluding in an arbitration that reciprocal compensation is appropriate in certain instances not addressed by section 251(b)(5), as long as there is no conflict with governing federal law.[354] At this writing, petitions for review of the FCC's order are pending before the D.C. Circuit.

The FCC has been less reticent as to other issues. Of particular importance, the Commission held that transport and termination should be treated as two distinct functions. The Commission defined "transport" as the transmission of terminating traffic that is subject to section 251(b)(5) from the interconnection point between the two carriers to the terminating carrier's end office switch that directly serves the called party (or equivalent facility provided by a nonincumbent carrier).[355] "Termination" is defined as "the switching of traffic that is subject to section 251(b)(5) at the terminating carrier's end office switch (or equivalent facility) and delivery of that traffic from that switch to the called party's premises."[356] The Commission stated that because alternative arrangements existed for the provision of transport between two networks, but "are not likely to exist in the near term" for termination, the forward-looking costs for transport and termination should be calculated differently.[357]

---

[354] *Id.* at ¶26.
[355] *Local Competition Order,* 11 F.C.C. Rec. at 16,015 ¶1039; 47 C.F.R. §51.701(c).
[356] *Local Competition Order,* 11 F.C.C. Rec. at 16,015 ¶1040; 47 C.F.R. §51.701(d).
[357] *Local Competition Order,* 11 F.C.C. Rec. at 16,015 ¶1040.

The Commission further concluded that the statutory pricing standards for interconnection and unbundled elements were "sufficiently similar" to those for transport and termination that use of the same general methodology made sense for establishing rates under these statutory provisions. The Commission accordingly adopted the same forward-looking pricing standard that it established for interconnection and unbundled elements. The Commission then gave the states three options for establishing transport and termination rate levels. First, a state commission could conduct a thorough review of economic studies prepared using the TELRIC-based methodology provided by the Commission.[358] Second, in the first months after the 1996 Act's passage, the state could adopt a default price pursuant to default proxies outlined in the *Local Competition Order,*[359] although it is doubtful that a state could still rely on these proxies today. Third, in some circumstances, states could order a "bill and keep" arrangement.[360]

"Bill-and-keep" is defined as an arrangement in which neither of two interconnecting carriers charge the other for terminating traffic that originated on the other carrier's network. Instead, each carrier recovers from its own end users the cost of both originating traffic delivered to the other carrier's network and terminating traffic received from the other carrier's network. A bill-and-keep approach for termination of traffic does not, however, preclude a positive flat-rated charge for transport of

---

[358] *Id.* at 16,024 ¶1055.

[359] *Id.* at 16,026–16,028 ¶¶1060–1062. The proxies were not intended for permanent use. *Id.* at 16,026 ¶1060 ("As with unbundled network elements, [the FCC] recognize[d] that it may not be feasible for some state commissions conducting or reviewing economic studies to establish transport and termination rates using [their] TELRIC-based pricing methodology within the time required for the arbitration process, particularly given some states' resource limitations. Thus, *for the time being,* [the Commission] adopt[ed] a default price range.") (emphasis added). As the FCC conceded before the Supreme Court, these "temporary and optional 'default proxies' . . . were designed for a past period in which no cost studies could have been made available to the state commissions." Government Reply Br. at 7 n.5, AT&T v. Iowa Utils. Bd., Nos. 97-826 et al. (S. Ct. filed June 17, 1998).

[360] *Local Competition Order,* 11 F.C.C. Rec. at 16,024 ¶1055.

traffic between carriers' networks.[361] The Commission found that the use of such bill-and-keep arrangements was appropriate when neither carrier had rebutted the presumption of symmetrical rates and the volume of terminating traffic that originates on one network and terminates on another is approximately equal to the volume of terminating traffic flowing in the other direction and is expected to remain so.[362]

On appeal, the Eighth Circuit concluded that the FCC lacked jurisdiction to issue these pricing rules for the same reason that it lacked authority to issue pricing rules governing access to unbundled elements and resale. In light of the Supreme Court's decision reversing the Eighth Circuit on that jurisdictional question, the issue now will return to the court of appeals, where incumbents now have an opportunity to challenge the merits of the FCC's pricing rules.

§5.5.3 Duties of Incumbent LECs

Under section 251(c), incumbent LECs have a duty (1) to negotiate interconnection agreements in good faith; (2) to provide interconnection for the transmission and routing of exchange and exchange access services "at any technically feasible point within the carrier's network" that is at least equal in quality to the interconnection provided to any affiliate, subsidiary, or other party and on rates, terms, and conditions that are just, reasonable, and nondiscriminatory; (3) to provide unbundled access to network elements at any technically feasible point on just, reasonable, and nondiscriminatory terms; (4) to offer for resale, at wholesale rates, any services provided to subscribers who are not carriers; the incumbent LEC may not impose any unreasonable or discriminatory conditions on resale, although a state may prohibit a reseller that obtains a service available at retail only to a particular category of subscribers

[361] *Id.* at 16,045 ¶1096.
[362] *Id.* at 16,054 ¶1111.

from offering that service to a different category of subscribers; (5) to provide reasonable notice of changes to the incumbent LEC's network that may affect a connecting carrier's ability to provide service; and (6) to provide physical collocation of equipment necessary for interconnection or unbundled access on rates, terms, and conditions that are just, reasonable, and nondiscriminatory; an incumbent LEC may provide virtual collocation if it demonstrates to a state commission that physical collocation is not practical, either for technical reasons or because of space limitations.

§5.5.3.1   Carriers to Whom These Duties Apply

The threshold question raised by these obligations is, of course, to whom they apply. Congress defined an incumbent LEC as a carrier that "on February 8, 1996, provided telephone exchange service in such area" *and* either "on February 8, 1996, was deemed to be a member" of the National Exchange Carrier Association (NECA) or "is a person or entity that, on or after February 8, 1996, became a successor or assign of a member of that association."[363]

One federal court has read the literal language of this requirement straightforwardly to mandate that, to qualify as an incumbent, the carrier must have provided telephone exchange service in the relevant area on February 8, 1996, *and* it must have been a NECA member on that date or must be a successor or assign of an entity that was itself a NECA member on that date: "Only if a telecommunications carrier satisfies *both* of these conditions can it be an ILEC subject to the 'additional obligations' under §251(c), including the resale obligation of §251(c)(4)."[364]

The FCC's rulings to date, however, have assumed that any carrier that qualifies as a "successor or assign" of a carrier that provided service on February 8, 1998, also qualifies as an incumbent. The FCC has made plain, however, that the fact that an

[363] 47 U.S.C. §251(h)(1).

[364] MCI v. Southern New England Tel. Co., 27 F. Supp. 2d 326, 337 (D. Conn. 1998) (citing Guam Public Utilities Commission Petition for Declaratory Ruling

affiliate of an incumbent provides local service is not sufficient for that affiliate to qualify as a "successor or assign"; rather, that affiliate must take actual ownership of the incumbent's network facilities.[365] Nor do states have the authority to expand the reach of the 1996 Act by relying on state law authority to apply these rules to companies that do not qualify as incumbents.[366] Because many incumbent LECs have created CLEC affiliates that are intended to provide, among other things, local telephone service in the incumbent's traditional region, the scope of the statute's "successor or assign" language has been a matter of significant controversy. CompTel, a trade association of interexchange carriers, has filed a petition with the FCC asking the Commission to conclude that essentially *any* affiliate of an incumbent carrier that offers local exchange service in the incumbent's territory is subject to all the obligations imposed on incumbents.[367]

Even if a company does not qualify as a successor or assign of an incumbent, under section 251(h)(2), the FCC may treat that carrier as an incumbent if it "occupies a position in the market for telephone exchange service within an area that is comparable to the position occupied by an incumbent"; it has "substantially replaced an incumbent"; and "such treatment is consistent with

---

Concerning Sections 3(37) and 251(h) of the Communications Act, Declaratory Ruling and Notice of Proposed Rulemaking, 12 F.C.C. Rec. 6925, 6935 ¶14 (1997) (hereinafter *Guam Public Utilities Commission*)).

[365] 47 C.F.R. §53.207; *see* Implementation of the Non-accounting Safeguards of Sections 271 and 272 of the Communications Act of 1934, as amended, First Report and Order and Further Notice of Proposed Rulemaking, 11 F.C.C. Rec. 21,905, 22,055 ¶312 (1996). "We also agree . . . that a BOC affiliate should not be deemed an incumbent LEC subject to the requirements of Section 251(c) solely because it offers local exchange services." *Id.* at 22,054 ¶309 (BOC affiliate becomes an "assign" only "if a BOC transfers . . . *ownership* of any network elements that must be provided on an unbundled basis pursuant to Section 251(c)(3)") (emphasis added).

[366] "[A]llowing states to impose on non-incumbent LECs obligations that the 1996 Act designates as [obligations on incumbent LECs] *would be inconsistent with the statute.*" *Local Competition Order,* 11 F.C.C. Rec. at 16,109 ¶1247 (emphasis added). "[S]tates may not unilaterally impose on non-incumbent LECs obligations the 1996 Act expressly imposes only on incumbent LECs." *Id.* at 16,110 ¶1248.

[367] CompTel Petition on Defining Certain Incumbent LEC Affiliates as Successors, Assigns, or Comparable Carriers Under Section 251(h) of the Communications Act, CC Docket No. 98-39 (FCC Mar. 23, 1998).

the public interest, convenience, and necessity and the purposes of [section 251]." Applying these principles, the FCC has made it plain that a party qualifies as a comparable carrier if it "control[s] the . . . local exchange network" and possesses substantial "economies of density, connectivity, and scale" such that, in the absence of "compliance with the obligations of Section 251(c), [it] can impede the development of telephone exchange service competition."[368]

Rural telephone companies[369] obtain an automatic exemption from all these obligations of incumbent LECs. This exemption lasts unless and until the rural LEC receives a bona fide request for interconnection/unbundling and the state commission determines that the request is "not unduly burdensome, is technically feasible," and will not interfere with universal service requirements.[370] A state commission may also suspend or modify the requirements of section 251(b) and (c) as to a local carrier that has less than 2 percent of the nation's subscriber lines if that action is "necessary" to avoid (i) a "significant adverse economic impact on users of telecommunications services generally," (ii) a "requirement that is unduly economically burdensome," or (iii) a "requirement that is technically infeasible," and if such action is consistent with the public interest.[371]

In its *Local Competition Order,* the FCC published rules discussing the exemption for rural LECs. The Eighth Circuit vacated those same rules in the *Iowa Utilities* decision, citing the

---

[368] *Guam Public Utilities Commission,* 12 F.C.C. Rec. at 6941 ¶27.

[369] The statute defines a "rural telephone company" as a local exchange carrier operating entity to the extent that such entity "(A) provides common carrier service to any local exchange carrier study area that does not include either—(i) any incorporated place of 10,000 inhabitants or more, or any part thereof, based on the most recently available population statistics of the Bureau of the Census; or (ii) any territory, incorporated or unincorporated, included in an urbanized area, as defined by the Bureau of the Census as of August 10, 1993; (B) provides telephone exchange service, including exchange access, to fewer than 50,000 access lines; (C) provides telephone exchange service to any local exchange carrier study area with fewer than 100,000 access lines; or (D) has less than 15 percent of its access lines in communities of more than 50,000 on February 8, 1996." 47 U.S.C. §153(37).

[370] *Id.* §251(f)(1).

[371] *Id.* §251(f)(2).

FCC's lack of authority to do so.[372] The Supreme Court reversed the court of appeals' determination.[373] The FCC rules are now subject to review on the merits before the Eighth Circuit. In substance, the FCC's rules require rural LECs wishing an exemption to "offer evidence" to the state commission of "undue economic burdens" resulting from competitive entry[374] and specifically identify as relevant "rural LECs" those with "fewer than two percent of subscriber lines nationwide."[375]

§5.5.3.2　Procedure for Implementing the Obligations Imposed on Incumbent LECs

For companies that are subject to the obligations imposed by section 251(c), those obligations are not generally self-executing. Rather, incumbents are required to enter into voluntary, good-faith negotiations with prospective entrants to implement these obligations. The statute permits those parties to reach an agreement "without regard" to the specific statutory obligations placed on incumbents by section 251.[376] A negotiated agreement must contain a detailed schedule of itemized charges for interconnection and for each service or network element included.[377] The FCC has emphasized that Bell Operating Companies are entitled to require a competing carrier to agree to an implementation schedule committing to a date to begin providing service.[378]

---

[372] *Iowa Utils. Bd.*, 120 F.3d at 801–803.

[373] AT&T v. Iowa Utils. Bd., 119 S. Ct. 721 (1999).

[374] *Local Competition Order,* 11 F.C.C. Rec. at 16,118 ¶¶1262–1263.

[375] *Local Competition Order,* 11 F.C.C. Rec. at 16,118 ¶1264. The FCC further stated: "any other interpretation would permit almost any company, including Bell Atlantic, Ameritech, and GTE affiliates, to take advantage of the suspension and modification provisions in section 251(f)(2). Such a conclusion would render the two percent limitation virtually meaningless." *Id.*

[376] 47 U.S.C. §252(a)(1).

[377] *Id.*

[378] Application by SBC Communications Inc., Pursuant to Section 271 of the Communications Act of 1934, as amended, to Provide In-Region, Inter-LATA Services in Oklahoma, Memorandum Opinion and Order, 12 F.C.C. Rec. 8685, 8706 n.109 (1997) ("BOCs are free to negotiate implementation

At any point during interconnection negotiations, either the incumbent or the prospective entrant may ask the relevant state commission to mediate disputes between the parties.[379] If the parties reach a complete agreement solely through such voluntary negotiations—and more than 5,400 have been reached on that basis[380]—they must submit the agreement to the state commission (or, if the state commission declines to participate in this process, to the FCC).[381] The state commission may reject the agreement in whole or in part only if it discriminates against a third-party telecommunications carrier or if it is inconsistent with the public interest.[382]

If the parties *cannot* reach a complete agreement, any party may petition the relevant state commission to arbitrate the unresolved issues.[383] Such a petition must be filed during the period between the 135th and the 180th days after the initial request for negotiation, and it must be accompanied by "all relevant documentation" as to the unresolved issues, the positions of the parties with respect to those issues, and any other issues discussed and resolved by the parties.[384] The commission must then give other parties an opportunity to respond to the petition and must resolve each disputed issue not later than nine months after the date of the first request for negotiation.[385] The complete agreement—containing the terms agreed to both as a result of negotiation and as a result of arbitration—is then presented to the commission for approval.[386] The commission may reject the agreement within 30 days,[387] but only if the agreement does not

---

schedules for their interconnection agreements."); *see also* SBC Communications Inc. v. FCC, 138 F.3d 410, 419–420 (D.C. Cir. 1998) (affirming FCC position).

[379] 47 U.S.C. §252(a)(2).

[380] United States Telephone Association, USTA Fact Sheet on Local Competition <http://www.usta.org/blileyft.html>.

[381] 47 U.S.C. §252(e)(1), (5).

[382] *Id.* §252(e)(2).

[383] *Id.* §252(a)(2).

[384] *Id.* §251(b)(1)–(2).

[385] *Id.* §252(b)(3).

[386] *Id.* §252(e).

[387] *Id.* §252(e)(4).

meet the obligations imposed by section 251 (including regulations prescribed by the FCC to implement section 251) or the pricing standards of section 252(d).[388] Any party that is aggrieved by a state commission determination may then seek review in federal district court.[389]

In addition to negotiating with individual new entrants, a Bell Operating Company may file with the state commission a statement of the terms and conditions that the company will offer within a state to comply with the substantive requirements of section 251.[390] That plan will be reviewed by the state commission under the same criteria as are applied to arbitrated interconnection/unbundling agreements.[391] Unless the BOC agrees to extend the time for consideration by the state commission, the commission must complete its review of any statement of terms and conditions within 60 days or the statement will become effective.[392] This provision applies only to Bell Operating Companies, rather than incumbent LECs generally, because the filing of such a statement may—in lieu of a signed interconnection agreement—provide the basis for a Bell Company application under section 271 for entry into long-distance markets. The requirements for long-distance approval are discussed at length at section 9.6.2.3(v).

While there is no doubt that the tasks that Congress gave to state commissions in arbitrating and approving agreements and statements are daunting, those entities do have the benefit (or perhaps the curse) of FCC regulations as a guide. Congress provided that, "[w]ithin 6 months after the date of enactment of the Telecommunications Act of 1996, the Commission shall complete all actions necessary to establish regulations to implement the requirements of this Section [251]."[393]

---

[388] *Id.* §252(e)(2)(B).
[389] *Id.* §252(e)(6).
[390] *Id.* §252(f).
[391] *Id.* §252(f)(2).
[392] *Id.* §252(f)(3).
[393] *Id.* §251(d)(1).

As we have discussed,[394] the scope of the FCC's authority to promulgate such rules—and its coexistence with specific statutory provisions (such as section 252(c) and (d)) that appear to give state commissions exclusive authority over pricing and other particular matters—has been the subject of extensive litigation. The Eighth Circuit determined that the FCC lacks authority to issue pricing rules, as well as rules involving the rural exemption, dialing parity, and the need to submit preexisting interconnection agreements to state commissions for approval.[395] The Eighth Circuit also found that the FCC could not use its section 208 authority to hear complaints to review state commission determinations.[396] In January 1999, the Supreme Court reversed those jurisdictional determinations (as to the section 208 issue, however, the Court concluded that the matter was not ripe).[397] The Eighth Circuit now will have an opportunity to review on the merits the FCC rules that it previously vacated on jurisdictional grounds.

§5.5.3.3 Duty to Negotiate in Good Faith

In accord with the 1996 Act's heavy reliance on private negotiation as a means of opening local markets to competition, the first substantive obligation that section 251(c) places on incumbent LECs is the "duty to negotiate in good faith in accordance with Section 252 the particular terms and conditions of agreements to fulfill the duties described" in section 251(b) and (c). Section 251(c)(1) further provides that a "requesting telecommunications carrier"—that is, a prospective local market entrant —"also has the duty to negotiate in good faith the terms and conditions of such agreements."

In its *Local Competition Order,* the FCC established minimum requirements of good-faith negotiation in order to "balance . . .

---

[394] *See* §3.3.1.
[395] Iowa Utils. Bd. v. FCC, 120 F.3d at 794–805; California v. FCC, 124 F.3d 934, 938 (8th Cir. 1997).
[396] Iowa Utils. Bd. v. FCC, 120 F.3d at 803.
[397] AT&T v. Iowa Utils. Bd., 119 S. Ct. 721.

the incentives between the bargaining parties" and to "guide parties and state commissions."[398] Those requirements are generally unsurprising and noncontroversial. For instance, negotiating parties may not "intentionally obstruct [ ] negotiations" through "duress or misrepresentation."[399] Additionally, in designating a representative to negotiate, a carrier must appoint someone "with authority to make binding representations on behalf of the party," although not necessarily on every issue — *i.e.*, a person may reasonably be an agent of limited authority.[400]

Incumbents are required to provide information necessary to reach an agreement. Thus, while an incumbent LEC does not have to hand over proprietary information about its network that is not necessary for interconnection, an incumbent "may not deny a requesting carrier's reasonable request for cost data during the negotiation process, because . . . such information is necessary for the requesting carrier to determine whether the rates offered by the incumbent LEC are reasonable."[401] Incumbent LECs also may not require requesting carriers to satisfy a "bona fide request" process.[402]

Agreements may not preclude a party from providing information requested by the FCC, by a state commission, or in support of a request for arbitration.[403] Other nondisclosure requirements do not necessarily constitute a violation of the good-faith negotiation duty, but such requirements do pose a "concern and any complaint alleging such tactics should be evaluated carefully."[404]

Furthermore, a party may voluntarily agree to limit its legal rights or remedies in order to obtain a valuable concession from another party. A party may not, however, demand that another party waive its legal rights. Parties must generally refrain from

---

[398] *Local Competition Order*, 11 F.C.C. Rec. at 15,570 ¶141.
[399] *Id.* at 15,574 ¶148.
[400] *Id.* at 15,577 ¶154.
[401] *Id.* at 15,577–15,578 ¶155.
[402] *Id.* at 15,578 ¶156.
[403] *Id.* at 15,575–15,576 ¶151.
[404] *Id.*

actions that are intended to delay negotiations or resolution of disputes.[405]

Finally, the Commission's "pick-and-choose" rule supports requesting carriers' ability to choose among individual provisions contained in publicly filed interconnection agreements. Section 51.809 of the FCC rules provides that an "incumbent [local exchange carrier] shall make available . . . any individual interconnection, service, or network element arrangement contained in any agreement to which it is a party . . . [to any requesting telecommunications carrier] . . . upon the same rates, terms and conditions as those provided in the agreement."[406] The pick-and-choose provision was stayed and then vacated by the Eighth Circuit, which held that it "would frustrate the Act's design to make privately negotiated agreements the preferred route to local telephone competition."[407] This obligation does not apply where the incumbent proves to the state commission that it would cost more to provide the service to the requesting carrier than the carrier that originally negotiated the agreement. The Supreme Court reinstated it in *Iowa Utilities*,[408] however, and it is therefore presently applicable.

---

[405] *Id.* at 15,576 ¶152.

[406] 47 C.F.R. §51.809; 47 U.S.C. §252(i). *See also Local Competition Order,* 11 F.C.C. Rec. at 16,138 ¶1310 ("Congress drew a distinction between 'any interconnection, service or network element[s] under an agreement,' which the statute lists individually, and agreements in their totality. Requiring requesting carriers to elect entire agreements, instead of the provisions relating to specific elements, would render as mere surplusage the words 'any interconnection, service, or network element.'").

[407] Iowa Utils. Bd. v. FCC, 120 F.3d at 792.

[408] AT&T v. Iowa Utils. Bd., 119 S. Ct. at 738 ("It is hard to declare the FCC's rule unlawful when it tracks the pertinent statutory language almost exactly. . . . And whether the Commission's approach will significantly impede negotiations (by making it impossible for favorable interconnection-service, or network-element terms to be traded off against unrelated provisions) is a matter eminently within the expertise of the Commission and eminently beyond our ken.").

§5.5.3.4   Interconnection

Section 251(c)(2) of the Act requires an incumbent LEC to provide "interconnection" to "any requesting telecommunications carrier" (A) for the transmission and routing of telephone exchange service and exchange access; (B) at any technically feasible point within the carrier's network; (C) that is at least equal in quality to that provided by the local exchange carrier to itself or to any subsidiary, affiliate, or any other party to which the carrier provides interconnection; and (D) on rates, terms, and conditions that are just, reasonable, and nondiscriminatory, in accordance with the terms and conditions of the agreement and the requirements of section 252.[409]

The 1996 Act does not define "interconnection." In its *Local Competition Order,* the Commission defined interconnection under section 251 as the "physical linking of two networks for the mutual exchange of traffic."[410] Under that ruling, when a LEC "transports and terminates" the traffic of another carrier, it is not providing interconnection under the Act. Consequently, carriers that wish to obtain transport and termination services from the LEC may not do so pursuant to section 251 and therefore are not entitled to cost-based rates for use of the LEC's network. For example, interexchange carriers may not obtain "interconnection" in lieu of purchasing interstate access service for the purpose of routing long-distance traffic.

The FCC's decision that interconnection does not include transport and termination was affirmed by the Eighth Circuit in its *CompTel* decision.[411] The court of appeals held that the FCC's conclusion was not inconsistent with the textual reference to interconnection "for the transmission and routing" of traffic: that language merely identified what the physical link of interconnection would be used for; it did mean that interconnection

---

[409] *See also* 47 C.F.R. §51.305(a)(1)–(5).
[410] *Local Competition Order,* 11 F.C.C. Rec. at 15,590 ¶176.
[411] Competitive Telecomms. Assn. v. FCC, 117 F.3d 1068, 1071–1073 (8th Cir. 1997).

included that transmission and routing.[412] Nor was the FCC's conclusion contrary to the 1996 Act's goal of creating cost-based rates. As the circuit court explained, the 1996 Act does not mandate a flash-cut to cost-based rates. On the contrary, section 251(g) explicitly preserves the current access charge regime until the FCC supersedes it.[413]

(i) "For the Transmission and Routing of Telephone Exchange Service and Exchange Access."   Section 251(c)(2)(A) of the Act requires incumbent LECs to provide interconnection to a requesting carrier only "for the transmission and routing of telephone exchange service and exchange access." The Commission has clarified that this imposes a threefold obligation on LECs to provide interconnection for purposes of transmitting and routing (1) telephone exchange traffic, (2) exchange access traffic, or (3) both.[414]

The FCC found that IXCs are telecommunications carriers under the 1996 Act.[415] They are thus permitted to obtain interconnection pursuant to section 251(c)(2). However, the FCC concluded that traditional interexchange carriers like AT&T may not obtain interconnection under section 251(c)(2) solely for the purpose of originating or terminating their interexchange traffic or interstate traffic.[416] Such a carrier "is not offering access, but rather is only obtaining access for its own traffic."[417] Only IXCs that offer "access services" in competition with an incumbent LEC—"[f]or example, when an IXC interconnects at a local switch bypassing the incumbent LEC's transport network"[418]— are eligible to obtain interconnection pursuant to section 251(c)(2). Thus, interexchange carriers are not entitled to cost-based rates for interstate access; they must instead obtain such services

---

[412] *Id.* at 1071–1072.
[413] *Id.* at 1072–1073.
[414] *Local Competition Order,* 11 F.C.C. Rec. at 15,594 ¶184. *See also* 47 C.F.R. §51.305(a)(1).
[415] *See Local Competition Order,* 11 F.C.C. Rec. at 15,598 ¶190.
[416] *Id.* at 15,598 ¶191. *See also* 47 C.F.R. §51.305(b).
[417] *Local Competition Order,* 11 F.C.C. Rec. at 15,599 ¶191.
[418] *Id.*

under the Commission's access-charge regime, which is discussed in section 2.3.2.

(ii) "At Any Technically Feasible Point."   The Act requires an
incumbent LEC to provide interconnection at any "technically
feasible point."[419] In the *Local Competition Order,* the Commission
has interpreted "technically feasible" to refer only to "technical
or operational concerns, rather than economic, space, or site
considerations."[420] As a result, the Commission concluded that
it was not appropriate to consider costs in determining technically feasible points of interconnection.[421] The Commission also
held that "existing space or site restrictions" should not be
included within a technical feasibility analysis, at least where
there is the possibility of site expansion in a particular instance.[422] Space considerations are relevant, however, to whether
an incumbent must allow physical (rather than virtual) collocation of equipment, a topic discussed below in section 5.5.3.7.
Requesting carriers seeking "technically feasible," but expensive
interconnection are required to bear the cost of that interconnection, including a reasonable profit.[423]

On appeal, the Eighth Circuit upheld the FCC's understanding of the technical feasibility requirement—and, in particular,
the Commission's understanding that cost was irrelevant to
the analysis. The court held that the FCC's interpretation was
"reasonable and entitled to deference": "Although economic
concerns are not to be considered in determining if a point of
interconnection or unbundled access is technically feasible, the
costs of such interconnection or unbundled access will be taken
into account when determining the just and reasonable rates,
terms, and conditions for those services."[424] That portion of the
Eighth Circuit's *Iowa Utilities* decision was not affected by the
Supreme Court's decision on review of the Eighth Circuit's order.

---

[419] *See also* 47 C.F.R. §51.305(a)(2).
[420] *Local Competition Order,* 11 F.C.C. Rec. at 15,602 ¶198.
[421] *Id.* at 15,603 ¶199.
[422] *Id.* at 15,604 ¶201.
[423] *Id.* at 15,603 ¶199.
[424] *Iowa Utils. Bd.,* 120 F.3d at 810.

The FCC has also addressed several other aspects of technical feasibility. First, the Commission determined that in providing technically feasible interconnection an incumbent LEC must accept "the novel use of, and modification to, its network facilities to accommodate the interconnector or to provide access to unbundled elements."[425] The Commission stated that, because incumbent LEC networks were not originally designed for interconnection with third parties, the absence of such a requirement would frustrate the purposes of the statute. A LEC may, however, consider any "legitimate threats to network reliability and security" before providing interconnection, since each carrier "must be able to retain responsibility for the management, control, and performance of its own network."[426] Incumbent LECs bear the burden of proving to the relevant state commission, "with clear and convincing evidence, that specific and significant adverse impacts would result from the requested interconnection or access."[427]

The FCC further directed state commissions to consider, in determining if a certain requested point of interconnection is technically feasible, whether successful interconnection has been achieved in the past either at the requested point "or at substantially similar points in networks employing substantially similar facilities."[428] Incumbent LECs bear the burden of proving to the appropriate state commission that interconnection or access at a point is not technically feasible.[429]

Finally, the FCC defined a minimum set of technically feasible points of interconnection. Incumbent LECs must provide interconnection at (1) the line side of a local switch, (2) the trunk side of a local switch, (3) the trunk interconnection points for a tandem switch, (4) central office cross-connect points, (5) out-of-band signaling transfer points necessary to exchange traffic and access call-related databases, and (6) points of access to unbundled elements.[430] The Commission acknowledged that there may be

---

[425] *Local Competition Order,* 11 F.C.C. Rec. at 15,605 ¶202.
[426] *Id.* at 15,605–15,606 ¶203.
[427] *Id.*
[428] *Id.* at 15,606 ¶204.
[429] *Id.* at 15,606 ¶205. *See also* 47 C.F.R. §51.305(c).
[430] *Local Competition Order,* 11 F.C.C. Rec. at 15,608 ¶210. *See also* 47 C.F.R. §51.305(a)(2).

"rare circumstances" where interconnection at these points is not feasible and placed the burden on incumbents to demonstrate the existence of such circumstances.[431]

(iii) "At Least Equal in Quality."   The Commission defined the "at least equal in quality" requirement of section 251(c)(2) as requiring an incumbent LEC to provide interconnection "at a level of quality that is at least indistinguishable from that which the incumbent provides itself, a subsidiary, an affiliate, or any other party."[432] Incumbent LECs are required to "design interconnection facilities to meet the same technical criteria and service standards, such as probability of blocking in peak hours and transmission standards, that are used within their own networks."[433] Under the FCC's ruling, moreover, the equal in quality obligation is not to be measured merely by how end users perceive service. More objective measures are to be used to ensure that incumbent LECs do not discriminate against competitors "in a manner imperceptible to end users, but which still provides incumbent LECs with advantages in the marketplace."[434]

The FCC also purported to require incumbents to provide entrants with interconnection of a quality *superior* to that which an incumbent LEC currently provides to itself so long as such an arrangement is technically feasible.[435] Under the FCC's regime, the requesting carrier would have been obligated to pay the cost of this superior interconnection.

The Eighth Circuit, however, determined in *Iowa Utilities* that such a requirement (and the FCC's analogous attempt to require incumbents to provide superior-quality unbundled elements) was inconsistent with the terms of section 252(c). The court explained that while the statutory reference to interconnection

---

[431] *Local Competition Order,* 11 F.C.C. Rec. at 15,609 ¶211.

[432] *Id.* at 15,614–15,615 ¶224.

[433] *Id.*

[434] *Id.* at 15,615 ¶224. *See also* 47 C.F.R. §51.305(a)(3).

[435] *Local Competition Order,* 11 F.C.C. Rec. at 15,615 ¶225. This requirement, the Commission held, will "permit new entrants to compete with incumbent LECs by offering novel services that require superior interconnection quality." *Id. See also* 47 C.F.R. §51.305(a)(4).

"at least equal in quality" "leaves open the possibility" that incumbent LECs may *agree* to provide interconnection that is superior in quality when the parties are negotiating agreements under the Act, this phrase *mandates* only that the quality be equal, not superior. In other words, the statute "establishes a floor beneath which the quality of interconnection may not go," but does not authorize the Commission to "*require*[ ] superior quality interconnection when requested."[436] In simple terms, the 1996 Act "does not mandate that incumbent LECs cater to every desire of every requesting carrier."[437]

The FCC did not seek review in the Supreme Court of this aspect of the Eighth Circuit's ruling. Accordingly, the Supreme Court's decision should have no effect on the validity of this aspect of the circuit court's ruling. Nevertheless, several parties have suggested that the Supreme Court's ruling calls the Eighth Circuit's decision on this point into question, and that issue will be briefed before the Eighth Circuit on remand.

(iv) "On Rates, Terms, and Conditions That Are Just, Reasonable, and Nondiscriminatory." The Commission's national interconnection rules included minimum national standards for the establishment of just, reasonable, and nondiscriminatory terms and conditions of interconnection. The Commission stated that such national standards "will tend to offset the imbalance in bargaining power between incumbent LECs and competitors and encourage fair agreements in the marketplace between parties."[438]

In promulgating those rules, the Commission explained that, unlike the requirement in section 202 of the Communications Act, the nondiscrimination requirement in section 251(c)(2) is not qualified by the language "unjust or unreasonable." The Commission therefore concluded that Congress intended the 1996 Act requirement to be "a more stringent standard."[439]

---

[436] *Iowa Utils. Bd.*, 120 F.3d at 812 (emphasis in original).
[437] *Id.* at 813.
[438] *Local Competition Order*, 11 F.C.C. Rec. at 15,611 ¶216.
[439] *Id.* at 15,612 ¶217.

The Commission also rejected the so-called historical interpretation of nondiscriminatory—that is, "a comparison between what the incumbent LEC provided other parties in a regulated monopoly environment"—and instead interpreted the term to apply "to the terms and conditions an incumbent LEC imposes on third parties *as well as on itself.*"[440]

The Commission deferred much of its additional discussion of nondiscriminatory access to its analysis of the related statutory obligation to provide physical or virtual collocation pursuant to section 251(c)(6) (a topic that we address below as well).[441] It did, however, address one particular aspect of nondiscriminatory access. It concluded that when it is technically feasible, incumbents must provide requesting carriers with two-way trunking where a carrier requesting interconnection pursuant to section 251(c)(2) does not carry a sufficient amount of traffic to justify separate one-way trunks.[442] At the same time, however, the Commission refused to adopt an MCI proposal that would have permitted interconnecting carriers, both competitors and incumbent LECs, to designate points of interconnection on each other's networks. The Commission stated that this practice would, for the time being, be "best addressed in negotiations and arbitrations between parties."[443]

§5.5.3.5 Access to Unbundled Network Elements

Section 251(c)(3) requires an incumbent LEC to provide "to any requesting telecommunications carrier for the provision of a telecommunications service, nondiscriminatory access to network elements on an unbundled basis at any technically feasible point on rates, terms, and conditions that are just, reasonable, and nondiscriminatory in accordance with the terms and conditions of the agreement and the requirements of this section

---

[440] *Id.* at 15,612 ¶218 (emphasis added).
[441] *See* §5.5.3.7.
[442] *Local Competition Order,* 11 F.C.C. Rec. at 15,612 ¶219.
[443] *Id.* at 15,613 ¶220.

and section 252."[444] An incumbent LEC must provide such un-bundled network elements "in a manner that allows requesting carriers to combine such elements in order to provide such tele-communications service."[445]

As with interconnection, the FCC determined in its *Local Competition Order* that it needed to create national rules to implement the duties imposed by section 251(c)(3) in order to further the procompetitive purposes of the 1996 Act.[446] The FCC left the states with the authority to add to these rules as necessary. The FCC then proceeded to define each aspect of the obligations that subsection (c)(3) places on incumbents and to identify a minimum list of network elements that incumbents must make available immediately. The Commission also stated that it had the "authority to identify additional, or perhaps different, un-bundling requirements that would apply to incumbent LECs in the future."[447]

We discuss below the obligations that the FCC placed on incumbents in this regard in its *Local Competition Order,* as well as subsequent developments that have altered and supplemented those obligations. Of particular importance, the Supreme Court's decision in early 1999 vacated all of the FCC rules requiring access to specifically identified parts of the incumbent's network (e.g., loops and switches). The Court's decision requires the agency to rethink those determinations giving added meaning to section 251(d)(2)'s injunction that the agency consider whether access to proprietary elements is "necessary" and whether lack of access to any element would "impair" a new entrant's ability to provide service.[448] Further proceedings as to those issues were ongoing before the FCC in mid-1999.

(i) Network Elements. The Act defines a "network element" as a "facility or equipment used in the provision of a telecom-

---

[444] 47 U.S.C. §251(c)(3). *See also* 47 C.F.R. §51.307(a).
[445] 47 U.S.C. §251(c)(3). *See also* 47 C.F.R. §51.309(a).
[446] *See Local Competition Order* 11 F.C.C. Rec. at 15,624 ¶¶241–242.
[447] *Id.* at 15,626 ¶246.
[448] AT&T v. Iowa Utils. Bd., 119 S. Ct. 721.

munications service. Such term also includes features, functions, and capabilities that are provided by means of such facility or equipment, including subscriber numbers, databases, signaling systems, and information sufficient for billing and collection or used in the transmission, routing, or other provision of a tele-communications service."[449]

The Commission concluded that a "network element" should include the "physical facilities of the network, together with the features, functions, and capabilities associated with those facilities."[450] For some elements, especially the local loop, a requesting carrier that obtains access to the element necessarily gets the exclusive right to use that facility for a period of time. For other, shared facilities, such as common transport, a requesting carrier purchases access on a minute-by-minute basis. In either case, the requesting carrier's use of the element does not affect the incumbent LEC's physical control or duty to repair and maintain network elements.[451]

The Commission further determined that the fact that a feature may be sold directly to end users as a retail service does not mean that the same feature cannot also be part of a network element under the 1996 Act. The Commission stated that if it were to conclude that such features could not be defined as a network element, then incumbent LECs could provide local service to end users by selling them unbundled loops and switching elements and thereby entirely evade the unbundling requirement in section 251(c)(3).[452] Under the Commission's determination, incumbents must make vertical services such as Caller ID—which are features of the incumbent's switch—available both at the statutory rates for resale of complete services sold at retail to end users *and* at the statutory rates for unbundled network elements.

Incumbents challenged that determination in *Iowa Utilities*. They contended primarily that if finished services were available

---

[449] 47 U.S.C. §153(29). *See also* 47 C.F.R. §51.5.

[450] *Local Competition Order,* 11 F.C.C. Rec. at 15,611 ¶258. *See also* 47 C.F.R. §51.307(c).

[451] *Local Competition Order,* 11 F.C.C. Rec. at 15,611 ¶258. *See also* 47 C.F.R. §51.309(c).

[452] *Local Competition Order,* 11 F.C.C. Rec. at 15,633 ¶263.

both as network elements and under the separate resale pricing methodology, entrants would take advantage of the 1996 Act by obtaining the same service at one of two different rates, depending on which was more attractive in a particular context. Incumbents also pointed to legislative history showing that "services" were originally included in the definition of network elements, but that that term was removed before the 1996 Act was passed.

The Eighth Circuit rejected that argument. It concluded that "[w]hile Section 251(c)(4) does provide for the resale of telecommunications services, it does not establish resale as the exclusive means through which a competing carrier may gain access to such services."[453] The court further "agree[d] with the FCC that [the incumbent's interpretation] would allow the incumbent LECs to evade a substantial portion of their unbundling obligation" by making unbundled elements available at retail.[454]

The Supreme Court was similarly unpersuaded by the incumbents' argument. The Court concluded that "vertical switching features, such as Caller I.D., are 'functions . . . provided by means of' the switch, and thus fall squarely within the statutory definition" of a network element.[455]

(ii) For the Provision of a Telecommunications Service. Under section 251(c)(3), a requesting carrier may obtain unbundled access from an incumbent LEC "for the provision of a telecommunications service."[456] That language is broader than the reference to interconnection "for the transmission and routing of telephone exchange and exchange access" in section 251(c)(2), and the FCC has accordingly concluded that unbundled elements obtained pursuant to section 251(c)(3) may be used for a broader range of services than subsection (c)(2) allows for interconnection.[457]

---

[453] *Iowa Utils. Bd.*, 120 F.3d at 809.
[454] *Id.*
[455] AT&T v. Iowa Utils. Bd., 119 S. Ct. at 734.
[456] *See* 47 C.F.R. §51.315(a).
[457] *Local Competition Order,* 11 F.C.C. Rec. at 15,636 ¶270.

The Commission defined "provision" for purposes of section 251(c)(3) to include not only the physical delivery through network facilities, but also the delivery "through information (such as billing information) that enables incumbents to offer services on a commercial basis to consumers." This includes, for example, "information required for pre-ordering, ordering, provisioning, billing, and maintenance and repair services."[458]

The Commission further ruled that incumbents may not restrict the types of telecommunications services requesting carriers may offer through unbundled elements, nor may they restrict requesting carriers from combining elements with any technically compatible equipment the requesting carriers own.[459] Moreover, incumbents must provide requesting carriers with all of the functionalities of a particular element so that the requesting carriers can provide any telecommunications services that can be offered by means of the element—even if that service is different from the one that the incumbent currently provides.[460]

(iii) Access Standards.   Under section 251(d)(2) of the Act, the Commission, in determining what UNEs should be made available, is required to "consider, at a minimum," whether "(A) access to such network elements as are proprietary in nature is necessary; and (B) the failure to provide access to such network elements would impair the ability of the telecommunications carrier seeking access to provide the services that it seeks to offer."[461]

The FCC interpreted these standards in an extremely relaxed way. Indeed, before it ever even reached the issue of the limitations that these standards placed on incumbents' unbundling obligations, the FCC determined that other language in section 251(c)(3) created very broad duties for incumbents. Drawing on section 251(c)(3)'s statement that unbundled elements must be

---

[458] *Id.* at 15,633 ¶¶261–262.
[459] *Id.* at 15,646–15,647 ¶292. *See also* 47 C.F.R. §51.309(a).
[460] *Local Competition Order,* 11 F.C.C. Rec. at 15,647 ¶292.
[461] *Id.* at 15,616 ¶227, 15,637–15,644 ¶¶271–272, 15,640–15,642 ¶¶277–282.

made "available at any technically feasible point," the Commission held that a determination that it is technically feasible to unbundle a particular facility generally *requires* the conclusion that the element should be made available on an unbundled basis.[462] Technical feasibility thus created a strong presumption that an element should be unbundled.[463]

Turning to the "necessity" and "impairment" standards themselves, the Commission determined that they do little, if anything, to undermine the heavy presumption that it thought was created by the "at any technically feasible point" language. Most important, the Commission concluded that in determining whether those standards are met, both the federal agency itself and state commissions in subsequent arbitration proceedings need look only to the alternative functionalities available *within the incumbent's own network.*[464] To the Commission, any evaluation of whether an entrant could obtain an element from any other source would "nullify" section 251(c)(3).[465] Then, in determining whether it was "necessary" to obtain a particular proprietary element, the FCC determined that the relevant standard for itself and for state agencies is whether the entrant's ability to compete "would be significantly impaired or thwarted."[466] And an entrant's ability to provide service is "impaired"—thus mandating that the incumbent turn over nonproprietary elements—if "the quality of the service the entrant can offer, absent access to the requested element, declines, and/or the cost of providing the service rises."[467]

In its *Iowa Utilities* decision, the Eighth Circuit overturned the FCC's understanding that technical feasibility creates a presumption that an element should be unbundled. The court of

[462] *Id.* at 15,640–15,641 ¶¶278–280.
[463] *Id.* at 15,616 ¶227, 15,637–15,644 ¶¶271–288; *see also* 47 C.F.R. §51.317 (b); AT&T v. Iowa Utils. Bd., 119 S. Ct. at 736.
[464] *Local Competition Order,* 11 F.C.C. Rec. at 15,643 ¶285, 15,644 ¶¶287–288; *see also* 47 C.F.R. §51.317(b)(1)(ii); AT&T v. Iowa Utils. Bd., 119 S. Ct. at 735.
[465] *Local Competition Order,* 11 F.C.C. Rec. at 15,644 ¶287.
[466] *Id.* at 15,641–15,642 ¶282.
[467] *Id.* at 15,643 ¶285. *See also* 47 C.F.R. §51.317(b)(2).

appeals concluded that "[b]y its very terms," the statutory reference to access at a "technically feasible point" "only indicates *where* unbundled access may occur, not *which* elements must be unbundled."[468] The FCC's contrary understanding was thus inconsistent with the plain language of the statute and could not be upheld.[469]

The court of appeals, however, found no fault with the FCC's conclusion that any evaluation of "necessity" and "impairment" need not consider whether the entrant could obtain the element from sources other than the incumbent. Echoing the Commission's reasoning, the court concluded that "[a]llowing incumbent LECs to evade their unbundling duties whenever a network element could be obtained elsewhere would eviscerate unbundled access as a means of entry and delay competition."[470] The court of appeals then concluded that the FCC's definitions of the words "necessary" and "impair" accorded with some prior usages and dictionary definitions and thus were reasonable.[471]

The Supreme Court disagreed with the Eighth Circuit as to the lawfulness of the FCC's interpretation of the necessary and impair standards (the technical feasibility issue was not before the Court). The Court explained:

> The Commission cannot, consistent with the statute, blind itself to the availability of elements outside the incumbent's network. That failing alone would require the Commission's rule to be set aside. In addition, however, the Commission's assumption that *any* increase in cost (or decrease in quality) imposed by denial of a network element renders access to that element "necessary," and causes the failure to provide that element to "impair" the entrant's ability to furnish its desired services is simply not in accord with the ordinary and fair meaning of those terms.[472]

Elaborating on these points in his concurrence, Justice Breyer explained that, "given the Act's basic purpose, [section 251(c)]

---

[468] *Iowa Utils. Bd.*, 120 F.3d at 810.
[469] *Id.*
[470] *Id.* at 811.
[471] *Id.* 811–812.
[472] AT&T v. Iowa Utils. Bd., 119 S. Ct. at 735.

requires a convincing explanation of why facilities should be shared (or 'unbundled') where a new entrant could compete effectively without the facility, or where practical alternatives to that facility are available."[473] Justice Breyer noted that there were three main objections to too much unbundling. First, sharing entails significant administrative costs because "someone must oversee the terms and conditions of that sharing." Second, "a sharing requirement may diminish the original owner's incentive to keep up or to improve the property by depriving the owner of the fruits of value-creating investment, research, or labor." Third, "[i]ncreased sharing by itself does not automatically mean increased competition. It is in the *un*shared, not in the shared, portions of the enterprise that meaningful competition would likely emerge. Rules that force firms to share *every* resource or element of a business would create, not competition, but pervasive regulation, for the regulators, not the marketplace, would set the relevant terms."[474]

Because the FCC had applied an incorrect standard in determining that incumbents must provide access to specific network elements (determinations we address further below), the Supreme Court vacated all of the Commission's requirements for access to specific elements, which were contained in 47 C.F.R. §51.319; the FCC must now revisit all these rules. It would also seem that, by necessary implication, moreover, the Supreme Court's decision also invalidates 47 C.F.R. §51.317, which directs states to apply the now-discredited necessary and impair standards in determining whether additional elements should be made available. The Eighth Circuit is to receive briefing of that issue on remand.

(iv) Provision of Combined Elements and Access to All the Network Elements Necessary to Duplicate an Incumbent's Local Service.   One of the thorniest issues to arise in the wake of the 1996 Act has been the ability to use network elements as a substitute

[473] *Id.* at 753 (Breyer, J., concurring in part and dissenting in part).
[474] *Id.* at 753.

for resale—but *without* adhering to the resale pricing methodology, *without* adhering to the joint marketing restrictions that under 47 U.S.C. §271(e)(1) applied for three years from passage of the Act to the big long-distance carriers if they sold an incumbent's local service, *without* having to pay access charges as resellers do, and *with* the capacity to offer additional capabilities and services.

The basic problem is as follows. If entrants may obtain all the elements necessary to provide service and may request those elements in a precombined format, they obtain the same functionality from the incumbent that a reseller obtains. Accordingly, a duty to provide access to all the precombined elements necessary to provide service is, in the minds of many, substantively indistinguishable from an incumbent's separate duty to provide access to complete services for resale. As noted above, however, an entrant using such combined elements avoids the pricing and other limitations associated with resale. Incumbents argued strenuously that such access destroys the statutory distinction between resale and access to network elements, undermines Congress's intent to encourage competing facilities-based networks, leads inevitably to massive losses for incumbents, and undermines universal service.[475] With respect to this last point, incumbents have argued that such losses will place enormous pressure on the basic service rates of rural and residential customers, which, as discussed in sections 2.1 and 6.1, are often below cost and subsidized with revenues from more profitable services. On the other hand, AT&T and other new entrants have argued that access to this so-called "platform" of all the precombined elements needed to provide local service is crucial to jump-starting local competition.

The FCC sided with the entrants. In its *Local Competition Order,* the Commission determined that new entrants should be able to obtain all the network elements necessary to replicate an incumbent's existing local service—or, put differently, that a carrier did not need to own any local facilities in order to obtain

---

[475] *See Local Competition Order,* 11 F.C.C. Rec. at 15,661–15,664 ¶¶318–322.

unbundled elements from an incumbent.[476] The FCC also required incumbents not to separate unbundled elements that are already combined in the incumbent's network and even to create new combinations of elements for the benefit of entrants.[477] Simply put, under the FCC's order, there was no limit on the ability of entrants to use preassembled, but nominally "unbundled," network elements interchangeably with resale—but without the statutory limitations that Congress had placed on resellers.

Unlike the Commission, however, the Eighth Circuit largely agreed with the incumbents. In its *Iowa Utilities* decision, it determined that the statute did not permit such an end run on the statutory resale rules. In the court's words: "To permit such an acquisition of already combined elements at cost based rates for unbundled access would obliterate the careful distinction Congress has drawn in subsections 251(c)(3) and (4) between access to unbundled network elements on the one hand and the purchase at wholesale rates of an incumbent's telecommunications retail services for resale on the other."[478]

Thus, although the court of appeals concluded that the FCC acted reasonably in determining that entrants could receive all the elements necessary to provide service,[479] it simultaneously determined that entrants could not receive those elements on a *combined* basis. Relying on section 251(c)(3)'s statement that "requesting carrier[s]"—not incumbents—will "combine" elements, the court of appeals determined that the FCC's conclusion that incumbents must provide precombined sets of network elements was inconsistent with the plain language of the 1996 Act.[480] Under the Eighth Circuit's ruling, therefore, incumbents may disassemble parts of their networks and require an entrant to reassemble those parts if the entrant wants to receive all the

---

[476] *Id.* at 15,666–15,671 ¶¶328–341.

[477] *Local Competition Order,* 11 F.C.C. Rec. at 15,647 ¶¶293–294; 47 C.F.R. §51.315(b)–(f).

[478] *Iowa Utils. Bd.,* 120 F.3d at 813.

[479] *Id.* at 814–815.

[480] *Id.* at 813.

advantages of obtaining access to a complete service under the network element rules, and not the statutory resale rules. As a practical matter, since the Eighth Circuit clarified in an October 1997 rehearing order that it intended to allow incumbents to disassemble these combinations before turning them over to entrants and vacated the contrary FCC regulation (47 C.F.R. §51.315(b)), the platform approach, which was initially a significant part of the local entry strategy of AT&T and other carriers, has been moribund.

The Supreme Court's January 1999 decision may or may not revive the platform. The Court rejected incumbents' arguments as to both whether an entrant had to have some of its own facilities to obtain network elements and whether the FCC could prohibit incumbents from separating elements before turning them over to new entrants. On the first point, the Court explained that in its view the FCC "reasonably omitted a facilities-ownership requirement. The 1996 Act contains no such limitation; if anything, it suggests the opposite, by requiring in §251(c)(3) that incumbents provide access to 'any' requesting carrier."[481] On the combination issue, the Court concluded that "§251(c)(3) is ambiguous on whether leased network elements may or must be separated, and the rule the Commission has prescribed is entirely rational, finding its basis in §251(c)(3)'s nondiscrimination requirement."[482]

The Court expressly acknowledged, however, that both these issues may be rendered largely "academic" because of the need for a remand as to what network elements must be made available.[483] As the Court correctly understood, the "combination" and "all elements" issues are relevant largely because they relate to whether new entrants may obtain a full platform of all the elements necessary to provide service. If, under a proper application of the necessary and impair standards, incumbents need not provide all the basic network pieces that make up the platform, that issue becomes mooted for reasons wholly independent of

[481] AT&T v. Iowa Utils. Bd., 119 S. Ct. at 736.
[482] *Id.* at 737.
[483] *See id.*

whether an incumbent must provide combined elements or whether the statute permits an entrant without facilities of its own to purchase all the network elements necessary to provide service. The fate of the platform thus remains very much an open question.

(v) Specific Unbundling Requirements. The following sections describe the specific network elements that the Commission required incumbent LECs to unbundle in its *Local Competition Order.* As we have already explained, the Supreme Court has vacated these specific requirements and required the FCC to reconsider them. Nonetheless, at least some of these obligations may be reimposed on remand, and in any event, the FCC's initial set of rules on these issues provides important background to any understanding of the post-1996 Act landscape.

(a) Local loops. Under the *Local Competition Order,* incumbent LECs were required to provide local loops on an unbundled basis to requesting carriers.[484]

The Commission has refused to define the loop element "in functional terms" and instead defined a loop "in terms of the facility itself."[485] It defined the local loop element "as a transmission facility between a distribution frame, or its equivalent, in an incumbent LEC central office, and the network interface device at the customer premises."[486] The Commission stated that an "appropriate access point" for an unbundled loop would be the main distribution frame in a LEC central office.[487]

---

[484] *Local Competition Order,* 11 F.C.C. Rec. at 15,689 ¶377. "Without access to unbundled local loops, new entrants would need to invest immediately in duplicative facilities in order to compete for customers. Such investment and building would likely delay market entry and postpone the benefits of local telephone competition for consumers. Moreover, without access to unbundled loops, new entrants would be required to make a large initial sunk investment in loop facilities before they had a customer base large enough to justify such an expenditure." *Id.* at 15,690 ¶378. *See also* 47 C.F.R. §51.319(a).

[485] *Local Competition Order,* 11 F.C.C. Rec. at 15,693 ¶385.

[486] *Id.* at 15,691 ¶380; 47 C.F.R. §51.319(a).

[487] *Local Competition Order,* 11 F.C.C. Rec. at 15,690–15,691 ¶379.

The *Local Competition Order* further provided that the definition of an unbundled loop includes two-wire and four-wire analog voice-grade loops and two-wire and four-wire loops that are conditioned to transmit the digital signals needed to provide advanced data services, such as digital subscriber lines (DSLs).[488] The Commission noted that this aspect of its loop definition would in some instances require the incumbent LEC to take affirmative steps to condition existing loop facilities to enable requesting carriers to provide services not currently provided over such facilities. Requesting carriers would, however, be required to bear the cost of compensating the incumbent LEC for such conditioning.[489]

The Commission's suggestion that incumbents would have to alter their loops in order to allow entrants to provide services over these facilities that the facilities do not currently support has been the subject of controversy. Elsewhere in its *Local Competition Order,* the FCC specifically stated that this conditioning obligation was an "example" of a "superior quality" requirement."[490] But as discussed above (section 5.5.3.4), on review of that order, the Eighth Circuit held that the 1996 Act does not permit the FCC to require incumbents to provide "superior quality" interconnection or network elements.[491]

Despite the Eighth Circuit's unequivocal holding, the FCC again concluded in its 1998 *Advanced Services Order* that incumbents must condition their loops to make them usable for these advanced data services.[492] Several petitions for reconsideration raising this issue are pending before the Commission.[493]

The Commission also required incumbent LECs to offer unbundled access to its network interface device (NID), a piece of

[488] *Id.* at 15,691 ¶380.

[489] *Id.* at 15,692 ¶382.

[490] *Id.* at 15,659 ¶314 n.680.

[491] *Iowa Utils. Bd.,* 120 F.3d at 813.

[492] Deployment of Wireline Services Offering Advanced Telecommunications Capability, Memorandum Opinion and Order and Notice of Proposed Rulemaking, 13 Comm. Reg. (P & F) 1 ¶53 (Aug. 7, 1998) (hereinafter *Advanced Services Order*).

[493] *See, e.g.,* Deployment of Wireline Services Offering Advanced Telecommunications Capability, Petition for Reconsideration of SBC Communications, CC Docket No. 98-147 et al. (FCC Sept. 8, 1998).

equipment used to connect loop facilities to the wiring inside a customer's premises.[494] The Commission stated that a requesting carrier is entitled to connect its loops, via its own NID, to the incumbent LEC's NID. The Commission rejected suggestions that would require an incumbent LEC to permit a new entrant to connect its loops directly to the incumbent LEC's NID. The Commission left it to the states to determine whether direct connection to the NID can be achieved in a technically feasible manner in the context of specific requests by competitors.[495]

The Commission also declined to adopt a requirement that incumbent LECs provide subloop unbundling—that is, access to some discrete parts of the local loop element. The Commission found that proponents of subloop unbundling had not addressed certain technical issues raised by incumbent LECs including, for instance, the network security issues raised when new entrants' technicians tried to access parts of the local loop.[496] The Commission thus left the technical feasibility of subloop unbundling to be addressed "at the state level on a case-by-case basis."[497] The Commission also said that it would revisit the specific issue of subloop unbundling sometime in 1997, but it has yet to do so.[498]

Subsequently, state commissions have reached varying decisions regarding subloop unbundling, and decisions reaching opposing conclusions based on the particular records presented in state proceedings have been affirmed by federal courts.[499] The states that have required subloop access may be required to revisit that issue in light of the FCC's forthcoming "impairment" regulations.

---

[494] *See* 47 C.F.R. §51.319(b)(1).
[495] *Local Competition Order,* 11 F.C.C. Rec. at 15,697–15,699 ¶¶392–396. *See also* 47 C.F.R. §51.319(b).
[496] *Local Competition Order,* 11 F.C.C. Rec. at 15,696 ¶391.
[497] *Id.*
[498] *Id.*
[499] *Compare, e.g.,* MCI Telecomms. v. Bell Atlantic-Va., No. 3:97CV629 (E.D. Va. July 1, 1998) (upholding denial of subloop unbundling) *with* Southwestern Bell Tel. Co. v. AT&T, No. A 97-CA-132 SS at 10 (W.D. Tex. Aug. 31, 1998) (upholding approval of subloop unbundling).

(b) Local switching capability. Under the *Local Competition Order,* incumbent LECs were also required to provide local switching as an unbundled network element.[500] The Commission defined the local switching element to encompass "line-side and trunk-side facilities plus the features, functions, and capabilities of the switch."[501] The line-side facilities include "the connection between a loop termination at, for example, a main distribution frame (MDF), and a switch line card."[502] Trunk-side facilities include "the connection between, for example, trunk termination at a trunk-side cross-connect panel and a trunk card."[503] The "features, functions, and capabilities" of the local switch include "the basic switching function of connecting lines to lines, lines to trunks, trunks to lines, trunks to trunks. [Those features] also include [ ] the same basic capabilities that are available to the incumbent LEC's customers, such as a telephone number, directory listing, dial tone, signaling, and access to 911, operator services, and directory assistance."[504]

As noted above (section 5.5.3.5(i)), the *Local Competition Order* further mandated that the local switching element include "all vertical features that the switch is capable of providing, including custom calling, CLASS features, and Centrex."[505] As we further explained above, both the Eighth Circuit and the Supreme Court rejected incumbents' objections to the FCC's determination that such features constitute network elements.[506] It remains to be seen, however, whether access to such features is consistent with the necessity and impairment tests that the FCC must apply on remand from the Supreme Court's decision.

[500] *See* 47 C.F.R. §51.319(c).

[501] *Local Competition Order,* 11 F.C.C. Rec. at 15,706 ¶412.

[502] *Id. See also* 47 C.F.R. §51.319(c)(1)(i)(A).

[503] *Local Competition Order,* 11 F.C.C. Rec. at 15,706 ¶412. *See also* 47 C.F.R. §51.319(c)(1)(i)(B).

[504] *Local Competition Order,* 11 F.C.C. Rec. at 15,706 ¶412. *See also* 47 C.F.R. §51.319(c)(1)(i)(C)(1).

[505] *Local Competition Order,* 11 F.C.C. Rec. at 15,706 ¶412. *See also* 47 C.F.R. §51.319(c)(1)(i)(C)(2).

[506] *Iowa Utils. Bd.,* 120 F.3d at 808; AT&T v. Iowa Utils. Bd., 119 S. Ct. at 728–729.

Finally, the FCC determined that "customized routing"—a feature that permits requesting carriers to designate the particular outgoing trunks that will carry certain classes of traffic and thus will allow entrants to self-provide operator services and directory assistance—is technically feasible on many incumbent switches and must be provided where feasible.[507]

(c) Tandem switching capability.   Tandem switches connect only trunks, not lines, and perform switching between end office switches. Under the *First Local Competition Order,* incumbent LECs were required to provide access to their tandem switches unbundled from interoffice transmission facilities. The Commission defined the tandem switch element to include "the facilities connecting the trunk distribution frames to the switch, and all the functions of the switch itself, including those facilities that establish a temporary transmission path between two other switches."[508] The FCC's definition of the tandem switching element also includes the "functions that are centralized in tandems rather than in separate end office switches, such as call recording, the routing of calls to operator services, and signaling conversion functions."[509]

(d) Packet switching capability.   Packet switches are used to provide a wide variety of data services. In its *Local Competition Order,* the FCC, citing the inadequacy of the record, refused to require incumbent LECs to make their packet switches available as network elements.[510] In a subsequent Notice of Proposed Rulemaking in its Advanced Services Docket, however, the FCC has suggested that it intends to require unbundling of packet switching.[511] The Commission may well be required to alter that

---

[507] *Local Competition Order,* 11 F.C.C. Rec. at 15,709 ¶418.

[508] *Id.* at 15,713 ¶426. *See also* 47 C.F.R. §51.319(c)(2)(i)–(ii).

[509] *Local Competition Order,* 11 F.C.C. Rec. at 15,713 ¶426. *See also* 47 C.F.R. §51.319(c)(2)(iii).

[510] *Local Competition Order,* 11 F.C.C. Rec. at 15,713 ¶427.

[511] *See* Deployment of Wireline Services Offering Advanced Telecommunications Capability, Memorandum and Order, and Notice of Proposed Rulemaking, 13 F.C.C. Rec. at 24011 (1998).

view to accord with the Supreme Court's recent decision requiring the Commission to consider the availability of elements outside the incumbent's network in carrying out the statutorily mandated necessity and impairment inquiries. We discuss unbundling of elements necessary for advanced services further both below and in Chapter 11.[512]

(e) Interoffice transmission facilities.   Under the *Local Competition Order,* incumbent LECs were also required to provide interoffice transmission facilities on an unbundled basis to requesting carriers.[513] This duty required incumbent LECs to provide unbundled access to (1) shared transmission facilities between end offices and the tandem switch and (2) dedicated transmission facilities between LEC central offices or between such offices and those of competing carriers. The Commission stated that "at a minimum" incumbent LECs would have to provide access to "interoffice facilities between end offices and serving wire centers (SWCs), SWCs and IXC [points of presence], tandem switches and SWCs, end offices or tandems of the incumbent LEC, and the wire centers of incumbent LECs and requesting carriers."[514] In addition, incumbent LECs were required to provide "all technically feasible transmission capabilities, such as DS1, DS3, and Optical Carrier levels (e.g., OC-3/12/48/96) that the competing provider could use to provide telecommunications services."[515]

In a subsequent order, the FCC also specifically identified "shared transport"—which it defined as all shared interoffice transport facilities—as a network element that incumbents were required to provide.[516] Under the FCC's understanding, an entrant who buys shared transport could obtain access to the *undifferentiated* whole of the incumbent's transport facilities and thus

[512] *See* §11.4.2.
[513] *Local Competition Order,* 11 F.C.C. Rec. at 15,717 ¶439. *See also* 47 C.F.R. §51.319(d).
[514] *Local Competition Order,* 11 F.C.C. Rec. at 15,718 ¶440.
[515] *Id.*
[516] Implementation of Local Competition Provisions in the Telecommunications Act of 1996, Third Order on Reconsideration and Further Notice of Proposed Rulemaking, 12 F.C.C. Rec. 12,460 (1997).

would not need to purchase access to specifically enumerated facilities.

Several incumbents challenged that conclusion as inconsistent both with the statutory definition of a "network element" (because shared transport, as the FCC understood it, did not refer to a particular "facility or equipment") and with the Eighth Circuit's prior *Iowa Utilities* (later invalidated) holding that incumbents could not be required to provide combinations of network elements (because shared transport as the FCC understood it could be provided only when precombined by the incumbent with switching and with the routing functions of the switch).

Despite those arguments, the Eighth Circuit affirmed the FCC's order as consistent with both the text of the 1996 Act and the Circuit court's own *Iowa Utilities* decision.[517] Subsequently, however, the Supreme Court vacated the Eighth Circuit's order and remanded the matters for further proceedings consistent with the revised necessity and impairment guidelines that the FCC must create in response to the Court's 1999 *Iowa Utilities* decision.[518]

(f) Databases and signaling systems. (1) Signaling links and signaling transfer points. In parallel to their voice networks, incumbent LECs operate signaling networks that are used to transport information associated with individual calls. In the *Local Competition Order,* the Commission required LECs to provide access to their signaling links and signaling transfer points (STPs)—packet switches that connect these links—on an unbundled basis.[519] The Commission refused to require that incumbent LECs permit requesting carriers to link their own STPs directly to the incumbent's switch or call-related databases.[520]

---

[517] Southwestern Bell Tel. Co. v. FCC, 153 F.3d 597 (8th Cir. 1998).

[518] Ameritech Corp. v. FCC, 1999 WL 116994 (U.S. June 1, 1999) (No. 98-1381).

[519] *Local Competition Order,* 11 F.C.C. Rec. at 15,738 ¶479. *See also* 47 C.F.R. §51.319(e)(1)(i).

[520] *Local Competition Order,* 11 F.C.C. Rec. at 15,739 ¶480. *See also* 47 C.F.R. §51.319(e)(1)(iv).

(2) Call-related databases.   Under the *Local Competition Order,* incumbent LECs were also required to provide access to their call-related databases—signaling databases used for billing and collection or used in the transmission, routing, or other provision of a telecommunications service—for the purpose of switch query and database response through the signaling network.[521] In particular, the Commission expressly found that it was technically feasible for incumbent LECs to provide access to the line information database (LIDB), the toll free calling database, and number portability downstream databases.[522] The Commission required incumbent LECs to provide this access to their call-related databases by means of physical access at the STP linked to the unbundled database.[523] The FCC refused, however, to require that LECs provide direct access to call-related databases by unbundling the service control point (SCP) from its associated STP.[524]

The Commission also required LECs to provide access to call-related databases used in the incumbent's advanced intelligent network (AIN)—that is, the capabilities that allow telephone companies to perform advanced functions (such as playing recorded announcements) using computers and software that are completely independent of the central office switch that traditionally has performed such functions.[525] The Commission noted that although access to incumbent AIN SCPs is technically feasible, "such access may present the need for mediation mechanisms to, among other things, protect data in incumbent AIN SCPs and ensure against excessive traffic volumes. In addition, there may be mediation issues a competing carrier will need to address before requesting such access."[526] The Commission

---

[521] *Local Competition Order,* 11 F.C.C. Rec. at 15,741 ¶484. *See also* 47 C.F.R. §51.319(e)(2)(i).
[522] *Local Competition Order,* 11 F.C.C. Rec. at 15,741 ¶484. *See also* 47 C.F.R. §51.319(e)(2)(ii).
[523] *Local Competition Order,* 11 F.C.C. Rec. at 15,742 ¶484.
[524] *Id.* at 15,742 ¶485.
[525] *Id.* at 15,742 ¶486. *See also* 47 C.F.R. §51.319(e)(2)(v).
[526] *Local Competition Order,* 11 F.C.C. Rec. at 15,743 ¶488.

stated that "if parties are unable to agree to appropriate mediation mechanisms through negotiations," the states should resolve these problems in arbitration, where they "must consider whether such mediation mechanisms will be available and will adequately protect against intentional or unintentional misuse of the incumbent's AIN facilities."[527] The Commission encouraged incumbent LECs and competitive carriers "to participate in industry fora and industry testing to resolve outstanding mediation concerns. Incumbent LECs may establish reasonable certification and testing programs for carriers proposing to access AIN call related databases in a manner similar to those used for SS7 certification."[528]

In the *Local Competition Order,* the Commission further recognized the concern that requiring incumbent LECs to provide unbundled access to AIN call-related databases at cost "may reduce the incumbent's incentive to develop new and advanced services using AIN."[529] The Commission stated that this concern was outweighed by the fact that "requiring entrants to bear the cost of deploying a fully redundant network architecture, including AIN databases and their application software, would constitute a significant barrier to market entry for competitive carriers."[530] The Commission stated that it would "revisit the proper balance between providing unbundled access and maintaining the incentives of incumbent LECs to innovate" at a later date, for example, when competition "reduce[s] the incumbent LEC's control over bottleneck facilities and increase[s] the importance of innovation."[531] As discussed in Chapter 12, the FCC has subsequently revisited that general issue, but without granting extensive relief to incumbents, in its advanced services proceeding. It will be required to consider it again in light of the Supreme Court's *Iowa Utilities* decision.

[527] *Id.*
[528] *Id.*
[529] *Id.* at 15,744 ¶489.
[530] *Id.*
[531] *Id.*

(3) Service management systems. Under the *Local Competition Order,* incumbent LECs were also required to provide access to the service management systems (SMSs) that allow competitors to create, modify, or update information in call-related data-bases.[532] Incumbent LECs must allow competitors to input information into the SMS database by the same means that the incumbents use, be it magnetic tapes or through an electronic interface.[533]

The Commission required that competitors be given access to the incumbent LEC's AIN through the incumbent LEC's service creation environment (SCE), an interface used to design, create, and test AIN-supported services.[534] The SCE is where software is tested before it is transferred to the SMS, where it is then downloaded into an SCP database for active deployment on the network. The Commission recognized in this regard that, "although technically feasible, providing nondiscriminatory access to the SMS and SCE for the creation and deployment of AIN services may require some modifications, including appropriate mediation, to accommodate such access by requesting carriers."[535]

(4) Third-party call-related databases. In the *Local Competition Order,* the Commission found "that there is not enough evidence in the record to make a determination as to the technical feasibility of interconnection of third party call-related databases to the incumbent LEC's signaling system."[536] The Commission held that "state commissions could find such an arrangement to be technically feasible" and that it did "not intend to preempt such an order through these rules."[537] The Commission stated that it

[532] *Local Competition Order,* 11 F.C.C. Rec. at 15,746 ¶493. *See also* 47 C.F.R. §51.319(e)(3)(i).
[533] *Local Competition Order,* 11 F.C.C. Rec. at 15,746 ¶494. *See also* 47 C.F.R. §51.319(e)(3)(ii).
[534] *Local Competition Order,* 11 F.C.C. Rec. at 15,747 ¶495. *See also* 47 C.F.R. §51.319(e)(3)(iii).
[535] *Local Competition Order,* 11 F.C.C. Rec. at 15,748 ¶496. *See also* 47 C.F.R. §51.319(e)(3)(iv).
[536] *Local Competition Order,* 11 F.C.C. Rec. at 15,750 ¶501.
[537] *Id.* at 15,750–15,751 ¶502.

would revisit the issue in 1997,[538] but instead, in December 1998, it decided to terminate the intelligent networks proceeding where this issue had been assigned.[539] In doing this, the Commission reserved the ability to institute proceedings "[i]f a need for consideration of these issues should arise in the future."[540]

(5) Operation support systems.   In the *Local Competition Order,* the FCC ruled that an incumbent LEC must provide access to its operation support systems (OSSs)—the computerized preordering, ordering, provisioning, maintenance and repair, and billing systems that incumbents employ—as well as the information those systems contain.[541] In the FCC's view, Congress recognized that "the massive operations support systems employed by incumbent LECs, and the information such systems maintain and update to administer telecommunications networks and services, represent a significant potential barrier to entry" that should be addressed by unbundling these capabilities.[542]

In reaching that conclusion, the Commission reasoned that access to OSSs was authorized by the 1996 Act in several different ways. First, the support systems could be characterized as "databases" or "facilit[ies] . . . used in the provision of a telecommunications service," and the functions performed by such systems could be characterized as "features, functions, and capabilities that are provided by means of such facilit[ies]" within the meaning of 47 U.S.C. §153(29), the statutory provision that defines network elements.[543] Second, the information contained in, and processed by, operations support systems can be classified as "information sufficient for billing and collection or used in the transmission, routing, or other provision of a telecommunications service" within the meaning of the same statutory

---

[538] *Id.*
[539] Intelligent Networks, Order, CC Docket No. 91-346, ¶7 (Dec. 4, 1998).
[540] *Id.* ¶6.
[541] *Local Competition Order,* 11 F.C.C. Rec. at 15,763 ¶516. *See also* 47 C.F.R. §51.319(f)(1).
[542] *Local Competition Order,* 11 F.C.C. Rec. at 15,763 ¶516.
[543] *Id.* at 15,763 ¶517.

definition.[544] Third, nondiscriminatory access to the functions of operations support systems, which would include access to the information they contain, could be viewed as a "term or condition" of nondiscriminatory access to other network elements under section 251(c)(3) or of resale under section 251(c)(4).[545]

The Commission required incumbent LECs to provide nondiscriminatory access to their OSS functions for preordering, ordering, provisioning, maintenance and repair, and billing available to the LEC itself, which "necessarily includes access to the functionality of any internal gateway systems the incumbent employs in performing the above functions for its own customers."[546] An incumbent that provides network resources electronically does not meet its duty to provide nondiscriminatory access by offering competitors access that requires human intervention.[547]

In the *Iowa Utilities* proceedings, incumbent LECs challenged the FCC's decision to mandate such broad access to OSSs. The Eighth Circuit, however, rejected the claim that the FCC's decision was inconsistent with the 1996 Act. Emphasizing section 153(29)'s definition of a network element as a "facility or equipment used in the provision" of a "telecommunications service," a term that in turn is defined by section 153(46) to mean the "offering of telecommunications for a fee directly to the public," the court of appeals held that an OSS qualifies as a network element because it is necessary to the provision of telecommunications to the public. The court thus believed that it was reasonable to understand the statutory term "network element" to "include all of the facilities and equipment that are used in the overall commercial offering of telecommunications."[548]

The Supreme Court affirmed the Eighth Circuit's decision on that issue, although it stressed a different point. In the Court's view, "Section 153(29)'s reference to 'databases . . . and information sufficient for billing and collection or used in the transmission, routing, or other provision of a telecommunications

---

[544] *Id.*
[545] *Id.*
[546] *Id.* at 15,766–15,767 ¶523.
[547] *Id.*
[548] *Iowa Utils. Bd.,* 120 F.3d at 808–809.

service' provides ample basis for treating [OSS] as a 'network element.'"[549] Despite that ruling on the definitional issue, however, the Supreme Court's ruling on the necessity and impairment issues—and its vacation of all the FCC's specific unbundling requirements—will require the FCC to reconsider whether and to what extent incumbents must provide access to OSSs.

The obligation to provide nondiscriminatory access to OSSs has repeatedly been a major issue in the FCC's decision to reject the BOCs' petitions under section 271 to provide in-region long-distance service. In the context of those petitions, the FCC has looked exhaustively and in extraordinary detail at the specific level of OSS access that the BOC has offered to its competitors and in every instance to date has found that access insufficient to satisfy its understanding of the statutory requirements. The FCC has repeatedly concluded that incumbents have failed either to "deploy[ ] the necessary systems and personnel to provide sufficient access to each of the necessary OSS functions and . . . adequately [to] assist[ ] competing carriers to understand how to implement and use all of the OSS functions available to them" or to make these OSS functions "operationally ready, as a practical matter."[550]

(g) _Operator services and directory assistance._   Under the _Local Competition Order,_ incumbent LECs were also required to

---

[549] AT&T v. Iowa Utils. Bd., 119 S. Ct. at 734.

[550] Application of Ameritech Michigan Pursuant to Section 271 of the Communications Act of 1934, as Amended, to Provide In-Region IntraLATA Services, Memorandum Opinion and Order, 12 F.C.C. Rec. 20,543, 20,612 ¶136 (1997); Application of BellSouth Corporation, et al. Pursuant to Section 271 of the Communications Act of 1934, as Amended, to Provide In-Region IntraLATA Services in South Carolina, Memorandum Opinion and Order, 13 F.C.C. Rec. 539, 589 ¶88 (1997) (hereinafter _South Carolina Order_); Application by BellSouth Corporation, et al. Pursuant to Section 271 of the Communications Act of 1934, as Amended, to Provide In-Region IntraLATA Services in Louisiana, Memorandum Opinion and Order, 13 F.C.C. Rec. 6245, 6258 ¶22 (1998) (hereinafter _First Louisiana Order_); Application by BellSouth Corporation, et al. Pursuant to Section 271 of the Communications Act of 1934, as Amended, to Provide In-Region IntraLATA Services in Louisiana, Memorandum Opinion and Order, 13 F.C.C. Rec. 20,599, 20,604–20,605 ¶9 (1998) (hereinafter _Second Louisiana Order_).

provide access to their operator services and directory assistance facilities.[551] If a carrier requested an incumbent LEC to unbundle the facilities and functionalities providing operator services and directory assistance as separate network elements, the incumbent LEC was required to provide the competing provider with nondiscriminatory access to such facilities and functionalities at any technically feasible point.[552] The incumbent LEC was also required to rebrand or unbrand these services—that is, the incumbents' employees or facilities used to provide the service were obliged to identify the service as being provided by the competing carrier or not identify any carrier at all.[553]

Finally, incumbents were required to make available directory assistance databases in a manner that allows both entry of a requesting carrier's customer information into the database and the ability to read such a database so as to enable requesting carriers to provide operator services and directory assistance concerning the customers of the incumbent.[554] Whether that obligation required incumbents to allow so-called carry-out access to these databases—that is, whether the entrants may obtain a copy of the database or merely a physical "read-only" link to that database is an issue that has divided state commissions,[555] and the FCC has yet to provide a definitive answer.[556]

---

[551] 47 C.F.R. §51.217(c).

[552] *Local Competition Order,* 11 F.C.C. Rec. at 15,771–15,772 ¶534. Access to operator services and directory assistance must accord with the privacy protections accorded CPNI under 47 U.S.C. §222, a topic discussed in detail in §14.5.2. *See also* 47 C.F.R. §51.319(g).

[553] *See* 47 C.F.R. §51.217(d).

[554] *Local Competition Order,* 11 F.C.C. Rec. at 15,774 ¶538.

[555] *See* Order Resolving Non-pricing Arbitration Issues and Requiring Filing of Interconnection Agreement, Petition of AT&T Communications of Virginia, Inc. for Arbitration of Unresolved Issues from Interconnection Negotiations with GTE South, Inc. Pursuant to §252 of the Telecommunications Act of 1996, No. PUC960117 at 10-12 (Va. Corp. Commn. Dec. 11, 1996); Order, Telecommunications Arbitration Case 4—In the Matter of Petition of MCI Telecommunications Corp. for Arbitration of Unresolved Issues with Bell Atlantic—Washington, D.C., Inc. Pursuant to Section 252 of the Telecommunications Act of 1996, No. 8 at 26-29 (D.C.P.S.C. Dec. 26, 1996).

[556] *See Second Louisiana Order,* 13 F.C.C. Rec. at 20,744–20,745 ¶248.

(vi) Pricing of UNEs. Of course, the question that underlies all these unbundled access issues is the one of price. It is the price for access to network elements that determines whether that access is attractive to an entrant or, alternatively, whether the entrant will decide to build its own facilities. The 1996 Act specifies that unbundled elements must be made available at "just and reasonable rate[s]" that are "based on the cost (determined without reference to a rate-of-return or other rate-based proceeding) of providing" the network element and that "may include a reasonable profit."[557] In its *Local Competition Order,* the FCC purported to implement those statutory guidelines by adopting a detailed series of regulations establishing its total element long run incremental cost (TELRIC) methodology.[558] That methodology assumes the "use of the most efficient telecommunications technology currently available and the lowest cost network configuration," given the actual location of the incumbent's wire centers.[559]

We discuss the details of this pricing methodology in Chapter 2. It is important to note, however, that as of early 1999 the FCC's pricing rules had essentially never been in effect. Those rules were stayed on jurisdictional grounds by the Eighth Circuit within months after they were issued and ultimately were vacated on that same basis by the court.[560] Although the Supreme Court determined in January 1999 that the FCC had jurisdiction to issue these rules under section 201(b),[561] the Eighth Circuit must still decide whether those rules are substantively consistent with the 1996 Act.

In the absence of FCC regulations, it was left to state commissions around the country to determine appropriate pricing methodologies in the context of arbitrating agreement terms. While the states have generally adopted forward-looking methodologies, they have not uniformly adopted the FCC's specific TELRIC approach (at least as some have interpreted it). Some

---

[557] 47 U.S.C. §252(d)(1).
[558] *Local Competition Order,* 11 F.C.C. Rec. at 15,844 ¶672.
[559] 47 C.F.R. §51.505(b)(1).
[560] *Iowa Utils. Bd.,* 120 F.3d at 796.
[561] AT&T v. Iowa Utils. Bd., 119 S. Ct. at 729.

states, for instance, have assumed that not only the wire centers, but also the location of the local loops would remain unchanged in the future. To date, federal district courts have affirmed state commission decisions as consistent with the 1996 Act even where they arguably do not follow the FCC in all aspects of its methodology.[562]

§5.5.3.6　Resale

In addition to all local exchange carriers' general obligation to allow resale pursuant to section 251(b)(1), section 251(c)(4) provides a specific resale obligation on incumbent carriers. Section 251(c)(4) mandates that incumbent LECs have the duty "to offer for resale at wholesale rates any telecommunications service that the carrier provides at retail to subscribers who are not telecommunications carriers." Incumbent LECs have an additional duty "not to prohibit, and not to impose unreasonable or discriminatory conditions or limitations on, the resale of such telecommunications service."[563]

As noted in section 5.5.2.1 above, the FCC has concluded that this obligation differs from the one imposed by section 251(b)(1) in two respects. First, while subsection (b)(1) applies to all "telecommunications services," subsection (c)(4) applies only to telecommunications services provided at retail to subscribers who are not telecommunications carriers.[564] Second, in section 252(d)(3), the 1996 Act prescribed a specific pricing methodology for access to an incumbent's services.[565] That methodology requires incumbents to offer their services for resale "on the basis of retail rates charged to subscribers for the telecommunications service requested, excluding the portion thereof attributable to any marketing, billing, collection, and other costs that will be avoided by the local exchange carrier."[566]

---

[562] *See, e.g.,* MCI v. GTE Northwest, No. C97-067051, at 6–7 (W.D. Wash. Jul. 7, 1998); MCI v. Pacific Bell, No. C97-1756SI, at 6–11 (N.D. Cal. Sept. 29, 1998); AT&T v. Bell South, 20 F. Supp. 2d 1097 (1998).

[563] 47 U.S.C. §251(c)(4)(A)–(B).

[564] *Local Competition Order,* 11 F.C.C. Rec. at 15,981 ¶976.

[565] *Id.*

[566] 47 U.S.C. §252(d)(3).

We discuss both of these issues below, and the pricing issue is covered in greater detail in Chapter 2. We also discuss below the law regarding what resale limitations are considered "unreasonable and discriminatory" for purposes of both statutory subsections.

(i) *Services to Which the Section 251(c)(4) Resale Obligation Applies.* The statute itself provides significant guidance as to the scope of incumbents' resale duty. Under section 251(c)(4), that duty applies to (1) "telecommunications service[s]" (2) that "the carrier provides at retail to subscribers who are not telecommunications carriers." Because that test is largely self-explanatory, the FCC has largely declined to provide additional guidance on this point except to note that the statute does not limit the resale duty to basic telephone service.[567]

The FCC did hold, however, that exchange access services are not subject to this resale requirement. The Commission reached this conclusion for several reasons. First, "these services are predominantly offered to, and taken by, IXCs, not end-users."[568] Second, because access services are "an input component to the IXC's own retail service, LECs would not avoid any 'retail' costs when offering these services at 'wholesale' to these same IXCs."[569] Finally, "Section 251(c)(4) does not entitle subscribers to obtain services at wholesale rates for their own use. Permitting IXCs to purchase access services . . . would be inconsistent with this requirement."[570]

(ii) *Pricing of Services for Resale.* Section 252(d)(3) requires that incumbents make their services available "on the basis of retail rates charged to subscribers for the telecommunications service[s] requested, excluding the portion thereof attributable to any marketing, billing, collection, and other costs that will be avoided by the local exchange carrier." The import of this

---

[567] *Local Competition Order,* 11 F.C.C. Rec. at 15,934 ¶971; 47 C.F.R. §51.605(a).
[568] *Local Competition Order,* 11 F.C.C. Rec. at 15,935 ¶874.
[569] *Id.*
[570] *Id.*

pricing rule is discussed in greater depth in section 2.4.4.1. For present purposes, the key point is that this statutory provision creates a "top-down" methodology grounded in an incumbent's current retail prices. This methodology thus carries over all the implicit universal service subsidies contained in those rates. That rule stands in stark contrast to the "bottom-up" cost-based pricing that section 252(d)(1) mandates for access to network elements. Of course, it is this difference in pricing methodology (as well as the ability to avoid access charges and to make money on vertical services) that, as discussed above (section 5.5.3.5(iv)), has led the large interexchange carriers to try to engage in resale by another name—the so-called unbundled network element platform—and thus to obtain complete, finished services, while avoiding universal service burdens (at least until alternative, explicit universal service subsidy schemes are put in place). As we noted in discussing this issue previously, the viability of the platform still remains a live issue in light of the Supreme Court's January 1999 decision requiring the FCC to reconsider which specific elements must be made available by incumbents.

The Supreme Court's decision, however, does resolve the jurisdictional issue as to resale pricing. As discussed, the Court concluded that section 201(b) grants the FCC authority to issue rules governing pricing issues under the 1996 Act.[571] Incumbents are now free to challenge the substance of the FCC rules before the Eighth Circuit. In general, the key attribute of the FCC's rules is that they do not set rates based on the costs that actually *"will be avoided"* by the incumbent, as the statute indicates. Instead, the Commission concluded that avoided retail costs shall be those that are "avoidable" by a hypothetical company that provides only wholesale services.[572]

In the absence of FCC rules, states were free to determine their own ideas of an appropriate resale pricing methodology—of course, within the confines of the statutory language, of course. Where state commissions followed the FCC in applying

[571] *See* AT&T v. Iowa Utils. Bd., 119 S. Ct. at 730.
[572] *Local Competition Order,* 11 F.C.C. Rec. at 15,956 ¶¶911–912; 47 C.F.R. §51.609(b).

an "avoidable" cost methodology, that determination has been affirmed as consistent with the statute.[573]

The FCC has also held, in a decision that was never jurisdictionally controversial, that when an incumbent LEC resells services under section 251(c)(4), the incumbent is entitled to continue to receive interstate access-charge revenues: "IXCs must still pay access charges to incumbent LECs for originating or terminating interstate traffic, even when their end user is served by a telecommunications carrier that resells incumbent LEC retail services."[574] To ensure that this requirement is enforced, the Commission stated that "[n]ew entrants that purchase retail local exchange services from an incumbent LEC at wholesale rates are entitled to resell only those retail services, and not any other services —such as exchange access—the LEC may offer using the same facilities."[575]

(iii) Conditions and Limitations on Resale.   Given the many types of limitations that incumbents might place on resale of their services—and the fact that in a particular context those restrictions may serve legitimate procompetitive ends—the FCC's *Local Competition Order* did not attempt to provide encyclopedic rules as to whether each particular kind of restriction is or is not permissible. Rather, the FCC established a "presumption" that such restrictions are unreasonable, but allowed incumbents to rebut that presumption by demonstrating to a state commission "that [a particular] restriction is reasonable and nondiscriminatory."[576] The FCC suggested that any attempt to show that a resale restriction is reasonable must demonstrate that the limitation is "narrowly tailored" to serve appropriate goals.[577] That rule applies to limitations derived both from a

---

[573] MCI Telecomms. v. Bell Atlantic-Va., No. 3:97CV629, at 22–23; Southwestern Bell Tel. Co. v. AT&T, No. A 97-CA-132 SS, at 26–29; MCI v GTE Northwest, No. C97-742WD, No. C97-905WD, No. C97-928WD, at 6 (E.D. Wash. Jul. 1, 1998); MCI v. Pacific Bell, No. C 97-0670 SI, No. C 97-1756 SI, No. C 97-1757 SI, at 14–18 (N.D. Cal. Sept. 29, 1998).

[574] *Local Competition Order,* 11 F.C.C. Rec. at 15,982–15,983 ¶980.

[575] *Id.*

[576] 47 C.F.R. §51.613(b).

[577] *Local Competition Order,* 11 F.C.C. Rec. at 15,966 ¶939.

particular resale agreement and from the LEC's underlying tariff.[578]

The *Local Competition Order* followed a similar course in addressing the specific issues raised by resale of incumbents' promotional and discounted offerings. The FCC concluded that there was no basis to conclude that such offerings were generally exempt from statutory resale requirements,[579] but recognized that at least some promotions serve procompetitive purposes that would be undermined if they had to be made available at the promotional rate minus the statutory avoided cost discount.[580] In particular, promotions that are limited in length "enhanc[e] marketing and sales-based competition."[581] To preserve incumbents' incentives to offer such promotions, the Commission held that short-term promotional prices—those that last for no more than 90 days—do not constitute retail prices and thus are not subject to the statutory wholesale rate obligation.[582] Accordingly, the underlying service must still be made available for resale, but only at the normal retail rate minus the statutory wholesale discount. Incumbents may not evade the 90-day limitation by, for example, offering consecutive discounts.[583]

In the same vein, the FCC concluded that volume discounts must generally be made available to resellers—although perhaps at a different wholesale discount—and that end-user restrictions attached to a service could not be applied automatically to resold services.[584] Again, however, the Commission declined to create a bright-line rule and deferred resolution of specific issues to the states: "We conclude that the substance and specificity of rules concerning which discount and promotion

---

[578] *Id.*

[579] *Id.* at 15,970 ¶948. The FCC similarly found no statutory basis to exempt services offered at below-cost rates from the statutory resale requirement. *Id.* at 15,973 ¶956.

[580] *Id.* at 15,970 ¶949.

[581] *Id.*

[582] *Id.* at 15,970 ¶¶949–950; 47 C.F.R. §51.613(a)(2).

[583] *Local Competition Order,* 11 F.C.C. Rec. at 15,970–15,971 ¶950; 47 C.F.R. §51.613(a)(2)(ii).

[584] *Local Competition Order,* 11 F.C.C. Rec. at 15,971 ¶¶951–952.

restrictions may be applied to resellers in marketing their services to end users is a decision best left to state commissions, which are more familiar with the particular business practices of their incumbent LECs and local market conditions."[585] The FCC did conclude, however, that rules that prevent resellers from aggregating traffic from multiple end-users to reach the minimum usage requirements for volume discounts are presumptively unreasonable.[586]

In *Iowa Utilities*, the Eighth Circuit found that the FCC's decisions on resale of discounted and promotional offerings were (1) within the Commission's jurisdiction and (2) reasonable interpretations of the 1996 Act. The circuit court pointed to section 251(c)(4)(B) as "authoriz[ing] the Commission to issue regulations regarding the incumbent LECs' duty not to prohibit, or impose unreasonable limitations on, the resale of telecommunications services."[587] On the merits, the court found that the FCC's rules on these issues were valid because they "restric[t] the ability of incumbent LECs to circumvent their resale obligations under the Act."[588] Neither of those conclusions was affected by the Supreme Court's subsequent decision in the *Iowa Utilities* case.

Because the *Local Competition Order* left it to state commissions to determine whether particular resale limitations are reasonable, there has been repeated skirmishing on these issues in those fora. One area of dispute that has arisen repeatedly is whether so-called contract service arrangements (or CSAs)—customer-specific rates that incumbents negotiate to address a particular competitive circumstance—must be made available for resale and, if so, whether any restrictions on such resale are appropriate. Incumbents argued that if they were required to make their negotiated CSAs available at a wholesale discount on top of the negotiated discount, their competitors could always undercut those special rates, thus undermining any incentive that the incumbents had to offer these discounts in the first place. Incumbents were willing, however, to make the underlying

[585] *Id.* at 15,971 ¶952.
[586] *Id.* at 15,971 ¶953.
[587] *Iowa Utils. Bd.*, 120 F.3d at 819.
[588] *Id.*

527

service that was subject to the CSA available at the normal whole-sale discount. State commissions in Louisiana, Georgia, and Minnesota, among other places, were convinced of the validity of that argument and placed significant limitations on the resale of CSAs.[589]

But in something of a bait-and-switch, the FCC—after first stating that it would defer to the states' judgment as to the propriety of particular resale limitations—subsequently indicated that it believed that at least those state decisions that flatly exempted CSAs from resale requirements were per se unlawful and would prevent a BOC from obtaining section 271 approval to provide long-distance service. The Commission concluded that such an exemption could not be considered to be "narrowly tailored" and would encourage incumbents to shift customers to CSAs in order to evade their statutory resale obligations.[590] At least one federal court has also agreed that a broad limitation on reselling CSAs is not permissible.[591]

More recently, however, the FCC has suggested that contract provisions limiting resale of CSAs to parties who are similarly situated to the party with whom the incumbent negotiated the original CSA may well be appropriate. In a section 271 decision,

[589] Interconnection Agreement Negotiations Between AT&T and BellSouth Telecommunications, No. U-22145, at 4 (La. P.S.C. Jan. 15, 1997) ("[r]equiring BellSouth to offer already discounted CSAs for resale at wholesale prices would create an unfair competitive advantage"); Petition by AT&T for Arbitration of Interconnection Rates, Terms, and Conditions with BellSouth Telecommunications, Inc., No. 6801-U, at 25 (Ga. P.S.C. Mar. 4, 1997) ("it would be reasonable and competitively neutral to make CSAs available for resale at no discount"); AT&T's, MCIMetro's and MFS's Consolidated Petition for Arbitration with U S WEST Communications, Inc., Nos. P-442,221/M-96-855, at 24 (Minn. P.U.C. Nov. 5, 1996) ("contract services . . . which are specifically packaged to provide volume or term discounts should be limited to the same class of customers eligible to purchase the service from USWC"); Petition by AT&T for Arbitration of Certain Terms and Conditions of a Proposed Agreement with GTE Concerning Interconnection and Resale, No. 96-478, at 5 (Ky. P.S.C. Feb. 14, 1997) ("[t]he Commission has decided in previous orders that CSAs . . . will not be required to be made available for resale").

[590] *South Carolina Order,* 13 F.C.C. Rec. at 662–663 ¶¶223–224; *First Louisiana Order,* 13 F.C.C. Rec. at 6284–6285 ¶64.

[591] MCI Telecomms. v. BellSouth Telecomms., 7 F. Supp. 2d 674, 678 (E.D.N.C. 1998).

the FCC stated that "limiting the resale of CSAs to similarly situated customers, on a general basis, may be a reasonable and non-discriminatory resale restriction because it is sufficiently narrowly tailored. CSA offerings, by their nature, are priced to a specific set of customer needs, sometimes based on a competitive bidding process. To this extent, it is reasonable to assume that [the incumbent's] ability to offer a CSA at a given price will be dependent on certain end-user characteristics."[592]

The FCC's approach to cross-selling limitations follows a pattern similar to its other determinations in this area. Section 251(c)(4)(B) specifically provides that "[a] state commission may, consistent with regulations prescribed by the Commission under this Section, prohibit a reseller that obtains at wholesale rates a telecommunications service that is available at retail only to a category of subscribers from offering such service to a different category of subscribers." The FCC concluded that this provision authorizes states to prohibit resale of residential services to non-residential users and to prevent the resale of means tested services such as Lifeline to customers who do not meet the income qualifications for those services.[593] Those limitations are obviously crucial because, as discussed in more depth in the chapter on universal service,[594] residential services are generally priced below cost; incumbents are expected to make up the resulting revenue shortfall by pricing nonresidential (that is, business) services above cost. If resellers could obtain a discount off the subsidized residential rate and sell those services to the same business customers that incumbents must currently serve at above-cost rates, resellers could undermine existing rate structures before a new, explicit-subsidy-based rate scheme was put in place. Outside of these specific areas, however, the FCC determined that cross-selling restrictions are presumptively improper, but could be authorized where an incumbent proves to a state commission that a particular cross-selling restriction is reasonable.[595]

---

[592] *Second Louisiana Order,* 13 F.C.C. Rec. at 20,781–20,782 ¶316.

[593] *Local Competition Order,* 11 F.C.C. Rec. at 15,975 ¶962; 47 C.F.R. §51.613(a)(1).

[594] *See* §6.1.1.2.

[595] *Local Competition Order,* 11 F.C.C. Rec. at 15,975–15,976 ¶¶962–963.

Finally, the FCC determined that services available for resale must be at least equal in quality to the service the incumbent offers to itself or to end-users.[596]

§5.5.3.7 Collocation

Under section 251(c)(6), an incumbent LEC is required to allow other carriers to place their own network transmission equipment within the LEC's buildings. Here, Congress to some degree has returned to the approach the FCC unsuccessfully tried several years ago. As noted above (section 5.3.2), in *Bell Atlantic Telephone Cos. v. FCC* the D.C. Circuit invalidated two administrative orders in which the FCC had required local telephone companies to set aside space in their central offices for competitors' telephone network equipment.[597]

The *Bell Atlantic* case turned on the court's inability to find in the Communications Act any express or necessarily implied grant of takings authority to the Commission.[598] The new Act appears to cure that problem, at least in part, by specifying in section 251(c)(6) that incumbents must permit "physical collocation of equipment necessary for interconnection or access to unbundled network elements" or provide for virtual collocation if "the local exchange carrier can demonstrate to the state commission that physical collocation is not practical for technical reasons or because of space limitations." Under virtual collocation, interconnectors are allowed to designate central office transmission equipment dedicated to their use, as well as to monitor and control their circuits terminating in the LEC central office.[599] Interconnectors, however, do not pay for the incumbent's floor space under virtual collocation arrangements and have no right to enter the LEC central office.[600] Under virtual collocation, LECs must install, maintain, and repair interconnector-designated

---

[596] *Id.* at 15,979 ¶970.
[597] Bell Atlantic Tel. Cos. v. FCC, 24 F.3d 1441 (D.C. Cir. 1994).
[598] *Id.* at 1446–1447.
[599] *Local Competition Order,* 11 F.C.C. Rec. at 15,785 ¶559.
[600] *Id.*

equipment under the same intervals and with the same or better failure rates for the performance of similar functions for comparable LEC equipment.[601]

(i) Where Collocation May Occur. The FCC determined in its *Local Competition Order* that the "premises" where collocation must be permitted under the 1996 Act covers a broader range of facilities than the Commission's prior expanded interconnection rules had covered. The prior rules had required collocation at end offices, wire centers, and tandem switches, as well as at remote distribution nodes and other "rating points." In contrast, under the 1996 Act, the FCC has concluded that, to the extent technically feasible, collocation must be permitted at *all* "buildings or similar structures owned or leased by the incumbent LEC that house LEC network facilities," as well as all LEC structures on public rights-of-way that house such facilities.[602]

(ii) What Facilities May Be Collocated. The FCC further concluded that the statutory requirement that incumbents permit collocation of equipment "necessary for interconnection or access to unbundled network elements" should be understood broadly. In particular, in the FCC's view, the word "necessary" should be understood to mean not "indispensable," but rather "used or useful," because the latter interpretation was thought more likely to promote fair competition.[603] This broad construction of statutory language that evidently implicates takings issues is, to say the least, in considerable tension with both the D.C. Circuit's *Bell Atlantic* decision and with the Supreme Court's more restrictive understanding of that term in *Iowa Utilities.* The FCC did, however, recognize that the statutory reference to interconnection necessary for "interconnection or access to network elements" does place some limitations on the incumbents' duties.

---

[601] Expanded Interconnection with Local Telephone Company Facilities, Report and Order and Notice of Proposed Rulemaking, 7 F.C.C. Rec. 7369, 7393–7394 ¶45 (1992); Expanded Interconnection with Local Telephone Company Facilities, Second Report and Order and Third Notice of Proposed Rulemaking, 8 F.C.C. Rec. 7374, 7393 ¶31 (1993).

[602] *Local Competition Order,* 11 F.C.C. Rec. at 15,791 ¶573.

[603] *Id.* at 15,794 ¶579.

The Commission concluded that an incumbent need not allow collocation of equipment for enhanced services or of switching equipment, since that equipment is not used for interconnection or access to network elements.[604]

One issue that has arisen repeatedly in the wake of the FCC's *Local Competition Order* is whether incumbents must permit remote switching modules (or RSMs) to be collocated. RSMs are facilities that may be used for access and/or interconnection *and* for switching, a function for which neither the 1996 Act nor the FCC's current rules permit collocation. And RSMs may take up additional collocation space because they can be used for switching. State commissions have taken both sides on the question of whether collocation of RSMs must be permitted and have been affirmed by federal courts in their contrasting conclusions.[605]

In its recent *Advanced Services* proceedings, the FCC has taken up this question.[606] The FCC interpreted its "existing rules . . . to require incumbent LECs to permit collocation of all equipment that is necessary for interconnection or access to unbundled elements regardless of whether such equipment includes a switching functionality, provides enhanced services capabilities, or offers other functionalities."[607] [T]his rule requires incumbent LECs to permit competitors to collocate such equipment as DSLAMs, routers, ATM multiplexes, and remote switching modules.[608] Incumbents, moreover, may not place any limitation on a competitor's ability to use the functionalities inherent in these facilities.[609]

---

[604] *Local Competition Order,* 11 F.C.C. Rec. at 15,795 ¶581, 15,795 n.1417; 47 C.F.R. §51.323(c).

[605] *Compare* MCI Telecomms. v. Bell Atlantic-Va., No. 3:97CV629 at 18–19, *with* MCI Telecomms. v. U S WEST Communications, Inc., No. C97-1508R, 11–13 (W.D. Wash. 1998).

[606] *Deployment of Wireline Services Offering Advanced Telecommunications Capability,* First Report and Further Notice of Proposed Rulemaking, CC Docket No. 98-147, F.C.C. 99-48 (Mar. 31, 1999).

[607] *Id.* ¶28.

[608] *Id.*

[609] *Id.*

(iii) Allocation of Collocation Space. Under the *Local Competition Order,* incumbents are required to make space available to requesting carriers on a first-come, first-served basis.[610] Collocators seeking to expand their collocated space are also allowed to use contiguous space where available.[611] Incumbents are not required to lease or construct additional space to provide physical collocation to interconnectors when existing space has been exhausted.[612] Incumbent LECs are required, however, to take collocator demand into account when renovating existing facilities and constructing or leasing new facilities, just as they consider demand for other services when undertaking such projects.[613] Incumbents may impose reasonable restrictions on the "warehousing" of space for future use by collocators.[614] Under the new *Advanced Services Collocation Order,* incumbents must remove obsolete equipment and offer collocation in adjacent space (such as controlled environmental vaults where feasible.[615]

(iv) Space Constraints and Virtual Collocation. The *Local Competition Order* recognizes that Congress expressly contemplated that incumbents could provide virtual collocation where space constraints or other technical barriers prevent physical collocation.[616] In the Commission's view, these issues are best handled by state commissions on a case-by-case basis.[617] The Commission did note, however, that incumbent LECs may retain a limited amount of floor space for defined future uses as long as they do not reserve such space "on terms more favorable than those that apply to other telecommunications carriers seeking to hold collocation space for their own future use."[618] Moreover, the

[610] *Local Competition Order,* 11 F.C.C. Rec. at 15,797 ¶585; 47 C.F.R. §51.323(f)(1).
[611] *Local Competition Order,* 11 F.C.C. Rec. at 15,797–15,798 ¶585.
[612] *Id.* at 15,798 ¶585.
[613] *Id.*; 47 C.F.R. §51.323(f)(3).
[614] *Local Competition Order,* 11 F.C.C. Rec. at 15,798 ¶586; 47 C.F.R. §51.323(f)(6).
[615] *Advanced Services Collocation Order,* ¶¶44, 60.
[616] *Local Competition Order,* 11 F.C.C. Rec. at 15,805 ¶602.
[617] *Id.*
[618] *Id.* at 15,805–15,806 ¶604; 47 C.F.R. §51.323(f)(4).

Commission determined that incumbent LECs are not required to provide virtual collocation that is equal in all functional aspects to physical collocation.[619] Where an incumbent claims it does not have sufficient space, the *Local Competition Order* requires that it provide the relevant state commission with detailed floor plans or diagrams of any premises where the incumbent alleges that there are space constraints; under the Commission's more recent order, incumbents must also allow a requesting carrier a tour of the premises.[620]

The Commission recognized that, given its expansive understanding of the premises where collocation is permitted under the 1996 Act, space constraints might also preclude virtual collocation at certain incumbent LEC premises.[621] The Commission again left it to state commissions to make case-by-case judgments on this issue, but noted that incumbents must relinquish space held for future use before denying virtual collocation due to a lack of space.[622] When virtual collocation is not feasible, an incumbent LEC is required to provide other forms of interconnection and access to unbundled network elements to the extent technically feasible.[623]

In the *Advanced Services Order,* the Commission sought comment on further rules governing space exhaustion and virtual interconnection. Among other things, the Commission is considering whether incumbents should be required to provide, upon request, a report indicating where collocation space is available.[624] That proceeding also involves consideration of proposed modifications to the FCC's rules allowing incumbents to reserve some amounts of space for their own future use.[625]

(v) Security Arrangements for Collocation. The Commission's *Local Competition Order* permitted LECs "to require reasonable security arrangements to separate an entrant's collocation

---

[619] *Local Competition Order,* 11 F.C.C. Rec. at 15,807 ¶607.
[620] *Id.* at 15,805 ¶602; Advanced Services Collocation Order ¶57.
[621] *Local Competition Order,* 11 F.C.C. Rec. at 15,806 ¶606.
[622] *Id.;* 47 C.F.R. §51.323(f)(5).
[623] *Local Competition Order,* 11 F.C.C. Rec. at 15,806 ¶606.
[624] 13 Comm. Reg. (P & F) 1 ¶147.
[625] *Id.* ¶149.

space from the incumbent LEC's facilities."[626] Under that order, incumbents could place competitors' equipment in "collocation cages" that protect both the incumbent's and the competitor's equipment from interference by unauthorized parties.[627]

In the *Advanced Services Collocation Order,* however, the FCC "has concluded" that incumbents should be required to offer alternative arrangements that minimize space usage, including "cageless collocation."[628] The Commission noted that "the use of a caged collocation space results in the inefficient use of the limited space in a LEC premises."[629] Incumbents must also permit the use of "shared cage" collocation and may not impose more stringent security requirements on entrants than they impose on themselves.[630]

§5.5.4 Antitrust Litigation in the Wake of the 1996 Act

A new wave of antitrust cases is just now being brought against the incumbent local telephone companies. One competitor doing business in California filed a section 2 monopolization case against Pacific Bell.[631] The allegedly monopolizing conduct was Pacific Bell's inability to process substantial numbers of incoming orders for resale of Pacific Bell's service. "PACBELL's internal processes to handle customer migration are so intentionally and seriously flawed that, assuming PACBELL converted customers at what it represents to be its full stated capacity (4000 orders per business day), PACBELL will be able to process less than one million migration orders in 1997 which would mean that by January 1998, PACBELL would still have at least 93% of the local

---

[626] *Local Competition Order,* 11 F.C.C. Rec. at 15,803 ¶598; 47 C.F.R. §51.323(i).

[627] *Local Competition Order,* 11 F.C.C. Rec. at 15,803 ¶598.

[628] *Advanced Services Collocation Order* ¶42.

[629] *Id.*

[630] *Id.* ¶¶27, 41.

[631] Complaint, Caltech Intl. Telecomm Corp. v. Pacific Bell, No. C97-2105 PJH (N.D. Cal. June 5, 1997).

exchange market . . . ."[632] The CLEC is claiming $85 million in pre-trebled damages. The Antitrust Division of the U.S. Department of Justice also has taken notice of the same conduct.[633]

Another competitor, Electric Lightwave, Inc. (ELI), filed a monopolization case against U S WEST Communications, Inc.[634] ELI alleges that U S WEST (1) failed to provide interconnection facilities needed to handle ELI's traffic, (2) failed to provide "ordering procedures and facilities equivalent to those that [U S WEST] provides to itself," (3) hampered ELI's provision of ISDN service, (4) refused to lease inner ducts in conduits, (5) refused to provide sufficient switch ports for ELI to connect to U S WEST's end offices, and (6) discriminated against ELI in competitive bids. In addition, U S WEST allegedly told a customer that U S WEST could install service in two weeks, but that it would take ELI over a month to obtain the necessary U S WEST facilities if ELI won the contract. ELI seeks damages beginning in 1994, when it first gained state regulatory approval to offer local service.

§5.6 Conclusion

A simple fact is now clear: competition flourishes wherever competitors are assured the same rights of carriage as any other plain old customer. Competition used to be officially impossible, in markets for phones, faxes, and private switches, as it was in markets for long-distance and for wireless telephony. As soon as competitors won rights to interconnect with landline networks, competition thrived. All the theories about natural monopoly and the inherent efficiencies of exclusive franchises collapse when common carrier rules guarantee carrier-to-carrier

---

[632] *Id.* at 6.

[633] *See* Evaluation of the United States Department of Justice, Application of SBC Communications Inc., et al. Pursuant to Section 271 of the Telecommunications Act of 1996 to Provide In-Region, InterLATA Services in the State of Oklahoma, CC Docket No. 97-121 (FCC May 16, 1997).

[634] Complaint, Electric Lightwave, Inc. v. U S WEST Communications, Inc., No. C97-1073 (W.D. Wash. June 30, 1997).

interconnection. Those rules make competition not only possible, but also inevitable.

The Commission that spent many decades protecting the end-to-end anticarriage hegemony of the integrated phone network will spend the next decade undoing the handiwork of its own past. Market forces would do the job better, and probably almost as fast. But the political pressure to get on with things has created a slew of federal and state mandates, often with mind-numbing detail, which the FCC and its state counterparts have now been charged with implementing.

Regulators have been directed not only to enforce common carriage, but also to define every station at which the telecom train must stop and start. If market forces had been left alone for the last half century, none of this would now be necessary.

6

Universal
Service*

§6.1 Introduction

"Universal service" has long been a goal of federal telecommunications law. In the 1934 Communications Act, Congress
assigned to the Federal Communications Commission (FCC) the
task of "regulating interstate and foreign commerce in communication by wire and radio so as to make available, so far as possible, to all the people of the United States a rapid, efficient,
Nation-wide, and world-wide wire and radio communication service with adequate facilities at reasonable charges."[1] But the 1934

---

*This chapter was co-authored by Rebecca A. Beynon, Associate, Kellogg,
Huber, Hansen, Todd & Evans; University of Texas (B.S., with high honors,
1984); University of Lund, Sweden (1984–1985); University of California
(M.S. Chem. E., 1987); University of Texas School of Law (J.D., *summa cum
laude*, 1994); Chancellors; Order of the Coif; Law Clerk, Honorable A. Ray-
mond Randolph, U.S. Court of Appeals, D.C. Circuit, 1994–1995; Law Clerk,
Honorable Sandra Day O'Connor, U.S. Supreme Court, 1996–1997.

[1] 47 U.S.C. §151; *see also id.* §307(b) ("[T]he Commission shall make such
distribution of licenses . . . among the several States and communities as to
provide a fair, efficient and equitable distribution of radio service to each of

Act prescribed no mechanism for subsidizing any kind of universal service program, and the legislative history gives no clue how Congress intended for the Commission to carry out this mandate.[2] In fact, the original impetus for "universal service" subsidies came from state regulators rather than from the FCC.[3]

It was not until it enacted the 1996 Telecommunications Act that Congress gave the Commission express directions regarding universal service. It assigned the FCC the task of conducting, in collaboration with a new Federal-State Joint Board, a thorough review and restructuring of the existing federal universal service guarantees.[4] The relief was long overdue: the universal service guarantee had devolved into a tangle of implicit subsidies and accounting sleights of hand utterly unsuited to a competitive marketplace. The Act directs the Commission to rip apart and rebuild this structure so that "any support mechanism continued

the same."). In 1984, the Court of Appeals for the D.C. Circuit rejected MCI's contention that universal service is exclusively a local issue on the basis of the plain language of 47 U.S.C. §151. National Assn. of Regulatory Util. Commrs. v. FCC, 737 F.2d 1095, 1108 n.6 (D.C. Cir. 1984) (NARUC v. FCC).

[2] M. Mueller, Universal Service: Competition, Interconnection, and Monopoly in the Making of the American Telephone System 157–158 (1997) (hereinafter Mueller, *Universal Service: Competition, Interconnection, and Monopoly*); L. Gasman, Cato Institute, Universal Service: The New Telecommunications Entitlements and Taxes 4 (1998) (hereinafter *New Telecommunications Entitlements*). In fact, there is some dispute whether Congress even intended to create a universal service subsidy. *Compare* Glen O. Robinson, The "New" Communications Act: A Second Opinion, 29 Conn. L. Rev. 289, 321 (1996) ("There is no [Communications Act of 1934] legislative history showing that Congress intended by the act to do anything more than transfer to a new agency the extant regulatory regime that had been established by the Mann-Elkins Act and allowed to languish under the ICC's administration.") *with* A. Hammond, Universal Service in the Digital Age: The Telecommunications Act of 1996: Codifying the Digital Divide, 50 Fed. Comm. L.J. 179, 206 n.124 (1997) ("[O]thers have seen universal service as a logical and fundamental purpose of the 1934 Act—an Act designed to assure basic telephone service, even to those in remote areas, as the country was emerging from economic disaster.").

[3] Mueller, *Universal Service: Competition, Interconnection, and Monopoly* at 158. From 1935 to 1945, as the Commission achieved long-distance rate decreases, the Bell System and independent telcos sought rate increases for intrastate services. *Id.*

[4] 47 U.S.C. §254(a).

or created under the new [47 U.S.C. §254 will] . . . be explicit, rather than implicit as many support mechanisms are today."[5]

The 1996 Act authorizes the Commission to define universal service on an ongoing basis.[6] The Commission is also directed to ensure that interexchange rates for rural and high-cost users are no higher than rates for urban and low-cost users.[7] The Act does not preempt state guarantees of universal service as long as the state measures do not conflict with the federal commitments.[8] The 1996 Act also requires all providers of interstate telecommunications services to contribute in an equitable and nondiscriminatory fashion to universal service.[9]

§6.1.1 Defining Universal Service

Neither "universal" nor "service" is self-defining, and the more technology offers, the harder the definitions become. As originally conceived, "universal service" meant a single provider offering a single network to which all customers are connected. Over time, the term acquired a new meaning: the provision of some set of basic local services to all customers at an affordable price supported by implicit subsidies. Now, with the 1996 Act, Congress has directed that all subsidies become both explicit and portable so that competition can flourish.

---

[5] H.R. Conf. Rep. No. 458, 104th Cong., 2d Sess. 131 (1996), *reprinted in* 1996 U.S.C.C.A.N. 10, 142.

[6] 47 U.S.C. §254(c). The Commission must also ensure that rural healthcare providers, schools, and libraries have affordable access to telecommunications services. 47 U.S.C. §254(h). The Senate bill sought not only to preserve universal service, but also to advance it, granting preferential rates to schools, libraries, and rural healthcare facilities. The conference agreement, in modifying the Senate's approach, expanded universal service to include insular areas and low-income consumers. A. Campbell, Universal Service Provisions: The "Ugly Duckling" of the 1996 Act, 29 Conn. L. Rev. 187, 190–191 (1996).

[7] 47 U.S.C. §254(g).

[8] *Id.* §254(f).

[9] *Id.* §254(d).

§6.1.1.1   Universal Service as a Single Network

In 1907, "universal service" was the Bell System's answer to competition. Bell's original patents had expired, and competitors were rushing in to serve customers previously ignored by Bell. Around this time, Theodore Vail, a brilliant administrator, took charge of the declining Bell empire. Independent companies served half of the nation's telephones; 57 percent of cities were served by two providers.[10] Vail believed passionately in universal service, to be supplied by one company—his own. His objective was not a telephone in every home, or even an exchange in every community, but a nationally interconnected network.[11] Western Union had used its power over interconnection to destroy its rivals, and Vail chose the same approach.

Although the Bell System had lost its original patents on the telephone, it had acquired new ones, which gave it an edge in providing quality long-distance connections. Bell offered its superior long-distance service to its own local affiliates, but not to others. The company also refused to sell equipment or to provide interconnection to unaffiliated companies—even to those independents that did not directly compete with it. Vail rejected the idea of interconnection as unfair because it permitted Bell's smaller competitors to capture the benefits of Bell's expansion.[12] In rapid succession, phone companies not affiliated with the Bell System either folded or were acquired.[13] In 1876, Western Union—at that time the largest corporation in the world—had declined to purchase Bell's patent. In 1910, it was Vail's turn to buy Western Union—for the then astronomical sum of $30 million.

[10] M. Mueller, Universal Service in Telephone History: A Reconstruction, Telecommunications Poly., July 1993, at 362–363.

[11] See Mueller, *Universal Service: Competition, Interconnection, and Monopoly* at 96–103.

[12] Mueller, Universal Service in Telephone History at 362–363.

[13] See Mueller, *Universal Service: Competition, Interconnection, and Monopoly* at 107–113; G. Robinson, The Federal Communications Act: An Essay on Origins and Regulatory Purpose, *reprinted in* A Legislative History of the Communications Act of 1934, at 8 n.25 (M. D. Paglin ed., 1989).

Vail's slogan, announced in 1908, had an Orwellian ring to it: "One System, One Policy, Universal Service." A year later an AT&T Annual Report asserted that "no aggregation of isolated independent systems not under common control, however well built or equipped, could give the public the service that the interdependent, intercommunicating, universal system could give."[14]

§6.1.1.2 Universal Service as Local Service at Reasonable Rates

As the Bell monopoly grew, the term "universal service" took on a new meaning. A paramount objective of regulators became making local telephone service available to all consumers at a reasonable cost: a telephone within arm's reach of the chicken in every pot.

In their effort to push local telephone rates down to affordable levels, regulators focused primarily on rates and overall carrier costs. Neither the FCC nor state regulators sought to align prices of individual services with their corresponding costs. Long-distance rates were used to subsidize local rates, business rates to subsidize residential rates, and urban rates to subsidize rural rates. As long as telephone service remained an end-to-end monopoly, schisms between price and cost were immaterial. A large New York brokerage firm making heavy use of long-distance service had no choice but to subsidize the local services of homeowners in Fishkill.

But with the arrival of competition in some segments of the industry came the significant problem of "cream-skimming,"[15] which in turn disturbed the web of subsidies used to support universal service. Competing long-distance providers targeted low-cost, high-priced services, such as high-density routes between major cities. If the Bell System responded by lowering its long-distance prices to competitive levels, there would be no money

---

[14] Mueller, *Universal Service: Competition, Interconnection, and Monopoly* at 98 (citing AT&T 1909 Annual Report).
[15] "Cream-skimming" or "cherry-picking" is the problem of unregulated competitors undercutting an incumbent's price with respect to the customers who provide the subsidies.

available for subsidies. If the Bell System did not lower its prices, however, the outcome would be the same. It would lose the business and with it the subsidy. At the same time, of course, fledgling competitors had to be protected from the potentially overwhelming might of the Bell System. The company that could arbitrarily set prices above costs could also ruin the competition by lowering its prices below costs.

Thus, the system of implicit subsidies that had been worked out to support universal service worked only as long as telephone service remained a monopoly, and the advent of competition became a pernicious problem.[16] The system of universal service suppressed competition by forcing regulators to act to prevent competitors from cream-skimming the high-revenue, low-cost customers because cream-skimming by the market leaves no cream to be skimmed by the regulator. This means that competitors will be discouraged from pursuing the low-revenue, high-cost customers because the regulator is already delivering cream at a depressed price that no one else can match.

The next step is a war of governmental agency against governmental agency, fought through a single, hapless, regulated intermediary. The agency committed to universal service—the FCC or its state counterpart—anoints and defends a monopolist by promoting cross-ownership, vertical integration, bigness, and all the tax-and-spend possibilities that monopoly makes possible. The agency committed to dismantling monopoly—the Department of Justice or a state attorney general—attacks the monopolist. The premises from which the governmental arms operate are irreconcilably at odds. One operates from the notion that universal service is just, and the other from the idea that competition is efficient. Both sides are right. Collectivism is equal, universal, and fair, but often impoverishing. Competition is productive and efficient, but does not promise equality at the finish line.

---

[16] Competition also brought for the first time an express discussion of universal service into the public discourse. Robinson, The "New" Communications Act at 322.

§6.1.1.3   Developing Universal Service Subsidies

Implicit in the debate over universal service is the notion that, within some defined territory, some basic package of service will be offered on the same terms to all consumers. Thus, the first question is the map—the geographic area over which services should be made generally available. The objectives of universal telephone and cable service have typically been pursued one franchise area (normally a county or a municipality) at a time. But smaller territories are possible, and larger ones, too.

The "service" component—or the contents of the package—must also be defined. For telephone, broadcast, and cable, regulators did not step in to mandate service to all until the services had already substantially developed. Thus, the minimums—basic telephone, basic cable, and so on—were informed first by market demand, and regulators had some assurance that they were mandating something that people actually wanted.

The final key component of universal service is price, or at least price-averaging. At a fundamental level, underlying costs define price. But regulators have considerable power to spread costs across both services and their consumers, particularly when a monopoly is maintained either by economic imperatives or by franchise regulation. Customers that are cheaper to serve end up paying above-cost rates so that high-cost customers can pay less.[17]

---

[17] E. Bailey & W. Baumol, Deregulation and the Theory of Contestable Markets, 1 Yale J. on Reg. 111, 115–116 (1984). Telephone companies are required to price-average over broad geographic areas. See §6.2.1.4. The 1992 Cable Act likewise requires a cable operator to establish a uniform rate structure throughout the cable system's "geographic area." 47 U.S.C. §543(d); see J. Thorne, P. Huber & M. Kellogg, Federal Broadband Law §6.6.3 (1995) (hereinafter *FBL*). Broadcasters are required to provide uniformly "free" TV in every geographic area, but may price-discriminate at will among advertisers. See *id.* §6.5.1. "Direct broadcast satellite" (DBS), "multichannel multipoint distribution services" (MMDS), "local multipoint distribution service" (LMDS), and "satellite master antenna television" (SMATV) face no price-averaging requirements—but have cost structures that favor averaging. See *id.* §6.7.

§6.1.2   The Case for More

Regulators plainly can define territories, service packages, and cost-averaging procedures, but should they? Taking the question a step further and assuming that universal service is appropriate at some level, does the rapid advance of technology mean that territories should be reaffirmed, service packages expanded, and prices averaged more ambitiously than ever before?

One frequently raised justification for universal service subsidies is that they avoid the otherwise inevitable prospect of the "haves" versus the "have-nots."[18] Most Americans own and use telephones and televisions, but for now, personal computers belong to around one-third of the population.[19] Left unregulated, advocates of universal service assert, telephone and cable companies will supply service only to high-income areas.[20] Without government help, less-affluent families and institutions

---

[18] For example, the Clinton administration's Information Infrastructure Task Force states that, "as a matter of fundamental fairness, this nation cannot accept a division of our people among telecommunications or information 'haves' and 'have-nots.'" Information Infrastructure Task Force, The National Information Infrastructure: Agenda for Action, 58 Fed. Reg. 49,025, 49,028 (1993); R. Reich, The Work of Nations: Preparing Ourselves for 21st Century Capitalism (1991) (predicting dire social consequences if information "haves" leave the "have-nots" farther behind).

[19] Penetration rates for various technologies are as follows: television, 98 percent; telephone, 94 percent; videocassette recorders (VCRs), 82 percent; cable TV, 65 percent; personal computers, 37 percent; modems, 26 percent; and e-mail, 17 percent. *See* Bureau of the Census, U.S. Dept. of Commerce, Statistical Abstract of the United States: 1998 at tbl. 915 (television, VCRs, and cable TV statistics for 1996; VCR and cable TV statistics are percentages of TV households); National Telecommunications Information Administration, U.S. Dept. of Commerce, Falling Through the Net II: New Data on the Digital Divide at chart 1 (July 1998) (telephone, computer, modem, and e-mail statistics for 1997).

[20] Comments of the National Cable Television Association, Inc., at 2, Inquiry into Policies and Programs to Assure Universal Telephone Service in a Competitive Market Environment, RM-8388 (FCC Dec. 16, 1993) (subsidies are necessary to ensure that telephone service remains affordable to low-income and rural subscribers). Without universal service subsidies, local telephone service costs would increase dramatically. For example, local service in Carney, Michigan, would cost $52 per month, rather than $9; in Bluffton,

---

will simply be cut out of the Information Age and all the income, education, and services supplied within the new telecosm.[21]

A second rationale for a universal service policy derives from the economics of public goods. A network entails high fixed costs, which must be borne by many users. By paying for a share of these overhead costs, each additional user benefits not only himself, but also everyone else on the network.[22] Ideally, each user should bear only that portion of the fixed cost that he is willing to pay, with those willing to pay the most bearing the largest share and the least eager subscribers paying less. Without a government mandate along these lines, so this theory goes, the network will not grow to its economically optimal size.[23] The

---

South Carolina, it would cost $44 per month, instead of $7; and in Alpine, Texas, $90 per month, instead of $9. R. Neel, Speech: The Good, the Bad, and the Ugly of Telecom Reform, 45 Depaul L. Rev. 995, 1001–1002 (1996).

[21] The U.S. Advisory Council on the National Information Infrastructure found that, by 2000, 60 percent of jobs "will require a working knowledge of information technologies." United States Advisory Council on the National Information Infrastructure, Kickstart Initiative: Connecting America's Communities to the Information Superhighway 11 (1996). *See* James Walter Grudus, Local Broadband Networks: A New Regulatory Philosophy, 10 Yale J. on Reg. 89 (Winter 1993) (public benefits); B. Egan & S. Wildman, Funding the Public Telecommunications Infrastructure 4 <http://www.benton.org/library/fundtelecom/working5.html> (higher productivity); S. Hadden, Universal Service: Policy Options for the Future 1–2 (1993), *presented at* From Public TV to Universal Access: Bringing Home the Electronic Highway, Lyndon B. Johnson Library, Austin, Texas (Nov. 4–5, 1993) (cheaper health care); Alliance for Public Technology, Connecting Each to All: A Telecommunications Platform for the Information Age 2 (1993) <http://www.apt.org/publica/each2all.html> (citizen empowerment); B. O'Connor, Universal Service and NREN, 6 Edge 75 (Dec. 2, 1991); M. Ethan Katsh, Communications Revolutions and Legal Revolutions: The New Media and the Future of Law, 8 Nova L. Rev. 631, 639 (1984) (a "more democratic" democracy); W. Stone, Technology Offers Route Around Freeway Gridlock, Columbus Dispatch, Apr. 27, 1994, at 8A (lower pollution due to telecommuting).

[22] *But see* New Telecommunications Entitlements at 17–18 ("The network effect argument is not an example of a market externality, because there is no evidence that it would, broadly speaking, benefit everyone to more or less the same degree.").

[23] E. Noam, NetTrans Accounts: Reforming the Financial Support System for Universal Service in Telecommunications (draft Sept. 1993) <http://www.ctr.columbia.edu/vi/papers/nettrans.htm>.

same may hold true for some services offered over the network, such as educational services. Suppliers of information and education may be unable to capture the true social benefits of their services in the marketplace; government-mediated subsidies will cure this market failure.[24]

§6.1.3 The Case for Less

Objections to governmental promotion of universal service range equally broadly. Some agree that there is a need to subsidize some consumers, but believe that the universal service program is not directed specifically enough at the needs of truly needy consumers.[25] For example, the rural subsidy benefits all rural dwellers, wealthy and poor alike.[26] Rural businesses, such as ranching, farming, mining, timber production, and vacation resorts, choose their locations as a business matter and should no more be entitled to subsidies than would businesses that locate in urban areas.[27] In this vein, some experts and industry representatives contend that universal service does not address the underlying reasons poor consumers lack phone service.[28] Many of these critics support the idea of replacing the universal

---

[24] Cf. Hadden, Universal Service at 7 (regulators could "help avoid creation of an information underclass" by establishing technical minimum standards that service providers must meet).

[25] D. Kaserman & J. Mayo, Cross-Subsidies in Telecommunications: Roadblocks on the Road to More Intelligent Telephone Pricing, 11 Yale J. on Reg. 119, 140–141 (1994) ("[R]aising the price of a relatively price elastic service (long-distance) to lower the price of a relatively price inelastic service (local usage) tends to reduce the overall demand for access. Moreover, the demand for customer access itself is extremely price-inelastic. Therefore, any policy that attempts to increase subscribership levels by reducing the price of customer access is likely to have only limited success, particularly if the program does not target specific beneficiaries.") (hereinafter *Cross-Subsidies in Telecommunications*).

[26] New Telecommunications Entitlements at 22.

[27] See M. Einhorn, Recovering Network Subsidies Without Distortion 12–13 <http://www.benton.org/library/recovering/wp4.html> (hereinafter *Recovering Network Subsidies Without Distortion*).

[28] See, e.g., New Telecommunications Entitlements at 15–16.

service system with a system that pays subsidies directly to consumers, perhaps through tax deductions, "telephone stamps," or prepaid debit cards, rather than to providers.[29]

Other criticisms of universal service go deeper. Some deride the system as merely "pork."[30] Others complain it is paternalistic.[31] At the heart of these objections is the notion that market forces can ascertain both supply and demand better than the government can and that, whatever form it takes, government intervention will skew the market. Thus, these critics maintain that universal service distorts the market, skews companies' investments in service and geographic markets, and diminishes incentives for competitors.[32] As a result, they conclude, universal service reduces incentives to invest in emerging technologies, thereby ensuring that a technological status quo will be maintained.[33]

It is quite clear that developing universal telephone service by regulation is "very much in conflict" with developing specialized services by competition.[34] Subsidizing any segment of a market

[29] *See* Recovering Network Subsidies Without Distortion at 12–13; A. Kahn, A Free Ticket to Rich Telecom Markets, Wall St. J., Nov. 10, 1995, at A15 (letter to the editor); Comments of Bell Atlantic at 5–6, Inquiry into Policies and Programs to Assure Universal Telephone Service in a Competitive Market Environment, RM-8388 (FCC Dec. 16, 1993); New Telecommunications Entitlements at 11–13; M. Mueller, Telecommunications Access in the Age of Electronic Commerce: Toward a Third-Generation Universal Service Policy, 49 Fed. Com. L.J. 655, 670–671 (1997) (hereinafter *Third-Generation Universal Service*) (a report analyzing the use of prepaid debit cards in the United Kingdom's electric industry found that the cards caused a substantial decrease in the rate of disconnection).

[30] New Telecommunications Entitlements at 22 ("We must conclude that support for subsidies for rural telephone service, which comes largely from lawmakers from rural states, reflects political realities, not economic justifications."). *See also* E. Noam, Will Universal Service and Common Carriage Survive the Telecommunications Act of 1996, 97 Colum. L. Rev. 955, 956 (1997) (asserting that the "politically mandated support for universal service will increase in the age of information.").

[31] *See, e.g.*, T. Krattenmaker, Responses, 29 Conn. L. Rev. 373, 377 (1996) (querying "Why do we know better than low income consumers what are those consumers' most compelling unfulfilled wants?") .

[32] New Telecommunications Entitlements at 30–31.

[33] *Id.* at 23–25, 31–35.

[34] L. Pressler & K. Schieffer, A Proposal for Universal Telecommunications Service, 40 Fed. Comm. L.J. 351, 367 (1988).

distorts the market not once, but twice. First, subsidy reduces incentives for the market to find its own way of providing the subsidized service. As one analyst put it, "In a competitive market, companies could and would seek higher profits in high-cost areas by developing technology that would reduce the costs of serving those areas."[35] Second, universal service curtails the supply of the services that are being "milked" to fund other, higher-cost services. Even if all suppliers are milked equally, marginal ones may find the burden more than they can bear.[36]

Unrestrained competition, it is argued, can deliver universal service, too, and better than the government.[37] At the turn of the century, competition between Bell and the independents spurred each to wire as many homes as possible. If the private sector begins by wiring the most profitable communities first, those communities will also underwrite the cost of developing the technology and pushing production down the cost curve. Flushable toilets, cars, and many other essentials of life that we all—both rich and poor—take for granted today began as luxuries, not as universal staples. The theory is that telecommunications will evolve that way, too, if market forces are unleashed. Markets will find ways of producing public goods without help from the government.[38]

[35] New Telecommunications Entitlements at 19.

[36] Comments of the National Cable Television Association, Inc., at 3, Inquiry into Policies and Programs to Assure Universal Telephone Service in a Competitive Market Environment, RM-8388 (FCC Dec. 16, 1993); A. Barrett, Shifting Foundations: The Regulation of Telecommunications in an Era of Change, 46 Fed. Comm. L.J. 39, 60–61 (1993); see also J. Browning, Universal Service (An Idea Whose Time Is Past), Wired, Sept. 1994, at 102.

[37] Hearing on H.R. 3636 Before the Telecommunications and Finance Subcomm., Energy and Commerce Comm., 103d Cong., 2d Sess. (Feb. 3, 1994) (statement of James Crowe, CEO and Chairman, MFS Communications Company); id. (statement of Mark Cooper, Director of Research, Consumer Federation of America).

[38] See generally Public Goods and Market Failures: A Critical Examination (Tyler Cowan ed., 1992). For example, Microtel Communications has filled a niche market in New York City: for $23 per month, subscribers can make local, directory assistance, and 911 calls, but subscribers must prepay for calls outside the metropolitan area. New Telecommunications Entitlements at 18–19.

The final objection to universal service in the form of advanced broadband service is also the boldest: too much bandwidth is simply bad. The contention is that broadcasting will give way to "narrowcasting" by segregating audiences by class, race, religion, sex, and so on. A single, national culture will vanish; people will talk only to their clones. "Faction—the scourge of democracy feared by its critics from James Madison to Walter Lippmann—is given the support of technology; compromise, mutualism, and empathy—indispensable to effective democratic consensus—are robbed of their national medium."[39] These critics fear that the "global village" will give way to the Tower of Babel: "a hundred chattering mouths bereft of any common language."[40]

§6.2   Universal Service Prior to the 1996 Act

In the simplest sense of the word, telephone service today is as close to universal as one can get: some 94 percent of households have service.[41] Before the enactment of the 1996 Act, a number of subsidies had developed to support this system. These subsidies were largely implicit; implemented at the state level; and designed to shift costs from rural to urban areas, from residential to business customers, and from local to long-distance services.[42]

---

[39] B. Barber, The Second American Revolution, Channels, Feb./Mar. 1982, at 23–24.

[40] *Id.*

[41] Industry Analysis Division, FCC, Telephone Subscribership in the United States 3 (July 27, 1998) (hereinafter *Telephone Subscribership*). To be sure, among some sex, race, age, income, and geographic groups, access to phone service is significantly lower. *See generally* National Telecommunications Information Administration, U.S. Dept. of Commerce, Falling Through the Net II: New Data on the Digital Divide (July 1998); *see also* Benton Foundation, Losing Ground Bit by Bit: Low-Income Communities in the Information Age (1998) <http://www.benton.org/library/low-income>. Over six million homes are without telephones. Telephone Subscribership at tbl. 1.

[42] Federal-State Joint Board on Universal Service, Report and Order, 12 F.C.C. Rec. 8776, 8784 ¶10 (1997) (hereinafter *Universal Service Order*), *appeal pending sub nom.* Texas Office of Pub. Util. Counsel v. FCC, No. 97-60421 (5th Cir.).

§6.2.1 Implicit Subsidies

In general, a subsidy is implicit when a single company is required to obtain revenues from certain sources at above-competitive prices and to charge below-competitive prices for other services.[43] Before the 1996 Act, regulators had developed three implicit subsidy mechanisms to keep basic local telephone rates low: interstate access charges (designed to shift costs from local services to long-distance ones), geographic rate-averaging (designed to shift costs from rural users to urban ones), and subsidization of residential lines via business lines. Of these mechanisms, only interstate access charges are regulated by the FCC.[44] We describe below how the interstate access charge subsidy mechanism evolved. Bear in mind, however, that state regulators have devised their own very important implicit subsidy mechanisms.[45]

§6.2.1.1 Separations[46]

The 1934 Communications Act divided jurisdiction between federal and state authorities, which meant that the regulatory turf—the "rate base"—had to be divided between them.[47] In

---

[43] *Universal Service Order*, 12 F.C.C. Rec. at 8784 ¶10 n.15.

[44] *Id.* at 8784–8785 ¶12.

[45] States have subsidized basic local service by permitting phone companies to charge above-cost rates to businesses. They have also allowed phone companies to charge above-cost prices for various "nonessential" services, such as intraLATA (local access and transport area) long-distance and intrastate access charges, and for vertical service, such as Call Waiting. Finally, state regulators have ensured that residential users across the state pay the same rates by requiring "geographic rate averaging," a concept described in Cross-Subsidies in Telecommunications at 129–130.

[46] *See* 47 C.F.R. Part 36; M. Kellogg, J. Thorne, & P. Huber, Federal Telecommunications Law §§9.3.1–9.3.3, 9.4 (1992) (hereinafter *FTL1*).

[47] *See* 47 U.S.C. §221(c). In 1930, the Supreme Court held that costs of interstate and intrastate plant had to be separated before the adequacy of rates could be assessed, reasoning that "unless an apportionment is made, the intrastate service to which the exchange property is allocated will bear an undue burden." Smith v. Illinois Bell Tel. Co., 282 U.S. 133, 150–151 (1930), *conformed to,* Illinois Bell Tel. Co. v. Gilbert, 3 F. Supp. 595 (N.D. Ill. 1933),

1947, the FCC and the National Association of Regulatory Utility Commissioners (NARUC) developed a Separations Manual for assigning non-traffic-sensitive (NTS) common costs[48] to the federal or state rate bases.[49] This initial approach assigned common costs to each jurisdiction based on relative usage. Over time, however, both state and federal regulators came to embrace the idea that long-distance rates should be used to subsidize local service. This policy was formalized in the Ozark Plan of 1970.[50] The subsidies grew rapidly thereafter. By 1980, roughly 26 percent of the cost of access lines was paid for by long-distance tolls, even though long-distance calls accounted for only 8 percent of access line usage.[51] Recognizing that the interstate contribution to local NTS costs was grossly overinflated, the Commission froze at the 1981 percentage the *total* interstate contribution to non-traffic-sensitive plant.[52] In 1983, the FCC extended the freeze until 1986, after which it was replaced by a 25 percent interstate allocation factor.[53]

---

rev'd sub nom. Lindheimer v. Illinois Bell Tel. Co., 292 U.S. 151 (1934). *See FTL1* §§2.5, 9.3.1.

[48] *I.e.,* costs that are incurred in providing both intrastate and interstate services.

[49] MCI v. FCC, 750 F.2d 135, 137–138 (D.C. Cir. 1984).

[50] Prescription of Procedures for Separating and Allocating Plant Investment, Operating Expenses, Taxes and Reserves Between the Interstate and Intrastate Operations of Telephone Companies, Report and Order, 26 F.C.C.2d 247 (1970). The Ozark Plan was the fifth revision to the Separations Manual. MCI v. FCC, 750 F.2d 135, 137 (1984). In 1971, Congress added a new section 410(c) to the 1934 Act requiring the FCC to refer separations proceedings to a "Federal-State Joint Board."

[51] Gerald Faulhaber, Telecommunications in Turmoil: Technology and Public Policy 73 (1987).

[52] Amendment of Part 67 of the Commission's Rules and Establishment of a Joint Board, 89 F.C.C.2d 1, 4–5 ¶7, *modified,* 90 F.C.C.2d 52, *recons. denied,* 91 F.C.C.2d 558 (1982), *aff'd sub nom.* MCI v. FCC, 750 F.2d 135; MCI v. FCC, 712 F.2d 517, 523 n.4 (D.C. Cir. 1983).

[53] Amendment of Part 67 of the Commission's Rules and Establishment of a Joint Board, Decision and Order, 96 F.C.C.2d 781, 782 ¶2 (1983). The D.C. Circuit rejected challenges to the interim freeze. MCI v. FCC, 712 F.2d 517.

§6.2.1.2   Access Charges[54]

The AT&T divestiture and the emergence of long-distance competition in the 1980s forced the FCC to overhaul its long-distance-to-local subsidy.[55] Since they were now out of the long-distance business, the Bell companies no longer were able to pay for below-cost local rates by pricing long-distance calls above cost. The 1982 AT&T divestiture Decree required the Bell companies to file tariffs for exchange access (i.e., access to the local networks for the purpose of originating and terminating long-distance traffic) that were cost-based and equal for all carriers.[56] The Decree also contained a clause that gave the new long-distance competitors a right to receive traffic at the same unit cost as AT&T in any exchange area, even if that traffic were delivered to facilities more distant than AT&T's.[57]

In 1983, the FCC issued rules phasing in a system in which all interexchange carriers pay charges for access to the local telephone companies' networks, with the same price to be charged for originating and terminating long-distance traffic.[58] These charges, however, included not only the actual cost of providing originating and terminating access, but also the line costs that previously had been allocated to the federal rate base.[59] In other words, the FCC replaced its existing subsidy system, in which a

---

[54] *See generally FTL1* §9.6. Current regulations governing access charges are contained in the Commission's rules. *See* 47 C.F.R. Part 69.

[55] At first, the new entrants to the long-distance market, such as MCI, simply leased a local telephone company's unswitched private lines, mostly at flat, non-traffic-sensitive rates, since the interstate subsidy of local NTS costs was recovered almost entirely from traffic-sensitive (TS) charges on switched long-distance services.

[56] Modification of Final Judgment app. B ¶B(2), *reprinted in* United States v. AT&T, 552 F. Supp. 131, 233 (D.D.C. 1982) (hereinafter *Decree*).

[57] *Decree* app. B ¶B(3), 552 F. Supp. at 233.

[58] *See* §2.3.3.3; *FTL1* §§9.5.–9.6.

[59] Federal-State Joint Board on Universal Service, Report to Congress, 13 F.C.C. Rec. 11,501, 11,572 ¶146 (1998) (hereinafter *Report to Congress*) ("Interstate access charges . . . have traditionally been set above the economic cost of access, which has permitted [incumbent local exchange carriers] to charge lower rates for local service in high-cost areas.").

single company shifted costs from local to long-distance services, to an access-charge regime, in which all long-distance companies paid above-cost prices for access to the local networks, thereby enabling the local telephone companies to pay for below-cost local service.

§6.2.1.3 SLCs and CCLCs[60]

In designing its access-charge system, the Commission tried to implement a more sensible method for recovering non-traffic-sensitive common costs. Ideally, the Commission hoped to establish a regime in which traffic-sensitive costs would be recovered from interexchange carriers according to actual usage and NTS costs would be recovered through a flat charge paid by end users.[61] The Commission's first proposal was to recover NTS costs through a $6-a-month "subscriber line charge" (SLC) that would be imposed directly on each subscriber. This proposal would have eliminated much of the inefficiency created by the Ozark Plan's subsidy-laden system. Non-traffic-sensitive costs would have been shifted directly to end users, and there would then have been no further debate about how to allocate any of those costs among interexchange carriers. But the $6-a-month SLC did not survive; it was forcefully opposed by consumer advocacy groups, state regulators, Congress, and (astonishingly) Judge Harold Greene.[62]

The Commission compromised on a plan that imposed a more acceptable $3.50 SLC on residential users and higher SLCs

---

[60] See generally FTL1 §§9.6.4–9.6.7.

[61] See MTS and WATS Market Structure, Third Report and Order, 93 F.C.C.2d 241, 297–315 ¶¶197–249 (1983) (hereinafter Access Order).

[62] United States v. Western Elec. Co., 569 F. Supp. 990, 998–1000 (D.D.C. 1983) (criticizing FCC decision to impose end-user charges for recovery of non-traffic-sensitive plant); see also United States v. Western Elec. Co., 627 F. Supp. 1090, 1096 n.18 (D.D.C. 1986) ("The assumption that high-quality, low-cost telephone service would be provided by the local companies was an essential ingredient in the Court's determination that the consent decree was in the public interest. . . ."); United States v. Western Elec. Co., 592 F. Supp. 846, 861–867 (D.D.C. 1984) (in considering waiver requests, court will take into account effects on local ratepayers).

on certain other users.[63] But the Commission still had to find a way to collect the remainder of NTS costs. It decided to continue to recover these costs from interexchange carriers, via usage-based access charges, and it required certain carriers to pay a metered carrier common line charge (CCLC) for exchange access.[64] The D.C. Circuit rejected an attack on the CCLC brought by new entrants to the interexchange business, unpersuasively declaring that "[r]ecovery of the balance of NTS costs through the usage-based carrier common line charge and special access surcharge, is not inconsistent with the decision to impose flat-rate end user charges."[65] In the end, as was the case before 1983, the new regime recovered a large portion of non-traffic-sensitive costs from per-minute charges assessed on long-distance calls.

To keep carrier common line charges roughly uniform from local telephone company to local telephone company, the Commission implemented a "pooling" mechanism. As explained above, before divestiture AT&T recovered local plant costs allocated to the interstate jurisdiction by charging above-cost per-minute charges for long-distance calls. If it had returned those

[63] MTS and WATS Market Structure, Report and Order, 2 F.C.C. Rec. 2953, 2954–2955 ¶13, 2956 ¶27 (1987) (hereinafter *MTS and WATS Market Structure Report and Order*). The D.C. Circuit upheld the imposition of an SLC. NARUC v. FCC, 737 F.2d 1095. The monthly residential and business line SLCs have been $3.50 since 1989. *MTS and WATS Market Structure Report and Order*, 2 F.C.C. Rec. at 2954–2955 ¶13, 2957 ¶27; 47 C.F.R. §§69.104(e), 69.203(a). Since May 1984, multiline business SLCs have been $6.00 a month. *MTS and WATS Market Structure Report and Order*, 2 F.C.C. Rec. at 2968 n.10; 47 C.F.R. §69.104(d).

[64] *See Decree* app. B ¶B(3), 552 F. Supp. at 233. Local exchange carriers have been required to average interstate access charges throughout their state service areas. *Access Order*, 93 F.C.C.2d at 330 ¶¶323, 326; 47 C.F.R. §69.3(e)(7). *See* Policy and Rules Concerning Rates for Dominant Carriers, Second Report and Order, 5 F.C.C. Rec. 6786, 6793–6799 ¶¶55–102 (1990) (discussing common-line formula adjustment under price caps).

[65] NARUC v. FCC, 737 F.2d at 1134. The appellate court went on to hold: "The portion of costs which temporarily or permanently will not be borne by the end users, which forms the basis for carriers' access charges, is essentially a subsidy. This subsidy is not logically attributable to a particular class of carriers. The Commission's decision to recover NTS costs from end users on a flat-rate basis therefore does not require it also to assess the subsidized balance of those costs on a flat-rate basis from the interexchange carriers." *Id.*

long-distance revenues to local telephone companies in proportion to the amount of long-distance traffic they actually generated, smaller and rural telephone companies would have fallen steadily behind, since they usually generated little long-distance traffic. Instead, therefore, AT&T placed the revenues in an interstate "pool" and distributed them to local telephone companies in proportion to their investment.[66]

Pooling remained necessary even after the FCC's 1983 line-charge reforms. If each local telephone company simply kept for itself the access-charge revenues it collected, telcos in urban areas might collect more than their costs, while those in rural ones might collect less. The result would be a system in which rural carriers were forced to increase the carrier common line charges assessed on long-distance companies in order to recover their costs. Therefore, to maintain geographically uniform CCLCs, access-charge revenues still had to be pooled nationwide—and then distributed back to individual telcos in proportion to their contribution to the aggregate interstate rate base.

The upshot is that individual telcos continued to recover the interstate part of their local loop costs not directly from end users and interexchange carriers, but from a common, federally supervised fund into which local exchange carriers are required to deposit SLCs and CCLCs. The FCC established what would become the National Exchange Carrier Association (NECA) to administer this fund.[67] Initially, participation in the pool was mandatory, but in 1989, carriers were permitted to opt out, though they must still make so-called long-term support (LTS) payments.[68] The LTS payments are distributed to high-cost local exchange carriers, which enables them to charge lower access

[66] *See id.* at 1104 n.5; MTS and WATS Market Structure, Second Supplemental Notice of Inquiry and Proposed Rulemaking, 77 F.C.C.2d 224, 226–229 ¶¶13–22 (1980). This was called the "division of revenues" process and was required to be terminated upon divestiture of the Bell System. *Decree* app. B ¶B(1), 552 F. Supp. at 233.

[67] *See* 47 C.F.R. §§69.601–69.613.

[68] *MTS and WATS Market Structure Report and Order*, 2 F.C.C. Rec. at 2955–2956 ¶¶23–25, 2957 ¶27. Carriers that opt out of the pool must provide the difference between the CCLC revenue requirement of NECA participants and the projected CCLC revenue of the NECA participants. 47 C.F.R.

rates than their interstate revenues would otherwise justify and permits them to recover all of their interstate line costs.[69]

§6.2.1.4   Rate-Averaging

In addition to its access-charge regime, the Commission has adopted certain "rate-averaging" practices that are effectively urban-to-rural subsidies. First, it has interpreted section 202(a)'s prohibition on unreasonable price discrimination as requiring local exchange carriers to charge the same "averaged" access-charge rates to all interexchange carriers throughout specified areas.[70] It has also encouraged long-distance carriers to file tariffs that reflect nationally averaged rates, so that users are billed the same rates for calls that cover the same distance, regardless of the actual access charges associated with those calls.[71] (States have also developed their own rate-averaging policies, which typically require telephone companies to average local rates, so that urban areas subsidize rural areas.[72])

§6.2.2   Explicit Subsidies

Before 1996, in addition to its mechanisms for implicitly subsidizing universal service, the FCC had developed several

---

§69.612(a). NECA participants' CCLC rate is based on price-cap local exchange carriers' average CCLC rate. Policy and Rates Concerning Rates for Dominant Carriers, Order on Reconsideration, 6 F.C.C. Rec. 2637, 2712 ¶164 (1991); 47 C.F.R. §69.105(b)(2), (3).

[69] Universal Service Task Force, FCC, Preparation for Addressing Universal Service Issues: A Review of Current Interstate Support Mechanisms 71 (1996) (hereinafter *Review of Current Interstate Support Mechanisms*).

[70] 47 C.F.R. §69.3(e)(7); *see* Southwestern Bell Tel. Co. v. FCC, 100 F.3d 1004 (D.C. Cir. 1996) (remanding as unlawful the Commission's rejection of a Southwestern Bell access tariff offering services at rates below its geographically averaged rates).

[71] MTS and WATS Market Structure, Report and Third Supplemental Notice of Inquiry and Proposed Rulemaking, 81 F.C.C.2d 177, 192–195 ¶¶63–79 (1980).

[72] *Universal Service Order,* 12 F.C.C. Rec. at 8784 ¶11.

programs explicitly to fund universal service, including those described below.

§6.2.2.1   The Universal Service Fund

Until recently local exchange carriers with higher-than-average local loop costs (above 115 percent of the nationwide average) could assign an additional percentage of their costs to the interstate jurisdiction over the 25 percent allocation factor.[73] These carriers could then recover their additional costs from a federal Universal Service Fund (or high-cost assistance fund). Interexchange carriers with more than 0.5 percent of the nation's presubscribed lines were required to contribute based on their number of presubscribed lines.[74] In 1995, the Universal Service Fund was nearly $750 million.[75]

§6.2.2.2   Dial Equipment Minute Weighting

The FCC has also established an explicit subsidy that helps rural carriers cover their switching costs, which, on a per-line basis, are often higher than those of larger carriers.[76] The FCC's "Dial Equipment Minute (DEM) Weighting" rules allow small LECs (those with fewer than 50,000 access lines) to assign a disproportionally large part of their switching costs to the federal

---

[73] Amendment of Part 67 of the Commission's Rules and Establishment of a Joint Board, Decision and Order, 96 F.C.C.2d 781, 782 ¶3 (1984); 47 C.F.R. §69.116. *See* 47 C.F.R. §§36.631–36.641 (expense adjustments). LECs with less than 200,000 lines per study area (the area within a single jurisdiction where a local exchange carrier provides local phone service) were the focus of the fund. *Review of Current Interstate Support Mechanisms* at 50.

[74] 47 C.F.R. §69.116(a).

[75] *Review of Current Interstate Support Mechanisms* at 52.

[76] Because rural LECs typically serve fewer lines than urban LECs, they are often forced to use smaller switches. Thus, rural LECs tend to have not only above-average loop costs, but also above-average switching costs. The Bell Operating Companies serve some 121 million access lines from about 9,000 switches, averaging over 13,000 lines per switch. All other LECs serve about 37 million lines from 13,000 switches, averaging fewer than 3,000 lines per switch. *See* FCC, Trends in Telephone Service at tbls. 6.2, 18.2 (Feb. 1998).

rate base.[77] Small LECs that receive LTS payments from NECA
assign the additional costs to NECA's switching rate element;
other LECs recover the costs through their own CCLCs.[78] The
Dial Equipment Minute Weighting subsidy for 1995 was estimated to be $311 million.[79]

§6.2.2.3 Lifeline Assistance and Link Up America Plans

The FCC's Lifeline Assistance[80] and Link Up America[81] programs are intended to assist low-income Americans in obtaining
access to the public switched network and to some local calling.
The Lifeline program helps poor subscribers pay their monthly
telephone bills; Link Up helps them cover the costs of installing
phone service.[82] States have administered the programs, and
NECA has supervised the Lifeline and Link Up funds. Interexchange carriers support the programs based on a flat-rate, per-
line basis.[83]

Although the Commission originally developed two Lifeline
plans in the mid-eighties, nearly all of the 44 participating states
have adopted the program in which the subscribers' SLCs are
waived up to the amount matched by the state.[84] In 1994, about
4.4 million households received $123 million in Lifeline sup-
port.[85] The Commission asserts that about 80 percent of Lifeline

---

[77] 47 C.F.R. §36.125.

[78] *Review of Current Interstate Support Mechanisms* at 66.

[79] *Id.*

[80] 47 C.F.R. §§69.104(j)–(l), 69.117, 69.203(f)–(g).

[81] *Id.* §§36.701–36.741, 69.117.

[82] Lifeline was originally developed to counteract the imposition of the
SLC and was expanded despite the fact that there was no indication that the
SLC had an adverse impact on subscribership. *See Access Order,* 93 F.C.C.2d at
243–244 ¶¶3–4; *Review of Current Interstate Support Mechanisms* at 36–37.

[83] Interexchange carriers with .05 percent or more of the country's presubscribed lines are required to participate. 47 C.F.R. §69.117.

[84] *Id.* §69.104(k). Forty-three states including the District of Columbia and
the Virgin Islands participate in this plan. *Universal Service Order,* 12 F.C.C.
Rec. at 8957 ¶341 n.847. Only California participates in the other. See 47
C.F.R. §69.104(j) for a description of the plan.

[85] *Review of Current Interstate Support Mechanisms* at 35.

subscribers "depend on the subsidy to make telephone service affordable."[86] Other studies, however, conclude that "the monthly price of basic local service is not the most important factor affecting the affordability of telephone service. . . . [A] household's ability to pay usage-related costs is usually the most important."[87]

To qualify for the Link Up America program, which pays half of the first $60 in connection fees, subscribers must meet their state's needs-based test.[88] All states but California participate in the Link Up America program.[89]

§6.3   The 1996 Act

The 1996 Act, in which Congress expressly referred to the term "universal service" for the first time, significantly changed the universal service landscape. The Act sets forth detailed guidelines that the Commission and states are to consider in their efforts to preserve and advance universal service. In addition, the statute directs regulators to make existing and future universal service support mechanisms "explicit,"[90] and it provides that schools, libraries, and rural healthcare providers will receive discounts on services.

[86] *Id.* at 4. *But see* C. Garbacz & H. Thompson, Do Lifeline Programs Promote Universal Telephone Service for the Poor?, Pub. Util. Fort., Mar. 15, 1997, at 30 ("[T]he overwhelming majority of lifeline subscribers would have taken network service even if the assistance program were not available. For these customers, the program simply redistributes income.").

[87] Mueller, Universal Service: Competition, Interconnection, and Monopoly at 172; *see also* Third-Generation Universal Service at 660 ("For the poor, the main barriers are the unrecoverable fixed costs of establishing the account relationship (deposits, installation fees), the cost of usage, and the risk of losing control over the level of usage, which can lead to a poor credit record or disruption or destruction of the account relationship.").

[88] *Universal Service Order,* 12 F.C.C. Rec. at 8959 ¶344. The Commission established Link Up in 1987. *MTS and WATS Market Structure Report and Order,* 2 F.C.C. Rec. at 2958 ¶35.

[89] *Universal Service Order,* 12 F.C.C. Rec. at 8966 ¶359 n.903.

[90] 47 U.S.C. §254(e). Eligible carriers must use universal service support "for the provision, maintenance, and upgrading of facilities and services for which the support is intended." *Id.*

In companion orders released on the same day, the Commission has taken steps to implement section 254's universal service mandates. In the *Universal Service Order*,[91] it established the definition of services to be supported by federal universal support mechanisms; it replaced existing federal subsidy programs with a new fund; it adopted rules that established funding methods to provide schools, libraries, and rural healthcare providers with support; and it decided which carriers would contribute to these funds and which carriers would receive support.

In the *Access Charge Reform Order*,[92] the Commission purported to address the subsidy mechanisms implicit in its access-charge regime. The Commission significantly reformed the way in which access charges are recovered. It did not, however, make much progress in transforming its existing regime's implicit subsidies into the "explicit" subsidies required by the 1996 Act.

§6.3.1   Definition of Universal Service

The Act directed the FCC, within one month after enactment of the 1996 Act, to "institute and refer to a Federal-State Joint

---

[91] *Universal Service Order*, 12 F.C.C. Rec. 8776. As of mid-1999, a petition for review of numerous aspects of the *Universal Service Order* was still pending. The Fifth Circuit Court of Appeals heard oral argument on the consolidated petitions on December 1, 1998. Texas Office of Pub. Util. Counsel v. FCC, No. 97-60421 (5th Cir.). Among other things, parties have asserted that the Commission violated the 1996 Act by failing immediately to make all existing implicit subsidies explicit (the "date certain" argument), by relying on the forward-looking methodology (also known as the "total element long run incremental cost" or "TELRIC" methodology) to calculate the costs of implicit subsidies, and by impermissibly concluding that schools and libraries were to receive internal connections at discounted rates. The Eighth Circuit has already addressed the "date certain" argument in the access reform proceeding, where it held that the 1996 Act does not require that implicit subsidy mechanisms immediately be made explicit. Southwestern Bell Tel. Co. v. FCC, 153 F.3d 523, 537 (8th Cir. 1998). "Rather, the rules enacted by the FCC must establish 'a specific timetable for implementation.'" *Id.*

[92] Access Charge Reform, First Report and Order, 12 F.C.C. Rec. 15,982 (1997) (hereinafter *Access Charge Reform Order*).

Board"[93] a proceeding to recommend changes to the Commission's regulations in order to implement universal service in accordance with the Act.[94] The Act required the Joint Board to be composed of three FCC Commissioners; four state commissioners, nominated by NARUC and approved by the FCC; and a state-appointed utility consumer advocate, nominated by the National Association of State Utility Commissioners.[95]

On March 8, 1996, the Commission named the members of the Joint Board and asked it to address a number of issues, including defining the services to be supported by federal universal service and the mechanisms that would support those services.[96] The Act charged the Joint Board with submitting its recommendations to the Commission, after notice and comment, within nine months of the statute's enactment.[97] After a series of open meetings,[98] the Joint Board issued a recommended decision on the statutory deadline, November 8, 1996.[99] The Commission ultimately adopted virtually all of the Joint Board's recommendations.[100]

In the 1996 Act, Congress prescribed general principles on which the Joint Board and the Commission were "to base policies for the preservation and advancement of universal service:"[101]

Quality services should be available at just, reasonable, and affordable rates;

---

[93] The duties and power of Federal-State Joint Boards are described in 47 U.S.C. §410(c).

[94] 47 U.S.C. §254 (a)(1). Universal service is addressed in section 254, in addition to section 214(e), which governs the "Provision of Universal Service."

[95] 47 U.S.C §§254(a)(1), 410(c). The Act provided that the Commission Chairman or a Commissioner designated by the Commission would serve as the Joint Board's Chairman. *Id.* §410(c).

[96] Federal-State Joint Board on Universal Service, Notice of Proposed Rulemaking and Order Establishing a Joint Board, 11 F.C.C. Rec. 18,092 (1996).

[97] 47 U.S.C. §254(a)(1).

[98] *See Universal Service Order,* 12 F.C.C. Rec. at 9612 app. K.

[99] Federal-State Joint Board on Universal Service, Recommended Decision, 12 F.C.C. Rec. 87 (1996).

[100] *Universal Service Order,* 12 F.C.C. Rec. at 8781 ¶3.

[101] 47 U.S.C. §254(b)(1)–(6).

All regions of the nation should have access to advanced telecommunications and information services;

Consumers throughout the nation, including low-income consumers and those in rural, insular, and high cost areas, should
have access to telecommunications services that are reasonably
comparable to those offered in urban areas at rates that are reasonably comparable to the rates charged in urban areas;

All providers of telecommunications services should contribute
on an equitable and nondiscriminatory basis to preservation and
advancement of universal service;

Both the states and the federal government should develop specific, predictable, and sufficient support mechanisms to preserve
and advance universal service;

Schools, health care providers, and libraries should have access
to advanced telecommunication services.

In addition to these specific considerations, Congress authorized the Joint Board and the Commission to establish any additional guidelines that "are necessary and appropriate for the
protection of the public interest, convenience and necessity and
are consistent with this Act."[102] Upon the Joint Board's recommendation, the Commission adopted "competitive neutrality" as
an additional principle, to ensure that universal service support
mechanisms "neither unfairly advantage nor disadvantage one
provider over another, and neither unfairly favor nor disfavor
one technology over another."[103] The Commission has concluded
that its universal service policies should strike a "fair and reasonable balance" among all of these guiding tenets.[104]

The Act assigns the Joint Board and the FCC the task of developing a definition of the services to be supported by federal support mechanisms.[105] In determining which telecommunications
services should be federally supported, Congress directed the
Joint Board and the Commission to consider four factors.[106]

[102] *Id.* §254(b)(7).
[103] *Universal Service Order,* 12 F.C.C. Rec. at 8801 ¶¶46–47.
[104] *Id.* at 8803 ¶52.
[105] 47 U.S.C. §254(a)(1).
[106] *Id.* §254(c)(1).

First, is the service essential to education, public health, or public safety?[107] Second, has the service, through the operation of market forces, been subscribed to by a majority of residential customers?[108] Third, is the service being deployed in public telecommunications networks by telecommunications carriers?[109] And finally, would the inclusion of this particular service be consistent with the public interest, convenience, and necessity?[110]

The set of services included under the universal service definition is not intended to be static. Congress recognized that "[u]niversal service is an evolving level of telecommunications services."[111] Accordingly, the Act contemplates that the Commission periodically will evaluate the services that constitute universal service, "taking into account advances in telecommunications and information technologies and services."[112] In addition, the Joint Board may recommend to the Commission that additional services be added.[113] Conceivably, then, universal service may someday include features that today only a small percentage of subscribers have, such as Caller ID or digital subscriber line (DSL) services. The Commission also promised to establish a Joint Board to reconsider the definition of services by January 1, 2001.[114]

In its *Universal Service Order,* the Commission concluded that universal service support mechanisms will now subsidize "single-party service; voice grade access to the public switched network; DTMF [Dual Tone Multifrequency] signaling, or its functional equivalent; access to emergency services; access to operator services; access to interexchange service; access to directory assistance; and toll limitation service for qualifying low-income consumers."[115] The Commission also decided that, in addition to

---

[107] *Id.* §254(c)(1)(A).
[108] *Id.* §254(c)(1)(B).
[109] *Id.* §254(c)(1)(C).
[110] *Id.* §254(c)(1)(D).
[111] *Id.* §254(c)(1).
[112] *Id.*
[113] *Id.* §254(c)(2).
[114] *Universal Service Order,* 12 F.C.C. Rec. at 8834–8835 ¶104.
[115] *Id.* at 8809 ¶61. *See id.* 8810–8812 ¶¶62–64, 8814–8822 ¶¶71–82 for definitions and descriptions of these services. *See also* Federal-State Joint Board

subsidizing access to local service, some amount of local usage should be supported. It committed to determining that amount by the end of 1997, although it has postponed that date.[116]

§6.3.2 Phasing In Explicit Subsidies

In its *Universal Service Order*, the Commission recognized the need to convert its existing support programs for high-cost areas and for low-income subscribers to "explicit competitively neutral federal universal support mechanisms."[117] It also developed rules to implement section 254(h)'s requirements that schools and libraries receive discounted services and that rural health-care providers receive services at rates comparable to those for similar services in urban areas.

§6.3.2.1 Modifications to Existing Programs

(i) Low-Income Subscribers.   Observing that the Act "evinces a renewed concern for the needs of low-income citizens," the Commission took steps to expand its Lifeline Assistance and Link Up America programs.[118] It increased funding for the Life-

---

on Universal Service, Fourth Order on Reconsideration, Report and Order, 13 F.C.C. Rec. 5318, 5324–5329 ¶¶8–16 (1997) (hereinafter *Fourth Order on Reconsideration*) (technical clarifications to services included within universal service support). Section 254(k) of 47 U.S.C. directs the Commission to develop rules to prevent overassignment of joint and common costs to interstate universal services. The Commission implemented "section 254(k) by codifying its prohibitions in Part 64 of our rules" and committed to, "from time to time, re-evaluate our rules to determine whether additional rule changes are necessary." Implementation of Section 254(k) of the Communications Act of 1934, as Amended, Order, 12 F.C.C. Rec. 6415, 6415 ¶1 (1997).

[116] *Universal Service Order*, 12 F.C.C. Rec. at 8812–8814 ¶¶65–70. In October 1998, the FCC sought comment "on whether some amount of minimum local usage should be included in the basic services packages, and if so, how to determine that local usage requirement." Federal-State Joint Board on Universal Service, Memorandum Opinion and Order and Further Notice of Proposed Rulemaking, 13 F.C.C. Rec. 21,252, 21,279–21,280 ¶50 (1998).

[117] *Universal Service Order*, 12 F.C.C. Rec. at 8782 ¶6.

[118] *Id.* at 8955 ¶335. As an initial matter, the Commission concluded that section 254(j)'s directive that the 1996 Act's universal service provisions not

line program; made the program available in all states, irrespective of state participation; and required all eligible carriers to provide it.[119] The Commission found that Lifeline services should include single-party service; voice grade access to the public switched network; DTMF or its functional digital equivalent; access to emergency services, operator services, interexchange service, and directory assistance; and toll limitation.[120] The Commission concluded, however, that the Lifeline program would not be used to support low-income consumers' access to interexchange or advanced services.[121] With respect to the Link Up program, the Commission maintained support at its current level, but amended the program so that eligible carriers could more easily qualify for support.[122]

The Commission ruled that consumer eligibility for the Lifeline and Link Up programs will be based on the same criteria, and it directed states to base eligibility on income or factors directly related to income.[123]

(ii) Rural, Insular, and High-Cost Areas.

In the *Universal Service Order*, the Commission promised to change the way in which

---

"affect" the Lifeline Assistance program did not prevent it from modifying this program. *Id.* at 8953–8957 ¶¶331–340.

[119] *Id.* at 8952 ¶326, 8961–8964 ¶¶347–353. The Commission also increased federal support to $5.25 (previously $3.50), requiring no state matching support, but merely the state's approval of the intrastate rate reduction, and "'provide[d] for additional federal support equal to one half of any support generated from the intrastate jurisdiction, up to a maximum of $7.00 in federal support.'" *Id.* at 8962–8963 ¶¶350–352 (quoting Joint Board Recommended Decision).

[120] *Id.* at 8952 ¶328, 8979–8983 ¶¶384–389. *See also Fourth Order on Reconsideration,* 13 F.C.C. Rec. at 5388–5389 ¶¶114–117. Local carriers may not require up-front deposits from subscribers using toll limitation, nor may they disconnect Lifeline subscribers for nonpayment of long-distance bills. *Universal Service Order,* 12 F.C.C. Rec. at 8952 ¶328, 8983–8990 ¶¶390–402. The Commission determined that "PICCs attributable to all qualifying low-income customers who have toll blocking" should be supported and recoverable by all eligible carriers. *Fourth Order on Reconsideration,* 13 F.C.C. Rec. at 5393–5395 ¶¶122–125.

[121] *Universal Service Order,* 12 F.C.C. Rec. at 8991–8992 ¶404.

[122] *Id.* at 8976–8977 ¶¶379–380.

[123] *Id.* at 8973–8974 ¶¶373–374, 8977–8978 ¶381.

it administers the three programs it has previously used to support high-cost and small telephone companies—the Universal Service Fund (or high-cost assistance fund), the DEM weighting program, and the LTS program. The Commission decided to replace these separate funds with a single fund that will support carriers providing service in rural, insular, and high-cost areas. The amount of support these carriers will receive will be the difference between a "benchmark" amount, based on the nationwide average revenue per line, and the cost of service in the carrier's geographic area.[124] The carrier's cost of service will be determined by a forward-looking economic cost model.[125] The federal share of the difference between the national benchmark and a carrier's forward-looking cost of providing supported services will be 25 percent.[126] States will be responsible for implementing universal support mechanisms to cover the remaining costs.[127]

---

[124] *Id.* at 8893–8894 ¶214, 8895 ¶217, 8919–8924, ¶¶257–267.

[125] *Id.* at 8893 ¶214. The Commission stated that "the proper measure of cost for determining the level of universal service support is the forward-looking economic cost of constructing and operating the network facilities and functions used to provide the supported services. . . ." *Id.* ¶224. The Commission explained that "[i]n using the term 'forward-looking economic cost,' we mean the cost of producing services using the least cost, most efficient, and reasonable technology currently available for purchase with all inputs valued at current prices." *Id.* ¶224 n.573. The Commission adopted a model platform "to estimate the cost of providing the supported services," committed to selecting cost inputs, and referred many non-rural-carrier support issues to the Joint Board. Federal-State Joint Board on Universal Service, Fifth Report and Order, 13 F.C.C. Rec. 21,323, 21,324–21,325 ¶2 (1998). *See* New Telecommunications Entitlements at 20–21 (discussing the problems inherent in forward-looking cost methodology). *See also* §5.5.3.5. As of mid-1999, a petition for review was still pending in the Fifth Circuit, in which parties have asked the court to invalidate the Commission's use of the TELRIC methodology. *See supra* note 91.

[126] *Universal Service Order,* 12 F.C.C. Rec. at 8925 ¶269.

[127] *Id.* at 8924–8925 ¶¶268–269, 8926 ¶¶271–272. In its April 1998 *Report to Congress,* the Commission stated its intent to initiate a proceeding to reconsider that allocation. *Report to Congress,* 13 F.C.C. Rec. at 11,605 ¶224. Furthermore, the Commission provided that "additional federal universal service support should be provided to any high cost areas where state mechanisms, in combination with baseline federal support, are not sufficient to maintain rates at affordable levels." *Id.* at 11,606 ¶227. Upon referral of

The Commission will permit states, in the first instance, to conduct the forward-looking cost studies necessary to determine the cost of providing service in high-cost, rural, and insular areas.[128] States must submit proposed studies to the Commission for a determination whether the proposed methodologies conform to the Commission's criteria for forward-looking cost studies. If a state elects not to conduct its own forward-looking economic cost study or if a state-conducted study does not meet the Commission's criteria, then the Commission will decide on the forward-looking cost to be used.[129] Since the forward-looking methodologies for determining eligible carriers' costs are not yet in place, the Commission has decided to continue to use the existing support mechanisms for nonrural carriers until July 1999.[130] The Commission concluded that rural carriers will need more time to adjust to changes in universal service support, and it ruled that a forward-looking cost mechanism for rural carriers would not become effective before January 1, 2001.[131] The FCC indicated that it would seek comment on the use of competitive bidding to set universal service support levels for rural, insular, and high-cost areas.[132]

---

the issue by the FCC, the Joint Board recommended that the Commission develop a new methodology for determining the jurisdictional division for high-cost areas. Federal-State Universal Service Joint Board, Second Recommended Decision, CC Docket No. 96-45 (Nov. 25, 1998).

[128] *Universal Service Order,* 12 F.C.C. Rec. at 8912 ¶248.

[129] *Id.* at 8890 ¶206, 8899 ¶223, 8912–8917 ¶¶248–251. The Commission established ten criteria that states should follow in developing a methodology to calculate forward-looking costs. *Id.* at 8912–8916 ¶250.

[130] Federal-State Joint Board on Universal Service, Order and Order on Reconsideration, 13 F.C.C. Rec. 13,749, 13,753 ¶8 (1998) (hereinafter *Referral Order*). Originally, this date was December 31, 1998. *Universal Service Order,* 12 F.C.C. Rec. at 8927 ¶273.

[131] *See Universal Service Order* 12 F.C.C. Rec. at 8889 ¶204, 8894–8895 ¶216, 8917–8918 ¶¶252–256, 8934–8944 ¶¶291–310; *Referral Order,* 13 F.C.C. Rec. at 13,749 ¶1, 13,753–13,754 ¶¶8–10. Pursuant to the Commission's suggestion, the Joint Board established a Rural Task Force to study a forward-looking cost methodology for rural carriers. *Universal Service Order,* 12 F.C.C. Rec. at 8917 ¶253; Federal-State Joint Board on Universal Service Announces Rural Task Force Members, Public Notice, CC Docket No. 96-45 (July 1, 1998).

[132] *Universal Service Order,* 12 F.C.C. Rec. at 8890 ¶207, 8918 ¶256, 8947–8951 ¶¶319–325. The Commission also promised to revisit the question

(iii) Rate-Averaging.   Section 254(g) directs the Commission and states to adopt rules to ensure that the rates charged by providers of interexchange telecommunications services are no higher for subscribers in rural and high-cost areas than the rates charged in urban areas. By directing regulators to require, in essence, an implicit urban-to-rural subsidy, section 254(g)'s requirements are in significant tension with section 254(e)'s mandate that universal service support mechanisms be made "explicit." To implement section 254(g)'s requirements, the Commission merely codified the section's language and its own "existing policies."[133] The Commission requires "rate integration across affiliates," but does not "require a carrier to integrate an interstate interexchange CMRS [commercial mobile radio service] service with other interstate interexchange service offerings.[134] The Commission also noted that "Congress intended the states to play an active role in enforcing Section 254(g) with respect to intrastate geographic rate averaging."[135]

§6.3.2.2   New Programs Required by the 1996 Act

(i) Schools and Libraries.[136]   The 1996 Act requires telecommunications carriers to offer discounted rates to elementary and secondary schools and libraries.[137] Section 254(h)(1)(B) provides

---

whether to provide support for toll-free access and access to information services in the insular areas of the Commonwealth of the Northern Mariana Islands and Guam. *Id.* at 8995–9001 ¶¶410–423.

[133] Policy and Rules Concerning the Interstate, Interexchange Marketplace, Report and Order, 11 F.C.C. Rec. 9564, 9568–9569 ¶9, 9588 ¶52 (1996).

[134] Policy and Rules Concerning the Interstate, Interexchange Marketplace, First Memorandum Opinion and Order on Reconsideration, 12 F.C.C. Rec. 11,812, 11,819 ¶14, 11,821 ¶18 (1997).

[135] Policy and Rules Concerning the Interstate, Interexchange Marketplace, Report and Order, 11 F.C.C. Rec. 9564, 9585 ¶46 (1996).

[136] *See* 47 C.F.R. §§54.500–54.517.

[137] 47 U.S.C. §254(h)(1)(B). *See also* Hammond, Universal Service in the Digital Age at 210–214 (questioning the wisdom of excluding community-based organizations (CBOs) and urban healthcare organizations from the funding scheme and noting that the California Public Utilities Commission included CBOs in its discount structure).

that this discount shall be an amount that the Commission (for interstate services) and the states (for intrastate services) determine "is necessary to ensure affordable access to and use of such services by such entities."[138] In its *Universal Service Order*, the Commission concluded that it was not precluded from providing federal support to fund intrastate discounts.[139] Moreover, it decided that it could condition that federal support on a requirement that states establish intrastate discounts at least equal to the interstate discounts.[140]

The Commission determined that schools and libraries would receive discounts of 20 to 90 percent on "commercially available telecommunications services," Internet access, and internal connections.[141] The size of the discount applicable to a school or library will be based on indicators of economic disadvantage and on the price of telecommunications services in the relevant location.[142] Schools and libraries must seek competitive bids for all services eligible for the section 254(h) discount to ensure that they are not charged needlessly high prices.[143] Carriers that provide the discounted services[144] will receive payment either through an offset to their universal service contribution obligations or

---

[138] 47 U.S.C. §254(h)(1)(B).

[139] *Universal Service Order*, 12 F.C.C. Rec. at 9065 ¶550.

[140] *Id.*

[141] *Id.* at 9006–9023 ¶¶431–462, 9026–9050 ¶¶473–521. The discount program was effective for the 1997–1998 school year and support was available January 1, 1998. *Id.* at 9092 ¶607. *See also* R. Cook, All Wired Up: An Analysis of the FCC's Order to Internally Connect Schools, 50 Fed. Comm. L.J. 215 (1997) (discussing congressional intent to fund internal connections). Parties have petitioned for review of the Commission's internal connections discount. *See supra* note 91.

[142] *Universal Service Order*, 12 F.C.C. Rec. at 9035–9054, ¶¶493–528; 47 C.F.R. §54.505(c). *See also* Hammond, Universal Service in the Digital Age at 208–209 (stating that funding "without regard to the current disparity in — and pressures on — educational allocations, may exacerbate rather than ameliorate the disparity" and noting budgetary closures of local libraries).

[143] *Universal Service Order*, 12 F.C.C. Rec. at 9029–9030 ¶¶480–481, 9031–9032 ¶484. Schools and libraries may form consortia to get better deals on these discounted services. *Id.* at 9027–9029 ¶¶476–479.

[144] The carrier need not be a telecommunications carrier. *Id.* at 9084–9089 ¶¶589–599.

directly from the universal service administrator.[145] The Commission determined that requiring schools and libraries to pay service providers directly could create cash-flow problems for these disadvantaged schools and libraries.[146]

The Commission originally set an annual cap of $2.25 billion on universal service support for schools and libraries.[147] Later, however, it reduced this cap to $1.9 billion for 1998 and the first half of 1999, even though 30,000 schools and libraries had asked for around $2 billion by the third quarter of 1998.[148] The Commission concluded that its earlier allotment could cause consumer rates to rise precipitously and might result in rate churn.[149] Recognizing that its "revised collection rates will not fully satisfy the estimated support requested by schools and libraries," the Commission devised rules that would ensure that "schools and libraries with the greatest level of economic disadvantage will have priority."[150]

---

[145] *Id.* at 9083 ¶586.

[146] 47 U.S.C. §254(h)(1)(B); *Universal Service Order,* 12 F.C.C. Rec. at 9083 ¶586. The Commission declined to set up a separate fund. *Id.* at 9082–9083 ¶585.

[147] *Universal Service Order,* 12 F.C.C. Rec. at 9054 ¶529.

[148] Federal-State Joint Board on Universal Service, Fifth Order on Reconsideration and Fourth Report and Order, 13 F.C.C. Rec. 14,915, 14,917–14,918 ¶3, 14,925–14,926 ¶17 (1998) (hereinafter *Fifth Order on Reconsideration*). The Commission revised the authorized collections for the first half of 1998, from $1 billion to $625 million, based on schools' and libraries' initial demand and logistics. *See* Federal-State Joint Board on Universal Service, Third Order on Reconsideration, 12 F.C.C. Rec. 22,801, 22,802–22,803 ¶3, 22,804 ¶6 (1997) (hereinafter *Third Order on Reconsideration*). The Commission authorized maximum collections of $325 million per quarter for the second half of 1998 and first half of 1999, noting that those collections would "not increase interstate telecommunications carriers' cost of providing service" and would "ensure that long distance rates, overall, will continue to decline." *Fifth Order on Reconsideration,* 13 F.C.C. Rec. at 14,928 ¶20.

[149] *Fifth Order on Reconsideration,* 13 F.C.C.Rec. at 14,928–14,929 ¶22.

[150] *Id.* at 14,917–14,918 ¶¶3–4, 14,936–14,940 ¶¶34–38. The Commission also revised its prioritization rules because it had dropped the "first-come, first-served" method in favor of a "filing window period," in which all applications are considered filed simultaneously. Federal-State Joint Board on Universal Service, Third Report and Order, 12 F.C.C. Rec. 22,485, 22,486 ¶2 (1997).

(ii) Rural Health Care.[151]   Section 254(h)(1)(A) requires telecommunications carriers to provide rural healthcare providers with "telecommunications services which are necessary for the provision of health care services in a state, including instruction relating to such services . . . at rates that are reasonably comparable to rates charged for similar services in urban areas in that state."[152] The Commission has interpreted this mandate broadly. It concluded that "health care services" are "health-related services, including non-clinical, informational, and educational public health services, that local public health departments or agencies are charged with performing under federal and state laws."[153] Services that are "necessary for the provision of health care services . . . including instruction relating to such services" are those services "reasonably related to the provision of health care services or instruction."[154] All public and nonprofit healthcare providers located in rural areas are eligible to receive supported services.[155] The Commission found it unnecessary to expand or elaborate on the definition of "health care provider," which is set forth in 47 U.S.C. §254(h)(5)(B).[156]

The Commission determined that universal service support mechanisms for rural healthcare providers should support those commercially available services of bandwiths up to 1.544 megabits per second that are necessary for the provision of healthcare services.[157] In addition, the Commission authorized support for "limited toll charges incurred by health care providers that cannot

---

[151] *See* 47 C.F.R. §§54.601–54.623.

[152] 47 U.S.C. §254(h)(1)(A). Furthermore, section 254(c)(3) provides that "the Commission may designate additional services for such support mechanisms for . . . health care providers." See *Universal Service Order,* 12 F.C.C. Rec. at 9119–9129 ¶¶657–675 for a discussion of determining rural and urban rates for the purpose of the rural healthcare provider provision.

[153] *Universal Service Order,* 12 F.C.C. Rec. at 9098–9100 ¶617.

[154] *Id.* at 9100 ¶618.

[155] *Id.* at 9115–9117 ¶¶649–652 (defining rural areas in accordance with a methodology developed by the Office of Management & Budget).

[156] *Id.* at 9117–9118 ¶¶653–654.

[157] *Id.* at 9101 ¶620; 47 C.F.R. §54.601(c)(1). The speed of a T-1circuit is 1.544 Mbps, the standard for digital transmission in the United States. Newton's Telecom Dictionary 1009 (7th ed. 1994).

obtain toll-free access to an Internet service provider."[158] The Commission will reconsider the scope of supported services in 2001.[159]

In its *Universal Service Order*, the Commission determined that the annual cost of support to rural healthcare providers should be no more than $400 million annually.[160] Subsequently, however, the Commission reconsidered this figure and concluded that, based on demand, $100 million was adequate for 1998.[161] Even though demand had not exceeded the $100 million figure, the Commission decided to implement an allocation system and instituted a pro rata system that would decrease all applicants' support by equal amounts.[162]

Like schools and libraries, rural healthcare providers are required to seek competitive bids for all services eligible for support.[163] Telecommunications carriers will recover the cost of providing eligible services to rural healthcare providers through offsets to their universal service support contributions.[164]

---

[158] *Universal Service Order*, 12 F.C.C. Rec. at 9107–9108 ¶631, 9158–9161 ¶¶744–749; 47 C.F.R. §§54.601(c)(2), 54.621. The Commission committed to investigating "whether and how to support infrastructure development needed to enhance . . . health care providers' access to advanced telecommunications and information services." *Universal Service Order*, 12 F.C.C. Rec. at 9109–9110 ¶635.

[159] *Universal Service Order*, 12 F.C.C. Rec. at 9110 ¶637.

[160] *Id.* at 9141 ¶705.

[161] *Third Order on Reconsideration*, 12 F.C.C. Rec. at 22,804 ¶5; *Fifth Order on Reconsideration*, 13 F.C.C. Rec. at 14,917 ¶3, 14,928 ¶21. The *Universal Service Order* had authorized collection of $100 million in the first quarter of 1998. *Universal Service Order*, 12 F.C.C. Rec. at 9145 ¶715.

[162] *Fifth Order on Reconsideration*, 13 F.C.C. Rec. at 14,940–14,941 ¶¶39–41. The Commission adopted the filing window procedure, which precluded a chronological prioritization system. *See supra* note 150.

[163] *Universal Service Order*, 12 F.C.C. Rec. 9133–9134 ¶¶686–689. Rural healthcare providers are also permitted to form consortia to acquire services. *See id.* at 9146–9148 ¶¶719–722.

[164] *Id.* at 9154–9156 ¶¶734–737.

§6.3.2.3   Who Will Receive Universal Service Support?[165]

Under the 1996 Act, only "eligible telecommunications carriers," as designated by the state commissions, are entitled to receive universal service support.[166] The Commission concluded that the plain language of section 214(e)(1) precluded it or states from adopting additional criteria for designating carriers as eligible telecommunications carriers. It therefore adopted the statutory criteria contained in section 214(e)(1) as the rule for determining whether a carrier is eligible to receive universal service support.[167] Once a carrier is determined to be eligible, it must provide the minimum package of services defined by the FCC.[168] After defining service areas, state commissions assign universal service providers to them upon either request or its own motion.[169] "Any telecommunications carrier, using any technology" may become an eligible telecommunications carrier if it offers the universal service package and does not simply resell another carrier's services.[170]

State commissions in rural areas are authorized to, and in urban areas are required to, designate more than one eligible telecommunications carrier "upon request and consistent with the public interest, convenience, and necessity."[171] In areas not served by any carrier, the Commission is empowered to designate an essential telecommunications carrier (a carrier of last resort) for interstate services, and the states are similarly empowered

---

[165] *See* 47 C.F.R. §§54.201–54.207.

[166] 47 U.S.C. §214(e).

[167] *Universal Service Order,* 12 F.C.C. Rec. at 8791 ¶24.

[168] 47 U.S.C. §§254(c)(1), 214(e)(1)(A).

[169] *Id.* §214(e)(2). The term "common carrier" is defined at *id.* §153(10). The term "service area" is defined at *id.* §214(e)(5); *see also Universal Service Order,* 12 F.C.C. Rec. at 8879–8884 ¶¶184–193.

[170] *Universal Service Order,* 12 F.C.C. Rec. at 8858–8859 ¶145. Section 214 also requires that, to be eligible, the telecommunications carrier advertise the package of services and prices. 47 U.S.C. §214(e)(1)(B); *Universal Service Order,* 12 F.C.C. Rec. at 8860 ¶148. *See id.* at 8861–8876 ¶¶150–180 (discussing the facilities requirement).

[171] 47 U.S.C. §214(e)(2).

with respect to the provision of intrastate services.[172] The 1996
Act permits telecommunications carriers to relinquish their status as eligible telecommunications carriers under certain circumstances if their area is served by more than one carrier.[173]

Carriers are required to use the universal service funds they
receive to provide, maintain, and upgrade the facilities and services for which the support is received.[174] Carriers are prohibited
from using noncompetitive services to subsidize competitive
services.[175] Additionally, the Commission and the states are permitted to establish certain cost-allocation rules and other safeguards to ensure that telecommunications services included in
the definition of universal service bear no more than a reasonable share of the joint and common costs used to provide those
services.[176]

§6.3.2.4 Who Will Pay for Universal Service?

The 1996 Act requires every carrier that provides interstate
telecommunications services "to contribute, on an equitable and
nondiscriminatory basis, to the specific, predictable, and sufficient mechanisms established by the Commission to preserve
and advance universal service."[177] However, the Commission
may exempt a carrier (or class of carriers) from the contribution
requirement if the Commission determines that the carrier's
contribution would be de minimis.[178] Additionally, "[a]ny other

---

[172] *Id.* §214(e)(3). *See Universal Service Order,* 12 F.C.C. Rec. at 8885–8886
¶¶194–197.
[173] 47 U.S.C. §214(e)(4). The state commission is charged with requiring
the remaining eligible carrier(s) to guarantee that all customers of the relin-
quishing carrier are served. *Id.; see also Universal Service Order,* 12 F.C.C. Rec.
at 8860 ¶149.
[174] 47 U.S.C. §254(e).
[175] *Id.* §254(k). *See supra* note 115.
[176] 47 U.S.C. §254(k).
[177] *Id.* §254(d). Some argue that a means-tested, general tax revenue-
funded universal service mechanism would be more economically efficient.
See New Telecommunications Entitlements at 12–13, 15; A. Kahn, The Road
to More Intelligent Telephone Pricing, 1 Yale J. on Reg. 139, 146–147 (1984).
[178] 47 U.S.C. §254(d). The Commission originally interpreted the statutory
de minimis clause to exclude all carriers whose cost of collecting universal

provider of interstate telecommunications may be required to contribute . . . if the public interest so requires."[179]

In its *Universal Service Order,* the Commission concluded that all interstate carriers must contribute to universal service. It ruled that "all telecommunications carriers that provide interstate telecommunications services" would be treated as mandatory contributors to universal service.[180] The Commission also determined that it was in the public interest to require non-common-carrier interstate telecommunications providers, such as pay phone aggregators and private service providers that offer their service to others for a fee, to contribute to universal service.[181]

The Commission determined that "it has jurisdiction to assess contributions for the universal service support mechanisms from intrastate as well as interstate revenues and to require carriers to seek state (and not federal) authority to recover a portion of the contribution in intrastate rates," although it declined to exercise the entirety of this jurisdiction.[182] Each carrier's contribution to universal service will be based on its end-user telecommunications revenues.[183] Contributions to rural, insular,

---

contributions exceeds the contribution itself. *Id.*; *Universal Service Order,* 12 F.C.C. Rec. at 9186–9189 ¶¶801–805. The Commission later determined that if a contributor's annual contribution was less than $10,000, it would be exempt. *See Fourth Order on Reconsideration,* 13 F.C.C. Rec. at 5482 ¶297.

[179] 47 U.S.C. §254(d).

[180] *Universal Service Order,* 12 F.C.C. Rec. at 9173 ¶777. The Commission provided a list of services that meet the definition of interstate telecommunications: "cellular telephone and paging services; mobile radio services; operator services; PCS; access to interexchange service; special access; wide area telephone service (WATS); toll-free services; 900 services; MTS; private line; telex; telegraph; video services; satellite services; and resale services." *Id.* at 9175 ¶780.

[181] *Id.* at 9182–9186 ¶¶793–800. The Commission found that "'other providers of telecommunications' that provide telecommunications solely to meet their needs should not be required to contribute." *Id.* at 9185 ¶799. The Commission excluded systems integrators; broadcasters; and nonprofit schools, universities, libraries, and rural healthcare providers from its permissive authority. *Fourth Order on Reconsideration,* 13 F.C.C. Rec. at 5471–5472 ¶277.

[182] *Universal Service Order,* 12 F.C.C. Rec. at 9192 ¶813; *Report to Congress,* 13 F.C.C. Rec. at 11,594–11,602 ¶¶198–218.

[183] *Universal Service Order,* 12 F.C.C. Rec. at 8797 ¶40, 9206 ¶843. The Commission concluded that interstate carriers' foreign telecommunications revenues

and high-cost and low-income support mechanisms will be based on interstate revenues alone; such a method fosters "comity" and "partnership" between state and federal governments and keeps basic residential service affordable.[184] In addition, these contributions will be recovered entirely through interstate rates.[185] In contrast, contributions to support mechanisms for schools, libraries, and rural healthcare providers will be based on both intrastate and interstate revenues, but again will be recovered entirely through rates for interstate services.[186]

The Commission has concluded that it will neither require nor prohibit carriers from recovering the contributions they make to universal service through surcharges imposed on end users,[187] a conclusion it reiterated in a report it submitted to Congress in May 1998.[188] Moreover, the Commission concluded that section 332(c)(3)(A) "does not preclude states from requiring commercial mobile radio service ("CMRS") providers to contribute to state support mechanisms."[189] The Commission ruled that

---

are included in the revenue base. *Id.* at 9173–9174 ¶779. "[E]nd-user telecommunications revenues includes revenues derived from SLCs. End-user revenues would also include revenues derived from other carriers when such carriers utilize telecommunications services for their own internal uses. . . ." *Id.* at 9206–9207 ¶844. The Commission establishes quarterly contribution factors for carriers. *See, e.g.,* Proposed Fourth Quarter 1998 Universal Service Contribution Factors Announced, Public Notice, 13 F.C.C. Rec. 15,588 (1998).

[184] *Universal Service Order,* 12 F.C.C. Rec. at 9198–9203 ¶¶824–836; *Report to Congress,* 13 F.C.C. Rec. at 11,599–11,602 ¶¶213–218.

[185] *Universal Service Order,* 12 F.C.C. Rec. at 8895–8896 ¶218.

[186] *Id.* at 8797 ¶40, 9203–9205 ¶¶837–840.

[187] *Id.* at 9210–9211 ¶853.

[188] Report in Response to Senate Bill 1768 and Conference Report on H.R. 3579, Report to Congress, 13 F.C.C. Rec. 11,810, 11,821–11,822 ¶18 (1998) (hereinafter *May Report to Congress*). The Commission stressed its desire that carriers "includ[e] complete and truthful information regarding the contribution amount." *Id.* at 11,822–11,823 ¶¶19–20; *see also Universal Service Order,* 12 F.C.C. Rec. at 9211–9212 ¶855. Upon referral by the Commission, the Joint Board recommended that the FCC ensure that carriers do not "overrecover" their universal service contributions from consumers and do not mislead consumers about universal service charges on their bills. Federal-State Universal Service Joint Board, Second Recommended Decision, 13 F.C.C. Rec. 24,744, 24,771–24,773, ¶¶69–73.

[189] *Fourth Order on Reconsideration,* 13 F.C.C. Rec. at 5485–5487 ¶¶301–305; *Universal Service Order,* 12 F.C.C. Rec. at 9181–9182 ¶791.

CMRS providers can recover their contributions from rates for intrastate and interstate services.[190]

Initially, the Commission ruled that Internet service providers (ISPs)[191] were not required to fund universal service.[192] At Congress's direction, it revisited this decision. The Commission reaffirmed its conclusions that telecommunications and information

---

[190] *Fourth Order on Reconsideration,* 13 F.C.C. Rec. at 5489 ¶309; *Report to Congress,* 13 F.C.C. Rec. 11,601–11,602 ¶218. The Commission adopted interim guidelines for CMRS reporting of interstate and intrastate wireless telecommunications revenues and sought comment on permanent mechanisms. Federal-State Universal Service Joint Board, Memorandum Opinion and Order and Further Notice of Proposed Rulemaking, 13 F.C.C. Rec. 21,252, 21,254–21,275 ¶¶5–41. Additionally, the Commission sought "comment on the extent to which the Commission's universal service rules facilitate the provision of supported services by service providers, such as wireless telecommunications providers and cable operators, that historically have not provided services eligible for universal service support." *Id.* at 21,253–21,254 ¶3, 21,275–21,277 ¶¶42–45.

[191] See generally §12.6.2.

[192] *Universal Service Order,* 12 F.C.C. Rec. at 9179–9181 ¶¶788–790. *See* Jamie N. Nafziger, A Cyberspace Perspective on Governance, Standards, and Control: Time to Pay Up: Internet Service Providers' Universal Service Obligations Under the Telecommunications Act of 1996, 16 J. Marshall J. Computer & Info. L. 37 (1997) (discussing the ISP exemption and advocating that it be eliminated). The Commission issued a Notice of Inquiry on the treatment of Internet access and other information service providers. Usage of the Public Switched Network by Information Service and Internet Access Providers, Notice of Inquiry, 11 F.C.C. Rec. 21,354 (1996). The Commission concluded that "any telecommunications carrier, even one that does not qualify as an 'eligible telecommunications carrier,' should be eligible for support for services provided to schools and libraries. We anticipate that Internet service providers may subcontract with [interexchange carriers] and [local exchange carriers] that were not already providing Internet access to begin to provide such access to the Internet. . . ." *Universal Service Order,* 12 F.C.C. Rec. at 9015 ¶449 (footnote omitted). *See* S. Foley, The Brewing Controversy Over Internet Service Providers and the Universal Service Fund: A Third Generation Interpretation of Section 254, 6 CommLaw Prospectus 245 (1998) (proposing that the Commission adopt one of two solutions: exempting ISPs from receiving and contributing to universal service support or permitting ISPs to receive and requiring them to contribute to universal service support); *see also* R. Frieden, Dialing for Dollars: Should the FCC Regulate Internet Telephony?, 23 Rutgers Computer & Tech. L.J. 47, 72–73 (1997) (stating that "the potential shortfall in universal service funding resulting from traffic migration to the Internet . . . suggest[s] the need to consider changes in funding universal service goals and the possible elimination of usage insensitive pricing including the prospect for imposing USF payments by Internet service providers for local exchange services") (footnote omitted).

services are "mutually exclusive" and that Internet access services are information services rather than telecommunications services.[193] The Commission decided, however, to reexamine in a subsequent proceeding its initial decision not to require ISPs that own transmission facilities to contribute to universal service.[194] As non-common carriers providing telecommunications, such ISPs could be required to contribute to universal service if the public interest so requires.[195]

With respect to Internet telephony (or IP telephony), the Commission again refused to make any definitive pronouncements.[196] It tentatively concluded that an ISP that provides subscribers access to the Internet to engage in "computer-to-computer" IP telephony "do[] not appear to be 'provid[ing]' telecommunications to its subscribers."[197] However, "phone-to-phone" IP telephony comes closer to telecommunications service, and ISPs providing these services thus may be subject to access charges and universal service contributions.[198] In the end, though, the Commission does not believe these interpretations will "create significant shifts in contribution obligations,"[199] since retail revenues of ISPs are small compared to overall long-distance revenues. "More importantly, however, Internet access generates additional telecommunications revenue to support universal service in the form of thousands of business lines," such that ISPs will contribute significant amounts to universal service indirectly.[200]

The Commission also has concluded that rates for interconnection, network elements, and access to network elements may

---

[193] *Report to Congress,* 13 F.C.C. Rec. at 11,536–11,540 ¶¶73–82.
[194] *Id.* at 11,534–11,536 ¶¶69–72.
[195] *Id.* at 11,534–11,535 ¶69.
[196] *Id.* at 11,541 ¶83.
[197] *Id.* at 11,541 ¶83, 11,543 ¶87.
[198] *See id.* at 11,543–11,545 ¶¶88–92.
[199] *Id.* at 11,547–11,548 ¶97.
[200] *Id.* at 11,532 ¶66 n.130; *see also id.* at 11,547–11,548 ¶97. For instance, America Online informed the FCC that it anticipates spending about $1.2 billion for telecommunications services in fiscal 1999, and the Commission notes that "[t]he prices that it pays for those services incorporate universal service contributions." *Id.* at 11,532 ¶66 n.130.

not include any funding for universal service. In the Commission's view, such a requirement would be inconsistent with the 1996 Act's mandate that universal service be recovered from providers of telecommunications service in an "equitable and nondiscriminatory" manner. In addition, such a requirement would conflict with section 252(d)(1)'s provision that rates for interconnection, network elements, and access to network elements be cost-based.[201]

§6.3.2.5 Administrative Mechanisms

In its *Universal Service Order,* the Commission designated the National Exchange Carrier Association (NECA) as the temporary administrator of the universal service support mechanisms and asked a Federal Advisory Committee to propose a permanent administrator.[202] In July 1997, the Commission instructed NECA to establish an independent, not-for-profit subsidiary (the Universal Service Administrative Company (USAC)). USAC was temporarily to manage the high-cost area and low-income support mechanisms and to bill, collect, and distribute the funds necessary to support schools, libraries, and rural healthcare providers.[203] The Commission also directed NECA to set up two unaffiliated, not-for-profit corporations (the School and Libraries Corporation (SLC) and the Rural Health Care Corporation (RHCC)); these corporations would perform administrative functions connected with the schools, libraries, and rural health-

[201] Implementation of Local Competition Provisions in the Telecommunications Act of 1996, First Report and Order, 11 F.C.C. Rec. 15,499, 15,860–15,861 ¶¶712–713 (1996); *see also Access Charge Reform Order,* 12 F.C.C. Rec. at 16,129–16,130 ¶¶337–338. The Eighth Circuit Court of Appeals upheld a challenge to this aspect of the *Access Charge Reform Order.* Southwestern Bell Tel. Co. v. FCC, 153 F.3d 523, 540–541 (8th Cir. 1998).

[202] *Universal Service Order,* 12 F.C.C. Rec. at 9171 ¶774, 9216–9217 ¶866.

[203] Changes to the Board of Directors of the National Exchange Carrier Association, Inc., Report and Order and Second Order on Reconsideration, 12 F.C.C. Rec. 18,400, 18,401 ¶1, 18,415 ¶25, 18,420–18,428 ¶¶33–51, 18,438 ¶71 (1997). The Commission also called for a USAC High Cost and Low Income Committee. *Id.* at 18,401–18,402 ¶2, 18,415 ¶25, 18,428–18,430 ¶¶52–56.

care providers programs, with the exception of billing, collecting, and distributing funds.[204]

Congress instructed the Commission to reconsider its universal service administrative structure and to establish a single administrator for the schools, libraries, and rural healthcare providers support programs.[205] Accordingly, the Commission named the USAC as the permanent administrator of all federal universal service support, effective January 1, 1999.[206]

§6.3.3   Phasing Out Implicit Subsidies

§6.3.3.1   A Market-Based Approach to Phasing Out Subsidies

A key change implemented by the 1996 Act was the requirement that universal support mechanisms be made "explicit and sufficient."[207] As discussed above, while some subsidies were explicit before 1996, most were not. Federal and state regulators simply required that certain users be charged uneconomically high rates for certain services so that the extra money could be used to allow other users to pay uneconomically low prices for other services.

As the Commission has acknowledged, a system of implicit subsidies is sustainable only if there is a way to ensure that all the carriers providing a given service are subject to the same subsidy

---

[204] *Id.* at 18,401–18,402 ¶2, 18,415–18,416 ¶26, 18,430–18,438 ¶¶57–70, 18,438–18,439 ¶¶72–73.

[205] The Conference Report of the supplemental appropriations legislation passed April 30, 1998, directed the Commission to designate a single entity as administrator of the schools, libraries, and rural healthcare programs and to comply with the General Accounting Office's finding that the FCC did not have the authority to condition NECA's appointment as temporary administrator on its establishment of SLC and RHCC. *May Report to Congress,* 13 F.C.C. Rec. at 11,810–11,811 ¶1.

[206] Changes to the Board of Directors of the National Exchange Carrier Association, Inc., Third Report and Order, Fourth Order on Reconsideration, and Eighth Order on Reconsideration, CC Docket Nos. 97-21, 96-45 (Nov. 20, 1998).

[207] 47 U.S.C. §254(e).

requirements. In a competitive environment, if only some carriers are required to support certain activities, the entire subsidy system will deteriorate. For example, a requirement that some carriers (e.g., incumbent carriers) charge some customers above-cost rates so as to charge below-cost rates to others will permit competitors not subject to this requirement to target the most profitable customers—those being charged above-cost rates. By undercutting an incumbent's rates, competitors will be able selectively to serve those customers, thereby depleting the revenue source needed to support below-cost rates for the other customers (which the new competitors have no interest in serving). The incumbent could respond by lowering its rates for the desirable customers, but that, too, would eliminate the revenue that previously was used to fund below-cost rates for some customers. As the FCC itself described the problem with respect to the subsidies implicit in access charges:

> The 1996 Act removes barriers to entry in the local market, generating competitive pressures that make it difficult for incumbent LECs to maintain access charges above economic cost. . . . [W]here existing rules require an incumbent LEC [i.e., local exchange carrier] to set access charges above cost for a high-volume user, a competing provider of exchange access services entering into a market can lease unbundled network elements at cost, or construct new facilities, to circumvent the access charge. In this way, a new entrant might target an incumbent LEC's high volume access customers, for whom access charges are now set at levels significantly above economic cost. As competition develops, incumbent LECs may be forced to lower their access charges or lose market share, in either case jeopardizing the source of revenue that, in the past, has permitted the incumbent LEC to offer service to other customers, particularly those in high-cost areas, at below-cost prices.[208]

In light of this problem, the FCC has interpreted section 254 (e)'s requirement that subsidies be made "explicit and sufficient"

---

[208] *Access Charge Reform Order,* 12 F.C.C. Rec. at 15,996–15,997 ¶32; *see also Universal Service Order,* 12 F.C.C. Rec. at 8786–8787 ¶17.

not merely as a mandate to identify and disclose currently existing implicit subsidies.[209] In the Commission's view, Congress also intended to ensure that subsidies are both "measurable" and "portable."[210] Measurable, in that any competing carrier, not just an incumbent, can assess the profitability of serving the subsidized end user. And portable, in that the carrier who actually serves the subsidized customer ends up pocketing the subsidy.[211] (In theory, this is all very well, but there remains one very large practical problem. Among the many sources of subsidy, only interstate access charges fall directly under the Commission's control.[212] The remaining subsidy mechanisms are administered by the states.)

Although the Commission recognized that a competitive environment would erode the implicit subsidy regime it had developed over the years, it concluded that it could not immediately remove and make explicit all universal service costs from interstate access charges.[213] "We cannot remove universal service costs from interstate access charges until we can identify those costs, which we will not be able to do even for non-rural incumbent carriers . . . before January 1, 1999."[214] And even assuming that accurate cost information were available, drastically cutting access charges to bring them to cost-based levels could prove disruptive to business operations.[215] Thus, the Commission declined to implement any dramatic changes to its access-charge regime, ruling that "the existing system of largely implicit subsidies" would have to "continue to serve its purpose."[216]

To bring access charges gradually to competitive levels, the Commission decided instead to rely on a "market-based approach."[217] The Commission reasoned that the introduction of

---

[209] *Access Charge Reform Order,* 12 F.C.C. at 15,997 ¶33.
[210] *Id.*
[211] *Id.*
[212] *Universal Service Order,* 12 F.C.C. Rec. at 8784–8785 ¶12.
[213] *Id.* at 8785 ¶13.
[214] *Id.*
[215] *Access Charge Reform Order,* 12 F.C.C. Rec. at 16,002 ¶46.
[216] *Universal Service Order,* 12 F.C.C. Rec. at 8786–8787 ¶17.
[217] *Access Charge Reform Order,* 12 F.C.C. Rec. at 16,002 ¶45.

competition to the market for interexchange access would bring access rates closer to actual cost. With competition, price-cap local exchange carriers will eventually no longer be able to charge interexchange carriers the maximum amounts prescribed by the Commission, but will instead have to decrease their rates to meet the competition. The result: subsidies will be squeezed out of the system.[218]

§6.3.3.2 Modifications to the Access-Charge Regime

The Commission went on to modify its access-charge regime. As in earlier access-charge proceedings, its primary goal was to bring access charges into line with cost-causation principles so that costs are recovered in the same way that they are incurred. Non-traffic-sensitive costs (e.g., common line costs) are to be recovered through flat charges, whereas traffic-sensitive costs (e.g., switching and transport charges) are to be recovered through usage-based, or per-minute, charges.[219]

As explained above, the Commission previously required incumbent carriers to recover non-traffic-sensitive common line costs both through a flat subscriber line charge and through a usage-based carrier common line charge. The Commission, however, had put a ceiling on SLCs, which virtually ensured that incumbent LECs could not "recover their average per-line interstate-allocated common line costs" from the SLC alone.[220] "As a result of the SLC ceilings, . . . incumbent LECs" were required to "recover the shortfall through usage-sensitive [carrier common

---

[218] *Id.* at 16,001–16,003 ¶¶44–49. Of course, if access charges are brought to economic levels, incumbent LECs will no longer have extra money in their pockets to fund the subsidies of local services required by state commissions. And nothing in the FCC's *Universal Service Order* or *Access Charge Reform Order* requires state commissions to modify their requirements that incumbent carriers provide below-cost services to certain subscribers. Conceivably, then, the FCC's access-charge reform will result in a system in which states require incumbent carriers to subsidize local services, but do not enable LECs to recover the costs of those subsidies.

[219] *Id.* at 15,998–16,001 ¶¶36–41.

[220] *Id.* at 16,013 ¶76.

line or CCL] charges assessed on interexchange carriers."[221] This system created an implicit subsidy whereby high-volume users would underwrite part of the costs of providing service to low-volume users.

To bring cost recovery closer in line with the way costs are incurred, the FCC determined that it would increase flat-rate charges and phase out usage-sensitive CCL charges.[222] Numerous parties, including the United States Department of Justice, recommended increasing the SLC to allow the full costs of interstate service to be recovered directly from end users of local service.[223] The Commission declined to do so, citing affordability concerns, even though it recognized that inflation had rendered the SLC ceiling significantly lower, in real dollars, than it had been initially.[224] Instead, the Commission left the SLC for primary residential and single business lines capped at $3.50 per month.[225]

The Commission did, however, provide for a gradual, phased-in increase in the SLC for second-line residential and multiple-line business customers.[226] The SLC ceiling for multiline business lines was increased to $9.00 per month, and the nonprimary residential line ceiling was increased by $1.50 in the first year, and $1.00 per year thereafter, until it reached the same level as the multiline business rate.[227]

In addition to these new SLC charges, the Commission established a series of additional flat-rate charges, known as presubscribed interexchange carrier charges or PICCs. PICCs are imposed on the presubscribed long-distance carrier.[228] There are PICCs for primary residential and single business lines (capped initially at $.53 per month), for nonprimary residential

[221] Id.
[222] Id. at 16,013–16,014 ¶77.
[223] See id. at 16,010–16,011 ¶73 n.77.
[224] Id. at 16,010–16,011 ¶73, 16,015–16,016 ¶82.
[225] Id. at 16,010–16,011 ¶73.
[226] See id. at 16,008–16,009 ¶70, 16,010–16,011 ¶73.
[227] Id. at 16,014 ¶78.
[228] Long-distance carriers are free to recover PICCs from end users in a variety of ways, including flat charges and increased per-minute fees. See supra notes 188 and 189 and accompanying text.

lines (capped at $1.50 per month), and for multiline business lines (capped at $2.75 per month).[229] Incumbent LECs, the Commission held, would be permitted to seek to recover interstate costs not recovered through the SLC through these various PICCs.[230]

The Commission acknowledged that as a result of the caps it imposed, even the combination of all these various SLC and PICC charges would not necessarily allow incumbent LECs to recover all of their interstate costs.[231] Accordingly, it decided to permit incumbents to recover the remainder, as they had in the past, through a per-minute CCLC imposed on interexchange carriers.[232] The FCC ruled, however, that incumbent LECs would generally not be permitted to recover those costs on charges for *terminating* calls.[233] Instead, incumbent LECs would, in the first instance, have to seek to recover those costs from *originating* calls, even though those were subject to the greatest amount of competition.[234] A number of parties challenged various aspects of the Commission's *Access Charge Reform Order,* but the United States Court of Appeals for the Eighth Circuit upheld the Commission's order on review.[235]

[229] *Access Charge Reform Order,* 12 F.C.C. Rec. at 16,022 ¶99.
[230] *Id.* at 16,019 ¶91.
[231] *Id.* at 16,022 ¶99.
[232] *Id.* at 16,022–16,023 ¶¶99–100.
[233] *Id.* at 16,022–16,023 ¶100.
[234] *Id.* The Commission's rationale for moving subsidies to the most competitive services was that it believed that market forces would drive rates down to actual costs. *Id.*
[235] Southwestern Bell Tel. Co. v. FCC, 153 F.3d 523 (8th Cir. 1998). Some incumbent carriers contended, among other things, that the Commission had impermissibly delayed in making implicit subsidies explicit, that it had created new implicit subsidies, and that it had unlawfully exempted ISPs and purchasers of unbundled network elements (UNEs) from access charges. *Id.* at 536–544. Interexchange carriers asserted that the Commission immediately should have set access charges at cost-based levels, eliminated the transport interconnection charge (TIC) and the tandem switching charge, and abolished the unitary and interim rate structures for tandem-switched transport. *Id.* at 546–554. The Texas Office of Public Utility Counsel claimed that the Commission's new regime would result in an inadequate intrastate revenue base and that the secondary residential and multiline business SLC increase was impermissible. Southwestern Bell Tel. Co. v. FCC, 153 F.3d at 554–559. The Eighth Circuit rejected these challenges, holding that the

In addition, the Commission modified its LTS system. As explained above, to ensure that CCLCs remained uniform across the country, the Commission had established an LTS fund.[236] Larger, lower-cost LECs were required to make LTS payments, which were used to keep the CCLCs of smaller, higher-cost LECs from rising above the national average. Carriers making LTS payments were permitted to recover these costs by raising their own CCLC rates, thereby increasing their own access charges.[237]

In the *Universal Service Order,* the Commission concluded that the LTS system was "an impermissibly discriminatory universal service support mechanism."[238] It therefore removed the LTS system from the access-charge regime, but ruled that rural LECs would continue to receive payments comparable to LTS from the new universal service support mechanisms.[239]

§6.3.4 State-Level Regulation of Universal Service

As noted above, states have developed their own, enormously important mechanisms to keep rates for basic local service affordable.[240] The Act does not preempt states from adopting regulations to preserve and advance universal service as long as the state measures are "not inconsistent" with the Commission's regulations.[241] Likewise, a state may adopt additional definitions

---

Commission had acted within its discretion as authorized by Congress in the 1996 Act and that it had not acted arbitrarily, capriciously, or contrary to the law. *Id.* at 559–560.

[236] *Universal Service Order,* 12 F.C.C. Rec. at 9163–9164 ¶754.

[237] *Id.*

[238] *Id.* at 9165 ¶757.

[239] *Access Charge Reform Order,* 12 F.C.C. Rec. at 16,145 ¶374; *Universal Service Order,* 12 F.C.C. Rec. at 9164–9166 ¶¶756–759, 9169–9170 ¶¶769–771.

[240] *See supra* note 48 and accompanying text. For a thorough review of individual state universal service funding mechanisms and policies before and after the 1996 Act, see E. Rosenberg & J. Wilhelm, National Regulatory Research Institute, State Universal Service Funding and Policy: An Overview and Survey (Sept. 1998).

[241] 47 U.S.C. §254(f). Section 253, which prohibits state or local barriers to entry and which itself has a broad preemption provision, states that "[n]othing in this section shall affect the ability of a state to impose, on a competitively

and standards to advance universal service, but only to the extent such measures "do not rely on or burden Federal universal service mechanisms."[242]

The 1996 Act imposes several affirmative duties on the states with respect to universal service. The Act provides that there "should be specific, predictable and sufficient Federal and state mechanisms to preserve and advance universal service."[243] It directs states to determine the manner in which "[e]very telecommunications carrier that provides intrastate telecommunications services shall contribute on an equitable and non-discriminatory basis" to the preservation and advancement of universal service in that state.[244] The Act requires state commissions to designate the telecommunications carriers eligible to receive support in exchange for their provision of the universal service package.[245]

The Commission did not in its *Universal Service Order* attempt to identify state-level implicit universal service support mechanisms, nor did it try to convert such implicit mechanisms to explicit federal universal service support.[246] In the Commission's view, such an undertaking would be an unwarranted intrusion into the local rate-setting process, precluded by section 152(b). Thus, "States, acting pursuant to sections 245(f) and 253 of the Communications Act, must in the first instance be responsible for identifying intrastate implicit universal service support."[247] The Commission also reasoned that the introduction of competition to the local markets will itself identify intrastate implicit universal service support, compelling states to move to explicit support mechanisms consistent with section 254(f).[248]

---

neutral basis and consistent with Section 254, requirements necessary to preserve and advance universal service." *Id.* §253(b).

[242] *Id.* §254(f).

[243] *Id.* §254(b)(5).

[244] *Id.* §254(f).

[245] *Id.* §214(e)(2); *see FTL1* §6.8.

[246] *Universal Service Order,* 12 F.C.C. Rec. at 8785–8786 ¶14.

[247] *Id.*

[248] *Id.*

7

Mergers and Acquisitions*

§7.1 Introduction

The original Bell System monopoly was created largely through merger and acquisition almost a century ago. Domestically and globally, mergers are now restructuring the industry for the new era of competition. Critics say "the old Ma Bell" will be recreated. It will indeed, but it won't be a monopoly. It will be recreated instead by four to six major competitors, each with the resources and reach to compete end to end in every major market in the United States and around the globe.

Four main factors account for the fundamental restructuring of the industry now under way.

*This chapter was co-authored by Rachel E. Selinfreund, Associate, Kellogg, Huber, Hansen, Todd & Evans; Northwestern University (B.A., with distinction, 1993); Harvard Law School (J.D., *magna cum laude*, 1996); Phi Beta Kappa; Sears Prize; Law Clerk, Honorable Laurence Silberman, U.S. Court of Appeals, D.C. Circuit, 1996–1997; Law Clerk, Honorable Antonin Scalia, U.S. Supreme Court, 1997–1998.

First: the vagaries of antitrust, regulatory, and legal history. The 1984 decision to divide the old Bell System into a long-distance carrier and seven regional holding companies was made by AT&T and reflected little more than Bell's own traditional practice of dividing up the nation into local operating companies and regional marketing territories.[1] At the time, the regulated monopoly franchise granted to local exchange carriers in most states severely limited any competition in local markets.[2] The 1982 Decree assumed that local exchange was a natural economic monopoly and resolutely quarantined the presumptive monopolists.[3] Because they believed so firmly in local monopoly, the architects of the Decree did not believe it was desirable to permit integration of (monopoly) local service with competitive long-distance, wireless, or information services. The 1996 Telecommunications Act assumes the opposite: local competition is

---

[1] As summarized by the United States Telecommunications Suppliers Association in 1983, "Western Electric's existing 'Bell Sales' operation performs a wide variety of procurement related functions for the BOCs through a highly integrated network of facilities, organized into seven regions which are virtually identical to the areas covered by AT&T's proposed 'regional holding companies.'" Comments of United States Telecommunications Suppliers Association Concerning AT&T's Proposed Plan of Reorganization at 7–8, United States v. Western Elec. Co., Inc., Civ. Act. No. 82-0192 (D.D.C. Feb. 14, 1983). The divestiture Decree itself did not call for seven regional holding companies, *see* Modification of Final Judgment §I, *reprinted in* United States v. AT&T, 552 F. Supp. 131, 226–227 (D.D.C. 1982) (hereinafter Decree), *aff'd sub nom.* Maryland v. United States, 460 U.S. 1001 (1983), and both Assistant Attorney General William Baxter and AT&T's then-general counsel testified before Congress that the Decree would not have precluded AT&T from spinning off all of the BOCs into a single holding company. *See* United States v. Western Elec. Co., Inc., 797 F.2d 1082, 1091 (D.C. Cir. 1986) (citing AT&T Proposed Settlement: Hearings Before the Senate Committee on Commerce, Science and Transportation, 97th Cong., 2d Sess. 73 (1982) (testimony of William F. Baxter)), *cert. denied,* 480 U.S. 922 (1987). No public official expressed any strongly held views regarding how many or few Regional Bells there would be, since no one anticipated any competition by, among, or (least of all) against the Bells.

[2] Indeed, the divestiture Decree was first interpreted to prohibit the BOCs from competing in local markets outside their own regions. *See* United States v. Western Elec. Co., Inc., 627 F. Supp. 1090, 1108 (D.D.C.), *rev'd in relevant part,* 797 F.2d 1082 (D.C. Cir. 1986), *cert. denied,* 480 U.S. 922 (1987).

[3] *See* Decree §II(D), 552 F. Supp. at 227–228.

not only possible, but inevitable; quarantines are to be phased out; exclusive franchises have been eliminated; and vertical re-integration of the industry is considered both likely and (under competitive conditions) desirable.

Second: the competitive impacts of technological change. Even as the legal barriers to competition erode, rapid technological advance is propelling fundamental changes in the price, quality, and variety of telecommunications services. Telephone, cable, and data services are converging, and the 1996 Act includes a range of initiatives to facilitate that process. There is no reason that the old industry structure, erected on the pillars of exclusive local franchise, regulated monopoly, and analog technology, should endure in the new environment. AT&T, for example, has merged with three different providers of "local" service — McCaw (wireless), TCG (competitive, business-market urban fiber), and TCI (residential cable). At all levels of the network, from customer premises to transoceanic calling, the basic economics of competition are being transformed by rapid technological advances, changing cost structures, the rise of data networks, and soaring demand for new bandwidth and services.

Third: the powerful economies of scale and scope that characterize network industries.[4] Large buyers of equipment are able to negotiate large discounts with hardware and software vendors.[5] Purchases of bulk services, like wholesale interexchange

---

[4] The Federal Communications Commission (FCC) has recognized that firms that can take advantage of scale economies by spreading development costs over a larger customer base are more likely to invest in infrastructure upgrades. *See, e.g.,* Bell Atlantic Mobile Systems, Inc. and NYNEX Mobile Communications Co., Order, 10 F.C.C. Rec. 13,368, 13,384–13,385 ¶46 (1995) (hereinafter *BA Mobile/NYNEX Mobile*) ("[T]he alleged efficiencies will improve service to customers by promoting technological innovation and new or improved service offerings for consumers."); Competition, Rate Deregulation and the Commission's Policies Relating to the Provision of Cable Television Services, Report, 5 F.C.C. Rec. 4962, 5003 ¶71 (1990) ("[I]ncreased concentration [in the cable industry] has provided economies of scale and fostered program investment.").

[5] Procurement savings "are as desirable as any other economies" for purposes of competitive analysis. 5 P. Areeda & D. Turner, Antitrust Law ¶1104a, at 11 (1980). The Commission has noted that procurement savings tend to lower marginal costs and "thereby counteract the merged firm's incentive to

transport or Internet backbone access, also become much less expensive with scale. Larger providers of service can distribute the costs of funding the development of new technology over an extended base of operations. Scale also eliminates many duplicative general and administrative costs, providing selling and maintenance efficiencies.[6] These economies are all particularly important for companies that are seeking to enter new geographic markets from scratch, gaining a competitive foothold against well-established incumbents.

Fourth: globalization. The Basic Telecommunications Agreement of the World Trade Organization (WTO)[7] has put other countries on a track toward opening up their telecom markets.[8]

---

elevate price." Applications of NYNEX Corp. and Bell Atlantic Corp. for Consent To Transfer Control of NYNEX Corp., Memorandum Opinion and Order, 12 F.C.C. Rec. 19,985, 20,066–20,067 ¶169 (1997) (hereinafter *BA/NYNEX*).

[6] *See* M. J. Renegar et al., ABN AMRO Chicago Corp., Investext Rpt. No. 2617676, CLEC Fourth Quarter and 1998 M&A Outlook—Industry Report at *1 (Dec. 30, 1997); B. Garrahan et al., Lehman Brothers, Inc., Investext Rpt. No. 3312761, Telecom Services: 1998 Consolidation—Industry Report at *14 (Nov. 25, 1997) (estimating that horizontal mergers can generate up to a 10–15 percent reduction in combined sales, general, and administrative expenses).

[7] The WTO's Basic Telecommunications Agreement was signed on February 15, 1997. Sixty-nine countries, including the United States, signed this agreement, by which "most of the world's major trading nations committed to move from monopoly provision of basic telecommunications services to open entry and pro-competitive regulation of these services." The Merger of MCI Communications Corp. and British Telecommunications plc, Memorandum Opinion and Order, 12 F.C.C. Rec. 15,351, 15,355–15,356 ¶7 & n.14 (1997) (hereinafter *BT/MCI II*). The Agreement "covers 95% of the global market for basic telecommunications services." Rules and Policies on Foreign Participation in U.S. Telecommunications Market, Order and Notice of Proposed Rulemaking, 12 F.C.C. Rec. 7847, 7849 ¶1 (1997). *See also* WTO Press Release, Ruggiero Congratulates Governments on Landmark Telecommunications Agreement (Feb. 17, 1997) <http://www.wto.org/wto/press/press67.htm>.

[8] Around the globe, "liberalization and the introduction of facilities-based competition" are "accelerating a shift from single national champion carriers, whether government- or privately-owned, to multiple carriers and more diverse markets." Douglas Galbi & Chris Keating, International Bureau, FCC, Global Communication Alliances 1 (Feb. 1996) (hereinafter *Global Communication Alliances*). *See also* K. Wallace, Lehman Brothers, Inc., Investext Rpt. No. 3312188, Controlled Chaos of Telecommunications—Industry Report at *1

It is now possible for major providers of telecom services to follow their largest, most profitable customers—the providers of financial services, cars, consumer products, etc.—as those customers go global. Each major provider must pursue such customers or risk losing them to others that do. Thus, MCI is now aligned with WorldCom, MFS, Brooks, and UUNet; Sprint has formed an alliance with France Telecom and Deutsche Telekom; AT&T has followed up its acquisitions of McCaw and TCG with the acquisition of TCI and Vanguard Cellular and a joint venture with BT. The financial challenge is enormous; viewed in the perspective of the considerably larger market that spans the Americas, Europe, Asia, and Africa, even the largest U.S. carriers still look quite small.[9] Only a handful of companies will emerge from the competitive fray with enough financial bulk to compete on a global scale.

§7.2 Unpredictable Markets

Whether analyzed under the rubric of conventional antitrust law or a "public interest" inquiry, the review of a merger centers on a predictive judgment about how markets will unfold if the transaction is approved and how they will unfold if it is not.[10]

(Dec. 22, 1997) (finding that "the deregulatory process is providing new, potentially advantageous investment opportunities").

[9] The global telecommunications market generated an estimated $700 billion in revenues in 1996, and it has been growing 20 percent per year. *See* International Telecommunication Union, World Telecommunication Development Report 1996/97, at 7 (1997). Telephone service revenue accounted for an estimated $472 billion of this revenue; within this category, an estimated $69 billion was generated by international telephone service. Mobile services generated an estimated $118 billion. Other services, including leased circuits, data communications, telex, and telegraph, generated an estimated $80 billion. *Id. See* Telegeography 1997/98 at fig. 1 (1997) (noting a nearly 30 percent growth rate based on projected figure for 1997). As the Commission's International Bureau has noted, multinational businesses alone accounted for "several billion dollars" in international traffic in 1996. Other analysts see that segment growing to $25 billion by the year 2000. *See* Global Communications Alliances at 5.

[10] "In evaluating the potential impact of the proposed merger on telecommunications markets . . . we will necessarily be making predictions of future

The problem for regulators, however, is that while a few major market trends are clear enough, all the details and timetables elude confident prediction. Time and again, important regulatory calls have been based on market predictions that turned out to be far off the mark.

For example, part of the theory of divestiture was that AT&T would become IBM's main competitor in computer markets;[11] at the same time, it was thought that IBM would become a major telecom competitor.[12] The Department of Justice accordingly abandoned its 13-year-old antitrust suit against IBM on the same day that it announced the Bell breakup. AT&T bought a computer subsidiary (NCR);[13] IBM bought a switch manufacturer (ROLM),[14] a satellite long-distance business,[15] and a stake in MCI.[16] All these quite logical competitive moves failed and were eventually abandoned; they had no effect at all on the competitive evolution of either industry.

---

market conditions and the likelihood of success of individual competitors." *BA/NYNEX*, 12 F.C.C. Rec. at 20,011–20,012 ¶41.

[11] "AT&T is likely to be an especially potent competitor [in the manufacture of computers and other electronic equipment] given its manufacturing expertise and the resources of Bell Laboratories." United States v. AT&T, 552 F. Supp. at 178–179 n.199. Richard Levine, an attorney with the Department of Justice and one of the drafters of the Decree, has stated that the Department believed that "[t]he best relief in the IBM case was to release AT&T from the 1956 Consent Decree, so that AT&T could provide a significant competitive challenge in computers." P. Temin and L. Galambos, *The Fall of the Bell System* 282 (1987) (citing T. Bell, The Decision To Divest: Incredible or Inevitable?, IEEE Spectrum, Nov. 1985, at 49).

[12] *See, e.g.,* F. Ringling, AT&T: The UnBelled Underdog?, Computer Decisions, Oct. 1983, at 102.

[13] *See* J. Auerbach, Purchase of NCR Just Didn't Ring True; The Break-Up of AT&T: The Sequel, Boston Globe, Sept. 21, 1995, at 54.

[14] *See* D. Clark, IBM Sells Off Its ROLM Stake; Move Affects 6,100 Workers, S.F. Chron., May 8, 1992, at B1. In 1989, IBM sold a half interest in ROLM to Siemens AG. In 1992, IBM sold Siemens its remaining interest. IBM Deals Seen on 2 Fronts, Chi. Trib., May 8, 1992, at C1.

[15] *See* Application for Consent To Transfer Control of Satellite Business Systems from International Business Machines Corporation to MCI Communications Corporation, Order and Authorization, File No. 18-DSS-TC-86(6), 1986 FCC LEXIS 3963 (Feb. 14, 1986).

[16] *See* IBM Will Sell Its MCI Stake for $400 Million, L.A. Times, Oct. 19, 1991, at D3.

Similarly, in 1982, Judge Harold Greene was equally sure that AT&T's entry into the field of electronic publishing would drive out all other competition.[17] When AT&T was finally allowed into the market seven years later, it had no visible impact. The Department originally believed that the Regional Bell Operating Companies (RBOCs) would dominate information services markets if allowed to enter,[18] and Judge Greene held that belief as recently as 1991, when the Bells were at last allowed into that business.[19] According to the original theory, Bell companies should today dominate every last corner of the Internet. In fact, their presence is hardly noticed.

If there is one point of near universal agreement among policymakers today, it is that predictions of this sort are always speculative and rarely reliable. The Department has acknowledged that "the complex and rapidly changing telecommunications industry" produces "unanticipated circumstances."[20] The FCC has likewise recognized that the "technologies, structure, and regulation of the communications industry" generally "are changing dramatically."[21] The FCC "cannot anticipate all of the changes that will occur as a result of technological advancements, competitive developments, and practical experience, particularly at the state level."[22] "None of us can accurately predict precisely

---

[17] United States v. AT&T, 552 F. Supp. at 182.

[18] Response of the United States to Public Comments on Modification of Final Judgment at 65, United States v. Western Elec. Co., Inc., No. 82-0192 (D.D.C. May 20, 1982).

[19] *See* United States v. Western Elec. Co., Inc., 767 F. Supp. 308, 326 (D.D.C. 1991) (lifting restriction with stay pending appeal), *stay vacated,* United States v. Western Elec. Co, Inc., No. 91-5263 (D.C. Cir. Oct. 7, 1991), *aff'd,* 993 F.2d 1572, *cert. denied,* 510 U.S. 984 (1993).

[20] Brief for Appellee United States of America at 16, United States v. Western Elec. Co., Inc., No. 94-5252 (Oct. 18, 1994).

[21] Establishment of Rules and Policies for the Digital Audio Radio Satellite Service in the 2310-2360 MHz Frequency Band, Report and Order, Memorandum Opinion and Order, and Further Notice of Proposed Rulemaking, 12 F.C.C. Rec. 5754, 5769 ¶33 (1997).

[22] Implementation of the Local Competition Provisions in the Telecommunications Act of 1996; Interconnection Between Local Exchange Carriers and Commercial Mobile Radio Service Providers, First Report and Order, 11 F.C.C. Rec. 15,499, 15,529–15,530 ¶58 (1996).

how the market will develop, either in terms of what new services will be offered or how consumers will respond to them."[23]

Predictions about local exchange markets are even more speculative than most. As of 1994, the Department was prepared to "watch" and "hope," but insisted it could not "credibly assert" or "confidently predict" how competition might—or might not—unfold.[24] "One can conceive scenarios" involving wireless or cable competition, but "there is neither technological nor economic experience which yet warrants the prediction that these systems can be expected."[25] "[S]ignificant local service competition may come . . . within [a] foreseeable time," but the "ultimate advent, let alone [the] early advent" of such a fundamental change in the telecommunications marketplace cannot "be confidently predicted."[26] In a September 1996 speech, the Assistant Attorney General for Antitrust observed that fiber optics, co-axial cable, digital compression, satellite, and other wireless technologies had all had observable impacts on wireline markets, but noted that "[n]obody can speak with certainty" about the future direction of this convergence.[27] Until quite recently, the Department took the position that it would make no competitive difference whether there were one, four, or ten Regional Bell

[23] FCC Oversight, Hearing of the Senate Commerce, Science and Transportation Committee, Federal News Service, June 18, 1996 (testimony of James Quello).

[24] Lawrence A. Sullivan, The MFJ Restriction on RBOC Interexchange Service: Determining When the Restriction Can Be Lifted, and What Can Be Done To Facilitate Local Exchange Competition at 11 (Feb. 10, 1994), *attached to* Motion of the United States, United States v. Western Elec. Co., Inc., No. 82-0192 (D.D.C. May 1, 1995).

[25] *Id.* at 10.

[26] *Id.* at 9.

[27] Anne K. Bingaman, Assistant Attorney General, Antitrust Division, U.S. Department of Justice, Competition and Innovation: Bedrock of the American Economy, Remarks Before the University of Kansas Law School (Sept. 19, 1996) (viewed Nov. 18, 1998) <http://www.usdoj.gov/atr/public/speeches/960919ks.htm>. Ms. Bingaman posed the following questions regarding these technologies, questions she noted no one could readily answer: "How will these technologies be deployed . . . [I]n what proportions will they be used? Which will be dominant? Which will be complementary? Which will be rendered obsolete?" *Id.*

companies[28] and that Regional Bells should, in any event, be *forbidden* to compete with one another for exchange services out-of-region.[29]

The FCC has noted that it is equally unable to predict the evolution of the technologies most likely to compete directly against local wireline phone service. In cable markets, the Commission anticipates "new technology and capacity expansion," but "accurate predictions of these developments are difficult."[30] In wireless markets, the Commission is unable even to estimate the value of new spectrum, "[g]iven that a range of services may be provided on [it]."[31] "The future," one FCC Commissioner remarks,

---

[28] AT&T Proposed Settlement: Hearings Before the Senate Committee on Commerce, Science and Transportation, 97th Cong., 2d Sess. 73 (1982) (testimony of William F. Baxter); Department of Justice Oversight of the United States v. American Telephone and Telegraph Lawsuit: Hearings Before the Senate Committee on the Judiciary, 97th Cong., 2d Sess. 112, 141–142 (1982) (prepared statement of William F. Baxter and testimony of Howard J. Trienens).

[29] After losing the fight to prevent any out-of-region RBOC competition for purely local services, the Department continued to oppose out-of-territory RBOC offerings of bundled local and long-distance services. For example, when Bell Atlantic initially sought a decree waiver in connection with the proposed TCI acquisition to offer a bundled package of local and long-distance services using the out-of-region TCI cable systems, the Department's staff informed Bell Atlantic that such a waiver raised serious concerns and Bell Atlantic should simply abandon that portion of the request. (Bell Atlantic did so.) Similarly, the Department refused even to respond to SBC's request for a waiver to offer out-of-region long-distance services. SBC had sought this relief in order to provide "the full complement of telecommunications services over Cable TV Montgomery, its cable television property in Montgomery County, Maryland, in competition with Bell Atlantic, AT&T, MCI, Sprint, and other carriers." Motion of Southwestern Bell Corporation for an Expedited Waiver at 3 (submitted to DOJ July 11, 1994). The Department argued before the Court of Appeals for the D.C. Circuit that "stringent[ly]" confining the Bell companies to their original territories was necessary to protect against the "evils" that led to the antitrust case. Brief for the Appellee United States of America at 48, United States v. Western Elec. Co., Inc., No. 86-5118 (D.C. Cir. Apr. 18, 1986).

[30] Implementation of Section 26 of the Cable Television Consumer Protection and Competition Act of 1992; Inquiry into Sports Programming Migration, Further Notice of Inquiry, 9 F.C.C. Rec. 1649, 1651 ¶15 (1994).

[31] Amendment of the Commission's Rules To Establish Part 27, the Wireless Communications Service, Report and Order, 12 F.C.C. Rec. 10,785, 10,870 ¶174 (1997).

"will be full of surprises."[32] Predictions of market evolution are all the more difficult, the FCC observes, "when, as now, competition in a key portion of the marketplace, local exchange and exchange access services, is in the earliest stages."[33] Thus, the Commission's merger rulings typically begin with a sonorous declaration about the "considerable uncertainty" surrounding the future of the markets under review.[34]

Nevertheless, the Commission frames its merger reviews as quite scientific: the Commission claims to "isolate the effect of the merger from all other factors affecting the development of the relevant markets over time. This is achieved by framing the analysis in a way that holds constant the effects of all changes in market conditions other than those directly caused by the merger."[35] The analysis may include the "trends within, and needs of, the telecommunications industry, the factors that influenced Congress to enact specific provisions of the Communications Act, and the nature, complexity, and rapidity of change in the telecommunications industry."[36] In evaluating "transitional markets,"[37] the Commission follows an "analytical framework" that

---

[32] Susan Ness, Commissioner, Federal Communications Commission, Predictions, Remarks Before the New York Chapter Federal Communications Bar Association (June 4, 1996) <http://www.fcc.gov/commissioners/ness/spmain.htm>.

[33] BA/NYNEX, 12 F.C.C. Rec. at 20,011–20,012 ¶41.

[34] See, e.g., id. at 20,011 ¶40; BT/MCI II, 12 F.C.C. Rec. at 15,354–15,355 ¶5.

[35] BA/NYNEX, 12 F.C.C. Rec. at 20,036–20,037 ¶97.

[36] Applications of Teleport Communications Group Inc. and AT&T Corp. for Consent to Transfer Control of Corporations Holding Point-to-Point Microwave Licenses and Authorizations to Provide International Facilities-Based and Resold Communications Services, Memorandum Opinion and Order, 13 F.C.C. Rec. 15,236, 15,242–15,243 ¶11 (1998) (footnotes omitted) (hereinafter Teleport/AT&T).

[37] The Commission defines "transitional markets" as those that "have experienced significant recent, or ongoing, changes." Application of WorldCom, Inc. and MCI Communications Corp. for Transfer of Control of MCI Communications Corp. to WorldCom, Memorandum Opinion and Order, 13 F.C.C. Rec. 18,025, 18,036–18,037 ¶18 (1998) (hereinafter MCI/WorldCom). For example, the Commission treats the markets for local exchange telephony services as transitional because they were "historically [] regulated as monopolies," but "are now in transition to becoming competitive as envisioned by the 1996 Act." Id.

"treats as 'most significant market participants' not only firms that already dominate transitional markets, but also those that are more likely to enter soon, effectively, and on a large scale once a more competitive environment is established."[38] Although the Commission's analysis sounds precise and mechanistic, the underlying inquiry is anything but; predicting market trends in telecom has proven to be tricky guesswork indeed.

§7.3 Jurisdictional and Procedural Overview

§7.3.1 The Department of Justice and the FCC

As discussed in section 7.4 below, the Department of Justice has broad general antitrust authority to review major mergers and acquisitions.[39] The 1996 Act repealed section 221(a) of the Communications Act, which previously permitted local phone companies to merge without facing antitrust scrutiny if the FCC approved.[40] In other respects, existing antitrust laws were left unchanged.[41]

The FCC's authority to review telecommunications mergers is even greater than the Department's, and far less constrained by either statute or precedent. The Commission has concurrent jurisdiction with the Department under sections 7 and 11 of the

---

[38] *Id.* at 18,038 ¶21.

[39] Most telecom mergers are "cleared" to the Department, rather than to the Federal Trade Commission, which has concurrent merger review authority.

[40] Telecommunications Act of 1996 §601(b)(2) (repealing 47 U.S.C. §221(a)). The Commission was empowered to immunize mergers from "any Act or Acts of Congress making the proposed transaction unlawful." Communications Act of 1934 §221(a) (codified at 47 U.S.C. §221(a)). Had it not been repealed, section 221(a) might have undercut several provisions of the new Act. Section 221(a) does not define "telephone company." As competition unfolds, any number of new competitors may earn the label. Section 221(a) might then have been invoked to circumvent the cable-telco buyout provisions of the new law.

[41] Telecommunications Act of 1996 §601(b)(1) ("Except as provided in paragraphs (2) and (3), nothing in this Act or the amendments made by this Act shall be construed to modify, impair, or supersede the applicability of any of the antitrust laws.").

Clayton Act to disapprove acquisitions of "common carriers engaged in wire or radio communications or radio transmission of energy" where "in any line of commerce or in any activity affecting commerce in any section of the country, the effect of such acquisition may be substantially to lessen competition, or to tend to create a monopoly."[42] In reviewing mergers, however, the Commission invariably notes this authority and then declares that it doesn't need it and won't rely on it.[43] The Commission much prefers to review all issues, competitive issues included, under its still broader, still less constrained "public interest" authority of the Communications Act.[44] "The competitive analysis applied under the public interest standard is necessarily broader than the standard applied to ascertain violations of the antitrust laws."[45] The Commission's "public interest" review authority also extends, symmetrically, to divestitures and spin-offs—transactions that rarely, if ever, engage the interest of the Department.

The Department usually takes the first swing at major telecom mergers; the Commission bats second. But the upshot is a double-layered review of all major telecom deals. "[O]ne of the underlying themes of the bill," the Conference Statement to the 1996 Act declares, is to get both the FCC and the Department of Justice "back to their proper roles."[46] The Act did shrink the Department's role as a shadow FCC for Bell Company operations.

---

[42] 15 U.S.C. §§18, 21(a) (1997). The D.C. Circuit has held that the FCC has discretion whether to enforce its Clayton Act authority. *See* United States v. FCC, 652 F.2d 72, 82–83 (D.C. Cir. 1980) (en banc).

[43] *See, e.g., MCI/WorldCom,* 13 F.C.C. Rec. at 18,032–18,033 ¶12; *BT/MCI II,* 12 F.C.C. Rec. at 15,364–15,365 ¶28; *BA/NYNEX,* 12 F.C.C. Rec. at 20,005 ¶33; Applications of Pacific Telesis Group and SBC Communications, Inc., for Consent To Transfer Control of Pacific Telesis Group, Memorandum Opinion and Order, 12 F.C.C. Rec. 2624, 2631 ¶13 (1997) (hereinafter *SBC/PacTel*).

[44] "Because our public interest authority under the Communications Act . . . is sufficient to address the competitive issues raised by the proposed merger . . . we decline to exercise our Clayton Act authority in this case." *BT/MCI II,* 12 F.C.C. Rec. at 15,364–15,365 ¶28. *See also BA/NYNEX,* 12 F.C.C. Rec. at 20,005 ¶33; United States v. FCC, 652 F.2d at 88.

[45] *BT/MCI II,* 12 F.C.C. Rec. at 15,365–15,366 ¶30 (citing United States v. FCC, 652 F.2d at 88 (The Commission's "determination about the proper role of competitive forces in an industry must therefore be based, not exclusively on the letter of the antitrust laws, but also on the 'special considerations' of the particular industry.")).

[46] S. Rep. No. 230, 104th Cong. 2d Sess. 201 (1996).

But the 1996 Act stopped short of directing the FCC to leave competitive considerations out of its own reviews of mergers conducted in connection with its responsibilities under the Communications Act.[47] Indeed, if anything, the Act has had an opposite effect: the Commission relies on the 1996 Act to justify its duplication of the Department's effort. In its order approving the merger of MCI and WorldCom, the Commission interpreted the 1996 Act, which establishes a clear national policy of "competition leading to deregulation, rather than continued regulation of dominant firms," as requiring it to focus on the merger's effect on future competition.[48] Because antitrust agencies "are required to approve mergers unless they substantially lessen competition," the Commission reasons that "it is possible that the antitrust agencies might well approve a merger that does not decrease the *current* level of competition but that does impede the development of *future* competition."[49] Thus, the Commission insists on conducting its own review of the competitive effects.

The result is that, in the context of mergers and acquisitions, there is now more duplication than ever. Dual review means lengthy delays[50] and the expenditure of substantial resources at both the FCC and the Department.[51] At least one FCC Commissioner has begun to question why such duplication is necessary.[52]

§7.3.2 Federal and State Authority

Except in those areas preempted by federal authority—wireless (in large part) and "information" services being the two most

[47] *Id.* at 200–201.

[48] *MCI/WorldCom,* 13 F.C.C. Rec. at 18,034–18,035 ¶14.

[49] *Id.* (emphasis added).

[50] For example, the Commission received the first petition for review in the MCI/WorldCom merger on October 1, 1997; the Department approved it on July 15, 1998; and the Commission did not sound in until September 14, 1998.

[51] *See* Separate Statement of Commissioner Harold Furchtgott-Roth in *MCI/WorldCom,* 13 F.C.C. Rec. at 18,158.

[52] "[H]ow exactly does the Commission's definition of relevant markets and its analysis of the competitive effects of the merger on those markets differ from the Department of Justice's analysis? To the extent that it is materially

notable examples[53]—telecom carriers generally must also obtain state licenses and state approval of any transfers of those licenses. Thus, state regulators get an independent crack at reviewing most major mergers (and spin-offs).[54] Often, however, this review is asymmetric: only authorities in the *acquired*-company states are engaged, not those in the acquiring-company states. The details of state-level reviews are outside the scope of this treatise. Suffice it to say that many consumer advocates and some state attorneys general view mergers as an opportunity to extract new concessions on rates on the ostensible ground that the claimed efficiencies and synergies of the merger should go to ratepayers rather than shareholders.[55]

---

different, what is the Commission's express statutory authority or unique expertise to perform such a review? If the analysis is not materially different, then why is it not redundant for this agency to repeat an analysis that numerous experts at the Department of Justice already perform? . . . Under the precluded competitor framework, is our analysis of potential competitors too speculative—especially since we do not seem to require the same type of evidence as the Department of Justice's merger guidelines would require of intent to enter the market by another means?" Separate Statement of Commissioner Harold Furchtgott-Roth in *Teleport/AT&T,* 13 F.C.C. Rec. at 18,158. *See also* Separate Statement of Commission Harold Furchtgott-Roth in *MCI/WorldCom,* 13 F.C.C. Rec. at 18,159 ("Even with our expertise in telecommunications, I question whether we can make such assumptions [about potential competitors] and whether they are even relevant to a narrow public interest analysis."); Separate Statement of Harold Furchtgott-Roth in Applications for Consent to the Transfer of Control of Licenses and Section 214 Authorizations from Southern New England Telecommunications Corp., Transferor, to SBC Communications Inc., Transferee, Memorandum Opinion and Order, 13 F.C.C. Rec. 21,292, 21,321 (1998) (hereinafter *SNET/SBC*) ("I continue to be frustrated by this agency's unwieldy review of mergers and the length of time that we take to do so.").

[53] *See* §§11.3, 12.3.

[54] Some states also have statutes that govern mergers and acquisitions. *See* 1 American Bar Association, Antitrust Section, Antitrust Law Developments 636 (3d ed. 1992) (hereinafter Antitrust Law Developments).

[55] *See, e.g.,* Proceeding on Motion of the Commission as to the Joint Petition of New York Telephone Company, a NYNEX Corporation, and Bell Atlantic Corporation for a Declaratory Ruling That the Commission Lacks Jurisdiction To Investigate and Approve a Proposed Merger Between NYNEX and a Subsidiary of Bell Atlantic, or, in the Alternative, for Approval of the Merger, et al., Opinion and Order, 1997 N.Y. PUC LEXIS 327, *51–*53 (May 30, 1997); Pacific Telesis Group, Opinion and Order, 177 P.U.R.4th 462, 1997 WL 406220, at *79–*81 (Cal. P.U.C. Mar. 31, 1997).

Here again, the effect is to add an additional layer of review rather than to substitute one regulator's review authority with another's. Sections 2(b) and 221(b) of the Communications Act[56] limit the FCC's jurisdiction to interstate matters.[57] But the Commission rejects the argument that it lacks authority to disapprove mergers because of concerns over intrastate wireline services: "[T]he public interest analysis necessarily includes a review of the nature and extent of local competition," the FCC maintains.[58]

§7.3.3 Presumptions, Procedures, and Burdens of Proof

Because predictions about the future of telecom markets are highly speculative, process, rules of evidence, and burdens of proof become very important.

The basic framework of review by the Justice Department centers on the procedures and burdens of ordinary civil litigation, with the Department in the role of prospective plaintiff. The Department's only real edge is procedural. The Hart-Scott-Rodino Antitrust Improvements Act of 1976[59] requires parties engaged in larger mergers to file a premerger notification with the Department and establishes some mandatory waiting periods during which the Department may exercise its investigative authority.[60]

---

[56] Communications Act of 1934 §§2(b), 221(b).

[57] Both of the 1934 Act's jurisdictional limits, sections 2(b) and 221(b), apply to the Commission's authority under section 11 of the Clayton Act — despite the language of the codified (but never congressionally enacted) 47 U.S.C. §§152(b), 221(b), referring only to "this chapter." The Commission was added to section 11's list of enforcement authorities by section 602(d) of the Communications Act of 1934. Act of June 19, 1934, 48 Stat. 1064, 1102. Section 2(b) of the 1934 Act applies to the whole of that "Act," as does section 221(b), thus including section 602(d). See 48 Stat. 1064, 1080. (The Statutes at Large, not the United States Code, provide the controlling law. See 1 U.S.C. §112; American Bank and Trust Co. v. Dallas County, 463 U.S. 855, 864 n.8 (1983).) Congress thus made the section 11 authority subject to these two broad exclusions of the Commission from intrastate matters.

[58] *BA/NYNEX*, 12 F.C.C. Rec. at 20,006–20,007 ¶35.

[59] 15 U.S.C. §18a (1994).

[60] *Id.*

If it does not like what it finds, the Department goes to court to enjoin the merger.[61]

Before the FCC, telecom merger applicants are in just the opposite procedural position: they are the supplicants; they have the burdens of proof; and if they cannot persuade the FCC of their right to merge, it is they who have to persuade a court to force the Commission to act and overrule its previous determination. They must persuade an appellate court, no less, which will inevitably give deference to the Commission's findings of fact, however speculative they may be.[62] The FCC frequently requires the merger parties to make available for public inspection some of the same documents submitted in private to the Department of Justice.[63] Unlike the Department, however, which has strict deadlines for seeking an injunction to block a merger

---

[61] Hart-Scott-Rodino (HSR) review that culminates in no action by the Department does not preclude a later lawsuit by the Department, another federal or state agency, or a private party. But absent concurrent jurisdiction like the FCC's, the HSR process usually takes care of federal government concerns, one way or another.

[62] *See* 47 U.S.C. §402(b)(3).

[63] *See, e.g., BA/NYNEX,* 12 F.C.C. Rec. at 20,000 ¶28; Application of Craig O. McCaw & Amer. Tel. & Tel. Co. for Consent to the Transfer of Control, Memorandum Opinion and Order, 9 F.C.C. Rec. 5836, 5842–5843 ¶6 (1994) (hereinafter *McCaw/AT&T*), *recons. denied on other grounds,* 10 F.C.C. Rec. 11,786 (1995), *affirmed sub nom.* SBC Comm., Inc. v. FCC, 56 F.3d 1484 (D.C. Cir. 1995); Application of GTE Corp. and Southern Pacific Co. for Consent To Transfer Control, Memorandum Opinion and Order, 94 F.C.C.2d 235, 240–241 ¶17 (1983); Application of General Telephone and Electronics Corporation To Acquire Control of Telenet Corporation and Its Wholly-Owned Subsidiary Telenet Communications Corp., Memorandum Opinion and Order, 72 F.C.C.2d 111, 162–169 ¶¶156–169 (1979) (hereinafter *GTE/Telenet*). The Commission has held that the confidentiality protections applicable to such documents when produced to the Justice Department or Federal Trade Commission, *see* 15 U.S.C. §§18a(h), 1313(c)(3), 1314(g), do not limit the Commission's ability to require merger parties to make those documents available for public inspection subject to protective order. *See* Application of WorldCom, Inc. and MCI Communications Corp. for Transfer of Control of MCI Communications Corp. to WorldCom, Inc., Order Adopting Protective Order, 13 F.C.C. Rec. 11,166, 11,167 ¶3 (1998); Applications of TCI Satellite Entertainment, Inc. and PRIMESTAR, Inc. for Consent To Transfer of Control, Order Adopting Protective Order, 13 F.C.C. Rec. 10,927, 10,928 ¶3 (1998).

that it does not like, the Commission is not subject to similar time constraints and can block a merger by inaction. The Commission's power to do nothing gives it enormous bargaining leverage over companies that want to merge.[64]

These procedural differences can make all the difference with mergers that do not contravene well-established guidelines or decisional norms. The Department can certainly block a merger that increases market concentration beyond the thresholds set out in its Merger Guidelines, and it is as likely to succeed in such blocking as the FCC. But the FCC has far more power to block mergers that threaten to undermine *potential* competition rather than actual. The FCC can get away with a lot more airy speculation about the future than can the Department. And the Commission insists it need not speculate at all—it need only explain why it is unpersuaded by the scenarios of the future set out by the petitioners.

The Commission is convinced that uncertainty about the future weighs *against* the approval of any merger, or at least against any merger that involves present or former monopolists.[65] In the Commission's view, it seems, everything is unpredictable about the future except that the competitive news is more likely to be bad than good. This is logically untenable, of course: if we simply don't know what the future holds, there is no less reason to expect good news as bad. In a further logical leap, the Commission goes on to state that because the outlook is so very uncertain, the Commission must "strictly enforce [its] requirement that the applicants demonstrate that, on balance, the

---

[64] As FCC Chairman Hundt explained, "No one benefits from protracted uncertainty that freezes business zeal into a state of suspended animation, while government authorities mull proposed combinations." Reed E. Hundt, Chairman, Federal Communications Commission, Thinking About Why Some Communications Mergers Are Unthinkable, Speech Before The Brookings Institution (June 19, 1997) <http://www.fcc.gov/Speeches/Hundt/spreh735.html>.

[65] "As a result of this uncertainty about the pace with which competition will develop in various telecommunications markets, we must be particularly concerned about mergers between companies that are potential rivals, especially where one of the merging parties is or was the incumbent monopoly provider." *BT/MCI II*, 12 F.C.C. Rec. at 15,354–15,355 ¶5.

proposed merger will be pro-competitive."[66] But how are applicants to "demonstrate" what "will be" (to a "strict" Commission no less) when the Commission is persuaded from the get-go that the future is unknowable? All the while, the Commission is as lenient with itself as it is strict with applicants. "In making our predictions, we are not bound by the rules of evidence that may apply in judicial contexts," the Commission insists.[67]

§7.3.4 Conditional Approvals

Most merger reviews are not all-or-nothing propositions; both the Department and the FCC commonly approve a merger subject to conditions, such as the divestiture of certain assets, new commitments to interconnect, unbundling, and so forth.

If Justice Department conditions cannot be implemented summarily (e.g., by divesting offending assets) prior to closing, they are commonly incorporated into a consent decree. A lawsuit is filed along with a proposed settlement, and a trial court must then conduct a public interest evaluation. (See section 4.8.) These days, however, the Department disfavors highly regulatory consent decrees that transform the Department and decree court into shadow FCCs with ongoing supervisory responsibilities.

For its part, the Commission does not have reservations about imposing conditions. Section 214, Title II's general licensing clause for common carriers, authorizes the Commission to attach to the certificate "such terms and conditions as in its judgment the public convenience and necessity may require."[68] Section

---

[66] *Id.* Applicants "must demonstrate not only the efficiency benefits of the merger, but how the merger would enhance or not retard competition." *BA/ NYNEX,* 12 F.C.C. Rec. at 20,007–20,008 ¶36.

[67] *Id.* at 20,011–20,012 ¶41 (citing FCC v. RCA Communications, Inc., 346 U.S. 86, 96–97 (1953)) ("To restrict the Commission's action to cases in which tangible evidence appropriate for judicial determination is available would disregard a major reason for the creation of administrative agencies, better equipped as they are for weighing intangibles by specialization, by insight gained through experience, and by more flexible procedure. In the nature of things, the possible benefits of competition do not lend themselves to detailed forecast.").

[68] 47 U.S.C. §214(c) (1997). *See, e.g.,* Request of MCI Communications Corporation British Telecommunications plc Joint Petition for Declaratory

303(r) likewise authorizes the Commission to incorporate conditions in wireless licenses.[69]

The Commission has apparently never invoked section 11 of the Clayton Act to disapprove a merger outright that has cleared review by the Department.[70] But the Commission has instead eagerly invoked its powers of review to impose a wide range of

---

Ruling Concerning Section 310(b)(4) and (d) of the Communications Act of 1934, as Amended, Declaratory Ruling and Order, 9 F.C.C. Rec. 3960, 3968 ¶39 (1994) (hereinafter *BT/MCI I*); Sprint Corporation, Petition for Declaratory Ruling Concerning Section 310(b)(4) and (d) and the Public Interest Requirement, 11 F.C.C. Rec. 1850, 1867–1872 ¶¶100–133 (1996); *GTE/Telenet*, 72 F.C.C.2d at 135 ¶76; *see also* Atlantic Tele-Network, Inc. v. FCC, 59 F.3d 1384, 1389–1390 (D.C. Cir. 1995); GTE Service Corp. v. FCC, 782 F.2d 263, 268 (D.C. Cir. 1986); Western Union Tel. Co. v. FCC, 541 F.2d 346, 355 (3d Cir. 1976), *cert. denied*, 429 U.S. 1092 (1977).

[69] 47 U.S.C. §303(r) (1997). *See, e.g.*, CBS, Inc. v. FCC, 453 U.S. 367, 386 (1981) (rules requiring access to broadcast time by political candidates properly adopted pursuant to section 303(r)); FCC v. National Citizens Comm. for Broad., 436 U.S. 775, 793–794 (1978) (broadcast-newspaper cross-ownership rules properly adopted pursuant to section 303(r)); United States v. Southwestern Cable Co., 392 U.S. 157, 178 (1968) (section 303(r) powers permit FCC to order cable company not to carry broadcast signal beyond station's primary market); United Video, Inc. v. FCC, 890 F.2d 1173, 1182–1183 (D.C. Cir. 1989) (syndicated exclusivity rules adopted pursuant to section 303(r) powers); Tele-Communications, Inc. and TeleCable Corp. Transfer of Control, Memorandum Opinion and Order, 10 F.C.C. Rec. 2147, 2147–2148 (1995); *McCaw/AT&T*, 9 F.C.C. Rec. at 5929–5930 ¶¶174–189; Application of Viacom, Inc. for Consent to the Transfer of Control of Paramount Communications, Inc., Memorandum Opinion and Order, 9 F.C.C. Rec. 1577, 1577–1578 ¶3 (1994).

[70] To the contrary, the Commission has repeatedly relied on that agency's conclusions after awaiting such review. AT&T summarized and endorsed the Commission's practice in its Opposition to Petitions To Deny and Reply to Comments at 11–12, AT&T and McCaw, File No. ENF-93-44 (Dec. 2, 1993): "[A]lthough the Commission is also separately authorized to enforce Section 7 of the Clayton Act with respect to mergers of 'common carriers,' the Commission has not done so in Section 310(d) proceedings. Rather, the Commission 'consider[s] competitive consequences as one part of [its] public interest calculus and leaves enforcement of Section 7 of the Clayton Act as such to the Justice Department, or the FTC.'" (footnotes omitted). *See also SBC/PacTel*, 12 F.C.C. Rec. at 2637–2638 ¶25; *BA Mobile/NYNEX Mobile*, 10 F.C.C. Rec. at 13,383–13,384 ¶43; *McCaw/AT&T*, 9 F.C.C. Rec. at 5922 ¶158 ("we are neither obligated nor equipped to duplicate in full the DOJ's review"; relying on DOJ review and DOJ lack of opposition to FCC approval); Applications of Centel Corporation and Sprint Corporation for Consent to the Transfer of Control of Authorizations in the Domestic Public Cellular Radio Telecommunications Service and Other Common Carrier Services, Memorandum Opinion and

conditions on mergers, including conditions with little, if any, direct relation to the actual license transfers before it. The Commission quite commonly negotiates elaborate commitments from merging parties to comply with all sorts of regulatory mandates that the FCC will not or cannot (for jurisdictional or statutory reasons) promulgate in the form of rules generally applicable to all. With the industry now undergoing fundamental restructuring, this backdoor regulatory tool gives the FCC almost unlimited—though little noted—power to regulate as it pleases, outside the ambit of Administrative Procedure Act (APA) process and judicial review.

We discuss how the Commission has exercised its power of conditional approval in section 7.5.4.7 below. Students of how the industry is regulated must recognize that it no longer suffices to read the Code of Federal Regulations: much of the de facto rulemaking is now incorporated in sweeping "conditions" and "commitments." They may appear to be merger specific, but they are easily replicated in all subsequent merger orders. With most major players likely to be involved in mergers or acquisitions in the next five years, regulation by condition may well evolve into one of the most significant bodies of "regulation" on the Commission's books.

§7.4 Substantive Merger Standards

§7.4.1 Media-Specific Standards Codified by Congress and the FCC

Congress and the Commission have codified various rules putting limits on the total number of broadcast stations a single company may own nationwide.[71] In the 1992 Cable Act, Congress

---

Order, 8 F.C.C. Rec. 1829, 1832 ¶18 & n.42 (1993) (hereinafter *Centel/Sprint*); Applications of Contel Corporation and GTE Corporation for Consent to the Transfer of Control of Authorizations Held by Contel Subsidiaries, Memorandum Opinion and Order, 6 F.C.C. Rec. 1003, 1005 ¶18 (1991) (hereinafter *Contel/GTE*).

[71] Until passage of the 1996 Act, cross-ownership of television and radio stations was limited to 20 AM, 20 FM, and 12 television stations, with a limit

likewise ordered the Commission to prescribe rules limiting the number of cable subscribers any one multisystem operator is authorized to reach.[72] And as discussed in section 10.8.4, the Commission has promulgated analogous rules to limit cross-ownership of wireless licenses within a single geographic market.[73] No comparable limits have been codified for wireline carriers.

§7.4.1.1 Section 7 of the Clayton Act

Today, most mergers are generally analyzed under section 7 of the Clayton Act.[74] Section 7 incorporates the policies underlying sections 1 and 2 of the Sherman Act, which prohibit combinations in restraint of trade and actual or attempted monopolization.[75] Section 7 proscribes acquisitions "where in any line of

---

of 25 percent on aggregate national audience reach. Radio station ownership was limited to an in-market audience reach of 25 percent for large markets (more than 15 stations). *See* 59 Fed Reg. 62,609 (1994). Section 202 of the 1996 Act directs the Commission to loosen further these restrictions, in part by raising audience reach limitations to 35 percent. The Commission abolished its multiple-ownership rules applicable to the top 50 television markets in 1979, Amendment of Section 73.636(a) of the Commission's Rules (Multiple Ownership of Television Stations), Report and Order, 75 F.C.C.2d 585, 597 ¶37 (1979), and its regional concentration rules in 1984, Repeal of the "Regional Concentration of Control" Provision of the Commission's Multiple Ownership Rules, Report and Order, 101 F.C.C.2d 402, 403 ¶2 (1984). This allowed broadcasting companies to expand the size of their markets beyond previous limits.

[72] 47 U.S.C. §533(f)(1)(A). The Commission established a 30 percent limit on the number of homes passed nationwide that any one entity can reach through cable systems in which it has an attributable interest and a 40 percent limit on the number of channels that can be occupied by programming in which the operator has an interest. Implementation of Sections 11 and 13 of the Cable Television Consumer Protection and Competition Act of 1992, Horizontal and Vertical Ownership Limits, Second Report and Order, 8 F.C.C. Rec. 8565, 8567 ¶¶3–4, 8592–8600 ¶¶64–78 (1993).

[73] In mergers that would have the effect of combining prohibited numbers of wireless licenses under single ownership, the parties routinely commit to divest properties as necessary to put themselves into compliance with these rules if the merger is otherwise approved.

[74] 15 U.S.C. §18 (1997).

[75] *See* 15 U.S.C. §§1, 2, 18 (1997). *See also* United States v. Penn-Olin Chemical Co., 378 U.S. 158, 170–171 (1964); Antitrust Law Developments at 275–276 & n.4.

commerce or in any activity affecting commerce . . . in any section of the country the effect of such acquisition may be substantially to lessen competition, or to tend to create a monopoly."[76]
Section 7 is concerned with probabilities—not certainties or
"ephemeral possibilities."[77] In determining what the probable
effects will be, courts first define the relevant product and geographic markets,[78] and then they evaluate the impact of the acquisition on competition in those markets.[79]

Though rarely noted, the fourth unnumbered paragraph of
section 7 sets out a "common-carrier proviso," which expressly
limits section 7 insofar as it might otherwise prevent a "common
carrier"[80] from "extending any of its lines"[81] through the acquisition of stock "of any other common carrier where there is no

---

[76] 15 U.S.C. §18 (1997).

[77] *See* Brown Shoe Co. v. United States, 370 U.S. 294, 323 (1962) ("Congress used the words '*may be* substantially to lessen competition' (emphasis
supplied) to indicate that its concern was with probabilities, not certainties.
Statutes existed for dealing with clear-cut menaces to competition; no statute
was sought for dealing with ephemeral possibilities. Mergers with a possible
anticompetitive effect were proscribed by this Act.") (footnote omitted).

[78] *See* Antitrust Law Developments at 282–298.

[79] *Id.* at 298–299.

[80] "Common carrier" clearly encompasses local telephone companies. Only
a few years before enactment of the Clayton Act, the Mann-Elkins Act of 1910
had included telephone companies in the definition of "common carriers" of
the Interstate Commerce Act, which was known as the Act to Regulate Commerce. The House bill that became the Clayton Act originally limited this proviso to railroads. On the Senate floor, the bill was amended to substitute
"common carrier" for "railroad." The conference committee adopted the Senate version, saying: "The House provision in this section that nothing contained therein shall be construed to prohibit any railroad corporation from
aiding in the construction of branch or short-line railroads so located as to
become feeders to the main line, etc., is amended so as to apply to any common carrier, *thus including telephone* and pipe *lines,* the committee believing
that all common carriers should be given the same rights in this respect and
that the extension of the rights to telephone and pipe lines would inure to the
benefit of the public." Earl Kinter, 2 The Legislative History of the Federal
Antitrust Laws and Related Statutes, Part 1, at 1748 (1978) (emphasis added).

[81] The acquisition of a neighboring carrier clearly constitutes the "extending" of lines. *See* Metropolitan Trust Co. v. Columbus S. & H. Ry. Co., 95 F. 18,
20 (S.D. Ohio 1899) ("Railroad companies, by the statutes of Ohio (sections
3300 and 3306), are given the power to extend their lines, either by their own
construction, or by the purchase or lease of other lines."); Rogers v. Nashville,
C. & St. L. Ry. Co., 91 F. 299, 323 (6th Cir. 1898) (quoting Tennessee statute

substantial competition" between the acquiring and acquired companies. The proviso's phrase "*is* no substantial competition" uses the present, not the future, tense, seeming to suggest that only actual (not potential) competition matters, and only *substantial* actual competition at that.[82] The legislative history of the Clayton Act suggests that one purpose of this proviso may have been to facilitate phone company mergers.[83]

§7.4.1.2 Section 2 of the Sherman Act

The Sherman Act condemns monopolization, combinations, and conspiracies to monopolize. The prevailing section 2 standards for monopolization liability require (1) monopoly power in the relevant market plus (2) "anticompetitive" conduct that "willfully" creates, increases, or maintains such power.[84] It is generally more difficult to establish that a merger is an antitrust

---

authorizing railroads to "acquire the line or lines of any other railroad companies . . . which may connect with and form . . . extensions").

[82] It appears that, for purposes of determining whether there is "substantial competition," one must compare the territory where lines overlap with the territory where there is no competition between the two carriers. This latter limitation is the holding of Navajo Terminals, Inc. v. United States, 620 F.2d 594, 601 (7th Cir. 1980), which is the sole case interpreting the common carrier proviso. "Congress must have contemplated a public benefit from line extensions, through gains in efficiency or the like, sufficient to outweigh the destruction of minor instances of competition between the carriers." *Id.*

[83] During debate on the Clayton Act, Congressman Vaughan complained: "I happen to live in a town where we have two systems, one exchange is located in Texas and the other in Arkansas, and I wish to make it certain that my people will not always be compelled to patronize and maintain two telephone systems." Kinter, 2 The Legislative History of the Federal Antitrust Laws and Related Statutes, Part 1, at 1633. To ameliorate this problem, Vaughan introduced an amendment that would have permitted the "selling [of] local exchanges to competitors for local business." *Id.* The amendment was rejected, perhaps because it was deemed unnecessary. *See* Remarks of Rep. Webb ("If [a sale] does not substantially lessen competition, [the Clayton Act] does not apply . . . at all. That is already in the bill."). *Id.*

[84] *See, e.g.,* Eastman Kodak Co. v. Image Technical Services, Inc., 504 U.S. 451, 481 (1992); Aspen Skiing Co. v. Aspen Highlands Skiing Corp., 472 U.S. 585, 600–605 (1985); United States v. Grinnell Corp., 384 U.S. 563, 570–571 (1966); United States Football League v. National Football League, 842 F.2d 1335, 1358–1359 (2d Cir. 1988).

violation under section 2 of the Sherman Act than under section 7 of the Clayton Act.[85] To begin with, the "willfully" requirement gives greater play to the reasons supporting a monopolist's conduct. Under the prevailing standards of *Eastman Kodak*[86] and *Aspen*,[87] legitimate business reasons play a dominant role: they validate challenged conduct even if there are some anticompetitive results that unavoidably flow from the conduct.[88]

---

[85] Areeda and Hovenkamp briefly suggest that section 2 of the Sherman Act might proscribe some potential-competition mergers that would pass muster under section 7 of the Clayton Act. 3 P. Areeda & H. Hovenkamp, Antitrust Law ¶701d, at 134–135 (rev. ed. 1996). The argument is that a merger by an incumbent monopolist or near-monopolist with a potential competitor may constitute Sherman Act "monopolization," actual or attempted, even though it cannot "substantially lessen" competition in the already monopolized market as section 7 of the Clayton Act requires. Ultimately, however, Areeda and Hovenkamp do not subscribe to the view that section 2 is more stringent than section 7. *See id.* ¶701a, at 132. *See also* 5 P. Areeda & D. Turner, Antitrust Law ¶1145b, at 257 (1980) ("[I]t would be surprising, to say the least, to find that the 1890 Sherman Act prohibits a merger whose effects are insufficient to satisfy the Clayton Act as amended in 1950."). Moreover, the one case cited by the Areeda and Hovenkamp treatise to support the view that section 2 is more stringent, United States v. El Paso Nat. Gas Co., 376 U.S. 651 (1964), was a section 7 case, not a section 2 case, and "was in reality . . . an actual-competition case rather than a potential-competition case." United States v. Marine Bancorporation, Inc., 418 U.S. 602, 623 & n.24 (1974). *But see* Antitrust Law Developments at 275–276 & n.4 ("[C]ourts are split as to whether the required showing under the Sherman Act is higher than that under Section 7.") (citing cases).

[86] Eastman Kodak Co. v. Image Technical Services, Inc., 504 U.S. at 483.

[87] Aspen Skiing Co. v. Aspen Highlands Skiing Corp., 472 U.S. at 600–605.

[88] There is a subjective component to this "legitimate business reasons" inquiry, looking to whether the challenged conduct was "'designed primarily to further any domination of the relevant market.'" *Id.* at 597 (quoting approved jury instruction). *See also id.* at 608–611; United States Football League v. National Football League, 842 F.2d at 1358–1359 (requiring that both intent *and* effect be proven). The "reasons" standard also inquires into whether the challenged conduct has harmful effects on consumer choices (price, output) and whether those effects are justified by legitimate business objectives. That inquiry focuses on the same anticompetitive effects as does section 7, and the established role of legitimate business objectives in justifying any such effects under the cited section 2 decisions is at least equal to the role of efficiencies in the section 7 analysis.

Section 2 is also rarely used to condemn mergers because of the difficulty in establishing "monopoly power." Initially, antitrust law reflected the old populist tradition and its generalized aversion to "bigness" in and of itself.[89] The kinds of companies that spawned the outcry against bigness were Standard Oil and Carnegie Steel—enterprises with virtually complete monopolies. In the 1940s, Judge Learned Hand could state confidently that while 90 percent market share was enough to constitute monopoly under the Act, "it is doubtful whether sixty or sixty-four [percent] would be enough; and certainly thirty-three [percent] is not."[90] Today, few courts will find monopolization (or even *attempted* monopolization) possible by a firm with a market share of less than 25 percent.[91] In the monopsony context, the Department of Justice has taken the position that a 35 percent market share is the safe-harbor boundary within which size is not an antitrust concern.[92] Moreover, courts today also consider other factors, such as ease of entry, because simple percentages fail to tell the whole competitive story. For example, if entry is extremely easy, courts are reluctant to find monopoly power because the threat of entry prevents price increases.[93]

[89] H. Hovenkamp, Federal Antitrust Policy §2.1(a), at 51–52 (1994) (hereinafter *Federal Antitrust Policy*). *See also* MCI Communications Corp. v. AT&T, 708 F.2d 1081, 1110 (7th Cir.), *cert. denied*, 464 U.S. 891 (1983). *Cf.* United States v. AT&T, 552 F. Supp. at 167 (in approving the Bell breakup, Judge Greene referred to the "goal of deconcentrating AT&T's vast economic power").

[90] United States v. Aluminum Co. of America, 148 F.2d 416, 424 (2d Cir. 1945).

[91] *See, e.g.,* M&M Medical Supplies and Service, Inc. v. Pleasant Valley Hospital, Inc., 981 F.2d 160, 168 (4th Cir. 1992) (en banc), *amended slip op.* M&M Medical Supplies and Service, Inc. v. Pleasant Valley Hosp., Inc. (4th Cir. W. Va. Jan. 20, 1993), *cert. denied*, 508 U.S. 972 (1993) (articulating common test presumptively rejecting claims where market share is less than 30 percent); Valley Liquors, Inc. v. Renfield Importers, Ltd., 822 F.2d 656, 666–667 (7th Cir.) (citing cases), *cert. denied*, 484 U.S. 977 (1987).

[92] Business Review Letter to Utilities Service Alliance, July 3, 1996, 6 Trade Reg. Rep. (CCH) ¶44,096 (Letter No. 96-18).

[93] Antitrust Law Developments at 217 (citing cases).

§7.4.2 The Merger Guidelines and Antitrust Case Law

The 1992 Horizontal Merger Guidelines and the 1997 revisions[94] set out the Federal Trade Commision's and the Department of Justice's general criteria for assessing mergers. The FCC claims to be informed by the guidelines, too,[95] though insists it is not bound by them.[96]

A general review of the Guidelines and case law is beyond the scope of this treatise. We include here only a brief review of those principles most relevant to an industry in transition from monopoly to competition.

§7.4.2.1 Concentrated Markets

The 1992 Guidelines take a case-specific approach to horizontal mergers, continuing the trend of the 1984 Guidelines away from simple rules for condemning mergers. The 1992 Guidelines indicate that while a presumption of harm arises from a 100-point change in the Herfindahl-Hirschman Index in a highly concentrated market,[97] that is subject to rebuttal by examination of the ease of entry, the capacity of other rivals, any changes under way in the market, and other factors that may make present market-share numbers misleading as reliable predictors of likely future market share or future power to raise price or reduce output.[98] More generally, the Guidelines recognize that unnecessary interference with mergers has its costs and that relevant information is often incomplete. The Guidelines therefore contemplate reasonable and flexible application of the standards "to the particular facts and circumstances of each proposed merger."[99]

[94] Antitrust Div., United States Dept. of Justice & Federal Trade Commn. 1992 Horizontal Merger Guidelines, 57 Fed. Reg. 41,552 (1992) (hereinafter 1992 Horizontal Merger Guidelines), *revised*, 4 Trade Reg. Rep. (CCH) 13,104 (Apr. 8, 1997).
[95] *See BT/MCI II*, 12 F.C.C. Rec. at 15,367–15,368 ¶34.
[96] *See MCI/WorldCom*, 13 F.C.C. Rec. at 18,035–18,038 ¶¶15–21.
[97] 1992 Horizontal Merger Guidelines §1.51.
[98] *Id.* (referring to §§2–5 of the Horizontal Merger Guidelines).
[99] 1992 Horizontal Merger Guidelines §0.

The Supreme Court, in *United States v. Philadelphia National Bank*,[100] articulated a legal presumption of lessened competition in circumstances presenting an "undue" market share and a "significant increase" in concentration by the merger of actual competitors.[101] But that rule is also only a presumption, and the courts have increasingly insisted on a full examination of relevant evidence—such as the ability of rivals to increase capacity, the ease of entry of potential rivals, and changing conditions that make present shares misleading as to future power—to determine whether lessening of competition would be likely to occur in the face of high market shares.[102] For example, in *Baker Hughes*, where the market at issue was highly concentrated,[103] the D.C. Circuit sharply rebuffed even a limited curtailing of a full-fledged analysis of the circumstances that might undermine a finding of competitive harm. It held that the analysis could not properly be limited to ease of entry.[104] "Predicting future competitive conditions in a given market, as the statute and precedents require, calls for a comprehensive inquiry" that precludes a rule narrowing the section 7 inquiry so as to close off a concrete market analysis of likely effects.[105]

§7.4.2.2 Potential Competition

The potential-competition doctrine has become increasingly important in the context of telecommunications mergers because the Commission has adopted a variant of it to analyze

---

[100] 374 U.S. 321 (1963).

[101] *Id.* at 363.

[102] *See, e.g.,* United States v. General Dynamics Corp., 415 U.S. 486, 503–504 (1974); R. C. Bigelow, Inc. v. Unilever N.V., 867 F.2d 102, 108 (2d Cir.), *cert. denied,* 493 U.S. 815 (1989); United States v. Waste Management, Inc., 743 F.2d 976, 981–983 (2d Cir. 1984); United States v. Baker Hughes, Inc., 908 F.2d 981, 982–992 (D.C. Cir. 1990) (per Thomas, J., joined by Ginsburg, R.B., and Sentelle, JJ.); United States v. Syufy Enters., 903 F.2d 659, 664 (9th Cir. 1990); United States v. Gillette Co., 828 F. Supp. 78, 84–85 (D.D.C. 1993); United States v. Calmar, Inc., 612 F. Supp. 1298, 1301 (D.N.J. 1985).

[103] United States v. Baker Hughes, Inc., 908 F.2d at 983 n.3.

[104] *Id.* at 983–987.

[105] *Id.* at 988.

"transition markets."[106] The potential-competition doctrine seeks to achieve future improvements in competition rather than to avoid the lessening of existing competition. The doctrine addresses mergers involving companies that are poised to become horizontal competitors, but haven't quite done so yet.[107] Mergers are scrutinized under this rubric only when the market in question is highly concentrated;[108] when few other potential entrants are "equivalent" to the company that proposes to enter the target market by merger;[109] when the entering company was reasonably likely to have entered the market but for the merger;[110] when the entering company has feasible means of entry other than merger; and when those other means offer a substantial likelihood of ultimately producing deconcentration in the target market.[111]

The potential-competition doctrine adds major additional levels of speculation to section 7 cases: whether the acquiring firm would enter; the scale, form, and timing of such entry; what other firms might enter or otherwise become new competitive forces, and in what ways and in what period and with what commitments; the extent to which existing price and output conditions in the market would be improved by the projected entry of

---

[106] See MCI/WorldCom, 13 F.C.C. Rec. at 18,036–18,039 ¶¶18–22.

[107] See Antitrust Div., United States Dept. of Justice, 1984 Merger Guidelines, 49 Fed. Reg. 26,823, §4.11 (hereinafter 1984 Merger Guidelines).

[108] United States v. Marine Bancorporation, Inc., 418 U.S. at 630–631; United States v. Siemens Corp., 621 F.2d 499, 505 (2d Cir. 1980); Antitrust Law Developments at 323 n.284.

[109] Antitrust Law Developments at 323–324 n.286. See also 1984 Merger Guidelines §4.132. Cf. Mercantile Texas Corp. v. Board of Governors of the Federal Reserve System, 638 F.2d 1255, 1267 (5th Cir. 1981).

[110] Concerning this element, there is case law holding that such entry must be certain. See FTC v. Atlantic Richfield Co., 549 F.2d 289, 294–295 (4th Cir. 1977). Most cases, however, hold that entry need only be reasonably likely. See, e.g., Tenneco, Inc. v. FTC, 689 F.2d 346, 352 (2d Cir. 1982); Yamaha Motor Co. v. FTC, 657 F.2d 971, 977–979 (8th Cir. 1981), cert. denied, 456 U.S. 915 (1982); Mercantile Texas Corp. v. Board of Governors of the Fed. Reserve Sys., 638 F.2d at 1268–1269; United States v. Siemens Corp., 621 F.2d at 506–507; BOC Intl. Ltd. v. FTC, 557 F.2d 24, 28–29 & n.7 (2d Cir. 1977).

[111] United States v. Marine Bancorporation, Inc., 418 U.S. at 633; B.A.T. Indus., Ltd., 104 F.T.C. 852, 924 (1984) (hereinafter B.A.T.); Antitrust Law Developments at 324–325 nn.291–293.

the acquiring firm amidst other new competitive forces; and the extent to which any substantial price-and-output benefits attributed to the projected entry of the acquiring firm would be achieved by other forces if no such entry occurred. Yet an additional layer of speculation is demanded if, at the initial step of the analysis, the product market is defined in such a way that today that market is not concentrated and the merging firms are not even participants. By contrast, when actual competitors merge, rather than comparing two future hypothetical worlds (the future market if the potential entrant were still independent and the future market without such independence), the inquiry compares the known present market with the postmerger market to detect lessening of competition (rather than the diminished possibility of improvements). There are no questions about whether and how and when and with what effect the merging firms would be in the market.

For these reasons, both commentators and courts have stressed the great importance of the distinction between the existing and the merely potential.[112] The general principle is this: eliminating a present market benefit is on a different plane from—and is categorically more subject to antitrust condemnation than—precluding a possible improvement in a market by some as yet nonexistent new structure. That principle rests on a sensible assessment. What has won its way into the market is presumptively beneficial. What has not won its way into the market carries no such presumption. Moreover, judicial scrutiny of the universe of all "could be" possibilities would require substantial additional speculation, with an accompanying increase in the costs of antitrust intervention into markets.

Courts have recognized two theories of potential competition: actual potential competition and perceived potential competition. The perceived potential entrant doctrine addresses cases where "the acquiring firm was perceived by competitors in a concentrated market as a likely potential entrant, and this

---

[112] *See, e.g.,* Aspen Skiing Co. v. Aspen Highlands Skiing Corp., 472 U.S. at 603–604 & n.31. *See* 3 P. Areeda & H. Hovenkamp, Antitrust Law ¶¶772c2–c3, at 189–194.

perception exerted a procompetitive effect on their behavior."[113] This doctrine has been recognized and accepted by the Supreme Court.[114]

A far more speculative theory of potential competition is the "actual potential competition" doctrine, which addresses cases where one of the merging firms had actual plans to enter the other's market—but plans not perceived by its proposed merger partner or the market participants[115]—before the two firms decided to merge instead.[116] The doctrine requires proof that the outside-the-market merger partner would, but for the merger, have offered an otherwise unavailable substantial improvement to the competitive state of the market.[117] The Department's 1984 Merger Guidelines (§4.1) lay out standards for the application of the doctrine—standards that take account of the degree of concentration,[118] the relative ease of entry into the market,[119] the number of other firms with similar entry advantages,[120] the presence or absence of "significant investments demonstrating an

---

[113] Antitrust Law Developments at 322; *see also B.A.T.,* 104 F.T.C. at 919–922.

[114] *See* United States v. Marine Bancorporation, Inc., 418 U.S. at 639–640.

[115] The Supreme Court has reserved judgment on the actual potential competition doctrine. *See id.* at 625, 639; United States v. Falstaff Brewing Corp., 410 U.S. 526, 537–538 (1973). The FCC, however, has adopted a variant of the actual potential competition doctrine in its analysis of "mergers involving carriers that had been prevented or deterred from entering the relevant market because of the legal, regulatory, economic and operational barriers that the 1996 Act seeks to lower." *MCI/WorldCom,* 13 F.C.C. Rec. at 18,036–18,037 ¶18, 18,038 ¶20.

[116] Such cases should be rare. *See, e.g., B.A.T.,* 104 F.T.C. at 919–922; Federal Antitrust Policy §13.4b, at 512–513.

[117] *See, e.g.,* United States v. Marine Bancorporation, Inc., 418 U.S. at 625, 632–639.

[118] 1984 Merger Guidelines §4.131.

[119] *Id.* §4.132.

[120] *Id.* §4.133. The Guidelines pointedly focus only on the number of other firms with "the same or a comparable advantage," *id.,* whether or not those firms actually will enter the market. This reflects the hazards of predicting actual future conduct of other firms and the present price-disciplining effects "other similarly situated" firms may exercise even if they have not entered. Moreover, marginal differences between different firms' ability to enter are irrelevant. *See id.* §4.132 ("If entry to the market is generally easy, the fact that entry is marginally easier for one or more firms is unlikely to

actual decision to enter,"[121] the market share of the inside-the-market merger partner,[122] and efficiencies.[123]

Roughly comparable standards are reflected in the decisions of courts, which—after generally reserving the question of the doctrine's validity—have applied the doctrine with extreme caution. For example, under the actual potential competition doctrine, the standard of proof has been variously formulated: the predicted entry "would have" occurred,[124] entry "would likely have" occurred,[125] entry was "reasonably probable,"[126] and "clear proof that independent entry would have occurred but for the merger."[127] Any such entry, moreover, must occur in "the near future, with 'near' defined in terms of the entry barriers and lead time necessary for entry in the particular industry."[128] Unsurprisingly, government attempts to invoke the doctrine have met with a stunning lack of success.[129]

---

affect the behavior of the firms in the market."). In making the required assessment of irreplaceable economic effects, the Department and the courts must proceed beyond mere market-share projections to an inquiry into what the firms are doing, how the market is changing, whether other firms can fill any particular gaps left by one of the merging parties, how regulation affects prices and entry, and so on. *See, e.g.,* United States v. Marine Bancorporation, Inc., 418 U.S. at 627; United States v. General Dynamics Corp., 415 U.S. at 498–504 (1974); Brown Shoe Co. v. United States, 370 U.S. at 322 n.38; 1992 Horizontal Merger Guidelines §1.52.

[121] 1984 Merger Guidelines §4.133 n.28.

[122] *Id.* §4.134.

[123] *Id.* §4.135.

[124] *B.A.T.,* 104 F.T.C. at 925; *SBC/PacTel,* 12 F.C.C. Rec. at 2634 ¶18.

[125] Tenneco, Inc. v. United States, 689 F.2d at 352; *see* United States v. Siemens Corporation, 621 F.2d at 506–507.

[126] BOC Intl., Ltd. v. FTC, 557 F.2d at 28–29.

[127] *B.A.T.,* 104 F.T.C. at 926; *see also* FTC v. Atlantic Richfield Co., 549 F.2d at 294–295.

[128] BOC Intl., Ltd. v. FTC, 557 F.2d at 29.

[129] *See, e.g.,* FTC v. Atlantic Richfield Co., 549 F.2d at 291; BOC Intl., Ltd. v. FTC, 557 F.2d at 25; United States v. Siemens Corp., 621 F.2d at 501; Tenneco, Inc. v. FTC, 689 F.2d at 348–349; Mercantile Texas Corp. v. Board of Governors of the Fed. Reserve Sys., 638 F.2d at 1259 (vacating and remanding); Republic of Tex. Corp. v. Board of Governors of the Fed. Reserve Sys., 649 F.2d 1026, 1044–1046 (5th Cir. 1981); United States v. First Nat'l State Bancorporation, 499 F. Supp. 793, 814–815 (D.N.J. 1980); United States v. Consolidated Foods Corp., 455 F. Supp. 108, 138–139 (E.D. Pa. 1978); FTC v. Tenneco, Inc., 433 F. Supp. 105, 114 (D.D.C. 1977); United States v. Black

621

There are good reasons for courts' reluctance to accept the actual potential competition doctrine: the balance of considerations—reliably proven competitive harms, likely competitive benefits, costs of enforcement—does not support a more aggressive anti-merger approach. A merger that does no more than eliminate a nonperceived potential competitor does not allow prices to be increased above premerger levels because it has no worsening effect at all on premerger competition. Moreover, the 1984 Guidelines' adoption of the theory,[130] which has not been updated, stands in considerable tension with the test for validity of horizontal mergers underlying the 1992 Guidelines: "the government's 1992 Merger Guidelines approve mergers that could not

---

& Decker Mfg. Co., 430 F. Supp. 729, 755–769 (D. Md. 1976); United States v. Hughes Tool Co., 415 F. Supp. 637, 645–646 (C.D. Cal. 1976); *cf.* United States v. Penn-Olin Chem. Co., 246 F. Supp. 917, 919–934 (D. Del. 1965), *aff'd,* 389 U.S. 308 (1967) (extensively reviewing evidence of numerous vigorous middle-management recommendations and nevertheless rejecting assertion of likely entry). *See generally* Antitrust Law Developments at 322–328 (citing cases).

The Supreme Court and Second Circuit have several times pointedly reserved judgment on whether to accept the actual potential competition theory at all, the theory has met with lack of success in almost all of the cases where it has been invoked, and the theory has been severely criticized as simply requiring too much speculation to be appropriate. *See, e.g.,* United States v. Marine Bancorporation, Inc., 418 U.S. at 639 (reserving judgment); United States v. Falstaff Brewing Corp., 410 U.S. at 537–538 (same); Tenneco, Inc. v. FTC, 689 F.2d at 355 (same); United States v. Siemens Corp., 621 F.2d at 504, 506 (same); *B.A.T.,* 104 F.T.C. at 919–930 (surveying cases); Federal Antitrust Policy §13.4b, at 512–513. In fact, there may not be a single court decision, at least in modern times, blocking a merger on such grounds where the potential entrant was not also an obvious perceived potential competitor, in which case the doctrine is unnecessary. Notably, in Yamaha Motor Co., Ltd. v. FTC, 657 F.2d at 977, which relied on the actual potential competition doctrine to uphold an FTC challenge to a merger, the reliance was evidently unnecessary: as the Eighth Circuit opinion indicates, *id.* at 975, there was no doubt that the potential entrant was a perceived potential competitor already having present market effects—as the FTC expressly concluded. *See* Brunswick Corp. et al., 94 F.T.C. 1174, 1273–1274 (1979). Similarly, in United States v. Phillips Petroleum Co., 367 F. Supp. 1226 (C.D. Cal. 1973), *aff'd without op.,* 418 U.S. 906 (1974), the district court expressly noted that the outside-the-market firm was a perceived potential entrant with a substantial present competitive impact on the market. *Id.* at 1234, 1255–1257.

[130] 1984 Merger Guidelines §4.1.

profitably increase prices above premerger levels without inviting entry."[131]

There is a fundamental policy objection to any expansive "actual potential competition" doctrine: the required predictions that are at the core of the doctrine involve profoundly unreliable prognostication, all in the face (by definition) of a lack of perception of the outside-the-market firm's significant near-term entry by those most likely to know.[132] The objection is especially strong in telecom, where intensive state and federal regulation substantially weakens any argument for such an intrusive antitrust principle.[133]

§7.5 Merger Review by the FCC

Roughly speaking, the FCC's merger analysis duplicates the Department's—but without any effective discipline of standards, law, or judicial review. The basic merger presumption of

---

[131] 2A P. Areeda, H. Hovenkamp, & J. Solow, Antitrust Law ¶420, at 62–63 (1995) (footnote omitted).

[132] See 3 P. Areeda & H. Hovenkamp, Antitrust Law ¶701d, at 135 (rev. ed. 1996) ("The 'potential competition' doctrines [of section 7] . . . are rightfully criticized for involving courts in undue speculation and for demanding excessive speculation about the nature of the oligopoly market at issue."). Many courts have sought to address this fundamental problem by expressly or in fact demanding clear proof of actual company-adopted and resource-backed plans, insisting repeatedly on the distinction between lower-level proposals and plans adopted at the decision-making levels of the company. See, e.g., United States v. Siemens Corporation, 621 F.2d at 508; United States v. Penn-Olin Chemical Co., 246 F. Supp. at 919 ("[I]t is essential to distinguish between the views and actions of those in the Olin organization who were charged with decision making responsibility, and those whose function it was to make preliminary studies and recommendations."); see also R. R. Donnelley & Sons Co. et al., 5 Trade Reg. Rep. (CCH) ¶23,876, 23,663 (19XX); B.A.T., 104 F.T.C. at 930; 1984 Merger Guidelines §4.133 n.28.

[133] When a market is actively regulated for the benefit of both consumers and competitors, there is good reason to relax even existing rules of antitrust intervention because the risk of harm from refraining from antitrust intervention is diminished. See, e.g., Concord v. Boston Edison Co., 915 F.2d 17, 25 (1st Cir. 1990) (Breyer, J.), cert. denied, 499 U.S. 931 (1991); Kartell v. Blue Shield of Mass., Inc., 749 F.2d 922, 931 (1st Cir. 1984) (Breyer, J.), cert. denied, 471 U.S. 1029 (1985).

the 1934 Act, unchanged (in this regard) by the 1996 Act, is that (1) every telecom merger entails de jure entry by a new name-plate into new markets, (2) every entry into every market is prohibited until the FCC permits it, (3) the FCC permits what it deems to be "in the public interest," and (4) the FCC has the flexibility under the public interest test to do whatever it pleases.

The Commission always insists that its analysis of the competitive effects of a proposed transaction is "informed by antitrust principles, but it is not governed by the scope of the antitrust laws."[134] It is likewise informed by "the broad aims of the (1934) Communications Act"[135] and the myriad, diverse, often conflicting policies expressed in the 1996 Act. It is further "informed" by the Commission's own prior merger rulings, which the Commission always takes pains to review and cite. But the Commission's important merger orders are so long, itemize so many issues that the Commission claims to have weighed, and contain so many carefully phrased qualifications and disclaimers that no binding precedent is ever established and no coherent body of principle ever emerges. There are so many dimensions of scrutiny and analysis that every merger can readily be distinguished from every other. There is, in sum, a glut of "information" to guide the Commission in its rulings—such an overload, in fact, that it adds up to no guidance at all. No matter how many mergers it decides, the Commission always writes things in a manner that leaves it free to decide the next merger differently if it so wishes.

---

[134] *Teleport/AT&T,* 13 F.C.C. Rec. at 15,243–15,244 ¶12 (citing FCC v. RCA Communications, Inc., 346 U.S. at 94; United States v. FCC, 652 F.2d at 81–82, 88).

[135] *BA/NYNEX,* 12 F.C.C. Rec. at 20,002–20,003 ¶31 (citing Western Union Div., Commercial Telegraphers' Union, A.F.L. v. United States, 87 F. Supp. 324, 335 (D.D.C. 1949), *aff'd,* 338 U.S. 864 (1949)). "These broad aims include those expressed in Section 1 of the Communications Act, to 'make available . . . to all the people of the United States a rapid, efficient, Nation-wide, and world-wide . . . communication service,' and those expressed in the 1996 Act, to establish a 'pro-competitive, deregulatory national policy framework designed to . . . open[ ] all telecommunications markets to competition.'" *Id.* (quoting 47 U.S.C. §151 (1997)); *see also* H.R. Rep. No. 104-458 at 1; Telecommunications Act of 1996, Pub. L. No. 104-404 (preamble), 110 Stat 56 (1996).

§7.5.1 The Public Interest Standard

Section 214(a), the Communications Act's general licensing provision for wireline common carriers, provides that no common carrier shall acquire any line "unless and until there shall first have been obtained from the Commission a certificate that the present or future public convenience and necessity require or will require" the operation of the line.[136] Section 310(d), the corresponding provision for wireless licenses, provides that no construction permit or station license may be transferred, assigned, or disposed of in any manner except upon a finding by the Commission that the "public interest, convenience, and necessity will be served thereby."[137] Both provisions are typically engaged in major telecom mergers, as the merging parties almost invariably hold both wireline and wireless licenses of some kind.

Here, in the Commission's own words, is what the Commission does with the public interest standard: The public interest standard "is a flexible one that encompasses the 'broad aims of the Communications Act.'"[138] Those aims include, "among other things," promoting a "'pro-competitive, de-regulatory national policy framework'"; promoting "the competition policies of the Sherman and Clayton Acts"; promoting "'access to advanced telecommunications and information services . . . in all regions of the Nation'"; and assessing likely impacts on "the quality of telecommunications services," including "the provision of new or additional services to consumers."[139] The Commission will assess whether a merger is "likely" to result in harmful or beneficial effects on competition in any affected market.[140] Its "assessment takes into account any pro-competitive commitments made by the parties."[141] The Commission also considers "merger-specific efficiencies, such as cost reductions, productivity enhancements, or improved incentives for innovation" and whether the merger

---

[136] 47 U.S.C. §214(a) (1997).
[137] *Id.* §310(d).
[138] *Teleport/AT&T,* 13 F.C.C. Rec. at 15,242–15,243 ¶11.
[139] *Id.* (footnotes omitted).
[140] *BT/MCI II,* 12 F.C.C. Rec. at 15,371–15,372 ¶41.
[141] *Id.*

"will support the general policies of opening markets and lowering entry barriers that underlie the 1996 Act and the WTO Basic Telecom Agreement."[142]

Neither the Commission nor the courts have built up a body of precedent to imbue the public interest "standard" with any concrete, durable meaning. The Commission chooses not to, and the courts have little opportunity to do so. As a practical matter, large mergers cannot be consummated in an appellate court after years of litigation with a hostile agency—such a process takes too long and is too uncertain for an industry that is evolving as fast as this one.

§7.5.2 Small Conglomerate Mergers

Between the Bell System divestiture in 1984 and the end of 1996, the number of telephone companies has fallen by nearly 8 percent, from 1,432 to 1,332.[143] Many mid-sized LECs[144] have either been bought by large LECs or merged with other mid-sized LECs (e.g., as United Telephone and Central Telephone did). Many mid-sized local exchange carriers have been taken over by larger companies (e.g., Contel by GTE and SNET by SBC), have merged with peers (e.g., Centel with Sprint/United, PTI with Century, SNET with Woodbury Telephone), and have bought smaller independents (e.g., six small LECs by Century). Some 8 million—45 percent—of the 20 million independent LEC lines in service have been involved in a consolidation of

---

[142] *Id.*

[143] USTA, Phone Facts 1997, at 3 (1997).

[144] The incumbent local exchange carriers in the United States come in roughly three sizes: small, medium, and large. The Bell companies and GTE each serve over 15 million lines. There are approximately 1,300 independent telephone companies that serve under 100,000 lines each (90 percent of these in fact serve under 10,000 lines). There are ten or so companies in the middle that serve between 200,000 and 2 million lines. (One exception: Sprint serves over 7 million lines.) The Bell Operating Companies (BOCs) and GTE together serve 75 percent of U.S. access lines, the 1,300 small independents serve another 15 percent, and the mid-sized LECs serve 10 percent. *Id.* at 3, 14–19.

some kind. The FCC has approved these small consolidations routinely and swiftly. The orders have typically been quite brief.[145] The FCC's recent approval of SBC's merger with SNET is typical. The Commission concluded that the merger is "unlikely to produce any meaningful public interest harms" and "is likely to produce at least some tangible public interest benefits,"[146] including enhanced research and technical design capabilities.[147] Thus, the Commission approved the merger in short order.[148]

In approving such mergers so easily, the Commission accepts, at least implicitly, the central economic rationale for all conglomerate mergers, including very big ones like SBC/PacTel/Ameritech or Bell Atlantic/NYNEX/GTE: size matters. Bigger is more efficient and more viable in light of: new regulatory and market conditions and the increasing consumer appetite for seamless, bundled, end-to-end service. And more and more mergers can be anticipated as formerly separate media and industries converge, as telecommunications continues to become a global marketplace, as the infrastructure of telecommunications networks increasingly benefits from economies of scale and

---

[145] *See, e.g., Pacific Telecom and Century Telephone Enterprises:* Applications of PacifiCorp Holdings, Inc. and Century Telephone Enterprises, Inc. for Consent To Transfer Control of Pacific Telecom, Inc., a Subsidiary of PacifiCorp Holdings, Inc., Memorandum Opinion and Order, 13 F.C.C. Rec. 8891 (1997); *Centel Corporation and Sprint: Centel/Sprint,* 8 F.C.C. Rec. 1829; *Contel Corporation and GTE: Contel/GTE,* 6 F.C.C. Rec. 1003; Application of Ameritech Illinois Metro, Inc., To Purchase and Provide Service over Certain Local Exchange Facilities Located in Northwest Chicago and Nearby Communities Pursuant to 47 U.S.C. §214, Order and Certificate, 13 F.C.C. Rec. 8006 (1997).

[146] *SNET/SBC,* 13 F.C.C. Rec. at 21,318 ¶50.

[147] *Id.* at 21,315 ¶45 (listing among the benefits improved wireless competition, improved research capabilities, and improved technical design capabilities, including the fact that "'Connecticut customers are likely to see the benefits of ADSL [asymetrical digital subscriber line] technology more quickly as a result of SNET's merger with SBC'" (quoting the Connecticut Department of Public Utility Control) (citation omitted)).

[148] As is also typical for the Commission, *see* §7.5.4.7, the Commission imposed conditions on the merger. *See SNET/SBC,* 13 F.C.C. Rec. at 21,318 ¶51.

scope, and as consumer demand—from both corporate customers (who themselves are going national and global) and residential users (who have now added wireless and data usage on top of their traditional demand for landline voice service)—for bundled services intensifies.

§7.5.3 Large Conglomerate Mergers

§7.5.3.1 SBC/PacTel

SBC/PacTel was the first merger of Regional Bell Operating Companies reviewed by the FCC. The Department of Justice concluded its HSR review and initiated no action against the merger. The Commission had little trouble with it, too, finding that the arguments that the merger might reduce competition "lack[ed] merit."[149] The Commission chose to emphasize that *opponents* to the merger had "failed to establish the elements needed to satisfy the doctrine of actual potential competition"[150]—a view of the burden of proof in merger matters quite at odds with what the Commission has said in subsequent mergers, where all the talk has been about the burden of proof faced by the merging parties. The Commission further concluded that the merger would reduce competition "only slightly, if at all."[151] There were quite enough "other potential entrants that are 'equivalent' to SBC . . . including five other RBOCs, GTE, and Sprint," as well as AT&T, MCI, LDDS, Cable & Wireless, TCI, and Time/Warner.[152] "Some of these companies have capabilities or assets comparable to those of SBC. . . . Some have assets that SBC lacks. . . . In conclusion, we find that there are more than a few other potential entrants into the markets in question that are at least equivalent to SBC in competitive capabilities. Certainly, there are more than the three that DOJ uses as a benchmark in

---

[149] *SBC/PacTel*, 12 F.C.C. Rec. at 2626–2627 ¶2.
[150] *Id.*
[151] *Id.*
[152] *Id.* at 2637 ¶24.

applying the actual potential competition doctrine."[153] The Commission further found that the merged SBC/PacTel would possess no monopsony power in the purchase of long-distance service for resale,[154] as MCI had alleged, and that the merged company would not be able to suppress competition by jiggering charges for terminating switched access or by engaging in other forms of nonprice discrimination against long-distance carriers.[155]

On the positive side, the Commission noted that the merger "may result in some modest improvements to the competitiveness and performance of some markets."[156] But a demonstration of benefits from the merger "is not, however, a prerequisite to [FCC] approval, provided that no foreseeable adverse consequences will result from the transfer."[157] Combining SBC and PacTel's mobile services would positively enhance competition in that market "by placing more territories under unified control."[158] And the merged company would "be a stronger competitor against AT&T, MCI, Sprint, and others"[159] when it was eventually permitted to enter long-distance markets.

The Commission was, in sum, quite casual about matters that it would later take very seriously in reviewing subsequent mergers—burdens of proof, the impact on potential competition, and the demonstration of procompetitive benefits most significantly among them.

§7.5.3.2   Bell Atlantic/NYNEX

Bell Atlantic/NYNEX followed close on the heels of SBC/PacTel. This second RBOC merger was of roughly comparable scope, but the Commission gave it a much more hostile look, on the ground that these two Bells were geographic neighbors and that Bell Atlantic had previously explored the possibility of competing in New York.

[153] *Id.* (footnote omitted).
[154] *See id.* at 2644–2645 ¶¶43–44.
[155] *See id.* at 2648–2650 ¶¶51–57.
[156] *Id.* at 2626–2627 ¶2.
[157] *Id.*
[158] *Id.* at 2658 ¶72.
[159] *Id.* at 2659 ¶74.

The Commission ended up approving the deal, but subject to a number of significant conditions, mostly related to unbundling and interconnection with competitors.[160] In effect, the Commission insisted that the merging companies surrender much of what they had previously won in court challenges to the Commission's own unbundling authority.[161]

The Commission wrote a lengthy opinion explaining how it viewed the merger and was ultimately able to approve it. The elaborate framework set out by the Commission was intended to be a general template for analyzing all major telecom mergers. It can readily serve: every possible issue is flagged, and every possible basis for fact-specific discretion is noted and reserved. The opinion is a verbose, sweeping, and unspecific, exhaustive analytical checklist. The one thing it does not do is give future petitioners any useful, intelligible guidance as to whether their merger will be approved.

The public interest standard, the Commission declared, requires a balancing of the overall costs and benefits of the merger. Beneficial effects in a number of markets or promotion of the overall policies of the Communications Act can overcome potential harms to competition in a specific market.

In assessing the potential for competitive harm, the analysis begins by defining the relevant product[162] and geographic markets.[163] For this merger, the Commission defined three relevant product markets for analysis: local exchange and exchange access service, long-distance (interLATA) service, and local exchange and exchange access service bundled with long-distance

---

[160] *See* §7.5.4.7.

[161] *See id.*

[162] The Commission has defined a relevant product market as "a service or group of services for which there are no close demand substitutes." *BA/NYNEX,* 12 F.C.C. Rec. at 20,014–20,015 ¶50 (citing Regulatory Treatment of LEC Provision of Interexchange Services Originating in the LEC's Local Exchange Area, Second Report and Order, 12 F.C.C. Rec. 15,756, 15,774–15,775 ¶27 (1997) (hereinafter *LEC In-Region Interexchange Order*)); *cf.* 1992 Horizontal Merger Guidelines §1.11.

[163] The Commission has defined a relevant geographic market as aggregating "those consumers with similar choices regarding a particular good or service in the same geographical area." *BA/NYNEX,* 12 F.C.C. Rec. at 20,016–20,017 ¶54; *cf.* 1992 Horizontal Merger Guidelines §1.21.

service ("bundled services").[164] Next, the Commission identified what it considered to be the most important participants in those markets. The universe of participants, the Commission declared, included *actual* competitors and also—a brand new term in the antitrust literature—"precluded competitors." Precluded competitors are those "firms that are most likely to enter but have until recently been prevented or deterred from market participation by barriers to entry the 1996 Act seeks to lower."[165] The Commission would separately assess the effects of the merger in three separate customer segments with "similar patterns of demand": residential customers and small businesses, medium-sized businesses, and large business/government users.[166]

The Commission claimed to weigh a variety of different market impacts and possibly anticompetitive stratagems. It considered both unilateral effects of the merger and coordinated effects. The analysis of unilateral effects, the Commission noted, was generally like the analysis called for in section 2.21 of the 1992 Horizontal Merger Guidelines,[167] though even here the Commission's inquiry was not to be limited by antitrust law or precedent. The Commission would also consider whether the merger would support the general policies of market-opening and barrier-lowering that underlie the 1996 Act.[168] In that regard, the Commission also would consider the merger's effect on dynamic market performance and, in particular, whether out-of-region entry into a local market by an incumbent local carrier would affect the process of opening local markets to competition.[169] The Commission would further weigh the merger's effect on the Commission's own ability to regulate in the future.[170] Finally, the Commission would consider whether efficiencies, cost reductions, productivity enhancements, improved incentives for innovation, and other procompetitive benefits of a merger were

---

[164] *BA/NYNEX,* 12 F.C.C. Rec. at 20,014–20,015 ¶50.
[165] *Id.* at 20,020 ¶60.
[166] *Id.* at 20,016 ¶53.
[167] *See id.* at 20,038–20,039 ¶102.
[168] *See id.* at 20,008–20,009 ¶37.
[169] *See id.* at 20,048–20,049 ¶¶125–127.
[170] *See id.* at 20,058–20,063 ¶¶147–156.

sufficient to outweigh any diminution in competition that might otherwise occur in some markets.[171]

The details of what the Commission said about these things in the specific context of Bell Atlantic/NYNEX hardly matter. The Commission said too much. With quite modest changes in wording here and there, with just slightly more emphasis on some facts and slightly less on others, the whole tenor of the opinion could have been altered to say whatever the Commission pleased. Quite minor editing in the final stages would have supplied an opinion to support anything from unconditional approval to outright rejection. Suffice it to say that the Commission opted to declare that New York markets were losing a likely and significant potential competitor and that the Commission didn't buy the merging parties' claims of efficiencies, but that the demanding unbundling conditions the Commission imposed would increase competition more than the merger itself would reduce it.

§7.5.4   The "Analytical Framework" Applied

§7.5.4.1   Conglomerate Mergers by Local Wireline Incumbents

From BA/NYNEX and its subsequent applications, one can begin to glean some general impression of how the Commission views the competitive facts and prospects of telecom markets and local exchange markets in particular. One must emphasize, however, that these views are only as durable as the economic predilections of the Commissioners themselves.

The Commission will assume orderly implementation of the 1996 Act and WTO Agreement.[172] But the Commission does not "assume that merely writing the rules called for by the 1996 Act eliminates concerns about potentially harmful effects of some

---

[171] *See id.* at 20,069 ¶178, 20,076 ¶192.

[172] *See BT/MCI II,* 12 F.C.C. Rec. at 15,356–15,357 ¶9, 15,370 ¶38; *BA/NYNEX,* 12 F.C.C. Rec. at 20,037 ¶98.

mergers."[173] The Commission's inquiry will gaze far into the future: the Commission will evaluate not only current impacts, but also impacts after the 1996 Act is implemented in the United States and the WTO Agreement is implemented abroad.[174]

As to *serious* potential competitors in local exchange markets, the Commission believes them to be few in number.[175] Only a handful "have, or are likely to speedily gain, the greatest capabilities and incentives to compete most effectively and soonest."[176] Entry barriers will remain high, even as unbundling and resale arrangements are implemented.[177] Brand name is important, and few potential entrants have a substantial brand.[178] The Commission will weigh every actual and potential competitor, one by one, to determine how real it really is.[179] AT&T, MCI, and Sprint, for example, rank as "previously precluded competitors that [are] among the most significant potential participants in the market for local exchange and exchange access services provided

[173] *Id.* at 19,989 ¶6.

[174] *See Teleport/AT&T,* 13 F.C.C. Rec. at 15,243–15,244 ¶13, *see also BA/ NYNEX,* 12 F.C.C. Rec. at 19,989–19,990 ¶7; *BT/MCI II,* 12 F.C.C. Rec. at 15,369 ¶36. "[T]he appropriate time frame . . . includes not only the period during the implementation of the 1996 Act and the WTO Basic Telecom Agreement, but also the period after the competitive entry obligations of the WTO Basic Telecom Agreement and the local competition provisions of the 1996 Act have been more fully implemented, and after the Bell Operating Companies (BOCs) have received authorization to provide in-region interLATA (including international) services pursuant to Section 271 of the Communications Act." *Id.* at 15,356–15,357 ¶9 (citing 47 U.S.C. §271 (1997)).

[175] *See BA/NYNEX,* 12 F.C.C. Rec. at 19,991 ¶10.

[176] *Id.* at 20,020–20,021 ¶62.

[177] *See id.* at 20,020 ¶61.

[178] *See id.* at 19,989 ¶6, 20,012 ¶42, 20,024–20,025 ¶70.

[179] "[A] firm may be likely to be among the most significant market participants even though it has not yet entered the relevant market. As we indicated in *BA/NYNEX,* these capabilities include access to the necessary facilities, 'know how,' and operational infrastructure such as sales, marketing, customer service, billing and network management. They also include less tangible capabilities such as brand name recognition in the mass market, a reputation for providing high quality, reliable service, existing customer relationships, or the financial resources to obtain these intangible assets. Another factor is whether the actual or precluded competitor had plans to enter the relevant market or was engaged in such planning." *BT/MCI II,* 12 F.C.C. Rec. at 15,380– 15,381 ¶65 (footnote omitted).

to residential and small business customers, because each has 'the capabilities and incentives to acquire a critical mass of customers in the relevant markets and to do so relatively rapidly.'"[180] Other competitive LECs (CLECS), by contrast, do not rank among the most significant market participants in this market "'because they lack[ ] the financial resources and brand name reputation necessary to enter the residential and small business market quickly.'"[181] And geographic contiguity can boost a company's status as a significant potential competitor.[182]

Local exchange and exchange access services occupy one relevant product market; interstate, interexchange, long-distance service occupies another.[183] But relevant product markets may change over time. Bundling is likely to become more important than it currently is,[184] and the Commission fully intends to analyze competitive impacts even in markets that don't yet exist.[185] Product markets can and must be subdivided to distinguish mass market customers from medium and large businesses.[186] Further subdivision by class of customer or type of service may be necessary: "certain carriers may target particular types of customers, provide specialized services or control independent facilities in specific geographic areas."[187] International services (which the

---

[180] *Teleport/AT&T,* 13 F.C.C. Rec. at 15,249–15,250 ¶25 (citing *BA/NYNEX,* 12 F.C.C. Rec. at 20,029–20,030 ¶82).

[181] *Id.* (citing *BA/NYNEX,* 12 F.C.C. Rec. at 20,032–20,033 ¶¶87–88).

[182] *See, e.g., BA/NYNEX,* 12 F.C.C. Rec. at 20,024 ¶69, 20,029 ¶79. In LATA 132, the Commission declares that "five companies—NYNEX, Bell Atlantic, AT&T, MCI, and Sprint—are the most significant market participants." *Id.* at 20,024–20,025 ¶70, 20,035 ¶94. "[A]lthough many other companies are precluded competitors, and some may be actual market participants in one or both of the relevant markets, no other company is among the most significant market participants in either of the relevant markets." *Id.* at 20,035 ¶94.

[183] *See id.* at 20,015 ¶51.

[184] *See id.* at 20,015–20,016 ¶52; *BT/MCI II,* 12 F.C.C. Rec. at 15,374–15,375 ¶49.

[185] "[T]he bundled product offerings may well become a separate relevant product market even if, today, such offerings are nascent or nonexistent in most markets." *Id.* (citing *BA/NYNEX,* 12 F.C.C. Rec. at 20,015–20,016 ¶52).

[186] *See BA/NYNEX,* 12 F.C.C. Rec. at 20,016 ¶53; *BT/MCI II,* 12 F.C.C. Rec. at 15,375 ¶50; *MCI/WorldCom,* 13 F.C.C. Rec. at 18,040 ¶25.

[187] *BA/NYNEX,* 12 F.C.C. Rec. at 20,016–20,017 ¶54 (citing *LEC In-Region Interexchange Order,* 12 F.C.C. Rec. at 15,771 ¶21).

Commission addressed in its 1997 BT/MCI order) add a number of additional markets to the list: outbound international service and "global seamless services," in particular.[188] And "[i]n defining the relevant product markets," the Commission "will examine not just the markets as they exist today, but as [it] expect[s] they will exist after a Bell Company receives authorization to provide in-region interLATA services pursuant to Section 271 of the Communications Act."[189]

Geographic markets may be defined in lots of different ways. Local markets are sort of local; long-distance markets may be point-to-point (e.g., city pairs)[190] or perhaps national.[191]

The Commission notes that mergers may depress competition by increasing concentration, but that they may also boost competition by turning two weak competitors into one stronger one.[192] A merger between actual or potential horizontal rivals may depress competition in two ways: directly, by increasing a dominant firm's *unilateral* power to behave anticompetitively, or indirectly, by making it easier for a (diminished) number of competitors to exercise market power through *coordinated interaction*.[193] But a merger that strengthens a "maverick firm" can

---

[188] *BT/MCI II,* 12 F.C.C. Rec. at 15,376 ¶52.

[189] *BA/NYNEX,* 12 F.C.C. Rec. at 19,989–19,990 ¶7.

[190] *See id.* at 20,016–20,017 ¶54. In the *LEC In-Region Interexchange Order,* the Commission found that each point-to-point market constituted a separate relevant geographic market. *Id.* (citing *LEC In-Region Interexchange Order,* 12 F.C.C. Rec. at 15,792–15,793 ¶64).

[191] *BT/MCI II,* 12 F.C.C. Rec. at 15,375–15,376 ¶51. "Because of the existence of ubiquitous calling plans and geographic rate averaging, however, . . . 'when a group of point-to-point markets exhibit sufficiently similar competitive characteristics (i.e., market structure), [the Commission] will examine that group of markets using aggregate data that encompasses all point-to-point markets in the relevant area, rather than examine each individual point-to-point market separately.'" *Id.* (citing *LEC In-Region Interexchange Order,* 12 F.C.C. Rec. at 15,794 ¶66).

[192] "[I]f, as a result of the merger, the merged entity either enters the relevant market or becomes a stronger and more significant competitor in the relevant market, then the merger may have the effect of reducing the market power of the dominant firm in that market." *BT/MCI II,* 12 F.C.C. Rec. at 15,398 ¶124.

[193] *See id.* at 15,398–15,399 ¶¶124–125; *BA/NYNEX,* 12 F.C.C. Rec., at 20,038–20,039 ¶101, 20,046–20,047 ¶121.

undermine coordinated interaction and therefore be procompetitive.[194]

In addition to "end user" markets, the Commission examines "input" markets. In its BT/MCI order, for example, the Commission identifies no fewer than six input markets for scrutiny.[195] The Commission considers whether the merger may increase market power in the provision of an input to rivals.

The Commission also examines vertical competitive effects — and here, too, allows that they may be either positive or negative. Vertical integration can be quite efficient.[196] But it can give a firm market power over upstream inputs that can be used to harm downstream end-user rivals.[197] In focusing on the extent to which a proposed merger is likely to increase adverse vertical effects, the Commission pays careful attention not to include adverse vertical effects that likely would arise even in the absence of the merger.[198] The Commission considers whether and to what extent the merged company will be able to raise rivals' costs[199] or engage in a predatory price squeeze.[200]

§7.5.4.2 Conglomerate Wireless Mergers

By contrast, the Commission has been strongly disposed to favor conglomerate mergers that expand the footprint of wire-

---

[194] *BT/MCI II,* 12 F.C.C. Rec. at 15,398–15,399 ¶125.

[195] *Id.* at 15,372–15,373 ¶43. These are (1) international transport between the United States and United Kingdom, (2) U.K. cable landing station access, (3) U.K. backhaul, (4) U.K. intercity transport, (5) U.K. terminating access services, and (6) U.K. originating access services.

[196] "Vertical effects that benefit competition refer to various types of efficiencies arising from vertical integration, especially efficiencies that reduce the costs of producing the relevant goods and services, improve the quality of products, or increase the variety of alternatives available to consumers." *Id.* at 15,409–15,410 ¶154.

[197] "These downstream effects could harm consumers through increases in prices, decreases in quality, or a reduction in alternatives in end-user markets." *Id.* (citing Thomas G. Krattenmaker & Steven C. Salop, Anticompetitive Exclusion: Raising Rivals' Costs To Achieve Power over Price, 96 Yale L.J. 209 (Dec. 1986)).

[198] *BT/MCI II,* 12 F.C.C. Rec. at 15,409–15,410 ¶154.

[199] *Id.* at 15,410–15,411 ¶¶156–157.

[200] *Id.* at 15,413–15,414 ¶162.

less carriers. Without exception, it has approved transfers of wireless licenses that had the effect of creating larger, contiguous service territories.[201] The Commission views the development of larger regional systems as procompetitive.[202] This benign view of wireless conglomerate mergers extends to those involving the wireless affiliates of Regional Bell Operating Companies, too.

§7.5.4.3 Vertical Mergers Between Long-Distance Carriers and CLECs

The Commission is readily persuaded that vertical integration by almost any company that competes against an incumbent LEC is procompetitive. It readily approved the $11 billion AT&T/ TCG merger which united the largest (long-distance) carrier in the country with a large CLEC.[203] In all likelihood, it will readily approve the AT&T/TCI merger as well. MCI/WorldCom was

---

[201] *See, e.g., BA Mobile/NYNEX Mobile,* 10 F.C.C. Rec. 13,368; Application of Corpus Christi Cellular Telephone Co. for Commission Consent To Transfer of Control of the Corpus Christi, Texas Non-Wireline Cellular Permit to McCaw, Memorandum Opinion and Order, 3 F.C.C. Rec. 1889 (1988) (hereinafter *Corpus Christi/McCaw*); Application of Madison Cellular Telephone Company for Consent To Transfer of Control, Memorandum Opinion and Order, 2 F.C.C. Rec. 5397 (1987). *See* Applications of MMM Holdings, Inc. for Transfer of Control of Lin Broadcasting Corporation, Memorandum Opinion and Order, 4 F.C.C. Rec. 8243 (1989); *Contel/GTE,* 6 F.C.C. Rec. 1003.

[202] *See, e.g., SBC/PacTel,* 12 F.C.C. Rec. at 2658 ¶72 (noting that the creation of wide-area commercial mobile radio service (CMRS) combinations, "by placing more territories under unified control, is likely to increase uniformity and reduce the occurrence of uncoordinated offerings and pricing"); *Corpus Christi/McCaw,* 3 F.C.C. Rec. at 1891 ¶19 (noting that regional systems are in the public interest and can result in marketing and personnel efficiencies and lower costs); *SNET/SBC,* 13 F.C.C. Rec. at 21,315 ¶45 ("We disagree with MCI and find that Applicants have demonstrated that the proposed merger is likely to produce at least some tangible public interest benefits. We find that the merger will provide Applicants with an increased wireless calling area that may result in improved wireless competition in the relevant markets.") (footnotes omitted).

[203] *Teleport/AT&T,* 13 F.C.C. Rec. at 15,262 ¶48 ("[A]s a result of the merger, the combined entity likely will be able to expand its operations and enter local markets more quickly than either party could do absent the merger. . . . AT&T has a strong brand name reputation in the provision of telephone service to the mass market, as well as a substantial base of residential, long-distance customers. These capabilities will now be combined with Teleport's local facilities

approved, too, despite significant horizontal overlaps in the long-distance operations of the two companies.[204]

§7.5.4.4 Merger Efficiencies

As to the claimed economic efficiencies that will result from a merger, the Commission is skeptical and not easily persuaded[205]—except when it wishes to be, and then it is.[206] The Commission will consider whether claimed efficiencies "are unlikely to be achieved through less competitively-harmful means than the merger,"[207] such as a joint venture. The applicants bear

---

and expertise and knowledge in providing local services. Even though the record is sparse, we believe these benefits warrant approval of the merger in light of our finding that the merger is unlikely to result in any anticompetitive effects.") (footnotes omitted).

[204] Some, but not all, of those overlaps were eliminated before the merger was completed. Under pressure from European and Justice Department regulators, MCI spun off its Internet backbone affiliate. See *MCI/WorldCom*, 13 F.C.C. Rec. at 18,103–18,104 ¶142.

[205] See, e.g., *BT/MCI II*, 12 F.C.C. Rec. at 15,431 ¶208 ("Although it appears that no party to this proceeding has challenged the BT/MCI assessment of the potential merger-specific efficiencies, we find that the evidence presented by the petitioners on this point so meager that the efficiency benefits are either non-cognizable or entitled to very little weight in our public interest analysis."); *BA/NYNEX*, 12 F.C.C. Rec. at 20,066 ¶168 ("Applicants have not carried their burden of demonstrating that the proposed merger will create verifiable merger-specific efficiencies that offset the merger's competitive harms.").

[206] See, e.g., *MCI/WorldCom*, 13 F.C.C. Rec. at 18,138 ¶198 ("Although we do not believe that Applicants have provided sufficient evidence to support all of their claims, we conclude that Applicants have made a sufficient showing here of potential benefits to find that, on balance, the merger is in the public interest, convenience, and necessity."); *Teleport/AT&T*, 13 F.C.C. Rec. at 15,262 ¶48 ("Although Applicants have not quantified or substantially supported the public interest benefits that may result from the merger, we are persuaded that, as a result of the merger, the combined entity likely will be able to expand its operations and enter local markets more quickly than either party could do absent the merger. . . . Even though the record is sparse, we believe these benefits warrant approval of the merger in light of our finding that the merger is unlikely to result in any anticompetitive effects."); *SBC/PacTel*, 12 F.C.C. Rec. at 2661 ¶83 ("We conclude that, on balance, the proposed transfer may result to a modest degree in efficiencies, in increases in the competitiveness of SBC/PacTel in a few markets, and in other public interest benefits. SBC/PacTel should be able to achieve some savings in overhead and support systems, and to offer 'one-stop shopping' of some services that is now impossible.").

[207] *BT/MCI II*, 12 F.C.C. Rec. at 15,430 ¶205.

the burden of proof and cannot "carry their burden if their efficiency claims are vague or speculative, and cannot be verified by reasonable means."[208]

§7.5.4.5 Foreign Ownership and National Security

Telecom mergers are going global, of course, and transnational mergers present yet another cluster of factors for the FCC's review.[209] When a foreign entity seeks to enter U.S. markets by forming a joint venture with, or investing in, a U.S. carrier that owns a radio license of some kind or another, it must meet the requirements of section 310(b)(4),[210] which contains the familiar "public interest" test.[211] And section 214's public interest test applies also to foreign carriers that seek wireline authorizations.

Before 1997, the test for entry by all foreign carriers was "whether effective competitive opportunities exist[ed] for U.S. carriers in the destination markets of foreign carriers seeking to enter the U.S. international services market through affiliation with a new or existing U.S. carrier."[212] After the United States

---

[208] *Id.* (citation and internal quotes omitted).

[209] For an extensive discussion of foreign investment in U.S. telecommunications, see Gregory Sidak, Foreign Investments in American Telecommunications (1997).

[210] 47 U.S.C. §310(b)(4) (1997). A "foreign carrier" is defined in section 63.18(h)(1)(ii) as "any entity that is authorized within a foreign country to engage in the provision of international telecommunications services offered to the public in that country within the meaning of the International Telecommunication Regulations, *see* Final Acts of the World Administrative Telegraph and Telephone Conference, Melbourne, 1988 (WATTC-88), Art.1." *Id.* §63.18(h)(1)(ii). *See also id.* §§34–39 (1997).

[211] *See, e.g.,* Application of PrimeMedia Broadcasting, Inc., Memorandum Opinion and Order, 3 F.C.C. Rec. 4293, 4295 ¶12 (1988).

[212] Market Entry and Regulation of Foreign-Affiliated Entities, Report and Order, 11 F.C.C. Rec. 3873, 3875–3876 ¶2 (1995). *See, e.g.,* Sprint Corporation, Petition for Declaratory Rules Concerning Section 310(b)(4) and (d) and the Public Interest Requirements of the Communications Act of 1934, as Amended, Declaratory Ruling and Order, 11 F.C.C. Rec. 1850 (1996) (applying the effective competitive opportunities test to the global alliance among Sprint, France Telecom, and Deutsche Telekom and approving the alliance subject to conditions).

entered into the WTO Basic Telecom Agreement, however, the Commission established an open entry standard for WTO members,[213] while still maintaining its effective competitive opportunities test in the context of non-WTO member countries. Although WTO members enjoy a presumption in favor of participation, the Commission "recognize[s] the possibility that circumstances might arise in which [its] safeguards might not adequately constrain the potential for anticompetitive harm in the U.S. market for telecommunications services."[214] Thus, "the Commission reserves the right to attach additional conditions to a grant of authority, and in the exceptional case in which an application poses a very high risk to competition, to deny an application."[215]

Although the standards are different, the Commission's concerns for both WTO members and nonmembers remain the same: whether the foreign country is open to U.S. competition and whether the merger will adversely affect competition in the United States.[216] The Commission has addressed these factors most prominently in its consideration of the BT/MCI merger.[217] The Commission approved the merger, subject to conditions, after concluding that the U.S.-U.K. route is one of the most competitive in the world because of the substantial liberalization of the U.S. and U.K. telecommunications markets.

---

[213] Rules and Policies on Foreign Participation in the U.S. Telecommunications Market, Report and Order and Order on Reconsideration, 12 F.C.C. Rec. 23,891, 23,897–23,898 ¶13 (1997) (hereinafter *Foreign Participation Proceeding*).

[214] *Id.*

[215] *Id.*

[216] The executive branch commonly weighs in on such mergers, too, flagging national security, law enforcement, and trade concerns. In the *Foreign Participation Proceeding,* the Commission pledged to continue to consider executive branch concerns in the context of foreign carrier applications to enter the U.S. market, either independently or by merger with existing U.S. carriers. *Foreign Participation Proceeding,* 12 F.C.C. Rec. at 23,919–23,921 ¶¶61–66.

[217] *See BT/MCI II,* 12 F.C.C. 15,351; *BT/MCII,* 9 F.C.C. Rec. 3960.

§7.5.4.6 Benchmark Regulation

Finally, the Commission apparently reserves the right to disapprove a merger on the ground that having fewer competitors makes the market harder to regulate. The warden needs to be able to compare and contrast its wards, the Commission maintains.[218] With this argument securely in hand, the Commission need never treat a subsequent merger the same way it treated a prior one. "Because we approve this merger with conditions, thereby reducing the number of independently controlled large incumbent LECs, future applicants bear an additional burden in establishing that a proposed merger will, on balance, be procompetitive and, therefore, serve the public interest, convenience and necessity."[219]

§7.5.4.7 Imposing Conditions: A Plenary Power to Regulate

As noted in section 7.3.4, the Commission has the power to condition its approval of license transfers, and thus of mergers in general. As described below, it exercises that power freely and aggressively. In a static industry, an industry with little to gain from restructuring, this would be of little consequence. But we

---

[218] "[W]e are concerned about the impact of the declining number of large incumbent LECs, on this Commission's ability to carry out properly its responsibilities to ensure just and reasonable rates, to constrain market power in the absence of competition, and to ensure the fair development of competition that can lead to deregulation." *BA/NYNEX*, 12 F.C.C. Rec. at 19,994 ¶16. *See also* Response of the United States to Comments on Its Report and Recommendations Concerning the Line-of-Business Restrictions Imposed on the Bell Operating Companies by the Modification of Final Judgment at 81–82, 98–99, 105, 115, United States v. Western Elec. Co., Inc., No. 82-0192 (D.D.C. Apr. 27, 1987); Hearings Before the Senate Subcommittee on Communications of the Committee on Commerce, Science, and Transportation on S. 1981, 101st Cong., 2d Sess. 186, 190–192 (1990) (statement of Alfred C. Sikes, Chairman, FCC). The D.C. Circuit has held that benchmarks "make it far easier to regulate the BOCs than the old Bell System." United States v. Western Elec. Co., Inc., 900 F.2d 283, 299 (D.C. Cir), *cert. denied*, 498 U.S. 911 (1990).

[219] *BA/NYNEX*, 12 F.C.C. Rec. at 19,994 ¶16.

are dealing here with an industry in which there are huge economic surpluses to be captured through consolidation. The plenary power of "public interest" effectively gives the FCC complete control to allocate or dissipate those surpluses as it sees fit. The Commission can load up mergers with any amount of prospective regulation that it pleases. And for all practical purposes, it can do so without worrying at all about the procedural requirements of the APA or the mandates of the 1996 Act—jurisdictional, procedural, substantive, or as interpreted by the courts.[220]

In its review of the Bell Atlantic/NYNEX merger, for example, the Commission brazenly lists its own recent defeat in the Eighth Circuit—a ruling that overturned major parts of the Commission's 1996 unbundling order[221]—as something that adds to market "uncertainty" and requires the Commission to be all the more cautious in approving mergers between incumbent monopoly providers and possible rivals.[222] To get their merger approved, the Commission concluded (though did not say it quite so boldly) that Bell Atlantic and NYNEX must give back to the Commission what they had won from it in the Eighth Circuit. The companies then duly filed a "commitment letter" with the

---

[220] *cf.* Separate Statement of Commissioner Michael K. Powell in *MCI/WorldCom*, 13 F.C.C. Rec. at 18,166: "Fundamentally, I believe that the Commission's public interest authority to review transfers of authorizations is not a license to sweep into the review every possible goal that one could argue is supported by or consistent with the statute. Nor should we allow our public interest authority to degenerate—in reality or impression—into serving as a 'back door' to achieve results the Commission is unable (or unwilling) to accomplish more directly, through traditional rulemaking.

Powell would therefore have the Commission engage in a three-step review in determining whether to weight a particular factor in the public interest merger review. First, the Commission should ask if it has authority even to consider the factor. Second, the Commission should evaluate whether the action the Commission would take is part of its "core function of setting telecommunications policy." And finally, the Commission's query should include an analysis of whether the action relies on its expertise in setting policy and "is not more readily handled by other processes or other institutions vested with Congressional authority." *Id.* at 18,167.

[221] *See* §5.1.2.3.

[222] *See BA/NYNEX*, 12 F.C.C. Rec. at 19,988 ¶4: "We must be especially concerned about mergers between incumbent monopoly providers and possible

Commission promising to do so—and more. Because the Commission believed the merger could undercut competition in Manhattan, Bell Atlantic and NYNEX were required to commit to entry-barrier-reducing conditions across their entire region, from Maine to West Virginia.[223] Then—and only then—was the merger approved.

The companies committed "to provid[ing] detailed performance monitoring reports to competing carriers, states and this Commission, regarding network performance and the performance of their operating support systems ("OSS")."[224] They "commit[ted] to negotiate performance standards and enforcement mechanisms, including private or self-executing mechanisms, covering all five aspects of OSS (pre-ordering, ordering, provisioning, repair and maintenance, and billing) and network performance."[225] They agree[d] to implement, within 15 months, "uniform OSS interfaces covering the entire Bell Atlantic/NYNEX combined regions, and to develop uniform interfaces within their current respective regions within 120 days."[226] They committed to "engage in carrier-to-carrier testing of OSS systems with any carrier that requests such testing" and to provide evidence of their "ability to handle reasonably expected demand for all OSS functions with respect to resold services, unbundled network elements and combinations of unbundled network elements."[227] They "commit[ted] to offer interconnection, unbundled network elements and transport and termination at rates based on forward looking economic cost."[228] They agreed to provide for "purchase, in conjunction with unbundled switching, shared transport offered on a minute-of-use basis, routed in the same manner as Bell Atlantic and NYNEX route their own

---

rivals during this initial period of implementation of the 1996 Act. . . . Key portions of [the Local Competition Orders] recently were vacated, which created even greater uncertainty as to the pace of development of competition."

[223] *Id.* at 19,993 ¶14, 20,070–20,079 ¶¶181–200.
[224] *Id.* at 19,992–19,993 ¶13.
[225] *Id.*
[226] *Id.*
[227] *Id.*
[228] *Id.*

traffic, and without the imposition of access charges."[229] They "agree[d] to offer an optional plan that assesses non-recurring charges on a recurring basis, and an installment payment plan for collocation and certain other large non-recurring charges."[230] They "agree[d] to offer, in interconnection negotiations and arbitrations, payment mechanisms for common construction costs and interconnector-specific construction and equipment costs related to collocation that apportion costs among the incumbent LEC and collocating carriers consistent with the Commission's decision in its Second Physical Collocation Order."[231]

The Commission's approvals of other, smaller mergers have also incorporated a wide array of conditions, ranging from the minor to the quite significant. In approving the AT&T/McCaw merger, for example, the Commission required the companies to offer local cellular and interexchange service on an unbundled basis[232] and to abide by certain customer proprietary network information (CPNI) rules.[233] The Commission further ordered AT&T to "not unreasonably discriminate" in McCaw's favor in the development of proprietary technology or in the supply of cellular equipment under contracts signed prior to the FCC's order.[234] In the Commission's July 1994 order permitting British Telecom to take a 20 percent ownership share in MCI, the Commission subjected the parties to certain reporting requirements.[235] In a follow-up order, approving BT's purchase of the remaining 80 percent of MCI, the Commission reaffirmed these safeguards and added requirements designed to preserve competition on the U.S.-U.K. route, including that MCI offer for sale some of its capacity on this route.[236] The Commission conditioned its approval of the MCI/WorldCom merger on two conditions: that

[229] Id.
[230] Id.
[231] Id. (footnotes omitted).
[232] McCaw/AT&T, 9 F.C.C. Rec. at 5928 ¶176.
[233] Id. at 5928–5929 ¶178.
[234] Id. at 5929 ¶¶182–184.
[235] BT/MCI I, 9 F.C.C. Rec. at 3965–3972 ¶39.
[236] BT/MCI II, 12 F.C.C. Rec. at 15,461–15,462 ¶286, 15,465–15,466 ¶297.

MCI complete the divestiture of its Internet assets prior to the close of its merger and that the transfer of MCI's direct broadcast satellite (DBS) license to WorldCom be subject to the outcome of pending applications for review of the initial license grant to MCI.[237]

Industry participants have quickly realized the importance of the merger review process. Each new license transfer application sparks a flood of comments asking for various new rules and requirements under the Commission's power to "condition." For example, the recent merger application of AT&T and TCI prompted a multitude of comments asking the Commission to impose local broadband unbundling, resale, interconnection, and collocation requirements.[238] In the local telephony context, this was done through bicameral legislation and notice-and-comment rulemaking; in the context of cable, commentators

---

[237] *MCI/WorldCom,* 13 F.C.C. Rec. at 18,026–18,027 ¶1.

[238] *See, e.g.,* Comments of America Online, Inc., at 45, Joint Applications of AT&T Corp. and Tele-Communications, Inc. for Transfer of Control to AT&T of Licenses and Authorizations Held by TCI and Its Affiliates or Subsidiaries, CS Docket No. 98-178 (FCC filed Oct. 29, 1998) (hereinafter *AT&T/TCI*) (arguing that "the fact that the specific safeguard proposed herein [an open access requirement] has not been promulgated pursuant to a formal notice-and-comment rulemaking or applied in a previous transfer application is of little consequence"); Petition of U S West To Deny Applications or To Condition Any Grant at iii–iv, *AT&T/TCI* (requesting the imposition of nine conditions, including local broadband unbundling, interconnection, and resale requirements); Comments of MCI WorldCom, Inc., at 4, *AT&T/TCI* ("[T]he Commission should condition approval of this merger on the implementation of equal access requirements, and compliance with obligations under sections 251(a) and (b) [of the 1996 Act] as well as the unbundling of the cable infrastructure."); Comments of Ameritech at 3, *AT&T/TCI* ("[T]he Commission should require AT&T: (1) to provide unbundled access to its fiber optic distribution network and to its hybrid-fiber-coaxial (or HFC) facilities; (2) to allow collocation of cable-modem termination equipment and fiber optic transmission interface equipment at *AT&T/TCI* headends; (3) to provide access to 'last mile' infrastructure to unaffiliated ISPs on a nondiscriminatory basis; (4) to offer for resale at wholesale rates advanced services and other programming services offered on an integrated basis using *AT&T/TCI* cable network facilities; and (5) to provide access to ducts, conduits, and rights-of-way controlled by *AT&T/TCI*. . . . The Commission should require *AT&T/TCI* and Liberty to provide alternative multichannel video programming distributors ("MVPDs") with access to video programming.").

argued it could be effectuated by nothing more than the Commission's unilateral power to impose conditions.

§7.6 Conclusion

The 1984 architects of the divestiture Decree assumed that AT&T would remain the leading manufacturer of telecom equipment and become a major rival of IBM's in the computer industry. But, in fact, AT&T made no headway in computers (it acquired and then spun off NCR) and recently divested its equipment arm, Lucent. Meanwhile, the number of central office switch manufacturers fell from 18 in the 1980s to six in the early 1990s.[239] Since the completion of its spin-off from AT&T in September 1996, Lucent has acquired seven smaller companies in order to consolidate and bundle its telecom equipment product and service offerings.[240] Nortel has pursued a similar strategy, purchasing or aligning with data, broadband, and wireless switch manufacturers.[241] Yet these trends notwithstanding, equipment

---

[239] See K. Hoyt, Decision Resources, in The World's Leading Telecommunications Equipment Companies 21-2 (Mar. 21, 1991); Michael Arellano & Gerald Arcari, Northern Business Information, in U.S. Central Office Equipment Market: 1994 Edition 127 (Oct. 1994). A study conducted by Arthur D. Little in the early 1990s concluded that "the 27 nameplates extant in 1980 have dwindled to 6 power centers in 1990." Hoyt, Decision Resources at 21-1.

[240] These companies include TKM Communications and Triple C Call Center Communications (call center integration), Octel Communications (voice mail), Livingston Enterprises (Internet connectivity), Prominent Corporation (LAN switches and routers), the LMDS Wireless Business of Hewlett-Packard (microwave radio technology), and Yurie Systems (ATM access technology and equipment for data, voice, and video networking).

[241] In January 1997, Nortel purchased 20 percent of Israel's largest telecom equipment manufacturer, Telrad. In November 1997, the company began its acquisition of Broadband Networks, a leading provider of broadband fixed wireless technology. In December 1997, Nortel purchased Sixtel, a supplier of enterprise network solutions in Italy, from Olivetti. In March 1998, the company bought Aptis Communications, a manufacturer specializing in access switches for network service providers, carriers, and Internet service providers. In May 1998, Nortel and Microcell, a Canadian personal communications service (PCS) provider, announced a joint venture to provide bureau services, software, hardware, and applications to wireless operators, enabling them to offer wireless Internet access and messaging. In the same

markets are more competitive than ever before. The old order maintained a one-to-one balance between monopoly providers of equipment and monopoly vendors of service; the new order permits a much smaller number of manufacturers to compete against each other worldwide. Lucent, Nortel, and Siemens compete fiercely for every sale to the U.S. market.

The service sector of the telecom industry has now entered a period of similar, equally profound restructuring. Even as the old monopolists are privatized, broken up, and unbundled, they themselves, and their upstart competitors, are forging new alliances to extend their networks geographically and their services vertically. Many niche players will continue to thrive in the new competitive environment. But it seems equally certain that there will emerge a fairly small number of truly global players—companies with the vast resources required to manage networks that span the globe. In terms of sheer bulk, these new transnational behemoths may well make yesterday's monopolists look quite small and tame. But the new network giants will not be monopolists; they will compete aggressively against each other.

The Commission occasionally acknowledges these trends. Large, national, and transnational business customers already occupy a discrete market of their own—as the Commission noted in its first BT/MCI order, a market for "Global Seamless Services"—that is of worldwide geographic scope.[242] Few enterprises will have the resources, scale, and international presence to compete on a truly global scale. The global-seamless-services market is necessarily limited to "only a handful of major competitors world-wide," the Commission acknowledges, because "[c]ompetition in these markets requires significant resources, which must extend throughout the world."[243] The Commission approved British Telecom's original investment in MCI and Deutsche Telekom's and France Telecom's investment in Sprint on the grounds, *inter alia*, that each of these alliances would add

---

month, the company acquired 33 percent of Photonic Technologies, an Australian optical network manufacturer.

[242] *BT/MCI I*, 9 F.C.C. Rec. at 3971 ¶51.

[243] *BT/MCI II*, 12 F.C.C. Rec. at 15,388 ¶¶91, 15,401 ¶130.

an additional player into the global seamless services market.[244] What is now becoming clear is that the global-seamless-services market is not just the market for transnationals like Daimler-Chrysler; it is the market for everyone. MCI started life as the provider of specialized services to large businesses, but it ended up redefining service for the mass market, too, and it is now the MCI/WorldCom/MFS/Brooks Fiber/UUNet conglomerate.

As was true of the equipment markets three decades ago, the structure of the telecom service industry today and the high market shares that some companies still hold are legacies of past regulation.[245] The existing separation of many of the major players in the industry is likewise a legacy of nonmarket forces, a reflection of bygone government choices, not of free-market evolution. The 1996 Act specifically removes barriers to entry and mandates competitor access in a host of well-considered, detailed ways based on Congress's predictive judgment that it is these prescribed steps that will make local markets as competitive as the underlying economics allow.

The antitrust laws place burdens of proof squarely on the government or private plaintiffs. This reflects the general presumption that it is harmful to condemn free-market transactions, including transactions that transfer control of business enterprises. In particular, freedom to change ownership has many benefits, including the capturing of operating and capital efficiencies and the securing of better management.[246] Such benefits readily include mergers involving monopolists; indeed, they

---

[244] See BT/MCI I, 9 F.C.C. Rec. at 3971 ¶51 (as "arguably . . . [the] first entrant" into the global-seamless-services market, the new BT/MCI alliance will have a "procompetitive . . . effect"); Sprint Corporation, Petition for Declaratory Ruling Concerning Section 310(b)(4) and (d) and the Public Interest Requirements of the Communications Act of 1934, 11 F.C.C. Rec. 1850, 1864 ¶¶84, 86 (joint venture among Sprint, FT, and DT will have a procompetitive effect as it will "add another significant competitor to this market").

[245] And for this reason, the history of concentration is a misleading predictor of the future. See 1992 Horizontal Merger Guidelines §1.521.

[246] See P. Areeda & L. Kaplow, Antitrust Analysis ¶503, at 801–806 (4th ed. 1988); 4 P. Areeda, H. Hovenkamp, & J. Solow, Antitrust Law ¶905d, at 32–33 (1998).

may be particularly important to a monopolist who is suddenly facing new competition in an industry with rapidly changing technology and market structures. Society loses by hampering such mergers in the absence of reliable proof of competitive harm.

The firms' judgments about their mergers, of course, as about all of their business options, may turn out to be wrong. But until there is reason to think that the government or courts can make these judgments better than market participants—whose individual employees may stake their careers on commitments to produce the benefits they have projected—the freedom to be incorrect is a vital part of what it means to have a free-market economy. Delaying and deterring such presumptively beneficial mergers in the absence of reliable bases for finding harm should be avoided.

8

Telecommunications Equipment[*]

§8.1 Introduction

The Bell System monopoly originated in patents on the telephone itself. Fittingly, equipment—the telephone itself—was
also the origin of the monopoly's demise. The equipment story
was mirrored in markets for enhanced services and replayed in
the market for long-distance service. Each of those markets is
discussed in a separate chapter, though the reader will notice significant overlap, particularly in the discussions of equipment
and enhanced services.

The deregulation of equipment has implications in service
markets, too. Local carrier services originate in equipment, of
course. Customer premises equipment is increasingly able to duplicate, and at competitive cost, the functionality that is available
from a carrier's central office equipment.

[*]This chapter was co-authored by Aaron M. Panner, Associate, Kellogg,
Huber, Hansen, Todd & Evans; Yale University (B.S., *summa cum laude,* 1986);
Harvard Law School (J.D., *magna cum laude,* 1995); Phi Beta Kappa; Law
Clerk, Honorable Michael Boudin, U.S. Court of Appeals, First Circuit,
1995–1996; Law Clerk, Honorable Stephen Breyer, U.S. Supreme Court,
1996–1997.

§8.2   Definitions

§8.2.1   Customer Premises Equipment (CPE)

Today, when a telephone may be bought for $10 in the corner drugstore, the definition of CPE and its separation from "the network" seems entirely natural and intuitive. It wasn't always so. When the Federal Communications Commission (FCC) first began to require the Bell System to permit competitive CPE to be interconnected with its network in the 1960s, the Commission balked at expanding the interconnection mandate to portions of the telephone "system": a system that included "the telephone set, usually located on the customer's premises."[1] It would take a decade before this initial effort to divide the network from customer-controlled terminal equipment would reach fruition once and for all.[2]

The 1996 Telecommunications Act provides that "[t]he term 'customer premises equipment' means equipment employed on the premises of a person (other than a carrier) to originate, route, or terminate telecommunications."[3] This definition was taken from the Bell Divestiture Decree, which defined CPE as "equipment employed on the premises of a person (other than a carrier) to originate, route, or terminate telecommunications, but [it] does not include equipment used to multiplex, maintain, or terminate access lines."[4]

Under the Decree (and presumably today), CPE included "complex" equipment, like private branch exchanges (PBXs) and key systems,[5] and computers that are "interconnectable to telecommunications facilities or used for communications functions"[6]

---

[1] American Telephone & Telegraph Co. "Foreign Attachment" Tariff Revisions in AT&T Tariff FCC Nos. 263, 260, and 259, Memorandum Opinion and Order, 15 F.C.C.2d 605, 606 (1968). *See* §8.4.1.2.

[2] *See* §8.4.1.

[3] 47 U.S.C. §153(14).

[4] Modification of Final Judgment §IV(E), *reprinted in* United States v. AT&T, 552 F. Supp. 131, 228 (D.D.C. 1982) (hereinafter Decree).

[5] *See* United States v. AT&T, 1982-2 Trade Cas. (CCH) ¶64,980, at 73,150 & n.4, 1982 U.S. Dist. LEXIS 15,262 (D.D.C. 1982).

[6] *See* Further Response of the United States to Motion of NYNEX Corporation to Provide Office Equipment and Related Services at 5, United States

—but only so long as the "customer" in question is not another carrier. A carrier, however, becomes an approachable "customer" when purchasing strictly for internal, noncarrier uses. A reseller of services is not considered a "carrier" if it uses equipment "in substantial part" for its own purposes.[7]

The development of a new generation of advanced services—for example, broadband access—may place renewed pressure on the equipment/service distinction as it is now understood. The capacity of the wires to carry information depends largely on the electronics placed at either end of the local loop. After industry standards have settled into place, it is perhaps not difficult to insist that the bandwidth-boosting electronics located on the customer premises be obtained quite independently from the complementary equipment located in the carrier's central office. But to keep pushing bandwidth higher and higher, carriers must keep venturing beyond what is standard. That quest will certainly be slowed by requirements that unnecessarily impede close coordination between providers of equipment at the two ends of the wire.[8] So far, however, the Commission has resolved to hold

---

v. Western Elec. Co., No. 82-0192 (D.D.C. Nov. 16, 1984). Judge Greene refused to say whether computers may be CPE and instead granted waivers permitting the BOCs to market computers. *See* United States v. Western Elec. Co., 604 F. Supp. 256, 265 & n.40 (D.D.C. 1984); Memorandum at 3–5, United States v. Western Elec. Co., No. 82-0192 (D.D.C. Apr. 22, 1985).

[7] Memorandum Order at 5–6, United States v. Western Elec. Co., No. 82-0192 (D.D.C. Apr. 11, 1985) (footnotes omitted). On the other hand, Judge Greene held that a BOC may not "sell telecommunications equipment to carriers or resellers which it has reason to know will be used for the performance of interexchange functions." *Id.* at 6 n.8.

[8] The 1996 Act imposes a similar dichotomy on cable providers. Section 629 of the Act requires the Commission to adopt regulations to ensure that cable converter boxes and interactive communications equipment can be offered by competitive vendors. Cable providers may continue to offer such devices, but only "if the system operator's charges to consumers for such devices and equipment are separately stated and not subsidized by charges for any such service." 47 U.S.C. §629. The Commission has compared section 629 to its *Carterfone* decision (discussed below at §8.4.1.2), stating that both embody policies "intended to result in the widest possible variety of [equipment] being commercially available to the consumer." Implementation of Section 304 of the Telecommunications Act of 1996, Report and Order, 13 F.C.C. Rec. 14,775, 14,785 ¶26 (1998). The Commission has indicated, however, that it will read this section 629 narrowly, such that it will not apply to

the regulatory line, which prevents the BOCs from providing equipment as part of a regulated, tariffed service.[9]

Semantic appearances notwithstanding, CPE need not actually be located on "customer premises"; by the same token, equipment on customer premises may not rank as CPE. A noncarrier, such as an information service provider, may collocate equipment in the telco central office that nonetheless remains "CPE." And phone companies are quite often called on to locate and operate full-fledged network switches on the premises of their very largest customers. Such switches are still "central office" equipment, not CPE.

§8.2.2 Inside Wiring

The dividing line between "inside" and "outside" wiring does not in fact depend on whether the wiring is inside or outside. Instead, the question is whether the wiring lies on the customer side or the telco side of the "demarcation point," a somewhat arbitrary point of interconnection between the network and the customer's equipment.

Under current regulations, the telco has some latitude in defining the demarcation point. In the case of single-unit installations, the demarcation point "shall be a point within 30 cm (12

---

cable providers that face effective competition. *See id.* at 14,812–14,813 ¶¶90–92. The cited order contains a discussion of the equipment aspects of cable regulation; for further discussion, see Implementation of Section 17 of the Cable Television Consumer Protection and Competition Act of 1992 Compatibility Between Cable Systems and Consumer Electronics Equipment, First Report and Order, 9 F.C.C. Rec. 1981 (1994).

[9] Confronted with an analogous problem in the late 1980s, the Commission decided to maintain the equipment/service line. The issue was whether BOCs would be required to detariff network channel terminating equipment (NCTE), complex equipment used to perform transmission, signaling, and network maintenance functions located on the customer's premises. The Commission decided to detariff, *i.e.*, treat the equipment as CPE. *See* Procedures for Implementing the Detariffing of Customer Premises Equipment and Enhanced Services (Second Computer Inquiry), Eighth Report and Order, 3 F.C.C. Rec. 477, 482, ¶38 (1988).

in) of the protector or, where there is no protector, within 30 cm (12 in) of where the telephone wire enters the customer's premises, or as close thereto as practicable."[10] In the case of multiunit installations, the requirements for the demarcation point depend in part on whether the wiring was in place as of August 13, 1990: if so, the sole requirement is that if there are multiple demarcation points within the premises, "the demarcation point for a customer shall not be further inside the customer's premises than a point twelve inches from where the wiring enters the customer's premises, or as close thereto as practicable."[11] For newer wiring, the telco may choose to set the demarcation point at the "minimum point of entry," that is, where the wiring crosses the property line or enters the building.[12] Otherwise, the premises owner may determine the location of the demarcation point or points for each customer so long as the demarcation point is not more than 12 inches inside the customer's premises.[13]

§8.2.3 Manufacturing

For purposes of its restrictions on BOC equipment manufacturing, the 1996 Act provides that "'manufacturing' has the same meaning as such term has under the AT&T Consent Decree."[14] The Court of Appeals for the D.C. Circuit ruled under the Decree that "manufacturing" covered much more than mere fabrication or assembly: it included design and development of equipment and development of software "integral to" the hardware.[15] This construction, the appellate court reasoned, advanced the "contemporaneous understandings of [the Decree's] purposes."[16]

---

[10] 47 C.F.R. §68.3.
[11] Id.
[12] Id.
[13] Id.
[14] 47 U.S.C. §273(h).
[15] United States v. Western Elec. Co., 894 F.2d 1387, 1390–1393, 1394 (D.C. Cir. 1990).
[16] Id. at 1389.

This 1990 ruling addressed what had been a long-running dispute. As early as 1985, AT&T had complained to the Department of Justice about BOC design and development of equipment.[17] The Department took no action until 1987, when Judge Greene demanded a report.[18] The Department then responded that AT&T's complaints presented "difficult[ ] definitional issues,"[19] because "there was no clear answer to the question of what activities—other than fabrication . . . —constituted 'manufacturing' under the decree."[20] Software presented a particularly difficult issue. The Plan of Reorganization (POR) gave BOCs the right to take over from AT&T the development of central-office switch software under certain circumstances,[21] and the BOCs had also been granted waivers to develop software of any type.[22] The Department itself would later argue to the appellate court that "the manufacturing prohibition does not apply to software, i.e., that the BOCs may engage in computer programming,

---

[17] See Letter from Jim Kilpatric, AT&T, to Kevin Sullivan, Dept. of Justice (Apr. 29, 1985).

[18] Order, United States v. Western Elec. Co., No. 82-0192 (D.D.C. May 19, 1987).

[19] Response of the United States Concerning Its Enforcement of the Modification of Final Judgment at 31, United States v. Western Elec. Co., No. 82-0192 (D.D.C. May 27, 1987).

[20] Id. at 37.

[21] See Plan of Reorganization at 339, United States v. Western Elec. Co., No. 82-0192 (D.D.C. Dec. 16, 1982) (assigning 2,000 software development and computer personnel to the BOCs' central staff organization); id. at 348–349 (provisions for BOCs to assume from AT&T continued software development for central office switches); id. at 429 (BOCs may "provide such software support for themselves"). In responding to comments on the POR, AT&T observed that the BOCs could "develop new computer based systems" after divestiture. AT&T Response to Objections at 512–523, United States v. Western Elec. Co., No. 82-0192 (D.D.C. Mar. 14, 1983). Judge Greene ultimately approved the POR—including the BOCs' software development activities—"as being consistent with the provisions and principles of the decree." Divestiture Decree §VIII(J), 552 F. Supp. at 232.

[22] See, e.g., Order at 1, United States v. Western Elec. Co., No. 82-0192 (D.D.C. May 24, 1985) (permitting BellSouth "to provide and market software and associated services . . . through a separate subsidiary"); id at 1–2, (permitting BellSouth's telephone companies "to provide software, operational support systems (including the use of data processing facilities to provide such systems), related services, and technical information, acquired or developed by the operating companies for their own use").

even where those programs are essential to the functioning of a telecommunications product."[23] AT&T has likewise agreed that BOCs may "work with manufacturers on ancillary modifications of commercially deployed software, as other customers do, to meet particular operating needs and feature requirements."[24]

In sum, the Decree definition, which has presumably been in some sense incorporated into the 1996 Act, seemed to pivot on the difference between software that is "integral" to the operation of hardware and software that is not. The distinction, however, may be more meaningful to lawyers than to software designers.

§8.2.4 Providing CPE

To provide CPE is to sell or lease it to a noncarrier end user. While the BOCs have always been permitted to provide CPE, the circumstances under which they may do so have been steadily liberalized. Restrictions remain, however; in particular, telecommunications carriers are still barred from bundling CPE with telecommunications service.

§8.3 Jurisdiction and Federal Preemption

It might seem obvious that nothing could be more local in the telecommunications world than customer premises equipment

---

[23] Brief for Appellee United States of America at 23, United States v. Western Elec. Co., No. 88-5050 (D.C. Cir. Sept. 1989). The earliest interpretation by the Department of Justice regarding the BOCs' authority to develop software held that the BOCs may develop software for their "own use," and even sell the software to others, provided they do not "provide ongoing maintenance or enhancement of the software to the third party." Memorandum of the United States at 22 n.*, United States v. Western Elec. Co., No. 82-0192 (Feb. 21, 1984).

[24] AT&T's Reply to Oppositions to Motion for Declaratory Ruling on Meaning of Manufacturing at 20 n.*, United States v. Western Elec. Co., No. 82-0192 (D.D.C. Sept. 8, 1987).

and inside wiring. In fact, the FCC has comprehensively pre-empted state regulation of CPE with the approval of the courts. The FCC also attempted to preempt state regulation of inside wiring, with somewhat less success.

As described in detail below, the FCC moved decisively in the mid-1970s to ensure that competitive providers of CPE would be permitted to interconnect their equipment to the public network. In so doing, the FCC was required to address state regulations that restricted connection of CPE to the local network. In *Telerent Leasing Corp.*,[25] the Commission preempted intrastate tariffs restricting interconnection of CPE. At issue were regulations in North Carolina and Nebraska that would have had the effect of restricting the interconnection of customer-owned equipment to the telephone network.[26] The Commission held that it had "primacy in authority over the terms and conditions governing the interconnection of customer-provided equipment to the nationwide telephone network. No State regulation can oust this Commission from its clear jurisdiction over interstate regulation of the terms and conditions governing such communication, including the right of subscriber interconnections."[27] The Commission rejected the argument that sections 2(b) and 221(b) of the Communications Act reserved to the states authority over use of CPE with intrastate services.[28] The Commission noted that

> because of the commonality of telephone company plant and facilities used to provide intrastate and interstate services and the indivisibility of such plant and facilities, rules governing

[25] Telerent Leasing Corp. et al., Petition for Declaratory Rulings on Questions of Federal Preemption of Regulation of Interconnection of Sub-scriber-Furnished Equipment to the Nationwide Switched Public Telephone Network, Memorandum Opinion and Order, 45 F.C.C.2d 204 (1974) (hereinafter *Telerent Leasing Corp.*).

[26] *Id.* at 204 ¶2. The proposed rule of the North Carolina Utilities Commission would have prohibited interconnection of customer-owned equipment with the telephone company's network. The Nebraska provision at issue was a letter from the state attorney general opining that the FCC's prior rulings did not prevent the telephone company from prohibiting the interconnection of customer-provided equipment for intrastate use. *Id.*

[27] *Id.* at 220 ¶38.

[28] *Id.* at 217 ¶32.

interconnection of customer-owned equipment must be the same for interstate and intrastate services. Here it is to be stressed that customer-owned equipment which is now available and in demand is either incapable of distinguishing between intrastate and interstate calls, or where such capability technically exists, it would make no sense from an economic or operational standpoint for the customer to arbitrarily confine its use to interstate service.[29]

As described above,[30] the Fourth Circuit affirmed.[31] Noting that if state regulations were permitted to restrict the use of CPE "contrary to the provisions of . . . any . . . interstate tariff, the commission w[ould] be frustrated in the exercise of that plenary jurisdiction over the rendition of interstate and foreign communication services that the Act has conferred upon it. The Commission must remain free to determine what terminal equipment can safely and advantageously be interconnected with the interstate communications network and how this shall be done."[32]

Soon thereafter, the FCC set up a registration program for CPE that established a highly permissive and exclusively federal standard for the equipment that could be connected to the public switched network.[33] This had the effect of preempting all state regulations and intrastate tariffs setting CPE network protection standards.[34] This was challenged in the Fourth Circuit, and while the court had ruled on the same issue a year earlier, it reached

---

[29] *Id.* at 218 ¶35.

[30] *See* §3.5.

[31] North Carolina Utils. Commn. v. FCC, 537 F.2d 787 (4th Cir. 1976).

[32] *Id.* at 793.

[33] *See* Proposals for New or Revised Classes of Interstate and Foreign Message Toll Telephone Service (MTS) and Wide Area Telephone Service (WATS), First Report and Order, 56 F.C.C.2d 593 (1975); Proposals for New or Revised Classes of Interstate and Foreign Message Toll Telephone Service (MTS) and Wide Area Telephone Service (WATS), Memorandum Opinion and Order, 58 F.C.C.2d 716 (1976); §8.4.1.2.

[34] Note that tariffs may still set forth interoperability standards. As described below, registration is intended to ensure that CPE will not harm the network; it does nothing to ensure that CPE will function as intended.

the merits of the jurisdictional issue again. And, again, the court ruled that the FCC had acted within its authority.[35]

To ensure that the market for CPE would be competitive, it was not enough to permit the connection of competitively provided CPE to the network; so long as the Bell System required customers to purchase certain equipment in conjunction with service, competitors faced a barrier to entry into significant portions of the CPE market. So in its *Second Computer Inquiry*, the Commission ordered the unbundling and detariffing of CPE, preempting any contrary state regulations.[36] On review, the D.C. Circuit upheld the Commission's broad preemption. Most CPE is used interchangeably for both interstate and intrastate communication; state regulation of CPE would therefore frustrate the Commission's decision that unfettered competition was in the public interest. "[W]hen state regulation of intrastate equipment or facilities would interfere with achievement of a Federal regulatory goal," the Court held, "the Commission's jurisdiction is paramount and conflicting state regulations must necessarily yield to the federal regulatory scheme."[37] And this principle holds even where the federal "regulatory scheme" is one of deregulation. "[W]e perceive no critical distinction," the Court explained, "between preemption by Title II regulation and preemption by the exercise of ancillary jurisdiction."[38] Although the Cheshire cat of federal regulation of CPE has faded, its preemptive grin remains.

As discussed below, following its *Second Computer Inquiry*, the FCC also unbundled and detariffed inside wiring.[39] The court of appeals overturned the FCC's order in part on jurisdictional

[35] *See* North Carolina Utils. Commn. v. FCC, 552 F.2d 1036 (4th Cir. 1977).
[36] *See* §8.4.3.1.
[37] Computer & Communications Indus. Assn. v. FCC, 693 F.2d 198, 214 (D.C. Cir. 1982).
[38] *Id.* at 217.
[39] Review of §§68.104 and 68.213 of the Commission's Rules Concerning Connection of Simple Inside Wiring to the Telephone Network and Petition for Modification of §68.213 of the Commission's Rules, Filed by the Electronic Industries Association, Report and Order and Further Notice of Proposed Rule Making, 5 F.C.C. Rec. 4686 (1990).

grounds.[40] The court held that the first half of this preemption order (requiring the states to "unbundle" the charges) had been sufficiently justified, but that the second (precluding the states from setting tariffs for inside wiring) had not.[41] On remand, the Commission decided to preempt state regulation that requires or allows telcos to bundle charges for simple inside wiring services with charges for tariffed services, but not to preempt state regulation that requires telcos to act as providers of last resort for inside wiring services.[42]

When CPE was first detariffed, the Bell System could provide CPE only through a separate subsidiary, but the Commission relaxed these restrictions after divestiture.[43] When the Commission granted the BOCs relief from the separate subsidiary requirements, the Commission also decided to preempt the states' ability to impose structural separation requirements on the CPE operations of the BOCs or other telcos.[44] The Commission explained that "because of the integrated nature of the telecommunications network, the services it supports, and the CPE used to originate and terminate both interstate and intrastate communications for customers, it is impossible for this Commission and a state to establish two conflicting regulatory regimes over structural arrangements for BOC provision of CPE."[45] Nor was the Commission willing to permit the states to impose more stringent safeguards on the independents than the Commission was imposing on the BOCs. The Commission did not, however, preempt the states from imposing on the independents nonstructural safeguards for customer proprietary network information

[40] NARUC v. FCC, 880 F.2d 422 (D.C. Cir. 1989).

[41] For a detailed discussion and criticism of this ruling, see §2.11.

[42] Detariffing the Installation and Maintenance of Inside Wiring, Second Further Notice of Proposed Rule Making, 5 F.C.C. Rec. 3407 (1990). *See also* Detariffing the Installation and Maintenance of Inside Wiring, Third Report and Order, 7 F.C.C. Rec. 1334 (1992) (adding additional refinements to scope of preemption ruling).

[43] *See* §8.4.3.

[44] Furnishing of Customer Premises Equipment by the Bell Operating Telephone Companies and the Independent Telephone Companies, Report and Order, 2 F.C.C. Rec. 143, 160 (1987), *on recons.*, 3 F.C.C. Rec. 22 (1987), *aff'd*, Illinois Bell Tel. Co. v. FCC, 883 F.2d 104 (D.C. Cir. 1989).

[45] *Id.* at 161.

(CPNI), network information disclosure, nondiscriminatory access to network services, and sales agency arrangements that are no more stringent than those developed for the BOCs.

Several states challenged the Commission's preemption order. The D.C. Circuit easily disposed of their contentions. The court noted that the intrastate and interstate elements of Centrex and like services "cannot be severed into discrete packages so as to permit separate state and federal regulation of the manner in which these services are marketed jointly with CPE."[46] Accordingly, the court concluded that "the Act permits the Commission to assert plenary jurisdiction over such marketing practices in service of a valid interstate objective, even to the point of preempting conflicting state regulation."[47]

§8.4 Interconnection of CPE

The market for CPE is largely deregulated. Equipment purchased from any source may be connected to the network so long as the equipment complies with certain basic safeguards. Regulatory protections have been put in place to ensure that local telephone companies cannot leverage whatever market power they possess to gain an unfair advantage in the market for equipment.

§8.4.1 The Slow Demise of Protective Tariffs

§8.4.1.1 The Establishment of the CPE Monopoly

For many decades, no competitive provider of telephone equipment was able to make a dent in the monopoly held by the Bell System and other local providers. The reason for this had

---

[46] Ill. Bell Tel. Co. v. FCC, 883 F.2d 104, 116 (D.C. Cir. 1989). For a full discussion of this aspect of the court's decision and the broader issue of preemption, see Chapter 2.

[47] Ill. Bell Tel. Co. v. FCC, 883 F.2d. at 116.

nothing to do with intellectual property rights, for Bell's patent on the telephone—perhaps the most valuable patent ever issued—expired in 1893. Indeed, the equipment side of telephony might have become vigorously competitive at that time: the technology was still in its infancy, telephone service was itself a competitive business, and end users were hungry for every possible improvement.

The Bell System, however, never cared to recognize the equipment market as a separate market. Bell did not sell equipment; it sold service. Its customers in turn bought service, and service alone—end-to-end service. Thus, Bell supplied not only the wires and switches of the network, but also all CPE and inside wiring. To freeze out alien CPE, Bell included within its tariffs various "foreign attachment" provisions that prohibited any non-Bell System product from being interconnected with Bell's network.[48] Such provisions were first incorporated in Bell company tariff schedules in 1913, but they appeared in private contracts with telephone subscribers as early as 1899.[49] The ostensible purpose of these provisions was to protect the physical integrity of the network.[50] Their practical effect, of course, was to eliminate all competitive suppliers of CPE.

---

[48] A typical such provision read as follows:

> No equipment, apparatus, circuit, or device not furnished by the Telephone Company shall be attached to or connected with the facilities furnished by the Telephone Company, whether physically, by induction or otherwise, except as provided in this tariff. In case any such unauthorized attachment or connection is made, the Telephone Company shall have the right to remove or disconnect the same; or to suspend the service during the continuance of said attachment or connection; or to terminate the service.

Jordaphone Corp. of America and Mohawk Business Machines v. American Telephone & Telegraph et al., Decision, 18 F.C.C. 644, 647 (1954) (hereinafter *Jordaphone*).

[49] Hush-A-Phone Corporation and Harry C. Tuttle, Complainants, American Telephone and Telegraph Company, et al., Defendants, Decision, 20 F.C.C. 391, 413 (1955).

[50] "Among the possible dangers to 'system integrity' posed by defective equipment might be erratic voltage generation on telephone lines, improper network control signaling, and poor service due to distortion of signals." Note,

For many years, the FCC accepted these provisions with hardly a murmur. Other telephone companies did the same thing after all—they had captive equipment affiliates, or they relied on long-term exclusive contracts for supply. The equipment and service halves of telephony were thus linked—if one was to be a monopoly, the other was, too.

Efforts to crack the monopoly by applying conventional antitrust law were unsuccessful so long as the FCC gave the system its imprimatur. For example, *Pastor v. AT&T*,[51] the first private antitrust case involving CPE, was decided summarily in favor of the Bell System in 1940. An inventor, Santos Pastor, had obtained a patent on an automatic dialer, which allowed "certain preselected call stations [to] be signalled by a single manipulation, pressing a button."[52] Pastor's 1927 offer to license his patent to Bell had been declined.[53] Twelve years later Pastor sued, claiming antitrust violations in Bell's policy against the "foreign attachment" of devices like his dialer to the network. The district court disagreed. Bell did not have a duty to deal with Pastor, and since Pastor had never manufactured any of his devices, he had not demonstrated any actual injury.[54] The court did state, however, that Pastor was "free to sell his patent [to] any other corporation or organization which may be interested in it or able to utilize it"[55] and suggested that others might then be able to press an antitrust claim further. But the court also stated that the next challenge to the foreign attachments policy should be presented to the regulatory commissions that had approved Bell's tariffs.[56] A series of subsequent CPE cases ended in much the same way.[57]

Competition in the Telephone Equipment Industry: Beyond *Telerent*, 86 Yale L.J. 536, 546 n.33 (1977).

[51] 76 F. Supp. 781 (S.D.N.Y. 1940).

[52] *Id.* at 782. At that time, about half of Bell System subscribers could dial their own calls directly rather than going through an operator.

[53] *Id.* at 784.

[54] *Id.* The district court also found that Pastor's suit was barred by the relevant statute of limitations. *Id.* at 784–785.

[55] *Id.* at 784.

[56] *Id.*

[57] *See, e.g.*, Carter v. AT&T, 365 F.2d 486, 498 n.23 (5th Cir. 1966) (citing Marcom, Inc. v. AT&T, No. 43215 (N.D. Cal. July 28, 1965); Western States

Plaintiffs repeatedly alleged that telcos had used foreign attachment and interconnection tariffs to block their businesses. Courts repeatedly ruled that regulatory agencies had "primary jurisdiction," so that the issues should be resolved first by the FCC and state commissions.

It took some time before the FCC seriously questioned the equipment monopoly. Instead, while the FCC had suggested as early as 1948 that the link between provision of equipment and provision of service might not be inextricable,[58] in the mid-1950s, the FCC took the foreign attachment provisions to ridiculous extremes.[59] In 1956, the Commission issued what was probably its most comical order: at issue was the "Hush-A-Phone," a metal device (packed with sound-muffling asbestos) that snapped onto the mouthpiece of the phone to provide some privacy and quiet in crowded office environments. Bell complained to the Commission that the Hush-A-Phone might muffle voices and lower the overall quality of telephone service; moreover, there was "no appreciable public demand" for the product.[60] The FCC agreed: "the unrestricted use of foreign attachments . . . may result in impairment to the quality and efficiency of telephone service,

---

Tel. Co. v. AT&T, No. 64-175-PH (S.D. Cal. July 28, 1964); Secra-fone v. Illinois Bell Tel. Co., No. 60C-1022 (N.D. Ill. 1961)), *cert. denied,* 385 U.S. 1008 (1967).

[58] In 1948, the Commission struck down foreign attachment provisions that required any device used to record a telephone call to be furnished, installed, and maintained (but not supplied, since Bell did not make any such devices) by the telephone company. *See* Use of Recording Devices in Connection with Telephone Services, Report to the Commission, 11 F.C.C. 1033 (1947). The Commission found that recording devices could in fact be used without causing "any perceptible effect on the functioning of the telephone apparatus or the quality of the telephone service"; all federal tariffs purporting to bar the use of recording devices were therefore rejected. *See id.* at 1036, 1053–1054.

[59] First, the Commission refused to extend the reasoning of the recording devices decision to the Jordaphone, a prototype answering machine. Unlike ordinary recording devices, the Jordaphone "opens and closes the telephone circuit." *Jordaphone,* 18 F.C.C. 644, 669. Although Bell had made no showing that the Jordaphone could harm the network, the FCC nonetheless determined that the Jordaphone would be used primarily with intrastate calls and should thus be left to state jurisdiction. *Id.* at 669.

[60] Hush-A-Phone Corporation and Harry C. Tuttle, Complainants, American Telephone and Telegraph Company, et al., Defendants, Decision, 20 F.C.C. 391, 397 (1955).

damage to telephone plant and facilities, or injury to telephone company personnel."[61] Foreign attachments would have to be analyzed one case at a time.[62] And after lengthy analysis, the Commission concluded that this particular snap-on cup would "be deleterious to the telephone system and injure the service rendered by it."[63] As a general principle, "telephone equipment should be supplied by and under control of the carrier itself."[64]

The D.C. Circuit sensibly reversed in a brief per curiam. The court found no support for the Commission's suggestion "that the use of a Hush-A-Phone affects more than the conversation of the user—that its influence pervades, in some fashion, the whole telephone system."[65] But the court went on to establish a principle of much wider significance: it affirmed "the telephone subscriber's right reasonably to use his telephone in ways which are privately beneficial without being publicly detrimental."[66] Moreover, the court explained, "[t]he mere fact that the telephone companies can provide a rival device would seem to be a poor reason for disregarding Hush-A-Phone's value in assuring a quiet line." And in a prescient observation, the court noted that "[t]he Commission's approach is well calculated to raise those very questions under the antitrust laws which petitioners seek here to raise, but which, in view of our decision, we do not reach."[67]

---

[61] *Id.* at 419.
[62] *Id.* at 420.
[63] *Id.*
[64] *Id.*
[65] Hush-A-Phone v. United States, 238 F.2d 266, 268 (D.C. Cir. 1956). In a passage tinged with sarcasm, the court explained:

> "Receiving impairment" is the term the Commission gives to the fact that the size and shape of some heads is such that if a Hush-A-Phone is held sealed to the mouth, the receiver will not be "well seated on the ear," so that the user will not hear as well what is said by the other party. The Commission does not indicate why a Hush-A-Phone user would keep the phone glued to his lips when listening rather than speaking. Nor does it appear why the user may not, as a matter of his own choice, impair his ability to hear in order to attain privacy of speech.

Id. at 269 n.10.
[66] *Id.* at 269.
[67] *Id.* at 268 n.9.

On remand, the FCC recognized the potential significance of the court's opinion. It accordingly directed Bell to permit its customers to use the Hush-A-Phone device and any other similar device that "does not injure defendants' employees or facilities, the public in its use of defendants' services, or impair the operation of the telephone system."[68] Future tariffs, the Commission warned, must distinguish "between the harmful and harmless" and avoid "encroach[ing] upon the right of the user to make reasonable use of the facilities furnished by the defendants."[69]

§8.4.1.2   The Crumbling of the Monopoly Edifice

The full implications of *Hush-A-Phone* were not realized for over a decade, when the Commission handed down its 1968 *Carterfone* decision.[70] At issue was a device permitting direct communication between a mobile radio and the landline network.[71]

---

[68] Hush-A-Phone Corp. and Harry C. Tuttle, Complainants v. American Telephone & Telegraph et al., Defendants, Decision and Order on Remand, 22 F.C.C. 112, 114 (1957).

[69] *Id.* at 113.

[70] Use of the Carterfone Device in Message Toll Telephone Services, Decision, 13 F.C.C.2d 420 (1968) (hereinafter *Carterfone*), *recons. denied,* 14 F.C.C.2d 571 (1968).

[71] When callers on the radio and on the telephone were both in contact with the base station operator, the handset of the operator's telephone was placed on a cradle in the Carterfone device. A voice control circuit in the Carterfone automatically switched on the radio transmitter when the telephone caller was speaking; when he stopped speaking, the radio returned to a receiving mode. A separate speaker was attached to the Carterfone to allow the base station operator to monitor the conversation, adjust the voice volume, and hang up the telephone when the conversation had ended.

Tom Carter, the inventor of the device, had sued the Bell System and GTE, seeking treble damages and an injunction establishing his customers' right to interconnect. He insisted he had "not attacked the reasonableness or validity" of telco tariffs "as a regulatory measure" and was "quite content to assume . . . that the tariff is valid under agency standards"; it was nonetheless a violation of antitrust standards. Carter v. AT&T, 365 F.2d 486, 492 (5th Cir. 1996) (quoting Appellants' Br. at 31). But a federal district court ruled that the FCC had primary jurisdiction "to resolve all questions relating to the justness, reasonableness, validity, and effect of the tariff and practices complained of." Carter v. AT&T, 250 F. Supp. 188, 192 (N.D. Tex. 1966). The Fifth Circuit

True to form, the Bell System objected to the device, but failed to demonstrate that it would harm the network. The Commission rejected Bell's argument. Instead, the Commission ruled that the basic principle of *Hush-A-Phone* applied: any form of CPE could be attached to the network "so long as the interconnection does not adversely affect the telephone company's operations or the telephone system's utility for others."[72] Unvarnished claims of threatened harm to the network would no longer suffice.

Technical problems aside, Bell had also argued that interconnection would have adverse economic effects and undercut universal service. But it had made no substantial effort to document the likelihood of such harms. "[E]conomic effects upon the carriers' rate structure might well be a public interest question," the Commission acknowledged, but "it is an issue, if a carrier seeks to raise it, to be decided upon the facts, i.e., will there be a 'cream skimming' effect, what will be the extent of it, and how does it weigh against the benefits of interconnection."[73] Thus, the Commission put Bell on notice that if it wanted to rely on such claims, it would have to document them thoroughly. Absent such support, Bell's tariffs forbidding attachments like the Carterfone would be rejected as unreasonable and (because Bell's own interconnecting equipment was approved for use) unduly discriminatory.

Even after *Carterfone*, the competitive providers of CPE did not have unfettered access to the network for a decade. Bell and other carriers responded to *Carterfone* by filing new tariffs, which permitted customers to connect *indirectly* to the telephone network an array of terminal equipment (including PBXs, key systems, computers, and private microwave systems) but only through telco-supplied interconnecting devices or "protective connecting

---

affirmed, Carter v. AT&T, 365 F.2d 486, and Carter then brought his complaint in the FCC.

[72] *Carterfone*, 13 F.C.C.2d at 424.

[73] Use of the Carterfone Device in Message Toll Telephone Service, Memorandum Opinion and Order, 14 F.C.C.2d 571, 573 (1968).

arrangements" (PCAs).[74] And any "network control signalling" devices — including the ordinary dial telephone — still had to be furnished, installed, and maintained by the telco.[75] The Commission turned aside the immediate challenges to these tariffs on the ground that although *Carterfone* permitted the interconnection of competitive CPE with the "telephone system," that "system" included "(1) the telephone set, usually located on the customer's premises; (2) the pair of wires, or loop, and its supporting structures, which connect the telephone set to the central office; (3) the switching equipment in the central office; and

---

[74] AT&T developed over 100 types of protective couplers between 1969 and 1976; over one million were installed before the FCC began its Part 68 registration program.

These PCAs became the focus of extensive antitrust litigation. In Litton Systems, Inc. v. AT&T, 700 F.2d 785 (2d Cir. 1983), *cert. denied,* 464 U.S. 1073 (1984), Litton had attacked the Bell System's PCA tariffs: Litton's principal argument was that "AT&T's bad faith opposition to certification standards drove Litton out of the telephone terminal equipment market in the interim period between the filing and the ultimate rejection of the tariff." *Id.* at 789 (citation omitted). The jury awarded Litton $276.8 million after trebling, and the appellate court affirmed, rejecting Bell's claims of antitrust immunity. The court held that Bell's PCA tariff filing had been a mere "sham," calculated to delay regulatory policies that had already been clear since *Hush-A-Phone* and *Carterfone. Id.* at 809–812.

This prompted a raft of me-too suits, with many plaintiffs hoping to invoke offensive collateral estoppel against Bell. For the most part, however, easy victories did not materialize. The D.C. Circuit declined to apply offensive collateral estoppel in a 1984 ruling. *See* Jack Faucett Assocs., Inc. v. AT&T, 744 F.2d 118, 124–126 (D.C. Cir. 1984), *cert. denied,* 469 U.S. 1196 (1985). Most other courts arrived at similar positions. Only one other court ended up giving preclusive effect to *Litton. See* Selectron, Inc. v. AT&T, 587 F. Supp. 856, 863–867 (D. Ore. 1984).

Ironically, the last PCA case reembraced the logic of the early cases and vindicated AT&T completely. Phonetele, Inc. v. AT&T, 889 F.2d 224 (9th Cir. 1989), *cert. denied,* 503 U.S. 914 (1992), worked its way through the courts in the late 1980s. Phonetele had manufactured a call-restricting device. The Ninth Circuit upheld the trial court's finding that Bell reasonably believed in the need for PCAs and had reasonably relied on regulatory decisions permitting them, even though those decisions were subsequently reversed.

[75] The particular services affected by the new tariffs were long-distance message telecommunications service or message toll telephone service, private line service, and wide area telecommunications service or WATS. American Telephone & Telegraph Co. "Foreign Attachment" Tariff Revisions in AT&T Tariff FCC Nos. 263, 260, and 259, Memorandum Opinion and Order, 15 F.C.C.2d 605, 605 (1968).

(4) the trunk facilities that connect central offices to each other."[76] *Carterfone* (the Commission reasoned) permitted interconnections with — but not substitutions or replacements for — the "system," expansively defined.[77] This substantially eviscerated *Carterfone*.

The Commission did not expressly approve the new tariffs, but it did not find them to violate *Carterfone* either. Instead, the Commission instructed the chief of the Common Carrier Bureau to begin informal discussions with telcos, interested manufacturers, user groups, and government agencies about the need for the various tariff restrictions.[78] These informal discussions quickly grew complicated with the convening of a Joint State-Federal Board, the commissioning of a scientific study on the requirements for network protections, and the commencement of a formal rulemaking proceeding.

In 1975, after this process had dragged on for seven years, the Commission abandoned definitional demarcations of the boundaries between the telephone system and the competitive world and finally set off seriously down the road to competition.[79] The vehicle was a request by a small carrier for a declaratory ruling that it need not permit the interconnection of customer-provided PBXs and key systems to the network.[80] The basic question, the Commission declared, is "whether any public interest reasons *now* exist for the applicability of our customer interconnection policy to depend on a distinction between interconnection devices which may constitute a substitution for telephone system equipment, such as PBX's and key systems, and other interconnected devices such as the Carterfone device."[81] Competition, the Commission now reasoned, would provide more

[76] *Id.* at 606.

[77] *Id.* at 609–610.

[78] *Id.* at 610–611.

[79] American Telephone & Telegraph Co.'s Proposed Tariff Revisions in Tariff F.C.C. No. 263 Exempting Mebane Home Telephone Co. of North Carolina from the Obligation to Afford Customers the Option of Interconnecting Customer-Provided Equipment to Mebane's Facilities, Memorandum Opinion and Order, 53 F.C.C.2d 473 (1975).

[80] *Id.* at 473–474. Mebane, as a connecting carrier, was included within the tariffs filed by Bell, and those tariffs required such interconnection.

[81] *Id.* at 476.

choice and lower prices. The Commission thus concluded that "the customer's right to interconnect" should not be limited "merely because the device he seeks to interconnect can be defined to constitute a substitution for telephone system equipment."[82] Thus, "the only question . . . is whether such interconnection would be harmful to the telephone company's operations."[83] And the affected telco had failed to allege any facts showing that interconnection of PBXs or key systems would be technically harmful.[84]

Later that same year the Commission solidified this progress by adopting Part 68 of its rules, discussed in the subsection to follow.[85] In essence, Part 68 provides that Commission standards for protective circuitry, rather than any protective tariff provisions limiting foreign attachments, will protect the integrity of the network. Various telcos and state utility commissions immediately challenged the new rules. The FCC was plainly wrong, they argued, in concluding that the costs of the registration program would be "minimal" and that the public benefits of liberalized interconnection would exceed the costs of implementing and complying with the program.[86] The loss of revenues from CPE would force major changes in rates for residential service presently subsidized by way of inflated prices for CPE.[87]

The Commission was affirmed, however, in a split decision by the Fourth Circuit.[88] The appellants were "confus[ing] the economic impact of the interconnection policy, which has been in effect since 1969, with the economic impact of the registration program."[89] The new registration program would merely do away

[82] *Id.*

[83] *Id.* at 477.

[84] *Id.*

[85] *See* Proposals for New or Revised Classes of Interstate and Foreign Message Toll Telephone Service (MTS) and Wide Area Telephone Service (WATS), First Report and Order, 56 F.C.C.2d 593 (1975); Proposals for New or Revised Classes of Interstate and Foreign Message Toll Telephone Service (MTS) and Wide Area Telephone Service (WATS), Memorandum Opinion and Order, 58 F.C.C.2d 716 (1976).

[86] North Carolina Utils. Commn. v. FCC, 552 F.2d 1036, 1052 (4th Cir. 1977). *See* §2.9.

[87] *North Carolina Utils. Commn.*, 552 F2d. at 1053.

[88] *Id.* at 1036.

[89] *Id.* at 1053.

with PCAs and network control signaling units (NCSUs).[90] There was no evidence that the underlying interconnection policy, in effect since 1969, had any adverse impact, and carriers had long insisted that PCAs and NCSUs were being priced at cost. It was therefore impossible to see how the registration program would have any significant economic impact.[91]

Early in the history of Part 68, the Commission permitted competitive installation and maintenance of complex inside wiring, defined at the time as wiring installations involving more than two access lines.[92] And in 1984, the Commission adopted section 68.213 of its rules, which allowed customers to connect simple inside wiring to the network.[93]

The particular regulations applicable to inside wiring have received some attention over the past few years as the Commission struggles to reconcile the differences between treatment of telephone inside wiring, on the one hand, and cable inside wiring, on the other. Historically, the two services have been treated differently.[94] The Commission has noted, however, that these differences may cause confusion and impede the development of

[90] *Id.*

[91] *Id.* at 1054.

[92] The Commission has since modified that definition to include installations involving more than four access lines. *See* Review of Sections 68.104 and 68.213 of the Commission's Rules Concerning Connection of Simple Inside Wiring to the Telephone Network, Order on Reconsideration, 12 F.C.C. Rec. 11,897, 11,899 ¶1 n.2 (1997).

[93] Originally, the Commission included several precautions in section 68.213, including requiring the subscriber to notify the telephone company in advance of any changes to inside wiring, requiring special testing to modified inside wiring, and giving the telco power to invoke special procedures if it believed that the Commission's rules were being violated. *See* Petitions Seeking Amendment of Part 68 of the Commission's Rules Concerning Connection of Telephone Equipment, Systems and Protective Apparatus to the Telephone Network, First Report and Order, 97 F.C.C.2d 527, 567–569 (1984). These special requirements were dropped in 1990. *See* Review of Sections 68.104 and 68.213 of the Commission's Rules Concerning Connection of Simple Inside Wiring to the Telephone Network, Report and Order and Further Notice of Proposed Rule Making, 5 F.C.C. Rec. 4686, 4701 (1990).

[94] For example, the demarcation point—that is, the point dividing the carrier's network from the customer's premises—has been set at a different point (in the case of cable, 12 inches outside the subscriber's premises; in the case of telephone, 12 inches inside). More significant, access to telephone inside

competition when cable operators and telephone companies are able to compete in the provision of both telephone and cable service—not to mention advanced services for broadband access to the Internet. The Commission has yet to resolve these issues.

§8.4.2   Part 68 Rules

Part 68 of the Commission's rules governs the terms and conditions under which CPE and premises wiring may be connected to the telephone network. The scope of the rules is very broad: with only limited exceptions, they purport to cover the direct connection of *all* terminal equipment used in conjunction with *all* services provided over the public switched telephone network (PSTN), as well as equipment used in conjunction with many private line services.[95] Notably, Part 68 is exclusively concerned with protection of the network. The operability, compatibility, and reliability of CPE are left to the market and may be addressed in carrier tariffs.

Part 68 also places obligations on carriers to disclose network information relevant to the interconnection of CPE. Thus, section 68.110(a) requires the telephone company[96] to provide "upon request" "[t]echnical information concerning interface parameters not specified in this part."[97] Section 68.110(b) requires carriers to inform customers of any network changes that might affect continuity of service; section 68.110(c) requires disclosure of information concerning customer premises wiring.

---

wiring is deregulated; cable operators may assert continued control over cable inside wiring prior to termination of service. *See* Matter of Telecommunications Services Inside Wiring; Customer Premises Equipment, Notice of Proposed Rulemaking, 11 F.C.C. Rec. 2747, 2748–2749 ¶3 (1996).

[95] *See* 47 C.F.R. §68.2(a). Private line services refer to services provided over lines that are leased to a particular party for nonswitched (i.e., point-to-point) use.

[96] This has been read to refer to all carriers. This is one example of the way that the language of Part 68 reflects the environment in which it was first drafted: the "telephone company" that the Commission had in mind was clearly the Bell System.

[97] 47 C.F.R. §68.110(a).

Under Part 68, before any equipment can be attached to the network, it must be registered.[98] Equipment is tested by the manufacturer or assembler itself; test results are submitted to the Commission along with the application for registration.[99] The Commission then issues a public notice of the application with a brief (five-day) period for public comments.[100] The application may be granted, granted with conditions, dismissed (if the application is defective, incomplete, or withdrawn or if the applicant refuses to provide requested information), or denied.[101] In addition, the Commission recently added procedures for revocation of registration in those cases where equipment registration was obtained through misrepresentation, where the registered equipment is shown to cause harm to the network, or where the registrant has "willfully or repeatedly" violated the terms or conditions of its registration or any other FCC rule or provision of the Communications Act.[102] In addition, the rules establish complaint procedures for violations of Part 68.[103]

The guts of Part 68 are technical parameters for the signals generated by terminal equipment.[104] These parameters are in-

---

[98] *See* 47 C.F.R. §68.102. Alternatively, the equipment may be connected through registered protective circuitry. The option of registering only discrete protective circuitry, rather than all terminal equipment, eliminates unnecessary documentation relating to total system design and performance criteria and thus removes the need for filing proprietary information with the Commission.

[99] *See* 47 C.F.R. §68.200. The FCC produces an extensive guide to application for registration of telephone and data terminal equipment, which is available on the FCC web site, <http://www.fcc.gov/Forms/Form730/730guide.pdf>.

[100] 47 C.F.R. §§68.202, 68.204.

[101] *Id.* §§68.206–.210.

[102] *Id.* §68.211.

[103] *See id.* §§68.400 et seq. Note that the complaint rules of section 1.700 of the Commission's rules are applicable only to complaints brought against common carriers. In the case where a common carrier discontinues service because of alleged harm to the network, the customer may bring a complaint pursuant to the Part 68 complaint procedure.

[104] *See* 1998 Biennial Regulatory Review—Modifications to Signal Power Limitations Contained in Part 68 of the Commission's Rules, Notice of Proposed Rulemaking, 13 F.C.C. Rec. 17,974 (1998). Equipment must comply with these rules even after being subjected to "environmental simulation"—

tended to ensure that those signals do not harm the network.[105] Potential harms to the network include electrical hazards to telephone company personnel and equipment, degradation of services, and malfunctioning of billing equipment. The technical parameters of Part 68 fall into three broad categories: signal power limitations;[106] transverse balance requirements;[107] and billing protection provisions in Section 68.314. In addition, Part 68 contains parameters governing the installation of simple and complex inside wiring in sections 68.213 and 68.215, respectively. Finally, Part 68 requires the use of standard plugs and jacks and sets forth those standards.[108]

The registration of conventional customer premises equipment that complies with the Part 68 parameters is entirely routine. Over 300,000 equipment models made by 11,000 different manufacturers have been granted registration since the program started in 1976.[109] In late 1998, the Commission decided that the process was sufficiently routine that it could be accomplished by an outside party, and the FCC accordingly adopted an order

---

vibration, shock, electrical charge, and other tests. *See* 47 C.F.R. §68.302. Notably, there is no requirement that the equipment still function after being subjected to those simulations.

[105] Strictly speaking, compliance with Part 68 creates a presumption that equipment will not harm the network and permits its use. If the telco finds that equipment harms the network or "reasonably determine[s]" that such harm is imminent, it may temporarily discontinue service, subject to certain procedural safeguards. *See* 47 C.F.R. §68.108.

[106] *See* 47 C.F.R. §68.308. Signal power limitations are designed to protect the network from crosstalk, noise, and other interference caused by excessive voltage or pulse amplitudes.

[107] *See* 47 C.F.R. §68.310. These limitations are also intended to prevent interference between adjacent channels sharing the same transmission path, i.e., "crosstalk."

[108] 47 C.F.R. §§68.104, 68.500 et seq.

[109] According to the FCC, about half of the registrations, representing $5 billion in factory sales, are for terminal equipment manufactured in the Pacific Rim countries; about 38 percent of the registrations, representing $2 billion in factory sales, are for equipment made in the United States. "Very few registrations are for equipment made in Europe, possibly the result of their higher labor costs." W. H. von Alven, The Federal Communications Commission's Telephone Equipment Registration Program Part 68—An Update <http://www.fcc.gov/Forms/Form730/730guide.pdf>.

permitting accredited private organizations—dubbed "Telecommunication Certification Bodies" or "TCBs"—to perform equipment authorizations "in essentially the same manner as the Commission."[110] At the same time, the Commission implemented "Mutual Recognition Agreements" on equipment testing with the European Union (EU) and the Asian Pacific Economic Cooperation (APEC) forum, which will permit equipment to be tested in the EU or in APEC countries for compliance with U.S. technical requirements. "To ensure parity between U.S. and [foreign] manufacturers, we will not permit parties in [a foreign] country to test and approve products to U.S. requirements until that country permits U.S. parties to test and approve products to its requirements."[111]

More complicated is the situation when customer premises equipment falls outside one or more of these parameters, either because it offers a new capability using existing network services or because it is designed to work with new network services. Under such circumstances, a manufacturer may seek a waiver, under section 1.3 of the Commission's rules, of the specific portion of Part 68 with which it will fail to comply.[112] The party requesting the waiver must demonstrate that no harm will come to the network through attachment of equipment for which a waiver is sought.[113] If the waiver is granted, the applicant must comply with all other provisions of Part 68.

In some cases, when new network services are offered and the equipment used in conjunction with such services does not

---

[110] *See* 1998 Biennial Regulatory Review, Report and Order, GEN Docket No. 98-68, ¶10 (Dec. 23, 1998). The Commission stated that its goal "is to discontinue granting routine non-controversial applications under Parts 2 and 68 of our rules when TCBs are available to perform the work," but the Commission declined to set a date for doing so. *Id.* ¶48.

[111] *Id.* ¶56; *see id.* ¶57.

[112] *See, e.g.*, Part 68 Waiver Request of Alameda Engineering, Inc., Order, 10 F.C.C. Rec. 12,135 (1995) (hereinafter *Alameda Engineering*). The usual "good cause" standard for a waiver applies. *See* WAIT Radio v. FCC, 418 F.2d 1153, 1157 (D.C. Cir. 1969). An applicant for a waiver must demonstrate that special circumstances warrant a deviation from the general rule and explain how the deviation will serve the public interest. *See* Northeast Cellular Tel. Co. v. FCC, 897 F.2d 1164, 1166 (D.C. Cir. 1990).

[113] *See Alameda Engineering*, 10 F.C.C. Rec. at 12,139 ¶21.

comply with some aspect of Part 68, the waiver procedure is cumbersome, and the registration procedures may be best honored in the breach. Ideally, the FCC attempts to keep Part 68 up to date, striving "to promote, on a nationwide and worldwide basis, rapid exploitation of [new] technology with minimum mandatory criteria for connection of CPE."[114] At the same time, given the pace of technological change (and of administrative proceedings), Part 68 has not remained current with changes in the network. Given the scope of Part 68, any equipment used in conjunction with any network service must be registered,[115] yet it may be impossible to produce customer premises equipment that complies with the current rules to be used in conjunction with new network services.

Although there is nothing in writing, the FCC has made a practice of looking the other way when equipment that does not comply fully with Part 68 is deployed in conjunction with new network services. Instead, the FCC has left it to the telco to include in its tariffs (intrastate tariffs usually) equipment standards that will protect the network. The reasoning behind this policy has been that the Part 68 rules are intended to open the market for equipment to competition, while protecting the network; public disclosure of standards by the telco keeps the equipment market open on an interim basis,[116] and the telco can presumably be relied on to protect its own network. Eventually, the Commission catches up, adopting new rules to cover CPE to be used in conjunction with the new service.[117]

---

[114] Proposed Rules, Connection of Customer-Provided Terminal Equipment to the Telephone Network, 59 Fed. Reg. 5166 (Feb. 3, 1994).

[115] *See* 47 C.F.R. §§68.2(a)(1), 68.102.

[116] The BOCs, for their part, are required to disclose relevant network information under the terms of the BOC Structural Relief Order, 2 F.C.C. Rec. 143 (1987), and the 1996 Act, 47 U.S.C. §§251(c)(5), 273(c)(1). *See* §§8.4.3.2, 8.7.1. In addition, all carriers are required under the terms of the FCC's rules and regulations to disclose to the public any information relating to network design affecting the manner in which CPE operates. *See* Amendment of Section 64.702 of the Commission's Rules and Regulations (Second Computer Inquiry), Memorandum Opinion and Order, 84 F.C.C.2d 50, 82–83 (1981); *see also* 47 C.F.R. §68.110(b).

[117] *See, e.g.,* Petition to Amend Part 68 of the Commission's Rules to Include Terminal Equipment Connected to Basic Rate Access Service Provided

The current situation with asymmetrical digital subscriber line (ADSL) and other digital subscriber line (xDSL) services is illustrative. There are no rules currently in place governing xDSL modems.[118] The appropriate standards are the subject of continuing discussions in industry fora, including the Part 68 industry meetings. Once the industry reaches a consensus on the appropriate standard,[119] it may petition the FCC for a rulemaking. At the same time, at least one manufacturer has already sought a waiver so that it may register an ADSL modem under Part 68.[120]

Part 68 also contains regulations, adopted pursuant to congressional mandate,[121] requiring certain telephones to be hearing aid compatible[122] and requiring most telephones to have volume control.[123] In a related vein, section 255(b) of the 1996 Act requires manufacturers of telecommunications equipment to "ensure that the equipment is designed, developed, and fab-

---

via Integrated Services Digital Network Access Technology, Report and Order, 11 F.C.C. Rec. 5091 (1996).

[118] *See* FCC Form 730 Application Guide, at A-2. By contrast, Part 68 (47 C.F.R. §68.308(b)(1)(viii)) has been applied to the much slower 56 kbps modems. U.S. Robotics was required to slow down its 56 kbps modem to operate no faster than 53 kbps. A. Rogers, *56-Kbps Modems Rarely Deliver 56 Kbps,* Communications Week (Feb. 1, 1997). U.S. Robotics has been in discussions with the FCC since January 1997 concerning relief to allow its modems to operate at a full 56 kbps. *U.S. Robotics Releases Preliminary Performance Data On Its High-Speed X2 Modem Technology,* http://www.3com.com/usrhistory/releases/103_82.html (Jan. 2, 1997).

[119] The standard in question is solely the signal characteristics required to protect the network, not the protocols to make equipment interoperable or compatible with various networks.

[120] *See* Northern Telecom Files Petition for Waiver, Public Comment Invited, Public Notice, NSD-L-98-135 (Dec. 11, 1998). The waiver application noted that xDSL systems "employ high-frequency spectral energy that can cause crosstalk interference in the PSTN" and therefore do not comply with section 68.308(e)(1) of the Commission's rules. Nortel's application states that its modem employs "power spectral density masks" that manage the potential for crosstalk. *Id.*

The catch to adjudication of this sort of a waiver is that the Commission must proceed with particular care because such a waiver is tantamount to a new rule: other manufacturers can seek the same waiver, and the Commission must apply the waiver standard in a consistent fashion.

[121] *See* 47 U.S.C. §610.

[122] *See* 47 C.F.R. §§68.4, 68.112, 68.316.

[123] *See id.* §§68.6, 68.317.

ricated to be accessible to and usable by individuals with disabilities, if readily achievable."[124]

§8.4.3 Beyond Part 68: Unbundling and Nonstructural Safeguards

When the Bell System was first permitted to provide nontariffed customer premises equipment, the Commission imposed a structural separations requirement to ensure that AT&T would be unable to cross-subsidize its equipment sales with its regulated communications services. In time, the separate subsidiary requirements were relaxed, and the Commission began to see that it could in large measure address the possibility that the BOCs might favor their own equipment operations over those of competitors by ensuring that all CPE providers had an equal ability to interconnect with the network.[125]

§8.4.3.1 Unbundling

One of the FCC's first tasks, however—and a policy that remains in place (for the time being)—was the unbundling of the provision of CPE from the provision of local service. In *Computer II,* the Commission concluded that the bundling of charges for CPE with rates for interstate services was thwarting the competitive provision of CPE. The provision of CPE, the Commission held, is simply not "communications common carriage," and CPE offered by common carriers should therefore be unbundled from transmission service. CPE costs were accordingly to be removed from a carrier's rate base and ultimately excluded from

---

[124] 47 U.S.C. §255(b). The FCC has initiated a rulemaking under this section of the Act. *See* Implementation of Section 255 of the Telecommunications Act of 1996, Access to Telecommunications Services, Telecommunications Equipment, and Customer Premises Equipment by Persons with Disabilities, Notice of Proposed Rulemaking, 13 F.C.C. Rec. 20,391 (1998).

[125] For an account of the rise and fall of structural separation in the CPE market, see M. Kellogg, J. Thorne, & P. Huber, Federal Telecommunications Law §§10.6–10.7 (1992) (hereinafter *FTL1*).

the jurisdictional separations process.[126] Once unbundled, the Commission determined that CPE should be detariffed to allow the provision of CPE to evolve on a competitive basis. The Commission declined to distinguish among various types of CPE. Deregulation was to be across the board to avoid any "artificial, uneconomic constraint on the design and use of CPE."[127] CPE was thus to be unbundled from transmission services; no carrier could sell CPE and transmission services as an indivisible package.[128]

Since its *Computer II* decision, the FCC has reduced the scope of the "network" (and correspondingly expanded the arena of competition) still further by unbundling and detariffing inside wiring.[129] Originally, all wiring, like all CPE, was owned, installed,

[126] Amendment of §64.702 of the Commission's Rules and Regulations (Second Computer Inquiry), Final Decision, 77 F.C.C.2d 384, 388 (1980) (hereinafter *Computer II*).

[127] "The continuation of tariff-type regulation over carrier-provided CPE," the Commission held, "neither recognizes the role of carriers as competitive providers of CPE, nor does it reflect the severability of CPE from transmission services. We conclude that CPE is a severable commodity from the provision of transmission services and that regulation of CPE under Title II is not required and is no longer warranted." *Id.* at 388.

[128] *Id.* The FCC has initiated a rulemaking to consider whether to modify the restrictions on the bundling of telecommunications services with CPE and enhanced services. *See* Policy and Rules Concerning the Interstate, Interexchange Marketplace, Further Notice of Proposed Rulemaking, 13 F.C.C. Rec. 21,531 (1998). That notice contained the Commission's tentative conclusion that "both the CPE market and the interstate, domestic, interexchange services market demonstrate sufficient competition that it is unlikely that non-dominant interexchange carriers could engage in anticompetitive behavior should the Commission allow the bundling of CPE" with domestic long-distance service. *Id.* at 21,538 ¶13. The details of any new FCC rules—for example, whether to allow package discounts, whether to require carriers to offer unbundled service, how to treat the provision of equipment for purposes of calculating universal service contributions, and even the reconciliation of any new rules with U.S. treaty obligations under the General Agreement on Trade in Services and the North American Free Trade Agreement (NAFTA)—are to be determined.

The Commission has also sought comment on whether it should make any changes with respect to bundling of CPE and local service. *Id.* at 21,536–21,547 ¶¶11–30.

[129] Review of §§68.104 and 68.123 of the Commission's Rules Concerning Connection of Simple Inside Wiring to the Telephone Network and Petition for Modification of §68.213 of the Commission's Rules, Filed by the Electronic

and maintained by the phone company, and the costs of the wiring were allocated between intrastate and interstate communications and then bundled into the respective rates for those services. The FCC order sought to open up inside wiring to competition by unbundling those charges and by detariffing inside wiring. Thus, as with the provision of CPE, the cost of installing and maintaining the phone wires in one's house is no longer included in the cost of your phone service, and when new wires are needed or the old ones wear out, competitive vendors may vie for the business.

The restrictions on bundling of CPE with services remain in place for all carriers, though the Commission appears poised to ease or eliminate some of these restrictions, at least in the case of interexchange carriers.[130] The bundling restrictions take on a heightened significance in the case of advanced services. For example, in the case of ADSL, the telephone company is barred from providing the CPE required to provide service as part of the service, thereby building the cost of the CPE into the cost of service.[131] Cable companies, which provide competing broadband service, may face similar restrictions under section 629 of the Act.

As an economic matter, if the service is competitive, all bundling should be permitted because there is no threat that dominance in a protected or regulated market can be transferred to the competitive marketplace.[132] It is for this reason that the effort to maintain the equipment/service distinction in the market for broadband access may itself be misguided: to the extent that incumbent local exchange carriers (LECs), competitive LECs, cable companies, and wireless companies offer genuine

---

Industries Association, Report and Order and Further Notice of Proposed Rule Making, 5 F.C.C. Rec. 4686 (1990).

[130] *See supra* note 128.

[131] Because the BOCs are required to disclose the network information required to build compatible ADSL equipment, the design of the CPE may be more complicated than necessary to protect the proprietary elements of the network. Several BOCs have sought relief from regulations that hamper their ability to compete on equal footing in the provision of "advanced services."

[132] For example, there is no restriction on bundling wireless telephones with wireless service.

choices to consumers in the market for broadband access, there is no purpose to be served by requiring one of those competitors to market its "service" and the equipment used to provide it separately. It would appear to be better for the consumer simply to permit all parties to compete to provide the best "turn-key" service at the lowest price.

§8.4.3.2 Nonstructural Safeguards

As noted, *Computer II* also included a structural separation requirement, but relief from that portion of the order was not long in coming. In 1987, the FCC explicitly predicated relief from separate subsidiary requirements for the BOCs on the adoption of "an effective set of nonstructural safeguards."[133] Aside from the accounting requirements, which it left to the joint cost proceeding, the FCC established such safeguards in four areas. The network information disclosure requirements and the requirement that all CPE providers have nondiscriminatory access to the network are designed to protect competitors' interconnection rights. In addition, safeguards related to the disclosure of CPNI—which are now imposed on all carriers by statute—and to the joint marketing of CPE and telecommunications services are intended to provide competitors with marketing opportunities equivalent to those of the BOCs.

(i) Disclosure of Network Information. The Commission established two sets of requirements concerning the disclosure of information about new or modified network services that might affect the interconnection of CPE.[134] A BOC that certifies that

---

[133] Furnishing of Customer Premises Equipment and Enhanced Services by the Bell Operating Telephone Companies and the Independent Telephone Companies, Report and Order, 2 F.C.C. Rec. 143 (1987) (hereinafter *BOC Structural Relief Order*), on recons., 3 F.C.C. Rec. 22 (1987), *aff'd,* Illinois Bell Tel. Co. v. FCC, 883 F.2d 104 (D.C. Cir. 1989).

[134] In *Computer II,* the Commission had required the BOCs to disclose network information when it was provided to their separate subsidiaries or to other entities for the benefit of their separate subsidiaries. 47 C.F.R. §64.702(d); Computer & Business Equipment Manufacturers Assn., Report and Order, 93 F.C.C. 2d 1226, 1244 ¶58 (1983). The BOCs were also required

it will not engage in CPE research, development, or design may not disclose such information to any unaffiliated entities that will engage in the research, development, design, or manufacture of CPE for the benefit of the BOC without making the information available to its CPE competitors at the same time and on the same terms and conditions. In addition, regardless of whether it discloses any information to an unaffiliated entity, the BOC must disclose such information to the public at a time reasonably in advance of implementation of the new or modified network service.[135]

Noncertifying BOCs are required to notify the CPE industry that a new or modified network service is under development when the BOC reaches the "make or buy" decision point on any product whose design affects or relies on the network interface. The notification must indicate that relevant technical and market information will be made available to any entity directly involved in the manufacture, design, lease, or sale of CPE.[136] Noncertifying BOCs must also publicly disclose technical network information and market information relating to a new or modified network service 12 months before its introduction.[137]

---

to disclose network technical and market information involving joint research and development by their network service providers and separate subsidiaries when the BOC decided to manufacture itself or procure from an unaffiliated entity any product the design of which affected or relied on the network interface—the so-called make/buy point. *Id.* at 1238, 1244–1245 ¶¶36, 58–59; Policy and Rules Concerning the Furnishing of Customer Premises Equipment, Enhanced Services and Cellular Communications Services by the Bell Operating Companies, Report and Order, 95 F.C.C. Rec. 1117, 1140 ¶60 (1983).

[135] *BOC Structural Relief Order,* 2 F.C.C. Rec. at 151 ¶53. These are equivalent to the safeguards established in *Computer II. See id.*

[136] The FCC decided to permit noncertifying BOCs to require the execution of nondisclosure agreements by entities receiving the network information after the make/buy point and before public disclosure. The FCC concluded that "the proprietary interests of network equipment manufacturers in the technical information supplied to the BOCs in connection with the development of new network services cannot be protected without such agreements." *Id.* at 151 ¶52.

[137] When the make/buy point occurs less than 12 months before the introduction of a new or modified network service, however, there will be only one disclosure obligation. When the BOC is able to introduce the service between 6 and 12 months after the make/buy point, public disclosure must occur at the

The BOCs' network disclosure obligations are not limited to those imposed in the structural relief orders; the latest word on network disclosure came in the Commission's rulemaking under section 251(c)(5) of the 1996 Act, which requires incumbent LECs to "provide reasonable public notice of changes in the information necessary for the transmission and routing of services using that local exchange carrier's facilities and networks, as well as of any other changes that would affect the interoperability of those facilities and networks."[138] The relationships of the various network disclosure obligations, primarily as they relate to enhanced services, are discussed in section 12.5.3 below.

(ii) Nondiscriminatory Access to the Network. The Commission placed great reliance on centralized operations groups (COGs) to ensure that the BOCs would not use their control over local bottleneck facilities to provide superior treatment to their CPE customers in the installation and maintenance of their network services.[139] The Commission required that COGs be maintained as organizations available to the entire CPE vendor community and to customers with non-BOC CPE as optional points for contact, installation, coordination, and administration with the BOC. The Commission required the BOCs to file non-discrimination compliance plans describing in detail the specific procedures they proposed using to ensure they would not discriminate in their provision of basic network services, including both installation and maintenance, to customers with non-BOC

---

make/buy point. When the BOC is able to introduce the service less than 6 months after the make/buy point, public disclosure must occur 6 months before the introduction of the service. Under the Commission's rules adopted pursuant to section 251(c)(5) of the 1996 Act, the planned changes may be provided less than 6 months before implementation if additional requirements set forth in section 51.333 of the Commission's rules are met. *See* 47 C.F.R. §51.331(a); Implementation of the Local Competition Provisions of the Telecommunications Act of 1996, Second Report and Order and Memorandum Opinion and Order, 11 F.C.C. Rec. 19,392, 19,490 ¶214 (1996). The timing requirements were adopted from the timing requirements for public notice under *Computer III*. *Id.* at 19,490 ¶214.

[138] 47 U.S.C. §251(c)(5).

[139] *BOC Structural Relief Order,* 2 F.C.C. Rec. at 155 ¶¶80–83.

CPE. These plans had to describe the operation of the COGs and how COG procedures prevent discrimination, as well as other procedures being proposed by the BOCs to prevent discrimination in the timing of their installation and maintenance of network services and in the quality of the circuits they provide. Finally, the Commission required the BOCs to file quarterly installation and maintenance reports, with installation and maintenance data segregated according to whether the end user possesses BOC-provided CPE or CPE provided by an independent vendor.[140]

On reconsideration, the Commission modified this last requirement somewhat after concluding that "there is little apparent likelihood that the BOCs can or will discriminate on the basis of the identity of the CPE vendor in the maintenance of network services."[141] Specifically, the Commission decided that each BOC could choose to file either the quarterly maintenance reports specified in the *BOC CPE Relief Order* or an annual affidavit, signed by one of its officers, attesting that the BOC has followed the maintenance procedures described in its compliance plan filings and that the company has not in fact discriminated in the provision of network maintenance on the basis of a customer's CPE vendor. The Commission noted that the BOCs' databases do not contain the CPE data necessary to generate the maintenance reports and that it would be counterproductive to institute a tracking or survey mechanism to obtain this information. In any event, the Commission reasoned, maintenance usually occurs well after the sale of CPE; there is therefore "little CPE marketing advantage to be gained by discriminating at the time when maintenance occurs. . . . While the BOCs conceivably could hope to gain some advantage in the CPE market place by establishing a reputation for providing superior network service maintenance to their CPE customers, it is highly improbable that

---

[140] *Id.* at 155 ¶84.

[141] Furnishing of Customer Premises Equipment by the Bell Operating Telephone Companies and the Independent Telephone Companies, Memorandum Opinion and Order on Reconsideration, 3 F.C.C. Rec. 22, 26 ¶29 (1987).

such a strategy could be made known to CPE customers without being discovered by their CPE competitors and this Commission."[142]

(iii) CPNI. Following the same model it used for AT&T, the Commission required the BOCs to make proprietary information concerning network customers available to competing CPE suppliers at the customer's request on the same terms and conditions as it is made available to BOC CPE personnel. When customers requested confidential treatment of their CPNI, the BOCs were required to limit access to this information to network services personnel with no involvement in CPE sales. The Commission also required the BOCs to notify their multiline business customers annually of the BOCs' CPNI obligations to ensure that these customers are aware of their rights.[143] Finally, to the extent that aggregate CPNI was provided to BOC CPE personnel and that such aggregated information did not disclose proprietary information, the Commission required the BOCs to make such aggregated CPNI available to independent CPE vendors on the same terms and conditions.[144]

These regulations were superseded by the 1996 Act and by the Commission's implementing regulations. Section 222 of the Act defines three categories of customer information—CPNI, which is individually identifiable information relating to a customer's use of services; aggregate customer information, which does not identify the characteristics of any individual user; and subscriber list information. Section 222 emphasizes privacy concerns in the case of CPNI and the free flow of information in the case of aggregate customer and consumer list information. In broad outline, section 222 and the implementing regulations prohibit

---

[142] *Id.*

[143] On reconsideration, the Commission explained that while it required the BOCs to notify their customers annually of their CPNI rights, a customer's request for confidential treatment of its CPNI need not be renewed annually to remain effective. The Commission also explained that a customer's request for confidential treatment of its CPNI may be made prior to the receipt of its first annual notification of its CPNI rights from the BOC. *Id.* at 22 ¶1.

[144] *BOC Structural Relief Order,* 2 F.C.C. Rec. at 153 ¶70.

the use of CPNI without the customer's permission except in limited circumstances. On the other hand, section 222 requires carriers to make aggregate and subscriber list information available on a nondiscriminatory basis.[145]

§8.4.3.3   Sales Agency Agreements

Finally, the *BOC Structural Relief Order* required the BOCs to provide independent CPE vendors with a meaningful opportunity to market their CPE jointly with Centrex and other BOC network services.[146] The Commission noted that the BOCs had portrayed their ability to offer their customers integrated CPE/network services packages "as one of the principal benefits of structural relief and their inability to offer 'one-stop shopping' as one of the most debilitating costs of the structural separation requirements."[147] If this was a benefit for the BOCs, the Commission concluded, then "the public will benefit by a requirement ensuring that similar opportunities be made available to independent CPE vendors."[148]

§8.4.4   *Pay Phone Interconnection*

When CPE was fully deregulated and detariffed in *Computer II*, the Commission made an exception for pay telephones. The Commission reasoned that while other CPE could be unbundled from basic exchange service, coin-operated pay phones were still integrated with the LECs' network facilities, and it concluded that pay phones should remain part of regulated basic communications service. This was because, at the time of the *Computer II* order, all coin-operated pay phones were controlled by the

---

[145] These rules are discussed in detail in §§5.4.3.1 and 14.5.2.

[146] The precedent for such a requirement had already been set in sales agency programs and in various other *Computer II* waivers that allowed the BOCs to engage in limited joint marketing if they provided independent CPE vendors with meaningful opportunities to engage in the same activities.

[147] *BOC Structural Relief Order,* 2 F.C.C. Rec. at 156 ¶90.

[148] *Id.* at 156 ¶91.

central office switch — the pay phones were "dumb," simply carrying out the instructions provided over the "smart" line from the switch. In other words, the switch, not the pay phone, determined how much money would be required to complete the call, how long the call could continue before additional coin deposit was required, and so on.[149] The Commission later extended this determination to coinless pay phones. Pay phones, in other words, were considered a service provided by the telco, not CPE.

At the time of divestiture, the Bell System pay phones were classified as exchange facilities installed by the BOCs for the provision of local service. The Decree therefore assigned all Bell System pay phones to the BOCs rather than to AT&T. However, the Decree court also required the BOCs to provide interconnection to pay phones provided by the interexchange carriers (IXCs). The occasion for the court's ruling was PacBell's effort to deny AT&T the opportunity to install pay phones at the Los Angeles airport during the 1984 summer Olympics.[150] Judge Greene ruled that such pay phones were an integral part of *interexchange* operations, and therefore the Decree required the BOCs to grant nondiscriminatory access.[151]

After divestiture, technology began to put pressure on the Commission's decision to except pay phones from the definition of CPE. Manufacturers developed "smart" pay phones, instruments that contain coin control and other supervision functions in on-board computers. Such telephones can be attached to the equivalent of an ordinary business line; the fact that the subscriber chooses to attach a pay phone to the line, rather than an ordinary telephone, makes little difference from the point of view of the network.[152] The Commission thus rightly revisited its

[149] Many local exchange carriers' pay phone operations continue to use dumb pay phones. Few independent providers do, for both historical and competitive reasons. Some LEC pay phone service providers (PSPs) have begun to make the transition to smart pay phones, but at least half the pay phones in use today are traditional dumb sets.

[150] United States v. Western Elec. Co., 583 F. Supp. 1257 (D.D.C. 1984).

[151] *Id.* at 1259.

[152] As we shall see, it does make *some* difference, but almost entirely because of regulatory restrictions that Congress has imposed on this market, not because of any fundamental difference in required network functions. Most states require pay phones to be connected to specially designated pay phone

decision to exclude all pay phone service from Part 68; Part 68 would apply to smart pay phones, and non-LEC providers would be permitted to interconnect smart pay phones with the public switched telephone network (PSTN).[153] The independent pay phone industry was born.

Until relatively recently, however, pay phones owned by LECs remained part of the network—that is, pay phones remained part of the local service rate base and were restricted (in most states) in what rates they could charge. Section 276 of the 1996 Act changed that by prohibiting LECs from subsidizing pay phone service from either intrastate or interstate basic telephone services[154] and prohibiting the BOCs from discriminating in favor of their own pay phone operations.[155] In addition, the Act explicitly preempts state regulations to the extent they are inconsistent with the regulations adopted by the Commission.[156]

Based on this mandate, the Commission has deregulated the pay phone industry. First, the Commission reclassified LEC-owned pay phones as CPE and required their transfer to unregulated status.[157] The Commission required LECs to tariff both

---

lines; rather than ordinary business lines. *See* Implementation of the Pay Telephone Reclassification and Compensation Provisions of the Telecommunications Act of 1996, Third Report and Order, CC Docket No. 96-128, n.389 (Feb. 4, 1999).

[153] The FCC determined in a later proceeding that the states, rather than the FCC, would regulate the rates and terms of pay phone interconnection. *See* Universal Payphone Corp., Memorandum Opinion and Order, 58 Rad. Reg. 2d (P & F) 76 (1988). The Commission also determined that the states retained authority over the rates, terms, and conditions of local and intrastate pay phone service. *Id.* at 80.

[154] 47 U.S.C. §276(a)(1) (as to BOCs), (b)(1)(B) (all LECs). The Act also directs the Commission to consider whether public interest pay phones should be maintained and to ensure that any such pay phones are supported "fairly and equitably." *Id.* §276(b)(2). The Commission left decisions about public interest pay phones to the states, requiring that any support for such pay phones be explicit—not based on subsidies—and competitively neutral. Implementation of the Pay Telephone Reclassification and Compensation Provisions of the Telecommunications Act of 1996, Report and Order, 11 F.C.C. Rec. 20,541, 20,677–20,683 ¶¶277–286 (1996) (hereinafter *Pay Telephone First Report and Order*).

[155] 47 U.S.C. §276(a)(2), (b)(1)(C).

[156] 47 U.S.C. §276(c).

[157] *Pay Telephone First Report and Order,* 11 F.C.C. Rec. at 20,611 ¶142.

"smart" and "dumb" pay phone lines at the state level[158] and to unbundle the features and functions necessary for pay phone service pursuant to the procedures established in the *Computer III* and open network architecture (ONA) proceedings.[159] BOCs were required to impose accounting safeguards and the other nonstructural safeguards of *Computer III* on their pay phone operations, but were not required to create separate affiliates[160] (though some have done so).[161] These determinations were affirmed in court.[162]

---

[158] Implementation of the Pay Telephone Reclassification and Compensation Provisions of the Telecommunications Act of 1996, Order on Reconsideration, 11 F.C.C. Rec. 21,233, 21,307–21,308 ¶¶162–163 (1996) (hereinafter *Pay Telephone Reconsideration Order*).

[159] *Id.* For a discussion of the tariffing and unbundling requirements contained in the *Computer III* and ONA proceedings, see §§12.5.1–12.5.3. Pay phone features and function are also required to satisfy the "new services test" under price caps. *See Pay Telephone Reconsideration Order,* 11 F.C.C. Rec. at 21,308 ¶163, n.492; 47 C.F.R. §61.49(g)(2). There has been controversy over whether certain elements of the tariff charges paid by PSPs must satisfy this test; in particular, independent PSPs have argued that local usage charges must satisfy the test, even when PSPs pay for local usage according to the same tariffs as other business subscribers. This issue is being litigated principally before state utility commissions and has yet to be resolved.

[160] *See Pay Telephone First Report and Order,* 11 F.C.C. Rec. at 20,640–20,644 ¶¶199–207. The FCC declined to apply nonstructural safeguards, aside from Part 64 cost allocation rules and Part 32 affiliate transaction rules, to non-BOC LECs. *Id.* at 20,641 ¶201.

[161] The Commission ruled that LECs transferring their pay phone assets to separate affiliates were required to value the assets at the higher of fair market value and net book value; according to the Commission, fair market valuation would "effectively capture[] on the carrier's books any appreciation in value of those assets, thus ensuring that any eventual gains would accrue to the benefit of the ratepayers and shareholders." *Pay Telephone First Report and Order,* 11 F.C.C. Rec. at 20,625 ¶166. The D.C. Circuit reversed. It held that because BOCs and GTE are subject to price caps, it was the shareholders, not the ratepayers, who bore the risk of a decline in asset value; they should therefore reap the benefit of increases in the value of such assets. Illinois Pub. Telecomm. Assn. v. FCC, 117 F.3d 555, 569–570 (D.C. Cir. 1997), *cert. denied,* 118 S. Ct. 1361 (1998).

[162] Illinois Pub. Telecomm. Assn. v. FCC, 117 F.3d 555; *see also* §8.6.2.

§8.5   Privacy and Law Enforcement—Equipment Issues

The preceding sections address rules aimed at facilitating the interconnection of communications equipment with the network. A mirror-image set of rules is aimed at making connections more difficult for unofficial snoopers, and easier for official ones. Chapter 13 discusses privacy and piracy laws that address human miscreants. But an additional body of laws and rules addresses how equipment must be designed to advance the twin, often contradictory, objectives of maintaining privacy and facilitating law enforcement.

§8.5.1   Surveillance

New technologies—including widely available wireless telephony and burgeoning digital telephony—have made surveillance both easier and more difficult. Congress has accordingly taken steps both to protect individuals' privacy from unauthorized snooping and to ensure that law enforcement can continue to snoop.

§8.5.1.1 Antisnooping

Section 2512 of the U.S. Criminal Code, the Electronic Communications Privacy Act (ECPA), makes it unlawful for any person to manufacture, assemble, possess, or sell any device "knowing or having reason to know that the design of such device renders it primarily useful for the purpose of the surreptitious interception of wire, oral, or electronic communications."[163] ECPA has been used to prosecute purveyors of bugs and other listening devices in the case of at least two chains of "spy shops" in recent years.[164] The statute's focus on those devices whose *design*

---

[163] 18 U.S.C. §2512.

[164] *See* United States v. Biro, 143 F.3d 1421 (11th Cir. 1998) (upholding conviction of purveyors of clandestine listening devices against challenge that

renders them *primarily useful* for surreptitious purposes indicates that "[t]he statute was not intended to prohibit the use of a device merely because it may be adapted to wiretapping or eavesdropping; by the same token, however, a device does not fall outside the ambit of the statute merely because it may have innocent uses."[165]

Specific antisnooping protections for cellular communications are contained in the Telephone Disclosure and Dispute Resolution Act of 1992.[166] That law required the FCC to promulgate rules making it unlawful to manufacture or import any radio scanner capable of intercepting cellular radio transmissions.[167] The Commission accordingly amended Parts 2 and 15 of its rules; it will no longer certify any devices of that kind.[168]

The efficacy of these measures is questionable. All cellular handsets are "scanners" in that they are designed to operate on different frequency channels as they move from cell to cell; cellular phones can therefore be converted to listening devices very easily. Ultimately, the conversion of all wireless systems to digital technology and the use of encryption will result in greater security for wireless communications.

---

the statute was vague as applied to them); United States v. Spy Factory, Inc., 951 F. Supp. 450 (S.D.N.Y.), *recons. denied,* 960 F. Supp. 684 (S.D.N.Y. 1997).

[165] United States v. Pritchard, 745 F.2d 1112, 1123 (7th Cir. 1984). *Compare* United States v. Schweihs, 569 F.2d 965 (5th Cir. 1978) (holding that an "ordinary amplifier" that "can be used in conjunction with radios, phonographs, and other audio equipment . . . is *not* primarily useful for the purpose of surreptitious interception of wire or oral communications) *with* United States v. Wynn, 633 F. Supp. 595, 603, 605 (C.D. Ill. 1986) (sale of telephone line amplifier modified with alligator clip hook-up leads supports conviction under section 2512).

[166] Pub. L. No. 102-556, 106 Stat. 4181 (codified at 15 U.S.C. §§5701, 5711–5712, 5714, 5721–5724, 47 U.S.C. §§227, 228, 302(a)).

[167] *See* 47 U.S.C. §302(d).

[168] The FCC declined, however, to extend the ban to frequencies occupied by similar services — for example, specialized mobile radio (SMR). The Commission also created exceptions for legitimate use by law enforcement personnel and for cellular operators who use them to test their systems. Amendment of Parts 2 and 15 to Prohibit Marketing of Radio Scanners Capable of Intercepting Cellular Telephone Conversations, Report and Order, 8 F.C.C. Rec. 2911 (1993).

§8.5.1.2   Government Snooping—CALEA

In the early 1990s, the FBI began to complain that certain technological developments were making law enforcement interception of telephone communications more difficult.[169] According to congressional testimony, among the problems—which are becoming more marked with the advent of digital switches—are interception of calls rerouted through call forwarding services, the inability to identify the destination of "speed-dialed" calls, and increasing trouble in isolating the communication stream associated with a particular target.[170]

In response, Congress passed the Communications Assistance for Law Enforcement Act of 1994 (CALEA).[171] CALEA requires telecommunications carriers to ensure that their "equipment, facilities, or services" used to originate, terminate, or direct communications are capable of enabling the government—pursuant to court order—to intercept, to the exclusion of any other communications, "all wire and electronic communications carried by the carrier within a service area" in real time.[172] The law also requires carriers to ensure that their equipment is capable of providing the government (again pursuant to court order) "call-identifying information that is reasonably available to the carrier."[173]

The House Report that accompanied CALEA stated that the intention of Congress was to preserve a balance among law enforcement needs, privacy interests, and technological innovation,[174] and a number of provisions in the Act are designed to

---

[169] *See* James X. Dempsey, Communications Privacy in the Digital Age: Revitalizing the Federal Wiretap Laws to Enhance Privacy, 8 Alb. L.J. Sci. & Tech. 65, 89 (1997).

[170] *Id.* at 90.

[171] Pub. L. No. 103-414, 108 Stat. 4279 (codified at 47 U.S.C. §§1001–1010 and scattered sections of 18 and 47 U.S.C.).

[172] *See* 47 U.S.C. §1002(a)(1).

[173] *Id.* §1002(a)(2). The law further provides that, with regard to information acquired under a pen register order, the call-identifying information "shall not include any information that may disclose the physical location of the subscriber."

[174] H.R. Rep. No. 827, pt. 1, 103d Cong., 2d Sess. 22 (1994).

limit the ability of the FBI to use CALEA as a license to reengineer the telephone network. Section 103(b) of CALEA explicitly states that the Act does not authorize "any law enforcement agency or officer" to require any specific equipment design or configuration or to prohibit the adoption of any equipment or service.[175] Instead, the Act calls for a process of consultation among law enforcement agencies and the telecommunications industry to establish safe-harbor compliance standards.[176] And the government or a private party may petition the Commission to establish such standards by rule.[177]

Following enactment of CALEA, the FBI attempted to have the dominant role in development of safe-harbor standards, but the industry has largely resisted the FBI's demands.[178] In late 1997, the Telecommunications Industry Association (TIA) and Committee T1, sponsored by the Alliance for Telecommunications Industry Solutions, published interim standards, declining to incorporate the FBI recommended changes.[179] In response to petitions for rulemaking and comments responding to a public notice, the Commission established a proceeding to evaluate whether the interim standard satisfied the statute's assistance capability requirements.[180] Additionally, the Commission extended

[175] 47 U.S.C. §1002(b)(1).

[176] Id. §1006(a)(2).

[177] Id. §1006(b).

[178] According to one commentator, the most significant concessions that the industry has made in the implementation of CALEA have been (1) to design cellular systems to provide information on customers' locations and (2) to provide the entire content of a packet-switched message to the government, even when the government is authorized to intercept only addressing or signaling data. See Dempsey, Communications Privacy in the Digital Age at 96–98. But cellular systems have to be designed to provide subscribers' locations under other FCC orders, see infra n.184 and accompanying text and the industry's agreement to provide the entire content of the packet-switched message appears to be a convenience for the industry—which is thereby relieved of the need to segregate the signaling information from the message content—rather than a concession to law enforcement.

[179] See Communications Assistance for Law Enforcement Act, Further Notice of Proposed Rulemaking, 13 F.C.C. Rec. 22,632, 22,639–22,643 ¶¶11–15 (1998).

[180] See id. at 22,643–22,645 ¶¶16–21. Congress explicitly gave the Commission this authority. 47 U.S.C. §1006(b). The Center for Law and Democracy (CLD), DOJ and the FBI, TIA, and the Cellular Telecommunications Industry Association filed petitions. The Commission also has initiated a rulemaking

the statutory compliance deadline for telecommunications carriers from October 25, 1998, to June 30, 2000.[181] A further obstacle to implementation of CALEA has been Congress itself. Section 109 of CALEA authorizes the FBI to pay for modifications to equipment to establish greater monitoring capabilities, but only "subject to the availability of appropriations."[182] Although the Act authorized appropriations of up to $500 million from 1995 to 1998 for implementation, in 1997 Congress refused to appropriate the allotted $100 million absent an acceptable implementation plan.[183]

Although CALEA does not require it, the FCC has required wireless service providers to modify their systems to enable them to relay to public safety authorities the cell site location of 911 callers. The FCC also ordered carriers to take steps over the next five years to deploy the capability to provide latitude and longitude information locating wireless telephone callers within 125 meters. Finally, the FCC proposed that, by the end of the same five-year period, covered carriers develop the capability to locate a caller within a 40-foot radius for longitude, latitude, and altitude, thereby permitting pinpointing a caller's location within a tall building.[184]

§8.5.1.3   More Government Snooping— Encryption Standards

One of the technological changes that has threatened the ability of law enforcement to gain access to communications is the

---

to establish implementing regulations. Communications Assistance for Law Enforcement Act, Notice of Proposed Rulemaking, 13 F.C.C. Rec. 3149 (1997).

[181] Petition for the Extension of the Compliance Date Under Section 107 of the Communications Assistance for Law Enforcement Act by AT&T Wireless Services, Inc., Lucent Technologies, Inc., and Ericsson, Inc. et al., Memorandum Opinion and Order, 13 F.C.C. Rec. 17,990 (1998). Again, the statute expressly authorizes this Commission action. 47 U.S.C. §1006(c)(1)–(4).

[182] 47 U.S.C. §1008.

[183] J. McGee, FBI Calls for Greater Wiretap Capability, Wash. Post, Apr. 30, 1997, at C13.

[184] *See* Revision of the Commission's Rules to Ensure Compatibility with Enhanced 911 Emergency Calling Systems, Report and Order and Further

development of so-called strong encryption. Encryption is the process by which data are transformed into an unintelligible series of bits—"ciphertext"—that can be read only by the use of a deciphering key. Encryption is accomplished by applying a mathematical algorithm to plain text.

With digital commerce making up an ever-increasing portion of the economy, the legitimate need for strong encryption is obvious. For example, encryption is vital to the banking system: by 1995, relying on a U.S. government-approved encryption system, the banking system processed daily "more than 350,000 messages with an estimated value of between $1 and $2 trillion."[185] Likewise, encryption is vital to ensure the security of electronic transactions carried over the Internet and to protect trade secrets and other confidential business—and personal—communications. Private access to strong encryption causes concern to the government on two levels, however. First, strong encryption can shield criminals' records and communications from the prying eyes and ears of law enforcement. Second, access to strong encryption technology may make the targets of intelligence efforts less vulnerable to U.S. signal intelligence capabilities.

Since 1993, the government has struggled to reconcile the needs of commerce and individual privacy with the needs of law enforcement. The focus of the Clinton administration's efforts has been the promotion of "key escrows," a system where the key to a code is deposited with a third-party escrow agent, where it is accessible to law enforcement under appropriate conditions. The Administration's initial effort to promote such a system was the so-called Clipper Chip,[186] but subsequent Clinton administration proposals have moved away from the promotion of a particular technology or encryption device or protocol. The main

---

Notice of Proposed Rulemaking, 11 F.C.C. Rec. 18,676, 18,682–18,664 ¶¶10–14 (1996).

[185] A.M. Froomkin, The Metaphor Is the Key: Cryptography, the Clipper Chip, and the Constitution, 143 U. Penn. L. Rev. 709, 719 (1995).

[186] The Clipper Chip used a secret algorithm and unique keys. The fact that the algorithm was kept secret raised suspicions that the algorithm was not well designed. In June 1998, however, the National Security Administration (NSA) released the algorithm—known as Skipjack—as well as the algorithm that permitted two Clipper-Chip-equipped devices to exchange keys in order to communicate.

manifestation of these policy developments has been changes in export controls over cryptographic equipment and software. Prior to 1996, most encryption was regulated under the Arms Export Control Act[187] and the International Traffic in Arms Regulations.[188] Most strong cryptographic products were placed on the United States Munitions List and could not be exported without a license. In 1996, however, the Clinton administration decided to significantly liberalize exports of strong crypto and permitting export of systems utilizing key lengths of up to 56 bits[189] with a license. In many cases, however, the granting of such a license was conditioned on the deposit of the key with a government-approved key escrow agent. In 1998, the administration decided to liberalize these rules further, permitting the export under license of cryptographic systems utilizing key lengths of up to 56 bits without any key escrow. For certain financial applications (and for overseas subsidiaries of U.S. firms), export of systems utilizing keys of unlimited lengths is authorized by the new interim regulations.[190]

While there are no explicit limits on cryptographic items produced for domestic consumption, some commentators have argued that because it is impractical for U.S. information technology companies to develop one cryptographic system for domestic use and one for overseas use, the government has used export controls as a way of creating de facto domestic limitations and key escrow requirements.[191]

A divided Ninth Circuit has struck down the Department of Commerce's export restrictions on cryptography[192] as an unconstitutional prior restraint on speech. In *Bernstein v. United States*,[193]

---

[187] 22 U.S.C. §2788.

[188] 22 C.F.R. §§120–130.

[189] The bit length of the key—the number of 1s and 0s that make it up—along with the complexity of the encryption algorithm, determines the strength of the encryption.

[190] *See* Interim Rule, Request for Comments, 63 Fed. Reg. 72,156–72,167 (Dec. 31, 1998).

[191] *See* Bernadette Barnard, Note, Leveraging Worldwide Encryption Standards via U.S. Export Controls: The U.S. Government's Authority to "Safeguard" the Global Information Infrastructure, 1997 Colum. Bus. L. Rev. 429, 445.

[192] 15 C.F.R. §730 et seq.

[193] 1999 U.S. App. LEXIS 8595 (9th Cir. May 6, 1999).

a computer scientist who wanted to publish—hence to export—an encryption program, challenged the export regulations. The district court held in his favor,[194] and the court of appeals affirmed. It held that "cryptographers use source code to express their scientific ideas" and that therefore "encryption software, in its source code form and as employed by those in the field of cryptography, must be viewed as expressive for First Amendment purposes.[195] The court went on to rule that the export regulations at issue—which permitted Bureau of Export Administration officials to deny an export license whenever "export might be inconsistent with 'U.S. national security and foreign policy interest'"[196]—constituted an unconstitutional prior restraint on speech because they "allow the government to restrain speech indefinitely with no clear criteria for review."[197] And the court warned that "[t]o the extent the government's efforts are aimed at interdicting the flow of scientific ideas (whether expressed as source code or otherwise), as distinguished from encryption products, these efforts would appear to strike deep into the heartland of the First Amendment."[198] Moreover, the court noted that "[g]overnment efforts to control encryption . . . may implicate not only the First Amendment rights of cryptographers intent on pushing the boundaries of science, but also the constitutional rights of each of us as potential recipients of encryption's bounty."[199]

[194] See Bernstein v. United States Dept. of State, 974 F. Supp. 1288 (N.D. Cal. 1997).

[195] Bernstein v. United States, 1999 U.S. App. LEXIS 8595, at **21–22 (footnote omitted).

[196] Id. at *16 (quoting 15 C.F.R. §742.15(b)).

[197] Id. at *33.

[198] Id. at **34–35.

[199] Id. at *36. The court invalidated the regulations in their entirety because it held that they were inseverable. Id. at ¶39.

Judge Nelson dissented because he was "inevitably led to conclude that encryption source code is more like conduct than speech" and that the plaintiff was therefore not entitled to bring a facial challenge to the regulation. Id. at ¶43.

The Ninth Circuit's decision is at odds with two prior district court decisions. In Junger v. Daley, 8 F. Supp. 2d 708 (N.D. Ohio 1998), the court held that "although encryption source code may occasionally be expressive, its export is not protected conduct under the First Amendment." Id. at 715. And the D.C. District Court had determined that the export control regulations were

§8.5.2   Antipiracy Regulations

The security of telecommunications not only matters for protection of the parties' privacy, but also is significant to protect communications and technologies that are in themselves valuable intellectual property. The issue arises most obviously in the context of cable and satellite television descramblers, but the law that has developed in these areas will inevitably develop a counterpart in the world of telephony, as valuable content is increasingly distributed over telephone lines to video monitors and computers.[200] Signal piracy already has its counterpart in the world of wireless telephony, where counterfeiters have gained unauthorized access to cellular service using cloned cellular phones.

The chief target of law enforcement efforts against cable piracy has been manufacturers and distributors of unauthorized signal decoders. Such cable pirates are subject to civil and criminal sanctions under section 605 of Title 47 and criminal sanctions under the Electronic Communication Privacy Act.[201]

Section 605(a) provides that "no person receiving, assisting in receiving, transmitting, or assisting in transmitting, any interstate or foreign communication by wire or radio shall divulge or

---

"narrowly tailored to the goal of limiting the proliferation of cryptographic produts and . . . . is justified." Karn v. Department of State, 925 F. Supp. 1, 10 (D.D.C. 1996), *remanded for further proceedings,* U.S. App. LEXIS 3123 (D.C. Cir. Jan. 21, 1997).

[200] Likewise, the well-publicized V-chip regulations will be of interest to the telecommunications industry. In the 1996 Act, Congress determined that "an apparatus designed to receive television signals" should be "equipped with a feature designed to enable viewers to block display of all programs with a common rating." 47 U.S.C. §303(x); *see id.* §330(c). In 1998, the FCC endorsed the television industry's voluntary "TV Parental Guidelines" and adopted technical rules requiring television sets with screens larger than 13 inches to be equipped with V-chip blocking technology. *See* Implementation of Section 551 of the Telecommunications Act of 1996, Report and Order, 13 F.C.C. Rec. 8242 (1998).

[201] 18 U.S.C. §§2510–2521. In one reported case, the government attempted to prosecute the distributor of unauthorized descramblers under 18 U.S.C. §1029, which prohibits traffic in "counterfeit access devices." The court of appeals overturned the conviction on this count, reasoning that use of the device did not result in a debit to any legitimate cable subscriber's account. United States v. McNutt, 908 F.2d 561 (10th Cir. 1990), *cert. denied,* 498 U.S. 1084 (1991).

publish" that communication, except as authorized.[202] Courts
have found that the prohibition against "assisting in receiving"
communications reaches the activity of those who manufacture
and sell unauthorized decoders.[203] Likewise, courts have accepted that the seller of a decoder "divulges" or "publishes" what
the device is used to intercept.[204]

The 1984 amendments to section 605 strengthened the sanctions against manufacturers of illegal decoders and created
section 605(e)(4), which provides a cause of action against manufacturers independent of section 605(a).[205] The 1984 and 1988
amendments to section 605 enhanced both civil and criminal

---

[202] 47 U.S.C. §605(a).

[203] See United States v. Beale, 681 F. Supp. 74 (D. Me. 1988) (no requirement that plaintiff prove interception); Communications Inc. v. Mogel, 625
F. Supp. 1194 (S.D. Fla. 1985) (same). The category of conduct deemed to
"assist" an unauthorized interception is broad; one defendant was convicted
for providing funds and equipment that enabled others to manufacture pirate
chips, as well as for encouraging them by his words and demonstrations.
Cable/Home Communications v. Network Productions, 902 F.2d 829, 849
(11th Cir. 1990) (holding that the First Amendment did not protect such conduct, as it was commercial speech related to illegal activity); ON/TV of
Chicago v. Julien, 763 F.2d 839, 843–844 (7th Cir. 1985) (defendant's intent
"to violate section 605 by actively encouraging the unauthorized interception
of . . . signals" need not be established in a civil case).

[204] National Subscription Television v. S& H TV, 644 F.2d 820, 826 (9th Cir.
1981); Chartwell Communications v. Westbrook, 637 F.2d 459, 465, 467 (6th
Cir. 1980).

[205] This amendment today is codified at 47 U.S.C. §605(e)(4):

> Any person who manufactures, assembles, modifies, imports, exports,
> sells, or distributes any electronic, mechanical, or other device or equip-
> ment, knowing or having reason to know that the device or equipment
> is primarily of assistance in the unauthorized decryption of satellite
> cable programming, or is intended for any other activity prohibited by
> [§605(a)], shall be fined not more than $500,000 for each violation, or
> imprisoned for not more than 5 years for each violation, or both. For
> purpose of all penalties and remedies established for violations of this
> paragraph, the prohibited activity established herein as it applies to
> each such device shall be deemed a separate violation.

Under "existing section 605 . . . those who 'assist' (including sellers and
manufacturers [of pirate devices])" are liable under section 605, and "this liability will remain undisturbed by [the] amendment"). H.R. Rep. No. 934, 98th
Cong., 2d Sess. (1984) (A-496 Ferris, Lloyd, & Casey).

penalties for intercepting scrambled (or otherwise privatized) video programming.[206] The standing of private parties to sue was expanded to "any person aggrieved."[207] Private actions may be brought by "any person with proprietary rights in intercepted programming," including "wholesale or retail distributors of satellite cable services."[208] The intent is to "encourag[e] inter-industry efforts to deal with piracy."[209] Nonetheless, the FCC estimated in 1991 that about 500,000 home dish owners still use illegal descramblers.[210]

---

[206] Any violation of section 605(a) is punishable by a fine of not more than $2,000, or imprisonment for not more than six months, or both. 47 U.S.C. §605(e)(1). If the violation of section 605(a) was for "purposes of direct or indirect commercial advantage or private financial gain," first offenders are subject to a fine of not more than $50,000, or imprisonment for not more than two years, or both. Subsequent offenses are punishable by a fine of not more than $100,000, or imprisonment for not more than five years, or both. 47 U.S.C. §605(e)(2).

A separate provision describes criminal penalties to be imposed on the manufacturer or seller of devices he knows are used primarily to violate section 605(a). Section 605(e)(4) stipulates that any such person shall be fined not more than $500,000 for each violation, or imprisoned for not more than five years, or both. 47 U.S.C. §605(e)(4).

Injunctive relief is available for any violation of section 605(a), upon bringing a civil suit in a United States district court or other court of competent jurisdiction. 47 U.S.C. §605(e)(3)(A).

For any violation of section 605(a), civil damages may be awarded.

The court may award actual damages and disgorgement of profits or statutory damages (up to $100,000), punitive damages of up to $100,000, attorney's fees, and costs.

[207] 47 U.S.C. §605(e)(3)(A); National Football League v. McBee & Bruno's, Inc., 621 F. Supp. 880, 887 (D. Mo. 1985) (discussing standing of copyright owners to sue under section 605).

[208] 47 U.S.C. §605(d)(6). This definition of "any person aggrieved" was added to clarify the standing of cable operators under section 605. See Showtime/The Movie Channel v. Covered Bridge Condo Assn., 881 F.2d 983, 985 (11th Cir. 1989) (explaining history of cable operators' standing under section 605).

[209] H.R. Rep. No. 887(II), 100th Cong., 1st Sess. 29 (1998), *reprinted in* 1988 U.S.C.C.A.N. at 5658.

[210] *See* Imposing Syndicated Exclusivity Requirements on Satellite Delivery of Television Broadcast Signals to Home Satellite Earth Station Receivers, Report and Order (Proceeding Terminated), 6 F.C.C. Rec. 725, 727 ¶14 (1991) (about "500,000 units have been modified to receive encrypted signals without authorization"). This number had grown rapidly since 1988, when Congress

The one major limit on liability concerns devices that can be used for both legal and illegal purposes.[211] Liability under both section 605(a)[212] and section 605(e)(4) requires intent; for instance, a violation of section 605(e)(4) depends on "knowing or having reason to know" that equipment will be used for piracy.[213] But if the only likely or plausible use of a gadget is piratical, the seller may not escape responsibility simply by exhorting buyers to be good, or pretending to hope that they will be.[214]

In addition to civil and criminal enforcement under section 605(a), producers and distributors of illegal signal descramblers are subject to prosecution under sections 2511 and 2512 of the U.S. Criminal Code. Section 2511 prohibits the intentional interception of "any wire, oral, or electronic communication," as

---

suggested that there were about 330,000 descrambler units "compromised by black market decoding chips." H.R. Rep. No. 887(II) at 28–29, *reprinted in* 1988 U.S.C.C.A.N. at 5657–5658. Unauthorized descramblers cost the satellite industry an estimated $100 million dollars per year. FBI: Turn in Illegal Satellite Decoders, Chi. Trib., Dec. 25, 1990, at 3. As of 1990, estimates indicated that from 50 to 80 percent of dish owners did not pay for the satellite programming they received. Inquiry into the Need for a Universal Encryption Standard for Satellite Cable Programming, Report, 5 F.C.C. Rec. 2710, 2714 ¶39 (1990); *see also* P. Lambert, SBCA: Programmers, Piracy, Compression, Broadcasting, Jan. 28, 1991, at 54 (a large, but unknown, number of dish owners pirate signals).

[211] Air Capital Cablevision, Inc. v. Starlink Communications Group, Inc., 601 F. Supp. 1568 (D. Kan. 1985) (dish antenna seller did not violate section 605 simply by selling a device capable of receiving unauthorized programs; salesman had no duty to tell the customer that he would violate the law by receiving unauthorizing signals).

[212] Shenango Cable TV, Inc. v. Tandy Corp., 631 F. Supp. 835 (W.D. Penn. 1986) (device that enabled subscriber to tape cable program on one channel while viewing another and restored remote control ability did not violate section 605(a) because it did not enable the user to receive channels he had not paid for or unscramble a cable signal.

[213] 47 U.S.C. §605(e)(4).

[214] ON/TV of Chicago v. Julien, 907 F.2d 152 (7th Cir. 1990) (use of disclaimer by seller of decoder kits does not defeat liability—defendant "could not simply include a disclaimer with the decoder kits when he sold them and thereby close his eyes to the fact that they were being used for an illegal purpose." Similarly, the claim that the decoders could be used for legal purposes did not defeat Julien's liability under section 605 when decoder kits were almost certainly assembled with illegal purpose).

well as the use or procurement of any interception device.[215] Section 2512 makes it illegal to "manufacture[], assemble[], possess[], or sell[] any electronic, mechanical, or other device, knowing or having reason to know that the design of such device renders it primarily useful for the purpose of the surreptitious interception of wire, oral, or electronic communications."[216] Uniform authority from the courts of appeals establishes that use and distribution of unauthorized descramblers can constitute a violation of sections 2511[217] and 2512.[218] Courts have rejected the argument that because cloned television descramblers are identical to legitimate descramblers, their design cannot be said to be primarily useful for the purpose of surreptitious interception of communications. "By cloning the computer chip of a legitimate descrambler and putting it into another descrambler, Defendant altered the design of the descrambler by making it non-unique. . . . [T]he sole purpose of the modification is to

---

[215] 18 U.S.C. §2511(1).

[216] *Id.* §2512(1)(b).

[217] United States v. Shriver, 989 F.2d 898, 901–902 (7th Cir. 1992) ("Based on this unambiguous language, one can only conclude that the use or encouragement of use of modified descramblers, if intentional, violates §2511."); United States v. One Macom Video Cipher II, 985 F.2d 258, 260 (6th Cir. 1993) (hereinafter *One Macom Video Cipher II*) ("[A]s claimant manufactured and used modified descramblers for the purpose of intentionally intercepting satellite television programming, he violated §2511."); United States v. Lande, 968 F.2d 907, 909–910 (9th Cir. 1992) ("A person who views satellite television programming by use of a modified descrambler and a satellite dish 'intentionally intercepts' the satellite television signal, which is an 'electronic communication.'") (footnote omitted).

[218] Two courts of appeals initially ruled that section 2512 did not apply to modified descramblers owned by or sold to owners of home satellite dishes, but both decisions have been overturned. *See* United States v. Hux, 940 F.2d 314 (8th Cir. 1991), *overruled by* United States v. Davis, 978 F.2d 415 (8th Cir. 1992); United States v. Herring, 933 F.2d 932 (11th Cir. 1991), *vacated,* 977 F.2d 1435 (11th Cir. 1992), 993 F.2d 784 (11th Cir. 1993) (en banc). *See also* United States v. Shriver, 989 F.2d at 905; *One Macom Video Cipher II,* 985 F.2d at 260–261; United States v. Harrell, 983 F.2d 36, 38 (5th Cir. 1993) ("We now join several other circuits who have previously found that the modified [Video-Cipher II] modules are primarily designed for electronic eavesdropping proscribed by §2512(1)(b)."); United States v. Splawn, 982 F.2d 414 (10th Cir. 1992); United States v. Lande, 968 F.2d at 910–911. *But see* United States v. Hochman, 809 F. Supp. 202 (E.D.N.Y. 1992).

permit the surreptitious interception of satellite television transmissions."[219]

Both sections 2511 and 2512 carry punishment of fines and imprisonment of up to five years.[220] In addition, section 2513 authorizes seizure and forfeiture of any device used, manufactured, possessed, or sold in violation of section 2511 or 2512.[221]

§8.5.2.1   Cellular Phone Piracy

Two types of cellular telephone piracy have been subject to prosecution under section 1029 of the Criminal Code, which prohibits the use of or traffic in "counterfeit access devices"[222] and which likewise prohibits use of or traffic in "a scanning receiver[ ] or . . . hardware or software used for altering or modifying telecommunications instruments to obtain unauthorized access to telecommunications services."[223] One type of piracy was known as "tumbling," a technique whereby a cellular phone would transmit a mobile identification number that did not correspond to an actual account, but that would nonetheless be put through. The second type of piracy involves the production of cloned cellular phones, in which a cellular phone's chip is erased and reprogrammed with the mobile identification number and electronic serial number of a legitimate subscriber's account, resulting in calls being billed to that legitimate subscriber.

Courts were divided on whether "tumbling" was subject to prosecution under that portion of section 1029 that prohibits use of a "counterfeit access device."[224] Congress therefore added section 1029(a)(8) in 1994 to close any loophole in the statute's coverage.[225] As for the use or production of cloned cellular phones,

---

[219] United States v. Splawn, 982 F.2d at 417.

[220] 18 U.S.C. §§2511(4)(a), 2512(1).

[221] *Id.* §2513.

[222] *Id.* §1029(a)(1).

[223] *Id.* §1029(a)(8).

[224] *Compare* United States v. Bailey, 41 F.3d 413 (9th Cir. 1994) (holding that tumbling falls within proscription on use of counterfeit access devices) *with* United State v. Brady, 13 F.3d 334 (10th Cir. 1993) (holding that tumbling does not involve access to an account).

[225] P.L. 103-414, §9; *see* H.R. Rep. No. 827, 103d Cong., 2d Sess. 31(1994), *reprinted in* 1994 U.S.C.C.A.N. 3489, 3511.

courts have held that such activity is prohibited by the statute's provision relating to counterfeit access devices, as well as by the provisions added by the 1994 amendments.[226]

§8.6 Equipment Pricing Issues and Pay Phone Compensation

§8.6.1 Interconnection Tariffs

As noted above,[227] in its Computer II inquiry, the Commission ordered the unbundling and detariffing of CPE—which means that equipment falls entirely outside of the tariffing mandate of Title II of the Communications Act. Though equipment is outside the ambit of tariffed prices, the interface itself is not. In sharp contrast with the policy for long-distance services (and also with pre-*Carterfone* Bell tariffs), regulators have opted not to impose interconnection charges in proportion to how much CPE a customer hangs onto the end of his or her telephone line. The customer may add any number of extension jacks, telephones, answering machines, and modems; the price of the line and its CPE interface does not change.[228]

One exception to this general rule is where the tariffs impose special charges to reflect CPE capabilities that may permit subscribers to avoid certain charges that they would otherwise incur. The classic example of this is the special-access surcharge imposed on users of PBXs to reflect their capacity to "patch" an interstate call to off-network destinations in the local exchange. Where a PBX is connected to an interexchange private line, the user has the capacity to carry interstate traffic without payment of access charges—a so-called leaky PBX. A special-access

---

[226] *See, e.g.,* United States v. Watson, 118 F.3d 1315 (9th Cir. 1997); United States v. Yates, 914 F. Supp. 152 (E.D. Ky. 1995).

[227] *See* §8.4.3.1.

[228] As a practical matter, the Commission would probably draw the line—as it has in the case of "private" cable service—if a subscriber attempted to create a do-it-yourself party line by connecting multiple dwellings to the same line. *Cf.* J. Thorne, P. Huber, & M. Kellogg, Federal Broadband Law §1.6.2.

charge is applied in such situations in lieu of per-minute access charges.[229] Another example is the FCC's tacit approval of state tariffs that require pay phone providers to purchase special pay phone access lines, rather than business lines, for the provision of pay phone service.[230]

Other proposals (not yet accepted by any regulator) have urged surcharges or usage-sensitive charges for customers who connect modems to residential phone lines because such equipment often entails much heavier usage of the line (and the switch beyond) than ordinary voice-related equipment.

§8.6.2 Pay Phone Compensation

Prior to the deregulation of pay phones in 1996, the coexistence of LEC and independent pay phones made little difference in the market for *local* pay phone calls. In most states, independent PSPs were required to charge the same rates as the LEC provider, so it made little difference to the caller whether the pay phone happened to be branded with a Bell or not.[231] When it came to the use of pay phones to make *long-distance calls,* however, independent PSPs, non-BOC LEC PSPs, and BOC PSPs were all treated differently. Independent PSPs generally presubscribed their pay phones to an interexchange carrier of their choice. The IXC would provide operator services to the pay phone for collect calls and calls billed to a calling card or a third party. The IXC in turn paid the pay phone provider a commission for all such calls. The independent provider might in turn

---

[229] *See* MTS and WATS Market Structure, First Order on Reconsideration, 97 F.C.C.2d 682, 868 (1984).

[230] *See* Implementation of the Pay Telephone Reclassification and Compensation Provisions of the Telecommunications Act of 1996; Implementation of the Pay Telephone Reclassification and Compensation Provisions of the Telecommunications Act of 1996, Third Report and Order, CC Docket No. 96-128, ¶183 (Feb. 4, 1999).

[231] It did mean, however, that in certain states where local rates were kept at $.10 into the 1990s—including many New England states—the independent pay phone industry was much slower to develop than in those states where the regulated rate was $.25 or where rates had been deregulated.

pass on a portion of this commission to the owner of the property where the pay phone was located, the "location provider."

BOC PSPs, on the other hand, were barred by the MFJ from receiving any compensation for interLATA (local access and transport area) calls, lest they run afoul of the interLATA line of business restriction. Thus, the presubscribed IXC would negotiate a commission arrangement directly with the location provider; the BOC PSP would receive no direct compensation for interLATA calls made using its pay phones. Non-BOC LEC PSPs, who had no interLATA restriction to contend with, could negotiate commission arrangements with IXCs for long-distance calls. And all LECs, BOCs, and non-BOCs received compensation through the carrier common line (CCL) charges; such CCL elements were intended to compensate the LEC for providing access to facilities used for interexchange traffic by the IXCs.

Non-BOC PSPs received commissions on all traffic sent from their pay phones to the presubscribed IXC, but this did not mean that they received compensation for all calls. By the mid-1980s, it was possible to reach an IXC other than the presubscribed IXC from a pay phone by dialing an access code (sometimes a five-digit 10XXX code, sometimes a seven-digit number beginning with 950, sometimes an 800 number). IXCs paid no compensation on such "dial-around" traffic. PSPs understandably began to block such access codes so that all long-distance traffic would be routed through the presubscribed IXC. The presubscribed provider, often a small operator services provider (OSP) who resold long-distance transmission services, would all too frequently charge exorbitant rates for such traffic. This led to a proliferation of complaints to the Commission and prompted the Commission to undertake a rulemaking to consider policies concerning OSPs.

The Commission's deliberations were interrupted by the passage, in 1990, of the Telephone Operator Consumer Services Improvement Act (TOCSIA).[232] In TOCSIA, Congress addressed the worst perceived abuses of the new, partially deregulated pay

---

[232] *See* 47 U.S.C. §226.

phone regime by imposing certain restrictions on both OSPs and pay phone providers and other "aggregators,"[233] such as hotels and hospitals. OSPs are required to identify themselves at the beginning of each call and to disclose, upon request, the rates that they charge.[234] Aggregators are required to post information regarding the provider of operator services and the address at the FCC where complaints can be made and to ensure that all the aggregator's phones permit access to 950 and 800 long-distance access code numbers. Moreover, the law requires that aggregators charge no more for such access "than the amount the aggregator charges for calls placed using the presubscribed provider of operator services."[235] Finally, TOCSIA requires OSPs to file informational tariffs.[236] TOCSIA also directed the FCC to engage in a rulemaking to enact regulations to protect consumers from abuses.[237]

---

[233] TOCSIA defines an "aggregator" as "any person that, in the ordinary course of its operations, makes telephones available to the public or to transient users of its premises, for interstate telephone calls using a provider of operator services." *Id.* §226(a)(2).

[234] *See id.* §226(b)(1)(A)–(C). An OSP is also required to bill only for completed calls (where this is possible) to ensure that it pays commissions only to aggregators who comply with their obligations under the Act and to avoid passing off calls to other OSPs who may be unable to determine the originating location of the call (a practice known as "call splashing"). *See id.* §226(b)(1)(D)–(I).

[235] *Id.* §226(c)(1)(C).

[236] *See id.* §226(c)(1)(A). The Commission designated several of these informational tariffs for investigation because they did not appear just and reasonable, but the investigations were dropped after the OSPs under investigation dropped their rates. *See* Billed Party Preference for InterLATA 0+ Calls, Second Report and Order on Reconsideration, 13 F.C.C. Rec. 6122, 6124–6125 ¶4 & n.13 (1998) (hereinafter *Billed Party Preference Order*).

[237] This led to the adoption of a report and order in 1991 that elaborated on TOCSIA's informational requirements, prohibitions on call blocking, and restriction on charges related to operator services. *See* Policies and Rules Concerning Operator Service Providers, Report and Order, 6 F.C.C. Rec. 2744 (1991) (adopting 47 C.F.R. §§64.703–.707, 68.318).

Later, after adoption of the 1996 Act, the Commission further strengthened the informational requirements by requiring OSPs to disclose orally to away-from-home callers how to obtain the total cost of a call before the call is connected. *Billed Party Preference Order,* 13 F.C.C. Rec. at 6123–6124 ¶1. The

In addition, TOCSIA directed the FCC to engage in a separate rulemaking to ensure that all aggregators would allow callers to "obtain access to the [OSP] desired by the consumer through the use of an equal access code," such as 10288 (10ATT), and/or that all OSPs should have a 950 or 800 access code number available for use anywhere in the United States. TOCSIA was not entirely one-sided, however. It also recognized for the first time that if independent pay phone providers were making their pay phones available to the long-distance companies, the FCC should at least consider the need to compensate the pay phone providers for the service. Congress therefore directed the FCC to "consider the need to prescribe compensation (other than advance payment by consumers) for owners of competitive public payphones for calls routed to providers of operator services that are other than the presubscribed provider of operator series for such telephones."[238]

In response, the FCC adopted a flat-rate compensation mechanism, in the amount of $6 per phone per month, divided among the carriers according to their shares of the interLATA toll market.[239] The FCC noted that a per-call mechanism would be preferable, but technically infeasible.[240] Subsequently, Sprint and AT&T certified that they could track calls and pay compensation on a per-call basis, and were permitted to do so, at the rate of $.25 per call.[241] In a subsequent notice of proposed rulemaking, the Commission tentatively concluded that all large IXCs were capable of paying compensation on a per-call basis.

Commission thus rejected the possibility of adopting a "billed party preference" approach, which would have permitted a person signing up for a calling card to select the OSP that would carry that customer's interstate pay phone traffic whenever that customer used the calling card. *Id.* at 6142–6143 ¶35. Of course, using access codes, callers can already accomplish this on their own.

[238] 47 U.S.C. §226(e)(2).

[239] *See* Policies and Rules Concerning Operator Service Access and Pay Telephone Compensation, Second Report and Order, 7 F.C.C. Rec. 3251, 3257 ¶41, 3262 App. B (1992).

[240] *Id.* at 3253 ¶13.

[241] *See* Policies and Rules Concerning Operator Service Access and Pay Telephone Compensation, Memorandum Opinion and Order, 10 F.C.C. Rec. 1590 (1994); Policies and Rules Concerning Operator Service Access and Pay

In adopting this compensation mechanism, the Commission concluded that subscriber 800 calls — calls made to 800 numbers assigned to a subscriber, rather than 800 access code numbers — were not within the class of calls for which Congress in TOCSIA directed the Commission to consider compensation.[242] The D.C. Circuit reversed this aspect of the Commission's order.[243] The court found no reason to distinguish the routing of access code and subscriber 800 calls and therefore remanded the issue to the FCC. Before the FCC could address the issue on remand, however, Congress again intervened by passing section 276 of the 1996 Act.

The TOCSIA compensation scheme had substantial gaps. It covered only interstate calls, leaving the question of compensation for intrastate calls to state regulators. As noted, it did not provide compensation for 800 calls. Moreover, access code calls routed to long-distance carriers that did not provide operator services fell outside the scope of the Commission's order.

§8.6.3   The 1996 Act and the Pay Phone Orders

Section 276 of the 1996 Act addresses the problems of compensation and competitive equity that existed under TOCSIA by requiring the FCC to establish regulations to ensure that "all payphone service providers are fairly compensated for each and every completed intrastate and interstate call using their payphone."[244] The Act gives the BOCs and all other LECs the right to negotiate on behalf of the location provider the terms of the contract with the presubscribed interLATA provider for the pay

---

Telephone Compensation, Memorandum Opinion and Order, 10 F.C.C. Rec. 5490 (1995).

[242] Policies and Rules Concerning Operator Service Access and Pay Telephone Compensation, First Report and Order, 6 F.C.C. Rec. 4736, 4764 (1991).

[243] Florida Pub. Telecomm. Assn. v. FCC, 54 F.3d 857 (D.C. Cir. 1995).

[244] 47 U.S.C. §276(b)(1)(A). Congress created exceptions to this rule only for emergency calls and telecommunications relay service calls for hearing disabled individuals. *Id.*

phone,[245] but preserves preexisting contracts between location owners and interLATA carriers.[246]

Based on this mandate, the Commission determined that to the extent possible the market should set the rate of compensation for all pay phone calls; only where the market cannot function properly should the Commission intervene.[247] The Commission therefore deregulated the local coin rate and preempted any state rate caps;[248] both decisions were upheld on appeal.[249]

The Commission similarly determined that PSPs should be compensated for long-distance calls pursuant to private agreement.[250] However, because of the limitations that TOCSIA places on the blocking of access code calls, the Commission determined that it was required to put in place a default compensation rate for such calls, especially access code and subscriber 800 calls, which would apply in the absence of a negotiated agreement.[251] The Commission decided that, in keeping with its deregulatory approach, it would attempt to set a per-call default based on a market surrogate.[252] It chose the local coin rate, reasoning that

[245] *Id.* §276(b)(1)(D), (E).

[246] *Id.* §276(b)(3). Prior to the passage of the Act, BOC PSPs were barred from negotiating for commissions from IXCs.

Recently, a group of small companies that provide long-distance service to Bell pay phones brought an antitrust case against Bell Atlantic for replacing their concededly high-priced long-distance services with MCI's lower-priced services. *See* IPSPCC v. Bell Atlantic Corp., No. 98-0127 (TPH) (D.D.C. filed Jan. 16, 1998). The district court denied a temporary restraining order and later a preliminary injunction on the basis that the Telecommunications Act of 1996 "contemplated" that the Bell companies, although prohibited from providing long-distance service at their pay phones, may nonetheless select and arrange for such service from other providers. *See* Order, IPSPCC v. Bell Atlantic Corp., No. 98-0127 (TPH) (D.D.C. Mar. 4, 1998).

[247] *Pay Telephone First Report and Order,* 11 F.C.C. Rec. at 20,564 ¶49.

[248] *Id.* at 20,572 ¶60.

[249] Illinois Pub. Telecomm. Assn. v. FCC, 117 F.3d at 561–563.

[250] *See* 47 C.F.R. §64.1300(a).

[251] *Pay Telephone First Report and Order,* 11 F.C.C. Rec. at 20,567 ¶49. The Commission noted that as a practical matter TOCSIA prevents PSPs from blocking subscriber 800 calls because there is no way for the PSP to distinguish between a subscriber 800 number (1-800-FLOWERS) and an 800 access code (1-800-COLLECT). *Id.*

[252] *Id.* at 20,577 ¶70.

"[i]f a rate is compensatory for local coin calls, then it is an appropriate compensation amount for other calls as well, because the cost of originating the various type of payphone calls are similar."[253] The Commission turned aside objections that the costs of local calls and coinless calls—like access code and subscriber 800 calls—are different.[254] The D.C. Circuit was not convinced. "The FCC failed to respond to any of the data showing that the costs of different types of payphone calls are not similar. Rather the FCC's Order proclaims that local coin calls versus 800 and access code calls are 'similar,' *without even acknowledging any of the contrary data*. . . . [This] epitomizes arbitrary and capricious decisionmaking."[255]

On remand, the Commission duly considered the data concerning cost differences and determined that the per-call costs of coinless calls were 6.6 cents less than for local calls; it accordingly set the default rate at the local coin rate minus 6.6 cents, $.284 during the first two years of the compensation scheme. The D.C. Circuit again reversed (though this time it left the rate in place pending the Commission's decision on remand), complaining that the Commission had failed adequately to explain the logic behind its avoided-cost methodology. In particular, the court questioned the Commission's failure to state explicitly that competition was keeping the local coin rate close to costs so as to ensure that the subtraction of avoided costs from the local coin rate was not a subtraction of "apples from oranges."[256]

The D.C. Circuit's decision in *Payphones II* is hard to reconcile with its decision in *Payphones I*. The court had concluded in the earlier decision that the Commission had reasonably decided that "market forces generally will keep prices at a reasonable level."[257] There is no difference, economically speaking, between

---

[253] *Id.* The Commission set the default rate initially at $.35, the deregulated local coin rate in four of the five states where the rate was set by the market. Since the local coin rate was deregulated in 1997, $.35 has become the predominant rate across the country.

[254] *Pay Telephone Reconsideration Order,* 11 F.C.C. Rec. at 21,268 ¶71.

[255] Illinois Pub. Telecomm. Assn. v. FCC, 117 F.3d at 564 (*Payphones I*) (emphasis in original).

[256] MCI v. FCC, 143 F.3d 606, 608 (D.C. Cir. 1998) (*Payphones II*).

[257] Illinois Pub. Telecomm. Assn. v. FCC, 117 F.3d at 562.

the conclusion that market forces keep prices at a "reasonable level" and the conclusion that prices will be close to costs. Thus, the court's statement that "this holding went to the Commission's decision to deregulate the coin call market, *not* to the question of whether coin call rates converge with costs,"[258] is, economically speaking, incoherent.

Nonetheless, the FCC backed down and calculated a per-call rate using a bottom-up methodology in its Third Report and Order.[259] The FCC now calculated the rate at $.24 per call[260] and observed that if it had calculated the rate using its former top-down methodology, it would have calculated an even lower rate—only $.23 per call.[261] In addition, the FCC "strongly encourage[d] the IXCs to develop targeted call blocking,"[262] which might permit a transition to a true market compensation rate, under which a PSP would presumably be free to charge IXCs whatever it wished for access to its pay phones (within the limits set by TOCSIA) and IXCs would be free to accept or reject calls from such pay phones. The Commission stopped short, however, of holding that it would mandate a transition to a market regime following the expiration of the current rate in 2002.

The problems with the per-call compensation mechanism do not end with the effort to set the rate. The FCC decided that IXCs, as the "principal economic beneficiary" of access code and subscriber 800 calls, should be responsible for tracking and paying compensation on all such calls.[263] However, in many cases, there is not a single IXC that handles a call; the call may be sent to one IXC's switch, transmitted on another IXC's lines, and routed through another IXC's POP. The FCC has never made it clear who has the obligation to pay on calls that are routed to resellers; while it has provided that "facilities-based" carriers are

---

[258] MCI v. FCC, 143 F. 3d at 608.
[259] Implementation of the Pay Telephone Reclassification and Compensation Provisions of the Telecommunications Act of 1996, Third Report and Order, CC Docket No. 96-128 (Feb. 4, 1999).
[260] *Id.* ¶191.
[261] *Id.* ¶193.
[262] *Id.* ¶67.
[263] *Pay Telephone First Report and Order,* 11 F.C.C. Rec. at 20,584 ¶83.

responsible for tracking and paying compensation,[264] it has also said that resellers with "switching capability" are responsible,[265] without defining these terms with any clarity. The issue is sure to generate controversy as IXCs and PSPs attempt to reconcile the per-call compensation payments.

§8.7   Industry Structure

Efforts to restrict local carriers' participation in the markets for equipment and enhanced services have not only raised intractable definitional problems, but also, more important, entailed unacceptably high costs in efficiency and innovation. Experience has shown that in many of these markets the local exchange carrier's position as the dominant provider of local service provides no advantage in parallel markets so long as certain relatively minor safeguards are in place. Accordingly, although the FCC long followed a pattern of placing strict structural restrictions on BOC participation in certain markets, these restrictions have eased over time and continue to ease.

The BOCs' relative freedom to provide equipment contrasts with severe restrictions on BOC manufacturing. Under the terms of the Decree, the BOCs were barred from manufacturing telecommunications equipment, but not from the provision of CPE. Section 273 of the 1996 Act takes the place of the Decree's manufacturing restriction. Section 273 makes explicit reference to the Decree and its interpretation,[266] and parties are sure to argue that even where no explicit reference is made, section 273 should be interpreted in light of the Decree restrictions. This section thus gives the history of the manufacturing restriction before describing section 273.[267]

---

[264] *Id.* at 20,586 ¶86.

[265] *Pay Telephone Reconsideration Order,* 11 F.C.C. Rec. at 21,277 ¶92.

[266] *See* 47 U.S.C. §273(h) ("As used in this section, the term 'manufacturing' has the same meaning as such term has under the AT&T Consent Decree.").

[267] *See also* §8.2.3 (discussing definition of terms under the Decree).

The history matters also because one cannot imagine any other reason for current manufacturing restrictions than perpetuation of some version of the status quo ante 1996. It is hard to take seriously the argument that the BOCs are in a position to gain any competitive advantage in the market for equipment, or that they could successfully engage in unfair self-dealing, in the absence of legal restrictions. But when the Bell System was intact, this was not the case; section 273—not unlike the Decree before it—thus visits on the sons the sins of the mother.

The exclusion of the BOCs from the market for central office equipment looks particularly odd in view of the tremendous concentration of that market over the last few years. This concentration has given rise to litigation over anticompetitive practices by equipment makers, though as yet none of the cases has proceeded to judgment. All of these suits related to concerns about carriers being locked into the equipment and proprietary software of the dominant manufacturers. In light of such concerns, a policy of discouraging new entry into the market seems increasingly anachronistic.

§8.7.1   The Origin of Manufacturing Restrictions

Like the market for CPE, the market for network equipment (the complicated switches and transmission facilities used to transport traffic between end users) might have become vigorously competitive right from the start. But Theodore Vail, master architect of the Bell System, was also a great master of exclusive dealing, and he brought the same philosophy to equipment that he brought to the network. The Bell exchanges, local or long-distance, were not going to interconnect with any other company's exchanges; by the same token, they were not going to buy anyone else's equipment. Manufacturing would be done in house. In time, the larger independent companies adopted similar isolationist philosophies for themselves.

In 1882, Bell acquired Western Electric, a successful manufacturer of telephone equipment and thereafter maintained the company as a separate, wholly owned subsidiary. Bell and Western immediately entered into a contract by which Western obtained the exclusive right to manufacture telephone equipment under the Bell patents and obliged itself to sell only to Bell. Between 1901 and 1913, Western also entered into standard supply contracts with the local Bell companies, contracts that facilitated Western manufacturing, purchasing, and supplying for the Bell System. In short order, Western Electric became Bell's principal developer, storekeeper, installer, repairer, salvager, and junker. In time, Bell and Western Electric eliminated competition from even foreign equipment manufacturers through agreements appointing Western Electric as exclusive sales agent for such manufacturers in the United States.

With these arrangements in place, Western Electric was positioned to dominate the telephone equipment markets to precisely the same extent that Bell succeeded in dominating the telephone network. It could hardly be otherwise. Every telephone line deployed or acquired by Bell would mean another telephone manufactured by Western Electric. All Bell traffic was to be routed over Bell lines, so Western Electric would also dominate the manufacture of cable and switches. As Bell extended and consolidated its monopoly over the network, Western Electric did precisely the same in the manufacture of telephone equipment. As the independent telephone companies folded, so, too, did the independent manufacturers of telephone equipment.[268]

---

[268] Ironically, the one procurement case to result in a finding of liability was brought by ITT against GTE, the largest independent telco, not against Bell. ITT v. GTE Corp., 351 F. Supp. 1153 (D. Haw. 1972) (*ITT v. GTE I*), aff'd in part and rev'd in part, 518 F.2d 913 (9th Cir. 1975) (*ITT v. GTE II*). (ITT also sued Bell, but the case was dismissed. ITT v. AT&T, 444 F. Supp. 1148 (S.D.N.Y. 1978).) ITT was then the world's second largest manufacturer of telecommunications equipment. GTE was the second largest manufacturer in the United States and the major supplier to non-Bell telcos. ITT attacked GTE's acquisitions of several equipment manufacturers and claimed that exclusive dealing between GTE's equipment arm and its telco subsidiaries had foreclosed the market for independent manufacturers like ITT.

A federal district court found GTE liable and ordered divestiture of various telephone companies. *ITT v. GTE I*, 351 F. Supp. at 1242–1248. The Ninth Circuit vacated this order on the ground that divestiture was not a remedy available to private plaintiffs under the Clayton Act, *ITT v. GTE II*, 518

There was thus established, from the very beginning, a fateful link between competition in the networks and competition in the manufacture of telephone equipment. There almost certainly was no "natural" monopoly for telephone equipment then, nor is there one today. Vail believed otherwise. "We found out that every manufacturer and every exchange man, if left to himself, would run off in different lines of development. . . . We found that by standardizing the apparatus, and having it as nearly alike as possible for all places, it would be a great advantage to the business generally."[269]

Vail's considerable early successes in expanding his network and freezing out competitors amplified the impact of his decision to deal nearly exclusively with the in-house Bell manufacturer. The government went along, either oblivious to what was happening or actively encouraging it. The exclusive dealing arrangements between Bell and Western Electric were not seriously attacked. And when the government tacitly endorsed monopoly in telephone operations, both local and long-distance, it unconsciously sealed the fate of competition in equipment

---

F.2d at 920–925, an interpretation of the Clayton Act subsequently rejected in California v. American Stores Co., 495 U.S. 271, 283–285 (1990). The Ninth Circuit also rejected the district court's definition of the relevant market as encompassing only the equipment purchases of non-Bell companies. *ITT v. GTE II*, 518 F.2d at 930–932. According to the Ninth Circuit, the market included Bell companies; nontelco customers, such as industrial and government users; and microwave common carriers. *Id.* at 932–934.

On remand, the district court found that GTE's self-dealing had foreclosed 7.4 percent of that market, too large a share under the circumstances. ITT v. GTE Corp., 449 F. Supp. 1158, 1178 (D. Haw. 1978) (*ITT v. GTE III*). The court noted that the market was already highly concentrated; that the foreclosure problem was not declining; that GTE intended to continue purchasing its own equipment exclusively, regardless of price or quality; that competitors had no alternative markets; and that entry barriers were high. Accordingly, the district court held GTE liable to ITT for damages. *Id.* at 1179–1184.

GTE has since sold its switch manufacturing operations to AT&T, which in turn spun off its equipment operations, creating Lucent Technologies.

[269] *See* Deposition of T. N. Vail, Exhibit C, Evidence for the Defendant, Western Union Tel. Co. v. AT&T (Boston 1909), *reprinted in* I Defendants' Third Statement of Contentions & Proof at 122, United States v. AT&T, No. 74-1698 (D.D.C. Mar. 10, 1980).

manufacture as well. Government authorities had worried end-lessly about the problem of two or more phone lines leading into each house, connecting to competing exchanges that did not connect with each other. In solving that problem, such as it was, government officials quite casually accepted equipment monop-olies as well.

§8.7.1.1 The 1956 Suit

Protected by franchise, the Bell System grew rapidly in strength and influence. Demand for telephone services mushroomed. Competition against the Bell System was against the law. Secure in its government embrace, the Bell System was operated in a benign spirit of public service and technological development. The years from 1913 until about 1950 were remarkably good for Bell.

Too good, in fact. The Bell System was already huge when Vail signed on with the government in the Kingsbury Commit-ment.[270] It continued growing inexorably thereafter.[271] While it was a fairly benign monopoly, it was a monopoly nonetheless and could be more than heavy-handed in its dealings with both com-petitors and customers. This attracted hostility, and inevitably government attention. Shortly after the FCC's formation in 1934, independent manufacturers caught at least one ear in the agency, which launched a massive investigation of the Bell Sys-tem. A report issued nearly five years later was sharply critical of Western Electric and recommended new efforts to open up Bell's equipment purchases to competitive bidding. In 1949, the Justice Department launched a major new attack on Bell's hege-mony.[272] Bell, the government claimed, had unlawfully monop-olized telephone equipment markets of every description. The company should be required to split Western Electric into three parts and to spin them all off into independent firms.

---

[270] For a discussion of the Kingsbury Commitment, see §4.2.
[271] *See* §1.6.
[272] *See* §4.3.

The federal government, however, was faced with a powerful opponent—itself. By 1949, the FCC had become a thoroughly servile agent of Bell's monopoly. Indeed, as discussed earlier in this chapter, only a year earlier the Hush-A-Phone company had approached the FCC for permission to sell a plastic telephone cup that would fit over the mouthpiece of a telephone receiver. The FCC gravely weighed the matter for seven years and then endorsed Bell's position that such a device threatened the integrity of the network.

This sort of thing was not going to help lawyers down the street at the Antitrust Division. After all, if "foreign attachments" truly threatened the reliable operation of the vast Bell network when they consisted of a cup that slipped on the mouthpiece of a telephone, who could question the Bell System's need to maintain absolute control over the manufacture of highly complex switches and high-capacity transmission trunks? If the FCC was even arguably right in its *Hush-A-Phone* decision, then the Department of Justice was almost surely wrong in its claim that non-Bell equipment could be mixed and matched in the heart of the network without difficulty. The nominal defendant in the antitrust suit was the Bell System, but the unnamed and unindicted co-conspirators were clearly the FCC and its siblings in state regulatory circles. The government was really suing itself.

The government was thus assured of one victory and one defeat, both of which materialized on January 24, 1956, after seven years of wasted effort. The Bell corporate empire—network, manufacturing, and all—was left intact. All the government had won was two new quarantines, which—at that time—had no substance and served no purpose other than to save face for Justice Department lawyers. One of these covered equipment. The Bell telephone companies could continue to buy any and all of their equipment from Western Electric. There was not even any mention of competition in terminal equipment of the kind that brought Hush-A-Phone to court the following year. Bell was, however, required to grant nonexclusive licenses under all existing and future Bell equipment patents to all applicants—in exchange for "reasonable" royalties and reciprocal licenses. The 1956 Decree allowed any applicant that was unable to secure reasonable licensing terms to apply to the district court "for the determination of reasonable royalties and other terms. . . ."[273] Bell was also solemnly prohibited from acquiring any other telephone equipment manufacturer, a laughable restriction for a company that already owned an all but absolute and unchallengeable monopoly in the business.

Finally, subject to a few specific exceptions, Western Electric was barred from manufacturing any type of equipment not sold or leased for use within the Bell System's regulated domain. Since telephone regulation had already been extended to the manufacture of plastic cups that fitted on the end of telephones and to plastic slipcovers that could be used to improve the appearance of the "official" telephone book, this did not look like much of a restraint. Even so, this concession would prove to be hugely important. In 1956, three Bell Labs scientists would travel to Stockholm to collect a Nobel Prize for their discovery of the transistor. The transistor would create the modern computer industry. But Bell, the discoverer of the device, would have to leave that industry to others. The ultimate result was a second near-monopoly, this time in the computer industry, and a second (equally futile) antitrust suit by the Department that sought to break up IBM.[274]

In the years after the 1956 settlement, the FCC would make no further attempt to promote competition in the provision of central office and network equipment. What little it did was aimed at containing the monopoly and at checking up on the prices paid by service companies to their equipment manufacturing affiliates. With the FCC's tacit approval, Bell rejected competitive bidding for central office and other major communication equipment items: nonprice factors, such as product performance, features, design, and quality, were accepted as essential in making procurement decisions. The FCC did claim the

---

[273] 1956 Decree §X(B), United States v. Western Elec. Co., 1956 Trade Cas. (CCH) ¶68,246 (D.N.J. 1956). In such a proceeding, the burden of proof was to be on AT&T to defend the reasonableness of its proposed royalties or other terms requested by it. *Id.* In fact, *no* applicant ever sought the district court's assistance.

[274] For a discussion of the FCC's policies regarding the computer industry, see Chapter 11.

authority to impose competitive bidding requirements as an inherent part of ratemaking.[275] But the Commission chose not to impose such a requirement. It required only that Bell give the BOCs more purchasing autonomy,[276] a rather modest step in the direction of eliminating the otherwise almost complete foreclosure of this market. It was not a step with any significant result.

§8.7.1.2 Divestiture and the 1982 Decree[277]

Section II(D)(2) of the Decree forbade the BOCs to "[m]anufacture or provide telecommunications products or customer premises equipment (except for the provision of customer premises equipment for emergency services)." The Decree did not define telecommunications products, and Judge Greene took the term to be equivalent to "telecommunications equipment," which was defined as "equipment, other than customer premises equipment, used by a carrier to provide telecommunications services."

Judge Greene approved this restriction, at least insofar as it applied to equipment used by telcos, as "an outgrowth of the government's case."[278] The government had claimed that "a combination of vertical integration and rate-of-return regulation . . . tended to generate decisions by the Operating Companies to purchase equipment produced by Western [Electric] that is more expensive or of less quality than that manufactured by the general trade."[279] Moreover, theory held that BOCs manufacturing central office equipment would cross-subsidize and discriminate

---

[275] *See* American Telephone & Telegraph, the Associated Bell System Companies, Charges for Interstate Telephone Service, AT&T Transmittal Nos. 10989, 11027, 11657, Phase II Final Decision and Order, 64 F.C.C.2d 1, 41–43, 105 (1977).

[276] *Id.*

[277] For an overview of the circumstances surrounding the adoption of the 1982 Decree, see §4.4.3. This discussion is condensed from §6.5 of *FTL1*.

[278] United States v. AT&T, 552 F. Supp. at 190.

[279] *Id.* (quoting United States v. AT&T, 524 F. Supp. 1336, 1373 (D.D.C. 1981)).

in favor of their affiliated manufacturers and thereby foreclose competition.[280]

§8.7.2   The 1996 Act Restrictions

The 1996 Act eliminated the Decree and the manufacturing restrictions contained therein. As with the Decree's interLATA restriction, however, these provisions of the Decree were replaced with a statutory analog—with an escape hatch. Section 273 of the 1996 Act provides a route to manufacturing relief for the BOCs; in addition, it immediately authorizes the BOCs to engage in a range of research and collaborative activities with other manufacturers.

Section 273(a) of the 1996 Act provides that "a Bell operating company may manufacture and provide telecommunications equipment, and manufacture customer premises equipment, if the Commission authorizes that Bell operating company or any Bell operating company affiliate to provide interLATA services under section 271(d), subject to the requirements of [section 273] and the regulations prescribed thereunder."[281] Unlike the interLATA prohibition, 47 U.S.C. §271(a), the manufacturing restriction by its terms does not apply to "affiliates." Neither the FCC nor the courts have considered the significance of that omission. The meaning of "manufacturing" is the same "as such term has under the AT&T Consent Decree."[282] BOCs may engage in such activities only through a separate affiliate;[283] this restriction expires three years after the FCC authorizes the BOC to engage in these activities unless the FCC extends the restriction.[284] The FCC has tentatively concluded that a BOC will gain

[280] *Id.* at 191 (footnote omitted) (citing United States v. AT&T, 524 F. Supp. at 1373).

[281] 47 U.S.C. §273(a).

[282] *Id.* §273(h); *see* §8.2.3.

[283] *Id.* §272(a)(2)(A). Such affiliate must operate independently from the BOC; maintain separate books; have separate officers, directors, and employees; and conduct all transactions, including credit transactions, with the BOC at arm's length. *Id.* §272(b).

[284] *Id.* §272(f)(1).

manufacturing relief once it has obtained in-region interLATA authority in any of its states.[285]

Section 273(a) also prohibits a BOC or its affiliates from engaging in any manufacturing joint venture with another, unaffiliated BOC or BOC affiliate, presumably to reduce the risk of a group of Bell companies exerting monopsony power in the equipment markets.

While the BOCs remain barred from manufacturing, section 273(b) explicitly authorizes the BOCs to engage in the sort of activities that large customers in technology-driven industries routinely undertake with their suppliers. The companies may participate in research activities relating to manufacturing, royalty agreements with otherwise unaffiliated manufacturers, and "close collaboration" in the design and development of telecommunications equipment or CPE. This relief may encompass most of the manufacturing activities in which the Bell companies wish to engage.[286] The FCC has tentatively concluded that the Act does not permit collaboration between unaffiliated BOCs,[287] but such a limitation does not appear in the language of the act, which authorizes collaboration with "*any* manufacturer of customer premises equipment or telecommunications equipment."[288]

The FCC has also suggested that the BOCs' statutory right to enter into royalty agreements might be circumscribed to "protect against potential anticompetitive abuses."[289] According to the

---

[285] Implementation of Section 273 of the Communications Act of 1934, as Amended by the Telecommunications Act of 1996, Notice of Proposed Rulemaking, 11 F.C.C. Rec. 21,784, 21,790 ¶8 (1996) (hereinafter *Equipment NPRM*). As of the date of this writing, the Commission had taken no action in this docket.

[286] The Act also purports to limit the "provision" of telecommunications equipment by a Bell Company (i.e., the sale of such equipment to third parties). 47 U.S.C. §273(a). The Bell companies, however, already received a waiver from the Decree court to provide telecommunications equipment, subject to certain safeguards. Order, United States v. Western Elec. Co., No. 82-0192 (D.D.C. Sept. 10, 1987). Under a general "grandfather" provision of the Act, such relief continues in force. *See* 47 U.S.C. §271(f).

[287] *Equipment NPRM*, 11 F.C.C. Rec. at 21,791 ¶11.

[288] 47 U.S.C. §273(b)(1) (emphasis added).

[289] *Equipment NPRM*, 11 F.C.C. Rec. at 21,792 ¶12.

FCC, royalties based on sales volumes might give BOCs incentives to purchase inferior equipment not only because it will receive royalties, but also in the hope of encouraging other carriers to purchase the same equipment to maintain full interoperability with the BOC network.[290] The suggestion that royalty agreements could be circumscribed in this way runs contrary to the most obvious reading of the statute, however: Congress moroeever was aware that volume-based royalty arrangements are the rule, not the exception.[291]

Section 273(c) requires BOCs—at least BOCs who have been authorized to engage in manufacturing[292]—to disclose information concerning network standards. Section 273(c)(1) requires a BOC "in accordance with regulations prescribed by the Commission [to] maintain and file with the Commission full and complete information with respect to the protocols and technical requirements for connection with and use of its telephone exchange service facilities."[293] The BOC is also required to report to the Commission any anticipated changes in such protocols or requirements.[294] Despite existing rules requiring disclosure of network information, the Commission has tentatively concluded that its existing rules may be inadequate to meet the needs of manufacturers in particular and asked for comment on how to consolidate the various disclosure requirements.[295] Other issues that the Commission will try to resolve in its rulemaking

---

[290] *Id.*

[291] In other places in the Act, Congress limited the scope of permitted royalty arrangements expressly. *See* 47 U.S.C. §274(c)(2)(C), (i)(8).

[292] The FCC has noted that although the information disclosure requirements of section 273(c) apply on their face to all BOCs, section 273(c) is contained within a provision that otherwise addresses BOC obligations *in the manufacturing context. See Equipment NPRM,* 11 F.C.C. Rec. at 21,795 ¶17. See n.299 *infra* and accompanying text.

[293] 47 U.S.C. §273(c)(1).

[294] *Id.* Section 273(c)(4) requires disclosure of the "planned deployment of telecommunications equipment" in a timely fashion to interconnecting carriers. This requirement closely tracks the requirements of section 251(c)(5). *See* §8.4.3.2(i).

[295] *Equipment NPRM,* 11 F.C.C. Rec. at 21,794 ¶15, 21,795–21,796 ¶18.

under section 273(c)(1) include the manner and timing of disclosure of network changes.[296]

Section 273(c)(2) prohibits BOCs from disclosing any information required to be filed with the Commission under section 273(c)(1) before such information is filed. The Commission noted that this section stands in tension with section 273(b)(1), which permits "close collaboration" with manufacturers in the design of telecommunications equipment.[297] The Commission has not yet determined how to permit "close collaboration" while preventing the communication of technical information in advance of public disclosure.[298]

Section 273(e) contains certain restrictions on BOC procurement activities.[299] Section 273(e)(1) prohibits BOCs, for the period during which they are required to operate a separate manufacturing subsidiary, to "discriminate in favor of equipment or supplies by an affiliate or related person."[300] Section 273(e)(2) more broadly requires BOCs to make procurement and supply contracts "for equipment, services, and software on the basis of an objective assessment of price, quality, delivery, and other commercial factors."[301] Section 273(e)(3) requires BOCs "to the extent consistent with the antitrust laws to engage in joint network planning and design with local exchange carriers in the same area of interest."[302] The Commission has tentatively concluded that these obligations, unlike the infrastructure sharing required by section 259 of the Act,[303] "specifically contemplate[] joint network planning and design between a BOC and other

---

[296] *Id.* at 21,797 ¶22.

[297] *Id.* at 21,799 ¶27.

[298] *Id.*

[299] Again, it is not clear whether this provision applies to BOCs generally or only to BOCs engaged in manufacturing. *See id.* at 21,817 ¶63.

[300] 47 U.S.C. §273(e)(1).

[301] *Id.* §273(e)(2). It is not clear whether subsection (e)(1) imposes any obligation beyond that imposed by subsection (e)(2).

[302] 47 U.S.C. §273(e)(3).

[303] *See id.* §259(b)(6) (providing that an incumbent LEC shall not be required to "engage in any infrastructure sharing agreement for any services or access which are to be provided or offered to consumers by the qualifying carrier in such local exchange carrier's telephone exchange area").

LECs that may be the BOC's competitors."[304] Section 273(e)(4) prohibits BOCs engaged in manufacturing from restricting sales to other LECs; section 273(e)(5) requires BOCs and the entities owned by them to protect proprietary information submitted for procurement purposes.

Section 273(d)(2) through (d)(8) contains restrictions on the manufacturing activities of standard-setting organizations.[305] As a general matter, such standard-setting bodies are prohibited from taking advantage of their privileged access to proprietary information and their ability to set equipment standards to gain a leg up in the manufacture of equipment. They are required to engage in the manufacturing of equipment they certify through a separate subsidiary and may not discriminate in favor of an affiliate.[306] Moreover, any nonaccredited standards development organization must provide public notice of any standard-setting activities and perform such activity only pursuant to published, auditable, and industry-accepted criteria.[307] These requirements remain in place only until "alternative sources of industry-wide standards, industry-wide generic requirements, or product certification for a particular class of telecommunications equipment" exist.[308] The Commission, as the Act requires, established dispute resolution procedures when technical disputes arise between nonaccredited standards development organizations and their funding parties.[309]

---

[304] *Equipment NPRM,* 11 F.C.C. Rec. at 21,821 ¶71.

[305] Section 273(d)(1) barred Bell Communications Research, Inc. (Bellcore) from engaging in manufacturing so long as it was an affiliate of any BOC. The BOCs sold Bellcore—which has been renamed as Telecordia Technologies—to Science Applications International Corporation; the sale was completed in November 1997. Indeed, many of the provisions of section 273(d) appear to have been adopted with Bellcore in mind.

[306] 47 U.S.C. §273(d)(3).

[307] *Id.* §273(d)(4).

[308] *Id.* §273(d)(6).

[309] *See* Implementation of Section 273(d)(5) of the Communications Act of 1934, as Amended by the Telecommunications Act of 1996—Dispute Resolution Regarding Equipment Standards, Report and Order, 11 F.C.C. Rec. 12,955 (1996).

§8.7.3   Concentration in the Central Office
Equipment Market and Lock-In

The decision to separate equipment manufacturing functions from local exchange functions in the MFJ was directed chiefly at concerns about self-dealing—the worry that LECs would buy inferior, overpriced equipment from themselves and pass the cost on to ratepayers. But another concern is emerging—that equipment manufacturers themselves may have market power that is subject to abuse due to concentrated central office equipment (and other switching equipment), and in particular as a result of the need to acquire continual upgrades to existing equipment.

The concern first presented itself in connection with AT&T's acquisition of cellular provider McCaw.[310] AT&T was at that time the nation's largest manufacturer of switches, cell site radios, and related network equipment used by cellular telephone systems.[311] Cellular providers that purchased equipment from AT&T (or another manufacturer) are "locked in"[312] to that manufacturer's standards. AT&T customers either had to keep buying from AT&T or had to undertake a disruptive and expensive changeout of their network to another manufacturer.[313] The

---

[310] For discussions of this acquisition, see §4.4.5. *See also* Complaint, United States v. AT&T Corp. and McCaw, No. 94-01555 (D.D.C. July 15, 1994) (*McCaw Complaint*). Concurrent proceedings by the FCC and the California Public Utilities Commission were also held. *See* Opinion and Order, Joint Application of AT&T, Ridge Merger Corp. and McCaw for Authorization To Transfer Indirect Control of Airsignal of California, et al., from McCaw to AT&T, Dec. 94-04-0402 (Cal. P.U.C. Apr. 6, 1994) (approving transfer of licenses subject to conditions).

[311] *See* Competitive Impact Statement at 2–3, United States v. AT&T and McCaw, No. 94-01555 (D.D.C. July 15, 1994) (*AT&T/McCaw Competitive Impact Statement*).

[312] *See generally* Eastman Kodak Co. v. Image Technical Servs., 504 U.S. 451, 476 (1992).

[313] With cell sites costing $750,000 and switches approximately $7 million, changing manufacturers is extremely expensive. Southwestern Bell Mobile Systems, McCaw's competitor in the Dallas area, estimated that it would cost over $1.2 billion to replace all the AT&T equipment it currently uses. *See* Affidavit of John T. Stupka ¶¶16–18, *attached to* Comments of SBC Communications on Proposed Final Judgment, United States v. AT&T and McCaw, No. 94-01555 (D.D.C. Oct. 25, 1994).

lock-in also applied to the computer software needed to operate the equipment and to ongoing software upgrades that enhance performance and allow new services. The government claimed that the merger would give AT&T an incentive to abuse its position as a locked-in equipment supplier to McCaw's competitors. By withholding equipment and services or raising its prices, AT&T had the power to increase the costs and decrease the capabilities of its equipment customers.[314] Cellular subscribers would likely bear the brunt of AT&T's market power, in the form of lower-quality and higher-cost cellular services.[315]

Simultaneously with the filing of its complaint, the government proposed a consent decree that would, for ten years after the merger, place substantial restrictions on the operations of AT&T/McCaw.[316] AT&T agreed to abide by the terms of the decree while the court conducted its Tunney Act review.[317] Judge Greene, however, never conducted the Tunney Act review, never entered the proposed decree, and never otherwise acted on the pending antitrust case. A year and a half later, when Congress passed the 1996 Act, AT&T had announced its plan to spin off its equipment business to Lucent Technologies Inc., and Congress eliminated the decree.[318]

Lucent's independence has not eliminated concerns about abuse of market power. In 1996, Bell Atlantic and DSC Communications sued AT&T and its equipment spin-off, Lucent, for delaying and sabotaging industry-standard switch interfaces needed to connect competing products to Lucent switches.[319]

---

[314] *AT&T/McCaw Competitive Impact Statement* at 10.

[315] *Id.*

[316] Proposed Final Judgment, United States v. AT&T and McCaw, No. 94-01555 (D.D.C. July 15, 1994) (*Proposed Final Judgment*).

[317] *See* 15 U.S.C. §16.

[318] Telecommunications Act of 1996, §601(a)(3). The Conference Statement noted that "[s]ince the passage of the original bills in both the House and Senate, AT&T has announced that it will spin off its manufacturing business, and so the manufacturing aspects of the decree will soon become moot." H.R. Conf. Rep. No. 458, 104th Cong., 2d Sess. 199 (1996), *reprinted in* 1996 U.S.C.C.A.N. 10,231.

[319] Complaint, Bell Atlantic Corp. v. AT&T Corp., Civ. Act. No. 5-96CV45 (E.D. Tex. Feb. 14, 1996).

Plaintiffs complained about sabotage of two interfaces: the TR-303, which was needed by transmission equipment competitors, and the advanced intelligent network (or AIN) triggers, which were needed for competitive provision of applications software for the switch. The district court denied the defendants' motions for dismissal and summary judgment.[320] The parties then settled the case on confidential terms.[321]

§8.8 Conclusion

Thirty years ago the Bell System was a vertically integrated monopoly that provided a single product — telephone service, in all its varieties. The efforts of competitors to chip away at the edges of this monopoly, by gaining the opportunity to provide equipment used in the provision of service in a competitive market, had been rebuffed by the Bell System and, for many years, by the FCC and by the courts. Independent telephone companies followed the Bell System model. The winds of change were just beginning to blow with the *Carterfone* decision.

Today, the picture could hardly be more different. The Bell System is gone, competition is the clarion call of the day, and the market for consumer premises equipment is so competitive that no single manufacturer can even arguably claim any power in the market. AT&T has spun off its manufacturing operations into Lucent Technologies, and GTE has abandoned network equipment manufacturing entirely. From the perspective of 15 years' distance, the manufacturing restrictions in the MFJ appear more apt to protect AT&T/Lucent from competition in manufacturing than to protect competition or to prevent cross-subsidy.

Yet the manufacturing restrictions remain, and restrictions on provision of bundled CPE threaten to impede consumers' access to advanced services like ADSL. It is always easy to articulate the

[320] Memorandum Opinion and Order, Bell Atlantic Corp. v. AT&T Corp., Civ. Act. No. 5-96CV45 (E.D. Tex. June 26, 1996); Order, Bell Atlantic Corp. v. AT&T Corp., Civ. Act. No. 5-96CV45 (E.D. Tex. Feb. 25, 1997).

[321] The economics of the software issues are discussed in §3.9.8.2.

reasons for such restrictions by invoking the shibboleths of cross-subsidy, discriminatory access to information, and self-dealing. In a world of price caps and rapid innovation, where access to the local loop is assured to all (at least on paper) and where the real value comes from the electronics placed on either end of that loop, it is fair to wonder whether these restrictions still have their place. No one disputes that restrictions have real economic costs. The only question is whether they offer sufficiently important economic benefits to make them worthwhile. For now, Congress and the FCC still believe the answer is yes; but the pressure of innovation may force a reevaluation soon.

9

Long-Distance Services*

§9.1 Introduction

Once divorced from local services by the Modification of Final Judgment (MFJ) and AT&T's divestiture of the BOCs, long distance became a major telecommunications market in its own right. During the 1980s and 1990s, interstate long-distance calling volume increased by about 11 percent each year; by the end of 1996, approximately 158 million lines in the United States were "presubscribed" to a designated long-distance carrier.[1] Americans were making more than 300 billion minutes of switched

---

*This chapter was co-authored by Austin C. Schlick, Partner, Kellogg, Huber, Hansen, Todd & Evans; Princeton University (A.B., *magna cum laude* in History, 1985); Yale Law School (J.D., 1990); Phi Beta Kappa; Law Clerk, Honorable Abner Mikva, U.S. Court of Appeals, D.C. Circuit, 1990–1991; Law Clerk, Honorable Sandra Day O'Connor, U.S. Supreme Court, 1991–1992.

[1] *See* Industry Analysis Division, FCC, Long Distance Market Shares: Third Quarter 1998 at tbl. 2.1 (Dec. 1998). Special-access lines, WATS lines, and other specialized lines are not included in the counts of presubscribed lines. *Id.* at 4 ("A telephone line is said to be presubscribed to the long distance carrier that receives the ordinary long distance calls placed on that

731

interstate calls annually by the late 1990s,[2] generating revenues of over $100 billion per year.[3] Other long-distance services are intrastate or international or use dedicated (i.e., unswitched) lines or the airwaves.

Deregulation and growth of the long-distance market have gone hand in hand. From the 1930s until the late 1970s, almost every aspect of interstate telephony was comprehensively regulated. The regulatory environment has changed rapidly in the last two decades, however. Much of this market has now been essentially deregulated. Indeed, the most important regulation of the market in recent years has been directed at a group of local carriers—the Bell companies—that merely are seeking to become long-distance carriers.

§9.2 Jurisdiction: The Advent of Regulation

"Long-distance" services include both interstate and intrastate toll services. The former are regulated by the Federal Communications Commission (FCC), the latter by state regulators.[4] As discussed in section 9.7, until recently the states exercised their jurisdiction over intrastate toll services to limit competition as part of a larger plan for preserving affordable local telephone service.[5] The FCC, on the other hand, embarked beginning in the 1960s on a long and halting drive toward competition in interstate long distance.

The Communications Act of 1934 reflected Congress's belief that telephone service was and would remain a monopoly.[6] Unlike almost all other countries around the world, the United States left ownership of that monopoly in private hands. But com-

---

line. . . . By the end of 1996, more than 600 companies were providing long distance service to their own presubscribed customers.").

[2] *Id.* at 4 (interstate terminating minutes). This total "excludes calls made on private telecommunications systems, on leased lines, and minutes on the 'closed end' of WATS-like calls." *Id.* at 2.

[3] *Id.* at tbl. 3.1.

[4] *See* §3.3.

[5] *See also* §6.1.

[6] *See* Chapter 2.

prehensive regulation was in order.[7] Accordingly, the Act vested the FCC with broad powers to "regulat[e] interstate and foreign commerce in communication by wire and radio so as to make available, so far as possible, to all people of the United States a rapid, efficient, Nation-wide, and world-wide . . . communication service with adequate facilities at reasonable charges."[8] The FCC used these powers, first, to institutionalize the Bell System's long-distance monopoly,[9] later to protect Bell from incipient competition,[10] next to help dismantle Bell's long-distance monopoly when competitive pressures became too great,[11] and finally to regulate local telephone competition as the quid pro quo for long-distance entry.[12]

§9.3 Early Competitive Entry

The FCC's most basic power is to grant or deny licenses.[13] A would-be provider of long-distance service needs either airwave or terrestrial transmission systems; it may not lawfully operate either without express FCC permission.[14] Section 214 of the Communications Act specifically prohibits construction of new lines unless the FCC concludes the new facilities will serve the "public convenience and necessity."[15] This regulatory structure reflects the assumption that long-distance telephone service was a natural monopoly like local service. From 1934 until about

---

[7] *See* Wiley, The End of Monopoly: Regulatory Change and the Promotion of Competition, *in* Telecommunications and the Law 147–148 (W. Sapronov ed., 1988).

[8] 47 U.S.C. §151.

[9] *See* §9.3.

[10] *See* §9.4.1.

[11] *See* §§9.4.2, 9.4.4.

[12] *See* §9.6.2.

[13] *See* Chapter 3.

[14] 47 U.S.C. §214.

[15] *Id.* §214(a). A carrier seeking to construct new lines or to extend existing lines must submit an application to the FCC describing the proposed construction or extension, the service to be provided, cost estimates, proposed tariff changes, and the factors showing public need. *See* 47 C.F.R. §63.01 (1998).

1960, the FCC embraced that assumption uncritically. Competition certainly would have been possible during that period, if only because Bell (with the Commission's full approval) inflated the price of long-distance service to subsidize local connections.[16] But competition was considered to be inefficient in the short run and not economically viable in the long, so the Commission did nothing to encourage it.

§9.3.1   Technological Advances

The development of microwave and satellite technologies radically changed that picture, making competition both practical and inevitable.[17] Microwave was first developed just prior to World War II; it was improved during the war, largely through military applications.[18] During this same period, RCA and others developed television, and when the war ended, the television market exploded. Since television signals could not be carried over twisted-pair copper wires and since laying a new set of coaxial cables to do this job appeared (at first) prohibitively expensive, microwave technology provided an ideal medium for transmitting television signals between cities.[19] The Commission dedicated almost 70 percent of nongovernmental assignments of microwave frequencies to the burgeoning television industry.[20] Most of these assignments went to the Bell System, as the principal common carrier of television signals, with Western Union in a largely supporting role.[21]

During the late 1940s, however, the Commission received several applications for private microwave construction permits.

---

[16] See §2.3.5.

[17] See §1.4.

[18] See generally Gerald W. Brock, The Telecommunications Industry 180–187 (1981) (tracing the development of competition in microwave for audio and visual transmissions).

[19] See id. at 180–181.

[20] See Public Notice, 39 F.C.C. 236 (1946) (allocating microwave frequencies to the various nongovernmental radio services from 25,000 to 30,000,000 kilocycles).

[21] See Brock, The Telecommunications Industry at 182.

The Commission initially was inhospitable to these applications. Although the Commission authorized construction and use of private microwave systems for video transmission to areas where common carrier service was unavailable, private users were required to abandon their microwave systems once common carrier service was made available to them.[22] This made a certain amount of sense, since the FCC did not want supposedly scarce spectrum squandered on duplicate facilities. But having largely limited microwave spectrum to common carrier use, the Commission refused to require common carriers to interconnect with other carriers' microwave facilities.[23] This made no sense, since once spectrum had been allocated to a private system, the most efficient use of that system required interconnection with the much more extensive common carrier networks, including the Bell System.[24]

---

[22] *See* Allocation of Frequencies to the Various Classes of Non-government Services in the Radio Spectrum from 10 Kilocycles to 30,000,000 Kilocycles, Report of the Commission with Respect to Frequency Service—Allocations to the Non-government Fixed and Mobile Services Between 1000 Mc and 13200 Mc, 39 F.C.C. 298, 300 (1948). *See also* AT&T, Charges and Regulations for Television Transmission Services and Facilities, Report of the Commission, 42 F.C.C. 1, 22–24 (1949) (authorizing non-common-carrier intercity relaying until common carrier transmission became available); Brock, The Telecommunications Industry at 185.

[23] *See* Establishment of Physical Connections and Through Routes and Charges Applicable Thereto, Decision, 17 F.C.C. 152 (1952) (holding that mandatory interconnection between Bell and Western Union served no public purpose). Although the Commission protested that its decision was "not intended to support any claim which the Bell System may have made to a monopoly in the field of intercity video transmission," dissenting Commissioner Hyde pointed out that, "in the absence of interconnection, or in the absence of a service substantially paralleling the existing and proposed Bell System, no common carrier can compete with Bell in the intercity video transmission field." *Id.* at 175.

[24] *See* Jeffrey Rohlfs, A Theory of Interdependent Demand for a Communications Service, Bell J. Econ. 16–37 (Spring 1974) ("The utility that a subscriber derives from a communications service increases as others join the system."); William J. Baumol & J. Gregory Sidak, Toward Competition in Local Telephony 109–110 (1994) ("an individual consumer's demand for use of the network increases with the number of other users on the network"). In J.E. Belknap and Associates, Applications for Construction Permits for Experimental Microwave Relay Stations at Osceola, Arkansas, and Kennett, Missouri, Memorandum Opinion and Order, 18 F.C.C. 642 (1954), the Commission permitted an applicant to offer specialized common carrier microwave relay facilities for intercity video relay because "[t]he applicant . . . appears

Outside the sphere of television, the FCC initially foreclosed competitive entry of any sort.[25] In its MacKay Radio & Telegraph Co. Report and Order, the FCC stated bluntly that it would not sacrifice frequency to uses that can adequately be performed by wire.[26] "[I]n view of the limited availability of frequencies, resulting in great difficulty in maintaining provision even for the various public and safety devices," the FCC declared that "devotion of radio facilities to a private use capable of rendition by wire lines is not in the public interest unless future developments should conclusively demonstrate the sufficiency of frequencies for such purposes over and above the requirements of the public services."[27]

The Commission's first tentative move away from this position came in its *Three Circuits* decision.[28] Citing a "national policy in international communications favor[ing] competition,"[29] the FCC authorized a radiotelegraph company to open new circuits to Portugal and the Netherlands in direct competition with another company that already provided similar service.[30] Yet the

---

to have no present need for interconnection with the services of any other carrier" and because the service would be offered "in an area where, and under conditions which, make it appear that there is no diversion of traffic or substantial basis upon which to conclude that duplication of investment or operating expenses, or establishment of harmful competition will result from a grant." *Id.* at 642–643.

[25] *See, e.g.,* MacKay Radio & Tel. Co., Statement of Facts and Grounds for Decision, 2 F.C.C. 592 (1936), *aff'd,* MacKay Radio & Tel. Co. v. FCC, 97 F.2d 641 (D.C. Cir. 1938) (denying applicant a license to operate a direct public radio telegraph service between the United States and Norway, a route already served by RCA Communications).

[26] MacKay Radio & Tel. Co., Inc., Report and Order of the Commission, 39 F.C.C. 1, 11 (1939). Here, the FCC refused frequency for IBM's experimental development of "radiotype," which involved a machine like a standard typewriter that was actuated and controlled automatically by a radio transmitter and could accurately transmit up to 100 words per minute. *Id.*

[27] *Id.*

[28] MacKay Radio & Tel. Co., Applications for Radiotelegraph Circuits Between the United States and Finland, Portugal, Surinam and the Netherlands, Decision, 15 F.C.C. 690 (1951) (hereinafter *Three Circuits*), *rev'd sub nom.* RCA Communications, Inc. v. FCC, 201 F.2d 694 (D.C. Cir. 1952), *cert. granted,* 345 U.S. 902, *vacated and remanded,* 346 U.S. 86 (1953).

[29] *Three Circuits,* 15 F.C.C. at 699.

[30] *Id.* at 691.

court of appeals reversed, and its decision was upheld by the Supreme Court.[31] The "encouragement of competition as such has not been considered the single or controlling reliance for safeguarding the public interest," the Supreme Court stated.[32] "To say that national policy without more suffices for authorization of a competing carrier wherever competition is reasonably feasible," the Court continued, "would authorize the Commission to abdicate what would seem to us one of the primary duties imposed on it by Congress."[33] Thus, while FCC's mandate was broad enough to permit the introduction of competition as economic and technological developments warranted, the Commission would have to articulate just how competition would comport with the public interest.[34]

In due course, the FCC did just that. The Commission's strategy for bringing competition to the long-distance market was largely to avoid difficult questions of markets and subsidies and to focus instead on technologies. Competitors were first allowed to use microwave systems, then satellites, to provide competitive services. Before long, the specific technologies were forgotten, and the principle of competition was firmly established.[35]

§9.3.2 Microwave

The Commission's first major, sustained break from the old monopoly paradigm came with its *Above 890* decision in 1959.[36] Here, the Commission concluded that its earlier concerns about the scarcity of available frequency were exaggerated.[37] The Com-

---

[31] RCA v. FCC, 346 U.S. at 86.

[32] *Id.* at 93.

[33] *Id.* at 95.

[34] *Id.* at 93.

[35] *See generally* H. E. Marks, Two Decades of Telecommunications Regulation: An Historical Perspective, *in* Telecommunications and the Law 111, 116 (W. Sapronov ed., 1988); Wiley, Telecommunications and the Law at 149.

[36] Allocation of Frequencies in the Bands Above 890 MHz, Decision, 27 F.C.C. 359 (1959) (hereinafter *Above 890*), *recons. denied*, 29 F.C.C. 825 (1960) (hereinafter *Above 890 Reconsideration Order*).

[37] *Id.* at 413. The FCC decided that "there are now available adequate frequencies above 890 MHz to take care of the present and reasonably foreseeable

mission accordingly allocated spectrum to private microwave users who would use it for their own end-to-end private connections, completely bypassing the established long-distance network. Thus, in a fundamental change of policy, the Commission concluded that the availability of adequate frequency was reason enough to license private systems without regard to whether common carrier facilities were available to serve those routes. "[E]ven in areas where common carrier facilities and personnel are readily available," the Commission explained, "there appears to be a need for private systems."[38] Private systems would allow users to customize their transmission capacity to meet their particular needs and provide better control and more flexibility in administering the system.[39] The Commission also concluded that expanding eligibility for licenses would afford a "competitive spur in the manufacturing of equipment and in the development of the communications art."[40] The FCC found no basis for concluding that "substantially adverse economic effects would flow from the licensing of private point-to-point systems as proposed herein";[41] therefore, it was "unnecessary to consider whether such licensing is contrary to the public interest."[42] The Commission explained: "A finding on adverse economic effects cannot be based upon a speculative possibility of future adverse effects."[43]

---

future needs of both the common carriers and private users for point-to-point communications systems." *Id.* at 404. Indeed, the Commission awkwardly confessed that "[a]t the present time, under current policies, only a limited use is being made of microwave frequencies." *Id.* at 413.

[38] *Id.*

[39] *Id.*

[40] *Id.* at 414.

[41] *Id.* at 411.

[42] *Id.* at 412.

[43] *Id.* On reconsideration, the FCC acknowledged that the establishment of private communication systems would result in a loss to the common carriers of "some" message toll and private line revenues. Still, the Commission stated that there was no basis on which to conclude that the probable economic losses will be "of such a nature and magnitude, when viewed in relation to the total resources and communications market of the communications common carrier industry, as to impair the ability of the industry to furnish an adequate nationwide service at reasonable charges." *Above 890 Reconsideration Order,* 29 F.C.C. at 850.

The *Above 890* decision established an important principle, radical in its time: the established monopoly phone companies enjoyed no presumptive right to carry all long-distance traffic and collect all long-distance revenues. In practical terms, however, the impact of *Above 890* was quite limited. Only a small fraction of users had a need for the kinds of dedicated, high-capacity, point-to-point transmission services that privately owned microwave systems provided.[44]

But soon this ripple began to spread. The market distortions that made bypassing Bell with private microwave systems attractive — nationwide price averaging and subsidization of local service by long distance — also provided an irresistible lure for new entry by "specialized common carriers." These companies sought to provide competitive common carrier service exclusively on high-density routes where per unit costs were low but rates were high.[45]

In 1963, the newly formed Microwave Communications, Inc. (destined to become MCI, which later merged into MCI World-Com), applied to the FCC for construction permits for microwave facilities between Chicago, St. Louis, and nine intermediate points.[46] The proposed service was limited to point-to-point transmissions between MCI's microwave sites, leaving each subscriber to obtain a communications link (loop service) to MCI's sites.[47] This was an advance from *Above 890*, in that the new company would operate as a common carrier, not just a private system. Microwave bypass services would thus become available to smaller users and to users who did not care to operate their own telecommunications facilities.

[44] Since shared usage of private microwave systems was largely prohibited, "customers whose communication demand was not large enough to justify the creation of their own end-to-end microwave system did not benefit from this decision." Knieps & Spiller, Regulating by Partial Deregulation: The Case of Telecommunications, 35 Admin. L. Rev. 391, 398 (1983).

[45] *See generally* J. Hillman, Telecommunications Deregulation: The Martyrdom of the Regulated Monopolist, 79 Nw. U. L. Rev. 1183, 1187–1193 (1984–1985) (discussing the opening of private line markets to competition).

[46] Application of Microwave Communications, Inc. for Construction Permits to Establish New Facilities in the Domestic Public Point-to-Point Microwave Radio Service at Chicago, Ill, St. Louis, Mo., and Intermediate Points, Decision, 18 F.C.C.2d 953 (1969), *recons. denied,* 21 F.C.C.2d 190 (1970).

[47] *Id.* at 953–954 ¶1.

After six years of opposition by Bell and other existing carriers, the FCC voted 4-3 to grant MCI's application.[48] The FCC noted that MCI proposed to offer its subscribers lower rates than those charged by the incumbent carriers and that subscribers who did not require full-time communication services would receive additional savings through the channel sharing and half-time use services offered by the tariff.[49] In addition to lower cost, MCI promised its subscribers greater flexibility of use, especially in terms of channel bandwidth, split channels for voice and data transmissions, and the installation of customer equipment.[50] Despite the duplication of facilities that would be involved, "MCI's offering would enable . . . subscribers to obtain a type of service not presently available and would tend to increase the efficiency of operation of the subscribers' businesses."[51]

Opponents of MCI's proposal—existing carriers and dissenting Commissioners—argued that MCI's so-called cost saving was merely a form of "cream-skimming."[52] The carriers argued that in order to compete with MCI on low-cost routes, they would be forced to abandon cost-averaging policies and increase their rates for subscribers on lightly used routes. The Commission dismissed these concerns by noting that MCI's service would appeal only to a few subscribers with "unique and specialized characteristics."[53] "In these circumstances," the Commission asserted, "we cannot perceive how a grant of the authorizations requested would pose any serious threat to the established carriers' price averaging policies."[54]

Thus, with rather cursory analysis, the Commission had begun the process of introducing competitive long-distance service. The Commission was looking, as Commissioner Johnson said in his separate statement, "for ways to add a little salt and pepper

[48] Id.
[49] Id. at 954 ¶2, 958 ¶15.
[50] Id. at 954 ¶2, 959 ¶17.
[51] Id. at 959 ¶17.
[52] Id. at 960 ¶21. Cream-skimming occurs when a company operates on high-density routes where lower fixed costs per channel permit lower rates with higher profits, while leaving other carriers to provide higher-cost, lower-profit universal service.
[53] Id. at 960 ¶22.
[54] Id.

of competition to the rather tasteless stew of regulatory protection that this Commission and Bell have cooked up."[55] What it got was a different meal altogether.

Following MCI's successful application on the St. Louis-Chicago route, and even before MCI opened for service in January 1972, the FCC received a flood of new applications from MCI and companies associated with it, as well as from other new, would-be carriers.[56] The Commission accordingly initiated a rulemaking to establish an overall policy concerning new entry into the "specialized communications field."[57] In its 1971 *Specialized Common Carriers* decision, the Commission announced a new, even more general policy favoring competition in the provision of intercity private line connections.[58] The Commission found that there was a public need and demand both for the proposed facilities and services and, more generally, for new and diverse sources of supply resulting from new entry. The Commission also decided that competition in the specialized communications field was feasible and likely to have beneficial effects that outweighed any adverse impacts on service to the public by existing carriers.[59] Accordingly, the Commission held that "a general policy in favor of the entry of new carriers in the specialized communications field would serve the public interest, convenience and necessity."[60] Furthermore, it was "not necessary

---

[55] *Id.* at 978.

[56] As of March 15, 1971, the FCC had received proposals from 33 different applicants for the operation of 1,877 microwave stations. Establishment of Policies and Procedures for Consideration of Application to Provide Specialized Common Carrier Services in the Domestic Public Point-to-Point Microwave Radio Service, First Report and Order, 29 F.C.C.2d 870, 871 n.1 (1971) (hereinafter *Specialized Common Carriers*), *aff'd,* 31 F.C.C.2d 1106 (1971), *aff'd sub nom.* Washington Util. & Transp. Commn. v. FCC, 513 F.2d 1142 (9th Cir.), *cert. denied,* 423 U.S. 836 (1975). One company, Data Transmission Corporation (Datran), proposed to build a switched network dedicated exclusively to data transmission. *Specialized Common Carriers,* 29 F.C.C.2d at 872 ¶3.

[57] Establishment of Policies and Procedures for Consideration of Application to Provide Specialized Common Carrier Services in the Domestic Public Point-to-Point Microwave Radio Service, Notice of Inquiry to Formulate Policy, Notice of Proposed Rulemaking, 24 F.C.C.2d 318, 327 ¶22 (1970).

[58] *See generally Specialized Common Carriers,* 29 F.C.C.2d 870.

[59] *Id.* at 917 ¶94, 920 ¶103.

[60] *Id.* at 920 ¶103; *see* Washington Utils. & Transp. Commn. v. FCC, 513 F.2d 1142 (9th Cir. 1975).

---

or desirable in the public interest to hold comparative hearings for the purpose of restricting new entry in any particular area to only one private line applicant."[61]

In short order, the Commission granted new licenses to various microwave carriers who would now be competing against AT&T's Bell System.[62] MCI quickly expanded its network by constructing new facilities and acquiring other small microwave carriers. Within two years, its network reached 40 cities and both coasts. Another entrant, Southern Pacific Communications Co. (forerunner of Sprint), also had established a bicoastal microwave system by the end of 1973.

MCI and Sprint have since abandoned their microwave beginnings for fiber optics. Yet microwave transmission technology was crucial to the development of competition in the long-distance marketplace. It reduced the overall entry costs for new firms, while simultaneously allowing carriers to enter with geographically mobile fixed assets rather than the traditional telephone cables that were literally sunk costs.[63]

§9.3.3 Satellite Common Carriage

Satellite technology was being developed during the same period; rapid progress under government sponsorship after the launching of the Explorer in 1958 reduced launching and operating costs, thereby making economically feasible the use of satellites for communications purposes.[64] Codified under the

---

[61] *Specialized Common Carriers,* 29 F.C.C.2d at 926 ¶120.

[62] The boundaries of the new long-distance market in which competition was to be permitted were clear enough. Competition was being approved for "specialized," "private line," point-to-point services, not for switched long-distance service generally. Nevertheless, in *Execunet I,* discussed in detail below, the Court of Appeals for the D.C. Circuit would subsequently argue that the FCC had failed to make the definition of private line service set out in 47 C.F.R. §21.2 expressly applicable to the licenses granted to specialized carriers. MCI Telecommunications Corp. v. FCC, 561 F.2d 365, 373–374 (D.C. Cir. 1977) (*Execunet I*), *cert. denied,* 434 U.S. 1040 (1978).

[63] *See* D. L. Kaserman & J. W. Mayo, Long-Distance Telecommunications Policy—Rationality on Hold, Pub. Util. Fort., Dec. 22, 1988, at 21–22.

[64] *See* Competition in the Interstate Interexchange Marketplace, Notice of Proposed Rulemaking, 5 F.C.C. Rec. 2627, 2629 ¶15 (1990).

Communications Act, the Communications Satellite Act of 1962[65] authorized the creation of the Communications Satellite Corp. (COMSAT)—a private corporation subject to government regulation.[66] COMSAT was given authority to "provide communications links with the INTELSAT space segment, to provide end to end services . . . to serve as a carrier's carrier . . . [and] to provide end to end services between domestic carriers."[67]

In its 1970 Report on Domestic Communication-Satellite Facilities (*DOMSAT I*), the FCC adopted an "open skies" policy and allowed legally, financially, and technologically qualified applicants to apply for domestic satellite permits.[68] By opening up this market to nongovernmental entities, the FCC hoped to spur efficiency, lower costs, increase public welfare, and encourage a larger array of services.[69]

In 1972, *DOMSAT II*[70] solidified and enhanced these objectives by removing most of the institutional barriers that still blocked satellite development; the flexible licensing procedures introduced by *DOMSAT II* encouraged competitive entry in domestic and international satellite markets[71] and extended to the ground segments as well as those in space.[72] At this point, how-

[65] Pub. L. No. 87-624, §102, 76 Stat. 419 (1962) (codified as amended at 47 U.S.C. §§701–757 (1988)).

[66] 47 U.S.C. §§701(c), 731.

[67] Note, The Satellite Competition Debate: An Analysis of FCC Policy and an Argument in Support of Open Competition, 40 Syracuse L. Rev. 867, 870–871 (1989).

[68] Establishment of Domestic Communication-Satellite Facilities by Non-governmental Entities, Report and Order, 22 F.C.C.2d 86, 93 (1970) (hereinafter *DOMSAT I*); AT&T, Extension of the Moratorium on Use of Comstar Satellite Systems for Non-government Private Line Services, Memorandum Opinion and Order, 72 F.C.C.2d 895 (1979) (hereinafter *Satellite Private Line Services*).

[69] Note, The Satellite Competition Debate at 874 n.53.

[70] Establishment of Domestic Communications-Satellite Facilities by Non-governmental Entities, Second Report and Order, 35 F.C.C.2d 844 (1972) (hereinafter *DOMSAT II*), recons. denied, 37 F.C.C.2d 184, 38 F.C.C.2d 665 (1972), aff'd sub nom. Network Project v. FCC, 511 F.2d 786 (D.C. Cir. 1975).

[71] See Establishment of Satellite Systems Providing International Communications, Report and Order, 101 F.C.C.2d 1046, 1066 ¶44 (1985) ("The domestic satellite industry exemplifies all the benefits of a competitive market.").

[72] *DOMSAT II*, 35 F.C.C.2d at 855 ¶33 ("Our broad policy objective is to aim toward a flexible ground environment which would permit a variety of

ever, the FCC faced a paradox regarding its open entry policy: in order to encourage competition and promote new entry by specialized common carriers, the FCC found it necessary to limit Bell's involvement in the domestic satellite market.[73] Bell was strictly forbidden to use its satellite facilities for competition in the "non-governmental private line services" for three years, beginning in 1972.[74]

These satellite policies reflected the Commission's determination that a competitive, Bell-free marketplace could best identify the merits of satellite technology as a communications medium and the kinds of uses to which it could be put.[75] The first domestic common carrier satellite (Westar) was launched by Western Union on April 13, 1974.[76] As a result of the FCC's initiatives, many new satellite carriers quickly entered the market—including RCA; Western Union; GTE; Sprint's predecessor, Southern Pacific Communications Corp.; and United States Satellite Systems, Inc.[77]

By the late 1970s, satellite operators had found a ready market for their services among distributors of cable television programming. These distributors found satellite services cost-effective

---

earth station ownership patterns and afford diversified access to space segments except where this is impractical."). *See generally* Wiley, Telecommunications and the Law at 158–159.

[73] This restriction arose from the Commission's concern that specialized common carriers (offering private line services pursuant to the authority granted the year before in *Specialized Common Carriers*) would not be able to compete with AT&T if AT&T immediately gained permission to use satellite transmission for private line services. The Commission's policy was essentially intended to give other satellite carriers the chance to establish themselves and develop a customer base before facing competition from AT&T. *See DOMSAT II,* 35 F.C.C.2d at 847–850 ¶¶8–15.

[74] Competition in the Interstate Interexchange Marketplace, Notice of Proposed Rulemaking, 5 F.C.C. Rec. 2627, 2629 ¶16(1990). *See also DOMSAT II,* 35 F.C.C.2d at 851–853 ¶¶21–26.

[75] *See* Licensing of Space Stations in the Domestic Fixed-Satellite Service, Notice of Inquiry and Proposed Rulemaking, 88 F.C.C.2d 318, 321 ¶9 (1981).

[76] *See* Application of Western Union Telegraph Co. for Authority to Launch and Operate a Domestic Communications Satellite, Memorandum, Opinion, Order, and Authorization, 46 F.C.C.2d 162 (1974) (authorizing WESTAR I launch).

[77] See W. Bolter, Telecommunications Policy for the 1990s and Beyond 255 (1990).

because one-way, point-to-multipoint video transmission required the use of only one large earth station to put up the signal with multiple, much less expensive, receive-only earth stations to bring it down. Once these satellite operators were well established, the Commission removed the restrictions on the Bell System in 1979.[78]

§9.3.4 Cable, Mobile, and Broadcast Services

Cable companies arrived next in the long-distance market. At first, there was little apparent overlap between their one-way broadcast video services and the two-way voice services traditionally supplied by phone companies. But as discussed in Chapter 11, by the 1970s cable operators were beginning to carry data traffic, too. Since then, the FCC has generally encouraged such initiatives.[79] Two wireless technologies that originally were conceived as competitors to cable systems—multichannel multipoint distribution service (MMDS) and local multipoint distribution service (LMDS)—also are being adapted to offer Internet and other data services.[80]

---

[78] See Satellite Private Line Services, 72 F.C.C.2d at 900–902 ¶¶20–26.

[79] See, e.g., Heritage Cablevision Associates of Dallas, L.P. v. Texas Utilities Elec. Co., Memorandum Opinion and Order, 6 F.C.C. Rec. 7099 (1991) (asserting jurisdiction to regulate pole attachments used for nonvideo services, such as data transmission, in addition to video and other traditional cable television services); Cox Cable Communications, Inc., Memorandum Opinion and Order, Declaratory Ruling, and Order, 58 Rad. Reg. 2d (P & F) 1235, 1236 (1985) (preempting a Nebraska Public Service Commission order requiring cable operator to obtain a certificate of public convenience and necessity before providing high-speed digital transmission services), vacated as moot, 1 F.C.C. Rec. 561 (1986).

[80] See §11.2.2.3; Amendment of Parts 21 and 74 to Enable Multipoint Distribution Service and Instructional Television Fixed Service Licensees to Engage in Fixed Two-Way Transmission, Report and Order, 13 F.C.C. Rec. 19,112 (1998) (Commission permitting MMDS providers to offer wireless two-way services); see also Annual Assessment of the Status of Competition in Markets for the Delivery of Video Programming, Fifth Annual Report, CS Docket No. 98-101, ¶87 (Dec. 23, 1998) (hereinafter Video Competition Report) (discussing LMDS provider CellularVision discontinuing its video programming services, selling part of its spectrum to Winstar's wireless data network, and

Cable systems constitute a second "last mile" into nearly 70 percent of American homes.[81] Once interconnected with a global or nationwide information infrastructure (e.g., the Internet), these systems are capable of carrying data and voice traffic over local access and transport area (LATA) boundaries at a minimal marginal cost.[82] Indeed, Congress recognized cable providers as potential providers of telecommunications services when it drafted the Telecommunications Act of 1996.[83]

Competitive mobile radio services likewise flowered in the late 1970s and in the 1980s. The FCC's long-standing policies favoring competitive provision of paging, mobile telephony, and related services resulted in vigorously competitive markets. As discussed in Chapter 13, providers of radio services have rapidly knit together their operations with little regard to traditional boundaries between "local" and "long-distance" operations.

In the 1990s, the growth of mobile services led the FCC back once again to satellite use. During 1993 and 1994, the Commission completed rulemaking proceedings on two types of low earth orbiting (LEO) mobile satellite services.[84] In November 1993, the Commission adopted final rules for LEO systems operating at frequencies below 1 GHz.[85] These rules streamlined the

---

using its deployed facilities and remaining spectrum to offer Internet-based data services).

[81] National Cable Television Association, Cable Television Facts-at-a-Glance 1998 <http://www.ncta.com/overview98_7.html>.

[82] See §11.2.2.3.

[83] S. Conf. Rep. No. 230, 104th Cong., 2d Sess. 148 (1996).

[84] LEO systems differ from "geostationary" satellites in that they use many small satellites orbiting the earth at much lower altitudes. See Amendment of the Commission's Rules to Establish Rules and Policies Pertaining to a Mobile Satellite Service in the 1610–1626.5/2483.5–2500 MHz Frequency Bands, Notice of Proposed Rulemaking, 9 F.C.C. Rec. 1094, 1105 ¶20 (1994) (hereinafter *MSS Notice*).

[85] Amendment of the Commission's Rules to Establish Rules and Policies Pertaining to a Non-voice, Non-geostationary Mobile-Satellite Service, Report and Order, 8 F.C.C. Rec. 8450 (1993) (hereinafter *NVNG Report and Order*). These systems are variously referred to as Little LEOs or nonvoice, non-geostationary (NVNG) mobile satellite services. Little LEOs are capable of providing nationwide, two-way data communications and position location services using low-cost, portable transceivers. See generally id.

licensing procedures for little LEOs, allowing operators to acquire a single license that covers all LEOs in any given system.[86]

In October 1994, the FCC adopted final rules for "Big LEOs,"[87] which operate above 1 GHz and provide a wider array of services than Little LEOs.[88] The FCC classified Big LEOs as a commercial mobile radio service (CMRS) and ruled that because they provide capacity to CMRS providers, and not directly to end users, licensees will be regulated as private, rather than common, carriers.[89]

Big LEOs must be able to provide continuous coverage "throughout the fifty states, Puerto Rico and the U.S. Virgin Islands."[90] The Commission adopted a "strict" financial qualification standard for Big LEO applicants identical to the one used in the domestic fixed-satellite service.[91] As of 1998, four companies were licensed to operate Big LEO systems.[92] Two of the four

[86] 47 C.F.R. §25.115(d) (1997). NVNG transceivers operating in the United States must communicate with or through U.S.-authorized space stations only, and such communications must first be authorized by the space station licensee or an authorized vendor. *Id.* §25.135(c). License terms are for ten years, commencing on the date that the licensee certifies that its first satellite is operational. *Id.* §25.121(d)(2).

[87] Amendment of the Commission's Rules to Establish Rules and Policies Pertaining to a Mobile Satellite Service in the 1610–1626.5/2483.5–2500 MHz Frequency Bands, Report and Order, 9 F.C.C. Rec. 5936 (1994) (hereinafter *Big LEO Report and Order*).

[88] The Commission has claimed that Big LEOs ultimately will offer "an almost limitless number of services, including ubiquitous voice and data mobile services, position location services, search and rescue communications, disaster management communications, environmental monitoring, paging services, facsimile transmission services, cargo tracking, and industrial monitoring and control." *Id.* at 5940 ¶3.

[89] *See Big LEO Report and Order,* 9 F.C.C. Rec. at 6001 ¶172; Implementation of Sections 3(n) and 332 of the Communications Act, Second Report and Order, 9 F.C.C. Rec. 1411, 1457–1458 ¶¶108–109 (1994).

[90] 47 C.F.R. §25.143(b)(2)(iii).

[91] *Big LEO Report and Order,* 9 F.C.C. Rec. at 5948–5954 ¶¶26–42; 47 C.F.R. §25.143(b)(3).

[92] *See* Application of Motorola Satellite Communications, Inc., Order and Authorization, 10 F.C.C. Rec. 2268 (1995); Application of Loral/Qualcomm Partnership, L.P., Order and Authorization, 10 F.C.C. Rec. 2333 (1995); Application of Mobile Communications Holdings, Inc., Order and Authorization, 12 F.C.C. Rec. 9663 (1997); Application of Constellation Communications, Inc., Order and Authorization, 12 F.C.C. Rec. 9651 (1997).

licensees—Motorola (operating under the name Iridium) and Loral/Qualcomm (operating under the name Globalstar)—had launched a substantial number of satellites and were beginning to roll out their services.[93]

In addition to authorizing service through new technologies, the FCC also began to blur the once-rigid regulatory lines between broadcast and carrier services. In 1982, the Commission authorized direct broadcast satellite (DBS) providers to provide video broadcast services via satellite to customers on a subscription basis.[94] As a result, there are currently four satellite providers offering DBS service to 7.2 million subscribers.[95] These providers also are beginning to deploy interactive data and telecommunications services, putting them in competition with terrestrial and other satellite carriers.[96]

Thus, competition has come to the long-distance market step by step, technology by technology. There was no direct assault on the Bell System's venerable long-distance monopoly. The erosion came on the technological flank with microwaves, satellites, coaxial cables, glass fibers, and lasers, and finally a new generation of mobile radio services.[97] As will be seen below, once the FCC authorized these new technologies, it was hard-pressed to keep up with the inevitable competitive consequences.

§9.3.5   License Conditions and the Right to Compete

When the FCC began licensing competitive long-distance technologies, an obvious question arose: how would these new systems be used? Section 214(c) of the Communications Act permits

[93] Wireless Telecommunications Bureau, FCC, Third Annual Report and Analysis of Competitive Market Conditions with Respect to Commercial Mobile Radio Services at G-2 (June 1998) (hereinafter *Third Annual CMRS Competition Report*).

[94] Inquiry into the Development of Regulatory Policy in Regard to Direct Broadcast Satellites, Report and Order, 90 F.C.C.2d 676 (1982).

[95] *Video Competition Report* ¶¶61–79.

[96] *Id.* ¶75.

[97] *See* J. R. Haring & K. B. Levitz, The Law and Economics of Federalism in Telecommunications, 41 Fed. Comm. L.J. 261, 263 (1989).

the Commission to place conditions on licenses—to limit the services that may be provided over authorized facilities.[98] The speed at which competition was allowed into long-distance markets can be traced largely to this clause—or, more precisely, to one federal court's avoidance of it.

The FCC's *Specialized Common Carriers* ruling in 1971 clearly stated that the new microwave facilities would be used to provide "private line" services. In September 1974, however, MCI filed revisions to the tariff under which it furnished its interstate private line services and announced a new class of "metered use" services, including one called "Execunet."[99] Using Execunet, a subscriber would be able to reach any telephone in any city served by MCI simply by dialing a local MCI number followed by an access code and the number of the desired location. Execunet customers would be billed for each call on a time and distance basis very much like regular users of AT&T's long-distance service.[100]

At the direction of FCC Chairman Richard Wiley, and after heavy ex parte lobbying by the Bell System, the Common Carrier Bureau drafted a letter rejecting MCI's tariff. The full FCC adopted the letter on circulation, without a meeting.[101] *Special-*

---

[98] 47 U.S.C. §214(c) (Commission may attach to the issuance of the certificate such terms and conditions as in its judgment the public convenience and necessity may require). For the seminal explanation of the public convenience and necessity standard, see RCA v. FCC, 346 U.S. 86. *See also* Phonetele, Inc. v. AT&T, 664 F.2d 716, 722 (9th Cir. 1982), *cert. denied,* 459 U.S. 1145 (1983); Mid-Texas Communications Sys., Inc. v. AT&T, 615 F.2d 1372, 1379 (5th Cir. 1980), *cert. denied,* 449 U.S. 912 (1980); Hawaiian Tel. Co. v. FCC, 498 F.2d 771, 776 (D.C. Cir. 1974); Northeastern Tel. Co. v. AT&T, 477 F. Supp. 251, 253 (D. Conn. 1978); NAACP v. FPC, 425 U.S. 662, 669 (1976) ("the use of the words 'public interest' in a regulatory statute . . . take[s] meaning from the purposes of the regulatory legislation"); New York Cent. Sec. Corp. v. United States, 287 U.S. 12, 25 (1932) ("the term 'public interest' as thus used [in a statute] is not a concept without ascertainable criteria"); Business Roundtable v. SEC, 905 F.2d 406, 413 (D.C. Cir. 1990) (broad public interest mandates "must be limited to the purposes Congress had in mind when it enacted [the] legislation").

[99] MCI, Tariff F.C.C. No. 1 (1974).

[100] *Execunet I,* 561 F.2d at 367, 367 n.3.

[101] MCI Telecommunications Corporation, Investigation into the Lawfulness of Tariff FCC No. 1 Insofar as It Purports to Offer Execunet Service,

ized Common Carriers had authorized only "private line" communications, the Commission said, whereas Execunet was "essentially a switched public message telephone service."[102] MCI immediately went to court and argued that the Commission had followed illegal procedures in rejecting Execunet. Before the case was briefed, the FCC sought and obtained a voluntary remand for further consideration. The Commission then initiated a truncated proceeding on the lawfulness of MCI's tariff. Following an en banc oral argument, the Commission rejected Execunet a second time.[103]

The matter went back to the D.C. Circuit Court of Appeals, which ruled in MCI's favor in *Execunet I,* an opinion made up of equal parts legal legerdemain and heavy-handed policymaking.[104] Many of the construction permits under which MCI was operating contained no express limitation to the provision of private line services. The filing of a tariff, the court of appeals declared, is the usual mechanism under the Communications Act for initiating new services over previously authorized facilities.[105] "[C]arriers should in general be free to initiate and implement new rates or services over existing communications lines, unless and until the Commission, after hearing, determines that such rates or practices are unlawful, subject only to a limited period of suspension set out in the statute."[106] Thus, a carrier can usually tell if it is subject to service restrictions simply by examining the instruments of authorization issued to it by the Commission.[107]

Decision, 60 F.C.C.2d 25, app. B at 62–64 (1976) (letter order of July 2, 1975 (FCC 75-799)).

[102] *Id.* at 63.

[103] *Id.* at 58 ¶116, *rev'd sub nom. Execunet I,* 561 F.2d 365.

[104] *Execunet I,* generally. The court found that the Commission refused to consider whether the Execunet service should be permitted, regardless of the scope of the *Specialized Common Carriers* decision, and further indicated that it had intended to confer on AT&T a monopoly over MTS and WATS by that ruling.

[105] *Id.* at 374; *see* AT&T v. FCC, 487 F.2d 865, 870–881 (2d Cir. 1973).

[106] *Execunet I,* 561 F.2d at 374.

[107] *Id.* at 373.

If the Commission wanted to restrict the services a carrier could provide over already authorized facilities, the court held, Section 214 required an express determination that restrictions were required by the "public convenience and necessity."[108] And although the Commission's entire discussion in *Specialized Common Carriers* had focused on private line services, there had been no express, "affirmative finding"[109] to that precise effect. Thus, any facilities authorizations granted under that decision could not be limited to private line services.[110] "In so holding," the court blandly disclaimed, "we have not had to consider, and have not considered, whether competition like that posed by Execunet is in the public interest."[111]

§9.4 Interconnection and Equal Access

Having won in *Execunet I* the right to challenge the Bell System, the new entrants found that they required Bell's help in doing so. The new microwave systems were well suited for the long-distance wholesale end of telephony, but the new entrants also needed distribution plant—retailers, so to speak—at both ends of their microwave networks.

The FCC had anticipated this issue of local interconnection in *Specialized Common Carrier;* it had decided that "established carriers with exchange facilities should, upon request, permit interconnection or leased channel arrangements on reasonable terms and conditions to be negotiated with the new carriers, and also afford their customers the option of obtaining local distribution service under reasonable terms set forth in the tariff sched-

---

108

[I]t is readily apparent that failure to consider the public interest ramifications of a service—either pro or con—during resolution of a Section 214(a) application is simply not the same thing as an affirmative determination that the "public convenience and necessity may require" a restriction on a facility authorization. . . .

Id. at 378.
[109] *Id.*
[110] *Id.*
[111] *Id.* at 380.

ules of the local carrier."[112] The Commission had concluded, however, that "[i]n view of the representations of AT&T and GT&E in this proceeding . . . and the self-interest of other independent telephone companies in not losing potential new business, there appears to be no need to say more on this question at this time."[113]

Despite the Commission's relatively clear holding that existing carriers were required to offer interconnection to specialized common carriers, the Bell System continued to resist. Bell and MCI had begun negotiating for the provision of interconnection services, but Bell broke off negotiations in the late summer of 1973 and submitted tariffs to public utility commissions in each of the states in which MCI sought interconnection. Interconnection facilities are entirely intrastate, Bell reasoned, and were therefore matters of state, not federal, regulation.[114] Bell announced that it would provide no interconnection to MCI pending of these tariffs.[115] The state tariffs filed by Bell permitted specialized carriers like MCI to interconnect for ordinary private line service, but not for more elaborate (and valuable) private line services such as foreign exchange (FX) service and common control switching arrangements (CCSA).[116]

MCI complained to the Commission, and in *Bell System Tariff Offerings,* the Commission agreed that MCI was entitled to receive from local telephone companies various types of inter-

[112] *Specialized Common Carriers,* 29 F.C.C.2d at 940.

[113] *Id.* ("[s]hould any future problem arise . . . we will act expeditiously to take such measures as are necessary and appropriate in the public interest to implement and enforce the policies and objectives of this Decision").

[114] Bell System Tariff Offerings of Local Distribution Facilities for Use by Other Common Carriers, Decision, 46 F.C.C.2d 413, 416 (1974) (hereinafter *Bell System Tariff Offerings*), *aff'd sub nom.* Bell Tel. Co. of Pa. v. FCC, 503 F.2d 1250 (3d Cir. 1974).

[115] Bell Tel. Co. of Pa. v. FCC, 503 F.2d 1250, 1256 (3d Cir. 1974), *cert. denied,* 422 U.S. 1026 (1975).

[116] *Bell System Tariff Offerings,* 46 F.C.C.2d at 418. FX is a private line service that is partially switched. It allows a business located in one state to, in effect, maintain a local phone in another state. CCSAs are private line systems for linking the various offices of a company through large switches on a local telephone company's premises instead of through PBX switches on the customer's premises. *Id.* at 418 n.5.

connection, including connection for furnishing FX and for insertion of its facilities into a telephone company's CCSA.[117] The ruling also established that interconnection of long-distance and local facilities are matters for federal, not state, jurisdiction.[118] It was plain that interconnection was technologically feasible; Bell was already providing FX and CCSA interconnection to its own Long Lines Department and to numerous independent telephone companies. Specialized common carriers therefore were to enjoy full interconnection rights of similar type[119] for any interstate services authorized either "presently or hereafter."[120] The Commission likened its decision to an earlier ruling involving the interconnection of customer premises equipment.[121] The Third Circuit affirmed.[122]

---

[117] *Id.* at 426–427. The ruling to that effect was initially set out in a letter dated October 19, 1973, from Bernard Strassburg, Chief of the Common Carrier Bureau. *Id.* at 430.

[118] *See* California v. FCC, 567 F.2d 84, 86 (D.C. Cir. 1977) (authorizing the FCC to regulate facilities used in both local and long-distance communications, including FX and CCSA facilities), *cert. denied,* 434 U.S. 1010 (1978). *See also* Interconnection with Special Carriers in Furnishing Interstate Foreign Exchange (FX) Service and Common Control Switching Arrangements (CCSA), Memorandum Opinion and Order, 56 F.C.C.2d 14, 21 (1975) ("The key issue . . . is the nature of the communications which pass through the facilities, not the physical location of the lines.").

[119] *Bell Tel. Co. of Pa.,* 503 F.2d at 1254–1259.

[120] *Bell System Tariff Offerings,* 46 F.C.C.2d at 438.

[121] *See* Use of the Carterfone Service in Message Toll Telephone Service, Decision, 13 F.C.C.2d 420 (1968) (permitting any attachment of CPE to the telephone network as long as it does not have any negative effect on the operations of the telephone company or utility of its network), *recons. denied,* 14 F.C.C.2d 571 (1968). *See* §8.4.1.2.

Parallel issues arose in the newly competitive satellite industry. *See* §9.3.3. In the *Domestic Satellite* decision, the Commission required Bell and the other telephone carriers to submit descriptions of the kinds of interconnection arrangements they proposed to make available to other domestic satellite systems as a prerequisite to favorable action on their own applications. Thereafter, the Commission conditioned Bell's applications for domestic satellite authorizations on Bell's provision of effective access arrangements. Application of AT&T for Authorization to Construct & Operate Five Earth Stations to Provide Domestic Communications Satellite Services, Memorandum, Opinion, Order, and Authorization, 42 F.C.C.2d 654 (1973) (hereinafter *Domestic Satellite*), *recons. denied,* 45 F.C.C.2d 93 (1974).

[122] *See Bell Tel. Co. of Pa.,* 503 F.2d 1250.

§9.4.1   Execunet II

Meanwhile, MCI was moving ahead with its Execunet service. The service immediately raised a cluster of new questions about interconnection—which AT&T had anticipated in its Third Circuit challenge to the FCC's *Bell System Tariff Offerings.* In that appeal, AT&T had specifically complained that the FCC's order imposed an unreasonably "unbounded" interconnection obligation,[123] and the appellate court had specifically concluded otherwise. "On its face," the Third Circuit had conceded, the FCC's order gave "little guidance as to the types of services that AT&T will be required to provide 'hereafter.'" However, "[o]rders are not to be read in a vacuum, but rather must be read and interpreted in the context in which they appear."[124] And as the Third Circuit read the order, the Commission had required AT&T to provide interconnection only for elements of *private line* services.[125]

Hours after the Supreme Court denied AT&T's application for certiorari in *Execunet I,* AT&T announced it would stop providing additional interconnection for Execunet or similar services and filed with the Commission a petition for a declaratory ruling that it was under "no obligation" to furnish any specialized carrier with connections for Execunet-type services. On February 23, 1978—scarcely a month later, after expedited review—the Commission agreed with AT&T.[126]

The matter then returned to the D.C. Circuit, which once again sided with MCI.[127] In its *Execunet II* decision, the appellate court now denounced the FCC for having done precisely what

[123] *Bell System Tariff Offerings,* 46 F.C.C.2d at 424–427.
[124] *Bell Tel. Co. of Pa.,* 503 F.2d at 1273.
[125] *Id.* at 1273–1274.
[126] Petition of AT&T for a Declaratory Ruling and Expedited Relief, Memorandum Opinion and Order, 67 F.C.C.2d 1455 (1978) (hereinafter *AT&T Petition*). The petition was denied only "insofar as it requests a determination with respect to the scope of petitioner's interconnection obligations to specialized common carriers, if any, under the Sherman Act, the common law, or any federal or state statute other than the Communications Act." *Id.* at 1480 ¶83.
[127] MCI Telecomms. Corp. v. FCC, 580 F.2d 590 (D.C. Cir. 1978) (*Execunet II*).

Execunet I had reproached it for failing to do—making an explicit finding that competitive provision of switched services was not within the public interest determination of the FCC's original *Specialized Common Carriers* order.[128] Now, the court of appeals said that its *Execunet I* decision clearly contemplated—"by virtue of AT&T's representations and actions—that AT&T would provide interconnections for Execunet service."[129] The court based this remarkable conclusion on the fact that AT&T had made such a fuss about MCI's service: if AT&T was not going to provide interconnection, then MCI's Execunet service could not have done AT&T any harm.[130] Neither AT&T nor the Commission would be permitted to "renounce a position and obligation which they assumed throughout the course of the Execunet proceedings."[131] Any limits on interconnection rights would be "clearly inconsistent with the basic themes" of *Execunet I*.[132] "[T]he expansive interpretation of *Specialized Common Carrier* we advanced in [*Execunet I*] clearly mandates an equally expansive view of the scope of [Bell's] interconnection obligations."[133] Three years later the court of appeals extended identical interconnection obligations to all independent local exchange telephone companies.[134]

---

[128] *Id.* at 596–597.

[129] *Id.* at 595.

[130]

   Never in the proceedings before this court did AT&T even suggest that it was not required to provide these connections, or that the question of MCI's authority to provide or expand its Execunet service was, as a practical matter, of no consequence since AT&T could and would refuse to provide the essential interconnections. . . .

Id.

[131] *Id.*

[132] *Id.* at 597. Even though the interconnection order did speak in terms of "private line service," the Commission recognized "that the *Specialized Common Carrier* decision encompassed specialized communication services other than those which theretofore had been described as 'private line services'" and acknowledged that "private line" had emerged as shorthand for the broader term "specialized communication service" because of the particular context in which the interconnection issues were most frequently raised. *Id.* at 596 (citing *AT&T Petition,* 67 F.C.C.2d at 1474).

[133] *Execunet II,* 580 F.2d at 597.

[134] Lincoln Tel. & Tel. Co. v. FCC, 659 F.2d 1092 (D.C. Cir. 1981) (*Execunet III*). See Wiley, Telecommunications and the Law at 161.

The *Execunet* decisions had profound practical implications. MCI and other carriers had their licenses in hand, and these licenses had now, by judicial declaration, become licenses to compete unconditionally wherever facilities had been authorized.[135] Yet so far as current law is concerned, *Execunet* can be viewed as a historical curiosity. The FCC retains its section 214(c) power to issue conditional licenses and need only exercise that power in ways that will pass muster in the D.C. Circuit (which has exclusive jurisdiction under section 402(b)).

Happily, however, the Commission's policy preferences have been in quite the opposite direction. The Commission has become increasingly *unwilling* to place conditions of any kind in operating licenses. Prodded by the various *Execunet* decisions, the Commission opened a new rulemaking and in 1980 formally adopted an open-entry policy for all interstate services.[136] Similarly, in 1982, the Commission began to allow satellite carriers to sell transponder capacity; previously only common carrier services were permitted.[137]

§9.4.2 The Right to Resell

Interconnection with Bell's local exchanges was essential for the new specialized carriers, but they needed still more. They wanted to provide every kind of interstate service, yet the cost of

---

[135] *Execunet I*, 561 F.2d at 365.

[136] MTS and WATS Market Structure, Phase I, Report and Third Supplemental Notice of Inquiry and Proposed Rulemaking, 81 F.C.C.2d 177 (1980), Third Report and Order, 93 F.C.C.2d 241 (1983) (hereinafter *Access Order*), *modified on recons.*, 97 F.C.C.2d 682 (1983), *modified on further recons.*, 97 F.C.C.2d 834(1984), *aff'd in principal part and remanded in part*, NARUC v. FCC, 737 F.2d 1095 (D.C. Cir. 1984), *cert. denied*, 469 U.S. 1227 (1985). *See also* MTS and WATS Market Structure, Phase III, Notice of Proposed Rulemaking, 94 F.C.C.2d 292 (1983).

[137] Domestic Fixed-Satellite Transponder Sales, Memorandum, Opinion, Order, and Authorization, 90 F.C.C.2d 1238, 1255 ¶41 (1982) ("[T]he record shows that the certification of noncommon carrier domsat systems is consistent with our policies fostering multiple satellite entry. They encourage additional entry, additional facility investment, more efficient use of the orbital and frequency spectrum and allow for technical and marketing innovation in the provision of domsat services.").

deploying a nationwide long-distance network in a single step remained prohibitive, even with microwave. The solution, from the new entrants' perspective, was to compete with Bell over some parts of the network, while using Bell's long-distance facilities elsewhere. In effect, the specialized carriers wanted to interconnect with Bell's *long-distance* facilities, too. Stated another way, they wanted the right to resell Bell's long-distance services as an adjunct to their own facilities-based services, just as they had won the right (in effect) to resell Bell's local exchange connections.

When the FCC issued its *Specialized Common Carriers* decision in 1971, AT&T's private line tariff expressly prohibited "piece out" and "resale." The piece-out prohibition was intended to prevent precisely what the new entrants intended to do, which was to build the easy and cheap parts of a private line network (over flat terrain, for example) and rely on Bell to carry traffic in the difficult and expensive places. AT&T therefore declared it would connect its private line services to any other carrier's network only on the premises of the ultimate customer, where the customer had a "regular and continuing requirement to originate or terminate communications."[138] "Customers" and "end users" could buy AT&T's services, but "carriers," "resellers," and the like could not.[139]

In July 1976, the FCC correctly concluded that restrictions of this kind prevented normal economic activities, such as arbitrage, and therefore helped sustain price discrimination and maintain rates at variance with true costs.[140] Accordingly, the

---

[138] AT&T, Restrictions on Interconnection of Private Line Services, Memorandum Opinion and Order, 60 F.C.C.2d 939, 940 ¶2 (1976) (hereinafter *Interconnection Restrictions*). The resale prohibition in Tariff 260 read in pertinent part: "Private line service shall not be used for any purpose for which a payment or other compensation shall be received by either the customer or any authorized or joint user, or in the collection, transmission, or delivery of any communications for others." AT&T Tariff F.C.C. No. 260, Private Line Service, §2.6.3(A)(1) (1984).

[139] For a general overview of resale and sharing restrictions and regulations during this period, see Resale and Sharing of Private Line Communications Services: AT&T Restriction and FCC Regulation, 61 Va. L. Rev. 679 (1975).

[140] Regulatory Policies Concerning Resale and Shared Use of Common Carrier Domestic Public Switched Network Services, Report and Order, 83 F.C.C.2d 167, 175–176, ¶¶15–16 (1980) (hereinafter *Switched Network Resale*).

Commission directed AT&T and other carriers to eliminate all piece-out[141] and resale restrictions[142] from their interstate private line tariffs.

In 1980, on the heels of the *Execunet II* ruling, the Commission directed AT&T to remove similar restrictions from its message toll service (MTS) and WATS tariffs.[143] WATS—AT&T's "wide area telecommunications services"—was a discount service for volume users; MCI and other specialized carriers were now targeting those same users.[144] The new entrants viewed WATS as their most difficult competition[145] and frequently complained that WATS prices were being manipulated and artificially depressed to thwart the new competitive challenges.[146] The FCC addressed these allegations by ordering AT&T to permit others to resell WATS services without hindrance.[147] In 1983, the Com-

[141] AT&T Restrictions on Interconnection of Private Line Services, Memorandum Opinion and Order, 60 F.C.C.2d 939, 946 ¶19 (1976).

[142] Regulatory Policies Concerning Resale and Shared Use of Common Carrier Services and Facilities, Report and Order, 60 F.C.C.2d 261 (1976) (hereinafter *Facilities Resale*), *modified on recons.*, 62 F.C.C.2d 588 (1977) (hereinafter *Resale and Shared Use*), *aff'd*, AT&T v. FCC, 572 F.2d 17 (2d Cir.), *cert. denied*, 439 U.S. 875 (1978). Resale was defined as "the subscription to communications services and facilities by one entity and the reoffering of communications service and facilities to the public (with or without 'adding value') for profit." *Facilities Resale*, 60 F.C.C.2d at 263 ¶4.

[143] *Switched Network Resale*, 83 F.C.C.2d at 194 ¶73.

[144] *Id.* at 169–171, ¶¶4–6. WATS was introduced by AT&T in the 1960s as a way to fight end-to-end bypass in which both the LEC and interexchange carriers were cut out of the transmission. Using WATS, a firm could lease a line from its place of business to the local switch, over which a call to anyplace in the United States could be made. WATS cost a fixed amount per month, with a marginal price of zero per call. This service was used by firms with large, unconcentrated calling volumes. *See* NARUC v. FCC, 746 F.2d 1492, 1495 (D.C. Cir. 1984).

[145] Gerald R. Faulhaber, Telecommunications in Turmoil: Technology and Public Policy 69 (1987).

[146] *Switched Network Resale*, 83 F.C.C.2d at 170 ¶4; NARUC v. FCC, 746 F.2d at 1495–1496.

[147] In so doing, it rejected AT&T's argument that increases in long-distance telephone rates for customers would result if MTS users switched to WATS. AT&T also argued that a "change in the restrictions on WATS would lead to a decrease in MTS revenues, shifting costs from interstate operations to intrastate." The FCC discounted this claim as well. *Resale and Shared Use*, 62 F.C.C.2d at 596 ¶15.

mission extended resale rights to *intrastate* WATS used for "access" to interstate communication.[148] In parallel with these initiatives, resellers were classified as common carriers under 47 U.S.C. §153(h).[149] Like other carriers, they had to offer nondiscriminatory service at reasonable rates,[150] but if they owned no facilities, they were not required to file tariffs or receive permission to begin or terminate service.[151]

The right to resell WATS immediately attracted hundreds of new long-distance resellers. They built their networks not out of wires and switches, but out of tariffs, assembling packages of WATS and private lines supplied by other carriers.[152] As the FCC anticipated, this created steady, strong pressure toward cost-based pricing in the long-distance market.[153] At the same time, entry barriers into the market, particularly capital requirements, were markedly reduced.[154]

---

[148] AT&T, Restrictions on Resale and Sharing of Switched Services, Memorandum Opinion and Order, 53 Rad. Reg. 2d (P & F) 112 (1983), *aff'd sub nom.* NARUC v. FCC, 746 F.2d at 1492. *See* R. R. McKenna, Pre-emption Under the Communications Act, 37 Fed. Comm. L.J. 1, 37–38 (1985). The Commission had also established a docket to examine the terms and conditions under which exchange carriers must interconnect with shared tenant service (STS) providers. It ordered that exchange carriers interconnect STS systems to interstate networks without regard for any state commission restrictions on STS resale of local exchange services. *See* International Business Machines Corp., Request for Declaratory Ruling re State Regulation of Shared Telecommunications Services Systems, Memorandum Opinion and Order, 59 Rad. Reg. 2d (P & F) 964, 967 (1985).

[149] *See Resale and Shared Use,* 62 F.C.C.2d at 600 ¶20 ("'Resale carriers,' whether they be brokers or 'value added' carriers . . . are equally subject to the requirements of Title II of the Communications Act.").

[150] Resellers affiliated with dominant carriers would, however, be regulated in the same way as their dominant affiliates. Policy and Rules Concerning Rates for Competitive Common Carrier Services and Facilities Authorizations Therefor, Second Report and Order, 91 F.C.C.2d 59, 73 n.37 (1982) (hereinafter *Competitive Carrier Second Report*).

[151] *See id.* at 73 ¶30. Entities that shared interstate private lines and private networks ("sharers") were not considered to be common carriers at all; therefore, their actions are monitored, but not regulated by the FCC. AT&T v. FCC, 572 F.2d at 21.

[152] Faulhaber, Telecommunications in Turmoil at 71.

[153] Competition in the Interstate Interexchange Marketplace, Notice of Proposed Rulemaking, 5 F.C.C. Rec. at 2630 ¶¶26–28.

[154] R. M. Atkinson, G. M. Neely, & S. Drumming, Testing AT&T's Dominance in the Long Distance Market, Pub. Util. Fort., Aug. 30, 1990, at 23, 25.

Today, there are hundreds of resellers in the long-distance market. Entry has been easier than winning market share, however. In an industry where carriers with names as familiar as AT&T spend billions of dollars per year to woo and keep customers, upstart resellers without brand recognition remain niche players. The combined revenues of all resellers still account for less than 20 percent of total industry revenues.[155]

§9.4.3 Market-Opening Litigation

New entrants were not content merely to advance their cause before the FCC. Again led by MCI, would-be interconnectors fought the Bell System in the courts as well, with the critical support of the Department of Justice.

§9.4.3.1 MCI Communications Corp. v. AT&T

In March 1974, as carriers were exercising the licensing rights afforded by *Specialized Common Carrier*[156] and concurrent with the introduction of its new Execunet intercity service offering,[157] MCI sued the Bell System for monopolizing intercity communications.[158] The complaint alleged 22 forms of misconduct.[159] Of

---

See also Regulatory Policies Concerning Resale and Shared Use of Common Carrier Domestic Public Switched Network Services, Report and Order, 83 F.C.C.2d 167 (1980) (Commission prohibited tariff restrictions on the resale and shared use of MTS and WATS services); Competition in the Interstate Interexchange Marketplace, Notice of Proposed Rulemaking, 5 F.C.C. Rec. 2627, 2630 ¶25 (1990) (1980 tariff decision "reduced entry barriers for the long-distance marketplace," in part by "reduc[ing] the capital requirements necessary for entry by permitting new entrants to offer regional or even nationwide service without constructing their own facilities").

[155] FCC data aggregate all long-distance carriers other than AT&T, MCI WorldCom, and Sprint, including some small facilities-based carriers, and hence overstate actual resale market share. Industry Analysis Division, FCC, Long Distance Market Shares: Third Quarter 1998 at tbl. 3.2. Resellers have established a greater presence as providers of business services than of residential services. *Id.* at tbl. 4.1.

[156] *Specialized Common Carriers,* 29 F.C.C.2d 870.

[157] *See* §9.4.1.

[158] MCI v. AT&T, 708 F.2d 1081.

[159] Perhaps an indication of how out of touch Bell's legal strategies had become, Bell itself filed a counterclaim against MCI, alleging that MCI attempted

the 15 allegations of misconduct that went to the jury, the jury found for MCI on 10, including predatory pricing[160] and refusal to interconnect as part of an attempt to maintain a long-distance monopoly.[161] The jury awarded $600 million. Trebled to $1.8 billion,[162] this was, at the time, the largest money verdict ever awarded.

On appeal, the Seventh Circuit agreed with the trial court's ruling that Bell enjoyed no general immunity from the antitrust laws, there being no "plain repugnancy" between antitrust and regulatory provisions.[163] Because Bell's predatory pricing and refusal to interconnect had not been *required* by the FCC, the FCC's failure to disapprove Bell's initiatives was not a defense.[164] There likewise was no immunity by virtue of state regulation. The jury had found that Bell had filed state tariffs in bad faith to delay MCI's entry into the market; the appellate court agreed that these filings had been a "sham."[165]

---

and conspired to monopolize and actually monopolized the St. Louis-Chicago market, conspired to restrain trade in that market, and wrongfully acquired stock or share capital of other corporations, which substantially lessened competition. The district court did not permit any of these allegations to go to the jury.

[160] When the FCC first allowed competition in some segments of the long-distance market, Bell slashed prices for services in which new competition seemed imminent. Four months after the FCC's decision in *Above 890,* Bell filed a new tariff, called Telpak, that offered substantial discounts for bundles of 60 channels (Telpak C) or 240 channels (Telpak D). Telpak was designed to eliminate the incentive for entities to construct private microwave systems for their own use where Bell facilities were available. Following the *Specialized Common Carriers* decision, Bell filed a new tariff, called Hi/Lo, that substantially reduced the rate for single-channel lines connecting high-density centers, where the specialized common carriers were likely to compete. Two years later the FCC found Hi/Lo to be unreasonable. *See* MCI v. AT&T, 708 F.2d at 1081 n.32. Bell then filed a replacement tariff, known as the Multi-Schedule Private Line (MPL) tariff, that offered similarly low rates on high-density routes.

[161] MCI v. AT&T, 708 F.2d at 1093.

[162] *Id.*

[163] *Id.* at 1102 (quoting *Gordon,* 422 U.S. at 682, and *Philadelphia Natl. Bank,* 374 U.S. at 350-351).

[164] *Id.* at 1103-1105.

[165] *Id.* at 1153-1159. The *Noerr-Pennington* doctrine provides that a person cannot suffer antitrust liability for exercising the First Amendment right to petition the government. Eastern R. R. Presidents Conference v. Motor Freight,

The Seventh Circuit further agreed that Bell had attempted to preserve a monopoly by refusing to interconnect its local switching facilities with MCI for the purpose of providing FX and CCSA services. There was no dispute that the local switches were "essential facilities" in providing these services and were infeasible to duplicate.[166] The dispute centered on whether Bell had both sincerely and reasonably interpreted the FCC's 1970 *Specialized Common Carriers* ruling as forbidding MCI to provide FX and CCSA services. The appellate court noted that while *Specialized Common Carriers* was "extremely opaque,"[167] both the FCC and the courts had subsequently interpreted that ruling to require interconnection.[168] The jury also had sufficient evidence, from such sources as internal company memos, to conclude that Bell had taken an indefensibly narrow view of the FCC's mandate so as to "buy time" in meeting MCI's competition.[169] Implicit in the Seventh Circuit's analysis was the assumption that interexchange services do in fact occupy a separate market than local services. Thus, liability arose from Bell's use of its essential facility to "impede or destroy competition in other markets."[170]

On the other hand, the court ruled that MCI had not presented sufficient evidence to support a finding that the Bell System unlawfully denied MCI "multipoint connections" to complete MCI's intercity coverage in areas where MCI had no service facilities at all.[171] *Specialized Common Carriers* could not be

---

Noerr 365 U.S. 127 (1961); United Mine Workers of Am. v. Pennington, 381 U.S. 657 (1965). The Seventh Circuit approved a jury instruction that "stressed that MCI's burden on this claim is higher (clear and convincing evidence) because of these First Amendment concerns." MCI v. AT&T, 708 F.2d at 1155.

[166] MCI v. AT&T, 708 F.2d 1132–1133.

[167] *Id.* at 1133.

[168] *Id.* at 1134 (citing *Bell System Tariff Offerings,* 46 F.C.C.2d 413, and *Execunet I,* 561 F.2d 365).

[169] *Id.* at 1139–1141. The court also upheld jury findings that Bell had unreasonably insisted on connecting with MCI only at the customer's premises; provided physical connections that were inefficient for high traffic volumes; and failed to maintain sufficient trouble-reporting procedures. *Id.* at 1133, 1139–1141.

[170] *Id.* at 1144.

[171] *Id.* at 1147–1150. "Multipoint service described the situation where AT&T provided a private line to a customer between city A and city B, and

read as imposing any such "extraordinary obligation to fill in the gaps in [Bell's] competitor's network."[172] MCI likewise had failed to prove that Bell's *intercity* network was an essential facility[173] or that Bell's denial of interconnections to its intercity network constituted an antitrust violation under any other theory.[174] The court thus distinguished the case in which a competitor needs to pass through an essential facility to reach the ultimate customer from the case in which the need is simply to resell a complementary service (in this instance, AT&T's ubiquitous long-distance service).

On the predatory pricing issues, the Seventh Circuit ruled that the appropriate cost measure was a question of law and should not have been given to the jury.[175] The court then held that the test for below-cost pricing should look to "long run incremental costs" (LRIC), defined as "the average cost of adding an entire new service or product rather than merely the last unit of production."[176] The jury had used "fully distributed cost" (FDC), a method by which all of a firm's costs are allocated over all of its products according to an arbitrary formula that assigns to the new product part of the costs of producing existing products.[177]

MCI provided a private line between city B and city C. MCI sought an interconnection in city B between its own line and AT&T's line so that MCI's customer in city C could have uninterrupted service between city C and city A." *Id.* at 1147.

[172] *Id.* at 1149.

[173] *See id.* at 1148.

[174] *Id.* at 1149.

[175] *Id.* at 1111–1112.

[176] *Id.* at 1115, 1119–1123.

[177] *Id.* at 1116; *see also id.* at 1175–1176 (Harlingtonwood, J., concurring in part and dissenting in part). As the Seventh Circuit explained, "There are countless FDC methods, each allocating costs by a different mathematical formula." As a result, "FDC cannot purport to identify those costs which are *caused* by a product or service, and this is fundamental to economic cost determination." *Id.* at 1116. "A simple example helps to highlight the arbitrariness of FDC methodology. Imagine a railroad line that simultaneously transports three different products: gold, lead and feathers. If the railroad attempted to calculate, on a fully distributed cost basis, the cost of shipping each of these products, it would reach radically different results depending on whether it allocated joint and common costs on the basis of the value, weight, or bulk of the respective commodities shipped." *Id.* at 1116 n.48.

Because the evidence showed that Bell's charges for the new services were well above LRIC,[178] this appellate pricing ruling devastated MCI's case, notwithstanding other favorable rulings on the issues of interconnection and essential facilities. After the court of appeals remanded the case for a recalculation of damages, a new jury awarded $113 million after trebling—less than 7 percent of the prior judgment.[179]

§9.4.3.2 *Southern Pacific Communications Co. v. AT&T*

Southern Pacific Communications (later Sprint) filed another major long-distance interconnection case against the Bell System in 1978. After a 33-day bench trial, the district court found for Bell on the merits and dismissed the case.[180] Most of Judge Richey's lengthy opinion was copied verbatim from Bell's proposed findings and conclusions.[181] In the original portions of his opinion, moreover, Judge Richey embraced Bell's view that the FCC's decisions opening the telecommunications industry to competition were contrary to the public interest.[182]

The D.C. Circuit affirmed, although it disagreed with Judge Richey's findings in several respects. The appellate court held, contrary to Judge Richey, that Bell possessed no implied immunity from the antitrust laws because of FCC regulation.[183] But on the issue of interconnection, the appellate court (breaking with the Seventh Circuit's *MCI* decision) upheld Judge Richey's find-

---

[178] And perhaps even above FDC as well, though the jury had not so found. *Id.* at 1125–1128.

[179] Daniel F. Cuff, MCI and AT&T in Accord, N.Y. Times, Nov. 19, 1985, at D6.

[180] Southern Pacific Communications Co. v. AT&T, 556 F. Supp. 825 (D.D.C. 1983), *aff'd*, 740 F.2d 980 (D.C. Cir. 1984), *cert. denied*, 470 U.S. 1005 (1985).

[181] *See* Southern Pacific Communications Co. v. AT&T, 740 F.2d 980, 988 (D.C. Cir. 1984).

[182] *E.g.*, Southern Pacific Communications Co. v. AT&T, 556 F. Supp. at 1096–1099.

[183] Southern Pacific Communications Co. v. AT&T, 740 F.2d at 999–1000. Citing Judge Greene's decision in United States v. AT&T, the court held that the FCC could have prevented the problems that led to the antitrust cases had it not been completely ineffectual. *Id.* at 1000.

ing that Bell's refusal to provide interconnections after the *Specialized Common Carriers* decision was excusable because Bell had a "reasonable basis in regulatory policy" to believe that it was not required to interconnect, and Bell actually believed, in good faith, that it did not have to interconnect.[184]

The treatment of subsidy and pricing issues in *Southern Pacific* was more favorable still for the Bell System.[185] Judge Richey flatly ruled that FCC regulation prevented Bell from exercising power over price. The D.C. Circuit overruled him on this point,[186] but upheld his bottom-line finding that Bell's challenged prices were above both LRIC and FDC.[187] The appellate court also recorded its "serious doubts about the usefulness of FDC as a measure of cost to be used in distinguishing lawful from predatory pricing."[188]

---

[184] *Id.* at 1010. In a separate opinion, the D.C. Circuit refused to give collateral estoppel effect to MCI v. AT&T, 708 F.2d 1081, and United States v. AT&T, 552 F. Supp. 131 (D.D.C. 1982) (*Decree Opinion*), *aff'd sub nom.* Maryland v. United States, 460 U.S. 1001 (1983), holding that Southern Pacific had waived most of its collateral estoppel claims and that the *AT&T* decision specifically renounced collateral effect. Southern Pacific Communications Co. v. AT&T, 740 F.2d 1011 (D.C. Cir. 1984).

In another case against Bell, a federal district court ruled against the Bell System when it refused to provide *long-distance* interconnection to an independent telephone company seeking to provide *local* service. Woodlands Telecomms. Corp. v. AT&T, 447 F. Supp. 1261 (S.D. Tex. 1978), *rev'd and remanded,* Mid-Texas Communications Sys., Inc. v. AT&T, 615 F.2d 1372 (5th Cir.), *reh'g denied,* 618 F.2d 1389 (5th Cir.), *cert. denied sub nom.* Woodlands Telecomms. Corp. v. Southwestern Bell Tel. Co., 449 U.S. 912 (1980). While it upheld the verdict's assessment of Bell's long-distance network as an "essential facility," Mid-Texas Communications Sys., Inc. v. AT&T, 615 F.2d 1372, 1375–1376 (Fifth Cir. 1980), the Fifth Circuit reversed because it found that the jury had not been sufficiently instructed to take regulation into account and to consider that federal regulation formed part of the market environment in which the Bell companies operated, *id.* at 1385–1390. Specifically, the Fifth Circuit found that the trial court had erred by instructing the jury that Bell had monopoly power (since the FCC might have deprived Bell of such power by ordering it to provide interconnections) and by failing to instruct the jury to consider whether Bell's refusal to interconnect was "reasonable" in light of applicable regulations. *Id.* at 1387, 1390.

[185] Southern Pacific Communications Co. v. AT&T, 556 F. Supp. 825.

[186] Southern Pacific Communications Co. v. AT&T, 740 F.2d at 1001.

[187] *Id.* at 1006.

[188] *Id. See also Aeronautical Radio,* 642 F.2d at 1222; 3 P. Areeda & D. Turner, Antitrust Law ¶719 (1978); 1 A. Kahn, The Economics of Regulation 150–158 (1988).

§9.4.3.3   Divestiture of the Bell System/ The MFJ Regime

These private antitrust suits against Bell were, in retrospect, of secondary importance to the U.S. Department of Justice's own case. Dissatisfied with the antitrust consent decree that had been entered in 1956 against AT&T,[189] the Department filed a separate action under the Sherman Act in 1974.[190] Much like MCI and Sprint, the Department alleged that the Bell System was stifling competition in long-distance markets using a two-pronged strategy of discriminatory interconnection and exchange access practices, together with predatory pricing subsidized by regulated local exchange revenues. Discovery in the new case began in 1975. The trial started on January 15, 1981, and continued with interruptions for almost a year, until the parties presented a proposed settlement that would supplant the 1956 Decree.[191]

As discussed in section 4.3, the resulting 1982 Decree—known as the Modification of Final Judgment or simply "the MFJ"— had four basic provisions: AT&T's divestiture of its local telephone operating companies; a requirement that the divested Bell Operating Companies (BOCs) provide all long-distance carriers and information providers with "equal access"; a prohibition of the BOCs from competing in markets other than local services; and release of AT&T from the 1956 Decree.[192]

§9.4.4   Equal Access Regulation

One upshot of the FCC's interconnection decisions and the 1982 Decree was that the local Bell Operating Companies would

---

[189] Under that decree, the Bell System agreed to provide only common carrier communications services and not to enter any other markets. Bell's equipment subsidiary, Western Electric, agreed to provide licenses and technical information to all comers wishing to manufacture Bell-patented products and manufacture only equipment used in providing telephone service. *See* United States v. Western Elec. Co., 1956 Trade Cas. (CCH) ¶68,246 (D.N.J. 1956); §4.4.2.

[190] *See Decree Opinion*, 552 F. Supp. at 139 & n.18.

[191] *Id.* at 139–141.

[192] *Id.* at 226–227.

have to engage in the extremely complex task of interconnecting entire networks. Fortunately for regulators and Judge Harold Greene, however, it is not necessary to police interconnection rights in minute detail; it suffices to insist on equal treatment. This is hardly a radical concept in telecommunications or in common carrier law generally.[193] What it comes down to is that "carriers" can be "customers," too, and when buying carriage from others, a carrier is entitled to service on nondiscriminatory terms like any other purchaser.

The principle of "*equal* access" first entered the modern regulatory lexicon close on the heels of the access right—that is, the right to interconnect. In *Specialized Common Carriers,* the FCC declared for the first time: "[W]here a carrier has monopoly control over essential facilities we will not condone any policy or practice whereby such carrier would discriminate in favor of an affiliated carrier or show favoritism among competitors."[194] After 1970, the Commission and the MFJ court steadily elaborated on that core principle.

Like everything else in telephony, the equal access principle has two halves, one (so to speak) for each end of the telephone line. For providers—long-distance carriers—equal access means a right to reach consumers. For consumers—people who make or receive calls—equal access means a right to select among carriers.

§9.4.4.1 Equal Access for Carriers

The specialized carriers did not win a right to fully equal interconnection overnight, and it is unlikely that they could have afforded to exercise that right if they had won it. Following *Execunet II,* the Bell System filed a new set of interconnection tariffs: the Exchange Network Facilities for Interstate Access (ENFIA) Agreements. These went into effect in 1979 and lasted until the

---

[193] A right to interconnect on more or less equal terms can be traced back to the telegraph statute in the 1800s. *See generally* §5.1.1; section 5.1.2.2 addresses equal access regulation as it applied to the BOCs' local operations under the MFJ.

[194] *Specialized Common Carriers,* 29 F.C.C.2d at 940 (quoting *Specialized Common Carriers,* Notice of Inquiry to Formulate Policy, Notice of Proposed Rulemaking, and Order, 24 F.C.C.2d 318, 347 (1970)).

Bell breakup in 1984.[195] The tariffs set out four different types of connections that the new long-distance carriers could buy from Bell's local exchange companies; these have since evolved into four standardized "feature groups." Depending on which access package they buy, carriers may connect on the "line side" or the "trunk side" of a local exchange switch; they may be accessed with shorter (1+) or longer (950-IXXX) access codes; and they may receive more or less additional electronic information.[196] The prices of the feature groups vary according to the sophistication of the interconnection supplied.[197]

When divestiture separated AT&T from the Bell System's local exchange operations, the divested Bell companies assumed the common carrier's traditional obligations to tariff their long-distance access services and treat all long-distance carriers equally.[198] As of January 1, 1984, AT&T, MCI, and all the other new carriers became (in principle, at least) similarly situated customers of the Bell companies, entitled to equal treatment.

The express equal access obligations in the Divestiture Decree created a firm and independent timetable for moving the Bell companies toward equal access[199] and spurred the FCC to fur-

---

[195] *See* Exchange Network Facilities for Interstate Access (ENFIA), Memorandum Opinion and Order, 71 F.C.C.2d 440, 443 (1979) (hereinafter *ENFIA Agreement*), *aff'd in part*, MCI v. FCC, 712 F.2d 517 (D.C. Cir. 1983).

[196] Feature Group A (formerly ENFIA A) provides carriers with a line-side connection to the local switch and a local 7-digit access number. Feature Group B (formerly ENFIA B and C) provides carriers with a trunk-side connection to the local switch and a 950-IXXX access number. Feature Group C, available only to AT&T, provides a trunk-side connection and 1+ service. Feature Group D provides every carrier with 1+ service and a 10XXX access code, a trunk-side connection to the switch, and several additional features. Feature Groups C and D are regarded as "premium access." National Exchange Carrier Association Tariff F.C.C. No. 1, at 157–159.

[197] *See* §5.2.1.2.

[198] *See Decree Opinion*, 552 F. Supp. at 195–200. *See also* §5.1.2.2.

[199] According to the divestiture agreement, the BOCs had to begin offering equal access by 1984; interexchange carriers had to be able to obtain equal access for one-third of their subscribers by 1985; and such access had to be furnished to all subscribers "upon bona fide request" by 1986. *Decree Opinion*, 552 F. Supp. at 196. *See generally* §5.1.2.2.

The GTE Consent Decree similarly required GTE's operating companies to "offer equal access through end offices serving at least two thirds of its

ther action. By 1985, scarcely a year after divestiture, the Commission had adopted and implemented its own administrative equal access rules.[200] The Commission directed all local exchange carriers (not just the former Bell affiliates) to undertake equal access conversions.[201] By 1996, 99.42 percent of all access lines in the United States (including 99.99 percent of Bell lines) had been converted to equal access.[202]

Although the FCC did not insist on "absolute technical equality," it did undertake to monitor the quality and price of access offered by the exchange carriers. The Commission did this in part through the Bell companies' semiannual progress reports filed with the Department of Justice.[203] In addition, the Exchange Carrier Standards Association (later renamed the Alliance for Telecommunications Industry Solutions), composed of both exchange and interexchange carriers, was organized in early 1985 under the auspices of the American National Standards Institute; its Carrier Liaison Committee provides an open forum for the resolution of equal access interconnection problems.[204] The Committee's Network Operations Forum resolves provisioning problems (matters involving installation, repair, and

---

exchange access lines by September 1, 1987, and through all Operating Companies end offices serving more than 10,000 lines by December 31, 1990." United States v. GTE, 603 F. Supp. 730, 744 (D.C. 1984). Unlike the Bell companies, however, GTE's local telephone companies were permitted to provide long-distance service, and to do so without structural separation obligations. *Id.* at 752–753.

[200] MTS and WATS Market Structure, Phase III, Report and Order, 100 F.C.C.2d 860 (1985) (hereinafter *Phase III*); Investigation into the Quality of Equal Access Services, Memorandum Opinion and Order, 60 Rad. Reg. 2d (P & F) 417, 419 (1986) (hereinafter *Equal Access Quality Investigation*).

[201] *Phase III*, 100 F.C.C.2d 860; Equal Access Quality Investigation, 60 Rad. Reg. 2d at 419.

[202] Industry Analysis Division, FCC, Distribution of Equal Access and Presubscribed Lines 2 (Nov. 1997).

[203] United States v. Western Elec. Co., 569 F. Supp 1057, 1062 (D.D.C. 1983); Modification of Final Judgment §II(C), *reprinted in* United States v. AT&T, 552 F. Supp. 131, 227 (D.D.C. 1982) (hereinafter *Decree*).

[204] *Phase III*, 100 F.C.C.2d at 861 ¶4, 880–886 ¶¶66–82, 882 n.72; MTS and WATS Market Structure, Phase III, Memorandum Opinion and Order, 58 Rad. Reg. 2d (P & F) 731, 733 (1985) (hereinafter *MTS and WATS Market Structure, Phase III*).

maintenance), while its Interexchange Customer Service Center resolves exchange access ordering problems.[205] These forums address national issues; local problems are resolved bilaterally.[206] The FCC monitors the entire process and provides regulatory review when necessary.[207] In particular, the Commission has continued to grapple with the question of how equal is "equal."[208] Investigations have examined such matters as call blocking frequencies, the sufficiency of access trunks, trunk selection methods, and the transmission quality of access services.

The FCC additionally ordered owners of basic transmission facilities to provide equal access to planned changes in network design or intercarrier connections.[209] Thus, AT&T and the BOCs were required publicly to disclose all technical information concerning proposed new or changed network design at the "make/buy" point[210]—the point at which they decide to manufacture themselves or to purchase from another company any product that affects the network interface.[211] The FCC lifted this requirement in 1999, finding that it had been superseded by the net-

---

[205] *MTS and WATS Market Structure, Phase III,* 58 Rad. Reg. 2d at 733–734, 740; *Phase III,* 100 F.C.C.2d at 883–884 ¶77.

[206] *MTS and WATS Market Structure, Phase III,* 58 Rad. Reg. 2d at 733.

[207] *See Phase III,* 100 F.C.C.2d at 884 ¶78. *See also MTS and WATS Market Structure, Phase III,* 58 Rad. Reg. 2d at 739 ("In striking a balance between minimizing our regulatory presence in matters that are better resolved within the private sector and, at the same time, promoting our statutory objectives, our staff shall participate only as an observer . . . of the Carrier Liaison Committee.").

[208] *See, e.g., Equal Access Quality Investigation,* 60 Rad. Reg. 2d at 417.

[209] *See* Amendment of §64.702 of the Commission's Rules and Regulations (Second Computer Inquiry), Memorandum Opinion and Order, 84 F.C.C.2d 50, 82–83 ¶95 (1981) (hereinafter *Computer II Reconsideration Order*). *See* §§5.2.4, 8.4.3.2.

[210] Amendment of §64.702 of the Commission's Rules and Regulations (Third Computer Inquiry), Report and Order, 104 F.C.C.2d 958, 1086 ¶255 (1986) (hereinafter *Computer III*).

[211] *Computer II Reconsideration Order,* 84 F.C.C.2d at 81–83 ¶¶92–95 (ordering carriers owning basic transmission facilities to disclose all areas of information (network design, technical standards, research and development, customer proprietary, etc.) to "all interested parties on the same terms and conditions insofar as such information affects either intercarrier connection or the manner in which interconnected CPE operates"). *See also Computer III,* 104 F.C.C.2d at 1080–1086 ¶¶46–255.

work disclosure rules of 47 U.S.C. §251(c)(5) (for incumbent LECs) and by market changes (for AT&T).[212]

§9.4.4.2 Equal Access Under the Bell Divestiture and GTE Decrees

As discussed in section 9.6.1, the 1982 Divestiture Decree required the BOCs to provide "exchange access" and "exchange services for such access" to all interexchange carriers on equal terms.[213] An interexchange carrier was required to establish one or more points of presence in any LATA it wished to serve. The BOC was to act as the local collector and distributor of calls to and from those "points of presence."[214] Each BOC was required to provide "exchange access" "on an unbundled, tariffed basis, that is equal in type, quality, and price to that provided to AT&T."[215]

---

[212] Computer III Remand Proceedings: Bell Operating Company Provision of Enhanced Services, Report & Order, CC Docket No. 95-20 (Mar. 20, 1999) at ¶¶41–52.

[213] *Decree Opinion,* 552 F. Supp. at 225–226; Decree §II(B), 552 F. Supp. at 227. Exchange access may include "any activity or function performed by a BOC in connection with the origination or termination of interexchange telecommunications." *Id.* §IV(F), 552 F. Supp. at 228. *See also* §9.8.

[214] *Decree* §IV(F), 552 F. Supp. at 228. *See also* Competitive Impact Statement at 32, United States v. Western Elec. Co., No. 74-1698 (D.D.C. Feb. 10, 1982) (hereinafter *Competitive Impact Statement*). Although the definition of exchange access stated that the interexchange carriers may establish a "point or points" of presence, it was understood that the BOCs were required to provide access only from one point per LATA. *See* United States v. Western Elec. Co., 569 F. Supp. 990, 1027 n.192 (D.D.C. 1983).

[215] *Decree* §II(A), app. B §A(1), 552 F. Supp. at 227, 232. Section II(B) similarly directed: "No BOC shall discriminate between AT&T and . . . other persons . . . in the . . . interconnection and use of the BOC's telecommunications service and facilities or in the charges for each element of service." *Id.* §II(B), 552 F. Supp. at 227. Section IV(F) stated that "exchange access" was to be provided via connections "with signal quality and characteristics equal to that provided similar traffic of AT&T." Those "characteristics" were defined to include "equal probability of blocking, based on reasonable traffic estimates supplied by each interexchange carrier." *Id.* §IV(F), 552 F. Supp. at 229. Appendix B of the Decree provided a timetable for implementing "nondiscriminatory access" and defined the term in more detail.

Judge Greene allowed the Bell companies to exercise their independent judgment regarding the technical details of access.[216] Under the Decree, equality was tested *functionally*.[217] The BOCs were not required to rip out AT&T's existing connections after divestiture; functionally similar connections were provided to the new long-distance carriers via "access tandems." Judge Greene further agreed that "technically different" access[218] was acceptable so long as the functions ultimately provided were comparable. He expressly accepted the BOCs' position that "equal access" should be defined as access whose "overall quality in a particular area is equal within a reasonable range which is applicable to all carriers" and declined to require absolutely identical technical quality, which would have meant identical values for loss, noise, echo, and probability of blocking.[219]

In order to further the goals of equal access on the customer side, the Decree required each BOC to offer a service that "permits each subscriber automatically to route, without the use of

---

[216] In approving the Decree, the district court stated that the first "principle" of equal access was that "the Operating Companies should have latitude to provide access in the manner they deem most efficient." *Decree Opinion*, 552 F. Supp. at 142 n.46. "[S]ince the Bell System network is both vast and complex, a variety of approaches will in all probability be necessary to achieve equal access. Imposition by the Court of a single procedure applicable to all areas and all interconnection requirements is likely to create inefficiencies and impose added costs on the Operating Companies without achieving superior results." *Id.* at 197.

[217] The same principle has been adopted by the FCC respecting comparably efficient access afforded enhanced service providers. *See* §12.5.

[218] United States v. Western Elec. Co., 569 F. Supp. at 1063.

[219] Unduly rigid demands for technical equality, Judge Greene concluded, "would necessitate substantial dismantling and reconstruction of local telephone networks without any real benefits either to the consuming public or to AT&T's intercity competitors." *Id.* (footnote omitted). The court also noted that "[t]he Operating Companies are not responsible, of course, for correcting any quality deficiencies that may result from an interexchange carrier's own facilities." *Id.* at 1063 n.15. Similar issues arose with respect to the shared use of space and facilities. At divestiture, the BOCs and AT&T still shared many facilities; their respective switches were sometimes located on adjacent floors of the same building or even in adjacent parts of the same room. The BOCs were not, however, required to offer similar sharing arrangements to other carriers. *See Decree Opinion*, 552 F. Supp. at 198 n.278. *See also Decree* §II(A), app. B §C(1), 552 F. Supp. at 234.

access codes, all the subscriber's interexchange communications to the interexchange carrier of the customer's designation."[220] This was a departure from the prior system of double-dialing, whereby a caller using MCI would dial 7 (or even 11 digits) just to get a second dial tone. Although never described this way, the Decree required BOCs to implement (in effect) a single-key automatic dialing system, much like those built into countless telephones, so that when "1" is dialed as the first digit of an interLATA call, the call is automatically handed off to the carrier previously specified by the subscriber. The Decree also required the BOCs to enable customers to select interexchange carriers call-by-call by dialing "the minimum number of digits" feasible.[221]

As equal access capabilities were deployed, however, competing interexchange carriers and the architects of divestiture discovered to their chagrin that many customers were not the least bit interested in exercising the power of choice that had been won on their behalf. What was to be done with customers who declined to designate a preferred carrier? Judge Greene ruled that while a BOC could assign such customers at random, it was equally free to leave them all with AT&T[222] or to block interexchange calls not preceded by the five-digit access code (e.g., 10-222 for MCI) for per-call designation of a long-distance carrier.[223] *New* subscribers, however, would have to designate or be blocked or allocated by the BOC at random.[224]

When the Commission applied equal access rules to independent LECs in 1985,[225] it mandated a balloting and allocation

---

[220] *Decree* §II(A), app. B §A(2)(ii), 552 F. Supp. at 233.

[221] *Id.* app. B §A(2)(i), 552 F. Supp. at 233. Per-call carrier designation must use "the minimum number of digits necessary at the time access is sought to permit nationwide, multiple carrier designation for the number of interexchange carriers reasonably expected to require such designation in the immediate future." *Id.*, 552 F Supp. at 233. Currently a five-digit access code of the form 10XXX is required.

[222] United States v. Western Elec. Co., 578 F. Supp. 668, 676 (D.D.C. 1983).

[223] *Id.* at 677.

[224] *Id.*

[225] *See* Investigation of Access and Divestiture Related Tariffs, Memorandum Opinion and Order, 101 F.C.C.2d 911 (1985) (hereinafter *Allocation Order*), *recons. denied*, 102 F.C.C.2d 503 (1985); Investigation of Access and

plan so that customers could choose, if they wished, to which interexchange carrier they would be presubscribed.[226] The Commission modified its procedures for presubscribed interexchange carrier (PIC) changes in 1992, following lawsuits between AT&T and MCI regarding customer complaints of slamming.[227] The new rules were designed to reduce confusion among customers when they changed their primary interexchange carrier and to help eliminate fraudulent telemarketing practices by carriers.[228] Among other things, they required verification and auditing of PIC change orders, as well as quality assurance programs to assure that telemarketers do not mislead customers.[229]

Equal access also required nondiscriminatory pricing.[230] The Decree required that BOC access prices be "unbundled" such that no interexchange carrier need "pay for types of exchange access that it does not utilize."[231] But this solemn demand for nondiscriminatory pricing proved empty. Access charges may be aver-

---

Divestiture Related Tariffs, Memorandum Opinion and Order, 101 F.C.C.2d 935 (1985).

[226] *Allocation Order,* 101 F.C.C.2d at 924–927, app. B.

[227] Policies and Rules Concerning Changing Long Distance Carriers, Report and Order, 7 F.C.C. Rec. 1038 (1992).

[228] *Id.*

[229] *Id.* at 1039 ¶4. In December 1998, the Commission further revised its presubscription rules to combat slamming. In that Order, the Commission directed telcos planning to implement "PIC freezes" (a safeguard against slamming that requires the local carrier involved in switching a consumer's long-distance carrier to confirm the switch with the customer) to explain to the customer how such a freeze may be lifted. Policies and Rules Concerning Unauthorized Changes of Consumers' Long Distance Carriers, Second Report and Order and Further Notice of Proposed Rulemaking, CC Docket No. 94-129 (Dec. 23, 1998). The Commission also rejected the "welcome package" (a package sent by the new carrier to the customer, which contains a postcard the customer can send back to cancel the switch to the new carrier) as a sufficient means of verifying a PIC change. *Id.*

[230] *See also* §2.3.3.6.

[231] *Decree* §II(A), app. B §B(1), 552 F. Supp. at 233. Charges for each unbundled element of service must be "cost justified." *Id.* §II(A), app. B §B(2), 552 F. Supp. at 233. In approving the Decree, Judge Greene expressly declared that "[t]he decree would leave state and federal regulators with a mechanism—access charges—by which to require a subsidy from intercity service to local service." *Decree Opinion,* 552 F. Supp. at 169 & n.161; *see also* United States v. Western Elec. Co., 569 F. Supp. at 999; *Competitive Impact Statement* at 48.

aged, Judge Greene held.[232] Regulators, he also declared, could engage in "value pricing" of access services that require AT&T to pay a premium for superior access, regardless of underlying costs.[233]

§9.4.4.3 Equal Access Under the 1996 Act

Although the AT&T and GTE Decrees were superseded by the 1996 Act on a prospective basis,[234] the Decrees' equal access requirements and the law interpreting these requirements survived intact. Congress expressly preserved equal access obligations on local exchange carriers wrought by the AT&T and GTE Decrees and subsequent Commission rulemakings, as they were in effect at the time of the Act's passage.[235] This provision

---

[232] *See* United States v. Western Elec. Co., 569 F. Supp. at 1007 n.79 (approving geographically averaged access rates and declining to require "that higher-than-average-cost areas [not be] combined with lower-than-average-cost areas"). At the time of divestiture, Judge Greene permitted certain BOCs to continue providing interexchange service in two high-density corridors on the Eastern Seaboard. The BOCs were not, however, required to impute to their corridor services the same access charges that they would assess competing carriers. *See* United States v. Western Elec. Co., 569 F. Supp. at 1018 n.144. Some inequality in access charges was "reasonable" because the BOCs' services in the corridors "were sanctioned specifically to preserve for interstate callers in these areas the advantages of the existing local networks." *Id.* at 1107.

[233] *Decree Opinion,* 552 F. Supp. at 199 n.287. Judge Greene declined to impose the premium charges himself, reasoning that a court "lacks the expertise and flexibility to determine the amount of such a premium." The Decree itself incorporated a clause (which expired by its own terms in September 1991) that equalized access rates notwithstanding the lower costs of providing service to AT&T. *Decree* §II(A), app. B §B(3), 552 F. Supp. at 233. This clause was intended to neutralize temporarily the cost advantage AT&T would otherwise have enjoyed as a result of its legacy of sharing arrangements and collocation with the BOCs. *See id.* at 197 n.278; Response to Comments on Proposed MFJ 101 (May 20, 1982). In August of 1991, however, the FCC ordered the BOCs to maintain the status quo on pricing. The BOCs' adherence to this Order after the Decree's contrary provision became effective essentially confirmed that the Decree's pricing requirements were toothless. *See* MTS and WATS Market Structure, Transport Rate Structure and Pricing, Order and Further Notice of Proposed Rulemaking, 6 F.C.C. Rec. 5341, 5344 ¶¶12–13 (1991); *see also* §2.3.3.3(ii).

[234] 47 U.S.C. §601(a).

[235] *Id.* §251(g) (providing that local exchange carriers "shall provide exchange access, information access, and exchange services for such access to

ensured that termination of these Consent Decrees would not turn back the clock to a pre-equal access regime.

While the 1996 Act preserved the Divestiture Decree's equal access requirements, new section 251(b)(3) of the Communications Act independently requires that customers be able to choose presubscribed carriers for their interLATA toll calls. The FCC reaffirmed its approach to presubscription for toll calls and attempted to apply these presubscription rules to intrastate, in addition to interstate, calls.[236] That effort was rebuffed initially by the Eighth Circuit on jurisdictional grounds, but later reinstated by the Supreme Court.[237] In the same FCC proceeding, the Commission also considered whether to require presubscription specifically for international calls.[238] Although the Commission stated that a separate presubscription choice for international calling would be "consistent with the intent of the 1996 Act because it could foster additional carrier competition," the Commission refrained, for the time being, from making this a "nationwide requirement," citing concerns about technical feasibility.[239]

---

interexchange carriers and information service providers in accordance with the same equal access and nondiscriminatory interconnection restrictions and obligations (including receipt of compensation) that apply to such carrier . . . under any court order, consent decree, or regulation, order, or policy of the Commission, until such restrictions and obligations are explicitly superseded by regulations prescribed by the Commission" and that "such restrictions and obligations shall be enforceable in the same manner as regulations of the Commission").

[236] Implementation of the Local Competition Provisions of the Telecommunications Act of 1996, Second Report and Order and Memorandum Opinion and Order, 11 F.C.C. Rec. 19,392, 19,412 ¶34 (1996) (hereinafter *Second Local Competition Order*) ("the dialing parity requirement for toll calling can best be achieved through presubscription because that method would enable customers to route a particular category of traffic to a preselected carrier without having to dial access codes"), *vacated in part sub nom.* California v. FCC, 124 F.3d 934 (8th Cir. 1997), *cert. granted sub nom.* AT&T v. FCC, 118 S. Ct. 879 (argued Oct. 13, 1998).

[237] *See* §9.7.2. AT&T v. Iowa Utils. Bd., 119 S. Ct. 721 (1999), *reversing in part, affirming in part, and remanding* 120 F.3d 753 (8th Cir. 1997), *reversing in part and remanding* 124 F.3d 934 (8th Cir. 1997).

[238] *Second Local Competition Order,* 11 F.C.C. Rec. at 19,416–19,417 ¶¶43–45.
[239] *Id.* at 19,417 ¶45.

§9.4.4.4 Equal Access for Adjunct Interstate Services

Similar clusters of equal access issues have surrounded discrete interstate services, such as "800" numbers, calling cards, and operator services.[240] Indeed, because these services require additional steps to process through the network—from an extra database query to a live operator's intervention—implementing equal access has been particularly vexing.

(i) "700," "800," and "900" Services. With 800-number services,[241] the party receiving the call pays the phone bill, at least initially, and is thus most likely designated as the "customer."[242] But because the routing of a call must begin where the call originates, not where it ends, equal access is possible only if the caller's LEC has a means to decide which long-distance carrier should be handed the 800 call.

Prior to divestiture, equal access to 800-number services did not exist. The Bell System had provided the service exclusively since 1967.[243] Under the 800-NXX numbering plan that was accepted by Judge Greene to provide equal access,[244] the second three-digit group would indicate the carrier chosen by the entity subscribing to the 800 service. BOCs would check this coding and hand off 800 traffic in much the same way as all other long-distance calls. While affording all interexchange carriers the ability to provide the service, this kept 800 numbers carrier specific. A business that had signed up with AT&T, for example, found it

---

[240] Pay phones and the equal access issues they raise are discussed in §8.6.

[241] The prefixes "888" and "877" have been added to the roster of toll-free dialing codes and are interchangeable with traditional "800" numbers.

[242] *See* Provision of Access for 800 Service, Memorandum Opinion and Order on Reconsideration and Second Supplemental Notice of Proposed Rulemaking, 6 F.C.C. Rec. 5421 (1991) (hereinafter *800 Access*). The price of a call is routed back to the caller indirectly (for example, in the price of the sweater purchased from Land's End over an 800 number).

[243] Provision of Access for 800 Service, Notice of Proposed Rulemaking, 102 F.C.C.2d 1387, 1388 ¶3 (1986); *see also* Provision of Access for 800 Service, Supplemental Notice of Proposed Rulemaking, 3 F.C.C. Rec. 721 ¶5 (1988) ("AT&T remained the sole interstate 800 service provider until late 1986").

[244] United States v. AT&T, 604 F. Supp. 316 (D.D.C. 1985).

very difficult to change carriers later, especially after the number in question had been widely advertised. An 800 number was not "portable" from one carrier to another. Furthermore, as a practical matter, only AT&T had the facilities needed to translate 800 numbers back into the ordinary area-code-and-number essential for routing (800) CAR-RENT to the leasing company in Chicago. Nonetheless, the NXX plan provided AT&T and its competitors identical signals, and that was enough.[245] In this context at least, the "purpose" of the Decree was "a limited one: to remove barriers."[246] The BOCs also were planning to deploy their own database systems, which would solve the number-translation difficulty.

By the end of 1986, all BOCs were providing access for 800 service using the NXX plan.[247] By that time, however, MCI had developed its own capability for performing 800-number translations. It immediately sought an injunction to stop the BOCs from performing the translations for other carriers.[248] Without deciding the merits of the Decree issues, Judge Greene ruled that the BOCs could deploy the databases as permitted by the FCC.[249]

---

[245] *Id.* at 323. The Decree's equal access provisions were not intended to "punish AT&T or to compensate for the . . . economic and technological deficiencies" of competitors by "granting them free access to AT&T technology, equipment, and information." *Id.* at 324 (footnote omitted).

[246] *Id.* at 324.

[247] Report of the United States to the Court Concerning the Status of Equal Access at 12, United States v. Western Elec. Co., No. 82-0192 (D.D.C. Oct. 31, 1986).

[248] MCI's Motion to Cease Deployment of Interexchange and Information Service Capabilities in BOC 800 Service Database, United States v. Western Elec. Co., No. 82-0192 (D.D.C. Mar. 17, 1987). The Department of Justice took the position that the BOC database functions were permissible exchange access services. Further Response of the United States to MCI's Motion to Cease Deployment of Interexchange and Information Service Capabilities in BOC 800 Service Database at 3, United States v. Western Elec. Co., No. 82-0192 (D.D.C. July 15, 1987).

[249] Memorandum and Order, United States v. Western Elec. Co., No. 82-0192 (D.D.C. Mar. 3, 1992). Previously Judge Greene had suggested that allowing the BOCs to use AT&T's database facilities "might conceivably" involve the prohibited provision by the BOCs of interexchange services. United States v. AT&T, 604 F. Supp. at 323.

The FCC had more ambitious plans to boost 800-number competition by exceeding mere equal treatment. In 1991, the Commission concluded that number portability was an essential predicate to full competition in 800-number services.[250] In a series of orders, the FCC therefore set out a plan for 800-number portability and, upon its implementation by LECs in 1993, eliminated price-cap regulation and otherwise "streamlined" its regulation of AT&T's 800-service offerings.[251]

A collateral benefit of 800-number portability was that blocks of 10,000 800 numbers sharing the same NXX[252] code now could be broken up, making it easier for end users to obtain "vanity" 800 numbers. In part for this reason, the FCC in 1996 used the rules promulgated for 800-number assignment as the basis for assigning new 888 numbers.[253] In March 1998, the Commission established apportionment rules for 877 numbers similar to those it had adopted for 800 and 888 numbers.[254]

[250] Competition in the Interstate Interexchange Marketplace, Report and Order, 6 F.C.C. Rec. 5880, 5903–5904 ¶133 (1991) (hereinafter *1991 Report on Interexchange Competition*) ("the fact that 800 numbers are not 'portable' reduces the competitiveness of the 800 services market").

[251] *See 800 Access*, 6 F.C.C. Rec. at 5425–5427. *See also 1991 Report on Interexchange Competition*, 6 F.C.C. Rec. at 5906 ¶¶149–151 (barring AT&T from including any inbound service in new Tariff 12 options until 800 numbers became portable, but grandfathering existing Tariff 12 options containing inbound services); Competition in the Interstate Interexchange Marketplace, Second Report and Order, 8 F.C.C. Rec. 3668 (1993) (hereinafter *1993 Report on Interexchange Competition*) (forbearing from price-cap regulation of AT&T's 800 services after 800-number portability had been implemented).

[252] The NXX code in an 800 number is the fourth, fifth, and sixth digits of the ten-digit number.

[253] Toll Free Service Access Codes, Report and Order, 11 F.C.C. Rec. 2496 (1996).

[254] Toll Free Service Access Codes, Fourth Report and Order and Memorandum Opinion and Order, 13 F.C.C. Rec. 9058, 9060 ¶3 (1998) ("[V]anity numbers in the 877 toll free code and future toll free codes shall be assigned on a first-come, first-served basis as each code is opened for calling.") The Commission also instituted for numbers using newer codes (in this case, 888 or 877) the "right of first refusal," which automatically reserved a seven-digit vanity number in the newer codes to the owner of the number in an older code. *See id.* ("If, however, the current 800 subscriber with the number corresponding to the 888 set-aside vanity number declines to reserve that 888 set-aside number, the number shall be assigned on a first-come, first-served basis. The 888 set-aside numbers will be available for assignment 90 days after the 877 code is deployed.").

A cluster of parallel issues have arisen with calls prefixed by "700" or "900." Carriers use 900 numbers to provide audio-information services, chat lines, and the like; the calling party pays for the call at a rate set by the called party, which covers both the call and the value of the information provided.[255] The 700 numbers are used to provide other specialized pay-per-call services.[256]

Although 900-number services have been offered since 1988, the FCC did not begin to investigate the portability of 900 numbers until 1996, when it decided (pursuant to the number portability requirements in the 1996 Act) that portability should be mandatory for LECs providing 900-number services.[257] While

[255] Telephone Number Portability, First Report and Order and Further Notice of Proposed Rulemaking, 11 F.C.C. Rec. 8352, 8449–8450 ¶188 (1996). The 500-number service, which provides subscribers with a 500 "area code" number that can be programmed to deliver calls wherever the consumer travels in the United States and in many locations around the world, has similar underpinnings to 900-number service and is regulated in the same manner as 900-number services. *Id.*

[256] While 700 numbers can be used for any purpose designated by the carrier, a caller can generally access only the 700 services offered by the caller's presubscribed interexchange carrier (or by dialing a 10XXX access code), unlike 900 numbers. Therefore, 700 numbers "lack the ability to conveniently and universally market an information service." Policies and Rules Concerning Interstate 900 Telecommunications Services, 6 F.C.C. Rec. 6166, 6180 n.129 (1991). After divestiture, AT&T wanted 700 numbers available immediately at all end offices and maintained that the BOCs had a duty under the Decree "to provide exchange access for any interexchange carrier's offering of new or improved services." AT&T's Response to NYNEX's Motion for Clarification at 4, United States v. Western Elec. Co., No. 82-0192 (D.D.C. Nov. 13, 1984). Smaller interexchange carriers, however, wanted 700 numbers made available office-by-office as equal access was deployed. Judge Greene ruled that because the BOCs were not in competition with AT&T for 700 services, they could exercise ordinary business judgment in making the 700 numbers available. Opinion at 3–4, United States v. Western Elec. Co., No. 82-0192 (D.D.C. May 7, 1985) ("[T]he decree does not prohibit the offering of new or improved services until after implementation of full equal access. This does not mean, however, that the Operating Companies are required to offer the 700 Service Access Code immediately in all end offices."). *See also* United States v. Western Elec. Co., 569 F. Supp. at 1009 n.92 ("the decree does not require . . . that an Operating Company provide service to areas which it may serve").

[257] Telephone Number Portability, First Report and Order and Further Notice of Proposed Rulemaking, 11 F.C.C. Rec. 8352, 8454 ¶198 (1996); *see*

the Commission suggested that it *may* have the authority to require 900-number portability for interexchange carriers,[258] it put off ruling on this issue pending determination whether 900-number portability for these carriers is technically feasible.[259]

Portability is not possible for services using 700 numbers. For example, AT&T's EasyReach 700 service, which assigns customers a number for life, gives customers a carrier for life, too. There was no orderly assignment of 700 numbers among carriers; carriers may thus use overlapping 700 numbers for different services. To reach the right service, a caller must use the right carrier, by either calling on a line presubscribed to that carrier or dialing the right access code. This has prevented local telcos from creating an equal access database for the 700 services as they have done for 800 numbers.

(ii) Calling Cards. Equal access also has been implemented with regard to calling card services and their associated billing. Initially, Judge Greene took the lead, particularly by requiring the Bell companies to make available to all interexchange carriers the validation data needed for billing services, which they had previously provided only to AT&T.[260] In April 1992, however,

---

also Telephone Number Portability, Second Memorandum Opinion and Order on Reconsideration, 13 F.C.C. Rec. 21,204, 21,221 ¶34 (1998) ("The number portability requirements of section 251(b)(2) apply only to LECs. Specifically, section 251(b)(2) imposes a duty on 'each local exchange carrier . . . to provide, to the extent technically feasible, number portability in accordance with requirements prescribed by the Commission.' Thus, we cannot rely on section 251 for authority to require IXCs or other non-LECs to provide number portability for . . . 900 number service").

[258] Telephone Number Portability, Second Memorandum Opinion and Order on Reconsideration, 13 F.C.C. Rec at 21,221–21,223 ¶¶35–36. The Commission acknowledged that the majority of 900 numbers have been provisioned by interexchange carriers rather than LECs. *Id.* at 21,222–21,223 ¶36.

[259] *Id.* at 21,223 ¶37.

[260] United States v. Western Elec. Co., 698 F. Supp. 348, 355 (D.D.C. 1998); Opinion at 28–29, United States v. Western Elec. Co., No. 82-0192 (D.D.C. May 8, 1990).

the FCC intervened in the context of joint-use calling cards.[261] It required local telephone companies to offer all interexchange carriers nondiscriminatory access to LEC card-validation data and screening data and prohibited the LECs from favoring any interexchange carrier when contracting to accept interexchange carrier calling cards as a form of payment for the LEC's services.[262]

In 1993, the Commission further required LECs to make the billing name and address (BNA) information of all of their calling card customers available to all interexchange carriers on a tariffed basis, thus allowing interexchange carriers directly to bill LEC calling card customers for interexchange services.[263] Three years later the Commission addressed potential abuses by the recipients of this customer information, clarifying that BNA was being made available to further equal access, not for marketing purposes.[264]

(iii) Operator Services.   Before divestiture, all operator-assisted calls were routed directly to the bank of operators maintained by

[261] *See* Policies and Rules Concerning Local Exchange Carrier Validation and Billing Information for Joint Use Calling Cards, Report and Order and Request for Supplemental Comment, 7 F.C.C. Rec. 3528 (1992).

[262] The FCC also amended its rules to allow interexchange carriers access to the LEC's line information database (LIDB) for collect or third-party calls. This allows interexchange carriers to detect fraudulent use of numbers to which these calls cannot be charged (such as public telephones). *See* Final Report to Congress of the FCC Pursuant to the Telephone Operator Consumer Services Improvement Act of 1990 (Nov. 13, 1992). The FCC subsequently required that incumbent LECs make the LIDB available to all comers on an unbundled basis, pursuant to section 251 of the 1996 Act. Implementation of the Local Competition Provisions in the Telecommunications Act of 1996, First Report and Order, 11 F.C.C. Rec. 15,499, 15,741 ¶484 (1996). The Supreme Court, however, required the Commission to reconsider that decision. AT&T Corp. v. Iowa Utils. Bd., 119 S. Ct. 721, 734–736 (1999).

[263] Policies and Rules Concerning Local Exchange Carrier Validation and Billing Information for Joint Use Calling Cards, Second Report and Order, 8 F.C.C. Rec. 4478 (1993); Policies and Rules Concerning Local Exchange Carrier Validation and Billing Information for Joint Use Calling Cards, Second Order on Reconsideration, 8 F.C.C. Rec. 8798 (1993).

[264] Policies and Rules Concerning Local Exchange Carrier Validation and Billing Information for Joint Use Calling Cards, Third Order on Reconsideration, 11 F.C.C. Rec. 6835, 6853 ¶30 (1996).

the end user's single phone company. Following divestiture, with equal access in place, operator-assisted interLATA calls from private phones were expected to be delivered to the end user's presubscribed interexchange carrier.[265] But carriers other than AT&T did not *have* operators. Accordingly, the Department of Justice in 1986 permitted the BOCs to make their operators available to the new carriers for operator-assisted interexchange calls.[266] The 1996 Act converted this authorization to a mandate, requiring all local exchange carriers, including the BOCs, to make their operator services available to other carriers, including interexchange carriers, on a nondiscriminatory basis.[267]

Making the operator services business into a competitive market, with numerous carriers and others vying to provide service, has had its drawbacks, however. In October 1990, Congress addressed the problems of fraudulent practices, misleading rates, and confused customers by passing the Telephone Operator Consumer Services Improvement Act (TOCSIA),[268] which requires interstate operator services providers (OSPs) to file informational tariffs "specifying rates, terms, and conditions, and including commissions, surcharges, any fees which are collected from consumers, and reasonable estimates of the amount of traffic priced at each rate, with respect to calls for which operator

---

[265] Directory assistance service (411) calls were handled the same way. After divestiture, directory assistance was split between the BOCs and AT&T; the BOCs handle requests for local numbers. AT&T and other interexchange carriers handle requests for numbers in other LATAs or area codes by "retailing" the BOCs' local services. *See* Policies and Rules Concerning Operator Service Providers, Notice of Proposed Rulemaking, 5 F.C.C. Rec. 4630, 4630 ¶2 (1990).

[266] Letter from Douglas H. Ginsburg, Assistant Attorney General, Antitrust Division, DOJ, to Kenneth E. Millard, Ameritech, at 2 (July 18, 1986). In October 1992, Judge Greene, without explanation or comment, denied AT&T's six-year-old request for a declaratory ruling that the BOC could not provide operator call handling for interLATA telephone calls without a modification of the Decree. Order, United States v. Western Elec. Co., No. 82-0192 (D.D.C. Oct. 1, 1992) (denying AT&T's Motion for Declaratory Ruling on Operator Call Handling, United States v. Western Elec. Co., No. 82-0192 (D.D.C. Aug. 20, 1986)).

[267] *See* 47 U.S.C. §§251(b)(3), 271(c)(2)(B)(vii); *see also* §5.5.3.5.

[268] 47 U.S.C. §§226(a) et seq.

services are provided."[269] TOCSIA also provides that the Commission may require the OSP to provide cost justification for its rates if these rates appear to be unjust and unreasonable.[270] Pursuant to the FCC rules implementing TOCSIA,[271] OSPs are now required to identify themselves and to provide additional information on request.[272] Aggregators must display calling instructions and consumer protection information near the telephone;[273] they are also prohibited from blocking 800 and 950 access codes.[274]

The Commission also has attempted to foster competition in the operator services market by simplifying dialing requirements and establishing a new routing methodology for interLATA operator-assisted calls.[275] Under a "Billed Party Preference" (BPP) system, operator-assisted interexchange calls would be routed not to the OSP chosen by the owner of the telephone (or the owner of the premises on which the telephone was located), but to the OSP predetermined by the party being billed for the call.[276] In 1994, the Commission declared that BPP would enhance competition for operator services, improve service quality for consumers, increase network usage, and help create an advanced telecommunications infrastructure for the future.[277] The fly in the ointment was expense: "substantial network modifications" by local exchange carriers and OSPs costing billions

---

[269] *Id.* §226(h)(1)(a).

[270] *Id.* §226(h)(2).

[271] Policies and Rules Concerning Operator Service Providers, Report and Order, 6 F.C.C. Rec. 2744 (1991), *recons.,* 7 F.C.C. Rec. 3882 (1992).

[272] *Id.* at 2756–2760 ¶¶24–41.

[273] *Id.*

[274] *Id.* at 2761–2762 ¶¶42–46. For a discussion of 950 access, see §9.4.4.1. In 1992, the FCC concluded that because consumer information requirements and open access rules were fulfilling TOCSIA's objectives, further regulation of OSPs was unnecessary. Final Report to Congress of the FCC Pursuant to the Telephone Operator Consumers Services Improvement Act of 1990 (Nov. 13, 1992).

[275] Billed Party Preference for 0+ InterLATA Calls, Notice of Proposed Rulemaking, 7 F.C.C. Rec. 3027 (1992).

[276] *Id.* at 3027 ¶1.

[277] Billed Party Preference for 0+ InterLATA Calls, Further Notice of Proposed Rulemaking, 9 F.C.C. Rec. 3320 ¶2 (1994).

of dollars would be required.[278] After further rounds of comment[279] and a total of six years of deliberation, the Commission eventually declined to adopt BPP. Choosing a decidedly low-tech alternative, the FCC instead required operators to disclose rate information for long-distance calls orally and directed OSPs to submit more detailed information in their tariff filings, all in the hope of addressing consumer complaints.[280]

§9.4.5 Expanded Interconnection and Exchange Access Services

As discussed above, long-distance competition was built on the right to interconnect—with other long-distance carriers for the most efficient long-distance routing via resale and with local carriers for origination and termination of traffic.[281] That meant that the prices consumers would pay for long distance, and the quality of their service, would depend on the development of competition in long-distance resale and the provision of access to local networks. Within the long-distance market, competitive entry (albeit limited) and regulatory reforms addressed the issue. The market would respond to demand. But at the ends of the long-distance call, within the local exchange, competition remained very limited even after the FCC preempted barriers to competitive termination of interstate traffic.[282]

Strong competition did develop in some market segments. Most particularly, competitive access providers (CAPs) quickly deployed their own advanced, fiber-optic networks (or, in some

[278] *Id.* at 3325–3327 ¶¶20–35. LECs would have to install new software in all of their end offices and increase their operator services capacity to handle the additional traffic BPP would bring; OSPs would have to modify their networks. *Id.*

[279] Billed Party Preference for 0+ InterLATA Calls, Second Further Notice of Proposed Rulemaking, 11 F.C.C. Rec. 7274 (1996); Billed Party Preference for 0+ InterLATA Calls, Public Notice, 11 F.C.C. Rec. 12,830 (1996).

[280] Billed Party Preference for 0+ InterLATA Calls, Second Report and Order on Reconsideration, 13 F.C.C. Rec. 6122 (1998).

[281] *See* §§9.4.1–9.4.3.

[282] *See* §1.9.2.

cases, microwave systems) to serve high-usage business customers in compact downtown districts.[283] Large revenues could be gained from carrying access traffic over these geographically small networks. Regulators helped out new entrants as well, by keeping the incumbent LECs' access prices well above cost to subsidize other services. This created an artificially high price ceiling that the CAPs, who had no universal service obligations, easily could stay under.[284]

But even with these opportunities, the CAPs still could not provide local services unless state regulators and municipalities allowed, and they could interconnect with incumbent LECs only in the same manner as the interexchange carriers themselves, that is, as customers of the LECs' call-termination services.[285] Having established the rules it thought necessary for competitive long-distance service—and being jurisdictionally barred from opening local markets[286]—the FCC turned to addressing these limitations on the development of competition in the "in between" access market.

What was effectively the next chapter in the *Execunet* saga was opened in November 1989, when Metropolitan Fiber Systems (MFS)—a major CAP—petitioned the Commission for broader authority to interconnect its facilities with those of the BOCs.[287]

---

[283] *See* Industry Analysis Division, FCC, Local Competition 5 (Dec. 1998) ("[M]any CLECs began as competitive access providers (CAPs) concentrating on providing special access type services to business customers when they first entered the market and . . . these services continue to represent significant parts of their businesses."). As of 1994, dozens of CAPs were operating fiber-optic networks in 78 cities. Paul S. Brandon & Richard Schmalensee, The Benefits of Releasing the Bell Companies from the Interexchange Restrictions, *in* Deregulating Telecommunications: The Baby Bells' Case for Competition 81 (Richard S. Higgins et al. eds., 1995). *See also* Industry Analysis Division, FCC, Fiber Deployment Update: End of Year 1997 at tbl. 14 (Apr. 1998) (CAPs had deployed approximately 396,000 fiber miles of cable as of year-end 1994).

[284] For a discussion of interstate access pricing, see §2.3.3.3.

[285] *See* §5.3.2.

[286] *See* §3.3.

[287] Petition for Interconnection of Competitive Access Carrier Facilities, Public Notice, 5 F.C.C. Rec. 726 (1990) (hereinafter *MFS Petition*). MFS operates metropolitan fiber-optic systems and is now a subsidiary of MCI World-Com, along with MCImetro forming the foundation of MCI WorldCom's local entry initiatives.

MFS sought rights to cobble together bits and pieces of service and facilities from two or more local carriers in any way that may be cheap or convenient, without having to take the entirety of the incumbent LEC's end-to-end service offering.[288] In 1991, the Commission tentatively supported these efforts,[289] and in September 1992, it established the terms by which competitive providers at large would interconnect with local facilities.[290]

The Commission concluded that expanded interconnection should be made available to all parties who wished to terminate their own special (i.e., unswitched) access transmission facilities at the incumbent LEC's premises, including CAPs, inter-exchange carriers, and end users.[291] The Commission also required local telcos to provide physical collocation of other carriers' transmission equipment on the incumbent LEC's premises if space was available[292] unless state regulators mandated virtual collocation instead.[293] If physical collocation was not offered due to space constraints, virtual collocation had to

---

[288] *Id.*

[289] Expanded Interconnection with Local Telephone Company Facilities, Notice of Proposed Rulemaking and Notice of Inquiry, 6 F.C.C. Rec. 3259, 3259 ¶1 (1991) (announcing intention to "remove the barriers that currently impede the development of greater competition in the provision of interstate access transmission facilities").

[290] Expanded Interconnection with Local Telephone Company Facilities, Report and Order and Notice of Proposed Rulemaking, 7 F.C.C. Rec. 7369 (1992).

[291] *Id.* at 7403 ¶65. The Commission concluded that incumbents should be required to offer interconnection at serving wire centers (SWCs), end offices, remote distribution nodes, and any other points that the LEC treats as rating points (points used in calculating the length of interoffice special access links). *Id.* at 7417 ¶113.

[292] In the interest of saving time and resources, the Commission later allowed LECs to limit their initial tariffs to only those central offices in which expanded interconnection is most likely to be requested. Expanded Interconnection with Local Telephone Company Facilities, Memorandum Opinion and Order, 8 F.C.C. Rec. 127, 128 ¶9 (1992). The Commission also held, however, that LECs must include in their tariffs provisions establishing procedures to add central offices upon receiving a bona fide request for interconnection. *Id.* at 129 ¶16.

[293] Expanded Interconnection with Local Telephone Company Facilities, Report and Order and Notice of Proposed Rulemaking, 7 F.C.C. Rec. 7369, 7389–7394 ¶¶39–46 (1992).

be.[294] AT&T and any other parties already located in the same buildings as a LEC central office were to interconnect in the same manner as other parties.[295] Having learned the lesson of *Execunet I* and *Execunet II*,[296] the Commission specifically and expressly banned "ratcheting"—the carriage of switched access traffic over special-access facilities interconnected pursuant to this Order.[297]

The FCC established similar rules for switched access: first, by allowing basic interconnection so that competitive providers of unswitched access could compete for the provision of interstate switched transport and, second, by adopting broader measures for removing barriers to the development of competitive interstate switched access networks.[298] The FCC in this manner opened up access to various LEC functionalities (such as signaling), thereby "open[ing] the door to a robust 'network of networks.'"[299]

Several telcos challenged the new physical collocation requirements as exceeding the Commission's statutory authority. In *Bell Atlantic v. FCC,* the D.C. Circuit vacated the physical collocation aspects of the expanded interconnection regime and remanded the virtual collocation issues back to the Commission.[300] Specif-

---

[294] *Id.* at 7407 ¶77.

[295] *Id.* at 7403–7404 ¶66.

[296] *See* §§9.4.1, 9.4.2.

[297] Expanded Interconnection with Local Telephone Company Facilities, Report and Order and Notice of Proposed Rulemaking, 7 F.C.C. Rec. 7369, 7420–7421 ¶¶108–109 (1992), *recons.,* 8 F.C.C. Rec. 127 (1992), *further recons.,* 8 F.C.C. Rec. 7341 (1993), *vacated in part and remanded sub nom.* Bell Atlantic Tel. Cos. v. FCC, 24 F.3d 1441 (D.C. Cir. 1994). The FCC granted interconnectors that were already collocated in a LEC's central office and were providing such services a limited waiver of the prohibition on ratcheting. Emergency Petition for Declaratory Ruling, or, Alternatively, Petition for Waiver Filed by Teleport Communications Group, Order, 8 F.C.C. Rec. 2578 (1993).

[298] *See generally* Expanded Interconnection with Local Telephone Company Facilities, Report and Order and Notice of Proposed Rulemaking, 7 F.C.C. Rec. 7369 (1992).

[299] Expanded Interconnection with the Local Telephone Company Facilities, Second Notice of Proposed Rulemaking, 7 F.C.C. Rec. 7740, 7741 ¶4 (1992).

[300] *See* Bell Atlantic Tel. Cos. v. FCC, 24 F.3d 1441 (D.C. Cir 1994).

ically, the appellate court concluded that the Commission's statutory authority to order "physical connections with other carriers" under section 201(a) of the Communications Act did not empower the Commission to "grant third parties a license to exclusive physical occupation of a section of the LECs' central offices."[301] In so finding, the court relied heavily on the "takings" implications, under the Fifth Amendment, of physical collocation. Unwilling to infer that the FCC had the power to authorize takings of LEC property that would subject the government to paying compensation, the court took a narrow view of the Commission's statutory powers.[302]

On remand, the Commission expanded its virtual collocation requirements and made physical collocation an option for incumbent local carriers if they preferred it.[303] The Commission defined virtual collocation in some detail.[304] Interconnectors could specify the kind of transmission equipment they wanted; LECs would then buy or lease the equipment and submit a tariff to cover it.[305] The Commission reaffirmed, however, that only physical collocation of circuit-terminating equipment in LEC offices would meet all of the Commission's regulatory objectives.[306]

The Commission went to some length to establish that its virtual collocation mandate was not a "taking."[307] Several Bell companies nevertheless challenged the order in the D.C. Circuit, arguing that the FCC's new rules made virtually collocated equipment the property of the incumbent LEC in name only and thus raised the same problem of Commission authority to authorize a taking as the original physical collocation requirement. The LECs' challenge, however, was dismissed as moot in light of the

---

[301] *Id.* at 1445–1447.

[302] *Id.*

[303] Expanded Interconnection with Local Telephone Company Facilities, Memorandum Opinion and Order, 9 F.C.C. Rec. 5154 (1994).

[304] *Id.* at 5169–5174 ¶¶41–66.

[305] *Id.* at 5170–5171 ¶¶49–53.

[306] *Id.* at 5159–5160 ¶12 ("if physical collocation is unavailable, however, we conclude that virtual collocation is the best alternative").

[307] *Id.* at 5163–5165 ¶¶22–30.

1996 Act's express authorization of physical and virtual colloca-tion.[308]

The 1996 Act addressed these same issues by establishing a sweeping new set of unbundling and interconnection mandates that benefit interexchange access providers and all other tele-communications carriers.[309] Congress not only ratified the FCC's expanded interconnection initiatives, but also largely super-seded them, folding access to incumbents' local networks for ter-minating long-distance calls into broader rights of access for the provision of local services.[310] What had been an "in-between" market straddling local and long distance thus became the com-petitive vanguard of the local services market. Indeed, interex-change carriers (particularly AT&T and MCI WorldCom) quickly gobbled up many of the smaller CAPs after passage of the 1996 Act, thus making the CAPs' exchange access operations the local piece of their new end-to-end networks. The integrated services of the old Bell System were recreated by AT&T, MCI WorldCom, and the like, leaving only the Bells themselves bound by the Decree's division of markets.

§9.5 Carriage and Rate Regulation

§9.5.1 Regulation of Nondominant Carriers

As competition increased in the interexchange market during the 1970s and 1980s, the FCC became increasingly convinced that regulation should be scaled back. As an initial step, in 1979 the Commission launched its Competitive Carrier rulemaking.[311]

---

[308] Pacific Bell v. FCC, 81 F.3d 1147 (D.C. Cir. 1996); *see* 47 U.S.C. §251(c) (6); H.R. Rep. No. 204, 103d Cong., 1st Sess. 73 (1995) ("[T]his provision is necessary . . . because a recent court decision indicates that the Commission lacks the authority under the Communications Act to order physical colloca-tion.") (citing Bell Atlantic Tel. Cos. v. FCC, 24 F.3d 1441).

[309] 47 U.S.C. §251(c).

[310] *See* §5.3.2.

[311] Policy and Rules Concerning Rates for Competitive Common Carrier Services and Facilities Authorizations Therefor, Notice of Inquiry and Pro-posed Rulemaking, 77 F.C.C.2d 308 (1979); First Report and Order, 85

This rulemaking divided the world into two spheres—"dominant" carriers and "nondominant" ones. AT&T, local telephone companies, domestic satellite carriers, and resellers of satellite transmission facilities were considered dominant carriers.[312] Nondominant carriers were defined to be those unable to raise price, curtail overall output, or engage in predatory or discriminatory pricing[313]—in short, those firms that lacked market power.[314] All specialized common carriers and resellers were classified as nondominant.[315] In the following years, the FCC systematically dismantled most regulatory demands imposed on nondominant carriers.

Regulation of nondominant carriers under Title II[316] first was streamlined; tariffs could be filed on 14 rather than 90 days' notice and would rarely be suspended and investigated.[317] The FCC then announced a policy of permissive "forbearance":[318] it

---

F.C.C.2d 1 (1980) (hereinafter *Competitive Carrier First Report*); Further Notice of Proposed Rulemaking, 84 F.C.C.2d 445 (1981) (hereinafter *Competitive Carrier Further NPRM*); Second Report and Order, 91 F.C.C.2d 59 (1982), *recons.*, 93 F.C.C.2d 54 (1983); Second Further Notice of Proposed Rulemaking, 47 Fed. Reg. 17,308 (1982); Third Further Notice of Proposed Rulemaking, 48 Fed. Reg. 28,292 (1983); Third Report and Order, 48 Fed. Reg. 46,791 (1983); Fourth Report and Order, 95 F.C.C.2d 554 (1983) (hereinafter *Competitive Carrier Fourth Report*); Fourth Further Notice of Proposed Rulemaking, 96 F.C.C.2d 922 (1984) (hereinafter *Competitive Carrier Fourth Further NPRM*); Fifth Report and Order, 98 F.C.C.2d 1191 (1984) (hereinafter *Competitive Carrier Fifth Report*); Sixth Report and Order, 99 F.C.C.2d 1020 (1985) (hereinafter *Competitive Carrier Sixth Report*), *rev'd and remanded sub nom.* MCI Telecomms. Corp. v. FCC, 765 F.2d 1186 (D.C. Cir. 1985).

[312] *Competitive Carrier First Report,* 85 F.C.C.2d at 20.

[313] *Id.* at 10.

[314] "[A] firm without market power," the Commission explained, "does not have the ability or incentive to price its services unreasonably, to discriminate among customers unjustly, to terminate or reduce service unreasonably or to overbuild its facilities." *Id.* at 20–21. "[A] competitive firm, lacking market power, must take the market price as given, because if it raises price it will face an unacceptable loss of business, and if it lowers price it will face unrecoverable monetary losses in an attempt to supply the market demand at that price." *Id.* at 21.

[315] *Id.* at 20.

[316] 47 U.S.C. §§201–226. *See also* §§2.12–2.13.

[317] *Competitive Carrier First Report,* 85 F.C.C.2d at 35–38.

[318] An alternative considered, but rejected, would have been to "redefin[e] the term common carrier so as to exclude most currently regulated communication providers." Note, Redefining "Common Carrier": The FCC's Attempt

would refrain from subjecting nondominant carriers to various procedural requirements, though their rates would ostensibly still have to be just, reasonable, and nondiscriminatory.[319] In 1982, the Commission announced it would forbear from applying the tariff filing requirements of section 203 and the entry and exit requirements of section 214 of the Communications Act to re-sellers of terrestrial services;[320] a year later the Commission extended forbearance to specialized common carriers and all re-maining resellers[321] and, in 1984, to all remaining domestic non-dominant carriers.[322]

In 1985, the Commission resolved to eliminate tariffs of non-dominant carriers root and branch; these carriers would instead deal with their customers through bilateral contracts like unreg-ulated businesses.[323] The FCC reasoned that this would prevent delay in introducing new offerings, reduce opportunities for col-lusive pricing, and stimulate more customer-specific arrange-ments.[324] Forbearance was now mandatory, not permissive; any nondominant carrier with tariffs on file would have to eliminate them within six months.[325] MCI, however, went to court and won the right to continue being regulated.[326] The Communications

---

at Deregulation by Definition, 1987 Duke L.J. 501, 502; *see Competitive Carrier Further NPRM,* 84 F.C.C.2d at 471.

[319] 47 U.S.C. §§201–202; *Competitive Carrier Further NPRM,* 84 F.C.C.2d at 471–491. *See Competitive Carrier Fourth Report,* 95 F.C.C.2d at 556.

[320] *Competitive Carrier Second Report,* 91 F.C.C.2d at 73. Other Title II requirements continued to apply to all carriers.

[321] *See Competitive Carrier Fourth Report,* 95 F.C.C.2d at 557. Nondominant carriers included international record carriers, other record carriers, long-distance carriers affiliated with certain non-Bell local telephone companies, and miscellaneous common carriers (which relayed video signals and their corresponding audio components by terrestrial microwave).

[322] *Competitive Carrier Fifth Report,* 98 F.C.C.2d at 1193, 1209. These re-maining nondominant carriers included domestic satellite carriers and cer-tain carriers providing DEMS (a form of high speed, two-way digital transmission service).

[323] *Competitive Carrier Fourth Further NPRM,* 96 F.C.C.2d at 923–924; *Com-petitive Carrier Sixth Report,* 99 F.C.C.2d at 1034.

[324] *Competitive Carrier Sixth Report,* 99 F.C.C.2d at 1030–1032.

[325] *Id.* at 1034.

[326] MCI v. FCC, 765 F.2d 1186 (D.C. Cir. 1985). MCI putatively opposed forbearance because of the "increased administrative costs" associated with

Act, the D.C. Circuit ruled, leaves the Commission with "no statutory authority to prohibit the filing of tariffs that, by statute, every common carrier 'shall' file."[327]

In holding that the FCC could not *preclude* the filing of tariffs by nondominant carriers,[328] the court of appeals initially declined to rule on the validity of the FCC's forbearance from *requiring* nondominant carriers to file tariffs.[329] In August 1989, however, AT&T filed a complaint against MCI, claiming that MCI was violating section 203(a) by offering negotiated rates to certain customers, without putting them on file with the FCC.[330] AT&T claimed that this practice put it at a significant competitive disadvantage because MCI could delay AT&T price cuts by opposing AT&T's newly filed tariffs, while offering its own negotiated rates without any similar risk.[331] MCI, on the other hand, argued that the Commission had removed all of MCI's filing obligations in 1983.[332] AT&T countered that the FCC order in question was a statement of enforcement policy and did not exempt nondominant carriers from the obligation to file rates.[333]

In October 1991, 25 months after filing its complaint, AT&T sought a writ of mandamus from the D.C. Circuit ordering the FCC to issue a cease and desist order against MCI. The court dismissed AT&T's petition after the Commission announced that it would conclude its investigation by January 30, 1992.[334]

---

negotiating customer-specific pricing arrangements rather than using generic tariffs. *Competitive Carrier Sixth Report,* 99 F.C.C.2d at 1024 ¶6.

[327] MCI v. FCC, 765 F.2d at 1186. Section 203(a) of the Communications Act states: "Every common carrier, except connecting carriers, shall, within such reasonable time as the Commission shall designate, file with the Commission and print and keep open for public inspection schedules showing all charges for itself and its connecting carriers . . . and showing the classifications, practices, and regulations affecting such charges." 47 U.S.C. §203(a).

[328] MCI v. FCC, 765 F.2d at 1195–1196.

[329] *Id.* at 1196.

[330] *See* AT&T Communications v. MCI Telecomms. Corp., Memorandum Opinion and Order, 7 F.C.C. Rec. 807 (1992), (hereinafter *AT&T v. MCI*).

[331] *Id.* at 808 ¶¶7–8.

[332] *Id.* at 808 ¶9. *See also Competitive Carrier Fourth Report,* 95 F.C.C.2d 554 (1983).

[333] AT&T v. MCI, 7 F.C.C. Rec. at 808 ¶8.

[334] *See* AT&T v. FCC, 978 F.2d 727, 731 (D.C. Cir. 1992).

Two days before the court-imposed deadline, the Commission dismissed AT&T's complaint, stating that the FCC's 1983 Order was a substantive rule on which MCI had properly relied.[335] It also stated that the issue raised in AT&T's complaint—whether forbearance was still a legitimate policy in light of the D.C. Circuit's decision in *MCI v. FCC*—implicated broader policy issues that were more properly the subject of a rulemaking proceeding than an adjudication. The Commission announced such a rulemaking the same day.[336]

AT&T then appealed the dismissal of its complaint to the D.C. Circuit.[337] In that proceeding, the court chastised the Commission for delaying so long before putting off the central issue altogether.[338] Turning to the underlying policy, the court followed *MCI v. FCC* and held that section 203(a)—which states that "every" carrier "shall" file its tariffs with the Commission—means what it says. The Commission's section 203(b) authority to "modify any requirement" of the section "in particular instances or by general order applicable to special circumstances or conditions" does not extend to eliminating the tariff requirement altogether. The court noted that while it did "not quarrel with the Commission's policy objectives," it suggested that the Commission "obtain congressional sanction for its desired policy course."[339]

Less than two weeks after the decision in *AT&T v. MCI*, the Commission completed the rulemaking proceeding it had commenced in response to AT&T's earlier complaint. The Commission affirmed its permissive detariffing policy as a valid exercise of its authority to modify tariff filing requirements under section

[335] AT&T v. MCI, 7 F.C.C. Rec. at 809 ¶13.

[336] Tariff Filing Requirements for Interstate Common Carriers, Notice of Proposed Rulemaking, 7 F.C.C. Rec. 804 (1992).

[337] AT&T v. FCC, 978 F.2d at 734.

[338] *Id.* at 733 ("We have little difficulty in concluding . . . that it was arbitrary and capricious for the Commission to dismiss AT&T's complaint with only a promise to address the legal issue it raised in a future rulemaking. To the extent that the Commission thought it had discretion to postpone a decision to a rulemaking, it misunderstood its role as an adjudicator.").

[339] *Id.*

203(b).[340] Acknowledging the D.C. Circuit's contrary order, however, the decision ordered MCI to file tariffs that complied with section 203 by stating actual rates, not just maximum rates for services.[341] When MCI failed to amend its tariff, AT&T sought enforcement of the Commission's order.[342] The district court granted AT&T's request and clarified that section 203 requires tariffs to specify the actual rates a carrier charges to each customer.[343] MCI's tariff, the court held, allowed MCI to charge customers rates that were not specified in the tariff.[344] Accordingly, the court ordered MCI to "file promptly with the FCC tariffs setting forth all rates for its interstate common carrier services; all rates charged shall be either 'published in' or 'readily ascertainable from' the published schedule."[345] The D.C. Circuit affirmed.[346] In an unpublished per curiam opinion, the court simply noted that its decision in *AT&T v. FCC* "conclusively determined that the FCC's authorization of permissive detariffing violates section 203(a) of the Communications Act."[347]

The Supreme Court granted certiorari and affirmed the appellate court's order. The Commission's modification authority is very limited, the Court held, and certainly does not allow the FCC to disregard direct congressional mandates.[348] Writing for a 5-3 majority, Justice Scalia reasoned that "modify" implies a power to make incremental changes only.[349] Tariff requirements

---

[340] Tariff Filing Requirements for Interstate Common Carriers, Report and Order, 7 F.C.C. Rec. 8072 (1992), *stayed pending further notice,* 7 F.C.C. Rec. 7989 (1992), *rev'd sub nom. . . .* AT&T v. FCC, 1993 U.S. App. LEXIS 21516 (D.C. Cir. June 4, 1993), *aff'd,* 512 U.S. 218 (1994).

[341] Tariff Filing Requirements for Interstate Common Carriers, Report and Order, 7 F.C.C. Rec. 8072, 8075-8076 ¶19 (1992).

[342] AT&T v. MCI, 1993 U.S. Dist. LEXIS 9084, slip op. (D.D.C. July 7, 1993).

[343] *Id.*

[344] *Id.* at 2.

[345] *Id.* at 3.

[346] AT&T v. MCI, 1994 U.S. App. LEXIS 19414 (D.C. Cir. filed Apr. 25, 1994) (per curiam).

[347] *Id.* (citing AT&T v. FCC, No. 92-1628 (D.C. Cir. June 4, 1993)).

[348] *See* MCI v. AT&T, 114 S. Ct. 2223, 2231-2233 (1994).

[349] *Id.* at 2230-2231.

are the "heart of the common carrier section of the Communications Act";[350] the Commission's order exempting 40 percent of the long-distance industry from complying with these requirements was just too much.[351] The Court "sympath[ized]" with the argument that tariff filings by nondominant carriers might actually limit competition,[352] but held that only Congress can eliminate tariffing wholesale.

Having thus been ordered to continue taking delivery of tariffs from nondominant carriers, the FCC stopped reading them. In a new rulemaking, the Commission "streamlined" review of tariff filings by nondominant carriers.[353] Requiring nondominant carriers to file tariffs, the Commission reiterated, was "not only unnecessary to ensure just and reasonable rates, but [was] actually counterproductive" because "the sharing of pricing information can facilitate price fixing."[354] Under the streamlined rules, nondominant carriers filed their tariffs one day before they were to go into effect, without supporting cost information.[355] The tariffs were presumed lawful.[356] A nondominant carrier also was allowed to submit tariffs that provided for a "reasonable range of rates."[357]

[350] *Id.* at 2232.

[351] *Id.* ("What we have here, in reality, is a fundamental revision of the statute, changing it from a scheme of rate regulation in long distance common-carrier communications to a scheme of rate regulation only where effective competition does not exist. That may be a good idea, but it was not the idea Congress enacted into law in 1934.").

[352] *Id.* at 2233 ("[Petitioners] contend that filing costs raise artificial barriers to entry and that the publication of rates facilitates parallel pricing and stifles price competition. We have considerable sympathy with these arguments.").

[353] Tariff Filing Requirements for Nondominant Common Carriers, Memorandum Opinion and Order, 8 F.C.C. Rec. 6752 (1993).

[354] *Id.*; MCI v. AT&T, 114 S. Ct. 2233 (citing Sugar Institute, Inc. v. United States, 297 U.S. 553 (1936)); American Column & Lumber Co. v. United States, 257 U.S. 377 (1921)).

[355] 47 C.F.R. §§61.23(c), 61.38.

[356] 47 C.F.R. §1.773(a)(ii).

[357] Tariff Filing Requirements for Nondominant Common Carriers, Memorandum Opinion and Order, 8 F.C.C. Rec. 6752, 6757–6760 ¶¶27–38 (1993) (hereinafter *Range Tariff Order*); 47 C.F.R. §61.22(b). The filing of tariffs based

The dominant common carriers, AT&T and all the Bell companies, opposed the FCC's attempt to allow nondominant common carriers to file only a range of rates in their tariffs, arguing that it violated section 203(a) of the Communications Act, which requires all common carriers to file "schedules showing all charges."[358] The Commission defended itself by arguing that section 203(a)'s mandate did not preclude the use of a range of rates because the Communications Act did not define "schedules of charges."[359] The FCC also contended that "even if section 203(a) cannot reasonably be interpreted to allow some common carriers to file range tariffs, the Commission could adopt the Range Tariff Order under section 203(b), which grants the Commission authority to 'modify any requirement' of the section."[360]

The D.C. Circuit disagreed with the Commission, holding that the *Range Tariff Order* "violates the clear mandate of section 203(a), that every common carrier file 'schedules showing all charges'. . . . [The] clear and definite language of the rate-filing provision does not encompass the concept of ranges."[361] The Supreme Court's decision in *MCI v. AT&T*, moreover, had established that the Commission's modification power under section 203(b) was modest.[362] "Congress enacted the Communications Act and the mandates of the Act are not open to change by the Commission or the courts."[363]

In 1996, Congress intervened to end this back-and-forth between the FCC and the courts. New section 10 of the Communications Act, added by the Telecommunications Act of 1996, provides the Commission with the power to forbear from enforcing regulations it determines no longer necessary to protect

---

on a "reasonable range of rates" obviated the need for carriers to file additional tariffs when they instituted rate changes that fell within the range specified by the initial tariff.

[358] Southwestern Bell Corp. v. FCC, 43 F.3d 1515–1517 (D.C. Cir. Jan. 20, 1995).

[359] *Id.*

[360] *Id.*; 47 U.S.C. §203(b)(2).

[361] Southwestern Bell Corp. v. FCC, 43 F.3d at 1517, 1520.

[362] *Id.* at 1526.

[363] *Id.* at 1519.

carriers or consumers and do not serve the public interest.[364] Based on this provision, the FCC concluded that it now had "express authority to eliminate unnecessary regulation and to carry out the pro-competitive, deregulatory objectives that it pursued in the Competitive Carrier proceeding for more than a decade."[365] The Commission explained that as long as it can determine that its enforcement of such regulation on a carrier meets the "three statutory forbearance criteria" set forth in the Act, the Commission is authorized to forbear from requiring them to file tariffs.[366] The Commission thereupon prohibited nondominant interexchange carriers from filing tariffs for interstate, domestic interexchange services and ordered that these carriers cancel all such tariffs already on file.[367]

§9.5.2 Regulation of Dominant Carriers

While the FCC was steadily cutting back on regulation of nondominant carriers, it simultaneously was trimming the group of carriers and services that continued to be subject to full "dominant carrier" regulation. Before divestiture, the Bell System was indisputably "dominant" wherever it operated: the Department

---

364

> [T]he Commission shall forbear from applying any regulation or any provision of this Act to a telecommunications carrier or telecommunications service, or class of telecommunications carriers or telecommunications services, in any or some of its or their geographic markets, if the Commission determines that—(1) enforcement of such regulation or provision is not necessary to ensure that the charges, practices, classifications or regulations by, for, or in connection with that telecommunications carrier or telecommunications service are just and reasonable, and are not unjustly or unreasonably discriminatory; (2) enforcement of such regulation or provision is not necessary for the protection of consumers; and (3) forbearance from applying such provision or regulation is consistent with the public interest.

47 U.S.C. §160.

[365] Policy and Rules Concerning the Interstate, Interexchange Marketplace, Implementation of Section 254(g) of the Communications Act of 1934, as Amended, Second Report and Order, 11 F.C.C. Rec. 20,730, 20,738 ¶13 (1996) (hereinafter *Forbearance Order*).

[366] *Id.*

[367] *Id.* at 20,773 ¶77.

of Justice and the FCC agreed on that. But after divestiture, the agreement disappeared. The Divestiture Decree had been built on the bedrock assumption that divestiture would quickly eliminate AT&T's market power in the long-distance market.[368] To be sure, the decree had allowed for a few years of adjustment while the BOCs implemented equal access and new long-distance carriers deployed new facilities.[369] From then on, however, AT&T was to bear no special burdens, and the BOCs were to provide equal interconnection to all long-distance carriers.

The FCC was unable to shift gears quite as quickly, in part because the long-distance market remained stubbornly concentrated after divestiture. AT&T remained dominant in the FCC's eyes, as did all local operating companies in their home territories, including GTE, its then-subsidiary Contel, and other independent local telephone companies.[370] Consistent with the half-bound, half-free policy it had been pursuing, the FCC continued to subject these carriers to full-bore regulation under Title II into the 1990s.

On September 16, 1991, after conducting a long-awaited investigation into the effects of increased competition in long-distance services, the Commission affirmed that steadily rising competition in interstate business services had made further deregulation appropriate.[371] The high-end business segment of the long-distance market still was not perfectly competitive, the

---

[368] See Decree Opinion, 552 F. Supp. at 171–175.

[369] See, e.g., Decree §I(C), 552 F. Supp. at 227 (requiring AT&T to provide the BOCs with "all research, development, manufacturing, and other support services to enable [them] to fulfill the requirements" of the MFJ until "September 1, 1987"); id. §VIII(D), 552 F. Supp. at 231 (prohibiting AT&T from engaging in electronic publishing for seven years).

[370] See, e.g., Policies and Rules Concerning Rates for Dominant Carriers, Memorandum Opinion and Order, 6 F.C.C. Rec. 4819 (1991). The FCC has also treated some carriers as dominant in particular, narrow situations. For example in 1991, it subjected Atlantic Tele-Network (ATN) to disclosure requirements for its U.S.-bound traffic from Guyana because ATN held a majority interest in the local exchange carrier there. Atlantic Tele-Network, Inc., Application for Authority to Acquire and Operate Facilities for Direct Service Between the United States and Guyana, Order, Authorization, and Certificate, 6 F.C.C. Rec. 6529 (1991).

[371] 1991 Report on Interexchange Competition, 6 F.C.C. Rec. 5880, 5881–5882 ¶¶8–9 (1991) (hereinafter *1991 Report on Interexchange Competition*).

Commission conceded, but it was competitive enough. There was abundant capacity to serve this end of the market; indeed, MCI and Sprint at that time could have absorbed as much as 15 percent of AT&T's business day traffic without expanding their networks.[372] Such excess capacity imposed a significant (theoretical) constraint on AT&T's prices.[373] The costs of detailed advance tariff reviews therefore outweighed the benefits; privately negotiated contracts, if generally available to other subscribers on similar terms, would provide better service all around.[374]

Thus, regulation for all of AT&T's Basket 3 services[375] except for analog private line services,[376] as well as all services not originally placed in one of the three price-cap baskets,[377] was officially streamlined, meaning that they would no longer be subject to price-cap regulation and tariff filings for these services would be exempted from traditional advance screening by the Commission.[378] After a short transitional period, these services would be subject to the rules developed for nondominant carriers.[379] Price-cap regulation would be retained, however, for all services in Basket 1, and these services could not be included in any contract-based tariffs.[380] AT&T thus became a regulatory oxymoron—both dominant (i.e., possessing market power) and nondominant (i.e., lacking market power) in the very same market.[381]

---

[372] *Id.* at 5888 ¶46.

[373] *Id.*

[374] *Id.* at 5882 ¶9 ("[T]he public interest will be best served by more limited advance review of AT&T's business service filings, coupled with current post-effective review procedures, including the complaint process and our authority to initiate investigations and find tariffs unlawful after they take effect.").

[375] *See* §9.5.2.2 (discussing price-cap baskets).

[376] *1991 Report on Interexchange Competition*, 6 F.C.C. Rec. at 5895 ¶81 ("[A]nalog private line services are of diminishing importance in the marketplace and these services are consequently less subject to competition than other business services. Under the circumstances, we are concerned that elimination of the price cap restraints for analog private line services could lead to higher prices for these services.").

[377] E.g., Tariff 12 services. *See id.* at 5893 ¶72. *See also* §9.5.3.

[378] *1991 Report on Interexchange Competition*, 6 F.C.C. Rec. at 5893–5895 ¶¶72–76.

[379] *Id.* at 5902–5903 ¶¶126–128.

[380] *Id.* at 5908 ¶165.

[381] In 1995, in connection with the merger of AT&T and McCaw Cellular Communications, the FCC determined that all interexchange services in the

In 1993, AT&T petitioned the FCC to end this paradox and to be reclassified as nondominant for all its interstate and international services.[382] After a year passed without action by the Commission, AT&T offered to cut rates for low-income and low-volume callers—and to guarantee those rates until 1998—if the Commission would classify AT&T as nondominant.[383] This "price protection" deal was designed to appease FCC Chairman Reed Hundt, who had earlier expressed fear that AT&T would raise rates for those groups if dominant carrier regulations were eased.[384]

In October 1995, the Commission took AT&T up on its offer. The FCC ruled that "AT&T lacks market power in the interstate, domestic, interexchange market" and accordingly reclassified AT&T as a nondominant carrier for that market.[385] AT&T was relieved of the obligation to file tariffs weeks or even months before it actually planned to offer those services.[386] AT&T also became exempt from price-cap regulation for its residential long-distance, operator, 800 directory assistance, and analog private line services, in addition to the business services that already were regulated as nondominant.[387] AT&T's financial, network construction, and cost-support reporting obligations also were substantially reduced.[388] But AT&T was ordered to satisfy its supposedly "voluntary" commitments for low-income and low-volume customers.[389] In exchange for being dubbed a non-

---

United States comprised a relevant economic market. Applications of Craig O. McCaw and AT&T Corp., Memorandum Opinion and Order, 9 F.C.C. Rec. 5836, 5845–5848 ¶¶10–15, *aff'd sub nom.* SBC Communications Inc. v. FCC, 56 F.3d 1484 (D.C. Cir. 1995).

[382] Motion for Reclassification of American Telephone & Telegraph Company as a Nondominant Carrier, Public Notice, 8 F.C.C. Rec. 7581 (1993).

[383] *See* Letter from Alex J. Mandl, Executive Vice President, AT&T, to Reed E. Hundt, Chairman, Federal Communications Commission (Oct. 4, 1994).

[384] *See* AT&T Offers FCC Deal: Price Protection in Return for Less Regulation, Common Carrier Week, Oct. 10, 1994, at 1.

[385] Motion of AT&T Corp. to Be Reclassified as a Non-dominant Carrier, Order, 11 F.C.C. Rec. 3271 ¶1, 3356 ¶164 (1995). The Commission withheld judgment as to AT&T's dominance in international markets, resolving to rule on that matter in a separate proceeding. *Id.* at 3271 ¶2.

[386] *Id.* at 3281 ¶12.

[387] *Id.*

[388] *Id.* at 3281–3282 ¶¶12–13.

[389] *Id.* at 3346 ¶136.

dominant carrier, AT&T had, in effect, agreed to subject itself to price regulation, the very necessity of which confirmed that — more than a decade after divestiture — AT&T had not lost its market power after all.

§9.5.2.1   Dominant Carrier Regulation in International and Satellite Markets

International long-distance service, like its domestic counterpart, is a common carrier service subject to Title II rate and entry regulation.[390] Before the Bell divestiture in 1984, AT&T collected more than 70 percent of the gross revenues for U.S. international telephone services.[391] AT&T's international rates, like its rates for domestic long-distance services, were subject to rate-of-return regulation administered by the FCC. MCI and Sprint did not provide international service before divestiture; the few small carriers that did provide such service faced the same tariff and licensing requirements as AT&T.[392]

In 1985, in the midst of its domestic reforms, the FCC began to streamline regulation of international carriers in an analogous fashion.[393] The Commission divided the market into four segments: international message telephone service (IMTS), non-IMTS (telex, telegraph, etc.), "the provision of multi-purpose satellite earth station services," and "the provision of international space segment services."[394] Within each of these segments, the Commission identified dominant carriers who could restrict output and maintain prices above competitive levels without losing sales.[395] Among U.S. carriers, AT&T and certain providers

---

[390] See §7.5.4.5 for a general discussion of the regulation of entry into U.S. telecommunications markets by foreign carriers.

[391] See Industry Analysis Division, FCC, Trends in the U.S. International Telecommunications Industry at fig. 19 (Aug. 1998).

[392] Such carriers resold AT&T's service, leased circuits on AT&T's undersea cables, or both. MCI and Sprint began their international service the same way.

[393] International Competitive Carrier Policies, Report and Order, 102 F.C.C.2d 812 (1985) (hereinafter *International Competitive Carrier Policies Order*).

[394] *Id.*

[395] International Competitive Carrier Policies, Petition for Reconsideration, 60 Rad. Reg. 2d (P & F) 1435 (1986) (hereinafter *International Competitive Carrier Policies Reconsideration*).

of service to Alaska, Hawaii, and Guam were dominant in the IMTS market,[396] and all "foreign owned" carriers were categorized as dominant in all market segments.[397] Dominant firms would be held to full Title II regulation.[398] Nondominant carriers, on the other hand, would be subject to streamlined tariff and licensing requirements.[399]

The Commission's 1989 decision to regulate AT&T by way of price caps instead of rate-of-return regulation applied to international services, too.[400] In December 1991, moreover, the FCC again tracked domestic regulation (this time, entry regulation) by requiring dominant carriers to allow foreign carriers to resell the domestic end of international private line service, provided that the foreign carrier's home country provides similar resale opportunities to U.S.-based carriers.[401] The Commission expressed its belief that resale would "yield the same public benefits" in international telecommunications that it had in domestic interexchange service.[402]

---

[396] *International Competitive Carrier Policies Report,* 102 F.C.C.2d at 830 ¶44 ("AT&T is still the only provider of IMTS between the U.S. mainland and the majority of foreign countries. In those countries where there are other IMTS providers, AT&T still has an overwhelming market share."). The Commission classified all other IMTS providers (e.g., Sprint and MCI) as nondominant. The Commission determined that all providers of non-IMTS, including AT&T, would be treated as nondominant. *Id.* at 829 ¶39.

[397] *Id.* at 842 n.74. United States carriers were treated as foreign owned if they were "over 15% directly or indirectly foreign owned by a foreign telecommunications entity or [an entity] on whose board of directors an employee, agent or representative of a foreign telecommunications [entity] sits." *Id.*

[398] *Id.* at 829 ¶39; *see* 47 U.S.C. §§201 et seq.

[399] *International Competitive Carrier Policies Reconsideration,* 60 Rad. Reg. 2d 1435.

[400] Rates for Dominant Carriers, 54 Fed. Reg. 19,836 (1989); 47 C.F.R. §§61.41 et seq. In 1996, the Commission removed AT&T's international services from price-cap regulation upon determining that AT&T was a nondominant carrier in the international telecommunications services market. Motion of AT&T Corp. to Be Declared Non-dominant for International Service, Order, 11 F.C.C. Rec. 17,963 (1996); *see also id.* at 17,964–17,965 ¶4 ("domestic competition prevents AT&T from leveraging control over its domestic network to shut out competition on the international segment").

[401] Regulation of International Accounting Rates, First Report and Order, 7 F.C.C. Rec. 559 (1991).

[402] *Id.* at 560 ¶8; *see* §9.4.3.

The Commission conducted a major review of its regulation of U.S. international carriers in 1992.[403] In the resulting Order, the Commission relaxed its prior stance that foreign-affiliated carriers always should be treated as dominant and decided instead to regulate these carriers as dominant "only on those routes where a foreign affiliate of the carrier has the ability to discriminate in favor of its U.S. affiliate in the provision of services or facilities used to terminate U.S. international traffic."[404]

Just four years later the Commission adopted rules aimed at further reducing regulatory burdens on U.S. international service providers, which included streamlined tariff-filing requirements on nondominant international resale and facilities-based carriers.[405] In 1997, the Commission streamlined the tariff requirements that applied to U.S. carriers classified as dominant due to affiliation with a foreign carrier[406] that has market power.[407]

[403] Regulation of International Common Carrier Services, Notice of Proposed Rulemaking, 7 F.C.C. Rec. 577 (1992).

[404] Regulation of International Common Carrier Services, Report and Order, 7 F.C.C. Rec. 7331, 7334 ¶19 (1992) ("(1) carriers that have no affiliation with a foreign carrier in the destination market will presumptively be considered nondominant for that route; (2) carriers affiliated with a foreign carrier that is a monopoly in the destination market will presumptively be classified as dominant for that route; and (3) carriers affiliated with a foreign carrier that is not a monopoly on that route will receive closer scrutiny by the Commission. We will place the burden of proof on any party, applicant or petitioner, that seeks to defeat the presumptions in the first two categories.").

[405] Streamlining the International Section 214 Authorization Process and Tariff Requirements, Report and Order, 11 F.C.C. Rec. 12,884, 12,915 ¶80 (1996); *see also* 47 C.F.R. §63.12.

[406] In 1995, the Commission had eased its 15 percent test of foreign affiliation, adopting "a greater than 25 percent interest" test instead. Market Entry and Regulation of Foreign-Affiliated Entities, Report and Order, 11 F.C.C. Rec. 3873, 3967–3968 ¶249 (1995); *see also* 47 C.F.R. §63.18(h)(1)(i).

[407] *See* Rules and Policies on Foreign Participation in the U.S. Telecommunications Market, Report and Order and Order on Reconsideration, 12 F.C.C. Rec. 23,891 (1997) (hereinafter *Foreign Participation Proceeding*). *See* 47 C.F.R. §63.10(c)(1) (shortened tariff filing notice period); *id.* §63.10(b) (tariff filings accorded a presumption of lawfulness); *id.* §63.10(c) (prior-approval requirement for circuit additions or discontinuances removed); *id.* (degree of structural separation between a U.S. carrier and its foreign affiliate reduced); *id.* (reduced reporting requirements).

The Commission also addressed "co-marketing agreement[s] [and] other non-equity arrangement[s]" that fall short of foreign affiliation, applying dominant carrier regulation to U.S. carriers on routes where these arrangements

The Commission carried its theme of regulatory forbearance through to satellite services as well. Under the FCC's initial dominant carrier framework for international services, COMSAT was a dominant provider of multipurpose satellite earth station services and international space segment services, subject to full Title II regulation.[408] In 1996, COMSAT petitioned the Commission for streamlined tariff relief for all of its international common carrier services. The Commission partially granted COMSAT's petition, waiving the tariff requirements applicable to COMSAT's switched voice and private line services and effectively treating COMSAT as nondominant for these services. The Commission did not excuse COMSAT from dominant carrier regulation for its video transmission services, however.[409] The Commission granted COMSAT this and other relief two years later, reclassifying COMSAT as nondominant in the provision of all INTELSAT services (e.g., switched voice, private line, and video services between the United States and foreign countries) in all "competitive markets."[410] In those markets, COMSAT would no longer be subject to rate regulation.[411] In February 1999, the Commission further extended incentive-based price regulation to COMSAT's provision of services in "noncompetitive markets" in exchange for rate reductions and the promise of no future rate increases for these services.[412]

"present[ ] a substantial risk of anticompetitive harm in the U.S. international market." *Foreign Participation Proceeding,* 12 F.C.C. Rec. at 23,992 ¶224; *see also id.* at 23,944–23,947 ¶¶124–132 (discussing open entry standard for carriers based in WTO member nations); §7.5.4.5 (same).

[408] *International Competitive Carrier Policies Report,* 102 F.C.C.2d at 838–839, ¶¶65–66.

[409] *See* Comsat Corporation Petition for Partial Relief from the Current Regulatory Treatment of Comsat World Systems' Switched Voice, Private Line, and Video and Audio Services, Order, 11 F.C.C. Rec. 9622 (1996).

[410] *See* Comsat Corporation, Order and Notice of Proposed Rulemaking, 13 F.C.C. Rec. 14,083 (1998). The Commission created a list (*see id.* at 14,176–14,177 app. A, 14,178–14,183 app. B) of all countries that would be deemed "noncompetitive markets." COMSAT remains dominant in the provision of service to these noncompetitive markets, most of which are lesser-developed countries.

[411] *See id.* at 14,087 ¶4.

[412] Comsat Corporation, Policies and Rules for Alternative Incentive Based Regulation of Comsat Corporation, Report and Order, IB Docket No. 98-60

§9.5.2.2 Price-Cap Regulation

That AT&T remained dominant even after spinning off the BOCs perhaps justified continued regulation, but provided no assurance that FCC accountants would get the regulation right.[413] Given the new competition in long distance, however, the risks of getting it wrong were now quite serious. It was important not only to prevent AT&T from crushing the competition, but also to prevent an army of accountants from stifling innovation and efficiency within AT&T (and, indirectly, other carriers affected by AT&T's pricing). To address these concerns, the FCC turned to price-cap regulation as of July 1, 1989.[414]

The new price-cap tariffs divided AT&T's services into three "baskets": Basket 1 services covered residential and small business services; Basket 2 services included "toll-free" services; and Basket 3 was composed of all other business services.[415] The plan

---

(Feb. 9, 1999). *See also id.* n.2 ("Specifically, 'thin-route' and 'occasional-use single-carrier' markets are considered 'non-competitive', whereas, 'thick-route' and 'occasional-use multiple-carrier' markets are considered 'competitive.'").

[413] *See* §§9.2, 9.6.9, 9.10.

[414] AT&T had been required to file new tariffs in May 1989. Policy and Rules Concerning Rates for Dominant Carriers, Report and Order and Second Further Notice of Proposed Rulemaking, 4 F.C.C. Rec. 2873, 3094 ¶442 (1989) (hereinafter *AT&T Price-Cap Order*). For a description of the transition from rate-of-return regulation to price-cap regulation, see Levitz, Loosening the Ties That Bind: Regulating the Interexchange Services Market for the 1990s, 62 Rad. Reg. 2d (P & F) 618 (1987).

[415] Basket 1 services were generally plain old telephone services (POTS) plus international message telephone service (IMTS), Reach Out America, and operator-assisted and credit card calling; services in Basket 3 included ProAmerica, WATS, Megacom, Software-Defined Network, voice-grade private lines, wide-band private line services, and other switched services. *See also* FCC Shakes Off Past, OKs Caps for AT&T, Network World, Mar. 20, 1989, at 1, 53.

Not included in the 1989 price-cap plan were AT&T's customer-specific plans—Tariffs 12, 15, and 16—or private line channels obtained by AT&T from other telcos under Tariff 11. Tariffs 12, 15, and 16 represented customized arrangements for which price caps were "superfluous." Tariff 11 was excluded from the plan because the LEC special-access prices, which formed the bulk of the tariff's costs, were beyond AT&T's control. *AT&T Price-Cap Order*, 4 F.C.C. Rec. at 3033–3037 ¶¶327–336.

established AT&T's existing rates as a starting point,[416] but required annual tariff filings to demonstrate that proper adjustments to the price-cap index for each basket were being made.[417] Under the new scheme, prices could rise with inflation,[418] but only after the inflation rate had been discounted by an annual "productivity offset" factor[419] and by what might be called a "political factor" (set at 0.5 percent), ostensibly included to make sure that AT&T's anticipated gains were shared with its customers.[420] Certain other direct changes in costs — such as reductions in access charges, for example — might also result in separate price adjustments.[421] Finally, there were "bands" on price changes of individual services within each basket.[422]

"The attractiveness of incentive regulation," the FCC explained, "lies in its ability to replicate more accurately than rate

[416] *AT&T Price-Cap Order,* 4 F.C.C. Rec. at 3084–3089 ¶¶424–430.

[417] *Id.* at 3094 ¶¶442–444.

[418] The Gross National Product Price Index (GNP-PI) was chosen over other alternatives (Consumer Price Index, Producer Price Index) as a measure of inflation because its lower volatility and resistance to atypical price changes most closely reflected the changes in production costs faced by dominant carriers. Policy and Rules Concerning Rates for Dominant Carriers, Further Notice of Proposed Rulemaking, 3 F.C.C. Rec. 3195, 3389–3393 ¶¶346–355 (1988); *AT&T Price-Cap Order,* 4 F.C.C. Rec. at 2969–2974 ¶¶189–197.

[419] The Commission found that the productivity of the telecommunications industry had exceeded that of the general economy by 2 to 3 percent over the past 40 years. Policy and Rules Concerning Rates for Dominant Carriers, Further Notice of Proposed Rulemaking, 3 F.C.C. Rec. 3195, 3403 ¶373 (1988). Because the GNP-PI reflected productivity gains in the economy in general, but not necessarily gains experienced by carriers, the productivity offset factor was included to make up for this difference. *AT&T Price-Cap Order,* 4 F.C.C. Rec. at 2989–2997 ¶¶221–239.

[420] This factor was termed the consumer productivity dividend (CPD); it was implemented to ensure that ratepayers received lower rates under price-cap regulation than they did under the rate-of-return system. *AT&T Price-Cap Order,* 4 F.C.C. Rec. at 2894 ¶41. *See also id.,* at 3001 ¶248 ("The CPD ensures that consumers are the first beneficiaries of added efficiency under price caps, since prices will be 0.5 percent lower than otherwise.").

[421] These "exogenous costs" reflected administrative, judicial, and legislative changes beyond the carrier's control. Other exogenous costs include Separations Manual changes, Uniform System of Account changes, and changes in international accounting rates. *Id.* at 3003 ¶254.

[422] Upper bands promoted rate stability and protected consumers from unduly high rate increases; lower bands were implemented to prevent predatory behavior. *Id.* at 3065–3067 ¶¶387–391.

of return the dynamic, consumer-oriented process that characterizes a competitive market."[423] Because incentive regulation places limits on prices rather than on profits (as in traditional rate-of-return regulation), AT&T would have strong incentives to cut costs and operate efficiently.[424] The basket system provided AT&T some flexibility to meet competition,[425] but separation of different categories of services into different baskets also erected a safeguard against cross-subsidy of more competitive services with less competitive services.[426] Rate bands further prevented rate shocks for customers and predatory pricing against competitors.[427]

The FCC decided to initiate a comprehensive review of the plan's performance after three years of price-cap regulation.[428] Although the Commission acknowledged that periodically reviewing whether the price-cap levels were too high or too low could produce the same investment-padding incentives caused by rate-of-return regulation, the Commission suggested that such monitoring was needed to ensure that AT&T's performance stayed within the prescriptions of the Communications Act under the new regulatory approach.[429]

MCI petitioned the Commission for clarification concerning treatment of AT&T's promotional prices when calculating average prices. The FCC ruled that "in general, promotional pricing should not be credited in price index calculations."[430] The court

---

[423] *Id.* at 2893 ¶36. *See generally* Price Caps: An Alternative Regulatory Framework for Telecommunications Carriers, Pub. Util. Fort., Jan. 18, 1990, at 44.

[424] *AT&T Price-Cap Order,* 4 F.C.C. Rec. at 2893 ¶36, 2964–2965, ¶¶175–176.

[425] The basket and band approach gives "AT&T less flexibility in its pricing of residential and various less competitive services, and greater flexibility to price efficiently in more competitive areas." *AT&T Price-Cap Order,* 4 F.C.C. Rec. at 3052 ¶360.

[426] *Id.*

[427] *Id.* at 3065 ¶387.

[428] *Id.* at 3138–3143 ¶¶552–562.

[429] *Id.* at 3141 ¶557 ("[W]e run the risk that the regulatory controls that we have carefully crafted will produce unintended and unexpected results.").

[430] Policies and Rules Concerning Rates for Dominant Carriers, Memorandum Opinion and Order on Reconsideration, 6 F.C.C. Rec. 665, 670 ¶48 (1991).

of appeals disagreed, holding that the Commission's clarification was contrary to its original price-cap order.[431] On remand, the Commission instituted a new rulemaking (never completed) with the tentative goal of excluding promotional rates from price-cap calculations.[432]

The Commission conducted its first triennial review of AT&T's price caps in 1993, having previously streamlined regulation of several Basket 3 services as part of the interexchange competition proceeding.[433] The report concluded that price caps had performed as hoped, yielding lower rates and improved efficiency and innovation.[434] Nevertheless, the Commission concluded that ending price regulation for AT&T altogether would be premature: even though AT&T had been deemed nondominant for most business services,[435] it still maintained "by far the largest market share," and its prices had remained "at or near the price cap maximum."[436] The Commission therefore proposed only minor adjustments to AT&T's price-cap plan.[437]

In January 1995, the Commission removed Basket 1 commercial services from price-cap regulation, but for the time being left analog private line services and 800 directory assistance

---

[431] AT&T v. FCC, 978 F.2d 727 (D.C. Cir. 1992).

[432] Policy and Rules Concerning Rates for Dominant Carriers, Order and Notice of Proposed Rulemaking, 8 F.C.C. Rec. 3715 (1993); Policy and Rules Concerning Rates for Dominant Carriers, Order, 11 F.C.C. Rec. 19,664 (1996).

[433] Price Cap Performance Review for AT&T, Report, 8 F.C.C. Rec. 6968 (1993) (hereinafter *AT&T Price-Cap Review*). The Commission in 1991 streamlined regulation of most of AT&T's Basket 3 business services, removing them from price-cap regulation. After this, only analog private line services remained in Basket 3. *See 1991 Report on Interexchange Competition*, 6 F.C.C. Rec. at 5893–5895 ¶¶72–78.

[434] *AT&T Price-Cap Review*, 8 F.C.C. Rec. at 6968 ¶¶1, 4.

[435] *See* §9.5.2.

[436] *AT&T Price-Cap Review*, 8 F.C.C. Rec. 6970. While AT&T's pricing of Basket 1 was near the price-cap maximum, its pricing of services in Baskets 2 and 3 was well below the maximum. The latter baskets thus demonstrated prices set "in response to competition, not regulation" and, unlike Basket 1 services, warranted streamlined regulation. *Id.*; *1991 Report on Interexchange Competition*, 6 F.C.C. Rec. at 5893–5895 ¶¶72–78.

[437] *See* Revisions to Price Cap Rules for AT&T Corp., Notice of Proposed Rulemaking, 8 F.C.C. Rec. 5205 (1993); *see also AT&T Price-Cap Review*, 8 F.C.C. Rec. at 6973 (terminating general review of AT&T's behavior under price caps).

under price-cap regulation.[438] This would not last long, however; in October, AT&T was reclassified as a nondominant carrier by the Commission.[439] The remaining analog private line and 800 directory assistance services, among others, became exempt from price-cap regulation.[440]

§9.5.3   From Public Tariffs to Private Contracts

Whether under a traditional rate-of-return regime or price caps, price regulation revolved around the tariff—a public statement of terms and conditions of service—with an implicit commitment of service on demand without discrimination and with a regulator behind the scenes making sure that price is (to at least some extent) connected to cost and that one buyer is treated the same as the next. At the other pole lies the purely private contract, a bilateral, individually negotiated deal. Contracts need not be averaged across consumers; they need not lump together traffic-sensitive and traffic-insensitive costs; they need not guarantee a reasonable price, nondiscriminatory treatment, or a fair rate of return. In an unregulated market, private contracts will gravitate toward terms of this kind only when market forces favor them. When market conditions change, contract terms will change, too. As competition infiltrated AT&T's long-distance monopoly, the inevitable shift from tariffs to flexible contracts occurred. This shift occurred not just in flash cuts from price regulation to nondominant status, but also in the creation of a new form of tariffs that were themselves closer to being contracts.

§9.5.3.1   AT&T and the One-Customer Tariff

When MCI and other new rivals first appeared, AT&T attempted to meet the competition's business-grabbing deals,

[438] Revisions to Price Cap Rules for AT&T Corp., Report and Order, 10 F.C.C. Rec. 3009 (1995).
[439] *See* Motion of AT&T Corp. to Be Reclassified as a Non-dominant Carrier, Order, 11 F.C.C. Rec. 3271 (1995).
[440] *Id.* at 3281 ¶12. *See also* §9.8.2.

while also hewing to its obligation to provide service under tariff. But as competition became firmly rooted and telecommunications systems more sophisticated, complex, and variable, this became impossible. In 1987, AT&T finally attacked the problem head on, filing its Tariff 12 as a one-customer tariff, the ultimate regulatory oxymoron. The tariff was filed specifically and explicitly to permit AT&T to supply a private network to General Electric.[441] The tariff integrated a variety of separately tariffed services into a single contract or "option" and set a single five-year price for the customized whole. MCI and Sprint rushed in to protest. The integrated, customer-specific service offering was discriminatory, they pointed out. They were right, but complex, privately negotiated contracts always are discriminatory in a sense. Da Vinci may commit to paint one Mona Lisa, but rarely two.

The FCC required AT&T to make the customized services available not only to General Electric, but also to similarly situated customers, without geographical restrictions.[442] AT&T made the change, and the FCC then approved the first four Tariff 12 contracts.[443] AT&T quickly filed dozens of additional one-customer arrangements under Tariff 12.[444]

In 1990, however, the D.C. Circuit overturned the FCC's approval of Tariff 12, finding fault with the logic underlying the Commission's determination that the integrated service packages offered under Tariff 12 were not "like" the aggregation of their constituent parts and that AT&T hence was not prohibited from selling its Tariff 12 offerings at a lower price.[445] The court conceded that one way or another the FCC would "undoubtedly

[441] AT&T Request for Waiver of Rules Regarding Proposed Custom-Designed Integrated Service, Public Notice, 2 F.C.C. Rec. 3915 (1987).

[442] AT&T, Revisions to Tariff F.C.C. No. 12, Memorandum Opinion and Order, 4 F.C.C. Rec. 4932, 4934 ¶18 (1989) (hereinafter *Tariff 12 Order*), *recons. denied*, 4 F.C.C. Rec. 7928 (1989), *rev'd and remanded*, MCI v. FCC, 917 F.2d 30 (D.C. Cir. 1990).

[443] AT&T, Revisions to Tariff F.C.C. No. 12, Custom-Designed Integrated Services, Memorandum Opinion and Order, 4 F.C.C. Rec. 5430 (1989).

[444] By January 1991, AT&T had 77 such service packages filed under Tariff 12. AT&T, Revisions to Tariff F.C.C. No. 12, Order, 6 F.C.C. Rec. 740, 741 n.1 (1991).

[445] MCI v. FCC, 917 F.2d at 37–40. The court held that the FCC based its "likeness" determination on cost differentials and competitive necessity, both of which are "forbidden considerations." *Id.* at 39 (citing American Broad. Co.

permit AT&T to compete effectively against its competitors in the large user market," but required that the Commission "do so by turning square corners of administrative law."[446]

On remand, as the court of appeals had anticipated, the FCC again approved Tariff 12.[447] The Commission found that, in terms of customer perceptions and service functionalities, the integrated service packages offered under Tariff 12 are not "like" the individually tariffed services of which they are constituted. "Like" services have to be offered without unreasonable discrimination on similar terms to all comers.[448] But services that are not "like" their constituent elements may be priced on a customer-specific basis.[449]

This time the court of appeals upheld Tariff 12.[450] It agreed with the FCC that a Tariff 12 package was not "like" the combination of its component services and that different service packages offered under the general rubric of Tariff 12 were not "like" each other for purposes of section 202(a) of the Communications Act.[451]

---

v. FCC, 663 F.2d 133, 139 (D.C. Cir. 1980); Western Union Intl. Inc. v. FCC, 568 F.2d 1012, 1019 n.15 (2d Cir. 1977), *cert. denied,* 436 U.S. 944 (1978)) ("Pricing differences *a fortiori* cannot be a basis for finding the services unlike—otherwise, the very discrimination Section 202 [of the Act] attempts to prevent would be the grounds for finding that section inapplicable . . . [i]t would seem that the Commission committed legal seppuku.").

[446] MCI v. FCC, 917 F.2d at 42.

[447] *AT&T, Revisions to Tariff F.C.C. No. 12,* Memorandum Opinion and Order on Remand, 6 F.C.C. Rec. 7039 (1991).

[448] 47 U.S.C. §202(a).

[449] *Id.*

[450] Competitive Telecomms. Assn. v. FCC, 998 F.2d 1058 (D.C. Cir. 1993).

[451] Another dispute over AT&T's Tariff No. 12 arose in 1995, when AT&T demanded that Public Service Enterprises of Pennsylvania, a customer under the tariff that was reselling AT&T's service to others, furnish AT&T with detailed information about each customer to whom it was reselling the tariffed service. When Public Service refused to provide the information sought by AT&T, AT&T refused to provide its service, arguing that it was entitled to deny tariff-based service to customers it believes "are not similarly situated" to the customer for whom the tariff had been designed. The Commission rejected this claim and AT&T's demand for detailed information, Public Service Enterprises of Pa., Inc. v. AT&T Corp., Memorandum Opinion and Order, 10 F.C.C. Rec. 8390 ¶1 (1995), but the D.C. Circuit overturned this ruling on appeal, AT&T v. FCC, 86 F.3d 242 (D.C. Cir. 1996). In particular, the

§9.5.3.2   Tariff 15

AT&T followed Tariff 12 with Tariff 15. Tariff 15 gave AT&T additional flexibility when courting large customers, allowing AT&T to meet competition by offering special pricing outside of its general tariffs. The notion of nondiscriminatory "competitive" discounts to specific customers raised a paradox similar to Tariff 12's customized service packages. Indeed, FCC rejected AT&T's initial attempts to offer services under Tariff 15 because AT&T did not make its "Competitive Pricing Plans" available to all customers and would not make a discount available until one of AT&T's competitors approached the customer with a lower-priced offering.[452]

In 1991, the Commission broadly determined that AT&T's Tariff 15 plans were unreasonably discriminatory and suspended them.[453] AT&T quickly revised its plans by eliminating the requirement that the customer disclose competitive offers to AT&T and making them available to similarly situated customers; the Commission accepted these changes and approved the plans.[454] After these initial disputes, AT&T's Tariff 15 filings were generally routinely approved by the Commission over MCI's protests.[455]

---

court decided that the Commission had not sufficiently explained its reasons for denying AT&T's request for customer information. *Id.* at 245. The court also questioned whether AT&T's requirements truly placed a substantial burden on resale customers as a group. *Id.* at 247.

[452] *See* AT&T Communications, Revisions to Tariff FCC No. 15, Competitive Pricing Plans—Holiday Rate Plan, Memorandum Opinion and Order, 4 F.C.C. Rec. 7933, 7934 (1989), *recons. denied,* 5 F.C.C. Rec. 1821 (1990); AT&T, Competitive Pricing Plan 2—Resort Condominiums International, Memorandum Opinion and Order, 6 F.C.C. Rec. 5648, 5649 ¶12 (1991).

[453] AT&T Communications, Tariff F.C.C. No. 15, Memorandum Opinion and Order, 6 F.C.C. Rec. 5648 (1991), *app. for stay denied,* AT&T v. FCC, No. 91-1504 (D.C. Cir. Dec. 2, 1991), *app. for stay granted,* AT&T v. FCC, No. 91-1504 (D.C. Cir. Dec. 17, 1991), *remand granted,* AT&T v. FCC, No. 91-1504 (D.C. Cir. Jan. 21, 1992); AT&T Communications, Tariff F.C.C. No. 15, Order Designating Issue for Investigation, 6 F.C.C. Rec. 6656 (1991).

[454] AT&T Communications, Tariff F.C.C. No. 15, Transmittal Nos. 3498 and 3823, Order, 7 F.C.C. Rec. 818 (1992).

[455] *See* AT&T Communications, F.C.C. No. 15, Contract Tariff No. 40, Order, 7 F.C.C. Rec. 4650 (1992); AT&T Communications, Tariff F.C.C. No. 15,

§9.5.3.3   Tariff 16

Tariff 16, also rolled out by AT&T in 1988, was the equivalent of Tariff 12, but for "government or government supported customers."[456] Section 201(b) of the Communications Act allows a separate pricing classification for services provided to government.[457] This tariff suffered from some of the same internal inconsistencies found in Tariffs 12 and 15, as well as controversies regarding the "governmental" nature of the services offered.[458] AT&T first proposed Tariff 16 after winning a competitive bid for a contract solicited by the Department of Defense.[459] In 1989, Tariff 16 became the "umbrella tariff" under which AT&T provided 60 percent of the world's largest private network—the Federal Telecommunications System 2000 (FTS-2000) to federal government agencies.[460]

§9.5.3.4   Forbearance Under the 1996 Act

As part of its implementation of the 1996 Act, the FCC decided in October 1996 that nondominant interexchange carriers would no longer be required (or permitted) to file tariffs for their

---

Competitive Pricing Plan 22, Order, 7 F.C.C. Rec. 4636 (1992); AT&T Communications, Tariff F.C.C. No. 1, et al., Memorandum Opinion and Order, 9 F.C.C. Rec. 299 (1994).

[456] Tariff 16 was entitled "Competitively Bid Government Services."

[457] 47 U.S.C. §201(b).

[458] For example, in 1989, AT&T proposed a tariff for outbound services that it planned to provide to the University of Texas at Austin. The Commission rejected the proposal, asserting that AT&T, by offering this service exclusively to the University, was discriminating against other government customers. AT&T, Revisions to Tariff F.C.C. No. 16, Memorandum Opinion and Order, 5 F.C.C. Rec. 700 (1990).

[459] See AT&T, Tariff F.C.C. No. 16, Order, 4 F.C.C. Rec. 2231 (1989); AT&T, Revisions to Tariff F.C.C. No. 16, Memorandum Opinion and Order, 5 F.C.C. Rec. 468 (1990).

[460] AT&T, Tariff F.C.C. No. 16, Order, 4 F.C.C. Rec. 2231 (1989); AT&T Transmittal Nos. 1555 and 1623, Tariff F.C.C. No. 16, Memorandum Opinion and Order, 4 F.C.C. Rec. 5043 (approving AT&T's tariffed rates for FTS-2000 services); Pa. Chooses AT&T's Tariff 16 Calling Services, Comm. Week, Nov. 6, 1989, at 60.

domestic interstate services.[461] The paradox of contract tariffs was thus resolved in favor of contract over tariff, signaling another step in the march to competitive interstate markets.

§9.6 Structural Regulation: Bell Company Entry

While the FCC gradually deregulated interstate markets throughout the 1980s and early 1990s, a glaring exception was the continued prohibition against participation of the Bell companies in these markets. Initially, this prohibition was caused by the FCC's lack of power to authorize BOC entry: during the 1980s, the MFJ court twice rejected the FCC's view that the Bell companies should be allowed to compete against their old parent, AT&T, in long distance.[462] More recently the FCC itself has used its new power to grant the BOCs interLATA authority as a means of advancing its goal of promoting competition in local markets. Accordingly, callers who used the BOCs as their local telephone company (approximately 80 percent of all U.S. telephone customers) have had no choice but to use a different company—usually AT&T—for their interLATA calls. The result has been not merely to exclude a handful of potential entrants from the long-distance business, but also to keep out the very companies that, with their established customer bases and familiar names, could credibly challenge the "Big Three" of AT&T, MCI WorldCom, and Sprint.

---

[461] Policy and Rules Concerning the Interstate, Interexchange Marketplace; Implementation of Section 254(g) of the Communications Act of 1934, as Amended, Second Report and Order, 11 F.C.C. Rec. 20,730, 20,733 ¶3 (1996) ("We conclude that a policy of complete detariffing (i.e., not permitting nondominant interexchange carriers to file tariffs) for [interstate, domestic] services would further advance the statutory objectives of the forbearance provision, Section 10. We therefore order all nondominant interexchange carriers to cancel their tariffs for interstate, domestic, interexchange services within nine months from the effective date of this Order."). *See also* §9.5.1.

[462] *See* §§9.6.1, 9.6.2.1.

§9.6.1 The Divestiture Decree

With respect to regulation of long-distance services, the key provision of the Divestiture Decree was section II(D)(1), which prohibited the divested BOCs from providing "interexchange telecommunications services." This restriction went to the heart of the government's antitrust case. The strongest evidence marshalled by the government involved anticompetitive conduct in long-distance markets, and competing interexchange carriers had won their private antitrust verdicts against the Bell System on the strength of similar claims.[463] Indeed, the entire division of the Bell System's assets at divestiture was rationalized as a separation of "local" from "long-distance" operations.[464]

The FCC had opposed all of the Decree's line-of-business restrictions on the BOCs, including the prohibition on BOC provision of interLATA services.[465] In comments filed with Judge Greene during the district court's Tunney Act hearings,[466] the Commission maintained that the Department of Justice's concerns about discrimination and cross-subsidy by the local monopolies were exaggerated.[467] Indeed, the Commission argued that it "would be particularly unwise" from the perspective of interLATA competition "to preclude entry by any qualified entrant such as the divested BOCs."[468] In approving section

---

[463] See §§3.4., 9.4.4.

[464] See §9.4.4.3.

[465] From the outset, the Commission believed that these "post-divestiture restrictions" were "unnecessary and unwise." Brief of the Federal Communications Commission as Amicus Curiae on Stipulation and Modification of Final Judgment at 30, United States v. Western Elec. Co., No. 82-0192 (D.D.C. Apr. 22, 1982). "[T]he proposed restrictions on the divested BOCs," the Commission stated emphatically, "would do more harm than good and thus are not 'in the public interest.'" See also Brief of the Federal Communications Commission as Amicus Curiae on Question No. 1 on Stipulation and Modification of Final Judgment at 11, United States v. Western Elec. Co., No. 82-0192 (D.D.C. June 14, 1982).

[466] See 15 U.S.C. §16(e).

[467] Brief for FCC as Amicus Curiae at 29, 32–33, 35–36, United States v. Western Elec. Co., No. 82-0192 (D.D.C. Apr. 20, 1982).

[468] Id. at 36.

II(D)(1), however, Judge Greene agreed with the Department that if the BOCs provided interexchange services, "they would stand to gain business if other carriers were disadvantaged by poor access arrangements and high tariffs."[469] They would "have substantial incentives to subvert [the Decree's] equal access requirements" and would find ways to "provide to their own interexchange service more favorable treatment than that granted to the other carriers."[470]

The scope of the Decree's "interexchange telecommunications services" prohibition was defined by three separate clauses of the Decree. "Interexchange" transmissions were (for Decree purposes) transmissions between local access and transport areas, or LATAs.[471] "Telecommunications" were electromagnetic transmissions of customer information.[472] "Services" were transmissions offered to customers "for hire."[473] Taken together, these definitions described the common carrier business of carrying customer messages between LATAs.[474] Inevitably, however, the MFJ's prohibition on this activity precipitated controversy and still more litigation.

---

[469] *Decree Opinion*, 552 F. Supp. at 188.

[470] *Id.*

[471] *Decree* §IV(K), 552 F. Supp. at 229, defined "interexchange telecommunications" as "telecommunications between a point or points located in one exchange telecommunications area and a point or points located in one or more other exchange areas or a point outside an exchange area." The definition thus also included transmissions from a LATA to any point that is not within any LATA, such as a point within the territory of an independent telephone company. *See* §9.8.2.

[472] *Decree* §IV(O), 552 F. Supp. at 229, defined "telecommunications" as "the transmission, between or among points specified by the user, of information of the user's choosing, without change in the form or content of the information as sent and received, by means of electromagnetic transmission, with or without benefit of any closed transmission medium, including all instrumentalities, facilities, apparatus, and services (including the collection, storage, forwarding, switching, and delivery of such information) essential to such transmission."

[473] *Decree* §IV(P), 552 F. Supp. at 229.

[474] "Most simply, a LATA marks the boundaries beyond which a Bell Operating Company may not carry telephone calls." United States v. Western Elec. Co., 569 F. Supp. 990, 994 (D.D.C. 1983) (footnote omitted). The relevant Decree definitions were transported largely intact to the 1996 Act and now are

§9.6.1.1   Creation of LATAs

Judge Greene's first task after entering the Decree was to complete the separation between local and long-distance services.[475] Although the divested BOCs were to confine their telephone operations to "exchanges," this term was not intended to coincide with the small territories served by individual end offices, which are also called "exchanges." To avoid confusion, the service areas allocated to BOCs under the Plan of Reorganization were renamed LATAs. The two principal services provided by BOCs after divestiture would be "transport" among end users within a LATA and "access" to long-distance carriers that carried calls to or from a LATA. LATAs were not, however, intended to separate "local" from "toll" calls; the BOCs could continue to provide toll service within individual LATAs.[476]

Section IV(G) of the Decree defined a LATA as "one or more contiguous local exchange areas serving common social, economic, and other purposes, even where such configuration transcends municipal or other local governmental boundaries."[477] Absent special approval, no LATA was to encompass more than one standard metropolitan statistical area (SMSA) or cross state boundaries.[478]

The threshold size for LATAs was based on the Department of Justice's estimate of the minimum size necessary to attract competitive interexchange service. The Department initially adopted 100,000 telephone stations as the "guideline minimum size" for

---

interpreted by the FCC. *See* 47 U.S.C. §153(21) (definition of "interLATA service"); *id.* §153(25) (definition of "LATA"); *id.* §153(43) (definition of "telecommunications"); *id.* §153(46) (definition of "telecommunications service").

[475] United States v. Western Elec. Co., 569 F. Supp. 990.

[476] United States v. Western Elec. Co., 569 F. Supp. at 995 ("The distance at which a local call becomes a long distance toll call has been, and will continue to be, determined exclusively by the various state regulatory bodies. After divestiture, calls placed within any one LATA may still be either 'local' or 'toll' depending upon the requirements or rates established by state regulators.") (footnote omitted).

[477] *Decree*, 552 F. Supp. at 229.

[478] *Id.*

a LATA, based on the assumptions that an interexchange carrier would need to capture a 5 percent market share to compete and that interexchange carriers would find it economic to establish facilities to serve 5,000 or more subscribers.[479] "As a general proposition," the Department further suggested, "no [LATA] should be smaller than the geographic region . . . served by an existing AT&T Class 4 office."[480]

AT&T agreed that each LATA should be large enough to "present an attractive market for potential new entrants" and to "assure that there will be multiple interexchange carriers actually or potentially able to serve all telephone subscribers in the area."[481] AT&T also backed the Department of Justice's decision to enlarge various LATAs because "larger LATAs give potential new entrants the right to offer service to larger numbers of subscribers with a lesser investment" and "larger LATAs promote competition by encouraging new entry."[482]

In the ensuing debate over appropriate LATA boundaries, regulators and others concerned with keeping down local rates argued for larger LATAs (to allow the local companies to carry additional profitable intraLATA toll traffic). So did the smaller interexchange carriers, which wanted to avoid the expense of building separate facilities to reach their thinly dispersed customer bases in numerous small LATAs. But the two largest competitive interexchange carriers, MCI and Sprint, wanted smaller LATAs.[483] Indeed, MCI challenged all the BOC LATAs on the

---

[479] Response of the United States to Comments Received on the BOC LATA Proposals at 16–17, United States v. Western Elec. Co., No. 82-0192 (D.D.C. Mar. 23, 1982). *See* United States v. Western Elec. Co., 569 F. Supp. at 1019 n.149. Judge Greene subsequently criticized the 5 percent assumption, but nonetheless approved almost all of the Department's recommendations. *Id.* at 1020 n.150.

[480] *Competitive Impact Statement* at 30.

[481] AT&T Response to Comments and Objections Relating to the Proposed LATA Boundaries at 7, United States v. Western Elec. Co., No. 82-0192 (D.D.C. Nov. 23, 1982).

[482] *Id.* at 5 (emphasis omitted).

[483] This was a marked change, of course, for MCI at least. Well before divestiture, the FCC in its *Specialized Common Carriers* decision had ordered Bell to provide access within territories known as local distribution areas (LDAs). In its private antitrust case against Bell, MCI complained that the

ground that they were honeycombed by the territories of independent telcos and therefore not "contiguous," as required by the Decree. Judge Greene rejected the argument; "contiguity," for Decree purposes, ignored the territories of independent telcos.[484]

Judge Greene readily accepted that the size of the LATAs "implicate[d] significant policy choices."[485] He noted that larger LATAs would leave the BOCs enough toll traffic to "augment[ ] their financial viability" and "decreas[e] the pressure for rate increases" and to avoid "significant rearrangement costs that would otherwise be incurred if integrated local networks were severed by LATA boundaries."[486] He also recognized that "large LATAs also have some procompetitive features (e.g., they tend to reduce the number of facilities AT&T's competitors will have to build as well as the number of telecommunications facilities AT&T will own after divestiture)."[487] Finally, Judge Greene emphasized the importance of establishing some parity between the

---

LDAs had been drawn by Bell too narrowly as an impediment to long-distance competition. *See* MCI v. AT&T, 708 F.2d at 1145–1146; United States v. AT&T, 524 F. Supp. at 1355 ("defendants attempted to deny competitors meaningful access to local distribution facilities . . . by making the local distribution area arbitrarily small") (footnotes omitted).

[484] United States v. Western Elec. Co., 569 F. Supp. at 1010–1011. Although the Decree did not impose any obligations on independent telephone companies, it did affect what traffic neighboring BOCs could carry to and from their service areas. This presented a potentially serious problem, as many smaller independent telcos relied on the BOCs for connection to long-distance carriers. Various independent service areas were therefore "assigned" to one or another BOC as "shadow" LATAs. *See Decree* §IV(G)(2), 552 F. Supp. at 229; United States v. Western Elec. Co., 569 F. Supp. at 1008 n.85.

[485] United States v. Western Elec. Co., 569 F. Supp. at 995.

[486] *Id.* at 995 & n.23.

[487] *Id.* at 995–996 n.24. *See also id.*, at 996 & n.27 ("the Court necessarily must consider" policies including "competition"; "Operating Company viability"; "the minimization of service disruption to telephone subscribers; the avoidance of costly network rearrangement; and the establishment of LATAs of sufficient size to attract several interexchange carriers").

Elsewhere the court reiterated that "large LATAs could promote competition in the long distance market." *Id.* at 1004 n.62. The court explained:

No carrier has as many existing points of presence as AT&T. If a LATA were so small as to leave room for only one interexchange carrier efficiently to serve that region through its own facilities, and if AT&T had a point of presence already established in that region, there would be

BOCs and AT&T, which, "even after divestiture, will be far larger and more powerful than any of the individual Operating Companies."[488]

The Decree required the district court's approval only for LATAs that crossed state or metropolitan-area boundaries, but Judge Greene nevertheless decided that his general supervision of the reorganization necessitated review of all proposed LATAs.[489] The subsequent bargaining on LATA boundaries was worthy of an Arabian bazaar.[490] Many of Judge Greene's calls on LATA boundaries seemed to turn on highly impressionistic factors. For example, in rejecting a Bell request to consolidate six SMSAs in a single Birmingham LATA in northern Alabama, Judge Greene observed that "Florence and Huntsville identify with each other more than either does with Birmingham."[491] He decided a similar dispute involving the Southeast Florida LATA the other way,[492] largely because of "a letter to the Court from the Governor of Florida . . . indicat[ing] that failure to consolidate the area

---

little incentive to a competitor to undertake the expense involved in establishing its own point of presence in this small market area. Hence, the objective of competition would be defeated and AT&T might be left in control of facilities or markets having bottleneck monopoly characteristics.

Id.

[488] *Id.* at 996 n.26. *See also* Response of the United States to Comments Received on the BOC LATA Proposals at 7 (Nov. 23, 1982) ("where the choice is between retaining an element of AT&T's monopoly and potentially adding in a marginal way to that of a BOC, the Department believes that the choice the decree takes is to remove the risk of continued AT&T monopoly power").

[489] The court had a responsibility to ensure that none of the proposed LATAs "depart[ed] from the letter and the spirit of the decree." United States v. Western Elec. Co., 569 F. Supp. at 1001 (footnotes omitted). The district court had previously noted that "[i]t is nowhere spelled out" how the LATAs "would be established, defined, or demonstrated. AT&T would thus be wholly free to draw the exchange area boundaries so as to further its own interests" absent supervision by the district court. *Decree Opinion*, 552 F. Supp. at 214 n.345.

[490] *See, e.g.,* United States v. Western Elec. Co., 569 F. Supp. at 1020–1028 (ruling on LATA disputes).

[491] *Id.* at 1030 n.204. South Central Bell "reluctantly accept[ed]" splitting Florence and Huntsville from the Birmingham LATA, even though this would cost an additional $1.485 million in reconfiguration costs. *Id.* at 1029–1030 & n.201.

[492] *Id.* at 1032.

into a single LATA would entail rate increases which would adversely affect the large number of retired persons living in Florida on fixed incomes."[493] Judge Greene similarly agreed to approve the consolidation of Syracuse with Utica and Albany with Glens Falls,[494] in part because Glens Falls relied on Albany for its airport and "much of its transportation and medical needs" and Albany residents "turn to the Glens Falls area for many recreational opportunities."[495]

Carving up the Bell System territories inevitably collided with established network and tariff realities. These conflicts were handled ad hoc, by waiver, adjustment, or exception. For example, Judge Greene approved two corridors for high-density traffic between New York City and northern New Jersey and between Philadelphia and Camden, New Jersey, even though these corridors connected multiple SMSAs and crossed state boundaries.[496]

Ultimately, Judge Greene accepted most of the LATAs approved by the Department of Justice, including those that crossed

---

[493] *Id.* In addition, the court noted that "Florida has already licensed an intrastate carrier, Microtel, Inc., to compete with Southern Bell for intercity, intra-LATA calls. The State Public Service Commission, in its filings with the Court, has persuaded the Court that it is a strong body and one committed to promoting competition." *Id.*

[494] *Id.* at 1019, 1057, 1104.

[495] *Id.* at 1020 n.151.

[496] The court found this exception to be so significant that it required a modification of the Decree pursuant to section VII. *Id.* at 1019. "Limited corridor exceptions represent the most extreme departure from the provisions of the decree of all the exceptions requested by AT&T. A corridor exception is justifiable only when an entire network arrangement reflects such a high investment and such entrenched usage that it would be irrational to order the fragmentation of the network." *Id.* at 1017 n.136. Similarly, Judge Greene generally permitted BOCs to continue providing established nonoptional extended area service (EAS) arrangements (free calling to nearby local exchanges) even across LATA boundaries, but he rejected the suggestion of some state regulators that the BOCs be permitted to continue providing *optional* EAS arrangements. *Id.* at 1002 n.54. Judge Greene likewise rejected the request of the West Virginia Public Service Commission to preserve an optional in-state discount calling service known as "circle calling." United States v. Western Elec. Co., 569 F. Supp. at 1026 & n.189.

state or metropolitan lines.[497] The Bell System's territory was divided into a total of 163 LATAs with an average population of roughly 500,000. The New York Metropolitan LATA included nearly 6 million stations; the Los Angeles LATA, over 4 million. At the low end, the very smallest LATAs served only about 10,000 subscribers.

§9.6.1.2 Post-divestiture Modifications

For all the complexity of the task, initial division of the Bell System turned out to be the easy part. It immediately was clear that the Decree's restrictions on the divested local companies were impractical, unnecessarily broad, or simply exceptionally onerous, and a steady stream of requests for relief ensued.[498] These requests quickly led to outright elimination of the Decree's most sweeping, but also most peripheral, line-of-business restriction.[499] And even with respect to the Decree's three "core" restrictions,[500] numerous waivers—and full relief from the information services prohibition—were granted.[501]

---

[497] In approving the exceptional LATAs, the court also stated it would require BOCs to provide some form of equal access for intraLATA toll traffic. *See* §9.7.

[498] In 1987, Judge Greene complained that "[a]lmost before the ink was dry on the decree, the Regional Companies began to seek the removal of its restrictions." United States v. Western Elec. Co., 673 F. Supp. 525, 601 (D.D.C. 1987); *aff'd in part and rev'd in part*, 900 F.2d 283 (D.C. Cir.), *cert. denied*, 498 U.S. 911 (1990).

[499] *See id.* at 599 (lifting section II(D)(3)'s prohibition against BOC provision of services other than telecommunications and exchange access).

[500] *See* United States v. Western Elec. Co., 673 F. Supp. 525, 529 (D.D.C. 1987) (listing "interexchange services," "manufacturing," and "information services" as "core restrictions").

[501] *See* United States v. Western Elec. Co., 767 F. Supp. 308 (D.D.C. 1991) (lifting section II(D)(1)'s prohibition against BOC provision of information services), *aff'd*, 993 F.2d 1572 (D.C. Cir. 1993). Judge Greene would consider a BOC's request for a waiver of the Decree's line-of-business restrictions only after an initial evaluation by the Department of Justice. United States v. Western Elec. Co., 592 F. Supp. 846, 873 (D.D.C. 1984), *appeal denied*, 777 F.2d 23 (D.C. Cir. 1985). When a proposed modification was uncontested by both the Department and AT&T, a "public interest" test governed. *See Decree* §VII, 552 F. Supp. at 231. In 1990, after Judge Greene had been ruling on waiver

Universal service had been an important factor in the court's approval of relatively large LATAs,[502] and maintaining universal service was the single most constant theme in Judge Greene's waiver jurisprudence.[503] Further adjustments in LATA boundaries were required every year to maintain service to individual households, most of them rural, that were for some reason thought to be on the wrong side of some LATA boundary. Such waivers were approved BOC-by-BOC, sometimes household-by-household.[504]

Judge Greene viewed local telcos as integral arms of the regulatory state. Their principal mission was not competition or profit, but service — universal service. The BOCs were thus permitted to provide free time and weather service,[505] relay services

---

requests for six years, the D.C. Circuit clarified that under the public interest standard the Decree court could reject an uncontested waiver request only if "the proposed modification would be certain to lessen competition in the relevant market." United States v. Western Elec. Co., 900 F.2d 283, 308 (D.C. Cir.), *cert. denied,* 498 U.S. 911 (1990). Under section VIII(C) of the Decree, however, a waiver contested by the Department or AT&T had to be denied if there was a "substantial possibility that [the BOC] could use its monopoly power to impede competition." *Id.* at 295.

[502] *See, e.g.,* United States v. Western Elec. Co., 569 F. Supp. at 997 n.33; *see also id.* at 1022 n.162 (consolidation of Delaware and Philadelphia area into a single LATA).

[503] *See id.* at 1091; *Decree Opinion,* 552 F. Supp. at 169, 224 n.376.

[504] *E.g.,* Order, United States v. Western Elec. Co., No. 82-0192 (D.D.C. Mar. 22, 1985) ("Pacific Bell is permitted to provide telephone service to Mrs. Mary Campbell, who lives in the Plymouth exchange in the Stockton, California LATA, via the Placerville central office in the Sacramento, California LATA."); Order, United States v. Western Elec. Co., No. 82-0192 (D.D.C. Sept. 10, 1991) ("Wisconsin Bell may provide interLATA cross-boundary foreign exchange service to Ms. Vicki Millard and Mr. Ricky Schultz, as directed by the Wisconsin Public Service Commission."). At the height of his power, Judge Greene approved 20 or so such requests every year.

[505] United States v. Western Elec. Co., 578 F. Supp. 658 (D.D.C. 1983) (BOCs may provide time and weather announcements so long as no alternative providers are present); Memorandum at 1 n.1, 8, United States v. Western Elec. Co., No. 82-0192 (D.D.C. Feb. 8, 1988) (a BOC "may provide such announcements to its customers as a public service"—that is, without "special additional charges to the public"—"regardless of the existence of alternative service providers").

for hearing-impaired persons across LATA boundaries,[506] emergency 911 service,[507] ordinary directory assistance,[508] and directory assistance for customers of independent telephone companies.[509] Next-generation information service gateways and modern network signaling systems, however, were strictly confined within LATA boundaries.[510] Similarly, the BOCs were permitted to sell services to government entities much more readily than to the private sector.[511]

The strongest rationale Judge Greene recognized for permitting a BOC to provide an interLATA service was that nobody else would. In the same vein, and despite his frequent criticism of regulators and their efficacy,[512] Judge Greene consistently granted all waivers that BOCs needed to comply with direct regulatory mandates.[513]

---

[506] Memorandum, United States v. Western Elec. Co., No. 82-0192 (D.D.C. Sept. 11, 1989).

[507] Order, United States v. Western Elec. Co., No. 82-0192 (D.D.C. Feb. 2, 1989) (authorizing the BOCs "to provide, using their own facilities, 911 emergency service across LATA boundaries to any 911 customer whose jurisdiction crosses a LATA boundary").

[508] United States v. Western Elec. Co., 569 F. Supp. at 1097–1101, 1101 n.175.

[509] Memorandum at 5–6 & nn.9, 10, United States v. Western Elec. Co., No. 82-0192 (D.D.C. Feb. 6, 1984).

[510] See Opinion, United States v. Western Elec. Co., No. 82-0192 (D.D.C. Jan. 24, 1989), aff'd, 907 F.2d 160 (D.C. Cir. 1990); Opinion, United States v. Western Elec. Co., No. 82-0192 (D.D.C. Sept. 6, 1990), aff'd, 969 F.2d 1231 (D.C. Cir. 1992).

[511] E.g., Memorandum, United States v. Western Elec. Co., No. 82-0192 (D.D.C. Nov. 6, 1987) (waiver granted for switching services to be offered the government; status of BOC nongovernment customers left uncertain).

[512] Decree Opinion, 552 F. Supp. at 223 ("For a great many years, the Federal Communications Commission has struggled, largely without success, to stop practices of this type through the regulatory tools at its command."); United States v. Western Elec. Co., 675 F. Supp. at 660 (accusing then-FCC Chairman Dennis Patrick of inciting "noncompliance" amongst the BOCs).

[513] See, e.g., United States v. Western Elec. Co., 578 F. Supp. at 657 (BOC services not under tariff); Order, United States v. Western Elec. Co., No. 82-0192 (D.D.C. Dec. 23, 1986) (detariffing billing and collection services); Memorandum and Order, United States v. Western Elec. Co., No. 82-0192 (D.D.C. Sept. 28, 1990) (detariffing exchange access from cellular radio systems); Order, United States v. Western Elec. Co., No. 82-0192 (D.D.C. Apr. 20, 1989) (interexchange lifeline services).

Over time, the BOCs' requests for relief shifted from narrow, customer-specific or service-specific proposals to generic and categorical proposals. Waivers for international services provide an example of this pattern. Beginning in 1984, the BOCs and their affiliates gained permission to provide a wide array of services overseas.[514] Initially, however, the "interexchange" prohibition applied to foreign markets where the BOCs did not even have any local telephone facilities: BOCs could provide telephone service within Switzerland, for example, but not "long-distance" service between Switzerland and France.[515] In 1986, Judge Greene ended this nonsensical extension of the LATA concept by removing all quasi-LATA lines outside of the United States.[516] Communications between the United States and foreign countries, however, were still "interexchange."[517] In 1993, Judge Greene eased this restriction as well. The court granted a generic waiver permitting any BOC (subject to certain restrictions) to provide end-to-end international traffic between the United States and any other foreign country and to own minority interests in international satellite and submarine cable facilities.[518]

---

[514] *See* United States v. Western Elec. Co., 604 F. Supp. 256, 261–262 (D.D.C. 1984) (foreign consulting and cellular services); Memorandum, United States v. Western Elec. Co., No. 82-0192 (D.D.C. June 26, 1986) (foreign manufacturing, telecommunications between foreign nations, and foreign nontelecommunications businesses); Memorandum, United States v. Western Elec. Co., No. 82-0192 (D.D.C. Feb. 13, 1989) (transpacific cable).

[515] *E.g.,* Order at 4, United States v. Western Elec. Co., No. 82-0192 (D.D.C. Dec. 14, 1984) (permitting Pacific Telesis to provide "[t]elecommunications services and information services within a foreign nation, including originating or terminating telecommunications from or to other nations, provided, however, that the foreign business shall not provide or have a financial interest in telecommunications services between nations").

[516] Order at 3, United States v. Western Elec. Co., No. 82-0192 (D.D.C. June 26, 1986) (granting waiver to permit a BOC to carry calls between nations, but "solely outside of the United States, Canada, and the islands at this date included in the 809 area code").

[517] *Id.*

[518] Order, United States v. Western Elec. Co., No. 82-0192 (D.D.C. Feb. 4, 1993). The court also allowed the BOCs to provide interexchange service in, and manufacture telecommunications products and equipment for sale in, Canada and the islands included in the 809 area code, areas that had been

The Bell companies likewise sought sweeping relief for wireless services. In 1991, consolidating 23 then-pending waiver requests, they petitioned the MFJ court for blanket authority to provide long-distance services to the millions of BOC customers served out of competitive cellular systems rather than bottleneck wireline exchange networks.[519] Judge Greene approved the waiver in April 1995, but placed extensive preconditions and restrictions on the BOCs' relief.[520] While the Bell companies' appeal of those qualifications was pending, the 1996 Act, which included a provision granting the unrestricted relief sought by the BOCs, became law.[521]

The process of chipping away at the Decree's interexchange restriction continued with the BOCs' efforts to gain permission to offer information services. Removal of the Decree's information services restriction in 1991 freed the Bell companies to provide information services to consumers.[522] Nonetheless, the Bell

---

omitted from prior international relief. *Id.* Conditions imposed on this relief included a nondiscrimination requirement in allocating traffic among U.S. carriers. *Id.*

[519] Bell Companies' Motion for a Modification of Section II of the Decree to Permit Them to Provide Cellular and Other Wireless Services Across LATA Boundaries, United States v. Western Elec. Co., No. 82-0192 (DOJ June 20, 1994).

[520] United States v. Western Elec. Co., 890 F. Supp. 1 (D.D.C. 1995). Conditions included equal access and nondiscrimination for competing interexchange carriers, separate subsidiary requirements for the BOCs' wireless affiliates, resale requirements, and a requirement that BOCs separately market their local and long-distance wireless services. *Id.* at 7–8. In addition, before a BOC could take advantage of the relief at all, it had to show that competitively provided exchange access services were available in the area for which relief was requested. *Id.* at 9.

[521] *See* 47 U.S.C. §271(b)(3), (g)(3) (allowing BOCs to provide "incidental interLATA services," including "commercial mobile services").

[522] *See* United States v. Western Elec. Co., 767 F. Supp. 308 (D.D.C. 1991), *aff'd,* 993 F.2d 1572 (D.C. Cir.), *cert. denied,* 114 S. Ct. 487 (1993). *See also Decree* §IV(J), 552 F. Supp. at 229 (defining "information services" as "the offering of a capability for storing, transforming, processing, retrieving, utilizing, or making available information which may be conveyed via telecommunications, except that such service does not include any use of any such capability for the management, control, or operation of a telecommunications system or the management of a telecommunications service"). The Decree's restrictions on BOC provision of information services are further discussed in §12.7.5.

companies' ability to participate fully in the information services market remained constrained by the interLATA restriction.[523] Accordingly, the BOCs petitioned Judge Greene in 1993 for a waiver to allow them to provide certain categories of information services, such as access to computer databases, across LATA boundaries.[524] Although endorsed by the Department of Justice,[525] the waiver languished in the district court[526] until the Telecommunications Act of 1996 superseded the Decree and granted the BOCs much of the relief they had sought.[527]

As the 1990s progressed, the BOCs' requests for relief went to the heart of the Decree's restrictions. In 1994, four BOCs petitioned the Decree court to vacate the Decree in its entirety.[528] And in 1995, Ameritech and the Department of Justice negotiated a plan that would have waived the interexchange restriction for certain of Ameritech's service areas.[529] With its proposed

---

[523] Unlike all other information services providers, the Bell companies could provide information services only within LATAs except to the extent that service-specific waivers of the interexchange restriction had been granted. *See* United States v. Western Elec. Co., 1989-1 Trade Cas. (CCH) ¶68,400, *aff'd* 907 F.2d 160 (D.C. Cir. 1990), *cert. denied,* 498 U.S. 1109 (1991). In 1991, the D.C. Circuit confirmed that "when information services are . . . bundled with leased interexchange lines, the activity is covered by the decree." United States v. Western Elec. Co., 907 F.2d 160, 163 (D.C. Cir. 1990).

[524] Motion of the Bell Companies for a Waiver of the Interexchange Restriction to Permit Them to Provide Information Services Across LATA Boundaries, United States v. Western Elec. Co., No. 82-0192 (D.D.C. June 25, 1993).

[525] Memorandum of the United States in Support of the Motion of the Bell Operating Companies for a Waiver to Permit Them to Provide Information Services Across LATA Boundaries, United States v. Western Elec. Co., No. 82-0192 (D.D.C. May 8, 1995).

[526] Order, United States v. Western Elec. Co., No. 82-0192 (D.D.C. Sept. 8, 1995) (court declaring it would address the interLATA information services waiver request "in due course").

[527] 47 U.S.C. §271(g)(4); *see* §9.6.4.

[528] Motion of Bell Atlantic Corporation, BellSouth Corporation, NYNEX Corporation, and Southwestern Bell Corporation to Vacate the Decree, United States v. Western Elec. Co., No. 82-0192 (D.D.C. Jul. 6, 1994).

[529] Motion of the United States for a Modification of the Decree to Permit a Trial, Supervised by the Department of Justice and the Court, in Which Ameritech Could Provide Interexchange Service for a Limited Geographic Area, with Appropriate Safeguards, When Actual Competition and Substantial Opportunities for Additional Competition in Local Exchange Service Develop, United States v. Western Elec. Co., No. 82-0192 (D.D.C. filed Apr.

unbundling of local loops and other network elements, interconnection with other local exchange carriers, dialing parity, and number portability, Ameritech's plan in many respects foreshadowed the requirements of section 251 of the 1996 Act.[530] Before Judge Greene acted on these requests, however, the 1996 Act became law, rendering the Decree's judicial restrictions obsolete.[531]

Throughout this process, erosion of the Decree progressed inexorably. Where the BOCs were successful in obtaining waivers, they filed further requests in an effort to expand the scale and scope of these victories. Waivers were filed faster than they were processed, leading to growing backlogs before the Department of Justice and Judge Greene: by 1994, the average age of waivers pending before the DOJ and Judge Greene was two and a half years.[532] This breakdown of Judge Greene's oversight of the telecommunications industry was of serious concern to legislators when they drafted the 1996 Act. Offended that a single judge had effectively supplanted Congress and the FCC as the policymaker for interLATA services, and was not even filling that role very effectively, legislators decried the "ossified perspective of an industry structure . . . lack of expertise and understanding

---

3, 1995) (final negotiated proposal) (hereinafter *DOJ/Ameritech Proposal*). *See also* §5.4.8.

[530] *See DOJ/Ameritech Proposal;* 47 U.S.C. §251. Both NYNEX and PacTel submitted similar waiver requests for New York and California, respectively. Memorandum in Support of Request of NYNEX Corporation for a Waiver to Provide Interexchange Services in New York, United States v. Western Elec. Co., No. 82-0192 (D.D.C. Aug. 25, 1994); Memorandum of Pacific Telesis Group in Support of Its Motion for a Waiver to Provide Interexchange Services to Customers in California, United States v. Western Elec. Co., No. 82-0192 (D.D.C. Jan. 31, 1995).

[531] *See* §9.6.4.

[532] Affidavit of Paul M. Rubin, *attached* to Motion of Bell Atlantic Corporation, BellSouth Corporation, NYNEX Corporation and Southwestern Bell Corporation to Vacate the Decree, United States v. Western Elec. Co., No. 82-0192 (D.D.C. July 6, 1994); Antitrust Division, United States Department of Justice, Line of Business Waiver Requests Submitted to the Department Pursuant to Section VIII(C) of the Modification of Final Judgment (Dec. 23, 1994). By contrast, in 1986, the average age of waivers pending before the court was five months.

of the way telecommunications markets operate; and the lack of an orderly procedure to ensure that waiver requests are timely passed" that were the hallmarks of the Decree era.[533]

§9.6.2 Bell Company Entry Under the 1996 Act

Congress thus had the Bell companies' efforts to secure inter-LATA relief very much in mind when, in 1996, it finalized its long-awaited overhaul of telecommunications regulation.

As long as the BOCs' local markets were closed to competitors, there was at least a rough sense of justice in preventing the BOCs from offering interLATA service. If the BOCs were able to offer interLATA service, they alone could provide one-stop shopping for local and long-distance services. But once Congress opened the BOCs' local markets to new entrants in 1996, that rationale for the Decree restrictions disappeared. Congress accordingly lifted the Decree's old restrictions on BOC entry in order to "foste[r] competition in" interexchange markets[534] and "lower prices in long distance calls through competition."[535]

Congress did not declare an open market overnight, however. Instead, it set up a set of Byzantine rules granting immediate relief for some long-distance services and establishing criteria for the FCC to use to grant eventual relief for the remaining services. Implementation of these provisions has been as arcane as application of the old Decree rules, but at least the end point is now clear. The question now is not whether the progression toward full, uncabined competition will continue in long-distance markets—it will—but whether imaginary lines between

---

[533] H. Rep. 204, pt. 1, 104th Cong., 1st Sess. 207–208 (1995).

[534] Southwestern Bell Tel. Co. v. FCC, 153 F.3d 597, 600 (8th Cir. 1998).

[535] 142 Cong. Rec. S686–S687 (daily ed., Feb. 1, 1996); *see id.* at S713 (daily ed., Feb. 1, 1996) (Sen. Breaux) ("removing all court ordered barriers to competition—including the MFJ interLATA restriction—will benefit consumers by lowering prices and accelerating innovation"); *id.* at S704 (daily ed., Feb. 1, 1996) (Sen. Ford) (estimating savings of $333 billion from greater long-distance competition as a result of the 1996 Act).

different classes of "long-distance" services will continue to have any relevance.

§9.6.2.1 Exclusion of the BOCs

As late as 1987, the FCC had again advocated allowing the BOCs to provide interLATA services and promised to fashion appropriate regulations to prevent discrimination and cross-subsidy.[536] Judge Greene again rejected the Commission's advice and refused to allow wholesale BOC entry into the long-distance market.[537] And even though the court of appeals was more sympathetic to arguments for BOC entry, it, too, was concerned with the "persistence of [the BOCs'] local exchange monopoly—upon which interexchange carriers rely for access to ultimate consumers" and was fearful of discrimination and cross-subsidy that could accompany this monopoly.[538] While the D.C. Circuit acknowledged that the Commission had developed nondiscrimination safeguards and cost-separation principles in the context of BOC provision of customer premises equipment and enhanced services, the court pointed out that these rules had not yet been expressly applied to BOC provision of interLATA services. "[U]ntil those regulations are adjusted to take account of BOC entry into the interexchange market," the court concluded, "equal access and proper cost allocation cannot be assured."[539]

In effect, the court of appeals proposed to resolve concerns about discrimination and cross-subsidy by suggesting that the Commission set, in advance, express terms and conditions under which BOC entry into interLATA service would be accomplished. Although the BOCs asked the Commission to undertake

[536] Comments of the Federal Communications Commission as Amicus Curiae on the Report and Recommendations of the United States Concerning the Line of Business Restrictions Imposed on the Bell Operating Companies by the Modification of Final Judgment at 2, United States v. Western Elec. Co., No. 82-0192 (D.D.C. May 22, 1987).

[537] United States v. Western Elec. Co., 673 F. Supp. at 546–547.

[538] United States v. Western Elec. Co., 900 F.2d 283, 300–301 (D.C. Cir. 1990), *cert. denied*, 498 U.S. 911 (1990).

[539] *Id.* at 301. *See also id.* (noting "the danger of allowing entry before the FCC's regulations are designed to deal with the problem").

a comprehensive review and any necessary overhaul of existing safeguards,[540] the Commission never acted on that request. In February 1996, however, Congress itself provided the terms and conditions of BOC entry into interLATA service.

The Telecommunications Act of 1996 drastically reshaped the entire telecommunications industry, and especially the operations of the Bell companies. The most fundamental change was in the local market, where the 1996 Act requires incumbent LECs to permit requesting competitors to interconnect with the incumbent LECs' local networks, to provide competitors with "unbundled" access to network elements, and to offer competitors telecommunications services at wholesale rates in order to allow the competitors to resell these services.[541]

In exchange for providing this access, the Bell companies received the opportunity to provide long-distance service both inside and outside their regions. In section 601(a)(1) of the 1996 Act, Congress directed that "[a]ny conduct or activity that was . . . subject to any restriction or obligation imposed by the AT&T Consent Decree" no longer shall be subject to that Decree, but instead shall be subject to the restrictions and obligations of the 1996 Act.[542] Congress then granted out-of-region relief that is relatively straightforward and without conditions; in-region relief, on the other hand, was made available only after a BOC has satisfied numerous conditions—principally concerning the local market.[543]

---

[540] See Petition for Rulemaking to Determine the Terms and Conditions Under Which Tier 1 LECs Should Be Permitted to Provide InterLATA Telecommunications Services, No. RM-8303 (FCC July 15, 1993).

[541] 47 U.S.C. §251(c); see Chapter 5.

[542] Pub. L. No. 104-104, 110 Stat. 143. Section 601(a)(2) makes an identical substitution of jurisdiction with respect to the GTE Consent Decree, which was entered in 1984 in connection with GTE's acquisition of Sprint.

[543] Congress also sought to maintain a level playing field while the Bell companies were in the process of complying with the new local requirements of the 1996 Act by precluding carriers serving more than 5 percent of the nation's access lines (i.e., AT&T, MCI WorldCom, and Sprint) from jointly marketing resold Bell Company local service with their long-distance service until the Bell Company gained the right to sell interexchange service in the relevant or until three years had passed from the date of the 1996 Act's enactment. 47 U.S.C. §271(e)(1). This three-year period expired in February 1999, before any BOC obtained section 271 relief.

§9.6.2.2 Out-of-Region and Incidental Interexchange Relief

The Bell companies could immediately offer interexchange services outside their in-region states after passage of the 1996 Act.[544] Because the Act does not distinguish between calls originating out-of-region that terminate in-region and calls that take place entirely out-of-region, the Bell companies can terminate within their regions calls that originate out-of-region.[545] There is no limitation on the use of in-region facilities for the termination of such calls. Thus, calls that originate out-of-region need not be handed off to some unaffiliated interexchange carrier for delivery in-region, but can be handled entirely by the Bell Company itself.

There are some qualifications. Out-of-region relief does not apply to 800 and private line services that originate out-of-region and terminate in-region where the in-region party selects the carrier. Such services are treated as in-region services.[546] The Commission has also concluded that out-of-region, interLATA information services are subject to the "separate affiliate" requirements set out in section 272 of the 1996 Act.[547]

---

[544] 47 U.S.C. §271(b)(2). The 1996 Act speaks of in-region "States," which include any states in which a Bell Company was authorized to provide wireline telephone exchange service under the AT&T Consent Decree as of the date of enactment of the 1996 Act. *Id.* §271(i). Thus, even if the Bell Company traditionally provided service in only a portion of a state, the entire state is considered "in-region."

[545] *Id.* §271(b)(4).

[546] In 1996, the Commission ruled that calling card calls originating outside of a BOC's region and terminating within a BOC's region would not be considered "in-region" services because they do not allow the called party to determine the interexchange carrier. *See* Bell Operating Company Provision of Out-of-Region Interstate, Interexchange Services, Report and Order, 11 F.C.C. Rec. 18,564, 18,585–18,586 ¶¶45–47 (1996); 47 U.S.C. §271(j).

[547] Implementation of the Non-accounting Safeguards of Sections 271 and 272 of the Communications Act of 1934, as Amended, First Report and Order and Further Notice of Proposed Rulemaking, 11 F.C.C. Rec. 21,905, 21,946–21,947 ¶¶85–87 (1996) (hereinafter *Non-accounting Safeguards Order*); 47 C.F.R. §53.201(c). *See* §9.6.2.3.

Despite these limitations, the Bell companies can provide a full range of services—including bundled local and long-distance service—outside their current in-region states.[548] This freedom is less significant than it sounds, however. One of the Bell companies' most significant advantages as interexchange carriers is their strong brand names in telephony, but those brand names have vastly less cachet outside the areas where the Bell Company is the incumbent local service provider. Pacific Bell is unlikely to be a strong contender in New York City, just as Bell-South will have a hard time signing up customers in Minneapolis. Not surprisingly, therefore, Bell companies generally have provided out-of-region long-distance services only in areas where they have some local presence (for instance, as cellular carriers).

The 1996 Act also allowed the Bell companies immediately to offer interexchange transport for certain "incidental" interLATA services, which are defined in section 271(g).[549] The most important authorization contained in this section is the grant to Bell companies of full authority to provide long-distance services

---

[548] The Commission has found the BOCs nondominant in the provision of out-of-region, domestic interexchange services and international services originating out-of-region, as well as in-region. Regulatory Treatment of LEC Provision of Interexchange Services Originating in the LEC's Local Exchange Area, Policy and Rules Concerning the Interstate, Interexchange Marketplace, Second Report and Order and Third Report and Order, 12 F.C.C. Rec. 15,756, 15,763–15,764 ¶8, 15,876 ¶210 (1997) (hereinafter *BOC Nondominance Order*); *see also* NYNEX Long Distance Co. et al., Application for Authority Pursuant to Section 214 of the Communications Act of 1934 to Provide International Services from Certain Parts of the United States to International Points Through Resale of International Switched Services, Memorandum Opinion and Order, 12 F.C.C. Rec. 11,654, 11,660 ¶12 (1997) (finding that BOCs will be unable to use their local exchange monopolies to "raise the price of international services by restricting their output of such services, even if they were to offer such services on an integrated basis with their local exchange and exchange access services").

Before providing international services, the BOCs must obtain section 214 authority. *See* 47 U.S.C. §214; Application of BellSouth Corporation, et al. Pursuant to Section 271 of the Communications Act of 1934, as Amended, to Provide In-Region, InterLATA Services in South Carolina, Memorandum Opinion and Order, 13 F.C.C. Rec. 539, 542 ¶3 n.4 (1997) (hereinafter *South Carolina Order*).

[549] 47 U.S.C. §271(g).

over their cellular and personal communications service (PCS) systems or in conjunction with those wireless services, without any requirement to provide competing long-distance providers equal access.[550] Bell companies own four of the ten largest cellular carriers in the United States and are major players in PCS as well.[551] Thus, this "incidental" relief provided Bell companies with the means to offer interexchange service to millions of wireless customers without prior FCC approval, both in their home regions and in other areas where the BOCs have wireless systems.

The Act's "incidental" interexchange relief also includes delivery of video and audio programming across LATA boundaries.[552] Prior to the Act, Bell companies had already gained substantial freedom to deliver video services over cable and radio-based systems and to distribute programming to those individual systems by satellite.[553] Under the 1996 law, similar relief was afforded without regard to the particular distribution technology used, so that Bell companies could send video programming to their subscribers over cable, radio, or satellite systems and distribute their own programs to other system operators using any technology.

Also as "incidental" services, the Bell companies were allowed to offer "a service that permits a customer that is located in one LATA to retrieve stored information from, or file information for storage in, information storage facilities of such company that are located in another LATA."[554] This "stored information"

---

[550] *Id.* §§271(g)(3), 332(c)(8).

[551] Third Annual CMRS Competition Report at tbls. 4, 7A (listing Bell Atlantic, BellSouth, SBC, and Ameritech as among the top ten mobile telephony providers in the United States, based on population covered and subscribership). U S WEST also was in the top ten until it sold its cellular holdings to AirTouch in April 1998. *Id.* at n.8.

[552] 47 U.S.C. §271(g)(1).

[553] *See, e.g.*, Order, United States v. Western Elec. Co., No. 82-0192 (D.D.C. Mar. 16, 1995) (Bell Atlantic waiver to provide video programming services); Order, United States v. Western Elec. Co., No. 82-0192 (D.D.C. June 26, 1995) (waivers to provide video programming services); Order, United States v. Western Elec. Co., No. 82-0192 (D.D.C. Aug. 14, 1995) (U S West waiver for interLATA video programming delivery).

[554] 47 U.S.C. §271(g)(4). The 1996 Act separately authorizes the BOCs to provide interexchange services incidental to the provision of "Internet services

provision allows the Bell companies to arrange for interLATA connections between customers and BOC information databases, so that, for example, a customer could check for voice mail or e-mail messages when out of town by calling a local or toll-free number, instead of incurring separate long-distance charges.

Other "incidental" interLATA services that were permitted immediately under the 1996 Act include remote monitoring of alarm systems[555] and delivery of telephone (network control) signaling information across LATA boundaries.[556] The Act also allowed the Bell companies to continue offering any interexchange services authorized under the waiver provisions of the MFJ prior to the enactment of the new law.[557]

§9.6.2.3   In-Region Interexchange Relief

The traditional rationale for the MFJ's line-of-business restrictions was the BOCs' "bottleneck" power over local exchange facilities.[558] The district court believed that "[p]articipation in these [prohibited] fields carries with it a substantial risk that the Operating Companies will use the same anticompetitive techniques used by AT&T in order to thwart the growth of their own competitors."[559] By eliminating local exchange monopolies,

---

over dedicated facilities to or for elementary and secondary schools." *Id.* §271 (g)(2).

[555] While section 271(g)(1)(D) allows the BOCs immediate entry into interLATA remote monitoring, section 275(a)(1) prohibits a BOC or BOC affiliate from engaging in alarm monitoring for five years from the date of the 1996 Act's passage; this limitation does not apply to those alarm monitoring services that were being provisioned on November 30, 1995. *Id.* §275(a); Implementation of the Telecommunications Act of 1996: Telemessaging, Electronic Publishing, and Alarm Monitoring Services, 12 F.C.C. Rec. 3824, 3839 ¶¶29–33 (1997); *see also* Alarm Industry Commun. Comm. v. FCC, 131 F.3d 1066 (D.C. Cir. 1997) (applying section 275(a)(1)).

[556] 47 U.S.C. §271(g)(1)(D), (5).

[557] *Id.* §271(f).

[558] *Decree Opinion*, 552 F. Supp. at 223–224 (divestiture would give the BOCs the local networks that had been "[t]he key to [AT&T's] power to impede competition").

[559] *Id.* at 224.

however, the Telecommunications Act of 1996 put an end to the local bottleneck.

Yet Congress was not content with its de jure termination of the BOCs' local monopolies. To ensure that the bottleneck was actually eliminated in practice before the BOCs receive authority to provide long-distance service to their local customers, Congress imposed "special provisions" on the Bell companies (and only the Bell companies) that must be satisfied before a Bell Company can offer interLATA service to its local customer base.[560]

Not surprisingly, these and other "special" restrictions on the BOCs have been a source of great controversy. Two Bell companies—BellSouth and SBC—brought suits challenging their constitutionality.[561] The Bells contended that the special provisions violate the bill of attainder clause, which prohibits Congress from singling out private parties for punishment without a judicial trial.[562] There is no dispute that the 1996 Act singles out BOCs by name.[563] The closer question is whether Congress's insistence that the BOCs satisfy special conditions not required of other incumbent LECs in order to provide certain interLATA services is punishment. Divided panels of the Fifth and D.C. Circuits rejected the Bell companies' argument that the 1996 Act's special restrictions on the BOCs are punishment and upheld the constitutionality of these provisions.[564] According to the Fifth Circuit, the in-region, interLATA services rules and other special provisions are merely "prophylactic" regulations designed to prevent future harms.[565] In rejecting BellSouth's challenge to

---

[560] 47 U.S.C. §§271–272.

[561] BellSouth Corp. v. FCC, 144 F.3d 58 (D.C. Cir. 1998) (electronic publishing), *cert. denied,* 119 S. Ct. 889 (1999); SBC Communications, Inc. v. FCC, 154 F.3d 226 (5th Cir. 1998) (interLATA entry and other restrictions), *cert. denied,* 119 S. Ct. 889 (1999). *See also* BellSouth Corp. v. FCC, No. 98-1019 (D.C. Cir. filed January 13, 1998) (interLATA entry).

[562] Selective Serv. Sys. v. Minnesota Pub. Interest Research Group, 468 U.S. 841, 846 (1984).

[563] *See* 47 U.S.C. §153(4).

[564] *See generally* BellSouth Corp. v. FCC, 144 F.3d 58; SBC Communications, Inc. v. FCC, 154 F.3d 226, *cert. denied,* 1999 U.S. LEXIS 736, *cert. denied, motion granted,* 1999 U.S. LEXIS 735.

[565] SBC Communications, Inc. v. FCC, 154 F.3d at 243.

section 274 of the Act, the D.C. Circuit also concluded (in the context of restrictions on BOC electronic publishing) that the separation requirements imposed on Bell companies are a permissible regulatory tool, with "the earmarks of a rather conventional response to commonly perceived risks of anticompetitive behavior."[566] In a subsequent decision, the D.C. Circuit rejected BellSouth's attack on section 271 on similar grounds, adding that while section 274 "added restrictions on the BOCs that had been lifted from the MFJ in 1991," section 271 "is merely a revised version of the MFJ restrictions covering the provision of long-distance services that were still in effect when the Act was passed."[567]

Thus, despite its general thrust of opening the doors of previously closed markets, the 1996 Act contains a sui generis limitation against a BOC or any of its affiliates providing in-region interLATA services.[568] In order to offer these services, a BOC must apply to the FCC for authorization, identify each state for which it is seeking interLATA relief, and satisfy four general requirements. First, a BOC must show that it has satisfied either section 271(c)(1)(A) (Track A) or section 271(c)(1)(B) (Track B). Second, a BOC must demonstrate compliance with the 14-point "competitive checklist" for open local markets.[569] Third, a BOC must demonstrate that it will provide interLATA services in accordance with a set of regulatory safeguards enumerated in section 272.[570] Fourth, a BOC must show that its application is "consistent with the public interest, convenience, and necessity."[571]

(i) Track A and Track B.   Under Track A, a BOC must demonstrate that it is providing interconnection and network access

---

[566] BellSouth Corp. v. FCC, 144 F.3d at 65.
[567] BellSouth Corp. v. FCC, 162 F.3d 678, 683 (D.C. Cir. 1998).
[568] 47 U.S.C. §271(a).
[569] *Id.* §271(c)(2)(B).
[570] *Id.* §271(d)(3)(B).
[571] *Id.* §271(d)(3)(C).
[572] *Id.* §271(c)(1)(A).

to one or more "competing providers of telephone exchange service" through state commission-approved interconnection agreements.[572] A "competing provider" must be providing telephone exchange service—other than exchange access or cellular service—"to residential and business subscribers" and must "offer" local service either "exclusively" or "predominantly" over its own facilities (as opposed to reselling the BOC's services).[573]

Under Track B, a BOC must show that, as of three months before the BOC's application, no competing provider of facilities-based telephone service had requested access and interconnection.[574] In a Track B application, a BOC must further demonstrate that it has filed a statement of generally available terms and conditions for access and interconnection and that this statement has been approved or permitted to take effect by the relevant state commission.[575]

(ii) The Competitive Checklist. Regardless of whether a BOC's application relies on Track A or Track B, a BOC must demonstrate that the agreement(s) or statement of terms and conditions on which its application relies complies with the 14

---

[573] Although Track A was written with wireline local telephone competitors (particularly cable companies) principally in mind, the Commission concluded that the presence of active PCS wireless carriers in a state could satisfy Track A where the BOC applicant can show that PCS competes with the telephone exchange service offered by the applicant in the relevant state. Application of BellSouth Corporation, et al., Pursuant to Section 271 of the Communications Act of 1934, as Amended, to Provide In-Region, InterLATA Services in Louisiana, Memorandum Opinion and Order, 13 F.C.C. Rec. 20,599, 20,620–20,631 ¶¶25–43 (1998) (hereinafter *Second Louisiana Order*). The Commission also concluded that unbundled network elements are a competing provider's own facilities for purposes of determining whether the competitor is providing service "over [its] own telephone exchange service facilities" under section 271(c)(1)(A). Application of Ameritech Pursuant to Section 271 of the Communications Act of 1934, Amended, to Provide In-Region, InterLATA Services in Michigan, Memorandum Opinion and Order, 12 F.C.C. Rec. 20,543, 20,598 ¶102 (1997) (hereinafter *Michigan Order*).

[574] 47 U.S.C. §271(c)(1)(B).

[575] *Id.* Track B relief became available beginning ten months after the date of the 1996 Act's enactment (i.e., on December 8, 1996). *Id.*

[576] 47 U.S.C. §271(c)(2)(B).

checklist items set out in section 271's competitive checklist.[576] This competitive checklist is Congress's determination of "what . . . [local] competition would encompass."[577] Largely tracking section 251 of the Communications Act, the checklist contains requirements for network unbundling; access to emergency, operator, and directory services; access to telephone numbers; number portability; dialing parity; reciprocal compensation; and resale.[578] Congress expressly prohibited the Commission from expanding or contracting this checklist.[579]

(iii) Structural Separation and Nondiscrimination Requirements. The Act further requires Bell companies to establish separate subsidiaries for certain competitive activities.[580] These activities include in-region interLATA telecommunications services; certain information services, such as voice mail, e-mail, and computer database services across LATA boundaries;[581] and manufacturing activities.[582]

Section 272 requires a BOC to demonstrate that it has created a separate long-distance affiliate that will operate independently from the BOC; that it has established nondiscriminatory safeguards for its long-distance affiliate; that it will comply with audit requirements; and that it will not provide any of its facilities, services, or information concerning its provision of exchange access to its long-distance affiliate unless it also provides these facilities,

---

[577] 141 Cong. Rec. S7972, S8009 (daily ed., June 8, 1995) (statement of Sen. Hollings).

[578] 47 U.S.C. §271(c)(2)(B), (d)(2)(B).

[579] *Id.* §271(d)(4) ("The Commission may not, by rule or otherwise, limit or extend the terms used in the competitive checklist.").

[580] *Id.* §272.

[581] *Id.* §272(a)(2)(C). The FCC has ruled that even out-of-region interLATA information services are subject to the separation requirement. *Non-accounting Safeguards Order,* 11 F.C.C. Rec. at 21,946–21,947 ¶¶85–87. The restrictions applicable to interLATA information services expire in February 2000 unless extended by the Commission. *See id.* §272(f)(2).

[582] *Id.*

services, and information to other providers of interLATA services on the same terms and conditions.[583]

(iv) The Public Interest Test. When these statutory preconditions are satisfied, the FCC must then apply the ordinary test for approval of a new service under the Communications Act—whether the service is broadly consistent with the public interest.[584] This requirement tracks section 214 of the Communications Act, which requires all common carriers to obtain prior FCC approval for new interstate communications facilities and services.[585]

(v) The Role of State Commissions and Department of Justice. When deciding on a section 271 application, the Commission must give "substantial weight" to the Attorney General's evaluation of the application, which may be based on "any standard the Attorney General considers appropriate."[586] Thus, while the Decree court lost its place as the principal federal regulator of local telephone companies, the Department kept a hand in regulating the Bell companies after the death of the Consent Decree it had negotiated. This was bad news for the BOCs, for the Department soon made clear its preference for imposing

---

[583] 47 U.S.C. §272(a)–(e). In separate rulemakings, the Commission established both accounting and nonaccounting safeguards that it believed necessary to ensure BOC compliance with the separate affiliate requirements of section 272. *See* Accounting Safeguards Under the Telecommunications Act of 1996, Report and Order, 11 F.C.C. Rec. 17,539 (1996); *Non-accounting Safeguards Order,* 11 F.C.C. Rec. 21,905. Bell Atlantic appealed the *Non-accounting Safeguards Order,* arguing that the "plain meaning" of section 272(e)(4) (which states that a BOC may provide interLATA facilities or services to its long-distance affiliate so long as these services also are provided on nondiscriminatory terms to nonaffiliated carriers) permits BOCs to carry interLATA traffic for their separated affiliate. Bell Atlantic Tel. Co. v. FCC, 131 F.3d 1044, 1045 (D.C. Cir. 1997). The D.C. Circuit rejected this reading, holding that Bell Atlantic's "literalis[t]" interpretation of the "ambiguous" clause did not hold true to the context of the 1996 Act and that the Commission's interpretation (that this provision addresses interLATA services the BOC is otherwise authorized to provide) was reasonable. *Id.*

[584] *Id.* 47 U.S.C. §271(d).

[585] *See Michigan Order,* 12 F.C.C. Rec. at 20,743–20,744 ¶384.

[586] 47 U.S.C. §271(d)(2)(A).

extensive interconnection and unbundling requirements as a condition of section 271 relief and took the position that long-distance entry should be awarded only upon a finding that the local market is "fully and irreversibly open to competition"—a standard not found in the 1996 Act, and one that freed the Department from the statutory mooring of the competitive checklist.[587]

The FCC also must "consult" with the relevant state commission "in order to verify the compliance" of the BOC with the local-market requirements of section 271.[588] The FCC has acknowledged the "unique ability" of state commissions to evaluate section 271 applications, given their knowledge of local conditions and ability to gather a comprehensive, factual record.[589] On the other side of the coin, though, the views of state commissions that provide "only a cursory review of BOC compliance with section 271" will receive little deference.[590]

(vi) Deadline for Decision.   Another major difference from the days of the MFJ is the speed with which Bell Company requests for interLATA relief must be processed. Under the MFJ, Judge Greene would take months and often years to rule on a BOC motion for relief. The 1996 Act, by contrast, requires the Commission to approve or deny a request for in-region relief not later than 90 days after it receives the BOC's application.[591] If a section 271 application is denied, the applicant may appeal to the D.C. Circuit.[592] Any other party "who is aggrieved or whose interests are adversely affected" by the Commission's decision may also appeal to that court.[593]

---

[587] *See, e.g.,* Evaluation of the United States Department of Justice, Second Application by BellSouth Corporation, et al., Pursuant to Section 271 of the Communications Act of 1934, as Amended, to Provide In-Region, InterLATA Services in Louisiana, CC Docket No. 98-101 (FCC Aug. 19, 1998).

[588] 47 U.S.C. §271(d)(2)(B).

[589] *Michigan Order,* 12 F.C.C. Rec. at 20,559 ¶30.

[590] *Id.* The D.C. Circuit has affirmed the Commission's assertion that it is not obligated to defer to the state commission's determination of a BOC's compliance with section 271. SBC Communications, Inc. v. FCC, 138 F.3d at 416.

[591] 47 U.S.C. §271(d)(3).

[592] *Id.* §402(b)(9).

[593] *Id.* §402(b)(6).

§9.6.2.4 The FCC's Application of Section 271

Interpretation of Track A and Track B was the central issue raised by the first Bell Company section 271 application considered by the FCC. In April 1997, the regional Bell company SBC Communications applied for section 271 relief in Oklahoma.[594] SBC contended that it satisfied the requirements of section 271(c)(1)(A) (Track A) because Brooks Fiber Communications, a competitive LEC (CLEC) with which SBC had signed a state-approved interconnection agreement, had begun providing local exchange service to business customers and a small number of residential customers "exclusively or predominantly over its own network" within the preceding three months.[595]

SBC further argued that it could qualify for interLATA entry under Track B whether or not Brooks Fiber qualified as a facilities-based provider of business and residential local service within the definition of section 271(c)(1)(A) because no competing local carrier had begun providing facilities-based service to business and residential customers prior to "the date which is three months before the date the company [SBC] ma[de] its application."[596]

The FCC denied SBC's application. First, the Commission stated that SBC was not eligible to pursue interLATA authorization under Track A because facilities-based residential competition had not sufficiently developed in Oklahoma.[597] The FCC

---

[594] The first company actually to file an application was Ameritech for Michigan in January 1997. However, Ameritech withdrew its application because Ameritech's interconnection agreement with AT&T, on which Ameritech relied for purposes of Track A, had not yet been approved by the Michigan Public Service Commission. *See* Application of Ameritech Michigan Pursuant to Section 271 of the Communications Act of 1934, as Amended, to Provide In-Region, InterLATA Services in Michigan, Order, 12 F.C.C. Rec. 3309 (1997).

[595] Brief for SBC at ii, Application by SBC Communications Inc., Pursuant to Section 271 of the Communications Act of 1934, as Amended, to Provide In-Region, InterLATA Services in Oklahoma, CC Docket No. 97-121 (FCC Apr. 11, 1997).

[596] *Id.* at 14–15 (footnotes omitted).

[597] Application by SBC Communications Inc., Pursuant to Section 271 of the Communications Act of 1934, as Amended, to Provide In-Region, InterLATA Services in Oklahoma, Memorandum Opinion and Order, 12 F.C.C. Rec. 8685, 8694–8699 ¶¶13–22 (1997) (hereinafter *Oklahoma Order*).

rejected SBC's reliance on Brooks Fiber's four residential customers because these customers were Brooks Fiber employees being served on a test basis without charge and Brooks Fiber did not offer residential service to the general public.[598] The Commission reasoned that while the competitors used by a BOC to establish Track A compliance did not have to have any specific number of customers, they must nonetheless constitute an "actual competitive alternative" to BOC local service.[599]

The FCC also read Track B differently than SBC. In its Order, the Commission stated that Track B is foreclosed by a "qualifying request . . . for negotiation to obtain access and interconnection that, if implemented, would satisfy the requirements of section 271(c)(1)(A)."[600] The FCC thus adopted the stance that a Bell Company cannot request interLATA relief under Track B if it has received a request for interconnection by a "potential competing provider" of facilities-based service.[601] This effectively ruled out reliance on Track B for all BOCs, since AT&T, shortly after the passage of the 1996 Act, strategically requested negotiations toward an agreement for potential facilities-based interconnection in every state.

The D.C. Circuit Court of Appeals upheld the FCC's rejection of SBC's application.[602] Given ambiguous statutory language, the court held that the Commission's readings of Track A and Track B were within its zone of interpretative discretion.[603]

The FCC's second denial of a Bell Company request for inter-LATA authority came in response to Ameritech's application for relief in Michigan. The Commission ruled that although Ameritech satisfied the requirements of Track A in Michigan,[604] it had

[598] *Id.* at 8696–8699 ¶¶17–22.
[599] *Id.*
[600] *Id.* at 8701–8702 ¶27.
[601] *Id.* at 8704–8705 ¶34. In a subsequent decision, the Commission concluded Track B could be foreclosed if a BOC received a "qualifying request" for interconnection, even if the requesting carrier took no "reasonable steps" to offer local service. *South Carolina Order,* 13 F.C.C. Rec. at 571–581 ¶¶58–76.
[602] 47 U.S.C. §401(b)(6), (9).
[603] SBC Communications, Inc. v. FCC, 138 F.3d at 421.
[604] The Commission concluded that Brooks Fiber, through its use of fiber-optic rings and unbundled loops, was providing facilities-based service to

not demonstrated satisfaction of the competitive checklist items covering to OSS, interconnection, and access to 911 services and had not shown that it would comply with section 272.[605]

Having denied Ameritech's application on the basis of these specific items, the Commission declined to evaluate whether Ameritech had complied with the remaining checklist requirements.[606] Yet the *Michigan Order* was anything but a narrow, fact-specific ruling. To the contrary, the Commission purported to "provide substantial guidance for future applications."[607] In hundreds of pages and more than a thousand footnotes, the Commission offered a self-styled "roadmap" for Bell Company entry into the long-distance market.

The touchstone of the *Michigan Order* was the Commission's contention that section 271 was "designed to ensure that local telecommunications markets are open to competition."[608] The Commission thus did not view the 1996 Act's competitive checklist as an exclusive set of criteria for the BOCs' local markets, but asserted that the checklist "prescribes certain minimum access and interconnection requirements" and that "compliance with the checklist will not necessarily assure that all barriers to entry to local telecommunications market[s] have been eliminated."[609] For example, the Commission asserted that it had the authority to require a BOC to agree to ongoing performance measurements as part of a section 271 application—essentially establishing a fifteenth checklist item under the guise of its public interest review.[610]

The Commission justified its expansion of the competitive checklist—in apparent violation of section 271(d)(4)—on the grounds that the 1996 Act's public interest evaluation required

---

business and residential customers in Michigan. *Michigan Order,* 12 F.C.C. at 20,598 ¶102.

[605] *Id.* at 20,547 ¶¶5–6, 20,577–20,599 ¶¶62–104 (Track A), 20,599–20,724 ¶¶105–343 (competitive checklist), 20,724–20,737 ¶¶344–373 (section 272).

[606] *Id.*

[607] *Id.* at 20,751–20,752 ¶403.

[608] *Id.* at 20,551 ¶15.

[609] *Id.* at 20,747 ¶390.

[610] *Id.* at 20,659 ¶217.

a much broader inquiry than simply assessing the public bene-fits of BOC entry into the interLATA market.[611] In fact, the Commission asserted that the public interest requirement of the 1996 Act would not be satisfied until the Commission concluded that "the BOC has undertaken all actions necessary to assure that its local telecommunications market is, and will remain, open to competition."[612] The Commission did not explain precisely how a BOC could satisfy this vague standard, but it did contend that any additional requirements imposed as a result of this test would not be viewed as necessary "preconditions to BOC entry"—an unconvincing semantic distinction that limited in word only the Commission's expansion of the competitive checklist.[613]

The Commission further used the public interest test to justify imposing national pricing standards for BOC provision of local facilities and service to competitors.[614] This claim of pricing authority, in the face of a prior ruling by the Eighth Circuit Court of Appeals that the Commission lacked jurisdiction to impose national pricing rules,[615] was an unusually aggressive assertion of power. The Eighth Circuit (which had not yet been reversed on the underlying jurisdictional issue by the Supreme Court) rebuffed the Commission in an unusually assertive decision of its own. It issued a writ of mandamus ordering the Commission "to confine its pricing role under section 271(d)(3)(A) to determining whether applicant BOCs have complied with the pricing methodology and rules adopted by the state commissions and in effect in the respective states in which such BOCs seek to provide in-region, interLATA services."[616]

More than a year later, in its *Second Louisiana Order,* the Commission revisited the "roadmap" of the *Michigan Order.* Adopting a far less aggressive tone than in 1997, the FCC reviewed all 14 checklist items and set out in workmanlike fashion what it

[611] *Id.* at 20,745 ¶386.
[612] *Id.* at 20,745–20,746 ¶386.
[613] *Id.* at 20,747–20,748 ¶391.
[614] *Id.* at 20,696 ¶286.
[615] *See Iowa Utils. Bd.,* 109 F.3d 418 (8th Cir. 1997); Chapter 5.
[616] *Iowa Utils. Bd.,* 135 F.3d 535, 543 (8th Cir. 1997), *vacated and remanded* 119 S. Ct. 721 (1999).

believed to be the necessary elements of section 271 compliance. The Commission nominally reaffirmed its perceived legal authority to undertake expansive public interest review, but in fact suggested a narrow review focused principally on the existence of performance measurements and standards for provisioning local facilities and services to competitors.[617] Indeed, the Commission's Chairman sought to reassure BOCs—and no doubt Congress—that the Commission had not turned section 271 into an insurmountable barrier to BOC interLATA entry.[618]

Throughout all of its section 271 evaluations, the Commission has consistently emphasized its belief that the provisions of section 271 are a means to ensure not merely that the local market is open, but also that the local market is open to a degree that satisfies the Commission. In its quest for an irreversibly open market, however, the Commission has been willing to sacrifice a more competitive long-distance market. The Commission, which had supported BOC entry into the long-distance market since the imposition of the MFJ, thus found itself as the primary force preventing this entry. Whether the blame lies with the BOCs— for delaying compliance with section 271—or with the Commission—for misusing section 271 to accomplish backdoor regulation of the local market—is open to debate. What cannot be seriously debated, however, is that in its initial comprehensive review, the *Michigan Order*, the Commission was guilty of the worst kind of overreaching in an attempt to "coerce" state commissions and the BOCs into accepting the Commission's national agenda.[619] This overzealousness created an atmosphere of distrust and uncertainty that has been difficult to dissipate and left the BOCs with the distinct impression that the Commission would keep the "carrot" of long-distance entry just out of their reach for years to come. Subsequent Commission orders started

---

[617] *Second Louisiana Order,* 13 F.C.C. Rec. at 20,806–20,808 ¶¶361–366.

[618] Separate Statement of Chairman William E. Kennard, *Second Louisiana Order,* 13 F.C.C. Rec. at 20,812 ("As to the remaining items that BellSouth did not meet in this application, I believe BellSouth can and will remedy the deficiencies we identify in our Order. While the deficiencies that remain are significant, they are not insurmountable.").

[619] *Iowa Utils. Bd.,* 135 F.3d at 540.

repair of this damage, but only after consumers of long-distance services collectively had lost billions of dollars from delay in BOC interLATA entry.

§9.6.2.5 Other Paths to In-Region InterLATA Service

The Commission has itself acknowledged the likely benefits of Bell Company entry into the long-distance market.[620] Nevertheless, the Commission has been willing to forego such benefits, even when they are arguably consistent with section 271, in order to maintain pressure on the BOCs to fulfill the local-market requirements the FCC seeks to impose through section 271's competitive checklist and public interest test.

For example, the Commission has rejected BOC marketing alliances with long-distance carriers. In May 1998, U S West announced an agreement with the long-distance carrier Qwest Communications, in which U S West would market Qwest's inter-LATA services as part of a bundled package that would include local exchange services and intraLATA toll services.[621] Ameritech announced a similar arrangement with Qwest a short time later.[622]

These arrangements offered consumers long-distance service through their local carrier at rates significantly below the average rates offered by the major interexchange carriers.[623] But the FCC

---

[620] *BOC Nondominance Order,* 12 F.C.C. Rec. at 15,809 ¶92 ("We find that the entry of the BOC interLATA affiliates into the provision of interLATA services has the potential to increase price competition and lead to innovative new services and marketing efficiencies."); *accord* Evaluation of the United States Department of Justice at 3–4, Application of SBC Communications Inc., for Provision of In-Region, InterLATA Services in Oklahoma, CC Docket No. 97-121 (FCC May 16, 1997) ("additional entry, particularly by firms with the competitive assets of the BOCs, is likely to provide additional competitive benefits").

[621] AT&T Corp. v. Ameritech Corp., Memorandum Opinion and Order, 13 F.C.C. Rec. 21,438, 21,447–21,454 ¶¶8–16 (1998) (hereinafter *Qwest Order*), *aff'd sub nom.* U S West v. FCC, No. 98-1468, 1999 U.S. App. LEXIS 11,777 (D.C. Cir. Jun. 8, 1999).

[622] *Id.*

[623] The rates established as part of the Qwest/Ameritech alliance were $0.07 per minute for off-peak residential service and $0.15 per minute for

was unmoved. In the Commission's view, allowing Ameritech and U S West to provide comprehensive "one-stop shopping" would improperly enable them to "compete in the combined services market" prior to "demonstrating compliance with the market opening provisions in section 271."[624] This ability would undermine the "carefully balanced incentive structure" of the 1996 Act.[625]

The Commission has further rejected BOC requests for authority to offer high-speed data services across LATA boundaries, notwithstanding that the Act directs the Commission to "encourage the deployment on a reasonable and timely basis of advanced telecommunications capability to all Americans."[626] Rejecting arguments that forbearance would allow new high-speed networks and services, the Commission concluded that Congress had not provided it with "the statutory authority to forbear from [section 271's] critical market-opening provisions of the Act until their requirements have been fully implemented."[627]

The Commission likewise declined to exercise its power under the 1996 Act to move or erase LATA boundaries for high-speed data services, which would allow the BOCs to carry—as "intra-LATA" traffic—data traffic that would otherwise be off limits to them.[628] To the contrary, the Commission has declared that the BOCs "are likely to be shaped by LATA boundary restrictions for a period of unforeseeable duration," which will include "at least the near-term."[629]

---

peak residential service. *Id.* at 21,449–21,450 ¶10 & n.45. The average price paid by residential customers enrolled in AT&T's discount plans during this same time period was nearly $0.17 per minute. *See* Industry Analysis Division, FCC, Reference Book of Rates, Price Indices, and Household Expenditures for Telephone Service at tbl. 2.4 (July 1998).

[624] *Qwest Order,* 13 F.C.C. Rec. at 21,466–21,467 ¶39.

[625] *Id.*

[626] 47 U.S.C. §706.

[627] Deployment of Wireline Services Offering Advanced Telecommunications Capacity, Memorandum Opinion and Order and Notice of Proposed Rulemaking, CC Docket No. 98-147, ¶12 (Aug. 7, 1998). Further discussion of this proceeding may be found in Chapter 11.

[628] *Id.* ¶¶80–82.

[629] *Second Local Competition Order,* 11 F.C.C. Rec. at 19,400 ¶5, 19,414 ¶37.

§9.7   Regulation of IntraLATA Toll Services

As the FCC gradually opened *inter*state toll markets during the 1970s, 1980s, and early 1990s, *intra*state toll markets remained generally closed to full, presubscribed competition. This was principally because intraLATA long-distance services, aside from the small percentage of intraLATA traffic that crossed state boundaries, were outside federal jurisdiction. From the creation of LATAs in the MFJ, intraLATA long distance was in the hands of state regulators who were wary of tampering with the intrastate competitive landscape. As recently as 1997, most states still allowed LECs to route all "1+" intraLATA toll traffic to themselves; to use another carrier, the customer had to dial an additional five or seven digits.[630] Incumbent LECs carry the overwhelming share of the profitable intraLATA toll market in each of these states, and these revenues provide a substantial part of the surplus needed to subsidize local service to high-cost customers.[631]

§9.7.1   IntraLATA Toll Access Under the Bell
Divestiture Decree

It has been clear since divestiture that competition is eminently possible in carrying intraLATA toll traffic.[632] Some

---

[630] Callers may reach a long-distance carrier in states where such dialing arrangements are authorized by dialing a five-digit carrier access code ("10XXX," with "XXX" representing a three-digit carrier identification code) or a seven-digit carrier access code ("101XXXX," with "XXXX" representing a carrier identification code).

[631] Federal-State Joint Board on Universal Service, Report and Order, 12 F.C.C. Rec. 8776, 8785 ¶14 (1997) (acknowledging the role of higher intrastate toll service rates in maintaining low basic local service rates).

[632] As of June 1984, five states allowed intraLATA toll competition. *See* Pearce, Plenty to Get Steamed About, Computerworld, June 6, 1984, at 12. By August 1986, 16 states allowed competition. IntraLATA Competition: LATA Barrier Falls, Network World, Aug. 25, 1986, at 11. By 1990, 24 states allowed competition. As of year-end 1997, all states permitted some degree of intraLATA toll competition. NARUC, Telecommunications Competition 1997, at 213–222 (1998).

LATAs span entire states, and even at divestiture, the largest LATAs encompassed millions of customers. Indeed, while the Decree surrendered intraLATA transport to state regulation, Judge Greene "always contemplated" the prospect of full intra-LATA competition and equal access for those services.[633] He announced that any BOC that failed to commit to equal access for intraLATA toll service would not be granted otherwise routine Decree waivers for efficiency-driven adjustments of the initial LATA boundaries.[634] The BOCs were thus effectively compelled to provide equal access "for intra-LATA as well as for inter-LATA traffic"[635] unless "affirmatively prohibited from granting such access by a command of a state regulatory body acting under state law."[636]

Judge Greene stopped short of requiring 1+ access to intraLATA toll competitors, however, and made it clear that other aspects of the definition of "equality" in this context would not

[633] United States v. Western Elec. Co., 569 F. Supp. at 1005 n.72. Judge Greene conceded that he had no power to require equal access in this sphere directly. *Decree Opinion,* 552 F. Supp. at 159 n.117. *See also* United States v. Western Elec. Co., 569 F. Supp. at 1005 ("The Court has previously noted that intrastate as well as intraLATA regulation is not preempted by the decree and, hence, that state regulatory bodies will control traffic within the LATAs themselves. The Court, therefore, lacks the authority to require the opening-up of states and LATAs to internal competition over the objections of the states or their regulatory agencies") (footnotes omitted). *See also id.* at 1005 ("the lack of competition in this market would constitute an intolerable development").

[634] United States v. Western Elec. Co., 569 F. Supp. at 1006 & n.54. Whatever power the district court might or might not have had to withhold the approval of exceptional LATA boundaries as a lever to require intraLATA equal access, it plainly did have the power to enforce the BOCs' commitments to provide such access. *See* Local 93, Intl. Assn. of Firefighters v. Cleveland, 478 U.S. 501, 522 (1986) (the parties may agree to enforceable decree provisions that the court would be powerless to impose in a litigated judgment: "it is the agreement of the parties, rather than the force of the law upon which the complaint was originally based, that creates the obligations embodied in a consent decree").

[635] United States v. Western Elec. Co., 569 F. Supp. at 1006. The BOCs supplied the commitment demanded in Response of the Bell System Operating Companies to the Court's Opinion Establishing BOC LATAs, Appendix C: Commitment of the Bell Operating Companies, United States v. Western Elec. Co., No 82-0192 (D.D.C. May 5, 1983).

[636] United States v. Western Elec. Co., 569 F. Supp. at 1006 n.74.

be particularly stringent.[637] Presubscription to a carrier other than a customer's telephone exchange service provider thus was not an option for either interstate intraLATA toll calls or, in most states, for intrastate intraLATA toll calls.[638]

§9.7.2 IntraLATA Toll Equal Access Under the 1996 Act

In the 1996 Act, Congress set in motion a process to address these dialing limitations and open intraLATA toll markets to full and level competition. Requiring immediate intraLATA toll dialing parity was infeasible: local toll revenues still provided significant support for below-cost basic local service. Furthermore, immediate opening of the markets would give the interexchange carriers a dramatic advantage in providing these services, insofar as the long-distance incumbents could then provide 1+ dialing for all toll calls regardless of LATA boundaries, whereas the most prominent group of incumbent LECs—the BOCs—could, for the time being, carry only toll calls that stayed within LATA boundaries.[639]

Congress addressed this problem with a prospective rule and a pragmatic exception. Section 251(b)(3) of the Act makes it a duty of all local exchange carriers "to provide dialing parity to competing providers of telephone exchange service and telephone toll service."[640] At the same time, however, Congress provided a specific exception for BOC intraLATA toll dialing parity:

---

[637] Id. at 1108.

[638] An interstate intraLATA toll call is a call that (1) crosses a state boundary, but does not cross a LATA boundary, and (2) is subject to a charge. A call from Philadelphia, Pennsylvania across the Delaware River to Cherry Hill, New Jersey is an example of such a call.

[639] See §9.6.2.1.

[640] 47 U.S.C. §§153(39), 251(b)(3). The Act further defines "dialing parity" to mean "that a person who is not an affiliate of a local exchange carrier is able to provide telecommunications services in such a manner that customers have the ability to route automatically, without the use of any access code, their telecommunications to the telecommunications services provider of the customer's designation from among two or more telecommunications services providers (including such local exchange carrier)."

the BOCs must provide intraLATA dialing parity upon their receipt of permission to provide interLATA services in a given state, but states that had not yet ordered dialing parity as of December 19, 1995, could not do so until February 8, 1999.[641] Thus, although all LECs had a general duty to provide dialing parity, the BOCs alone—since they alone continue to be subject to the interLATA prohibition—were given a specific exemption from that duty.

In 1996, as part of its omnibus proceeding on the local competition provisions of the 1996 Act, the FCC promulgated extensive rules to implement the requirement that LECs provide dialing parity to competing intraLATA toll carriers.[642] The Commission rules required incumbent LECs that provided interLATA or interstate services to implement dialing parity by August 8, 1997, except that BOCs had to implement dialing parity by February 8, 1999 (absent prior section 271 relief for the state).[643] These federal requirements were promptly struck down by the Eighth Circuit.[644] The court held that the FCC has no right to prescribe rules for dialing parity on calls that are intrastate.[645] While the court of appeals agreed that the Act requires intraLATA toll dialing parity, it held that the Act nowhere calls for FCC involvement in enforcing that requirement.[646] Nor did section 251(g)—which continues equal access obligations[647]—give the FCC jurisdiction over intrastate matters within the jurisdiction of the states on the basis that the MFJ had discussed intraLATA as well as interLATA dialing parity. The Supreme Court reversed as part of the broad jurisdictional holding of its *Iowa Utilities Board* decision.[648] The Court found that intraLATA toll dialing parity, as a matter expressly addressed

---

[641] 47 U.S.C. §271(e)(2). No BOC received in-region interLATA relief in time for that provision to take effect.

[642] *Second Local Competition Order,* 11 F.C.C. Rec. at 19,400 ¶4.

[643] 47 C.F.R. §51.211.

[644] California v. FCC, 124 F.3d 934 (8th Cir. 1997), *rev'd sub nom.* AT&T Corp. v. Iowa Utils. Bd., 119 S. Ct. 721 (1999).

[645] *Id.* at 939–943.

[646] *Id.* at 942–943.

[647] *See* §9.4.5.3.

[648] AT&T Corp. v. Iowa Utils. Bd., 119 S. Ct. at 733.

within the Act, also fell within the FCC's rulemaking powers under section 201(b) of the Communications Act.[649] The Court therefore returned the matter to the Eighth Circuit and the FCC. The court and the Commission thus faced the problem of reconciling administrative deadlines that called for gradual implementation of intraLATA toll dialing parity by February 8, 1999,[650] with the practical reality that most states were not implementing dialing parity as of the Supreme Court's decision in late January 1999. The FCC resolved this problem in favor of a workable implementation schedule, giving the BOCs that had not yet implemented intraLATA toll dialing parity until May 7, 1999, to comply.[651]

Once both LECs and interexchange carriers are permitted to carry all toll calls without regard to LATA boundaries, it becomes senseless to force customers to pick (and LECs to spend the millions of dollars necessary to allow customers to pick) different carriers for intraLATA and interLATA toll calls. From the consumer's perspective, a toll call that crosses LATA boundaries is indistinguishable from one that does not. That callers in most states still use a different carrier depending on whether they are calling a point inside or outside of their LATA is just another respect in which artifacts of what was arguably the central development in the history of long-distance competition, the breakup of the Bell System in 1984, have become impediments to a rational competitive market.

---

[649] *Id.* ("None of the statutory provisions that these rules interpret displaces the Commission's general rulemaking authority. . . . And since the provision addressing dialing parity, §251(b)(3), does not even mention the States, it is even clearer that the Commission's §201(b) authority is not superseded.").

[650] *See* 47 C.F.R. §§51.205–.215.

[651] Interexchange carriers had attempted by various means to force immediate implementation of intraLATA toll dialing parity with mixed success. For example, the Virginia State Corporation Commission found that the "compressed time frame" and "inconvenience" caused by the FCC's attempt to assert jurisdiction over intraLATA dialing parity necessitated suspension of the deadline and the establishment of a new one. Implementation of IntraLATA Toll Dialing Parity Pursuant to the Provisions of 47 U.S.C. §251 (b)(3), Order on Motion of Bell Atlantic-Virginia, Inc. to Clarify Its Obligation to Implement IntraLATA Toll 1+ Presubscription, Case No. PUC970009 (Va. St. Corp. Commn. Nov. 6, 1998), *aff'd sub nom.,* AT&T of Va. v. Bell Atlantic of Va., 35 F. Supp. 2d 493 (E.D. Va. 1999).

§9.8 Industry Outlook: The Limits of Competition

Two decades after the idea was first seriously advanced, the principle of competition in long-distance markets is now solidly and irrevocably established. The market has gradually responded to the profound regulatory changes discussed above. Essentially all Bell Company local telephone lines and more than 99 percent of all local lines support 1+ dialing.[652] More than 30 different long-distance carriers have annual toll revenues that exceed $100 million.[653] More than 600 carriers compete in one segment or another of the long-distance market.[654]

AT&T's share of the interstate interLATA market has fallen steadily. In 1987, AT&T's share of presubscribed lines was 83.7 percent, while MCI's and Sprint's were 8.2 and 4.8 percent, respectively.[655] In 1990, AT&T's share was 75.6 percent, while MCI's and Sprint's were 13.2 and 6.6 percent.[656] By December 1996, AT&T served 63.3 percent of the 158.6 million presubscribed lines in service areas with equal access; MCI, Sprint, and all other long-distance carriers served 14.5, 7.4, and 12.1 percent, respectively.[657] In terms of dollars of revenue, AT&T's share declined from just over 90 percent in 1984 to less than 45 percent in 1997.[658] AT&T's share of calling minutes fell from 84 percent in 1984 to less than 51 percent in the third quarter of 1998.[659]

---

[652] Industry Analysis Division, FCC, Trends in Telephone Service at tbl. 6.1 (July 1998).

[653] Industry Analysis Division, FCC, Toll Carrier Revenue in 1997 (1998).

[654] Industry Analysis Division, FCC, Trends in Telephone Service at tbl. 6.1 (1998).

[655] Industry Analysis Division, FCC, Long Distance Market Shares: Fourth Quarter 1998 at tbls. 2.1–2.2 (1999).

[656] *Id.*

[657] *Id.*

[658] These figures exclude the toll revenues of local exchange carriers. *Id.* at tbl. 3.2.

[659] *Id.* at tbl. 1.1. Overall, AT&T's market share has declined far more quickly among larger users than lower-volume residential callers. *See id.* at tbls. 4.1–4.3.

The emergence of a large number of carriers (generally resellers) and the whittling down of AT&T's share of the long-distance market should not be confused with full competition, however.[660] Facilities-based entry into the interstate market has been minimal since divestiture. WorldCom was by far the most significant newcomer, but it merged with MCI in 1998. Consequently, AT&T has lost its market share almost totally to the two carriers that had substantial rival facilities at divestiture — MCI and Sprint.[661]

This ongoing concentration reflects a profound shift in the economics of telecommunications.[662] Facilities-based competition in long distance could have blossomed with the advent of microwave radio in the 1950s. With radio, a carrier's costs increase substantially as traffic volumes increase because new towers and transceivers must be added. This makes it feasible for small carriers to target a market segment and compete with large incumbents in that segment. Not so with fiber-optic cables, which became the dominant technology during the 1980s. The upfront costs of deploying fiber-optic cable are very high. Rights-of-way must be secured, and deploying cable is enormously labor intensive. These costs are the same whether the fiber-optic cable contains one pair of optical fibers or a dozen, whether the fiber is "lit" (i.e., connected to functioning electronics) or "dark," and whether the lit fiber carries a million telephone calls or none at

---

[660] *See* Evaluation of the United States Department of Justice at 3–4, Application of SBC Communications Inc., for Provision of In-Region, InterLATA Services in Oklahoma, CC Docket No. 97-121 (FCC May 16, 1997) ("[i]nterLATA markets remain highly concentrated and imperfectly competitive"); Paul W. MacAvoy, *Testing for Competitiveness of Markets for Long Distance Telephone Services: Competition Finally?*, 13 Rev. Ind. Org. 295, 319 (1998) ("Rather than competition increasing since AT&T divestiture, it has been decreasing. The usual tests in industrial economics disprove hypotheses as to growing competitiveness in long distance telephone services."). Indeed, enhancing competition in this market was one of the key goals of the 1996 Act. *Michigan Order,* 12 F.C.C. Rec. at 20,602 n.252 ("the goal of the Act is to bring robust competition not only to the local market but to all telecommunications markets").

[661] At the end of 1996, AT&T, MCI, and Sprint together controlled nearly 88 percent of the nation's presubscribed access lines. Industry Analysis Division, FCC, Long Distance Market Shares: Third Quarter 1998 at tbl. 2.2.

[662] *See* §1.14.

all. Costs are incurred at the front end, and they are fixed. And because wireline networks have almost zero (or even negative) salvage value, costs are irrevocably sunk before they generate a single dollar of revenue.

Once the up-front costs of deploying fiber are sunk, however, the marginal cost of carrying an additional minute of traffic is just a fraction of a penny. Furthermore, the capacity of fiber networks can be increased and at relatively little cost;[663] the capacities of the long-distance fiber-optic networks already exceed demand by a large margin.[664]

These basic industry economics are reflected in long-distance prices. Using resellers to arbitrage on their behalf as necessary, large customers are able to obtain prices of pennies per minute, without surcharges or pricing gimmicks. For the carriers, putting additional traffic through the (underused) network is everything, since average costs fall as volume increases.

Small business and residential customers, by contrast, have relatively little traffic to send, but require a monthly bill and customer service just like large corporate accounts. From the perspective of these low-usage customers, moreover, comparison shopping might not be worth the hassle even if they knew of all carriers and pricing plans from which they could choose. Accordingly, these customers generally pay roughly 15 to 20 cents a minute for long-distance calls, either in the form of high "basic" rates or as a result of monthly fees associated with lower per-minute prices.[665]

---

[663] New technologies enabling carriers to transmit data over fiber channels using multiple wavelengths, new types of higher-capacity fiber-optic cable (e.g., "dispersion-shifted fiber"), and newer and better optical amplification techniques have continuously increased the capacity of fiber networks. *See* Industry Analysis Division, FCC, Fiber Deployment Update: End of Year 1997, at 3 (1998).

[664] *See* Revisions to Price Cap Rules for AT&T Corp., 10 F.C.C. Rec. 3009, 3017 ¶23 (1995) ("AT&T's competitors appear to have sufficient network capacity to serve a significant portion of AT&T's commercial long-distance traffic . . . [they] have a greater supply of unused fiber capacity than AT&T.").

[665] *See* Affidavit of Richard L. Schmalensee ¶18, Second Application of BellSouth Corporation, et al. Pursuant to Section 271 of the Communications Act of 1934, as Amended, to Provide In-Region, InterLATA Services in Louisiana, CC Docket No. 98-121 (FCC July 9, 1997) (average rate of $0.18 per

Overall prices for long-distance service have indeed fallen by roughly 50 percent against the Consumer Price Index since divestiture,[666] as the long-distance carriers are quick to point out. But for residential and small business customers, virtually all the drop has come from regulation, not the market. Peel off the (declining) access charges long-distance companies pay to local exchange carriers and interstate toll rates in fact fell faster *before* 1984 than after.[667] Allowing for inflation, AT&T's overall prices in real dollars have (at best) inched down a couple of percentage points a year, and low-volume customers have experienced significant price increases. That is disappointingly small progress for a period in which fiber-optic technology has supplied thousandfold gains in transmission efficiencies.

Sunk costs of entry and economies of scale are largely to blame for the lackluster competition in long distance, but not entirely. Bell companies that have networks in the ground want to carry interLATA calls in their home regions, yet the FCC will not let them do so until local markets show stronger signs of competition. Relatedly, many state regulators were receptive to the argument that as long as the local Bell Company cannot offer interLATA services, interexchange carriers should not be given the advantage of offering intraLATA toll service (in addition to their interLATA service) on a presubscribed 1+ basis.

---

minute). The discount plans offered by the Big Three provide little respite from high basic prices. *See* Industry Analysis Division, FCC, Reference Book of Rates, Price Indices, and Household Expenditures for Telephone Service at tbl. 2.4 (July 1998) (showing that the average price across calling volumes of residential customers enrolled in AT&T's discount plans was nearly $0.17 per minute).

[666] Industry Analysis Division, FCC, Reference Book of Rates, Price Indices, and Household Expenditures for Telephone Service at tbl. 4.1.

[667] W. E. Taylor, Effects of Competitive Entry in the U.S. Interstate Toll Markets: An Update 1 (May 28, 1992), *cited in* Paul S. Brandon & Richard Schmalensee, The Benefits of Releasing the Bell Companies from the Interexchange Restrictions, *in* Deregulating Telecommunications: The Baby Bells' Case for Competition 73 (Richard S. Higgins et al. eds., 1995) ("Even if AT&T's prices had remained constant (net of access charges), the rate of decline of real toll prices (net of access charges) would have been about half the rate at which they declined (net of separations charges) in the decade prior to divestiture.").

The resulting sacrifice of toll competition in the interests of prodding local competition represents a 180-degree turn for regulators. For three decades, the whole idea had been separating toll from local so that toll could be competitive even if local was not. In a sense, however, this turnabout was inevitable after 1996, when Congress embraced the notion of competition in all telecommunications markets. Arbitrary distinctions between local and long-distance calls may have made pragmatic sense when the question was where Bell's monopoly should end. But when the question became where competition should start, LATAs and other arbitrary regulatory lines became indefensible. Unless there is some clear economic distinction between local and long distance—and carriers' emphasis on one-stop shopping and bundled services suggests there is not—competition (and regulation) should be consistent from one end of the call to the other. It only remains to be seen whether this leveling process will cause the competitive waters on the long distance side to rise further or fall.

10

Wireless Services*

§10.1 Introduction

A hundred years ago, Guglielmo Marconi successfully sent and received signals over radio waves.[1] He planned to use his new invention as a mobile telephone on seagoing vessels.[2] For Marconi and his contemporaries, the primary aim for the radio—which was named for what it lacked, "the wireless"—was to sever telephony from the landline umbilical.[3] The idea of using radio to broadcast entertainment came some 20 years later[4] and

*This chapter was co-authored by Courtney Simmons Elwood, Partner, Kellogg, Huber, Hansen, Todd & Evans; Washington and Lee University (B.A., *summa cum laude,* 1990); Yale Law School (J.D., 1994); Phi Beta Kappa; Law Clerk, Honorable J. Michael Luttig, U.S. Court of Appeals, Fourth Circuit, 1994–1995; Law Clerk, Honorable William H. Rehnquist, Chief Justice, U.S. Supreme Court, 1995–1996.

[1] PBS Online, A Science Odyssey: People and Discoveries <http://www.pbs.org/wgbh/aso/databank/entries/btmarc.html>.

[2] *Id.*

[3] "Federal regulation of radio" in this country "beg[an] with the Wireless Ship Act of June 24, 1910 . . . which forbade any steamer carrying or licensed to carry fifty or more persons to leave any American port unless equipped with efficient apparatus for radio communication, in charge of a skilled operator." National Broad. Co. v. United States, 319 U.S. 190, 210 (1943).

[4] PBS Online, A Science Odyssey: Radio Transmission <http://www.pbs.org/wgbh/aso/tryit/radio/earlyyears.html>.

may be regarded as merely a detour on the way toward an array of competitive, global wireless telecommunication services.

Radio's first land-to-land telecommunications use in the United States was by the Detroit Police Department in the 1920s.[5] Other uses developed during World War II.[6] In 1945, the Federal Communications Commission (FCC) granted experimental radio licenses for a broad range of private users,[7] and, in 1949, permanently allocated frequencies to mobile services.[8] Although the first mobile telephone service connected to the public network was introduced in 1946, most mobile radio systems of the day did not interconnect to the landline network.[9]

Pagers as we now know them took a different path. In 1946, the Bell System offered on an experimental basis a one-way signaling service to vehicles, and later to pocket-sized receivers.[10] By one account, the first page was sent on October 15, 1950, to a doctor on a New York golf course.[11] By another account, the British invented paging to replace noisy hospital public address systems, and the first page was sent in London's St. Thomas Hospital in 1956.[12] The first units were the size of bricks, almost as heavy, and about as informative. And until 1965, no company

[5] AT&T Consumer Products Supplies Buick with Mobile, PR Newswire, Sept. 13, 1983.

[6] H. Rosenberg, Mobile Telephones: No Place to Hide, Fin. World, Nov. 30, 1983, at 14.

[7] Allocation of Frequencies to the Various Classes of Non-governmental Services in the Radio Spectrum from 10 Kilocycles to 30,000,000 Kilocycles, 39 F.C.C. 68 (1945); Allocation of Frequencies to the Various Classes of Non-governmental Services in the Radio Spectrum from 10 Kilocycles to 30,000,000 Kilocycles, Report of the Commission, 39 F.C.C. 257 (1946).

[8] General Mobile Radio Service, Report and Order of the Commission, 13 F.C.C. 1190 (1949).

[9] G. Calhoun, Digital Cellular Radio 30 (1988).

[10] Amendment of Part 21 of the Commission's Rules with Respect to the 150.8–162 Mc/s Band to Allocate Presently Unassignable Spectrum to the Domestic Public Land Mobile Radio Service by Adjustment of Certain of the Band Edges, Report and Order, 12 F.C.C.2d 841, 845 ¶8 (1968), *recons. denied*, 14 F.C.C.2d 269 (1968), *aff'd sub nom.* Radio Relay Corp. v. FCC, 409 F.2d 322 (2d Cir. 1969).

[11] H. Peterson, Paging Progress, Network World, May 2, 1984, at 71.

[12] P. Purton, From a Quiet Beginning Paging Finds New Fields, Times, Feb. 19, 1990.

offered selective paging to an individual pager.[13] But paging technology has improved dramatically in recent years, and paging use has increased exponentially. There were one million pagers in use nationwide in the late 1970s, 2.2 million in 1983, and 49.8 million in 1997.[14] That number is expected to jump to 80 million within a few years.[15]

Two-way voice communication by radio requires more spectrum and more sophisticated technology, and so has developed more slowly. The original single-cell transmitters that provided mobile telephony until cellular systems were put into place in the 1980s could typically support a total of 25 channels,[16] only about

[13] H. Peterson, Paging Progress, Network World, May 2, 1984, at 71.

[14] L. Wood, There's No Escaping Beepers, Chi. Trib., Mar. 18, 1990, at 20; G. Ozanich, Trafficking in Cellular Radio Technology, Network World, Jan. 18, 1984, at 15; Implementation of Section 6002(b) of the Omnibus Budget Reconciliation Act of 1993, Third Report, 13 F.C.C. Rec. 19,746, 19,753 (1998) (hereinafter *Third Annual CMRS Competition Report*). Other forecasts for year-end 1997 statistics ranged from 44.48 million (Insight Research Corporation) to 52.7 million (WinterGreen Research Inc.). Having dropped dramatically over the last ten years, subscription fees are now often less than $10 a month for local service and less than $30 a month for national coverage. Increase in Bundled Minutes Leads Dramatic Declines in Wireless Telephony Prices, PR Newswire, Feb. 23, 1998 (According to The Strategis Group, since 1992, local numeric paging service with a customer-owned page fell 23 percent, averaging $9.23 per month. Local numeric paging service with a rental pager fell 35 percent, averaging $12.33 per month.); New Study Finds Paging, SMR Prices Vary by Market, Carrier, Land Mobile Radio News, May 8, 1998 ("The three best rates for local one-way alphanumeric service are AirTouch Paging . . . in Phoenix, at 300 messages for $8.95 per month; American Paging Inc. in Milwaukee, at 250 messages for $8.95; and AT&T Wireless in Dallas, at 100 messages for $8.95." One-way regional paging services can run up to $48 per month. "The best deals for nationwide alpha service are American Paging in Chicago at 200 messages for $29.95, and in Salt Lake and Phoenix at 125 messages for $29.95, and in Phoenix at 200 messages for $24.95; Paging Network Inc. in Phoenix at 200 messages for $29.95; and TSR in San Francisco at 200 messages for $26.95."); *Third Annual CMRS Competition Report* app. C, tbl. 7 (June 11, 1998) (prices for narrowband personal communications services (PCS) range from $19.95 to $34.95 and include the leased paging unit and 200–600 or unlimited messages per month; SkyTel offers two-way paging for $39.95 per month).

[15] Paging Profitability Hinging on Increasing Bandwidth, Services, Land Mobile Radio News, Jan. 16, 1998.

[16] AT&T Consumer Products Supplies Buick with Mobile, PR Newswire, Sept. 13, 1983.

half of which could be used at a time. Since 30 subscribers might
be licensed for every channel, calls often could not be completed. Of 23 channels supporting 700 users in New York City,
for example, only 12 could be used simultaneously.[17] The available spectrum supported only 140,000 subscribers nationwide,
including police departments and other special users.[18] Demand
far exceeded supply. By 1976, Bell mobile service in the New
York metropolitan area served 543 customers and had a waiting
list of 3,700,[19] often leaving would-be subscribers waiting six
years for service.[20]

Almost three decades earlier, in 1947, Bell Labs had developed the concept of cellular communications. As the FCC has
explained, the spectrum is "divided into discrete channels which
are assigned in groups to small geographical cells covering a
defined service area. The key to the cellular system's high capacity is its ability to shrink the size of those cells while holding
the total amount of spectrum used by the system constant. What
results is a multiple re-use of channels throughout a given geographical area."[21] Although the technology was understood for
decades, the licensing of cellular properties did not get under
way until the early 1980s.

But by 1992, the FCC had recognized a "revolution" in mobile
telephony.[22] The Commission observed the "steadily increasing
consumer and business interest in new mobile services," particularly for those that "facilitate contacting an individual instead
of a particular station."[23] The FCC therefore sought to encourage new wireless technologies, including the development of

[17] Godin, The Cellular Telephone Goes on Line, Electronics, Sept. 22,
1983, at 121. *See also* M. Schneider, Cellular Communications Service: Wireline Delivery or Delay?, 72 Geo. L.J. 1183 (1984).
[18] Godin, The Cellular Telephone Goes on Line at 121.
[19] Calhoun, Digital Cellular Radio at 31.
[20] C. Mayer, Walkie Talkie Telephoning, Wash. Post, June 6, 1982, at K1.
[21] An Inquiry Relative to the Future Use of the Frequency Band 806–960
MHz, Second Report and Order, 46 F.C.C.2d 752, 753–754 ¶5 (1974).
[22] *See* Amendment of the Commission's Rules to Establish New Personal
Communications Services, Notice of Proposed Rule Making and Tentative
Decision, 7 F.C.C. Rec. 5676, 5678 ¶3 (1992).
[23] *Id.* at 5687–5688 ¶25.

"personal communications services" ("PCSs").[24] Citing market projections, the Commission predicted that "there could be over 60 million PCS users in the United States" by 2002.[25] Those projections may be met. PCS had roughly 6.4 million subscribers at the end of 1998,[26] and in its early stages at least, the market is growing faster than predicted.[27]

By the year 2000 — or roughly 100 years after Guglielmo Marconi first sent signals over radio waves — five or more significant competitors will be offering mobile telephony in every market. Through new allocations of spectrum, the introduction of digital radio, and the shrinking of cell sites, the overall transmission capacity of wireless-service spectrum bands will continue to expand, increasing by at least 10-fold over the next five years and at least 100-fold over the course of the next decade.[28]

§10.2 Jurisdiction: Federal Versus State

The Radio Act of 1927 nationalized all wireless spectrum and placed all aspects of radio broadcasting under the ultimate

---

[24] *See id.* at 5678 ¶3.

[25] *Id.* at 5688 ¶26.

[26] Third Annual CMRS Competition Report tbl. 5D (June 11, 1998). The Third Report estimates that there are 60 million cellular subscribers and 2.3 million digital specialized mobile radio (SMR) subscribers. *Id.*

[27] *See* Wireless Replacing Wireline in Some Applications, Mobile Comm. Rep., Mar. 23, 1998.

[28] *See, e.g.,* T. Foley, A Space Odyssey, Part 1, Comm. Week Intl., Mar. 2, 1998, at 19 ("Satellite companies are planning to make greater use of new technologies, such as spot-beam antennas and intersatellite links, to increase the number of times the spectrum could be used by 20 or 40, or even 100."); G. Gilder, The Bandwidth Tidal Wave, Forbes ASAP, Dec. 5, 1994, *reprinted at* <http://www.forbes.com/asap/gilder/telecosm10b.htm> ("For the last five years, communications processors have indeed been improving their price/performance tenfold every two years — more than three times as fast as microprocessors. . . . Soaring DSP [digital signal processing] capabilities have already made possible the achievement of many new digital technologies previously unattainable. Among them are digital video compression, video teleconferencing, broadband digital radio pioneered by Steinbrecher . . . digital echo cancellation and spread-spectrum cellular systems that allow 100 percent frequency reuse in every cell.").

control of the newly created Federal Radio Commission.[29] The Commission was empowered to license every last transmitter in the land. It would assign frequencies for public use and decide who could use them. It would classify radio stations, prescribe service limits, assign wavelengths, regulate networks, and approve the locations and power levels of transmitters. Its power to grant, deny, renew, or revoke licenses was unlimited. Congress had instructed the Commission simply to advance the "public interest, convenience or necessity."[30]

Seven years later, the 1927 Radio Act was folded intact into the Communications Act of 1934, and the Federal Radio Commission was absorbed into the new Federal Communications Commission. The FCC thus acquired plenary jurisdiction over the issuance of licenses for all forms of radio telecommunications.[31] There was (and is) no separate state authority for licensing purely intrastate transmissions.

Section 301 of the 1934 Act expressly prohibits private ownership of radio spectrum.[32] The critical terms of that provision—

---

[29] *See, e.g.,* Thomas W. Hazlett, The Rationality of U.S. Regulation of the Broadcast Spectrum, 33 J.L. & Econ. 133 (1990). *See* National Broadcasting Co. v. United States, 319 U.S. 190, 210–213 (1943), for history of federal regulation of radio leading up to the enactment of the Radio Act of 1927.

[30] Radio Act of 1927, ch. 169, 44 Stat. 1163.

[31] 47 U.S.C. §301.

[32] "It is the purpose of this Act, among other things, to maintain the control of the United States over all the channels of radio transmission; and to provide for the use of such channels, but not the ownership thereof, by persons for limited periods of time, under licenses granted by Federal authority, and no such license shall be construed to create any such right, beyond the terms, conditions and periods of the license." *Id.* On its face, section 301 confines spectrum rights to the transient conditions of a temporary license, which, under section 304 of the Act, has no "legal or proprietary right to a renewal." FCC v. National Citizens Comm. for Broad., 436 U.S. 775, 805 n.25 (1978). However, "both the Commission and the courts have recognized that a licensee who has given meritorious [or substantial] service has a 'legitimate renewal expectanc[y]' that is 'implicit in the structure of the Act' and should not be destroyed absent good cause." *Id.* (quoting Greater Boston Television Corp. v. FCC, 444 F.2d 1201, 1213 & n.35 (1971)). These provisions apply to all licenses, whether originally obtained by application, lottery, or purchase at auction.

that the government shall "maintain the control" over and that licensees shall not have "ownership" of radio channels—leave the Commission with close to absolute authority over the structure of the industry, the geographic markets it serves, and the services it provides.

Traditionally the FCC classified land mobile radio services into two categories: public mobile services and private land mobile services.[33] Public mobile services, such as a radio telephone service interconnected with the public telephone network, were subject to all of the burdens of federal common carrier regulation, as well as state regulation of intrastate services.[34] Private land mobile services, on the other hand, were initially defined as the class of radio services that did not interconnect with the public switched network, except by direct agreement with a local carrier.[35] A radio dispatch service, such as that operated by police departments, fire departments, and taxicab companies, was one example. Such services were exempt from common carrier regulation.

---

[33] National Assn. of Regulatory Util. Commrs. v. FCC, 525 F.2d 630, 634 (D.C. Cir. 1976) (*NARUC I*); Implementation of Sections 3(n) and 332 of the Communications Act, Second Report and Order, 9 F.C.C. 1411, 1414 ¶3 (1994) (hereinafter *Communications Act Second Report*).

[34] *NARUC I*, 525 F.2d at 634; *Communications Act Second Report*, 9 F.C.C. Rec. at 1414 ¶3.

[35] Communications Amendments Act of 1982, Pub. L. No. 97-259, §120(a), 96 Stat. 1087, 1096–1097 (1982). *See also id.* §120(b), 96 Stat. 1087, 1097 ("'Private land mobile service' means a mobile service which provides a regularly interacting group of base, mobile portable, and associated control and relay stations (whether licensed on an individual, cooperative, or multiple basis) for private one-way or two-way land mobile radio communications by eligible users over designated areas of operation."). "The primary test for inclusion in the private land mobile radio service . . . [was] that a licensee not resell interconnected telephone service for profit." Request of Fleet Call, Inc. for Waiver and Other Relief to Permit Creation of Enhanced Specialized Mobile Radio Systems in Six Markets, Memorandum Opinion and Order, 6 F.C.C. Rec. 1533, 1537 ¶31 (1991), *recons. dismissed*, 6 F.C.C. Rec. 6989 (1991). If providers satisfied this test, and hence passed any landline costs through to their customers without markup, they remained private carriers exempt from common carrier regulation. *Id.;* Communications Amendments Act of 1982, Pub. L. No. 97-259, §120(a), 96 Stat. 1087, 1097.

In 1993, Congress scrapped this dichotomy and replaced it with two newly defined categories of mobile services: commercial mobile radio service (CMRS) and private mobile radio service (PMRS).[36] More important, Congress devised a "comprehensive, consistent regulatory framework" for CMRS providers.[37] Congress instructed that CMRS providers be treated as common carriers under the Act and thereby subject to all the requirements of Title II.[38] However, Congress authorized the Commission to designate any provision of Title II (other than sections 201, 202, and 208) to be "inapplicable" to CMRS providers if the Commission found such provision unnecessary to ensure "just," "reasonable," and nondiscriminatory practices in commercial mobile service.[39] Pursuant to this authority, the Commission has announced that it will forbear from enforcing many of the Title II provisions to CMRS providers.[40] While generally forbearing from tariff and rate regulation, the Commission nonetheless continues to examine some of the particulars of how rates are charged. It has, for example, opened an inquiry on "Calling Party

[36] Omnibus Budget Reconciliation Act of 1993, Pub. L. No. 103-66, Title VI, §6002(b)(2)(A), 107 Stat. 312, 393–396 (1993); *Communications Act Second Report,* 9 F.C.C. Rec. at 1417 ¶11. "Commercial mobile service" is defined in the Act as "any mobile service . . . that is provided for profit and makes interconnected service available (A) to the public or (B) to such classes of eligible users as to be effectively available to a substantial portion of the public." 47 U.S.C. §332(d)(1). "Private mobile service" is defined as "any mobile service . . . that is not a commercial mobile service or the functional equivalent of a commercial mobile service, as specified by regulation by the Commission." *Id.* §332(d)(3).

[37] *Communications Act Second Report,* 9 F.C.C. Rec. at 1417 ¶11.

[38] 47 U.S.C. §332(c)(1)(A).

[39] *Id.*

[40] *Communications Act Second Report,* 9 F.C.C. Rec. at 1418–1419 ¶16, 1463–1493 ¶¶124–219. Specifically, the Commission chose to forbear from imposing any tariff filing obligations on CMRS providers and from establishing any market entry or exit requirements. *Id.* at 1418 ¶16, 1478–1479 ¶¶174–175. But the Commission chose not to forbear from enforcing certain provisions related to the complaint process and remedy, as well as sections containing specific consumer related provisions (e.g., protections against obscene and harassing calls and obligations for the disabled). *Id.* at 1418–1419 ¶16, 1475 ¶164.

Pays" wireless service,[41] and it is examining the propriety of billing in whole-minute increments.[42]

Until 1993, the states retained, as part of their general power to regulate common carriers, the power to regulate "charges, classifications, practices, services, [and] facilities" of purely *intrastate* wireless services.[43] State commissions occasionally exercised that authority to curb abuses,[44] but for the most part, state

---

[41] Calling Party Pays Service Option in the Commercial Mobile Radio Services, Notice of Inquiry, 12 F.C.C. Rec. 17,693 (1997). Calling Party Pays (CPP) is a service whereby the party placing the call or page pays all airtime charges and any applicable charges for calls transported within the local access and transport area (LATA). Without this service, the party who receives the call incurs charges for incoming calls. *Id.* at 17,694 ¶3. While rarely found in this country, CPP is common in many countries throughout Europe and Latin America and in Israel. According to an industry study, the international experience shows that CPP billing "spurs wireless usage, promotes acceptance of wireless service, allows greater cost control by consumers, and increases the proportion of traffic on wireless networks relative to wireline networks." *Third Annual CMRS Competition Report*, 13 F.C.C. Rec. at 19,760–19,761, (citing CTIA Service Report, The Who, What, and Why of "Calling Party Pays," July 4, 1997).

[42] In November 1997, Southwestern Bell Mobile Systems (SBMS) petitioned the Commission for a declaratory ruling that rounding up to the next minute and charging for incoming calls are common industry practices that are not unjust or unreasonable. Wireless Telecommunications Bureau Seeks Comment on a Petition for a Declaratory Ruling Regarding the Just and Reasonable Nature of, and State Law Challenges to, Rates Charged by CMRS Providers When Charging for Incoming Calls and Charging for Calls in Whole-Minute Increments Filed by Southwestern Bell Mobile Systems, Public Notice, 12 F.C.C. Rec. 19,670 (1997). SBMS's petition was precipitated by a series of class action lawsuits alleging that CMRS carriers' billing practices violate section 201(b) of the Communications Act of 1934. *Id.* One such suit was filed against SBMS in the District of Massachusetts. Smilow v. Southwestern Bell Mobile Sys., Inc., 1997 U.S. Dist. LEXIS 19,453 (D. Mass. July 11, 1997). The court stayed the suit until the Commission made an initial determination of the lawfulness of SBMS's practices. *Id.* The Commission has sought public comment, but has not yet issued an opinion on the matter.

[43] 47 U.S.C. §152(b). *See* §3.3, discussing limits on the FCC's authority to regulate intrastate aspects of radio common carriage.

[44] Centel, for example, reportedly charged its customers AT&T rates to deliver wide-area traffic, but in fact used Sprint's cheaper service. In June 1990, the North Carolina Utilities Commission ordered Centel to "cease and desist immediately from charging its customers more than it actually pays for long distance service." The Commission also considered imposing fines or other sanctions against Centel based on the fact that Centel filed tariffs that

regulation of radio services was minimal.[45] In the 1993 Budget Act, however, Congress preempted even this limited grant of authority. Congress barred the states from regulating "the entry of or the rates charged by" any CMRS or PMRS provider and left to the states only an undefined authority to regulate "the other terms and conditions" of commercial mobile service.[46]

Accordingly, to the extent that state and local municipalities can still exercise their regulatory will over wireless operations, they do so by restricting the placement of radio towers, cell sites, and other facilities. Indeed, section 332(c)(7) of the 1996 Act expressly reserves to the states and local governments the authority "over decisions regarding the placement, construction, and modification of personal wireless service facilities."[47] A state or municipality may not, however, invoke this authority either to "unreasonably discriminate among providers" of equivalent services or to effectively prohibit the provision of personal wireless services; in addition, all decisions under section 332(c)(7) must be in writing and supported by substantial evidence.[48] The Act

---

referred to the AT&T rate. *See* T. Lanning, N.C. Commission Probes Centel Cellular, Telephony, June 4, 1990, at 10.

[45] *See, e.g.,* Telocator, Report on State Regulation of Common Carrier Paging Companies (Jan. 1991); CTIA, State by State Regulatory Update (June 1990); NARUC, NARUC Annual Report on Utility & Carrier Regulation 646 (Dec. 1989).

[46] Omnibus Budget Reconciliation Act of 1993, Pub. L. No. 103-66, Title VI, §6601(a), 107 Stat. 312 (1993) (codified at 47 U.S.C. §332(c)(3)(A)). By "other terms and conditions," Congress was referring to things like customer billing information and practices, billing disputes, consumer protection matters, and facilities siting issues. *See also* Connecticut Dept. of Pub. Util. Control v. FCC, 78 F.3d 842, 845–846 (2d Cir. 1996) *and* GTE Mobilnet of Ohio v. Johnson, 111 F.3d 469, 473–474 (6th Cir. 1997) (both discussing preemption provision). *See* §10.3.5 for a discussion of CMRS and PMRS.

[47] 47 U.S.C. §332(c)(7)(A). "Personal wireless service facilities" means "facilities for the provision of commercial mobile services, unlicensed wireless services, and common carrier wireless exchange services." *Id.* §332(c)(7)(C).

[48] *Id.* §332(c)(7)(B)(i), (iii). According to some courts, the requirement that a state or local regulation may not effectively prohibit the provision of wireless services applies only to "blanket prohibitions" and "general bans or policies," and not to individual zoning decisions. *See, e.g.,* AT&T Wireless PCS v. City Council of Va. Beach, 155 F.3d 423, 428–429 (4th Cir. 1998); Cellco Partnership v. Town Plan and Zoning Commn. of the Town of Farmington, 3 F. Supp. 2d 178, 184–185 (D. Conn. 1998).

further provides that "[a]ny person adversely affected" by a decision of state or local government that is inconsistent with these provisions may commence an action in any court of competent jurisdiction.[49] This private cause of action has spawned a rash of lawsuits challenging the decisions of the state and local planning commissions.[50]

The 1993 Act also authorizes a state to petition the FCC for permission either to regulate the rates charged by CMRS providers or, if the state already had such regulation in effect, to continue such regulation.[51] Congress instructed the Commission to grant a state's petition to regulate if "(i) market conditions with respect to such services fail to protect subscribers adequately from unjust and unreasonable rates or rates that are unjust or unreasonably discriminatory; or (ii) such market conditions exist and such service is a replacement for land line telephone

---

[49] 47 U.S.C. §332(c)(7)(B)(v).

[50] See, e.g., AT&T Wireless PCS v. City Council of Va. Beach, 155 F.3d 423 (4th Cir. 1998) (city council's decision denying application for construction of tower on church's property did not unreasonably discriminate against providers, did not effectively prohibit wireless services, and was properly in writing and supported by substantial evidence); Cellular Tel. Co. v. Zoning Bd. of Adjustment of the Borough of Ho-Ho-Kus, 24 F. Supp. 2d 359 (D.N.J. 1998) (upholding decision of zoning board denying plaintiffs' application for variances to construct wireless communication facility); Omnipoint Communications Enter. v. Zoning Hearing Bd. of Chadds Township, 1998 U.S. Dist. LEXIS 17403 (E.D. Pa. Oct. 28, 1998) (denying defendant's motion to dismiss lawsuit challenging, under section 332(c)(7)(B), the zoning board's decision denying application to build tower); Cellco Partnership v. Russell, 1998 U.S. Dist. LEXIS 11639 (W.D.N.C. June 23, 1998) (upholding county's moratorium suspending the issuance of new permits for constructing wireless facilities and dismissing as unripe challenge to city tower ordinance); Sprint Spectrum v. Pintauro, 12 F. Supp. 2d 247 (D. Conn. 1998) (factual issues precluded summary judgment on plaintiffs' claim that decision denying special permit to construct tower was unsupported by substantial evidence); Cellco Partnership v. Town Plan and Zoning Commn. of the Town of Farmington, 3 F. Supp. 2d 179 (D. Conn. 1998) (local commission's decision denying special permit to reconstruct church steeple in order to install cellular facility within was not supported by substantial evidence as required by 47 U.S.C. §332(c)(7)(B)(iii)).

[51] 47 U.S.C. §332 (c)(3)(A), (B).

exchange service for a substantial portion of the telephone land line exchange service within such state."[52]

Pursuant to this provision, Connecticut, which had regulated wholesale cellular providers since 1986, petitioned the FCC for continued regulatory authority over cellular rates. An investigation by Connecticut's Department of Public Utility Control (DPUC) had concluded that continued regulation of rates was necessary because of the lack of market competition, although its findings on whether the rates were unreasonable or discriminatory were inconclusive.[53] The FCC denied the DPUC petition. It found that section 332 "express[es] an unambiguous congressional intent to foreclose state regulation in the first instance" and that Connecticut had not sustained its burden of demonstrating that market conditions (including the pending competition from PCS) failed to protect consumers.[54] The Commission's decision was affirmed on appeal.[55] The FCC has denied petitions of at least seven states, in addition to Connecticut, that sought to continue regulating wireless rates.[56]

---

[52] *Id.* §332(c)(A). In its 1994 order implementing section 332, the Commission promulgated detailed rules for state petitions seeking to institute or retain rate regulatory authority. *Communications Act Second Report,* 9 F.C.C. Rec. at 1504–1507 ¶¶250–257 (1994) (codified at 47 C.F.R. §20.13).

[53] *Connecticut Dept. of Pub. Util. Control,* 78 F.3d at 847.

[54] Petition of the Connecticut Department of Public Utility Control to Retain Regulatory Control of the Rates of Wholesale Cellular Service Providers in the State of Connecticut, Report and Order, 10 F.C.C. Rec. 7025, 7030 ¶8, 7055 ¶67 (1995).

[55] *Connecticut Dept. of Pub. Util. Control,* 78 F.3d at 849–851.

[56] *See, e.g.,* Petition of the State of Ohio for Authority to Continue to Regulate Commercial Mobile Radio Service, Order on Reconsideration, 10 F.C.C. Rec. 12,427 (1995); Petition of the People of the State of California and the Public Utilities Commission of the State of California to Retain Regulatory Authority over Intrastate Cellular Service Rates, Report and Order, 10 F.C.C. Rec. 7486 (1995), *recons. denied,* 11 F.C.C. Rec. 796 (1995); Petition on Behalf of the Louisiana Public Service Commission for Authority to Retain Existing Jurisdiction over Commercial Mobile Radio Services Offered Within the State of Louisiana, Report and Order, 10 F.C.C. Rec. 7898 (1995); Petition of Arizona Corporation Commission to Extend State Authority over Rate and Entry Regulation of All Commercial Mobile Radio Services, Report and Order on Reconsideration, 10 F.C.C. Rec. 7824 (1995); Petition of New York State Public Service Commission to Extend Rate Regulation, Report and Order, 10 F.C.C. Rec. 8187 (1995); Petition on Behalf of the State of Hawaii, Public Utility

But conceivably states may regain jurisdiction when wireless providers begin to provide fixed wireless services that compete directly with wireline service. Section 332(c)(3)(A) expressly provides that a state may once again regulate CMRS to ensure the provision of universal service where CMRS is "a substitute for landline telephone exchange service for a substantial portion of the communications within such State."[57]

In any event, the long-term implications of the preemption provision (and the Commission's interpretation of it) will be far-reaching. All regulatory trends point toward a wireless industry that is not subject to any significant degree of rate regulation. And projections cited by the FCC suggest that wireless services will become a major competitor to landline in the local loop.[58] If these two trends continue, we may expect the rise of wireless technology eventually to propel across-the-board rate deregulation of the local exchange.

§10.3 Spectrum Allocation: General Considerations

§10.3.1 License Terms and Renewal Expectancy

Under section 301 of the Communications Act, licensees are granted spectrum rights for a fixed period of time, with no vested

---

Commission, for Authority to Extend Its Rate Regulation of Commercial Mobile Radio Services in the State of Hawaii, Report and Order, 10 F.C.C. Rec. 7872 (1995). *See also* Progress in the Year of the Rat and What's Hot in the Year of the Ox, Remarks of Commissioner Rachelle Chong Before the Cellular Telecommunications Industry Association, San Francisco, Mar. 4, 1997 (Commission addressed 12 state preemption petitions in 1996); GTE Mobilnet of Ohio v. Johnson, 111 F.3d 469 (6th Cir. 1997) (cellular companies moved to enjoin state from regulating rates on grounds of section 332(c)(3)(A) preemption; appellate court held the district court should have abstained under principles of *Younger* abstention from considering the carriers' motion for relief).

[57] 47 U.S.C. §332(c)(3)(A). *See* §10.8.3.

[58] *See, e.g., Third Annual CMRS Competition Report,* 13 F.C.C. Rec. at 19,776–19,778.

right to renewal.[59] Prior to 1993, licenses for common carrier mobile services were granted for ten-year terms, and, generally speaking, licenses for private land mobile services were granted for five years.[60] In 1993, Congress required uniform treatment; all CMRS licenses are now issued for ten years.[61] So are licenses for local multipoint distribution service,[62] wireless communications service,[63] and direct broadcast satellite.[64]

While technically provisional, these licenses are, for all practical purposes, permanent. Spectrum has been privatized—de facto property rights have been created—without anyone ever using such politically delicate terms. The Commission and the courts instead have affirmed that licensees have a "renewal expectancy."[65] Licenses will be renewed upon a largely pro forma demonstration that the renewal applicant (1) has provided "substantial" service during the past license term and (2) has substantially complied with applicable FCC rules and policies and the Communications Act, as amended.[66]

[59] 47 U.S.C. §301 ("It is the purpose of this Act . . . to provide for the use of such channels . . . by persons for limited periods of time."); Victor Broad., Inc. v. FCC, 722 F.2d 756, 760–761 (D.C. Cir. 1983).

[60] Implementation of Sections 3(n) and 332 of the Communications Act, Further Notice of Proposed Rulemaking, 9 F.C.C. Rec. 2863, 2892 ¶139 (1994).

[61] 47 C.F.R. §22.144(a); Implementation of Sections 3(n) and 332 of the Communications Act, Third Report and Order, 9 F.C.C. Rec. 7988, 8157 ¶386 (1994) (hereinafter *Communications Act Third Report*).

[62] Rulemaking to Amend Parts 1, 2, 21, and 25 of the Commission's Rules to Redesignate the 27.5–29.5 GHz Frequency Band, to Reallocate the 29.5–30.0 GHz Frequency Band, to Establish Rules and Policies for Local Multipoint Distribution Service and for Fixed Satellite Services, Second Report and Order, Order on Reconsideration, and Fifth Notice of Proposed Rulemaking, 12 F.C.C. 12,545, 12,656–12,657 ¶259 (1997).

[63] Amendment of the Commission's Rules to Establish Part 27, the Wireless Communications Service ("WCS"), Report and Order, 12 F.C.C. Rec. 10,785, 10,840 ¶106 (1997); 47 C.F.R. §27.13.

[64] Revision of Rules and Policies for the Direct Broadcast Satellite Service, Report and Order, 11 F.C.C. Rec. 9712, 9762 ¶130 (1995).

[65] "The renewal expectancy is based on a concept that 'the public itself will suffer if incumbent licensees cannot reasonably expect renewal when they have rendered superior service.'" Victor Broad., Inc. v. FCC, 722 F.2d 756, 760 (D.C. Cir. 1983) (quoting Citizens Communications Ctr. v. FCC, 447 F.2d 1201, 1213 n.35 (D.C. Cir. 1971)). *See also* FCC v. National Citizens Comm. for Broad., 436 U.S. 775, 805 n.25 (1978).

[66] *Communications Act Third Report,* 9 F.C.C. Rec. at 8157 ¶386; *see, e.g.,* 47 C.F.R. §22.940(a)(1). "Substantial" means that the service was "sound, favorable,

The creation of property rights in spectrum by way of the administrative conceit of "renewal expectancy" can be traced back to 1970, when the Commission first adopted such a policy for certain broadcast licenses.[67] In 1991, the Commission extended the "expectancy" to the renewal of cellular licenses[68] and then "to all CMRS services" in 1994.[69] Two years later Congress codified the practice for broadcast licenses, but failed to do the same for CMRS licenses.[70]

---

and substantially above a level of mediocre service which would barely warrant renewal." *Id.* In order to establish its right to renewal, the licensee must file a description of its current services, an explanation of its record of expansion, a description of its investments, and copies of any FCC orders finding violations of the Commission's rules. 47 C.F.R. §22.940(a)(2).

[67] Within a decade after Congress passed the 1934 Act, extensive renewal proceedings were the norm; the proceedings came to involve difficult and lengthy determinations about the relative merits of competing applicants. *See* Citizens Communications Ctr. v. FCC, 447 F.2d 1201, 1211–1213 (D.C. Cir. 1971) (comparative-hearing requirements were consistently applied). *See also* Robert A. Anthony, Towards Simplicity and Rationality in Comparative Broadcast Licensing Proceedings, 24 Stan. L. Rev. 1 (1971) (describing FCC licensing and requirements up through the 1960s). Indeed, prior to 1952, the Communications Act required that decisions on renewal applications "be limited to and governed by the same considerations and practice which affect the granting of original applications." Communications Act of 1934, §307(d), 48 Stat. 1084. In 1952, however, Congress recognized that it was fanciful to ask the Commission to evaluate a renewal application without reference to the applicant's past performance. *See* H.R. Rep. No. 1750, 82d Cong., 2d Sess. 8 (1952) (previous standard "is neither realistic nor does it reflect the way in which the Commission actually handle[s] renewal cases"). Congress therefore amended the statute to provide simply that renewal "may be granted . . . if the Commission finds that public interest, convenience, and necessity would be served thereby." Communications Act Amendments, §55, 66 Stat. 714 (1952). In 1970, the FCC adopted a new policy: an incumbent's license would be renewed if it could show that its service has been "substantially attuned to meeting the needs and interests of its area" and that its operation has been free of "serious deficiencies." Policy Statement Concerning Comparative Hearings Involving Regular Renewal Applicants, Public Notice, 22 F.C.C.2d 424, 425 (1970).

[68] Amendment of Part 22 of the Commission's Rules Relating to License Renewals in the Domestic Public Cellular Radio Telecommunications Service, Report and Order, 7 F.C.C. Rec. 719, 719–722 ¶¶3–18 (1991).

[69] *Communications Act Third Report*, 9 F.C.C. Rec. at 8156 ¶386.

[70] 47 U.S.C. §309(k).

§10.3.2 Geographic Area Licensing

For years, the Commission required licensees to secure permission to locate each and every transmitter. That approach has generally given way to "geographic area licensing," whereby a licensee is permitted to occupy a defined bubble of space, on a defined frequency band, at a defined power.[71] Licensees are then permitted to construct transmission towers anywhere within their designated geographic area.

§10.3.3 Zoning[72]

As the ultimate owner of all spectrum, the FCC has broad authority to "zone" wireless licenses for specific uses. CMRS frequencies are "zoned" for wireless telephony and data services, not conventional broadcast. UHF spectrum is zoned for the broadcast of the *licensee's* programs, not for common carriage.[73]

---

[71] For example, the Commission adopted rules in 1997 to make the transition from site-by-site licensing to geographic area licensing for all exclusive, nonnationwide paging channels. Revision of Part 22 and Part 90 of the Commission's Rules to Facilitate Future Development of Paging Systems, Second Report and Order and Further Notice of Proposed Rulemaking, 12 F.C.C. Rec. 2732 (1997). *See also Communications Act Third Report,* 9 F.C.C. Rec. at 8044 ¶98 (adopting geographic area licensing for 800 MHz SMR service based on so-called Major Trading Areas (MTAs) because it will be easier to administer, will provide licensees and the public with greater certainty about what area is covered by each authorization, and will make it easier to resolve conflicts between applicants seeking to provide service to a common area); 47 C.F.R. §22.909 (geographic area licensing for cellular service based on so-called Metropolitan Statistical Areas (MSAs) and Rural Service Areas (RSAs); 47 C.F.R. §24.202 (geographic area licensing for broadband PCS service based on Rand McNally's MTAs and Basic Trading Areas (BTAs)).

[72] This section is adapted from Peter W. Huber & Howard A. Shelanski, Administrative Creation of Property Rights to Radio Spectrum, 41 J.L. & Econ. 581 (1998), which demonstrates how substantive and procedural changes in the FCC's administration of radio frequencies have gradually strengthened licensees' rights to keep, alienate, use, and protect the exclusivity of spectrum even without any underlying legal shift from licensing to private ownership.

[73] Conservative calculations suggest that the opportunity costs of zoning licenses to particular services are very high. The FCC's Office of Plans and

For the first half century or so of its existence, the Commission exercised its zoning powers aggressively. But digital technology has rendered obsolete the logic and utility of zoning. The rapid and inexorable trend today is toward dezoning wireless media.

The FCC has traditionally restricted how radio licensees may use their spectrum in two principal ways. First, the Commission prescribed—and for the most part continues to prescribe—what types of services (e.g., cellular telephony or broadcast television) may be transmitted over certain spectrum bands.[74] Second, the Commission prohibited—and for a few services continues to prohibit—radio licensees to slice up spectrum (into either geographic or frequency sub-bands[75]) or to allocate it to different

---

Policy estimates the net welfare loss from preventing UHF broadcasters in Los Angeles from converting spectrum to cellular telephony to be $660 million to $783 million (in 1991 dollars) for the years 1992–2000. Evan Kwerel & John R. Williams, Office of Plans and Policy, FCC, Changing Channels: Voluntary Reallocation of UHF Television Spectrum (OPP Working Paper No. 27, Nov. 1992).

[74] Before PCS, the Commission tended to allocate spectrum "for specific services, such as mobile telephone, dispatch, or paging." *See* Implementation of Section 6002(b) of the Omnibus Budget Reconciliation Act of 1993, Second Report, 12 F.C.C. Rec. 11,266, 11,288 (1997). *See, e.g.,* Amendment of Parts 2 and 22 of the Commission's Rules to Permit Liberalization of Technology and Auxiliary Service Offerings in the Domestic Public Cellular Radio Telecommunications Service, Notice of Proposed Rule Making, 2 F.C.C. Rec. 6244, 6245 ¶¶7–8 (1987) (specifying operational and technical requirements that limited the use of the cellular spectrum to voice telephony and "permit[ting] data transmissions, but the transmitted signals must conform to the characteristics of voice transmissions").

[75] Each cellular licensee, for example, may now geographically partition its license within the MSA or RSA, 47 C.F.R. §22.947(b), but is still prohibited from disaggregating its spectrum, Geographic Partitioning and Spectrum Disaggregation by Commercial Mobile Radio Services Licensees, Report and Order and Further Notice of Proposed Rulemaking, 11 F.C.C. Rec. 21,831, 21,875 ¶93 (1996). However, the Commission is currently seeking comment on whether to allow spectrum disaggregation for cellular service. *Id.* at 21,876 ¶95; *see infra* note 88. Already cellular providers may obtain multiple licenses and may buy and sell their licenses freely so long as licensing provisions regarding the location and power of transmitters are respected. *See* An Inquiry into the Use of the Bands 825–845 MHz and 870–890 MHz for Cellular Communications Systems, Report and Order, 86 F.C.C.2d 469, 487 ¶37 (1981).

uses.[76] Thus, the Commission's standard allocation was static: it bound the licensee to a specific use of allotted spectrum—a use the licensee could not freely alter even as technology and market demand change over the life of the license. Broadcasters, for example, were barred early on from using their main frequencies and facilities to transmit private messages to specific receivers— essentially telephone or telegraph services.[77] Indeed, even after the deregulatory trend of the 1980s, it could be said that "the Commission has never permitted an existing licensee to voluntarily discontinue providing the service for which it was licensed and to provide a completely different service."[78]

Until recently, the most rigid zoning division maintained by the Commission separated "broadcast" from "common carrier" uses of spectrum. Out of concern that stations are responsible for operating in the public interest, not for the private benefit of a licensee or other programmer,[79] the Commission has historically

---

[76] See, e.g., Revision of Radio Rules and Policies, Report and Order, 7 F.C.C. Rec. 2755, 2787 n.124 (1992) ("[broadcast] licensees must maintain control of their facilities") (hereinafter Radio Rules Revision); 47 C.F.R. §73.3555(a)(3)(ii). See also Use of Special Signals for Network Purposes Which Adversely Affect Broadcast Service, Public Notice, 22 F.C.C.2d 779 (1970); Digital Data Transmission Within the Video Portion of Television Broadcast Station Transmissions, Notice of Proposed Rulemaking, 10 F.C.C. Rec. 4918, 4918 ¶3 (1995) ("we have generally not allowed the transmission of ancillary telecommunications services within the video portion of broadcast television signals without prior Commission consent").

[77] Application of Scroggin & Company Bank (Station KFEQ), St. Joseph, Missouri, Statement of Facts and Grounds for Decision, 1 F.C.C. 194 (1935); Bremer Broadcasting Company (WAAT), Jersey City, New Jersey, Statement of Facts and Grounds for Decision, 2 F.C.C. 79 (1935).

[78] Kwerel & Williams, Changing Channels.

[79] Radio stations have long sold blocks of advertising time to brokers who then supply commercial messages to fill them. See Petition for Issuance of Policy Statement or Notice of Inquiry on Part-Time Programming, Policy Statement, 82 F.C.C.2d 107, 107 n.2, 108–109 ¶3 (1980) (hereinafter Part-Time Programming); 47 C.F.R. §73.3555(a)(3)(iv). In the 1920s, AT&T ran its radio operations like its phone business, selling carriage slots at posted hourly rates for any purchaser to fill with whatever programs or commercials it wanted. The FCC, however, has distinguished acceptable "time brokerage" from impermissible transfer of control of airtime by a broadcast licensee to an outside party. Part-Time Programming, 82 F.C.C.2d at 108–109 ¶3 (some "block" programming has "contributed variety . . . to broadcasting"); see Application of

drawn a strict line between "broadcast" and "carriage," has generally barred broadcasters from transferring control over time blocks to third parties,[80] and has continued to insist that a broadcast licensee must not "assume[ ] the passive role of a common carrier."[81]

Yet even with respect to broadcasters, the Commission has increasingly recognized that subdivision of time brings certain efficiencies.[82] Conventional broadcasters have been permitted to overlay some very modest carrier-like services on top of their

---

Cosmopolitan Broadcasting Corporation, Newark, New Jersey, for Renewal of License for Station WHBI-FM, Decision, 59 F.C.C.2d 558 (1976) (refusing to renew an FM radio license because the station sold most of its airtime, through brokers, to numerous foreign-language programmers), *petition for recons. denied,* 61 F.C.C.2d 257 (1976) (licensee's sale of pure airtime—broadcasting in more than 20 languages—free of programming control by the station, crossed the line from allowable brokerage to carriage and violated the policy that licensees must be ultimately responsible for programming, regardless of the source); Application of Continental Broadcasting, Inc., Newark, N.J. for Renewal of License of Station WNJR, Newark, N.J., Decision, 15 F.C.C.2d 120, 127 ¶20 (1968) (licensee did not exercise adequate control and supervision); Metropolitan Broadcasting Corporation (WMBQ), Brooklyn, N.Y. for Renewal of License, Findings of Fact and Conclusions of the Commission, 8 F.C.C. 557, 563–564 ¶¶20–27, 570 ¶3 (1941) (denying application for construction permit because applicant had sold considerable airtime to time brokers).

[80] *See* Howard Shelanski, The Bending Line Between Conventional Broadcast and Wireless Carriage, 97 Colum. L. Rev. 1048 (1997).

[81] Fresno FM Limited Partnership, Decision, 6 F.C.C. Rec. 1570, 1572 ¶12 (1991). *See also* Silver Star Communications-Albany, Inc. Licensee of Radio Stations WMJM and WFAV-FM Order to Show Cause Why the Licenses of WMJM and WFAV-FM, Cordele, Georgia Should Not Be Revoked, Decision, 3 F.C.C. Rec. 6342 (1988).

[82] *See Part-Time Programming,* 82 F.C.C.2d at 120 ¶32 ("[B]rokerage can often represent both a less expensive program source for the individual licensee and an appropriate market response to the audience's fragmentation into preference groups too small to support an entire station.") In 1992, the FCC reduced limits on subdivision and classified time brokering as a "joint venture" that would generally be approved. *Radio Rules Revision,* 7 F.C.C. Rec. at 2787–2789 ¶¶63–67. Joint ventures between separately owned stations allow efficient joint advertising sales, shared technical facilities, and joint programming arrangements, i.e., "time brokerage." Broadcast licensees must still, however, "maintain control of their facilities and . . . ensure that their stations program in the public interest and serve the needs of their communities." *Id.* at 2787 n.124; 47 C.F.R. §73.3555(a)(2)(ii).

basic broadcast operations, such as allowing radio stations to offer paging services[83] or television stations to transmit stereo sounds.[84] The 1996 Telecommunications Act also permits broadcasters to offer "ancillary or supplemental services"—e.g., wireless voice or data—on the new channels, but only if they do so alongside advanced television (for which they are the only eligible licensees).[85]

§10.3.4   Dezoning

All wireless telecom services are moving toward substantial or complete dezoning. The trend started with Direct Broadcast Satellite (DBS) services.[86] The FCC under the Reagan administration allowed DBS operators great freedom to subdivide and

---

[83] The Commission deregulated radio stations' use of the "subcarrier" portions of their assigned frequencies, and they now offer paging, utility load signaling, and other services on those bands. Spectrum can be subdivided into a main channel and a number of "subchannels" or "subcarriers," which can be transmitted simultaneously. Amendment of Parts 2 and 73 of the Commission's Rules Concerning Use of Subsidiary Communications Authorizations, First Report and Order, 53 Rad. Reg. 2d (P & F) 1519 (1983); The Use of Subcarrier Frequencies in the Aural Baseband of Television Transmitters, Second Report and Order, 55 Rad. Reg. 2d (P & F) 1642 (1984) (hereinafter *Television SCA Use*); Amendment of Parts 2 and 73 of the Commission's AM Broadcast Rules Concerning the Use of the AM Carrier, Report and Order, 100 F.C.C.2d 5 (1984).

[84] Television, too, may transmit on subcarrier frequencies, which are mostly used for stereo sound purposes. *Television SCA Use,* 55 Rad. Reg. 2d 1642. Television operators also transmit electronic newspapers, data, computer software, and paging services within the unused "vertical blanking interval"—the momentary blank between picture frames—of their signals. Amendment of Parts 2, 73, and 76 of the Commission's Rules to Authorize the Offering of Data Transmission Services on the Vertical Blanking Interval by TV Stations, Report and Order, 101 F.C.C.2d 973 (1985).

[85] *See* 47 U.S.C. §336(a)(2).

[86] For a discussion of DBS and its perceived advantages over conventional broadcast, see National Assn. of Broadcasters v. FCC, 740 F.2d 1190, 1195 (D.C. Cir. 1984). The Commission first granted an application to construct a DBS system in 1982. Application of Satellite Television Corporation for Authority to Construct an Experimental Direct Broadcast Satellite System, 91 F.C.C.2d 953 (1982); National Assn. of Broadcasters v. FCC, 740 F.2d 1190, 1197 (D.C. Cir. 1984).

sublet their spectrum—to cross at will the regulatory line between "broadcast" and "carriage." The owner of a DBS could
lease under contract, or outright sell, transmission space to private users—so-called customer-programmers. The owner thus
could operate, and be subject to regulation, as a common carrier
for independent programmers. Or it could transmit its own programming, either scrambled and paid for by subscribers or "in
the clear" and paid for by advertisers, and be subject to regulation as a broadcaster. The operator had unprecedented freedom
to use its satellite spectrum rights for any mix of carriage, broadcast, subscription services, or private transport.[87]

Most other nonbroadcast wireless licensees have gained comparable freedom to subdivide their spectrum (i.e., disaggregate)
and subdivide the geographic area of their license (i.e., partition), as they see fit.[88] The Commission has allowed licensees to
slice spectrum into increments of any size and to occupy or lease
those increments more or less as they see fit.

[87] *See* National Assn. of Broadcasters, 740 F.2d at 1200. Remarkably, "no
one challenged the Commission's decision that a satellite owner that acts as
a common carrier, offering satellite transmission services 'indiscriminately to
the public . . .' is not also subject to regulation as a broadcaster." National
Cable Television Assn. v. FCC, 33 F.3d 66, 73 (D.C. Cir. 1994). But an alliance
of traditional broadcasters did challenge the FCC's determination that
customer-programmers, who controlled the content of the programming transmitted by a DBS carrier, were not engaged in broadcasting and hence were
not subject to Title III regulation. The D.C. Circuit agreed that the Commission had failed to explain adequately its decision to exempt customer-programmers from broadcast regulation. *National Assn. of Broadcasters,* 740 F.2d
at 1199–1206. In a later rulemaking, the FCC supplied the missing explanation, Subscription Video, Report and Order, 2 F.C.C. Rec. 1001 (1987), and
the court upheld its decision, National Assn. for Better Broad. v. FCC, 849
F.2d 665 (D.C. Cir. 1988). As of February 1998, all DBS licensees had chosen
to be regulated as subscription services. Policies and Rules for the Direct
Broadcast Satellite Service, Notice of Proposed Rulemaking, 13 F.C.C. Rec.
6907, 6911–6912 ¶5 (1998).

[88] The FCC presently permits spectrum disaggregation and geographic
partitioning of licenses for broadband PCS, Geographic Partitioning and
Spectrum Disaggregation by Commercial Mobile Radio Services Licensees,
Report and Order and Further Notice of Proposed Rulemaking, 11 F.C.C.
Rec. 21,831 (1996) (hereinafter *Geographic Partitioning Order*); 800 MHz and
900 MHz SMR, Amendment of Part 90 of the Commission's Rules to Facilitate Future Development of SMR Systems in the 800 MHz Frequency Band,

From the beginning, wireless common carriers have been permitted—indeed required—to "broker" time on their spectrum.
Wireless telephone carriers create not a single, broad, one-way
program channel, but thousands of narrow, two-way audio circuits. They use those channels to do precisely what broadcasters

---

Second Report and Order, 12 F.C.C. Rec. 19,079, 19,127–19,153 ¶¶138–227
(1997); 39 GHz fixed point-to-point microwave, Amendment to the Com-
mission's Rules Regarding the 37.0–38.6 GHz and 38.6–40.0 GHz Bands,
Report and Order and Second Notice of Proposed Rule Making, 12 F.C.C.
Rec. 18,600, 18,634–18,636 ¶¶70–74 (1997); wireless communications service,
Amendment of the Commission's Rules to Establish Part 27, the Wireless
Communications Service ("WCS"), Report and Order, 12 F.C.C. Rec. 10,785,
10,834–10,839 ¶¶92–103 (1997); local multipoint distribution service, Rule
Making to Amend Parts 1, 2, 21, and 25 of the Commission's Rules to Redes-
ignate the 27.5–29.5 GHz Frequency Band to Reallocate the 29.5–30.0 GHz
Frequency Band, to Establish Rules and Policies for Local Multipoint Distri-
bution Service and for Fixed Satellite Service, Fourth Report and Order, 13
F.C.C. Rec. 11,655 (1998); and maritime services, Amendment of the Commission's Rules Concerning Maritime Communications, Third Report and
Order and Memorandum Opinion and Order, PR Docket No. 92-257 (July
9, 1998). The Commission allows only partitioning of cellular licenses, *see*
Geographic Partitioning Order, 11 F.C.C. Rec. at 21,875 ¶93; and multipoint distribution service licenses, *see* Amendments of Parts 21 and 74 of the Commission's Rules with Regard to Filing Procedures in the Multipoint
Distribution Service and in the Instructional Television Fixed Service, Report
and Order, 10 F.C.C. Rec. 9589, 9614–9615 ¶¶46–47 (1995). But it is currently considering a proposal to permit disaggregation of cellular licenses.
Geographic Partitioning Order, 11 F.C.C. Rec. at 21,876 ¶95. In addition, the
Commission is seeking comment on partitioning and disaggregation proposals for all paging services, Revision of Part 22 and Part 90 of the Commission's Rules to Facilitate Future Development of Paging Systems, Second
Report and Order and Further Notice of Proposed Rulemaking, 12 F.C.C.
Rec. 2732, 2815–2818 ¶¶188–194, 2821–2825 ¶¶203–218 (1997) (adopting partitioning for certain paging licenses and proposing partitioning and
disaggregation for all paging licenses); general wireless communications services, *Geographic Partitioning Order,* 11 F.C.C. Rec. at 21,876 ¶96; and narrowband PCS, Amendment of the Commission's Rules to Establish New Personal
Communications Services, Narrowband PCS, Report and Order and Further
Notice of Proposed Rulemaking, 12 F.C.C. Rec. 12,972, 13,014–13,018,
¶¶87–99 (1997). The Commission has also proposed allowing licensees of
218–219 MHz service (formerly interactive video and data service or IVDS)
to partition and disaggregate their spectrum. Amendment of Part 95 of the
Commission's Rules to Provide Regulatory Flexibility in the 218–219 MHz
Service, Order, Memorandum Opinion and Order and Notice of Proposed
Rulemaking, 13 F.C.C. Rec. 19,064, 19,092 ¶51 (1998) (hereinafter *218–219
MHz Service*).

may not: to sell retail slots over which buyers transmit what they please. But cellular and PCS operators are also free to provide their own (audio) programming, just as conventional radio broadcasters do, although we are perhaps not accustomed to thinking about telephony that way. Any phone company can set up weather, sports, or other information and entertainment lines and own 976 or 1-900 dial-in services, in addition to merely carrying the signals of its customers. Cellular and PCS carriers, however, have no broadcaster-like obligations to serve the Commission's view of the "public interest." On the whole, these licensees have been relatively free to permit use and occupancy of their systems for a variety of purposes.[89] Cellular and PCS technologies have so far been used mostly for voice, but wireless data networks are in wide use, too, and the Commission has approved video applications.[90]

The Commission has permitted the digitization of existing analog cellular networks[91] and has already removed some restrictions on the types of services that cellular, PCS, and other

---

[89] Cellular operators may, under some circumstances, be required to refrain from providing use of their facilities to parties whom they know are transmitting obscene or harassing material. 47 U.S.C. §223; Sable Communications of Cal., Inc. v. FCC, 492 U.S. 115, 124 (1989). Extension of the rule to "indecent material" under 47 U.S.C. §223(d)(2) was recently held unconstitutional by the Supreme Court. *See* Reno v. ACLU, 521 U.S. 844 (1997).

[90] Rulemaking to Amend Part 1 and Part 21 of the Commission's Rules to Redesignate the 27.5–29.5 GHz Frequency Band and to Establish Rules and Policies for Local Multipoint Distribution Service, Notice of Proposed Rulemaking, Order, Tentative Decision, and Order on Reconsideration, 8 F.C.C. Rec. 557, 565–566 ¶¶57–65 (1993); Rulemaking to Amend Parts 1, 2, 21, and 25 of the Commission's Rules to Redesignate the 27.5–29.5 GHz Frequency Band, to Reallocate the 29.5–30.0 GHz Frequency Band, to Establish Rules and Policies for Local Multipoint Distribution Service and for Fixed Satellite Services, Second Report and Order, Order on Reconsideration, and Fifth Notice of Proposed Rulemaking, 12 F.C.C. Rec. 12,545, 12,553–12,554 ¶¶5–6 (1997).

[91] *See* Implementation of Section 6002(b) of the Omnibus Budget Reconciliation Act of 1993, Second Report, 12 F.C.C. Rec. 11,266, 11,277 & n.32 (1997) (CDMA/TDMA); Report and Plan for Meeting State and Local Government Public Safety Agency Spectrum Needs Through the Year 2010, Report and Plan, 10 F.C.C. Rec. 5207, 5241 (1995) (CDMA/TDMA); *Communications Act Third Report,* 9 F.C.C. Rec. at 8030–8033 ¶74 (CDPD).

CMRS licensees may provide.[92] In 1996, the Commission included fixed wireless services within the set of permissible CMRS services in order "to encourage innovation and experimentation through a broader, more flexible standard."[93] CMRS licensees, however, are still prohibited from providing video broadcast services.[94]

The Commission has given similar flexibility to several new wireless services, including 218–219 MHz service (formerly called interactive video and data service)[95] and wireless communica-

---

[92] In 1996, for example, the Commission modified its rules to allow all CMRS licensees—including providers of cellular, narrowband and broadband PCS, specialized mobile radio, and certain paging services; 220 MHz service; and for-profit interconnected business radio services—to provide fixed wireless services in addition to mobile services on their assigned spectrum. Amendment of the Commission's Rules to Permit Flexible Service Offerings in the Commercial Mobile Radio Services, First Report and Order and Further Notice of Proposed Rulemaking, 11 F.C.C. Rec. 8965, 8967 ¶2 (1996).

[93] Amendment of the Commission's Rules to Permit Flexible Service Offerings in the Commercial Mobile Radio Services, First Report and Order and Further Notice of Proposed Rule Making, 11 F.C.C. Rec. 8965, 8973–8977 ¶¶17–24 (1996). Industry analysts predict that fixed wireless services will be used as a "safety net" to existing local wireline service, which may be interrupted due to weather or other emergencies, or as a separate "wireless local loop" to provide service to apartment buildings, office buildings, or older homes where rewiring costs are particularly high. *Id.* at 8973–8974 ¶18. Previously, fixed services (except for broadcast services) were permitted only if provided ancillary, auxiliary, or incidental to mobile operations. *Id.* at 8973 ¶17.

[94] *Id.* at 8977 ¶25.

[95] Amendment of Parts 0, 1, 2, and 95 of the Commission's Rules to Provide Interactive Video and Data Services, Report and Order, 7 F.C.C. Rec. 1630, 1637 ¶54 (1992) (hereinafter *IVDS Report*); Amendment of Parts 0, 1, 2, and 95 of the Commission's Rules to Provide for Interactive Video Data Services, Memorandum Opinion and Order, 7 F.C.C. Rec. 4923, 4924 ¶9 (1992). IVDS licensees (now designated as 218–219 MHz licensees) are treated as private carriers, not common carriers, and will not be required to file tariffs of any kind. *IVDS Report,* 7 F.C.C. Rec. at 1637 ¶54. Also, the FCC has granted IVDS licensees authority to use their spectrum for "other applications"— beyond the interactive text-based services initially planned for IVDS—"without Commission approval" as long as the services do not run afoul of prior FCC rules. Annual Assessment of the Status of Competition in Markets for the Delivery of Video Programming, Fourth Annual Report, 13 F.C.C. Rec. 1034, 1098–1099 ¶107 (1998). The Commission sua sponte redesignated IVDS as 218–219 MHz service in September 1998 in order to reflect the breadth of

tions service.[96] Each of these digital services—like CMRS—will remain free of any serious regulatory obligations. Congress appears to commend regulatory flexibility. In 1997, Congress provided that the Commission may allocate spectrum to provide for flexibility of use as long as the use is consistent with international agreements, required by public safety allocations, and in the public interest.[97]

§10.3.5 *"Public" and "Private" Carriers: Parity Among Comparable Wireless Providers*

Private land mobile services initially were defined in the Communications Act as a class of radio services that do not interconnect with the public switched network except by direct agreement with a local carrier.[98] Radio dispatch services were an example. These services were exempt from federal common carrier regulation, as well as from state and local regulation.

---

services offered in the 218–219 MHz band. *218–219 MHz Service,* 13 F.C.C. Rec. at 19,075–19,076. *See also* §10.4.6.2.

[96] Amendment of the Commission's Rules to Establish Part 27, the Wireless Communications Service ("WCS"), Report and Order, 12 F.C.C. Rec. 10,785, 10,797–10,802 ¶¶25–36 (1997). WCS licensees may provide any fixed, mobile, audio broadcast satellite, or radiolocation service consistent with international allocations and technical limitations. *Id.* at 10,797–10,798 ¶25.

[97] Balanced Budget Act of 1997, amending the Communications Act of 1934, §3304, Pub. L. No. 105-33 (1997).

[98] Communications Amendments Act of 1982, Pub. L. No. 97-259, §120(a), 96 Stat. 1087, 1096–1097 (1982). *See also id.* §120(b), 96 Stat. 1097 ("'Private land mobile service' means a mobile service which provides a regularly interacting group of base, mobile portable, and associated control and relay stations (whether licensed on an individual, cooperative, or multiple basis) for private one-way or two-way land mobile radio communications by eligible users over designated areas of operation."). "The primary test for inclusion in the private land mobile radio service . . . [was] that a licensee not resell interconnected telephone service for profit." Request of Fleet Call, Inc. for Waiver and Other Relief to Permit Creation of Enhanced Specialized Mobile Radio Systems in Six Markets, Memorandum Opinion and Order, 6 F.C.C. Rec. 1533, 1537 ¶31 (1991) (hereinafter *Fleet Call Order*), *recons. dismissed,* 6 F.C.C. Rec. 6989 (1991). If providers satisfied this test, and hence passed any landline costs through to their customers without markup, they remained private

As companies like Nextel developed technology to boost system capacity and improve transmission quality, interconnection with the landline network became much more attractive. Just as MCI began with private line connections and ended up as a "public" long-distance carrier, companies such as Nextel introduced technologies and developed business strategies that made the transition from private networks to public carriage inevitable.

During the 1980s, Nextel (formerly Fleet Call) amassed SMR licenses that were traditionally used for taxi dispatch service. It then sought permission from the FCC to digitize its analog SMR spectrum to provide enhanced SMR (ESMR) service, including all types of voice and data applications. The Commission granted Nextel's request in 1991.[99] Despite the remarkable similarities between the proposed ESMR service and cellular service, the Commission permitted Nextel to remain "private," and thus beyond the reach of Title II's common carrier requirements.[100]

This had major regulatory consequences. Cellular companies had been regulated as common carriers by the FCC, as well as by some state regulatory commissions. As to PCS, nobody quite knew whether it should be categorized as public or private. The 200-odd experimental PCS providers that had been licensed were, in practice, subject to neither federal nor state regulation. The FCC asked for public comments on whether PCS should be regulated as a common carrier or a private land mobile service.[101]

---

carriers exempt from common carrier regulation. *Id.*; Communications Amendments Act of 1982, Pub. L. No. 97-259, §120(a), 96 Stat. at 1097.

[99] *Fleet Call Order*, 6 F.C.C. Rec. 1533.

[100] *Id.* at 1537 ¶31.

[101] *See* Amendment of the Commission's Rules to Establish New Personal Communications Services, Notice of Proposed Rule Making and Tentative Decision, 7 F.C.C. Rec. 5676, 5712 ¶¶94–95 (1992). As with SMR service, the FCC suggested that PCS providers would get the benefit of being treated as a private land mobile service simply by refraining from reselling interconnected telephone service for a profit. *Id.* at 5712 ¶95. In other words, the regulatory status of PCS would be determined by the part of the service that PCS did *not* provide. *See also* Amendment of Part 90 of the Commission's Rules to Prescribe Policies and Regulations to Govern the Interconnection of Private Land Mobile Radio Systems with the Public Switched Telephone Network in the Bands 806–821 and 851–866 MHz, Memorandum Opinion and Order, 93 F.C.C.2d 1111, 1114–1115 ¶9 (1983), *on recons.*, 49 Fed. Reg. 26,066 (1984),

Congress stepped in. Unhappy with the regulatory disparity between new digital services like ESMR and traditional cellular service,[102] Congress ordered the Commission to regulate similar services similarly.[103] Congress defined a new class of service—commercial mobile service—and ordered that any provider of such services would henceforth "be treated as a common carrier."[104] This put both Nextel and PCS companies on a regulatory par with cellular carriers. True "private mobile services," by contrast, continued to be exempt from common carriage regulation.[105]

The Commission accordingly reclassified a broad body of wireless services—including former private services—as CMRS[106] and declared that "virtually all CMRS services are actually or potentially competitive with each other to some degree."[107]

---

aff'd by judgment sub nom. Telocator v. FCC, 764 F.2d 926 (D.C. Cir. 1985); Amendment of Part 90, Subparts M and S, of the Commission's Rules, Report and Order, 3 F.C.C. Rec. 1838, 1840 ¶¶24–25 (1988), *recons. denied,* 4 F.C.C. Rec. 356 (1989); Paul Kelley d/b/a/American Teltronix, Licensee of Station WNHM 552, Memorandum Opinion and Order, 3 F.C.C. Rec. 5347, 5437 ¶6 (1988), *recons. denied,* 5 F.C.C. Rec. 1955, 1956 ¶¶9–10 (1990).

[102] *See* Lewis J. Paper, Getting Personal: The Politics of the Wireless Revolution, 21, 24–32 (Institute for Information Studies 1996).

[103] *See* Omnibus Budget Reconciliation Act of 1993, Pub. L. No. 103-66, Title VI, §6001(a), 107 Stat. 312 (1993) (codified at 47 U.S.C. §332). Congress noted that "'private' carriers have become indistinguishable from common carriers but [they] were subject to inconsistent regulatory schemes." H.R. Rep. No. 111, 103d Cong., 1st Sess. 260 (1993). Congress amended section 332(c) of the 1934 Act so that all commercial mobile service providers would be treated as common carriers and subject to the provisions of Title II of the 1934 Act unless the Commission determined provisions were inapplicable. For a general discussion of the background behind section 332, see Connecticut Dept. of Pub. Util. Control v. FCC, 78 F.3d 842, 845–846 (2d Cir. 1996).

[104] 47 U.S.C. §332(c)(1).

[105] *Id.* §332(c)(2).

[106] Implementation of Sections 3(n) and 332 of the Communications Act, Second Report and Order, 9 F.C.C. Rec. 1411, 1448–1459 ¶¶81–115 (1994) (hereinafter *Communications Act Second Report*). The FCC, for example, classified the following as CMRS: 220–222 MHz land mobile services, certain business radio services, SMR services, private and common carrier paging, 800 MHz air-ground services, and existing cellular services.

[107] Action in Docket Case, Regulatory Framework for CMRS Completed, News, GN Docket No. 93-252, 1994 LEXIS 3946 (Aug. 9, 1994). Congress

The criteria that define CMRS are straightforward. The service must be "provided for profit."[108] It must be "interconnected" with the public switched network.[109] It must be made available "to the public" (without restriction)[110] or "to such classes of eligible users as to be effectively available to a substantial portion

---

provided a three-year transition period for any private service reclassified as CMRS. Omnibus Budget Reconciliation Act of 1993, Pub. L. No. 103-66, Title VI, §6002(c)(2)(B) (1993). Accordingly, providers that were licensed to provide a private land mobile service as of August 10, 1993, and were then reclassified as CMRS were not subject to Title II until August 10, 1996. These "grandfathered" licensees were allowed to modify and expand their existing systems and acquire new licenses in the same service for which they were licensed. *Communications Act Second Report,* 9 F.C.C. Rec. at 1513-1514 ¶¶280-283. The same holds for wide-area SMR services and all private paging licensees on frequencies allocated as of January 1, 1993. *Id.* at 1514 ¶284. Providers licensed after August 10, 1993, were regulated as CMRS immediately.

[108] 47 U.S.C. §332(d)(1). The Commission interprets this to mean offered with the "intent of receiving compensation or monetary gain." *Communications Act Second Report,* 9 F.C.C. Rec. at 1427-1428 ¶43. If a private mobile carrier offers some portion of its capacity for hire, it is then a "for profit" carrier to that extent. *Id.* at 1427-1429 ¶¶43-46.

[109] 47 U.S.C. §332(d)(1)-(2). The Commission defines the interconnection requirement to apply to any service that allows subscribers to "send or receive messages to or from anywhere on the public switched network." *Communications Act Second Report,* 9 F.C.C. Rec. at 1434-1435 ¶55. The Commission has determined that incidental use of the public switched network for internal control purposes (for example, to control transmitters) does not constitute interconnection. *Id.* But "direct or indirect connection" will suffice, and the use of "store and forward technology" will also subject the carrier to CMRS regulation. *Id.* at 1435-36 ¶¶56-58. To ensure regulatory symmetry, the Commission has concluded that "even a mobile service that is not yet interconnected, but has requested [to be] interconnect[ed], [will be] considered an interconnected service" for the purposes of the statutory definition. *Id.* at 1434-1435 ¶55 (internal citation omitted).

[110] 47 U.S.C. §332(d)(1)(A). A service is available "to the public" if it is "offered to the public without restriction on who may receive it." *Communications Act Second Report,* 9 F.C.C. Rec. at 1439 ¶65. The Commission recognized, however, that "[t]he terms and conditions for different classes of customers may . . . vary. Whether such differences are lawful would be a question of whether there is unreasonable discrimination under Section 202(a) of the Act." *Id.* at 1439 n.130. Thus, individualized or customized service offerings made by CMRS providers to individual customers will be treated as CMRS offerings, "regardless of whether such offerings would be treated as common carriage under existing case law, if the service falls within the definition of CMRS." *Id.*

of the public."[111] Any service that is functionally equivalent[112] to a CMRS service will be treated as one;[113] others will not.[114] As part of this flexible approach, the Commission adopted a rebuttable presumption that PCS should be classified as CMRS unless a PCS provider demonstrates that its intended use does not meet the criteria for CMRS.[115] The Commission has retained this presumption in its ongoing regulation of PCS.[116]

§10.3.6   Reallocating Spectrum

In 1993, Congress ordered the United States Secretary of Commerce to reallocate at least 200 MHz of additional spectrum

---

[111] 47 U.S.C. §332(d)(1)(B). The Commission has concluded that the legislative intent was to ensure that the definition of "'commercial mobile services' encompass[ed] all providers who offer their services to broad or narrow classes of users so as to be effectively available to a substantial portion of the public." *Communications Act Second Report*, 9 F.C.C. Rec. at 1439–1440 ¶66. "Service is *not* 'effectively available to a substantial portion of the public' if it is provided exclusively for internal use or is offered only to a significantly restricted class of eligible users." *Id*. at 1440–1441 ¶67.

[112] To determine functional equivalence, the Commission said it will consider a "variety of factors." *Communications Act Second Report*, 9 F.C.C. Rec. at 1447–1448 ¶80. The "principal inquiry" will be whether the offering in question is a close substitute for any CMRS offering as evidenced, inter alia, by the cross-price elasticity of demand. *Id*. "Market research information identifying the targeted market for the service under review also will be relevant." *Id*. The Commission stated it would "refine this examination in the context of the individual cases that may arise based on a showing by any interested party." *Id*.

[113] 47 U.S.C. §332(d)(3). The Commission noted, however, that because it had "broadly interpreted the definitional elements of CMRS," it would "anticipate that very few mobile services that do not meet the definition of CMRS will be a close substitute for a commercial mobile radio service." *Communications Act Second Report*, 9 F.C.C. Rec. at 1447 ¶79.

[114] The Commission, for example, classified all existing government and public safety services as private mobile radio services. *Id*. at 1448 ¶82.

[115] *Id*. at 1460–1463 ¶¶118–123.

[116] *See* Personal Communications Industry Association's Broadband Personal Communications Services Alliance's Petition for Forbearance for Broadband Personal Communications Services, Memorandum Opinion and Order and Notice of Proposed Rulemaking, 13 F.C.C. Rec. 16,857 ¶111 (1998).

previously reserved for government use to new wireless services.[117] The legislation directed the Department of Commerce to identify 50 MHz for "immediate reallocation" by the FCC to the private sector, with the balance to be allocated over a ten-year period.[118] The Commerce Department promptly recommended for reallocation 50 MHz among three frequency bands—2,390–2,400 MHz, 2,402–2,417 MHz, 4,660–4,685 MHz.[119] The Commission assessed the nature of these bands and existing needs to designate them, respectively, by unlicensed PCS devices, by other unlicensed devices operating in accordance with Part 15 of the Commission's rules, and by fixed and mobile services.[120]

The Balanced Budget Act of 1997 required the Secretary of Commerce to identify "a band or bands of frequencies that in the aggregate span not less than 20 MHz" of spectrum reserved for government use for reallocation to commercial use.[121] In addition, Congress required the Commission to assign an additional 55 MHz of spectrum using competitive bidding procedures no later than September 30, 2002.[122]

§10.3.7 *Administrative Law Constraints on Spectrum Allocations*

Section 303 of the Communications Act gives the Commission general authority to allocate and assign spectrum. In 1943, the

[117] Omnibus Budget Reconciliation Act of 1993, Pub. L. No. 103-66, Title VI, §6001, 107 Stat. 312, 380–384 (1993).
[118] Omnibus Budget Reconciliation Act of 1993, Pub. L. No. 103-66, Title VI, §6001, 107 Stat. 312, 383, 385 (1993).
[119] Allocation of Spectrum Below 5 GHz Transferred from Federal Government Use, First Report and Order and Second Notice of Proposed Rule Making, 10 F.C.C. Rec. 4769, 4771 ¶3 (1995).
[120] *Id.* at 4773 ¶6.
[121] Balanced Budget Act of 1997, Pub. L. No. 105-33, §3002(e), 111 Stat. 251, 264–265 (1997).
[122] Balanced Budget Act of 1997, Pub. L. No. 105-33, §3002(c), 111 Stat. 251, 261–262 (1997). In addition, Congress specified that spectrum located at 2,110–2,150 MHz and 15 MHz from within the 1,990–2,110 MHz band must be reallocated unless the Commission and the President determined

Supreme Court upheld Congress's general right to delegate to the Commission the essentially unbounded authority to enact any rule pertaining to the use and management of spectrum that the Commission deems to be required by "public convenience, interest, or necessity."[123] However, standard principles of administrative law circumscribe, to some degree, the Commission's discretion in allocating spectrum for a particular service or technology, in establishing the rules that govern the particulars of how the spectrum is used, and in assigning licenses to specific licensees.

In the context of rulemaking, the Administrative Procedure Act (APA) imposes the usual requirements of notice,[124] opportunity to comment, a statement of reasons for adopting a rule, and publication of the rule adopted.[125] The Commission must compile a suitable record and ensure that all interested parties are afforded an opportunity to be heard. The final rule must be a logical outgrowth of the rule initially proposed; otherwise, the Commission must solicit additional rounds of comments.[126]

The Negotiated Rulemaking Act of 1990[127] and the Federal Advisory Committee Act[128] empower the Commission to establish advisory committees. These committees may be instructed, for example, to search for "consensus on the language or substance of the appropriate rules"[129] or to develop the technical

---

that allocation of other spectrum would better serve the public interest and would yield comparable or greater receipts at auction. *Id.*

[123] National Broad. Co. v. United States, 319 U.S. 190 (1943).

[124] 5 U.S.C. §553. The notice must contain either the terms or substance of the proposed rule or a description of the subjects and issues involved. Buckeye Cablevision, Inc. v. FCC, 387 F.2d 220 (D.C. Cir. 1967). The requirements of notice and opportunity to comment do not apply to "interpretative rules"—rules that do "not contain new substance but merely express[] the agency's understanding of a congressional statute," National Latino Media Coalition v. FCC, 816 F.2d 785 (D.C. Cir. 1987)—or general statements of policy. 5 U.S.C. §553(b)(3)(A).

[125] *See generally* 5 U.S.C. §553.

[126] Omnipoint v. FCC, 78 F.3d 620, 631 (D.C. Cir. 1996).

[127] 5 U.S.C. §§561 et seq.

[128] 5 U.S.C. App. §§1 et seq.

[129] FCC Asks for Comments and Nominations for Membership Regarding the Establishment of an Advisory Committee to Negotiate Regulations, Public Notice, 9 F.C.C. Rec. 6706, 6706 ¶3 (1994).

standards rules that will govern spectrum allocations.[130] The Commission has, for instance, relied on negotiated rulemaking to address the proposed allocation of frequency spectrum to small and large low-earth orbit (LEO) satellites.[131] Advisory committees include representatives of the interested parties that may be significantly affected by the outcome of proposed rules.[132]

The assignment of licenses is an essentially adjudicatory process. Section 309 of the 1934 Act requires the Commission to hold a formal hearing to resolve any "substantial or material question of fact with respect to a pending application."[133] In addition, the APA generally requires notice, submission of written evidence, testimonial evidence, and cross-examination.[134]

---

[130] FCC Asks for Comments Regarding the Establishment of an Advisory Committee to Negotiate Proposed Regulations, Public Notice, 7 F.C.C. Rec. 5241, 5241 ¶1 (1992) (hereinafter *Request for Comments on Advisory Committee*). Negotiated rulemaking, in this context, attempts to encourage negotiations, in a less adversarial setting than comparative hearings, by developing regulations "that will facilitate the shared use of the spectrum by the maximum number of . . . providers." *Id.* An advisory committee's report is only a proposed rule; the report must still receive the FCC's approval through the notice-and-comment rulemaking process. Peter M. Shane, Symposium: The New Public Law: Structure, Relationship, Ideology, or, How Would We Know a "New Public Law" If We Saw It?, 89 Mich. L. Rev. 837, 844 n.26 (1991).

[131] *Request for Comments on Advisory Committee,* 7 F.C.C. Rec. at 5241 ¶5.

[132] *Id.* Before adopting negotiated rulemaking to develop new regulations, the FCC must consider whether the following factors have been met: (1) there is a need for a rule, (2) a limited number of interests have been identified that will be significantly affected by the rule, (3) there is a reasonable likelihood that a committee can be convened with a balanced representation of persons who can adequately represent those interests and the parties are willing to negotiate in good faith to reach a consensus on the proposed rules, (4) there is a reasonable likelihood that a committee can reach a consensus within a fixed period of time, (5) the negotiated rulemaking will not cause an unreasonable delay in the issue of notice and the new rules, (6) the agency has adequate resources to commit to the committee, and (7) the agency commits to using the consensus of the committee as the basis for rules proposed by the agency. *Id.* at 5241 ¶¶4, 5; 5 U.S.C. §583(a).

[133] 47 U.S.C. §309(e).

[134] 5 U.S.C. §§554, 556. *But see* United States v. Storer Broad. Co., 351 U.S. 192, 202 (1956) (under section 309 of the Communications Act, every party "shall have the right to present his case or defense by oral *or* documentary evidence, to submit rebuttal evidence, and to conduct cross-examination *as may be required for a full and true disclosure of the facts*" (emphasis added)); Cellular

The Commission's decision must be "supported by and in accordance with the reliable, probative, and substantial evidence."[135] The Commission initially issued "block A" cellular licenses through a lengthy process of comparative hearings that adjudicated the relative merits of competing applications.[136] But Congress has since authorized the Commission to replace the burdens and formalities of comparative hearings with a lottery or auction system to award licenses.[137] Applicants merely submit written evidence that they satisfied the minimum requirements to participate in the process.[138]

License revocations are also adjudicatory proceedings, subject to a variety of procedural protections. The Commission bears the burden of proceeding and of proof.[139] The 1934 Act expressly invokes the procedures of the APA for cease and desist orders, requiring notice and the opportunity to demonstrate compliance.[140] But the Commission has broad discretion to determine whether and under what conditions it will permit oral arguments.[141]

Before transferring a license, a licensee must obtain the Commission's permission, based on its determination that such a

---

Mobile Sys. of Pa. v. FCC, 782 F.2d 182, 197, 198 (D.C. Cir. 1985) (The requirement of a "'[f]ull hearing'" under the APA "does not vouchsafe an inalienable right to cross-examination"; "[c]ross-examination is . . . not an automatic right conferred by the APA; instead, its necessity must be established under specific circumstances by the party seeking it."). For any adjudication for which the Commission has designated a hearing, the authority conducting the hearing must issue a recommended decision to which any party may file exceptions. 47 U.S.C. §409.

[135] 5 U.S.C. §556(d).

[136] MobileTel Inc. v. FCC, 107 F.3d 888, 891 (D.C. Cir. 1997) ("often drawn-out comparative hearings" for block A licenses).

[137] 47 U.S.C. §309(i) (random selection), (j) (competitive bidding).

[138] An interested party may object to a license granted by lottery or auction if "substantial or material" issues of fact exist concerning the qualifications of the licensee. 47 U.S.C. §309(i)(2), (j)(5). See 47 C.F.R. §§1.823(b), 1.2108.

[139] 47 C.F.R. §1.91(d).

[140] 47 U.S.C. §312(e); 5 U.S.C. §558(c).

[141] FCC v. WJR, The Goodwill Station, 337 U.S. 265, 281–283 (1949) (neither the Constitution nor the Communications Act requires the Commission to offer an opportunity for oral argument).

transfer is in the "public interest."[142] The Commission will generally seek comment and may hold a formal hearing before rendering its determination.[143] This power to approve or deny transfers gives the Commission broad-ranging authority to review—and, if it chooses, to block—mergers and acquisitions that it deems uncompetitive or otherwise inimical to the public interest. When AT&T sought to acquire McCaw, for example, the Commission decided not to invoke its Clayton Act jurisdiction,[144] but rather considered antitrust issues (i.e., "the competitive impact of the proposed merger") in connection with the application to transfer the radio licenses.[145]

Section 402(b) of the 1934 Act provides for the appeal of license grants or denials to the D.C. Circuit.[146] A notice of appeal must be filed with the court within 30 days of the date the public notice is issued for the order complained of.[147] All other final orders of the Commission may be appealed to the circuit in which the petitioner resides or has its principal office.[148] Prior to

---

[142] 47 U.S.C. §310(d) (permit or license may be transferred, or otherwise disposed of, only if the Commission finds such a transfer or disposition serves the "public interest, convenience, and necessity," just as if the proposed transferee "were making application under section 308 for the permit or license in question"). A change in ownership or control of the licensee also triggers the provisions of section 309. Interested parties generally have 30 days in which to file petitions to deny the transfer. 47 U.S.C. §309(d). For a discussion of procedures to transfer licenses of companies subject to hostile takeovers, see Stephen F. Sewell, Hostile Tender Offers for Companies Holding Licenses Issued by the Federal Communications Commission, 49 Fed. Com. L.J. 167 (1996).

[143] 47 U.S.C. §309(e).

[144] Applications of Craig O. McCaw, Transferor, and American Telephone & Telegraph Company, Transferee, for Consent to the Transfer of Control of McCaw Cellular Communications, Inc. and Its Subsidiaries, Memorandum Opinion and Order, 9 F.C.C. Rec. 5836, 5844 ¶9 & n.25 (1994).

[145] Id. at 5843 ¶7, 5849–5850, ¶20.

[146] 47 U.S.C. §402(b); Waterway Communications Sys., Inc. v. FCC, 851 F.2d 401, 403 (D.C. Cir. 1988). Cf. Freeman Engg. Assocs. v. FCC, 103 F.3d 169, 178 (D.C. Cir. 1997) (denial of a pioneer's preference is neither a denial of a license nor ancillary thereto, and thus is not appealable under section 402(b)).

[147] 47 U.S.C. §402(c).

[148] Id. §402(a); 28 U.S.C. §2342(1). Petitions for review under section 402(a) may be brought "to enjoin, set aside, annul, or suspend" final orders.

appeal, any party to a proceeding or any party adversely affected may petition the Commission for reconsideration of any order or action of the Commission.[149] In accordance with the APA, the appellate court may set aside rules that conflict with the plain meaning of a statute, are unreasonable interpretations of ambiguous statutes, or are the product of arbitrary or capricious action by the agency.[150] The appellate court may not substitute the court's judgment for that of the agency; it must instead ascertain that the Commission "has examined the relevant data and articulated a satisfactory explanation for its action."[151]

§10.3.8 Constitutional Constraints on Spectrum Allocations

The Constitution requires due process when the government deprives an individual of "life, liberty, or property."[152] Due process demands notice of the proposed action, the right to present evidence, the right to cross-examine adverse witnesses, and a decision based on the evidence presented.[153]

Petitions or appeals under section 402(a) and section 402(b) are mutually exclusive. Friedman v. FCC, 263 F.2d 493, 494 (D.C. Cir. 1959).

[149] 47 U.S.C. §405. Petitions for reconsideration must be filed within 30 days from the date on which the public notice is given of the order. 47 U.S.C. §405(a); 47 C.F.R. §1.106(f). The filing of a petition is not a precondition to judicial review unless the petitioning person was not a party to the proceeding or relies on questions of law or fact that the Commission has not yet considered. 47 U.S.C. §405(a). The Commission has 90 days to grant or deny a petition for reconsideration. *Id.* §405(b)(1).

[150] California v. FCC, 124 F.3d 934, 939 (8th Cir. 1997); 5 U.S.C. §706(2).

[151] Omnipoint v. FCC, 78 F.3d 620, 632 (D.C. Cir. 1996) (internal quotation marks and citations omitted); *see also* Cincinnati Bell Tel. v. FCC, 69 F.3d 752, 758 (6th Cir. 1995) ("The agency must articulate a satisfactory explanation for its action including a 'rational connection between the facts found and the choice made.'" (quoting City of Brookings Mun. Tel. Co. v. FCC, 822 F.2d 1153, 1165 (D.C. Cir. 1987)).

[152] U.S. Const. amend V.

[153] Goldberg v. Kelly, 397 U.S. 254 (1970). In addition, due process may require an unbiased tribunal, an opportunity to present reasons against taking the agency action, the right to see the opposing evidence, the right to counsel, a record of the evidence, and written findings of facts and reasons.

In its 1945 decision in *Ashbacker Radio Corp. v. FCC,* the Supreme Court held that if two bona fide applications are mutually exclusive, they are entitled to a comparative hearing.[154] *Ashbacker* involved a challenge to the Commission's decision to grant a construction permit for a broadcasting station without a hearing, while at the same time setting a hearing for another permit that was mutually exclusive with the first. Thus, the circumstances drew into conflict two provisions of section 309(a)—the first, which grants the Commission authority to grant a permit without a hearing, and a second, which gives applicants a right to a hearing. Writing for the Court, Justice Douglas held that "where two bona fide applications are mutually exclusive the grant of one without a hearing to both deprives the loser of the opportunity which Congress chose to give him."[155] *Ashbacker* applies only to parties whose license applications have been declared mutually exclusive; it does not apply to prospective applicants. In 1956, in *United States v. Storer Broadcasting,* the Supreme Court held that the Commission may summarily screen applicants for eligibility based on threshold standards, provided the standards are adequately supported by the record in a rulemaking proceeding.[156]

The FCC's discretion in licensing is also constrained by the equal protection clause. In 1995, the Supreme Court limited an agency's discretion to provide race-based preferences. *Adarand Constructors v. Pena* (discussed in more detail in section 10.4.3 below) held that a federal program that makes distinctions on the basis of race must serve a compelling government interest and must be narrowly tailored to serve that interest.[157] The following Term, the Court held that a state program that classifies on the basis of sex must demonstrate an "exceedingly persuasive justification" to withstand constitutional scrutiny.[158] In light of

---

In Mathews v. Eldridge, 424 U.S. 319 (1976), the Supreme Court introduced a balancing test by which a court can determine upon review what process was due based on the circumstances.

[154] 326 U.S. 327 (1945).

[155] *Id.* at 332.

[156] 351 U.S. 192 (1956).

[157] 515 U.S. 200 (1995).

[158] United States v. Virginia, 518 U.S. 515 (1996).

these decisions, the Commission eliminated all preferential terms for businesses owned by women or minorities.[159] In all future auctions, any Commission preferences will be race- and gender-neutral; they will be targeted instead at various tiers of small businesses.[160]

The takings clause of the Fifth Amendment may impose a third set of constraints on any Commission action that zones or revokes a license. To be sure, the Commission continues to insist that the original granting of a license creates no property rights. This was quite clear to the Supreme Court, too—in 1940.[161] But as noted in section 10.3.1 above, the "renewal expectancy" creates de facto property rights. When one adds to the renewal expectancy the fact that today's licensees pay billions of dollars to acquire their licenses at auction, it seems safe to predict that a takings case will be prosecuted successfully, sooner or later.

§10.4   Spectrum Allocation: Specific Bands and Applications

The Commission first allocated frequencies for land mobile services in 1949.[162] The Commission allocated one block of frequency to "the conventional telephone company" and another to "miscellaneous" or "limited" common carriers, which are also commonly known as radio common carriers (RCCs).[163] In 1970,

[159] *See, e.g.,* Implementation of Section 309(j) of the Communications Act—Competitive Bidding, Tenth Report and Order, 11 F.C.C. Rec. 19,974, 19,979–19,980 ¶10 (1996) (IVDS rules).

[160] *Id.* at 19,980 ¶11.

[161] FCC v. Sanders Bros. Radio, 309 U.S. 470, 475 (1940) ("The policy of the Act is clear that no person is to have anything in the nature of a property right as a result of the granting of a license."). *See also* Longshore v. United States, 77 F.3d 441 (Fed. Cir. 1996) (finding no taking in violation of the Fifth Amendment where Congress requires a fee as a price for participating in the lottery for cellular radio system licenses).

[162] General Mobile Radio Service, Report and Order of the Commission, 13 F.C.C. 1190, 1228–1231 (1949).

[163] *Id.* at 1228–1229. A "miscellaneous," "limited," or "radio" common carrier is one that "is engaged in the business of providing the radio-link portion of the service, but generally without interconnection to the public message

the Commission allocated additional spectrum for the provision of land mobile service and again split the allocation of new frequencies between local exchange carriers (LECs) and RCCs.[164] The FCC expressed the hope that "AT&T, as well as others" would aggressively develop and implement new services.[165] A year later the FCC promulgated rules with respect to certain of the new frequencies.[166] The Commission announced that the new licenses would be awarded on an "open entry" basis to the best applicants, thereby expressly rejecting the argument (from already established carriers) that "ruinous competition" might result from such unrestricted entry.[167]

§10.4.1   *Allocation of Spectrum for Paging*

The Commission first allocated spectrum for common carrier paging (CCP) in 1949.[168] Responding to rapid growth in the

---

landline telephone system." *Id.* at 1228. *See also* Applications of ITT Mobile Telephone, Inc., (Assignee) and Walter F. Corbin (Assignor), Memorandum Opinion and Order, 1 Rad. Reg. 2d (P & F) 957 n.2 (1963) (hereinafter *ITT Mobile Telephone, Inc.*) ("A miscellaneous common carrier is one which is not engaged in the business of providing either a public landline message telephone service or public message telegraph service. Typically, at the present time, such miscellaneous common carrier services are not interconnected with telephone landline facilities.").

[164] An Inquiry Relative to the Future Use of the Frequency Band 806–960 MHz, First Report and Order and Second Notice of Inquiry, 19 Rad. Reg. 2d (P & F) 1663, ¶¶9, 31, 33 (1970); Amendment of Parts 2, 89, 91, and 93, First Report and Order, 23 F.C.C.2d 325, 338–339 ¶31 (1970).

[165] An Inquiry Relative to the Future Use of the Frequency Band 806–960 MHz, 19 Rad. Reg. 2d (P & F) 1663 ¶37 (1970).

[166] Amendment of Parts 21, 89, 91 and 93 of the Rules to Reflect the Availability of Land Mobile Channels in the 470–512 MHz Band in the 10 Largest Urbanized Areas of the United States, Second Report and Order, 30 F.C.C.2d 221 (1971).

[167] *Id.* at 234 ¶30.

[168] *See* General Mobile Radio Service, Report and Order of the Commission, 13 F.C.C. 1190, 1215 (1949). For some time to follow, pages were delivered without identifying the caller's telephone number, and the recipient had to call an answering service to retrieve a message. Revision of Part 22 and Part 90 of the Commission's Rules to Facilitate Future Development of Paging

industry,[169] the Commission, in 1982, allocated 40 new paging channels to CCP in the 931 MHz band and dedicated three channels for use by nationwide systems.[170]

At the same time, the Commission allocated 40 channels in the 929 MHz band for private carrier paging (PCP).[171] PCP was established as a distinct service from CCP. PCP licensees were only "authorized either to operate systems for their own internal use or to provide service to limited categories of eligible users."[172] In 1982, however, with increase in demand for paging spectrum, the Commission authorized PCP licensees to use some of the newly allocated channels in the 929 MHz band to provide commercial paging services.[173] Throughout the 1980s, PCP operators were allowed to provide service to an expanding pool of eligible users,[174] culminating in a 1993 FCC order allowing them to provide service on virtually the same basis as CCP providers.[175] In 1994, responding to the mandate of the 1993 Budget Act, the Commission found that PCP services were substantially similar to CCP services and therefore reclassified PCP services as a CMRS service.[176]

Systems, Notice of Proposed Rule Making, 11 F.C.C. Rec. 3108, 3109–3110 ¶4 (1996) (hereinafter *Revision of Part 22 and Part 90*).

[169] The use of pagers increased dramatically with the introduction, in 1982, of digital displays on pagers, which allowed for transmission of numeric messages and the recall of any message on demand. In 1984, alphanumeric pagers were introduced.

[170] Amendment of Parts 2, 22, and 90 of the Commission's Rules to Allocate Spectrum in the 928–941 MHz Band and to Establish Other Rules, Policies, and Procedures for One-Way Paging Stations in the Domestic Public Land Mobile Service, First Report and Order, 89 F.C.C.2d 1337 (1982). The Commission initially proposed designating specific channels for particular types of paging technology, but abandoned the plan upon realizing users and manufacturers had strong incentives to adopt various types of technologies.

[171] *Id.* at 1342 ¶14.

[172] Revision of Part 22 and Part 90, 11 F.C.C. Rec. at 3110 ¶5.

[173] *Id.*

[174] *Id.*

[175] Amendment of the Commission's Rules to Permit Private Carrier Paging Licensees to Provide Service to Individuals, Report and Order, 8 F.C.C. Rec. 4822 (1993).

[176] *Communications Act Second Report,* 9 F.C.C. Rec. at 1452–1453 ¶¶96–97 (1994); *Communications Act Third Report,* 9 F.C.C. Rec. 7988, 8026 ¶67, 8035 ¶77 (1994).

The 931 MHz CCP licenses were initially assigned by the Commission using a so-called notice and cut-off procedure, under which a public notice announcing the filing of an application would trigger a 60-day period during which other applicants could file for transmitters located within 70 miles of the first; the Commission staff would choose the frequency assignments, and if frequencies were not available for all applicants, a lottery would be held to determine who received the licenses.[177] In 1994, the Commission adopted new rules that reduced the "notice and cut-off" window to 30 days and provided for competitive bidding for mutually exclusive applications filed within that window.[178] In 1997, when the Commission made the transition to geographic area licensing for paging, it decided to offer all mutually exclusive licenses pursuant to competitive bidding rules.[179] The Commission planned to hold a series of auctions for a series of licenses, grouped together based on "interdependency and operational feasibility."[180] Incumbent (i.e., nongeographic) providers have been allowed to continue to operate under previous authorizations and to add internal sites without having to file another application.[181] Licensees of the nationwide channels in the 929–931 MHz band who had satisfied certain build-out requirements were exempted from competitive bidding and were granted a nationwide license outright.[182]

In recent years, digital technology has erased the functional lines between paging and two-way telecommunications services.

---

[177] Revision of Part 22 of the Commission's Rules Governing the Public Mobile Services, Further Notice of Proposed Rulemaking, 9 F.C.C. Rec. 2596, 2598 ¶¶13–14 (1994).

[178] Revision of Part 22 of the Commission's Rules Governing the Public Mobile Services, Report and Order, 9 F.C.C. Rec. 6513, 6517 ¶16 (1994). Applications for 931 MHz paging licenses had to specify the channel to be used, and the channel must be available. *Id.* at 6534 ¶98.

[179] Revision of Part 22 and Part 90 of the Commission's Rules to Facilitate Future Development of Paging Systems, Second Report and Order and Further Notice of Proposed Rulemaking, 12 F.C.C. Rec. 2732, 2735–2736 ¶2 (1997).

[180] *Id.* at 2781–2782 ¶97.

[181] *Id.* at 2746 ¶19.

[182] *Id.* at 2761–2762 ¶¶50–54.

The Commission is beginning to accommodate that evolution. PCS licensees (see below) are permitted to use their spectrum for one-way messaging, as well as two-way communication, and most do.[183] Indeed, the Commission's first allocations of PCS spectrum involved three narrow (1 MHz) slices of spectrum in the 900 MHz band, which were suitable mainly for messaging and data transmission and one limited form of wireless telephony (CT-2). The Commission auctioned off two of the three MHz bands in 1994 and reserved one MHz for development of newer PCS.[184] In addition to allocating more spectrum for paging services, the Commission has expanded the use of services in the 220 MHz band to include paging services.[185]

§10.4.1.1   Geographic Coverage of Paging Licenses

The early metropolitan paging services typically covered a 25-mile radius,[186] served by a single transmitter broadcasting at authorized power. As the amount of spectrum allocated to paging increased, paging companies expanded the scope of their

---

[183] Such services require no more than 50 kHz per licensee. *See* §10.4.3 for a complete discussion of narrowband PCS.

[184] Amendment of the Commission's Rules to Establish New Narrowband Personal Communications Services, First Report and Order, 8 F.C.C. Rec. 7162, 7165 ¶19 (1993).

[185] Prior to 1997, the Commission permitted 220 MHz licensees to offer paging services only if they were ancillary to the licensees' primary mobile operations. *See* Amendment of Part 90 of the Commission's Rules to Provide for the Use of the 220–222 MHz Band by the Private Land Mobile Radio Service, Second Memorandum Opinion and Order and Third Notice of Proposed Rulemaking, 11 F.C.C. Rec. 188, 200 ¶14 (1995). The Commission dropped the "ancillary" requirement in 1997 to allow one-way and two-way paging services. Amendment of Part 90 of the Commission's Rules to Provide for the Use of the 220–222 MHz Band by the Private Land Mobile Radio Service, Third Report and Order and Fifth Notice of Proposed Rulemaking, 12 F.C.C. Rec. 10,943, 10,990–10,991 ¶95, 11,013 ¶149 (1997). Use of the 220 MHz spectrum has been through a series of reallocations and reclassifications. *See* §10.4.6.7 for a discussion on 220 MHz licenses.

[186] FM Subcarriers Employed; Diversicom Introduces Nationwide Paging Service Using Satellite, Comm. Daily, Oct. 10, 1985, at 4.

coverage by acquiring contiguous licenses. In 1982, the Commission reserved separate channels for multiarea paging.[187] In 1983, the FCC decided to issue three licensees to provide nationwide paging networks.[188]

The 1982 Divestiture Decree barred the Bell Operating Companies from providing telecommunications service across LATA boundaries. But in 1989, Judge Harold Greene granted a blanket waiver that permitted the Bell companies to provide one-way paging, regardless of geographic scope.[189] The 1996 Act eliminates the Bell Company interLATA restriction entirely for the provision of "commercial mobile services."[190]

In 1997, the Commission moved from site-by-site licensing of non-nationwide paging licenses to geographic area licensing, with the geographic area defined by the 51 MTAs.[191] Common carrier paging services in the 35–36 MHz, 43–44 MHz, 152–159 MHz, and 454–460 MHz bands were granted licenses

---

[187] Amendment of Parts 2, 22, and 90 of the Commission's Rules to Allocate Spectrum in the 928–941 MHz Band and to Establish Other Rules, Policies, and Procedures for One-Way Paging Stations in the Domestic Public Land Mobile Service and the Private Land Mobile Radio Services, Second Report and Order, 91 F.C.C.2d 1214, 1225 ¶37 (1982). Recipients of these multiarea paging licenses were required to build a transmitter in at least three geographic areas within eight months of receiving the license. *Id.* at 1225 ¶38.

[188] Amendment of Parts 2 and 22 of the Commission's Rules to Allocate Spectrum in the 928–941 MHz Band and to Establish Other Rules, Policies and Procedures for One-Way Paging Stations in the Domestic Public Land Mobile Radio Service, Memorandum Opinion and Order on Reconsideration (Part 2), 93 F.C.C.2d 908 (1983).

[189] Memorandum and Order, United States v. Western Elec. Co., No. 82-0192 (D.D.C. Feb. 16, 1989). That order generally required the BOCs to provide exchange access and interconnection on an equal basis to both affiliated and nonaffiliated paging firms. *Id.* at 8–9.

[190] 47 U.S.C. §271(b)(3), (g)(3) (permitting Bell Operating Companies to provide "incidental interLATA services," which include "commercial mobile services"). Mobile services include paging services. *See id.* §153(27).

[191] Revision of Part 22 and Part 90 of the Commission's Rules to Facilitate Future Development of Paging Systems, Second Report and Order and Further Notice of Proposed Rulemaking, 12 F.C.C. Rec. 2732, 2735–2736 ¶2 (1997). The FCC designated MTAs as the geographic areas for most paging systems in the 929 and 931 MHz range because MTAs "mirror[ed]" the large geographic area of these paging systems. *Id.* at 2744 ¶16.

based on a geographic unit called an Economic Area (EA).[192] Incumbent paging providers were allowed to trade in their site-specific licenses for geographic area licenses.

§10.4.2 Allocation of Spectrum for Cellular

While Bell Labs developed the concept of cellular communications in 1947, the sophisticated radio and computer technologies needed to implement the idea did not then exist.[193] It took 15 years for AT&T to develop the technologies necessary to build the first experimental cellular system.[194] It then took another 15 years for regulation to catch up with the new technology. In 1977, the FCC finally granted Illinois Bell's application to construct and operate (with AT&T's assistance) a developmental cellular system in Chicago.[195] The Commission awarded a second developmental license to American Radio Telephone Service (a subsidiary of Motorola) to operate in the Washington, D.C.-Baltimore area.[196] The FCC allocated these

---

[192] *Id.* at 2748 ¶23. The Bureau of Economic Analysis of the Department of Commerce has divided the United States into 172 EAs. *Id.* Each EA consists of metropolitan areas or similar areas that serve as centers of economic activity—and the surrounding counties that are economically related to the nodes. EAs are typically bigger than BTAs but smaller than MTAs. *Id.*

[193] *See* AT&T Enters into Agreement with Southwestern Bell Mobile Systems, Business Wire, July 2, 1990; D. Huff, Cellular Radio, Technology Rev., Nov. 1983, at 53.

[194] AT&T Enters into Agreement with Southwestern Bell Mobile Systems, Business Wire, July 2, 1990.

[195] Application of Illinois Bell Telephone Company for Authority to Construct a Developmental Cellular System at Ten Sites at Various Locations in the State of Illinois with Control Point at 714 Lake Street, Oak Park, Illinois, Order, 63 F.C.C.2d 655 (1977), *aff'd sub nom.* Rogers Radio Communication Servs., Inc. v. FCC, 593 F.2d 1225 (D.C. Cir. 1978). Two years later the FCC expressly authorized Illinois Bell to charge customers for cellular service. Telocator Network of America v. Illinois Bell Tel. Co., Memorandum Opinion and Order, 70 F.C.C.2d 713, 716–717 ¶11 (1979).

[196] Application of American Radio Telephone Service, Inc. for Authority to Construct a Developmental Cellular Mobile and Portable Radio Telephone System in the Washington, D.C.-Baltimore, Maryland-Northern Virginia Area, Memorandum Opinion and Order, 66 F.C.C.2d 481 (1977) (hereinafter *American Radio Tel. Serv. Inc.*). The FCC apparently issued no other developmental

carriers 40 MHz of the 800 MHz frequency band for mobile radio cellular systems.[197]

In 1981, the Commission decided to license two blocks of cellular spectrum in each cellular geographic service area (CGSA), which was simply defined as the area that each applicant proposed to serve.[198] On reconsideration, the FCC revised its CGSA proposal to limit "somewhat" an applicant's "unfettered discretion" to define its CGSA. Under the revised ruling, each CGSA would, generally speaking, coincide with an SMSA or MSA.[199] A first license ("block B") would go to an affiliate of the incumbent wireline phone company in each area; a second ("block A") would go to an unaffiliated competitor. This was a departure from the long regulatory tradition of issuing only a single monopoly license—an exclusive franchise—for local wireline carriers.[200]

---

licenses. *See* P. McGuigan, D. Connors, & K. Cannon, Cellular Mobile Radio Telecommunications: Regulating an Emerging Industry, 1983 B.Y.U. L. Rev. 305, 314 n.42 (citing Inquiry into the Use of Certain Frequency Bands for Cellular Communications Sys., 46 Fed. Reg. 27,655, 27,656 & n.8 (1981)).

[197] *American Radio Tel. Serv. Inc.*, 66 F.C.C.2d at 481 ¶1. The FCC decided on the 800 MHz band because of severe spectrum limitations at lower frequency bands. *See* William C. Y. Lee, Mobile Cellular Telecommunications Systems 4–5 (1989). FM broadcasting operates in the vicinity of 100 MHz, television service ranges from 41 to 960 MHz, air-to-ground systems use 118–136 MHz, military aircraft use 225 to 400 MHz, maritime mobile service operates around 160 MHz, and fixed station services operate from 30 to 100 MHz. Because the lower spectrum was already crowded, the FCC was forced to allocate space to cellular services at the higher end. *Id.*

[198] An Inquiry into the Use of the Bands 825–845 MHz and 870–890 MHz for Cellular Communications Systems, Report and Order, 86 F.C.C.2d 469, 509 ¶97 (1981), *modified on recons.*, 89 F.C.C.2d 58 (1982), *petition for review dismissed sub nom.* United States v. FCC, No. 82-1526 (D.C. Cir. Mar. 3, 1983) (hereinafter *Cellular Report and Order*).

[199] An Inquiry into the Use of the Bands 825–845 MHz and 870–890 MHz for Cellular Communications Systems, Memorandum Opinion and Order on Reconsideration, 89 F.C.C.2d 58, 69–71 ¶24–28, 86–87 ¶62–63 (1982).

[200] For a brief period during 1974, the FCC concluded that telcos were the only organizations that had demonstrated that they possess the "resources and the expertise necessary" to provide cellular phone service and that "competing cellular systems would not be feasible." An Inquiry Relative to the Future Use of the Frequency Band 806–960 MHz, Second Report and Order, 46 F.C.C.2d 752, 760 ¶21 (1974). Accordingly, the FCC concluded that "only wireline carriers should be licensed to operate [cellular systems]." *Id.* Within a year, however, the FCC backed away from this no-competition decision and

The FCC said it would first issue licenses for the 30 largest MSAs, then licenses for the next 276 MSAs, and finally licenses for 428 RSAs.[201] But it took until 1989 for the Commission to issue at least one license in all 306 MSAs nationwide[202] and until 1990 for the Commission to award construction permits for cellular systems in the final two of the country's 428 rural service areas.[203]

---

opted to permit nonwireline providers to develop and operate cellular systems, though at that time the FCC still planned to authorize only one such system per market. An Inquiry Relative to the Future Use of the Frequency Band 806–960 MHz, Memorandum Opinion and Order, 51 F.C.C.2d 945, 946 ¶4, 953–954 ¶¶30–32 (1975). Then, in 1981, the Commission resolved to continue its dual-licensing competitive scheme by licensing two cellular systems, designated as block A and block B. *Cellular Report and Order,* 86 F.C.C.2d at 476 ¶15, 482–483 ¶¶27–29. The anticipated "diversity of technology, service and price" (*id.* at 478 ¶19) was soon realized when in 1984 the Commission touted "the highly competitive market structure" of the industry. Amendment of the Commission's Rules to Allow the Selection from Among Mutually Exclusive Competing Cellular Applications Using Random Selection or Lotteries Instead of Comparative Hearings, Report and Order, 98 F.C.C.2d 175, 195–196 ¶36 (1984) (hereinafter *Random Selection or Lotteries*). *See also* Schneider, Cellular Communications Service, 72 Geo. L.J. 1183.

[201] Applications for the first batch of MSAs were accepted through June 7, 1982. U.S. Dept. of Commerce, A Competitive Assessment of the U.S. Cellular Industry (Jan. 1989). As of December 1982, when comments on the Modification of Final Judgment (MFJ) were being filed with the Decree court, the Commission had received 586 applications for the 60 largest MSAs, 464 of which were from nonwireline carriers and 122 from wireline carriers. Advanced Mobile Phone Service, Inc. (AMPS), AT&T's cellular communications subsidiary, filed 55 of the 122 wireline applications. Reply Comments of Amicus Curiae FCC—On Application of AT&T and the Bell Operating Companies for Approval of Exchange Areas or Local Access Transport Areas Established Pursuant to the Modified Final Judgment at 3, United States v. Western Elec. Co., No. 82-0192 (D.D.C. Dec. 15, 1982) (hereinafter *FCC Reply*).

[202] It was not until 1986 that the FCC began its lottery allocation process for MSAs 91 to 305. The Commission received almost 100,000 applications for those licenses, plus an additional 288,000 applications for RSA licenses. CTIA, State of the Cellular Industry at 62. As of August 1991, both licenses in all MSAs had been issued with the exception of the nonwireline license in Jackson, Michigan. FCC, Status of MSA Cellular Markets (Aug. 1991).

[203] Nationwide Cellular Phone Service in View, Christian Science Monitor, Dec. 28, 1990, at 9. The permits require that the systems be operational within 18 months.

The Commission initially awarded the block A licenses through comparative hearings.[204] But the enormous expense, burden, and delay imposed by this process and the unexpected number of applicants led the Commission to switch tracks in 1984 and adopt a lottery system for distributing licenses in markets other than the 30 largest.[205] The Commission decided to maintain a separate allocation process for wireline and nonwireline carriers in markets 31–90.[206] Thousands of ostensible spectrum "providers" materialized out of thin air, entered the lottery, were awarded licenses, and resold them in short order, at tremendous profit, to companies with real resources to build and operate cellular systems.[207] In 1993, Congress authorized the Commission to award mutually exclusive spectrum licenses either by lottery or by auction (i.e., by "competitive bidding").[208] Congress repealed the Commission's lottery authority in 1997 for all applications other than for noncommercial educational and public interest broadcast stations.[209] Competitive bidding therefore is mandatory for nearly all licenses.

From the date it began offering service onward, a cellular licensee in an MSA market was required to have facilities capable of providing service to at least 75 percent of its geographic ser-

[204] *Cellular Report and Order,* 86 F.C.C.2d at 498–499 ¶¶62–66.

[205] *Random Selection or Lotteries,* 98 F.C.C.2d at 175 ¶1; FCC Wireless Telecommunications Bureau, FCC Report to Congress on Spectrum Auctions 6–7, WT Docket No. 97-150 (Oct. 9, 1997) (hereinafter *FCC Report to Congress on Spectrum Auctions*). In 1981, Congress added section 309(i) to the Communications Act of 1934 to authorize the Commission to assign licenses by "random selection," i.e., lottery. Omnibus Budget Reconciliation Act of 1981, Pub. L. No. 97-35, §1242, 95 Stat. 736–737 (1981), *amended,* Communications Amendments Act of 1982, Pub. L. No. 97-259, §115, 96 Stat. 1094–1095 (1982).

[206] *Random Selection or Lotteries,* 98 F.C.C.2d at 194–198 ¶¶34–41. License applicants were prescreened before entering the lottery. After the lottery, the winner's application was reviewed, and petitions to deny were accepted. For markets 91 and beyond, the Commission stayed with its notice and cutoff procedures modified slightly to permit only a one-day filing period. *Id.* at 202–203 ¶¶50–53.

[207] *FCC Report to Congress on Spectrum Auctions* at 7.

[208] Omnibus Budget Reconciliation Act of 1993, Pub. L. No. 103-66, §6002(a), 107 Stat. 312, 387–392 (1993).

[209] Balanced Budget Act of 1997, amending the Communications Act of 1934, Pub. L. No. 105-33 §3002(a), 111 Stat. 251, 258–260 (1997).

vice area.[210] The licensee was then given five years to "fill in" or "build out" any unserved area.[211] After five years, the licensed areas would be redefined to coincide with the areas where the licensee was actually offering service.[212] This process of shrinking licenses to areas actually served began in 1992. Through that process, the FCC defined unserved areas and offered them for relicensing. The Commission reauctioned 14 such licenses in early 1997; the ten winners paid over $1.8 million to U.S. Treasury for their licenses.[213]

Until the late 1980s, the Commission required that all cellular systems and telephones meet a specific analog technical standard.[214] In 1988, the Commission relaxed its rules somewhat, allowing cellular carriers to deploy new technologies and provide auxiliary services as long as carriers continued to support the current technical standard.[215] To deploy a new technology or service—such as code division multiple access (CDMA) or cellular digital packet data (CDPD)—a cellular licensee must

---

[210] *Cellular Report and Order,* 86 F.C.C.2d at 509 ¶97; Amendment of Part 22 of the Commission's Rules to Provide for Filing and Processing of Applications for Unserved Areas in the Cellular Service and to Modify Other Cellular Rules, Second Report and Order, 7 F.C.C. Rec. 2449, 2451–2452 ¶6 (1992). In MSA markets below the top 90, applicants could define their system to cover 75 percent of the area *or* 75 percent of the population of the desired cellular market. For RSA applications, there was no minimum coverage requirement. *Id.* at 2451 n.8.

[211] Amendment of Part 22 of the Commission's Rules to Provide for Filing and Processing of Applications for Unserved Areas in the Cellular Service and to Modify Other Cellular Rules, Third Report and Order and Memorandum Opinion and Order on Reconsideration, 7 F.C.C. Rec. 7183, 7183 ¶2 (1992).

[212] *See* Amendment of Part 22 of the Commission's Rules to Provide for Filing and Processing of Applications for Unserved Areas in the Cellular Service and to Modify Other Cellular Rules, Second Report and Order, 7 F.C.C. Rec. 2449 (1992).

[213] Auction of Cellular Unserved Area Licenses (Auction No. 12), Public Notice, 12 F.C.C. Rec. 25 (1997); Cellular Unserved Areas Auction Closes, Winning Bidders in the Auction of 14 Licenses to Provide Cellular Service in Unserved Areas, Public Notice, Rpt. No. AUC-97-12-F, 1997 FCC LEXIS 446 (Jan. 22, 1997).

[214] *Cellular Report and Order,* 86 F.C.C.2d at 505–509 ¶¶84–89.

[215] Amendment of Parts 2 and 22 of the Commission's Rules to Permit Liberalization of Technology and Auxiliary Service Offerings in the Domestic Public Cellular Radio Telecommunications Service, Report and Order, 3 F.C.C. Rec. 7033 (1988).

simply inform the FCC 30 days before its introduction.[216] In 1996, the Commission modified its rules to allow all CMRS licensees. including cellular, to provide fixed, in addition to mobile, services on their spectrum.[217]

§10.4.2.1 Geographic Coverage of Cellular Licenses

As discussed above, the FCC originally planned to allow each applicant to define the cellular geographic service area (CGSA) it proposed to serve.[218] The Commission emphasized that "nationwide availability of service" was "a primary goal" and that "a major basis of comparison [among license applicants] w[ould] be the geographic area that an applicant propose[d] to serve."[219] Such things as metropolitan areas, highways, "and areas likely to have high mobile usage characteristics" were noted only secondarily as "other significant factors to be considered."[220] A year later, however, the FCC concluded that this approach would be too cumbersome to administer. So the Commission defined the CGSA in terms of the SMSA or MSA.[221] But the FCC left licensees some latitude to go beyond the strict MSA boundaries

[216] 47 C.F.R. §22.390(b); *see also* Implementation of Section 6002(b) of the Omnibus Budget Reconciliation Act of 1993, Second Report, 12 F.C.C. Rec. 11,266, 11,277 & n.32 (1997) (CDMA/TDMA); *Communications Act Third Report,* 9 F.C.C. Rec. at 8030–8033 ¶74 (CDPD).

[217] Amendment of the Commission's Rules to Permit Flexible Service Offerings in the Commercial Mobile Radio Services, First Report and Order and Further Notice of Proposed Rule Making, 11 F.C.C. Rec. 8965 (1996).

[218] *Cellular Report and Order,* 86 F.C.C.2d at 509 ¶97.

[219] *Id.* at 502 ¶76.

[220] *Id.*

[221] An Inquiry into the Use of the Bands 825–845 MHz and 870–890 MHz for Cellular Communications Systems, Memorandum Opinion and Order on Reconsideration, 89 F.C.C.2d 58, 69–71 ¶¶24–28, 86–87 ¶¶62–63 (1982). A few months later the Commission dropped the SMSA standard for CGSAs in New England, determining that New England service areas would be based on New England County Metropolitan Areas (NECMAs). NECMAs covered larger areas and more closely paralleled natural markets in New England than did SMSAs. An Inquiry into the Use of the Bands 825–845 MHz and 870–890 MHz for Cellular Communications Systems, Memorandum Opinion and Order on Further Reconsideration, 90 F.C.C.2d 571, 579 ¶21 (1982).

and to file separate licenses for geographically contiguous service areas.[222]

From 1984 until 1993, wireless affiliates of Bell Operating Companies (BOCs) were subject to the MFJ's restrictions on interLATA services.[223] The FCC, however, issued licenses that covered geographic territories that crossed multiple LATA boundaries, particularly in rural areas.[224] Year by year, Judge Greene redrew the service areas in which wireless affiliates were permitted to offer "local" service.[225] Section 271(b)(3) of the 1996 Act eliminates the interLATA restriction entirely for Bell Company provision of "commercial mobile services," including cellular service.[226]

---

[222] An Inquiry into the Use of the Bands 825–845 MHz and 870–890 MHz for Cellular Communications Systems, Memorandum Opinion and Order on Reconsideration, 89 F.C.C.2d 58, 87 ¶63 (1982).

[223] *See* United States v. Western Elec. Co., 578 F. Supp. 643, 645–646, 647 (1983).

[224] These restrictions proved particularly onerous for U S WEST, which through a subsidiary acquired equity interests in 87 RSAs and held a non-managing minority interest in 67 other RSAs. At least 54 of those RSAs had boundaries that intersected more than one LATA boundary. U S WEST accordingly sought a waiver in December 1989 to provide interLATA cellular service within RSAs and to permit certain affiliated cellular systems to own interexchange links. When the Department of Justice failed to act on that request, U S WEST sought relief directly from the Decree court. In August 1990, the court denied U S WEST's request on the ground that Department had not yet taken a position on the issue. Memorandum and Order, United States v. Western Elec. Co., No. 82-0192 (D.D.C. Aug. 8, 1990).

[225] On February 18, 1993, Judge Greene permitted BOC cellular affiliates to provide interLATA service within any RSA. Decision, United States v. Western Elec. Co., No. 82-0192, at 1–2 (D.D.C. Feb. 18, 1993). Shortly before the 1996 Act was passed, Judge Greene also acceded to an agreement between the Department of Justice and the BOCs that allowed BOC affiliates to offer wireless interLATA services anywhere, subject to certain conditions. United States v. Western Elec. Co., 890 F. Supp. 1 (D.D.C. 1995) (limiting the resale of switched interexchange service provided by others, and the purchase of interexchange services from a single source to no more than 45 percent; also requiring separate subsidiaries, including physical and operational separation for the principal facilities used to provide wireless interexchange services, and unbundling of marketing and service operations).

[226] *See* 47 U.S.C. §271(b)(3), (g)(3) (permitting Bell Operating Companies to provide "incidental interLATA services," which include "commercial mobile services"). Under 47 U.S.C. §332(c)(2) and 47 U.S.C. §153(27), commercial mobile services include cellular services.

§10.4.3 Allocation of Spectrum for PCS— Narrowband, Broadband, and Unlicensed

Personal communications services (PCS) include wireless voice, data, and imaging services—an extended "family of mobile or portable radio communications services."[227] The Commission opened its first PCS docket in 1989, in response to petitions from two companies requesting spectrum for new wireless services.[228] The Commission envisioned PCS to be a general, all–purpose digital service that would compete directly with cellular, but would also provide a wide array of data services. PCS would be provided through "microcells," served by small, low-power, digital transceivers, providing wireless short-range links on one side and connection to the landline network and higher-powered cellular networks on the other.

In 1990, the Commission issued a Notice of Inquiry soliciting comments on a broad array of issues relating to PCS.[229] A year later came a Policy Statement in which the Commission announced a commitment to the "rapid development" of new wireless services.[230] To that end, the FCC proposed issuing licenses to multiple providers and giving licensees broad flexibility as to how they use allocated spectrum.[231]

True to its plan, the FCC has authorized PCS licensees to provide a wide range of services with the intention of "allow[ing] the market, rather than the Commission, to determine the best use

[227] Amendment of the Commission's Rules to Establish New Personal Communications Services, Notice of Proposed Rule Making and Tentative Decision, 7 F.C.C. Rec. 5676, 5689 ¶29 (1992) (hereinafter *New PCS Tentative Decision*).

[228] *See id.* at 5679–5680 ¶¶8–9.

[229] Amendment of the Commission's Rules to Establish New Personal Communications Services, Notice of Inquiry, 5 F.C.C. Rec. 3995 (1990).

[230] Amendment of the Commission's Rules to Establish New Personal Communications Services, Policy Statement and Order, 6 F.C.C. Rec. 6601 (1991).

[231] *Id.*

of this spectrum."[232] The Commission allocated PCS spectrum in three broad categories: narrowband, broadband, and unlicensed.[233]

The FCC allocated three megahertz in the 900 MHz band to narrowband PCS.[234] This initial allocation of spectrum was intended to provide advanced voice paging, two-way acknowledgment paging, data messaging, electronic mail, and facsimile services—services that generally require no more than 50 kHz per licensee.[235] The Commission licensed only two of the three megahertz of spectrum, leaving the third for future use as the service develops.[236] The two megahertz were sliced into 50 kHz and 12.5 kHz channels, which were paired in various configurations for licensing.[237]

---

[232] Implementation of Section 6002(b) of the Omnibus Budget Reconciliation Act of 1993, Second Report, 12 F.C.C. Rec. 11,266, 11,288 (1997) (hereinafter *Section 6002(b) Second Report*). "Broadband PCS licenses, for example, can be used for any mobile or fixed service." *Id.* The Commission also has permitted PCS licensees to disaggregate and partition their assigned spectrum and sell or otherwise transfer those segments freely. Geographic Partitioning and Spectrum Disaggregation by Commercial Mobile Radio Services Licensees, Report and Order and Further Notice of Proposed Rulemaking, 11 F.C.C. Rec. 21,831 (1996).

[233] *Section 6002(b) Second Report*, 12 F.C.C. Rec. at 11,288. In accordance with Congress's directive in the Omnibus Budget Reconciliation Act of 1993, the FCC allocated additional spectrum for OCS since the initial allocation.

[234] *See* Amendment of the Commission's Rules to Establish New Narrowband Personal Communications Services, First Report and Order, 8 F.C.C. Rec. 7162 (1993) (hereinafter *New Narrowband PCS*). Narrowband PCS "is broadly defined by the [FCC] as a family of mobile or portable radio services that may be used to provide wireless telephony, data, advanced paging, and other services to individuals and businesses, and which may be integrated with a variety of competing networks." FCC Wireless Telecommunications Bureau, Narrowband PCS Fact Sheet <http://www.fcc.gov/wtb/pcs/nbfctsh.html>.

[235] *New Narrowband PCS*, 8 F.C.C. Rec. at 7162 ¶1, 7165 ¶20.

[236] *Id.* at 7165 ¶19.

[237] Implementation of Section 309(j) of the Communications Act—Competitive Bidding, Third Report and Order, 9 F.C.C. Rec. 2941, 2945–2946 ¶10 (1994) (each license contains a single 50 kHz channel, a single 12.5 kHz channel, a 50 and a 12.5 kHz channel, *or* two 50 kHz channels).

In 1994, the Commission allocated broadband PCS[238] 120 MHz in the 1,850–1,990 MHz band.[239] This spectrum, which is suitable for mobile telephone and data services, was subdivided into six bands—three bands of 30 MHz (blocks A, B, and C) and three bands of 10 MHz (blocks D, E, and F). The 10 MHz blocks were expected to serve a variety of functions, including offering "niche" services, providing general mobile telephony service like that provided by existing cellular systems, and increasing the capacity of existing cellular, PCS, and SMR licensees.[240]

---

[238] The Commission defines broadband PCS as "[r]adio communications that encompass mobile and ancillary fixed communication services that provide services to individuals and businesses and can be integrated with a variety of competing networks." Amendment of the Commission's Rules to Establish New Personal Communications Services, Second Report and Order, 8 F.C.C. Rec. 7700, 7713 ¶24 (1993).

[239] Amendment of the Commission's Rules to Establish New Personal Communications Services, Memorandum Opinion and Order, 9 F.C.C. Rec. 4957, 4961 ¶10 (1994) (hereinafter *PCS Order*). The Commission had earlier divided spectrum for PCS between upper and lower portions of the 2 GHz band. Amendment of the Commission's Rules to Establish New Personal Communications Services, Second Report and Order, 8 F.C.C. Rec. 7700, 7725 ¶56, 7738 ¶88 (1993). A number of firms sought reconsideration, raising concerns that this allocation would be susceptible to signal interference and that the need to consolidate several different slivers of disparate spectrum to offer a commercially viable cellular-like service would create a license-swapping aftermarket following the auctions that would delay PCS implementation and drive up its costs. *See, e.g.*, Statement of Alex D. Felker, Vice President for Technology, Time Warner Telecommunications at 14–16, Amendment of the Commission's Rules to Establish New Personal Communications Services, Gen. Docket No. 90-314 (FCC Apr. 12, 1994) (en banc). Panel discussions among telecommunications industry analysts, manufacturers, and investors resulted in a plan to consolidate all PCS spectrum in the 1,850–1,990 MHz range. This was made possible by an agreement by the mobile satellite industry to swap part of its lower-band spectrum for the higher-frequency 2,100 MHz band allocation earmarked for PCS. The new spectrum allocation scheme returned the 2,180–2,200 MHz PCS allocation "to reserve status for future allocation potentially to MSS, as requested by the MSS interests," while removing "an equal amount of spectrum from potential consideration for MSS in the band 1,970–1,990 MHz." *PCS Order*, 9 F.C.C. Rec. at 4970 ¶26, 4995–4996 ¶¶94–97, 5082 app. D. The consolidation also allowed for the use of a single-band handset and thereby reduced the cost of PCS equipment to consumers. *Id.* at 4973–4974 ¶¶34–40.

[240] *PCS Order*, 9 F.C.C. Rec. at 4981 ¶60; Geographic Partitioning and Spectrum Disaggregation by Commercial Mobile Radio Services Licensees, Notice

In the same order, the Commission allocated 30 MHz of spectrum to unlicensed PCS services,[241] which, the FCC predicted, "w[ould] consist of terminal devices," such as "new cordless telephones, local area networks in offices, and other kinds of short-range communications."[242] Unlicensed PCS operations, which are not considered CMRS, must operate under very low power, which limits their range, but enables the spectrum to be reused many times.[243]

To encourage innovative uses of the PCS spectrum, the Commission adopted a policy of granting a "pioneer's preference." Recipients of such preferences were placed on a special licensing track, exempt from lotteries and comparative hearings; so long as they were otherwise qualified, they were guaranteed a license.[244] In October 1992, the Commission granted preferences for three of the more coveted broadband PCS licenses to Cox Enterprises, American Personal Communications (APC, an affiliate of the *Washington Post*), and Omnipoint Communications.[245]

---

of Proposed Rulemaking, 11 F.C.C. Rec. 10,187, 10,205 ¶39 (1996) ("10 MHz licensees may be able to provide services ranging from specialized, 'niche' applications to services comparable to those now provided by cellular systems, through the use of advanced digital techniques, such as Code Division Multiple Access (CDMA) and Time Division Multiple Access (TDMA), and microcellular technology.").

[241] *PCS Order,* 9 F.C.C. Rec. at 4990–4991 ¶¶84–87.

[242] *Section 6002(b) Second Report,* 12 F.C.C. Rec. at 11,288 n.82.

[243] *Id.*

[244] Establishment of Procedures to Provide a Preference to Applicants Proposing an Allocation for New Services, Report and Order, 6 F.C.C. Rec. 3488, 3492 ¶32 (1991). Under this program, the Commission had discretion to award a "preference" to any license applicant that had "developed an innovative proposal that leads to the establishment of a service not currently provided or a substantial enhancement of an existing service." *Id.* at 3494 ¶47. The purpose of the preference was to "foster the development of new services and improve existing services by reducing for innovators the delays and risks associated with the Commission's allocation and licensing processes." *Id.* at 3488 ¶1.

[245] *See* Amendment of the Commission's Rules to Establish New Personal Communications Services, Tentative Decision and Memorandum Opinion and Order, 7 F.C.C. Rec. 7794, 7797–7804 ¶¶6–23 (1992); Review of the Pioneer's Preference Rules, Memorandum Opinion and Order on Remand, 9 F.C.C. Rec. 4055, 4055–4056 ¶3 (1994). These tentative awards were finalized by the Commission in December of the following year. Amendment of the

The Commission also granted a pioneer's preference for a narrowband PCS license to Mobile Telecommunications Technologies Corporation (Mtel).[246]

In 1994, after several unsuccessful applicants challenged the preferences, the Commission amended its pioneer's preference regulations and ordered the "pioneers" to pay for their spectrum.[247] Mtel (which subsequently became Skytel) sued.[248] A few months later, in a rider on the General Agreement on Tariffs and Trade (GATT), Congress superseded the Commission's action.[249] Pioneers, Congress directed, were to pay 85 percent of the average per capita winning bid for the 20 most populous

---

Commission's Rules to Establish New Personal Communications Services, Third Report and Order, 9 F.C.C. Rec. 1337, 1339–1348 ¶¶7–74 (1994), *recons. pending, petitions for review filed,* Pacific Bell v. FCC, Nos. 94-1148 et al. (D.C. Cir.), *remanded on the FCC's own motion* (July 26, 1994).

[246] *New PCS Tentative Decision,* 7 F.C.C. Rec. at 5735–5736 ¶¶149–151.

[247] The decision impacted pioneer awards for broadband PCS, local multipoint distribution service (LMDS), and 1.6/2.4 GHz band low-earth orbital satellite systems (Big LEOs). Review of the Pioneer's Preference Rules, Memorandum Opinion and Order on Remand, 9 F.C.C. Rec. 4055, 4055 ¶1 (1994). The Commission decided that the pioneer grants were merely intended to "assure innovators that they would be able to obtain licenses so as to implement their innovations" rather than to "give the preference recipient a financial or competitive advantage over other licensees." *Id.* at 4058 ¶¶10–11. Uncertain of the true value of the licenses, the FCC offered the pioneers a choice: either pay 90 percent of the winning bid for the companion MTA license in the awarded service area or pay a sum equal to 90 percent of the adjusted value of the pioneer's preference license, as determined based on an average per population price for the 30 MHz licenses in the top ten MTAs. *Id.* at 4055 ¶1, 4060–4061 ¶¶20–25, 4064 ¶39.

[248] In 1996, the Court of Appeals for the District of Columbia remanded the case to the Commission. Mobile Communications Corp. of Am. v. FCC, 77 F.3d 1399 (D.C. Cir. 1996).

[249] Uruguay Round Agreements Act, Pub. L. No. 103-465, §801, 108 Stat. 4809, 5050–5053 (1994). Some small measure of controversy attended the lobbying for this bill. On September 29, 1994, the *Washington Post* ran an editorial endorsing passage of GATT. H. Rowen, The Raid on GATT, Wash. Post, Sep. 29, 1994, at A23. The *Post,* however, neglected to mention its 70 percent ownership of the broadband pioneer being awarded the Washington-Baltimore MTA. In a full-page ad that ran in the paper on October 4, Pacific Telesis accused the *Post* of trying to secure a "billion-dollar loophole" for itself. Representative John Dingell (D-Mich.) thereupon attacked the ad as "misleading and motivated by a desire to secure competitive advantage,"

license areas, excluding the pioneer's markets.[250] In the Balanced Budget Act of 1997, Congress terminated the FCC's authority to give preferential treatment to pioneers.[251]

§10.4.3.1 Geographic Coverage of PCS

The Commission based the geographic service area for PCS licenses on the Rand McNally Major Trading Areas (MTAs) and Basic Trading Areas (BTAs).[252] Such a fragmented approach, which created hundreds and hundreds of new licensing areas,

---

berating the tactic as "unknowing, ignorant, vicious and irresponsible." "Vicious, Irresponsible" Ad, Comm. Daily, Oct. 6, 1994, at 2; M. Mills, War over a "Pioneer" Provision, Wash. Post, Oct. 5, 1994, at F1. The *Washington Post* subsequently divested itself of all but a 1.5 percent minority interest in APC. Washington Post Company Divests Interest in PCS Partnership, PR Newswire, Jan. 9, 1995. In a letter to colleagues, Representative Dingell expressed the belief that the Commission did not in fact have the authority to charge for spectrum licenses and that, without legislative backing, any FCC effort to do so would be "quite possibly overturned in court," leaving government coffers empty. H. Kurtz, Post Taken to the Pillory, Wash. Post, Oct. 7, 1994, at B1. President Clinton signed GATT into law on December 8, 1994. Pub. L. 103-465, 108 Stat. 4809.

[250] Uruguay Round Agreements Act, Pub. L. No. 103-465, §801, 108 Stat. 4809, 5050–5052 (1994). The law included a price floor of $400 million for the broadband pioneer licenses. *Id.*, 108 Stat. 5052.

[251] Pub. L. No. 105-33, §3002(a)(1)(F), 111 Stat. 251 (1997). The Commission accordingly terminated the pioneer's preference program and dismissed all 13 pioneer's preference requests that remained pending before it. Dismissal of All Pending Pioneer's Preference Requests, Order, 12 F.C.C. Rec. 14,006 (1997), *recons. denied,* 13 F.C.C. Rec. 11,485 (1998).

[252] *PCS Order,* 9 F.C.C. Rec. at 4969 ¶24, 4987–4988 ¶¶75–79. Rand McNally partitions the 50 states and the District of Columbia into 47 MTAs and 487 BTAs. *See* Rand McNally, 1993 Commercial Atlas & Marketing Guide 38–39 (124th ed. 1993). MTAs serve as regional units "of wholesaling, distribution, banking, and specialized services such as advertising" and can sprawl across several states. *Id.* at 4, 38–39. Within each MTA are two or more BTAs, which represent community units of "specialized services, such as medical care, entertainment, higher education and a daily newspaper," serving as the areas in which consumers will generally remain for most shopping goods purchases; a BTA can thus include from a single to dozens of counties. *Id.* The Commission supplemented the Rand McNally list by defining additional MTAs and BTAs for Puerto Rico, the U.S. Virgin Islands, Guam, the Northern Mariana Islands, and American Samoa. *PCS Order,* 9 F.C.C. Rec. at 4969 n.23.

was likely to promote the statutory objective of "avoiding excessive concentration of licenses and . . . disseminating licenses among a wide variety of applicants."[253]

For narrowband PCS, the Commission created 11 channels providing nationwide service, 6 channels for each of 5 large regional subdivisions, 7 channels for each of 51 MTAs, 2 channels for each of 492 local BTAs, and 8 additional channels for existing paging licensees.[254] Thus, in total, the two megahertz of narrowband PCS spectrum created over 5,000 new licensing opportunities. The FCC initially imposed strict minimum coverage requirements on the narrowband licensees.[255] But, in 1997, the Commission proposed to relax these standards, requiring only that a licensee provide "substantial service" in the licensing area within five years.[256]

For broadband PCS, the Commission licensed two of the 30 MHz blocks (blocks A and B) in each of the 51 MTAs; the third 30 MHz block (block C) and the three 10 MHz blocks (blocks D, E, and F) were licensed in each of the 493 BTAs.[257] All broadband PCS licensees are subject to certain minimum construction (or "build-out") requirements.[258]

---

[253] 47 U.S.C. §309(j)(3)(B).

[254] Implementation of Section 309(j) of the Communications Act—Competitive Bidding, Third Report and Order, 9 F.C.C. Rec. 2941, 2945–2946 ¶10 (1994). Each license contains a single 50 kHz channel, a single 12.5 kHz channel, a 50 and a 12.5 kHz channel, *or* two 50 kHz channels. *Id.* In its first pass at drawing up narrowband service boundaries, the Commission did not adopt any large regional license areas; instead, these six spectrum blocks had been reserved for additional MTA licensing. Amendment of the Commission's Rules to Establish New Narrowband Personal Communications Services, First Report and Order, 8 F.C.C. Rec. 7162, 7167 ¶¶27–28 (1993).

[255] *Id.* at 7168 ¶37; Amendment of the Commission's Rules to Establish New Narrowband Personal Communications Services, Memorandum Opinion and Order, 9 F.C.C. Rec. 1309, 1313–1314 ¶¶27–34 (1994).

[256] Amendment of the Commission's Rules to Establish New Personal Communications Services, Narrowband PCS, Report and Order and Further Notice of Proposed Rulemaking, 12 F.C.C. Rec. 12,972, 12,995–12,996 ¶¶43–44 (1997).

[257] *PCS Order,* 9 F.C.C. Rec. at 4988 ¶78. This order modified the Commission's original plan for allocating broadband PCS spectrum. *See id.* at 4969–4970 ¶¶24–26.

[258] *Id.* at 5018–5020 ¶¶154–157.

§10.4.3.2   PCS Auctions

In the Omnibus Budget Reconciliation Act of 1993, Congress authorized the Commission to use competitive bidding procedures to award certain electromagnetic spectrum licenses, such as PCS.[259] The statute requires that the Commission, in designing a bidding system, "disseminat[e] licenses among a wide variety of applicants, including small businesses, rural telephone companies, and businesses owned by members of minority groups and women" (referred to collectively as "designated entities").[260] The Commission developed what it termed an "innovative methodology"—the "simultaneous multiple-round auction"—in the hopes that it would help achieve this objective and avoid over- or undervaluation of the licenses.[261]

With the same goal in mind, the Commission decided to allow applicants to form cooperative agreements in bidding. The Commission recognized that the formation of bidding consortia could "reduce entry barriers for smaller firms, and improve their

---

[259] Omnibus Budget Reconciliation Act of 1993, Pub. L. No. 103-66, Title VI, §6002(a), 107 Stat. 387–392 (1993).

[260] 47 U.S.C. §309(j)(3)(B); FCC Wireless Telecommunications Bureau, FCC Report to Congress on Spectrum Auctions at 21, WT Docket No. 97-150 (Oct. 9, 1997) (hereinafter *FCC Report to Congress on Spectrum Auctions*).

[261] *FCC Report to Congress on Spectrum Auctions* at 3; Implementation of Section 309(j) of the Communications Act—Competitive Bidding, Second Report and Order, 9 F.C.C. Rec. 2348, 2366–2367 ¶¶106–108 (1994) (hereinafter *Second Competitive Bidding Order*). In a simultaneous multiple-round auction, bidders submit offers electronically on one or more individual properties, assess the results of that round's bidding, and then continue adjusting their bids upward until no new bids are offered. Martin Spicer, FCC, International Survey of Spectrum Assignment for Cellular and PCS, Sponsored by the Wireless Telecommunications Bureau (Sept. 1996) <http://www.fcc.gov/wtb/auctions/papers/spicer.html>. The procedure is somewhat complicated by activity rules, stopping rules, bidding limitations (which are in turn contingent on upfront payment levels), and other mechanisms designed to aid the Commission in managing the auctions. *See* 47 C.F.R. §§24.701–24.708. According to auction theory, the tendency to inflate or deflate the bids for auctioned goods is lessened as participants are given feedback concerning other bidders' estimates of the goods' value. This increases certainty, which should raise bids all around and facilitate the efficient aggregation of interdependent licenses. *Second Competitive Bidding Order*, 9 F.C.C. Rec. at 2363–2364 ¶¶89–94.

ability to compete in the auction process and in the provision of service."[262] While the Commission withheld the bidders' identities during the auction, required disclosure of cooperative bidding arrangements, and prohibited discussions between bidders at certain times, it imposed no restrictions on the terms of cooperative agreements.[263] The Commission relied instead on antitrust law to limit undue levels of collusion among bidders.[264]

Conducted by the Commission in July 1994, the first PCS auction sold ten nationwide narrowband licenses for approximately $650 million dollars—about ten times preauction projections.[265] The 30 regional licenses (6 licenses in each of the five regions) were sold for more than $390 million in a second wave of auctions that began in October 1994.[266] Four companies won licenses in each of the five regions, thus providing them with national coverage.[267] As of yet, there have been no auctions for the

---

[262] *Id.* at 2387 ¶222.

[263] *See id.* at 2387–2388 ¶¶224–225; Implementation of Section 309(j) of the Communications Act—Competitive Bidding, Fifth Report and Order, 9 F.C.C. Rec. 5532, 5570–5571 ¶91 (1994) (hereinafter *Fifth Competitive Bidding Order*); Implementation of Section 309(j) of the Communications Act—Competitive Bidding Narrowband PCS, Third Memorandum Opinion and Order and Further Notice of Proposed Rulemaking, 10 F.C.C. Rec. 175, 188–190 ¶¶26–31 (1994) (hereinafter *Third Narrowband Order*). The FCC required only that bidders identify in their preauction applications "any parties with whom they have entered into any consortium arrangements, joint ventures, partnerships or other agreements or understandings which relate in any way to the competitive bidding process"; collaborate and discuss bidding only with parties who were named on their preauction applications; and if their bid was successful, disclose the terms and conditions of any such arrangements in their postauction application. *Second Competitive Bidding Order,* 9 F.C.C. Rec. at 2387–2388 ¶225.

[264] *Id.* Sanctions for bid-rigging, market allocation agreements, or other bidding arrangements that violate the antitrust laws may include license forfeiture and exclusion from future auctions. *Id.* at 2388 ¶226.

[265] *FCC Report to Congress on Spectrum Auctions* at 10. This total selling price includes the high bids from the auction, plus the price paid for a pioneer preference license.

[266] *Id.*

[267] PCS Development Corp., PageMart (backed by Morgan Stanley), MobileMedia PCS, and Advanced Wireless Messaging (a subsidiary of American Paging, which in turn is 85 percent owned by Telephone & Data Systems) each knit together nationwide coverage by winning a license in each of the

MTA and BTA narrowband licenses, nor have such auctions been scheduled.[268]

In compliance with congressionally imposed time constraints,[269] the FCC began auctioning broadband PCS licenses in the winter of 1994. The auction for A- and B-block 30 MHz licenses ran from December 1994 through March 1995. All block A and B licenses that were not already awarded to pioneers—99 licenses in all—were auctioned during that period.[270] At the outset of this auction, 62 entities had been accepted by the Commission to participate in the bidding.[271] This auction raised over $7.7 billion, including the price paid by the three pioneers.[272] The initial C-block auction was held from December 1995 to May 1996; in July 1996, the Commission held a second C-block auction to reauction several licenses on which the winning bidder

---

five regional areas. *See* Narrowband PCS Regional Auction Winners Re: Applications Accepted for Filing, Public Notice, Report No. CN-95-1, 1994 FCC LEXIS 6288 (Dec. 9, 1994). This aggregation strategy was not without some cost, however. The Commission calculated that, on average, bidders paid $3.10 per MHz per person in the nationwide narrowband auctions; in the regional auctions, this figure rose to $3.46. *FCC Report to Congress on Spectrum Auctions* at 10.

[268] Truth-in-Billing and Billing Format, Notice of Proposed Rulemaking, 13 F.C.C. Rec. 18,176, 18,198–18,199 ¶55 (1998).

[269] Omnibus Budget Reconciliation Act of 1993, Pub. L. No. 103-66, Title VI, §6002(d)(2)(B), 107 Stat. 396–397 (1993) (Commission must commence issuing PCS licenses within 270 days after the date of enactment, August 10, 1993).

[270] *FCC Report to Congress on Spectrum Auctions* at 10; Auction Notice and Filing Requirements for 99 MTA Licenses Located on the A and B Blocks for Personal Communications Services in the 2 GHz Band, Public Notice, Rpt. No. AUC-94-04, 1994 FCC LEXIS 4602 (Sept. 19, 1994).

[271] The identity and the identification numbers of these bidders were disclosed a month before the auction; thus, unlike the nationwide narrowband auction, broadband MTA licensee hopefuls knew in advance against whom they were to bid. 62 Applications Are Accepted to Participate in the December 5, 1994, Broadband PCS Auction, Public Notice, 1994 FCC LEXIS 5732 (Nov. 10, 1994). Roughly one-third of these entities applied to bid on at least 50 different MTA licenses. *Id.*

[272] *FCC Report to Congress on Spectrum Auctions* at 10; Commercial Mobile Radio Service Information: Announcing the Winning Bidders in the FCC's Auction of 99 Licenses to Provide Broadband PCS in Major Trading Areas, Public Notice, 1995 FCC LEXIS 1731 (Mar. 13, 1995).

had already defaulted.[273] In all, 493 30 MHz BTA licenses sold for well over $10 billion.[274] The D-, E-, and F-block auctions began in August 1996 and concluded in January 1997; almost 1,500 licenses were sold for a total $2.5 billion.[275] Thus, the broadband PCS auctions alone raised $20 billion for the U.S. Treasury—not all of which has been (or likely will be) collected.

As discussed in section 10.3.8, Congress directed that the auction of PCS spectrum allow for "small businesses, rural telephone companies, and businesses owned by members of minority groups and women" to participate.[276] For such "designated entities" participating in the first PCS auction (of nationwide narrowband licenses), the Commission adopted specific preferences, such as installment payment options, tax certificates, and bidding credits.[277] The Commission, however, was disappointed with designated entities' participation and success in the auction.[278] The FCC therefore relaxed the standards for qualifying as a "small business" in the regional narrowband auctions.[279] The Commission also proposed that four MTA blocks and two BTA blocks in each market be reserved exclusively for bidding by

[273] *FCC Report to Congress on Spectrum Auctions* at 10.
[274] *FCC Report to Congress on Spectrum Auctions* at 10.
[275] *Id.*
[276] 47 U.S.C. §309(j)(3)(B), (4)(D). To achieve this goal, the Commission was directed to consider the use of "tax certificates, bidding, preferences," "alternative payment schedules and methods of calculation, including lump sums or guaranteed installment payments, with or without royalty payments, or other schedules or methods." 47 U.S.C. §309(j)(4)(A), (D), 309(j)(4)(C)(ii).
[277] Implementation of Section 309(j) of the Communications Act—Competitive Bidding, Third Report and Order, 9 F.C.C. Rec. 2941, 2968–2979 ¶¶66–89 (1994). Installment payment options were extended to small businesses bidding in the BTA, MTA, or regional narrowband auctions, and tax certificates were to be issued to minority- and female-owned enterprises. *Id.* at 2968–69 ¶68. Minority- and female-owned businesses were also entitled to bidding credits of up to 25 percent. *Id.*
[278] *Third Narrowband Order,* 10 F.C.C. Rec. at 208 ¶73.
[279] Under the new limit, a small business was defined as any firm, together with its affiliates and certain investors, that had an average of less than $40 million in gross revenues during the preceding three years. *Id.* at 196 ¶46. The previous standard was $6 million in net income after federal income taxes. *Id.* at 194 ¶42.

designated entities and that additional preferences apply to these "entrepreneurs' blocks."[280] But in 1997, the Commission reversed course and decided against establishing entrepreneurs' blocks for narrowband licenses.[281] After the Supreme Court's decisions in *Adarand* and *VMI*,[282] the Commission expressed doubt whether any of its race- or gender-based preferences for narrowband services were constitutional.[283] It therefore proposed to offer preferences only to small businesses.[284]

The Commission pressed ahead with "entrepreneurs' blocks" for *broadband* PCS licenses. In 1994, the FCC designated the C and F blocks in each market as "entrepreneurs' blocks"—for these licenses, large companies with more than $125 million in annual gross revenues or $500 million or more in assets were prohibited from bidding.[285] Entities eligible to participate in the entrepreneurs' block auctions were to receive bidding credits of up to 25 percent, a tax certificate, and an installment payment option if they also qualified as a minority- and/or women-owned business, a small business, or both.[286]

But just before the start of the C-block auction, the Supreme Court issued its decision in *Adarand*.[287] Telephone Electronics Corp. (TEC) swiftly filed a lawsuit in the D.C. Circuit. The court stayed the auction pending a determination of the constitution-

---

[280] *Id.* at 208–209 ¶¶74–76.

[281] Amendment of the Commission's Rules to Establish New Personal Communications Services, Narrowband PCS, Report and Order and Further Notice of Proposed Rulemaking, 12 F.C.C. Rec. 12,972, 12,984 ¶¶19–20 (1997) (hereinafter *Narrowband PCS Order*).

[282] Adarand Constructors, Inc. v. Pena, 515 U.S. 200 (1995); United States v. Virginia, 518 U.S. 515 (1996).

[283] *Narrowband PCS Order,* 12 F.C.C. Rec. at 13,004–13,005 ¶¶61–63.

[284] *Id.* at 13,005 ¶64.

[285] *Fifth Competitive Bidding Order,* 9 F.C.C. Rec. at 5580 ¶113.

[286] *Id.* at 5581 ¶114. The FCC later clarified that designated entity provisions for women- and minority-owned businesses were distinct from those for small businesses in general; as a result, women- and minority-owned entities could qualify for their provisions regardless of size, and small businesses could qualify for their provisions regardless of ownership. Implementation of Section 309(j) of the Communications Act—Competitive Bidding, Second Memorandum Opinion and Order, 9 F.C.C. Rec. 7245, 7267 ¶131 (1994).

[287] Adarand Constructors, Inc. v. Pena, 515 U.S. 200 (1995).

ality of the FCC's designated entity rules.[288] In April 1995, the FCC authorized TEC to participate in the designated entity auctions; in return, TEC agreed to drop its suit against the Commission.[289] In light of this challenge and the decision in *Adarand,* the Commission eliminated all race- and gender-based provisions applicable to its C-block rules, defining all entrepreneur preferences solely in terms of a firm's revenue and assets.[290] That decision was upheld on appeal.[291]

Eighteen licensees from the initial C-block auction defaulted on their installment payments, and the Commission opted to reauction the licenses in July 1996.[292] After several more licensees informed the Commission in early 1997 of difficulty in making installment payments, the Commission suspended the deadline for payment of C-block installment payments on March 31, 1997.[293] The suspension was not enough to save one of the largest auction winners, Pocket Communications, Inc., from filing for bankruptcy protection the next day.[294] The Commission suspended payment obligations for F-block licenses on April 28,

[288] Telephone Elec. Corp. v. FCC, No. 95-1015, 1996 U.S. App. LEXIS 4942 (D.C. Cir. Mar. 15, 1996). The court dissolved the stay on May 1, 1995. Telephone Elec. Corp. v. FCC, No. 95-1015, 1995 U.S. App. LEXIS 15337 (D.C. Cir. May 1, 1995).

[289] *See* TEC Drops Court Suit Against FCC's Entrepreneurs Auction, Common Carrier Week, Apr. 24, 1995.

[290] Implementation of Section 309(j) of the Communications Act — Competitive Bidding, Sixth Report and Order, 11 F.C.C. Rec. 136 (1995).

[291] Omnipoint Corp. v. FCC, 78 F.3d 620 (D.C. Cir. 1996).

[292] Amendment of the Commission's Rules Regarding Installment Payment Financing for Personal Communications Services Licensees, Fourth Report and Order, 13 F.C.C. Rec. 15,743, 15,744–15,745 ¶2 & n.7 (1998). The Commission's regulations allow the Commission to either reauction the forfeited license or offer it to the next highest bidder. 47 C.F.R. §1.2109.

[293] Installment Payments for PCS Licenses, Order, 12 F.C.C. Rec. 17,325 (1997).

[294] Communications; Firms Tune In on Satellite Radio Licenses, Chi. Trib., Apr. 2, 1997, at 2. Pocket paid $1.4 billion for 43 C-block licenses. *Id.* As a result of heavy competitive bidding and inflated projections on the value of these licenses, several large bidders, including Pocket, paid considerably more for their licenses than bidders in the A- and B-block auctions. Amendment of the Commission's Rules Regarding Installment Payment Financing for Personal Communications Services (PCS) Licenses, Second Report and Order and Further Notice of Proposed Rule Making, 12 F.C.C. Rec. 16,436, 16,442

1997.[295] In October 1997, the Commission gave each C-block winner four options: resume payment on its debt in full;[296] disaggregate half of its spectrum (15 of the 30 MHz) and earn a credit for the returned portion;[297] surrender *all* of the licenses and, in return, have all outstanding debt forgiven;[298] or prepay selective licenses of its choosing and surrender the others to the Commission.[299] Each licensee was asked to choose among these options by January 15, 1998,[300] a deadline that was later extended to June 8, 1998.[301] Unhappy with the options, General Wireless Inc. and NextWave Telecom Inc., winners of 14 and 63 C-block licenses, respectively, filed for bankruptcy.[302]

¶10 (1997) (hereinafter *Second Report on Installment Payment*), *modified on recons.*, Order on Reconsideration of the Second Report and Order, 13 F.C.C. Rec. 8345, *further recons. pending*. General Wireless, Inc., and Pocket Communications both filed for bankruptcy protection, where General Wireless was relieved from almost all its payments to the Commission. The Commission's appeal is pending as of this writing.

[295] FCC Announces Grant of Broadband Personal Communication Services D, E, and F Block BTA Licenses, Public Notice, 13 F.C.C. Rec. 1286, 1287 (1997).

[296] *Second Report on Installment Payment*, 12 F.C.C. at 16,439–16,440 ¶6.

[297] *Id.* at 16,439 ¶6, 16,455–16,458 ¶¶38–45.

[298] *Id.* at 16,439–16,440 ¶6, 16,462–16,464 ¶¶53–58.

[299] *Id.* at 16,440 ¶6, 16,467–16,470 ¶¶64–69. The Commission declined to extend the same options to participants in the F-block auction. *Id.* at 16,439 ¶6. For the 800 MHz SMR and LMDS auctions, the Commission elected not to offer an installment payment option to winning bidders; however, bidding credits were extended to small businesses and entrepreneurs. Auction of 800 MHz Specialized Mobile Radio Service Licenses, Public Notice, 13 F.C.C. Rec. 1857 (1997); Rulemaking to Amend Parts 1, 2, 21, and 25 of the Commission's Rules to Redesignate the 27.5–29.5 GHz Frequency Band, Second Order on Reconsideration, 12 F.C.C. Rec. 15,082 (1997).

[300] *Second Report on Installment Payment*, 12 F.C.C. Rec. at 16,470 ¶70.

[301] Wireless Telecommunications Bureau Announces June 8, 1998 Election Date for Broadband PCS C Block Licensees, Public Notice, 13 F.C.C. Rec. 7413 (1998).

[302] Bankruptcy Court Reduces Value of PCS Licenses, Communications Today, Apr. 28, 1998 (General Wireless declared bankruptcy in October 1997); NextWave, Biggest C-Block Bidder, Declares Bankruptcy, Mobile Communications Report, June 15, 1998 (NextWave declared bankruptcy on June 8, 1998). In April 1998, a bankruptcy judge revalued General Wireless's 14 licenses at $166 million, reducing the company's payment obligation by $954 million. *Id.* The FCC's appeal of this decision was pending at the time of this

Other auction winners elected to return large chunks of spectrum to the Commission. At least 144 licenses have or will be returned in full, along with portions of another 119.[303] The Commission's resolution of C-block problems—problems created by the Commission's own mismanagement of the auctions—has been widely and properly criticized for subverting the fairness and purpose of the entire auction process.[304] The biggest losers are, of course, those who actually came up with the money for what they bid, paying a price driven sky high by deadbeat interlopers.

§10.4.4 Allocation of Spectrum for Specialized Mobile Radio

Specialized mobile radio (SMR) and enhanced SMR (ESMR, also known as wide-area SMR) compete directly with cellular and broadband PCS in the market for mobile telephony.[305] From its inception in 1974 until the mid-1990s, SMR was used almost exclusively to provide dispatch services.[306] But recent develop-

---

writing. But Congress may step in. The Clinton Administration has included among the initiatives in its fiscal 2000 budget plan a proposal that would remove all spectrum licenses (including paging, dispatch radio, cellular, PCS, and broadcast) from the protection of the bankruptcy laws. J. Silva, Kennard Denies Improper Bankruptcy Lobbying, Radio Comm. Report, Apr. 19, 1999, at 17.

[303] Telephony, Comm. Daily, July 6, 1998. Licenses belonging to Pocket Communications were not included. *Id.*

[304] *See, e.g.,* Statement of Commissioner Susan Ness Concurring in Part, Dissenting in Part, Amendment of the Commission's Rules Regarding Installment Payment Financing for Personal Communications Services (PCS) Licensees, Order on Reconsideration of the Second Report and Order, 13 F.C.C. Rec. 8345, 8390–8394 (1998).

[305] Implementation of Section 6002(b) of the Omnibus Budget Reconciliation Act of 1993, Third Report, 13 F.C.C. Rec. 19,746, 19,786–19,787 (1998). For a general discussion of SMR, see Cellnet Communications v. FCC, 149 F.3d 429, 433 (6th Cir. 1998).

[306] Amendment of Part 90 of the Commission's Rules to Facilitate Future Development of SMR Systems in the 800 MHz Frequency Band, Further Notice of Proposed Rule Making, 10 F.C.C. Rec. 7970, 7974–7975 ¶3 (1994) (hereinafter *SMR Further Notice*).

ments in digital technologies have enabled SMR providers to offer a competitive real-time, two-way switched voice service that is interconnected with the public switched network either on a stand-alone basis or packaged with other telecommunications services.[307]

The Commission initially allocated SMR services roughly 14 MHz of spectrum in the 800 MHz band; the spectrum was divided into 280 channels (of 50 kHz each), 200 of which are contained in a contiguous 10 MHz block, while the remaining 80 channels are divided into eight blocks with other mobile services in between.[308] Licensees of this first batch of SMR spectrum were awarded either one or five channels at a time on a station-by-station basis, with geographic coverage defined by location, antenna height, and transmitter power of the individual base station.[309]

In 1986, the Commission allocated 200 channel pairs in the 900 MHz band for SMR to alleviate congestion in the 800 MHz SMR band.[310] Four years later the Commission provided an additional 150 channels in the 800 MHz band for possible SMR use.[311]

In the 1993 Budget Act, Congress ordered that all substantially similar commercial mobile services be regulated alike. As explained above, Congress took this action in part because SMR

---

[307] *Id.; see also* Chadmoore Communications, Inc. v. FCC, 113 F.3d 235, 237 (D.C. Cir. 1997) ("In recent years, . . . emerging SMR technologies have enabled licensees to offer their customers sophisticated voice and data transmission services over extensive areas (e.g., two-way acknowledgment paging, credit card authorization, automatic vehicle location, remote database access, and voice mail).").

[308] *SMR Further Notice,* 10 F.C.C. Rec. at 7974 ¶3. Not all of the 14 MHz is available in the Canadian and Mexican border areas. *Id.* at 7974 n.5.

[309] *Id.* at 7975 ¶3.

[310] Amendment of Parts 2 and 90 of the Commission's Rules to Provide for the Use of 200 Channels Outside the Designated Filing Areas in the 896–901 MHz and the 935–940 MHz Bands Allotted to the Specialized Mobile Radio Pool, Second Order on Reconsideration and Seventh Report and Order, 11 F.C.C. Rec. 2639, 2647 ¶22 (1995). The actual bands appear at 896–901 MHz and 935–940 MHz, but are generally referred to as the 900 MHz SMR bands.

[311] *SMR Further Notice,* 10 F.C.C. Rec. at 7974–7975 ¶3.

providers were offering a service comparable to cellular and PCS, but were regulated under an entirely different set of rules.[312] As a result of Congress's action, the Commission ruled that all SMR systems providing interconnected service would be classified as CMRS, while all others would be classified as PMRS.[313]

Soon thereafter, the Commission proposed, and later adopted, a new comprehensive regulatory structure for licensing SMR providers. First, the Commission decided to relicense, by auction, the 900 MHz SMR band in 20 ten-channel blocks (five MHz) using MTAs as the geographic service areas.[314] The Commission then reapportioned the upper 10 MHz block of 800 MHz spectrum by dividing it into three licenses: block A was allocated one MHz (20 channels), block B three MHz (60 channels), and block C six MHz (120 channels).[315] Each set of these licenses covers one of the 175 Economic Areas (EAs).[316]

During the first SMR auction, held December 1995 to April 1996, the Commission sold 1,020 900 MHz licenses for over $200 million.[317] In December 1997, the FCC completed its auction of 525 SMR licenses of the upper 200 channels in the 800 MHz band, raising an additional $96 million for the U.S.

---

[312] *Communications Act Second Report,* 9 F.C.C. Rec. at 1415–1416 ¶7, 1417 ¶11; *see also* §10.2.

[313] *Communications Act Second Report,* 9 F.C.C. Rec. at 1417 ¶11.

[314] *Communications Act Third Report,* 9 F.C.C. Rec. at 8050–8051 ¶¶114–115. Incumbent 900 MHz licensees were required to obtain the relevant MTA license at auction, or obtain consent from the MTA licensee, to continue operating. *Id.* at 8052 ¶¶118–119.

[315] Amendment of Part 90 of the Commission's Rules to Facilitate Future Development of SMR Systems in the 800 MHz Frequency Band, First Report and Order, Eighth Report and Order, and Second Further Notice of Proposed Rule Making, 11 F.C.C. Rec. 1463, 1469 ¶3, 1489–1490 ¶37 (1995).

[316] *Id.* at 1484 ¶25. The Commission decided that EAs, which are geographic units devised by the Bureau of Economic Analysis of the Department of Commerce, were preferable because an EA is smaller than an MTA and hence will encourage small- and medium-sized firms to bid for areas where otherwise providers might have little interest to serve. *Id.* at 1468 n.3, 1483 ¶23.

[317] *FCC Report to Congress on Spectrum Auctions* at 11.

[318] 800 MHz SMR Auction Closes, Public Notice, 12 F.C.C. Rec. 20,417 (1997).

[319] See discussion of Nextel at §10.3.5.

Treasury.[318] Nextel[319] dominated this auction: spending over $88 million, it won 475 of the 525 available licenses to obtain all 10 MHz in almost every EA across the country.[320]

§10.4.5   Allocation of Spectrum for Mobile Satellite Service

The next generation of mobile services is now operational. Back in 1990, mobile satellite service (MSS) operators first proposed to use a low-earth orbit (LEO) satellite to provide global voice, data, and possibly video services to the public.[321] In January 1994, the FCC allocated 33 MHz of spectrum to MSS—one band from 1,610 to 1,626.5 MHz and another from 2,483.5 to 2,500 MHz.[322] The Commission ordered that 5.15 MHz of spectrum (1,621.35–1,626.5 MHz) operate using a frequency division multiple access/time division multiple access (FDMA/TDMA) system, while the remaining spectrum would operate

[320] 800 MHz SMR Auction Closes, Public Notice, 12 F.C.C. Rec. 20,417, 20,424–20,449 attachment A; Nextel News Release, Nextel Strengthens Spectrum Position in FCC Auction, Dec. 9, 1997.

[321] Amendment of the Commission's Rules to Establish Rules and Policies Pertaining to a Mobile Satellite Service in the 1610–1626.5/2483.5–2500 MHz Frequency Bands, Report and Order, 9 F.C.C. Rec. 5936, 5941–5942 ¶6 (1994).

[322] Amendment of Section 2.106 of the Commission's Rules to Allocate the 1610–1626.5 MHz and the 2483.5–2500 MHz Bands for Use by the Mobile-Satellite Service, Including Non-geostationary Satellites, Report and Order, 9 F.C.C. Rec. 536 (1994).

[323] Amendment of the Commission's Rules to Establish Rules and Policies Pertaining to a Mobile Satellite Service in the 1610–1626.5/2483.5–2500 MHz Frequency Band, Memorandum Opinion and Order, 11 F.C.C. Rec. 12,861, 12,863 ¶8 (1996) (hereinafter *MSS Order*). The future applicants for MSS licenses debated the virtues of the two technologies. With FDMA/TDMA, the available spectrum is subdivided into smaller bands allocated to individual users, i.e., frequency division; and each user is assigned two time slots—one for sending and one for receiving—within a repetitive time frame, i.e., time division. R. Nelson, Iridium: From Concept to Reality, Via Satellite, Sept. 1, 1998 (hereinafter Nelson, Iridium). "During each time slot, the digital data are burst between the mobile handset and the satellite." *Id.* With CDMA, "the signal from each user is modulated by a pseudo-random noise (PRN) code. All users share the same spectrum. At the receiver, the desired signal is extracted

using a code division multiple access (CDMA) technology.[323] This would allow the Commission to license up to five LEO systems.[324] Because spectrum is scarce, the Commission imposed rigorous technical and financial standards on MSS applicants.[325] To promote competition in the MSS market, the Commission adopted policies in 1997 that permit non-U.S. licensed satellites to provide services in the United States.[326]

MSS licensing began on January 31, 1995.[327] Projects currently under way include Iridium, Teledesic, Globalstar, and Ellipso. Iridium, an international consortium headed by Motorola, developed a 66-satellite system to offer services equivalent to those of PCS[328] and began providing commercial service on November 1, 1998.[329] Teledesic, backed by Bill Gates, Craig McCaw, Motorola, Saudi Prince Alwaleed Bin Talal, and Boeing, has proposed a $9 billion constellation of over 288 satellites to "provide broadband telecommunications services primarily to

---

from the entire population of signals by multiplying by a replica code and performing an auto-correlation process. The key to the success of this method is the existence of sufficient PRN codes that appear to be mathematically orthogonal to one another. Major advantages cited by CDMA proponents are inherently greater capacity and higher spectral efficiency. Frequency reuse clusters can be small because interference is reduced between neighboring cells." *Id.*

[324] *MSS Order,* 11 F.C.C. Rec. at 12,863 ¶8.

[325] The key qualifications were that all applicants must use nongeostationary orbits, must be capable of serving the entire world (excluding the poles), and must demonstrate sufficient committed capital to fund the project. Amendment of the Commission's Rules to Establish Rules and Policies Pertaining to a Mobile Satellite Service in the 1610–1626.5/2483.5–2500 MHz Frequency Bands, Report and Order, 9 F.C.C. Rec. 5936, 5944–5954 ¶¶11–42 (1994).

[326] Amendment of the Commission's Regulatory Policies to Allow Non-U.S. Licensed Space Stations to Provide Domestic and International Satellite Service in the United States, Report and Order, 12 F.C.C. Rec. 24,094 (1997).

[327] *See MSS Order,* 11 F.C.C. Rec. at 12,864 ¶11 (licenses granted to Iridium, Globalstar, and Odyssey, but withheld from Ellipso and Aries pending further evaluation of their financial qualifications). Ellipso and Aries received their licenses in June 1997. Nelson, Iridium. In December 1997, TRW dropped its Odyssey project. *Id.*

[328] For a detailed discussion of Iridium's history, technology, equipment, financing, and prospective market, see Nelson, Iridium.

[329] M. Mills, On Guard Against LEO, Wash. Post, Nov. 2, 1998, at F23.

fixed users—the satellite equivalent of a fiber-optic access link."[330] Teledesic plans to begin providing commercial services in 2003.[331] Globalstar, which plans to begin rolling out voice, data, fax, and other telecommunications services to users worldwide in late 1999, has already launched a portion of its satellite fleet.[332] Beginning in 2001, Mobile Communications Holdings' Ellipso system will, the company hopes, provide voice and data services to areas of the world with insufficient telecommunications infrastructure.[333]

§10.4.6 Allocation of Spectrum for Other Wireless Services

The Commission has auctioned spectrum for use in providing many other wireless services, including wireless communications service (WCS), 218–219 MHz service, digital audio radio service (DARS), direct broadcast satellite (DBS) service, multipoint/multichannel distribution service (MDS or MMDS), local multipoint distribution service (LMDS), and 220 MHz service. As of this writing, the Commission has auctioned over 4,300 such wireless licenses for over $22 billion.[334] How much of that total will actually be collected remains in doubt.

---

[330] Teledesic Press Release, Teledesic Applauds Launch of Iridium's Global Phone Service, Nov. 2, 1998; Teledesic, Fast Facts <http://www.teledesic.com/overview/fastfact.html>.

[331] *Id.*

[332] Globalstar, Global Star Press Releases, <http:www.globalstar.com/news/releases/index.htm>. First Globalstar Satellites in Orbit, PR Newswire, Feb. 17, 1998; Prepared Testimony of Betty C. Alewine, President and CEO, COMSAT Corporation, Before the Senate Commerce, Science, and Transportation Committee, Subcommittee on Communications, S. 3265: The International Satellite Communications Reform Act of 1998, Sept. 10, 1998. Funds for the $275 million project were raised through a consortium including Qualcomm, Alcatel Espace, Pacific Telesis, Alenia, Vodafone, Space Systems/Loral, Dacom, Deutsche Aerospace, and Hyundai. L. Manuta, Reaching the Ends of the Earth, Satellite Communications, June 1994, at 17.

[333] Ellipso, Ellipso Home Page <http://www.ellipso.com>.

[334] *FCC Report to Congress on Spectrum Auctions* at 11.

§10.4.6.1   Wireless Communications Service

The Commission defines WCS broadly as "a wireless service which can be used for fixed, mobile, radiolocation, and digital audio broadcasting satellite uses."[335] In fact, the FCC intentionally placed few restrictions on the use of the spectrum, concluding that allowing "a broad range of services to be provided on this spectrum" will encourage "the development and deployment of new telecommunications services and products to consumers."[336]

WCS operates in the 2.3 GHz frequency band (2,305–2,320 MHz and 2,345–2,360 MHz).[337] The Commission divided this spectrum into four blocks—two blocks (A and B) of 10 MHz and two blocks (C and D) of 5 MHz.[338] The FCC designed the geographic services area for WCS by aggregating EAs into Major Economic Areas (MEAs) and still larger Regional Economic Area Groupings (REAGs). Blocks A and B span the country's 52 MEAs, and blocks C and D cover the 12 REAGs.[339] In April 1997, the Commission auctioned all 128 WCS licenses for over $13

---

[335] Biennial Regulatory Review—Amendment of Parts 0, 1, 13, 22, 24, 26, 27, 80, 87, 90, 95, 97, and 101 of the Commission's Rules to Facilitate the Development and Use of the Universal Licensing System in the Wireless Telecommunications Services, Notice of Proposed Rulemaking, 13 F.C.C. Rec. 9672, 10,066 app. P ¶18 (1998); Amendment of the Commission's Rules to Establish Part 27, the Wireless Communications Service ("WCS"), Report and Order, 12 F.C.C. Rec. 10,785, 10,797–10,798 ¶25 (1997) (hereinafter *WCS Order*).

[336] *WCS Order,* 12 F.C.C. Rec. at 10,798 ¶26; *see also id.* at 10,797–10,798 ¶25 ("WCS licensees themselves will determine the specific services they will provide within their assigned spectrum and geographic areas.").

[337] *Id.* at 10,787 ¶2. The Appropriations Act of 1997 directed the Commission to reallocate the use of the frequencies at 2,305–2,320 MHz and 2,345–2,360 MHz to wireless services and to assign the use of these frequencies by competitive bidding. The Appropriations Act also required the Commission to hold competitive bidding no later than April 15, 1997, and to ensure that all proceeds of the competitive bidding were deposited in the U.S. Treasury by September 30, 1997. Omnibus Consolidated Appropriations Act, 1997, Pub. L. No. 104-208, 110 Stat. 3009 (1996).

[338] *WCS Order,* 12 F.C.C. Rec. at 10,787 ¶4, 10,807–10,808 ¶45.

[339] *Id.* at 10,814 ¶54.

million.[340] The licenses were granted for a ten-year term, with a renewal expectancy at the end of that term.[341]

§10.4.6.2   218–219 MHz Service

The Commission defines 218–219 MHz service, until recently called interactive video and data service or IVDS, as "a point-to-multipoint, multipoint-to-point, short distance communication service" that is capable of transmitting information, product, and service offerings to subscribers and receiving interactive responses.[342] Initially licensees planned to use the service for fixed "interactive text-based supplements" to television programming — for viewer polling, education, or home shopping.[343] But having since been granted unprecedented regulatory flexibility, 218–219 MHz licensees are now authorized to use their spectrum for mobile as well as fixed operations.[344] Licensees plan to provide a myriad of services, including home banking, remote meter reading, inventory monitoring, transmission of data between a bank's central computer and ATMs, alarm security functions, cable television theft deterrence, and stock transaction or quotation services.[345] The list of possible uses for this

---

[340] *FCC Report to Congress on Spectrum Auctions* at 11.

[341] *WCS Order,* 12 F.C.C. Rec. at 10,840 ¶106. The licenses are not subject to the CMRS spectrum cap. *Id.* at 10,832–10,834 ¶¶87–91. *See* §10.8.4.

[342] Annual Assessment of the Status of Competition in Markets for the Delivery of Video Programming, Fourth Annual Report, 13 F.C.C. Rec. 1034, 1098–1099 ¶107 (1998) (hereinafter *Annual Assessment of Video Programming*). In September 1998, the Commission on its own motion redesignated IVDS as "218–219 MHz Service" in order to reflect the regulatory flexibility that licensees have in offering services and the breadth of services they now offer in the 218–219 MHz band. Amendment of Part 95 of the Commission's Rules to Provide Regulatory Flexibility in the 218–219 MHz Service, Order, Memorandum Opinion and Order, and Notice of Proposed Rulemaking, 13 F.C.C. Rec. 19,064, 19,075–19,076 ¶16 (1998) (hereinafter *Regulatory Flexibility Order*).

[343] *Annual Assessment of Video Programming,* 13 F.C.C. Rec. at 1098–1099 ¶107.

[344] Amendment of Part 95 of the Commission's Rules to Allow Interactive Video and Data Service Licensees to Provide Mobile Service to Subscribers, Report and Order, 11 F.C.C. Rec. 6610 (1996).

[345] *Regulatory Flexibility Order,* 13 F.C.C. Rec. at 19,075–19,076 ¶16; *Annual Assessment of Video Programming,* 13 F.C.C. Rec. at 1098–1099 ¶107.

spectrum may expand even further in upcoming months because the Commission has tentatively decided to reclassify 218–219 MHz service "from a strictly private radio service to a service that can be used for both common carrier and private operations."[346] The Commission has also proposed to extend the term of all 218–219 MHz licenses from five to ten years,[347] to relax the licensees' construction or "build-out" requirements,[348] and to allow licensees to partition and disaggregate their spectrum.[349]

The FCC first allocated spectrum at 218–219 MHz in 1992, dividing that one megahertz of spectrum into two equal blocks.[350] Like cellular licenses, these licenses are defined geographically according to MSAs and RSAs.[351] And at least for the moment, both licenses within the same geographic area cannot be held by the same entity.[352] In September 1993, the Commission awarded the first 18 IVDS licenses by lottery (two winners in nine of the top ten MSAs).[353] The following year the FCC held an auction to

[346] *Regulatory Flexibility Order,* 13 F.C.C. Rec. at 19,082–19,083 ¶33.

[347] *Id.* at 19,084–19,085 ¶36.

[348] *Id.* at 19,088–19,089 ¶44. Presently a 218–219 MHz licensee must, within the first year, be providing service to at least 10 percent of the population or geographic area covered by the license, 30 percent within three years, and 50 percent within five years. *Id.* at 19,087 ¶40. The Commission has proposed to modify these standards to require only that the licensee provide "substantial service" within five years. *Id.* at 19,088–19,089 ¶44.

[349] *Id.* at 19,092 ¶51.

[350] Amendment of Parts 0, 1, 2 and 95 of the Commission's Rules to Provide Interactive Video and Data Services, Report and Order, 7 F.C.C. Rec. 1630, 1631–1633 ¶¶13–20 (1992) (hereinafter *IVDS Order*), *on recons.,* Memorandum Opinion and Order, 7 F.C.C. Rec. 4923 (1992), *further recons.,* Second Memorandum Opinion and Order, 8 F.C.C. Rec. 2787 (1993); 47 C.F.R. §95.803(b) (maximum of two IVDS systems per service area; two frequency segments available for each service area).

[351] 47 C.F.R. §95.803(c); *IVDS Order,* 7 F.C.C. Rec. at 1638 ¶62.

[352] 47 C.F.R. §95.813(b)(1). In its September 1998 Notice of Proposed Rulemaking, the Commission sought comment on whether to revise the restriction on owning both licenses in the same market. *Regulatory Flexibility Order,* 13 F.C.C. Rec. at 19,090–19,091 ¶¶48–50.

[353] Interactive Video and Data Service (IVDS) Applications Accepted for Filing, Public Notice, 1993 FCC LEXIS 5347 (Oct. 20, 1993). These licenses were granted in March 1994. Interactive Video and Data Service Licenses Granted, Public Notice, 1994 FCC LEXIS 1288 (Mar. 30, 1994).

award licenses for the remaining 297 MSAs (or 594 licenses).[354] Both licenses in each service area were offered for auction at the same time, with the highest bidder given a choice between the two available licenses and the second highest bidder winning the remaining license.[355] Nearly 94 percent of all IVDS licenses were won by small businesses.[356] Many of the winning bidders have since defaulted on their payment obligations.[357] A second round of auctions will eventually be held for an additional 981 licenses—two licenses in each of the 428 RSAs, plus 125 MSA licenses from defaulted winners—but as of this writing, all efforts to schedule the second round have failed.[358]

§10.4.6.3   Digital Audio Radio Service

Spectrum for DARS[359] ranges from 2,320 to 2,345 MHz. Because at least 12.5 MHz of spectrum is necessary for a viable DARS system and because there are only 25 MHz of spectrum allocated exclusively for DARS, the Commission decided to auction two licenses, with only four applicants that filed before the

---

[354] Interactive Video and Data Service (IVDS) Applications Accepted for Filing, Public Notice, 9 F.C.C. Rec. 6227 (1994). These licenses were granted to winning bidders in January and February 1995. *Regulatory Flexibility Order,* 13 F.C.C. Rec. at 19,069 ¶6.

[355] Implementation of Section 309(j) of the Communications Act—Competitive Bidding, Fourth Report and Order, 9 F.C.C. Rec. 2330, 2332 ¶13 (1994).

[356] Implementation of Section 309(j) of the Communications Act—Competitive Bidding, Sixth Memorandum Opinion and Order and Further Notice of Proposed Rulemaking, 11 F.C.C. Rec. 19,341, 19,346 ¶5 (1996).

[357] Auction of Interactive Video and Data Service (IVDS), Public Notice, 11 F.C.C. Rec. 20,950 (1996) (hereinafter *IVDS Auction Notice*). In an effort to prevent defaults, the Commission has repeatedly extended the periods for winning bidders to pay the principal and interest they owe and has offered licensees automatic "grace periods" when they fail to make a payment. *Regulatory Flexibility Order,* 13 F.C.C. Rec. at 19,070–19,072 ¶¶9–11.

[358] *IVDS Auction Notice,* 11 F.C.C. Rec. at 20,950. On January 29, 1997, the Commission postponed the auction for the second round of IVDS licenses. Wireless Telecommunications Bureau Postpones February 18, 1997 Auction Date for 981 Interactive Video and Data Service (IVDS) Licenses, Public Notice, 12 F.C.C. Rec. 1389 (1997).

[359] DARS promises to provide continuous nationwide radio programming with compact disc sound quality.

1992 cutoff date eligible to participate. Both licenses are nation-wide. The Commission conducted a simultaneous multiple-round auction for the two DARS licenses on April 1, 1997.

§10.4.6.4 Direct Broadcast Satellite

DBS service transmits video signals from the earth to satellites, which then beam the signals directly to individual homes and offices equipped to receive them.[360] There are essentially three types of DBS service—C-band, medium-power DBS (also known as Ku-band), and high-power DBS. C-band service is the grandfather of today's DBS services. Developed in the late 1970s, the service is capable of delivering programming directly to households, but requires that the subscriber purchase and install an enormous receiving dish measuring four to eight feet in diameter.[361] Most industry analysts agree that any C-band service that remains in operation today will soon be replaced by medium- and high-power service. Medium-power DBS operates in a different frequency band and requires a smaller (27- to 39-inch) dish. High-power DBS is capable of offering more TV channels than medium-power DBS, via an even smaller dish, only 18 inches in diameter.

Under international treaties, the United States has been allotted eight orbital positions from which to provide domestic service; only three of these positions have a signal footprint that allows a high-power DBS satellite to transmit programming to the entire continental United States.[362] Each orbital slot can

---

[360] For a discussion of DBS and its perceived advantages over conventional broadcast, see §10.3.4 and National Assn. of Broadcasters v. FCC, 740 F.2d 1190, 1195 (D.C. Cir. 1984).

[361] Policies and Rules for the Direct Broadcast Satellite Service, Notice of Proposed Rulemaking, 13 F.C.C. Rec. 6907, 6910–6911 ¶4 (1998) (hereinafter *DBS Notice*).

[362] Revision of Rules and Policies for the Direct Broadcast Satellite Service, Report and Order, 11 F.C.C. Rec. 9712, 9727 ¶39 (1995) (hereinafter *DBS Order*); Revision of Rules and Policies for the Direct Broadcast Satellite Service, Notice of Proposed Rulemaking, 11 F.C.C. Rec. 1297, 1299 ¶5 (1995) (hereinafter *DBS Revision Notice*).

accommodate 32 transponder frequencies (or analog channels), each with a 24 MHz bandwidth.[363]

The Commission first granted an application for a DBS system in 1982.[364] By 1989, the number of requests for DBS orbital slots and channels exceeded the remaining supply.[365] The Commission resolved the problem not by its usual course (at the time) of holding a lottery or engaging in comparative hearings. The Commission instead simply divided the number of available analog channels pro rata among the applicants.[366]

In 1995, the Commission reclaimed over 50 DBS channels when the Advanced Communications Corporation failed to meet the FCC's construction requirements.[367] The Commission was confronted again with how to best allocate the resource. This time the FCC decided to adopt a process of competitive bidding.[368] At the same time, the Commission imposed a four-year construction deadline and conditioned licenses on the licensee providing service to Alaska and Hawaii where "such service is technically feasible."[369] The Commission auctioned the reclaimed channels in January 1996 for over $700 million.[370]

---

[363] *DBS Notice*, 13 F.C.C. Rec. at 6912 ¶6. Each analog channel can carry multiple broadcast television channels.

[364] Inquiry into the Development of Regulatory Policy in Regard to Direct Broadcast Satellites for the Period Following the 1983 Regional Administrative Radio Conference, Report and Order, 90 F.C.C.2d 676 (1982); *see also* Application of Satellite Television Corporation for Authority to Construct an Experimental Direct Broadcast Satellite System, 91 F.C.C.2d 953 (1982); National Assn. of Broadcasters, 740 F.2d at 1197.

[365] *DBS Revision Notice*, 11 F.C.C. Rec. at 1299–1300 ¶7.

[366] Applications of Continental Satellite Corp. et al., Memorandum Opinion and Order, 4 F.C.C. Rec. 6292, 6299 ¶¶54–56 (1989).

[367] *DBS Revision Notice*, 11 F.C.C. Rec. at 1300 ¶8.

[368] *DBS Order*, 11 F.C.C. Rec. at 9714–9715 ¶7.

[369] *Id.* at 9715–9716 ¶¶8–10, 9761 ¶125.

[370] *DBS Notice*, 13 F.C.C. Rec. at 6913 ¶8; Federal Communications Commission 62nd Annual Report, FY1996, at 63 (Sept. 15, 1997), *available at* <http://www.fcc.gov/annual_report_96.html>. In February 1998, the Commission proposed to streamline its DBS rules and sought comment on developing limits for horizontal concentration in the multichannel video programming distribution market. *DBS Notice*, 13 F.C.C. Rec. at 6908 ¶1.

§10.4.6.5 Multipoint/Multichannel Distribution Service

The spectrum allocated for MMDS spans the 2,150–2,680 MHz band, providing a maximum of 13 channels of 6 MHz each.[371] The Commission auctioned all 493 MMDS licenses (one for each of the BTAs in the United States and its territories), between November 1995 and March 1996, for a total of over $216 million.[372] Until recently MMDS providers were allowed to provide only one-way broadband service; thus, the service — popularly referred to as "wireless cable" — was dedicated almost exclusively to offering subscribers video programming through microwave transmitting and receiving antennas.[373] In September 1998, the Commission lifted the "one-way" restriction.[374] MMDS therefore will now be able to offer fixed two-way voice, data, and video services.

§10.4.6.6 Local Multipoint Distribution Service

Like MMDS, LMDS is capable of offering subscribers one- and two-way broadband services, such as video programming, video teleconferencing, wireless local loop telephony, and high-speed data transmission (e.g., Internet access).[375] The FCC has allocated 1,300 MHz of spectrum (2,750–2,835 MHz, 2,910–2,925

---

[371] FCC Wireless Telecommunications Bureau, Multipoint/Multichannel Distribution Services Auction Fact Sheet <http://www.fcc.gov/wtb/auctions>.

[372] *FCC Report to Congress on Spectrum Auctions* at 11; FCC Wireless Telecommunications Bureau, Multipoint/Multichannel Distribution Services Auction Fact Sheet <http://www.fcc.gov/wtb/auctions>.

[373] FCC Wireless Telecommunications Bureau, Multipoint/Multichannel Distribution Services Auction Fact Sheet <http://www.fcc.gov/wtb/auctions>.

[374] Amendment of Parts 21 and 74 to Enable Multipoint Distribution Service and Instructional Television Fixed Service Licensees to Engage in Fixed Two-Way Transmissions, Report and Order, 13 F.C.C. Rec. 19,112 (1998).

[375] Rulemaking to Amend Parts 1, 2, 21, and 25 of the Commission's Rules to Redesignate the 27.5–29.5 GHz Frequency Band, to Reallocate the 29.5–30.0 GHz Frequency Band, to Establish Rules and Policies for Local Multipoint Distribution Service and for Fixed Satellite Services, First Report and Order and Fourth Notice of Proposed Rulemaking, 11 F.C.C. Rec. 19,005, 19,011 ¶15 (1996).

MHz, and 3,100–3,130 MHz) to LMDS.[376] The spectrum is divided into two blocks—one is 1,150 MHz and the other 150 MHz—and is licensed by BTAs, for a total of 986 LMDS licenses.[377] The Commission placed no restrictions on the number of licenses any one entity can acquire and expressly permitted the partitioning of LMDS licenses based on any geographic area defined by the parties and the disaggregation for any amount of spectrum.[378] The auction was held in February and March of 1998; 864 licenses were sold to a total of 104 LMDS carriers, who paid over $575 million for the spectrum.[379]

§10.4.6.7   220 MHz Service

Occupying the 220–222 MHz frequency band, 220 MHz service is a land mobile radio service that may be used for either

---

[376] Rulemaking to Amend Parts 1, 2, 21, and 25 of the Commission's Rules to Redesignate the 27.5–29.5 GHz Frequency Band, to Reallocate the 29.5–30.0 GHz Frequency Band, and to Establish Rules and Policies for Local Multipoint Distribution Service and for Fixed Satellite Services, Second Report and Order, Order on Reconsideration, and Fifth Notice of Proposed Rulemaking, 12 F.C.C. Rec. 12,545, 12,556 ¶13 (1997) (hereinafter *Second LMDS Order*). These extremely high frequencies allow LMDS to offer greater capacity than MMDS. N. Gohring, High-Speed Wireless Hits Market: MMDS Operators Are First to Develop Services, Telephony, Aug. 3, 1998; Will LMDS Become a Factor in Broadband Networking?, Broadband Networking News, Mar. 31, 1998. However, higher frequency bands exhibit significantly more rain fade than the MMDS bands. In addition, MMDS providers generally can reach more customers at less cost because MMDS channels offer a 30 mile line-of-sight range, compared to the one- or two-mile range of the LMDS frequency band. Spike Technologies' PRIZM BDS Compliant with FCC's New Two-Way Rules for Low Frequency Channels, PR Newswire, Oct. 15, 1998.

[377] *Second LMDS Order*, 12 F.C.C. Rec. at 12,556 ¶13.

[378] *Id. See also* Rulemaking to Amend Parts 1, 2, 21, and 25 of the Commission's Rules to Redesignate the 27.5–29.5 GHz Frequency Band, to Reallocate the 29.5–30.0 GHz Frequency Band, and to Establish Rules and Policies for Local Multipoint Distribution Service and for Fixed Satellite Service, Fourth Report and Order, 13 F.C.C. Rec. 11,655 (1998).

[379] FCC Wireless Telecommunications Bureau, FactSheet: Local Multipoint Distribution Service Auction (Auction No. 17) (Mar. 25, 1998) <http://www.fcc.gov/Bureaus/Wireless/Factsheets/lmds.html>. However, 122 licenses were not sold (109 did not receive minimum bids, and 13 are held by the Commission due to withdrawn bids). *Id.* Of the 864 licenses sold, 181 were won

commercial or private purposes.[380] Today, the spectrum is principally used to provide radio dispatch services; however, given the lack of regulatory restrictions on how the spectrum may be used, the service may eventually be employed to compete with PCS, cellular, or ESMR service. The frequency band was divided for licensing into 200 five kilohertz paired channels, some of which are licensed on a national basis and some of which are licensed on a local basis.[381] The licenses were granted in two phases. Phase I began in May 1991 and was not completed until 1993, when the last of approximately 3,800 licenses were issued by lottery.[382] In Phase II, the Commission switched from lottery to competitive bidding. The auction began on September 15, 1998, and was completed on October 22, 1998, raising (in net high bids) over $21 million for the U.S. Treasury. Of the 908 licenses auctioned (made up of 3 nationwide, 30 regional economic area grouping, and 875 economic area licenses), 693 were sold. A reauction of the 225 Phase II 220 MHz licenses began on June 8, 1999.[383]

§10.5   Interconnection

Like local wireline networks, wireless networks connect to other local wireline networks, to long-distance networks, and to

---

with a single bid. F. Dawson, LMDS Auction Brings Surprises, Multichannel News, Mar. 30, 1998, at 73.

[380] Auction of the Phase II 220 MHz Service Licenses, Public Notice, 13 F.C.C. Rec. 16,445 (1998); Implementation of Section 6002(b) of the Omnibus Reconciliation Act of 1993, Competition in the Commercial Mobile Radio Services, Second Report, 12 F.C.C. Rec. 11,266, 11,320–11,321 (1997); Implementation of Section 6002(b) of the Omnibus Reconciliation Act of 1993, Third Report, 13 F.C.C. Rec. 19,746, 19,805–19,806, 19,808 (1998).

[381] Amendment of Part 90 of the Commission's Rules to Provide for the Use of the 220–222 MHz Band by the Private Land Mobile Radio Service, Second Memorandum Opinion and Order and Third Notice of Proposed Rulemaking, 11 F.C.C. Rec. 188, 194–195 ¶4 (1995).

[382] *Id.* at 195 ¶5.

[383] FCC, 220 MHz Reauction Fact Sheet (Auction #24) <http://www.fcc.gov/wtb/auctions>.

each other. Chapter 2 discusses the basic economics of inter-connection to the wireline network, and Chapter 5 discusses the interconnection rules for wireline networks. We review here the major rules that bear on interconnection by and to wireless net-works and how (or if) prices for interconnection are set.

§10.5.1 Interconnecting Wireless Providers with Local Landline Networks

The early regulation of interconnection between local wireline providers and wireless start-ups focused on ensuring that LECs did not discriminate in favor of their affiliated wireless compa-nies and against unaffiliated ones.[384] Cellular companies were initially viewed as just another customer for the local wireline carrier. But when wireless service far outpaced expectations,[385] that view changed. Wireless providers demanded, and were quickly given, more efficient, higher capacity interconnection. They came to be viewed as the "co-carriers" that they are—com-peting local carriers that simply use a new transmission medium to reach their local exchange customers.

A 1968 paging proceeding was the first in which the FCC explicitly required local phone companies to supply unaffiliated wireless carriers with dial-up interconnection to the LEC's net-work in any community where such access is being used by the LEC affiliate.[386] Local carriers were directed to offer unaffiliated

---

[384] As discussed in §10.4.2, each cellular service area in the country was awarded two cellular licenses, with one license going to the local telephone company for that market.

[385] The Cellular Telecommunications Industry Association (CTIA) esti-mated that there were 91,600 cellular subscribers in January 1985. By June of that year, this number more than doubled to 203,600. In June 1998, the num-ber of wireless subscribers (including cellular, PCS, and ESMR) was estimated to be over 60 million. CTIA, CTIA's Semi-annual Data Survey Results <http://www.wow-com.com/ professional/reference/datasurvey/>.

[386] Amendment of Part 21 of the Commission's Rules with Respect to the 150.8–162 Mc/s Band to Allocate Presently Unassignable Spectrum to Domes-tic Public Land Mobile Radio Service by Adjustment of Certain of the Band Edges, Report and Order, 12 F.C.C.2d 841, 846 ¶11 (1968) (hereinafter *Amendment of Part 21 of the Commission's Rules*). In its 1949 order establishing

wireless carriers the same type of interconnection at the same tariffs and with access to the same discounts as they offered to their own wireless affiliates.[387] The Commission also announced other detailed requirements aimed to ensure "that a balance be established so that the wireline company will not be in a position, because of its control over dial access interconnection, to claim or enjoy advantages not available to the [unaffiliated wireless carriers]."[388]

During these early years, a memorandum of understanding (MOU) governed the relationship between mobile wireless providers and the Bell System. The MOU included general provisions establishing the wireless providers' status as co-carriers rather than end users. In addition, it outlined their right to share in interstate and intrastate toll message charges that involved their mobile radio systems and their right to obtain seven-digit numbers for assignment to paging and mobile radio units.[389]

The introduction of cellular service in the early 1980s provoked a new series of disputes on the types of cellular systems that could interconnect with the local exchange network and the price of such interconnection. The Commission intervened, but decided against prescribing a single, specific type of interconnection because the details of interconnection would depend on

---

a dual licensing system, the FCC had left open whether it would require the telephone facilities to interconnect with facilities belonging to so-called miscellaneous or radio common carriers. General Mobile Radio Service, Report and Order of the Commission, 13 F.C.C. 1190, 1229–1230 (1949).

[387] *Amendment of Part 21 of the Commission's Rules,* 12 F.C.C.2d at 849–850 ¶15.

[388] *Id.* at 850 ¶17. The Court of Appeals for the Second Circuit relied on these requirements in upholding the FCC's decision to permit wireline carriers to provide mobile paging services. Radio Relay v. FCC, 409 F.2d 322, 327 (2d Cir. 1969) (FCC's equal access requirements were "designed to obviate any advantages that may accrue and equalize the competitive situation").

[389] *See* Interconnection Between Wireline Telephone Carriers and Radio Common Carriers Engaged in the Provision of Domestic Public Land Mobile Radio Service Under Part 21 of the Commission's Rules, Memorandum Opinion and Order, 63 F.C.C.2d 87 (1977); Interconnection Between Wireline Telephone Carriers and Radio Common Carriers Engaged in the Provision of Domestic Public Land Mobile Radio Service Under Part 22 of the Commission's Rules, Memorandum Opinion and Order, 80 F.C.C.2d 352 (1980).

a cellular system's design.[390] The Commission therefore established only general guidelines for LECs to follow. The FCC ordered that interconnection arrangements be "reasonably designed so as to minimize unnecessary duplication of switching facilities and the associated costs" and emphasized its expectation that "all telephone companies . . . furnish appropriate interconnection to cellular systems upon reasonable demand . . . and upon terms no less favorable than those offered to the cellular systems of affiliated entities or independent telephone companies."[391]

This general guidance was not entirely effective. During the 1980s, several Bell companies simply refused to provide unaffiliated wireless carriers with a certain type of interconnection — Type 2.[392] A few BOCs even threatened to cut off interconnection

---

[390] *See* An Inquiry into the Use of the Bands 825–845 MHz and 870–890 MHz for Cellular Communications Systems, Report and Order, 86 F.C.C.2d 469, 496 ¶¶55, 57 (1981) (hereinafter *Cellular Report and Order*).

[391] *Id.* at 496 ¶¶56–57. To give practical effect to a wireless carrier's general right to equal connection, the FCC required affiliated carriers applying for an in-region license to "set forth in its application exactly how its system will interconnect with the landline network" so that a potential competitor could "design its system to connect with the landline network in exactly the same fashion if the competitor so chooses. Failure to provide such information [was] cause for denying the application. If a license [was] granted to [an affiliated] carrier for a cellular system serving the same area as its landline system, the license [was] conditioned on the carrier providing a competing cellular operator the option of obtaining interconnection in the manner set forth in its application." An Inquiry into the Use of the Bands 825–845 MHz and 870–890 MHz for Cellular Communications Systems, Memorandum Opinion and Order on Reconsideration, 89 F.C.C.2d 58, 81–82 ¶50 (1982). Where an unaffiliated wireless carrier sought interconnection arrangements different from those specified in the application of an affiliated carrier, the unaffiliated applicant could negotiate other interconnection arrangements with the landline carrier. *Id.* at 82 ¶51. "[R]easonable and appropriate" interconnection was required even in areas where the local incumbent telephone company did not apply for (or receive) cellular service. *Id.* at 81 n.41. To facilitate enforcement of equal interconnection requirements, the Commission also required incumbents to operate their cellular affiliates as fully separate subsidiaries. The Commission noted that this would "greatly simplif[y] the opportunity of other cellular operators to gain interconnection rights to the landline network on the same basis as the telephone subsidiary." *Cellular Report and Order*, 86 F.C.C.2d at 494 ¶50.

[392] In the beginning, there were three basic types of interconnection. Type 1 interconnection treated the mobile telephone switching office (MTSO) as a

altogether if nonaffiliates refused to adhere to proffered contracts for Type 1 interconnection.[393] As a result, unaffiliated carriers were forced to accept an inferior Type 1 interconnection or delay offering service until the issue was resolved. The unaffiliated carriers then turned to state utility commissions and the FCC to complain.[394]

---

private branch exchange (PBX) served primarily by a single end office. Type 1 interconnection offered inferior transmission quality, did not permit arrangements under which interexchange carriers bill cellular subscribers directly for toll calls, and made inefficient use of MTSO switching facilities. Type 2A interconnection treated the MTSO as a tandem switch with links to a number of telco end offices and other carriers. This provided cellular carriers with lower interconnection costs, flexible collection of customer-specific billing data, flexible administration of a numbering plan, and improved transmission. Type 2B interconnection offered, in addition, direct MTSO interconnection with specific, high-volume end offices. The MTSO routed the cellular traffic directly to other end offices and interexchange carriers and functioned as a co-carrier. *See generally* Equal Access and Interconnection Obligations Pertaining to Commercial Mobile Radio Services, Notice of Proposed Rule Making and Notice of Inquiry, 9 F.C.C. Rec. 5408, 5451–5452 ¶105 (1994) (hereinafter *Equal Access Notice*); *Cellular Report and Order,* 86 F.C.C.2d at 496 ¶55; The Need to Promote Competition and Efficient Use of Spectrum for Radio Common Carrier Services (Cellular Interconnection Proceeding), Memorandum Opinion and Order on Reconsideration, 4 F.C.C. Rec. 2369, 2374 ¶33 (1989).

[393] In 1984, Indiana Bell threatened to cut off the interconnection facilities if the Indianapolis Telephone Company did not enter into a Type 1 contract that it had on the table. The company filed interconnection complaints with the Indiana Public Service Commission and the FCC. As a result of its FCC complaint, the company received a partial settlement ten months later under which Indiana Bell acknowledged the company's right to Type 2 interconnection. *See* Indianapolis Telephone Company's Proposed Findings of Fact and Order, Emergency Petition of Indianapolis Telephone Company to Prevent Disconnection by Indiana Bell Telephone Company, Inc., Cause No. 37671 (Ind. P.S.C. Nov. 12, 1985); Stipulation of Partial Settlement—Technical Matters, filed with the Federal Communications Commission in E-55-5; 104 Pub. Util. Rep. 4th (PUR) 99, 110–111, 112–113 (July 15, 1989).

[394] For example, on November 13, 1985, six independent wireless companies filed a complaint with state public utilities commissions after Ohio Bell, Cincinnati Bell, and Wisconsin Bell held up negotiations for 12 months over Type 2 interconnection. In early 1986, both Cincinnati Bell and Ohio Bell formally acknowledged that Type 2 would be acceptable. In the interim, however, the Cleveland unaffiliated wireless provider was forced to go on line with Type 1 interconnection. In Milwaukee, the state commission required the wireless provider to use Type 1 arrangements while the issue was being considered by the state public service commission. *See* Peter Huber, The Geodesic

The FCC responded with a policy statement, resolving most of the interconnection disputes in favor of the unaffiliated carriers.[395] The Commission required that all wireline telephone companies provide (1) the type of interconnection the mobile carrier requested, (2) interconnection to the wireless carrier that was no less favorable than that furnished to the affiliated carrier, and (3) reasonable interconnection arrangements different from those used by the incumbent company if the wireless carrier chose to negotiate with the telephone company.[396] The Commission also prohibited local exchange carriers from imposing recurring charges on nonaffiliated carriers for the use of NXX codes and telephone numbers.[397] LECs were allowed to charge

---

Network: 1987 Report on Competition in the Telephone Industry §4.13 n.49 (1987). Subsequently, however, the Wisconsin commission recognized the "willingness on the part of the local exchange companies to work with the cellular companies in developing [Type 2] interconnection agreements." Application for Consent and Approval of a Cellular Tandem Interconnection Agreement Between Certain Wireline Local Exchange Carriers and Cellular Tel. Cos. Pursuant to Section 4905.31, Rev. Code, 1990 Ohio PUC LEXIS 892, at *2 (Aug. 8, 1990).

[395] The Need to Promote Competition and Efficient Use of Spectrum for Radio Common Carrier Services, Memorandum Opinion and Order, 59 Rad. Reg. 2d (P & F) 1275 (1986); The Need to Promote Competition and Efficient Use of Spectrum for Radio Common Carrier Services, Declaratory Ruling, 2 F.C.C. Rec. 2910 (1987) (hereinafter *Radio Services Ruling*).

[396] The Need to Promote Competition and Efficient Use of Spectrum for Radio Common Carrier Services, Memorandum Opinion and Order, 59 Rad. Reg. 2d (P & F) 1275 app. B (FCC Policy Statement on Interconnection of Cellular Systems). The Commission gave the telcos six months to fulfill an unaffiliated carrier's request for Type 2 interconnection. *Radio Services Ruling*, 2 F.C.C. Rec. at 2914 ¶32. The Commission advised wireless carriers to file complaints if they believed a telephone company unreasonably delayed the interconnection or charged an unreasonable amount. *Id.* at 2914 ¶35. The telephone company then bore the burden of justifying its delay or showing that its rates were reasonable. *Id.* The Commission reaffirmed and again clarified its interconnection policies in 1989. The Need to Promote Growth and Efficient Use of Spectrum for Radio Common Carrier Services, Cellular Interconnection Proceeding, Memorandum Opinion and Order on Reconsideration, 4 F.C.C. Rec. 2369 (1989).

[397] The Commission ruled that LECs do not "own" exchange codes (NXX codes) or telephone numbers. They simply administer them. Therefore, LECs "may not impose recurring charges solely for the use of numbers." The Need to Promote Competition and Efficient Use of Spectrum for Radio Common

only a reasonable initial connection fee to compensate for the costs associated with new numbers.[398]

In 1992, the FCC proposed to extend the "federally protected right to interconnection" to PCS providers.[399] Under the Commission's proposal, a PCS provider was "entitled to obtain a type of interconnection" with the public switched telephone network "that is reasonable for the particular PCS system and no less favorable than that offered by the LEC to any other customer or carrier."[400]

Before the Commission could promulgate its proposed rule, Congress stepped in. The 1993 Budget Act added a blanket requirement that, "[u]pon reasonable request of any person providing commercial mobile service, the Commission shall order a common carrier to establish physical connections with such service pursuant to the provisions of section 201 of this Act."[401] This requirement was watered down somewhat with the additional language that the requirement "shall not be construed as a limitation or expansion of the Commission's authority to order interconnection" "[e]xcept to the extent that the Commission is required to respond" to a demand for interconnection.[402] The

---

Carrier Services, Memorandum Opinion and Order, 59 Rad. Reg. 2d (P & F) 1275 app. B ¶4 (1986) (FCC Policy Statement on Interconnection of Cellular Systems).

[398] *Id.*

[399] Amendment of the Commission's Rules to Establish New Personal Communications Services, Notice of Proposed Rule Making and Tentative Decision, 7 F.C.C. Rec. 5676, 5714 ¶99 (1992).

[400] *Id.* at 5715 ¶101.

[401] Omnibus Budget Reconciliation Act of 1993, Pub. L. No. 103-66, §6002(b)(2)(A), 107 Stat. 393 (1993) (codified at 47 U.S.C. §332(c)(1)(B)). Section 201 reads, in relevant part: "It shall be the duty of every common carrier engaged in interstate or foreign communication by wire or radio to furnish such communication service upon reasonable request therefor; and, in accordance with the orders of the Commission, in cases where the Commission, after opportunity for hearings, finds such action necessary or desirable in the public interest, to establish physical connections with other carriers. . . ." 47 U.S.C. §201(a).

[402] Omnibus Budget Reconciliation Act of 1993, Pub. L. No. 103-66, §6002 (b)(2)(A), 107 Stat. 393 (1993) (codified at 47 U.S.C. §332(c)(1)(B)).

Commission interpreted this interconnection mandate as requiring that LECs provide "reasonable and fair interconnection" to all CMRS and PMRS providers.[403]

Also in 1993, the Commission established a policy of "mutual compensation," under which the LEC and the cellular carrier were required to pay each other "reasonable costs" for terminating traffic that originates on the other party's network.[404] Parties were expected to negotiate private interconnection agreements that set forth the details of such compensation and other terms of interconnection. In practice, the regime of negotiated "mutual compensation" was not very successful.[405] Cellular carriers often paid LECs three separate usage-sensitive

---

[403] *Communications Act Second Report,* 9 F.C.C. Rec. at 1497–1499 ¶¶227–236, 1511 ¶273. Such interconnection shall require (1) mutual compensation between LECs and CMRS providers, under which each shall compensate the other for the "reasonable costs" incurred in originating and terminating traffic on their respective facilities; (2) that LECs "establish reasonable charges for interstate interconnection provided to [CMRS] licensees," which shall not "vary from charges established by LECs for interconnection provided to other mobile radio service providers"; and (3) that "in determining the type of interconnection that is reasonable for a [CMRS] system, the LEC shall not deny to a CMRS provider any form of interconnection arrangement that the LEC makes available to any other carrier or other customer, unless the LEC meets its burden of demonstrating that the provision of such interconnection arrangement to the requesting commercial mobile radio service provider either is not technically feasible or is not economically reasonable." *Id.* at 1498 ¶¶232–234. The Commission also concluded "that separate interconnection arrangements for interstate and intrastate commercial mobile radio services are not feasible"; therefore, it preempted "state and local regulations of the kind of interconnection to which CMRS providers are entitled." *Id.* at 1498 ¶230. However, the Commission decided, as it did in the cellular context, that LEC costs associated with the provision of interconnection for interstate and intrastate cellular services are "segregable" and therefore decided not to preempt state regulation of LEC intrastate interconnection rates applicable to CMRS services. *Id.* at 1498 ¶231.

[404] *Communications Act Second Report,* 9 F.C.C. Rec. at 1498 ¶232; 47 C.F.R. §20.11(b).

[405] The Commission found that, "in many cases, incumbent LECs appear to have imposed arrangements that provide little or no compensation for calls terminated on wireless networks, and in some cases imposed charges for traffic originated on CMRS providers' networks, both in violation of section 20.11 of our rules." Implementation of the Local Competition Provisions in the Telecommunications Act of 1996, First Report and Order, 11 F.C.C. Rec. 15,499, 16,044 ¶1094 (1996) (hereinafter *Local Competition Order*).

charges for local calls made from a cellular subscriber to a local exchange subscriber, regardless of the physical interconnection facility used: (1) per-call charges for call set-up; (2) per-minute charges for usage; and (3) per-minute, per-mile charges for transport between the cellular carrier's mobile telephone switching office and the LEC's tandem or end-office switch.[406]

Because of the system's apparent inequity, the Commission revisited the compensation rules just prior to passage of the 1996 Act. It proposed that, "at least for an interim period, interconnection rates for local switching facilities and connections to end users should be priced on a 'bill and keep' basis (i.e., both the LEC and the CMRS provider charge a rate of zero for the termination of traffic)."[407]

But before the Commission could promulgate its rule, Congress again intervened. In section 251(b)(5) of the 1996 Act, Congress expressly requires that all LECs "establish reciprocal compensation agreements" with CMRS providers, as well as competing local exchange carriers, "for the transport and termination of telecommunications" traffic.[408] In implementing this provision, the FCC ruled that compensation between a LEC and a CMRS provider must be symmetrical. That is, the rates paid by a LEC to a CMRS provider for transport and termination of traffic originated by the LEC must be the same as the rates the LEC charges for transport and termination of traffic originated by the CMRS provider.[409] Any precise determination of the applicable

---

[406] Interconnection Between Local Exchange Carriers and Commercial Mobile Radio Service Providers, Notice of Proposed Rulemaking, 11 F.C.C. Rec. 5020, 5039–5040 ¶40 (1996) (hereinafter *LEC/CMRS Notice*). The Commission sought comment on whether interconnection arrangements should continue to be established on the basis of individually negotiated contracts or whether the Commission should impose a tariff system. *Equal Access Notice,* 9 F.C.C. Rec. at 5450–5457 ¶¶102–120.

[407] *LEC/CMRS Notice,* 11 F.C.C. Rec. at 5023 ¶3.

[408] 47 U.S.C. §251(b)(5). *See Local Competition Order,* 11 F.C.C. Rec. at 15,997 ¶1008 ("LECs are obligated . . . to enter into reciprocal compensation arrangements with all CMRS providers, including paging providers, for the transport and termination of traffic on each other's networks.").

[409] *Local Competition Order,* 11 F.C.C. Rec. at 16,031–16,032 ¶1069, 16,040–16,044 ¶¶1085–1093. The Commission decided against mandating the bill-and-keep method as "a single, nationwide policy that would govern all

transport and termination rate for CMRS calls would be virtually impossible because most CMRS subscribers are moving locations during the course of any particular call; the Commission therefore authorized parties to "calculate overall compensation amounts by extrapolating from traffic studies and samples."[410] In addition, because many CMRS providers had negotiated inequitable compensation agreements predating the 1996 Act, the FCC granted all CMRS providers the right to renegotiate any nonreciprocal compensation interconnection agreement entered into before these rules took effect.[411] From the moment that the CMRS provider requests renegotiation until a new agreement is finalized, the CMRS provider may charge the LEC the same rates the LEC is charging the CMRS provider under the old agreement.[412]

As discussed in Chapters 2 and 5, incumbent LECs (ILECs) challenged the Commission's jurisdiction to promulgate these wholly local pricing rules as they applied to competitive LECs (CLECs) and CMRS providers. While the Court of Appeals for the Eighth Circuit set aside the FCC's pricing rules as applied to CLECs, the court went out of its way to leave the reciprocal compensation rules intact as far as CMRS providers are concerned.[413]

LEC-CMRS transport and termination of traffic." *Id.* at 16,058 ¶1118. The Commission, however, authorized state commissions to impose bill-and-keep arrangements between LECs and CMRS providers "if traffic is roughly balanced in the two directions and neither carrier has rebutted the presumption of symmetrical rates." *Id.* at 16,055 ¶1112. The Commission also read section 251(b)(5) as forbidding a LEC from charging a CMRS provider for terminating traffic that originated on the LEC's network. *Id.* at 16,016 ¶1042.

[410] *Id.* at 16,016–16,018 ¶1044.

[411] 47 C.F.R. §51.717(a); *Local Competition Order,* 11 F.C.C. Rec. at 16,044–16,045 ¶¶1094–1095.

[412] 47 C.F.R. §51.717(b).

[413] Iowa Utils. Bd. v. FCC, 120 F.3d 753, 800 n.21 (8th Cir. 1997). *rev'd in part on other grounds,* 119 S. Ct. 721 (1999). Said the court: "Because Congress expressly amended section 2(b) to preclude state regulation of entry of and rates charged by Commercial Mobile Radio Service (CMRS) providers, see 47 U.S.C. §152(b) (exempting the provisions of section 332), 332(c)(3)(A), and because section 332(c)(1)(B) gives the FCC the authority to order LECs to interconnect with CMRS carriers, we believe that the Commission has the authority to issue rules of special concern to the CMRS providers, but only as these provisions apply to CMRS providers." *Id.; see also* Summary of Currently

The 1996 Act contains a second provision that is important to CMRS providers. Section 251(c)(2) requires that all incumbent LECs provide "any requesting telecommunications carrier" with interconnection with the LECs' networks "for the transmission and routing of telephone exchange service and exchange access" "on rates, terms and conditions that are just, reasonable, and nondiscriminatory."[414] The Commission held that CMRS providers were "telecommunications carriers" under the statutory definition and that, at a minimum, cellular, broadband PCS, and certain SMR carriers provide "telephone exchange service."[415] Therefore, CMRS providers are entitled to the rights established by section 251(c). According to the statutory language, the rates and terms for interconnection were to be worked out in individual agreements negotiated by the parties.[416] Nevertheless, the Commission believed that its "establishment of pricing methodologies and default proxies" could be used as interim rates to "help expedite the parties' negotiations and drive voluntary CMRS-LEC interconnection agreements."[417] The Eighth Circuit vacated the interconnection pricing rules, even with respect to CMRS providers.[418] As discussed in section 3.3.4, however, the Supreme Court reinstated the FCC's authority to issue such rules.

§10.5.2 Interconnecting Wireless Switches with Long-Distance Networks

As discussed in Chapter 5, disputes about the interconnection of long-distance networks to local landline networks spawned

---

Effective Commission Rules for Interconnection Requests by Providers of Commercial Mobile Radio Services, Public Notice, 12 F.C.C. Rec. 15,591 (1997). The ILECs did not challenge the court's distinction when seeking review by the Supreme Court.

[414] 47 U.S.C. §251(c).
[415] *Local Competition Order,* 11 F.C.C. Rec. at 15,998–16,000 ¶¶1012–1013.
[416] *See* 47 U.S.C. §252.
[417] *Local Competition Order,* 11 F.C.C. Rec. at 16,005 ¶1024.
[418] Iowa Utils. Bd. v. FCC, 120 F.3d at 819 n.39.

two decades of antitrust litigation and FCC regulation and precipitated the breakup of the Bell System. Wireless services missed all the opening rounds, however: the first cellular systems were just beginning to operate in 1984, when the Bell System was dismantled.

As a result, the Commission never prescribed rules for how wireless carriers should deal with long-distance carriers,[419] though the Commission once came close. In 1994, the Commission issued a Notice of Proposed Rulemaking addressing equal access and interconnection obligations for CMRS providers.[420] MCI, which had previously attempted to persuade the Commission that all mobile carriers should be required to provide 1+ access to their networks,[421] renewed its demands.[422] The FCC tentatively concluded that equal access obligations for cellular (although not for other CMRS) carriers would be in the public interest.[423] Congress was of a different view. Passage of the 1996 Act preempted further action along these lines by the Commission.[424]

---

[419] Mobile providers (whether or not affiliated with a landline telco) were not required by the FCC to give their customers 1+ access to the long-distance carrier of their choice. Unlike the local loop, the mobile switch was not an "essential" or "bottleneck" facility. It was a competitive facility; there was always a competing mobile provider down the road.

[420] Equal Access and Interconnection Obligations Pertaining to Commercial Mobile Radio Services, Notice of Proposed Rule Making and Notice of Inquiry, 9 F.C.C. Rec. 5408 (1994) (hereinafter *Equal Access and Interconnection NPRM*).

[421] MCI Petition, Policies and Rules Pertaining to the Equal Access Obligations of Cellular Licensees, RM-8012 (June 2, 1992).

[422] *See Equal Access and Interconnection NPRM,* 9 F.C.C. Rec. at 5415–5416 ¶13.

[423] *Id.* at 5417–5432 ¶¶16–49. Despite Congress's attempt to create regulatory parity for all CMRS providers in the 1993 Budget Act, the Commission addressed "the equal access question separately with respect to each of the various mobile services comprising the CMRS marketplace." *Id.* at 5424 ¶30. For services other than cellular, the Commission did not find evidence in the record to impose equal access, *id.* at 5429–5432 ¶¶44–49, since "all CMRS providers other than cellular licensees currently lack market power," *id.* at 5429 ¶44.

[424] Interconnection and Resale Obligations Pertaining to Commercial Mobile Radio Services, Order, 11 F.C.C. Rec. 12,456 (1996).

Until 1996, however, wireless affiliates of the Bell Operating Companies were subject to the Divestiture Decree and, as a result of certain decisions by Judge Greene, subject to its equal access obligations. The Decree itself did not specifically address whether its obligations and restrictions applied to BOC cellular affiliates.[425] From the beginning, however, the court made perfectly clear its view that mobile telephone and paging services were "exchange telecommunication services" within the meaning of the Decree and hence subject to the decree's prohibition on interexchange (or interLATA) service.[426] The court was willing, in certain circumstances, to waive the interLATA restriction for BOC affiliates; but Judge Greene required as a condition of all such waivers that the affiliates provide equal access.[427] In

---

[425] *Equal Access and Interconnection NPRM,* 9 F.C.C. Rec. at 5415 ¶12.

[426] United States v. Western Elec. Co., 578 F. Supp. 643, 645–646, 647 (D.D.C. 1983). In that case, the BOCs sought a waiver of LATA restrictions with respect to nine specific areas in which cellular systems (already operating and under development) crossed the newly defined LATA boundaries. Judge Greene granted the appropriate waivers, recognizing that LATA boundaries had been defined by reference to landline rather than mobile calling patterns and that "the technological and competitive issues implicated by mobile radio services were, in some locations, significantly different" from those relevant to landline services. *Id.* at 648, 649. AT&T argued vigorously that imposing LATA boundaries on BOC mobile services would make no economic or technical sense and would serve no legitimate competitive purpose. AT&T Response to Comments and Objections Relating to the Proposed LATA Boundaries at 26, 27, United States v. Western Elec. Co., No. 82-0192 (D.D.C. Nov. 23, 1982). The FCC likewise urged that LATA boundaries should not be applied to cellular service, noting that "there is virtually no competitive risk involved in making clear that the BOCs may engage in the cellular radio business to the same geographical extent as any other entity" and that imposing LATA boundaries on BOCs' mobile affiliates would put them at a "potentially serious" competitive disadvantage with competitors offering a "more geographically expansive service." *FCC Reply* at 2, 4 (Dec. 15, 1982). The Department of Justice, followed by Judge Greene, took the position that mobile services should be fully subject to restrictions on interLATA services. Initially advocating a case-by-case approach to LATA restrictions, the DOJ recommended in 1987 general geographic relief for mobile services. Report and Recommendations of the United States Concerning the Line of Business Restrictions Imposed on the Bell Operating Companies by the Modification of Final Judgment at 56, United States v. Western Elec. Co., No. 82-0192 (D.D.C. Feb. 2, 1987).

[427] *See, e.g., Western Elec. Co.,* 578 F. Supp. at 651; Order, United States v. Western Elec. Co., No. 82-0192, §3 (D.D.C. June 20, 1986).

1986, for example, several Bell companies filed motions with the court requesting that the Decree be interpreted to permit the BOCs to provide intraLATA cellular services outside their geographic region.[428] The court denied the motions.[429] Affirming its earlier ruling, the court held that the Decree forbid the BOCs from providing exchange services out of region.[430] But the D.C. Circuit reversed: it found that nothing in the Decree prohibited Bell companies from providing extraregional exchange services;[431] hence, nothing prohibited wireless affiliates from providing cellular service anywhere in the country as long as the service did not cross LATA boundaries. Forced to accept extraregional service, the district court conditioned that service, like all operations of a BOC wireless affiliate, on their abiding by the Decree's equal access obligations.[432]

All the while, the FCC was issuing licenses that covered geographic territories that crossed multiple LATA boundaries, particularly in rural areas.[433] Year by year, Judge Greene therefore redrew the service areas in which wireless affiliates were permitted to offer "local" service.[434] Shortly before the 1996 Act was

---

[428] United States v. Western Elec. Co., 627 F. Supp. 1090 (D.D.C. 1986).

[429] *Id.* at 1104–1109.

[430] *Id.* at 1106–1109.

[431] United States v. Western Elec. Co., 797 F.2d 1082, 1089–1091 (D.C. Cir. 1986).

[432] *See, e.g.,* Order at 3–4, United States v. Western Elec. Co., No. 82-0192 (D.D.C. Oct. 31, 1986) (granting waiver to BellSouth to provide voice storage and retrieval services to cellular customers on the condition that BellSouth provide equal access to competing providers); Opinion at 17, United States v. Western Elec. Co., No. 82-0192 (D.D.C. Sept. 12, 1990) (permitting BOC affiliates to offer automatic call delivery to their customers, but only on the condition that the call be carried by an interexchange carrier designated in advance by the customer).

[433] These problems were particularly acute for U S WEST, which sought a waiver to provide interLATA cellular service within RSAs and to permit certain affiliated cellular systems to own interexchange links. When the Department of Justice failed to act on that request, U S WEST sought relief directly from the Decree court. In August 1990, the court denied U S WEST's request on the ground that DOJ had not yet taken a position on the issue. Memorandum and Order, United States v. Western Elec. Co., No. 82-0192 (D.D.C. Aug. 8, 1990).

[434] Judge Greene granted almost 60 waiver requests for mobile services, the bulk of them after 1988. On February 18, 1993, Judge Greene permitted

passed, Judge Greene also acceded to an agreement between the Department of Justice and the BOCs that allowed BOC affiliates to offer wireless interLATA services, subject to the provision of equal access[435] and other conditions.[436] Similar equal access requirements were briefly extended to AT&T's cellular (though not to its other wireless) operations by way of a consent decree entered in connection with its 1994 purchase of McCaw.[437]

The 1996 Telecommunications Act superseded both the Bell and the McCaw decrees entirely.[438] In addition, section 705 ex-

---

BOC cellular affiliates to provide interLATA service within any RSA. Decision at 1–2, United States v. Western Elec. Co., No. 82-0192 (D.D.C. Feb. 18, 1993). Judge Greene imposed the usual conditions on this waiver. The BOCs had to provide exchange access on a nondiscriminatory basis and to lease all interexchange links from an unaffiliated interexchange carrier.

[435] United States v. Western Elec. Co., 890 F. Supp. 1 (D.D.C. 1995). A generic waiver request filed with the Department of Justice argued that the restriction itself was anticompetitive in that it prevented BOC affiliates from competing on an equal basis with independent competitors, who routinely bought long-distance service in bulk for their cellular customers. Motion of the Bell Companies for Removal of Mobile and Other Wireless Services from the Scope of the Interexchange Restriction and Equal Access Requirement of Section II(D) of the Decree, United States v. Western Elec. Co., No. 82-0192 (D.D.C. Dec. 13, 1991). After extensive discussions with the Department, the BOCs submitted a revised order and a model equal access plan based on MTAs rather than traditional LATA boundaries. See Letter from Michael K. Kellogg to Richard L. Rosen, Chief, Communications and Finance Section, Antitrust Div., Dept. of Justice (Nov. 12, 1993) (replying to comments on revised order). The DOJ subsequently filed a memorandum with the court, supporting in part and opposing in part the BOCs' motion. Memorandum of the United States in Response to the Bell Companies' Motions for Generic Wireless Waivers at 1–2, United States v. Western Elec. Co., No. 82-0192 (D.D.C. July 25, 1994).

[436] See Memorandum of the United States in Response to the Bell Companies' Motions for Generic Wireless Waivers, United States v. Western Elec. Co., No. 82-0192 (D.D.C. July 25, 1994).

[437] The Department concluded that the merger would eliminate McCaw as a competitor of AT&T in the cellular exchange market. Competitive Impact Statement at 13, United States v. AT&T Corp., No. 94-01555 (D.D.C. Aug. 5, 1994). The most notable difference between equal access under the McCaw decree and under the Bell Decree was that the McCaw decree allowed AT&T to continue operating on the long-distance side of the equal access lines. Proposed Final Judgment §IV, United States v. AT&T Corp., Inc., No. 94-01555 (D.D.C. July 15, 1994). The Bell Decree expressly prohibited the BOCs from doing so.

[438] 47 U.S.C. §271(b)(3), (g)(3).

pressly provides that CMRS providers "shall not be required to provide equal access to common carriers for the provision of telephone toll services."[439] The Act further granted the Commission the authority to require CMRS providers to unblock access to competing long-distance carriers where the Commission found that access was being denied to carriers of a subscriber's choice and such denial was "contrary to the public interest, convenience, and necessity."[440]

§10.5.3 Wireless-to-Wireless Interconnection

In conjunction with its 1994 NPRM on cellular carriers' equal access obligations, the Commission issued a Notice of Inquiry to consider a general rule requiring CMRS carriers to provide interconnection with other CMRS providers.[441] Months before, the Commission had punted on the issue.[442] One year after issuing the NPRM, the Commission deferred again: it concluded that CMRS-to-CMRS interconnection obligations might "promote the efficient provision of service to consumers at reasonable prices," but regulation along those lines was still premature.[443]

---

[439] *Id.* §332(c)(8).

[440] *Id.*

[441] *Equal Access and Interconnection NPRM,* 9 F.C.C. Rec. at 5458–5469 ¶¶121–143. Most commenters opposed any such rules. Bell Atlantic and Bell South urged the Commission to allow the marketplace and negotiation to determine the manner of CMRS-to-CMRS interconnection. Interconnection and Resale Obligations Pertaining to Commercial Mobile Radio Services, Second Notice of Proposed Rule Making, 10 F.C.C. Rec. 10,666, 10,673–10,674 ¶¶13–14 (1995). CMRS providers argued regulation was unnecessary, given the state of competition and the lack of any bottleneck facilities. *Id.* at 10,674 ¶16. MCI adopted the position that CMRS providers were presumptively common carriers and should be required to interconnect with any other common carrier. *Id.* at 10,678 ¶23.

[442] *Communications Act Second Report,* 9 F.C.C. Rec. at 1499 ¶237.

[443] Interconnection and Resale Obligations Pertaining to Commercial Mobile Radio Services, Second Notice of Proposed Rule Making, 10 F.C.C. Rec. 10,666, 10,681–10,682 ¶¶28–29 (1995). The uncertainty over the interoperability among the different wireless services and the time needed to construct the newly licensed PCS systems were two reasons for not requiring CMRS

The Act's section 251(b) obligations (number portability, dialing parity, access to rights-of-way, etc.) apply only to "local exchange carriers," and CMRS providers are not classified as such unless and until the Commission affirmatively concludes that they should be.[444]

But CMRS providers *are* "telecommunications carriers" under the 1996 Act and therefore are subject to the basic interconnection requirements of section 251(a).[445] That is, they are required to "interconnect directly or indirectly with the facilities and equipment of other telecommunications carriers" and have a duty "not to install network features, functions, or capabilities that do not comply with the guidelines and standards established pursuant to section 255 or 256."[446]

In 1996, the Telecommunications Resellers Association (TRA) sued the Commission on its initial 1994 decision not to resolve CMRS-to-CMRS interconnection[447]—a decision the Commission had refused to reconsider.[448] In April 1998, a panel of the

---

interconnection. *Id.* at 10,681–10,682 ¶¶29–30. The Commission also reasoned that CMRS providers' existing interconnections with users of other networks through the landline network provided a disincentive to behave anticompetitively against their CMRS competitors. *Id.* at 10,682 ¶31.

[444] *Local Competition Order,* 11 F.C.C. Rec. at 15,994 ¶1001, 15,995– 15,996 ¶1004. Section 3(26) defines a "local exchange carrier" as "any person that is engaged in the provision of telephone exchange service or exchange access," but "does not include a person insofar as such person is engaged in the provision of a commercial mobile service under section 332(c), except to the extent that the Commission finds that such service should be included in the definition of such term." 47 U.S.C. §153(26). Nor did the Commission choose to classify CMRS providers as LECs. *Local Competition Order,* 11 F.C.C. Rec. at 15,995–15,996 ¶1004. Since CMRS providers were not LECs, they obviously could not be treated as incumbent LECs, subject to the requirements of section 251(c). *See* 47 U.S.C. §251(h) (definition of incumbent LEC); *Local Competition Order,* 11 F.C.C. Rec. at 15,996 ¶1006.

[445] *See Local Competition Order* 11 F.C.C. Rec. at 15,989 ¶993.

[446] 47 U.S.C. §251(a)(1), (2).

[447] *Communications Act Second Report,* 9 F.C.C. Rec. at 1499–1500 ¶237.

[448] Implementation of Sections 3(n) and 332 of the Communications Act, Memorandum Opinion and Order on Partial Reconsideration of Second Report and Order, 11 F.C.C. Rec. 19,729, 19,736 ¶14 (1996). *See* Telecommunications Resellers Assn. v. FCC, 141 F.3d 1193 (D.C. Cir. 1998). The complainants were actually equipment manufacturers who were ready to provide the equipment for this type of interconnection.

D.C. Circuit upheld the Commission's decision to defer on the issue, although the court expressed "dismay" over the five years that had lapsed while the Commission investigated the issue.[449] The Commission refused to commit to a schedule for deciding the issue, but anticipated issuing a final order by the end of 1998.[450] As of mid-1999, however, no final order had been issued.

§10.5.4 Interconnection and Equal Access Requirements in Perspective

The interconnection mandates imposed on BOC-affiliated wireless carriers under the Divestiture Decree have been almost completely superseded. They remain of interest, however, as an instructive case study on how interconnection regulation can go haywire.

The divested BOCs were permitted to continue providing wireless services, but subject to the Decree's line-of-business restrictions and equal access requirements. This was inconsistent with the "quarantine" theory urged by the government:[451] wireless services were manifestly not monopolies. Extending the line-of-business restrictions and equal access requirements to wireless services provided by BOC affiliates was likewise inconsistent with the theory of the Decree:[452] wireless services are neither rate regulated nor a bottleneck. And the Decree failed to require BOCs to offer equal interconnection to unaffiliated providers of wireless services, even though wireless providers require interconnection with the local exchange in much the same way as providers of interexchange and information services. The parties, in short, placed the bottleneck restrictions and safeguards and obligations *on the wrong switch:* they focused on the wireless switch—which is not a bottleneck—instead of the wireline switch, which *was* thought to be one.

---

[449] Telecommunications Resellers Assn. v. FCC, 141 F.3d at 1197.
[450] *Id.*
[451] *See* §4.4.3.
[452] *See id.*

Soon after the Decree was entered, both the Department and Judge Greene recognized and set about correcting one-half of this mistake by creating new equal access safeguards on the wireline switch in the process of granting various waivers. But Judge Greene declined—except on a piecemeal basis in occasional waivers—to take the logical next step, which was to remove the restrictions and requirements imposed *at the level of the wireless exchange*. A decision to exclude BOC affiliates from wireless services altogether might have been at least theoretically consistent with the Decree. The decision to permit these same companies to provide an arbitrarily crippled form of wireless services has neither a theoretical nor a pragmatic justification.

The FCC took a different tack that at least has the virtue of being internally consistent. After considering and rejecting the polar options of wireless monopolies and complete telco exclusion from the market, the FCC opted for a balanced middle course. Telco mobile affiliates would compete according to the same rules as everyone else. Telcos themselves would be required to deal with affiliates and others on the same nondiscriminatory terms.

§10.6 Common Carriage

§10.6.1 Resale of Wireless Services

As discussed above, the Commission licensed only two blocks of cellular spectrum in each geographic market;[453] the B-block licensees (who were affiliates of wireline carriers) were awarded licenses significantly ahead of the A-block licensees (who were unaffiliated).[454] In order to encourage additional competition and deter price discrimination, the Commission forbade any

---

[453] An Inquiry into the Use of the Bands 825–845 MHz and 870–890 MHz for Cellular Communications Systems, Report and Order, 86 F.C.C.2d 469, 509 ¶97 (1981) (hereinafter *Cellular Report and Order*).
[454] *See* §10.4.2.

cellular licensee to restrict the resale of its cellular capacity.[455] In the beginning, this resale policy permitted the unaffiliated carriers to enter the market as soon as the facilities of the wireline carriers were operational, thus offsetting the "headstart" enjoyed by wireline carriers.[456]

In 1992, the Commission created an exception to the prohibition on resale restrictions. The FCC allowed the wireline affiliate to restrict the resale of its services by the unaffiliated cellular licensee in the same geographic area after the five-year "build-out" period had expired.[457] The rule was designed to address the problem of nonwireline licensees relying exclusively on resale service instead of building their own systems.

On June 12, 1996, the Commission extended resale rights to broadband PCS and certain kinds of SMR services (those that provide "real-time, two-way switched voice service that is interconnected").[458] The resale requirement does not require providers to structure operations or offerings in any particular

---

[455] *Cellular Report and Order,* 86 F.C.C.2d at 510–511 ¶¶103–107. *See also* Cellnet Communication, Inc. v. FCC, 965 F.2d 1106, 1108–1109 (D.C. Cir. 1992) (discussing cellular resale obligation; "the FCC's policy on resale barred facilities-based carriers from restricting resale to non-facilities-based resellers and from discriminating against purchasers for resale").

[456] *See* Petitions for Rule Making Concerning Proposed Changes to the Commission's Cellular Resale Policies, Report and Order, 7 F.C.C. Rec. 4006, 4007–4008 ¶11 (1992).

[457] *Id.* at 4006 ¶1. The rule, which was formerly codified at 47 C.F.R. §22.901(e), stated that "[e]ach cellular licensee must permit unrestricted resale of its service, except that a licensee may apply resale restrictions to licensees of cellular systems on the other channel block in its market after the five year build-out period for licensees on the other channel block has expired."

[458] Interconnection and Resale Obligations Pertaining to Commercial Mobile Radio Services, First Report and Order, 11 F.C.C. Rec. 18,455, 18,466 ¶19 (1996) (hereinafter *CMRS Interconnection and Resale Obligations Order*). The Commission concluded that the costs of regulation were outweighed by resale's many public benefits, including encouraging competitive pricing; discouraging unjust, unreasonable, and discriminatory practices; reducing the need for regulatory intervention and concomitant market distortions; promoting innovation; improving carrier management and marketing; generating increased research and development; and positively affecting the growth of the market. *Id.* at 18,461–18,462 ¶10. The Commission recodified the amended cellular rule at 47 C.F.R. §20.12(b).

way, such as to adopt separate wholesale/resale business structures or to offer resellers a discount margin of the price of service.[459] The Commission did not extend the resale prohibition to other CMRS providers based on its conclusion that, "in the immediate future, only cellular, broadband PCS and covered SMR licensees will compete for customers in the mass market for two-way switched voice services."[460] Furthermore, the Commission concluded that the competition that broadband PCS and SMR would bring to the market for mobile telephony would in the future obviate the need for an express resale requirement.[461] Therefore, by regulation, the resale requirement will sunset on November 24, 2002—five years after the award of the last group of initial broadband PCS licenses.[462]

§10.6.2 Roaming

The Commission's rules require that all cellular, broadband PCS, and covered SMR licensees provide mobile radio service upon request to any subscriber in good standing—even if that licensee has no preexisting relationship with that subscriber—while that subscriber is located in the licensee's geographical service area and if the subscriber is using mobile equipment that is

---

[459] *CMRS Interconnection and Resale Obligations Order,* 11 F.C.C. Rec. at 18,462 ¶12.

[460] *Id.* at 18,467–18,468 ¶21.

[461] *Id.* at 18,468–18,469 ¶24.

[462] *Id.* (codified at 47 C.F.R. §20.12(b)). The five-year period commenced as of November 25, 1997, the date on which the Commission completed its award of the last group of initial licenses for currently allocated broadband PCS spectrum. The CMRS resale rule therefore will terminate at the close of November 24, 2002. Commencement of Five-Year Period Preceding Termination of Resale Rule Applicable to Certain Covered Commercial Mobile Radio Service Providers, Public Notice, CC Docket No. 94-54 (July 2, 1998). A reseller of cellular service challenged the FCC's decision to include a sunset provision, but the Court of Appeals for the Sixth Circuit found the agency did not act arbitrarily, capriciously, or otherwise contrary to law in including the sunset provision. Cellnet Communications v. FCC, 149 F.3d 429 (6th Cir. 1998).

compatible with the licensee's base stations.[463] A licensee can provide such service, which is commonly called "roaming," in two basic forms: manual and automatic. Manual roaming is the only form available when neither the roaming subscriber nor the subscriber's home carrier have a contractual relationship with the roamed-on or "host" carrier. A manual roamer typically originates a call by giving a valid credit card number to the host carrier.[464] Automatic or "seamless" roaming occurs when the host carrier has a contractual relationship with the home carrier, and thus the roaming subscriber may originate a call without taking any action other than turning on his or her telephone. Generally speaking, before the subscriber can complete the roaming call, "the host system first identifies the subscriber's home carrier by means of the subscriber's telephone number, verifies that it has an agreement with that carrier, and queries the carrier to verify that the subscriber's account is current."[465] In December 1997, the Commission sought comments on whether it should require cellular, broadband PCS, and covered SMR to provide "automatic roaming."[466]

§10.6.3 Wireless Number Portability

Section 251(b)'s requirement that "local exchange carriers" provide number portability[467] does not, by the Act's express terms,

---

[463] See 47 C.F.R. §20.12(c) (cellular, broadband PCS, and certain kinds of SMR); id. §22.901 (cellular); see also Interconnection and Resale Obligations Pertaining to Commercial Mobile Radio Services, Second Report and Order and Third Notice of Proposed Rulemaking, 11 F.C.C. Rec. 9462 (1996) (hereinafter Second Interconnection Report).

[464] Second Interconnection Report, 11 F.C.C. Rec. at 9465 ¶5.

[465] Id. at 9465–9466 ¶6.

[466] Commission Seeks Additional Comment on Automatic Roaming Proposals for Cellular, Broadband PCS, and Covered SMR Networks, Public Notice, 12 F.C.C. Rec. 20,317 (1997). The Commission has yet to take action.

[467] The 1996 Act defines "number portability" as "the ability of users of telecommunications services to retain, at the same location, existing telecommunications numbers without impairment of quality, reliability, or convenience when switching from one telecommunications carrier to another." 47 U.S.C. §153(30).

apply to CMRS providers.[468] But the Commission claims to have found "independent authority under sections 1, 2, 4(i), and 332 of the Communications Act of 1934" to require it.[469] The Commission ordered cellular, broadband PCS, and covered SMR providers to have the capability of delivering calls from their networks to ported numbers by December 31, 1998, and to offer number local number portability by June 30, 1999.[470] The Commission affirmed its deadline in March 1997, refusing to yield to complaints that the requirements were too stringent.[471]

In December 1997, the Cellular Telecommunications Industry Association (CTIA) filed a petition requesting that the Commission employ its authority under section 10 of the Communications Act of 1934, as amended, to forbear from enforcing

---

[468] *See* Telephone Number Portability, First Memorandum Opinion and Order on Reconsideration, 12 F.C.C. Rec. 7236, 7315 ¶141(1997) (hereinafter *Number Portability Order on Reconsideration*). Section 251(b) obligations apply only to "local exchange carriers," and by statutory definition, CMRS providers are not classified as such unless and until the Commission affirmatively concludes that they should be. Section 3(26) defines a "local exchange carrier" as "any person that is engaged in the provision of telephone exchange service or exchange access," but "does not include a person insofar as such person is engaged in the provision of a commercial mobile service under section 332(c), except to the extent that the Commission finds that such service should be included in the definition of such term." 47 U.S.C. §153(26); *see also Local Competition Order,* 11 F.C.C. Rec. at 15,994 ¶1001, 15,995–15,996 ¶1004. The Commission has not elected to classify CMRS providers as LECs. *Id.*

[469] *Number Portability Order on Reconsideration,* 12 F.C.C. Rec. at 7315 ¶141; Telephone Number Portability, First Report and Order and Further Notice of Proposed Rulemaking, 11 F.C.C. Rec. 8352, 8431–8432 ¶153 (1996) (hereinafter *Number Portability Order*).

[470] *Number Portability Order,* 11 F.C.C. Rec. at 8439 ¶165. By the December 31, 1998, deadline, CMRS providers were "to have the capability to query the number portability databases nationwide, or arrange with other carriers to perform the queries . . . in order to route calls from wireless customers to customers who have ported their numbers." *Number Portability Order on Reconsideration,* 12 F.C.C. Rec. at 7313 ¶136. By June 30, 1999, they were to "(1) offer service provider portability in the 100 largest MSAs, and (2) be able to support nationwide roaming." *Id.*

[471] *Number Portability Order on Reconsideration,* 12 F.C.C. Rec. at 7315–7317 ¶¶140–142. *See also* Telephone Number Portability, Second Memorandum Opinion and Order on Reconsideration, 13 F.C.C. Rec. 21,204, 21,206–21,207 ¶4 (1998) (affirming the number portability deadlines and requirements).

number portability requirements for CMRS providers. CTIA requested that the Commission forbear from enforcing the June 30, 1999, implementation deadline for CMRS number portability at least until the completion of the five-year build-out period for broadband PCS carriers has expired. On February 8, 1999, the Commission granted CTIA's forbearance petition, extending to November 24, 2002, the deadline for CMRS providers to support service provider local number portability in the top 100 Metropolitan Statistical Areas (MSAs).[472]

§10.6.4 Unbundling Wireless Networks

Wireless carriers presently are not subject to the unbundling requirements of the 1996 Act. Those obligations, found in section 251(c)(3), apply only to "incumbent local exchange carriers." While today wireless providers are not considered to be "local exchange carriers,"[473] much less "incumbent" LECs, that might change when and if wireless becomes competitive with wireline service. Under such circumstances, the Commission might exercise its discretion to reclassify CMRS providers as LECs and/or incumbent LECs.[474] Wireless carriers would then be subject to the full range of access and interconnection obligations of section 251.

---

[472] In the Matter of Cellular Telecommunications Industry Association's Petition for Forbearance from Commercial Mobile Radio Services Number Portability Obligations and Telephone Number Portability, Memorandum Opinion and Order, WT Dkt. No. 98-229, FCC 99-19, 1999 FCC Lexis 641 (Feb. 9, 1999).

[473] Section 3(26) defines a "local exchange carrier" as "any person that is engaged in the provision of telephone exchange service or exchange access," but "does not include a person insofar as such person is engaged in the provision of a commercial mobile service under section 332(c), except to the extent that the Commission finds that such service should be included in the definition of such term." 47 U.S.C. §153(26); *see also Local Competition Order*, 11 F.C.C. Rec. at 15,994 ¶1001, 15,995–15,996 ¶1004. The Commission has not elected to classify CMRS providers as LECs. *Id.*

[474] 47 U.S.C. §§153(26), 251(h)(2).

§10.7   Universal Service

§10.7.1   Build-Out Requirements

The Commission has traditionally required licensees to construct their facilities and provide service to a minimum number of customers within a specified period; "warehousing" licenses was forbidden.[475] Warehousing usually occurred when a provider used only a portion of its allocated spectrum to provide service, leaving the remainder of the spectrum fallow. As the Commission described it, warehousing occurs when spectrum is "held out of use even though it would be profitable for a firm without market power to provide service using that spectrum."[476]

In its 1993 Budget Act, Congress codified that general build-out policy, expressly requiring the Commission to "include performance measurements, such as appropriate deadlines and penalties for performance failures, . . . to prevent stockpiling or warehousing of spectrum by licensees."[477] Congress was concerned that incumbents would acquire a license for a service that competes with its own service in an effort to impede competition.[478] In addressing this provision, the Commission concluded

---

[475] For example, cellular carriers in the top 90 markets were given five years to "fill in" their MSAs and three years to cover 75 percent of the geographic area. Implementation of Sections 3(n) and 332 of the Communications Act, Further Notice of Proposed Rule Making, 9 F.C.C. Rec. 2863, 2875–2876 ¶¶59–61 (1994) (providing former build-out requirements for cellular licenses; public land mobile service, conventional SMR, local 220–222 MHz, business radio, and paging licenses; nationwide 220 MHz and PCS licenses; and 800 and 900 MHz SMR licenses). As noted in §10.4.2, after the five-year deadline, the Commission proceeded to "shrink wrap" and then reauction licenses in those areas where the cellular licensee had failed to begin providing service.

[476] Implementation of Section 309(j) of the Communications Act Competitive Bidding, Notice of Proposed Rule Making, 8 F.C.C. Rec. 7635, 7650 ¶91 (1993).

[477] 47 U.S.C. §309(j)(4)(B) (ordering the Commission to impose such requirements as part of process of auctioning licenses).

[478] Implementation of Section 309(j) of the Communications Act—Competitive Bidding, Second Report and Order, 9 F.C.C. Rec. 2348, 2386 ¶216 (1994).

that, for most auctionable licenses, existing construction and coverage requirements would be sufficient to meet Congress's mandate.[479] In 1997, the Commission revised its build-out requirements for paging providers.[480]

Now that most licensees are paying dearly for their spectrum, the warehousing rules make no economic sense. Enforcement of normal antitrust principles should take care of attempts to monopolize—see section 10.8.1 below. Anticompetitive concerns aside, market forces will prescribe build-out schedules far more wisely than regulators. Not infrequently the most intelligent way to use a resource like spectrum is not to try to use it right away. The enormous investment required to begin providing service may make it entirely rational to wait to invest until uncertainty about technical standards, market demand, and other factors has been reduced.[481]

---

[479] *Id.* at 2386 ¶219. Examples of today's construction period and coverage requirements are as follows: a 30 MHz broadband PCS licensee must serve one-third of its area population within five years and two-thirds by the end of the ten-year license term (47 C.F.R. §24.203(a)); a 10 MHz broadband PCS licensee must serve one-quarter of the population within five years or show that it is providing "substantial service" (47 C.F.R. §24.203(b)); a DBS licensee has four years to construct its first satellite and six years to complete all satellite stations within its system (Revision of Rules and Policies for the Direct Broadcast Satellite Service, Report and Order, 11 F.C.C. Rec. 9712, 9715–9716 ¶¶8, 10 (1995); 47 C.F.R. §100.19(b)); WCS and LMDS licensees are required only to build out their systems so as to provide "substantial service" within ten years of receiving their license (Amendment of the Commission's Rules to Establish Part 27, the Wireless Communications Service ("WCS"), Report and Order, 12 F.C.C. Rec. 10,785, 10,843 ¶111 (1997); Rulemaking to Amend Parts 1, 2, 21, and 25 of the Commission's Rules to Redesignate the 27.5–29.5 GHz Frequency Band, to Reallocate the 29.5–30.0 GHz Frequency Band, and to Establish Rules and Policies for Local Multipoint Distribution Service and for Fixed Satellite Services, Second Report and Order, Order on Reconsideration, and Fifth Notice of Proposed Rulemaking, 12 F.C.C. Rec. 12,545, 12,659 ¶266 (1997)).

[480] Revision of Part 22 and Part 90 of the Commission's Rules to Facilitate Future Development of Paging Systems, Second Report and Order and Further Notice of Proposed Rulemaking, 12 F.C.C. Rec. 2732, 2766–2767 ¶¶63–64 (1997).

[481] Robert MacDonald & Daniel Siegel, The Value of Waiting to Invest, Q.J. Econ., Nov. 1986, at 707; *see also* John V. Leahy, Investment in Competitive Equilibrium: The Optimality of Myopic Behavior, Q.J. Econ., Nov. 1993, at 1105. For example, after paying billions of dollars for their spectrum rights,

The Commission seems willing at least to entertain such arguments. It has indicated that it will consider granting waivers to the build-out requirements for good cause shown. IVDS licensees (now 218–219 MHz licensees) were supposed to provide service to at least 10 percent of the population in their service area within one year of operation, but the Commission issued waivers for this requirement after a lawsuit challenging the lottery used to distribute the licenses impelled many licensees to delay construction.[482] The Commission dropped other antiwarehouse requirements in 1997.[483]

§10.7.2 Wireless Contribution to Universal Wireline Service

The 1996 Act was clear in requiring all telecommunications carriers to contribute to the universal service fund—including wireless carriers.[484] The Joint Board added as a guiding principle the notion that eligible telecom carriers—regardless of their technology—will be able to provide universal service and receive

---

successful broadband PCS bidders had to decide whether to invest in more advanced CDMA digital compression technology or more established TDMA technology. The large sunk investment at issue in such cases makes mistakes costly and may make delay efficient if technological uncertainty will diminish over time. Peter W. Huber & Howard A. Shelanski, Administrative Creation of Property Rights to Radio Spectrum, 41 J.L. & Econ. 581, 591–592 (1998).

[482] Interactive Video and Data Service (IVDS) Licenses Requests by Lottery Winners to Extend Construction Deadline, Memorandum Opinion and Order, 11 F.C.C. Rec. 9537 (1996).

[483] Users of the 220 MHz band complained about the so-called 40-mile rule, which barred them from acquiring identical channels within 40 miles of an existing location unless it was demonstrated that their existing channels were "fully loaded." Operators pleaded that the rule impaired their ability to provide CMRS-type services. The Commission concluded that market forces were sufficient to prevent the warehousing of spectrum. Amendment of Part 90 of the Commission's Rules to Provide for the Use of the 220–222 MHz Band by the Private Land Mobile Radio Service, Fourth Report and Order, 12 F.C.C. Rec. 13,453 (1997).

[484] See 47 U.S.C. §254(d).

support.[485] The Joint Board also concluded that section 332(c) does not preclude states from requiring CMRS providers to contribute to any state universal service support mechanism.[486]

§10.8   Industry Structure

The Commission's control over spectrum allocation, assignment, and license transfers gives it essentially complete power to control the competitive structure of the wireless industry. With power to allocate spectrum, the FCC has absolute power to dictate industry structure—everything from the geographic scope of service areas to who owns how much and in which markets.

The Commission established its authority to shape industries in this manner when it issued regulations in 1941 intended to force NBC to divest one of its radio networks.[487] The regulation in question prohibited a broadcast affiliate of a parent with more than one network from obtaining a second license if there would be substantial overlap in the territories served by the affiliated stations.[488] The regulations were based on the Commission's predictive judgment that the network's domination of the limited resource of the electromagnetic spectrum would be detrimental to the public interest.[489] The Commission likewise has used its authority to issue rules to restrict ownership of multiple

[485] Federal-State Joint Board on Universal Service, Recommended Decision, 12 F.C.C. Rec. 87, 101–102 ¶23 (1996) (hereinafter *Joint Board Recommended Decision*); *see also* Federal-State Joint Board on Universal Service, Report and Order, 12 F.C.C. Rec. 8776, 8932–8934 ¶¶286–290, 8944–8945 ¶¶311–313 (1997) (hereinafter *Joint Board Order*).

[486] *Joint Board Recommended Decision,* 12 F.C.C. Rec. at 484 ¶791; *see also Joint Board Order,* 12 F.C.C. Rec. at 9181–9182 ¶791. *See generally* §6.3.

[487] FCC, Report on Chain Broadcasting at 80–87, Commission Order No. 37, Docket No. 5060 (1941), *modified,* Supplemental Report on Chain Broadcasting (Oct. 1941), *appeal dismissed sub. nom.* National Broad. Co. v. United States, 47 F. Supp. 90 (S.D.N.Y. 1942), *aff'd,* 319 U.S. 190 (1943).

[488] *See* 47 C.F.R. §3.107 (1941).

[489] The Commission's regulations and reasoning were upheld by the Supreme Court. National Broad. Co. v. United States, 319 U.S. 190 (1943).

stations[490] and to restrict ownership of stations in certain concentrated markets.[491]

§10.8.1 Joint Ownership of Wireline and Wireless Properties

Committed from the outset to licensing more than one wireless carrier in each geographic market, the Commission had to

[490] In 1940, the Commission prohibited anyone from owning more than six FM radio stations. Rules Governing High Frequency Broadcast Stations, 5 Fed. Reg. 2382, 2384 (1940). The limit was raised to seven stations in 1953. Amendment of Sections 3.35, 3.240 and 3.636 of the Rules and Regulations Relating to the Multiple Ownership of AM, FM and Television Broadcasting Stations, Report and Order, 18 F.C.C. 288, 295 ¶17 (1953). In 1984, this rule was changed to limit ownership to 12 stations in each broadcast service. Amendment of Section 73.3555 [formerly Sections 73.35, 73.240, and 73.636] of the Commission's Rules Relating to Multiple Ownership of AM, FM and Television Broadcast Stations, Report and Order, 100 F.C.C.2d 17, 55 ¶110 (1984). On reconsideration of this 1984 order, the Commission added a restriction limiting the aggregate ownership interests in TV stations to no more than 25 percent of the national audience. Amendment of Section 73.3555, [formerly Sections 73.35, 73.240 and 73.636] of the Commission's Rules Relating to Multiple Ownership of AM, FM and Television Broadcast Stations, Memorandum Opinion and Order, 100 F.C.C.2d 74, 97 ¶52 (1985). The limit was raised to 14 stations if at least 2 stations were minority controlled, and the reach was increased to 30 percent of the national audience, provided that at least 5 percent of the aggregate reach is contributed by minority-controlled stations. Id. at 94–95 ¶45. In accordance with sections 202(a) and 202(c)(1) of the 1996 Act, the Commission amended its rules, eliminating the limit on the number of radio or television stations a person or entity could own and raising the television audience reach cap to 35 percent. Implementation of Sections 202(a) and 202(b)(1) of the Telecommunications Act of 1996 (Broadcast Radio Ownership), Order, 11 F.C.C. Rec. 12,368, 12,371 ¶6 (1996); Implementation of Sections 202(c)(1) and 202(e) of the Telecommunications Act of 1996 (National Broadcast Television Ownership and Dual Network Operations), Order, 11 F.C.C. Rec. 12,374, 12,377 ¶8 (1996). The Commission is examining the effects of its changes to the national television ownership rule. 1998 Biennial Regulatory Review—Review of the Commission's Broadcast Ownership Rules and Other Rules Adopted Pursuant to Section 202 of the Telecommunications Act of 1996, Notice of Inquiry, 13 F.C.C. Rec. 11,276, 11,281 ¶16 (1998).

[491] From 1977 to 1984, the Commission also restricted ownership of three broadcast stations of any type if two of them were within 100 miles of the third and there was overlap in the service areas. See Repeal of the "Regional

grapple with the question of whether LECs could be numbered among the licensees. For a time, the Commission tilted in favor of LECs rather than against them.[492] While not exclusive licensees, LECs or their affiliates were favored assignees of specific blocks of spectrum on the assumption that they were uniquely skilled in deploying wireless services. While not affirmatively tilting things in their favor, the Commission has likewise permitted cable operators to provide cellular and PCS service.[493]

When it first allocated frequencies for land mobile services in 1949, the Commission allocated separate blocks to telcos and to "miscellaneous common carriers," more commonly known as radio common carriers (RCCs).[494] In a 1963 order, the Commission reaffirmed the policy of allocating separate blocks of spectrum to telcos and RCCs.[495]

Concentration of Control" Provisions of the Commission's Multiple Ownership Rules, Memorandum Opinion and Order, 100 F.C.C.2d 1544, 1545 ¶2 (1985).

[492] An Inquiry Relative to the Future Use of the Frequency Band 806–960 MHz, Second Report and Order, 46 F.C.C.2d 752, 760 ¶21 (1974) (hereinafter *Future Use Inquiry, Second Order*) (FCC briefly concluded that telcos were the only organizations that had demonstrated that they possess the "resources and the expertise necessary" to provide cellular phone service and that "competing cellular systems would not be feasible").

[493] "The Commission has . . . found that the cross-ownership prohibition does not bar non-wireline cellular telephone carriers from providing video programming service within their cellular telephone service areas." Application of Teleport Communications—New York, for Transfer of Control of Stations WLU372, WLW316 and WLW317 from Merrill Lynch Group, Inc. to Cox Teleport, Inc., Memorandum Opinion and Order, 7 F.C.C. Rec. 5986, 5988 ¶16 (1992). *See also* Amendment of the Commission's Rules to Establish New Personal Communications Services, Tentative Decision and Memorandum Opinion and Order, 7 F.C.C. Rec. 7794, 7799–7802 ¶¶12–18 (1992) (tentatively granting PCS license to Cox Cable for use in connection with its cable service).

[494] General Mobile Radio Service, Report and Order of the Commission, 13 F.C.C. 1190, 1197, 1228 (1949). The Commission defined a "miscellaneous common carrier" as one "not engaged in the business of providing either a public landline message telephone service or public message telegraph service." ITT Mobile Telephone, Inc., Memorandum Opinion and Order, 1 Rad. Reg. 2d (P & F) 957 n.2 (1963).

[495] ITT Mobile Telephone, Inc., 1 Rad. Reg. 2d 957 ¶¶11–13.

In 1967, the FCC briefly considered excluding telco affiliates from the new cellular markets altogether.[496] But it ultimately decided not to impose any such quarantine.[497] In 1970, the

[496] Amendment of Part 21 of the Commission's Rules with Respect to the 150.8–162 Mc/s Band to Allocate Presently Unassignable Spectrum to the Domestic Public Land Mobile Radio Service by Adjustment of Certain of the Band Edges, Memorandum Opinion and Notice of Proposed Rulemaking, 9 F.C.C.2d 659, 664 ¶16 (1967) (questioning whether "the public interest [would] better be served by not making any assignment of [mobile] frequencies to wireline carriers").

[497] Amendment of Part 21 of the Commission's Rules with Respect to the 150.8–162 Mc/s Band to Allocate Presently Unassignable Spectrum to the Domestic Public Land Mobile Radio Service by Adjustment of Certain of the Band Edges, Report and Order, 12 F.C.C.2d 841 (1968). In a 1968 order, the Commission attempted to assuage concerns that AT&T or other telcos might eventually come to monopolize the provision of paging services, stating that "[s]ince we will retain at all times the power of the licensing function, we will have sufficient opportunity for appropriate scrutiny. We will in the exercise of our continuing regulatory authority inquire into any practices which may develop which appear to be unlawful, anticompetitive, or inimical to the public interest." Amendment of Part 21 of the Commission's Rules with Respect to the 150.8–162 M/c/s Band to Allocate Presently Unassignable Spectrum to the Domestic Public Land Mobile Radio Service by Adjustment of Certain of the Band Edges, Memorandum Opinion and Order, 14 F.C.C.2d 269, 271 ¶6 (1968). The Commission further explained:

> We have made available to wireline and non-wireline carriers the same number of frequencies; we insulated the non-wireline carriers from unfair practices; we retained the power of the licensing function to assure the adherence to the condition; . . . and each type of carrier is afforded an equal opportunity to compete. Under these circumstances, absent some specific showing there is no basis for us to assume that our rulemaking proceeding will result in the establishment of a coalition to suppress competition.

Id. at 273 ¶13 (citation omitted). *Cf.* Amendment of Part 90 of the Commission's Rules Governing Eligibility for the Specialized Mobile Radio Services in the 800 MHz Land Mobile Band, Order, 7 F.C.C. Rec. 4398 (1992) (banning telephone companies from acquiring enhanced specialized mobile radio (ESMR) licenses—in or out of their telephone service areas). Nonaffiliated common carriers are not barred from being licensed as SMR service providers. This is somewhat surprising because ESMR and cellular radio are used to provide very similar services—so similar in fact that the FCC formerly also barred cross-ownership of cellular and SMR licenses. *Future Use Inquiry, Second Order,* 46 F.C.C.2d at 787 §89.604 (prohibiting wireline telephone common carriers from holding SMR base station licenses); *id.* at 761 ¶25 (banning cellular systems from offering dispatcher-originated communications service with "fleet call" capability). In 1986, the Commission proposed to eliminate

Commission split the allocation of new frequencies between LEC affiliates and unaffiliated providers.[498] For cellular licenses, the FCC awarded "block A" licenses—first through comparative hearings and later by lottery—to "[c]ommon carriers *not* also engaged in the business of affording public landline message telephone service." By contrast, the FCC set aside "block B" licenses for common carriers that *were* already wireline licensees.[499]

The Commission eliminated its system of separate allocations for landline and nonlandline applicants in 1994.[500] With the proliferation of licenses for wireless services and the compelling logic of auctions as a means of assignment, it seems safe to assume that the era of either favoring or disfavoring LEC-affiliated

---

the SMR restriction. Amendment of Part 90 of the Commission's Rules Governing Eligibility for the Specialized Mobile Radio Services in the 800 MHz Band, Notice of Proposed Rulemaking, 51 Fed. Reg. 2910 (1986). But the proceeding was terminated in 1992 on the grounds that the record had become stale; the restriction was to be retained until the Commission could more fully evaluate the competitive impact of allowing wireline carriers into the SMR marketplace. *See* Amendment of Part 90 of the Commission's Rules Governing Eligibility for the Specialized Mobile Radio Services in the 800 MHz Land Mobile Band, Order, 7 F.C.C. Rec. 4398 (1992). The Commission's ban against wireline carriers holding SMR licenses was reviewed as a result of the 1993 Budget Act. *See* H.R. Rep. No. 111, 103d Cong., 1st Sess. 262 (stating that "[t]he Committee encourages the Commission to re-examine this restriction in light of the enactment of this section to determine the extent to which such a restriction is in the public interest"). In 1995, the Commission amended its rules to allow all mobile service common carriers to provide dispatch service, eliminating its restrictions prohibiting wireline common carriers from holding SMR and commercial 220 MHz licenses and the Commission's prohibition on the provision of dispatch service by common carriers. Eligibility for the Specialized Mobile Radio Services and Radio Services in the 220–222 MHz Land Mobile Band and User of Radio Dispatch Communications, Report and Order, 10 F.C.C. Rec. 6280, 6297 ¶29 (1995).

[498] An Inquiry Relative to the Future Use of the Frequency Band 806–960 MHz, First Report and Order and Second Notice of Inquiry, 19 Rad. Reg. 2d (P & F) 1663, ¶¶28–31 (1970).

[499] An Inquiry into the Use of the Bands 825–845 MHz and 870–890 MHz for Cellular Communications Systems, Report and Order, 86 F.C.C.2d 469, 476 ¶15, 491 ¶43, 565 §22.902(b) (1981) (hereinafter *Cellular Report and Order*).

[500] Revision of Part 22 of the Commission's Rules Governing the Public Mobile Services, 9 F.C.C. Rec. 6513 (1994); *see also* Revision of Part 22 of the Commission's Rules Governing the Public Mobile Services, Notice of Proposed Rule Making, 7 F.C.C. Rec. 3658, 3672–3673 §22.905 (1992).

wireless licensees has come to an end. Standard antitrust principles can and will take care of undue aggregations of licenses in particular markets.

But antitrust law has not completely taken over quite yet. In a 1997 rulemaking, the Commission barred incumbent LECs (and cable operators) from owning 1,150 MHz LMDS licenses on their home turf for three years from the date of the auction.[501] The idea was to encourage unaffiliated licensees to use LMDS licenses to compete in both local telephony and local subscriber video markets. A group of LECs, trade associations, and individuals unsuccessfully challenged the Commission's restrictions in the D.C. Circuit.[502] After the 1998 LMDS auction, a number of winning bidders asked the Commission to waive its restriction on incumbent LECs' and incumbent cable operators' right to use the licenses where they already provide service. In September 1998, the Commission denied ten such waiver requests.[503]

§10.8.2   Separate Affiliate Requirements for Wireline-Wireless Conglomerates

In 1974, the Commission required telcos to operate their mobile telephone affiliates as wholly separate subsidiaries.[504]

[501] Rulemaking to Amend Parts 1, 2, 21, and 25 of the Commission's Rules to Redesignate the 27.5–29.5 GHz Frequency Band, to Reallocate the 29.5–30.0 GHz Frequency Band, to Establish Rules and Policies for Local Multipoint Distribution Service and for Fixed Satellite Services, Second Report and Order, Order on Reconsideration, and Fifth Notice of Proposed Rulemaking, 12 F.C.C. Rec. 12,545, 12,614–12,634 ¶¶157–199 (1997). Incumbent LECs were not barred from acquiring the in-region 150 MHz LMDS license for which the Commission found incumbents would not have any anticompetitive incentives in using. *Id.* at 12,626 ¶182. *See also* Melcher v. FCC, 134 F.3d 1143, 1146–1149 (D.C. Cir. 1998) (discussing FCC order and background).

[502] Melcher v. FCC, 134 F.3d at 1149–1165.

[503] *See* Requests for Waiver of Section 101.1003(a) of the Commission's Rules Establishing Eligibility Restrictions on Incumbent LECs and Cable Operators in the Local Multipoint Distribution Service, Order, 13 F.C.C. Rec. 18,694 (1998).

[504] *Future Use Inquiry, Second Order,* 46 F.C.C.2d at 760 ¶23. The FCC also required that wirelines file all contracts between themselves and their

Separate subsidiary requirements and arm's-length dealing, the Commission reasoned, helped ensure that LECs offered interconnection on equal terms to unaffiliated wireless licensees.[505] In 1982, the Commission reaffirmed separate subsidiary requirements for AT&T's cellular operations, but eliminated them for other local exchange carriers[506] and for paging services.[507] The separate subsidiary requirements were then extended to the divested Bell companies in 1983.[508]

In general, the Bell Divestiture Decree permitted the divested BOCs to provide local wireless services, subject to the Decree's line-of-business restrictions. This was inconsistent with the "quarantine" theory urged by the government[509] because wireless services were manifestly not monopolies. In the decade after divestiture, there evolved in Judge Greene's courtroom a quite different and independent set of separate subsidiary requirements by way of the MFJ waiver process.[510] But those are now of

---

mobile telephone affiliates or subsidiaries, as well as records of all money flows and exchanges or flows of property of any kind. *Id.* at 760–761 ¶25. *See also Cellular Report and Order,* 86 F.C.C. Rec. at 493–495 ¶¶48–52 (promulgating 47 C.F.R. §22.903, requiring separate affiliate for LEC cellular affiliate).

[505] *Cellular Report and Order,* 86 F.C.C. Rec. at 491–492 ¶32, 494 ¶50 (separate subsidiary requirement will "reduc[e] the possibility that wireline carriers will behave anticompetitively").

[506] An Inquiry into the Use of the Bands 825–845 MHz and 870–890 MHz for Cellular Communications Systems, Memorandum Opinion and Order on Reconsideration, 89 F.C.C.2d 58, 78 ¶44 (1982).

[507] Amendment of Parts 2 and 22 of the Commission's Rules to Allocate Spectrum in the 928–941 MHz Band and to Establish Other Rules, Policies, and Procedures for One-Way Paging Stations in the Domestic Public Land Mobile Radio Service, First Report and Order, 89 F.C.C.2d 1337, 1345 ¶23 (1982).

[508] Policy and Rules Concerning the Furnishing of Customer Premises Equipment, Enhanced Services and Cellular Communications Services by the Bell Operating Companies, Report and Order, 95 F.C.C.2d 1117, 1120 ¶3 (1983).

[509] *See* §4.4.1.

[510] The Decree itself did not require any separation between radio and landline intraLATA services. But Judge Greene's waivers for interLATA BOC cellular services were made contingent on the use of separate subsidiaries. *See, e.g.,* United States v. Western Elec. Co., 578 F. Supp. at 643. Separate subsidiary requirements were erected in the same way for out-of-region paging operations by BOC affiliates. *See, e.g.,* Opinion and Order, United States v.

only historical interest, as the Decree was wholly superseded by the 1996 Act.[511]

In its 1993 PCS order, the Commission concluded that the public interest would not be served by a structural separation requirement for PCS operations of LECs.[512] The Commission, however, found the record insufficient to repeal the requirement that BOCs provide cellular service through a separate subsidiary.[513] On appeal, the Sixth Circuit later held that the Commission failed to properly justify its disparate treatment of cellular and PCS providers.[514] The Commission responded by requiring all incumbent LECs (other than rural ones) to provide CMRS, including cellular service and PCS, *in-region* through a separate CMRS affiliate.[515] At the same time, it somewhat loosened the level of separation required and eliminated separate-

---

Western Elec. Co., No. 82-0192 (D.D.C. May 14, 1986); Memorandum Opinion and Two (2) Orders, United States v. Western Elec. Co., No. 82-0192 (D.D.C. June 20, 1986). The upshot of all this was a remarkable patchwork of separate subsidiary demands. The Decree required nothing of a BOC affiliate offering in-region intraLATA cellular services; the FCC, however, demanded a separate subsidiary. The Decree required a separate subsidiary for a BOC affiliate offering out-of-region paging services; the FCC did not. There were in fact eight possible combinations in the separate-subsidiary matrix, depending on whether the radio service involved telephone or paging, was or was not affiliated with a BOC, and was in-region or out-of-region. The FCC required separate subsidiaries in four of these instances (for cellular services both in-region and out-of-region, by both BOC and non-BOC telco affiliates), the Decree in two (paging and cellular services, out-of-region only, for BOC affiliates only)—but the FCC rules and antitrust pronouncements agreed that a separate subsidiary was needed in only one of the eight possible combinations of circumstances (out-of-region cellular services by BOC affiliates).

[511] Telecommunications Act of 1996, §601(a)(1) (codified at 47 U.S.C. §152 note). The AT&T/McCaw decree likewise required McCaw and McCaw's wireless services affiliates to "be maintained as corporations or partnerships . . . separate from AT&T." But that decree, too, was superseded by the 1996 Act. *Id.* §601(a)(3).

[512] Amendment of the Commission's Rules to Establish New Personal Communications Services, Second Report and Order, 8 F.C.C. Rec. 7700, 7751–7752 ¶126 (1993).

[513] *Id.* at 7751–7752 n.98.

[514] Cincinnati Bell Tel. Co. v. FCC, 69 F.3d 752, 768 (6th Cir. 1995).

[515] Amendment of the Commission's Rules to Establish Competitive Service Safeguards for Local Exchange Carrier Provision of Commercial Mobile

subsidiary rules entirely for CMRS provided by an incumbent LEC outside its wireline service area.[516]

§10.8.3 Wireless-Wireline Competition

Until very recently wireless telephony was considered to be only a complement to wireline voice services. In its most recent report on the CMRS industry, however, the Commission recognized that many analysts now "believe that wireless and wireline technologies are increasingly competing for a single pool of minutes-of-use."[517]

Perhaps the most likely force behind the increasing substitution of wireless for wireline service is the ever decreasing price differential between the services. Wireline service costs between 5 and 20 cents per minute,[518] while a 1997 study estimated wireless service as ranging between 25 and 73 cents a minute,[519] and AT&T is today advertising rates as low as 10.7 cents a minute for a nationwide plan with a large bundle of minutes.[520]

Also important to the growing competition between the two services is new "wireless local loop" technology. This technology enables "fixed" wireless connections to be established between ordinary central office switches (equipped with wireless transceivers) and residences or businesses (also with wireless transceivers).[521] The Commission has already promulgated rules to

---

Radio Services, Report and Order, 12 F.C.C. Rec. 15,668, 15,692–15,693 ¶¶37–38 (1997).

[516] *Id.* at 15,692–15,694 ¶¶37–40.

[517] Implementation of Section 6002(b) of the Omnibus Reconciliation Act of 1993, Third Report, 13 F.C.C. Rec. 19,746, 19,776 (1998) (hereinafter *Section 6002(b) Third Report*).

[518] *Id.*

[519] Analysts Agree PCS Is Driving Down Wireless Prices, But Disparities Persist, PCS Week, Oct. 7, 1997.

[520] AT&T Wireless Services, AT&T Digital One Rate <http://www.attws.com/personal/onerate/index.html>.

[521] In February 1997, AT&T announced the development of a "revolutionary fixed wireless technology" that allows AT&T to offer local service to up to 2,000 homes with just 10 MHz of PCS spectrum. *See* AT&T News Release, AT&T's Breakthrough Wireless Technology New Alternative for Local Service,

allow cellular, PCS, and paging carriers to determine for themselves what mix of mobile and fixed services it will provide to the
public.[522] Although wireless local loop technology served only
about 1 million subscribers in 1997, an industry analyst predicts
that the number of subscribers worldwide will grow to approximately 8 million by 2000 and to 47 million by 2005.[523]

With additional PCS licensees building out their systems and
coming on line over the next few years, the price of wireless service can be expected to continue to drop. Wireless links will become competitive with wireline for voice and some kinds of data
in the last mile of the network. This last prediction does not look
to price alone. Wireless service offers consumers a better product—full mobility. That advantage will make wireless an attractive substitute even at higher prices. For decades, consumers were
happy enough with free broadcast. The FCC officially scoffed
at the idea that significant numbers of consumers would prefer
to pay $20 a month for cable. But most households in fact
did because cable was so much better than the free service it
replaced. Wireless and wireline telephony are now on a similar
competitive trajectory. If and when they do converge in a single
market, local exchange service will be certifiably competitive

---

Feb. 25, 1997. Another carrier, WinStar Communications, provides a wireless
fiber service using the 38 GHz band. Wireless local loop technology has
already succeeded as a landline alternative in countries seeking to rapidly
expand their telecom infrastructure without laying copper or installing
poles. *See Section 6002(b) Third Report,* app. F.

[522] Amendment of the Commission's Rules to Permit Flexible Service
Offerings in the Commercial Mobile Radio Services, First Report and Order
and Further Notice of Proposed Rulemaking, 11 F.C.C. Rec. 8965,
8973–8977 ¶¶17–24 (1996). Industry analysts predict that fixed wireless services will be used as a "safety net" to existing local wireline service, which may
be interrupted due to weather or other emergencies, in addition to its use as
a "wireless local loop" to provide service to apartment buildings, office buildings, or older homes where rewiring costs are particularly high. *Id.* at
8973–8974 ¶18. Previously, fixed services (except for broadcast services) were
permitted only if provided ancillary, auxiliary, or incidental to mobile operations. *Id.* at 8973 ¶17.

[523] Booming Market Expected for Global Wireless Local Loop After 2000:
Worldwide Demand Projected to Approach 50 Million by 2005, PR Newswire,
Sept. 16, 1998.

everywhere, and the deregulatory implications will be significant.[524]

§10.8.4 Ownership of Multiple Wireless Licenses in a Single Geographic Market

From the outset, the Commission prohibited wireless licensees in the same geographic market from buying up each other's licenses. In 1963, for example, the Commission reaffirmed its rule barring affiliated carriers from acquiring or using frequencies assigned to others.[525]

In 1994, the Commission set limits on the aggregation of CMRS licenses in a single market. The FCC imposed an overall 45 MHz CMRS "spectrum cap," forbidding any single entity from having an "attributable interest" in more than 45 MHz of cellular, PCS, and SMR spectrum "with significant overlap in any

---

[524] For purposes of BOC entry into in-region interLATA services under section 271, the Commission has indicated that a PCS provider in a particular state may qualify as a "facilities based competitor." In order to be a "competing provider" in the context of section 271(c)(1)(A), a PCS provider must "be an actual commercial alternative to the BOC." Application of Ameritech Michigan Pursuant to Section 271 of the Communications Act of 1934, as Amended, to Provide In-Region, InterLATA Services in Michigan, Memorandum Opinion and Order, 12 F.C.C. Rec. 20,543, 20,584–20,586 ¶¶76–78 (1997). While cellular service is expressly excluded from the definition of "telephone exchange service" under section 271, PCS service is not. See 47 U.S.C. §271(c)(1)(A) and §153(47)(A) (defining "telephone exchange service").

[525] ITT Mobile Telephone, Inc., 1 Rad. Reg. 2d (P & F) 957 ¶11 ("the establishment of separate frequency blocks was designed to foster competition" between affiliated and nonaffiliated carriers and the experience since 1949 has been "salutary"). The FCC thereafter barred any licensee from owning a significant interest in both cellular spectrum blocks in the same service area. See Amendment of the Commission's Rules to Allow the Selection from Among Mutually Exclusive Competing Cellular Applications Using Random Selection or Lotteries Instead of Comparative Hearings, Report and Order, 98 F.C.C.2d 175, 218 ¶79 (1984); An Inquiry into the Use of the Bands 825–845 MHz and 870–890 MHz for Cellular Communications Systems, Memorandum Opinion and Order on Reconsideration, 89 F.C.C.2d 58, 62 ¶7 (1982).

geographic area."[526] In addition, and by separate order, the Commission forbade any single entity (or affiliated entities) from acquiring more than 25 MHz of cellular spectrum in any geographic area or 40 MHz of PCS spectrum, and no cellular licensee was allowed to acquire more than 10 MHz of PCS spectrum in the same license area, or 15 MHz after January 1, 2000.[527] Surprisingly no similar limitation was placed on SMR licensees' ability to acquire PCS spectrum.[528]

In 1995, the Court of Appeals for the Sixth Circuit held that the cellular-PCS cross-ownership restrictions were arbitrary and capricious.[529] The court concluded that the FCC had "provided little or no support for its assertions that cellular providers, released from all regulatory shackles and given free reign to roam the wireless communications landscape, might engage in anticompetitive behavior or exert undue market power through, for example, predatory pricing schemes."[530] Lacking adequate justification, the eligibility rules were struck down.[531]

On remand, the Commission decided (and this time properly supported its decision) to maintain the 45 MHz spectrum cap, but to eliminate both the PCS and the cellular/PCS restrictions.[532] In November 1998, the Commission initiated a new rulemaking

---

[526] *Communications Act Third Report,* 9 F.C.C. Rec. at 8109–8110 ¶263 (1994) (codified at 47 C.F.R. §20.6 (a)). The rules on whether an interest is "attributable" are detailed and complex, *see* 47 C.F.R. §20.6(d); but in essence, the Commission will find an interest is "attributable" if it is a controlling interest or constitutes 20 percent or more of the equity or outstanding stock of the CMRS licenses. "Significant overlap" occurs when at least 10 percent of the population of the MTA or BTA is within the MSA or RSA. 47 C.F.R. §20.6(c).

[527] Amendment of the Commission's Rules to Establish New Personal Communications Services, Memorandum Opinion and Order, 9 F.C.C. Rec. 4957, 4983–4984 ¶¶66–67 (1994) (hereinafter *PCS Order*).

[528] The Court of Appeals for Sixth Circuit held that "the different characteristics" of the markets for cellular and SMR services provided a rational basis for the FCC to treat the services differently. Cincinnati Bell Tel. Co. v. FCC, 69 F.3d 752, 765 (6th Cir. 1995).

[529] *Id.* at 762–763.

[530] *Id.*

[531] *Id.* at 762–764.

[532] Amendment of Parts 20 and 24 of the Commission's Rules—Broadband PCS Competitive Bidding and the Commercial Mobile Radio Service Spectrum Cap, Report and Order, 11 F.C.C. Rec. 7824, 7869 ¶94 (1996).

proceeding to determine whether to maintain even the 45 MHz cap.[533]

§10.8.5 Geographic Consolidation

In the post-divestiture environment, one major challenge for the industry has been how to knit nationwide networks back together again. The Commission has both allowed and encouraged providers of wireless telephone services to assemble licenses across geographic boundaries.[534]

In its original decision to issue cellular licenses defined geographically by MSAs, the Commission expressly stated that it did *not* intend to limit any operator's service to a single MSA and that there would be "no bar to the number of [MSAs] for which an applicant may seek a license."[535] The Commission also emphasized that after a cellular license was granted, it could otherwise be bought and sold freely and thereafter integrated as operators saw fit so long as licensing provisions regarding the location and

---

[533] 1998 Biennial Regulatory Review—Spectrum Aggregation Limits for Wireless Telecommunications Carriers, Notice of Proposed Rulemaking, WT Docket No. 98-205 (Dec. 10, 1998). The NPRM offers five options for managing the CMRS spectrum cap: maintaining the existing cap, modifying the spectrum cap, forbearing from enforcing the spectrum cap, establishing a sunset for the spectrum cap, and eliminating the cap and proceeding on a case-by-case basis.

[534] *See, e.g.,* Implementation of Section 6002(b) of the Omnibus Budget Reconciliation Act of 1993, Third Report, 13 F.C.C. Rec. 19,746, 19,766–19,767 (1998) (mobile telephone operators "are acquiring new licenses to gain the efficiencies of larger and/or more cohesive footprints and the marketing possibilities of multiple product offerings"); An Inquiry into the Use of the Bands 825–845 MHz and 870–890 MHz for Cellular Communications Systems, Memorandum Opinion and Order on Reconsideration, 89 F.C.C.2d 58, 89 ¶65 (1982) (defining areas by MSAs, though not limiting to one per applicant); *PCS Order,* 9 F.C.C. Rec. at 4979 ¶¶53–54, 4987–4988 ¶¶74–79 (supporting consolidation in the PCS market and expressing need for larger cellular areas).

[535] An Inquiry into the Use of the Bands 825–845 MHz and 870–890 MHz for Cellular Communications Systems, Memorandum Opinion and Order on Reconsideration, 89 F.C.C.2d 58, 89 ¶65 (1982).

power of transmitters were respected.[536] Cellular incumbents are now allowed to bid for and consolidate PCS spectrum like everyone else as long as they comply with the 45 MHz CMRS cap.[537] In other rulings, the Commission has recognized that the scope of wireless service markets may be quite separate from the geographic boundaries contained in radio licenses and that licensees should generally be free to acquire licenses to consolidate service territories efficiently.[538] The Commission might have saved the industry the high transaction costs (estimated at as much as $1 billion for the cellular industry[539]) of combining geographically contiguous licenses by issuing national licenses at

---

[536] As the Commission explained in 1986:

> [T]he wireline/nonwireline dichotomy is in large part an application processing tool. . . . The Commission sought by the set-aside to give both wireline and nonwireline eligibles an opportunity to become involved in providing cellular service. . . . Thus, the transfer of control of a nonwireline franchise to a wireline carrier, or vice versa, is not contrary to the Commission's set-aside policy.

Applications of James F. Rill, Trustee for Comet Inc. & Pacific Telesis Group, Memorandum Opinion and Order, 60 Rad. Reg. 2d (P & F) 583 ¶32 (1986). *See also* Applications of Advanced Mobile Phone Service, Inc., Contel Mobilcom, Inc., & GTE Mobilnet of Los Angeles, Inc. for a Construction Permit to Establish a Cellular System to Operate on Frequency Block B in the Domestic Public Cellular Radio Telecommunications Service to Serve the Los Angeles-Long Beach, California, Modified Standard Metropolitan Statistical Area, Memorandum Opinion and Order Granting Application, 93 F.C.C.2d 683, 692–693 ¶¶23–29 (1983).

[537] *See* §10.8.4.

[538] *See, e.g., Section 6002(b) Third Report,* 13 F.C.C. Rec. at 19,766 ("Since the first cellular licenses were granted, mobile telephone operators have been accumulating licenses to expand their footprints into new regions in hopes of capitalizing on the various efficiencies associated with economies of scale."). The FCC has acknowledged other mobile-service communities of interest that transcend metropolitan areas. *See, e.g.,* Amendment of Parts 2 and 22 of the Commission's Rules to Allocate Spectrum in the 928–941 MHz Band and to Establish Other Rules, Policies and Procedures for One-Way Paging Stations in the Domestic Public Land Mobile Radio Service, Third Report and Order, 97 F.C.C.2d 900, 910–911 ¶¶18–19 (1984) (lottery for nationwide paging networks).

[539] Amendment of the Commission's Rules to Establish New Personal Communications Sevices, Notice of Proposed Rule Making and Tentative Decision, 7 F.C.C. Rec. 5676, 5699 ¶57 & n.41 (1992) (hereinafter *PCS NPRM*). The Commission recognized that the same efficiencies likely existed for PCS:

the outset. But it opted for geographically fragmented licensing to promote "broader participation" in the early phases and hence "a greater diversity and degree of technical and service innovation than would be expected from a few large firms."[540]

§10.9   The Airwaves as Commons?

Telecom visionary and free-market guru George Gilder has developed a cogent argument for deprivatizing the airwaves.[541] His case centers on the remarkable capabilities of new, spread-spectrum technology. In the old, analog world, communication breaks down when two users attempt to occupy the same piece of spectrum at the same time. But with new, intelligent, digital radios, interference problems are quickly mediated and resolved by the machines themselves. The computer behind the radio constantly monitors for open space, much as a pedestrian hurrying along on a crowded sidewalk uses his eyes with his feet. Trains, which aren't agile or intelligent, require exclusive use of separate tracks. Cars don't because steering wheels and drivers let them dodge and weave. Spread-spectrum digital radios have electronic eyes and the power to maneuver.

The intelligent digital radios are now at hand, and their prices are plummeting. With this kind of technology, Gilder argues,

---

"[L]icensing larger PCS service areas at the outset may minimize unproductive regulatory and transaction costs and associated delay." It also "may facilitate regional and nationwide roaming; allow licensees to tailor their systems to the natural geographic dimensions of PCS markets; reduce the costs of interference coordination between PCS licensees; and simplify the coordination of technical standards." *Id.* at 5700 ¶58. The Commission balanced these efficiencies against advantages of a smaller geographic area (namely, a broader range of possible participants and the development of niche services, *id.* at 5700 ¶59) to settle on service areas that were larger than cellular MSAs, but not nationwide licenses. *See PCS Order,* 9 F.C.C. Rec. at 4969 ¶24, 4987–4988 ¶¶75–79.

[540] *PCS NPRM,* 7 F.C.C. Rec. at 5700 ¶59. Such an approach was also consistent with Congress's mandate in the 1993 Budget Act to "avoid[ ] excessive concentration of licenses and . . . disseminat[e] licenses among a wide variety of applicants." 47 U.S.C. §309(j)(3)(B).

[541] G. Gilder, Telecosm, Forbes, Apr. 11, 1994, at 99.

exclusive private tracks just get in the way. In the old world of analog, narrowband radio, every transmitter could be effectively shut down, for a moment at least, by any passing spray of radiation.[542] The new, digital, broadband world is much more robust. Errors are corrected and lanes changed continuously to avoid other traffic. Instead of auctioning off any more exclusive lanes, the FCC should begin shutting down the high-powered, blind transmitters—the obsolete technology that demands the whole beach and excludes everyone else from the surf.

Whether or not Gilder is right, Congress was wrong when it nationalized all the spectrum in 1927 on the theory that spectrum is inherently "scarce." There is no inherent "scarcity" of spectrum; there is no law of physics that limits how much information can be transported through the air, or through any other medium. Since 1927, we have increased by at least a millionfold the amount of information moving through the airwaves—and still we have not run out of space. We would have increased the amount ten-million-fold, or a hundred, if the airwaves had been left in private hands all along.

With airwaves, as with all other media, the more you spend, the more you can send: it all comes down to engineering and smart management.[543]

---

[542] *Id.*

[543] *See generally* Mark S. Fowler & Daniel L. Brenner, A Marketplace Approach to Broadcast Regulation, 60 Tex. L. Rev. 207, 221–226 (1982).

11

Data Services and the Internet*

§11.1 Introduction

The Internet is the most important development in mass communications of our times. It promises to become a major driver of economic growth in the United States and around the globe.[1]

---

*This chapter was co-authored by Antonia M. Apps, Associate, Kellogg, Huber, Hansen, Todd & Evans; University of Sydney Law School (LL.B., *First Class Honors,* 1990); Oxford University (BCL, 1993); Harvard Law School (LL.M., 1994); Law Clerk, Honorable T. W. Waddell, Chief Judge of the Equity Division, New South Wales Supreme Court, 1991; Law Clerk, Honorable Fred I. Parker, U.S. Court of Appeals, Second Circuit, 1997–1998.

[1] *See* Comments of the United States Internet Providers Association at i, Usage of the Public Switched Network by Information Service and Internet Access Providers, CC Docket No. 96-263 (FCC Mar. 24, 1997) ("The explosion of the ISP industry and the Internet is resulting in significant new economic opportunities for businesses and a new mass communications medium for consumers."); *id.* at 3–4 ("No doubt, as one of the fastest growing communications media in the world, the Internet will be a driving force behind economic growth in the United States into the 21st century."); K. Werbach, Office of Plans and Policy, FCC, Digital Tornado: The Internet and Telecommunications Policy at iii (OPP Working Paper No. 29, Mar. 1997).

The Internet is, of course, a medium—both physical and virtual—that compiles, processes, stores, and distributes content of one kind or another. Online content has various origins and travels under various regulatory labels—e-mail, voice, videotext, graphics, and so forth. The content can move instantaneously, in "real time," or it can be stored and retrieved. It can be conveyed one-to-one (as it is with e-mail, video-conferencing or a private, two-way voice conversation) or one-to-many (as it is with online "publishing," online "radio," and online video "broadcasting").

The present chapter addresses the telecom infrastructure that operates beneath the online services, not the services themselves. The following chapter addresses the extensive body of law that is aimed at separating "basic" telecom services—or at least those supplied by incumbent local carriers—from the "content" layer. That we scarcely know even how to title these two chapters reflects the profound regulatory confusion in this field. For three decades, the Federal Communications Commission (FCC) attempted to address all "online services" under the rubric of "enhanced services." But the Bell Divestiture Decree spoke instead of "information services," as did Congress in the Telecommunications Act of 1996; that is the official label now; it is also the title of the chapter that follows this one. We note here two fundamental points. First, the definitional line between the "content" and "transport" layers of the Internet is neither sharp nor clear. Second, *a great deal of regulatory consequence turns on which way a service is categorized.*

However perplexing the definitional problems, there is little disagreement about the importance of the underlying issues. In the 1996 Act, Congress recognized the importance of the Internet and similar new technologies. Section 706(a) of the 1996 Act requires the FCC and state commissions to "encourage the deployment on a reasonable and timely basis of advanced telecommunications capability to all Americans (including, in particular, elementary and secondary schools and classrooms)."[2]

---

[2] Telecommunications Act of 1996 §706(a) (codified at 47 U.S.C. §157 note).

"Advanced telecommunications capability" is then defined in section 706(c)(i) as "high-speed, switched, broadband telecommunications capability that enables users to originate and receive high-quality voice, data, graphics, and video telecommunications using any technology."[3]

Yesterday's networks will not serve. Considerations of engineering efficiency have historically favored different architectures for different types of communications. The telephone network was optimized for narrowband, point-to-point voice communications between individuals. Broadcasting infrastructure was broad, but was designed for point-to-all transmissions. Cable began life as a "community antenna," distributing video from a local headend without two-way or switching capabilities. All of these architectures and capabilities originated in the day of analog technology. Only data networks, which arrived much later, were designed and optimized from the outset for the efficient transport of digital data. The ascent of high-speed data to the pinnacle of the telecosm has far-reaching regulatory implications.

In the past, basic engineering differences among telephone, cable, and broadcast media made it easy for regulators to maintain different regulatory regimes for different media and the communications companies that operated them. Drawing legal distinctions among a "common carrier," a "phone company," a "cable operator," and a "broadcaster" was straightforward. Until the advent of digital computers and modems, there was too little in the way of "data communications" to merit much regulatory attention at all. Data communication has long been the "incidental" service tagged onto something else older and more important.

Thus, "information" (or "enhanced") services were deliberately separated from the ambit of "basic" regulated telephony. They are exempt from access charges and almost completely free of most other forms of common carrier regulation. As we discuss at the end of this chapter, data services over cable are likewise exempt from rate regulation under the 1992 Cable Act and remain largely exempt from common carrier regulation

---

[3] *Id.* §706(c)(i).

under Title II of the Communications Act of 1934. Broadcast licensees are permitted to add data transport on the subcarrier and blanking interval portions of their radio and TV bands, largely free of both broadcast and common carrier regulation.[4] Operators of direct broadcast satellites (DBS) are already almost completely free to provide common carriage, broadcast, or contract services as they wish, subject to almost no rate, content, or carriage regulation.

But wires and radios alike will all soon be digital, and bandwidth is increasing rapidly in every medium. Data traffic is growing far faster than analog voice or video. And on broadband digital channels, "data" encompasses everything. In short, the data inmates are taking over the regulatory asylum.

§11.2 Data Networks and the Internet

Voice and data networks handle communications transmissions in very different ways. The basic transmission format for the traditional voice network is a 4 kHz analog signal. Higher levels of the voice network (e.g., interoffice links) use digital transmission, as do more sophisticated versions of the local loop (e.g., integrated services digital networks (ISDN)). Digitized voice signals simply mirror their analog counterparts. The traditional voice network is circuit-switched. Each call, whether in digital or analog form, travels on a dedicated circuit (or partial circuit). The voice network is also hierarchical: many of the routes between adjacent levels of the hierarchy are fixed, although dynamic routing among alternate routes is common on long-haul routes. Telephone traffic is routed using both in-band signaling (for functions such as request for service, dialing, disconnect, and delivering intraswitch calls) and out-of-band signaling (for long-distance and most interswitch local calls). All out-of-band signaling uses the SS7 protocol.

---

[4] The 1996 Act gives broadcasters new spectrum, ostensibly to be used for digital TV, but again calls for regulatory flexibility and promises broadcasters freedom to provide "ancillary or supplementary services" over these bands. 47 U.S.C. §336(a).

Data networks communicate much more efficiently via data packets. Each individual data packet is assembled at the computer that originates the data communication in a standard format (TCP on the Internet). Since any form of information can be digitized, all information can be encoded this way: spreadsheets, voice, or video. To route the data packet to its destination, the packet is combined with the destination address, which is encoded according to a protocol of its own (IP on the Internet). This address or routing information is transmitted in band. When the data packet is combined with the destination address, the combination is the data payload itself—a fragment of data, sound, or picture associated with a unique destination address. By converting a voice signal into a data packet and by identifying that packet with a particular destination address, a data network is capable of mimicking all functions that can be performed on the voice network.

"Routers"—specialized computers—perform functions for data networks that are roughly analogous to the role of a switch in the switched telephone network. For instance, routers determine the best route between any two networks, even if there are numerous networks in between. Routers also provide network management services, such as load balancing, traffic statistics, and prioritization.

Historically most data networks were dedicated networks that operated according to proprietary standards. The early mass-market services like CompuServe operated according to their own proprietary standards, as did all first-generation financial and order-processing networks. Many still do. But the overwhelming trend is to migrate online services onto Web servers— systems that are fully compatible with the Internet and that have Web standards, described in the sections that follow.

§11.2.1   Origins of the Internet

The Internet has no defined *physical* structure; it is best described as a network of networks, millions of computers joined together by wires and radios of varying bandwidth. At the *virtual* level, it is a common set of protocols: the transmission control program/internetworking protocol (TCP/IP) and hypertext transfer protocol (HTTP)—the code of the World Wide Web.[5]

The Internet's most distinctive characteristic is that it is virtually devoid of regulation. There is no centralized Internet governing authority. No state, federal, or international agency currently regulates the Internet. Instead, the Internet manages to thrive through bilateral contractual arrangements and through the efforts of user groups that set standards and allocate network addresses.

The guiding light of the Internet is a voluntary organization sponsored by the National Science Foundation, known as the Internet Society. It governs the technical management and direction of the Internet through the Internet Architecture Board, which has responsibility for approving changes in the technical standards of the Internet. Another voluntary organization, the Internet Engineering Task Force, routinely meets to discuss operational and technical problems associated with the Internet.

Originally most Internet backbone traffic passed over NSFNet, a backbone funded by the National Science Foundation. NSFNet ran at 1.5 Mbps and linked together 37 hosts located at four academic and government sites. MCI provided the trunk lines, IBM supplied the routing equipment, and Merit oversaw the network. As word spread of the resources available over this web of interlinked computers, a variety of state and regional networks arose to provide access to user organizations in their geographic areas. Most of these state and regional networks were nonprofit organizations affiliated with major research universities.

But as the popularity of internetworking increased, a number of commercial organizations formed to provide Internet access. Some of the regional networks also began offering commercial access. Commercial access, however, was severely hampered by the NSFNet's "acceptable use policy" (AUP), which reserved

---

[5] Other higher-level protocols include file transfer protocol (FTP), network news transport protocol (NNTP), and simple mail transfer protocol (STMP). *See* Werbach, Digital Tornado at 19.

NSFNet's facilities for research and educational uses. This policy prevented commercial access providers from exchanging traffic via the NSFNet backbone. In response, in 1991, several prominent Internet access providers (IAPs) formed an "AUP-free" interconnection point, the Commercial Internet Exchange (CIX), through which member organizations could interconnect. At the CIX, members could exchange traffic without having to adhere to the NSFNet's acceptable use policy.

Around this time, Internet usage exploded, and the National Science Foundation decided that the provision of backbone services would best be left to commercial backbone providers. The National Science Foundation decided to cut all funding for the NSFNet as of April 30, 1995, leaving commercial backbone providers such as Alternet, PSInet, SprintLink, InternetMCI, and ANS to take up the slack. Regional networks and large IAPs wishing to connect to a backbone now have to connect to one of these commercial backbones.[6]

As part of privatization, the National Science Foundation has proposed further restructuring of the Internet's architecture. To prevent the commercial backbones from setting up a hodgepodge of bilateral connection points—potentially creating routing chaos—the National Science Foundation funded three network access points (NAPs), where backbones, regional networks, and IAPs could interconnect without having to adhere to an acceptable use policy. NAPs and the network multiplied and grew from there. This architecture moved the national Internet structure from a noncommercial backbone with parallel commercial backbones to a more complex system of multiple commercial backbones with major exchange points.

---

[6] The National Science Foundation has funded a new very-high-speed backbone network (vBNS) to interconnect its five supercomputing centers at 155 Mbps. This network will not provide the IAPs and large regional networks with backbone service. Rather, it will have an acceptable use policy that emphasizes developing capabilities for high-definition remote visualization and video transmission. Various other government agencies continue to maintain backbones that are reserved for their own traffic, such as ESNet (Energy and Sciences Network) and NSI (NASA Science Internet).

§11.2.2 Data Networks: The Internet's Physical Infrastructure

The physical infrastructure of the Internet is divided (roughly) into five layers.[7]

1. Customer Premises Equipment (CPE): Some 80 million users (at last count)[8]—or, more precisely, their computers, serial ports, modems, ISDN adapters, cable modems, digital subscriber line (DSL) adapters, satellite dishes, wireless transceivers, and so forth.

2. Local access—wired or wireless, telephone, cable, terrestrial or satellite.[9]

3. Some 5,000 Internet service providers (ISPs) that connect high-speed business lines and individual dial-up connections to Internet terminal equipment.[10] These are mostly regional networks that serve a specific geographic area over a collection of dial-up lines and trunks that interconnect residential and small-business customers, larger-business LANs, and ISPs.

4. The ISPs link in turn to 39 North American Internet backbone networks.[11] They interconnect at 11 major NAPs.[12] The backbones provide cross-country carriage along with connections to other regional networks and other national and international backbones.

---

[7] See generally J. Rickard, Internet Architecture, Boardwatch Magazine's Directory of Internet Service Providers 8 (Winter 1998–Spring 1999).

[8] This figure is for the United States. It is estimated that the global Internet user population is 148 million, with 33.25 million users in Europe and 23.7 users in Asia/Pacific. See Infoseek.com Industry Watch, Africa Has Lowest Internet Usage Worldwide (visited Oct. 27, 1998) <http://www.industry watch.com/story/19981028/03/08/759353_st.html>.

[9] Bellcore, TR-EOP-000315, Local Exchange Routing Guide (LERG) (Dec. 1, 1997).

[10] B. McCarthy, Introduction, Boardwatch Magazine's Directory of Internet Service Providers 4 (Winter 1998–Spring 1999).

[11] See Rickard, Internet Architecture at 15–16.

[12] Id. at 11.

5. Around 40 million servers, the computers on which content is stored and transactions are executed.[13]

§11.2.2.1 Life at the Edge: Computers, Modems, and Servers

Computers, modems, and set-top boxes surround the Internet at its periphery. On the residential desktop stands the "client." This is typically a personal computer (PC), equipped with a modem or digital terminating equipment, like an ISDN device (frequently, but incorrectly, called a "modem," too). At the far end: the "host"—another computer that processes requests from its clients, whenever they come a-calling. At last count, there were about 80 million wired clients in the United States and about 40 million host servers.

§11.2.2.2 Local Access: Telephone Networks

The local telephone network currently provides ubiquitous voice service and mass-market access to the Internet. Most residential users still rely on analog voice grade modems to connect their computers to the telephone network.[14]

---

[13] Network Wizards, Internet Domain Name Survey (last modified July 1998) <http://www.nw.com/zone/WWW/report.html>.

[14] Analog modems convert the digital information generated by computers into a format that is identical to the analog voice signals produced by a telephone. At the central office, analog signals are received by another modem that digitizes the signal in order to send it through a digital switch. According to Ziff Davis Market Intelligence, in January 1998, nearly 45.6 million of the 100.6 million households in the United States had a PC, for a penetration rate of 45 percent. *See* Household PC Penetration Jumps to Nearly 45% in U.S., Ziff-Davis Finds, Business Wire, June 9, 1998. Approximately 80 percent of these (or one-third of all U.S. households) had modems attached to their PCs, and all but a minute fraction of those modems were analog. *See* International Data Corporation, Going Mainstream: The Internet and the U.S. Mass Market, Computer Industry Report, Jan. 15, 1998, at 4; G. Quick & T. Wasserman, Cable, ADSL Chasing 56K—Modem Technologies Vie for Users, Computer Retail Week, Feb. 9, 1998.

Although the telephone network was not designed to carry digital data, it is rapidly being upgraded to do so more quickly and efficiently. Existing copper plant is being upgraded to provide digital circuits. ISDN is already widely available, and prices are dropping.[15] More recently phone companies have begun deploying DSL technologies,[16] which support simultaneous digital transmission of voice and video over existing copper plant.[17]

---

[15] ISDN uses advanced electronics on either end of an ordinary copper wire to increase the bandwidth of the wire to two 64 kbps voice and data channels that can be bonded together to form one 128 kbps transmission path, together with one 16 kbps network signaling and data channel. *See generally* Bellcore, Special Report, SR-BDS-000828, Issue 7, A Guide to New Technologies and Services 4-1 to 4-18 (1993). By the end of 1997, the Bell Operating Companies (BOCs) had deployed ISDN in 39 percent of their central offices, making it available to 71 percent of their access lines. Industry Analysis Division, FCC, Trends in Telephone Service at tbl. 17.2 (July 1998). There were more than 1 million ISDN users in 1997, and as of January 1998, industry analysts were predicting that there would be nearly 1.895 million basic rate interface (BRI) ISDN lines by the end of 1998 and 5.165 million BRI lines by the end of 2001. *See* Phillips Business Information, Inc., Industry Experts Predict Continued Growth for ISDN in '98, ISDN News, Jan. 13, 1998.

[16] DSL lines have advanced electronics—DSL modems—installed on either end of the line that provide advanced signal processing, digital multiplexing, and compression algorithms to transmit a tremendous amount of information: 8 Mbps downstream (to the user) for asymmetric DSL (ADSL), expected to be the most commonly deployed, and up to 52 Mbps downstream for upcoming technologies (e.g., for very high speed DSL (VDSL)). DSL's greatest drawback is its limited geographic serving ability. For example, ADSL lines can be used only to connect subscribers at less than 18,000 feet from a central office, which only covers 80 percent of U.S. access lines. In addition, speed decreases with distance from the central office (at 18,000 feet, ADSL offers a data rate of around 2 Mbps). *See generally* ADSL Forum, Frequently Asked Questions (visited Nov. 16, 1998) <http://www.adsl.com/faq.html>; ADSL Forum, VDSL-Frequently Asked Questions (visited Nov. 16, 1998) <http://www.adsl.com/vadsl_faq.html>. *See also* A. Reinhardt, What Could Whip the World Wide Wait, Bus. Wk., Feb. 16, 1998, at 83.

[17] In the past year, Ameritech, Pacific Bell, U S WEST, Bell Atlantic, BellSouth, and GTE all announced initial deployment of ADSL technology for Internet access. *See* Ameritech News Release, Ameritech Launches High Speed Internet Service, Dec. 9, 1997; GTE Press Release, GTE Applauds FCC Ruling on Asymmetric Digital Subscriber Line (ADSL) Tariff, Oct. 30, 1998; Pacific Bell Launches ADSL Program (Sept. 2, 1998) <http://www.internet news.com/isp-news/1998/09/0201-bell.html>; U S WEST News Release, U S WEST Turns On Nation's First Mass-Market, Multi-city Deployment of

ADSL technology, a new modem technology, adds high-speed data capability to traditional local exchange service. This is accomplished by placing an ADSL modem at each end of the local exchange customer's copper local loop. Typically, one modem—the digital subscriber line multiplexer or DSLAM—is located in the local exchange customer's serving wire center and the other at the customer's premises. The combined ADSL modems create three transmission channels. One channel is used for traditional voice-grade, circuit-switched applications, while the other two channels are used for high-speed data communications (one "downstream" channel, one "upstream").

The data channels are connected to a fast packet switched network; the voice channel is connected to a traditional voice-grade switch. ADSL does not provide a dial-up capability. Instead, it creates a dedicated virtual circuit that is always active—a permanent virtual channel to a single (but changeable) destination specified by the customer—a corporate LAN or an ISP, for example. The end user places long-distance "calls" by entering or "dialing" the called party's Internet protocol (IP) address (e.g., 155.179.79.70) or its associated uniform resource locator (URL) name (e.g., www.khhte.com).

§11.2.2.3 Local Access: Cable and Wireless Alternatives

Cable modem service is one of the most prominent and rapidly expanding high-speed data services being offered in the targeted market for ADSL. As of this writing, cable modem service is commercially available to more than 20 million homes or

---

Ultra-Fast ADSL Internet Service, May 4, 1998; BellSouth News Release, BellSouth Announces Aggressive 30 Market Roll-Out of Ultra-high Speed BellSouth.Net FastAccess ADSL Service, May 20, 1998; R. Sykes, ADSL Goes to Limited U.S. Market (Oct. 7, 1998) <http:/cnn.com/TECH/computing/9810/07/adslusa/index.html>. MCI WorldCom also announced plans to offer DSL services nationwide by the second quarter of 1999 including such additional services as frame relay, ATM (asynchronous transfer mode—a high-speed cell-based data transmission protocol that may be run over ADSL), and voice. MCI WorldCom Press Release, MCI WorldCom Delivers DSL Integrated Local Access Services for the Enterprise, Jan. 26, 1999.

about 20 percent of all cable homes passed in North America. The number of cable modem subscribers in North America is estimated at more than 800,000 as of July 1, 1999, about 80 to 90 percent of the entire high-speed market.

Cable modem service is provided using two different methods—two-way cable modems that send and receive data exclusively over the cable company's coaxial cable running to the location (e.g., they do not use the local service or a loop provided by any local exchange carrier) and "telco-return" modems, which use an access line to provide the "upstream" transmission (all "downstream" transmissions are made through the coaxial cable). More than 85 percent of the cable modem subscribers are receiving service with two-way cable modems, with the remainder being served by telco-return modems. Two-way cable modem service is quite like ADSL from a customer's perspective—usually offered on a unlimited use, "always on," basis. Cable operators benefit from a basic network infrastructure that can provide a greater bandwidth than a twisted pair. Cable modem service thus typically starts at a rate of 10 Mbps downstream and often reaches 30 Mbps—as compared to typical ADSL downstream rates of 1.5 Mbps on LEC copper. Moreover, a two-way cable modem can offer an upstream rate as high as the downstream rate. Cable operators, unlike LECs, are generally free to bundle customer premises equipment, transport service, and Internet service—a very significant marketing advantage.

DBS operators have also introduced two-way services that use the telephone line as a return path.[18] Hughes Electronic Corp. offers its DirecDuo service, which provides both high-speed (400 kbps) Internet access and DBS video programming through the same satellite dish. There are currently 10 million DBS homes, although only a fraction use their dishes for DBS data services.[19]

---

[18] DBS providers began delivering online services and the Internet to their customers in 1996. S. Higgins, Direct Broadcast TV May Go Further than Many Predicted, Investor's Business Daily, Nov. 16, 1995, at A8.

[19] See Satellite TV Surpasses 10 Million Subscriber Mark, Business Wire, Nov. 13, 1998; see also M. Ribbing, Pizza-Size Satellite Dish Starts to Deliver, The Sun (Baltimore), Mar. 8, 1998, at 1D (predicting 30 million DBS subscribers by the end of 2007).

Although the two-way capabilities of DBS are limited, there are currently numerous outstanding proposals to deploy broadband satellite networks with much larger upstream bandwidth. The largest of these projects is Teledesic,[20] which will rely on low-earth orbit (LEO) satellites to build international satellite backbone networks.[21] In addition, there are several proposals to deploy narrow-to-mid-band satellite networks that would provide personal communications services (PCS) to end users, as

[20] Teledesic's current plan for building its "Internet in the sky" is to deploy 288 LEO satellites, which is significantly less ambitious than its original plan to deploy 840. The company plans to launch its first satellite sometime in 2001. When it actually begins service (expected in 2003), Teledesic states that "from day one" it will be able to offer "'fiber-like' . . . broadband telecommunications access for businesses, schools and individuals everywhere on the planet." *See* Teledesic, Teledesic Fast Facts (visited Dec. 1, 1998) <http:/www. teledesic.com/overview/fastfact.html>. Teledesic's network will operate in the Ka-band (28.6–29.1 GHz uplink and 18.8–19.3 GHz downlink) and will offer most users up to a 64 Mbps downstream connection and up to a 2 Mbps upstream connection. Users with "broadband terminals" will enjoy a two-way 64 Mbps connection. The terminals can interface with IP, ISDN, ATM, and other network protocols. In May 1998, Motorola announced that it would partner with Teledesic, abandoning its Celestri project, which was until that point the second largest broadband LEO project. *See* Teledesic Press Release, Teledesic, Motorola, Boeing, Matra Marconi Space to Partner on "Internet-in-the-Sky", May 21, 1998.

[21] Behind Teledesic, the most ambitious broadband LEO project is Sky-Bridge, which is being backed by Alcatel and Loral, among others. *See* Sky-Bridge Press Release, SkyBridge Will Expand Its Satellite Constellation from 64 to 80 Satellites to Meet Market Demand, June 1, 1998. The $4.2 billion SkyBridge proposal calls for 80 LEOs to be launched in time for operations to begin by the end of 2001. The SkyBridge network will operate in the Ku-band and will provide upstream connections of between 16 kbps and 2 Mbps and downstream connections of from 6 kbps to 20 Mbps. There are also a number of middle-earth orbit (MEO) satellite projects expected to be operational within the next few years, including Ellipso and ICO. The remaining broadband satellite proposals call for geostationary (GEO) satellites (LEOs and MEOs are nongeostationary satellites). Loral and Alcatel are backing a $1.6 billion project called Cyberstar. It relies on a yet-to-be-determined number of GEO satellites and will initially have land-based upstream paths. It would provide data and video services at speeds of 27 and 45 Mbps. Lockheed is backing Astrolink, which relies on nine GEO satellites to provide up to 10.4 Mbps "Major Enterprise" connections and up to 110 Mbps connections to regional gateways. The $4 billion Astrolink project is scheduled to begin operations in 2001. Finally, Hughes is backing the $3.5 billion Spaceway project, which would (initially) use nine GEO satellites to provide 6 Mbps connections.

opposed to backbone services to businesses and ISPs.[22] The largest of the narrow-to-mid-band LEO projects is Iridium.[23] Iridium became commercially available to customers in November 1998, offering satellite voice, cellular roaming, and calling card services through its network of 66 LEOs.[24]

Terrestrial wireless services are rapidly being converted to digital if they were not digital from the start. All-digital PCS networks are now being built in virtually every major metropolitan area in the United States.[25] Nextel has also converted much of its specialized mobile radio (SMR) spectrum into an all-digital, nationwide wireless network.[26] Fixed wireless technologies are expected to play an increasingly important role in the local loop, particularly for data services.[27] Local multipoint distribution ser-

---

[22] American Mobile Satellite has also launched a satellite service in the United States to offer fixed telephony and data. A report by the Federal Aviation Administration in May 1998 predicted that, at a minimum, four big LEOs and three little LEOs will be deployed between 1998 and 2010. GlobalStar, a consortium of telecommunications companies including Loral and Qualcomm, is backing a project to launch 52 LEO satellites, and has publicly projected subscriber counts of 19 million mobile voice and data users by 2012 for its satellite communications services.

[23] Iridium was conceptualized in 1987 by Motorola engineers as a LEO-based, wireless personal communications network "designed to permit any type of transmission—voice, data, fax, or paging—to reach its destination anywhere on earth." Iridium, The Iridium System (visited Dec. 1, 1998) <http://www.iridium.com/systm/systm.html>. Motorola is Iridium's primary investor and contractor. Other major investors include Lockheed Martin, Raytheon, and Sprint. The Iridium system interacts with end users over the L-band, and the satellites, gateways, and earth stations interact over the Ka-band.

[24] See Iridium Press Release, The World's First Wireless Communications Industry: Global Satellite Telephone and Paging Company Starts Service Today, Nov. 1, 1998.

[25] Unlike conventional cellular, PCS networks were designed from the start as digital networks, transmitting information in bits instead of analog waves. See Implementation of Section 6002(b) of the Omnibus Budget Reconciliation Act of 1993, Second Report, 12 F.C.C. Rec. 11,266, 11,290 (1997) (hereinafter *Omnibus Budget Report*).

[26] *Id.* at 11,306–11,307.

[27] J. A. Stern, Towering Above Us, N.J. Law J., Dec. 16, 1996, at 32. WinStar, the largest holder of radio spectrum in the United States, has launched its fixed wireless service, Wireless Fiber, to provide local, long-distance, and Internet access services over a network of roof-mounted access antennas that

vice (LMDS) is a digital microwave broadband service that operates at very high frequencies with capacious bandwidth.[28] In
March 1998, the FCC auctioned two licenses in each of nearly
500 markets (also known as Basic Trading Areas or BTAs).[29]
Although the deployment schedule for LMDS is highly uncertain, many major industry players—including AT&T, MCI,
Sprint, GTE Corp., and Ameritech—have expressed interest in
deploying the technology.[30] Another form of fixed wireless, multipoint multichannel distribution service (MMDS), also shows
promise as a broadband distribution system.[31] Finally, over the

terminate on a landline switch. *See generally* New Paradigm Resources Group
and Connecticut Research, 1998 Annual Report on Local Telecommunications Competition, Winstar 2–3 (9th ed. 1998). Other competitors, such as
Advanced Radio Telecom and AT&T, are expected to offer fixed wireless services. In February 1997, AT&T introduced a new fixed wireless system that will
provide households with the equivalent of an ISDN line, with two voice lines
and 128 kbps data speeds. *See* AT&T News Release, AT&T's Breakthrough
Wireless Technology New Alternative for Local Service, Feb. 25, 1997.

[28] LMDS enables customers to bypass overburdened phone lines to access
the Internet at 500 kbps, 4 times the speed of an ISDN line (128 kbps) and
20 times the speed of a 28.8 kbps modem. *See* J. Daponte, CellularVision
Offers Wireless High Service (June 23, 1997) <http://www.totaltele.com>.
"Generally, each cell in an LMDS system will contain a centrally located transmitter (hub), multiple receivers or transceivers, and point-to-point links interconnecting the cell with a central processing center and/or other cells." FCC
Wireless Telecommunications Bureau, LMDS Fact Sheet (last modified Sept.
17, 1997) <http://www.fcc.gov/wtb/auctions/lmds/lmdsfact.html>. CellularVision, which operates the only commercial LMDS site in the United States,
began marketing Internet access service in Manhattan and New York in June
1997. *See* V. Vittore, Cellular Vision Rolls Out LMDS Internet Access in NYC
(June 27, 1998) <http://www.mediacentral.com/Magazines/CableWorld/News
97/1997062708.htm>.

[29] There were 104 winning parties out of 139 eligible bidders. No bids were
made on 109 of the 986 licenses available, and the FCC indicated there would
likely be a second auction for these areas in 1999. At a minimum, the Commission requires licensees to provide "substantial service" during the 10-year
license term. 47 C.F.R. §101.1011.

[30] Total Telecom, U.S. Operators on Blocks for Wireless LMDS (Aug. 11,
1997) <http://www.totaltele.com/cgi-bin/disp.cgi?id=5530&type=article&
template=more.html>. Under Commission rules, incumbent local exchange
carriers (LECs) and cable companies were not permitted to bid on in-region
licenses. *See* FCC Adopts Service and Auction Rules for LMDS, Report, CC
Docket No. 92-297 (1997).

[31] MMDS is now being used for analog wireless cable-TV services, but is
being upgraded to provide residential and business Internet access at speeds

next decade, terrestrial analog television will give way to digital advanced television.[32] The top 10 television markets will go digital by May 1999.[33] Many broadcasters have already announced that they are deploying digital television broadcasts ahead of schedule.[34] Digital satellite television has been available since 1994.[35]

§11.2.2.4 Internet Service Providers

Nearly 5,000 ISPs comprise the next layer of the Internet. Some operate only packet switches (routers), leaving all the local hauling to others. Some do both. Some operate backbones, too. Smaller ISPs just link up with larger ones, but the regional and national ISPs link directly to the national backbones. The largest

---

up to 27 Mbps. *See* G. Blackwell, Wireless Access Enters Real-World Trials, Internet World, May 1997, at 15. Although operators are currently licensed only for one-way, the FCC recently granted a license to MMDS operator CAI Wireless Systems to offer two-way services in Boston.

[32] The FCC set a target date of 2006 for the completion of the transition from analog to digital television (DTV). *See* Advanced Television Systems and Their Impact upon the Existing Television Broadcast Service, Fifth Report and Order, 12 F.C.C. Rec. 12,809, 12,850 ¶99 (1997) (hereinafter *Advanced Television Systems Fifth Report and Order*). Congress subsequently made the date a statutory requirement. *See* Balanced Budget Act of 1997, 47 U.S.C. §309(j)(14) ("A broadcast license that authorizes analog television service may not be renewed to authorize such service for a period that extends beyond December 31, 2006."); Advanced Television Systems and Their Impact upon the Existing Television Broadcast Service, Memorandum Opinion and Order on Reconsideration of the Fifth Report and Order, 13 F.C.C. Rec. 6860, 6876 ¶45 (1998).

[33] These top 10 markets serve 30 percent of U.S. television households. By November 1, 1999, the top 30 markets—covering 53 percent of U.S. TV households—will convert to digital. *See Advanced Television Systems Fifth Report and Order*, 12 F.C.C. Rec. at 12,844 ¶85.

[34] At the time of the *Advanced Television Systems Fifth Report and Order*, 24 stations in the top 10 markets had voluntarily committed to build DTV facilities within 18 months. *Advanced Television Systems Fifth Report and Order*, 12 F.C.C. Rec. at 12,840–12,841 ¶76. By the November 1, 1998, due date, some 42 stations launched DTV. *See* William E. Kennard, Chairman, Federal Communications Commission, Remarks to the "Dawn of Digital Television" Summit Meeting, Washington, D.C. (Nov. 16, 1998).

[35] *See* Satellite TV Surpasses 10 Million Subscriber Mark, Business Wire, Nov. 13, 1998.

ISPs include AOL/Compuserve and MSN.[36] Most Bell companies also have ISP affiliates, but they have captured only modest market share.

§11.2.2.5 National Backbones and NAPs

ISPs hand their traffic off to some 39 North American Internet backbone networks.[37] Backbone providers install fast routers in a number of cities and then lease or deploy very-high-speed data lines to connect up the routers.[38] They also supply links to backbones in other countries. Although there are nearly 40 North American operators of backbone networks, three large ones dominate the business.

The major backbone providers are scrambling to deploy additional capacity. Despite all the talk of insufficient bandwidth for local access, the Internet frequently "chokes" in the backbones, too.[39] The federal government is working to deploy the Next Generation Internet, which will link government agencies to researchers through a new, high-speed network.[40] Industry analysts agree that the Internet backbones are very congested and offer unsatisfactory performance.[41]

The major backbones and ISPs traditionally operated on "peering" arrangements, under which they accepted and handed off traffic to each other at no charge. In May 1997, WorldCom/UUNet broke ranks and began charging smaller ISPs and backbone networks for interconnection; only ISPs that can "route traffic on a bilateral and equitable basis" to and from WorldCom

[36] R. Pegoraro, Internet Service, Please, Wash. Post, Oct. 30, 1998, at N40–N50. The next in line include AT&T WorldNet, IBB Internet Connection Services, Earthlink Networking, GTE Internetworking, and Prodigy. *Id.*

[37] *See* McCarthy, Introduction at 4.

[38] Rickard, Internet Architecture at 15–16.

[39] "Congestion on the current Internet hampers its use in research, teaching, and learning," according to the University of Michigan. *See* Group Formed for Faster Internet, AP Online, Oct. 8, 1997.

[40] *See* Next Generation Internet Initiative, Overview (visited Dec. 22, 1998) <http://www.ngi.gov/overview/fast_facts.html>.

[41] *See* J. Dvorak, Breaking Up the Internet Logjam, PC Magazine, Apr. 8, 1997, at 87.

are given free interconnection.[42] Several of the smaller back-bones complained,[43] but quickly capitulated. MCI, BBN, and Sprint then began charging smaller backbones, too.[44] The back-bone networks are now dominated by an elite, self-selected group of eight or nine "peers."[45] The nonpeers must pay up to several hundred thousand dollars per month in interconnection charges to one of the providers and must discontinue peering with the other backbones.[46] WorldCom/UUNet, for example, will not allow any provider that purchases interconnection from it to inter-connect freely with any other backbone. The group of nine, the self-defined peers, is the supplier of the true Internet backbone today. The rest are, in varying degrees and ways, their customers.

[42] R. Barrett, UUNet Sets Official Peering Requirements, Interactive Week Online (May 13, 1997) <http://www.zdnet.com/zdnn/content/inwo/0513/inwo 0001.html>.

[43] NetRail, a backbone headquartered in Atlanta, called WorldCom's deci-sion to stop peering "a restriction of free trade." *See* J. Poole, Midrange ISP Prices Climb, InfoWorld, May 5, 1997, at 10. CAIS Internet described it as "anti-competitive." *See* CAIS Internet Responds to New UUNet Peering Pol-icy, PR Newswire, May 1, 1997; *see also* UUNet Technologies to Cut Off Free Connections to Its Internet Backbone, Business Wire, Apr. 25, 1997 ("The move is seen as a power play designed to force smaller providers to pay for access—or possibly go out of business.").

[44] B. Riggs, Free Ride Is Over for Small ISPs, LAN Times, May 26, 1997, at 19. PSINet has announced that it will peer with smaller ISPs for free. *See* C. Macavinta, PSINT to Peer with Small Potatoes (Aug. 25, 1997) <http:// www.news.com/news/item/0,4,13703,000.html?latest>.

[45] J. Kornblum, Will WorldCom Own the Backbone Business? (Sept. 11, 1997) <http://www.news.com/News/Item/0,4,14171,00.html> (citing Nathan Stratton, CEO of NetRail). More generally, the number of backbone peers has declined sharply in recent years. In September 1997, WorldCom, the owner of UUNet, purchased the AOL and CompuServe backbones. S. Lohr, AOL to CompuServe's Customers in 3-Way Deal, N.Y. Times (Sept. 8, 1997) <http:// www.nytimes.com/library/cyber/week/090897compuserve.html>. WorldCom then acquired MCI, reducing the number of peers to seven. There have been other acquisitions—GTE purchased BBN; AT&T purchased Teleport Com-munications Group, owner of the TCG CERFnet backbone. AT&T to Merge with Teleport, CNET News.com (Jan. 8, 1998) <http://www.news. com/News/ Item/0,4,17952,00.html>.

[46] P. Lambert, UUNet Fees Threaten to Break Up Internet, Interactive Week, Apr. 30, 1997.

United States backbone providers connect their networks at 11 major "network access points" (NAPs).[47] For example, World-Com's MAE East in Washington, D.C., handles more than 60 percent of all worldwide traffic and an estimated 85 percent of all intra-European traffic.[48]

§11.2.3 Protocols and Links: The Internet's Virtual Structure

Every server on the Internet has a unique IP address, expressed as four sets of decimal numbers separated by periods.[49] This identifier is unique and is exactly analogous to a telephone number, complete with country code, area code, exchange code, and station identifier. The destination IP address is embedded in every individual TCP/IP data packet sent over the Internet. An ordinary home PC is assigned a new, temporary IP address by the end user's ISP each time it logs on to the Internet.

Routing on the Internet is dynamic. A communication is handed off to a series of routers. At each step, the router determines where the data packet goes next, until it finally reaches its destination.[50]

---

[47] Rickard, Internet Architecture at 10–11. The interconnection points are four official NAPs in San Francisco, Chicago, Washington, D.C., and Pennsauken, N.J.; four metropolitan area exchanges (MAEs) operated by MFS in Washington, D.C., San Jose, Calif., Los Angeles, and Chicago; two federal internet exchanges (FIXes) in Mountain View, Calif., and College Park, Md.; and a commercial interexchange (CIX) in Santa Clara, Calif. Backbones are also linked at hundreds of other interconnection points wherever more than one backbone has a router or point of presence (POP) in the same room.

[48] Dvorak, Breaking Up the Internet Logjam at 87.

[49] The Kellogg-Huber server, for example, has the address 208.212.245.129.

[50] Each router is programmed with a set of instructions (mathematical algorithms) that route traffic according to certain priorities—e.g., the quickest, simplest, or most reliable possible route. Routers maintain routing tables, which are continually updated from information (known as routing updates) provided by other routers. For example, a routing table might contain this instruction: "To reach network 10, send to node X." The router then computes variable X, based on the routing updates that it receives, and routes traffic accordingly. The same process is repeated at each subsequent router

For an ordinary computer-to-computer communication over the Internet, the originating computer can specify new IP addresses throughout the duration of the connection. Each new address results in a connection to a new server. "Surfing" is simply a series of data calls to different computers on the Net.[51]

The language that Web clients and servers use to communicate is called hypertext transfer protocol (HTTP).[52] Every Web page on the Internet has its own unique address, known as a uniform resource locator (URL).[53] HTTP is designed to run in conjunction with the Internet's TCP/IP protocol. All information that is actually transmitted over the Internet uses the TCP/IP protocol. Web browsers and servers translate information between the HTTP and TCP/IP protocols. Thus, a request by a client to access Big Yellow is created in HTTP (i.e., www.bigyellow. com), converted by the ISP into TCP/IP, sent over the Internet, received by the server, and converted by the server back into HTTP.

A "hypertext link" is an element in an electronic document (i.e., a Web page) that "links" that place in the document to another place in the same document, to a different document on the same Web site, or to a different document on an entirely different Web site. On the World Wide Web, a surfer can use links

---

that a data packet encounters. It is therefore possible that each individual packet in a given data transmission will travel the Internet over a different route.

[51] The calling computer does not typically specify a destination address as a 12-digit number. Instead, it specifies a mnemonic (e.g., khhte.com), and routing computers consult a look-up table that is updated several times a day to convert the mnemonic to the standard 12-digit format. This process is roughly analogous to translating 800 numbers to ordinary 10-digit numbers.

[52] HTTP specifies how information is exchanged between Web servers and client browsers, and it enables the exchange of files (text, graphic images, sound, video) between Web servers and client browsers. HTTP permits a browser to make only one request per connection. Thus, each time an end user wants to go to a different Web page, site, or server, the user's browser must initiate a new request and connection.

[53] A URL has three parts: the protocol, the host name, and the directory. The protocol is the language that the browser uses to request information from the server, which for the Web is always HTTP. The host name is the address of the server on which information is stored. The directory is the location of the file or other form of information on the server.

as shortcuts to jump to a second page or separate Web site referenced by that link.[54]

§11.2.4 The Meaning of "Inter" in "Internet"

A variety of different players—phone companies, cable companies, and satellite operators—now hold themselves out to end users as providing high-speed access to the Internet. Technically speaking, that is a promise to originate and deliver data traffic encoded and addressed according to the protocols of the Internet—which is to say, according to the TCP/IP protocol.

TCP/IP is a packaging and addressing system that is hardware independent, network independent, server independent, content independent. That is how TCP/IP provides seamless interconnection between Wintel and Apple PCs, Sun and IBM servers, and countless other hardware platforms. That is how it provides transparent connectivity between wired and wireless networks, copper and coax, phone networks operating on U.S. standards and those operating on European standards. Every packet is discretely addressed and encoded—with *both* the address on the "envelope" *and* the content within it completely under the control of the computer that generates the packet, i.e., the "client" or the "server." TCP/IP places *complete* control over routing, addressing, origin, destination, and content itself in the hands of the originating computer. The network itself need contain nothing but routing tables—the equivalent of a street map used by a Postal Service or Federal Express truck.

Thus, as a recent textbook explains, TCP/IP incorporates a "common addressing scheme that allows any TCP/IP device to uniquely address any other device in the entire network, even if

---

[54] *See* Implementation of the Telecommunications Act of 1996: Telemessaging, Electronic Publishing, and Alarm Monitoring , First Report and Order and Further Notice of Proposed Rulemaking, 12 F.C.C. Rec. 5361, 5381 n.114 (1997). When a user clicks on a hypertext link in a given Web site, the server on which that site is located transmits to the user's Internet browser the URL address of the linked Web page, which then initiates a new connection to the linked Web page.

the network is as large as the worldwide Internet."[55] The FCC likewise recognizes that "the interoperability of the Internet is made possible by the TCP/IP protocol, which defines a common structure for Internet data and for the routing of that data through the network."[56] That is the whole point of TCP/IP addressing. That is why we call the service the *Inter*net.

In the packetized TCP/IP environment that comprises the Internet, any forced routing of traffic of packets to a particular server or home page is precisely that—forced, artificial, concocted so as to undermine the intent and objective of the Internet protocol itself. *Any* bundling of content in connection with an "Internet" service *must* be clumsily contrived—it *must* be wholly incidental to the underlying TCP/IP carriage. The whole point of TCP/IP encoding is to *sever* all such links.[57] TCP/IP encoding implies the ultimate in unbundling, unbundling right down to the level of the individual data packet. It is not honestly possible to promise true "Internet access," but deliver a service that is locked preferentially to a particular server.

§11.2.5 *Voice/Data Gateways*

To connect an ordinary telephone with an Internet computer, the analog signal that contains the spoken words must be assembled into data packets. If the purpose is to reach another telephone, the destination number must likewise be assembled into data packets. So, too, must any other conventional call information—such as the calling party's number—that would ordinarily be embedded in the signaling system 7 (SS7) signal used to set up a conventional phone call. In addition, for an Internet

---

[55] C. Hunt, TCP/IP Network Administration 4 (1998).

[56] Werbach, Digital Tornado at 18. "When an end user sends information over the Internet, the data is first broken up into packets. Each of these packets includes a header which indicates the point from which the data originates and the point to which it is being sent, as well as other information. TCP/IP defines locations on the Internet through the use of 'IP numbers.'" *Id.*

[57] "TCP/IP can be run over an Ethernet, a token ring, a dial-up line, an FDDI net, and virtually any other kind of physical transmission medium." Hunt, TCP/IP Network Administration at 4.

computer to hand off a data communication to an ordinary telephone, the dialed number must be extracted from one or more suitably identified data packets, and subsequent packets must be disassembled into a conventional analog signal suitable for transmission through conventional phone switches over conventional lines.

Various companies are now offering "gateway services" that provide an interface between the public switched telephone network and the Internet, for fax and/or voice. These functions can be performed at both the originating and the terminating ends of the phone call. To originate a phone call that is to be carried over the Internet, an end user accesses the gateway by calling an ordinary local telephone number given to it by the ISP to which it subscribed. The end user transmits information to the gateway regarding the call's destination, and the gateway produces a packetized TCP/IP stream of data.[58] The gateway then routes these packets over the Internet to the destination gateway. There, the second gateway disassembles the packetized data and transmits it to a central office voice switch. The switch rings the called party's number and transmits the data as a standard analog signal to the number called.

With voice-data gateways multiplying, "click-to-dial" buttons and "surf and call" services are beginning to appear. Instead of containing the URL addresses of ordinary Web servers, a "click-to-dial" hypertext link contains the URL address of a gateway server that interconnects with the public switched telephone networks. When a Web surfer clicks on such a link, his browser is routed to a gateway that dials a voice number embedded in the button clicked. In effect, his browser instantly disconnects from the page he was browsing and initiates a new Internet connection to a voice-data gateway. The gateway in turn places the call.

---

[58] Specifically the gateway consults a look-up table that matches telephone numbers to the IP address of the gateway server that is nearest to the location of the destination number. The gateway includes this IP address along with the packetized voice conversation and other kinds of signaling information (e.g., basic line and trunk status (available, busy) or automatic number identification (used for Caller ID and other services)) that are required for an ordinary voice call.

At that point, the surfer's computer must turn on a microphone and speaker, and a voice conversation is under way.

§11.3 Jurisdiction

The state/federal division of authority to regulate the new data networks is far from clear. The FCC undoubtedly has at least partial jurisdiction over the data network services offered by phone companies and still broader authority over the competitive alternatives offered on cable- and radio-based systems. In all likelihood, the Commission will endeavor to assert plenary control over these networks, and it may well get away with doing so. If it does, the end is nigh for state regulation: digital data networks will inevitably eclipse, and eventually displace, all the rest.

§11.3.1 "Basic" Versus "Enhanced" Services

For jurisdictional purposes, the first issue is whether services are "basic" or "enhanced" or "information" services. As we discuss in the following chapter, the FCC has preempted the entire sphere of "enhanced" services. In addition, the 1996 Act imposes a number of specific (preemptive) federal regulations on specifically identified information services.

The Communications Act of 1934 divided the universe of electronic communications into two principal categories: (1) "common carrier" services, which were regulated in Title II of the 1934 Act, and (2) "broadcast" or "radio" services, which were regulated in Title III. It was not until the 1960s that the Commission began to grapple with the new phenomenon of computers connecting to telephone lines.[59]

---

[59] At around this time, the Commission was also grappling with how to regulate the emerging cable industry. At first, the Commission declined to assert federal jurisdiction over cable. *See generally* Frontier Broadcasting Co. v. Collier, Memorandum Opinion and Order, 24 F.C.C. 251 (1958); CATV and TV Repeater Services, Report and Order, 26 F.C.C. 403 (1959). Several years later

In its 1980 *Computer II* decision, the Commission adopted a regulatory scheme that distinguished between a common carrier's offering of "basic transmission services" and its offering of "enhanced services."[60] (*See* further discussion at section 12.7.4.) The Commission defined a "basic transmission service" as the offering by a common carrier of "pure transmission capability" for the movement of information "over a communications path that is virtually transparent in terms of its interaction with customer supplied information."[61] By contrast, the Commission defined "enhanced services" as "services, offered over common carrier transmission facilities used in interstate communications, which employ computer processing applications that act on the format, content, code, protocol or similar aspects of the subscriber's transmitted information; provide the subscriber additional, different, or restructured information; or involve subscriber interaction with stored information."[62] The common carrier offering of basic services was regulated under Title II of the 1934 Act, but enhanced services were not.[63]

---

the Commission exerted federal jurisdiction over cable, though it never precisely categorized cable as either a common carrier or a broadcasting service. After fighting over the jurisdictional status of cable for over 20 years, Congress, in 1984, ended the debate. The 1984 Cable Act granted the FCC jurisdiction over cable services, which the 1984 Act defined as a new service category, distinct from both common carriage and broadcasting. *See* 47 U.S.C. §522(6).

[60] *See* Amendment of Section 64.702 of the Commission's Rules and Regulations (Second Computer Inquiry), Final Decision, 77 F.C.C.2d 384 (1980) (hereinafter *Computer II*).

[61] *Id.* at 419–420 ¶¶93, 96.

[62] 47 C.F.R. §64.702(a).

[63] *Computer II*, 77 F.C.C.2d at 428–430 ¶¶114–118. In *Computer II*, the Commission determined that while it had jurisdiction over enhanced services under the general provisions of Title I, it would not serve the public interest to subject enhanced service providers to traditional common carriage regulation under Title II because, among other things, the enhanced services market was "truly competitive." *Id.* at 430 ¶119, 432 ¶124, 433 ¶128. Examples of services the Commission has treated as enhanced include voice mail, e-mail, fax store-and-forward, interactive voice response, protocol processing, gateway, and audiotext information services. *See* Bell Operating Companies Joint Petition for Waiver of Computer II Rules, Order, 10 F.C.C. Rec. 13,758, 13,770–13,774 app. (1995).

Although it implements fundamental change, the 1996 Act preserves this traditional regulatory taxonomy. Title I of the 1996 Act regulates common carrier services, while Title II addresses broadcasting. And although the 1996 Act does not use the Commission's nomenclature, it essentially codifies the *Computer II* regulatory distinction between "basic" and "enhanced" services, terming these services "telecommunications" and "information" services, respectively.[64] According to the Commission, "all of the services that the Commission has previously considered to be 'enhanced services' are 'information services.'"[65] But "information services," the Commission also concludes, sweeps somewhat more broadly than "enhanced services."[66] The Commission has sought comment on whether it should eliminate the

---

[64] *See* 47 U.S.C. §153(46) (defining "telecommunications service"); *id.* §153(20) (defining "information service"). The Commission has tentatively proposed that the terms "basic services" and "telecommunications services" be interpreted to extend to the same services. *See* Computer III Further Remand Proceedings: Bell Operating Company Provision of Enhanced Services; 1998 Biennial Regulatory Review—Review of Computer III and ONA Safeguards and Requirements, Further Notice of Proposed Rulemaking, 13 F.C.C. Rec. 6040, 6066–6067 ¶41 (1998) (hereinafter *Computer III Remand Further Notice*).

[65] *See* Implementation of the Non-accounting Safeguards of Sections 271 and 272 of the Communications Act of 1934, as Amended, First Report and Order and Further Notice of Proposed Rulemaking, 11 F.C.C. Rec. 21,905, 21,955–21,956 ¶102 (1996) (hereinafter *Non-accounting Safeguards Order*), *aff'd*, Bell Atlantic Tel. Cos. v. FCC, 131 F.3d 1044 (D.C. Cir. 1997).

[66] In its *Non-accounting Safeguards Order*, the Commission explained that "information services" are provided "via telecommunications," whereas "enhanced services" are only those that are "'offered over common carrier transmission facilities used in interstate communications,'" that apply computer processing applications. *Non-accounting Safeguards Order*, 11 F.C.C. Rec. at 21,956 ¶103 (citations omitted). Thus, the Commission stated, live operator telemessaging services that do not involve "computer processing applications" are information services, although they are not enhanced services. Another example would be the provision of a video service over broadcast or cable facilities, which might be considered an information service, but would not have been considered an enhanced service. This interpretation, the Commission reasoned, would provide "regulatory stability for telecommunications carriers and ISPs alike, by preserving the definitional scheme under which the Commission exempted certain services from Title II regulation." *Id.* at 21,955–21,956 ¶102.

basic/enhanced dichotomy and "conform its terminology to that used in the 1996 Act."[67]

So far, the Commission has declined to adopt a general rule as to whether Internet services are "information services." Instead, the Commission will make this determination on a "case-by-case basis," in reviewing specific comparably efficient interconnection (CEI) plans filed for each service.[68] But most Internet services, including Internet access services, would seem to fall squarely on the "enhanced/information" services side of the definitional line. The Commission has held that "end-to-end protocol processing services [are] enhanced services."[69] Similarly, Internet gateway services that provide conversion between voice and public-switched-telephone-network signaling (including routing and dialing information), on the one hand, and data encoded in the TCP/IP protocol, on the other, would seem to fall

---

[67] *Computer III Remand Further Notice*, 13 F.C.C. Rec. at 6067 ¶42. Under this proposal, all services would be deemed either telecommunications or information services.

[68] *Non-accounting Safeguards Order*, 11 F.C.C. Rec. at 21,967–21,968 ¶127. The Commission has, however, ruled that Internet access services are information services, at least when provided by ISPs. *See* Federal-State Joint Board on Universal Service, Report to Congress, 13 F.C.C. Rec. 11,501, 11,536 ¶73 (1998) (hereinafter *Report to Congress*).

[69] *Non-accounting Safeguards Order*, 11 F.C.C. Rec. at 21,957 ¶105. In the *Non-accounting Safeguards Order*, the FCC concluded that "both protocol conversion and protocol processing services constitute information services under the 1996 Act." *Id.* at 21,956 ¶104. The Commission explicitly rejected the argument that "information services" refers only to those services that transform or process the *content* of information transmitted by an end user. Rather, the Commission ruled that "an end-to-end protocol conversion service that enables an end-user to send information into a network in one protocol and have it exit the network in a different protocol clearly 'transforms' user information." *Id.* The Commission further noted that under *Computer II* and *Computer III*, three categories of protocol processing services were treated as basic, rather than enhanced, services "because they result in no net protocol conversion to the end-user." *Id.* at 21,957 ¶106. The Commission explained that "[b]ecause 'no net' protocol processing services are information service capabilities used 'for the management, control, or operation of a telecommunications system or the management of a telecommunications service,'" they constitute telecommunications services, rather than information services, under the 1996 Act. *Id.*

squarely on the "enhanced/information services" side of the line.[70]

With three decades of precedent on their side, service providers may be able to place themselves on the (largely deregulated) "enhanced" side of the line if they so choose. That precedent has uniformly held that even a peppercorn of change in content effected by the service provider converts the *whole* service from a "basic" service into an "enhanced." This absolutist approach was convenient to regulators when the main purpose of the definitions was to maintain a quarantine around the basic service monopoly. As discussed in more detail in section 11.7, however, regulators not quite ready for wholesale deregulation may soon find that strong line of precedent inconvenient, in that it readily permits any enterprise in the digital future to place itself on the deregulated side of the line if it chooses.

§11.3.2   Federal Regulation of "Basic" LEC Data Services

In May 1998, GTE filed an interstate access tariff with the FCC to establish a new offering of ADSL.[71] The Commission suspended the tariff for one day, imposed an accounting order,[72]

---

[70] Where Bell Atlantic gateways process *both* ends of a call made over the Internet (i.e., an originating gateway converts the voice signal to a data packet, and a destination gateway converts the data packet back into a voice signal), Bell Atlantic might be said to provide a "no net" protocol processing service. As a general matter, however, there is no guarantee that the voice signal converted into a data packet by the originating gateway will be turned back into voice conversation by a Bell Atlantic destination gateway. The data packet might simply be downloaded to a computer/server and never listened to at all, or it might be subjected to further digital processing. Since there is no assurance from Bell Atlantic's perspective that the data packet assembled by the originating gateway will be disassembled by a Bell Atlantic gateway, it is sensible to conclude that the entire operation will be treated as a net protocol conversion.

[71] GTE Telephone Operations, GTOC Tariff No. 1, GTOC Transmittal No. 1148 (filed May 15, 1998, to become effective May 30, 1998).

[72] GTE Telephone Operations, GTOC Tariff No. 1, GTOC Transmittal No. 1148, Order, 13 F.C.C. Rec. 13,798 (1998) (order suspending the transmittal

and subsequently issued an order designating for investigation the issue whether GTE's ADSL service was an interstate service that was properly tariffed at the federal level.[73] Five months later the Commission ruled that it was.[74]

More than 40 parties filed comments in response to GTE's direct case. At stake, many felt, was the possibility of not just ADSL connections to the Internet being classified as interstate, but dial-up connections to ISPs as well. This in turn has significant revenue implications for telephone companies under existing reciprocal compensation agreements.

Competitive LECs and ISPs argued that the Internet traffic delivered over GTE's ADSL service consists of one intrastate call that terminates at the ISP's local server, or point of presence (POP), followed by a second, separate interstate connection from the ISP's POP to the Internet Web site.[75] The Commission rejected this two-call approach, however, stating that "the communications at issue here do not terminate at the ISPs local server . . . but continue to the ultimate destination or destinations, very often at a distant Internet Web site accessed by the end user."[76] The Commission also rejected the argument that its

---

for one day and requiring GTE to keep an accounting for revenue from the service).

[73] GTE Telephone Operations, GTOC Tariff No. 1, GTOC Transmittal No. 1148, Order Designating Issues for Investigation, 13 F.C.C. Rec. 15,654 (1998). As of this writing, the Common Carrier Bureau has released three other orders designating this issue for investigation in response to tariffs filed by other BOCs seeking to offer ADSL service. *See* Bell Atlantic Telephone Companies, Bell Atlantic Tariff No. 1, Transmittal No. 1076, Order Suspending Tariff and Designating Issues for Investigation, 13 F.C.C. Rec. 17,883 (1998), as amended Sept. 30, 1998; Pacific Bell Telephone Company, Pacific Bell Tariff No. 128, Pacific Bell Transmittal No. 1986, Order Designating Issues for Investigation, 13 F.C.C. Rec. 16,326 (1998); BellSouth Telecommunications, Inc., BellSouth Tariff No. 1, BellSouth Transmittal No. 476, Order Suspending Tariff and Designating Issues for Investigation, 13 F.C.C. Rec. 16,286 (1998).

[74] GTE Telephone Operating Cos., GTOC Tariff No. 1, GTOC Transmittal No. 1148, Memorandum Opinion and Order, 13 F.C.C. Rec. 22,466 (1998) (hereinafter *GTE Tariff Order*).

[75] *Id.* at 22,474 ¶15.

[76] *Id.* at 22,476 ¶19. *See also id.* at 22,475 ¶17 ("[T]he Commission traditionally has determined the jurisdictional nature of communications by the

Universal Service Order ruling that ISPs do not offer "telecommunication services" and are not "telecommunications carriers,"[77] precluded a finding that the communication was a single call. The Commission pointed out that under the 1996 Act definition of information service, "an information service, while not a telecommunications service itself, is provided *via telecommunications*," and therefore "necessarily require[s] a transmission component in order for users to access information."[78]

Nor was the Commission persuaded by the argument that its *Access Charge Reform Order,* which treated enhanced service providers (ESPs) as end users for the purpose of applying access charges, mandated the two-call analysis.[79] As the Commission pointed out, "[t]hat the Commission *exempted* ESPs from access charges indicates its understanding that they in fact use interstate access service; otherwise, the exemption would not be

---

end point of the communication and consistently has rejected attempts to divide communications at any intermediate points of switching or exchanges between carriers."). The Commission cited its decisions on voice messaging and on 800 and credit card calls, which applied the same principle. *See* Petition for Emergency Relief and Declaratory Ruling Filed by the BellSouth Corp., Memorandum Opinion and Order, 7 F.C.C. Rec. 1619, 1620 ¶9 (1992) (holding that an incoming interstate transmission call to a switch serving a voice mail subscriber and an intrastate transmission of that message from the switch to a voice mail apparatus were a single interstate call). *See also* Teleconnect Company, Complainant v. Bell Telephone Company of Pennsylvania, Memorandum Opinion and Order, 10 F.C.C. Rec. 1626, 1629 ¶¶12–15 (1995) (800 travel service); Southwestern Bell Telephone Company, Transmittal Nos. 1537 and 1560, Revisions to Tariff No. 68, Order Designating Issues for Investigation, 3 F.C.C. Rec. 2339 (1988) (credit card calls).

[77] *See Report to Congress,* 13 F.C.C. Rec. at 11,536 ¶73 ("We find that Internet access services are appropriately classed as information, rather than telecommunications, services."); *id.* at 11,534 ¶69 n.138 ("[W]e do not treat an information service provider as providing a telecommunications service to its subscribers. . . . The information service provider, indeed, is itself a user of telecommunications.").

[78] *GTE Tariff Order,* 13 F.C.C. Rec. at 22,477–22,478 ¶20 (emphasis in original) (citing 47 U.S.C. §153(20)).

[79] *See* Access Charge Reform, First Report and Order, 12 F.C.C. Rec. 15,982, 16,133–16,134 ¶¶346–347 (1997) (hereinafter *Access Charge Reform Order*); Southwestern Bell Tel. Co. v. FCC, 153 F.3d 523, 542 (8th Cir. 1998) (holding that the Commission's decision to exempt ISPs from the application of access charges, other than subscriber line charges, was reasonable and lawful).

necessary."[80] Having determined that an Internet call was a single call, the Commission applied the "mixed-use facilities" or "ten percent rule" to determine whether the call was interstate.[81] Since GTE's ADSL service would carry more than 10 percent of "inseparable interstate traffic," federal tariffing was appropriate.[82]

It is not surprising that the Commission concluded that ADSL, to be used predominantly for high-speed access to the Internet, was an interstate access service. The Commission has repeatedly noted that Internet services are "jurisdictionally interstate."[83] The Commission simply put to rest contradictory

---

[80] *GTE Tariff Order,* 13 F.C.C. Rec. at 22,478 ¶21 (citing Access Charge Reform, Notice of Proposed Rulemaking, Notice of Inquiry, 11 F.C.C. Rec. 21,354, 21,478 ¶284 (1996) ("although [ESPs] may use incumbent LEC facilities to originate and terminate interstate calls, ESPs should not be required to pay interstate access charges")).

[81] In the MTS and WATS Market Structure Decision and Order, the Commission adopted the Joint Board's proposal that special-access lines carrying a de minimis amount of interstate traffic in addition to intrastate traffic be assigned to intrastate jurisdiction and that traffic be deemed de minimis when it amounts to 10 percent or less of the total traffic on a special-access line. MTS and WATS Market Structure, Amendment of Part 36 of the Commission's Rule and Establishment, Decision and Order, 4 F.C.C. Rec. 5660, 5660 ¶2 (1989). GTE also argued that because it was technologically impossible to segregate and measure intrastate and interstate Internet traffic, federal regulation was appropriate under the "inseparability doctrine." GTE Direct Case at 18. The Commission declined to address this argument. *See GTE Tariff Order,* 13 F.C.C. Rec. at 22,481 ¶28.

[82] *GTE Tariff Order,* 13 F.C.C. Rec. at 22,481 ¶27.

[83] *See* MTS and WATS Market Structure, Memorandum Opinion and Order, 97 F.C.C.2d 682, 715 ¶83 (1983) (enhanced service is "jurisdictionally interstate"); Amendments of Part 69 of the Commission's Rules Relating to Enhanced Service Providers, Notice of Proposed Rulemaking, 2 F.C.C. Rec. 4305, 4306 ¶7 (1987) ("[e]nhanced service providers . . . use the local network to provide interstate services"); Amendments of Part 69 of the Commission's Rules Relating to Enhanced Service Providers, Order, 3 F.C.C. Rec. 2631, 2631 ¶2 (1988) (describing companies that provide such services as "interstate service providers"); *Access Charge Reform Order,* 12 F.C.C. Rec. at 16,131 ¶341 (1997), *aff'd sub nom.* Southwestern Bell Tel. Co. v. FCC, 153 F.3d 523 (8th Cir. 1998). *See also GTE Tariff Order,* 13 F.C.C. Rec. at 22,478 ¶21 & nn.79, 80 (listing authorities); Bell Atlantic Telephone Companies Offer of Comparably Efficient Interconnection to Providers of Internet Access Service, Order, 11 F.C.C. Rec. 6919, 6936 ¶50 (1996) (concluding that Internet access service "like exchange access service . . . provides access to interLATA Internet

statements in past rulings that gave rise to the theories advanced by competitive LECs and ISPs in opposition to GTE's tariff.

Four months after issuing the *GTE Tariff Order,* the Commission applied the logic of that order to circuit-switched dial-up Internet connections and concluded that these services, like dedicated Internet connections, should be classified as interstate telecommunications services. But the FCC structured its decision so as not to upset the state commission rulings that require ILECs to pay CLECs reciprocal compensation for Internet-bound traffic that ILECs terminate on CLECs' networks—even where such agreements require reciprocal compensation only with respect to the termination of purely local traffic. The FCC states that "[a]lthough reciprocal compensation is mandated under section 251(b)(5) only for the transport and termination of local traffic, neither the statute nor our rules prohibit a state commission from concluding in an arbitration that reciprocal compensation is appropriate in certain instances not addressed by section 251(b)(5), so long as there is no conflict with governing federal law."[84] The FCC's order has been appealed in the D.C. Circuit.

§11.3.3   Federal Jurisdiction over Cable and Wireless Data Services

As discussed in section 11.8, other operators of other media are emerging rapidly as alternative providers of high-speed data services. For the most part, regulation of these new data media is minimal. Accordingly, jurisdictional lines remain unclear. With nobody much regulating the data services offered on these media, there is little occasion to resolve who owns the (unexercised)

---

providers that will complete connections to servers located in other LATAs"); *Report to Congress,* 13 F.C.C. Rec. at 11,533 ¶67 ("The provision of leased lines to Internet service providers, however, constitutes the provision of interstate telecommunications.").

[84] Implementation of the Local Competition Provisions in the Telecommunications Act of 1996, Inter-Carrier Compensation for ISP-Bound Traffic, Declaratory Ruling in CC Docket No. 96-98 and Notice of Proposed Rulemaking in CC Docket No. 99-68 ¶26 (rel. Feb. 26, 1999).

power to do so. Should these issues come to a head, however, it again seems very likely that the Commission will successfully assert close to plenary jurisdiction.

§11.4   Common Carriage

With a few important exceptions discussed below, the 1996 Act and all the FCC's general rules pertaining to common carriage apply equally to voice and data. Thus, Chapters 2, 5, 8, and 9 are the starting point in analyzing all obligations and restrictions imposed on the carriage of voice and data alike. The rules pertaining to franchise and open entry, customer premises equipment, rate regulation of service, separate subsidiaries (for BOC-affiliated interLATA (local access and transport area) services)—all the general requirements set out in or devolving from sections 251, 271, and 272 of the 1996 Act—presumptively apply to data networks just as they do to voice.

But the most important exception to this general rule threatens to swallow it whole. The exception concerns the regulatory division between "basic" data transport services (addressed in this chapter) and "information services" (addressed in the next). Two key points, easily overlooked in all that follows, are that (1) information services are almost completely deregulated and (2) even the *slightest* change in protocol or content converts "basic" data transport into "information" for regulatory purposes. This second point is the most important qualification here. With voice, the carrier's objective is generally to transmit the customer's call transparently and instantaneously—though 976-dial-it services, online directories, and so forth will quite often lift voice, too, from the "basic" to the "information" side of the regulatory divide. But changes in protocol, along with caching and storage, are commonplace in data networks—almost inevitable, in fact. Thus, most voice services look "basic" and in fact are. Many data services that look "basic" probably aren't.

With that key qualification noted, we survey in the following sections the main regulatory differences between "basic" common carriage of voice and "basic" common carriage of data.

§11.4.1   Resale

Local data services offered by LECs are subject to the same section 251(c)(4) resale requirements as voice services.[85] The Commission has initially ruled that advanced services such as ADSL, are telecommunications services and are therefore subject to the 1996 Act's resale requirements.[86] In the same proceeding, the Commission declined to rule specifically which planned xDSL services rank as "telephone exchange service" versus "exchange access."[87] Whether a service may be categorized as an "exchange access" service is crucial in the voice context. In the *Local Competition Order,* the Commission ruled that "[e]xchange access services are not subject to the resale requirements of section 251(c)(4)" because "[t]he vast majority of purchasers of interstate access services are telecommunications carriers, not end users."[88] Data services may end up being treated differently, however, because high-speed access services may end up being "offered predominantly to residential or business users or to Internet service providers."[89] Thus, the fact that LEC services like ADSL are styled as interstate *access* services[90] and will likely

[85] 47 U.S.C. §251(c)(4).

[86] *See* Deployment of Wireline Services Offering Advanced Telecommunications Capability, Memorandum Opinion and Order and Notice of Proposed Rulemaking, 13 F.C.C. Rec. 24,011, 24,040 ¶60 (1998) (hereinafter *Advanced Services Order*).

[87] *Id.* ¶40.

[88] *See* Implementation of the Local Competition Provisions in the Telecommunications Act of 1996, First Report and Order, 11 F.C.C. Rec. 15,499, 15,934–15,935 ¶873 (1996) (hereinafter *Local Competition Order*).

[89] *Advanced Services Order,* 13 F.C.C. Rec. at 24,040 ¶61. It is true that the Commission has treated ISPs as end users for the purposes of the ESP exemption, but this does not mean ISPs should be treated as end users for all purposes. *See GTE Tariff Order,* 13 F.C.C. Rec. at 22,477–22,478 ¶20 (rejecting the argument that the Commission's treatment of ISPs as end users for access-charge purposes meant that the call necessarily terminated at the ISP's POP). It could be argued that ISPs are more like carriers in some contexts or perform functions somewhere in between an end user and a carrier. If treated as carriers in the resale context, the question would be whether it may still be said that "advanced services [are] offered predominantly" to "subscribers who are not telecommunications carriers."

[90] *See GTE Tariff Order,* 13 F.C.C. Rec. 22,466 (holding that GTE's offering of Internet services over ADSL was an interstate access service).

be used mainly to carry interstate Internet traffic may not release LECs from the obligation to offer sharp discounts to resellers of those same services.[91]

§11.4.2 Unbundling and Interconnection

Pursuant to sections 251, 252, and 271, the Commission in the past two years has conducted extensive proceedings to define incumbent LECs' unbundling and interconnection obligations. *See* sections 2.4 and 5.5.

In its 1996 *Local Competition Order,* the Commission decided not to require incumbent LECs to unbundle or provide interconnection to high-speed data network equipment, but left open the possibility it might revisit unbundling requirements in the future.[92] As permitted by the Commission's rules adopted in 1996,[93] a handful of states then attempted to extend unbundling and interconnection obligations to such equipment in state arbitration proceedings and section 271 applications.[94]

[91] *See Advanced Services Order,* 13 F.C.C. Rec. at 24,040 ¶61 ("To the extent that advanced services are local exchange services, they are subject to the resale provisions of section 251(c)(4). . . . To the extent that advanced services are exchange services, we believe that advanced services are fundamentally different from the exchange access services that the Commission referenced in the Local Competition Order and concluded were not subject to section 251(c)(4).")

[92] *Local Competition Order,* 11 F.C.C. Rec. at 15,683 ¶366 (list of seven network elements that incumbent LECs had to make available to new entrants); *id.* at 15,626 ¶246 (noting the Commission's authority to identify additional unbundling requirements in the future). FCC Rule 319, 47 C.F.R. §51.319, which codified the unbundling of the seven network elements listed in the *Local Competition Order,* was vacated by the Supreme Court in AT&T Corp. v. Iowa Utilities Board, 119 S. Ct. 721 (1999).

[93] *Local Competition Order,* 11 F.C.C. Rec. at 15,499 ¶244 (tentatively adopting the conclusion that states could impose additional unbundling requirements pursuant to section 252(e)(3)). FCC Rule 319, 47 U.S.C. §51.319, which codified the specific unbundling requirements of the *Local Competition Order,* was vacated by the Supreme Court in AT&T Corp. v. Iowa Utilities Board, 119 S. Ct. 721 (1999).

[94] *See, e.g.,* MCI Telecomms. v. Bell Atlantic-Va., Civ. No. 3:97CV629 (E.D. Va. July 1, 1998) (denying access to dark fiber and denying subloop unbundling because of technical infeasibility); MCI Telecomms. v. U S WEST

In August 1998, the Commission returned to this issue and concluded that advanced telecommunications services provided by LECs (as distinct from wholly separate subsidiaries) must be unbundled.[95] The Commission ruled that, pursuant to section 251(c)(3), incumbent LECs must unbundle local loops capable of transporting high-speed digital signals.[96] "[I]f we are to promote the deployment of advanced telecommunications capability to all Americans, competitive LECs must be able to obtain access to incumbent LECxDSL-capable loops on an unbundled and nondiscriminatory basis."[97] The Commission further proposed to expand its unbundling requirements to allow competitive LECs to request "sufficient[ly] detailed information about the loop so that competitive LECs can make an independent determination about whether the loop is capable of supporting the xDSL equipment they intend to install."[98] For reasons discussed in the next section, the Commission has issued a notice of rulemaking to determine the extent and manner of unbundling for DSL-equipped local loops.[99]

As of this writing, we do not know just how far the Commission will try to push the unbundling of high-speed data networks deployed by LECs. One petitioner asked the Commission to adopt as federal requirements state policies that would (a) require ILECs to provide combinations of UNEs; (b) require sub-loop unbundling at four points: NID (network interface device),

---

Communications, Inc., No. C97-1508R (W.D. Wash. July 21, 1998) (holding that dark fiber is an unbundled network element (UNE) and ordering collocation of remote switching units); Southwestern Bell Tel. Co. v. AT&T Communications of the Southwest, Inc., No. A97-CA-13255 (W.D. Tex. Aug. 17, 1998) (holding that operational support systems were UNEs).

[95] *Advanced Services Order,* 13 F.C.C. Rec. at 24,035–24,039 ¶¶50–58. The Commission also concluded that "the availability of cost efficient collocation arrangements is essential for the deployment of advanced services by facilities-based competing providers" and that incumbent LECs had a "statutory obligation to offer cost efficient and flexible collocation arrangements" to competing providers. *Advanced Services Order* 13 F.C.C. Rec. at 24,041–24,042 ¶64.

[96] *Id.* at 24,036–24,037 ¶52.

[97] *Id.*

[98] *Id.* at 24,081–24,082 ¶157.

[99] *Id.* at 24,083–24,084 ¶162.

distribution cable, concentration electronics, and feeder cable; and (c) require performance measurements regarding the availability of DSL loops.[100] Others have sought similar results through challenges to the federal tariffs recently filed by LECs for ADSL services. They challenge BOC tariffs on the grounds that the tariffs improperly require customers to purchase both ADSL-based loop transmission and ATM transport between the central office and the Internet service provider/network service provider location, or that the tariffs improperly tie ADSL service to basic local exchange voice service, or that the tariffs fail to assign outside plant (local loop) costs to ADSL service, or that the tariffs improperly combine ADSL service and CPE. Failure to unbundle is also said to violate section 201(b) of the 1934 Act and section 251 of the 1996 Act. Section 201 bars the tying of less competitive services, such as ADSL, to a more competitive service such as ATM. Section 251 commands carriers to provide interconnection to their networks "at any technically feasible point."

At a minimum, the Commission will have to revise its approach to the unbundling of network elements in light of the Supreme Court's decision in *AT&T Corp. v. Iowa Utilities Board.*[101] As explained more fully in section 5.5.3.5, the Commission had essentially equated the "impairment" standard under the second prong of section 251(d)(2) with the "necessary" standard under the first prong.[102] The Court rejected the Commission's methodology, stating that section 251(d)(2) "require[d] the Commission

---

[100] *See* Petition of the Association for Local Telecommunications Services for a Declaratory Ruling at 36–45, Petition of the Association for Local Telecommunications Services (ALTS) for a Declaratory Ruling Establishing Conditions Necessary to Promote Deployment of Advanced Telecommunications Capability Under Section 706 of the Telecommunications Act of 1996, CC Docket No. 98-78 (FCC May 27, 1998).

[101] 119 S. Ct. 721 (1999).

[102] Section 251(d)(2) sets forth the standard for determining what network elements should be made available for unbundling pursuant to section 251(c)(3). Section 251(d)(2) directs the Commission to consider, "at a minimum, whether (A) access to such network elements as are proprietary in nature is necessary; and (B) the failure to provide access to such network elements would impair the ability of the telecommunications carrier seeking access to provide the services that is seeks to offer."

to determine on a rational basis *which* network elements must be made available, taking into account the objectives of the Act and giving some substance to the 'necessary' and 'impair' requirements. The latter is not achieved by disregarding entirely the availability of elements outside the network, and by regarding *any* 'increased cost or decreased service quality' as establishing a 'necessity' and an 'impair[ment]' of the ability to 'provide . . . services.'"[103]

§11.4.2.1 ADSL-Capable Unbundled Loops

One focal point of these unbundling controversies concerns the qualification of ADSL-capable unbundled loops. High-speed data services require clean, low-noise loops; many LEC loops are not suitable, and loops have to be qualified one by one. LECs have that process under way and are at least nominally committed to providing qualified loops through a nondiscriminatory and even-handed process as between the LECs themselves and requesting competitive LECs (CLECs). It is a complex process, all the more complicated because loops capable of supporting ADSL-speed services using one vendor's equipment may not perform up to speed with another vendor's. Worse still, ADSL equipment attached to one loop may undermine the performance of nearby loops on the same cable.

Assuming CLECs will continue to have nondiscriminatory access to suitably qualified local loops following the Supreme Court's decision in *AT&T Corp.*, it is unclear why CLECs should be entitled to more, in this context. Section 251(c) does not require the Commission to extend the unbundling and interconnection mandates to every service that any LEC might offer, at any point in the future. Section 251(c) was intended to open to competitors incumbent LECs' bottleneck facilities, not to provide competitors with access to investments in new technologies that incumbent LECs have not yet made and in which incumbent LECs will not be dominant providers.

---

[103] AT&T Corp. v. Iowa Utils. Bd., 119 S. Ct. at 736.

If CLECs that opt to use copper loop to provide high-speed data services continue to have access to the unbundled loop, and to have the right to collocate to attach their own electronics to incumbent LECs' unbundled loops, CLECs are in the same competitive position as incumbents in the contest to provide high-speed digital services over existing loops.[104] Cable modem and DBS providers operate their own, completely independent networks and distribution facilities in order to provide their high-speed data services without any unbundled access or interconnection to the local telephone network. And CLECs do not rely on incumbent LECs' facilities to serve many large business customers; CLECs serve those customers over their own competitive fiber-optic networks.[105]

§11.4.2.2 Spectrum Unbundling

For services like ADSL, LECs wish to be able to provide basic voice service and ADSL over the same loop. One is enough, and there isn't enough copper in the ground to waste it.

---

[104] For example, SBC LECs, Southwestern Bell Telephone Company, Pacific Bell, and Nevada Bell, have developed nondiscriminatory procedures to determine whether loops are ADSL-capable and, if so, to provide these loops to CLECs. All loops are checked and qualified on a "first asked, first qualified" basis between the SBC LEC and the other carrier. SBC LECs are also instituting an ordering process to ensure equivalent access to loop qualification. A carrier purchasing ADSL-compatible loops from SBC LECs may therefore integrate these loops with its own electronics to offer ADSL and other services in the same manner that SBC LECs will offer such services. *See* Petition of Southwestern Bell Telephone Company, Pacific Bell, and Nevada Bell for Relief from Regulation, Southwestern Bell Telephone Company, Pacific Bell, and Nevada Bell Petition for Relief from Regulation Pursuant to Section 706 of the Telecommunications Act of 1996 and 47 U.S.C. §160 for ADSL Infrastructure and Service, CC Docket No. 98-91 (FCC June 9, 1998).

[105] Incumbent LECs are not inherently in a better position to enter the market for high-speed data services, a market with respect to which Chairman Kennard noted that "[a]ll companies are new entrants." *See* William E. Kennard, Chairman, Federal Communications Commission, A Broad(band) Vision for America, Remarks before the Federal Communications Bar Association (June 24, 1998). Indeed, many competitive LECs and interexchange carriers, including AT&T/TCG and MCI/WorldCom/MFS, have been providing high-speed data services for many years.

This raises a fundamental unbundling question: must a LEC unbundle channels on a single wire? Must it be willing, for example, to allow an independent carrier to provide data service to the same customer, and over the same wire, that the LEC itself is using to provide voice service? This is "spectrum unbundling." A single loop is used to transport voice services provided by the LEC and data services provided by an unaffiliated data carrier. The Commission's *Advanced Services Order* seeks comment on questions of loop spectrum management; what standard, if any, should be adopted to minimize "crosstalk"; and whether two providers should be able to share the same loop for voice and data.[106]

A roughly analogous form of spectrum unbundling is already required of cable carriers, and (to a limited extent) of broadcasters, and may even be required of DBS providers. Over-the-air broadcasters are (or have been, or perhaps will be) required to surrender air time to reply to editorials (the now defunct "fairness doctrine") or to air political statements during elections.[107] Cable carriers are required to lease a certain number of channels to unaffiliated content providers and to "public, educational, and government" users.[108] More recently the Commission has adopted rules imposing certain public interest obligations on DBS providers, including an obligation to set aside channel capacity exclusively for noncommercial "educational or informational" programming.[109] However offensive all this may be to First Amendment principle, it is not technically different in those contexts.[110] Broadcasters simply accept a tape from whomever they are required to accommodate and play it at some designated time; cable companies begin with a capacious wire that is built for subdivision into multiple channels, so assigning some of

---

[106] *Advanced Services Order* at 13 F.C.C. Rec. at 24,083–24,084 ¶162.

[107] *See* J. Thorne, P. Huber, & M. Kellogg, Federal Broadband Law §5.4.3. (1995) (hereinafter *FBL*).

[108] *See id.* §§5.5.4, 5.5.5, 5.5.6.

[109] *See* Implementation of Section 25 of the Cable Television Consumer Protection and Competition Act of 1992, Report and Order, MM Docket No. 93-25 (Nov. 25, 1998).

[110] *See FBL* §§11.5.3, 11.5.6, 11.7.

those to others presents no technical challenge at all. And satellite has even greater capacity.

Existing telephone wires, by contrast, have limited capacity, and piggybacking data channels on top of voice is technically delicate. There is an ever present risk that one signal on the wire will interfere with the other or with other channels on adjacent wires bundled into the same telco cable.

§11.4.3   Local Data Services Offered by LECs Through Separate Affiliates

As a starting point, LECs are clearly entitled to provide basic data transport just as they provide basic voice. Many states now seem to be leaning to require no less; they do not want to see their local phone companies moving all the new capabilities outside the LEC itself, and thus (for the most part) outside the reach of state regulation, universal services mandates, and so forth.[111]

On the other hand, any data service that (through protocol conversion, caching, or otherwise) crosses the line into the realm of an "information service" is presumptively subject to the various separations requirements described in the next chapter. The Commission's *Advanced Services Order* makes clear that the Commission hopes to push as much service as possible in this direction. Whatever other good reasons there may be for doing this, there are attractive bureaucratic ones, too. The FCC has successfully asserted almost complete control over "information services"—its regulatory authority is far broader and more complete here than it is over basic services.

While moving services to the "information" side of the regulatory divide has many deregulatory advantages, there are some important disadvantages, too. If LECs offer high-speed data services like ADSL through a separate data affiliate, the affiliate would presumably have to enter into section 251/252 agreements with the LEC, which would need to be approved by the relevant

---

[111] *See, e.g.,* MCI Telecomms. Corp. v. Southern New England Tel. Co., 27 F. Supp. 2d 326 (D. Conn. 1998), discussed *infra.*

state commission. The agreement would then trigger "most favored nation" obligations and other federal and state nondiscrimination interconnection rules. By offering this kind of interconnection to its own data affiliate, the LEC would have to offer comparable interconnection to unaffiliated data carriers — spectrum unbundling, in other words — unless the Commission chose to waive, forbear, and preempt.

The Commission's *Advanced Services Order* is apparently written in the hope that Bell companies will develop even their *basic* data networks in separate subsidiaries, using existing LEC infrastructure and support only to supply unbundled loops on an arm's-length basis. The Commission's order claims to address advanced data services that are "telecommunications services" in that they do nothing more than "transport information of the user's choosing between or among user-specified points, without change in the form or content of the information as sent and received."[112]

But even these services, the Commission announces, will be wholly deregulated if a LEC's parent company opts simply to build the new networks under the umbrella of a wholly new and separate corporate entity. According to the Commission, "[A]n advanced services affiliate of an incumbent LEC that: (1) satisfies adequate structural separation requirements (i.e., is 'truly' separate); and (2) acquires, on its own, facilities used to provide advanced services (or leases such facilities from an unaffiliated entity) is generally not an incumbent LEC, and, therefore, is not subject to section 251(c) obligations with respect to those facilities."[113] Only the LEC subsidiaries will remain subject to unbundling, resale, and other section 251(c) obligations, not their separate data affiliates, whether the separate affiliates offer "basic" telecom services, information services, or anything else.[114]

It may be that a separate affiliate that does not meet all the conditions set forth in the Commission's *Advanced Services Order*

---

[112] *Advanced Services Order,* 13 F.C.C. Rec. at 24,029–24,030 ¶35.
[113] *Id.* at 24,054 ¶92.
[114] *Id.* at 24,050 ¶83.

can nevertheless escape at least some of the section 251(c) obligations. In one case, a state commission,[115] and subsequently a
federal district court,[116] approved a restructuring by an incumbent LEC whereby the incumbent transferred its retail services
to a subsidiary, while keeping the wholesale services within the
LEC. In *MCI Telecommunications Corp. v. Southern New England
Telephone Co.*, MCI and AT&T argued that the subsidiary of
Southern New England Telephone Company (SNET) should be
treated as its "successor or assign" and therefore subject to the
same resale obligations under section 251(c) as SNET was prior
to the restructuring. The court agreed that the claim that the
subsidiary should be considered a successor or assign had some
merit,[117] but relied on the language of section 251(h) to hold
that that was not enough to subject the subsidiary to section
251(c) obligations. Section 251(h) has two conditions: (1) the
LEC must have provided telephone exchange service on February 8, 1996; and (2) the LEC must have either been deemed
to be a member of the National Exchange Carrier Association
(NECA) pursuant to FCC Rule §69.601(b) on February 8, 1996,
or become a successor or assign of a NECA member thereafter.
Since it was undisputed that SNET's subsidiary did not provide
telephone exchange service on February 8, 1996, the subsidiary
was not subject to section 251(c).[118] Moreover, the court rejected

---

[115] *See* Decision, DPUC Investigation of the Southern New England Telephone Company Affiliate Matters Associated with the Implementation of Public Act 94-83, Docket No. 94-10-05 (Conn. D.P.U.C. June 25, 1997).

[116] *See* MCI Telecomms. Corp. v. Southern New England Tel. Co., 27 F.
Supp. 2d 326 (D. Conn. 1998) (*SNET*).

[117] Given that the *SNET* case involved a transfer of services and not a transfer of network elements, it is not clear that this statement by the court is correct. The Commission has defined "successor and assign" as an entity to which
a BOC has transferred "*ownership* of any network elements that must be provided on an unbundled basis pursuant to section 251(c)(3)." 47 C.F.R.
§53.207 (emphasis added). *See also Advanced Services Order,* 13 F.C.C. Rec. at
24,060 ¶105. In the *Advanced Services Order,* the Commission proposed a de
minimis exception to this rule, under which a limited transfer of advanced
services equipment—such as DSLAMs, packet switches, and transport facilities—would not make an advanced services affiliate a successor or assign. *Id.*
at 24,061 ¶108.

[118] *See SNET,* 27 F. Supp. 2d at 337.

piercing-the-corporate veil arguments, despite evidence that at least one objective of the restructuring was to escape resale obligations. In addition, the court was not concerned about the fact that the state commission had made "no secret of its aversion to the avoided cost methodology" and had expressed its willingness not to burden the subsidiary with the resale obligation.

If a transfer of retail services to a subsidiary is permissible, then a transfer of Internet and data services must be permissible, too. Indeed, in a similar restructuring proposed by Bell South, Bell South would offer integrated packages of services, including local, wireless, Internet, and even (once approved) interLATA long-distance services. It is difficult, then, to square the *Advance Services Order* with *MCI Telecommunications Corp. v. Southern New England Telephone Co.* The Commission assumed that anything less than full compliance with its structural separation conditions would render the "advanced services affiliate" merely a successor or assign, and that would be enough to render the entity subject to section 251(c) obligations.[119] The Commission glossed over the language of section 251(h),[120] the literal language of which does not support the Commission's position.[121]

§11.4.4 Interstate Access Services

LECs can provide "access" services to interstate data networks just as they provide "access" to interstate voice. The only important difference is that whereas voice is (roughly) three-quarters in-state, the lion's share of data traffic is interstate. As already noted, this has important implications in resolving questions about jurisdiction (state versus federal), resale discounts, and access charges, among others.

[119] *See Advanced Services Order,* 13 F.C.C. Rec. at 24,055–24,057 ¶96.
[120] *See id.* at 24,055 ¶95.
[121] The Commission could arguably get around this dilemma by designating all incumbent LEC (ILEC) subsidiaries that take on the ILEC's services as a "comparable carrier" within the meaning of section 251(h)(2) of the 1996 Act. Such an approach would, however, obliterate the distinction, clearly intended by the Act, between "affiliates" and "comparable carriers."

Properly structured, interstate *access* services do not run afoul of restrictions on Bell Company provision of interLATA service. Access must be offered LATA by LATA; intraLATA trunks must hand off traffic to unaffiliated interLATA carriers; the BOC may not provide transport across LATA boundaries. The BOC may route the traffic and translate addresses as needed—though in doing so it may transform the service from "basic" to "enhanced," which, as noted, may entail a slew of other regulatory (or deregulatory) consequences. Routing functions may draw on look-up tables that are located outside the LATA; interLATA transmission of routing information is expressly authorized by the "incidental interLATA service" under section 271(g).[122]

A Bell Company's right to *terminate* interLATA data traffic is broader still, just as its right to terminate voice traffic is broader than its right to originate.[123]

§11.4.5 BOC Obligations to Offer Equal Access to Interstate Data Carriers

A BOC providing basic data access services must offer interLATA carriers "equal access" to those services pursuant to section 251(g) of the 1996 Act.[124]

---

[122] Under the 1996 Act, Bell companies may provide signaling information associated with both intraLATA services and interLATA services on a centralized interLATA basis. *See* 47 U.S.C. §271(g)(5), (6). These provisions deliberately eliminated a restriction in the Bell Divestiture Decree that prohibited Bell companies from delivering or receiving SS7 information associated with an interLATA call. *See* H.R. Rep. No. 204, 104th Cong., 2d Sess. 79 (1995) ("Section[s 271(g)(5) and 271(g)(6)] allow a BOC to engage in interLATA services related to signaling information integral to the internal operation of the telephone network, including, for example, 'Signaling Systems 7' which sends information over the network prior to the completion of the call.").

[123] *See* §9.6.2.2.

[124] The Divestiture Decree also required the BOCs to provide exchange access services, which are necessary to originate or terminate an interexchange service, that are "equal in type, quality, and price" among the interexchange carriers. *See* United States v. Western Elec. Co., 552 F. Supp. 131, 196 (D.D.C. 1982) (citing §II.A of the Decree).

The line between access services that must be offered and interLATA services that must not be has long been far from clear,[125] and may be even more difficult to police for data because of the Internet's singular architecture (which was not in the mind of the Divestiture Decree's drafters). An arrangement whereby the Bell Company merely endorsed or marketed the interLATA services is currently being litigated.[126] The chances are that any such marketing activities will end up being viewed as prohibited entanglement that pushes the BOC to the forbidden side of the section 271 line, even though there is no express provision in the 1996 Act prohibiting BOCs from marketing the activities of an unaffiliated entity.[127] Equal access concerns have also been raised in connection with this litigation, although the Commission has been reluctant to address them.[128]

[125] See FTL1 §6.3.

[126] In AT&T Corp. v. Ameritech Corp., Memorandum Opinion and Order, 13 F.C.C. Rec. 21,438 (1998) (hereinafter *Qwest Order*), the Commission considered a section 271 and section 251(g) challenge to two separate business arrangements: one between Ameritech and Qwest and one between U S WEST and Qwest. Ameritech and U S WEST each agreed to market under their own brand names a combined package of services that included Qwest's long-distance service. The Commission ruled that Ameritech and U S WEST had "provided" interLATA services in violation of section 271. *See id.* at 21,466 ¶38.

[127] Under the Decree as interpreted by Judge Harold Greene, this was certainly prohibited. *See* United States v. Western Elec Co., 627 F. Supp. 1090, 1101–1102 (D.D.C. 1986) (*Shared Tenant Services Opinion*). But the 1996 Act did not codify the Decree; it terminated it. The only express restriction in the Act on marketing is section 272(g), which prohibits a BOC to market or sell interLATA services "provided by an *affiliate*." 47 U.S.C. §272(g)(2). In its *Qwest Order,* the Commission acknowledged that as a matter of statutory construction the word "provide" in section 271 must mean more than marketing; otherwise, the restrictions on marketing set forth in section 272(g)(2) would be superfluous. *See Qwest Order,* 13 F.C.C. Rec. at 21,463 ¶32. Nevertheless, the Commission regarded the business arrangements with Qwest as giving Ameritech and U S WEST the type of material competitive advantage that section 271 was meant to prohibit. *Id.* at 21,466 ¶38.

[128] In its *Qwest Order,* the Commission expressly declined to decide whether the business arrangements "violate[d] Ameritech's and U S WEST's equal access and nondiscrimination obligations under section 251(g)," *id.* at 21,477 ¶53, but later stated that "MFJ precedent, which would expressly control an analysis under section 251(g) prior to our future rulemaking, would appear to prohibit a BOC's endorsement or promotion of one IXC's services over another IXC's services." *Id.* at 21,477–21,478 ¶54.

Bell companies clearly may, however, provide data access services in the same manner as they provide voice access services — by allowing the customer to designate a data presubscribed interexchange carrier (PIC) and routing the data accordingly. Many BOCs have done precisely that. Bell Atlantic, for example, currently provides local Internet access services, but it does not provide or resell interLATA Internet carriage. Instead, Bell Atlantic Internet customers select a preferred interLATA Internet provider, just as Bell Atlantic local exchange customers select a presubscribed interexchange carrier for their home phone. Bell Atlantic bills the customer for the interexchange carrier's fees. In 1996, the Common Carrier Bureau approved Bell Atlantic's plan to provide Internet access service under this arrangement.[129] The Bureau noted that because Bell Atlantic was providing only access to intraLATA Internet servers and facilities and offering customers the choice to "PIC" an interLATA Internet carrier, it was not providing interLATA service at all.[130]

A data access service (at its originating end, at least) must be offered to all interLATA ISPs on equal terms. Each interLATA

[129] See Bell Atlantic's Offer of Comparably Efficient Interconnection to Providers of Internet Access Services, Order, 11 F.C.C. Rec. 6919 (1996). MFS had contended that Bell Atlantic would be "engaged in the unlawful resale of interLATA service through its proposed [Internet access service] offering," reasoning that "end users will use Bell Atlantic's proposed service to access computer servers that may be located in the same state, a different state, or another country." *Id.* at 6935 ¶48. The Bureau compared Bell Atlantic's approach to Internet access service to local exchange access service. In both instances, it is the interLATA carriers that "complete connections to servers located in other LATAs." *Id.* at 6936 ¶50. In the *Non-accounting Safeguards Order,* MFS again argued that "all Internet services are interLATA services and, hence, Internet services provided by the BOCs are interLATA information services" that a BOC may provide only through a section 272 affiliate after obtaining section 271 authorization. Implementation of the Non-accounting Safeguards of Sections 271 and 272 of the Communications Act, as Amended, First Report and Order and Further Notice of Proposed Rulemaking, 11 F.C.C. Rec. 21,905, 21,967 ¶126 (1996) (*Non-accounting Safeguards Order*). The Commission ruled that it will determine on a "case-by-case basis" whether specific Internet services provided by BOCs are "interLATA information services." *Id.* at 21,967 ¶127.

[130] See Bell Atlantic Telephone Companies Offer of Comparably Efficient Interconnection to Providers of Internet Access Services, Order, 11 F.C.C. Rec. 6919, 6936 ¶50 (1996).

ISP must be offered the opportunity to interconnect with the
data access service on the same terms. As discussed in section
9.6.2.5, a BOC may have some leeway in issuing requests for proposals on "teaming arrangements" with interested ISPs. Nondiscrimination or equal access concerns probably do not prohibit
the BOC from imposing some requirements on ISPs that wish to
interconnect with the BOC's access services.[131]

§11.4.6 BOC Provision of Basic InterLATA Data Services

Bell Operating Companies must comply with the restrictions
of section 271, which generally require BOCs and their affiliates
to obtain federal approval before providing certain "interLATA
services" in region.[132]

The Act expressly defines an "interLATA service" as "*telecommunications*" between points in two different LATAs.[133] The Act
defines "*telecommunications*" in turn as "the transmission . . . of
information of the user's choosing, without change in the form
or content of the information as sent and received."[134] Thus,
under the plain language of the Act, when section 271 proscribes
BOC provision of in-region "interLATA services," it clearly proscribes *only* the interLATA "transmission of information of the
user's choosing, without change in the form or content of the
information as sent and received." To the extent BOC data services meet that definition, they are clearly subject to the section
271(a) restriction.

---

[131] The Commission has generally acknowledged that "teaming arrangements" between a BOC and a nonaffiliate for the provision of interLATA
services are acceptable, provided that they comply with the equal access requirements that were imposed by the Decree. *See Non-accounting Safeguards
Order,* 11 F.C.C. Rec. at 22,047 ¶293. *See also Qwest Order,* 13 F.C.C. Rec. at
21,476–21,477 ¶53 & n.176 (noting that teaming arrangements previously
allowed under Decree precedent continue to be permissible under section
251(g)).

[132] *See* §9.6.2.3.

[133] 47 U.S.C. §153(21) (emphasis added).

[134] *Id.* §153(43) (emphasis added).

But as we discuss in detail in the following chapter, most data services involve at least some measure of "change in the form or content"—they are therefore *not* telecommunications services at all, but are instead "information services," under both long-standing FCC precedent and the unambiguous definitions of the 1996 Act. Whether section 271(a) applies to interLATA information services is less clear. Under the plain language of the Act, it does not. The FCC has reached the opposite conclusion, however. It has declared—in direct contradiction to the language of the Act—that "[i]f a BOC's provision of an Internet or Internet access service (or for that matter, any information service) incorporates a bundled, in-region, interLATA transmission component provided by the BOC over its own facilities or through resale, that service may only be provided . . . after the BOC has received in-region interLATA authority under section 271."[135] Courts will undoubtedly be called on to resolve the question soon enough. It is hard to see how the Commission's rewriting of the Act could be upheld.

§11.4.7   Deregulation of Internet Access Providers and Backbone Carriers

To date, the FCC has not treated Internet access providers that sell access services to end users as interexchange carriers— or at least it has not subjected them to any significant obligations under Title II. The Commission does not subject them to federal certification requirements under section 214 of the Communications Act, and it does not regulate them as providers of international services even though end users can establish international Internet connections. The FCC also does not require ISPs to file tariffs or to pay access charges, both of which are required of interexchange carriers.

As discussed below, however, there are signs that the Commission hopes to change this, at least insofar as necessary to

---

[135] *Non-accounting Safeguards Order*, 11 F.C.C. Rec. at 21,967 ¶127 (footnote omitted).

impose on interstate data carriers obligations to contribute to universal service funds and subsidies. The only alternative is to stand by and watch those funds and subsidies evaporate, as data networks progressively take over the transport of voice along with everything else.

§11.5 Rate Regulation

If the Internet's physical structure is ephemeral, its economics are downright deceptive. Most residential customers still use dial-up voice circuits to access their ISP, taking advantage of the flat-rate (all-you-can-eat) prices typically charged to residential users. As discussed in section 11.5.1 below, this is uneconomic all around and has begun to create significant problems.[136]

Residential users typically pay their ISP a flat fee to obtain an Internet connection of a specified bandwidth. For a time, this created significant overload problems on some of the more popular ISPs—AOL, in particular. Regional ISPs pay in turn for the connections on both sides of their switches. They typically pay the LEC for ordinary voice business lines on which the incoming circuit-switched calls terminate. And on the other side of their router, they pay to connect to backbone providers. Until recently, backbone providers have likewise charged regionals a flat fee to connect to their networks. But in the spring of 1997, the largest backbone providers began to change those arrangements, shifting to more traffic-sensitive charges.[137] In May 1997, WorldCom/ UUNet broke ranks and began charging smaller ISPs and back-

---

[136] *See* J. Gregory Sidak & Daniel F. Spulber, Cyberjam: The Law and Economics of Internet Congestion of the Telephone Network, 21 Harv. J.L. & Pub. Poly. 327 (1998).

[137] Now that MSFNet no longer obtains any subsidies, it is expected to dramatically increase its connection charges. This will have the greatest effect on the regional providers, who have obtained their backbone services from NSFNet. The National Science Foundation cushioned this blow by temporarily subsidizing the regionals; this support applied only to regional networks that obtained service from backbone providers that connected to all three priority NAPs and was phased out in 1998.

bone networks for interconnection.[138] MCI, BBN, and Sprint shortly followed suit,[139] resulting in the emergence of an elite, self-selected group of eight or nine true "peers."[140] The number of backbone providers will no doubt be further reduced as providers merge their operations. The nonpeers were forced to pay up to several hundred thousand dollars per month in interconnection charges to one of the providers and were re-quired to discontinue peering with the other backbones.[141]

In addition, ISPs, regional networks, and backbone service providers pay fees to connect to the NAPs or the CIX. The actual exchange of traffic between the backbone providers, regional networks, and other entities connected to the NAPs or the CIX is priced according to bilateral contractual agreements or exchanged without charge under "peering" agreements.

There have been numerous proposals to fundamentally re-evaluate the pricing of the Internet. Some applications are more delay-tolerant than others. Voice and video, for instance, do not tolerate delay nearly as well as data transmission. One possibility is to prioritize packets, putting a label in the header so that routers give priority to those who demand it. This would entail significant monitoring and billing costs, as the routers would have to measure the prioritized traffic and bill the originating party. A more plausible method would be to sell "priority chits" up front and have the routers prioritize the packets with the most chits.

Another possibility is to move to usage-based pricing, charging users for every packet sent. This approach also would involve

[138] Only ISPs that could "route traffic on a bilateral and equitable basis" to and from WorldCom would be given free interconnection. *See* R. Barrett, UUNet Sets Official Peering Requirements, Interactive Week Online (May 13, 1997) <http://www.zdnet.com/zdnn/content/inwo/0513/inwo0001.html>.

[139] *See* B. Riggs, Free Ride Is Over for Small ISPs, LAN Times, May 26, 1997, at 19.

[140] *See* AOL, WorldCom Asset Swap Sends Chill Down Backbone (Workgroup Computing Report, Sept. 23, 1997) (citing Nathan Stratton, CEO of NetRail).

[141] P. Lambert, UUNet Fees Threaten to Break Up Internet, Interactive Week (Apr. 28, 1997) <http://www.zdnet.com/zdnn/content/inwk/0413/inwk 0024. html>.

substantial monitoring costs—it would necessitate measuring the usage of every end user. Moreover, it might price voice and video out of the Internet entirely because each consumes many times the bandwidth of pure text. Usage-based pricing nevertheless has been adopted at several universities and throughout New Zealand and Chile, albeit at the cost of decreased usage.

New pricing schemes seem inevitable, and in all likelihood, they will vary widely as competitors and regulators try to thrash out what makes sense.[142] Sprint's recently announced ION service, for example, will allow customers to conduct multiple phone calls, receive faxes, and use the Internet simultaneously through a single connection. Using cell-based technology,[143] Sprint predicts the network cost to deliver a typical voice call will drop by more than 70 percent.[144] Whatever emerges from this cauldron of regulation and competition will, in time, supersede the pricing structures of traditional voice services, too.

§11.5.1   LEC Pricing of All-You-Can-Eat Voice Circuits

According to one study, the demand for some 6 million "second" residential subscriber lines in 1995—almost half of all "second" residential lines—can be attributed principally to online access.[145] This growth already has put pressure on the traditional

---

[142] *See generally* R. Frieden, Without Public Peer: The Potential Regulatory and Universal Service Consequences of Internet Balkanization, 3 Va. J.L. & Tech. 8 (1998).

[143] Combined with an asynchronous backbone network, the technology allows Sprint to integrate services rather than bundle different services together.

[144] Sprint Press Release, Sprint Unveils Revolutionary Network, June 2, 1998.

[145] Lee L. Selwyn & Joseph W. Laszlo, Economics and Technology, Inc., The Effect of Internet Use on the Nation's Telephone Network (Jan. 22, 1997) (prepared for the Internet Access Coalition), *attached to* Comments of the Internet Access Coalition, Usage of the Public Switched Network by Information Service and Internet Access Providers, CC Docket No. 96-262 (FCC Jan. 29, 1997). *See also* Joint Comments of Bell Atlantic and NYNEX on Notice of Inquiry at 11, Usage of the Public Switched Network by Information

landline phone network. In FCC filings, Bell companies and independents state that Internet use is overwhelming their voice network systems.[146] Most of this strain is caused by the very nature of data use. The average voice call lasts three minutes, and the probability that a call will last longer than 10 minutes is very low. In contrast, an average Internet call is 20 minutes, and calls of very long duration—12 hours and over—are not uncommon.[147]

§11.5.2 Access Charges Paid by ISPs to LECs

As discussed in Chapters 5 and 9, long-distance carriers and their customers pay "access charges" to originate and terminate voice calls on LEC networks. Providers and users of anything that can be styled as an "online service" do not.

Initially providers of enhanced services (ESPs) were treated as end users, paying local business rates, interstate subscriber line charges, and special-access surcharges for their local connections.[148] Given the high volumes of usage by providers of online services, these rates are significantly lower than the corresponding

---

Service and Internet Access Providers, CC Docket No. 96-262 (FCC Mar. 24, 1997); Pacific Bell Attacks Internet Access Exemption, Comm. Daily, Jan. 16, 1997 (reporting that new line installations in 1996 surged to 700,000 after declining from 500,000 in 1985).

[146] K. Cukier, Baby Bells Turn to the FCC as Internet Traffic Row Escalates; Internet Usage is Causing Problems with Telephone Service, Comm. Week Intl., Feb. 3, 1997, at 10. In Southwestern Bell Co. v. FCC, 153 F.3d 523, 542 (8th Cir. 1998), Bell Atlantic argued that, as a result of the expansion of traffic on the Internet, they have been required to spend billions of dollars to enhance network capacity.

[147] D. J. Edmonds et al., Bear, Stearns & Co., Investext Rpt. No. 2510862, Intermedia Communications Inc.—Company Report at *3 (Sept. 13, 1996). According to Pacific Telesis, 30 percent of all Internet calls last over 3 hours, and 7.5 percent last more than 24 hours. Firm: Internet Fees Too Low, Chattanooga Free Press, Mar. 26, 1997, at E10.

[148] See Amendments of Part 69 of the Commission's Rules Relating to Enhanced Service Providers, Order, 3 F.C.C. Rec. 2631, 2635 n.8, 2637 n. 53 (1988).

access charges would be.[149] In 1987, the Commission considered requiring ESPs to pay the same usage-sensitive access charges as voice long-distance carriers. The FCC recognized that the distinction it had adopted earlier made no sense—ESPs use precisely the same local lines that are used for voice calls, and indeed use them (on a per-customer basis) a lot more.[150] Faced with strong vocal opposition,[151] the Commission quickly abandoned the idea.[152] It revisited the idea again in early 1997, but again did nothing.[153] It opted instead only to raise monthly subscriber line charges on second-line residential service, second lines being most often used for data access.[154]

The Eighth Circuit upheld the Commission's decision to exempt ISPs from interstate access charges, "while continuing to investigate potential future changes in the area."[155] The court noted that ISPs had been exempted for 14 years,[156] that the decision to exempt did "not constitute the creation of a new, implicit and discriminatory subsidy,"[157] and that the Commission had "not foreclosed the possibility that ISPs would be subjected to

---

[149] See Access Charge Reform, First Report and Order, 12 F.C.C. Rec. 15,982, 16,132 ¶342 (1997) (hereinafter *Access Charge Reform Order*).

[150] Amendments of Part 69 of the Commission's Rules Relating to Enhanced Service Providers, Notice of Proposed Rulemaking, 2 F.C.C. Rec. 4305, 4306 ¶8 (1987) (noting that ESPs had had "ample notice of our ultimate intent to apply interstate access charges to their operations and ample opportunity to adjust their planning accordingly"). Further, the Commission expressed concerned that the ESPs were not paying their fair share of the costs of providing universal service. *Id.*

[151] See Immediate Hill Backlash, FCC Considers Linking ESP Access Charges to ONA, Comm. Daily, Nov. 17, 1988, at 1 (a "cyclone of protest from Congress, NTIA and hundreds of computer-service users" killed the FCC initiative).

[152] Amendments of Part 69 of the Commission's Rules Relating to Enhanced Service Providers, Order, 3 F.C.C. Rec. 2631, 2633 ¶17 (1988).

[153] See Access Charge Reform Order, 12 F.C.C. Rec. at 16,133 ¶344.

[154] *Id.* at 16,014 ¶78.

[155] See Southwestern Bell Co. v. FCC, 153 F.3d 523, 541 (8th Cir. 1998).

[156] *Id.*

[157] *Id.; see also id.* ("[T]he Commission's actions do not discriminate in favor of ISPs, which do not utilize LEC services and facilities in the same way or for the same purposes as other customers who are assessed per-minute interstate access charges.").

additional regulation under a scheme yet to be determined."[158]
The appellate court also affirmed the power of state regulators
to approve separate access tariffs for *intrastate* traffic.[159] This is
potentially significant in light of the Commission's conclusion
that it is unable to determine what fraction of traffic is intrastate.[160]

§11.5.3 LEC Pricing of High-Speed ADSL Services

So far, controversies about the pricing of LEC ADSL services
have focused on a few core issues. ADSL tariffs have been challenged for allegedly setting prices at rates that failed properly to
include costs for ATM transport services, or for improperly
merging ADSL service with voice service and improperly allocating costs to ADSL, or for failing to assign outside plant (local
loop) costs to their ADSL service.

Because LECs propose to offer ADSL over the same loops
they use to supply plain old telephone service (POTS) voice,
such disputes are inevitable. Allocating the cost of the loop to
one service or the other is inevitably arbitrary, especially in circumstances where the residential loop itself is subsidized by
overcharges loaded onto access services, business loops, and vertical services (like voice mail and Caller ID). Commission rules,
however, only require LECs to identify the direct cost to provide
the proposed new service.[161] When a new service is offered over
a loop already in service, there is no new loop cost. It is perfectly
reasonable to assert that loop costs contribute nothing to the
direct cost of ADSL service, though if all services were being

---

[158] *Id.* at 543.

[159] *Id.*

[160] *Id.* ("Because the FCC cannot reliably separate the two components
involved in completing a particular call, or even determine what percentage
of overall ISP traffic is interstate or intrastate, . . . the Commission has appropriately exercised its discretion to require an ISP to pay intrastate charges for
its line and to pay the [subscriber line charges] . . . but not to pay the per-
minute interstate access charge.").

[161] 47 C.F.R. §61.38.

retariffed from scratch, it would be equally reasonable to assert the opposite and to load all loop costs onto the data (ADSL) channel and none of them onto the voice. Commission precedent for lower-speed data-over-voice (DOV) supports the view that the later arrival—the data channel—need not be assigned loop costs already covered by the earlier tenant.[162]

Access charge issues will also have to be decided anew in the context of ADSL and other high-speed data services. The Commission's orders to date have not established a general access charge exemption for online services; they have merely affirmed the ISP's much narrower right to obtain interstate access using state-tariffed business lines.

§11.5.4 Reciprocal Compensation

Under the impetus of the 1996 Act, which demands as much, LEC-CLEC interconnection agreements routinely provide for carrier-to-carrier payments of "transport and termination" fees.[163] These "reciprocal compensation" fees, typically calculated on a minutes-of-use basis, are assessed whenever one company "terminates" "local telecommunications traffic" on another local carrier's network.[164]

---

[162] Significantly the Commission previously has been faced with similar objections about a similar, albeit slower, DOV service and found no basis for rejecting, suspending, or investigating those tariffs. In 1992, Southwestern Bell tariffed an interstate DOV service called "DovLink," which was provided over existing local loops. Although MFS objected to the pricing and costing of DovLink—on nearly identical grounds to those now being asserted against Pacific Bell's ADSL tariff—the Common Carrier Bureau concluded that it was not appropriate to reject or suspend and investigate Southwestern Bell's tariff. *See* Southwestern Bell Telephone Company, Revisions to Tariff F.C.C. No. 73, Transmittal No. 2211, Order, 7 F.C.C. Rec. 6336 (1992).

[163] Section 251(b)(5) imposes on LECs "[t]he duty to establish reciprocal compensation arrangements for the transport and termination of telecommunications."

[164] *See* 47 C.F.R. §51.701(a) (reciprocal compensation applies to local traffic); *id.* §51.701(b) (defining local traffic). Reciprocal compensation fees should not be confused with "access charges," which are the fees that interexchange carriers pay to LECs for connecting the end user to the long-distance carrier. *See Local Competition Order* 11 F.C.C. Rec. 15,449, 16,013 ¶1034 ("[A]s

Reciprocal compensation clauses raise unanticipated problems in connection with Internet services. Internet calling patterns are sharply asymmetrical—everyone seems to "originate" Internet traffic rather than terminate it; the home computer dials out frequently, but it almost never answers incoming Internet "calls." In addition, the "calls" that the computers place tend to last a long time. And for residential service at least, local regulators typically require ILECs to charge flat-rate, usage-insensitive fees for use of local lines. The upshot is that when local circuits are used to establish a dial-up Internet connection, from home computer through LEC to ISP, the LEC can collect only its usual flat-rate monthly fee from its residential customer, but may incur unlimited "reciprocal compensation" liability to the ISP, which is ostensibly "terminating" this arguably "local" call.

LECs have argued that Internet calls are "interstate" and not local for the purposes of reciprocal compensation agreements. Before the Commission issued its *GTE Tariff Order* on ADSL, several states[165] and two federal courts[166] had ruled to the contrary.[167] In the *GTE Tariff Order,* the Commission addressed whether calls made over dedicated ADSL lines, are local calls.[168] As discussed in sections 11.3.2 and 12.6.1, the Commission has

---

a legal matter, . . . transport and termination of local traffic are different services than access services for long-distance telecommunications.").

[165] Prior to the *GTE Tariff Order,* some 21 state commissions had ruled that LECs must provide reciprocal compensation for calls to the Internet.

[166] *See* Southwestern Bell Tel. Co. v. Public Util. Comm. of Texas, MO-98-CA-43, 1998 U.S. Dist. LEXIS 12938 (W.D. Tex. June 22, 1998) (holding that calls to ISPs are "local," not "interstate," and are therefore fully subject to reciprocal compensation obligations); Illinois Bell Tel. Co. v. WorldCom Techs., Inc., No. 98 C 1925, 1998 WL 419493 (N.D. Ill. July 23, 1998) (same).

[167] In Illinois Bell Telephone Co. v. WorldCom Technologies, Inc., which upheld the decision of the Illinois Commerce Commission (ICC) that Internet calls are "local traffic" as defined in Ameritech's interconnection agreements, the district court stated that "[a]fter reviewing relevant FCC precedent, this court finds that the FCC has not reached a coherent decision on the issue of compensation of LECs providing Internet access." 1998 WL 419493 at *8.

[168] *See GTE Tariff Order,* 13 F.C.C. Rec. 22,466, 22,466– 22,467 ¶2 (1998) ("This Order does not consider or address issues regarding whether local exchange carriers are entitled to receive reciprocal compensation when they deliver to information service providers, including Internet service providers, circuit-switched dial-up traffic originated by interconnecting LECs.") (foot

since made clear that its ruling on the nature of Internet calls applies equally to dial-up Internet connections.[169] The Commission's rejection of the two-call approach and invocation of the principle that the jurisdictional nature of communications is determined "by the end points of the communication" and should not be divided "at any intermediate points of switching or exchanges between carriers" precludes any further finding that Internet traffic over circuit-switched networks is still really local traffic.

§11.5.5   Charges Paid by ISPs to Connect to Internet Backbone Services

In May 1997, WorldCom/UUNet unilaterally announced that it would continue to peer only with ISPs that can "route traffic on a bilateral and equitable basis."[170] WorldCom unilaterally announced it would exchange traffic freely only with its largest competitors, who were of roughly the same size and scope.

§11.6   Universal Service

No one has any clear idea at this point what obligations, if any, LECs will have to extend high-speed data services to all customers. State regulators can be expected to press for new universal service obligations. Despite politic noises to the contrary,

---

note omitted). The Commission contended that the reciprocal compensation "controversy" implicated a "separate body of Commission rules and precedent regarding switched access service." *Id.*

[169] *See* Implementation of the Local Competition Provisions in the Telecommunications Act of 1996, Inter-Carrier Compensation for ISP-Bound Traffic, Declaratory Ruling in CC Docket No. 96-98 and Notice of Proposed Rulemaking in CC Docket No. 99-98, FCC 99-38 (rel. Feb. 26, 1999) (hereinafter *Reciprocal Compensation Order*).

[170] Randy Barrett, UUNet Sets Official Peering Requirements, Interactive Week Online (May 13, 1997) <http://www.zdnet.com/zdnn/content/inwo/0513/inwo0001.htm>.

FCC policy seems to be aimed in precisely the opposite direction: the policy is to strongly encourage the migration of high-speed data services into separate affiliates that are not subject to the LECs' traditional regulatory obligations.

If LECs themselves continue to deploy high-speed data services, one pressing problem in connection with universal service is that not all existing LEC copper plant can be upgraded to provide high-speed digital services like ADSL. Because of technical limitations, ADSL cannot be offered to every customer, even customers served by an ADSL-equipped central office. Customers must be located within the maximum acceptable standard distance of a suitably equipped central office, and their lines must meet certain transmission criteria. ADSL cannot be provided over a loop with load coils or any excessive bridged tap (multiple plant), nor can a DSLAM installed in a central office provide ADSL over a loop provisioned using any pair gain system (e.g., SLC, digital additional main line (DAML)). Some conditions can be successfully identified and removed to allow a loop to qualify, and other conditions can outright disqualify the loop for ADSL capability.[171] Moreover, there are often interference effects from other digital services in the loop's cable. ADSL is affected by interference from other digital services or technologies within the network.

As discussed in Chapter 6, in addition to restructuring the universal support funding mechanism that had existed under the pre-1996 Act regime (a largely state-run operation), the 1996 Act introduced a new subsidy scheme under which designated beneficiaries—including schools and libraries—are entitled to receive discounts for certain services.[172] The discounts apply to

[171] Some of the loops found with load coils and bridged taps can be "conditioned" or modified so that they can support ADSL service. Currently this conditioning would typically be performed on loops longer than 8,000 feet, but less than 16,000 feet. There are no guarantees that conditioning will provide an ADSL-capable loop, however, and each case must be evaluated individually.

[172] *See* Federal-State Joint Board on Universal Service, Report and Order, 12 F.C.C. Rec. 8776, 9002 ¶424 (1997) (hereinafter *Universal Service Order*), *appeal pending sub nom.* Texas Office of Pub. Util. Counsel v. FCC, No. 97-60421 (5th Cir.) ("For the first time, the 1996 Act includes schools and libraries

"telecommunications services, Internet access, and internal connections."[173] The Commission described Internet access as "a basic conduit, i.e., non-content access from the school or library to the backbone Internet network, which would include the communications link to the Internet service provider, whether through dial-up access or via a leased line, the links to other Internet sites via the Internet backbone, generally provided by an Internet service provider for a monthly subscription fee, if applicable, and electronic mail."[174] Rather than defining a set of services to be offered to schools, the Commission instead offered schools and libraries "the maximum flexibility to purchase from telecommunications carriers whatever package of commercially available telecommunications services they believe will meet their telecommunications service needs most effectively and efficiently."[175]

School administrators must negotiate with service providers to obtain the best and most cost-effective package of services, and they are then entitled to a discount of 20 to 90 percent, depending on the income level and whether the school or library is located in a rural area.[176] Funding for schools and libraries shall come from the same source of revenues used to support other universal service purposes under section 254.[177] Service providers, and not the schools and libraries, are required to seek

---

among the explicit beneficiaries of universal service support."). *See also* 47 U.S.C. §254(h)(1)(B); §6.3.2.2. The other designated beneficiary is rural healthcare providers. *See* 47 U.S.C. §254(h)(1)(A).

[173] 47 U.S.C. §254(c)(3). Section 254 defines the services that are to be supported for schools and libraries in terms of "telecommunications services," 47 U.S.C. §245(c)(1); "special" or "additional" services, *id.* §245(c)(3); and access to "advanced telecommunications and information services," *id.* §245(h)(2)(A). The Commission concluded that the "information services, e.g., protocol conversion and information storage, that are needed to access the Internet, as well as internal connections," could be classified as "additional services" that section 254(h)(1)(B), through section 254(c)(3), authorizes the Commission to support. *Universal Service Order,* 12 F.C.C. Rec. at 9010–9011 ¶439.

[174] *Universal Service Order,* 12 F.C.C. Rec. at 9004 ¶428.

[175] *Id.* at 9006 ¶431.

[176] *Id.* at 9002 ¶425.

[177] *Id.* at 9082–9083 ¶585.

compensation from the universal service administrator.[178] The Commission has said that it will provide discounts for Internet access and internal connection provided by nontelecommunications carriers, as well as those provided by telecommunications carriers. Thus, both telecommunications carriers and nontelecommunications carriers are eligible to be reimbursed for providing discounts.[179]

§11.7 Deregulating Data: Section 706 Petitions

Section 706(a) of the 1996 Act provides that "[t]he Commission and each State commission with regulatory jurisdiction over telecommunications services shall encourage the deployment on a reasonable and timely basis of advanced telecommunications capability to all Americans . . . by utilizing, in a manner consistent with the public interest, convenience, and necessity, price cap regulation, regulatory forbearance, measures that promote competition in the local telecommunications market, or other regulating methods that remove barriers to infrastructure investment."[180] The section defines "advanced telecommunications capability" to mean "high-speed, switched, broadband telecommunications capability that enables users to originate and receive high-quality voice, data, graphics, and video communications."[181]

Congress also commanded that the Commission undertake an inquiry, starting within 30 months of the 1996 Act's enactment and regularly afterwards, to determine "the availability of advanced telecommunications capability to all Americans."[182] If

---

[178] *Id.* at 9083 ¶586.

[179] *Id.* at 9085 ¶590; *see also id.* ("Section 254(h)(2), in conjunction with Section 4(i), authorizes the Commission to establish discounts and funding mechanisms for advanced services provided by non-telecommunications carriers, in addition to the funding mechanisms for telecommunications carriers created pursuant to sections 254(c)(3) and 254(h)(1)(B)."). A telecommunications carrier may either offset the discount against its universal service contribution obligations or be reimbursed for the amount of the discount. *Id.* at 9083 ¶586.

[180] 47 U.S.C. §157 note.

[181] *Id.* §706(c).

[182] *Id.* §706(b).

such capability is not "being deployed to all Americans in a reasonable and timely fashion," the Commission "shall take immediate action to accelerate deployment of such capability by removing barriers to infrastructure investment and by promoting competition in the telecommunications market."[183] The Commission has several times declared its commitment to this process.[184]

In 1997 and 1998, several Bell companies filed petitions pursuant to section 706 asking the Commission (1) to allow them to provide high-speed data services without regard to present LATA boundaries; (2) to affirm that xDSL and ISDN services are not subject to section 251(c)(3) unbundling obligations; (3) to relieve LECs from any obligation they might otherwise have to offer ADSL service for resale at a wholesale discount under section 251(c)(4); (4) to define LEC ADSL service as nondominant, thus relieving LECs of certain tariff filing requirements under section 203 and applicable rules in 47 C.F.R. Parts 61 and 69; and (5) to grant forbearance of the "most favored nation" obligation under section 252(i) to the extent that it might apply to certain interconnection, service, and network element agreements.[185] As discussed earlier in this chapter, the Commission

[183] *Id.* §706(a).

[184] *See, e.g.,* Access Charge Reform, Price Cap Performance Review for Local Exchange Carriers, Transport Rate Structure and Pricing, Usage of the Public Switched Network by Information Service and Internet Access Providers, Notice of Inquiry, 11 F.C.C. Rec. 21,354, 21,490–21,491 ¶¶311, 313 (1996) (the Commission expressed its commitment to "facilitat[ing] the development of the high-bandwidth data networks of the future" and to "creat[ing] incentives for the deployment of services and facilities to allow more efficient transport of data traffic to and from end users," such as removing obstacles to LECs' "deploying hardware to route data traffic around incumbent LEC switches" or "installing new high-bandwidth access technologies such as asymmetric digital subscriber line (ADSL) or wireless solutions.").

[185] Petition of Bell Atlantic, Petition of Bell Atlantic Corporation for Relief from Barriers to Deployment of Advanced Telecommunications Services, CC Docket No. 98-11 (FCC Jan. 26, 1998); Petition for Relief, Petition of U S WEST Communications, Inc., for Relief from Barriers to Deployment of Advanced Telecommunications Services, CC Docket No. 98-26 (FCC Feb. 25, 1998); Petition of Ameritech Corporation, Petition of Ameritech Corporation to Remove Barriers to Investment in Advanced Telecommunications Capability, CC Docket No. 98-32 (FCC Mar. 5, 1998); Petition of Southwestern Bell

declined to grant incumbent LECs relief, though it clearly had the power to do so,[186] from the unbundling and resale obligations of the 1996 Act, holding that "sections 251 and 252 apply to advanced telecommunications facilities and services offered by an incumbent [LEC]."[187] The Commission also denied relief from sections 251 and/or 271 through Commission forbearance or through interLATA boundary changes on the ground that it did "not have the statutory authority to do so."[188] This last conclusion requires some further analysis.

As discussed in section 9.5.3.4, section 10 of the Communications Act of 1934[189] gives the Commission general power to forbear from regulation if certain conditions are satisfied. But that power to deregulate expressly does not extend to sections 251(c) or 271.[190] The question is whether section 706 provides independent authority to deregulate all aspects of data services, including BOC provision of interLATA services.

On its face, section 706 appears to give the Commission plenary authority. This section does not narrowly restrict the permissible tools available to accomplish the stated objective. To the contrary, it lists specified types of deregulating methods, including "regulatory forbearance," and then, in a catchall provision, broadly directs the Commission to use any "regulating methods" to fulfill the statutory mandate, including ones "other" than those specifically listed. Despite this broad language, the Commission concluded that section 706 did not "constitute an independent

---

Telephone Company, Pacific Bell, and Nevada Bell for Relief from Regulation, Southwestern Bell Telephone Company, Pacific Bell, and Nevada Bell Petition for Relief from Regulation Pursuant to Section 706 of the Telecommunications Act of 1996 and 47 U.S.C. §160 for ADSL Infrastructure and Service, CC Docket No. 98-91 (FCC June 9, 1998).

[186] Under section 251(d), the Commission has the authority to "determin[e] what network elements should be made available for purposes of subsection (c)(3)." 47 U.S.C. §251(d).

[187] Advanced Services Order, 13 F.C.C. Rec. at 24,019 ¶18. The Commission also denied, without explanation, SBC's requests for relief from the dominant treatment of ADSL and from the obligations of section 252(i). *Id.* at 24,048 ¶79.

[188] *Id.* at 24,019 ¶18.

[189] 47 U.S.C. §160.

[190] *See id.* §160(d).

grant of forbearance authority," but merely directed the Commission to use the authority granted in other provisions . . . to encourage the deployment of advanced services."[191] The Commission's analysis involved a four-step process. First, the Commission found ambiguity in the language of section 706.[192] Second, the Commission imported the restriction in section 10, which precludes forbearance from the requirements of sections 251(c) and 271, on the ground that there was "no language in section 10 that carve[d] out an exclusion from this prohibition for actions taken pursuant to section 706."[193] Third, the Commission noted that there was nothing in the legislative history indicating that Congress gave the Commission independent authority to forbear from provisions of the Act.[194] Finally, the Commission concluded that as a matter of policy, because of the central importance of sections 251(c) and 271 in opening local markets to competition, the Commission's narrow interpretation of section 706 would better promote the objectives of the 1996 Act.[195]

The Commission left open the possibility that it might grant very limited, case-by-case relief from interLATA restrictions by way of LATA boundary modifications, as authorized by section 3(25)(B) of the Communications Act.[196] That section expressly permits the Commission to approve modifications of a LATA— consistent with the pre-1996 history of numerous district court LATA-boundary modifications.[197] The Commission declined to modify LATA boundaries wholesale for packet-switched services,[198] but said it would entertain petitions for more targeted modifications of LATA boundaries and sought comment on what

---

[191] *Advanced Services Order,* 13 F.C.C. Rec. at 24,044–24,045 ¶69.

[192] *Id.* at 24,045 ¶70.

[193] *Id.* at 24,045–24,046 ¶¶72–73.

[194] *Id.* at 24,046–24,047 ¶75.

[195] *Id.* ¶78.

[196] 47 U.S.C. §153(25)(B); *Advanced Services Order,* 13 F.C.C. Rec. at 24,096–24,097 ¶192.

[197] *See, e.g.,* Decision, United States v. Western Elec. Co., No. 82-0192 (D.D.C. Oct. 28, 1987); Order, United States v. Western Elec. Co., No. 82-0192 (D.D.C. Aug. 1, 1989); Order, United States v. Western Elec. Co., No. 82-0192 (D.D.C. Dec. 12, 1989).

[198] *Advanced Services Order,* 13 F.C.C. at 24,049–24,050 ¶82.

circumstances would warrant modification and how they should be evaluated.[199] The Commission has granted at least one request for LATA relief for ISDN service.[200]

The Commission has also launched an open-ended "inquiry" into advanced services in general, as required under section 706.[201] The Notice of Inquiry broadly covers the definition of terms such as broadband and high-speed, the use of the local loop for transmitting data, the availability of backbone facilities, and the availability and impact of wireless transmission of data. The Commission expects to issue a report by February 1999.

Whatever good for competition and CLECs it may do in the long term, the Commission's Order will certainly discourage new investment by ILECs in the short. Requiring ILECs to "unbundle" and sell to their competitors whatever new capabilities and services they add to their networks, at rates "based on the cost[s] of providing" them,[202] creates a strong disincentive to invest. The unbundling requirement creates a very real barrier to innovation and investment because an incumbent LEC bears all of the risks associated with investment and deployment, but gets few of the benefits. A competing carrier seeking unbundling of a successful innovation and investment can take exclusive control of that investment and pay no more than a cost-based rate plus a possible reasonable profit.[203] At the same time, unsuccessful innovations and investments are borne solely by the incumbent LEC. The result is a skewed, inequitable structure of risks and rewards.[204]

---

[199] *Id.* ¶¶190, 196.

[200] Southwestern Bell Telephone Company Petition for Limited Modification of LATA Boundaries to Provide Integrated Services Digital Network (ISDN) at Hearne, Texas, Memorandum Opinion and Order, 13 F.C.C. Rec. 13,166 (1998).

[201] Inquiry Concerning the Deployment of Advanced Telecommunications Capability to All Americans in a Reasonable and Timely Fashion, and Possible Steps to Accelerate Such Deployment Pursuant to Section 706 of the Telecommunications Act of 1996, Notice of Inquiry, 13 F.C.C. Rec. 15,280 (1998) (hereinafter *Advanced Services Inquiry*).

[202] 47 U.S.C. §252(d).

[203] *Id.* §252(d)(1).

[204] The Commission itself has made sympathetic noises along similar lines. Responding to assertions that the incentives for developing innovative new

Imposing unbundling and price regulation on new high-speed data capabilities deployed by incumbent LECs will have a second deleterious impact on investment and competition: it will suppress new investment by CLECs, too. Most states set prices below even the incremental cost of providing service and still further below the actual book cost including capital and depreciation. It makes no sense to build and deploy what you can buy more cheaply from others—least of all, to build and deploy innovative new technology that is to be offered in an already competitive market, where there is a real risk that it will not turn out to be what customers want.

§11.7.1 Deregulating Data

For over 20 years, the Commission has pursued a consistent policy of *not* regulating innovative services offered in competitive markets and—above all—of *not* regulating nondominant second-to-market providers of such services. It has been the Commission's unvarying policy carefully to demarcate less than fully competitive services and to regulate those services alone, while deregulating competitive services on the other side of the boundary. And within markets that are less than fully competitive, it has been the Commission's policy to regulate only the dominant provider, not its competitors.

Despite the Commission's ruling in the *Advanced Services Order,* this body of precedent strongly supports the deregulation of high-speed data services. And because the emerging market for high-speed data services is being served competitively, by providers who face no regulation at all in the provision of such services, Commission precedent supports complete deregulation of incumbent LECs in the provision of these competitive services.

---

services would be substantially harmed if an overly broad interpretation of the unbundling obligation were adopted, the Commission acknowledged "that prohibiting incumbents from refusing access to proprietary [network] elements could reduce their incentives to offer innovative services." *Local Competition Order,* 11 F.C.C. Rec. at 15,642 ¶282 (hereinafter *Local Competition Order*).

The case for deregulation is all the more compelling because the services at issue center on risky innovation and the deployment of cutting edge technology. Overregulation has the very real potential to stifle markets like these, as the Commission's former chief economist has recognized.[205] More recently, FCC Chairman William Kennard has declared that he sees no reason to impose discount resale and unbundling requirements on LECs that provide high-speed residential data services, provided the LECs have opened up access to their underlying network facilities.[206]

CLECs themselves are divided on the desirability of forcing ILECs to unbundle and/or offer advanced services to resellers at a discount.[207] Facilities-based CLECs like Teleport Communications Group acknowledge "a real and substantial risk that the development of facilities-based local competition can be adversely affected if wholesale or retail rates are priced inequitably relative to unbundled element costs, creating an uneconomic price squeeze. . . . [The FCC] must ensure that wholesale competition does not drive out or diminish the development of

---

[205] In 1997, Joseph Farrell called for the "[d]eregulation of innovation," specifically citing high-speed data services as an example. Innovative add-ons to the basic network should *not* themselves be subject to unbundling regulation, Farrell argued, so long as the core elements of the traditional monopoly network are. J. Farrell, Competition, Innovation and Deregulation, Remarks at the Merrill Lynch Telecommunications CEO Conference, New York (Mar. 19, 1997). *See also id.* ("[W]hen an ILEC invests in a 'parallel, better' infrastructure, such as fiber to the home, perhaps it should be able to keep that from competitors, for a while or even for as long as it wants, provided that the old infrastructure is still available on an unbundled basis, is properly maintained, and so on.").

[206] *See* William E. Kennard, Chairman, Federal Communications Commission, A Broad(band) Vision for America, Remarks before the Federal Communications Bar Association (June 24, 1998) (noting that the telcos "have rightly asked, 'Why should we make this new investment if we simply have to turn around and sell this new service—or the capabilities of these advanced electronics—to our competitors?' . . . If the telephone company has opened up its underlying network to competition, the competitors can invest in the same advanced services. Where networks are open, I see no reason to require discount resale or unbundling of these new services and advanced technologies that are available to all.").

[207] *See* §2.7.

1047

strong, facilities-based competition."[208] The CLECs who disagree are the ones who prefer regulatory arbitrage to building real networks. They insist that the Commission should unbundle and price-regulate everything, everywhere—new services no less than old, competitive services no less than uncompetitive ones, innovation no less than tried and true.[209]

§11.7.2 Accounting Safeguards for Deregulated Data Services

Data services will be progressively deregulated, but the regulation of voice services will linger on the scene for many years to come. In proposing deregulation of their high-speed data services, LECs have accordingly proposed to abide by the Part 64 accounting methods for nonregulated offerings to record the investment, expenses, and revenues associated with ADSL infrastructure and investment.[210]

---

[208] Comments of Teleport Communications Group Inc. at 58–59, Implementation of the Local Competition Provisions in the Telecommunications Act of 1996, CC Docket No. 96-98 (FCC May 16, 1996).

[209] See, e.g., Comments of the Telecommunications Resellers Association at 18, Implementation of the Local Competition Provisions in the Telecommunications Act of 1996, CC Docket No. 96-98 (FCC May 16, 1996) ("[R]esale of telecommunications services generates numerous public benefits, among which are the downward pressure resale exerts on rates and the enhancements resale produces in the diversity and quality of product and service offerings.").

[210] It is arguably unnecessary to adopt these accounting methods, given that ADSL is a telecommunications service and the FCC's price-cap regulation eliminates the ability to cross-subsidize ADSL service by raising the prices of the other access services. See Separation of Costs of Regulated Telephone Service from Costs of Nonregulated Activities; Amendment of Part 31, the Uniform System of Accounts for Class A and Class B Telephone Companies to Provide for Nonregulated Activities and to Provide for Transactions Between Telephone Companies and Their Affiliates, Report and Order, 2 F.C.C. Rec. 1298, 1299 ¶1 (1987) (the goal of Part 64 was to "develop a system of accounting separation that would inhibit carriers from imposing on ratepayers for regulated interstate services the costs and risks of nonregulated ventures"). See §2.2.2.6.

§11.8   Nontelco Data Services

§11.8.1   Interactive Cable Services

Title VI of the 1934 Communications Act imposes franchise requirements and rate regulations on the provision of "cable services."[211] It also subjects operators of "cable systems" to pseudo-carriage obligations.[212] But as noted in section 11.2.2.3 above, cable operators are beginning to offer a wide range of two-way, interactive "noncable" services, such as Internet access, data transport, telecom services, and so forth.[213] The FCC has been uncharacteristically quiet about how to regulate these services. The Commission's silence has created regulatory freedom by default.

The last time the Commission even seriously addressed two-way cable services was over a quarter century ago. In its sweeping 1972 cable rules, the Commission mandated that cable operators offer two-way nonvideo services and preempted the states from regulating such services.[214] The D.C. Circuit overturned the FCC on the ground that the 1934 Communications Act gave states exclusive authority to regulate intrastate, two-way, nonvideo cable communications that were of a "common carrier" nature.[215] Since then, the FCC has never formally declared how it would regulate two-way, interactive cable services.[216] Con-

[211] 47 U.S.C. §§541, 543, 522(6).

[212] *See, e.g., id.* §531 (allowing franchise authorities to condition cable licenses on the designation of channels for public, educational, or government use); *id.* §532 (requiring cable operators to carry channels for commercial use); *id.* §534 (requiring cable operators to carry local commercial television signals); *id.* §535 (requiring cable operators to carry noncommercial educational television).

[213] These services use cable's "back channel," a 5–40 MHz slice of radio frequency (RF) spectrum that is not otherwise occupied by video programming.

[214] Amendment of Part 74, Subpart K of the Commission's Rules and Regulations Relative to CATV, First Report and Order, 36 F.C.C.2d 143, 192–193 ¶¶128–129, 193 ¶131 (1972).

[215] NARUC v. FCC, 533 F.2d 601 (D.C. Cir. 1976) (*NARUC II*); *see also* FCC v. Midwest Video, 440 U.S. 689 (1979) (FCC rules improperly imposed common carrier obligations on cable operators).

[216] Interactive cable services are not included as part of "basic cable service" (*see* 47 U.S.C. §522(3)) or "cable service" (*id.* §522(6)) as such terms are

gress chose not to address the matter in either the 1984 or the 1992 Cable Acts.[217] The FCC has hinted that at the very least such services would not be subject to cable price regulation.[218] If the Commission wanted, it might be able to interpret new provisions of the 1996 Act in a way that threatens new Title VI regulation.[219] But at least so far, the Commission has chosen not to do so.[220]

---

defined in the 1996 Act. Interactive cable services would also not be considered either "video programming" (which is "comparable" to what a television broadcaster provides, *see id.* U.S.C. §522(20)) or "other programming service" (which is "information that a cable operator makes available to all subscribers generally," *see id.* §522(14)). A better, but still weak, case could be made that interactive services fit under the Commission's definition of a "cable programming service," which includes "any video programming provided over a cable system, regardless of service tier, including installation or rental of equipment used for the receipt of such video programming." *See id.* §76.901(b).

[217] The 1984 Cable Act merely stipulates that a state or the Commission may require cable systems offering intrastate communications services (other than cable service) to file "informational" tariffs if the same service would be subject to regulation by the Commission or state if it was offered by a common carrier subject to Title II. *Id.* §541(d). *See* H.R. Rep. No. 98-934, Cable Communications Policy Act of 1984, at 42 (1984), *reprinted in* 1984 U.S.C.C.A.N. 4655, 4679 ("In general, services providing subscribers with the capacity to engage in transactions or to store, transform, forward, manipulate, or otherwise process information or data would not be cable services.").

[218] *See, e.g.,* Implementation of Sections of the Cable Television Consumer Protection and Competition Act of 1992: Rate Regulation, Second Order on Reconsideration, Fourth Report and Order, and Fifth Notice of Proposed Rulemaking, 9 F.C.C. Rec. 4119, 4131 ¶21(1994) ("Cable systems that now offer regulated service without competition will have an incentive to upgrade their systems with new capabilities and will have an incentive to introduce enhanced functions, such as interactivity, that are not subject to rate regulation.").

[219] The 1996 Act expanded the 1984 Cable Act's definition of "cable service" to include subscriber interaction required for the "selection or *use* of video programming or other programming service." 47 U.S.C. §522(6) (emphasis added). The Conference Report states that the amendment was included "to reflect the evolution of cable to include interactive services such as game channels and information services made available to subscribers by the cable operator, as well as enhanced services," but that it "was not intended to affect Federal or State regulation of telecommunications service offered through cable system facilities, or to cause dial-up access to information services over telephone lines to be classified as a cable service." S. Rep. No. 230, 104th Cong., 2d Sess. 169 (1996).

[220] *See* Implementation of Cable Act Reform Provisions of the Telecommunications Act of 1996, Order and Notice of Proposed Rulemaking, 11 F.C.C. Rec. 5937 (1996).

The Commission has also been completely silent on what type of Title II regulation, if any, would apply to interactive cable services.[221] For now, cable operators do not need advance approval to provide such services and do not have to file tariffs for them. The Commission's investigation into the deployment of advanced telecommunications services questioned the type of regulatory model that should apply to advanced telecommunications services, leaving open the possibility that the Commission may require unbundling of data transport for cable companies, too.[222]

May high-speed Internet access services delivered via cable networks be treated as common carriage? This position seems to have been rejected in a recent FCC Working Paper, *Internet over Cable*, which projected that the Commission "could reasonably conclude that Internet access services. . . come within the revised definition of 'cable services.'"[223] The paper styles that

[221] It is clear, however, that the provision of "interactive on-demand services" over a common carrier facility does not render the facility a "cable system." *See* 47 U.S.C. §522(7). Such services are defined as "a service providing video programming to subscribers over switched networks on an on-demand, point-to-point basis, but does not include services providing video programming. . . ." 47 U.S.C. §522(12). An operator that provides only interactive, on-demand video services, not common carriage transport or ordinary broadcastlike cable service, would not then be regulated under either Title VI or Title II. It would be exempt from the latter by the FCC's rules regarding enhanced service providers, described above.

[222] Inquiry Concerning the Deployment of Advanced Telecommunications Capability to All Americans in a Reasonable and Timely Fashion, and Possible Steps to Accelerate Such Deployment Pursuant to Section 706 of the Telecommunications Act of 1996, Notice of Inquiry, 13 F.C.C. Rec. 15,280, 15,308–15,309 ¶77 (1998) ("It may be [] that . . . as discrete industries and services begin to converge, the application of different regulatory models to competing services will have effects on the marketplace."). A June 1999 Federal Court ruling upheld a local ordinance requiring AT&T to allow unaffiliated ISPs to connect their facilities to AT&T's cable modem platform. *See* AT&T Corp. v. City of Portland, CV-99-65-PA (D. Or. June 3, 1999).

[223] Barbara Esbin, Office of Plans and Policy, FCC, Internet over Cable: Defining the Future in Terms of the Past 87 (OPP Working Paper No. 30, Aug. 1998). The paper distinguishes cable-delivered services like @Home, which provide their own content, and other services "that may offer the subscriber nothing more than basic conduit access to the Internet." *Id*. With respect to the latter, it finds that the case for categorizing such services as cable service "becomes more attenuated" and "[t]he regulatory status of such a service may best be resolved on a case-by-case basis." *Id*. at 87–88. The paper also notes

conclusion as "relatively easy" to reach. Yet that conclusion is plainly wrong.

That conclusion is premised on the logic that any act of bundling content with the underlying transport, however contrived, is enough to set aside the obligations of a common carrier. If this were so, any carrier could deregulate itself at will. Before the advent of dial telephones and automatic switchboards, all phone calls were routed initially through the phone company's own operator and switchboard, the "Internet portal" of its day. No one thought to argue that this meant phone companies weren't really carriers because the first moments of every phone call were conducted with a phone company representative for the purpose of accessing a phone company database. Such an argument would have been ridiculous then.

Cable's high-speed Internet services are readily distinguished from those of other ISPs. The main business of most existing ISPs is *not* to provide local transport itself—they rely mainly on local phone companies to provide that in the form of dial-up connections. The economic core of their business is to provide access to the backbone network, along with some content. The vast majority of ISPs rely on established long-distance carriers to furnish backbone transport, just as they rely on local carriers for the local leg. Their business is to assemble the pieces and provide some additional content *via* carriage, not to provide the underlying carriage itself. As we discuss in section 12.2.3, they clearly fall within the 1996 Act's definition of an "information service."[224] There is no plausible way, by contrast, to characterize what cable operators offer in these same terms.

Technically speaking, cable's promise is to originate and deliver data traffic encoded and addressed according to the protocols of the Internet—which is to say, according to the TCP/IP protocol. And any service provider whose core business is to trans-

---

that cable modem services that use cable plant downstream and telephone lines for the return path "may present a somewhat different interpretative problem, as the service itself would not readily fall under the plain language of the statute." *Id.* at 88.

[224] *See* 47 U.S.C. §153(20).

mit TCP/IP-encoded traffic is—as a matter of pure technological definition—providing pure carriage. As described above, TCP/IP places *complete* control over routing, addressing, origin, destination, and content itself in the hands of the originating computer. Any forced bundling in this environment has to be contrived, concocted, and clumsily grafted onto the underlying carriage. TCP/IP is the universal protocol of *unbundled, equal access* carriage—a protocol that is content-neutral, network-neutral, medium-neutral. It is, in short, the purest form of "common carriage" ever devised.

Without exception, courts have concluded that cable operators take on the regulatory mantle of common carrier when they provide services that constitute common carriage. In its 1972 rules, the Commission directed cable operators to offer two-way nonvideo services and preempted state regulation of such services.[225] The D.C. Circuit overturned on that ground, holding that under the law then in effect the Commission lacked jurisdiction over two-way, nonvideo cable communications that were of a "common carrier" nature.[226] Not long after, the Supreme Court noted that a "cable system may operate as a common carrier with respect to a portion of its service only."[227] In 1985—at the cable operator's behest—the Commission conducted another common carrier inquiry to determine whether high-speed digital transmission services offered by Cox Cable in Omaha,

---

[225] Amendment of Part 74, Subpart K of the Commission's Rules and Regulations Relative to CATV, First Report and Order, 36 F.C.C.2d 143, 192–193 ¶¶128–129, 193 ¶131 (1972).

[226] *NARUC II*, 533 F.2d 601. In holding that the services at issue were common carrier services, the court acknowledged that a cable operator can provide both common carrier and non-common-carrier services simultaneously. (The court cited Frontier Broadcasting Co. v. FCC, 24 F.C.C. 251, 254 (1958), which held that one-way cable television was a non-common-carrier activity because the content of transmissions was not under the control of the subscriber. 533 F.2d at 609 n.36.) "[I]t is clearly possible for a given entity to carry on many types of activities," the appellate court expressly noted; "[o]ne can be a common carrier with regard to some activities but not others." *Id.* at 608.

[227] FCC v. Midwest Video Corp., 440 U.S. 689, 701 n.9 (1979) (citing *NARUC II*, 533 F.2d at 608).

Nebraska, constituted interstate common carriage that fell outside the jurisdiction of state regulators.[228]

Congress codified this logic in the 1984 Cable Act. A cable
operator may not be regulated as a common carrier "by reason
of providing any cable service,"[229] but *may* be so regulated if it
offers any other "intrastate communications service . . . that
would be subject to regulation by the Commission or any State
if offered by a common carrier."[230] The 1984 Act deliberately
confined its definition of "cable service" to the one-way transmission to subscribers of video programming[231] or other programming service,[232] along with subscriber interaction, if any,
that is required for the selection of such video programming or
other programming service. The House Report explained at
length that interactive services were *not* included in that definition.[233] The 1984 Act's definition of cable services was intended
to cover some two-way transmission capabilities, the Report notes,
but only a limited few. These included subscriber selection of

[228] *See* Cox Cable Communications, Inc., Commline, Inc. and Cox DTS,
Memorandum, Opinion, Declaratory Ruling, and Order, 102 F.C.C.2d 110
(1985).

[229] 47 U.S.C. §541(c).

[230] *Id.* §541(d). The legislative history indicates that Congress was well
aware of the potential for cable to offer both voice and data transmissions
over their networks. H.R. Rep. No. 934, 98th Cong., 2d Sess. 28 (1984). Congress stopped short of resolving the issues of "competitive equity and universal telephone service" raised by the "growing convergence of cable and
telephone industries" because proceedings were then under way to determine
these issues (citing, among others, the Cox case). *Id.* at 29. Congress opted
simply to "preserve[] the regulatory and jurisdictional status quo with respect
to non-cable communications services." *Id.*

[231] 47 U.S.C. §522(20).

[232] *Id.* §522(14) (1998).

[233] H.R. Rep. No. 934, 98th Cong., 2d Sess. 41–42 (1984). The Report gave
examples on both sides of the line. The transmission or downloading of computer software (such as computer or video games or statistical packages) to all
subscribers to this service for use on personal computers would be a cable service. *Id.* at 42. On the other hand, a cable service would not include "'active'
information services such as at-home shopping and banking that allow transactions between subscribers and cable operators or third-parties." *Id.* Further,
the "capacity to communicate instructions or commands to software programs
such as computer or video games or statistical packages that do not retrieve
information and that are stored in facilities off the subscribers' premises" is
beyond the meaning of "cable service."

video programming (i.e., sending a signal from the subscriber premises to the cable operator over the cable system).[234] And they also included "non-video programming" that all subscribers may retrieve without requiring off-premises data processing. While the exact boundaries of this "other programming" category are fuzzy, the Report made clear that "cable service" does *not* include "unlimited keyword searches of information stored in data bases. . . . Such unlimited interaction goes beyond providing information retrieval and becomes a variety of data processing."[235]

---

[234] *Id.* at 43.

[235] *Id.* The Committee also stated:

The Committee intends that the interaction permitted in a cable service shall be that required for the retrieval of information from among a specific number of options or categories delineated by the cable operator or the programming service provider. Such options or categories must themselves be created by the cable operator or programming service provider and made generally available to all subscribers. By contrast, interaction that would enable a particular subscriber to engage in the offpremises creation and retrieval of a category of information would not fall under the definition of cable service. This definition of interaction is necessary in order to ensure that providing subscribers with the capacity to retrieve information — capacity which may be part of a cable service — does not also provide [subscribers] with the capacity to engage in off-premises data processing — an additional capacity which may not be offered as part of a cable service. . . .

A programming service involving only simple menu-selection would be a cable service. A service in which a cable operator provided capacity to retrieve information by keyword by presorting a data base in accordance with a specific index of keywords would also be a cable service. . . .

Some examples of cable services would be: video programming, pay-per-view, voter preference polls in the context of a video program, video rating services, teletext, one-way transmission of any computer software (including, for example, computer or video games) and one-way video-tex services such [as] a news [service], stock market information, and on-line airline guides and catalog services that do not allow customer purchases.

Some examples of non-cable services would be: shop-at-home and bank-at-home services, electronic mail, one-way and two-way transmission on non-video data and information not offered to all subscribers, data processing, video-conferencing, and all voice communications.

Id. at 43–44.

The 1996 Act added only two words to the key definition: "cable service" now includes "subscriber interaction, if any, which is required for the selection *or use* of such video programming or other programming service."[236] The Conference Report states that this change was to "reflect the evolution of cable to include interactive services. . . [and] enhanced services," but is "not intended to affect . . . regulation of telecommunications service offered through cable system facilities." By the same token, that amendment is not intended "to cause dial-up access to information services over telephone lines to be classified as a cable service."[237] In an exchange on the Senate floor, Senator Pressler stated that a change in the 1996 Act's definition of "telecommunications service" was "intended to clarify that the carriers of broadcast and cable services are not intended to be classified as 'common carriers' under the Communications Act to the extent they provide broadcast services or cable services."[238] The "to the extent" phrasing merely leads back, however, to the difference between cable services and common carriage; it provides no further guidance as to which is which.

§11.8.2 Broadcast Data Services

The Communications Act of 1934 generally requires broadcast licensees to serve the "public interest, convenience, or neces-

---

[236] 47 U.S.C. §522(6)(B).

[237] H.R. Conf. Rep. No. 408, 104th Cong., 2d Sess. 169 (1996). Reference is sometimes also made to the statement of Representative Dingell made on the House floor, commenting on how the revised definition of cable services would affect local franchising authorities' revenues from cable franchise fees: "[t]his conference agreement strengthens the ability of local governments to collect fees for the use of public right of way. For example, the definition of the term 'cable service' has been expanded to include game channels and other interactive services. This will result in additional revenues flowing to the cities in the form of franchise fees." 142 Cong. Rec. H1156 (daily ed. Feb. 1, 1996) (statement of Rep. Dingell).

[238] 141 Cong. Rec. S7996 (daily ed. June 8, 1995). The sentence that was deleted from the earlier version was: "The term [telecommunications service] includes the transmission, without change in the form or content, of information services and cable services, but does not include the offering of those services." S. 652 PP, 104th Cong., 1st Sess. §8 (mm) (Mar. 30, 1995).

sity."[239] The Commission has spent decades enforcing this requirement with elaborate rules regarding what a licensee may transmit over its radio spectrum.[240] The Commission also has historically drawn a strict line between "broadcast" and "carriage" and has generally barred broadcasters from transferring control over their spectrum, or pieces of it, to third parties.[241]

In small increments, however, the FCC has carved out exceptions for data traffic piggybacked on broadcast media. In the 1970s, the Commission reinterpreted its rules to allow FM radio stations to provide "visual" services,[242] using the "subcarrier"

---

[239] *See* 47 U.S.C. §§302, 303.

[240] For example, the FCC's 1946 "Blue Book" described three categories of programs that broadcasters had to balance or face nonrenewal. *See* Public Service Responsibility of Broadcast Licensees, Report by Federal Communications Commission (Mar. 7, 1946). *See also* Simmons v. FCC, 169 F.2d 670 (D.C. Cir. 1948); Bay State Beacon, Inc. v. FCC, 171 F.2d 826 (D.C. Cir. 1948). The FCC's 1960 En Banc Programming Inquiry Report and Statement of Policy listed 14 categories of programming "usually necessary to meet the public interest, needs and desires of the community. . . ." Commission En Banc Programming Inquiry, Report and Statement of Policy, 44 F.C.C. 2303, 2314 (1960). In 1976, the FCC ordered any TV license application proposing less than 5 percent "local" and less than 5 percent "informational" programming to be referred to the full Commission. Amendment to Section 0.281 of the Commission's Rules: Delegations of Authority, Report and Order, 59 F.C.C.2d 491 (1976).

[241] For example, in 1976, the FCC refused to renew an FM radio license because the station sold most of its airtime, through brokers, to small foreign-language programmers. Application of Cosmopolitan Broadcasting Corp., Report and Order, 59 F.C.C.2d 558, *recons. denied*, 61 F.C.C.2d 257 (1976). In recent years, however, the Commission has increasingly recognized that subdivision of a licensee's time brings certain efficiencies. In 1992, for example, the Commission reduced limits on subdivision and classified time brokering as a "joint venture" that would generally be approved. Revision of Radio Rules and Policies, Report and Order, 7 F.C.C. Rec. 2755, 2784 ¶58 (1992). Broadcast licensees must still, however, "maintain control of their facilities and . . . ensure that their stations program in the public interest and serve the needs of their communities." *Id.* at 2787 n.124. *See generally* Howard Shelanski, The Bending Line Between Conventional "Broadcast" and Wireless "Carriage," 97 Colum. L. Rev. 1048 (1997).

[242] The Commission defined "visual transmissions" as "[t]ransmissions of a broadcast nature on a subcarrier modulated with a signal of such characteristics as to permit . . . visual presentation of the information so transmitted, e.g., on a viewing screen or a graphic record." *See* Amendment of Part 73 of the Commission's Rules and Regulations Concerning the Transmissions of Non-aural Signals on an FM Broadcast Subcarrier Pursuant to a Subsidiary

portions of their assigned frequency bands.[243] In the early 1980s, the Commission eliminated all limitations on FM-subcarrier transmissions, permitting "any legitimate communications purpose whether broadcast related or not."[244] The Commission expressly exempted these activities from traditional broadcaster regulation (such as the fairness doctrine and equal time rule) and other "public interest" obligations.[245] In theory, FM-subcarrier services (unless privately offered) can be subject to Title II obligations, but the FCC has never actively sought to enforce any such requirements.[246]

The FCC has similarly avoided imposing any regulatory obligations on data transmitted in the interstices of television bands, known as the vertical blanking interval (VBI).[247] In 1984, the Commission authorized television licensees to use their VBI to broadcast electronic newspapers, data, computer software, and paging services within this (otherwise unused) piece of their

---

Communications Authorization, Report and Order, 51 F.C.C.2d 484, 486 ¶10 (1975) (hereinafter *FM Non-aural Signals Order*).

[243] Application of WFTL Broadcasting Co., Memorandum Opinion and Order, 45 F.C.C.2d 1152 (1974) (permitting use of subcarrier channels to provide services in a visual as well as in usual aural format); *FM Non-aural Signals Order,* 51 F.C.C.2d 484 (same). *See also* The Use of Subcarrier Frequencies in the Aural Baseband of Television Transmitters, Second Report and Order, Docket No. 21323, 1984 FCC LEXIS 2956 (Apr. 23, 1984) (extending FM subcarrier rules to TV aural baseband subcarriers); Amendment of Parts 2 and 73 of the Commission's AM Broadcast Rules Concerning the Use of the AM Carrier, Report and Order, 100 F.C.C.2d 5 (1984) (extending to AM subcarriers). Spectrum can be subdivided into a main channel and a number of "subchannels" or "subcarriers," both of which can be transmitted simultaneously.

[244] FM Licensees, First Report and Order, BC Docket No. 82-536, 1983 FCC LEXIS 648, ¶54 (Apr. 7, 1983).

[245] *Id.* ¶20.

[246] *See id.* ¶25.

[247] The VBI is the momentary blank period between picture frames in a television broadcast. H. Newton, Newton's Telecom Dictionary 646 (11th ed. 1996). The first commercial use of VBI, teletext ("a data system for the transmission of textual and graphic information intended for display on viewing screens"), was authorized by the FCC in 1983 at the urging of the television broadcasting industry. Amendment of Parts 2, 73 and 76 of the Commission's Rules to Authorize the Transmission of Teletext by TV Stations, Report and Order, BC Docket No. 81-741, 1983 FCC LEXIS 649 (May 20, 1983).

licenses.[248] Although services delivered over the VBI, like those on FM-subcarrier bands, have been deemed common carrier, the Commission has chosen to forbear from imposing traditional Title II requirements.[249]

The Commission seems headed in the same regulatory direction with new rules that allow broadcast television licensees to transmit data within their main video signals. The rules allow virtually any type of data to be transmitted as long as such transmissions do not interfere with the video transmission itself.[250] The Commission has already stated that it would follow the VBI model in deciding how (not) to regulate these services.[251]

The Commission has been more systematic in deregulating data transmission via direct broadcast satellite. Since the genesis of DBS, the Commission has actively encouraged its use for digital data transmission and other nonvideo uses.[252] DBS does

[248] Amendment of Parts 2, 73, and 76 of the Commission's Rules to Authorize the Offering of Data Transmission Services on the Vertical Blanking Interval by TV Stations, Report and Order, 101 F.C.C.2d 973 (1984).

[249] *See id.* at 977–978 ¶¶13–21.

[250] *See* Digital Data Transmission Within the Video Portion of Television Broadcast Station Transmissions, Report and Order, 11 F.C.C. Rec. 7799 (1996).

[251] *See id.* at 7805.

[252] *See* Inquiry into the Development of Regulatory Policy in Regard to Direct Broadcast Satellites, Report and Order, 90 F.C.C.2d 676, 682 (1982) (DBS offers "a wide variety of potential uses other than entertainment programming, including educational programming, transmission of medical data, and the like. While we have not proposed reserving channels for such purposes, we would certainly allow them and we would expect them to be provided if sufficient demand exists."). *But see* Applications of CBS, Inc., Memorandum Opinion and Order, 92 F.C.C.2d 64, 67–68 ¶4 (1982) ("nonconforming" uses of DBS spectrum must be "secondary" to video transmissions); Petition of United States Satellite Broadcasting Company, Inc. for Declaratory Ruling Regarding Permissible Uses of the Direct Broadcast Satellite Service, Memorandum Opinion and Order, 1 F.C.C. Rec. 977, 979 ¶13 (1986) (DBS is "primarily" a "vehicle for direct-to-home video programming," and "non-confirming" uses of DBS are permissible so long as the DBS operator provides the services "only on those transponders on which it continues to provide DBS service, and . . . non-DBS use cannot exceed fifty percent of each 24-hour day on any such transponder."); Revision of Rules and Policies for the Direct Broadcast Satellite Service, Report and Order, 11 F.C.C. Rec. 9712, 9718 ¶17 (1995) (DBS operator may "provide non-DBS service so long as at least half of its total capacity at a given orbital location is used for DBS service.").

not fit the definition of "cable" and is therefore not subject to Title VI regulation.[253] DBS operators have instead been given the choice to operate under Title II or Title III for all or part of their service.[254] But as either carrier or broadcaster, a DBS operator faces only a minimalist set of regulations.[255] Although the 1992 Cable Act halfheartedly directed the FCC to impose broadcast's "public interest" duties on DBS operators,[256] today DBS operators have unprecedented freedom to use their satellite spectrum for any mix of services, including data.[257] In April

---

[253] *See* Definition of a Cable Television System, Memorandum Opinion and Order, 5 F.C.C. Rec. 7638 (1990), *remanded in part on other grounds sub nom.* Beach Communications, Inc. v. FCC, 959 F.2d 975 (D.C. Cir.), *further considered on other grounds,* 965 F.2d 1103 (D.C. Cir. 1992), *rev'd,* 508 U.S. 307 (1993).

[254] *See* Inquiry into the Development of Regulatory Policy in Regard to Direct Broadcast Satellites for the Period Following the 1983 Regional Administrative Radio Conference, Report and Order, 90 F.C.C.2d 676, 709 ¶86 (1982).

[255] As carriers, DBS operators are deemed nondominant and subject to only perfunctory tariffing requirements. *Id., aff'd in part,* National Assn. of Broadcasters v. FCC, 740 F.2d 1190, 1199–1206 (D.C. Cir. 1984). As broadcasters, DBS operators face no rate regulation, and very few of the content regulations that terrestrial broadcasters do. *See* Subscription Video, Report and Order, 2 F.C.C. Rec. 1001 (1986). In 1987, the Commission reclassified all "subscription" TV services, however delivered—everything that isn't wholly advertiser-supported—as "non-broadcast services." The Commission's action was a response to the D.C. Circuit's ruling that the Commission incorrectly exempted "customer programmers"—that is, customers of DBS carriers that lease channels to distribute programming directly to individual viewers—from both carrier and broadcast regulation. *See* National Assn. of Broadcasters v. FCC, 740 F.2d 1190 (D.C. Cir. 1984).

[256] 47 U.S.C. §335(a). At a minimum, this shall include the "access to broadcast time requirement of section 312(a)(7)" and "the use of facilities requirements of section 315," both of which require broadcasters to make broadcast time available for political candidates. DBS operators must also set aside 4 to 7 percent of their channel capacity for noncommercial, educational, or informational programming. 47 U.S.C. §335(b)(1). The D.C. Circuit upheld these statutory provisions and FCC implementing orders as constitutional, reversing a federal district court that found them violative of the First Amendment. Time Warner Entertainment v. FCC, 93 F.3d 957 (D.C. Cir. 1996), *rev'g* Daniels Cablevision, Inc. v. United States, 835 F. Supp. 1 (D.D.C. 1993).

[257] *See generally* Howard Shelanski & Peter Huber, Administrative Creation of Property Rights to Radio Spectrum, 41 J.L. & Econ. 581 (1998).

1995, for example, Hughes launched its DirecPC data transmission service, which provides a 400 kbps Internet downlink via DBS transponders.[258]

The DBS model is now being pushed down to the terrestrial level as well, with the advent of all-digital advanced television (ATV), or DTV. Pursuant to the 1996 Act, the Commission was authorized to hand over additional spectrum licenses for ATV to incumbent broadcasters, free of charge.[259] When broadcasters begin digital transmissions over these new bands, they will be free to deliver "ancillary or supplementary services" if consistent with the "public interest, convenience and necessity."[260] In its April 1997 *ATV Order,* the Commission defined these services quite broadly to include "subscription television programming, computer software distribution, data transmissions, teletext, interactive services, audio signals, and any other services that do not interfere with the required free service."[261] Pursuant to its mandate under the 1996 Act, the Commission has adopted rules that require broadcasters to pay a fee of 5 percent of gross revenues received from ancillary or supplementary uses of DTV.[262]

---

[258] DirecPC consists of a pizza-sized satellite dish (nearly identical to a DBS dish) connected to a PC through a standard plug-in adapter card and a coaxial cable. The service provides up to 12 Mbps transmission speeds per channel. Applications already developed by Hughes include a "digital package delivery" service that could distribute large electronic files from a central location to branch offices, a videoconferencing service, and high-speed Internet access. *See* Birds of a Feather, Business Communications Rev., July 1995, at 16.

[259] 47 U.S.C. §336.

[260] *Id.* §336(a)(2). In addition, ancillary or supplementary services must be "consistent with the technology or method designated by the Commission for the provision of advanced television services" and must "avoid derogation of any advanced television services." *Id.* §336(b)(1), (2).

[261] Advanced Television Systems and Their Impact upon the Existing Television Broadcast Service, 12 F.C.C. Rec. 12,809, 12,820–12,821 ¶29 (1997) (hereinafter *Advanced Television Systems Fifth Report and Order*); 47 C.F.R. §73.624(c). Such services may be provided on a broadcast point-to-point or point-to-multipoint basis. 47 C.F.R. §73.624(c). An ancillary or supplementary service shall not, however, include a "video broadcast signal provided at no direct charge to viewers." *Id.*

[262] Fees for Ancillary or Supplementary Use of Digital Television Spectrum Pursuant to Section 336(e)(1) of the Telecommunications Act of 1996, Report and Order, MM Docket No. 97-247, ¶20 (Nov. 19, 1998).

Also pursuant to the 1996 Act, the Commission has determined that "non-broadcast services provided by digital licensees will be regulated in a manner consistent with analogous services provided by other persons or entities."[263] The Commission immediately likened this to its policies regarding FM subcarrier and VBI.[264]

§11.8.3   Other Wireless Data Services

The FCC restricts how radio licensees may use their spectrum in two principal ways. First, the Commission prescribes what types of services may be transmitted over certain spectrum bands.[265] Second, the Commission generally prevents radio licensees from slicing up their spectrum (into either geographic[266] or frequency

---

[263] *Advanced Television Systems Fifth Report and Order,* 12 F.C.C. Rec. at 12,823 ¶36; 47 U.S.C. §336(b)(3).

[264] *Advanced Television Systems Fifth Report and Order,* 12 F.C.C. Rec. at 12,823 ¶36.

[265] Prior to PCS, "the Commission's earlier allocations. . . tended to be for specific services, such as mobile telephone, dispatch, or paging." *See* Implementation of Section 6002(b) of the Omnibus Budget Reconciliation Act of 1993, Second Report, 12 F.C.C. Rec. 11,266, 11,288 (1997) (hereinafter *Omnibus Budget Report*). With cellular, for example, the Commission established specific operational and technical requirements on the use of the spectrum that limited its use to voice telephony. *See* Amendment of Parts 2 and 22 of the Commission's Rules to Permit Liberalization of Technology and Auxiliary Service Offerings in the Domestic Public Cellular Radio Telecommunications Service, Notice of Proposed Rulemaking, 2 F.C.C. Rec. 6244, 6245 ¶8 (1987) (the rules "permit[ted] data transmissions, but the transmitted signals must conform to the characteristics of voice transmission").

[266] Each cellular license, for example, is limited to a particular Metropolitan Statistical Area or Rural Service Area. Inquiry into the Use of the Bands 825–845 MHz and 870–890 MHz for Cellular Communications Systems, Memorandum Opinion and Order, 90 F.C.C.2d 571, 579 ¶21 (1982). Cellular providers may, however, obtain multiple licenses, Inquiry Into the Use of the Bands 825–845 MHz and 870–890 MHz for Cellular Communications Systems, Report and Order, 86 F.C.C.2d 469, 487 ¶37 (1981), and may buy and sell their licenses freely so long as licensing provisions regarding the location and power of transmitters are respected, Applications of James F. Rill, Trustee for Comet Inc. & Pacific Telesis Group, Memorandum Opinion and Order, 60 Rad. Reg. 2d (P & F) 583 ¶32 (1986).

sub-bands) and allocating it for different uses.[267] But the Commission has not used these rules to prohibit the digitization of existing wireless networks and has been consistently lax in applying the rules to the new digital networks now being deployed.

Moreover, the Commission has so far kept to a bare minimum the regulation of services provided over these digital wireless networks. The Commission's first major decision along these lines involved Nextel, formerly Fleet Call. Nextel amassed SMR licenses that were traditionally used for taxi dispatch services. It then sought permission from the FCC to digitize its analog SMR spectrum to provide enhanced SMR (ESMR) service, including all types of voice and data applications. In 1991, the Commission granted Nextel's request.[268] Despite the remarkable similarities between the proposed ESMR service and cellular service, the Commission permitted Nextel to remain "private," and thus beyond the reach of Title II requirements.[269]

Largely because of the disparities that the Commission's deregulation of new digital services like those of Nextel created,[270] Congress stepped in and directed the Commission to regulate similar services similarly.[271] This forced the Commission to bring Nextel from the private to the carrier side of the regulatory divide, but it also gave the Commission the freedom to deregulate across the board. Pursuant to congressional mandate, the Commission accordingly announced that it would forbear from applying rate regulation and other Title II requirements to all

---

[267] See, e.g., Revision of Radio Rules and Policies, Report and Order, 7 F.C.C. Rec. 2755, 2787 n.124 ("broadcast licensees must maintain control of their facilities"); 47 C.F.R. §73.3555(a)(3)(ii). See also Use of Special Signals for Network Purposes Which Adversely Affect Broadcast Service, Public Notice, 22 F.C.C.2d 779 (1970) ("we therefore, hold that signals of the nature described [audio tones for signaling purposes] cannot be employed without specific authorization by the Commission").

[268] Request of Fleet Call Inc. for a Waiver and Other Relief to Permit Creation of Enhanced Specialized Mobile Radio System in Six Markets, Memorandum Opinion and Order, 6 F.C.C. Rec. 1533 (1991).

[269] Id. at 1537 ¶¶32–35.

[270] See L. J. Paper, Getting Personal: The Politics of the Wireless Revolution 21, 24–32 (1996).

[271] See Omnibus Budget Reconciliation Act of 1993, Pub. L. No. 103-66, Title VI, §6001(a), 107 Stat. 312 (1993).

forms of CMRS providers.[272] The Commission also broadly pre-empted state regulation of wireless rates.[273]

A prime beneficiary of the Commission's permissive regime was digital PCS. PCS was conceived as a general, all-purpose digital service that could compete directly with cellular, but also provide a wide array of other data-type services.[274] The PCS licenses issued by the FCC accordingly permit a wide range of services to be provided.[275] The FCC has so far accepted that all personal communications services would be regulated equally. Under the Commission's existing rules, this means that no rate or entry/exit regulations will apply.[276]

---

[272] Implementation of Sections 3(n) and 332 of the Communications Act Regulatory Treatment of Mobile Services, Second Report and Order, 9 F.C.C. Rec. 1411, 1450–1451 ¶¶88–93 (1994).

[273] *Id.* at 1504 ¶250. The Commission later rejected the petitions of seven states asking the FCC for permission to continue to regulate cellular carriers. *See, e.g.,* Petition of Arizona Corporation Commission to Extend State Authority over Rate and Entry Regulation of All Commercial Mobile Radio Services, Report and Order on Reconsideration, 10 F.C.C. Rec. 7824 (1995). *See also* Connecticut Dept. of Pub. Util. Control v. FCC, 78 F.3d 842 (2d Cir. 1996) (upholding FCC rejection of Connecticut petition).

[274] By contrast, until 1987, the Commission required that all cellular systems and telephones meet a specific analog technical standard. Inquiry into the Use of the Bands 825–845 MHz and 870–890 MHz for Cellular Communications Systems, Report and Order, 86 F.C.C.2d 469, 505–509 (1981), *modified on recons.,* 89 F.C.C.2d 58 (1982), *petition for review dismissed sub nom.* United States v. FCC, No. 82-1526 (D.C. Cir. Mar. 3, 1983). In 1988, the Commission relaxed its rules somewhat, allowing cellular carriers to deploy new technologies and provide auxiliary services, provided that carriers continued to support the current technical standard. Amendment of Parts 2 and 22 of the Commission's Rules to Permit Liberalization of Technology and Auxiliary Service Offerings in the Domestic Public Cellular Radio Telecommunications Service, Report and Order, 3 F.C.C. Rec. 7033 (1988). To deploy a new technology or service—such as CDMA or CDPD—a cellular licensee must simply inform the FCC 30 days before its introduction. 47 C.F.R. §22.390(b).

[275] The Commission notes that "[b]roadband PCS licenses, for example, can be used for any mobile or fixed service. . . ." *Omnibus Budget Report,* 12 F.C.C. Rec. at 12,188. The Commission has permitted PCS licensees to sell the rights to portions of their assigned spectrum. Geographic Partitioning and Spectrum Disaggregation by Commercial Mobile Radio Services Licensees, Report and Order and Further Notice of Proposed Rulemaking, 11 F.C.C. Rec. 21,831 (1996) (hereinafter *Geographic Partitioning Order*).

[276] *See* Implementation of Sections 3(n) and 332 of the Communications Act Regulatory Treatment of Mobile Services, Second Report and Order, 9 F.C.C. Rec. 1411, 1418 ¶16 (1994).

Other wireless networks that are already digital or that soon will be are being afforded similar liberties. The Commission has permitted the digitization of existing cellular networks[277] and has already removed restrictions on the types of services that cellular licensees may provide.[278] The Commission has given similar flexibility to several new wireless services, including interactive video and data services (IVDS)[279] and wireless communications service (WCS).[280] Each of these digital services—like ESMR and PCS—will remain free of any serious regulatory obligations.

§11.9 Structural Regulation of the Industry

Until August 1998, the FCC had made notably little attempt to regulate the structure of competition in the Internet market. For good reason. No provider yet dominates these markets, and it is quite possible that no dominant provider will ever emerge. And while the Commission's Common Carrier Bureau remains preoccupied with LECs, the broadcast and cable bureaus have

[277] *See Omnibus Budget Report,* 12 F.C.C. Rec. at 12,166 (CDMA/TDMA); Implementation of Sections 3(n) and 332 of the Communications Act, Third Report and Order, 9 F.C.C. Rec. 7988, 8030–8033 ¶74 (1994) (CDPD).

[278] In 1996, for example, the Commission modified its rules to allow CMRS licensees to provide fixed in addition to mobile services on their spectrum. Amendment of the Commission's Rules to Permit Flexible Service Offerings in the Commercial Mobile Radio Services, First Report and Order and Further Notice of Proposed Rulemaking, 11 F.C.C. Rec. 8965 (1996).

[279] Amendment of Parts 0, 1, 2, and 95 of the Commission's Rules to Provide Interactive Video and Data Services, Memorandum Opinion and Order, 7 F.C.C. Rec. 4923, 4924 ¶9 (1992). IVDS licensees are treated as private carriers, not common carriers, and will not be required to file tariffs of any kind. Amendment of Parts 0, 1, 2, and 95 of the Commission's Rules to Provide Interactive Video and Data Services, Report and Order, 7 F.C.C. Rec. 1630 (1992). Moreover, IVDS licensees are permitted to use their licenses for "other applications" that they develop, "without Commission approval," as long as the services do not run afoul of prior FCC rules. Annual Assessment of the Status of Competition in Markets for the Delivery of Video Programming, Fourth Annual Report, 13 F.C.C. Rec. 1034, 1089–1099 ¶107 (1998).

[280] Amendment of the Commission's Rules to Establish Part 27, the Wireless Communications Service, Report and Order, 12 F.C.C. Rec. 10,785 (1997). WCS licensees may provide any fixed, mobile, or radiolocation service consistent with international allocations and technical limitations.

cheerfully unleashed their charges to offer competitive data services, subject to little regulation of any kind from Washington or state regulators.

LECs remain dominant providers of the dial-up voice circuits still used by most residential subscribers to access the Internet. But voice circuits are available to customers on demand, and to resellers, too, and unbundled loops are available to other CLECs. Incumbent LECs provide these loops, but remain marginal players in the ISP segment of the market. And as noted at the beginning of this chapter, LECs are now running behind in the race with cable and wireless providers to bring affordable high-speed data services to the mass market.

LECs have an even smaller role in the higher reaches of the network. BOCs will remain excluded from the backbone (interLATA) layers of Internet transport until the Commission approves section 271 or section 706 petitions. Or until the BOCs' successfully assert (and defend in court) their right to provide interLATA *information* services without securing section 271 approval.

In its 1998 *Advanced Services Order,* the Commission set off on a new structural regulation mission. It is apparent—although not expressly stated—that the Commission hopes to steer future investment in high-speed data services out of the existing ILECs entirely. The investment, it is assumed, will come either from CLECs or from LEC affiliates—wholly separate subsidiaries that deal with the ILECs only at arm's length, in precisely the same manner as CLECs.

§11.9.1   Voice and Data: One Market or Two?

From both the supply and the demand sides, the market for high-speed data networks remains separate from the market for conventional POTS. On the supply side, all carriers—including incumbent LECs—must deploy new, very different networks and equipment in order to meet the demand for new services. On the demand side, consumer demand for high-speed data services is increasing, especially as compared to the analog facilities that carry ordinary voice calls. The demand for high-speed data services is growing at a staggering rate, far outpacing the demand for voice.

Today, substitution between data and voice networks is only at the margin. Accordingly, the Commission has taken the view that the markets are fairly distinct: ISPs are not telecommunications carriers (and are therefore not subject to mandatory universal service contributions) and offer information rather than tele-communications services.[281] The mere fact that the Internet could be used for both voice and data was not enough, the Commission determined, to treat Internet services like a traditional, regulated telecommunications service.[282] But this conventional wisdom will soon be outdated. Data networks will in due course carry all the voice traffic, too. Indeed, many local and regional ISPs are already offering—and many more plan to offer—some form of voice service over data networks.[283]

In the emerging new universe of data telecom, media and services will compete in ways that are unexpected and largely unfamiliar today. Caller ID, a very rudimentary "data" service, can significantly shorten phone calls; many businesses already combine it with "pop-screen" computer software for precisely that

---

[281] Report to Congress, 13 F.C.C. Rec. at 11,552–11,553 ¶¶105, 106 (1998). Indeed, the Commission has gone so far as to say that these services are "mutually exclusive" categories. *See id.* at 11,522–11,523 ¶69 n.138.

[282] Indeed, the Commission has stated that precisely "because IP packets carrying voice communications are indistinguishable from other types of packets," carriers that provided Internet data services could not be deemed to be involved in the "provision" or "offering" of telecommunications. *Id.* at 11,543 ¶87 (citing 47 U.S.C. §§153(46), 254(d)). The Commission further ruled that all "hybrid" services—i.e., ones that involve both a typical information service (e.g., Internet access) and a typical telecommunications service (e.g., voice)—would necessarily fall on the information services side of the line. *See id.* at 11,529 ¶57 ("hybrid services are information services, and are not telecommunications services.").

[283] According to one industry research report, 22 percent of local and regional ISPs were offering some form of voice-over-IP service in February 1998 and 43 percent plan to offer it by February of 1999. *See* B. Caulfield, Separating ISPs from the Telcos, Internet World (Oct. 12, 1998) <http://www.internetworld.com/print/1998/10/12/ispworld/19981012-separating.html>. Among CLECs, 10 percent were offering voice-over-IP service in April 1998, and 50 percent plan to offer it by April 1999. *Id.* A survey of national ISPs indicated that 54 percent plan to offer IP telephony by July 1999. *Id.*

purpose.[284] E-mail and fax can have a similar effect—more is said in writing, meaning there is less to talk about over the phone.[285] A great deal of "voice" traffic is already asymmetric and one-way. Voice mail, standard menu-driven recordings, 900/976 dial-it services, and most fax traffic can all easily migrate onto a broadband digital Internet. Commercial services already convey fax transmissions over the Internet, particularly to overseas destinations, to bypass long-distance charges. In sum, the convergence of traditional media will be economic, too, not just technological. WGBH, SprintNet, and TCI do not compete against Bell Atlantic today. Once their radios and wires are all digital, they very well may.

Whatever position they command in voice markets, incumbent LECs cannot plausibly be viewed as dominant providers of data services. Incumbent LECs arguably remain dominant providers of some analog voice services, some medium-band digital services like ISDN, and some traditional higher-speed data services (like T-1 lines) to businesses. But incumbent LECs are not, by any stretch of the imagination, today's dominant providers of "digital and broadband services and facilities." For residential and small-business consumers, the main providers of such services today are cable companies and satellite carriers, along with various other, noncable, wireline, and wireless CLECs.

[284] Substitutions of this sort can in fact be traced back to the development of the signaling (SS7) network, a dedicated signaling network built to carry the signaling information associated with each phone call in order to alleviate network capacity shortages. These dedicated signaling facilities substituted for voice circuits for two reasons. First, with common channel signaling, voice trunks are not actually connected until the call is answered. Thus, if the receiving line is busy, the trunks that would have been used to connect the call in the old system are instead freed for use by other calls. Second, the creation of a dedicated switching network allows for the concentration of signaling traffic on fewer trunks. Instead of adding overhead on each call over the voice network, the dedicated signaling facilities handle the traffic. This allows telephone companies to deploy fewer voice trunks. See R. F. Rey, ed., Engineering and Operations in the Bell System 292–293 (1984); Travis Russell, Signaling System #7, at 4–6 (1995).

[285] The Internet already delivers more "mail" than the U.S. Postal Service, and by the year 2000, the number of e-mail messages and users are expected to grow to 60 million and 40 million, respectively. S. Miller, E-mail's Popularity Poses Workplace Problems, Business First, Oct. 6, 1997.

Moreover, to the extent that incumbent LECs begin providing high-speed data services, they will almost certainly remain non-dominant and nonessential for the foreseeable future. For the transport of digital data, cable, broadband satellite, and terrestrial wireless will evolve at least as fast as phone networks for the foreseeable future.

§11.9.2   Open Access to High-Speed Cable Networks

Several ISPs and telcos have petitioned the Commission to gain access to high-speed cable networks in order to use cable bandwidth to provide Internet access and online services.[286] In the FCC policy paper, *Internet over Cable,* the FCC has stated that "if evidence indicated that cable high-speed data communications platforms themselves occupied a 'bottleneck' or 'essential facilities' position vis-à-vis ISP or online service provider access," then unbundled access to services and facilities may be required to level the playing field.[287] The FCC further recognized that the "fundamental communications policy goals" that should guide the regulatory treatment of Internet over cable are "competitive and technological neutrality."[288] These neutrality principles have in fact been repeatedly affirmed by Congress,[289] the Com-

---

[286] AOL, MCI WorldCom, GTE, U S WEST, and Ameritech asked the FCC to open access to TCI's cable system as a condition of the AT&T merger.

[287] B. Esbin, Office of Plans and Policy, FCC, Internet over Cable: Defining the Future in Terms of the Past 96–97 (OPP Working Paper No. 30, Aug. 1998).

[288] *Id.* at 87.

[289] Each of the Communication Act's main titles avoids overlap with other titles by reference to the nature of services provided, not the underlying technology. *See* 47 U.S.C. §153(10) ("a person engaged in . . . broadcasting shall not . . . be deemed a common carrier"). The 1984 Cable Act clarified the divide between cable services and telecommunications services by providing that a cable system would not be regulated as a common carrier "by reason of providing any cable service." Moreover, the 1996 Act expressly recognizes that phone companies may provide—over phone wires or any other medium—common carriage, cable service, or "open video system" service, each regulated differently under different provisions of the Communication Act. Section

mission,[290] and the courts.[291] But the FCC has not followed them with respect to Internet over cable.

As discussed in section 5.5.3.5, under the 1996 Act Bell companies are required to "unbundle" and sell to their competitors whatever new capabilities and services they add to their networks[292] at rates "based on the cost[s] of providing" them.[293] In August 1998, the FCC even declared that it intended to require incumbent telephone companies to unbundle their high-speed Internet services.[294] The FCC has not retreated from these policies, even though it has found that in the consumer broadband

---

571 of 47 U.S.C. sets forth the regulatory options for telco offerings of video/cable service; Title II regulates common carriage.

[290] The FCC has, for example, authorized television licensees to use their vertical blanking interval (VBI) to provide all manner of data services within this (otherwise unused) piece of their licenses and has deemed the services to be common carriage. *See* Digital Data Transmission Within the Video Portion of Television Broadcast Station Transmissions, Report and Order, 11 F.C.C. Rec. 7799 (1996). It has likewise invited operators of direct broadcast satellites to choose for themselves whether to operate individual transponders to provide private carriage, common carriage, public broadcast, or subscription broadcast over their communications channels. *See* Inquiry into the Development of Regulatory Policy in Regard to Direct Broadcast Satellites for the Period Following the 1983 Regional Administrative Conference, Report and Order, 90 F.C.C.2d 676 (1982). Pursuant to the 1996 Act, the Commission has stated that "non-broadcast services provided by digital broadcast licensees will be regulated in a manner consistent with analogous services provided by other persons or entities." Advanced Television Systems and Their Impact upon the Existing Television Broadcast Service, Fifth Report and Order, 12 F.C.C. Rec. 12,809, 12,823 ¶36 (1997) (the Commission likened this to its policies regarding FM subcarrier and VBI); 47 U.S.C. §336(b)(3).

[291] For example, in 1976, the D.C. Circuit stated: "A particular system is a common carrier by virtue of its functions, rather than because it is declared to be so." NARUC I v. FCC, 525 F.2d 630, 644 (D.C. Cir. 1976) (*NARUC I*) (upholding FCC orders that classified "Specialized Mobile Radio Systems" as non-common carriers beyond the reach of Title II, but rejecting the FCC's claim that that it may classify services as it pleases). And again in 1994: "Whether an entity in a given case is to be considered a common carrier or a private carrier turns on the particular practice under surveillance." Southwestern Bell Tel. Co. v. FCC, 19 F.3d 1475, 1481 (D.C. Cir. 1994).

[292] 47 U.S.C. §251(c)(3).

[293] 47 U.S.C. §252(d)(1)(A)(i).

[294] *Advanced Services Order,* 13 F.C.C. Rec. at 24,017–24,018 ¶11 ("all incumbent LECs must provide requesting telecommunications carriers with unbundled loops capable of transporting high-speed digital signals, and must

market "[t]he preconditions for monopoly appear absent" and that "no competitor has a large embedded base of paying residential consumers."[295]

Yet in approving the AT&T/TCI merger, the FCC rejected petitions to require TCI to permit unaffiliated ISPs to obtain unbundled access to TCI's cable network.[296] The FCC was persuaded by AT&T-TCI's statement that customers of TCI's cable Internet service would still be able to "click through" the initial TCI-@Home screens and thereby connect to alternative access providers, like AOL, and alternative content providers, like Yahoo.[297] The FCC also noted the emergence of "multiple methods of providing high-speed Internet access"[298] and the fact that a merger proceeding was not the best forum to address this issue.[299]

§11.10 Conclusion[300]

The 1934 Communications Act was written around the technological paradigms of its day: broadcasting and common carrier telephony. The Act distinguishes wire from wireless, carriage

offer unbundled access to the equipment used in the provision of advanced services"). The Commission noted that it might identify "additional, or perhaps different," unbundling requirements in the future. *Id.* at 24,036 ¶51 (citing *Local Competition Order,* 11 F.C.C. Rec. at 15,624–15,626).

[295] Inquiry Concerning the Deployment of Advanced Telecommunications Capability to All Americans in a Reasonable and Timely Fashion, and Possible Steps to Accelerate Such Deployment Pursuant to Section 706 of the Telecommunications Act of 1996, Report, CC Docket No. 98-146, ¶48 (Feb. 2, 1999).

[296] *See* Applications for Consent to the Transfer of Control of Licenses and Section 214 Authorizations from Tele-Communications, Inc. to AT&T Corp., Memorandum Opinion and Order, CS Docket No. 98-178 (Feb. 18, 1999).

[297] The FCC stated that, "[b]ased on this representation, we conclude nothing about the proposed merger would deny any customer (including AT&T-TCI customers) the ability to access the Internet content or portal of his or her choice." *Id.* ¶96.

[298] *Id.*

[299] The FCC stated that "the open access issues would remain equally meritorious (or non-meritorious) if the merger were not to occur." *Id.*

[300] *See* Peter Huber & Evan Leo, The Incidental, Accidental Deregulation of Data . . . and Everything Else, 6 Indus. & Corp. Change 807 (1997).

from broadcast, broadcast from cable, voice from video, and both voice and video from data. It draws lines based on the type of content conveyed, the prices charged or not charged for conveying it, the wealth of the conveying company, and the novelty of the service. Although digital, broadband services were beyond imagination at the time the 1934 Act was enacted, they are nevertheless subject to the Act's taxonomy and the regulations that have emerged thereunder.

How telecommunications services are regulated today depends in large part on what the FCC calls them. The categories adopted by the Commission center on the official identity or status of the company providing the service, the identity or status of the consumer or interconnected enterprise at the other end, the technology used in between, and the geographic location over which the service is provided. A complex regulatory taxonomy has grown up over many decades, and not surprisingly, it mirrors the distinctions and lines drawn under the 1934 Communications Act.

But the digital telecosm no longer conforms to these established regulatory categories, and there is no good reason to continue regulating broadband networks and services under the old regulatory paradigms. Today, voice, video, and data are converging on the same wireless and wireline networks. Step by step, regulation must be revised to reflect current technological and economic imperatives.

As media and services converge, the Commission should adopt a uniform and systematic policy of granting "most favored nation" status to all me-too applicants who propose to provide any kind of service already approved and provided by an earlier applicant of any kind, whether or not the second applicant seeks authority under the same title of the Communications Act as the first. Digital technology and high bandwidth obliterate engineering and economic distinctions between different types of electronic communication. Not simply because "a bit is a bit." The key point is that high-bandwidth digital networks, both wired and wireless, are extremely flexible. They can readily be configured and interconnected to mimic any of the capabilities of any of the old, analog systems.

Congress has already established the model for "MFN" deregulation. Until 1993, the Commission did not treat all competing providers of wireless services alike. Cellular providers were treated as "common carriers" subject to Title II regulation and other requirements. By contrast, ESMR providers, which competed with cellular, were exempt from most forms of regulation. In the Omnibus Budget Reconciliation Act of 1993, Congress required the FCC to accord similar regulatory status to all competing providers of mobile wireless services, regardless of the technology used to provide such services.[301] Since then, the FCC has afforded wireless services regulatory flexibility with few serious regulatory obligations to hinder their development. Yet broadband services today are regulated as unevenly as wireless services were before 1993. Cable operators face no regulation when they provide cable modem service. Local exchange carriers that offer competing DSL service are still strictly regulated.

The wireless industry boomed under this new environment of liberalized entry and deregulation. PCS networks have been deployed even more rapidly than expected. Subscribership has soared, and prices have fallen. Demand for other new wireless services has also exceeded expectations. Like the wireless industry in 1993, the broadband industry in 1999 is poised for enormous growth. DSL technology, cable modems, and low-earth satellites are bringing broadband to copper, coax, and the skies.

---

[301] *See* Omnibus Budget Reconciliation Act of 1993, Pub. L. No. 103-66, Title VI, §6001(a), 107 Stat. 312 (1993).

12

Information Services*

§12.1 Introduction

Why aren't companies that provide e-mail regulated as common carriers? They perform much the same function as a phone company, after all, but aren't regulated in any comparable manner. Nor are any of the other providers of online services and content—credit card companies, bank ATM networks, and every provider doing business in the upper tiers of the Internet and other data networks. Such enterprises file no tariffs with the FCC or state regulators. They discriminate among their customers, they negotiate discounts and special contracts with impunity, and they have no universal service obligation to provide service on the same terms to all comers in any particular franchise area. They may be owned by foreigners; they may even

*This chapter was co-authored by Sarah O. Jorgensen, Associate, Kellogg, Huber, Hansen, Todd & Evans; Swarthmore College (B.A., *with distinction*, 1990); Harvard Law School (J.D., *magna cum laude*, 1995); Phi Beta Kappa; Law Clerk, Honorable Laurence Silberman, U.S. Court of Appeals, D.C. Circuit, 1995–1996; Law Clerk, Honorable William H. Rehnquist, Chief Justice, U.S. Supreme Court, 1997–1998.

operate their servers from overseas. They may transmit content of their own creation over their own networks. When their service goes down, for an hour or a day, they file no apologetic reports with the Federal Communications Commission (FCC). Section 12.4 deals with the happily deregulated status of these "information service" providers.

But as discussed in the previous chapter, data networks themselves—including many of the lower transport and routing tiers of the Internet—are a different regulatory matter. While there is a push to deregulate data networks, too, those provided by phone companies at least remain very much subject to all the traditional regulatory obligations of common carriers.

At the federal level, the origins of this regulatory split can be traced to a seminal FCC initiative in 1966, the Commission's Computer I inquiry. It was there that the Commission made the basic decision to separate the online universe in two, keeping the basic physical transport layers regulated, but deregulating the virtual and content layers. The overarching regulatory objective: to keep the deregulated half of the universe sufficiently separate from the regulated half to prevent each one from corrupting the other, while ensuring smoothly functioning connections between the two. The Commission, courts, and Congress have been fiddling with the details ever since, but that conceptual approach has held.

Section 12.5 of this chapter explores how this basic wall was erected, modified, and maintained. And it addresses the mirror-image problem: how to make sure that the regulated side interconnects with, or provides common carriage for, the unregulated side on acceptable terms.

Section 12.6 focuses on a more narrow aspect of the interconnection of the two sides: rate regulation and access charges and the application of universal service obligations.

Section 12.7 deals with the labyrinth of special rules that apply to some of the companies that do business on both sides of the line, and most particularly to incumbent local carriers. These rules attempt to regulate the structural relations of the industry participants and focus on particular lines of business or types of service.

It is by no means easy to determine which services fall on which side of the regulatory line.[1] We have already discussed the line-drawing problem once. See section 6.3.2.4. We will return to the same issue repeatedly in this chapter. We reiterate here two fundamental points. First, the definitional line between the "content" and "transport" layers is neither sharp nor clear. Second, a great deal of regulatory consequence pivots on which way a service is categorized. And we add a third point: though the Commission is now laboring to disclaim it, a large body of Commission precedent establishes that even the smallest peppercorn of content modification places an *entire service* (not just the pep-percorn itself) on the "enhanced," or *deregulated*, side of the line.

§12.2 Definitions

The key words are "basic" or "telecommunications" services, on the one hand, and "enhanced" or "information" services, on the other. Truth be told, however, at this point, we cannot even be sure what to call them.

§12.2.1 "Enhanced" and "Information" Services

Although the Commission has customarily spoken in terms of "enhanced" services, the Bell Divestiture Decree and, more important, the 1996 Telecommunications Act have used the term "information service." In 1996, the Commission finally considered the overlap between these terms. It ruled that "information services" include all "enhanced services," although the converse is not true.[2] The category of "information services" is broader

---

[1] "Well ump," a batter once asked legendary umpire Bill Klem, "is it a ball or a strike?" "It ain't nothing 'till I call it," Klem growled.

[2] Implementation of the Non-accounting Safeguards of Sections 271 and 272 of the Communications Act of 1934, as Amended, First Report and Order, 11 F.C.C. Rec. 21,905, 21,955–21,956 ¶¶102–103 (1996) (hereinafter *Non-accounting Safeguards Order*), aff'd, Bell Atlantic Tel. Cos. v. FCC, 131 F.3d 1044 (D.C. Cir. 1997).

than that of "enhanced services." The former are provided "via telecommunications," whereas "enhanced services" are only those that are "offered over common carrier transmission facilities used in interstate communications."[3] There is now a proposal before the Commission to retire the term "enhanced" and use "information" from here on out. However, we will still use both terms because at this point both are current and it is not possible to quote or discuss the applicable authority any other way.

§12.2.2 "Basic" and "Telecommunications" Services

Pure transport services on the regulated side of the wall also are in the process of being renamed. The FCC called them "basic," but the 1996 Act called them "telecommunications services." The Commission has tentatively proposed that the terms "basic services" and "telecommunications services" be interpreted to extend to the same services, even though the two definitions are somewhat different.[4] But again, we will use both terms because we still have to. If the Commission completes the job of redefinition now under way in light of the 1996 Act, yesterday's division, "basic/enhanced," will be relabeled "telecommunications/information."

§12.2.3 "Information" Versus "Telecommunications" Services Under the 1996 Act

The 1996 Act's complementary definitions of "telecommunications service" and "information service" are drafted to cover mutually exclusive territory. A telecommunications service is the

---

[3] *Id.* at 21,956 ¶103. The Commission also determined that live operator telemessaging services that do not involve "computer processing applications" are information services, although they are not enhanced services.

[4] Computer III Further Remand Proceedings: Bell Operating Company Provision of Enhanced Services 1998 Biennial Regulatory Review of Computer

transmission of information between or among points with *no* "change in the form or content."[5] An "information service," by contrast, "means the offering of a capability for generating, acquiring, storing, transforming, processing, retrieving, utilizing, or making available information *via telecommunications*, and includes electronic publishing."[6] "Information services" convey content "*via*" telecommunications, but they are not themselves "telecommunications services." Domino's Pizza conveys pizzas "*via*" truck, but that does not make Domino's Pizza a "trucking service." If one were to allow for the possibility that something can be *both* a "telecommunications service" *and* an "information service," then the statutory definition of "information service" would become tautological—such a service must simultaneously *be* a "telecommunications service" and perform its function "*via* telecommunications." There is no hint in the Act that Congress expected the categories of telecommunications and information services to be anything other than mutually exclusive.

In November 1997, Congress directed the FCC to submit a report reviewing the 1996 Act's definitions of, among other things, the terms "telecommunications," "telecommunications

---

III and ONA Safeguards and Requirements, Further Notice of Proposed Rulemaking, 13 F.C.C. Rec. 6040, 6066–6067 ¶41 (1998).

[5] "The term 'telecommunications' means the transmission, between or among points specified by the user, of information of the user's choosing, without change in the form or content of the information as sent and received." 47 U.S.C. §153(43). The phrase "telecommunications *service*" has a slightly more limited definition: "the offering of telecommunications for a fee *directly to the public*, or to such classes of users as to be effectively available directly to the public, regardless of the facilities used." 47 U.S.C. §153(46) (emphasis added). The phrase "telecommunications service" also is limited to "telecommunications provided on a common carrier basis," whereas the broader term "telecommunications" is not so limited. Federal-State Joint Board on Universal Service, Report and Order, 12 F.C.C. Rec. 8776, 9177–9178 ¶785, 9182–9183 ¶793 (1997) (hereinafter *Universal Service Order*), *appeal pending sub nom.* Texas Office of Pub. Util. Counsel v. FCC, No. 97-60421 (5th Cir.).

[6] 47 U.S.C. §153(20) (emphasis added). Further, "information service" "includes electronic publishing, but does not include any use of any such capability for the management, control, or operation of a telecommunications system or the management of a telecommunications service." *Id.*

service," and "information service."[7] In its April 10, 1998, *Report to Congress*, the FCC confirmed that the categories of "telecommunications service" and "information service" are mutually exclusive under the 1996 Act, just as the categories of "basic" and "enhanced" services were mutually exclusive under prior Commission precedent.[8] The Commission further stated that "Congress intended to maintain a regime in which information service providers are not subject to regulations as common carriers merely because they provide their services 'via telecommunications.'"[9] Thus, if an entity offers transmission incorporating a simple "transparent transmission path, without the capability of providing enhanced functionality, [it] offers 'telecommunications.'"[10] By contrast, if a business offers "transmission incorporating the 'capability for generating, acquiring, storing, transforming, processing, retrieving, utilizing, or making available information,' it does not offer telecommunications."[11] Instead, "it offers an 'information service' even though it uses telecommunications to do so."[12]

The Commission thus rejected the argument that to the extent that a provider engages in transmission of information, the provider is simultaneously a "telecommunications service provider" and an "information service provider." The Commission supported its understanding of the Act both with the statutory text and with the legislative history.[13] It concluded that by defining "telecommunications" as a transmission of information "without

---

[7] Departments of Commerce, Justice, and State, the Judiciary, and Related Agencies Appropriations Act, 1998, Pub. L. No. 105-119, §623, 111 Stat. 2440, 2521–2522.

[8] Federal-State Joint Board on Universal Service, Report, 13 F.C.C. Rec. 11,501, 11,507–11,508 ¶13 (1998) (hereinafter *Report to Congress*). "[W]e conclude that Congress intended these new terms to build upon frameworks established prior to the passage of the 1996 Act." *Id.* at 11,511 ¶21.

[9] *Id.* at 11,507–11,508 ¶13 (footnote omitted).

[10] *Id.* at 11,520 ¶39.

[11] *Id.*

[12] *Id.*

[13] The Commission found that the drafters of the House and Senate bills intended for the categories of "telecommunications" and "information" services to be mutually exclusive. *Id.* at 11,522–11,523 ¶43.

change in the form or content of the information," Congress intended to ensure that an information service provider would not be deemed to be providing telecommunications.[14]

§12.2.4 Protocol Processing Services

In its *Non-accounting Safeguards Order,* the Commission made clear that both "protocol conversion" and "protocol processing services" are information services under the 1996 Act.[15] This interpretation was in keeping with the FCC's "existing practice of treating end-to-end protocol processing services as enhanced services."[16] Three categories of protocol processing services, however, are treated as telecommunications services: (1) communications between an end user and the network itself (e.g., for initiation, routing, and termination of calls) rather than between or among users, (2) the introduction of a new basic network technology (which requires protocol conversion to maintain compatibility with existing custom premises equipment (CPE)), and (3) internetworking (conversions taking place solely within the carrier's network to facilitate provision of a basic network service that result in no net conversion to the end user, i.e., the transmission is transparent to the end user).[17]

At Congress's direction, the Commission revisited the regulatory classification of protocol processing services in its *Report to Congress.*[18] The Commission noted that Congress had settled on a definition of "information service" that did not refer to protocol processing and concluded there was therefore a "substantial"

[14] *Id.* at 11,520–11,521 ¶40.

[15] *Non-accounting Safeguards Order,* 11 F.C.C. Rec. at 21,956 ¶104. "Protocol conversion" is the way in which different computers communicate; it is necessary, for example, to permit a personal computer to communicate via a packet-switched network with a database such as Lexis. "Protocol processing services" are the services necessary to provide protocol conversion.

[16] *Id.* at 21,957 ¶105.

[17] Implementation of the Non-accounting Safeguards of Sections 271 and 272 of the Communications Act of 1934, as Amended, Order on Reconsideration, 12 F.C.C. Rec. 2297 (1997).

[18] For a discussion of the prior regulatory treatment of protocol conversion, see §12.6.7.

question whether Congress intended to treat protocol processing services as information services.[19] In the end, the Commission decided that it would not resolve the matter based on the record before it.[20]

§12.2.5 Mixed or Hybrid Services

Also at Congress's specific direction, the Commission considered in its *Report to Congress* how to apply the Act's "telecommunications"/"information" dichotomy to "mixed or hybrid services," a term the Act does not define.[21] The FCC interpreted the term as referring to "services in which a provider offers a capability for generating, acquiring, storing, transforming, processing, retrieving, utilizing or making available information via telecommunications, *and* as an inseparable part of that service transmits information supplied or requested by the user."[22] It follows, reasoned the FCC, that "hybrid services are information services, and are not telecommunications services."[23] Because they are offered "via telecommunications," information services necessarily require a transmission component in order for users to access information.[24]

The Commission went on to consider Internet-based services as a category of hybrid services. The Commission separately evaluated three issues: (1) the provision of transmission capacity to Internet access and backbone providers, (2) Internet access

---

[19] *Report to Congress,* 13 F.C.C. Rec. at 11,526–11,527 ¶¶50–51.

[20] It concluded that in any event there was no need to reach the issue. "The regulatory classification of protocol processing is significant to the provision of universal service only to the extent that it affects the appropriate classification of Internet access services and IP [Internet protocol] telephony. We find, however, . . . that Internet access services are appropriately classed as information services without regard to our treatment of protocol processing. Similarly, our discussion of the regulatory status of phone-to-phone IP telephony is not affected by our resolution of the protocol processing issue." *Id.* at 11,527 ¶52 (footnote omitted).

[21] *Id.*

[22] *Id.* at 11,529 ¶56.

[23] *Id.* at 11,529 ¶57 (footnote omitted).

[24] *Id.*

services, and (3) IP (Internet protocol) telephony. Its conclusions indicate that most Internet access and data networking services probably fall on the information services side of the line.

§12.2.5.1 Provision of Transmission Capacity to Internet Access and Backbone Providers

The Commission described the ways in which Internet service providers use telecommunications inputs. They purchase lines from local exchange carriers to connect to their dial-in subscribers. They may also lease lines from telecommunications carriers, use their own facilities to provide such transmission, and/or enter into interconnection arrangements with Internet backbone providers. The Commission concluded that although information service providers do not offer telecommunications services to their subscribers, "[t]he provision of leased lines to Internet service providers . . . constitutes the provision of interstate telecommunications" by the telecommunications carrier.[25] Currently the Commission requires the carriers that lease lines to Internet service providers to include the revenues they derive from those lines in their universal service contribution base. These carriers pass their costs on to lessee Internet service providers.

Some Internet service providers own their own transmission facilities and transport data over those facilities. Unlike the telecommunications carriers that lease lines to Internet service providers, however, such providers currently do not contribute to universal service mechanisms.[26] Concerned that the different treatment of lessee and facilities-based Internet service providers may create an artificial incentive for information service providers to integrate vertically,[27] the FCC has decided to reexamine this result. While it has not yet finally resolved the matter, it has tentatively observed that the facilities-based Internet service provider is arguably "furnishing raw transmission capacity to

[25] *Id.* at 11,533 ¶67 (footnote omitted).
[26] *Id.* at 11,534–11,535 ¶69.
[27] *Id.* at 11,535 ¶70.

itself," albeit as a non-common carrier.[28] To the extent that "any of the underlying inputs [used by Internet access and backbone providers] constitutes interstate telecommunications, [the FCC] has authority under the 1996 Act to require that the providers of those inputs contribute to federal universal service mechanisms."[29]

The Commission also stressed that the concept that Internet service providers may be providing themselves with transmission is not inconsistent with its conclusion that "telecommunications service" and "information service" are mutually exclusive categories:[30]

> [U]nder our understanding of the 1996 Act, we do not treat an information service provider as providing a telecommunications service to its subscribers. The service it provides to its subscribers is not subject to Title II, and is categorized as an information service. The information service provider, indeed, is itself a user of telecommunications; that is, telecommunications is an input in the provision of an information service. Our analysis here rests on the reasoning that under this framework, in every case, some entity must provide telecommunications to the information service provider. When the information service provider owns the underlying facilities, it appears that it should itself be treated as providing the underlying telecommunications. That conclusion, however, speaks only to the relationship between the facilities owner and the information service provider (in some cases, the same entity); it does not affect the relationship between the information service provider and its subscribers.[31]

§12.2.5.2   Internet Access Services

The Commission ruled that Internet access services are properly classified as information services.[32] Subscribers who store

---

[28] *Id.* at 11,528 ¶55.
[29] *Id.* at 11,532–11,533 ¶66.
[30] *Id.* at 11,534 ¶69 n.138.
[31] *Id.*
[32] *Id.* at 11,536 ¶73.

files on the computers of an Internet service provider are using the provider's capability for storing or making information available.[33] Those who retrieve information from the Internet can do so because the Internet service provider offers the capability for acquiring, retrieving, and utilizing information.[34] Electronic mail similarly uses data storage as a key feature of the service offering.[35] Once again, the Commission concluded that even though the provision of Internet access services involves data transport elements, the offering cannot be classified as a telecommunications service because "it offers end users information service-capabilities inextricably intertwined with data transport."[36] "In offering service to end users, [Internet access providers] do more than resell those data transport services. *They conjoin the data transport with data processing, information provision, and other computer-mediated offerings, thereby creating an information service.*"[37]

§12.2.5.3 IP Telephony

IP telephony, the Internet service that "most closely resemble[s] traditional basic transmission offerings," presented the most challenging classification problem.[38] Although the record before the FCC did not enable it to make a definitive pronouncement, the FCC's initial view was that "phone-to-phone" IP telephony bore many of the characteristics of "telecommunications services."[39] "From a functional standpoint, users of these services obtain only voice transmission, rather than information services

[33] *Id.* at 11,537–11,538 ¶76.
[34] *Id.*
[35] *Id.* at 11,538–11,539 ¶78.
[36] *Id.* at 11,539–11,540 ¶80.
[37] *Id.* at 11,540 ¶81 (emphasis added).
[38] *Id.* at 11,541 ¶83 (footnote omitted). Internet protocol telephony (IP telephony) is use of the Internet for telephone calls.
[39] *Id.* at 11,544 ¶89. The Commission tentatively defined "phone-to-phone IP telephony" as services in which the provider (1) holds itself out as providing voice telephony or facsimile transmission service, (2) does not require the customer to use CPE different from that used to make an ordinary phone call, (3) allows the customer to call telephone numbers assigned in accordance with the North American Numbering Plan, and (4) transmits customer information without net change in form or content. *Id.* at 11,543–11,544 ¶88.

such as access to stored files. The provider does not offer a capability of generating, acquiring, storing, transforming, processing, retrieving, utilizing or making available information. Thus, the record currently before us suggests that this type of IP telephony lacks the characteristics that would render them 'information services' within the meaning of the statute, and instead bear the characteristics of 'telecommunications services.'"[40] Until it had a better-developed record before it, however, the agency deferred its resolution of this issue.

§12.2.6 None of the Above

To keep things interesting, many services are *neither* telecommunications nor information. "Customer premises equipment" occupies a category of its own, though for the most part the Commission has endeavored to deregulate it in parallel with enhanced services. Broadcast and cable services meet the 1996 Act's literal definition of "information services," but elsewhere are defined outside of it.[41] And in one important section, section 271, the 1996 Act creates a further definitional category of "incidental" services provided in conjunction with broadcast, storage equipment, wireless telecommunications, and other activities. See section 12.7.11 below.

§12.3 Jurisdiction and Federal Preemption

The scope of federal jurisdiction over telecommunications services and information services depends a good deal on which side of the wall one is standing.

---

[40] *Id.* (footnote omitted).
[41] *See* 47 U.S.C. §153(10) ("a person engaged in radio broadcasting shall not, insofar as such person is so engaged, be deemed a common carrier"). But broadcasters may also provide "carriage," as when radio stations transmit paging messages in the otherwise dead spaces of their frequency bands. *See, e.g.,* FM Licensees, First Report and Order, BC Docket No. 82-536, ¶54 (June 22, 1983).

On the side occupied by pure providers of information services, the Commission has been largely successful in preempting state authority and thereby ensuring deregulation. The Commission's *Computer II* decision largely accomplished this goal by continuing the deregulation of information services started in *Computer I* and by asserting in addition that the states could not impose any inconsistent regulation. This preemption of inconsistent state regulation is discussed more fully in the context of deregulation of information services. *See* section 12.4.2 below. And as discussed in Chapter 14, the First Amendment operates as a second source of preemptive, deregulatory federal authority, but state law still governs many of the outer limits of what can be said and how, e.g., obscenity and libel.

On the other side, occupied by pure providers of telecommunication services, the Commission's preemptive authority is more limited. The 1934 Communications Act left the states with a considerable measure of authority over intrastate telecom matters, so the Commission has the burden of demonstrating the interstate nature of the services over which it wants to assert federal jurisdiction. See section 3.3.

The differing extent of federal jurisdiction over information services and telecommunications services has created some thorny issues in the intersection between the two, i.e., in deciding both where the line between the two is drawn and how the two sides interconnect. As with telecommunication services, it has been up to the Commission to demonstrate that the interconnection rules are so inseparably intertwined with interstate communications that dividing them into in-state and interstate communications is impractical. *See* sections 12.5.1 and 12.6.1 below. Similarly, the Commission's regulation and preemption of structural separation has faced repeated court challenges, and the Commission has been forced to establish the need to preempt inconsistent state regulation. *See* sections 12.5.1 and 12.7.1 below. However, the Commission, backed by Congress in the 1996 Act, in the end has successfully asserted federal control over most of the wall-building, as well as over many of the rules governing interconnection.

§12.4 Federal Deregulation of Information Services

The FCC has generally treated enhanced services the same way it has treated CPE.[42] This is logical enough: CPE includes telephones, private branch exchanges (PBXs), computers, packetizers, and almost every other piece of equipment that a provider of information might use in delivering an online service. For many information services, a private exchange supplies the interface between the public phone network and an array of computers, disk drives, modems, and other components used to provide an information service. The same sorts of risks and benefits that accompany telco provision of CPE—potential discrimination in interconnection and cross subsidization, on the one hand, and economies of scale and scope, on the other—apply to telco provision of enhanced services.

The FCC's experience with CPE involved a long process of deregulation. Raised in the protective confines of the regulated monopoly, CPE was pushed out into the competitive marketplace to fend for itself. By contrast, computer-based communications, so-called enhanced services, grew up in the heady atmosphere of unfettered competition.[43] As data processing (computer services) and communications began to coalesce with the advent of remote computing and timesharing, the FCC was faced with the question of whether to pull this industry out of the wild and domesticate it with regulation. Resisting the usual empire-building impulses of most bureaucracies, the FCC chose to forbear extending its jurisdiction to cover the new technology.

---

[42] See §8.4.

[43] For a brilliant description of the personalities, economic forces, and technological developments behind the rise of computer hardware and software, see G. Gilder, Microcosm (1990). *See also* T. Kidder, The Soul of a New Machine (1981).

§12.4.1 Origins of the FCC's Policy to Deregulate Information Services: **Computer I**

The Commission first undertook to examine the convergence of computers and communications in 1966. In computing at that time, bigger was better. Computers occupied whole rooms, if not buildings, and had armies of attendants. Pundits believed in something called "Grosch's law," according to which the efficiency of computing increased in step with the size of the computer. The bigger (and more expensive) the machine was, the faster it worked, and the more capacity it had—too much capacity, often, for the needs of any one company, and certainly too much expense. Computing for the masses was therefore provided by "time sharing," which involved connecting small dumb terminals to large central mainframes over the phone lines.[44]

"[I]t is clear," the Commission confidently declared in 1966, "that data processing cannot survive, much less develop further, except through reliance upon and use of communication facilities and services."[45] Steve Jobs and Steve Wozniak, both youngsters at the time, apparently neglected to read this pronouncement from Washington, but their Apple computer still lay some years in the future.

So far as the Commission could see in 1966, it faced a fundamental choice: whether to regulate the burgeoning data processing field as an integral part of communications. If not, how was it to draw the line between regulated communications and

---

[44] The phone links and terminals replaced on-site electronic input and output devices. Previously, remote users had to mail or physically deliver data to the computer. *See* G. Dippel & W. House, Information Systems: Data Processing and Evaluation 67–68 (1969); Note, The FCC Computer Inquiry: Interfaces of Competitive and Regulated Markets, 71 Mich. L. Rev. 172, 173–174 (1972); Pierce, The Transmission of Computer Data, Scientific American, Sept. 1966, at 145. *See generally* Note, Computer Services and the Federal Regulation of Communications, 116 U. Pa. L. Rev. 328 (1967).

[45] Regulatory Pricing Problems Presented by the Interdependence of Computer and Communication Services and Facilities, Final Decision and Order, 28 F.C.C.2d 267, 269 (1971) (hereinafter *Computer I*), aff'd sub nom. GTE Serv. Corp. v. FCC, 474 F.2d 724 (2d Cir.), *decision on remand,* 40 F.C.C.2d 293 (1973).

unregulated data processing? And on what terms would common carriers be permitted to participate in unregulated data processing? The FCC contracted with the Stanford Research Institute (SRI) to examine these questions. In a five-volume report, SRI recommended against regulating the computer industry. But it provided little guidance on the question that had prompted all the concern in the first place: where the computer industry ended and the telecommunications industry began.

Undeterred, the Commission issued its *Computer I* decision in 1971.[46] Data processing, the Commission found, was a highly competitive industry and should remain so; the Commission therefore would not regulate "data processing as such."[47] This was simple; this was clear. Everything else, it turned out, would remain opaque.

The Commission concluded that computer services could be categorized as message-switching, data processing, or a combination of both, that is, a "hybrid service." Message-switching involved communications and therefore was to be regulated; data processing involved information services and was not to be regulated. However, as to combination services, the Commission concluded that some hybrids ("hybrid data processing") were mostly computing with some incidental messaging, while others ("hybrid communications") were mostly messaging with some incidental computing. The Commission thus defined four broad categories, two of which were to be regulated, two not.

---

[46] Regulatory and Policy Problems Presented by the Interdependence of Computer and Communications Services and Facilities, Tentative Decision, 28 F.C.C.2d 291 (1970) (hereinafter *Computer I, Tentative Decision*); *Computer I*, 28 F.C.C.2d 267.

[47] The Commission brushed aside suggestions by some commentators that it had no statutory authority to extend its common carrier regulatory jurisdiction to data processing services. A discussion of the scope of its jurisdiction was "neither relevant nor necessary" for purposes of its decision, the Commission stated, because it was not proposing to regulate data processing as such. The Commission warned, however, that "if there should develop significant changes in the structure of the data processing industry, or, if abuses emerge which require the exercise of corrective action by the Commission, we shall not hesitate to re-examine the policies set forth herein." *Computer I*, 28 F.C.C.2d at 268 ¶¶4–6 (footnote omitted).

As to the two intermediate categories, the Commission regrettably despaired of the ability to adopt "rules of general applicability sufficiently definitive to accommodate the variety of future service offerings" in such an innovative field.[48] It declined even to give illustrative examples to help map out the definitional territory. Instead, it would render "ad hoc evaluations" to determine on which side of the line "hybrid services" fell.[49] The Commission's decision was affirmed in large part on appeal.[50] One or two bits that served to limit telco involvement in these unregulated "computer" activities were rejected. Those bits, the Second Circuit concluded, served only to protect the data processing market—a market "beyond [the FCC's] charge and which the Commission itself has announced it declines to regulate."[51]

§12.4.2 Preemption of State Regulation of Information Services: Computer II

Beyond the FCC's charge? Not for long. Litigation over *Computer I* ended in 1973, seven years after the proceeding began. Three years later the Commission initiated the Second Computer Inquiry. And in May 1980, after four years of deliberation, the Commission issued *Computer II*.[52]

Computer II was mainly concerned with shutting AT&T out of information service markets. But *Computer II* also addressed and extended the deregulation of information services. Initially the

---

[48] *Computer I*, 28 F.C.C.2d at 276–279 ¶¶26–34.

[49] *Id.* at 276 ¶27.

[50] GTE Serv. Corp. v. FCC, 474 F.2d 724, 731 (2d Cir. 1973).

[51] *Id.* at 733.

[52] Amendment of Section 64.702 of the Commission's Rules & Regulations, Second Computer Inquiry, Final Decision, 77 F.C.C.2d 384 (hereinafter *Computer II*), *modified on recons.*, 84 F.C.C.2d 50 (1980) (hereinafter *Computer II Reconsideration Order*), *further modified on recons.*, 88 F.C.C.2d 512 (1981) (hereinafter *Computer II Further Reconsideration Order*), *aff'd sub nom.* Computer and Communications Indus. Assn. v. FCC, 693 F.2d 198 (D.C. Cir. 1982), *cert. denied*, 461 U.S. 938 (1983), *aff'd on second further recons.*, FCC 84-190 (May 4, 1984).

Commission proposed simply to redefine the sphere of data processing.[53] But it soon realized this was impossible. Transmission links for voice and data had previously been offered as discrete services, but with the incorporation of digital technology into the telephone network and the proliferation of communicating computers everywhere, the old distinctions were obsolete. Carriers were now simply providing bandwidth, which customers would then use at will for "voice, data, video, facsimile, or other forms of transmission."[54] It was now futile to search for any clear, stable point at which "communications" shaded into "data processing."[55] The respective technologies were too intertwined to draw an enduring line of demarcation.

So the Commission resolved instead to deregulate all computer-enhanced services, along with all forms of CPE.[56] Regulation under Title II of the Communications Act would end at a boundary defined by "basic" telephone services.

Basic services would be limited to switching and transmission. Carriers could maintain technical parameters of fidelity; they could likewise provide compression, error control, and such, but only to facilitate economical, reliable transport. Storage within the network was permitted only as needed to facilitate immediate transmission.[57] Thus, basic services would offer "a pure transmission capability over a communications path that is virtually transparent in terms of its interaction with customer supplied information."[58]

Any service that was not basic was "enhanced."[59] Such services "acted on the format, content, code, protocol or similar aspects

---

[53] *Id.* at 392 ¶3 n.3.
[54] *Id.* at 419 ¶94.
[55] *Id.* at 394 ¶¶25–26.
[56] *Id.* at 428 ¶114, 447 ¶160.
[57] *Id.* at 420 ¶95.
[58] *Id.* at 420 ¶96.
[59] *Id.* at 420–421 ¶97. Examples of services the Commission has treated as enhanced include voice mail, e-mail, fax store-and-forward, interactive voice response, protocol processing, gateway, and audiotext information services. *See* Bell Operating Companies Joint Petition for Waiver of Computer II Rules, Order, 10 F.C.C. Rec. 13,758, 13,770–13,774 (1995).

of the subscriber's transmitted information, or provided the subscriber additional, different, or restructured information, or involved subscriber interaction with stored information."[60] With basic services defined as narrowly as possible, everything else would be left to competitive markets.[61]

To make sure that regulation of enhanced services did not materialize at a local level, the Commission invoked "ancillary jurisdiction" under Title I of the Communications Act to preempt any inconsistent state regulation.[62] This meant no franchise, no tariffs, no traditional common carrier regulation of any kind. In *Computer I*, as the appellate court had noted, the FCC had concluded that the "data processing" market was "beyond its charge" and one "the Commission itself has announced it declines to regulate." By *Computer II*, the Commission was ready to assert jurisdiction over the entire sphere, so as to crowd out state regulators completely, and then to "forbear" from regulating the market at all.[63] The FCC's *Computer II* decision was affirmed "in its entirety" by a unanimous panel of the Court of Appeals for the D.C. Circuit.[64]

This jurisdictional line seems to have held.[65] In February 1991, 16 enhanced service providers petitioned the FCC for a declara-

[60] *Computer II,* 77 F.C.C.2d at 387 ¶5.

[61] *Id.* at 429 ¶116.

[62] Computer and Communications Industry Assn. v. FCC, 693 F.2d 198, 205 (D.C. Cir. 1982). "Section 152 gives the Commission jurisdiction over 'all interstate and foreign communication by wire or radio,' and Section 153 defines 'communication by wire' as 'the transmission of writing, signs, signals, pictures and sounds of all kinds . . . incidental to such transmission.' The Commission found that enhanced services fall within its ancillary jurisdiction as incidental transmissions over the interstate telecommunications network." *See id.* at 207. *See also* Comment, Storming the AT&T Fortress: Can the FCC Deregulate Competitive Common Carrier Services?, 32 Fed. Comm. L.J. 205, 217–219 (1980).

[63] *Computer II,* 77 F.C.C.2d at 428 ¶¶113–114.

[64] Communications Indus. Assn. v. FCC, 693 F.2d 198.

[65] As discussed in §12.5.1, the Ninth Circuit has circumscribed the Commission's authority to preempt state regulation of how local phone companies deal or interconnect with information services providers. But this is tied to the state's exercise of authority over traditional phone-company common carriers, not state authority over the new-generation providers of information services.

tory ruling that would preempt the states and the District of Columbia from applying state tariff regulation to enhanced service providers.[66] In their comments, they stressed that the information services market is characterized by three salient factors: the demand for information services is widely dispersed, the fixed costs for the provision of information services are very high, and the economies of scale are correspondingly great. As a result, enhanced service providers must seek a geographically broad market using centralized facilities, so it is not sensible or feasible to distinguish between "intrastate" and "interstate" aspects of their services.[67] The Commission finally denied their petitions as moot in 1995 when the District of Columbia withdrew the requirements.[68] Thus, under the Commission's watchful eye, state regulation of information services has not developed.

§12.4.3   Deregulation of Information Services Confirmed: Computer III and the 1996 Act

In its subsequent *Computer III* inquiry, the Commission's theory of regulation shifted significantly from precluding telco participation in the information services industry to establishing guidelines that would allow such participation on an equal access and nondiscriminatory basis. *See* sections 12.7.8–12.7.11 below.

[66] Petition for Declaratory Ruling That States and the District of Columbia Are Preempted from Imposing Public Utility Regulation on Enhanced Service Providers, 6 F.C.C. Rec. 1363 (1991).

[67] *See, e.g.*, Comments of ADAPSO at 18, Petition for Declaratory Ruling That States and the District of Columbia Are Preempted from Imposing Public Utility Regulation on Enhanced Service Providers, Docket No. 91-223 (Apr. 8, 1991); Comments of Prodigy Services Company at 26, Petition for Declaratory Ruling That States and the District of Columbia Are Preempted from Imposing Public Utility Regulation on Enhanced Service Providers, Docket No. 91-223 (Apr. 8, 1991).

[68] Petition for Declaratory Ruling That States and the District of Columbia Are Preempted from Imposing Entry and Exit Regulation and Tariff

But the premise of the Commission's regulatory inquiry remained the same: the information services industry was to be deregulated. The focus instead was on allowing telco participation without reducing any of the protections for the information services industry, i.e., protections against cross-subsidy or discrimination by the telcos. Indeed, the information services market not only was unregulated, but also enjoyed highly favorable access charges and tariff regulation. *See* sections 12.6.2 and 12.6.3 below. The 1996 Act, in effect, confirmed the Commission's position on these broad issues. It solidified the unregulated state of the information services market, maintained the industry's generally favorable regulatory status, and established terms on which telcos could participate in the information services industry. *See* section 12.7.11 below.

§12.5   Delivering Information Services over Phone Lines: Interconnection, Open Networks, Comparably Efficient Interconnection, and Unbundling

Information service providers deliver their product "via telecommunications"—that is, indeed, the definition of "information service" in the 1996 Act. To do so, they must connect their servers (computers) or human operators directly or indirectly to data networks, i.e., phone lines, cable, or radio.

They can, of course, deploy their own transport systems to do part of the job. If they use private networks that are entirely on private premises, that is the end of the regulatory matter; the networks are deregulated CPE or "inside wiring," and the services are deregulated information services. If they connect to the public phone network, however, they will generally do so under tariff, on regulated terms, under interconnection mandates of the 1996 Act.

Requirements on Carrier Affiliated and Noncarrier Affiliated Enhanced Service Providers, Order, 10 F.C.C. Rec. 12,128 (1995).

§12.5.1   Federal Jurisdiction over Interconnection Regulation

Most interconnection regulation is now federal. Over the past two decades, the Commission has repeatedly tried to preempt more of the field and has repeatedly failed, as we discussed in sections 3.3. We summarize here only those parts of it that arose in the specific context of information services regulation.

The FCC's 1980 *Computer II* decision preempted inconsistent state regulation of enhanced services (see section 12.3 and 12.4.2 above), and it barred states from eliminating the structural separation requirements the Commission had imposed on AT&T (see section 12.7.4 below). But it left state authorities free to add additional protections against anticompetitive conduct, including the terms of interconnection between phone companies and providers of enhanced services.[69]

In *Computer III,* the Commission went further and sought to preempt state regulation inconsistent with its unbundling and interconnection rules (ONA and CEI) and with other nonstructural safeguards applicable to AT&T and the Bell Operating Companies (BOCs).[70] Some "Basic Service Elements," the Commission allowed, would be subject to dual state and federal jurisdiction and would have to be tariffed accordingly. To promote uniformity, the Commission established a joint state/federal conference to address the issue.[71]

The Commission had difficulty defending this preemptive scope in the courts. Eventually the Ninth Circuit struck down the interconnection rules, not only on substantive and procedural grounds, but also as to the Commission's power to preempt.[72]

---

[69] Amendment of Section 64.702 of the Commission's Rules and Regulations (Third Computer Inquiry), Report and Order, 104 F.C.C.2d 958, 1125 ¶343 (1986) (hereinafter *Computer III*) (quoting *Computer II Further Reconsideration Order,* 88 F.C.C.2d at 541).

[70] *Id.* at 1125–1126 ¶¶343–344.

[71] This was pursuant to §410(b) of the Act. *See* §9.3.1.

[72] California v. FCC, 905 F.2d 1217 (9th Cir. 1990) (*California I*). Previously the Supreme Court had disapproved of the FCC's preemption of state depreciation practices. Louisiana Pub. Serv. Commn. v. FCC, 476 U.S. 355 (1986) (*Louisiana PSC*). For a detailed discussion, see §3.6.

See sections 12.7.8 and 12.7.10 below. On remand for the second time, the Commission reworked the substance of its *Computer III* interconnection rules, proposing to preempt only state regulation of intrastate communications that would necessarily thwart or impede federal regulation. While the Ninth Circuit balked yet again as to the substance of several of the rules,[73] it approved the Commission's preemption of inconsistent state regulation. The Commission's Remand Order preempted state requirements only for structural separation, customer proprietary network information (CPNI), and network disclosure.[74] Moreover, the Court found, the Commission this time had "presented adequate record support" that its preemption of state regulation fell within the narrow "impossibility exception," i.e., the Commission had "met its burden of showing that its regulatory goals of authorizing integration of services would be negated by the state regulations."[75] The Commission thus managed to retain the central thrust of its preemption of state interconnection regulation, even though it was forced to justify particular aspects and rules under a fairly strict standard.

§12.5.2 Open Networks and Comparably Efficient Interconnection Before 1996

Computer I and *II* were grounded on the idea that if phone companies were simply excluded from information service markets, interconnection would take care of itself under the normal tariffing process. A phone company excluded from this market presumably would have no incentive to discriminate against "customers" in it. However, *Computer III* began the process of relaxing this policy of "maximum separation." In *Computer III*, the Commission directed LECs to meet two conditions as prerequisites for the removal of structural separation requirements.

---

[73] California v. FCC, 39 F.3d 919 (9th Cir. 1994) (*California III*).

[74] *Id.* at 932. As the court described, the Commission had preempted "nearly all state regulation of enhanced services by communications common carriers." *Id.* at 931.

[75] *Id.* at 932–933.

They had to unbundle their local networks (open network architecture, or ONA) and to interconnect with unaffiliated providers on the same terms as they connected with their own information service affiliates (comparably efficient interconnection, or CEI).

The Commission's ONA mandate was the genesis of what would eventually be transformed into the unbundling mandate of the 1996 Act (section 251). As discussed in more detail in section 5.4, the Commission sketched the outlines of its program and left it to the BOCs to develop, in the first instance, detailed ONA plans in line with these general requirements. The BOCs duly filed initial ONA plans; the Commission approved some and disapproved others.[76] The BOCs then filed amended plans, which the Commission approved subject to certain further modifications.[77] In its 1990 Computer III remand proceedings,[78] the Commission reaffirmed the ONA policies developed in *Computer III* and subsequent orders that approved ONA plans submitted by various BOCs.[79]

---

[76] *Filing and Review of Open Network Architecture Plans,* Memorandum Opinion and Order, 4 F.C.C. Rec. 1 (1988). AT&T also filed its own streamlined ONA plan, as required in the *Computer II Reconsideration Order.* That plan was approved with only minor adjustments the same day.

[77] Filing and Review of Open Network Architecture Plans, Phase I, Memorandum Opinion and Order, 5 F.C.C. Rec. 3103 (1990). The Commission promised that structural separation requirements would be removed for each BOC when it filed a notice informing the Commission that (a) it was technically prepared to offer each of its initial ONA services, (b) federal tariffs for each of its initial interstate ONA services were in effect, and (c) it had filed state tariffs for each of its initial intrastate ONA services. The Commission did not require, however, that such state tariffs be effective for the removal of structural separation. On December 19, 1991, the FCC required a series of further amendments to the BOCs' already-approved ONA plans and a series of annual reports to "ensure continued BOC progress in the provision of new ONA services and new technical capabilities to enhanced service providers." Filing and Review of Open Network Architecture Plans, Memorandum Opinion and Order, 6 F.C.C. Rec. 7646, 7647 ¶1 (1991).

[78] Computer III Remand Proceedings, Report and Order, 5 F.C.C. Rec. 7719 (1990).

[79] *See* Filing and Review of Open Network Architecture Plans, Phase I, Memorandum Opinion and Order on Reconsideration, 5 F.C.C. Rec. 3084 (1990) (hereinafter *ONA Reconsideration Order*); Filing and Review of Open Network Architecture Plans, Phase I, Memorandum Opinion and Order, 5 F.C.C. Rec. 3103 (1990) (hereinafter *BOC ONA Amendments Order*); *Computer III Remand Proceedings,* Report and Order, 5 F.C.C. Rec. 7719 (1990).

In addition to unbundling basic services, the Commission required a carrier subject to the ONA obligations to provide competing providers with CEI.[80] This meant that all providers of enhanced services using "common interconnection facilities" were to be charged the same "Basic Interconnection Charge."[81] A BOC providing enhanced services was to pay this charge as well, even if it used a quite different and more efficient form of direct, on-premises connection. By mandating averaged pricing, the FCC aimed to encourage BOCs to deploy the most economic forms of interface facilities.[82]

Moreover, the Commission imposed several other nonstructural safeguards. BOCs with affiliates providing enhanced services were to keep separate the affiliates' costs by complying with the safeguards imposed in the joint cost proceeding.[83] Both AT&T and the BOCs were required to file quarterly reports comparing service provided to their enhanced service affiliates with service provided to competitors. The Commission also limited use of CPNI by BOC affiliates and by others. And the Commission promulgated network disclosure rules to prevent BOCs from designing new network services or changing network technical specifications to the advantage of their own enhanced service providers.[84] These safeguards, in combination with the ONA and CEI requirements, were intended to ensure equal and efficient interconnection between telecommunication and information service providers, with the goal of relaxing structural separation.

MCI challenged the FCC's order in the Computer III remand proceeding.[85] The Ninth Circuit agreed with MCI that the ONA plans as approved did not accomplish fundamental unbundling

---

[80] Amendment to Sections 64.702 of the Commission's Rules and Regulations (Third Computer Inquiry), *Phase II, Report and Order,* 2 F.C.C. Rec. 3072 (1987) (hereinafter *Phase II Order*).

[81] Amendment of Sections 64.702 of the Commission's Rules and Regulations (Third Computer Inquiry), Memorandum Opinion and Order, 2 F.C.C. Rec. 3035, 3051 ¶113 (1987) (hereinafter *Phase I Reconsidered*).

[82] *Computer III* 104 F.C.C.2d at 1051 ¶¶180–181.

[83] *See* §§12.7.3–12.7.4.

[84] *See* §5.4.3.2.

[85] *See* California v. FCC, 4 F.3d 1505 (9th Cir. 1993) (*California II*).

and that the FCC's approval of these plans constituted a change from its original position that complete ONA was a prerequisite to the elimination of structural separation.[86] The appellate court did not, however, set aside the orders implementing ONA.[87] MCI's challenge was directed at structural separation, and the orders in question "did not themselves lift structural separation or explain the conditions under which structural separation, after *California I,* could be lifted."[88] The court was "aware that the FCC has since ordered the lifting of structural separation," but noted "[t]hat order is not now before us."[89] This decision thus left in place the ONA requirements of Computer III remand proceeding and left the structural separation matters for later consideration. (See section 12.7.9 below.)

§12.5.3   Open Networks and Comparably Efficient Interconnection After 1996

It seems clear now that the 1996 Act replaced the unbundling/interconnection/resale parts of the various Computer inquiries with its own unbundling requirements in section 251. However, providers of information services are not the immediate beneficiaries of these requirements. Section 251(c)(3) requires local exchange carriers (LECs) to offer unbundled network elements only to "telecommunications carriers," which does not appear to include providers of information services.[90] But it is perfectly clear that information service providers can, if they choose, deal

[86] *Id.* at 1513.

[87] *Id.* at 1516. The Ninth Circuit's earlier decision in *California I (see* §12.7.8) rested in part on the ability of ONA to guard against discrimination once structural separation was lifted. Because the Commission's order in the Computer III remand proceeding came after this decision, it was not clear whether the newly approved (and slightly altered) ONA regime would, in the court's view, suffice in guarding against discrimination to the same degree that ONA as previously defined by *Computer III* would.

[88] *See California III,* 39 F.3d at 928.

[89] *California II,* 4 F.3d at 1513.

[90] The Act defines a "telecommunication carrier" as a provider of "telecommunications services," which in turn is defined as the "offering of telecommunications for a fee directly to the public, or to such classes of users

with LECs through intermediaries that *do* meet the definition of "telecommunications carrier" and thereby benefit from the unbundling requirements.

As to structural regulation, the Commission issued a January 1998 *Further Notice* to reconsider, "[i]n light of the 1996 Act and ensuing changes in telecommunications technologies and markets," the regulation of BOC provision of information services.[91] The time had arrived, the Commission stated, "not only to respond to the issues remanded by the Ninth Circuit, but also to reexamine the Commission's nonstructural safeguards regime governing the provision of information services by the BOCs."[92]

The Commission concluded that the 1996 Act does not expressly overrule or disturb its *Computer II, Computer III,* and ONA requirements, which will "continue to govern" the provision of data services by the Bell companies and other entities.[93] According to the Commission, these requirements remain "the only regulatory means by which certain independent [information service providers] are guaranteed nondiscriminatory access to BOC local exchange services used in the provision of intraLATA [local access and transport area] information services."[94] Although the 1996 Act "imposed a series of safeguards to prevent the BOCs from using their existing market power to engage in improper cost allocation and discrimination in their provision of interLATA information services," such safeguards "do not explicitly displace the safeguards established by the Commission in the *Computer II, Computer III,* and ONA proceedings."[95]

But the Commission nevertheless thought it should address the "issues raised by the interplay between the safeguards and

---

as to be effectively available directly to the public, regardless of the facilities used." 47 U.S.C. §153(46).

[91] *See* Computer III Further Remand Proceedings: Bell Operating Company Provision of Enhanced Services, Further Notice of Proposed Rulemaking, 13 F.C.C. Rec. 6040, 6045 ¶5 (1998) (hereinafter *Computer III Remand Further Notice*).

[92] *Id.*

[93] *Non-accounting Safeguards Order,* 11 F.C.C. Rec. at 21,969–21,970 ¶132.

[94] *Id.* at 21,970–21,971 ¶134.

[95] *Computer III Remand Further Notice,* 13 F.C.C. Rec. at 6045–6046 ¶5.

terminology established in the 1996 Act and the *Computer III* regime."[96] The Commission tentatively concluded that, "given the protections established by the 1996 Act and our ONA rules, we should eliminate the requirement that BOCs file Comparably Efficient Interconnection (CEI) plans and obtain Common Carrier Bureau approval for those plans prior to providing new intraLATA information services."[97] In the alternative, the Commission proposed "at a minimum" to "eliminate the CEI-plan requirement for BOC intraLATA information services provided through an Act-mandated affiliate under section 272 or 274."[98] The Commission also tentatively ruled that "the Commission's network information disclosure rules established pursuant to section 251(c)(5) should supersede certain, but not all, of the Commission's previous network information disclosure rules established in *Computer II* and *Computer III*."[99]

The Commission reiterated these tentative conclusions in early 1998, when it issued its first proposals to eliminate unnecessary regulations pursuant to the biennial review provisions of section 11 of the Act.[100] The Commission proposed to eliminate certain of its *Computer III* and ONA rules, including ONA and Nondiscrimination Reporting Requirements, Network Information Disclosure Rules, and rules governing the use of CPNI.[101] The Commission also sought comment on whether section 251 unbundling and the Commission's implementing regulations issued thereunder eliminate entirely the need for ONA.[102] The Commission acknowledged, however, that replacing ONA with

---

[96] *Id.*

[97] *Id.* at 6046–6047 ¶7; *see also id.* at 6076–6079 ¶¶60–65.

[98] *Id.* at 6046–6047 ¶7; *see also id.* at 6079–6082 ¶¶66–72.

[99] *Id.* at 6046–6047 ¶7; *see also id.* at 6111 ¶122.

[100] *See* 47 U.S.C. §161; *Computer III Remand Further Notice,* 13 F.C.C. Rec. at 6040.

[101] *Computer III Remand Further Notice,* 13 F.C.C. Rec. at 6085–6012 ¶¶78–124.

[102] "For example, is ONA unbundling still necessary for ISPs [information service providers] that are also telecommunications carriers for whom section 251 unbundling is available? As for pure ISPs, does the fact that they can obtain the benefits of section 251 by becoming telecommunications carriers, or by partnering with or obtaining basic services from competitive telecommunications providers, render ONA unnecessary?" *Id.* at 6091 ¶95.

section 251 unbundling might give information service providers greater access to LECs' networks than they need or deserve.[103]

The Commission has not yet made a final determination as to whether it will eliminate its previously existing ONA and *Computer III* regulations, which therefore continue to govern interconnection of telecommunication and information services. However, were the elimination of those rules to occur, it would, as the Commission suggests, constitute a significant shift toward increased unbundling and access by information service providers to basic telecommunication services.

§12.6 Rate Regulation and Access Charges

§12.6.1 State Versus Federal Jurisdiction

Most information services are largely interstate in nature, which means the rates for these services should be regulated, if at all, by the FCC, not state regulators. Most Internet access services are technically "information services" under the Commission's definition, and therefore fall under federal jurisdiction. And if Internet access services were not information services, they would presumably be classified as interstate access services, which likewise would be subject to federal, not state, jurisdiction.

The FCC appears to have affirmed this basic understanding in two recent orders, in which it has held that the provision of

---

[103]

[S]ection 251 provides a level of unbundling that pure ISPs do not receive under the Commission's current ONA framework. Unbundling under section 251 includes the physical facilities of the network, together with the features, functions, and capabilities associated with those facilities. Section 251 also requires incumbent LECs to provide for the collocation at the LEC's premises of equipment necessary for interconnection or access to unbundled network elements, under certain conditions. Unbundling under ONA, in contrast, emphasizes the unbundling of basic services, not the substitution of underlying facilities in a carrier's network. ONA unbundling also does not mandate interconnection on carriers' premises of facilities owned by others. These differences may be due to the different policy goals that the two regimes were designed to serve. *Id.* at 6090–6091 ¶93 (footnotes omitted).

Internet access is "largely interstate" and therefore within the FCC's jurisdiction.[104] The Commission rejected the analysis adopted by several state commissions—and by at least one federal district court—which had held that an Internet communication could be treated as two separate calls: a "local" telecommunications service provided by one or more local exchange carriers between the end-user and the ISP's point of presence, and an "interstate" information service, between the ISP and the Internet.[105] Instead, the FCC held that it would "analyze ISP traffic as a continuous transmission from the end user to a distant Internet website."[106]

§12.6.2   Access Charges for Enhanced Service Providers

As discussed in section 2.3.4, providers of enhanced services were categorized as "customers" of telcos at the outset and have clung tenaciously to that label ever since. The upshot is that they do not pay the steep access charges paid by ordinary (voice) long-distance companies for telecommunications transmission,

---

[104] GTE Telephone Operating Cos., GTE Tariff No. 1, GTOC Tariff No. 1148, Memorandum Opinion and Order, 13 F.C.C. Rec. 22,466 (1998); Implementation of the Local Competition Provisions in the Telecommunications Act of 1996, Inter-Carrier Compensation for ISP-Bound Traffic, Declaratory Ruling in CC Docket No. 96-98 and Notice of Proposed Rulemaking in CC Docket No. 99-98 (rel. Feb. 26, 1999) (hereinafter *Reciprocal Compensation Order*).

[105] These rulings generally involved interpretation of the scope of incumbent LECs' obligations under section 251(b)(5) of the Act and interconnection agreements entered into pursuant to the Act. By the terms of the FCC's *Local Competition Order*, incumbent LECs are required to pay reciprocal compensation only on "local traffic." *See Local Competition Order*, 11 F.C.C. Rec. at 16,012–16,013. Several state commissions ordered incumbent LECs to pay reciprocal compensation on calls that their subscribers placed to the Internet through ISPs served by CLECs on the ground that the call to the ISP was a local call.

[106] *Reciprocal Compensation Order* ¶13. The FCC held that a state commission may nonetheless require an incumbent LEC to pay reciprocal compensation to a CLEC in circumstances where the incumbent's subscriber accesses the Internet throught an ISP served by the CLEC. *See id.* ¶26. The FCC's Order is currently on appeal before the D.C. Circuit.

even though most Internet and other enhanced service traffic is in fact interstate.

The Commission preserved this access charge exemption for information service providers in its 1983 access charge proceeding[107] and again in its 1997 *Access Charge Reform Order.*[108] In its *Access Charge Reform Order,* the Commission faced the problem whether to impose interstate access charges on information service providers that use local exchange facilities to originate and terminate calls. The Commission ruled that LECs could not assess interstate access charges on information service providers. Thus, information service providers (including Internet service providers) are treated as end users for purposes of access charges—typically paying LECs a flat monthly rate for their connections, regardless of the amount of usage they generate.

The Commission reasoned that information service providers should not be subject to interstate access charges because the current access-charge system "includes non-cost-based rates and inefficient rate structures."[109] In addition, "it is not clear that [information service providers] use the public switched network in a manner analogous to [interexchange carriers]. . . . [M]any of the characteristics of [information service provider] traffic (such as large numbers of incoming calls to Internet service providers) may be shared by other classes of business customers."[110]

As many LECs pointed out, however, the Commission's notion that information service providers do not provide interstate services departs from numerous previous determinations that Internet communications are interstate communications. The Commission also discounted the LECs' argument that network congestion warranted the imposition of interstate access charges on information service providers. It decided to consider in a later proceeding other solutions to network congestion.

All in all, the Commission's enduring discrimination in favor of data (and against voice) makes no economic sense. Access charges for voice are too high; access charges for data are too

---

[107] MTS and WATS Market Structure, 48 Fed. Reg. 42,984, 42,997 (1983).
[108] Access Charge Reform, First Report and Order, 12 F.C.C. Rec. 15,982, 16,133 ¶344 (1997) (hereinafter *Access Charge Reform Order*).
[109] *Id.* at 16,133 ¶345.
[110] *Id.*

low. The federal resolution to subsidize universal service entirely out of one stream of traffic and not the other is yet another instance of regulators putting politics above economic efficiency.

In a report to Congress in April 1998, however, the Commission made an exception to this general policy. It suggested that "[c]ertain ISP telephony services lack the characteristics that would render them information services and instead bear the characteristics of telecommunications services." Such a characterization, as a basic telephone service, would make those services subject to access charges by BOCs, as well as to universal service obligations. Thus, as a result of this report, a few of the BOCs started assessing access charges on companies that use the local network and Internet protocol to complete long-distance calls. But the majority of data providers continue to benefit from low access charges.

§12.6.3 Contribution to Universal Service

The 1996 Act states that "[e]very *telecommunications carrier* that provides interstate telecommunications service" *must* contribute to universal service.[111] In addition, the Commission is authorized to require contributions from any "other provider of interstate telecommunications," should the public interest so require. The Commission faced the question of what constitutes a "telecommunications carrier," which must contribute to universal service, as opposed to some other "provider of interstate telecommunications" or an "information service provider," which need not. As discussed above (section 12.2.5), the Commission went to some lengths to assure that few information service providers would be required to contribute to universal service. The main exception is for those who provide unadorned interstate transport, to themselves or others. In the Internet context, that should mean for the most part the owner-operators of the Internet backbones and perhaps some of the facilities-based regional ISPs.

---

[111] 47 U.S.C. §254(d) (emphasis added).

§12.7 Structural Regulation: Companies Trying to Walk Both Sides of the Line

There are, in theory, two basic ways to monopolize online content. One is to merge competitors horizontally: AOL buys CompuServe, Yahoo, Amazon.com, and so on until a single company owns all the online content. The other is to extend monopoly vertically: the monopoly phone company (Bell), cable company (TCI), broadcaster (NBC), software vendor (Microsoft), or PC manufacturer (Compaq) extends its tentacles to monopolize all the content all the cyberservice. In practice, neither of these is likely to happen. But the theory, especially the vertical part of it, is remarkably tenacious.

In this section, we examine the labyrinthine details of how the theory of vertical integration has been applied to phone companies. We begin with a brief summary of how the theory of anticompetitive vertical integration historically has been applied in content-based industries (e.g., newspaper and broadcast). We then trace the development of the theory of maximum (vertical) separation in *Computer I* and *Computer II*, its codification in the Bell Divestiture Decree, its eventual demise in *Computer III*, and the apparent affirmation of that decision in the 1996 Act. One thing is clear from this history: a profound shift in thinking has occurred recently. Not long ago most authorities, the Commission foremost among them, were certain that local phone companies would take over online markets the moment they were allowed into them. (They believed much the same of video markets, as discussed in section 13.7.) Today, the main sources of vertical leverage are thought to be much lower in the network—on the desktop, in fact.

§12.7.1 Federal Preemption of Structural Regulation

The Commission's determination to separate phone service from computers originated two decades before the Bell breakup. No one much questioned the Commission's power to make

AT&T-specific structural calls at the federal level in its *Computer I* decision.[112] The Commission's 1980 *Computer II Order* barred states from eliminating the structural separation requirements the Commission had imposed on AT&T.[113] In *Computer III,* the Commission sought to preempt the states again in order to prevent them from imposing structural separation requirements on enhanced services provided by independent carriers.[114] This policy has prevailed in large part, although it has been subject to challenge. *See* section 12.5.1 above. More important, the 1996 Act generally strengthens the federal hand so far as structural regulation is concerned. And the Act incorporates such a mass of confusing detail that most state regulators may well be grateful to leave this particular field alone.

§12.7.2 *The Fear of Vertical Integration*

Computer I and *II* and the AT&T Divestiture Decree viewed providers of "information services" in the same light as providers of CPE and long-distance equipment—equally vulnerable to discrimination, price abuses, and cross-subsidy by local telco monopolists—and it therefore protected both from regulation. See section 12.4 above. But the historical context for government deregulation of the two types of providers was completely different. The government's treatment of network services and CPE cases developed on the heels of major private antitrust initiatives. In contrast, there had been no private cases addressing interconnection, subsidy, or predatory pricing in the market for information services.

The simplest explanation for this vacuum in the antitrust record is that there have been almost no abuses to allege in this particular area. There were indeed few online information

---

[112] *Computer I,* 28 F.C.C.2d at 274–275 ¶23.

[113] *Computer III,* 104 F.C.C.2d at 1125 ¶343 (quoting *Computer II Further Reconsideration Order,* 88 F.C.C.2d at 541 ¶83).

[114] Computer III Remand Proceedings: Bell Operating Company Safeguards and Tier 1 Local Exchange Company Safeguards, Report and Order, 6 F.C.C. Rec. 7571 (1991).

services to speak of at the time. The Internet didn't exist. The information services industry is a product of recent rapid technological development in the computer industry. That development occurred, for the most part, after the new regulatory principles of *Execunet* and *Carterfone* had been established, litigated, and finally accepted by the industry.[115] Relations between telcos and information service providers have thus been forged in a quite different climate from those between telcos and competing providers of CPE or long-distance service.

Moreover, reacting to the problems it struggled with in other areas, the FCC resolved from the beginning of the computer age to maintain equitable relations between telephony and the computer industry. As discussed below, that regulatory commitment effectively quarantined telcos from any direct involvement in the provision of online information services. The 1982 Decree reinforced the quarantine insofar as the BOCs were concerned. As a result of these various factors, there have been few opportunities for either the actuality or even the allegation of telco misconduct in markets for information services.[116]

Ironically trends under way since the 1980s now suggest that market power (if any is to be found at all) lies more with those who control the *content* of information services than those who control the *conduit*. Indeed, distribution media spanning the printing press and the Internet, the telephone network, radio and television, cable and satellite, personal computers and mainframes, compact disks, floppies, and game cartridges are growing increasingly competitive, more so year by year as the media

---

[115] *See* §§8.4.1, 9.4.1.

[116] The common tendency to "leave things to the regulators" shows in Business Aides, Inc. v. Chesapeake & Potomac Telephone Co. of Virginia, 480 F.2d 754 (4th Cir. 1973). The plaintiff was an answering service frustrated in its desire to expand by the telephone company's policy of refusing to give answering services the equipment to operate in more than one exchange of the local area without mileage charges. *Id.* at 756. The court held that the telephone company enjoyed state action immunity by virtue of the approval given the tariff by state regulators, even though the tariff did not expressly prohibit the service the plaintiff sought. *Id.* at 758. *See also* Penny v. Southwestern Bell Tel. Co., 906 F.2d 183 (5th Cir. 1990) (computer bulletin board owners' allegation that telephone company charged discriminatory rates should be heard first by state regulators under primary jurisdiction).

converge.[117] Information content, by contrast, is often a more unique asset. In some areas, it appears the "bottleneck" is created by the message, not the medium.[118]

As a result, the Commission and antitrust courts have been very active in regulating the structure of the *content* end of information services. News organizations consistently have been the subject of major federal antitrust actions[119] and congressional legislation.[120] Similarly, broadcast has been the target of much litigation and legislation. In the early days of broadcast, several antitrust suits concerned attempts to leverage content into distribution.[121] In 1943, Justice Frankfurter upheld FCC regulations[122] that in effect required NBC to divest one of its networks.[123] More recently a new generation of lawsuits directed at cable operators has attacked exclusive distribution deals between established cable companies and content producers as denying access to an "essential facility"—program content.[124] Congress

[117] *See* §1.10.

[118] P. Huber, M. Kellogg & J. Thorne, The Geodesic Network II: 1993 Report on Competition in the Telephone Industry §§5.1–5.107 (1992).

[119] In 1945, in one of the landmark "essential facilities" rulings, the federal government won a major antitrust action against the Associated Press (AP) on the theory that AP controlled news-gathering facilities of such importance that their benefits would have to be made available to competing newspapers in the same locality. Associated Press v. United States, 326 U.S. 1, 20 (1945).

[120] In 1970, Congress enacted the Newspaper Preservation Act, Pub. L. 91-353, 84 Stat. 466 (1970) (codified at 15 U.S.C. §§1801–1804), which overturned a 1969 Supreme Court antitrust ruling against two newspapers in Tucson, Arizona. Citizen Publishing Co. v. United States, 394 U.S. 131 (1969). The Act generally exempts "joint newspaper operating arrangements" from the reach of the antitrust laws. 15 U.S.C. §1803.

[121] *See, e.g.,* General Talking Pictures Corp. v. AT&T, 18 F. Supp. 650, 651–652 (D. Del. 1937); Stanley Co. of Am. v. AT&T, 4 F. Supp. 80 (D. Del. 1933); Philco Corp. v. Radio Corp. of Am., 186 F. Supp. 155, 158 (N.D. Ohio 1960); Radio Corp. of Am. v. Rauland Corp., 186 F. Supp. 704, 709 (N.D. Ill. 1956); AT&T v. Delta Communications Corp., 408 F. Supp. 1075 (S.D. Miss. 1976), *aff'd,* 579 F.2d 972 (5th Cir. 1978), *cert. denied sub nom.* Delta Communications Corp. v. National Broad. Co., 444 U.S. 926 (1979).

[122] FCC, Report on Chain Broadcasting 80–87 (1941).

[123] National Broad. Co. v. United States, 319 U.S. 190 (1943).

[124] *See* FCC Issues Report to Congress on the State of Cable TV, Executive Summary of Report No. DC-1690, MM Docket No. 89-600, 1990 FCC LEXIS 4061, at *32 (July 26, 1990) (citing "considerable anecdotal evidence" that cable operators denied competitors access to programming); NTIA, The NTIA

finally addressed the issue in the 1992 Cable Act;[125] in 1993, a civil action brought by the Department of Justice resulted in consent decrees in 1993 requiring cable affiliates to make available to competitors national and regional sports programming services on nondiscriminatory terms.[126] Other antitrust cases involving exclusionary conduct by cable companies have multiplied.[127] And similar litigation has arisen in connection with airline reservation computer systems.[128]

Infrastructure Report: Telecommunications in the Age of Information 239 (Oct. 1991); L. Malt, PacWest Cable Battling TBS, Electronic Media, Apr. 30, 1990, at 26. Even cable programmers have had difficulties obtaining access to copyrighted program content. United States v. American Socy. of Composers, Authors & Publishers, 1991-2 Trade Cas. (CCH) ¶69,504 (S.D.N.Y.), *aff'd,* 956 F.2d 21 (2d Cir.), *cert. denied,* 504 U.S. 914 (1992).

[125] The 1992 Cable Act requires the FCC to promulgate rules that prohibit practices, such as exclusive contracts, that prevent multichannel video programming vendors from obtaining programming. Pub. L. No. 102-385, §19 (codified at 47 U.S.C. §548). And as required by §536, the FCC adopted rules to prohibit practices by cable operators that interfere with program access, such as requiring a financial interest in a program service as a condition of carriage or coercing program vendors to provide exclusive rights as a condition of carriage. Implementation of Sections 12 and 19 of the Cable Television Consumer Protection and Competition Act of 1992, Further Report and Order, 8 F.C.C. Rec. 3359 (1993).

[126] United States v. Primestar Partners, L.P., 1994-1 Trade Cas. (CCH) ¶70,562 (S.D.N.Y. 1994); State of New York v. Primestar Partners, L.P., et al., 1993-2 Trade Cas. (CCH) ¶70,403 (S.D.N.Y. 1993). *See generally* J. Thorne, P. Huber & M. Kellogg, Federal Broadband Law Chs. 8 & 9 (1995) (hereinafter *FBL*).

[127] *See, e.g.,* Sunbelt Television, Inc. v. Jones Intercable, Inc., 795 F. Supp. 333 (C.D. Cal. 1992) (a jury found defendant monopolized local TV advertising by refusing to carry a local broadcast station); New York Citizens Comm. on Cable TV v. Manhattan Cable TV, Inc., 651 F. Supp. 802 (S.D.N.Y. 1986) (consumer antitrust suit over Time Warner's refusal to carry competing program services was ultimately settled when the cable company agreed to carry Bravo, a specialized premium service); Central Telecomms., Inc. v. TCI Cablevision, Inc., 800 F.2d 711 (8th Cir. 1986) (TCI was found guilty of monopolization for a "campaign, accompanied by numerous unethical and illegal acts," to coerce a city to grant it an exclusive cable franchise), *cert. denied,* 480 U.S. 910 (1987). One of the largest of these cases addressed TCI's merger with Liberty Media, which culminated in another consent decree. *See* Competitive Impact Statement, United States v. Tele-Communications, Inc. and Liberty Media Corp., No. 94-0948, 59 Fed. Reg. 24,723, 24,725–24,726 (May 12, 1994).

[128] For a summary, see Note, The Legal and Regulatory Implications of Airline Computer Reservation Systems, 103 Harv. L. Rev. 1930, 1934–1945

Early antitrust challenges to Bell monopolies of white and yellow pages directories were dismissed because courts found insufficient effect on interstate commerce and because, in the words of one court, the directory monopoly "is a natural incident of Bell's public utility character."[129] In the new competitive climate of the 1970s, however, antitrust actions aimed at freeing up listing information began to survive motions to dismiss.[130] The Supreme Court recently held that white pages listings are not protected by copyright because they are merely compilations of

---

(1990). In a 1984 antitrust complaint, several smaller airlines unsuccessfully alleged that American and United were monopolizing computer reservation services and leveraging that power into the airline business itself. Air Passenger Computer Reservations Sys. Antitrust Litig., 694 F. Supp. 1443 (C.D. Cal. 1988), aff'd sub nom. Alaska Airlines, Inc. v. United Airlines, Inc., 948 F.2d 536 (9th Cir. 1991), cert. denied, 503 U.S. 977 (1992). Similar antitrust allegations raised by about 100 travel agents against American Airlines were rejected in 1989 and 1990. See "Sabre" Air Passenger Computer Reservation System Antitrust and Contract Litigation, No. 761 (N.D. Tex. June 7, 1988).

[129] Best Advertising Corp. v. Illinois Bell Tel. Co., 229 F. Supp. 275, 277 (S.D. Ill. 1964), aff'd, 339 F.2d 1009 (7th Cir. 1965); see also Thornhill Publishing Co. v. GTE Corp., 594 F.2d 730, 735–739 (9th Cir. 1979).

[130] In one of the first major cases, a yellow pages competitor successfully claimed illegal tying. White Directory Publishers, Inc. v. New York Tel. Co., 1981-2 Trade Cas. (CCH) ¶64,268 (W.D.N.Y. 1981). Many other suits of this kind have followed, often revolving around an essential facility theory, with varying results. See, e.g., Directory Sales Management Corp. v. Ohio Bell Tel. Co., 833 F.2d 606, 612–613 (6th Cir. 1987) (business classifications are not an essential facility because they are unreliable and must be cross-checked); White Directory of Rochester, Inc. v. Rochester Tel. Corp., 714 F. Supp. 65, 70 (W.D.N.Y. 1989) (no denial of an essential facility when directory publisher could duplicate information from other sources and had done so in other areas); BellSouth Adver. & Publishing Corp. v. Donnelley Info. Publishing, Inc., 719 F. Supp. 1551, 1566–1567 (S.D. Fla. 1988) (essential facility claim presented factual disputes precluding summary judgment), rev'd in other part, 999 F.2d 1436 (11th Cir. 1993), cert. denied, 510 U.S. 1101 (1994); Direct Media Corp. v. Camden Tel. & Tel. Co., 989 F. Supp. 1211, 1218–1219 (S.D. Ga. 1997) (same); Great Western Directories, Inc. v. Southwestern Bell Tel. Co., 63 F.3d 1378 (5th Cir. 1995) (upholding jury finding that directory listing updates were essential), amended in other part, 74 F.3d 613 (5th Cir.), cert. dismissed, 518 U.S. 1048 (1996), vacated pursuant to settlement, Aug. 21, 1996. A recent lawsuit presents a variant on this theme by charging that defendants conspired to limit access to competing Internet yellow pages through collusion with Internet service providers. See GTE New Media Servs. Inc. v. Ameritech Corp., 21 F. Supp. 2d 27 (D.D.C. 1998).

facts without any claim to originality.[131] This ruling will further undermine any attempts to prove that white pages listings constitute an essential facility. Courts have likewise generally rejected tying and predatory pricing theories in this context.[132]

As in these other industries, control of content is also a key issue in the software industry. Many recent antitrust actions have involved charges of monopolization or tying.[133] And a 1987 dispute between the two dominant electronic publishers of legal materials revolved around matters of content.[134] The Ninth Circuit has gone so far as to declare that, in tying cases, copyright

---

[131] Feist Publications, Inc. v. Rural Tel. Serv. Co., 499 U.S. 340 (1991).

[132] *See, e.g., Directory Sales,* 833 F.2d at 613–614 (a telco's offer to customers of a free first listing was not predatory pricing because the telco had no intention of later selling first listings at a higher, monopoly price); Illinois Bell Tel. Co. v. Haines & Co., 905 F.2d 1081, 1087–1088 (7th Cir. 1990), *vacated on other grounds,* 499 U.S. 944, *remanded,* 932 F.2d 610 (7th Cir. 1991) (dismissed a discriminatory tying charge because the directory publisher had presented no evidence to show that the prices offered it were in fact higher than the prices offered to other publishers); *but see* Great Western Directories, Inc. v. Southwestern Bell Tel. Co., 63 F.3d 1378 (5th Cir. 1995) (a jury found that a telco had engaged in predatory pricing).

[133] *See, e.g.,* Atari Games Corp. v. Nintendo of Am., Inc., 897 F.2d 1572, 1574 (Fed. Cir. 1990); Virtual Maintenance, Inc. v. Prime Computer, Inc., 735 F. Supp. 231 (E.D. Mich. 1990); Nintendo of Am., Inc., Federal Trade Commission No. C-3350 (Nov. 15, 1991), *reported in* 61 Antitrust & Trade Reg. Rep. (BNA) 645 (Nov. 21, 1991). *See also* Settlement of States' Nintendo Suits Receives Final Approval of District Court, 61 Antitrust & Trade Reg. Rep. (BNA) 513 (Oct. 24, 1991) (describing settlement between Nintendo and all 50 states and the District of Columbia regarding resale price maintenance charges).

[134] In 1987, Mead Data Central charged West Publishing with abuse of an "essential facility" and maintenance of a monopoly "in the publication of the core source of judicial opinions of the lower federal courts and state courts and state statutes." Complaint at 4, Mead Data Cent., Inc. v. West Publishing Co., No. C-3-87-426 (S.D. Ohio Aug. 18, 1987). In a previous proceeding, West had sued Mead for infringing its copyright on the pagination used in such reporters as "F. Supp." and "F.2d." West Publishing Co. v. Mead Data Cent., Inc., 616 F. Supp. 1571 (D. Minn. 1985), *aff'd,* 799 F.2d 1219 (8th Cir. 1986), *cert. denied,* 479 U.S. 1070 (1987). The Second Circuit recently ruled that West's pagination system does not qualify for copyright protection. Matthew Bender & Co. v. West Publishing Co., 158 F.3d 693 (2d Cir. 1998). After protracted negotiations, the parties settled both suits with West agreeing to license its state statutes and pagination to Mead for undisclosed amounts.

protection of software creates a presumption of market power.[135] Other courts, however, have held that copyright protection is only one of several factors to consider in determining whether an antitrust defendant has market power in software.[136]

The failure of many content-based antitrust claims, particularly in the computer industry, is hardly surprising and for the most part quite lawful. In publishing, copyright usually confers a statutory monopoly. Software copyrights and process patents likewise protect the key value-creating components of information processing services of every kind. Even when copyrights and patents are not a factor, the economies of scope and scale applicable to the information content itself are far stronger than any economies of scope in the deployment of communications networks. The marginal costs of printing one more newspaper or deploying one more telephone line may be modest. But the marginal costs of sharing information content, software, or database indexes are zero. The owner of a Web site, a software program, or music CD can replicate the valuable information at virtually no cost at all. The economies of scale and scope thus hinge more on the content (which is expensive to generate, but costless to share) than the distribution (which even if comparatively cheap is never costless to extend). It is therefore perhaps not altogether

---

[135] Digidyne Corp. v. Data Gen. Corp., 734 F.2d 1336, 1341–1344 (9th Cir. 1984) (holding that refusal to license copyrighted operating system software except to purchasers of control processing unit (CPU) hardware constituted a per se unlawful tying arrangement), *cert. denied,* 473 U.S. 908 (1985); *see also* United States Steel Corp. v. Fortner Enters., Inc., 429 U.S. 610, 619 (1977) ("the copyright monopolies in United States v. Paramount Pictures, Inc., 334 U.S. 131 . . . and United States v. Loew's Inc., 371 U.S. 38 . . . represented tying products that the Court regarded as sufficiently unique to give rise to a presumption of economic power").

[136] *See, e.g.,* Digital Equip. Corp. v. Uniq Digital Techs., Inc., 73 F.3d 756, 762 (7th Cir. 1996) (rejecting *Digidyne's* position that "firms lose the right to design their product packages when one element is a copyrighted operating system"); Town Sound & Custom Tops, Inc. v. Chrysler Motors Corp., 959 F.2d 468, 479 n.11 (3d Cir.) (rejecting *Digidyne's* suggestion that defining the tying product market is unnecessary in a "per se" tying claim because power over a portion of the market is sufficient), *cert. denied,* 506 U.S. 868 (1992); A.I. Root Co. v. Computer/Dynamics, Inc., 806 F.2d 673, 676 (6th Cir. 1986) (rejecting claim that defendant possessed market power in a copyrighted software product).

surprising that most antitrust litigation relating to information services has originated well outside the telecommunications industry.

The ascendant theory today among those employed to foresee monopoly in telecommunications is that it is control of the desktop software—Microsoft's control—that presents the gravest threat of monopoly in the higher tiers of the Internet. As one industry observer wrote, "Some fear that as the digital future of the information superhighway emerges, an unchallenged Microsoft and Intel will wind up in total, undisputed control of the technology upon which the country's citizens and economy will depend."[137]

Perhaps it was this fear that prompted the Justice Department to challenge the manner in which Microsoft licenses its Windows operating system.[138] Microsoft required computer manufacturers to include Microsoft's Internet Explorer software on the desktop display. The Justice Department alleged that these licensing "restrictions exclude competing Internet browsers from the most important channels of distribution."[139] In addition, Microsoft's strategy included entering into "anticompetitive agreements with all of the nation's largest and most popular ISPs," whereby Microsoft supplied information about how to subscribe to certain ISP services in exchange for the ISP's offering on an exclusive basis of Microsoft's Internet browser as the browser of choice.[140] Microsoft has further leveraged its operating system monopoly by providing prominent "channel buttons" on the desktop, which

---

[137] G. Reback, S. Creighton, D. Killam, & N. Nathanson (Wilson, Sonsini, Goodrich & Rosati), with assistance from G. Saloner & W.B. Arthur, Technological, Economic and Legal Perspectives Regarding Microsoft's Business Strategy in Light of the Proposed Acquisition of Intuit, Inc. (Microsoft-Intuit White Paper, Feb. 1995). There was also a brief flurry of concern when Microsoft set up its own online network (MSN), but that abated quickly after it became clear that MSN was not taking over much of anything. *See generally* FBL §9.6.2 (Computers, Terminal Equipment, and Software).

[138] *See* Complaint, United States v. Microsoft Corp., Civ. Act. No. 98-1232 (May 18, 1998).

[139] *Id.* ¶27.

[140] *Id.* ¶¶28–30, 75. Microsoft had agreements with America Online, CompuServe, and the major Internet service providers—AT&T Worldnet, MCI, and Earthlink—to distribute Internet Explorer to their subscribers.

advertise and provide direct Internet access to select Internet content providers.[141] In exchange, these content providers agree not to promote or compensate competing browsers for the marketing or distribution of the content provider's material.[142] The fact that almost all personal computers manufactured and shipped to users in the United States are loaded with the Windows operating system provides Microsoft with a very powerful mechanism in the world of electronic commerce.

However, the difficulty of achieving integration is shown by the market's reaction. Not to be outdone, computer manufacturers are seeking to install their own features that automatically connect the computer to sites on the World Wide Web. Computer makers are including special quick-access buttons on keyboards to facilitate Internet access. These prewired connections lead the user to Web sites whose proprietors are paying the computer makers to funnel Internet traffic to their sites. Initially designed to be impossible to reconfigure, manufacturers backed off and provided instructions on how to reset the quick-access buttons.

§12.7.3   Excluding Phone Companies from Information Service Markets: The "Maximum Separation" Policy of Computer I

Based at least in part on fears of telco vertical integration into information services, in *Computer I,* the Commission instituted a policy of separation between the phone companies and the computer industry. As noted in section 12.4 above, the Commission decided not to regulate either pure or "hybrid" data processing and to regulate either pure or "hybrid" telecommunications, in effect regulating AT&T's phone companies out of the computer

---

[141] Microsoft has agreements with Disney, Hollywood Online, and CBS Sportsline. *Id.* ¶87.
[142] *Id.* ¶¶88–91.

business entirely.[143] The goal was to ensure no intermingling of costs and revenues between the two spheres by requiring "maximum separation" of regulated telco service and unregulated data processing services.[144] Any benefits of commingling the services would be "more than offset by the potential adverse effects of such an arrangement."[145]

Thus, telcos would be permitted to provide data processing services only through affiliates with separate books, officers, operating personnel, equipment, and facilities. Data processing affiliates, moreover, were forbidden to promote their products or services through association with the parent carrier, including use of the parent's name or symbol. Telcos would have to offer telecommunications services to both affiliates and nonaffiliates on scrupulously equal terms, as set out in public tariffs.[146] Telcos would not be permitted to buy data processing services from their own affiliates. Computer systems already operated by carriers would have to be dedicated exclusively to network functions and in-house needs.

With all this firmly established, the Commission then exempted about one-half of the 700 or so independent telephone companies from the new rules.[147] Imposing structural separation on smaller carriers, the Commission concluded, would suppress more competition than it promoted. Although the Commission

---

[143] The Commission nevertheless rejected an outright prohibition on the furnishing of computer services by any common carrier as "contrary to [its] policy of permitting the common carrier, directly or through affiliates, to engage in non-regulated activities so long as such activities are not repugnant to or in derogation of the economic and social objectives of the Act." *Computer I,* 28 F.C.C.2d at 270 ¶11.

[144] *Computer I,* 28 F.C.C.2d at 269–270 ¶10 (quoting *Computer I, Tentative Decision,* 28 F.C.C.2d at 302 ¶35). *See generally* Note, FCC Review of Regulation Relating to Provision of Data Processing Services by Communications Common Carriers, 15 B.C. Indus. & Com. L. Rev. 162 (1973).

[145] *Computer I,* 28 F.C.C.2d at 271 ¶15.

[146] To enforce its distinction between hybrid communications (to be offered by the carrier) and hybrid data processing (to be offered by the separate affiliate), the Commission held that before a common carrier could provide communication services to an affiliated data processing entity, it first had to submit a full description of the proposed hybrid service to the Commission.

[147] The exemption extended to carriers with combined operating revenues under $1,000,000. *Computer I,* 28 F.C.C.2d at 274–275 ¶23.

acknowledged that, irrespective of size, a carrier's influence is considerable within its operating franchise, it still concluded that "both the potential and motives for abuse by these smaller carriers is minimal at this time."[148]

The Commission's decision was affirmed in large part on appeal.[149] Even absent any explicit reference to computer services in the Communications Act, the Second Circuit reasoned, the FCC's rules were logically related to preserving efficient, low-cost phone service.[150] But, the court held, carriers could not be barred from purchasing data processing services from their own affiliates. Nor could the FCC forbid affiliates from using a telco's name or logo. These rules served only to protect the data processing market—a market "beyond [the FCC's] charge and which the Commission itself has announced it declines to regulate."[151] Thus, the Commission's maximum separation policy remained largely in place and continued to govern relations between telecommunication and information services providers.

So far as it went, the Commission's decision not to regulate computer services was a wise one. But in an apparent excess of caution, the Commission insisted that "enhanced services" should not under any circumstances be intermingled with "basic" phone service. Instead of permitting telcos to provide (and monopolize) everything, the Commission initially permitted them to provide nothing at all.

Viewed historically, the Commission's determination to ban the telcos from providing "enhanced services" was ironic, to say the least. Telephony originated as an "enhancement" of telegraphy, and an excellent enhancement it was, one that vaulted communications from Morse code to human conversation. So why isolate computer enhancements from the telephone company's network? Computers plainly offered many more opportunities for further improvement. The Internet has indeed

---

[148] *Id.*
[149] GTE Serv. Corp. v. FCC, 474 F.2d at 731.
[150] *Id.*
[151] *Id.* at 733.

improved telephony in subsequent years at least as much as telephony improved telegraphy.

What the Commission was really doing was protecting computers (and consumers) from . . . itself, and from its counterpart commissions in the states. As the Commission well understood, the phone service monopoly was largely a creation of regulation: regulation preserved the monopoly, and the monopoly justified still more regulation, until basic telephony was snarled in a stifling cocoon of bureaucracy. The way to protect the nascent computer industry from regulatory suffocation was to exclude it not only from the halls of the Commission, but also from the management, ownership, and participation of those who walked those same halls—the pervasively regulated, monopoly phone companies.

§12.7.4   Maximum Separation Continued: Computer II

Computer II[152] could, and should, have reversed course on structural separation, since technological developments since *Computer I* made it clear that such a divide was not tenable. In the seven years since *Computer I,* the world of computing had been radically transformed by the development of integrated circuits, the microprocessor, and the personal computer. Grosch's law had been repealed. Computers were fast becoming an integral part of all telecommunications equipment, from telephone handsets on up.[153] The *Computer I* definitions, unsatisfactory even in the 1960s when they were intended to protect the computer industry from regulation, were now hopelessly out of

---

[152] *Computer II,* 77 F.C.C.2d 384; *modified on recons., Computer II Reconsideration Order,* 84 F.C.C.2d 50, *further modified on recons., Computer II Further Reconsideration Order,* 88 F.C.C.2d 512, *aff'd sub nom.* Computer and Communications Indus. Assn. v. FCC, 693 F.2d 198 (D.C. Cir. 1982), *cert. denied,* 461 U.S. 938 (1983), *aff'd on second further recons.,* FCC 84-190 (May 4, 1984).

[153] *Computer II,* 77 F.C.C.2d at 391 ¶19. For a discussion of these developments, see generally Daniel Bell, The Coming of Post Industrial Society (1976); James Martin, Telecommunications and the Computer (1976); Symposium: Computers in Law and Society, Wash. U. L.Q. 371 (1977).

date.[154] The FCC therefore set out, yet again, to determine whether computer-driven services provided over phone lines should be regulated and, if so, to what extent.[155]

Initially, the Commission proposed simply to redefine the unregulated sphere of data processing.[156] In a Supplemental Notice, it proposed a modified definition of data processing in order to extend *Computer I* to distributed processing and to make it easier to distinguish carrier services from carrier-provided computer services.[157] But almost immediately it was faced with a question that challenged this approach. It had to decide whether computer capabilities built into the likes of a telephone could be included in a regulated service package.[158] *Computer I* did not even address this issue of "smart" CPE. After more than two years of delay, the Commission ruled in *Dataspeed 40/4* that AT&T could offer the data terminal in question under tariff, but announced that it would reexamine the issue in its Second Computer Inquiry.[159]

The Commission soon recognized that new definitions would not help. And so the Commission that once strained to define the telephone "system" as expansively as possible[160] now strained

---

[154] *See generally* Frieden, The Computer Inquiries: Mapping the Communications/Information Processing Terrain, 33 Fed. Comm. L.J. 55 (1981); Note, The Effect of the Second Computer Inquiry on Telecommunications and Data Processing, 27 Wayne L. Rev. 1537 (1981); Comment, Interdependence of Communications and Data Processing: An Alternative Proposal for the Second Computer Inquiry, 73 N.W.U. L.J. 307, 308 (1978).

[155] *Computer II*, 77 F.C.C.2d at 385–386 ¶1.

[156] *Id.* at 392 ¶20 n.3.

[157] Under the new proposal, "data processing" was defined as "the electronically automated processing of information wherein: (a) the information content or meaning, of the input information is in any way transformed, or (b) where the output information constitutes a programmed response to input information." *Id.* at 392–393 ¶22.

[158] AT&T Revisions to Tariffs FCC Nos. 260 and 267 Relating to Dataspeed 40/4, Memorandum Opinion and Order, 62 F.C.C.2d 21 (1977); *aff'd sub nom.* International Bus. Mach. Corp. v. FCC, 570 F.2d 452 (2d Cir. 1978). The Dataspeed 40/4 had data processing capabilities that enabled it to perform some functions that would have been performed in a central computer at the time the 1971 rules were adopted.

[159] *Computer II*, 77 F.C.C.2d at 392–393 ¶¶21–22.

[160] *See* §11.3.

in just the opposite direction. The telephone system was to provide "basic services," nothing more. All the rest was an exercise in freezing computer-related "enhancements" out of the telephone network, at least insofar as end users might be aware of them.

All of this elaborate definition and regulation, however, was aimed at keeping a single company out of data processing—AT&T. Only AT&T's telco affiliates would be limited to offering basic services; only AT&T would be required to maintain separate subsidiaries for any affiliate offering enhanced services.[161] As under *Computer I*, AT&T's affiliates would be required to adhere scrupulously to published tariffs in their dealings with both affiliated and unaffiliated providers of enhanced services. Only AT&T, the Commission concluded, was large enough and pervasive enough to have significant potential to cross-subsidize or to engage in other anticompetitive conduct.[162] The FCC's *Computer II* decision was affirmed "in its entirety" by a unanimous panel of the D.C. Circuit.[163] Shortly after the Bell divestiture, the FCC extended *Computer II*'s separate subsidiary mandate to the newly created BOCs.[164]

But by then, it was already quite clear that computers built into the telephone network could improve wonderfully network capabilities and the quality of service, just as computers were fast improving the performance of Cuisinarts, cars, and almost everything else. The Commission had indeed protected competition in the computer industry, but at the cost of crippling the improvement of service in the telephone industry. The Commission remarked that if "at some future time" evidence of serious inefficiencies were submitted, it would "reexamine the public interest ramifications and regulatory implications" of the boundaries

---

[161] The Commission's initial order applied to GTE as well, but this restriction was removed upon reconsideration, largely because GTE was at that time dependent on AT&T for the vast majority of its interstate transmission needs. *Computer II Reconsideration Order,* 84 F.C.C.2d at 72–73 ¶¶64–66.

[162] *Computer II,* 77 F.C.C.2d at 388–389 ¶12.

[163] Communications Indus. Assn. v. FCC, 693 F.2d at 203.

[164] *See* §12.4.2.

it had drawn.[165] In that remark, the seeds of *Computer III* were already sown.

§12.7.5   The Information Services Ban in the Bell Divestiture Decree

As happened with cable television,[166] Congress picked up on the FCC's quarantine and attempted to enact it into law. But the draft Senate bill incorporating the FCC's information services quarantine went nowhere in Congress.[167] Instead, the unenacted bill was noticed at the Department of Justice, which then incorporated its language in the Bell Divestiture Decree. Section IV(J) of the Decree barred the divested BOCs from providing information services, which were defined to include any service providing "the capability for generating, acquiring, storing, transforming, processing, retrieving, utilizing, or making available information which may be conveyed via telecommunications."[168]

Judge Harold Greene embraced the information services quarantine as his own. After five years, Justice changed its mind and supported removal of the information services restriction on the BOCs.[169] Judge Greene, however, resisted, and it took another five years of litigation to remove from the Decree what the FCC had long since repudiated.[170]

[165] *Computer II,* 77 F.C.C.2d at 421–422 ¶99.

[166] *See* §13.7.2.4.

[167] *See* S.898, 97th Cong., 1st Sess. (Oct. 20, 1981); *see* Kellogg, Thorne & Huber, *Federal Telecommunications Law* §6.4 (1992) *(FTL1)*.

[168] Modification of Final Judgment §IV(J), *reprinted in* United States v. AT&T, 552 F. Supp. 131, 229 (D.D.C. 1982) (hereinafter *Decree*).

[169] The Department of Justice expressly relied on the BOCs' experience distributing CPE in recommending removal of the information services restriction. *See, e.g.,* Report and Recommendations of the United States Concerning Line of Business Restrictions Imposed on the Bell Operating Companies by the Modification of Final Judgment at 131–132, United States v. Western Elec. Co., No. 82-0192 (D.D.C. Feb. 2, 1987); *see also* Motion of the United States for Removal of the Information Services Restriction of the Modification of Final Judgment at 23 n.30, United States v. Western Elec. Co., No. 82-0192 (D.D.C. Aug. 11, 1990).

[170] In 1987, the Department recommended removal of the information services restriction. The court rejected that recommendation, concluding that there was no basis for removing the restriction, since the BOCs retained

On May 28, 1993, the D.C. Circuit Court of Appeals issued a landmark opinion affirming the removal of the information services restriction.[171] The Department had concluded that (1) there was no substantial risk that removal of the ban would lessen competition, (2) regulation would minimize anticompetitive risks, and (3) removal of the ban would benefit consumers by enhancing competition. The appellate court agreed with each of these conclusions.

First, the court accepted that the BOCs still had local market power and "assume[d] *arguendo* that devices for avoiding the local loop altogether, such as satellite dishes, are inadequate."[172] It nevertheless found "strong support" in the record to conclude that BOCs will "be unable to discriminate against competing providers."[173] Competing providers can feed their signals into the telephone network through any number of competing telcos or bypass BOCs entirely with private networks.[174] At the customer end, "it is evidently difficult, if not impossible, for BOCs to distinguish between information service provider messages and others, as both may come over regular voice lines."[175]

---

monopoly control of the local telephone switches and wires. *See* United States v. Western Electric Co., 673 F. Supp. 525 (D.D.C. 1987). The court of appeals reversed and remanded on this issue, on the grounds that since none of the original parties to the Decree opposed removal of the restriction, the proper standard was a public interest standard that required only that the Department show it could reasonably conclude that removal of the ban was in the public interest. *See* United States v. Western Elec. Co., 900 F.2d 283, 289–293 (D.C. Cir.), *cert. denied sub nom.* MCI Communications Corp. v. United States, 498 U.S. 911 (1990). On remand, the district court grudgingly removed the prohibition against BOC provision of information services in deference to the court of appeals' opinion. *See* United States v. Western Elec. Co., 767 F. Supp. 308 (D.D.C. 1991).

[171] United States v. Western Elec. Co., 993 F.2d 1572 (D.C. Cir. 1993).

[172] *Id.* at 1578.

[173] *Id.*

[174] *Id.* at 1578–1579.

[175] *Id.* at 1579. Judge Greene had characterized the BOCs' evidence on these points as "halfhearted"; the appellate court in turn characterized Judge Greene's conclusion as "baffling[]." *Id.* (quoting *Western Elec. Co.,* 767 F. Supp. at 316). In the appellate court's view, the record was "persuasive" that BOCs would be unable to discriminate against competing information service providers. *Id.* at 1579–1580. Prognostications about risks of predatory pricing had not been backed by persuasive evidence and had indeed been contradicted by one of the appellants' own experts. *Id.* at 1580.

Second, the appellate court analyzed regulatory safeguards. Judge Greene had taken the position that since regulators had been unable to regulate the predivestiture AT&T effectively, they would be unable to regulate the BOCs.[176] The appellate court disagreed: "There is a lot of evidence that the break-up and other recent developments have enhanced regulatory capability."[177]

Finally, the appellate court addressed the competitive benefits of BOC entry. It noted that several segments of the information services market are highly concentrated and that in others BOCs might enjoy important economies of scope, with resulting consumer benefits.[178] Judge Greene had dismissed these arguments as "preposterous" and had foretold "a nightmare in which the BOCs would drive out the current competitors and perhaps 'extinguish' . . . competition altogether."[179] The appellate court, in contrast, concluded that BOCs can contribute positively to competition in new markets and that no BOC can "extinguish" competition simply by eliminating all but six other competitors. In any event, the extinction scenario depended on successful discrimination and cross-subsidy that the appellate court had already concluded was not likely.[180]

In contrast to his concerns with BOC competition, Judge Greene found no significant danger in allowing AT&T to provide data processing services at divestiture.[181] But he did decide

---

[176] *Id.*

[177] *Id.* The court noted that "[t]he seven independent BOCs are not the old AT&T." Now, the seven BOCs provide more regulatory benchmarks that regulators can use to detect discriminatory pricing. The FCC's shift toward price-cap regulation reduces any BOC's ability to shift costs from unregulated to regulated activities, and the FCC has tightened its accounting rules. Moreover, "information service giants operating throughout the country, such as IBM, AT&T and GE, will notice any discrepancies in treatment by the various BOCs and will have the capacity and incentive to bring anticompetitive conduct to the attention of regulatory agencies." Finally, BOCs would have a hard time conveying a reputation for predation to would-be competitors—purportedly to discourage entry—while keeping it a secret from regulators. The court thus concluded that it is "by no means valid" to assume that regulators are "captured" by regulatees in the telephone industry. *Id.* at 1580–1581.

[178] *Id.* at 1581.

[179] *Id.* (quoting 767 F. Supp. at 326).

[180] *Id.* at 1581–1582.

[181] United States v. AT&T, 552 F. Supp. at 179. The data processing industry was "already well established, [and] comprised of some of the nation's

that AT&T should be barred for an additional seven years (until 1989) from providing "electronic publishing over its own transmission facilities."[182] This moratorium embraced television, radio, and "electronic publications which appear either by audio means, on video screens, or in printed form," and it covered all types of information, including "news, business and financial reports, editorials, columns, sports, features, and electronic advertising."[183] Judge Greene reasoned that the "peculiar characteristics of the electronic publishing market" made that market uniquely vulnerable to discrimination by AT&T.[184] Were AT&T permitted to publish electronically, "there would be a substantial risk . . . that it would acquire a substantial monopoly over the generation of news in the more general sense."[185] Judge Greene concluded that a "seven-year period should be sufficient for the development of electronic publishing as a viable industry, for the acquisition of sufficient strength by individual publishers adequate to permit them to compete, and for the development of means other than the AT&T network for the transmission of the messages of electronic publishers."[186] The electronic publishing restriction on AT&T was lifted on schedule, seven years after it was imposed.[187]

---

leading corporate giants, as well as of many smaller concerns." In addition, "the growing demand for information services will necessarily increase the demand for transmission facilities for these services. Such an increase in demand is likely to stimulate AT&T's interexchange competitors to offer satisfactory alternatives to the AT&T network. . . ." *Id.* at 179–180.

[182] *Id.* at 225. Judge Greene defined electronic publishing as "the provision of any information which a provider or publisher has, or has caused to be originated, authored, compiled, collected, or edited, or in which he has a direct or indirect financial or proprietary interest, and which is disseminated to an unaffiliated person through some electronic means." *Id.* at 181. This definition was an amalgam of proposed legislative provisions that were pending at that time in the House and Senate. *Id.* at 180–181 n.206.

[183] *Id.* at 181 n.208.

[184] *Id.* at 182.

[185] *Id.* at 224.

[186] *Id.*

[187] *See* Memorandum, United States v. Western Elec. Co., No. 82-0192 (D.D.C. July 28, 1989).

§12.7.6   The Collapse of **Computer II**

Shortly before the Decree, the Commission had confidently asserted in *Computer II* that under its new definitions "the regulatory demarcation between basic and enhanced services becomes relatively clear-cut."[188] Perhaps it did, but only through a triumph of history over technology. The definition of "basic services," it turned out, was clear only if understood to mean "services actually provided by AT&T around 1982." However, AT&T plainly had no intention of freezing its technology in place. Through a series of waiver requests that systematically revealed flaws in the *Computer II* regime, AT&T began laying the groundwork for further change even before divestiture.

In 1981, AT&T requested a waiver that would permit BOCs to provide certain "custom calling" services directly to their customers instead of through a separate subsidiary.[189] These services, the predecessors of today's voice mail, included call answering and advance calling, together with an optional remote access feature.[190] AT&T, which had already designed and begun to install the services on an unseparated basis prior to *Computer II,* argued that any redesign effort would be costly and time consuming, resulting in a delay of the introduction of the services for at least three years.

The FCC was unmoved. "We cannot base a grant of the petition upon such a rationale," the Commission stated.[191] Rather, AT&T would have to demonstrate "that the application of the

---

[188] *Computer II,* 77 F.C.C.2d at 420–421 ¶97.

[189] AT&T Petition for Waiver of Section 64.702 of the Commission's Rules & Regulations, Memorandum Opinion and Order, 88 F.C.C.2d 1 (1981) (hereinafter *AT&T Petition for Waiver*).

[190] "Call answering" permits the automatic answering of simultaneous incoming calls when the customer's line is busy or, after a specified number of rings, when the customer does not answer. Callers are able to leave recorded messages for later retrieval by the customer. "Advance calling" permits customers to record messages for subsequent transmittal to designated telephones at specified or nonspecified times. "Remote access," an optional adjunct to the other two features, permits a CCS-II customer to access call answering and advance calling from touch-tone telephones at distant locations. *AT&T Petition for Waiver,* 88 F.C.C.2d at 1–2 ¶1.

[191] *Id.* at 17 ¶54.

separation rules will result in unreasonable costs to consumers because of technical impossibility or economic infeasibility."[192] Since AT&T conceded that "it is *technically* possible for it to provide call answering and advance calling through a fully separated subsidiary," the FCC concluded that there was no basis for a waiver. As AT&T had predicted, however, this decision dramatically delayed the availability of such services.[193]

The next challenge to *Computer II* involved "code and protocol conversion." Data transmissions often require low-level translation services that allow different machines to communicate in a common format.[194] These services were plainly "enhancements" under the *Computer II* definitions. The Commission therefore refused to treat such services as telecommunications services, stressing that no "compelling evidence" had been submitted to show that providing protocol conversion through a separate subsidiary would impose significant efficiency losses on the carrier or the public.[195] But it also later acknowledged that protocol conversion might well warrant different treatment from other enhanced services, since it was necessary (and in effect incidental) to basic transmission services.[196]

---

[192] *Id.* at 8 ¶22.

[193] *Id.* at 16–17 ¶53 (emphasis in original). AT&T ripped out the network capacity to offer these services, but before the services could be redesigned in keeping with *Computer II*, divestiture intervened. At that point, the BOCs were forbidden by the Decree to offer such services, even through separate subsidiaries. The district court did not grant a waiver to allow the BOCs to provide voice storage and retrieval until 1988. Thus, through a combination of regulatory and judicial restrictions, consumers were denied these services for almost a decade.

[194] Protocol conversion is necessary, for example, to permit a personal computer to communicate via a packet-switched network with a database such as Lexis. The communications protocol for the interface between the computer user and the regular telephone network (asynchronous) is different than the protocol for communications over a packet-switched network (X.25).

[195] Commissioner Fogarty's dissent was particularly critical of this treatment of protocol conversion: "It is difficult for me to see why protocol or code conversion is an *enhancement* to a communications service. It is, rather, as much a necessity to the provision of any communications service at all, for customers who happen to have disparate terminals, as is the presence of a local loop." *Computer II*, 77 F.C.C.2d at 512.

[196] Communications Protocols Under Section 64.702 of the Commission's Rules & Regulations, Memorandum, Opinion, Order, and Statement of Principles, 95 F.C.C.2d 584–585 ¶¶1–3 (1983).

If provision of such protocol conversion services was barred to AT&T, it would be limited in its ability to offer full-fledged data transmission. AT&T therefore sought an appropriate waiver. With the ink scarcely dry on *Computer II*, the FCC granted it. While the inefficiencies of separation were now plain, the FCC nevertheless declined to adopt any general change in the definition of enhanced services to move protocol conversion to the "basic" side of the line: "[A]ny inefficiencies which may flow from the application of these rules to carriers subject to structural separation," the FCC claimed, "are at this point minimal and are more than counterbalanced by the benefits of unregulated supply of enhanced services and marketplace certainty in maintaining the existing definition."[197] (The Department of Justice, by contrast, took the position that simple forms of protocol conversion were "basic" for purposes of the Decree.)

The FCC likewise declined to grant any general waiver to permit protocol conversion by the BOCs. But it did conclude that special treatment of particular services should be "addressed *ad hoc*."[198] "In this way," the Commission reasoned, "we will be able to assess the issues raised by a specific proposal to employ protocol conversions in connection with basic service in a narrow manner, with full appreciation of the circumstances and ramifications involved in any such proposal."[199]

Ad hockery, it soon became apparent, had problems of its own. By 1985, the Commission had before it eight protocol conversion petitions from the newly divested BOCs.[200] The Commission acknowledged that the BOCs "would avoid some economic costs" if permitted to collocate certain protocol conversion functions in their central offices, to the benefit of "[u]sers of the millions of

---

[197] *Id.* at 586–587 ¶¶4–5.

[198] *Id.* at 586–587 ¶5.

[199] *Id.* at 593 ¶20.

[200] Petitions for Waiver of Section 64.702 of the Commission's Rules (Computer II), Memorandum Opinion and Order, 100 F.C.C.2d 1057 (1985) (hereinafter *Petitions for Waiver*). "Collocation" of packet service nodes within the central offices would allow the BOCs to replace local loops with within-office wiring, thereby saving on transmission costs, materials, installation, and repair.

terminals and terminal-emulating personal computers."[201] But "a material portion of the savings" that the BOCs anticipated depended on the BOCs charging themselves less for interoffice transmission capacity than they charged to competing independent services. This "price squeeze" was unacceptable.[202] So the FCC granted waivers, but insisted that any lower prices offered to customers by BOCs reflect only true cost differences.[203]

Of more long-range importance, however, the Commission acknowledged that "the waiver process is insufficient to provide the stability needed by users, carriers, VANs, and other enhanced service providers, whose business planning and decision-making are affected by our decisions."[204] Accordingly, the FCC announced a forthcoming Notice of Proposed Rulemaking in which it would "seek to formulate general rules of future applicability to govern the treatment of protocol conversion and similar enhanced services."[205]

§12.7.7 Computer III *Emerges*

By June of 1986, the FCC was ready to abandon structural separation entirely.[206] The decision, however, took over a decade

---

[201] *Id.* at 1059–1060 ¶4.

[202] *Id.* at 1060 ¶5.

[203] *See id.* at 1099–1100 ¶107. The FCC also continued to require that marketing costs for protocol conversion be separated from marketing costs for basic services. *Id.* at 1100–1101 ¶109. It waived the ban on joint installation and maintenance, but only to the limited extent necessary to allow installation and repair of the protocol conversion equipment itself by unseparated telephone company employees. To ensure that subscribers to basic service do not cross-subsidize such operations, the Commission required that the operations be performed under express contract with the telco and that the contract be filed with the Commission and accepted beforehand. *Id.* at 1102–1103 ¶¶111–113.

[204] *Id.* at 1061–1062 ¶9.

[205] *Id.* at 1062 ¶10. As noted above, Congress subsequently asked the Commission to address the classification of protocol processing services in its *Report to Congress,* but the Commission concluded it was unable to resolve the matter on the record before it. *See* §12.2.3.

[206] Amendment of Section 64.702 of the Commission's Rules & Regulations (Third Computer Inquiry), Report and Order, 104 F.C.C.2d 958 (1986)

to implement—the job is not quite finished even today. It depended, to begin with, on final implementation of the *Joint Cost Order*[207] and on the approval of ONA plans by the BOCs, both of which required extensive proceedings. Moreover, the decision met with not one, but two hostile receptions from the Ninth Circuit. Then the 1996 Act intervened.

In reassessing its *Computer II* regime, the Commission for the first time recognized competition by AT&T and the BOCs as potentially beneficial. Accordingly, the Commission resolved to restrict their participation only to the extent needed to protect ratepayers and other competitors from inefficient practices.[208]

Structural separation, the Commission declared, had yielded more limited benefits than originally anticipated. It did indeed make cross-subsidy more difficult and highlighted any discrimination between a telco's own affiliates and unaffiliated competitors.[209] But divestiture had substantially attenuated these problems for both AT&T and the BOCs. AT&T no longer had an exclusive franchise or captive buyers of its equipment, and it faced growing competition in all its markets.[210] The funds it might have used for cross-subsidy were evaporating, and it was fast losing its ability to set discriminatory standards for interconnection.[211] Bypass and other new technologies were likewise placing some (albeit weaker) limits on the BOCs' ability to shift costs. More important, the BOCs faced persistent political and regulatory pressures to minimize rural, residential, and small business local exchange rates, even to below-cost levels. Their ability to discriminate in interconnection standards had eroded because they had to coordinate standards with each other and with other carriers.[212]

(hereinafter *Computer III*); *modified on recons.*, 2 F.C.C. Rec. 3035 (1987) (hereinafter *Phase I Reconsidered*), *further modified on recons.*, 3 F.C.C. Rec. 1135 (1988).

[207] *See* §2.2.2.6.
[208] *Computer III*, 104 F.C.C.2d at 1001–1002 ¶77.
[209] *Id.* at 1004–1006 ¶¶82–85.
[210] *Id.* at 1005 ¶83.
[211] *Id.* at 1006 ¶86.
[212] *Id.* at 1011 ¶97.

On the other side of the equation, the Commission found that the costs of structural separation had proved to be greater than initially believed. Protocol conversion, voice messaging services, and innovative routing and switching functions had all been inhibited.[213] Both the BOCs and AT&T had been discouraged from designing innovative enhanced services that used the public switched network.[214] And structural separation had denied both the BOCs and AT&T the opportunity to realize economies of scope in their research, development, and marketing.[215]

Initially the Commission proposed yet another set of definitions. *Computer II*'s two service categories would become three: "basic" services, as before; "services ancillary to communications," which would include enhanced services and CPE; and "non-communications services." Services falling in the new middle category would be regulated flexibly, depending on the market dominance of the carrier proposing to offer them, the economic characteristics of the service, and competitors' dependence on the carrier's "bottleneck facilities."[216] In effect, the Commission was preparing to resurrect the "hybrid" terminology of *Computer I*.

Wisely the Commission abandoned this tripartite scheme soon after it was proposed.[217] Instead, it decided to create the flexibility it desired by preserving the old line between "basic" and "enhanced" services, but abandoning structural separation entirely, with appropriate nonstructural safeguards.[218] An entirely new regulatory philosophy now began to take shape, the most fundamental change in eight decades of regulatory oversight.

---

[213] *Id.* at 985–986 ¶44.

[214] *Id.* at 1008–1009 ¶91.

[215] *Id.* at 1004, 1008–1009; *Phase I Reconsidered,* 2 F.C.C. Rec. at 3038 ¶25.

[216] *Computer III,* 104 F.C.C.2d at 1014–1015 ¶103.

[217] *Id.* at 1017–1018 ¶108.

[218] Amendment to Section 64.702 of the Commission's Rules & Regulations (Third Computer Inquiry), Report and Order, 2 F.C.C. Rec. 3072, 3078 (1987) (hereinafter *Phase II Order*), *modified on recons.,* 3 F.C.C. Rec. 1150 (1988) (hereinafter *Phase II Reconsidered*), *further modified on recons.,* 4 F.C.C. Rec. 5927 (1989) (hereinafter *Phase II Further Reconsidered*).

The old regulatory pair, exclusive franchise and strict quarantine, would give way to a new—equal access and competition all around. The FCC turned away from regulating access by or to corporate entities and began, at long last, to regulate access to the network itself. As discussed above (see section 12.5.2), *Computer III* implemented this new philosophy through the ONA and CEI requirements, which served as alternative safeguards to structural separation, and as prerequisites for its demise.

§12.7.8   *The Ninth Circuit Vacates* Computer III

A divided panel of the Ninth Circuit vacated *Computer III* and remanded the entire proceeding to the Commission.[219] The Commission had reversed course, the court noted, just 14 months after concluding in the BOC separation proceeding that divestiture had not reduced the need for structural separation. The court held that the Commission's explanation of its abrupt change of course was inadequate and its attempt to preempt contrary state rules beyond the scope of its authority.

The court acknowledged the Commission's "broad discretionary authority,"[220] but concluded that the agency had not "articulated a satisfactory explanation" for what it had done.[221] While the balancing of costs and benefits "must be left to the discretion of the FCC," "if the FCC's evaluation of any significant element in the cost/benefit analysis lacks record support, we cannot uphold the agency action."[222] The Commission's evidence concerning the high costs of structural separation was "marginal," but nevertheless "sufficient." Its finding that "changed

---

[219] California v. FCC, 905 F.2d 1217 (9th Cir. 1990) (*California I*). No one appealed the elimination of structural separation for AT&T or a number of other aspects of the *Computer III* regime. The Ninth Circuit, however, vacated the entire proceeding.

[220] *California I*, 905 F. 2d at 1230.

[221] *Id.* Judge Boochever dissented on this point, arguing that the court was engaged in blatant second-guessing of a policy judgment that necessarily involved a balancing of imponderables. *Id.* at 1251.

[222] *Id.* at 1231.

circumstances have made it more difficult for the BOCs to provide competitors with inferior access" was also reasonable in light of the emergence of powerful competitors such as IBM, the growing use of bypass technologies, and the FCC's ONA/CEI policies.[223] But the Commission had not provided adequate support for its conclusion that changed market and technological circumstances had reduced the danger that the BOCs would effectively subsidize their competitive activities with inflated monopoly revenues. Nor had it sufficiently explained why it had abandoned its original position that cost-accounting regulations are ineffective in preventing cross-subsidy.[224]

§12.7.9 The FCC's Response on Remand

On remand, the FCC prepared to lift structural separation requirements once again, to be replaced by a strengthened set of cost allocation and accounting safeguards.[225] The Commission also proposed to preempt state structural regulation that as a practical matter will prevent carriers from integrating their interstate operations.[226] "The enhanced services market generally is national or regional in scope," the Commission cautioned, "and a degree of certainty and uniformity may be necessary to enable the enhanced services market to develop in the way that both state commissions and this Commission desire."[227]

Accordingly, in late 1991, the Commission reinstated structural integration for the BOCs and, at the same time, revised in some respects the nonstructural safeguards it had originally proposed.[228] The Commission strengthened its existing accounting

[223] *Id.* at 1232–1233.
[224] *Id.*
[225] Computer III Remand Proceedings: Bell Operating Company Safeguards; and Tier 1 Local Exchange Company Safeguards, Notice of Proposed Rulemaking, 6 F.C.C. Rec. 174, 182–183 ¶54 (1990).
[226] *Id.* at 181 ¶48.
[227] *Id.* at 181 ¶47.
[228] Computer III Remand Proceedings: Bell Operating Company Safeguards and Tier 1 Local Exchange, Report and Order, 6 F.C.C. Rec. 7571 (1991), (hereinafter *Computer III Order on Remand*).

safeguards[229] and concluded that these safeguards—which include detailed cost allocation rules, the filing of cost allocation
manuals, independent audits, reporting requirements, the development of an automated system to store and analyze the data,
on-site audits by FCC staff, and the adoption of price caps—
were an effective alternative to structural separation in protecting
against cross-subsidy. The Commission essentially readopted its
other *Computer III* nonstructural safeguards against discrimination, including ONA requirements, which the Ninth Circuit had
concluded were adequate.[230]

§12.7.10   The Ninth Circuit's Second Decision and the FCC's Response

The FCC's second attempt to implement *Computer III* returned to the Ninth Circuit in 1994. The appellate court balked
again.[231] The court agreed that the Commission had "adequately responded to the concerns we expressed in *California I* by
increasing the nonstructural safeguards designed to prevent the
BOCs from passing on the costs of their enhanced services to
their telephone customers paying regulated rates."[232] But the

---

[229] *See* §2.2 for a discussion of some of these mechanisms.

[230] The Commission made one change: it revised its CPNI rules to require
that, for customers with more than 20 lines, BOC personnel involved in marketing enhanced services must obtain written authorization from the customer
before gaining access to its CPNI. This change eliminated the asymmetry in
the CPNI rules for large business customers, while leaving intact the efficiencies of joint marketing for smaller customers. The Commission concluded
that "large business customers" constituted a sufficiently "valuable market
segment" to make competitive equity worth pursuing even at the expense of
some efficiency. *Computer III Order on Remand*, 6 F.C.C. Rec. at 7612–7613
¶87.

[231] *California III*, 39 F.3d at 919.

[232] *Id.* at 923. Moreover, the implementation of price-cap regulation had
"reduce[d] any BOC's ability to shift costs from unregulated to regulated
activities, because the increase in costs for the regulated activity does not automatically cause an increase in the legal rate ceiling." *Id.* at 926–927 (citing
United States v. Western Elec. Co., 993 F.2d 1572, 1580 (D.C. Cir.), *cert. denied*,
114 S. Ct. 487 (U.S. 1993)).

Commission had retreated without adequate explanation from its *Computer II* position that only full ONA would prevent discrimination.[233] The FCC argued that other regulatory safeguards (CEI, nondiscrimination reporting requirements, and network disclosure rules) would prevent access discrimination even without full ONA, but the court found that it had not satisfactorily explained why it had taken a different position in *Computer III*.[234]

The Common Carrier Bureau responded by issuing an *Interim Waiver Order* granting the Bell companies a waiver of the *Computer II* rules to enable them to continue providing enhanced services on an integrated basis under existing CEI plans.[235] In October 1995, the Bureau denied petitions to reconsider its *Interim Waiver Order* and approved 12 CEI plans and 13 CEI plan amendments.[236] Meanwhile, in February 1995, the Commission opened a Computer III further remand proceeding to evaluate the nonstructural safeguards that were imposed on the BOCs in the *Computer III*/ONA framework to prevent discrimination.[237] This proceeding sat idle for over two years. Then Congress passed the 1996 Act.

§12.7.11 Structural Separation Under the 1996 Act

The 1996 Act says surprisingly little about information services in general. Indeed, as we discuss below, it says very much less than the Commission believes it says. And what it does say

---

[233] *California III,* 39 F.3d at 923.

[234] *Id.* at 929.

[235] *See* Bell Operating Companies' Joint Petition for Waiver of Computer II Rules, Memorandum Opinion and Order, 10 F.C.C. Rec. 1724 (1995) (hereinafter *Interim Waiver Order*).

[236] *See* Bell Operating Companies' Joint Petition for Waiver of Computer II Rules, Order, 10 F.C.C. Rec. 13,758 (1995).

[237] *See* Computer III Further Remand Proceedings: Bell Operating Company Provision of Enhanced Services, Notice of Proposed Rulemaking, 10 F.C.C. Rec. 8360 (1995).

flatly contradicts some key positions the Commission has taken in interpreting it.

The Act generally repeals the line-of-business restrictions imposed on BOCs by the Bell Divestiture Decree, including the information services ban. Precisely how Congress got to that point is important—essential, in fact—to interpreting the structural restrictions that the Act itself establishes as replacements for the Decree's.

The Senate proposed an original bill on March 30, 1995.[238] The Senate's basic approach was to leave the Decree restrictions in place and selectively remove or modify some of them. To that end, section 7(b) of the bill provided that the Communications Act was to supersede the Decree to the extent they are inconsistent.[239] This approach would have been more restrictive than the one that was ultimately adopted, which simply repealed the Decree.

Under the Senate's approach, the Decree's prohibition against the provision of information services by BOCs and BOC affiliates was to have remained in effect. The Senate bill merely stated that BOCs were to provide certain services, including information services, through separate affiliates.[240] This result is not as odd as it might at first seem. Judge Greene had the power to waive the restrictions related to information services and had done so on numerous occasions. The Senate bill simply authorized the Decree court to continue to enforce the Decree with respect to BOC provision of information services.

The House proposed a bill on May 3, 1995. The House's approach differed fundamentally from the Senate's. Instead of generally retaining the Decree's provisions, and then relaxing some of them, the House superseded the Decree in its entirety. The

[238] S. 652, 104th Cong., 1st Sess. (1995).

[239] *See* Joint Explanatory Statement of the Committee of Conference, H.R. Rep. No. 458, S. Rep. No. 230, 104th Cong., 2d Sess. 197 (1996).

[240] These services were (1) information services including alarm monitoring and cable services, other than those previously authorized information services; (2) manufacturing services; and (3) "interLATA services other than—(i) incidental services, not including information services; (ii) out-of-region services; or (iii) [previously authorized services]." S. 652, 104th Cong., 1st Sess. §102 (proposing new §252(a)(2)) (1995).

House then imposed on BOCs a new and different set of line-of-business restrictions. The bill did not impose restrictions on BOC provision of information services apart from requiring BOCs to provide those services through a separate subsidiary.

In the end, the House's conceptual approach prevailed. The Act "completely eliminate[d] the prospective effect of the AT&T Consent Decree."[241] The Act regulated all conduct that previously had been subject to the Decree's requirements, specifying that such conduct was no longer "subject to the restrictions and the obligations imposed by such Consent Decree."[242] Thus, the Act permits BOCs to engage in all activities that previously had been forbidden to them under the Decree, subject only to the Act's own explicit restrictions on that conduct.

§12.7.11.1 The Act's New Structural Requirements for Information Services Generally

The Act's new structural separation requirements are set out in sections 271–276,[243] which the Act collectively labels "Special Provisions Concerning Bell Operating Companies."[244] These new statutory line-of-business restrictions generally track the three categories of line-of-business prohibitions of the Divestiture Decree (although there are many differences in the details).

[241] Joint Explanatory Statement of the Committee of Conference, S. Conf. Rep. No. 230, 104th Cong., 2d Sess. 122 (1996).

[242] Pub. L. 104-104, Title VI, §601, 110 Stat. 143 (Feb. 8, 1996).

[243] 47 U.S.C. §§271–276.

[244] These "Special Provisions" twice have been attacked unsuccessfully as bills of attainder. BellSouth Corp. v. FCC, 144 F.3d 58 (D.C. Cir. 1998) (finding that the section 274 restriction on electronic publishing was "nothing more than a line-of-business restriction, comparable for example to the Glass-Steagall Act's limitation on the entry of commercial banks into investment banking, or to the cross-ownership restrictions on broadcasters upheld in FCC v. National Citizens Committee for Broadcasting" (citations omitted)); SBC Communications Inc. v. FCC, 1998 U.S. App. LEXIS 21646 (5th Cir. 1998) (holding that "the Special Provisions, viewed in terms of the type and severity of burdens imposed and the expressed intent of Congress, reasonably can be said to further nonpunitive legislative purposes such that the sanction at issue, a bar from participation in certain businesses, is neither historically nor functionally nor motivationally punitive," *id.* at *45.).

The Decree barred BOCs and their affiliates from (1) providing interexchange telecommunications services, (2) manufacturing or providing telecommunications products or customer premises equipment, and (3) providing information services.[245] Section 271 of the Act addresses BOC provision of "interLATA services." Section 273 addresses BOC "manufacturing" of telecommunications equipment and prohibits BOCs from engaging in these activities until they win section 271 interLATA relief. Sections 274 and 275 address two specific types of "information services"—electronic publishing and alarm services.

Buried in the middle of these line-of-business restrictions is section 272(a)(2), which addresses separate affiliate requirements for "interLATA telecommunications services," "manufacturing activities," and "interLATA information services."[246] Section 272(a)(2)(C) is the only clause that addresses structural separation for information services in general, and it requires such separation *only* for "*interLATA* information services" (other than electronic publishing and alarm monitoring services).[247] The Act makes no mention of intraLATA information services at all. Nor does the Act—unlike the Commission (see section 12.7.6 below)—draw any distinction between in-region and out-of-region interLATA information services. The Act plainly requires a separate subsidiary for both.[248] However, the separate subsidiary requirement will expire for all companies in 2000 unless the FCC extends it.[249]

As discussed in the following three sections, the 1996 Act imposes special structural safeguards on Bell companies that provide three categories of enhanced information services: electronic publishing, telemessaging, and alarm monitoring. Why did Congress single out these particular services? The FCC's explanation is that the local exchange market is not sufficiently

---

[245] *See Decree,* 552 F. Supp. at 227.

[246] 47 U.S.C. §272(a)(2)(A), (a)(2)(B), (a)(2)(C), respectively.

[247] *Id.* §272(a)(2)(C) (emphasis added).

[248] BOC interLATA information services already being offered when the Act was passed were exempted from the separate subsidiary requirement for a one-year "transition period."

[249] 47 U.S.C. §272(f)(2).

competitive to permit the Bell companies to provide these most important services without certain special safeguards.[250] A cynic might contend that the electronic publishing, telemessaging, and alarm monitoring industries mustered powerful lobbies and thus were able to extract extra measures of security from Congress. The Act's legislative history provides no good explanation as to why the *Computer II/III* rules, which essentially were retained elsewhere, could not adequately protect against anticompetitive conduct with respect to these services.

§12.7.11.2 The Act's Special Structural Requirements for Electronic Publishing

Section 274 of the 1996 Act separately addresses BOC provision of electronic publishing.[251] It defines what electronic publishing may include (things like the distribution of news, entertainment, and business information) and many other things that it may not (including voice mail, e-mail, Caller ID, and video programming).[252] The Act requires structural separation of Bell Company electronic publishing services *only* if those

---

[250] *See, e.g.,* Implementation of the Telecommunications Act of 1996: Telemessaging, Electronic Publishing, and Alarm Monitoring Services, First Report and Order and Further Notice of Proposed Rulemaking, 12 F.C.C. Rec. 5361 (1997) (hereinafter *Electronic Publishing Order*). "In enacting sections 260 and 274, Congress recognized that the local exchange market will not be fully competitive immediately. Congress therefore imposed requirements applicable to local exchange carriers' [ ] provision of telemessaging services in section 260, and a series of requirements applicable to Bell Operating Companies' (BOCs') provision of electronic publishing services in section 274. Collectively, these requirements are designed to prevent, or facilitate the detection of, improper cost allocation, discrimination, or other anticompetitive conduct." *Id.* at 5363 ¶3.

[251] 47 U.S.C. §274.

[252] *See id.* §274(h)(1), (2). Section 274(h)(2) sets forth a detailed list of services that are excluded from the definition of "electronic publishing": common carrier provision of telecommunications service, information access service, information gateway service, voice storage and retrieval, electronic mail, certain data and transaction processing services, electronic billing or advertising of a Bell Company's regulated telecommunications services, language translation or data format conversion, white pages directory assistance,

services are delivered over the BOC's own access lines.[253] The separation requirements for in-region electronic publishing differ slightly from those for interLATA information services, see section 12.7.6 below, simply because Congress wanted to codify agreements that had been struck between the Bell companies and publishers. For instance, the Commission may not extend the duration of the electronic publishing separation provisions beyond four years,[254] while it may extend the separation requirements for interLATA information services indefinitely.[255] And the BOCs are precluded from hiring or training personnel, engaging in equipment installation and maintenance, or conducting research and development on behalf of electronic publishing affiliates,[256] while for interLATA information services the BOCs need only maintain an arm's-length relationship with the affiliate.[257] Joint marketing for electronic publishing is forbidden, except in the case of ventures in which the Bell Company has a noncontrolling interest,[258] while there is no such prohibition for information services.[259] As with interLATA information services, however, existing electronic publishing services are grandfathered for the first year after enactment of the legislation.[260]

Section 274 does not require Bell Company electronic publishing (even if provided on an interLATA basis) to be provided through section 272 affiliates, but it does require a Bell Company that uses its own facilities to provide electronic publishing service to comply with certain specified separate affiliate requirements.[261] This left to the Commission the job of distinguishing

---

Caller ID services, repair and provisioning databases, and credit card and billing validation for telephone programming and full-motion video entertainment on demand.

[253] *Id.* §274(a),(b).
[254] *Id.* §274(g)(2).
[255] *Id.* §272(f)(2).
[256] *Id.* §274(b)(7), (c)(2)(C).
[257] *Id.* §272(b)(5).
[258] *Id.* §274(c).
[259] *Id.* §272(g).
[260] *Id.* §274(g)(1).
[261] *Id.* §274(b).

"information services subject to the Section 272 requirements from electronic publishing services subject to the Section 274 requirements."[262] The Commission opted for a process of ad hoc determinations. In making a determination, "the Commission may consider a number of factors, including whether the BOC controls, or has a financial interest in, the content of information transmitted to end-users."[263] The Commission did clarify that BOC provision of "introductory World Wide Web home pages, other types of introductory information, and software (such as browsers)" was not electronic publishing.[264]

The Commission has ruled that "electronic publishing services may include services provided through the Internet or through proprietary data networks."[265] But to be subject to section 274, a BOC must both (1) "disseminate the information via its basic telephone service (as defined by section 274(i)(2))"[266] and (2) "have control of, or a financial interest in, the content of the information being provided." "[C]ontrol of, or a financial interest in, the content of information alone, *without BOC dissemination of information,* is not electronic publishing under section 274."[267] Further, "'dissemination' means the transmission of information via a BOC or its affiliate's basic telephone service to the Internet, rather than the transmission of information to the end user. Thus, a BOC that is providing Internet access services to end users, and nothing more, is not engaged in the provision of electronic publishing pursuant to Section 274."[268]

Although the separate affiliate requirements of section 274 are not as stringent as those of *Computer II,* section 274 does turn

---

[262] *Non-accounting Safeguards Order,* 11 F.C.C. Rec. at 21,972–21,973 ¶138.
[263] *Id.*
[264] *Electronic Publishing Order,* 12 F.C.C. Rec. at 5379–5380 ¶46.
[265] *Id.*
[266] Section 274(i)(2) defines "basic telephone service" as any wireline telephone exchange service or facility provided by a BOC in a telephone exchange area, but not including a competitive wireline telephone exchange service or a commercial mobile service.
[267] *Electronic Publishing Order,* 12 F.C.C. Rec. at 5385 ¶56 (emphasis added).
[268] *Id.* at 5384 ¶54.

back the clock somewhat. Since the electronic publishing industry is vibrantly competitive today, requiring separate affiliates is far less appropriate than at the time of *Computer II*.

§12.7.11.3 The Act's Special Structural Requirements for Alarm Monitoring

Section 275 of the 1996 Act deals with the provision of "alarm monitoring services" by BOCs. "Alarm monitoring" is defined as a service that detects and transmits information about threats to personal or property safety to remote monitoring locations.[269] BOCs are generally prohibited from providing alarm monitoring for five years from enactment, although existing services are grandfathered.[270] The Act treats BOC alarm monitoring services as an "incidental" service, exempt from the in-region interLATA restriction and section 272 separate affiliate requirements. But unlike electronic publishing, BOC alarm monitoring operations are not subject to alternative separate affiliate requirements. Instead, like telemessaging, they are subject only to general prohibitions against discrimination and cross-subsidizing and the *Computer III* rules.[271]

§12.7.11.4 The Act's Special Structural Requirements for Telemessaging

Section 260 of the 1996 Act separately addresses the provision of "telemessaging service" by local exchange carriers. It defines "telemessaging" as "voice mail and voice storage and retrieval services, any live operator services used to record, transcribe, or relay messages (other than telecommunications relay services), and any ancillary services offered in combination with these services."[272] Section 260 prohibits LECs from subsidizing telemessaging with local exchange revenues and from discriminating in

---

[269] *See* 47 U.S.C. §275(e).
[270] 47 U.S.C. §275(a).
[271] 47 U.S.C. §275(b); Implementation of the 1996 Telecommunications Act: Telemessaging, Electronic Publishing, and Alarm Monitoring Services, Second Report and Order, 12 F.C.C. Rec. 3824 (1997).
[272] 47 U.S.C. §260(c).

favor of their own telemessaging operations. Unlike electronic publishing, section 260 does not have its own separate affiliate requirements to add teeth to these prohibitions. The Commission, however, has concluded that "telemessaging" is an information service that is subject to the section 272 separate affiliate requirements when provided on an interLATA basis.[273] Moreover, telemessaging, like all other enhanced services, is subject to restrictions imposed by *Computer III*.

§12.7.11.5 BOC Provision of IntraLATA Information Services Under the 1996 Act

In December 1996, the Commission announced "plan[s] to issue a Further Notice in [*Computer III*] to determine how to regulate BOC provision of intraLATA information services in light of the 1996 Act."[274] In January 1998, the Commission issued the long-awaited *Further Notice* to reconsider, "[i]n light of the 1996 Act and ensuing changes in telecommunications technologies and markets," the regulation of BOC provision of intraLATA information services.[275]

As noted in section 12.5.3 above, the Commission's *Further Notice* purported to conclude that its ONA/CEI interconnection rules still applied. But the Commission in effect acknowledged that they had been superseded by the unbundling and interconnection mandates of the 1996 Act.

The Commission went on to consider the impact of the 1996 Act on its structural separation rules. The Commission again noted, correctly, that the 1996 Act does not "explicitly displace the safeguards established by the Commission in the *Computer II, Computer III*, and ONA proceedings."[276] The Commission's *Further Notice* accordingly addressed the "issues raised by the interplay between the safeguards and terminology established in the

---

[273] *Non-accounting Safeguards Order,* 11 F.C.C. Rec. at 21,975–21,976 ¶¶144–145.
[274] *Id.* at 21,970 ¶133.
[275] *See Computer III Remand Further Notice,* 13 F.C.C. Rec. at 6045–6046 ¶5.
[276] *Id.*

1996 Act and the *Computer III* regime."[277] The Commission noted that the Act imposes no separate subsidiary requirements on Bell companies' provision of intraLATA information services. The Commission nevertheless concluded that it should continue to apply its nonstructural safeguards regime.[278] The Commission did, however, in light of the statutory omission of intraLATA information services, tentatively reject a proposal it had made in the Computer III further remand proceedings to reimpose some form of structural separation on BOC provision of intra-LATA information services.

§12.7.11.6   InterLATA Information Services

For the first seven years of Decree jurisprudence, BOCs were doubly prohibited from providing interLATA information services. Doing so ran afoul of both the information services restriction and the interLATA services restriction. Although the D.C. Circuit eliminated the former in 1991 (see section 12.7.5 above), the interLATA restriction remained. It barred BOCs from providing interLATA "telecommunications," which the Decree defined very broadly to cover every conceivable inter-LATA facility and service.[279] Judge Greene construed the inter-LATA restriction as precluding the BOCs from selecting an interexchange carrier for the delivery of some (but not all) information services to end users and from bundling interexchange transport with some (but not all) information services. That decision was affirmed on appeal.[280]

---

[277] *Id.*

[278] *Id.* at 6046–6047 ¶7; *see also id.* at 6067–6076 ¶¶43–59.

[279] "Telecommunications" means "the transmission, between or among points specified by the user, of information of the user's choosing, without change in the form or content of the information as sent and received, by means of electromagnetic transmission medium, including all instrumental-ities, facilities, apparatus, and services (including the collection, storage, for-warding, switching, and delivery of such information) essential to such transmission." *Decree* §IV(O), 552 F. Supp. at 229.

[280] *See* United States v. Western Elec. Co., 1989-1 Trade Cas. (CCH) ¶68,400, *aff'd,* 907 F.2d 160 (D.C. Cir. 1990), *cert. denied,* 498 U.S. 1109 (1991); *see also* United States v. Western Elec. Co., 12 F.3d 225, 232 (D.C. Cir. 1993) (Decree prohibits "arrangements, contractual or otherwise, in which the BOCs

When the 1996 Act was enacted, a request for an interLATA information services waiver that the seven BOCs had negotiated with the Department was pending before the Decree court. The waiver would have allowed Bell companies to resell interexchange services in connection with their provision of certain categories of information services, including electronic publishing, e-mail, purchase/reservation services, voice mail and audiotext services that use voice storage technology, and "live" operator services.[281] The district court declared it would address the waiver request "in due course," which appeared to be a signal that it would not act while Congress was debating telecom legislation.[282] Congress passed the 1996 Act, the Decree was superseded in its entirety, and that was the end of the waiver.

The 1996 Act does *not* expressly prohibit BOC provision of interLATA information services. The Commission has, however, read such a restriction into the Act. As a result, a BOC (or its affiliate) may not currently provide interLATA information services that originate within the BOC's region until it obtains section 271 authority. This result is arguably at odds with the Act itself, and with the Commission's other interpretations of the Act, though no court has yet made such a finding.

(i) The Language and Structure of the 1996 Act. Section 271(a) of the Act prohibits a BOC (or its affiliate) to "provide interLATA services" that originate within its region absent prior FCC approval. The scope of the section 271(a) prohibition is

---

have a direct and continuing share in the revenues of entities engaged in prohibited businesses").

[281] The waiver would have authorized BOCs to provide "the interexchange connections needed to connect the Bell company's information service customers with centralized facilities owned and operated by the Bell company and used for the provision of the [specified] information services. . . ." Proposed Order at 1, United States v. Western Elec. Co., No. 82-0192 (D.D.C. Apr. 24, 1995). This relief, the BOCs stated, would allow "BOC customers in one LATA [to] access BOC information services in another LATA by using the Internet." No party disputed that view in subsequent briefing on the BOCs' request.

[282] Order, United States v. Western Elec. Co., No. 82-0192 (D.D.C. Sept. 8, 1995) (approving Ameritech purchase of Guardian Corp.).

established by the Act's express definition of "interLATA services" as "telecommunications between a point located in a local
access and transport area and a point located outside such
area."[283] Thus, according to the plain language of the statute, the
prohibition of section 271(a) applies only when a BOC (or its
affiliate) *"provide[s]" "telecommunications."*[284]

As the Commission has recognized, "information services" do
not include "providing telecommunications." The two are mutually exclusive activities. In its *Report to Congress,* the Commission
conclusively established that a provider of information services
is *not* "providing telecommunications" when it acquires the necessarily included transmission capacity from another firm's
transmission facilities and bundles it into the end-user information service offered at a single price. Such an information service
provider is *using* telecommunications, not *providing* telecommunications. It is the company engaged in the provision of
transmission capacity *to* information service providers that is
providing telecommunications.[285] See section 12.2.3 above. Thus,

---

[283] 47 U.S.C. §153(21).

[284] This explicitly defined limitation of "interLATA services" to telecommunications is consistent with congressional intent. The legislative history
supports the conclusion that Congress intended section 271's restrictions to
apply only to interLATA telecommunications services. As noted above, the
Senate bill hardly addressed information services at all, other than requiring
separate subsidiaries. It was entirely silent on allowing BOCs to provide inter-
LATA information services. In addition, the Senate Report specified that
information service providers "do not *'provide'* telecommunications services;
they are *users* of telecommunications services." S. Rep. 230, 104th Cong., 2d
Sess. XX (1996) (emphasis added). The House bill, which Congress ultimately
adopted with some modifications, likewise contained no independent *general*
interLATA information services restriction, and it explicitly excluded information services from its definition of "telecommunications service."

[285] *Report to Congress,* 13 F.C.C. Rec. 11,501. "After careful consideration [in
the *Universal Service Order* and the *Non-accounting Safeguards Order*] of the
statutory language and its legislative history, we affirm our prior findings that
the categories of 'telecommunications service' and 'information service' in the
1996 Act are mutually exclusive. Under this interpretation, an entity offering
a simple, transparent transmission path, without the capability of providing
enhanced functionality, offers 'telecommunications.' By contrast, when an
entity offers transmission incorporating the 'capability for generating, acquiring, storing, transforming, processing, retrieving, utilizing, or making available information,' it does not offer telecommunications. Rather, it offers an

section 271's prohibition on BOC provision of "interLATA services" only prohibits the provision of interLATA telecommunications services and should not prevent the BOCs from providing interLATA information services.

This conclusion is reinforced in two ways by the structure of the Act. First, section 272(a)(2) breaks down the types of services for which a separate subsidiary is required: paragraph (A) covers "manufacturing activities," paragraph (B) covers origination of "interLATA telecommunications services," and paragraph (C) covers "[i]nterLATA information services." That breakdown itself confirms that Congress meant to distinguish between interLATA telecommunications services and interLATA information services.[286]

Second, section 272(f) establishes the "sunset" dates of the separate subsidiary requirements. Paragraph (1) sets sunset dates for manufacturing and "interLATA telecommunications services" three years after the date on which the BOC or its affiliate "is authorized to provide interLATA telecommunications services under section 271(d)" (unless the Commission extends the date). Paragraph (2) separately provides for a sunset for "interLATA information services" four years after enactment of the 1996 Act (unless extended). Paragraph (1)'s reference to section 271(d) confirms that "interLATA services" are only telecommunications—section 271(d) provides for a single application for authority to originate "interLATA services." In contrast, paragraph (2) ties the sunset of the restrictions on interLATA information services to the enactment of the 1996 Act, *not* to the date on which in-region entry is allowed under section 271 (as in paragraph (1)). This underscores Congress's intent that section 271 have no application to "interLATA information services."

'information service' even though it uses telecommunications to do so." *Report to Congress,* 13 F.C.C. Rec. 11,501, 11,520 ¶39 (footnote omitted); *see also id.* at 11,520–11,521 ¶40; §12.2.2.

[286] Moreover, only paragraph (B)'s "interLATA telecommunications services" category refers to section 271; paragraph (C)'s "interLATA information services" category makes no such reference. Similarly, only paragraph (B) speaks of "origination" as opposed to termination of services, a distinction that plays a vital role under section 271.

(ii) The Commission's Interpretation of Section 271(a) "Inter-LATA Services."   Despite the clear statutory language and structure, the Commission ruled in its *Non-accounting Safeguards Order* that the section 271(a) bar on BOC provision of "interLATA services" applies not only to telecommunications services, but also to information services.[287] It set forth its affirmative explanation for that conclusion in just one paragraph.[288]

First, the Commission concluded that since an interLATA information service must include a "bundled, interLATA transmission component," it follows that "interLATA information services are provided *via interLATA telecommunications* transmissions and, accordingly, fall within the definition of 'interLATA service.'"[289] But the Commission has now thoroughly and repeatedly explained, in the *Report to Congress,* that the "accordingly" does not follow at all. That information services are provided "via telecommunications" means that providers of such services *use* telecommunications, not that they *provide* telecommunications. And *providing* telecommunications is expressly required by the statutory definition of "interLATA services."

Second, the Commission said: "we believe that it is a more natural, common-sense reading of 'interLATA services' to interpret it to include both telecommunications services and information services." But it is well settled that a "natural, common-sense" meaning does not control when statutory terms are given express statutory definition.[290] Still less can such express definitions be

---

[287] *Non-accounting Safeguards Order,* 11 F.C.C. Rec. at 21,932–21,933 ¶¶55–57 (interpreting 47 U.S.C. §271(a)). However, the Commission did not comprehensively address BOC provision of Internet services. *Id.* at 21,967–21,968 ¶127. It went on to rule that if a BOC's provision of an Internet or Internet access service "incorporates a bundled, in-region, interLATA transmission component provided by the BOC over its own facilities or through resale, that service may only be provided through a section 272 affiliate, after the BOC has received in-region interLATA authority under section 271." It refused to consider whether various specific Internet services qualified as "interLATA information services," leaving such determinations to be made on a case-by-case basis. *Id.*

[288] *Id.* at 21,932–21,933 ¶56.

[289] *Id.* (emphasis added).

[290] The Commission elsewhere has recognized that "[t]he specific obligations of the 1996 Act depend on application of the statutory categories established in the Act's definitions section." Deployment of Wireline Services

ignored when they are in no sense anomalies in the statute, but accord with other provisions.

Third, the Commission found support in the fact that section 272(a)(2) uses the language "interLATA telecommunications services" and contrasts it with "interLATA information services." The FCC reasoned that since the Act distinguishes between the two terms, "[Congress] limited the term 'interLATA services' to transmission services when it wished to." Moreover, the Commission noted, "if Congress had intended the term 'interLATA services' to include only interLATA telecommunications services, its use of the term 'interLATA telecommunications services' in Section 272(a)(2) would have been unnecessary and redundant."[291]

The Commission's reasoning is obscure. Section 272(a)(2) supports the distinctness of information services and telecommunications services, as the Commission fully confirmed in the *Report to Congress*. And the most natural inference from the provision's use of "interLATA telecommunications services," rather than simply "interLATA services," is not that it chose a substantively narrower phrase, but that it was using a substantively equivalent phrase to highlight the contrast with "interLATA information services."

Moreover, the Commission's view that "interLATA information services" are "interLATA services" covered by section 271 produces an internal contradiction within section 272(a)(2). Section 272(a)(2)(B) specifically says that no separate subsidiary is required for out-of-region interLATA services covered by section 271. In contrast, section 272(a)(2)(C) requires a separate

---

Offering Advanced Telecommunications Capability, Memorandum Opinion and Order and Notice of Proposed Rulemaking, CC Docket No. 98-147, ¶33 (Aug. 7, 1998) (footnote citing 47 U.S.C. §153); *see Report to Congress,* 13 F.C.C. Rec. at 11,511 ¶21. And the law is settled that such definitions of what a term "means" have control even over what might otherwise be "natural" or "ordinary" meanings. *See, e.g.,* Gustafson v. Alloyd Co., 513 U.S. 561 (1995); FDIC v. Meyer, 510 U.S. 471 (1994); Smith v. United States, 508 U.S. 223 (1993); Colautti v. Franklin, 439 U.S. 379, 392 n.10 (1979) (quoting C. Sands, Statutes and Statutory Construction §47.07 (4th ed. Supp. 1982)); American Mining Congress v. EPA, 824 F.2d 1177, 1189 (D.C. Cir. 1987); National Wildlife Fedn. v. Gorsuch, 693 F.2d 156, 172 (D.C. Cir. 1982).

[291] *Non-accounting Safeguards Order,* 11 F.C.C. Rec. at 21,933 ¶56.

subsidiary in blanket fashion for all "interLATA information services" (except electronic publishing and alarm-monitoring services addressed in sections 274 and 275). The Commission's view reads the latter as immediately taking back a freedom just granted in the former—by requiring a separate subsidiary for out-of-region interLATA *information* services—even though there is no textual indication of any such relation between the provisions. Such a result is plainly to be avoided as unnatural and unlikely.[292]

(iii) "InterLATA Services" Under Section 271(g).   An additional argument supporting interpretation of "interLATA services" to include "interLATA information services" was raised in the few (unsolicited) comments that the Commission received in the *Non-accounting Safeguards Order.*[293] This argument was based on section 271's treatment of "incidental interLATA services." Section 271(b)(3) says that a BOC (or affiliate) may provide "incidental interLATA services (as defined in subsection (g))." Section 271(g) then defines "incidental interLATA services" to mean any of a fixed list of services. The argument made to the Commission was that since some items on the list are necessarily information

---

[292] The Commission saw no conflict, concluding "that the exception created by section 272(a)(2)(B)(ii) extends only to out-of-region interLATA services that are telecommunications services." *Id.* at 21,946–21,947 ¶86. The Commission went on to assert that, regardless of whether "interLATA services" include interLATA information services, section 271(a) *still* would bar BOCs from providing interLATA information services. The Commission maintained that "interLATA information service" "refers to an information service that incorporates as a necessary, bundled element an interLATA telecommunications transmission component provided to the customer for a single charge." *Id.* at 21,933 ¶57. According to the Commission, a BOC is "required to obtain section 271 authorization prior to providing, in-region, the interLATA telecommunications transmission component of an interLATA information service." *Id.* Again, this contradicts the distinction drawn in the *Report to Congress.* However, it allows BOCs to provide some types of information services without obtaining section 271 approval. For example, BOCs may offer an information service accessible across LATA boundaries, so long as the customers obtain the interLATA transmission necessary to access the service from an interexchange carrier not affiliated with the BOC. *Id.* at 21,963–21,965 ¶120–122. In the Commission's view, such a service is not an interLATA information service because it is unbundled. *Id.*

[293] *Id.* at 21,931–21,932 ¶53.

services, "interLATA services" must include information services. The Commission, however, wisely did not rely on this argument in explaining its conclusion. Indeed, the section 271(g) list could not justify the inference that the basic prohibition of section 271(a) encompasses information services, given the express congressional limitation to the contrary.[294]

In any event, the attenuated argument based on section 271(g) never gets off the ground. The argument requires, as its logical starting point, that there be no plausible interpretation of the section 271(g) items as addressing *telecommunications*. If section 271(g) plausibly can be so understood, then the entire chain of negative inference breaks at its very first link. In fact, section 271(g) is readily understood in just such a manner. Congress was making sure that certain services that might otherwise have been barred as the interLATA provision of telecommunications were excluded from section 271(a)'s prohibition. The Commission itself has recognized that, "[f]or the most part, the incidental interLATA services . . . are telecommunications services."[295]

---

[294] This type of indirect negative inference, even if it rested on a correct characterization of section 271(g), could not fairly justify overriding the expressly defined meaning of "interLATA services." After all, this argument is not offered to support one among several reasonable interpretations; it is offered simply to contradict the definition. Here, moreover, it would be especially implausible to rely on a provision that *authorizes* service to *tighten* the *prohibition* of section 271(a) beyond its explicit meaning.

[295] *Non-accounting Safeguards Order*, 11 F.C.C. Rec. at 21,950–21,951 ¶94 (footnote omitted). For example, wireless services (item (3)) are undoubtedly telecommunications. *See Universal Service Order*, 12 F.C.C. Rec. at 9175 ¶780. Network signaling (items (5), (6)), which is independently excluded from the definition of "information services," often would involve pure transmission of user-chosen information without change of form or content. Audio or video programming services (items (1)(A)–(C)) are generally treated as broadcast or cable services under Title III of the Communications Act and not as "information services"; they can easily be offered as common carrier transmission services. *See* Implementation of Section 302 of the Telecommunications Act of 1996, Open Video Systems, Second Order on Reconsideration, 12 F.C.C. Rec. 6258, 6259 ¶3 (1997); Bell Atlantic Video Services, Inc., 12 F.C.C. Rec. 9892, 9896 ¶10 & n.30 (1997). The Commission reserved the question whether video programming services are "information services" in Implementation of Section 302 of the Telecommunications Act of 1996, Second Report and Order, 11 F.C.C. Rec. 18,223, 18,347–18,348 ¶249 (1997).

§12.7.11.7   Services That Look "InterLATA" But Are Not

Though the Commission has broadly interpreted the Act's definition of "interLATA service" to include all interLATA information services, the Commission has been more cautious in determining what falls on the "interLATA" side of the line.

(i) BOC "Teaming Arrangements" with Unaffiliated InterLATA Carriers. The Commission ruled in the *Non-accounting Safeguards Order* that the 1996 Telecommunications Act does not, in principle, prevent a Bell Company and a nonaffiliate from entering into "teaming" activities in order to provide interLATA services before the Bell Company receives section 271 approval. Such "teaming" arrangements are acceptable, however, only if they comply with "any equal access requirements pertaining to 'teaming' activities that were imposed by the [Decree]."[296]

As a result, BOCs currently provide local Internet access services without providing or reselling interLATA Internet carriage, consistent with section 271(b)(1) and equal access requirements. In some arrangements, BOC Internet customers select a preferred interLATA Internet provider, just as BOC local exchange customers select a presubscribed interexchange (long-distance) carrier for their home phone. The BOC bills the customer for the interexchange carrier fees.[297] Commenters had contended that Bell Atlantic would be "engaged in the unlawful resale of interLATA service through its proposed [Internet access service] offering" because "end users will use Bell Atlantic's proposed service to access computer servers that may be located in the same state, a different state, or another country."[298] The Common Carrier Bureau rejected these arguments.[299] In the non-

---

[296] *Non-accounting Safeguards Order,* 11 F.C.C. Rec. at 22,047 ¶293.

[297] The Common Carrier Bureau approved BOC plans to provide Internet access service under this arrangement. *See, e.g.,* Bell Atlantic Telephone Companies Offer of Comparably Efficient Interconnection to Providers of Internet Access Services, 11 F.C.C. Rec. 6919 (1996).

[298] *See id.* at 6935 ¶48.

[299] Bell Atlantic's service would "not involve the resale of interLATA services," the Commission concluded, because "[t]o connect or transmit to Internet

accounting safeguards rulemaking, commenters asked the Commission to revisit the issue, but the Commission declined. Instead, it ruled that it would determine on a "case-by-case basis" whether specific Internet services provided by BOCs are "interLATA information services."[300]

(ii) Online Directories and Yellow Pages. Directories, reverse directories (for obtaining a name and address from a telephone number), and comparable Web-based services of natural interest to phone companies[301] and their competitors probably rank as "electronic publishing" subject to section 274. But since phone companies can place the servers that provide such directories out-of-region, they can then make a plausible argument that the service is not subject to section 274's structural separation requirements because information from the site is not "disseminated" via their "basic telephone service." And in the reverse situation, connecting a server to the Web (via an intraLATA trunk of some sort) is not in itself the provision of interLATA transmission, so it cannot possibly run afoul of section 271. End users, wherever located, may cross LATA boundaries to obtain access to these servers, i.e., the databases providing the information, but it is their Internet service provider that carries their transmission to the server. Thus, while the matter is not definitively settled, these directory services will likely be treated as intraLATA services.[302]

---

servers or facilities located in other LATAs, the end user customer must have a pre-existing arrangement with an interLATA Internet provider." *Id.* at 6936 ¶50.

[300] *Non-accounting Safeguards Order,* 11 F.C.C. Rec. at 21,967–21,968 ¶127.

[301] Many of these services have been provided on an interLATA basis by the BOCs directory since before the 1996 Act. *See* United States v. Western Elec. Co., 569 F. Supp. 1057, 1097–1101 (D.D.C.), *aff'd mem. sub nom.* California v. United States, 464 U.S. 1013 (1983). *See also* Bell Operating Companies' Joint Petition for Waiver of Computer II Rules, 10 F.C.C. Rec. 13,758, 13,769 ¶77 (1995) (NYNEX CEI plan for online yellow pages service); Pleading Cycle Established for Comments on Bell Atlantic's Request for Extension of Its Market Trial for Internet Electronic Yellow Pages, 11 F.C.C. Rec. 13,486 (1996) (describing service).

[302] The Commission has determined that an analogous arrangement is an intraLATA information service. Bell Operating Companies; Petitions for Forbearance from the Application of Section 272, 13 F.C.C. Rec. 2627 (1998).

(iii) Hypertext Links and "Surf and Call."   Hypertext links incorporated in Web pages maintained by BOCs should not involve BOCs in the provision of interLATA services. Each time a user clicks on a hypertext or a "surf and call" link, a new connection is established between the end user and the Web server that the user seeks to access. The connection is not routed through the owner of the page or the Web server that contains the hypertext link. The transmission of the link address from the page back to the user is no different in kind from the transmission to the end user of any other information from the Web site—it is the equivalent of handing out a directory number on the Web. The location of the Web server is not relevant; regardless of whether the server is located in- or out-of-region, the BOC provides no interLATA service.

BOC marketing of Web services that include surf-and-call links also should not be a problem. Under Decree precedent, Bell companies were prohibited from "engaging in activities that comprise the business of providing interexchange services."[303] Thus, BOCs were not to select a facilities-based carrier for end users, procure interexchange services for end users, or market interexchange services to end users.[304] But even assuming that these marketing restrictions remain in effect after the passage of the 1996 Act, marketing "surf and call" links to businesses would not involve a BOC in the business of providing interexchange services. No particular interexchange carrier would be associated with an individual link by the BOC. Each end user that establishes a connection as a result of a "surf and call" link will be

There, the Commission considered, among other things, a "regional electronic reverse directory service" provided by a centralized BellSouth database. *Id.* at 2655 ¶55, 2656–2657 ¶61. Subscribers obtain access to BellSouth's centralized database through a separate interexchange carrier, so BellSouth does not provide any interLATA transmission associated with the service. *Id.* at 2655 ¶57. The Commission concluded that since subscribers purchase the directory service "separately from the interLATA transmissions that allow the subscriber to communicate with BellSouth's centralized database," the reverse directory service was an "intraLATA information service that BellSouth need not provide through a separate affiliate." *Id.* at 2656–2657 ¶61.

[303] United States v. Western Elec. Co., 627 F. Supp. 1090, 1099–1101 (D.D.C.), *appeal dismissed in relevant part,* 797 F.2d 1082 (D.C. Cir. 1986).
[304] *Id.*

using its own ISP (and the Internet backbone provider that the ISP selects or, in the case of a Bell Company ISP, that the end user selects) to establish its Internet connection. Although the BOC would be involved indirectly in promoting the Internet as an alternative to traditional long distance, it would not promote any particular interexchange carrier over another, which is the activity at which the Decree's equal access provisions were directed.

§12.8   Outlook

The Communications Act of 1934 divided the universe of electronic communications into two categories: (1) "common carrier" services, which were regulated in Title II of the 1934 Act, 47 U.S.C. §§201 et seq., and (2) "broadcast" or "radio" services, which were regulated in Title III, *id.* §§301 et seq. In the 1960s, the FCC encountered the problem of how to regulate what was then a new phenomenon—the connection of computers to telephone lines.[305] *Computer II* adopted a regulatory scheme that distinguished between a common carrier's offering of "basic transmission services" and its offering of "enhanced services." Basic services were regulated under Title II of the 1934 Act, but enhanced services were not.[306] Although it implements fundamental change, the Telecommunications Act of 1996 preserves this traditional regulatory taxonomy. Title II of the 1996 Act continues to regulate common carrier services, while Title III ad-

---

[305] At around this time, the Commission also was grappling with how to regulate the emerging cable industry. At first, the Commission declined to assert federal jurisdiction over cable. *See* Frontier Broadcasting Co. v. Collier, Memorandum Opinion and Order, 24 F.C.C. 251 (1958); CATV and TV Reporter Services, Report and Order, 26 F.C.C. 403 (1959). Several years later the Commission exerted federal jurisdiction over cable, though it never precisely categorized cable as either a common carrier or a broadcasting service. After 20 years of fighting over jurisdiction, Congress passed the 1984 Cable Act granting the FCC jurisdiction over cable services as a new service category, distinct from both common carriage and broadcasting. *See* 47 U.S.C. §522(6)(A).

[306] *Computer II*, 77 F.C.C.2d at 428 ¶114; *see also id.* at 428–430 ¶¶114–118.

dresses broadcasting. Within Title II, "telecommunications services" continue to be separated from "information services."

Over the years, both Congress and the FCC have done what they could to maintain the lines between the various categories of service, subjecting each to very different regulations regarding the character, quality, and price of service offered; the content conveyed; and so forth. "Common carriage" and "broadcast," for example, remain quite separate regulatory categories;[307] carriers are strictly *required* to provide service in ways that are strictly *forbidden* to broadcasters. At the same time, a single company may be legally permitted to provide two or more separate services, subject to certain restrictions.

Within telecommunications regulation, the FCC has toiled to draw clear, stable lines between basic and enhanced services for over two decades. It has yet to meet with success. Indeed, the only clear lesson that has been learned is that all such lines are arbitrary, and become increasingly so year by year.

In the 1920s, the great "enhancement" in telephony was the dial telephone. People's names were replaced by numbers, and the whole system operated much faster and more efficiently. Telephone dialing must surely have seemed a remarkably sophisticated convenience at the time—a level of automation and transparency never dreamed of before. When touch-tone service was introduced in the 1960s, it, too, was a novel enhancement for which affluent users paid extra. Today, equipment located in computers, phone handsets, central office switches, or elsewhere will readily dial numbers in response to spoken commands. Callers are once again able to lift a handset, speak a name, and be connected without more ado. Telephony, in short, has become as convenient as it was in 1910, before telephones had dials. But the new convenience is, of course, an "enhancement," an "information service," or will certainly become one if offered in the network with enough fancy features piled on.

Similar issues arise again and again. Machines communicate with other machines through a vast array of different kinds of

[307] 47 U.S.C. §153(10) ("a person engaged in radio broadcasting shall not, insofar as such person is so engaged, be deemed a common carrier").

translators. We may anticipate in the not too distant future a machine that can serve as a passable translator between English and Japanese. And it will be possible, of course, to locate such a machine on either side of the Pacific, depending on which regulatory environment is more willing to accept it.

The convergence of computers and telephones, of broadcast and telephony, of basic and enhanced services, of local and interstate services will continue so long as the underlying technology continues to develop. Each important new technological development will be found to run afoul of some old regulatory line. The question each time will be whether it is technology or regulation that must give way.

13

Video Services[*]

§13.1 Introduction

The first and most obvious overlap between telephone service and cable television involved nothing more elaborate than the telephone pole. Running wires across communities is expensive, and local authorities invariably regulate—often very tightly—who may run wires where. Early cable operators thus sought to piggyback their networks on the poles and underground conduits already in place—owned, of course, by established telephone and electric companies.[1] Telcos already provided access

[*] This chapter was co-authored by Samuel L. Feder, Associate, Kellogg, Huber, Hansen, Todd & Evans; College of William and Mary (A.B., *cum laude*, 1992); University of Michigan (J.D., *summa cum laude*, 1995); Order of the Coif; Daniel H. Grady Prize; Class of 1908 Award; Maurice Weigle Award; Law Clerk, Honorable Edward R. Becker, U.S. Court of Appeals, Third Circuit, 1995–1996.
[1] Cable television in the United States originated in hilly, rural areas in the late 1940s and 1950s. The terrain made television reception poor or nonexistent; entrepreneurs therefore began to build large "community antennas" on hilltops, on tall buildings, and on masts to pull in distant signals and then distribute them by wire. The first commercial cable (or CATV) system originated in Lansford, Pennsylvania, in 1950. *See* Ferris, Lloyd, & Casey, 1 Cable Television Law: A Video Communications Practice Guide ¶5.03 n.6 (1989) (hereinafter *Cable TV Law*).

to their poles for Western Union's telegraph services, as well as for some governmental facilities.

In 1964, the Bell System concluded that cable presented a serious threat to its position as the nation's dominant communications carrier; an internal company report raised the specter of telephone service relegated "to an outmoded, voice-only equivalent of Western Union,"[2] while cable companies gradually seized control of video, then data, and finally an increasing share of voice transmissions. To prevent this, the Bell System would have to become a major participant in the provision of broadband communications facilities.[3]

Both the technology and the law, of both telephony and cable, have evolved a great deal since those days. On the technology side, telephone and cable are now converging in the common arena of two-way, digital transport.[4] Telephone companies are digitizing their networks and adding bandwidth. Digital technology and high bandwidth obliterate engineering and economic distinctions between different types of electronic communication. Not simply because "a bit is a bit." The key point is that high-bandwidth digital networks are extremely flexible. They can readily be configured and interconnected to mimic any of the capabilities of any of the old, analog systems.[5] They can also (as

[2] *See* Plaintiff's First Statement of Contentions and Proof at 203, 205, United States v. Western Elec. Co., No. 74-1698 (D.D.C. Nov. 1, 1978) (*Western Elec. Co., Plaintiff's First Statement*).

[3] *See id.* at 203, 206.

[4] As early as the 1960s, when cable operators were experimenting with pay-TV, FM music, closed circuit educational television, and some local television programming, they recognized that their systems would ultimately be capable of providing both one-way data services (like electronic publishing) and two-way services (like videotext, transactional services, telemetry, and ultimately ordinary voice phone service). *See, e.g.,* Noam, Towards an Integrated Communications Market: Overcoming the Local Monopoly of Cable Television, 34 Fed. Comm. L.J. 209, 235–236 ¶257 (1982). By 1970, the FCC was proposing to require that cable systems be built with two-way capabilities, as a "hybrid service" that incorporated both "broadcast" and "carrier" capabilities. The proposed order to that effect was largely overturned in National Assn. of Regulatory Utility Commissioners v. FCC, 533 F.2d 601 (D.C. Cir. 1976) (NARUC v. FCC).

[5] As early as 1992, the Commission recognized that with "technological developments and the digitization of the network, it will be increasingly

discussed in Chapter 11) be used to provide any array of new Internet and data services.

The law has evolved considerably, too. After almost three decades of legally imposed segregation, telephone and cable companies are now legally free to enter each other's markets.

§13.2   FCC Jurisdiction

In the early days of the new cable industry, the Federal Communications Commission (FCC) took the position that it had no jurisdiction at all over cable carriers.[6] Soon thereafter the FCC began to devise reasons why it should regulate cable carriers after all.[7] For a while, the FCC sought to win authority over cable television from Congress. No new legislation was forthcoming, however. Congress declined to pass a cable act in 1959 and again in 1966. Beginning in 1962, the FCC began to stitch together a different justification for regulating cable. The FCC had a mandate to advance "the public interest" in matters of broadcast, and cable undoubtedly had the power to affect the health of over-the-air broadcasting. The FCC thus asserted "ancillary jurisdiction" over cable operations; in 1968, the Supreme Court endorsed that extension of the FCC's regulatory reach.[8]

Since that time, the allocation of federal and state authority over cable television and related services has been hotly disputed. In 1976, the D.C. Circuit Court of Appeals overturned an

---

impractical to distinguish between voice, data, graphics or video transmissions." Telephone Company-Cable Television Cross-Ownership Rules, Sections 63.54–63.58, Second Report and Order, Recommendation to Congress, and Second Further Notice of Proposed Rulemaking, 7 F.C.C. Rec. 5781, 5828 ¶90 n.232 (1992) (hereinafter *Second Video Dialtone Order*).

[6] Frontier Broadcasting Co. v. Laramie Community TV Co., Memorandum Opinion and Order, 24 F.C.C. 251, 253–254 ¶7 (1958). For a general overview of the evolution of FCC jurisdiction, see Fogarty & Spielholz, FCC Cable Jurisdiction: From Zero to Plenary in Twenty-Five Years, 37 Fed. Comm. L.J. 113 (1985).

[7] Carter Mountain Transmission Corp. v. FCC, 321 F.2d 359 (D.C. Cir.), *cert. denied*, 375 U.S. 951 (1963).

[8] United States v. Southwestern Cable Co., 392 U.S. 157 (1968).

FCC claim of broad federal jurisdiction over nonvideo two-way services.[9] A unanimous 1984 decision by the Supreme Court, however, rejected Oklahoma's attempt to ban alcohol advertising on out-of-state signals retransmitted over cable systems.[10] Subsequent decisions have generally taken the view that the FCC has "broad preemptive authority" in this field.[11] The 1984 federal Cable Act attempted to settle these matters.[12]

The 1984 Act empowered the Commission to authorize state and local authorities to regulate cable rates.[13] The Commission retained authority to establish technical standards and to authorize local regulators to enact parallel regulations.[14] It was also empowered to preempt any requirement that cable systems operate as common carriers or utilities.[15] But the Act expressly barred any new FCC regulation of the content of cable programming.[16]

[9] NARUC v. FCC, 533 F.2d 601.

[10] Capital Cities Cable, Inc. v. Crisp, 467 U.S. 691 (1984).

[11] See Brenner, Price, & Meyerson, Cable Television and Other Nonbroadcast Video: Law and Policy 11-5 (1990) (hereinafter Cable Television); New York State Commn. on Cable Television v. FCC, 749 F.2d 804 (D.C. Cir. 1984) (upholding FCC preemption of state laws regulating satellite master antenna television systems); see also New York State Commn. on Cable Television v. FCC, 669 F.2d 58, 59 (2d Cir. 1982) (upholding FCC preemption of state laws regulating master antenna television systems); Brookhaven Cable TV, Inc. v. Kelley, 573 F.2d 765 (2d Cir. 1978) (upholding FCC preemption of state price regulation of special pay cable programming), cert. denied, 441 U.S. 904 (1979); North Carolina Utils. Commn. v. FCC, 552 F.2d 1036, 1040 (4th Cir.) (upholding FCC preemption of state regulation of customer-provided telephone terminal equipment), cert. denied, 434 U.S. 874 (1977). But see Louisiana Public Service Commission v. FCC, 476 U.S. 355 (1986), discussed in Chapter 3.

[12] Though section 556 of the 1984 Cable Act preempts any existing state laws inconsistent with the terms of the Act, it still confirms the states' right otherwise to regulate cable services. 47 U.S.C. §556(b).

[13] Cable Communications Policy Act of 1984, Pub. L. No. 98-549, §623 (originally codified at 47 U.S.C. §543(b)(1)). Under the current scheme, a local franchise authority may exercise limited regulatory jurisdiction upon approval by the FCC. See 47 U.S.C. §543(a).

[14] Pub. L. No. 98-549, §624 (originally codified at 47 U.S.C. §544(e)). The current provision requires the FCC to set technical standards. See 47 U.S.C. §544(e).

[15] 47 U.S.C §541(c).

[16] Id. §544(f)(1). Regulations already in effect were grandfathered. Id. §544 (f)(2). The Cable Act of 1984 was found by the Supreme Court to preempt

The 1992 Cable Act redefined federal jurisdiction over video services, including cable. Some provisions require the Commission to do things that had previously been discretionary.[17] The Commission is also empowered to oversee disputes concerning channel positioning arising under the must-carry rules[18] and to regulate program carriage agreements.[19] The Act directs the FCC to promulgate general rules defining "reasonable" cable rates.[20] The Commission is also required to maintain procedures for certifying local franchisors who will supervise enforcement of the rate rules.[21]

The 1992 Cable Act created a new category of service provider, the "multichannel video programming distributor": an entity that supplies multiple channels of video programming to end users.[22] This new category was defined principally to guide the analysis of when cable faces "effective competition."[23] It is also used to define marginal distributors of video programming who are to be protected from anticompetitive conduct by dominant cable operators or video programmers[24] and to define who may retransmit broadcast programming.[25]

The FCC has ruled that, for most purposes, multichannel video programming distributors include cable, multipoint multichannel distribution service (MMDS), direct broadcast satellite

---

state regulation of obscenity and indecency in cable programming. Community Television of Utah, Inc. v. Wilkinson, 611 F. Supp. 1099 (D. Utah 1985), *aff'd sub nom.* Jones v. Wilkinson, 800 F.2d 989 (10th Cir. 1986), *summarily aff'd,* 480 U.S. 926 (1987).

[17] The FCC is required to cap the rates cable operators charge subscribers and unaffiliated programmers for commercial access. It is also directed to promulgate rules restricting children's access to indecent programming. 47 U.S.C. §532(c)(4), (j). The Act specifically directs the FCC to enact technical standards, an area in which the Commission had long taken a relatively minimalist approach. *See id.* §544(e).

[18] *Id.* §§534(d), 535(g)(5).

[19] *Id.* §536.

[20] *Id.* §543(b).

[21] *Id.* §543(a). The FCC will administer rate regulations only when the franchisor's certification has been disapproved or revoked. *Id.* §543(a)(6).

[22] *Id.* §522(13).

[23] *Id.* §543(*l*)(1).

[24] *Id.* §548.

[25] *Id.* §325(b).

(DBS), distributors of video programming to home satellite dishes, and landlords that operate satellite master antenna systems. A telephone company that provides pure video transport qualifies, too, at least when the Commission is gauging "effective competition" against cable.[26] Customer-programmers that lease cable channels to distribute programming are not counted.[27] Neither are distributors of videocassettes.[28] Traditional TV broadcasters that offer only one channel of over-the-air programming don't count either, though they may when they begin offering multiplexed broadcast signals.[29] The Commission deferred ruling on whether to include local multipoint distribution service (LMDS) in the "effective competition" analysis.[30]

The 1996 Telecommunications Act slightly expands federal jurisdiction over video services by giving the Commission virtually exclusive authority over a new means of providing video services—the open video system (OVS).[31] As discussed below,[32] telephone companies and others that choose to operate as OVS providers are exempt from federally mandated local franchise requirements and from local rate regulation.[33]

---

[26] Implementation of Sections of the Cable Television Consumer Protection and Competition Act of 1992, Rate Regulation, Report and Order and Further Notice of Proposed Rulemaking, 8 F.C.C. Rec. 5631, 5649–5650 ¶¶20–21 (1993) (hereinafter *1993 Rate Order*).

[27] *See id.* at 5652 ¶23.

[28] *See* Implementation of Section 19 of the Cable Television Consumer Protection and Competition Act of 1992, Annual Assessment of the Status of Competition in the Market for the Delivery of Video Programming, First Report, 9 F.C.C. Rec. 7442, 7509–7510 ¶¶134–135 (1994).

[29] *See 1993 Rate Order,* 8 F.C.C. Rec. at 5652–5653 ¶24.

[30] *Id.* at 5653–5654 ¶25.

[31] 47 U.S.C. §§571, 573.

[32] *See* §13.3.1.3.

[33] 47 U.S.C. §573(c)(1)(C). Although the text of the 1996 Act appears to exempt OVS operators from all local franchise requirements, the Fifth Circuit held that the Act merely removes any federal requirement that localities impose such requirements. City of Dallas v. FCC, 165 F.3d 341 (5th Cir. 1999). According to the Fifth Circuit, localities may still apply franchise requirements if they choose to do so.

The states still, however, retain considerable oversight over cable. Local authorities have the power to issue franchises,[34] impose franchise fees,[35] require public access channels,[36] establish customer service requirements for cable operators,[37] and operate a cable system.[38] Franchise authorities may also request that operators provide specific facilities and equipment,[39] specify "broad categories" of programming,[40] and restrict obscene programming.[41] Under the 1992 Cable Act, franchise authorities still retain actual oversight of prices for basic cable service.[42] And as discussed in Chapter 11, intrastate *two-way* cable remains under state jurisdiction.

§13.3   Common Carriage of Video Signals

Restrictions directed at telephone company provision of video services can be, and have been, directed at either the transport or the content parts of the service because video service involves an integrated package of both. In this section, we focus on carriage regulation of telco transport. (We discuss carriage restrictions aimed at cable operator provision of data—which also may include video—in Chapter 11 (see section 11.4).)

[34] 47 U.S.C. §541(a)(1); *see also* 47 U.S.C. §§545 (franchise modification), 546 (franchise renewal).

[35] *Id.* §542.

[36] *Id.* §531.

[37] 47 U.S.C. §552(a)(1).

[38] *Id.* §541(f). *Cf.* Warner Cable Communications, Inc. v. City of Niceville, 911 F.2d 634 (11th Cir. 1990).

[39] 47 U.S.C. §544(b).

[40] *Id.* §544(b)(2)(B). Section 544 stipulates that federal authorities, franchisors, and states may not make requests concerning the provision or content of cable service, except as expressly provided in the Act. *Id.* §544(f).

[41] *Id.* §544(d). The Act did not preempt state law concerning libel, slander, obscenity, incitement, invasion of privacy, or false or misleading advertising. *Id.* §558. Nor did it take away from states the right to protect subscriber privacy in ways that overlap with federal standards. *Id.* §551(g).

[42] *Id.* §543(a)(2)(A).

§13.3.1   Telco Provision of Common Carrier Transport for Video

§13.3.1.1   Early Years

In 1966, the FCC ruled that the provision of cable service distribution facilities by a telephone company constituted a common carrier service and that telephone company tariffs covering cable television distribution facilities were a matter of federal jurisdiction.[43] In the Channel Service Tariffs subsequently filed, Bell offered cable operators broadband facilities capable of carrying 12 television signals.[44] Cable operators that leased their facilities from local telcos in some instances avoided the need to obtain a municipal franchise on the theory that the telco already had the necessary state authority to operate a communications network.[45]

Bell's share of new cable TV construction expanded from less than 1 percent in 1964 to 28 percent in 1967.[46] By 1967, Bell System companies were supplying channel transmission services to 178 communities; GTE and United Telecom subsidiaries and affiliates were likewise heavily involved in developing cable

---

[43] Commission Order, Dated April 6, 1966, Requiring Common Carriers to File Tariffs with Commission for Local Distribution Channels Furnished for Use in CATV Systems, Memorandum Opinion and Order, 4 F.C.C.2d 257 (1966) (hereinafter *Common Carrier Tariffs for CATV Systems*). To justify exercising federal jurisdiction over seemingly intrastate matters, the Commission reasoned that telco-provided cable facilities are links in a "continuous" interstate television network. General Telephone Co. of California et al., Applicability of Section 214 of the Communications Act with Regard to Tariffs for Channel Services for Use by Community Antenna Television Systems, Decision, 13 F.C.C.2d 448, 454–455 ¶13 (1968) (hereinafter *General Telephone Co. of California*), *aff'd sub nom.* General Tel. Co. of Calif. v. FCC, 413 F.2d 390 (D.C. Cir.), *cert. denied*, 396 U.S. 888 (1969).

[44] *See* The Associated Bell System Companies Tariffs for Channel Service for Use by Community Antenna Television System, Order, 5 F.C.C.2d 357 (1966), *adopted by* AT&T Communications, Tariff FCC No. 36 (Jan. 1, 1984) (hereinafter *Channel Service Tariffs*).

[45] *See Western Elec. Co., Plaintiff's First Statement* at 203, 215; 1 *Cable TV Law* ¶9.15 n.3.

[46] *See Western Elec. Co., Plaintiff's First Statement* at 203, 214.

channel services and cable services themselves, directly or through affiliates.[47]

Between 1970 and the late 1980s, the Commission approved hundreds of applications by telephone companies to provide bare-bones video channel service.[48] Telephone companies thus continued to provide video transport for much of the period during which the phone companies were themselves barred from having any interest in video content. As discussed in section 13.7.2.3, however, BOCs were barred by the Divestiture Decree from providing video transport on an interLATA basis, which limited their participation in video markets substantially.

§13.3.1.2 The FCC's Video Dialtone Regime

In 1987, the FCC began development of a new regulatory framework to permit incumbent local exchange carriers to offer video services over their existing networks.[49] Under the Commission's video dialtone (VDT) regime, telephone companies would offer a common carrier video transport service to multiple video programmers, one of which could be the telco itself.[50]

---

[47] *See General Tel. Co.*, 413 F.2d 390.

[48] For example, in January 1985, the FCC took just over three months to approve a section 214 application to provide broadband channel service in Washington, D.C. *See* Application of the Chesapeake and Potomac Telephone Co., Memorandum Opinion, Order and Certificate, 57 Rad. Reg. 2d (P & F) 1003 (1985), *recons. denied, id.* Rel. No. 85-279 (May 30, 1985).

[49] Telephone Company-Cable Television Cross-Ownership Rules, Sections 63.54–63.58, Notice of Inquiry, 2 F.C.C. Rec. 5092 (1987) (hereinafter *Telco Notice of Inquiry*); *see also id.*, Further Notice of Inquiry and Notice of Proposed Rulemaking, 3 F.C.C. Rec. 5849 (1988) (hereinafter *Telco Further Notice of Inquiry*).

[50] Telephone companies were permitted to hold up to a 5 percent voting or nonvoting interest in a video programmer that provided programming over the telco's network. *Second Video Dialtone Order,* 7 F.C.C. Rec. at 5801 ¶¶35–36. Telcos were barred, however, from "select[ing] video programming by determining how programming is presented for sale to consumers, including making decisions concerning the bundling or 'tiering,' or the price, terms and conditions of video programming offered to consumers." *Id.* at 5789 ¶14. Nor were telcos permitted to "have a cognizable financial interest in, or exercise editorial control over, video programming provided directly to subscribers within their telephone service areas." *Id.* The Commission's rules obligated the telco to expand the capacity of its network to accommodate all

To deploy VDT, telcos were not permitted to acquire existing cable facilities, but were instead required to use their own facilities or build new ones.[51]

In its 1991 First Report and Order, the FCC declared that "neither the LEC [local exchange carrier] providing video dialtone services nor its customer-programmer would be required to obtain a cable franchise in order to offer service."[52] A telco providing VDT services, the FCC found, would not be providing cable service and thus would not come within the definition of a cable operator subject to the franchise requirement.[53] Nor would the telco's customers be subject to the franchise requirement because they do not control the facilities required to qualify

---

programmers seeking access, where it appeared economically justifiable to do so. *Id.* at 5797–5798 ¶30. Indeed, the Commission rejected the first VDT application because the proposed service would not have provided sufficient capacity. Letter from the FCC to Edward D. Young III, New Jersey Bell (July 28, 1993). The FCC described video dialtone as an "enriched version" of traditional common carriage telephone service, Telephone Company-Cable Television Cross-Ownership Rules, Sections 63.54–63.58, Further Notice of Proposed Rulemaking, First Report and Order, and Second Further Notice of Inquiry, 7 F.C.C. Rec. 300, 306 ¶10 (1991) (hereinafter *First Video Dialtone Order*), which would be "offered over a broadband network analogous to the existing nationwide, switched narrowband network," *id.* at 306, and would provide "a platform through which subscribers can access video and other information services," *id.* at 307. It would, in other words, be traditional switched telephone service, but enriched by video and other information offerings from independent service providers. VDT services would be enhanced services subject to *Computer II* and *Computer III. Second Video Dialtone Order,* 7 F.C.C. Rec. at 5811–5812 ¶¶58–59.

[51] *Second Video Dialtone Order,* 7 F.C.C. Rec. at 5837–5838 ¶109. However, the Commission allowed telcos to use some existing facilities, such as cable wire drops. *See* Telephone Company-Cable Television Cross-Ownership Rules, Sections 63.54–63.58, Memorandum Opinion and Order on Reconsideration and Third Further Notice of Proposed Rulemaking, 10 F.C.C. Rec. 244, 259 ¶54 (1994).

[52] *First Video Dialtone Order,* 7 F.C.C. Rec. at 324–325 ¶50.

[53] *Id.* at 324–327 ¶¶50–52. The FCC concluded that "[a] LEC providing video dialtone service does not fall within [the definition of a cable operator] because the LEC itself is not providing the video programming service directly to the subscribers. Rather, the LEC is simply acting as a conduit in providing broadband common carrier-based service that enables its customers/programmers to provide video programming to subscribers." *Id.* at 327 ¶51.

as cable operators.[54] The D.C. Circuit upheld the Commission's position in August 1994.[55]

As of February 1995, 16 experimental VDT systems had been approved. The first nonexperimental system was also approved on July 28, 1994, after an 18-month wait. Bell Atlantic deployed the first and only commercial VDT network in Dover Township, New Jersey, in early 1996 to roughly 4,000 homes,[56] using SDV technology to offer voice, data, and video.[57]

§13.3.1.3   Telco Provision of Video Carriage Services Under the 1996 Act

New section 651, 47 U.S.C. §571, offers LECs four different regulatory options to provide video services. On July 23, 1996, the FCC required all telcos that were operating VDT systems to convert to one of the four options available under the 1996 Act.[58] The first two means of entry involve a common carrier framework. First, a LEC may choose to operate an open video system (OVS), a new regulatory regime that is somewhat similar to (though more LEC-friendly than) VDT.[59] Second, a LEC may provide "transmission of video programming on a common carrier basis," subject to Title II and section 652.[60] The last two options enable LECs to operate as a broadcaster and a cable operator, respectively.[61] We will focus on the first two here.

---

[54] *Id.* at 327 ¶52. A franchise, however, continues to be required when a cable operator leases channel service from a telco. *Id.* at 327 ¶52 n.84.

[55] National Cable Television Assn. v. FCC, 33 F.3d 66 (D.C. Cir. 1994).

[56] The Telco Line: Here's What Other Telco Players Are Up To, Electronic Media, Dec. 16, 1996, at 4.

[57] S. McCarthy, Telco Video Locomotion; Bell Atlantic Corp. and SBC Communications Inc.'s Plan to Deploy Fiber-to-the-Curb Switched Digital Video Systems, Telephony, Feb. 5, 1996, at 8.

[58] Implementation of Section 302 of the Telecommunications Act of 1996, Open Video Systems, First Order on Reconsideration, 11 F.C.C. Rec. 19,081 (1996).

[59] *See* 47 U.S.C. §571(a)(4).

[60] *See id.* §571(a)(2).

[61] A LEC may provide "video programming to subscribers using radio communication" subject to Title III and the buyout provisions of new section

(i) Open Video System.   Section 653 of the Act, 47 U.S.C. §573, lays out the basic regulatory framework for OVS and directs the Commission to develop OVS rules. OVS is similar to VDT in that the LEC must allow an unaffiliated programmer to provide video programming over the system to end users, for which the programmer pays the LEC a fee. Under the OVS regime, the LEC *is* permitted to provide its own video programming over its network; however, if the demand for carriage exceeds the capacity of the OVS, the OVS operator may only occupy one-third of its system's capacity with its own programming.[62]

The Act states that LECs providing OVS service are exempt from the federal requirement of obtaining a local franchise and from rate regulation requirements.[63] The Act also precludes the Commission from requiring LECs to obtain section 214 approval "with respect to the establishment or operation of a system for the delivery of video programming," which includes OVS.[64] The Commission adopted a "streamlined" certification process for LECs to obtain authority to operate an OVS, stating that it did not want to turn the OVS certification process into a "back-door" section 214 requirement.[65] The Commission's rules do not require extensive precertification submissions, but do specify the items that an applicant should submit and verify in order to facilitate the certification process.[66]

652, 47 U.S.C. §572. 47 U.S.C. §571(a)(1). Thus, LECs are now permitted to offer wireless cable service within their telephone service areas. A LEC may also provide video programming like a traditional cable operator. 47 U.S.C. §571(a)(3).

[62] *See id.* §573(b)(1)(B).

[63] *Id.* §573(c)(1)(C). Although this provision would appear to prevent localities from enforcing local franchise requirements, the Court of Appeals for the Fifth Circuit has held otherwise. See the discussion in the text below.

[64] *Id.* §571(c). In General Telephone Co. of California, Decision, 13 F.C.C.2d 448 (1968), the Commission determined that before a telephone company constructed, acquired, or operated distribution facilities to provide channel service to a cable television system, it had to obtain approval under 47 U.S.C. §214. *See Telco Further Notice of Inquiry,* 3 F.C.C. Rec. at 5849 ¶2.

[65] Implementation of Section 302 of the Telecommunications Act of 1996, Open Video Systems, Second Report and Order, 11 F.C.C. Rec. 18,223, 18,243 ¶29 (1996) (hereinafter *Second OVS Report and Order*).

[66] *See* 47 C.F.R. §76.1502.

As of this writing, the Commission has approved 24 OVS applications.[67] Only one incumbent LEC has received (or applied for) a certificate.[68]

In January of 1999, the Court of Appeals for the Fifth Circuit vacated several of the Commission's OVS rules.[69] Most important, the court invalidated the FCC's rule prohibiting localities from imposing franchise requirements on OVS operators.[70] The FCC's prohibition rested on its interpretation of 47 U.S.C. §573(c)(1)(C), which exempts OVS operators from, among other things, the rule that "a cable operator may not provide cable service without a franchise."[71] Based on the "clear statement" rule for preempting local authority and on the 1996 Act's express preservation of state and local law, the court held that section 573 deletes only "the *federal* requirement that cable operators get a franchise before providing service; it does not eviscerate the ability of local authorities to impose franchise requirements, but only their obligation to do so."[72] The court also invalidated the FCC's rule prohibiting cable operators that are also LECs from providing OVS unless they face effective competition,[73] vacated the rule prohibiting cable operators from obtaining capacity on an unaffiliated OVS absent a waiver by the OVS operator,[74] and overturned the rule requiring carriers to obtain Commission approval before constructing new physical plants needed to operate OVSs.[75]

On the other hand, the court refused to invalidate a number of the Commission's other OVS rules. The court upheld the FCC's rule limiting the fees collectible by localities to a percentage of the OVS operator's gross revenue (rejecting arguments

[67] *See* FCC, Filings for Certification of Open Video Systems (visited June 14, 1999) <http://www.fcc.gov/Bureaus/Cable/www/csovscer.html>.

[68] *See* Bell Atlantic-New Jersey, Inc., Certification to Operate an Open Video System, Order, 11 F.C.C. Rec. 13,249 (1996).

[69] City of Dallas v. FCC, 165 F.3d 341 (5th Cir. 1999).

[70] *Id.* at 347.

[71] 47 U.S.C. §541(b)(1).

[72] *City of Dallas,* 165 F.3d at 347 (emphasis added).

[73] *Id.* at 352–354.

[74] *Id.* at 356–358.

[75] *Id.* at 358–359.

that localities can also levy fees based on unaffiliated programmers' revenue),[76] agreed with the Commission that OVS operators are not required to provide institutional networks,[77] upheld
the rule that entities other than LECs may become OVS operators,[78] and sustained the rule making effective competition a
prerequisite to providing OVS for cable operators that are not
also LECs, even for those whose cable franchises have terminated.[79]

(ii) Common Carrier Video Transport Under the 1996 Act.
The 1996 Act preserves a LEC's right to use its facilities to provide video transport to others on a common carrier basis. Section 651(a)(2) of the Act, 47 U.S.C. §571(a)(2), states that a LEC
"providing . . . video programming on a common carrier basis"
shall be subject only to the requirements of Title II and the anti-
buyout provisions of section 652, but not to any of the other
requirements of Title VI.[80] The Act is careful to distinguish between, on the one hand, a common carrier that uses its common
carrier facilities to provide cable service (which *is* regulated as a
cable service under Title VI),[81] and, on the other hand, a common carrier that uses its facilities to provide common carriage
video transport (which is not).

The Commission has made clear that section 651(a)(2) covers
more than just the provision of channel service, which, by definition, involves the provision by a LEC of video distribution
facilities and services to franchised cable operators on a common
carrier basis.[82] A LEC may also provide common carrier video
transport to entities that do not qualify as cable operators—for

---

[76] *Id.* at 349–350.
[77] *Id.* at 350–351.
[78] *Id.* at 351–352.
[79] *Id.* at 354–356.
[80] *See* 47 U.S.C. §571(a)(2).
[81] *See id.* §571(a)(3)(A).
[82] The Commission has stated that channel service is the provision by a
telephone company of video distribution facilities and services to franchised
cable operators on a common carrier basis. *See Telco Further Notice of Inquiry,*
3 F.C.C. Rec. at 5849 ¶2 n.2; *Second Video Dialtone Order,* 7 F.C.C. Rec. at 5787
¶10 n.21.

example, entities that qualify for the private cable exemption of section 602(7)(B), which provides that "a facility that serves subscribers without using any public rights of way" does not constitute a cable system under section 602(7).[83] This has little direct regulatory significance for the LEC—it faces the same Title II regulation for the provision of channel service to a cable operator or common carrier video transport to a noncable operator. By contrast, noncable operators that purchase LEC transport for distribution of their own programming can escape both Title II and Title VI regulation.[84]

§13.4   Telco-Cable Interconnection

§13.4.1   Pole Attachments

In the early years of cable television, the Bell System and independent telcos had generally charged the infant cable operators only a modest "pole attachment" fee for the use of telco poles and conduits. When cable began to be perceived as a competitive threat, however, these policies were changed. Bell began restricting the types of services that could be delivered over any cables attached to its poles, prohibiting such services as pay TV, educational services, closed circuit transmissions, FM music, and all two-way services.[85] Bell also sharply increased the rates its affiliates charged for pole attachments and established a policy of permitting only a single cable company to attach to its poles.[86]

---

[83] 47 U.S.C. §522(7)(B).

[84] See Entertainment Connections, Inc.; Motion for Declaratory Ruling, Memorandum Opinion and Order, 13 F.C.C. Rec. 14,277 (1998).

[85] See Western Elec. Co., Plaintiff's First Statement at 203, 207; 2 Cable TV Law ¶16.02[3].

[86] Prospective cable companies sometimes challenged these practices in antitrust suits. In one such suit, brought in the mid-1960s, the district court denied an application for a preliminary injunction, holding that the cable company had not demonstrated irreparable injury. Radio Hanover, Inc. v. United Utils., Inc., 273 F. Supp. 709, 713 (M.D. Pa. 1967). The court went on to state that it viewed the cable company's case as weak on the merits, since the telco had offered to construct its own cable facilities and lease them to the

The independent telcos—which were not subject to the Bell System's 1956 quarantine and thus could act directly as cable providers—pursued similar policies, perhaps even more protectionist than the Bell System's.[87]

In a 1970 ruling on cable-telco relationships, the FCC took limited steps to regulate access to telephone poles and conduits.[88] Any telco seeking a section 214 waiver would have to demonstrate that independent cable operators had first been offered access to telco poles and conduits "at reasonable charges" and "without undue restrictions on the uses that may be made of the channel by the customer."[89] These requirements were engaged,

---

plaintiff at the same rate accepted by a rival cable company. *Id.* at 714. More than a decade later the Eighth Circuit held that a cable company denied pole attachments had standing to sue the telephone company and had demonstrated evidence of injury based on increased costs of construction incurred when it was forced to lay its cables underground. TV Signal Co. of Aberdeen v. AT&T, 617 F.2d 1302, 1310 (8th Cir. 1980).

[87] Between 1964 and 1966, for example, telco affiliates of GTE and United Telecom refused all new pole attachment requests by cable operators. 2 *Cable TV Law* ¶16.02[3]. *See also* Petition by Manatee Cablevision, Inc. to Stay Construction and Operation of CATV Distribution Facilities in Manatee County, Fla., Decision, 22 F.C.C.2d 841, 846 ¶17 (1970) (hereinafter *Manatee Cablevision*). Both GTE and United set up cable television subsidiaries to compete directly for local franchises. There were numerous complaints that the telcos engaged in anticompetitive and discriminatory practices to advance their own cable operations over those of the independent cable companies. *See, e.g., id.;* Warrensburg Cable, Inc. v. United Telephone Co. of Missouri, et al., Applications of United Transmission, Inc. and United Telephone Co. of Missouri for Certificate of Public Convenience and Necessity for Construction and Operation of CATV Channel Facilities in Warrensburg, Mo., Initial Decision of Administrative Law Judge David I. Kraushaar, 48 F.C.C.2d 910 (1973); Petition by TeleCable Corp. to Stay Construction and Operation of a CATV System in Bloomington and Normal, Ill., Decision, 19 F.C.C.2d 574 (1969). GTE's subsidiary, for example, almost always prevailed in competitive applications for cable franchisees in communities served by a GTE company. *See id.*

[88] *See generally* Siegel, The History of Cable Television Pole Attachment Regulation, 6 Comm. and the Law 9 (1984).

[89] Applications of Telephone Companies for Section 214 Certificates for Channel Facilities Furnished to Affiliated Community Antenna Television Systems, Final Report and Order, 21 F.C.C.2d 307, 326 ¶53 (1970) (hereinafter *Applications of Telcos*), *modified,* 22 F.C.C.2d 746 (1970), *aff'd sub nom.* General Tel. Co. of the Southwest v. United States, 449 F.2d 846 (5th Cir. 1971).

however, only if a telco applied for section 214 authorization to provide cable channel services; absent such application, the FCC (at that time) lacked general jurisdiction over pole attachments.[90] Thus, a telco had to surrender control over its poles and conduits as a precondition to even requesting permission to offer cable channel services.

Predictably, telco offering of such services declined sharply.[91] Now, the only effective way for a telco to meet the perceived competitive threat from cable television was to deny pole access altogether. The FCC, however, pressured the Bell System to reach an accommodation with cable operators, and in 1975, Bell and the National Cable Television Association accepted an agreement on pole attachment rates. Most other telephone and utility companies refused to join it; at that time, these other companies controlled 7 million of the 10 million available poles.[92]

Congress then enacted the 1978 Pole Attachment Act.[93] This legislation gave the FCC authority to regulate rates and terms of cable television pole attachments wherever states failed to impose such regulation themselves.[94] On this basis, the Commission established a mathematical formula for determining "just and reasonable" attachment rates[95] and set up a detailed complaint procedure to encourage private resolution of most disputes.[96] The Act did not provide an absolute right of pole access—access remains, in principle, a matter of contract nego-

---

[90] *See* California Water and Telephone Co. et al., Memorandum Opinion and Order, 64 F.C.C.2d 753, 758–759 ¶14 (1977).

[91] 1 *Cable TV Law* ¶9.15 n.1.

[92] Siegel, The History of Cable Television Pole Attachment Regulation at 13.

[93] 47 U.S.C. §224. "[T]he Commission shall regulate the rates, terms, and conditions for pole attachments to provide that such rates, terms, and conditions are just and reasonable. . . ." *Id.* §224(b)(1).

[94] *Id.* §224(c)(1) ("Nothing in this section shall . . . give the Commission jurisdiction with respect to rates, terms, and conditions for pole attachments in any case where such matters are regulated by a State.") In the 1984 Cable Act, Congress also amended the Pole Attachment Act to provide that a state would not be considered to be regulating pole attachments unless it had issued rules and was acting promptly on complaints. *See id.* §224(c)(3).

[95] 47 C.F.R. §1.1409(c).

[96] *Id.* §1.1404.

tiation.[97] In practice, however, cable companies have since been able to run wire to the doorsteps of over 90 percent of the nation's residences.[98]

One other and potentially explosive aspect of the pole attachment issue surfaced in a 1985 ruling by the Ninth Circuit Court of Appeals, in *Preferred Communications, Inc. v. City of Los Angeles*.[99] The court ruled that Preferred Communications, a disappointed applicant for a Los Angeles cable television franchise, had a First Amendment right to route its cables over "public facilities," including poles and underground conduit; the municipality could not prevent an unfranchised cable company from using such facilities to distribute electronic speech. The court interpreted the 1984 Cable Act as empowering the local authority to award one or more franchises within its local jurisdiction. While accepting that municipalities retained some leeway in awarding permits and franchises, the court rejected the notion that the Cable Act gave franchising authorities an absolute right to limit the number of cable operators allowed to provide service.[100] On review, the Supreme Court agreed that cable operators enjoy First Amendment rights, but remanded for fuller development of the facts.[101] The Ninth Circuit subsequently ruled that a city cannot "limit access . . . to a given region of the [c]ity to a single cable television company, when the public utility facil-

---

[97] *See* FCC v. Florida Power Corp., 480 U.S. 245, 251 n.6 (1987) ("The language of the Act provides no explicit authority to the FCC to require pole access for cable operators, and the legislative history strongly suggests that Congress intended no such authorization.") (citations to legislative history omitted).

[98] National Cable Television Association, Cable Television Developments 1-A (Sept. 1991). In upholding the FCC's rural exemption, the D.C. Circuit explained that the opportunities for telcos to use control over pole attachments to gain a monopolist's premium from providers of cable services decreased with passage of the Pole Attachments Act. *See* National Cable Television Assn. v. FCC, 747 F.2d 1503, 1505 n.1 (D.C. Cir. 1984); *see also Telco Notice of Inquiry*, 2 F.C.C. Rec. at 5093–5094 ¶13 (discussing ameliorating effect of the Pole Attachments Act).

[99] 754 F.2d 1396 (9th Cir. 1985), *aff'd in part and remanded*, 476 U.S. 488 (1986), *on remand*, 67 Rad. Reg. 2d (P & F) 366 (C.D. Cal. 1990), *aff'd in part and vacated in part*, 13 F.3d 1327 (9th Cir.), *cert. denied*, 512 U.S. 1235 (1994).

[100] *Id.* at 1409.

[101] *Preferred Communications*, 476 U.S. 488.

ities and other public property in that region necessary to the installation and operation of a cable television system are physically capable of accommodating more than one system."[102]

§13.4.2 Equal Access Under the Divestiture Decree

The Divestiture Decree required the BOCs to provide "exchange access, information access and exchange service for such access" to all interexchange carriers and information services providers.[103] BOCs that provided traditional cable service therefore were not required under the Decree to provide equal access to such services. The Decree defined exchange access with reference to functions of the traditional telephone network,[104] none of which was involved in the provision of cable service. These equal access obligations therefore did not have any coherent meaning outside the context of conventional exchange service.

[102] *Preferred Communications,* 13 F.3d at 1330.

[103] Modification of Final Judgment §II(A), *reprinted in* United States v. AT&T, 552 F. Supp. 131, 227 (D.D.C. 1982) (hereinafter *Decree*). Both "exchange access" and "information access" are defined in section IV of the Decree. *See id.* at 228–229. Both definitions make clear that such services revolve around "exchanges" (i.e., central telephone switches). *See id.* The Decree does not define, and does not prohibit, BOC involvement in radio stations, computer software, or the production of movies. These are not "exchange telecommunications" or "exchange access" services, nor are they "interexchange telecommunications services." The drafters of the Decree had no need to address radio, software, VCRs, movies, newspapers, compact disks, or skywriting, and in fact did not do so. It is not at all clear why the Justice Department believed that video signals are different from radio broadcasts, videocassettes, or CD-ROMs (all of which are "electromagnetic transmission media" under section IV(O), *see Decree,* 552 F. Supp. at 229). Perhaps it is simply that a cable wire "feels" a lot more like a telephone wire than does a floppy disk or VCR tape.

[104] The Decree defined exchange access to include "network control signalling, answer supervision, automatic calling number identification, carrier access codes, directory services, testing and maintenance of facilities and the provision of information necessary to bill customers." *Decree* §IV(F), 552 F. Supp. at 228–229. It also had numerous additional references to "switching," "routing," "probability of blocking," and so on. *See id.* All these references are to the functions of telephone switches (i.e., exchanges). Information access is defined in almost identical terms in §IV(I), 552 F. Supp. at 229. The Decree

It is in fact difficult to see how a BOC could have both provided traditional cable service and offered equal access to its
facilities at the same time. A cable network offers only a limited
(albeit rapidly increasing) number of channels. Cable providers
thus offer television programming on a contractual basis and of
necessity determine the content of that programming based on
commercial considerations, just as other information service
providers do. In contrast, common carriers receive traffic on a
tariffed basis and have no control over the content of the traffic.
A BOC providing a content-based product or service has to
determine the elements that go into that product or service. The
notion of equal access makes sense only when the BOC is acting
not as an information provider, but as a common carrier that
controls access to an exchange.

Although the Decree's equal access provision did not affect the
BOCs' provision of cable services, they did in at least one instance affect the provision of telephony services by a cable operator. In late 1993, U S WEST sought a Decree waiver in connection
with its investment in Time Warner Entertainment (TWE), the
nation's second largest cable operator.[105] As a condition of the
waiver, the Justice Department imposed equal access obligations
on TWE's two-way local telephony services.[106]

---

describes that function as the provision of "specialized" forms of "exchange
telecommunications services," which involve the BOC in "transmi[tting],
switching, forwarding or routing" information on behalf of a provider of
information services. *Id.* It includes, as does exchange access telecommunications, "network control signalling, answer supervision, automatic calling
number identification, carrier access codes, testing and maintenance of facilities, and the provision of information necessary to bill customers." *Id.*
Again, all these references are to the functions of telephone switches (i.e., exchanges).

[105] Motion for a Waiver of the Decree to Permit U S WEST, Inc. to Provide
Limited InterLATA Services and Engage in Limited Manufacturing Activities
Through Its Minority Partnership Investment in Time Warner Entertainment,
L.P., United States v. Western Elec. Co., No. 82-0192 (D.D.C. Dec. 10, 1993,
as revised, July 28, 1994). On September 15, 1993, U S WEST purchased a 25
percent limited partnership in Time Warner Entertainment (TWE). In order
to minimize potential Decree violations, Time Warner Inc. restructured TWE
to remove Decree-sensitive activities, including divesting all cable systems
located in U S WEST's territory.

[106] TWE must provide customers the ability to select their preferred carrier
for voice and data interexchange telecommunications between points in a

§13.4.3   Telco-Cable Interconnection Under the 1996 Act

§13.4.3.1   Telco's Duty to Provide Cable with Interconnection and Unbundling

As discussed in section 5.5, section 251 of the 1996 Act requires incumbent LECs to provide interconnection and unbundling to requesting "telecommunications carriers." To the extent that a cable operator is engaged in the provision of a "telecommunications service"—but not a "cable service"—it will be considered a telecommunications carrier and is entitled to obtain interconnection and unbundling like any other competitor.[107]

§13.4.3.2   Access to OVS Under the 1996 Act

Although a LEC operating an OVS must offer carriage to others, the Act contains the following provision: "Limitations on Interconnection Obligations.—A local exchange carrier that provides cable service through an open video system or a cable system shall not be required, pursuant to title II of this Act, to make capacity available on a nondiscriminatory basis to any other person for the provision of cable service directly to subscribers."[108]

---

cable system and points outside it; TWE must offer exchange access on equal type, quality, and price terms made available to all interexchange carriers, subject to any provisions regarding pricing practices in legislation or FCC regulations. Motion for a Waiver of the Decree to Permit U S WEST, Inc. to Provide Limited InterLATA Services and Engage in Limited Manufacturing Activities Through Its Minority Partnership Investment in Time Warner Entertainment, L.P., *United States v. Western Elec. Co.,* No. 82-0192 (D.D.C. Sept. 9, 1994).

[107] "Telecommunications service" is defined as offering for a fee, to the public, "the transmission, between or among points specified by the user, of information of the user's choosing, without change in the form or content of the information as sent and received." 47 U.S.C. §153(43), (46). "Cable service" is defined as "(A) the one-way transmission to subscribers of (i) video programming, or (ii) other programming service, and (B) subscriber interaction, if any, which is required for the selection or use of such video programming or other programming service." *Id.* §522(6).

[108] 47 U.S.C. §571(b).

In other words, an OVS provider's carriage obligations are limited to those contained in Title VI and cannot be expanded into the far broader obligations of a common carrier under Title II.[109] In this sense, OVS is quite different from the VDT model it replaces.[110]

The Commission has established detailed procedures to ensure that OVS operators provide nondiscriminatory access to video programming providers.[111] An OVS operator is required to file a "Notice of Intent" with the Commission that describes the proposed system's vital characteristics.[112] The Notice is then made public, and an enrollment process begins under which programmers request carriage on the OVS.[113] The OVS operator may establish its own terms and conditions of carriage, provided they are just and reasonable, and not unreasonably or unjustly discriminatory.[114] After the enrollment period, the OVS operator will determine whether demand for carriage, including its own demand, exceeds the system's channel capacity.[115] If demand for carriage does not exceed system capacity, the open video system operator should fill all video programming providers' demands for capacity, including its own.[116] If demand for carriage exceeds capacity, the open video system operator may select the programming services to be carried on no more than one-third of the system's activated channel capacity.[117] The remaining two-thirds of capacity must be allocated to unaffiliated

[109] 47 U.S.C. §553(c)(3); H.R. Conf. Rep. No. 458, 104th Cong., __ Sess. 172 (1996) (hereinafter *1996 Act Conference Report*) ("Open video systems are not subject to the requirements of title II for the provision of video programming or cable service.").

[110] As Congress noted, the VDT "rules implemented a rigid common carrier regime . . . and thereby created substantial obstacles to the actual operation of open video systems." *1996 Act Conference Report* at 179.

[111] *See* 47 C.F.R. §76.1503.

[112] *See id.* §76.1503(b)(1); *see also Second OVS Report and Order,* 11 F.C.C. Rec. at 18,248 ¶38.

[113] *See* 47 C.F.R. §76.1503(b)(1), (2).

[114] *See id.* §76.1504; *see also Second OVS Report and Order,* 11 F.C.C. Rec. at 18,249 ¶38.

[115] *See Second OVS Report and Order,* 11 F.C.C. Rec. at 18,249 ¶38.

[116] *See id.*

[117] *See* 47 U.S.C. §573(b)(1)(B); 47 C.F.R. §76.1503(c); *Second OVS Report and Order,* 11 F.C.C. Rec. at 18,249 ¶38.

video programming providers on a nondiscriminatory basis.[118] The Commission does not, however, require that a specific allocation methodology be used.[119] Aggrieved video programmers are permitted to file a complaint with the Commission, which places the burden on the OVS operator to establish that its allocation methodology was not discriminatory.[120] After service commencement, an open video system operator will be required to allocate open capacity, if any is available, at least once every three years on a nondiscriminatory basis, to the extent that there is demand.[121]

The Act subjects OVS operators to many of the same obligations that cable operators face regarding the carriage of local broadcast signals. For example, the Act directs the FCC to extend its rules concerning sports exclusivity, network nonduplication, and syndicated exclusivity to operators of open video systems.[122] OVS operators are also required to comply with the obligations regarding "must-carry" of commercial and noncommercial educational stations and carriage of channels for public, educational, or governmental (PEG) use.[123]

Imposing these signal carriage obligations on telco OVSs is not, however, as straightforward as it might seem. These obligations are defined with respect to cable system boundaries, which are quite different from the local exchange areas that define LEC operations. As one commentator notes, "To accomplish these straightforward objectives requires putting a jagged, but round, peg into a square, and equally jagged hole."[124] In the must-carry context, the Commission has addressed this problem by giving

[118] *See* 47 C.F.R. §76.1503(c)(2); *Second OVS Report and Order,* 11 F.C.C. Rec. at 18,249 ¶38.

[119] *See Second OVS Report and Order,* 11 F.C.C. Rec. at 18,249 ¶38.

[120] *See id.* at 18,268 ¶72.

[121] 47 C.F.R. §76.1503(c)(2)(ii); *Second OVS Report and Order,* 11 F.C.C. Rec. at 18,249–18,250 ¶38.

[122] *See* 47 U.S.C. §573(b)(1)(D); *see also id.* §§76.1506(m), 76.1508, 76.1509.

[123] *See* 47 C.F.R. §76.1506(a) (making applicable to OVSs the provisions of Subpart D, including the must-carry obligations for commercial and noncommercial educational stations, *see id.* §76.56); *id.* §76.1505 (making applicable to OVSs the PEG access requirements).

[124] *Cable Television* at 11-35.

OVSs that span multiple television markets a choice between providing to all subscribers every broadcast station eligible for must-carry status in any of the system's markets and providing subscribers only those broadcast stations eligible in their particular market.[125] In the PEG context, the FCC has ruled that an OVS operator's obligations will first be determined by negotiation between the local franchise authority and the OVS operator, and, where appropriate, the local cable operator.[126] If negotiations fail, the OVS operator must satisfy the same requirements as the local cable operator.[127]

In addition to its OVS provisions, the 1996 Act affects several other aspects of video services. The Act makes minor revisions to existing law on relationships among video programmers, video distributors, and manufacturers of customer-premises equipment.[128] It also makes technical adjustments to the must-carry

[125] *Second OVS Report and Order*, 11 F.C.C. Rec. at 18,311 ¶166. If the OVS operator chooses the former option and does not configure its system so that subscribers receive only the broadcast stations eligible in their particular market, the OVS operator is responsible for increased copyright fees. Implementation of Section 302 of the Telecommunications Act of 1996, Open Video Systems, Third Report and Order and Second Order on Reconsideration, 11 F.C.C. Rec. 20,227, 20,295 ¶157 (1996) (hereinafter *Third OVS Report and Order*).

[126] *Second OVS Report and Order*, 11 F.C.C. Rec. at 18,295 ¶137. Negotiation for PEG obligations "may include the local cable operator if the local franchising authority, the open video system operator[,] and the cable operator so desire." *Id.*

[127] *Id.* at 18,298 ¶141. The OVS operator "must match . . . the annual PEG access financial contributions of the local cable operator" and share with the local cable operator all costs related to PEG access services, facilities, and equipment. *Third OVS Report and Order*, 11 F.C.C. Rec. at 20,282 ¶130. If there is no local cable operator, the OVS operator must "make a reasonable amount of channel capacity available for PEG access." *Second OVS Report and Order*, 11 F.C.C. Rec. at 18,303 ¶151. If there was previously a local cable operator, the OVS operator may provide a "reasonable" amount of capacity by choosing either (1) the amount previously required under the cable operator's franchise agreement or (2) that amount "determined by comparison to the franchise agreement for the nearest operating cable system that has a commitment to provide PEG access and that serves a franchise area with a similar population size." *Third OVS Report and Order*, 11 F.C.C. Rec. at 20,286–20,287 ¶138. The local franchising authority may make such a choice every 15 years. *Id.*

[128] 47 U.S.C. §§549, 544, 544a. The Act also contains a section designed to foster video programming accessibility for the hearing and visually impaired.

rules—the rules that require cable operators, upon request, to transmit the signals of broadcasters operating in the same television market.[129] Finally, the new Act broadens the 1992 Cable Act's program access rules, which require video programmers affiliated with cable or satellite distributors to give other cable and satellite distributors nondiscriminatory access to their programming.[130] In a significant win for the local exchange carriers that are about to enter the business, the 1996 Act extends program access rights to all common carriers that provide video programming.[131]

The 1996 Act gave the Commission six months to investigate and report to Congress on "the level at which video programming is closed captioned." 47 U.S.C. §613(a). Eighteen months after that the Commission was required to issue regulations aimed at increasing the level of closed captioning, as it deemed necessary. *Id.* §613(b). The Commission also had six months to study and report to Congress on the use of video descriptions on video programming "in order to ensure the accessibility of video programming to persons with visual impairments"; but the new Act did not order any regulations on this subject. *Id.* §713(f). The Commission addressed these matters in Closed Captioning and Video Description of Video Programming, Implementation of Section 305 of the Telecommunications Act of 1996, Video Programming Accessibility, Report and Order, 13 F.C.C. Rec. 3272 (1997), and *id.*, Order on Reconsideration, 13 F.C.C. Rec. 19,973 (1998).

[129] 47 U.S.C. §§534–536. Under the old rule, the relevant market for purposes of must-carry obligations was specifically based on Arbitron's Area of Dominant Influence standard, a standard using the number of television households in the area where the relevant TV stations are located. Definition of Markets for Purposes of the Cable Television Mandatory Television Broadcast Signal Carriage Rules, Report and Order and Further Notice of Proposed Rulemaking, 11 F.C.C. Rec. 6201, 6203 ¶4 (1996). The 1996 Act adopts a more general standard using commercial publications that delineate television markets based on viewing patterns. 47 U.S.C. §534(h)(1)(C). The 1996 Act also alters the time the Commission has to make such market determinations from "expedited consideration" to "[w]ithin 120 days after the date on which a request is filed." 47 U.S.C. §534(h)(1)(C)(iv).

[130] 47 U.S.C. §548.

[131] *Id.* §548(j). This provision also extends the burdens of program access to common carriers and their programming affiliates. *Id.* But such burdens do not apply if a common carrier's interest in a programming vendor (or its parent company) arises solely as a result of the common carrier's holding, or having the right to appoint or elect, two or fewer common officers or directors. *Id.*

§13.4.3.3 Cable's Duty to Provide Interconnection Under the 1996 Act

When offering telecommunications service, cable operators are required to fulfill the duties that apply to all telecommunications carriers. First, they must interconnect directly or indirectly with the facilities and equipment of other carriers.[132] Second, they may not install network features that fail to comply with the requirements for disabled users and other standards established by the FCC.[133]

To the extent that a cable operator offers "telephone exchange or exchange access" to businesses or residences, it will be deemed a "local exchange carrier." As discussed in section 5.5.2, under section 251(b), all LECs, including cable-operated LECs, must comply with five duties: to permit the resale of their telecommunications services; to provide number portability to the extent "technically feasible"; to provide dialing parity; to provide access to their poles, ducts, conduits, and rights-of-way; and to establish reciprocal compensation arrangements for the transport and termination of traffic.

§13.5 Price Regulation

§13.5.1 Price Regulation of Telco Provision of Video Services

§13.5.1.1 Price Regulation of Telco Provision of Video Transport: Before 1996

The Commission treats the provision of a channel service by LECs as an interstate common carrier service, subject to federal tariff requirements[134] and to LEC price caps. The Commission

---

[132] 47 U.S.C. §251(a)(1).

[133] *Id.* §251(a)(2).

[134] *See* Common Carrier Tariffs for Local Distribution Channels Furnished for Use in CATV Systems, Memorandum Opinion and Order, 4 F.C.C. 2d 257

has never created a separate price-cap basket for LEC channel services; these services fall within the special access basket (Basket 3), which specifically includes audio and video services.[135]

LEC common carrier video transport provided in connection with now-defunct video dialtone service was also regulated as an interstate common carrier service[136] and subject to price caps.[137] After first declining to do so, the Commission required LECs to use a separate price-cap basket for VDT services in order to assure that telephone ratepayers did not subsidize VDT.[138] Bell Atlantic filed a request for a waiver of this requirement in February 1996, and the FCC granted it the following month, basing its decision on the fact that Bell Atlantic had no VDT revenues or demand in the base year, making it mathematically impossible to calculate the inflation adjustment required for the price-cap index.[139] This order did not address the issue of whether the separate basket requirement was negated by the 1996 Act's provisions doing away with VDT regulation.

§13.5.1.2 Price Regulation of Telco Provision of Video Transport: 1996 and After

The 1996 Act specifically repeals the Commission's video dialtone rules,[140] promulgated in 1992 under the Commission's Title

---

(1966). *See also* Bell Atlantic Operating Companies' Permanent Cost Allocation Manual for the Separation of Regulated and Nonregulated Costs, Memorandum Opinion and Order, 3 F.C.C. Rec. 109, 118 ¶¶87–88 (1988).

[135] *See* Policy and Rules Concerning Rates for Dominant Carriers, Second Report and Order, 5 F.C.C. Rec. 6786, 6788 ¶14 (1990).

[136] It therefore fell under 47 U.S.C. §203 (tariff or "schedule of charges" provisions).

[137] *Second Video Dialtone Order,* 7 F.C.C. Rec. at 5828 ¶91.

[138] Price Cap Performance Review for Local Exchange Carriers; Treatment of Video Dialtone Services Under Price Cap Regulation, Second Report and Order and Third Further Notice of Proposed Rulemaking, 10 F.C.C. Rec. 11,098 (1995).

[139] 1996 Annual Access Tariff Filing, Order, 11 F.C.C. Rec. 11,433 (1996).

[140] Telecommunications Act of 1996 §302(b)(3). Repeal of the Commission's video dialtone regulations is not intended to alter the status of any video dialtone service already in operation. *Id.*

II authority. The Act requires the Commission to "ensure that the rates, term, and conditions for [carriage on an OVS] are just and reasonable, and are not unjustly or unreasonably discriminatory."[141]

The Commission has refused to review the rates for OVS and has instead given OVS operators "maximum flexibility" to set their rates, so long as they are "just and reasonable and not unjustly or unreasonably discriminatory."[142] The Commission will rely on a "'presumption' approach" under which an OVS operator's rates are given a "strong presumption" of being just and reasonable "where at least one unaffiliated video programming provider, or unaffiliated programming providers as a group, occupy capacity equal to the lesser of one-third of the system capacity or that occupied by the open video system operator and its affiliates, and where the rate complained of is no higher than the average of the rates paid by unaffiliated programmers receiving carriage from the open video system operator."[143] Where these conditions are met, the complainant will have the burden of demonstrating that the rate is not just and reasonable.[144] Where these conditions are not met and a potential video programming provider files a complaint with the Commission, the burden shifts to the OVS operator to demonstrate "that the contested carriage rate is no greater than a carriage rate that could be imputed to the operator's affiliated video programming."[145]

§13.5.1.3 Price Regulation of Telco Provision of Video Content

To the extent that a LEC provides traditional cable service in competition with an incumbent, it is not likely to be subject to local cable rate regulation (nor, for reasons discussed in section 12.4, to common carrier rate regulation). Under such circumstances, the LEC would face "effective competition" from the

---

[141] 47 U.S.C. §573(b)(1)(A).
[142] *See Second OVS Report and Order,* 11 F.C.C. Rec. at 18,285 ¶114.
[143] *Id.; see also* 47 C.F.R. §76.1504(c).
[144] *See Second OVS Report and Order,* 11 F.C.C. Rec. at 18,285 ¶114.
[145] *Id.; see also* 47 C.F.R. §76.1504(d), (e).

incumbent cable operator and thus would be permitted to set its own rates.[146]

§13.5.1.4   Impact of Telco Entry on Cable Rate Regulation

Similarly, video competition from telcos provides relief from rate regulation for incumbent cable operators. Under section 543(l)(1)(D) of the 1996 Act, "effective competition" exists if a LEC or its affiliate (or any multichannel video programming distributor using its facilities) offers video programming services directly to subscribers by any means (other than direct-to-home satellite services) in the franchise area of an unaffiliated cable operator as long as the video programming services offered are comparable to the services provided by the unaffiliated cable operator.[147] The Commission defined comparable service to include at least 12 channels of video programming, including at least one channel of nonbroadcast service.[147]

---

[146] If the Commission finds that a cable system is subject to "effective competition," its rates "shall not be subject to regulation." 47 U.S.C. §543(a)(2). "Effective competition" can be found on one of four different bases: (A) fewer than 30 percent of the households in the franchise area subscribe to cable service (although such low-penetration cable systems may not in fact face any competition, Congress believed they should not be subject to the burden of price controls); (B) the franchise area is (i) served by at least two unaffiliated multichannel video programming distributors, each of which offers comparable video programming to at least 50 percent of the households in the franchise area, and (ii) the number of households subscribing to multichannel video programming distributors other than the largest multichannel video programming distributor exceeds 15 percent of the households in the franchise area; (C) a multichannel video programming distributor operated by the franchising authority for that franchise area offers video programming to at least 50 percent of the households in that franchise area; or (D) a LEC or its affiliate (or any multichannel video programming distributor using the facilities of such carrier or its affiliate) offers video programming services directly to subscribers by any means (other than direct-to-home satellite services) in the franchise area of an unaffiliated cable operator, as long as the video programming services offered by the LEC or through its facilities are comparable to the services provided by the unaffiliated cable operator. *Id.* §543(l)(1).

[147] Implementation of Cable Act Reform Provisions of the Telecommunications Act of 1996, Report and Order, CC Docket No. 96-85 (rel. Mar. 1999).

§13.5.2   Price Regulation of Cable Operator Provision of Telecom Services

Cable operators that provide competitive local exchange services are treated like any other new entrants. In nearly all states, they are required to file tariffs with the state commission,[148] but are treated as nondominant and not subject to rate regulation of any sort.[149]

§13.6   Universal Service

Many municipalities still make universal service of some sort a condition of a local cable franchise. Franchising authorities may require overbuilders—including telcos—to provide some degree of universal service as well,[150] although franchising authorities must give overbuilders a "reasonable period of time" in which to become "capable" of providing service throughout the franchise area.[151] Several states have passed laws that attempt to prevent cream-skimming by cable overbuilders.[152] These laws generally prevent a second cable franchise from being awarded on terms more favorable than was the first.[153]

---

[148] *See* National Association of Regulatory Utility Commissioners, Telecommunications Competition 1997, at 321–324 (1997).

[149] *See id.*

[150] The 1984 Act requires franchising authorities, in awarding a cable franchise, to "assure that access to cable service is not denied to any group of potential residential cable subscribers because of the income of the residents of the local area in which such group resides." 47 U.S.C. §541(a)(3). The D.C. Circuit has held that this section "manifestly does not require universal service," but is instead designed to require that "service not be denied to low income subscribers." ACLU v. FCC, 823 F.2d 1554, 1579–1580 (D.C. Cir. 1987), *cert. denied*, 485 U.S. 959 (1988); *see also* H.R. Rep. No. 934, 98th Cong., __ Sess. 59 (1984).

[151] 47 U.S.C. §541(a)(4)(A).

[152] *See Cable Television* at 3-58 (citing Fla. Stat. §166.046; Minn. Stat. §238.08[1][b]; Tenn. Code §§7-59-201 to 7-59-207; 65 ILCS §5/11-42-11; Cal. Govt. Code §53066.3(d)).

[153] *See id.* Florida and Minnesota permit franchising authorities to impose greater burdens on the second franchisee. *Id.*

Cable operators that provide local telephone service generally have no corresponding obligations to provide universal telephone service. In most states, universal service obligations extend only to incumbent LECs.[154] Indeed, the 1992 Cable Act prevents franchising authorities from imposing any requirement "that has the purpose or effect of prohibiting, limiting, restricting, or conditioning the provision of a telecommunications service by a cable operator or an affiliate thereof."[155]

§13.7   Industry Structure

§13.7.1   Telco Entry into Cable

Both state and federal regulators traditionally have regulated the entry of telephone companies and cable operators into each other's markets. At the state level, telephone companies seeking to provide cable service traditionally have been required to obtain a cable franchise.[156] It was common practice for municipalities to grant exclusive franchises—thereby precluding entry by telcos and others—until Congress in the 1992 Cable Act outlawed this practice.[157]

At the federal level, telephone companies—as common carriers—were required to obtain Commission approval under section 214 of the 1934 Act to deploy new facilities to deliver new

---

[154] *See, e.g.,* AT&T Communications of the Pac. Northwest, Inc. v. U S WEST Communications, No. Civ. 97-1578-JE, 1998 WL 897029, at *3 (D. Or. Dec. 11, 1998) ("U S WEST is required to provide service to anyone in its service area who requests it, whereas competitors . . . can solicit the most profitable customers while leaving the remainder for U S WEST to serve.").

[155] 47 U.S.C. §541(b)(3)(B).

[156] A cable franchise consists of a municipality's permission to string wires above or below the public streets within a defined area for a definite period. In return, a cable company typically commits to offer areawide service to all who want it at a uniform price.

[157] Under the 1992 Act, a franchisor "may not grant an exclusive franchise and may not unreasonably refuse to award an additional competitive franchise." 47 U.S.C. §541(a)(1). The 1984 Cable Act authorized municipalities to grant "one or more" franchises, which franchising authorities had interpreted as allowing them to grant one exclusive franchise.

video services.[158] Federal antitrust authorities also have seen fit to prevent or limit the ability of telephone companies to provide video services, out of the concern that local exchange carriers would improperly use their local monopolies to suppress competition in the adjacent video market. In the 1996 Act, Congress took several steps to end structural regulation of the industry, including creating the OVS regime (discussed in sections 13.3.1.3 and 13.4.3.2 above) and permitting LECs to provide cable service under Title VI, on the same terms as traditional cable operators.

As noted in section 13.3 above, entry restrictions directed at telephone company provision of video services divide between the transport and content parts of the service. Section 13.7.2 below discusses entry regulations aimed at telco provision of video content.

§13.7.2   Telco Entry into Cable: Video Content

§13.7.2.1   Impact of the 1956 Decree

By the terms of its 1956 Consent Decree,[159] the Bell System was prohibited from offering anything other than rate-regulated "common carrier" services, and the FCC had ruled in *Frontier Broadcasting Co.* that cable providers are not "common carriers" because they determine the content of what is being communicated.[160] So Bell began deploying cable systems for leasing to

---

[158] In 1968, the FCC announced that cable channel service, though seemingly local, was really interstate and that telephone companies would therefore need section 214 approval to build or operate cable facilities. *See* General Telephone Co. of California, Decision, 13 F.C.C.2d 488 (1968).

[159] United States v. Western Elec. Co., 1956 Trade Cas. (CCH) ¶68,246 (D.N.J. 1956).

[160] *Frontier Broadcasting Co.*, 24 F.C.C. at 253–254 ¶¶7–8. The case resulted from a complaint filed by 13 licensees of standard TV broadcast stations who requested that the Commission exercise jurisdiction over cable TV systems as communications common carriers under the amended Communications Act of 1934. *Id.* at 251 ¶1. The FCC determined that the traditionally accepted concept of a common carrier is an entity that furnishes communications facilities by wire or radio to all members of the public; the content of the communication is chosen by the customer, not the carrier. *Id.* at 253–254 ¶7. *See*

cable companies as a "common carrier" service permitted by the 1956 Decree.[161]

§13.7.2.2   The FCC's 1970 Cross-Ownership Ban

As tensions between cable carriers and telcos mounted in the 1960s, the FCC resolved to regulate their relationship.[162] The Commission initiated a first investigation of telco involvement in cable television in 1966 and that same year concluded that telco provision of broadband transmission for cable distribution was a "common carrier" function subject to federal tariffing.[163] Two years later the FCC required telcos to file for certificates of public convenience under section 214 of the Communications Act[164] before building facilities to support cable television service.[165] It

---

National Assn. of Broadcasters v. FCC, 740 F.2d 1190, 1199–1206 (D.C. Cir. 1984). Although cable systems send information by wire to any member of the public who wants to subscribe to the service, the specific signals received and distributed by the cable system are established by the cable operator and not the customer. *See Frontier Broadcasting,* 24 F.C.C. at 254–255 ¶8.

[161] 2 *Cable TV Law* ¶¶16.02[2]–16.02[3]. Here, the customer (i.e., the cable operator) chose the content, and the Bell System merely provided transmission.

[162] *See Applications of Telcos,* 21 F.C.C.2d at 307. A good overview of the history of cable-telco cross-ownership restrictions appears in Hart, The Evolution of Telco-Constructed Broadband Services for CATV Operators, 34 Cath. U. L. Rev. 697, 706–713 (1985). For an extensive description of various FCC rules limiting cross-ownership of mass media, see Emord, The First Amendment Invalidity of FCC Ownership Regulations, 38 Cath. U. L. Rev. 401 (1989).

[163] The Commission at first extended these requirements to AT&T and GTE only. Order Requiring Common Carriers to File Tariffs with Commission for Local Distribution Common Carrier Tariffs for Use in CATV Systems, Memorandum Opinion and Order, 4 F.C.C.2d 257, 257 ¶1 (1966).

[164] Section 214(a) provides in relevant part: "No carrier shall undertake the construction of a new line or of an extension of any line . . . unless and until there shall first have been obtained from the Commission a certificate that the present or future public convenience and necessity require . . . such additional or extended line. . . ." 47 U.S.C. §214(a).

[165] General Telephone Co. of California (formerly California Water & Telephone Company), The Associated Bell System Companies, The General Telephone System and United Utilities, Inc. Cos. Applicability of Section 214 of the Communications Act with Regard to Tariffs for Channel Service Use by Community Antenna Television Systems, Decision, 13 F.C.C.2d 448 (1968).

was on this jurisdictional and regulatory foundation that the FCC went on in 1970 to promulgate a general ban on cable/telco cross-ownership.[166]

The ban was precipitated by 17 section 214 cable system applications filed by entities owned in some degree by telcos offering phone service in the same areas.[167] Upon review, the FCC concluded that concentration of control in this way would be against the public interest.[168] The Commission accordingly ordered all telephone common carriers to stop providing video service "directly or indirectly" by early 1974.[169] Without specifically concluding that telcos had behaved anticompetitively, the FCC decided on a prophylactic ban aimed at "the prevention of . . . possible abuses. . . ."[170] No telco or telco "affiliate" would be granted section 214 certification to provide cable services within its telephone service area, nor would telcos be permitted to license pole or conduit space to their own cable affiliates.[171]

The cross-ownership ban extended not only to local telcos affiliated with the Bell System, but also to interexchange carriers like MCI and Sprint (within their "service areas") and to independent local telcos.[172] Independent telephone companies

---

[166] *Applications of Telcos,* 21 F.C.C.2d at 307.

[167] *See id.*

[168] *See id.* at 325 ¶48; *see also* Northwestern Indiana Tel. Co. v. FCC, 872 F.2d 465, 469 n.2 (D.C. Cir. 1989) ("[t]he need to eliminate favored treatment of telephone company affiliates is, of course, the cross-ownership rules' raison d'etre"), *cert. denied,* 493 U.S. 1035 (1990).

[169] *Applications of Telcos,* 21 F.C.C.2d at 325–326 ¶49. The FCC allowed for temporary authorizations under section 214(a) of the Act during a four-year period "to assure that existing CATV services would not be precipitously withdrawn from the public." *Id.* at 326 ¶50.

[170] *See id.* at 329 ¶58. *See also* Gordon, Levy, & Preece, Office of Plans & Policy, FCC, FCC Policy on Cable Ownership (Nov. 1981).

[171] *See Applications of Telcos,* 21 F.C.C.2d at 325–326 ¶49.

[172] The FCC's cross-ownership restrictions applied to "[a]pplications of *telephone common carriers* for construction and/or operation of CATV channel facilities in their service areas." *Applications of Telcos,* 21 F.C.C.2d at 330 app. A §I (emphasis added). There is some argument, however, that a proscription from cable operations within a telco's "telephone service area" should be taken to mean "local exchange service area," thus effectively exempting the interexchange carriers from the proscription. *See Telco Further Notice of Inquiry,* 3 F.C.C. Rec. at 5862–5863 ¶70; Winer, Telephone Companies Have First

were thus forced to divest their already established cable television service subsidiaries.[173] The concept of "affiliate" was broadly defined,[174] though the FCC over time narrowed its scope.[175]

The cross-ownership restrictions did not bar telcos from owning cable systems outside of their service areas.[176] Telcos were also permitted to continue to act as facilities providers for the in-area delivery of cable service, leasing channel services to fully independent cable operators, subject to advance approval under section 214.[177] And telcos were permitted to continue providing

---

Amendment Rights Too: The Constitutional Case for Entry into Cable, 8 Cardozo Arts & Ent. L.J. 257, 261 n.10 (1990). The FCC subsequently reversed itself and took this position. *First Video Dialtone Order,* 7 F.C.C. Rec. at 322–323 ¶46.

[173] *See Applications of Telcos,* 21 F.C.C.2d at 326 ¶50. *See, e.g., Manatee Cablevision,* 22 F.C.C.2d at 862–863 ¶63 (ordering General Telephone of Florida (GTF) and GTE Communications to cease any further cable television operations); *Warrensburg Cable,* 48 F.C.C.2d 910 (ordering United Telephone of Missouri to cease any further cable operations); Comark Cable Fund III v. Northwestern Indiana Tel. Co., 100 F.C.C.2d 1244 (1985) (cease and desist order against Northwestern Indiana Telephone Company and Northwest Indiana CATV, Inc., ordering termination of affiliation).

[174] *See Applications of Telcos,* 21 F.C.C.2d at 330 app. A §I.

[175] *See* Century Fed., Inc. v. FCC, 846 F.2d 1479, 1481–1482 (D.C. Cir. 1988) (upholding the FCC's position that installment payment plans for charges for communication services do not create a debtor-creditor relationship; hence, the two parties cannot be considered to be affiliated); Northwestern Indiana Tel. Co. v. FCC, 824 F.2d 1205, 1209–1210 (D.C. Cir. 1987) (citing the FCC's decision to exclude from the definition of affiliate an arrangement whereby the telephone company, C&P, constructed, maintained, and retained legal title to distribution facilities on telephone pole space leased by a cable operator who agreed in turn to pay construction costs and assume some of the risks and benefits of ownership, based on the assumption that, despite such an arrangement, C&P still had no control over either the cable company or its service), *following remand,* 872 F.2d 465, 468 (D.C. Cir. 1989) (the FCC stated that it did not consider "the leasing of pole space to be an indicator of affiliation"), *cert. denied,* 493 U.S. 1035 (1990).

[176] For a time, telcos were nonetheless required to obtain construction authority under section 214 for out-of-area cable operations. The Commission eliminated that requirement in 1984. *See* Blanket 214 Authorization for Provision by a Telephone Common Carrier of Lines for Its Cable Television and Other Non-common Carrier Services Outside Its Telephone Service Area, Report and Order, 98 F.C.C.2d 354 (1984); *id.,* 49 Fed. Reg. 21,333 (1984) (codified at 47 C.F.R. §63).

[177] *See Cable Television* at 11-23 to 11-28.

pole or conduit space to independent cable concerns. The Commission also preserved a waiver process, aimed principally at cable service in rural areas or other areas where cable service "demonstrably could not exist" without telco participation or upon "other showing of good cause" that a waiver would advance the public interest.[178] The Commission established a presumption in favor of waiving the cross-ownership ban in communities with population densities under 30 homes per cable mile.[179] In 1981, the FCC reaffirmed and extended its permissive waiver policy for rural areas.[180] As of April 1981, 96 waivers had been granted.[181] As of 1990, some 300 cable systems (out of about 8,400 nationwide) were operated by telcos.[182]

§13.7.2.3 Telco Provision of Video Service Under the 1982 Divestiture Decree

The 1982 Divestiture Decree arguably placed additional barriers between the BOCs and the provision of cable television services. From the time of divestiture, the Justice Department viewed cable television as an "information service" within the meaning of the Decree.[183] Although the Decree's information

[178] See Applications of Telephone Companies for Section 214 Certificates for Channel Facilities Furnished to Affiliated Community Antenna Television Systems, Memorandum Opinion and Order, 22 F.C.C.2d 746, 754–756 app. §2 (1970) (hereinafter Application of Telcos II), aff'd sub nom. General Telephone Company of the Southwest v. United States, 449 F.2d 846 (5th Cir. 1971).

[179] See Revision of the Processing Policies for Waivers of the Telephone Company-Cable Television Cross-Ownership Rules, Report and Order, 82 F.C.C.2d 233, 243 ¶24 (1979).

[180] The Commission created a cross-ownership exemption for carriers serving any locale that met the Census Bureau's definition of "rural area." Elimination of the Telephone Company-Cable Television Cross-Ownership Rules, Sections 63.54–63.56, for Rural Areas, Report and Order, 88 F.C.C.2d 564 (1981).

[181] See Noam, Towards an Integrated Communications Market at 243 n.152 (citing FCC Master Waiver Log, reported in National Cable Television Association Comments to the FCC, No. 80-767 (FCC Apr. 1981)).

[182] Hazlett, Should Telephone Companies Provide Cable TV?, Regulation 72 (1990).

[183] It was never altogether clear, however, that this view was consistent with the language of the Decree. A cable network transmits every channel of programming to every subscriber; only the terminal equipment (the decoder on

services restriction was removed in its entirety in late 1991,[184] the Decree's interLATA prohibition remained a significant obstacle to Bell Company provision of video services. The Department ruled that the transmission of video signals constitutes a "telecommunications service" subject to the interLATA restriction.[185] Whether the Department's position would stand up in court was never tested. Rather than challenge the Department's position head on, several BOCs sought Decree waivers. The Department also ruled that the Decree's interLATA restriction applied fully to BOCs' provision of video dialtone "to the extent video dialtone involves transmission of signals across LATA boundaries."[186] Several BOCs sought Decree waivers in connection with their in-region video dialtone experiments.[187]

---

the subscriber's premises) determines what is displayed on the subscriber's television. In that sense, then, cable is not conveyed via "telecommunications" within the meaning of the Decree because the information is not "of the user's choosing." *Decree,* 552 F. Supp. at 229. Prior to divestiture, the Justice Department discussed cable only in terms of its potential as a bypass medium. The one exception was in a 1982 response to comments, in which the Department stated that whereas cellular and public land radio services clearly fell under the Decree's definition of "exchange telecommunications," the provision of cable service "clearly involve[d] the generation, transformation and conveyance of information and is thus an information service." Response of the United States to Public Comments on Proposed Modification of Final Judgment at 52, United States v. Western Elec. Co., No. 82-0192 (D.D.C. May 20, 1982). Later in the same filing, the Department reaffirmed that "CATV would be treated as an information service." *Id.* at 116.

[184] *See* United States v. Western Elec. Co., 767 F. Supp. 308 (D.D.C. 1991), *aff'd,* 993 F.2d 1572 (D.C. Cir.), *cert. denied,* 510 U.S. 984 (1993).

[185] Letter from B. Grossman, Department of Justice, to A. Baker, Ameritech, May 14, 1987. Noting that "the MFJ makes no distinction between one-way (reception only) and two-way (reception and transmission) telecommunications," the Department concluded that even the operation of a receive-only satellite at the "head end" of a cable system would constitute "interexchange telecommunications services" in violation of §II(D). *Id.*

[186] *See* Reply Comments of the United States Department of Justice at 6, No. 87-266 (Mar. 13, 1992). A BOC provider of a VDT service, the Department concluded, would be providing an "exchange access" or "information access" service within the meaning of §II(A). *Id.* at 28.

[187] Motion of Bell Atlantic for Waivers for InterLATA Video Programming Delivery, United States v. Western Elec. Co., No. 82-0192 (D.D.C. Oct. 7, 1994); Bell Atlantic's Request for a Waiver to Provide Video Programming Service Without Regard to LATA Boundaries, United States v. Western Elec.

§13.7.2.4   The Video Ban in the 1984 Cable Act

Section 613(b) of the 1984 Cable Act[188]codified the FCC's 1970 cross-ownership rules[189] with only one key change in wording.[190] Congress's one change was to refer to "video programming" instead of "CATV service."[191] Although section 613(b) was commonly described as a "cross-ownership" prohibition,[192] the Act in fact addressed programming, not ownership. Section 613(b) prohibited a telco from "provid[ing] video programming directly to subscribers in its telephone service area"[193] and from providing "channels of communications" or other use of its facilities, to itself or its affiliates, in connection with their provision of video programming.[194] A telephone company's use of its *own telephone network* to provide video programming is clearly not

---

Co., No. 82-0192 (D.D.C. Feb. 26, 1993); Ameritech's Waiver Request for Video Dialtone, United States v. Western Elec. Co., No. 82-0192 (D.D.C. Oct. 20, 1994).

[188] Pub. L. No. 98-549, §613(b) (originally codified at 47 U.S.C. §533(b)).

[189] *See Telco Notice of Inquiry,* 2 F.C.C. Rec. at 5093 ¶¶2–7; H.R. Rep. No. 934, 98th Cong., 2d Sess. 55–58 (1984), *reprinted in* 1984 U.S.C.C.A.N. 4655, 4692–4695 (indicating congressional intent to codify FCC rules).

[190] Paragraph 1 forbade any common carrier from providing "video programming" in its own service area. Pub. L. No. 98-549, §613(b)(1). Paragraph 2 prohibited common carrier provision of channel facilities or pole attachments to a cable affiliate in its own service area. *Id.* §613(b)(2). Paragraph 3 codified the exemption for rural areas. *Id.* §613(b)(3). Paragraph 4 set out criteria for waiver of the ownership restrictions. *Id.* §613(b)(4).

[191] This change was intended to exclude from the restriction telco carriage of primarily textual information. *See* 130 Cong. Rec. S14,285 (daily ed. Oct. 11, 1984) (statement of Sen. Packwood). "[T]he term 'video programming' means programming provided by, or generally considered comparable to programming provided by, a television broadcast station." Pub. L. No. 98-549, §602 (16). Congress also indicated that it wished to provide an unqualified rural exemption, and the Commission complied. *See Telco Notice of Inquiry,* 2 F.C.C. Rec. at 5096 ¶7 n.12; H.R. Rep. No. 934, 98th Cong., 2d Sess. 56–57 (1984); *Telco Further Notice of Inquiry,* 3 F.C.C. Rec. at 5851 ¶8.

[192] *See, e.g., Second Video Dialtone Order,* 7 F.C.C. Rec. 5781 (addressing "Telephone Company-Cable Company Cross-Ownership Restrictions").

[193] Pub. L. No. 98-549, §613(b)(1).

[194] *Id.* §613(b)(2).

cross-ownership.[195] Section 613(b) was thus unusually strict;[196] most other telecommunications companies were not similarly restricted in what they could carry over their own core transmission facilities.[197]

The peculiar phrasing of section 613(b) created anomalous results that were frequently misunderstood. Section 613(b) quite plainly did *not* bar a telephone company from buying the facilities of a cable company in the telco's own service area as long as

[195] By contrast, for example, the FCC's television-radio-newspaper cross-ownership ban prohibits a holder of a television or radio license from "directly or indirectly *own[ing]*, operat[ing], or contoll[ing] a daily newspaper." 47 C.F.R. §73.3555(d) (emphasis added).

[196] The one, narrow legal opening for telcos came from the FCC's modification of when an "affiliation" triggers §613(b). The 1984 Act states that "the term 'affiliate' when used in relation to any person, means another person who owns or controls, is owned or controlled by, or is under common ownership or control with, such person." Pub. L. No. 98-549, §602 (1). The FCC traditionally defined affiliation broadly, as "any financial or business relationship whatsoever by contract or otherwise, directly or indirectly between the carrier and the customer, except only the carrier-user relationship." Revision of the Processing Policies for Waivers of the Telephone Company-Cable Television "Cross Ownership Rules," Sections 63.54 and 64.601, Memorandum Opinion and Order, 82 F.C.C.2d 254, 264 app. §2 (1980) (hereinafter *Cross-Ownership Rules Revision*). For its part, the Department of Justice took the position that a telco does not become an affiliate under the 1984 Act if it merely supplies video programming to a cable system or broadcaster. Government Defendants' Memorandum in Support of Their Motion at 66, Chesapeake and Potomac Telephone Co. v. United States, No. 92-1751-A (E.D. Va. May 22, 1993) (telcos "are free, for example, to offer their programming to television networks and local broadcasters"). Any telco ownership exceeding 1 percent created an affiliation. *Cross-Ownership Rules Revision*, 82 F.C.C.2d at 264 app. §2. In its 1992 video dialtone decision, however, the Commission loosened these criteria, permitting telcos to own up to 5 percent of any programmer, whether or not the programmer uses the telco's video dialtone service. *Second Video Dialtone Order*, 7 F.C.C. Rec. at 5801–5802 ¶36.

[197] Television broadcasters broadcast electronic newspapers, data, computer software, and paging services within the otherwise unused "vertical blanking interval" of their spectrum licenses. Amendment of Parts 2, 73, and 76 of the Commission's Rules to Authorize the Offering of Data Transmission Services on the Vertical Blanking Interval by TV Stations, Report and Order, 101 F.C.C.2d 973 (1985). Radio stations transmit paging services using the "subcarrier" portions of their assigned frequencies. 48 Fed. Reg. 28,445 (1983); 49 Fed. Reg. 18,100 (1984); Amendment of Parts 2 and 73 of the Commission's AM Broadcast Rules Concerning the Use of the AM Sub-Carrier, Report and Order, 100 F.C.C.2d 5 (1984).

the programming was provided by others.[198] It is also unclear whether section 613(b) applied at all to conventional airwave broadcasting or satellite services.[199]

The 1984 Act preserved the rural area exception to the video ban.[200] The Commission subsequently adopted new rules that made it easier for telcos to provide cable service to rural areas.[201] The FCC also declared that cross-ownership restrictions would not apply to cable services offered by telcos that did not own the

---

[198] *See, e.g.,* Application of C&P Telephone Co., Memorandum Opinion, Order, and Certificate, 57 Rad. Reg. 2d (P & F) 1003 (1985) (hereinafter *Application of C&P Telephone*) (approving construction of telephone company-owned cable facilities for lease to an unaffiliated programmer); *see also* H.R. Rep. No. 934, 98th Cong., 2d Sess. 57 (1984) (§613(b) does not "prevent a common carrier from constructing . . . a local distribution system that is capable of delivering video programming . . . [or] from leasing . . . such a system to a . . . cable operator").

[199] According to the Department of Justice, "[T]elephone companies can provide in-region video services, so long as they do so in ways other than as 'traditional cable operators.' They are free, for example, to offer their programming to television networks and local broadcasters whose signals reach [their own subscribers]. And they may even acquire local broadcast outlets for that purpose." Government Defendants' Memorandum in Support of Their Motion, and in Opposition to Plaintiffs' Motion for Summary Judgment at 66, Chesapeake and Potomac Tel. Co. of Va. v. United States, No. 92-1751-A (E.D. Va. May 22, 1993). It is unclear what the government's interpretation would imply for "nontraditional" forms of wireless delivery of video programming, including the oxymoronic "wireless cable" or direct broadcast satellite (DBS).

[200] Section 613(b)(3) granted an automatic waiver of the ownership ban to telcos providing service in any "rural" area, as defined by the Commission.

[201] The Commission abandoned its policy that telcos could not be independent cable owners in rural service areas without the grant of a waiver and abbreviated the process for granting section 214 waivers. Amendment of Parts 1, 63 and 76 of the Commission's Rules to Implement the Provisions of the Cable Communications Policy Act of 1984, Report and Order, 58 Rad. Reg. 2d (P & F) 1, 17–19 ¶¶66–68 (hereinafter *Cable Act Implementation*), *recons. denied,* 104 F.C.C. 2d 386 (1986), *remanded on other grounds sub nom.* ACLU v. FCC, 823 F.2d 1554 (D.C. Cir. 1987), *cert. denied,* 485 U.S. 959 (1988). The FCC eliminated the need to submit the information required by 47 C.F.R. §63.01 and instead required information on the system furnishing video programming and a certification that the proposed service area met the definition of "rural." Applications were then placed on public notice, and interested parties could file objections. The Commission stated, "We believe that this procedure will meet the requirement that we certify that a proposed cable system will serve a rural area without burdening either the telephone company or the Commission." *Cable Act Implementation,* 58 Rad. Reg. 2d at 19 ¶68.

landline telephone facilities in the same service area.[202] Thus, the cross-ownership restrictions did not apply to "non-wireline cellular operators and other radio common carriers,"[203] to resellers of interexchange services,[204] or to telcos operating cable systems outside their telephone service areas.[205]

The 1984 Act also preserved the "good cause" waiver exception. During the 1970s, few telcos sought waivers under this provision. This changed in the 1980s after the Bell System divestiture.[206] In 1984, the FCC allowed Wisconsin Bell to supply channel service to an independent cable operator[207]—the first section 214 grant to a divested BOC. Additional section 214 grants soon followed.[208] A landmark section 214 waiver in 1988 allowed GTE to build and maintain broadband transport facilities (550 MHz, 78-channel capacity, and bidirectional) to serve 5,000 homes in Cerritos, California.[209]

---

[202] Letter from Richard Firestone, Chief, Common Carrier Bureau, to Robert J. Butler, Esq., 5 F.C.C. Rec. 4547, 4548 (1990) (hereinafter *Firestone Letter*).

[203] *Cable Act Implementation*, 58 Rad. Reg. 2d at 16 ¶54.

[204] *Firestone Letter*, 5 F.C.C. Rec. at 4548.

[205] 47 C.F.R. §63.54 (1990).

[206] *Cable Television* §11.03, at 11-25.

[207] Application of Wisconsin Bell, Inc. for Authority Pursuant to Section 214 of the Communications Act of 1934, and Section 63.01 of the Commission's Rules and Regulations to Construct and Operate a Broadband Distribution System in Brookfield, Wisconsin, in Order to Provide Channel Service, Memorandum Opinion and Order, 56 Rad. Reg. 2d (P & F) 1262 (1984).

[208] In 1985, C&P Telephone filed a joint application with District Cablevision, Inc. (DCI). C&P would construct and operate the transmission lines using telephone ducts, while DCI would be responsible for the program service. *Application of C&P Telephone*, 57 Rad. Reg. 2d (P & F) at 1003. Ohio Bell received approval to build a cable fiber-optic system for Cleveland from the FCC in 1986. Application of Ohio Bell Telephone Co. for Authority Pursuant to Section 214 of the Communications Act of 1934, and Sections 63.01 and 63.07 of the Commission's Rules and Regulations to Construct and Maintain Broadband Transport Facilities in Cleveland, Ohio, Memorandum Opinion, Order, and Certificate, 1 F.C.C. Rec. 942 (1986). In 1989, Cincinnati Bell applied for approval to carry channel service for the trunk portion of Warner Cable's service in Cincinnati, while Warner provided the "coaxial drops" to the customers. Comm. Daily, Aug. 17, 1989, at 6.

[209] Application of General Telephone Co. of California for Authority Pursuant to Section 214 of the Communications Act of 1934, and Sections 63.01

§13.7.2.5   First Amendment Attacks on the Video Service Ban

On August 24, 1993, Judge Ellis of the U.S. District Court for the Eastern District of Virginia ruled that the ban on telco provision of programming is unconstitutional, both on its face and as applied to Bell Atlantic.[210] He found that although the government had identified a significant government interest supporting the statute (the promotion of diversity), the statute itself was not narrowly tailored to serve that interest. Noting that the alleged opportunities for cross-subsidization by telcos, which the government claimed would allow telcos to drive their competition out of business, all concerned the transport of programming (which the telcos are not precluded from providing), he

---

and 63.07 of the Commission's Rules and Regulations to Construct and Maintain Broadband Transport Facilities in Cerritos, California, Memorandum Opinion, Order, and Certificate, 3 F.C.C. Rec. 2317 (1988), aff'd, 4 F.C.C. Rec. 5693 (1989), remanded sub nom. National Cable Television Assn. v. FCC, 914 F.2d 285 (D.C. Cir. 1990). The National Cable Television Association objected, and in September 1990, the D.C. Circuit remanded the decision to the FCC. National Cable Television Assn., 914 F.2d 285. The court found that there was good cause for grant of a waiver of the cross-ownership rules to permit GTE Service Corp. to conduct the authorized tests, but remanded the case to the Commission because the Commission had not adequately explained why it was necessary for GTE California, Inc. (GTECA), to hire Robak—the corporate parent of the cable programming provider—to construct the system. Id. at 288–289. The court hypothesized that the benefits of the Cerritos system could have been achieved without the cross-ownership waiver if it were possible for GTECA to hire someone other than an affiliate of the cable programming provider for this construction project. Id. On remand, the Commission found that it was not necessary for GTECA to hire Robak to build the cable network and therefore rescinded GTECA's cross-ownership waiver and section 214 authorization. Application of General Telephone Co. of California for Authority Pursuant to Section 214 of the Communications Act of 1934, and Sections 63.01 and 63.07 of the Commission's Rules and Regulations to Construct and Maintain Broadband Transport Facilities in Cerritos, California, Memorandum Opinion and Order on Remand, 8 F.C.C. Rec. 8178, 8181–8182 ¶¶12–17 (1993). The Court of Appeals for the Ninth Circuit stayed the effectiveness of the remand order pending judicial review and then dismissed GTECA's challenge as moot because the original waiver granted by the FCC had expired. See GTE Cal., Inc., v. FCC, 39 F.3d 940 (9th Cir. 1994).

[210] Chesapeake & Potomac Tel. Co. of Va. v. United States, 830 F. Supp. 909 (1993), aff'd, 42 F.3d 181 (4th Cir. 1994), cert. granted, 515 U.S. 1157 (1995), judgment vacated, 516 U.S. 415 (1996).

found no justification for banning telcos from participating in the production of programming.

Other federal district courts followed Judge Ellis's ruling on section 613(b), also on First Amendment grounds.[211] On November 21, 1994, the Fourth Circuit affirmed Judge Ellis's ruling.[212] On December 30, 1994, the Ninth Circuit reached the same conclusion as the Fourth, acting on a challenge brought by U S WEST.[213] The Supreme Court granted certiorari on the Fourth Circuit case, which was argued on December 8, 1995; before the Court could rule, however, Congress passed the 1996 Act, which eliminated section 613(b) for good. The Solicitor General argued successfully that passage of the new Act mooted the case before the Supreme Court.

§13.7.2.6 Elimination of the Video Service Ban

While the legality of the video service ban was debated in the courts, the FCC and Congress were reexamining the policy wisdom of the ban. In 1981, the FCC first considered the possible efficiencies from telco entry into cable, but concluded that necessary safeguards against anticompetitive behavior were not yet in place.[214] In 1988, however, the FCC tentatively decided that greater telco involvement would assist rather than undermine competition.[215] Shortly thereafter the FCC initiated a full-scale

---

[211] *See, e.g.,* SNET v. United States, 886 F. Supp. 211 (D. Conn. 1995); NYNEX Corp. v. United States, No. 93-323-P-C, 1994 WL 779761 (D. Me. Dec. 8, 1994); Ameritech Corp. v. United States, 867 F. Supp. 721 (N.D. Ill. 1994); BellSouth Corp. v. United States, 868 F. Supp. 1335 (N.D. Ala. 1994); U S WEST, Inc. v. United States, 855 F. Supp. 1184 (W.D. Wash. 1994).

[212] Chesapeake & Potomac Tel. Co. of Va. v. United States, 42 F.3d 181 (4th Cir. 1994).

[213] U S WEST, Inc. v. United States, 48 F.3d 1092 (9th Cir. 1994). A similar decision was reached the same day in a challenge brought by Pacific Telesis against a district court order denying it a preliminary injunction. Pacific Telesis Group v. United States, 48 F.3d 1106 (9th Cir. 1994). The *Pacific Telesis* case was consolidated with the *U S WEST* case for oral argument; the one-page opinion remanding the district court's decision simply refers to the parallel decision reached in *U S WEST* and reiterates that §613(b) "violates the First Amendment." *Id.* at 1107.

[214] *Telco Further Notice of Inquiry,* 3 F.C.C. Rec. at 5850 ¶6 (describing Office of Plans and Policy, FCC, FCC Policy on Cable Ownership (1981)).

[215] *Id.* at 5849 ¶1.

review of the cable-telco cross-ownership restrictions.[216] The review led the FCC to recommend to Congress that the cross-ownership ban be repealed.[217] In the meantime, the FCC set about devising ways to loosen the ban.[218] The FCC decided to allow local telcos to provide video dialtone service, which the Commission believed would "stimulate robust competition in the video and nonvideo communications markets" and encourage investment in "modern telecommunications networks."[219]

[216] *Id.* The Commission suggested that the primary purpose of the cross-ownership restrictions—to promote the growth of an independent cable industry—had been fulfilled: cable companies by then were offering service to almost 80 percent of the nation's households. *Id.* at 5866 ¶84.

[217] *Id.* at 5860 ¶56. The Commission stated:

> The evidence before us to date suggests 1) the initial purpose of the cross-ownership ban—preventing telephone company preemption of competitive broadband services—has been accomplished; 2) the new and different services to the public the Commission hoped would emerge have not; 3) the ban restricts telephone companies from providing these services as well as competitive traditional services in cabled areas and any service in non-cabled areas; 4) the public interest generally is not served by this kind of consumer loss; 5) while telephone companies continue to have the ability to deny potential competitors access or to engage in anticompetitive cross subsidies, safeguards perhaps analogous to those devised in *Computer III* would avoid the costs to consumers caused by a ban and 6) even if such safeguards need to be supplemented by additional protective measures, those measures could be applied in an individual section 214 proceeding.

Id.

[218] The FCC recognized that the 1984 Cable Act constrained its power to modify cross-ownership rules, but noted that the Act allowed the Commission flexibility in defining "affiliation." Thus, the FCC "propose[d] to modify the standards of affiliation to permit the carrier to participate in provision of cable television service as long as its participation does not constitute ownership and/or control as contemplated by the Cable Act." *Id.* at 5866 ¶91. The FCC further proposed to establish more permissive standards for granting "good cause" waivers and specifically suggested that "construction and operation of technologically advanced, integrated broadband networks by carriers for the purpose of providing video programming and other services will constitute good cause for waiver." *Id.* at 5849 ¶1.

In 1991, the FCC determined that the telco-cable cross-ownership ban applies only to local exchange carriers within their "telephone service areas" and does not apply to long-distance carriers at all. *First Video Dialtone Order,* 7 F.C.C. Rec. at 322–323 ¶46.

[219] *Id.* at 330 ¶59.

In 1996, Congress finally finished the job, repealing the video service ban as part of the 1996 Act.[220] Under the 1996 Act, carriers need no longer secure an FCC license under section 214 of the Communications Act "with respect to the establishment or operation of a system for the delivery of video programming."[221] Thus, on March 11, 1996, the Commission terminated the video dialtone rulemaking proceeding in CC Docket No. 87-266, eliminated the video dialtone regulations and policies, and revoked the Common Carrier Bureau's order that had adopted subsidiary accounting and reporting requirements for video dialtone services.[222] Certain LECs already providing video dialtone service were "grandfathered" and permitted to convert their systems to new Open Video Systems.[223]

§13.7.3 Cable Entry into Telephony

Until the 1996 Telecommunications Act, many states still barred competitive entry into the provision of local exchange service.[224] In the states where such competition was permitted,

[220] 1996 Telecommunications Act §302(b) (repealing 47 U.S.C. §533(b)). The 1996 Act thus mooted another First Amendment case that phone companies had filed to challenge the applicability of section 214 to their cable operations. *See* United States Tel. Assn. v. FCC, No. 95-533-A (E.D. Va. July 31, 1995).

[221] 47 U.S.C. §571(c). The Conference Report notes: "[C]ommon carriers that establish video delivery systems, including cable and open video systems, are not required to obtain section 214 authority prior to establishing or operating such systems. This requirement has served as an obstacle to competitive entry and has disproportionately disadvantaged new competitors. Eliminating this barrier to entry will hasten the development of video competition and will provide consumers with increased program choice." *1996 Act Conference Report* at 172–173.

[222] Implementation of Section 302 of the Telecommunications Act of 1996 (Open Video Systems), Report and Order and Notice of Proposed Rulemaking, 11 F.C.C. Rec. 14,639 (1996).

[223] Bell Atlantic-New Jersey, Inc., Election of Open Video System Option and Motion for Extension of Time To Complete Open Video System Transition, Order, 11 F.C.C. Rec. 21,036 (1996).

[224] At least six states barred competition completely, and another four blocked entry into some form of local service. National Association of Regulatory Utility Commissioners, Telecommunications Competition 1997 (Sept. 1997).

cable operators and other potential new entrants were generally required to obtain from state regulators a Certificate of Public Convenience and Necessity (CPCN) to provide competitive local telephone services.[225] Meanwhile, while federal law barred incumbent local exchange carriers from providing video programming in their service areas, it did not bar cable companies from acquiring interests in new entrants that provide competing telephone service. The FCC ruled, for example, that in their own service areas cable operators could also provide competitive access services,[226] wireless telephone services such as PCS,[227] and long-distance telephone services.[228]

§13.7.4 Telco-Cable Mergers

The wide range of options that the 1996 Act creates for LECs to provide video services does not include the purchase of existing cable operators. While cable-telco mergers would generally

---

[225] See, e.g., GTE Sprint Communications Corp. v. Public Serv. Commn. of South Carolina, 341 S.E.2d 126, 129 (S.C. 1986) (discussing S.C. Code Ann. §58-9-280 (1976), which states, "No telephone utility shall begin the construction or operation of any telephone utility plant or system, or any extension thereof . . . without first obtaining from the Commission a certificate that public convenience and necessity require or will require such construction or operation. . . .").

[226] Application of Teleport Communications-New York for Transfer of Control of Stations WLU372, WLW316 and WLW317 from Merrill Lynch Group, Inc. to Cox Teleport, Inc., Memorandum Opinion and Order, 7 F.C.C. Rec. 5986, 5988 ¶¶16–18 (1992) (hereinafter Teleport Order). In this decision, the FCC approved Cox Cable's acquisition of Teleport, a competitive access provider (CAP) that provides alternative voice and data services in New York (among other cities). Section 613(b)'s ban, the Commission reasoned, is restricted to affiliation with incumbent local exchange telephone companies, the dominant owners of local poles and conduits and the dominant providers of switched service. A CAP like Teleport, the Commission reasoned, provides only "alternate" or redundant facilities to the dominant exchange carrier.

[227] See Amendment of the Commission's Rules to Establish New Personal Communications Services, Tentative Decision and Memorandum Opinion and Order, 7 F.C.C. Rec. 7794 (1992) (tentatively granting personal communications services (PCS) license to Cox Cable for use in connection with its cable service).

[228] Teleport Order, 7 F.C.C. Rec. at 5988 ¶16 (citing First Video Dialtone Order, 7 F.C.C. Rec. at 322–323 ¶46 (1991)).

be barred by existing antitrust laws anyway, the 1996 Act specifically bars most mergers, cross-ownership investments (exceeding a 10 percent threshold),[229] and joint ventures between phone companies and cable operators that serve the same local markets.[230] Certain limited-term agreements are permitted if they provide for sharing use of cable facilities "extending from the last multi-user terminal to the premises of the end user"— the cable "drop" that typically covers the last few hundred feet of a cable network.[231] Cable and telephone companies may also form joint ventures or partnerships of any kind if their home-turf service areas don't overlap.[232] Thus, a LEC wanting to provide cable service must either figure out a way of doing it over its existing copper-wire network or "overbuild" the existing cable operator with a second coaxial-cable network. Conversely, the Act prohibits a cable operator from acquiring more than a 10 percent interest "in any local exchange carrier providing telephone exchange service within such cable operator's franchise area."[233]

The Act contains an exception to each of the above prohibitions in rural areas.[234] The Act allows a local exchange carrier to buy[235] a cable system operator in nonurban[236] markets with fewer than 35,000 inhabitants[237] if the cable system serves less than 10 percent of the households in the telephone service

---

[229] The Act contains a "buy-out" provision that prohibits local exchange carriers from acquiring more than a 10 percent stake "in any cable operator providing cable service within the local exchange carrier's telephone service area." 47 U.S.C. §572(a).

[230] *Id.* §572(c). The 1996 Act also eliminates the antitrafficking restrictions that prohibited cable operators from selling or transferring ownership in a cable system within a 36-month period following the acquisition or initial construction of such system. 1996 Telecommunications Act §301(i). The Act retains provisions that give local franchising authorities 120 days to act on any request for approval of a sale or transfer of a franchise. 47 U.S.C. §537.

[231] *Id.* §572(d)(2).

[232] *See 1996 Act Conference Report* at 174.

[233] 47 U.S.C. §572(b).

[234] *See id.* §572(d)(1).

[235] This includes obtaining "a controlling interest in, management interest in, or enter[ing] into a joint venture or partnership." *Id.*

[236] More specifically, "outside an urbanized area, as defined by the Bureau of the Census." *Id.* §572(d)(1)(A)(ii).

[237] *Id.* §572(d)(1)(A)(i).

area.[238] A cable operator may likewise buy a local exchange carrier if the telco's facilities serve a nonurban market with fewer than 35,000 inhabitants.[239] There are a few other limited exceptions for rural markets.[240]

Another important exception to the general rule allows telephone companies to make "toe-hold" acquisitions of upstart cable challengers.[241] A telephone company may buy into a cable operator (Avis) in any non-top-25 cable market served by two or more cable systems[242] if (1) the dominant incumbent (Hertz) is owned by one of the top-10 cable system operators,[243] and (2) both Avis and Hertz are licensed to serve identical territories by the largest municipality in that television market,[244] and (3) Avis was not owned by any of the top-50 cable operators as of May 1,

---

[238] *Id.* §572(d)(1)(B).

[239] *Id.* §572(d)(1).

[240] Local exchange carriers are not precluded from purchasing (but are restricted from entering joint ventures with) cable operators that, as of June 1, 1995, (1) serve less than 17,000 cable subscribers, of which at least 8,000 live in an urban area and at least 6,000 in a nonurbanized area; (2) are not owned by any of the 50 largest cable system operators; and (3) are not in a top-100 television market. *Id.* §572(d)(4). Local exchange carriers with under $100 million in annual revenues may also buy or form joint ventures with any cable system that serves no more than 20,000 subscribers if no more than 12,000 of those subscribers live within an urbanized area. *Id.* §572(d)(5).

[241] *See id.* §572(d)(3).

[242] *Id.* §572(d)(3)(A). As of April 8, 1998, the top 25 cable markets were New York NY, Long Island NY, Orlando FL, San Diego CA, Bronx/Brooklyn NY, Phoenix AZ, Puget Sound WA, Chicago IL suburbs, Denver CO, Tampa/St. Petersburg FL, Cleveland OH, San Antonio TX, Los Angeles CA, Houston TX, New Orleans LA, Las Vegas NV, Palm Beach County FL, Broward/Dade County FL, Hampton Roads VA, Union NJ, Jacksonville FL, Orange County CA, Honolulu HI, Sacramento CA, and Fairfax VA. National Cable Television Association, Cable Television Developments 15 (Spring 1998).

[243] As such operators were ranked on May 1, 1995. 47 U.S.C. §572(d) (3)(D). As of February 28, 1995, the top ten cable operators were Tele-Communications, Inc. (TCI), Time Warner Cable, Comcast Corporation, Continental Cablevision, Inc., Cablevision Systems Corporation, Cox Communications, Newhouse Broadcasting Corporation, Adelphia Communications, Cablevision Industries, and Jones Intercable, Inc. National Cable Television Association, Cable Television Developments 14 (Spring 1995).

[244] As of May 1, 1995. 47 U.S.C. §572(d)(3)(B).

1995.[245] Although this statutory language is convoluted, it allows phone companies to buy into upstart wireline cable systems that are already beginning to challenge incumbents. Telco buyouts of terrestrial wireless cable systems are also permitted. Moreover, the buyout clauses of the Act apply only to mergers and joint ventures between local exchange companies and "cable" operators—a label that excludes most types of "wireless" cable.

The Act also empowers the Commission to grant waivers if the local franchising authority approves of the waiver and the Commission finds that either the cable operator or the LEC "(i) . . . would be subjected to undue economic distress by the enforcement of such provisions; (ii) the system or facilities would not be economically viable if such provisions were enforced; or (iii) the anticompetitive effects of the proposed transaction are clearly outweighed in the public interest by the probable effect of the transaction in meeting the convenience and needs of the community to be served."[246]

---

[245] *Id.* §573(d)(3)(C). Following the top-10 operators listed above, the next 40 were Times Mirror Cable Television, Viacom Cable, Sammons Communications Inc., Falcon Cable TV, Century Communications Corp., Crown Media, Inc., Colony Communications Inc., TeleCable Corporation, Scripps Howard Cable, Lenfest Group, KBLCOM, Inc. (Houston Industries), TKR Cable, Prime Cable, InterMedia Partner, Post-Newsweek Cable Inc., TCA Cable TV, Inc., Southern Multimedia Comm. (formerly Wometco), Charter Communications, Tele-Media Corporation, Multimedia Cablevision, Inc., Marcus Group, Triax Communications Corp., Rifkin & Associates, Inc., Western Communications, C-TEC Cable Systems, Columbia International, Inc., Service Electric Cable TV, Inc., SBC Media Ventures, Greater Media, Inc., Harron Communications Corp., Media General Cable, US Cable Corp., Bresnan Communications Company, Garden State Cable TV, Armstrong Utilities, Inc., Northland Communications Corporation, Summit Communications Group, Inc., Simmons Communications (American Cable Ent.), United Video Cablevision, Inc., and Insight Communications. National Cable Television Association, Cable Television Developments 14 (Spring 1995).

[246] 47 U.S.C. §572(d)(6).

14

Privacy, Intellectual Property, and Free Speech*

§14.1 Introduction

Shortly after the telephone first appeared, Ambrose Bierce called it "[a]n invention of the devil which abrogates some of the advantages of making a disagreeable person keep his distance."[1]

*This chapter was co-authored by Geoffrey M. Klineberg, Partner, Kellogg, Huber, Hansen, Todd & Evans; Princeton University (A.B., *magna cum laude*, in the Woodrow Wilson School for Public and International Affairs, 1985); Balliol College, Oxford University (M. Phil. in International Relations, with distinction, 1987); Yale Law School (J.D., 1990); Phi Beta Kappa; Law Clerk, Honorable José A. Cabranes, U.S. District Court, District of Connecticut, 1990–1991; Law Clerk, Honorable Patricia M. Wald, U.S. Court of Appeals, D.C. Circuit, 1991–1992; Law Clerk, Honorable Harry A. Blackmun, U.S. Supreme Court, 1992–1993. Special assistant to the Deputy Attorney General, U.S. Dept. of Justice, 1993–1995.

[1] Ambrose Bierce, The Devil's Dictionary 257 (1978).

Bierce was at least half right: a ringing telephone is the enemy both of domestic peace and of thoughtful reflection. The man from Porlock[2] is never more than 7 (or 11) digits away.

This chapter surveys three broad, overlapping, and often conflicting bodies of law: privacy, intellectual property, and free speech. These are large subjects that command an extensive literature of their own. But it is a literature that rarely addresses them from the perspective of the common carrier and its customer.[3] This chapter does. Section 14.2 surveys the law of wiretapping. Section 14.3 examines signal piracy. Section 14.4 discusses intellectual property from the common carrier's perspective. Section 14.5 addresses federal regulation of "informational privacy"—the protection of information acquired by carriers and others in connection with the operation and use of telecom networks. Section 14.6 covers a carrier's right to speak over its own network, its various obligations to censor the speech of others, its right to engage in such censorship on its own initiative, and its various obligations not to. Finally, section 14.7 surveys the use and abuse of telecom networks for purposes of solicitation and harassment. On several of these topics, much of the relevant law comes from the states rather than from federal authority; our discussion is therefore brief. And we devote no space at all to the important, evolving body of the common law concerned with invasions of privacy[4] and misappropriation of intellectual property.[5]

---

[2] See Samuel Taylor Coleridge, Preface, Kubla Khan (attributing the "fragmentary" nature of his great poem to the fact that he was interrupted in mid "vision" by a "person on business from Porlock").

[3] But see Richard Klingler, The New Information Industry: Regulatory Challenges and the First Amendment 139–163 (1996) (discussing interaction among First Amendment principles, antitrust enforcement, and common carrier regulation).

[4] One of the chief catalysts of the privacy right may have been the consternation felt by the wife of a turn-of-the-century Harvard law professor when her social activities were splashed across the pages of the Boston tabloids. See Arthur Miller, The Assault on Privacy: Computers, Data Banks, and Dossiers 170 (1971). The professor, Samuel D. Warren, and his (then-little known) colleague, Louis D. Brandeis, published an article in the Harvard Law Review advocating the recognition of a civil tort action for damages for the invasion of one's privacy. S. Warren & L. Brandeis, The Right to Privacy,

Whether state or federal in origin, the law of privacy, intellectual property, and free speech has traditionally drawn sharp distinctions between carriers and broadcasters. So long as those industries provided quite separate and distinct services, it was possible to regulate them differently and to treat them as quite separate creations for constitutional and other purposes. But the industries are now converging rapidly.

---

4 Harv. L. Rev. 193 (1890). In 1960, Dean Prosser identified four common-law privacy torts that were later adopted by the Restatement (Second) of Torts, including (1) publicity that unreasonably places the other in a false light before the public, (2) unreasonable intrusion upon seclusion of another, (3) unreasonable publicity given to the other's private life, and (4) misappropriation of the other's name or likeness. Restatement (Second) of Torts 652 (1977). W. Prosser & R. Keeton, Prosser & Keeton on the Law of Torts §117, at 849 (5th ed. 1984). By the end of the 1970s, only one state—Rhode Island—had still failed to recognize a tort for invasion of privacy. *See* Note, Tort Recovery for Invasion of Privacy, 59 Neb. L. Rev. 808, 809–810 (1980). The right to privacy is now explicit in some state constitutions. *See, e.g.,* Pa. Const. art. I, §§1, 8; Ark. Const. art. I, §22; Fla. Const. art. I, §23; S.C. Const. art. I, §10. The Restatement (Second) of Torts now lists at least four quite different tort actions generally subsumed under the rubric of "invasion of privacy." Restatement (Second) of Torts §652 (listing torts of unreasonable intrusion upon the seclusion of another, appropriation of another's name or likeness, unreasonable publicity given another's private life, and publicity that unreasonably places another in a false light before the public).

[5] The Supreme Court recognized the tort of misappropriation of intellectual property in International News Service v. Associated Press, 248 U.S. 215 (1918). While the Associated Press had no property right against the public, it could assert a "quasi-property" right against its competitor. *Id.* at 236. *See generally* Zechariah Chafee, Unfair Competition, 53 Harv. L. Rev. 1289, 1315 (1940); Leo J. Raskind, The Misappropriation Doctrine as a Competitive Norm of Intellectual Property Law, 75 Minn. L. Rev. 875 (1991); Michael Madow, Private Ownership of Public Image: Popular Culture and Publicity Rights, 81 Calif. L. Rev. 125 (1993). In American Television and Communications Corp. v. Manning, American Television and Communications purchased exclusive rights to display HBO programming in Denver. American Television and Communications Corp. v. Manning, 651 P.2d 440 (Colo. App. 1982) (*ATC*). ATC used a common carrier "multi-point distribution service" to transmit the signal from a satellite receiving dish to home subscribers equipped with a special antenna and converter. The defendants sold pirate antennas and converters. The Colorado Court of Appeals concluded that the elements of unfair competition and misappropriation had been established. *Id.* at 444 (applying *International News* and related precedent, KMLA Broadcasting Corp. v. 20th Century Cigarette Vendors Corp., 264 F. Supp. 35, 44 (C.D. Cal. 1967) (subscription music service could sue on misappropriation theory when defendant installed special receivers without authorization)).

Traditional broadcasters—newspapers—had complete control of what appeared in their newspapers, with concomitant responsibility for such things as libel, even libel placed in advertisements. But the new broadcasters (like cable companies) are now carriers, too, sometimes providing carriage under government must-carry mandates. Traditional common carriers offer service to all comers, regardless of what the customers have to convey. That posture has largely insulated carriers from libel, copyright, and other civil liabilities. Regulators have traditionally overseen what carriers do in microscopic detail, and no one much worried about First Amendment issues because carriers rarely, if ever, raised these matters on their own behalf. Now, high-bandwidth carriers also publish. On the new digital media, personals, commercial ads, mail, editorials, and news all move on the same conduits and are displayed on the same screen, combined at will, bit by bit, pixel by pixel.

The upshot is a tangle of irreconcilable rights and duties: obligations to carry, on the one hand, and duties to censor, on the other; rights to publish freely, on the one hand, and across-the-board accountability to regulators, on the other. The law is in a state of enormous flux. None of the old labels and legal pigeonholes work anymore; satisfactory new ones have not yet been invented.

§14.2   Wiretapping[6]

In the subsections that follow, the reader should bear in mind the many variations on the issues raised. Do the rules apply equally to all carriers, public and private, wireline and wireless, incumbent local exchange carrier (LEC) and competitive local exchange carrier (CLEC)? Do they apply to the whole length of the communication—from the cordless or cellular phone,

---

[6] *See generally* James X. Dempsey, Communications Privacy in the Digital Age: Revitalizing the Federal Wiretap Laws to Enhance Privacy, 8 Alb. L.J. Sci. & Tech. 65 (1997).

private branch exchange (PBX), or other customer premises equipment (CPE), onto the domestic wireline network, and (perhaps) onto foreign networks? Do they extend equally to voice alone, or data—paging beepers, e-mails, video signals? Do they cover all the ancillary information that can be gleaned from an aggressive tap: who placed the call, who answered it, the location of calling and called parties,[7] the duration of the call, billing information, credit history, calling patterns and statistics, and so forth? The answers are by no means uniform. They change from one Act of Congress to the next.

§14.2.1 Government Wiretaps and the Fourth Amendment

The Fourth Amendment cordons off a zone of privacy into which the government may not lightly tread: "The right of the people to be secure in their persons, houses, papers, and effects, against unreasonable searches and seizures, shall not be violated. . . ."[8]

Or so we know today. In 1928, in *Olmstead v. United States,*[9] the Supreme Court held that the interception by federal agents of messages passing over telephone wires did not constitute a "search" or "seizure" subject to the Fourth Amendment.[10] The Fourth Amendment applied only to the physical entry of a place and the seizure of tangible things. Dissenting, Justice Brandeis pointed out that constitutional "[c]lauses guaranteeing to the individual protection against specific abuses of power must have

---

[7] In United States v. Karo, the Supreme Court held that the monitoring of a beeper in a private location is a search subject to the Fourth Amendment warrant requirement. 468 U.S. 705, 706 (1984). By contrast, use of a beeper to follow an object being transported on the public roads or to monitor the general vicinity of an object does not. *See* United States v. Knotts, 460 U.S. 276 (1983); *Karo,* 468 U.S. at 714–716.

[8] U.S. Const. amend. IV.

[9] 277 U.S. 438 (1928).

[10] *Id.* at 464–466. The Court later held that electronic eavesdropping into a phone booth likewise did not constitute a Fourth Amendment "search" or "seizure." Goldman v. United States, 316 U.S. 129, 134–136 (1942).

a . . . capacity of adaptation to a changing world," in which "[s]ubtler and more far-reaching means of invading privacy have become available. . . ."[11]

In 1967, the Court overruled *Olmstead* in *Katz v. United States*,[12] holding that the Fourth Amendment did apply to recordings of the defendant's end of telephone conversations, which had been obtained by attaching an electronic listening device to the outside of a public telephone booth. Because the defendant had "justifiably relied on an expectation of privacy" in the telephone booth, "[t]he fact that the electronic device employed to [eavesdrop] did not happen to penetrate the wall of the booth" had "no constitutional significance."[13] The Court thus devised a flexible standard adaptable to changing technologies.

The Constitution governs state action, not action by private parties. The main federal wiretap laws discussed below cover both. They in fact reverse the constitutional balance by restricting private snooping considerably more strictly than the official variety. Private parties, unlike law enforcement officials, cannot get the search warrants that the wiretap laws authorize.

§14.2.2   Section 605[14]

Responding to the *Olmstead* Court's explicit invitation, Congress in 1934 included a provision in the new federal Communications Act prohibiting any person not authorized by the sender

---

[11] *Olmstead*, 277 U.S. at 472, 473 (Brandeis, J., dissenting).

[12] 389 U.S. 347 (1967). *See also* Berger v. New York, 388 U.S. 41 (1967).

[13] *Katz*, 389 U.S. at 353. The most famous expression of the *Katz* standard for Fourth Amendment coverage—whether one has a "reasonable expectation of privacy"—actually comes from Justice Harlan's concurring opinion. *Id.* at 360.

[14] Although this provision was originally enacted in 1912, Title VI, §605, 48 Stat. 1103, it was reenacted in 1934 as section 705 of the Communications Act. The provision is codified, however, at 47 U.S.C. §605. *See generally* Lavritz S. Helland, Section 705(a) in the Modern Communications World: A Response to Di Geronimo, 40 Fed. Comm. L.J. 115 (1988).

to intercept any communication.[15] Violators of this provision were subject to both civil liability and criminal sanctions.[16] The Communications Act likewise prohibits "assist[ing] in receiving" communications to which the recipients are not entitled. The provision was originally aimed at defendants who intercepted a private radio communication, such as a police or fire department dispatch, and then published the information by radio or newspaper.

As we discuss in section 14.3 below, section 605 has since served as the unintended, but sufficient, foundation for developing a new federal common law of "signal piracy."

§14.2.3 The Wiretap Act of 1968[17]

A year after the Supreme Court's decision in *Katz,* and in direct response to that ruling, Congress enacted Title III of the Omnibus Crime Control and Safe Streets Act of 1968.[18] The

---

[15] The Act provides:

No person receiving, assisting in receiving, transmitting, or assisting in transmitting, any interstate or foreign communication by wire or radio shall divulge or publish the existence, contents, substance, purport, effect or meaning thereof . . . ; [n]o person not being authorized by the sender shall intercept any communication . . . ; and [n]o person not being entitled thereto shall receive or assist in receiving any interstate or foreign communication by wire radio. . . . This section shall not apply to the receiving, divulging, publishing or utilizing the contents of any radio communication which is transmitted . . . for the use of the general public.

47 U.S.C. §605(a).

[16] 47 U.S.C. §501 ($10,000 or one year for first offense; $10,000 or two years for second offense). *See* United States v. Westbrook, 502 F. Supp. 588 (E.D. Mich. 1980); United States v. Stone, 546 F. Supp. 234 (S.D. Tex. 1982). Courts have also held that §605 creates a private cause of action for the sender to sue the one responsible for the unauthorized interception. *See, e.g.,* Reitmeister v. Reitmeister, 162 F.2d 691, 694 (2d Cir. 1947). *See generally* Ferris et al., Cable Television Law §26.02[1][a] (1989).

[17] *See generally* Clifford S. Fishman & Anne T. McKenna, Wiretapping and Eavesdropping §14.5, at 14-11 to 14-12 (2d ed. 1995).

[18] Wire Interception and Interception of Oral Communications, 18 U.S.C. §§2510–2521 (1970) (hereinafter *Wiretap Act*).

Wiretap Act was designed to "protect [ ] the privacy of wire and oral communications," while providing and specifying "circumstances and conditions under which the interception of wire and oral communications may be authorized."[19]

The Act generally prohibited the actual or attempted willful interception of "any wire or oral communication"; the use of any "electronic, mechanical or other device" to intercept any such communication; and the disclosure or use of the contents of such communications.[20] It provided both civil and criminal penalties for violators.[21] At the same time, the Act authorized wiretapping by law enforcement officials engaged in the investigation of specifically enumerated major crimes[22] and acting under a court order[23] issued upon a finding of probable cause. Wiretapping by federal law enforcement officials was to be authorized only as a last resort, when other investigative techniques would not work; surveillance was supposed to "minimize" the interception of

---

[19] S. Rep. 1097, *reprinted in* 1968 U.S.C.C.A.N. 2112, 2153.

[20] Former 18 U.S.C. §2511(1) (1988).

[21] *Id.* §§2520, 2511(1).

[22] The original list was generally limited to espionage and treason, violent crimes, and offenses typically associated with organized crime. The list of offenses for which wiretapping is permitted has been expanded steadily ever since—from the original 26 in 1968 to more than 100 in 1998. It currently includes crimes involving false statements on passport applications and loan applications or "any depredation" against any property of the United States. The government may seek a wiretap of *electronic* communications—as opposed to wire or oral communications—when investigating "any Federal felony." *Id.* §2516(3).

[23] 18 U.S.C. §2518. Before issuing such an authorization, the judge had to find probable cause that (a) the offense had been or was about to be committed, and (b) the surveillance would generate information concerning the offense; in addition, the court had to find that normal investigation would not succeed or would be too dangerous, (c) other investigative procedures had been tried and had failed or appeared likely to fail, and (d) a nexus existed between the location being monitored and the offense. *Id.* §2518(3). The number of federal court orders issued permitting electronic surveillance in criminal cases increased from 340 in 1992 to 672 in 1995. J. McGee, Wiretapping Rises Sharply Under Clinton: Drug War Budget Increases Lead to Continuing Growth Of High-Tech Surveillance, Wash. Post, July 7, 1996, at A1.

innocent conversations.[24] After concluding the investigation, law enforcement was required to provide notice to the defendant, who would have an opportunity prior to introduction of the evidence at any trial to challenge both the adequacy of the probable cause for and the lawfulness of the carrying out of the wiretap. The Act provided for continued court supervision after the surveillance had been authorized.[25] States could permit wiretapping under restrictions at least as comprehensive as the federal law,[26] and most have done so. Those same laws generally criminalize wiretapping and eavesdropping by private parties, and in many states, eavesdropping is also civilly actionable as an invasion of privacy.[27]

The 1968 law applied only to "wire" and "oral" communications; this limitation constituted "effectively planned obsolescence."[28] Microwave transmissions and fiber-optic systems did not seem to be covered by the Act at all.[29] Neither did the Act cover cordless or cellular telephones whose transmissions can be picked up by radio[30] or any communications other than those

---

[24] *See, e.g.,* Berger v. New York, 388 U.S. 41 (1967) (striking down a state wiretap statute because it permitted an impermissibly wide net capturing "any and all conversations").

[25] *See* former 18 U.S.C. §2518(8) (1982).

[26] 18 U.S.C. §2516(2).

[27] *See, e.g.,* Annotation, 49 A.L.R.4th 430 (1998); *see, e.g.,* Md. Code Ann. §10-402 (1997) (the law that Linda Tripp may have violated when taping her telephone conversations with Monica Lewinsky).

[28] Russell Burnside, The Electronic Communications Privacy Act of 1986: The Challenge of Applying Ambiguous Statutory Language to Intricate Telecommunications Technologies, 13 Rutgers Comp. & Tech. L.J. 451, 462–463 (1987).

[29] *Id.* at 463.

[30] With respect to mobile telephones, compare United States v. Hall, 488 F.2d 193 (9th Cir. 1973) (conversation with two cordless telephones not protected, but conversation with cordless and regular telephone fully protected), with Dorsey v. State of Florida, 402 So. 2d 1178 (1981) (under identical state statute, only that portion of conversation communicated by wire is protected), and State v. Howard, 235 Kan. 236, 679 P.2d 197 (1984) (same). *See generally* Note, Title III Protection for Wireless Telephones, 1985 U. Ill. L. Rev. 143, 148–151 (1985).

provided through common carriers.[31] A department store security officer thus escaped conviction for intercepting employee telephone calls on the store's in-house phone system.[32]

§14.2.4   The Electronic Communications Privacy Act of 1986

Congress passed the Electronic Communications Privacy Act of 1986 (ECPA)[33] to amend the 1968 Act in an effort to "update and clarify Federal privacy protections and standards in the light of dramatic changes in new computer and telecommunications technologies."[34]

The ECPA was made up of three parts, the first and most important of which extended protection for wire communications to include cellular communications and communications over private networks and intracompany systems.[35] Any human voice transmission now comes entirely under the definition of interception of a "wire communication."[36]

In addition, privacy protection was extended to "electronic communications" defined to include all communications not carried by sound waves, such as electronic mail or video teleconferences.[37] Consistent with this amended definition, Congress

---

[31] See former 18 U.S.C. §2510(1) (1982).

[32] United States v. Christman, 375 F. Supp. 1354 (N.D. Cal. 1974). It does seem at least questionable, in any event, whether Congress could constitutionally criminalize such local conduct in all circumstances, since the Wiretap Act was premised on its power to regulate interstate commerce.

[33] Pub. L. 99-508, 100 Stat. 1848 (codified at 18 U.S.C. §§2510–2521 (1988)).

[34] S. Rep. No. 541, Electronic Communications Privacy Act, 99th Cong., 2d Sess. (1986), reprinted in 1986 U.S.C.C.A.N. 3555 (hereinafter ECPA Senate Report).

[35] 18 U.S.C. §2510(1). Congress dropped the limitation that protection applied to transmission via common carriers only and further expressly protected communications carried by "any provider of wire or electronic communications service," a definition clearly broad enough to embrace all competitive local carriers and private carriers. See, e.g., id. §§2510(5)(a), 2511 (2)(a), 2518(4).

[36] Id. §2510(1).

[37] Id. §2510(12) (1988). "Electronic communications" refers to "any transfer of signs, signals, writing, images, sounds, data or intelligence of any nature

made it illegal to intercept the nonvoice portion of a communication, such as the digitized portion of some voice communications.[38] The ECPA amended the definition of "contents" so as to *exclude* from privacy protection the interception or disclosure of the existence of the communication, the identity of the parties, their location, their calling patterns, and so forth.[39]

Certain exclusions from the definitions of both "wire" and "electronic" communication created ambiguity about what the ECPA originally covered. The ECPA explicitly excluded from privacy protection "the radio portion of a cordless telephone communication that is transmitted between the cordless telephone handset and the base unit."[40] Yet technology has now developed such that the radio portions of cellular and cordless transmissions are easily intercepted.[41]

"Tone-only paging devices" were also excluded from protected communications,[42] but it is not immediately clear whether voice and display pagers qualify as either "wire" or "electronic" communications under the Act's definitions.

The ECPA added more felonies for which authorities were permitted to seek a wiretapping order[43] and set out a separate,

---

transmitted in whole or in part by a wire, radio, electromagnetic, photoelectronic or photo-optical system. . . ."

[38] *Id.* §2510(4).

[39] *Id.* §2510(8) ("contents . . . includes any information concerning the substance, purport, or meaning of that communication").

[40] *Id.* §2510(1), (12)(A). Congress noted that the ease with which a person could intercept cordless phone communications made it inappropriate to criminalize such interceptions. *ECPA Senate Report* 3566.

[41] Perhaps the most famous example of this activity occurred in late 1996, when a conference call involving House Speaker Newt Gingrich and other members of the House Republican leadership was intercepted and subsequently leaked to several major newspapers. *See* S. Levine, Eavesdropping on Cellular Calls Is Illegal but Easy, Wash. Post, Jan. 11, 1997, at A1. The illegal interception and disclosure of this cellular call resulted in the criminal prosecution of a Florida couple and a civil lawsuit filed against a Democratic lawmaker. *See* G. Gugliotta, A Congressman Takes It Personally—to Court; Boehner Sues McDermott over Leaked Tape of Phone Call on Gingrich's Ethics Woes, Wash. Post, Mar. 10, 1998, at A4.

[42] 18 U.S.C. §2510(12)(C).

[43] *Id.* §2516(1).

less restrictive standard for which authorities could intercept electronic (i.e., nonwire, nonoral) communications.[44] In addition,
separate minimization standards were required for oral versus electronic communications, given the differences in technology used
both to transmit and to intercept these communications.[45]

Finally, the ECPA dramatically increased the potential criminal and civil liability for violations.[46] Electronic communications
relating to criminal activity may be disclosed to law enforcement
officers if inadvertently intercepted by a service provider.[47]

Title II of the ECPA provided privacy protection to stored wire
and electronic communications and transactional records.[48]
This new chapter to Title 18 created a criminal offense for
"intentionally accessing without authorization a facility through
which electronic communication service is provided."[49] This chapter also prohibited the provider of an electronic communications

---

[44] A court order authorizing the interception of electronic communications
may be based on evidence of any federal felony. *See id.* §2516(3). In addition,
the statutory exclusionary rule included in the ECPA refers only to wire or
oral communications, not to electronic communications. *See id.* §2515.

[45] *Id.* §2518. Unlike listening to oral communications, it is rarely possible
to determine at what point to suspend surveillance of computer transmissions. The minimization standards therefore apply at the point where officials
initially review the transcript of an electronic communication and delete all
irrelevant materials before further dissemination. *See ECPA Senate Report* at
3585.

[46] The maximum criminal fine is now $250,000 for an individual and
$500,000 for an organization. 18 U.S.C. §3571(b). The maximum civil statu-
tory damages are $10,000. *Id.* §2520(c)(2)(B). And the person whose com-
munication was intercepted may recover not only his actual damages, but also
any profits gained by the perpetrator. *Id.* §2520(c)(2)(A).

[47] *Id.* §2511(3)(b)(iv).

[48] The Act makes it a crime to "intentionally access without authorization
a facility through which an electronic communication service is provided" or
to "intentionally [exceed] an authorization to access that facility." *Id.* §2701(a).
Other provisions governing stored electronic communications are similar to
those governing electronic communications in general — including significant
exceptions for interception and disclosure by law enforcement officers and
employees of service providers. *Id.* §2702(b). Indeed, the government can
obtain a court order to access stored electronic communications or computer
files on even a lesser showing — that the communications or the files "are relevant to an ongoing criminal investigation." *Id.* §2703(d).

[49] *Id.* §2701.

service from knowingly divulging the contents of any communication.[50] Rules were established for law enforcement access to information identifying a subscriber of an electronic communications service.[51]

Title III recognized the privacy implications of transactional data generated by communications systems. Congress established rules for the use of pen registers, which capture numbers identifying outgoing calls, and for trap and trace devices, which capture numbers identifying incoming calls.[52]

§14.2.5 Carrier Obligations to Assist Law Enforcement Officials in Conducting Wiretaps

In an interesting, entirely modern twist on search-and-seizure law, the Wiretap Act effectively requires carriers—private corporations—to supervise the public law-enforcement official. The law demands the "affirmative intervention" of the common carriers' personnel for switch-based interceptions,[53] and thus, law enforcement cannot remotely or independently activate interceptions within the switching premises of the carrier:[54] law enforcement agencies, such as the FBI, must continue to work through the phone company.[55]

In its original 1968 form, however, the Wiretap Act imposed no obligation on telecommunications carriers to cooperate. In 1970, the Ninth Circuit held that, absent a specific statutory mandate, federal courts could not require carriers to assist lawful

---

[50] *Id.* §2702.

[51] *Id.* §2703(c).

[52] *Id.* §3121.

[53] 47 U.S.C. §1004.

[54] H.R. Rep. No. 827, 103d Cong., 2d Sess. (1994), *reprinted in* 1994 U.S.C.C.A.N. 3489, 3506.

[55] 47 U.S.C. §1002(a)(3). Any interception of communications or access to call-identifying information "can be activated only . . . with the affirmative intervention of an individual officer or employee of the carrier. . . ." *Id.* §1004. Only in "emergency or exigent circumstances" may a carrier, at its discretion, allow "monitoring at its premises if that is the only means of accomplishing the interception or access." *Id.* §1002(c).

wiretaps.[56] Congress immediately amended the 1968 Wiretap
Act to require a provider of wire or electronic communication
service to furnish the applicant with all information, facilities,
and technical assistance necessary to accomplish an order authorizing the interception of a wire, oral, or electronic communication.[57] In addition, the amendment allowed compensation
for reasonable expenses incurred in providing such facilities or
assistance.[58]

In 1977, the Supreme Court interpreted this amending language to allow federal courts to require, upon request of the government, "any assistance necessary to accomplish an electronic
interception."[59] New York Telephone had refused to comply with
a court order authorizing the FBI to install and use pen registers
(which disclose only the telephone numbers that are dialed) in
order to identify members of an illegal gambling operation.[60]
The Court found that Congress's "prompt action in amending" the Wiretap Act following the Ninth Circuit's decision was
"'more in the nature of an overruling of that opinion'" than an
"unequivocal statement of its intent under Title III."[61] Further,
although the plain language of the amendment did not mention
"pen registers," cooperation in their installation was still covered
under the Act, as they "accomplish a far lesser invasion of
privacy."[62]

As discussed in the following section, Congress has continued
to expand the carrier's obligations to lend the wiretapping con-

---

[56] Application of the United States, 427 F.2d 639 (9th Cir. 1970).

[57] 18 U.S.C. §2518(4) (1993) (as amended, Pub. L. No. 91-358, 84 Stat. 654
(1970)).

[58] *Id.*

[59] United States v. New York Tel. Co., 434 U.S. 159, 177 (1977).

[60] *Id.* at 161. The district court ordered New York Telephone to furnish the
FBI "all information, facilities and technical assistance" and ordered the FBI
to compensate the company for its assistance. New York Telephone had
agreed only to identify the pairs of wires of the two telephone lines, but had
refused to lease lines to the FBI in order to install the pen registers. *Id.* at 162.

[61] *Id.* at 177 n.25. The Court's decision was also based in part on the All
Writs Act. Because the telephone company was a regulated utility with a duty
to serve the public, its facilities were being used in furtherance of a criminal
enterprise, and it did not have a substantial interest in not providing assistance, it was permissible to compel the company to cooperate with the FBI.
Id. at 172–175.

[62] *Id.* at 177.

stable a helping hand. The Communications Assistance for Law Enforcement Act (CALEA)[63] requires extensive and costly modifications to equipment to help law enforcement officials tap into the modern digital network and its cataracts of hyperentropic bits. The Act stops short of turning telephone companies into government investigators, however, by expressly exempting telcos from any responsibility for "decrypting, or ensuring the government's ability to decrypt," communications encrypted by customers.[64]

A 1996 Commission order requires providers of wireless services to modify their systems within 18 months to enable them to relay to public safety authorities the cell site location of 911 callers.[65] Carriers must now go further and deploy the capability to provide latitude and longitude information locating wireless telephone callers within 125 meters.[66] Finally, the Federal Communications Commission (FCC) proposed requiring that covered carriers be capable (within five years) of locating a caller within a 40-foot radius for longitude, latitude, and altitude; this would allow investigators to locate a caller within a tall building. Concern was raised over the conflict between this provision and the prohibition on government agents obtaining location information when using pen registers or trap-and-trace devices.[67] A Department of Justice Memorandum Opinion subsequently found that the wireless enhanced 911 (E911) rules requiring disclosure of calling party number, location, and other call-related information to emergency personnel do not violate the Wiretap Act or other applicable provisions of law.[68]

---

[63] Pub. L. No. 103-414, 108 Stat. 4279 (1994) (CALEA). The Act is also known as the Digital Telephony Act, taken from the Senate bill (S. 2375) preceding it. It is codified at 47 U.S.C. §§1001 et seq.

[64] 47 U.S.C. §1002(b)(3); *see also* T. Bunker, Overview of Clipper Security Chip Controversy, LAN Magazine, Aug. 1994, at 40.

[65] Revision of the Commission's Rules to Ensure Compatibility with Enhanced 911 Emergency Calling Systems, Report and Order and Further Notice of Proposed Rulemaking, 11 F.C.C. Rec. 18,676, 18,708 ¶63 (1996).

[66] *Id.*

[67] *See* 47 U.S.C. §1002(a)(2).

[68] Revision of the Commission's Rules to Ensure Compatibility with Enhanced 911 Emergency Calling Systems, Report and Order and Further Notice

§14.2.6   Communications Assistance for Law
Enforcement Act of 1994

In October 1994, Congress passed the Communications Assistance for Law Enforcement Act (CALEA), which amended sections of Title 18 and added a new chapter to the Communications Act.[69] The new law responded to complaints by law enforcement agencies that new telecommunications technology was impeding their ability to conduct wiretaps and trace messages during criminal investigations.[70] As discussed in Chapter 8, the Act requires telecommunications carriers to make it technically easier to conduct lawful wiretaps[71] and authorizes spending to compensate

---

of Proposed Rulemaking, 12 F.C.C. Rec. 22,665, 22,734 ¶142 (1997) (referring to Department of Justice Memorandum Opinion of J. Keeney, Acting Assistant Attorney General, Criminal Division, which is included in Docket No. 94-102 and available for review at the FCC).

[69] As reflected in the Act's title, the purpose of the new chapter 9 is "[t]o amend title 18, United States Code, to make clear a telecommunications carrier's duty to cooperate in the interception of communications for law enforcement purposes. . . ." 108 Stat. 4279 (1994).

[70] The FBI documented 183 instances in which wiretaps were frustrated by cellular phones, call forwarding, voice mail, call waiting, or other new phone services.

[71] 47 U.S.C. §1003. CALEA specifies capability and capacity requirements for "telecommunications carriers," which include LECs, interexchange carriers (IXCs), cellular and personal communications services (PCS) providers, and any other common carrier, but excludes online service providers and electronic mail providers. Carriers must have capabilities to enable the government to intercept wire and electronic communications and to access call-identifying information, as well as capabilities to deliver the required information to the government in any easily accessible format to a specified location and to facilitate interceptions and caller identifications unobtrusively. *Id.* §1002(a). In addition, carriers must ensure that their systems have enough capacity to accommodate "simultaneously the number of interceptions, pen registers, and trap and trace devices" specified by the government and that the capacity be expanded upon notice. *Id.* §1003(b)(1). CALEA does not, however, authorize law enforcement agencies to require any specific design of equipment, services, features, or system configurations to be adopted by either service providers or equipment manufacturers. *Id.* §1002 (b)(1). The standards used to make changes to the networks will be determined by an industry association or standard-setting organization on the basis of publicly available technical requirements or, in the absence of such requirements, set voluntarily by a private party. *Id.* §1006. Telecommunications carriers are also

them for making the changes.[72] Wiretapping capabilities must also be incorporated (at the carrier's expense) into the new technology created by those companies.[73] CALEA requires law enforcement officials to use the best available technology to wiretap, thus minimizing the extraneous information that can be obtained through "pen registers."[74] The Act further prohibits the use of trap-and-trace devices to obtain the physical location of a subscriber.[75]

Telecommunications carriers' equipment has to allow the government to access "call-identifying information" of a subscriber that can be transmitted over lines or facilities leased by law enforcement to a location away from the carrier's premises.[76] Call-

---

not responsible for "decrypting, or ensuring the government's ability to decrypt," communications encrypted by customers. *Id.* §1002(b)(3).

[72] *Id.* §§1008–1009.

[73] 47 U.S.C. §1008. The Attorney General can agree to pay the carriers for "additional reasonable costs of making compliance" with capability requirements in connection with equipment and facilities deployed on or before January 1995 or with those deployed after January 1995 in a situation in which compliance with the specified requirements is determined to be too costly for the carrier. *Id.* §1008(b)(2)(A). If no additional funds are allocated, the carriers are deemed to be in compliance with the law. *Id.* §1008(b)(2)(B). In spite of this provision, some critics argued that requiring telephone companies to pay for such expenses is "unprecedented," especially when the costs are uncertain and when the consumer may end up paying the bill. Both the Government Accounting Office (GAO) and the United States Telephone Association (USTA), an independent association representing telephone companies, said the legislation's cost will reach close to several billion dollars. *See* The Implementation of the Communications Assistance for Law Enforcement Act of 1994: Oversight Hearing Before the Subcomm. on Crime of the House Judiciary Committee, Testimony of Roy Neel, President of the United States Telephone Association, 105th Cong., 1st Sess. (Oct. 23, 1997), *available at* <http://www.usta.org/caleatst.html> or <http://www.house.gov/judiciary/3011.htm>.

[74] A "pen register" is a device "which records or decodes electronic or other impulses which identify the numbers dialed or otherwise transmitted on the telephone line to which such device is attached." 18 U.S.C. §3127(3); *see also* H. Newton, Newton's Telecom Dictionary 456 (11th ed. 1996) (defining "pen register" as a device that translates telephone dial pulses into ink and paper form, using dashes on paper tape).

[75] 47 U.S.C. §1002(a)(2), (4). "[C]all-identifying information shall not include any information that may disclose the physical location of the subscriber (except to the extent that the location may be determined from the telephone number)." *Id.* §1002(a)(2).

[76] *Id.* §1002.

identifying information is defined to include "dialing or signaling information that identifies the origin, direction, destination, or termination of each communication."[77] The law requires a court order prior to obtaining this information.[78] The legislation authorizing access was retained in Title 18, as amended by the ECPA and other sections of CALEA.

CALEA modified the ECPA by extending privacy protection to the radio transmission from cordless telephones to their base units.[79] It also added protection to data communications transmitted by radio.[80] Prior to passage of CALEA, law enforcement officials had been able to obtain from electronic communications providers transactional data, such as e-mail addresses of subscribers, through an "administrative subpoena."[81] CALEA disallowed the use of an "administrative subpoena" to obtain this information, but permitted such a subpoena for "the name, address, telephone toll billing records, telephone number or other

---

[77] *Id.* §1001(2).

[78] 18 U.S.C. §2516. It is unclear whether this new chapter to the Communications Act actually provides a new avenue for government access to such information or merely requires telecommunications carriers to enable their equipment to provide access. The law reads that telecommunications carriers must ensure that their equipment is capable of "expeditiously . . . enabling the government, pursuant to a court order . . . to intercept. . . . " 47 U.S.C. §1002(a)(1). The House Report accompanying CALEA explains that "the purpose of the legislation is to preserve the government's ability, pursuant to court order, to intercept communications." H.R. Rep. No. 827, 103d Cong., 2d Sess. (1994), *reprinted in* 1994 U.S.C.C.A.N. 3489. Thus, CALEA appears to provide no new authority for the government to obtain information; rather, it merely reinforces the requirement of a court order as specified in Title 18.

[79] *See* Pub. L. No. 103-414, §202(a) (striking out provision *excluding* radio portion of a cordless telephone communication that is transmitted between handset and base unit from the definitions of both wire communications (§2510(1)) and electronic communications (§2510(12))).

[80] 18 U.S.C. §2510(16).

[81] *Id.* §2703(c)(1)(B) ("A provider of electronic communication service . . . shall disclose a record or other information pertaining to a subscriber."). Information may be obtained through a warrant, permission of the subscriber, or court order. In order to obtain a court order, the government entity had to offer "specific and articulable facts showing that there are reasonable grounds to believe that the contents of a wire or electronic communication or the records or other information sought are relevant and material to an ongoing criminal investigation." *Id.* §2703(d).

subscriber number or identity, and length of service of a subscriber."[82]

The Commission issued an order in March 1999 establishing systems security and integrity regulations that telecommunications centers must follow to comply with section 105 of CALEA (47 U.S.C. §1004).[83] The new deadline for carriers to comply with CALEA is June 30, 2000.[84]

§14.2.7 Regulation of Snooping and Antisnooping Equipment

The Telephone Disclosure and Dispute Resolution Act of 1992 (TDDRA) extended the ECPA by directing the FCC to promulgate rules making it unlawful to manufacture or import any radio scanner capable of intercepting cellular radio transmissions.[85] See 8.5.1.1. The Commission accordingly amended its rules to provide that it would no longer certify any devices of that

---

[82] *Id.* §2703(c)(1)(C).

[83] Communications Assistance for Law Enforcement Act, Report and Order, CC Docket No. 97-213 (FCC Mar. 15, 1999) (adopting regulations — 47 C.F.R. §§64.2100–.2106 — to ensure that any interception or access to call-identifying information can be activated only according to appropriate legal authorization).

[84] Carriers were originally expected to comply with CALEA's capability requirements (§1002) by October 25, 1998. At the request of various equipment manufacturers and carriers, the FCC has now extended the deadline until June 30, 2000. The FCC rested its decision "on the determination that, although an industry standard has been developed, there is no technology available that will enable carriers to implement that standard." *See* Petition for the Extension of the Compliance Date Under Section 107 of the Communications Assistance for Law Enforcement Act, Memorandum Opinion and Order, 13 F.C.C. Rec. 17,990, 18,005 ¶25 (1998). Furthermore, in response to complaints by the FBI (among others) that the industry standard — known as "J-STD-025" — is deficient, the FCC announced that it would consider the issue of technical standards for CALEA compliance in a separate order. Communications Assistance for Law Enforcement Act, Further Notice of Proposed Rulemaking, 13 F.C.C. Rec. 22,632 (1998).

[85] Pub. L. No. 102-556, 106 Stat. 4181 (codified at 15 U.S.C. §5701, 15 U.S.C. §5714, 47 U.S.C. §227, 47 U.S.C. §228, 47 U.S.C. §302a, 15 U.S.C. §§5711–5712, 15 U.S.C. §§5721–5724).

kind.[86] And the law protects only transmissions in the cellular bands, not those in PCS and other commercial mobile radio service (CMRS) bands.[87] The Wiretap Act makes unlawful the sending of a device that is known to be designed primarily for the purpose of "surreptitious interception of wire, oral, or electronic communication."[88]

Encryption software and hardware—the "Clipper Chip," in particular—have likewise been the subject of much debate and of a variety of regulatory initiatives. See section 8.5.1.3.

§14.2.8   The Antiterrorism Act of 1996

The ECPA permitted interception of any electronic communication that was "readily accessible to the general public."[89] This qualification was defined to include radio communications that were not scrambled, modulated, carried on a subcarrier channel, or transmitted over a common carrier communication system. In 1994, Congress passed a provision making it clear that the privacy of data transfers was protected by the ECPA.[90] But less than two years later, in the Antiterrorism Act of 1996, Congress repealed the provision[91] on the basis of the Justice Department's claim that the 1994 amendment had been overbroad.[92]

---

[86] The FCC declined, however, to extend the ban to frequencies occupied by similar services (e.g., SMR). The Commission also created exceptions for legitimate use by law enforcement personnel, as well as for cellular operators who use them to test their systems. Amendment of Parts 2 and 15 to Prohibit Marketing of Radio Scanners Capable of Intercepting Cellular Telephone Conversations, Report and Order, 8 F.C.C. Rec. 2911, 2913 ¶19 (1993).

[87] 47 U.S.C. §302a(d) (1996).

[88] 18 U.S.C. §2512. "Surreptitious interception" has been interpreted to mean simply "secret listening." United States v. Bast, 495 F.2d 138, 138 (D.C. Cir. 1974).

[89] 18 U.S.C. §2511(g).

[90] Pub. L. 103-414, §203 (amending 18 U.S.C. §2510(16) (adding "electronic communications" as a category of radio communication covered by the wiretap statute)).

[91] Antiterrorism Act of 1996, Pub. L. 104-132, §731 (repealing 18 U.S.C. §2510(16)(F)).

[92] See Electronic Communications Provisions of the Administration Counter-Terrorism Proposal: Hearings on S.761 Before the Senate Judiciary Committee,

§14.2.9 The Foreign Intelligence Surveillance Act[93]

In 1978, Congress enacted a second law to govern wiretapping in national security cases: the Foreign Intelligence Surveillance Act (FISA).[94] This law authorizes the President, through the Attorney General, to conduct electronic surveillance in the United States after obtaining authorization from a judicial panel (composed of seven judges from seven of the U.S. judicial circuits designated by the Chief Justice of the Supreme Court). Authorization must be based on a probable cause finding that the target is a foreign power or an agent of a foreign power.[95] In its 20-year history, the FISA court has never turned down a government electronic surveillance request.[96]

Because it is aimed at foreign intelligence and counterintelligence, FISA does not offer some of the protections required in domestic electronic surveillance.[97] Most significant, FISA does not require that the target ever be given notice of the surveillance, even after the investigation is closed, unless the government seeks to use the results in a criminal prosecution.[98] If the target of the wiretap is not a U.S. citizen or permanent resident, the statute does not require probable cause to believe that the target is engaged in criminal conduct; it suffices that the target

---

Testimony of Jamie S. Gorelick, Deputy Attorney General, 104th Cong., 1st Sess. (May 24, 1995).

[93] See generally James X. Dempsey, Communications Privacy in the Digital Age: Revitalizing the Federal Wiretap Laws to Enhance Privacy, 8 Alb. L.J. Sci. & Tech. 65 (1997).

[94] Pub. L. No. 95-511, Title I, §101, 92 Stat. 1783 (1983) (codified at 50 U.S.C. §§1801–1811).

[95] 50 U.S.C. §§1801 et seq.

[96] J. McGee & B. Duffy, Someone to Watch over Us, Wash. Post, June 23, 1996 (Magazine), at 9, 12. See generally Jim McGee & Brian Duffy, Main Justice: The Men and Women Who Enforce the Nation's Criminal Laws and Guard Its Liberties (1996).

[97] Foreign Intelligence Surveillance Act: Oversight Hearings Before the Subcomm. on Courts, Civil Liberties, and the Administration of Justice of the House Comm. on the Judiciary, 98th Cong., 1st Sess. 2–18 (1983) (testimony of Mary Lawton, Counsel for the Office of Intelligence Policy and Review, U.S. Justice Department).

[98] 50 U.S.C. §1806(c).

be fingered as an agent of a foreign power.[99] Even if the target is a U.S. citizen, the statute allows surveillance on similar terms if there is probable cause to believe that the person is engaged in clandestine intelligence activities on behalf of a foreign power, "which activities involve or *may* involve a violation of the criminal statutes of the United States."[100]

§14.3   Signal Piracy

§14.3.1   Piracy of Cable Signals[101]

Cable piracy is another form of wiretapping.[102] Intercepting reruns of *I Love Lucy* may seem less objectionable than intercepting a real Lucy's phone calls. But in the digital environment now emerging, both cable and phone lines will carry Internet traffic, thereby indiscriminately intermingling entertainment and messaging.

In the Cable Communications Policy Act of 1984,[103] Congress added section 553 to Title 47 to deal with this kind of piracy: "[N]o person shall intercept or receive or assist in intercepting or receiving any communications service offered over a cable system, unless specifically authorized to do so by a cable operator or as may otherwise be specifically authorized by law."[104] The

[99] *Id.* §1801(b)(1) (defining an "agent of a foreign power").

[100] *Id.* §1801(b)(2)(A) (emphasis added).

[101] For additional discussion of state and federal laws applicable to cable piracy, see Ferris et al., Cable Television Law §26; Brenner & Price, Cable Television §5.08 (theft of cable service); United States v. Coyle, 63 F.3d 1239 (4th Cir. 1995) (upholding criminal conviction under mail fraud statute, 18 U.S.C. §1341, for selling devices to assist in violation of 47 U.S.C. §553).

[102] *See* Gardner F. Gillespie, Jeremy H. Stern, & David W. Karp, Cable Decoder Piracy, White Paper: A Summary of Federal Laws in the Cable Industry's Anti-piracy Arsenal (Mar. 15, 1991).

[103] Pub. L. No. 98-549, §2, 98 Stat. 2796 (1984).

[104] 47 U.S.C. §553(a)(1). Willful violations for personal use are subject to a fine of not more than $1,000, or imprisonment of up to six months, or both. *Id.* §553(b)(1). Willful violations for commercial gain are treated as felonies. *Id.* §553(b)(2). In addition to increasing penalties, the 1992 Cable Act made the sale or manufacture of each illegal device a separate violation. *Id.* §553(b)(3).

phrase "any communications service" includes audio, video, text, data, and interactive services.[105] Manufacturers of unauthorized descramblers are explicitly included among those who "assist in intercepting or receiving."[106] The 1984 Cable Act authorized civil actions for injunctive relief, actual damages, or damages prescribed by the statute.[107]

How does section 553 relate to section 605? Courts have reached different conclusions. Although section 553 clearly applies to cable systems and not to over-the-air broadcasts,[108] section 605 arguably applies to both. Before section 553 was enacted, courts had applied section 605 to the theft of cable programming;[109] Congress apparently did not intend to overturn that precedent.[110] But the 1988 amendments to section 605 permitted higher damages under section 605 than were subsequently provided for in section 553. Why then would anyone choose to sue under section 553?[111] A number of courts have held that section 553 is the exclusive remedy for piracy of wired services, while section 605 covers the air.[112] Other courts continue to apply sec-

---

[105] *See* H.R. Rep. No. 934, 98th Cong., 2d Sess. 8 (1984), *reprinted in* 1984 U.S.C.C.A.N. at 4720.

[106] 47 U.S.C. §553(a)(2). The distributor's intent is the dispositive factor under section 553. *See* H.R. Rep. No. 934, 98th Cong., at 83–84, *reprinted in* 1984 U.S.C.C.A.N. at 4720–4721.

[107] 47 U.S.C. §553(c)(3). *See, e.g.,* Cablevision Sys. Corp. v. Maxie's North Shore Deli Corp., 1991 U.S. Dist. LEXIS 4874 (E.D.N.Y. 1991).

[108] 47 U.S.C. §553. *See* H.R. Rep. No. 934, 98th Cong., at 83, *reprinted in* 1984 U.S.C.C.A.N. at 4720 (section 553 has no application to over-the-air signals).

[109] *See, e.g.,* Ciminelli v. Cablevision, 583 F. Supp. 158, 164 (E.D.N.Y. 1984), and cases cited therein.

[110] *See* H.R. Rep. No. 934, 98th Cong., at 84, *reprinted in* 1984 U.S.C.C.A.N. at 4721.

[111] *See Cablevision Sys. Corp.,* 1991 U.S. Dist. LEXIS 4874 (both section 553 and section 605 apply to theft of cable service, but court applied section 605 because of its greater penalties); American Cablevision of Queens v. McGinn, 817 F. Supp. 317, 320 (E.D.N.Y. 1993) (although both section 553 and section 605 applied to cable theft, court applied only section 553 because it more directly addressed the theft).

[112] *See, e.g.,* International Cablevision, Inc. v. Sykes, 997 F.2d 998, 1008–1009 (2d Cir. 1993); Joe Hand Promotions v. Rennard St. Enters., 954 F. Supp. 1046 (E.D. Pa. 1997); That's Entertainment, Inc., v. Anciano's Inc., 1996 U.S. Dist. LEXIS 13010 (N.D. Ill. 1996); International Cablevision, Inc., v. Noel, 859 F. Supp. 69 (W.D.N.Y. 1994); United States v. Norris, 833 F. Supp. 1392 (N.D. Ind. 1993), *aff'd,* 34 F.3d 530 (7th Cir. 1994).

tion 605 to cable pirates.[113] That makes section 553 completely superfluous, although such a result appears to be consistent with legislative intent. As under section 605(a), criminal liability under section 553 requires a willful violation of law.[114] Likewise, in a civil proceeding, a plaintiff must show that the supplier of a descrambler intended to assist in the piracy.[115] Having proved intent, the complainant need not prove that an end user actually intercepted anything.[116]

§14.3.2   Piracy of Wireless "Broadcasts"

As noted in section 14.2.2 above, section 605 of Title 47 prohibits the interception and publication of wire and radio transmissions, which include telephone, telegraph, and now television. The provision was originally aimed at defendants who intercepted a private radio communication, such as a police or fire department dispatch, and then published the information by radio or newspaper.[117] Picking up a broadcast intended from the outset "for the use of the general public" was expressly permit-

---

[113] *See, e.g.,* Kingvision v. Lovato, 1996 U.S. Dist. LEXIS 17632 (N.D. Cal. 1996); Time Warner v. Freedom Elecs., Inc., 897 F. Supp. 1454 (S.D. Fla. 1995); General Instrument Corp. of Del. v. Lake Sylvan Sales, 1993 U.S. Dist. LEXIS 16828 (E.D. Penn. 1993); Cablevision Sys. Corp. v. Frank de Palma, 1989 U.S. Dist. LEXIS 1087 (E.D.N.Y. 1989).

[114] 47 U.S.C. §553(b). *See* United States v. Gardner, 860 F.2d 1391 (7th Cir. 1988) (*Gardner*); H.R. Rep. No. 934, 98th Cong., at 84, *reprinted in* 1984 U.S.C.C.A.N. at 4721.

[115] Tandy Corporation escaped liability for selling the "Archer Converter," which allowed remote channel control and the use of a VCR to tape a cable channel while the owner viewed a different channel; it did not permit the subscriber to receive channels for which he had not paid. Thus, the converter was not an illegal "pirating device," and the defendant could not have had the requisite intent. Shenango Cable TV, Inc. v. Tandy Corp., 631 F. Supp. 835 (W.D. Pa. 1986); *see also* Storer Communications Inc., v. Mogel, 625 F. Supp. 1194 (S.D. Fla. 1985).

[116] *See Gardner,* 860 F.2d 1391; United States v. Beale, 681 F. Supp. 74, 75 (1988).

[117] *See* Lavritz S. Helland, Section 705(a) in the Modern Communications World: A Response to Di Geronimo, 40 Fed. Comm. L.J. 115 (1988).

ted.[118] But the literal language of section 605 can cover a great deal more.

The potential applicability of section 605 to signal piracy arrived in court as early as the 1960s, with the advent of subscription radio services.[119] Litigation increased in the late 1970s, when subscription television (STV) operators began offering pay TV service on scrambled UHF or VHF signals.[120] Multipoint distribution service (MDS) systems[121] were used to carry similar services on microwave frequencies; MDS signals were often not scrambled, but required a special antenna. MDS and STV operators attempted to invoke section 605 to block piracy. By its literal terms, however, section 605 permitted interception of any broadcast "for the use of the general public." The problem for MDS operators was that their signals were broadcast for the use

---

[118] In 1982, section 605(a) was amended to read: "This section shall not apply to the receiving, divulging, publishing or utilizing the contents of any radio communications which is transmitted by any station for the use of the general public." 47 U.S.C. §605(a). The change was to clarify the status of amateur radio transmissions, but not to change the application of the statute to television broadcasters. *See* 1982 U.S.C.C.A.N. 2244.

[119] The FCC determined that radio subscription services that provided background music to an industrial and mercantile clientele were not broadcasting. The FCC ruled that section 605 probably did apply. Amendment of Parts 2, 3 and 4 of the Commission's Rules and Regulations and the Standards of Good Engineering Practice, Report and Order, 11 Rad. Reg. (P & F) 1590, 1599 (1956); FCC, Public Notice No. 36067 (Aug. 3, 1969), *reprinted in* Unauthorized Reception of Subscription Television: Hearing on H.R. 4727 Before the Subcomm. on Telecommunications, Consumer Protection, and Finance of the House Comm. on Energy and Commerce, 97th Cong., 1st Sess. 227 (Nov. 17, 1981). *See* KMLA Broad. Corp. v. Twentieth Century Cigarette Vendors Corp., 264 F. Supp. 35 (C.D. Cal. 1967) (subscription radio broadcaster entitled to protection of section 605 as a nonbroadcaster because operator intended that only subscribers receive the signals and ordinary radio sets could *not* receive the signals).

[120] *See generally* Pay Television Piracy: Does Section 605 of the Federal Communications Act of 1934 Prohibit Signal Piracy—and Should It?, 10 Wm. Mitchell L. Rev. 531 (1984); J. Marshall, Stealing the Signals: Hackers Are Drawn to Satellite TV Industry, S.F. Chron., June 19, 1997, at B1; G. Beauchamp, Is FCC Paving the Way for Piracy, Multichannel News, Sept. 7, 1998, at 71.

[121] MDS was established by the FCC in 1974 as a common carrier service.

of the general public, and most of them did not scramble their signals.

In 1979, the FCC ruled that MDS operators were entitled to the protection of section 605 anyway[122] and reaffirmed as much in 1985.[123] Most courts have concurred, on the grounds that MDS operators clearly intended that only paying subscribers receive the signals.[124] Courts likewise ruled that STV operators were protected by section 605, even if these media were considered "broadcast" for other regulatory purposes.[125] In 1981, the Ninth Circuit reasoned that the key to determining whether an operator was entitled to section 605 protection turned on operator intent.[126] Scrambled signals are obviously not intended for receipt by the general public. As discussed below, proscriptions against piracy of less-than-public broadcast signals were first fleshed out in STV and MDS actions against sellers of decoders.

The same issues arose in a new context when satellites took over the long-distance transport of video for TV and cable in the 1970s.[127] The price of satellite receiving dishes then dropped quickly, and private dishes proliferated outside hotels, bars, and individual homes. As the cost of dishes dropped, unintended reception spread. Sales of dishes exploded in the early 1980s

---

[122] FCC, Public Notice No. 11850, Unauthorized Interception and Use of Multipoint Distribution Service (MDS) Transmissions (Jan. 24, 1979) (unauthorized interception of MDS signals violates §605). *See also* Amendment of Part 21 of the Commission's Rules, Memorandum Opinion and Order, 57 Rad. Reg. 2d (P & F) 1555 ¶4 n.4 (1985).

[123] FCC, Public Notice No. 1222 (Dec. 3, 1985) (extending protection to MDS signals, whether or not encrypted).

[124] *See* California Satellite Sys. v. Seimon, 767 F.2d 1364, 1367 (9th Cir. 1985) (unscrambled MDS signals protected; scrambling irrelevant to section 605), and cases cited therein. *See generally* Ferris et al., Cable Television Law §26.02[1].

[125] Chartwell Communications Group v. Westbrook, 637 F.2d 459, 465 (6th Cir. 1980).

[126] National Subscription Television v. S&H TV, 644 F.2d 820, 824–825 (9th Cir. 1981).

[127] Western Union's Westar I, launched in 1974, was the first domestic communications satellite capable of carrying television signals without shutting down its other channels. CBS began using the satellite the same year to broadcast pay programs. In 1975, HBO began transmitting regular programming via Westar I to its cable affiliates.

The legal status of this kind of interception under section 605 was unclear. Satellite transmissions are, of course, "radio communications" within the meaning of the Act.[128] But was the interception unauthorized? In 1978, the FCC declared that section 605 extended to "unauthorized uses" of intercepted satellite signals.[129] "Use" was not defined, and the meaning of "unauthorized" was unclear: at the time, the FCC licensed receive-only earth stations, which arguably "authorized" their use. But the Commission abandoned the licensing requirement in 1979.[130] Courts ruled that section 605 prohibited the interception of satellite transmissions by commercial establishments, such as sports bars,[131] but the status of interceptions for private use remained uncertain.[132]

In 1984, Congress amended section 605, sharpening the line between legal and illegal interceptions.[133] A new section, section

---

[128] 47 U.S.C §153(b) (defining radio communications).

[129] Federal Communications Commission Public Notice, 43 Fed. Reg. 46,581 (1978); *see* American Television and Communications Corp. v. Floken, 629 F. Supp. 1462, 1467–1468 (M.D. Fla. 1986) (describing cases extending protection of section 605 to televisions signals carried by satellite); Cable/Home Communication Corp. v. Network Productions, Inc., 902 F.2d 829, 847–848 (11th Cir. 1990) (applying section 605 to satellite signals by analogy to subscription television cases).

[130] The Commission suggested that although the interception of a non-broadcast signal by the home dish would probably violate section 605, licensing the antenna was not an effective method of enforcement. Regulation of Domestic Receive-Only Satellite Earth Stations, First Report and Order, 74 F.C.C.2d 205, 217 ¶31(1979).

[131] National Football League v. Cousin Hugo's, Inc., 600 F. Supp. 84, 87 (E.D. Mo. 1984); National Football League v. Alley, 624 F. Supp. 6, 9–10 (S.D. Fla. 1983).

[132] Inquiry into the Scrambling of Satellite Television Signals, Report, 2 F.C.C. Rec. 1669, 1681 (1987) (citing comments of NCTA); Note, Who Owns the Air? Unscrambling the Satellite Viewing Rights Dilemma, 20 Loy. L.A. L. Rev. 145, 145 (1986).

[133] Pub. L. No. 98-459, §§5(a), 6(a), 98 Stat. 2802, 2804 (1984). *See generally* Hearings Before the Subcomm. on Patents, Copyrights and Trademarks of the Comm. on the Judiciary on Privacy and Electronic Communications, 98th Cong., 1st Sess. 1266 (1984); Civil Liberties and the National Security State: Hearings Before the Subcommittee on Courts, Civil Liberties, and the Administration of Justice, 98th Cong., 1st & 2d Sess. 133 (1984).

605(b), expressly authorizes interception of "satellite cable programming"[134] for "private viewing" if "the programming involved
is not encrypted" and if the programmer has not established a
marketing system under which "an agent or agents have been
lawfully designated for the purpose of authorizing private viewing by individuals."[135]

This amendment did not modify the copyright law, however;[136] although an interception may not constitute piracy,
it may still be a copyright violation if the signal is then "performed" publicly. Section 605(b) contains a similar limit of its
own: interception for "private viewing" is covered, but commercial uses are not.[137] The statute defines "private viewing" as "the
viewing for private use in an individual's dwelling unit by means
of equipment owned or operated by such individual, capable of
receiving satellite cable programming directly from a satellite."[138]
Congress had in mind principally rural homeowners, for whom
a satellite dish was the only video link to the global village.[139]
The private viewing exception was not intended to cover "private cable systems"[140] (SMATV) or the "display of satellite cable

[134] The new provision defines "satellite cable programming" as "video programming which is transmitted via satellite and which is primarily intended
for the direct receipt by cable operators for their retransmission to cable subscribers." 47 U.S.C. §605(d)(1).

[135] *Id.* §605(b). *See also* 130 Cong. Rec. S14,286 (Oct. 11, 1984) (statement
of Sen. Packwood), *reprinted in* 1984 U.S.C.C.A.N. 4655, 4745 ("The main
purpose behind the enactment of section 605(b) was to '[make] it clear that
the manufacture, sale and home use of earth stations are legal activities.'"); *see
also* Sioux Falls Cable Television v. South Dakota, 838 F.2d 249, 252 (8th Cir.
1988) (*Sioux Falls CATV*) (quoting 130 Cong. Rec. H10,446 (Oct. 1, 1984)
(statement of Rep. Rose)).

[136] 47 U.S.C. §605(f).

[137] *See, e.g.,* American Television & Communications Corp. v. Floken, Ltd.,
629 F. Supp. 1462 (M.D. Fla. 1986).

[138] 47 U.S.C. §605(d)(4). The legislative history further describes a
"dwelling unit" as a place where generally the persons present are within the
normal circle of a family or its social acquaintances. 130 Cong. Rec. S14,286
(Oct. 11, 1984) (statement of Sen. Packwood), *reprinted in* 1984 U.S.C.C.A.N.
at 4749.

[139] *See* 130 Cong. Rec. S14,287 (Oct. 11, 1984) (statement of Sen. Packwood), *reprinted in* 1984 U.S.C.C.A.N. at 4746.

[140] *Id.* at S14,286, *reprinted in* 1984 U.S.C.C.A.N. at 4749–4750. Nor is it
contemplated that an individual may redistribute programming received by
his satellite equipment to the homes or residences of his neighbors. *Id.*

programming in the public area of an apartment building, condominium, or housing complex, or in taverns, restaurants, or fraternal halls."[141] Thus, a hotel falls outside section 605(b) and violates section 605(a) by retransmitting satellite signals to its guests.[142] A state prison does not violate section 605, apparently because there is no profit in that branch of the hospitality business.[143]

The 1984 amendments were intended to protect piracy of new satellite services, as well as that of STV or MDS;[144] the expansive readings of section 605 that have been accepted to protect STV and MDS operators will almost certainly be extended to direct broadcast satellite (DBS) services as well,[145] even though DBS is literally "broadcasting."[146]

---

[141] *Id.*

[142] *See, e.g.,* Showtime/The Movie Channel, Inc. v. Covered Bridge Condominium Assn., 881 F.2d 983, 988–989 (11th Cir. 1989) (Covered Bridge Condominium Assn.) (condominium could not rely on the private viewing exception because service had established a marketing system for SMATV systems); ESPN v. Edinburg Community Hotel, Inc., 623 F. Supp. 647, 652 (S.D. Tex. 1985) (retransmission to hotel rooms was not "private viewing").

[143] *Sioux Falls CATV,* 838 F.2d at 254 (distinguishing prison from institutions that provide programming for indirect financial gain, "in the sense that the availability of the system is an attraction to potential occupants or customers of the establishment, be it an apartment complex, a hotel, a dormitory, a bar, or a mobile home park.").

[144] "Section 605 not only prohibits unauthorized interception of traditional radio communications, but also communications transmitted by means of new technologies. For example, existing section 605 provided protection against the unauthorized reception of subscription television (STV), multipoint distribution services (MDS), and satellite communications. This amendment made by section 5 of the bill is intended to preserve this broad reach of existing section 605 and to make clear that all communications covered under section 605 will continue to be protected under new section 705(a)." 130 Cong. Rec. S14,287 (Oct. 11, 1984) (statement of Sen. Packwood), *reprinted in* 1984 U.S.C.C.A.N. at 4746.

[145] *See* American Television and Communications Corp. v. Floken, 629 F. Supp. 1462.

[146] To "broadcast" means "[t]o send information to two or more receiving devices simultaneously—over a data communications network, a voice mail, electronic mail system, a local TV or radio station or a satellite system." Newton's Telecom Dictionary 91 (11th ed. 1996). The FCC ruled in 1987 that subscription DBS services were not "broadcasting" within the meaning of the Communications Act. *See* Subscription Video, Report and Order, 2 F.C.C. Rec. 1001 (1987).

§14.3.3   Piracy of Scrambled Wireless Transmissions

The new section 605 invited distributors of cable programming to reprivatize their radio signals if they cared to, either by scrambling their signal or simply by establishing a formal plan to market their signals to owners of private dishes. By July 1986, most major cable networks were scrambling.[147] Sales of home dishes plummeted.[148]

Scrambling has now become so straightforward and so common that many of the old copyright and piracy assumptions accepted with in-the-clear broadcasts should be viewed as historical curiosities. Much copyright law could be rewritten and greatly simplified if "public performance," "fair use," and related doctrines were more closely tied to the presence or absence of scrambling. In a rough and indirect way, that is indeed what is happening.[149]

§14.3.4   Regulation of Scrambling and Decoding Equipment

As discussed in section 8.5, much of the protection provided by intellectual property law comes by way of regulating equip-

---

[147] HBO announced plans for scrambling by 1982. In 1986, HBO and Cinemax began scrambling, requiring home dish users to buy a $395 decoder, as well as to pay subscriber fees to receive the signals legally. Other pay channels followed. The major broadcast networks and PBS also use satellites to transmit their "network feeds"; many of these are now scrambled as well. *See* Inquiry into the Scrambling of Satellite Signals, Report, 2 F.C.C. Rec. 1669, 1689–1694 ¶¶149–185 (1987).

[148] While dish sales totaled 90,000 per month as of September 1985, by February 1986 they had dropped to 16,000. Nearly half of home earth station dealers went out of business in 1986. *See* D. Stover, The Satellite TV Puzzle: Legal Issues over Scrambling Telecommunications, Popular Science, Nov. 1986, at 71.

[149] *But see* Ferris et al., Cable Television Law §26.02[1]; *see also* California Satellite Sys. v. Seimon, 767 F.2d 1364 (1985) (scrambling irrelevant to interpretation of §705); FCC, Public Notice No. 1222 (Dec. 3, 1985) (extending protection to MDS signals, whether or not encrypted).

ment used to pirate or copy. For the most part, however, the Commission has left the evolution of scrambling technology to the market, and to state attorneys general and private civil claimants.[150] Periodically the Commission issues interpretive statements warning against unauthorized interception and use of satellite and MDS transmissions as a possible violation of section 605[151] or cautioning manufacturers and sellers of decoders not approved by the Commission that they may be violating the law.[152]

Market forces, lawsuits, and occasional updates of the copyright law by Congress have likewise dealt with the regulation

[150] Amendment of Part 21 of the Commission's Rules to Prohibit the Sale, Purchase, or Use of Facilities Designed for Reception Within the Range of 2150–2162 MHz, Memorandum Opinion and Order, 57 Rad. Reg. 2d (P&F) 1555 (1985) (rejecting MDS carrier's request to prohibit distribution of MDS receivers within the MDS service area unless registered with the MDS carrier, on the ground that section 605, as interpreted by the FCC and administered by the courts under the oversight of Congress, provided adequate protection from pirates); Amendment of Part 73 of the Commission's Rules and Regulations in Regard to Section 73.642(a)(3) and Other Aspects of the Subscription Television Service, Third Report and Order, 90 F.C.C.2d 341, 355–357 ¶¶38–45 (1982) (rejecting STV operator's concern that allowing sale of STV decoders would facilitate piracy).

[151] *See, e.g.,* FCC, Public Notice, 43 Fed. Reg. 46,581 (1978) (declaring that unauthorized interception of MDS violates section 605); FCC, Public Notice No. 11850, Unauthorized Interception and Use of Multipoint Distribution Service (MDS) Transmissions (Jan. 24, 1979) (same); FCC, Public Notice No. 7999, Unauthorized Interception and Use of Satellite Transmissions (Oct. 3, 1978) (unauthorized interception of satellite transmissions violates section 605); Inquiry into the Scrambling of Satellite Television Signals and Access to Those Signals by Owners of Home Satellite Dish Antennas, Report, 2 F.C.C. Rec. 1669, 1696 ¶194 (1987) (unauthorized interception of network television satellite feeds by home dish owners or the unauthorized sale of decoders could lead to civil or criminal actions under section 705(d)); *see also* Regulation of Domestic Receive-Only Satellite Earth Stations, First Report and Order, 74 F.C.C.2d 205, 216 ¶29 (1979).

[152] 47 C.F.R. §73.644; *see* FCC, Public Notice No. 34941, Manufacturers and Sellers of Non-approved Subscription Television (STV) Decoders Are Cautioned (Aug. 15, 1980) (manufacture, sale, or use of STV decoders not approved by the Commission unlawful under sections 302(a), 303(e), 303(r) of the Communications Act; notice does not mention section 605). For failure to heed the warnings, the FCC may impose a $2,000 forfeiture and other penalties. Public Notice No. 3876, FCC Issues Warning Against Theft of Satellite Programming, 65 Rad. Reg. 2d (P & F) 36 (1988); 47 U.S.C. §503(b)(2); Modified Cable Converter-Decoder, Public Notice, 9 F.C.C. Rec. 6436 (1994).

of consumer equipment and electronics that could "copy" or perform protected materials—everything from "player-pianos" to VCRs.[153]

§14.4   Misappropriation of Intellectual Property

A comprehensive treatment of copyright law lies outside the scope of this treatise. But in this age of all-digital conveyance and copying, telecommunications law and the law of intellectual property intersect on the premises of the carrier. As discussed in section 14.2 above, much of what copyright infringers commonly do is technically covered by the wiretap laws. By the same token, much of what carriers ordinarily do would seem to expose them to liability for contributory infringement of copyright laws.

§14.4.1   Carriage and Copyright

Copyright implicates the most proprietary end of the law of intellectual property; carriage implicates the least. Common sense suggests that carriers who provide transmission services to all comers without regard to content should not have to worry much about copyright. Their facilities can be used for all manner of copyright violation by providing connections to copiers of every sort, but carriers do not monitor transmissions against the possibility of infringements. Copyright infringement is a tort, however, and tort liability usually extends to every proximate cause and agent of a harm.[154] Nonetheless, telephone companies do not often get charged with copyright infringement. Why not?

---

[153] *See* Sony Corp. v. Universal Studios, 464 U.S. 417 (1984). *Sony Corp.* does not protect the manufacturer or owner of copying equipment when the final use is an infringement. *See* RCA Records v. All-Fast Sys., Inc., 594 F. Supp. 335 (S.D.N.Y. 1984) (owner of a retail copying service prohibited from selling blank audiocassette tapes, which he knew or should have known could be used to make unauthorized reproductions of copyrighted works, and from using a copying device to make reproductions).

[154] Alan Latman, Robert Gorman, & Jane Ginsburg, Copyright for the Nineties 666 (3d ed. 1989). As a partial remedy, a carrier may insist that its

First, it has been argued that the common carriage facilities the telephone company provides do not themselves "copy" the works transmitted over them. The electronic ghost of the message that actually passes through the telephone company's wires is too evanescent to be considered a copy in itself.[155] But modern telephone networks do, of course, copy and store—in central-office voice mail boxes, for example. Telephone companies even provide computer servers that can broadcast by phone a single message to many recipients.

The more cogent defense of passive carriers like telephone companies in a case of contributory infringement is that they are not active or knowledgeable enough about the copyright violations they may facilitate.[156] A common carrier is required to carry all comers;[157] it has neither control over nor knowledge of what it transmits.[158] But knowledge is not a necessary element of liability for direct infringement.

---

customers indemnify it against copyright liability in private contracts or tariffs, also a means of limiting the telephone company's liability in case of negligence. Investigation of Access and Divestiture Related Tariffs (Part 1 of 2), Memorandum Opinion and Order, 97 F.C.C.2d 1082, 1150–1151 (1984). *Cf.* Mr. Rooter Corporation v. Morris, 188 U.S.P.Q. (BNA) 392 (E.D. La. 1975) (requiring defendant in trademark infringement suit to indemnify telephone company).

[155] Latman, Copyright Law at 86–87 (discussing concept of "fixation"— when "[a] work that is fixed in a tangible medium of expression . . . to permit the work to be perceived, reproduced, or otherwise communicated for a period of more than transitory duration").

[156] The Supreme Court has described a contributory infringer as one who "was in a position to control the use of copyrighted works by others and had authorized the use without permission from the copyright owner." *Sony Corp.*, 464 U.S. at 437; *see id.* at 486–493 (Blackmun, J., dissenting). The contributory infringer must have "knowledge of the infringing activity [and then] induce, cause, or materially contribute to the infringing conduct of another." Gershwin Publishing Corp. v. Columbia Artists Management, Inc., 443 F.2d 1159, 1162 (2d Cir. 1971). *See* Latman, Copyright Law at 668.

[157] The common carrier's customers "transmit intelligence of their own design and choosing." National Assn. of Regulatory Util. Commrs. v. FCC, 525 F.2d 630, 641 n.58 (D.C. Cir. 1976) (quoting Industrial Radiolocation Service, Report and Order, 5 F.C.C.2d 197, 202 (1966)); Frontier Broadcasting Co. v. Collier, 24 F.C.C. 251, 254 (1958).

[158] The telephone itself is also arguably a "staple article of commerce," the sale of which, if "widely used for legitimate unobjectionable purposes," does not constitute contributory copyright infringement. *Cf. Sony Corp.*, 464 U.S.

Intellectual property laws provide numerous exemptions for carriagelike activities. Under trademark law, for example, printers who establish that they are innocent infringers of third-party trademarks are immune from damages liability and subject only to an injunction against future printing.[159] Libraries are exempt from liability for vicarious copyright infringements.[160] Under the Copyright Act, a carrier that retransmits a broadcast signal is innocent of infringement if it "has no direct or indirect control over the content or selection of the primary transmission or over the particular recipients of the secondary transmission" and provides only "wires, cables, or other communications channels for the use of others."[161] Similarly, cable companies that engage in secondary transmissions are entitled to a passive carrier exemption from infringement liability.[162] A cable system that is not truly "passive" will fall outside the scope of the exemption and violate the copyright owner's exclusive right to perform or display the copyrighted work publicly.[163] The cable system must be "merely retransmitting exactly what it receives" and must "exercise[ ] no control over the content or selection on the primary transmission, or over the particular recipients of its transmission."[164]

---

at 442 (an article of commerce "need merely be capable of substantial non-infringing uses"); Vault Corp. v. Quaid Software Ltd., 847 F.2d 255 (5th Cir. 1988) (software intended to defeat copyright protection encoded in other programs had substantial noninfringing use, such as the making of archival copies). *See* Henry H. Perritt, Jr., Tort Liability, the First Amendment, and Equal Access to Electronic Networks, 5 Harv. J. L. & Tech. 65 (1992). Logically this principle could be extended to telephone service as well as equipment, since, in telecommunications, equipment and service may often be substitutes.

[159] 15 U.S.C. §1114(2).
[160] 17 U.S.C. §108(a).
[161] *Id.* §111(a)(3).
[162] *Id.* §111(c)(2); *see also* 47 U.S.C. §558.
[163] *See* WGN Continental Broad. Co. v. United Video, Inc., 693 F.2d 622, 625 (7th Cir. 1982); National Assn. of Broadcasters v. Copyright Royalty Tribunal, 809 F.2d 172, 179 (2d Cir. 1986).
[164] Eastern Microwave, Inc. v. Doubleday Sports, Inc., 691 F.2d 125, 129 (2d Cir. 1982), *cert. denied,* 459 U.S. 1226 (1983); *see* 17 U.S.C. §111(a)(3) (1983); Hubbard Broad., Inc. v. Southern Satellite Sys., Inc., 593 F. Supp 808, 813 (D. Minn. 1984), *aff'd,* 777 F.2d 393 (8th Cir. 1985), *cert. denied,* 480 U.S.

§14.4.2 Passive Secondary Transmissions

Beginning in the late 1950s, subscription music services and cable television operators began leasing telephone lines to transport copyrighted works for retransmission to the public. When telephone companies lease private lines, they know who they are dealing with and probably have a pretty good idea of what they are carrying.

AT&T urged Congress to codify a "passive carrier" exemption to the copyright laws to protect common carriers "having no control over the selection of the works to be transmitted or communicated."[165] AT&T compared its services to the lease of an organ to a movie theater. The organ lessor should not be liable for every copyright infringement on the instrument because it does not control what is played on it. The Register of Copyrights held that a telephone company's "purely intermediate transmissions should be exempt, but that an express exemption [from copyright liability] is not necessary to exclude them."[166] The Register understood an intermediate transmission to be one intended for another carrier rather than for the public.[167] But at that time, AT&T typically owned and managed entire CATV distribution networks from the headend up to (but not including) each household's TV set; thus, AT&T, like a cable company, transmitted directly to the public.[168] AT&T was concerned that the new arrangements eroded the lines between the public performance and the "purely intermediate."[169]

---

932 (1987); David v. Showtime/The Movie Channel, 697 F. Supp. 752, 759 (S.D.N.Y. 1988).

[165] Allocating Copyright Liability to Telecommunications Common Carriers Supplying Cable Systems, 67 Minn. L. Rev. 963, 992 n.164 (1983) (quoting letter from Walter Derenberg, Counsel for AT&T, to Herbert Fuchs, Subcomm. No. 3 of the House Judiciary Comm. 7 (Jan. 27, 1966); letter from Walter Derenberg to Thomas C. Brennan, Senate Committee on the Judiciary (Apr. 25, 1967)).

[166] House Comm. on the Judiciary, Copyright Law Revision, Part 6, Supplementary Report of the Register of Copyrights on the General Revision of the U.S. Copyright Law: 1965 Revision Bill, 89th Cong., 1st Sess. 25 (Comm. Print. 1965).

[167] Id.

[168] Allocating Copyright Liability at 992 & n.163.

[169] Id. at 992 & n.162.

Influenced by these arguments, Congress drafted legislation in 1966 to insulate passive common carriers from copyright liability in these circumstances.[170] This passive carrier exemption was finally enacted in 1976.[171] Section 111(a)(3) of Title 17, enacted by the 1976 Copyright Act, exempts the "secondary transmissions" of a primary transmission[172] by a passive carrier from copyright liability. Transmission is defined broadly enough to include all communications media.[173] The secondary transmitter must have no direct or indirect control over the content or selection of the primary transmission or the recipients of the secondary transmission; it must provide only communications channels that are used by others.[174] The exemption does not apply to the carrier's transmission of its own programming over its own wires.[175]

The passive carrier exemption applies only to retransmissions of a primary transmission intended for the general public; as a

[170] H.R. Rep. No. 2237, 89th Cong., 2d Sess. 82 (1966) ("The general exception . . . extends to secondary transmitters that act solely as passive common carriers."). For discussion of the history of the passive carrier exemption, see generally Niels B. Schaumann, Copyright Protection in the Cable Television Industry: Satellite Retransmission and the Passive Carrier Exemption, 51 Fordham L. Rev. 637 (1983); see also Allocating Copyright Liability, 67 Minn. L. Rev. 963.

[171] 17 U.S.C. §111(a)(3).

[172] A "primary transmission" is "a transmission made to the public by the transmitting facilities whose signals are being received and further transmitted by the secondary transmission service." 17 U.S.C. §111(f). At the time the exemption was enacted, a "primary transmission" generally would have been an initial over-the-air television broadcast, but the Copyright Act's definition of "transmit" is broad enough to cover other types of initial distribution so long as the transmission is intended for the public at large. Hubbard Broadcasting, Inc. v. Southern Satellite Sys., Inc., 593 F. Supp. 808, 813–816 (D. Minn. 1984), aff'd, 777 F.2d 393 (8th Cir. 1985), cert. denied, 479 U.S. 1005 (1986).

A "secondary transmission" is "the further transmitting of a primary transmission simultaneously with the primary transmission" (or nonsimultaneously for certain cable systems outside the United States). See 17 U.S.C. §111(f).

[173] See H.R. Rep. No. 1476, 94th Cong., 2d Sess. 64 (1976), reprinted in 1976 U.S.C.C.A.N. at 5678 (quoting 17 U.S.C. §101).

[174] 17 U.S.C. §111(a)(3).

[175] Id.; see Eastern Microwave, Inc. v. Doubleday Sports, Inc., 534 F. Supp. 533 (N.D.N.Y.) (satellite carrier not entitled to exemption from liability for copyright infringement), rev'd, 691 F.2d 125 (2d Cir. 1982).

rule, when a telephone company leases its lines to a cable television service, the primary transmission will be an over-the-air television broadcast. The exemption does not, however, apply to the retransmission of signals that are specifically intended at the outset to reach only certain subscribers—for example, pay TV services or closed-circuit TV.[176] When a telephone company's lines are used to retransmit pirated software, for example, the company will have to defend itself under the general principles of copyright law discussed above, not under the passive carrier exemption of section 111(a)(3). Operators of computer bulletin boards (which provide services much like carriage) are already learning as much.[177]

§14.4.3 Intermediate Carriers

Telephone companies look and feel like traditional carriers; many other more specialized "carriers" do not. "Intermediate

---

[176] H.R. Rep. No. 1476, 94th Cong., 2d Sess. 92 (1976), *reprinted in* 1976 U.S.C.C.A.N. at 5707. The primary transmitter must intend and actually attempt to restrict the transmission. *Hubbard Broadcasting*, 777 F.2d at 399–400.

[177] *See* Sega Enterprises Ltd. v. MAPHIA, 857 F. Supp. 679 (N.D. Cal. 1994) (court issued preliminary injunction against bulletin board operator who made unauthorized copies of video games and encouraged others to upload and download them); Playboy Enters., Inc. v. Frena, 839 F. Supp. 1552 (M.D. Fla. 1993) (bulletin board operator found strictly liable for operating system in which users uploaded and downloaded copyrighted photographs without operator's knowledge). Two other recent cases, involving defamation rather than copyright, suggest a more lenient approach for unknowing contributory infringers. *See* Cubby, Inc. v. CompuServe, Inc., 776 F. Supp. 135, 139–140 (S.D.N.Y. 1991) (bulletin board operator was not liable for defamation unless it "knew or had reason to know" of the defamatory statements); Auvil v. CBS "60 Minutes," 800 F. Supp. 928 (E.D. Wash. 1992) (network affiliate that exercised no editorial control over the network broadcast—although it had the power to do so—served only as a conduit and was not liable for republishing defamatory statements). *See generally* John Carmichael, In Support of the White Paper: Why Online Service Providers Should Not Receive Immunity from Traditional Notations of Vicarious and Contributory Liability For Copyright Infringement, 16 Loy. L.A. Ent. L.J. 759 (1996); Christian Rieder, Personal Jurisdictions for Copyright Infringement on the Internet, 38 Santa Clara L. Rev. 367 (1998).

carriers," for example, feed broadcast programming to cable companies and others over microwave or satellite facilities. The FCC licensed the first such carrier, Intermountain Microwave, in 1958.[178] The business of hauling in distant broadcast signals for retransmission on cable networks grew rapidly thereafter.[179] The FCC has also licensed non-common-carrier microwave service, community antenna relay service (CARS),[180] which serves affiliated cable networks. Satellite operators, which generally lease transponders to other intermediate carriers, joined the club in 1976.[181] The first "superstation"[182] was WTBS of Atlanta; the broadcast licensee, Turner Broadcasting, encouraged cable operators to retransmit its signal. WTBS was thus a "willing" superstation. WGN of Chicago was (originally) an "unwilling" superstation.[183]

The copyright liability for cable companies that carried such signals was addressed first by the Supreme Court and then by compulsory license provisions of the 1976 Copyright Act.[184] Barred from suing the most obvious targets, some owners of copyrighted material have sued intermediate carriers instead.

[178] Application of Intermountain Microwave et al., Memorandum Opinion and Order, 24 F.C.C. 54 (1958).

[179] See Inquiry into the Impact of Community Antenna TV Systems, 26 F.C.C. 403, 409–410 ¶¶13–15 (1959); Amendment of Subpart L, Part II, to Adopt Rules and Regulations to Govern the Grant of Authorizations in the Business Radio Service, First Report and Order, 38 F.C.C. 683, 695 ¶¶30–31 (1965); Amendment of Subpart L, Part 91, to Adopt Rules and Regulations to Govern the Grant of Authorizations in the Business Radio Service, Second Report and Order, 2 F.C.C.2d 725, 772 (1966); Policy and Rules Concerning Rates for Competitive Common Carrier Services, Notice of Inquiry and Proposed Rulemaking, 77 F.C.C.2d 308, 321 ¶25 (1979).

[180] Amendment of Parts 2, 21, 74, and 91 of the Commission's Rules and Regulations, First Report and Order and Further Notice of Proposed Rulemaking, 1 F.C.C.2d 897 (1965).

[181] Schaumann, Copyright Protection at 638. See Application of Southern Satellite Systems, Inc., Memorandum Opinion and Certificate, 62 F.C.C.2d 153, 162 ¶21 (1976).

[182] A "superstation" is a television broadcast station, other than a network station, whose signal is retransmitted by satellite. 17 U.S.C. §119(d)(9).

[183] See Chicago Profl. Sports Ltd. Partnership v. National Basketball Assn., 754 F. Supp. 1336 (N.D. Ill. 1991).

[184] See Fortnightly Corp. v. United Artists, 392 U.S. 390 (1968); see also J. Thorne, P. Huber, & M. Kellogg, Federal Broadband Law §10.6 (1995).

True common carriers that provide passive microwave links are immune; they simply lease conduit to cable operators, who then have the intercepted broadcast signals carried through the system.[185] By the same logic, a truly passive satellite carrier is exempt from liability, even if it leases transponders to packagers and others who are actively involved in programming.[186]

Most satellites that are currently used for domestic communication transport video signals. The broadcast and cable networks feed in programming at one end of the satellite link and take it back at the other. Most satellite carriers are thus passive; they supply unadorned transport. As discussed above, "passive carriers" are almost wholly exempt from copyright liability.[187] The downstream cable system is subject to the 1976 Copyright Act (compulsory license) and the 1992 Cable Act (must-carry or re-transmission consent); the satellite carrier in this context is subject to neither.[188]

Many other carriers, however, supply more than completely unadorned transport. CARS, for example, is not a common carrier; it is affiliated with cable operators. And satellite operators that sell retransmitted broadcast signals directly to subscribers are exactly like traditional broadcasters — they are not "passive" in the eyes of the law, and so do not qualify for the carrier's copyright immunity. Many satellite resellers are a "new or mixed breed."[189] Unlike a telephone company, these intermediate carriers often carry signals at the request of receivers rather than

---

[185] *See* Inquiry into the Impact of Community Antenna Systems, Report and Order, 26 F.C.C. 403 (1959).

[186] In Eastern Microwave, Inc. v. Doubleday Sports, Inc., 691 F.2d 125, 133 n.19 (2d Cir. 1982), *cert. denied,* 459 U.S. 1226 (1983), the Second Circuit assumed that denial of the exemption to the resale carrier would require its denial to the underlying carrier, RCA. However, the court does not explain this piece of dictum, and it seems incorrect.

[187] *See generally* Stephen R. Barnett, From New Technology to Moral Rights: Passive Carriers, Teletext and Deletion as Copyright Infringement, 31 J. Copyright Socy. U.S.A. 427 (1984).

[188] *See* Implementation of the Cable Television Consumer Protection and Competition Act of 1992, Report and Order, 8 F.C.C. Rec. 2965, 2997 n.367 (1993).

[189] *Id.* at 2997 ¶131.

senders. And like many cable operators, they select which signals to retransmit[190]—favoring, for example, a superstation that carries a serious team like the Yankees over one that carries insignificant also-rans like the Red Sox.

Whether Congress originally intended to shelter such intermediate carriers is debatable.[191] Courts, however, have resolved most of the debate in their favor.[192] In its 1982 ruling in *Eastern Microwave,* the Second Circuit found a common carrier retransmission service entitled to the passive carrier exemption.[193] Doubleday owned the New York Mets and had licensed WOR-TV to broadcast their games. Eastern Microwave used both satellite and microwave to retransmit WOR's signal to cable operators nationwide. It had chosen WOR on the strength of a survey of demand for various independent signals and then conducted an extensive promotional campaign to sell the signal to distant cable systems.[194] Those cable systems made payments to the Copyright Royalty Tribunal as required by the 1976 compulsory license law, but Doubleday wanted more.

It did not get it. The Second Circuit noted that Eastern was selling only transmission services, with no editing of WOR's signal, to anyone who wanted to buy it. Any of the recipient cable companies could have operated its own microwave or satellite facilities in the same manner without incurring additional copyright liability. The result should not be different simply because

[190] *Id.* at 2999 ¶144.

[191] *Compare* Copyright Issues: Cable Television and Performance Rights: Hearings Before the Subcomm. on Courts, Civil Liberties, and the Administration of Justice of the House Comm. on the Judiciary, 96th Cong., 1st Sess. 23 (1979) (statement of Barbara Ringer, Register of Copyrights) (Congress did not consider the then-unanticipated activities of superstations and satellite relay services; section 111(a)(3) was intended to insulate the telephone company only) *with* H.R. Rep. No. 559, 97th Cong., 2d Sess. 4 (1982) (carriers are exempt from copyright liability when retransmitting television signals to cable systems via terrestrial microwave or satellite facilities).

[192] *See* Barnett, From New Technology to Moral Rights, 31 J. Copyright Socy. U.S.A. 427.

[193] Eastern Microwave, Inc. v. Doubleday Sports, Inc., 691 F.2d 125, 129–132 (2d Cir. 1982).

[194] *Id.* at 130.

Eastern was independent. That would "strangle" cable by "choking off" its supply of programs and would frustrate the compulsory copyright rules accepted by Congress.[195] Thus, an intermediate carrier may select any hapless broadcaster to be an "unwilling superstation" and still preserve its immunity from copyright liability so long as it retransmits exactly what it receives. This much "selection" is not enough to make the intermediate carrier "active."[196] Nor is the intermediate carrier's selection of which cable systems may receive the rebroadcast.

But any editing of the signal tips the scales decisively. United Video, a satellite common carrier, retransmitted WGN's signal from Chicago. First, however, it deleted material carried in the signal's vertical blanking interval (VBI). The Seventh Circuit ruled that this was too much. An intermediate satellite carrier is exempt from copyright liability only if it really is passive; but it may not even delete commercials.[197]

The Eighth Circuit addressed another wrinkle in its 1985 decision in *Hubbard Broadcasting*.[198] WTBS, a willing superstation, was "splitting its feed." It broadcast its signal to the general public on a UHF transmitter in Atlanta and simultaneously sent it by microwave to Southern Satellite, a satellite carrier, for nationwide distribution. The signals were not identical: WTBS replaced local advertising with national advertising on the microwave feed. Hubbard was a local broadcaster that carried the same programming in other markets. It sued both Southern Satellite and WTBS, arguing that the microwave signal was not a primary transmission "made for reception by the public at large." The appellate court disagreed. Under the Copyright Act's broad definition of "transmit," the microwave feed qualified as a primary transmission.[199] Furthermore, WTBS was broadcasting for the

---

[195] *Id.* at 132.

[196] *Id.* at 130.

[197] WGN Continental Broad. Co. v. United Video, Inc., 693 F.2d 622 (7th Cir. 1982). Although United Video retransmitted only to cable operators, that was a "public" enough performance to engage copyright liability.

[198] *Hubbard Broadcasting*, 777 F.2d 393.

[199] *Id.* at 401.

public at large. Unlike a typical subscription television service, WTBS was funded entirely by advertising revenues. The parallel, simultaneous UHF broadcast established that WTBS was indeed broadcasting to the general public. Since WTBS, not Southern Satellite, was substituting national for local commercials, Southern Satellite remained sheltered by the passive carrier exemption.[200] Because both WTBS and the satellite carrier were sued on a theory of contributory infringement, neither the court of appeals nor the district court ruled on the question of whether the superstation could be directly liable for copyright infringement.[201]

§14.4.4 Would-Be "Carriers" Who Are Not

The existence of a broad copyright exemption for "passive carriers," of course, encourages many unsuitable candidates to apply for the position. Programmers like Home Box Office (HBO) clearly do not qualify for any copyright exemption simply by virtue of the fact that they lease or own transponders on the satellites of common carriers.[202] Satellite operators may lose the exemption if they own programming, position themselves as direct broadcasters, or do business directly with selected subscribers who are equipped with suitable home dishes. Nor do they qualify for the cable operator's compulsory license.[203]

---

[200] *Id.* at 401–403.

[201] *Id.* at 404. The court ruled that WTBS was not liable for contributory infringement because its placement of national commercials on the microwave signal did not harm Hubbard, the broadcaster, or the copyright owners; these entities relied on local, not national, advertising.

[202] David v. Showtime/The Movie Channel, 697 F. Supp. 752, 759 (S.D.N.Y. 1988) (Showtime/The Movie Channel not entitled to the passive carrier exemption because it alone decided which movies to show and when to show them).

[203] *See* 17 U.S.C. §111. Some of these carriers, however, are entitled to a compulsory license under the Satellite Home Viewer Act (SHVA). The Satellite Home Viewer Act of 1988 created a compulsory license for satellite carriers engaged in the retransmission of superstations and network stations for private home viewing. *Id.* §119(a).

Despite their origins as "community antennas," cable companies clearly no longer qualify as "passive carriers" either. They exercise editorial control over the contents of their retransmissions. As drafted in 1966,[204] the passive carrier exemption protected a "common carrier." In 1975, however, the National Cable Television Association urged Congress to adopt clarifying language.[205] The Association pointed out that a cable operator may lease channel space to others, over whose programming decisions the operator has no control, even though cable operators are not technically common carriers in the broad definition of the word.[206] The passive carrier exemption protects "any carrier."[207] This is apparently broad enough to insulate a cable operator from copyright liability when it supplies services like a telephone company.

§14.4.5 Private Carriage

In a 1931 ruling, *Buck v. Jewell-LaSalle Realty,* the Supreme Court concluded that a hotel had unlawfully "performed" copyrighted music by piping it from a single master radio receiver to all rooms in the hotel.[208] Ironically the case seemed to turn on

---

[204] H.R. 4347, §111(a)(1)(C), *printed in* H.R. Rep. No. 2237, 89th Cong., 2d Sess. 7 (1966).

[205] *See* Copyright Law Revision: Hearings on H.R. 2223 Before the Subcomm. on Courts, Civil Liberties and the Administration of Justice of the House Comm. on the Judiciary, 94th Cong., 1st Sess. 508 (1975) (prepared statement of Rex A. Bradley, Chairman, National Cable Television Association).

[206] *See* Regulatory Policies Concerning Resale and Shared Use of Common Carrier Services and Facilities, Report and Order, 60 F.C.C.2d 261, 307–308 ¶101 (1976); Frontier Broadcasting Co., 24 F.C.C. 251, 254–255 ¶¶7–9 (1958).

[207] 17 U.S.C. §111(a)(3).

[208] 283 U.S. 191 (1931) (*Jewell-LaSalle*). Today, this result is precluded by 17 U.S.C. §111(a)(1) (a secondary transmission is not an infringement of copyright if it "consists entirely of the relaying, by the management of a hotel . . . of signals transmitted by a broadcast station licensed by the [FCC], within the local service area of such station, to the private lodgings of guests or residents of such establishment, and no direct charge is made to see or hear the secondary transmission").

the fact that the radio station had itself violated the copyright of the original performer: the broadcast was unauthorized. In a footnote, the Supreme Court suggested that the result would have been different if the broadcast had been with permission.[209] The implication seemed to be that you could steal from honest broadcasters, but not from thieves.

Jewell-LaSalle was virtually overruled by the Supreme Court in *Twentieth Century Music Corp. v. Aiken.*[210] A fast-food restaurant transmitted programs broadcast by a local radio station from four ceiling-mounted speakers in dining and working areas. The Supreme Court ruled that this did not infringe plaintiff's exclusive right to perform the work in public for a profit. The Court did not, however, overrule *Jewell-LaSalle* explicitly. It purported to distinguish it on the ground that the initial broadcast in *Jewell-LaSalle* was unauthorized. The interpretation of "performance" in *Aiken* was in turn superseded by the 1976 Copyright Act.[211]

§14.4.6 Internet Service Providers

Internet service providers have recently been the subject of two types of legislation: one extends criminal liability for nasty copyright infringers; the other limits the liability of nice ones. The No Electronic Theft (NET) Act, passed in late 1997, increased

---

[209] *Jewell-LaSalle*, 283 U.S. at 199 n.5. If the initial broadcast took place under unrestricted license, cases suggested that the license implicitly extended to others. *See* Buck v. Debaum, 40 F.2d 734 (S.D. Cal. 1929) (restaurant owner who played broadcast of plaintiff's copyrighted song over radio for his patrons not liable for infringement). ASCAP now expressly provides that broadcast licenses do not run in favor of persons picking up the broadcast for retransmission.

[210] 422 U.S. 151 (1975) (*Aiken*).

[211] Today, however, the result in *Aiken* would be the same, under a special exemption created for such situations in 17 U.S.C. §110(5) (providing that "communication of a transmission embodying a performance or display of a work by the public reception of the transmission on a single receiving apparatus of a kind commonly used in private homes" does not constitute an infringement of copyright so long as there is no direct charge and there is no further transmission to the public).

the liability of bulletin board operators.[212] Before passage of the Act, the "LaMacchia loophole" in copyright law exempted infringers from criminal liability if they did not profit from their actions. David LaMacchia, an MIT student, encouraged people to upload video games on his bulletin board for others to download. He was accused of violating both the Copyright Act and the federal wire fraud statute, but a federal court dismissed the prosecution on the grounds that copyright law didn't forbid his activity and that wire fraud statutes don't protect copyrights.[213] The 1997 law imposes criminal liability on anyone who "infringes a copyright willfully either for purposes of commercial advantage or private financial gain, or by the reproduction or distribution, including by electronic means, during any 180-day period, of 1 or more copies or phonorecords of 1 or more copyrighted works, which have a total retail value of more than $1,000."[214] Although evidence of reproduction or distribution is not enough to establish willful infringement,[215] the financial benefit to the infringer is not the only method of establishing liability under the amended Copyright Act. Online infringement continues to be an issue for courts.

One court has already concluded that providers of online services that offer space for storing copyrighted material, but subsequently allow access to the same material, may be liable.[216] A defendant had allowed a third party to store illegally copied material on its system, as well as to use its system for access and distribution of the material. The defendant was aware that the

---

[212] Pub. L. No. 105-147, §2(d), 111 Stat. 2678 (1997) (codified at 17 U.S.C. §506(a), 18 U.S.C. §2319(b), (c)).

[213] United States v. LaMacchia, 871 F. Supp. 535 (D. Mass. 1994). Criminal sanctions were not available under the Copyright Act without proof that LaMacchia received some type of commercial gain.

[214] 17 U.S.C. §506(a).

[215] *Id.* §506(a)(2) (to violate this subsection, a copyright infringement must be both willful *and* accomplished by "reproduction or distribution").

[216] Religious Tech. Ctr. v. Netcom On-Line Communication Servs., Inc., 907 F. Supp. 1361 (N.D. Cal. 1995) (*Netcom*) (denying summary judgment on the grounds that Netcom was not only leasing space for material that had been copyrighted, but also acting as a provider of access to the stored material). The case was settled in 1997.

material stored on its system had been illegally copied by a third party, but continued to accommodate that party in its distribution of the material.[217]

"Caching" presents a raft of new copyright concerns, none of which has been definitely resolved. The efficient design and operation of networks requires a considerable amount of intermediate storage at intermediate points in the network, particularly when the same material is being accessed repeatedly by many different users, as occurs with much of the publishinglike or broadcastlike content that moves on the Internet. Computers themselves repeatedly store (i.e., copy) material among different media—RAM,[218] hard drives, tape backups, and so forth.[219] However, a good argument can be made that caching serves the same function as a VCR,[220] but in this case instead of time shifting, a caching device shifts resources.[221]

In October 1998, the Digital Millennium Copyright Act[222] was signed into law. It provides that Internet providers are not liable for the "intermediate and temporary storage" of infringing material.[223] The exemption is limited to situations where the

[217] *See also* Sega Enters. v. Maphia, 948 F. Supp. 923 (N.D. Cal. 1996). Congress has proposed legislation to further limit the liability of online service providers for contributory infringement. On-Line Copyright Liability Limitation Act, H.R. 2180, 105th Cong. (1997); On-Line Copyright Infringement Liability Limitation Act, H.R. 3209, 105th Cong. (1998); Digital Copyright Clarification and Technology Education Act of 1997, S. 1146, 105th Cong. (1997). Two of the bills limit remedies to injunctive relief.

[218] Information stored in RAM has been found to meet the requirements of "copy" for purposes of copyright law. Mai Sys. Corp. v. Peak Computer, Inc., 991 F.2d 511 (9th Cir. 1993).

[219] The court in *Netcom* denied the claim that Netcom directly infringed plaintiff's copyrighted material by "caching" it. For a complete discussion of caching, see Richard Vermut, File Caching on the Internet: Technical Infringement or Safeguard for Efficient Network Operation?, 4 J. Intell. Prop. L. 273 (1997).

[220] *Sony,* 464 U.S. 417.

[221] *See* Vermut, File Caching on the Internet at 338.

[222] Title II of the Digital Millennium Copyright Act, Pub. L. No. 105-304, is the On-Line Copyright Infringement Liability Limitation Act. *See* 17 U.S.C. §512. The Digital Millenium Copyright Act was designed to implement both the World Intellectual Property Organization Copyright Treaty (1998) and the Performances and Phonograms Treaty (1998).

[223] 17 U.S.C. §512(b)(1).

storage and transmission are carried out through an "automatic technical process" pursuant to which the provider selects none of the material and the copy is retained only so long as necessary for the purpose of carrying out the transmission.[224]

§14.5 Informational Privacy

§14.5.1 Government Disclosure of Private Information

As highly engaged regulators of telecom networks, government officials have at least indirect access to a great deal of information about how people use their phones, whom they call, and what they call. Anything the phone company knows, the regulator may have occasion to find out, too.[225]

In three instances, the Supreme Court has indicated that the constitutional "right of privacy,"[226] such as it is, may extend to an individual's interest in controlling the extent to which personal information is disclosed to others. In 1977, the Court was faced with the question of whether that right was violated by a state's maintenance of centralized computer files with the names and addresses of all persons who have obtained, pursuant to a doctor's prescription, certain drugs for which there is both a lawful

---

[224] *Id.* §512(b)(1)(C).

[225] As Professor Miller warned 20 years ago:

[M]any people have voiced concern that the computer, with its insatiable appetite for information, its image of infallibility, and its inability to forget anything that has been stored in it, may become the heart of a surveillance system that will turn society into a transparent world in which our homes, our finances, and our associations will be bared to a wide range of casual observers, including the morbidly curious and the maliciously or commercially intrusive.

A. Miller, The Assault on Privacy: Computers, Data Banks, and Dossiers 3 (1971). *See also* D. Burnham, The Rise of the Computer State: The Threat to Our Freedoms, Our Ethics and Our Democratic Principles (1983).

[226] *See, e.g.,* Griswold v. Connecticut, 381 U.S. 479 (1965) (contraception); Loving v. Virginia, 388 U.S. 1 (1967) (marriage); Roe v. Wade, 410 U.S. 113 (1973) (abortion); Moore v. East Cleveland, 431 U.S. 494 (1977) (family relationships).

and an unlawful market.[227] In a second case the same year,[228] the Court heard a challenge to the public release of papers and tape recordings of former President Nixon. In a third decision,[229] the Court considered the effect of privacy on the Bank Secrecy Act of 1970,[230] which requires banks to make and retain copies of checks and other financial transfer instruments and to make these copies available to law enforcement agencies. The strength and parameters of this "informational privacy" right are unclear, for in all three cases the Court found that the government's interest outweighed the asserted right of privacy.

§14.5.2   Carrier Disclosure of Information About Customers

As the owners and operators of lines, phone companies might be said to be engaged in full-time "wiretapping" of the phones that connect to their lines. The wiretapping laws plainly extend to carriers insofar as carriers might attempt to listen in on phone calls or otherwise intercept the content of what they carry. But as we have seen, a great deal more information is acquired in setting calls and billing them. The wiretapping laws cannot include any blanket prohibition on the acquisition, storage, and use of such information; it is not possible to run a phone network without it.[231]

For many years, Judge Greene invoked concerns about misuse of customer information as an additional reason to bar phone companies from providing online information services of any

---

[227] Whalen v. Roe, 429 U.S. 589, 599 (1977).

[228] Nixon v. Administrator of Gen. Servs., 433 U.S. 425, 457 (1977).

[229] California Bankers Assn. v. Schultz, 416 U.S. 21 (1974). *See also* United States v. Miller, 425 U.S. 435 (1976).

[230] Pub. L. No. 91-508, 84 Stat. §§1114–1124 (1970).

[231] A communications provider may intercept, use, or disclose a communication while engaged in an activity that is a "necessary incident to the rendition of its service, except that a provider shall not utilize service observing or random monitoring except for mechanical or service quality control checks." 18 U.S.C. §2511(2)(a)(I).

kind. Through "control of its customers' lines of communication," a local phone company would "also have access to their lines of credit, travel plans, credit card expenditures, medical information, and the like. On the basis of a subscriber's telephone calling patterns with respect to information, an RBOC [Regional Bell Operating Company] could easily pinpoint that subscriber for the sale of RBOC-generated information and the sale of other products and services connected therewith, to the point where that company would have a 'Big Brother' type relationship with all those residing in its region."[232]

The ECPA contains no specific restriction against the collection of personal information gathered from transaction data, nor is there a restriction on the duration of storage of such data. The ECPA does not extend wiretapping restrictions to the collection of transmission profile data.[233] Indeed, the ECPA specifically allows the electronic service provider to divulge transaction records to any government entity without judicial intervention.[234]

Prior to the 1996 Act, the Commission had established requirements for handling customer proprietary network information (CPNI) as part of the enhanced services[235] operations of

[232] United States v. Western Elec. Co., 673 F. Supp. 525, 567 n.190 (D.D.C. 1987), *rev'd in part, aff'd in part,* 900 F.2d 283 (D.C. Cir. 1990); *see also* United States v. Western Elec. Co., 714 F. Supp. 1, 12 n.40 (D.D.C. 1988) (Bell companies barred from offering "user profile" services).

[233] A provider of public telecommunications services cannot disclose the contents of an e-mail message, for example, without the consent of at least one of the parties. *See* 18 U.S.C. §2511(3)(b). However, there is no specific restriction against the collection of personal information gathered from transaction data, nor is there a restriction on the duration of storage of such data.

[234] A communications provider must disclose the name, address, toll billing records, and other subscriber number or identity to the government when presented with an administrative, grand jury, or trial subpoena. 18 U.S.C. §2703(c)(1)(C).

[235] "Enhanced services" generally include such services as voice mail, electronic mail, electronic store-and-forward, fax store-and-forward, data processing, and gateways to online databases. Prior to the 1996 Act, enhanced services were defined as services "offered over common carrier transmission facilities used in interstate communications, which employ computer processing applications that act on the format, content, code, protocol or similar aspects of the subscriber's transmitted information; provide the subscriber additional, different, or restructured information; or involve subscriber interaction with stored information." 47 C.F.R. §64.702(a); *see also* North

AT&T, the BOCs, and GTE and the customer premises equipment (CPE) operations of AT&T and the BOCs. These requirements were contained in the Computer II,[236] Computer III,[237] GTE ONA,[238] and BOC structural relief[239] proceedings, but they were never codified in a comprehensive set of regulations.[240] The Commission had adopted these CPNI requirements, together with other nonstructural safeguards, purportedly to pro-

---

American Telecommunications Association Petition for Declaratory Ruling Under Section 64.702 of the Commission's Rules Regarding the Integration of Centrex, Enhanced Services and Customer Premises Equipment, 101 F.C.C.2d 349 (1985), *recons.*, 3 F.C.C. Rec. 4385 (1988).

[236] Amendment of Section 64.702 of the Commission's Rules and Regulations (Second Computer Inquiry), Final Order, 77 F.C.C.2d 384 (1980) *recons.*, 84 F.C.C.2d 50 (1980), *further recons.*, 88 F.C.C.2d 512 (1981), *aff'd sub nom.* Computer and Communications Indus. Assn. v. FCC, 693 F.2d 198 (D.C. Cir. 1982), *cert. denied,* 461 U.S. 938 (1983).

[237] Amendment of Section 64.702 of the Commission's Rules and Regulations (Third Computer Inquiry), 104 F.C.C.2d 958 (1986), *recons.*, 2 F.C.C. Rec. 3035 (1987), *further recons.*, 3 F.C.C. Rec. 1135 (1988), *second further recons.*, 4 F.C.C. Rec. 5927 (1989), *vacated sub nom.* California v. FCC, 905 F.2d 1217 (9th Cir. 1990) (*California I*); Computer III Remand Proceeding, 5 F.C.C. Rec. 7719 (1990), *recons.*, 7 F.C.C. Rec. 909 (1992), *petitions for review denied sub nom.* California v. FCC, 4 F.3d 1505 (9th Cir. 1993) (*California II*); Computer III Remand Proceedings: Bell Operating Company Safeguards and Tier I Local Exchange Company Safeguards, 6 F.C.C. Rec. 7571 (1991), *vacated in part and remanded sub nom.* California v. FCC, 39 F.3d 919 (9th Cir. 1994) (*California III*), *cert. denied,* 115 S. Ct. 1427 (1995); Computer III Further Remand Proceedings: Bell Operating Company Provision of Enhanced Services, Notice of Proposed Rulemaking, 10 F.C.C. Rec. 8360 (1995).

[238] Application of Open Network Architecture and Nondiscrimination Safeguards to GTE Corp., Report and Order, 9 F.C.C. Rec. 4922, 4944–4945 ¶45 (1994); Application of Open Network Architecture and Nondiscrimination Safeguards to GTE Corp., Memorandum Opinion and Order, 11 F.C.C. Rec. 1388, 1419–1425 ¶¶73–86 (1995) (hereinafter *GTE ONA Order*).

[239] Furnishing of Customer Premises Equipment by Bell Operating Telephone Companies and the Independent Telephone Companies, Report and Order, 2 F.C.C. Rec. 143 (1987) (hereinafter *BOC Structural Relief Order*), *recons. on other grounds,* 3 F.C.C. Rec. 22 (1987), *aff'd,* 883 F.2d 104 (D.C. Cir. 1989).

[240] *But see* 47 C.F.R. §22.903(f) (1997) (regulation that was part of the Commission's structural separation requirements in connection with the BOC provision of cellular services); *id.* §64.702(d)(3) (1997) (prior regulation prohibiting carriers from sharing customer information with their separate affiliates that provide CPE and enhanced services operations unless the information is made publicly available).

tect independent enhanced services providers and CPE suppliers by prohibiting AT&T, the BOCs, and GTE from using CPNI obtained from their provision of regulated services to gain a competitive advantage in the unregulated CPE and enhanced services markets, as well as to protect legitimate customer expectations of confidentiality regarding individually identifiable information.[241]

As part of the 1996 Act, Congress enacted a new section 222 governing the privacy of customer information.[242] Congress expressly provided that section 222 reflected a balance of "both competitive and consumer privacy interests with respect to CPNI."[243] On the one hand, Congress recognized the duty of all carriers to protect customer information and the principle that customers must be able to control information they view as sensitive and personal from use, disclosure, and access by carriers.[244] But, on the other hand, where customer information is not sensitive, the customer's interest lies more in choosing service from among a variety of competitors (necessitating access to the same information) than in prohibiting the sharing of information.

Section 222 sets forth three categories of customer information to which different privacy protections and carrier obligations apply—individually identifiable CPNI, aggregate customer information, and subscriber list information. CPNI includes information that is extremely personal to customers, as well as commercially valuable to carriers, such as to whom, where, and when a customer places a call, as well as the types of service offerings to which the customer subscribes and the extent the

[241] Implementation of the Telecommunications Act of 1996: Telecommunications Carriers' Use of Customer Proprietary Network Information and Other Customer Information, Notice of Proposed Rulemaking, 11 F.C.C. Rec. 12,513, 12,516 ¶4, 12,530 ¶40 (1996).

[242] 47 U.S.C. §222.

[243] Joint Explanatory Statement of the Committee of Conference, H.R. Rep. No. 458, S. Rep. No. 230, 104th Cong., 2d Sess. 205 (hereinafter *Conference Report*).

[244] 47 U.S.C. §222(c)(1) (section titled "Confidentiality of Customer Proprietary Network Information" embodies principle of customer control).

service is used.[245] Aggregate customer and subscriber list information, unlike individually identifiable CPNI, involves customer information that is not private or sensitive, but, like CPNI, is nevertheless valuable to competitors. Aggregate customer information is expressly defined as "collective data that relates to a group or category of services or customers, from which individual customer identities and characteristics have been removed."[246] Subscriber list information, although consisting of individually identifiable information, is defined in terms of public, not private, information, including the "listed names, numbers, addresses, or classifications . . . that the carrier or an affiliate has published, caused to be published, or accepted for publication in any directory format."[247]

As a general matter, a telecommunications carrier is limited to using CPNI only for the telecommunications service from which such information is derived or "services necessary to, or used in, the provision of such telecommunications service, including the publishing of directories."[248] There are, of course, some exceptions: customers may request in writing that their CPNI be disclosed to designated individuals,[249] and a telecommunications carrier may use, disclose, or permit access to CPNI in order to initiate, render, bill, and collect for telecommunications services;[250] to protect the rights or property of the carrier "from fraudulent, abusive, or unlawful use of, or subscription to, such services";[251] or to provide telemarketing, referral, or administrative services to the customer "if such call was initiated by the

---

[245] Congress defined CPNI as "information that relates to the quantity, technical configuration, type, destination, and amount of use of a telecommunications service subscribed to by any customer of a telecommunications carrier, and that is made available to the carrier by the customer solely by virtue of the carrier-customer relationship; and information contained in the bills pertaining to telephone exchange service or telephone toll service received by a customer of a carrier; except that such term does not include subscriber list information." *Id.* §222(f)(1).

[246] *Id.* §222(c)(3).
[247] *Id.* §222(f)(3).
[248] *Id.* §222(c)(1).
[249] *Id.* §222(c)(2).
[250] *Id.* §222(d)(1).
[251] *Id.* §222(d)(2).

customer and the customer approves of the use of such information to provide such service."[252]

The Commission promulgated rules implementing section 222 in February 1998.[253] The Commission's regulations generally permit carriers to use CPNI, without customer approval, to market offerings that are related to, but limited by, the customer's existing service relationship with their carrier.[254] Before carriers may use CPNI to market service outside the customer's existing service relationship, the Commission requires that carriers obtain express customer approval.[255] Such express approval may be written, oral, or electronic.[256] In order to ensure that customers are informed of their statutory rights before granting approval, the Commission has required carriers to provide a one-time notification of customers' CPNI rights prior to any solicitation for approval.[257] The Commission eliminated the Computer III CPNI framework in light of the comprehensive regulatory scheme Congress established in section 222.

Finally, the FCC recognized an apparent tension between section 222, which generally permits the sharing of CPNI only

[252] *Id.* §222(d)(3).

[253] Implementation of the Telecommunications Act of 1996; Telecommunications Carriers' Use of Customer Proprietary Network Information and Other Customer Information, Second Report and Order and Further Notice of Proposed Rulemaking, 13 F.C.C. Rec. 8061 (1998) (hereinafter *CPNI Order*).

[254] 47 C.F.R. §64.2005(a).

[255] *Id.* §64.2005(b). In a subsequent order, the Common Carrier Bureau clarified that when a customer purchases CPE or information services from a carrier that are bundled with a telecommunications service, the carrier subsequently may use any customer information independently derived from the carrier's prior sale of CPE or prior subscription to a particular information service. "Neither CPE nor information services constitute 'telecommunications services' as defined in the Act. Therefore, any customer information derived from the carrier's sale of CPE or from the customer's subscription to the carrier's information service would not be 'CPNI' because section 222(f) defines CPNI in terms of information related to a 'telecommunications service.'" Implementation of the Telecommunications Act of 1996: Telecommunications Carriers' Use of Customer Proprietary Network Information and Other Customer Information, Order, 13 F.C.C. Rec. 12,390, 12,393 ¶4 (1998) (footnotes omitted).

[256] 47 C.F.R. §64.2007(b).

[257] *Id.* §64.2007(f).

among entities with whom the customer has a prior service relationship, and section 272(c)(1), which prohibits a BOC from discriminating in favor of its own affiliate "in the provision or procurement of goods, services, facilities, *and information.*" The FCC resolved the tension by concluding that section 272 imposes "no additional obligations on the BOCs when they share CPNI with their statutory affiliates according to the requirements of section 222."[258] This is because "imposing section 272's nondiscrimination obligations when the BOCs share CPNI with their section 272 affiliates would not further the principles of customer convenience and control embodied in section 222, and could potentially undermine customers' privacy interests as well, while the anticompetitive advantages section 272 seeks to remedy are sufficiently addressed through the mechanisms in section 222 that seek to balance the competitive concerns regarding LECs' use and protection of CPNI."[259]

In the same manner as common carriers, most Web sites accumulate information about their online visitors, but few inform visitors they are doing so.[260] Some solicit consent via e-mail registration forms; others don't. Various congressional bills have recently proposed to limit use of "personally identifiable information" culled without express consent from consumers' visits to Internet Web sites.[261] In response to this potential regulation, a group of more than 60 global corporations and associations recently formed the Online Privacy Alliance, stating that it was

[258] *CPNI Order,* 13 F.C.C. Rec. at 8174–8175 ¶160.

[259] *Id.*

[260] Bureau of Consumer Information, Federal Trade Commission, Privacy Online: A Report to Congress, at iii (June 1998).

[261] *See* H.R. 98, 105th Congress, 1st Sess. (1997). The bill defined "written consent" narrowly, as "a statement—(A) in writing and freely signed by a subscriber; (B) consenting to the disclosures such service will make of the information provided; and (C) describing the rights of the subscriber under this Act"; H.R. 2368, 105th Congress, 1st Sess. (1997) (calling on interested parties to form an "industry working group" to create guidelines "which limit the collection and use" of similar consumer information). Both of these bills died in committee, although subcommittee hearings were held on H.R. 2368 in June 1998. *See* Electronic Commerce: Hearings of the Telecommunications, Trade and Consumer Protection Subcommittee of the House Commerce Committee (June 25, 1998).

their intention to establish a self-regulating framework for privacy guidelines and enforcement.[262]

§14.5.3 Caller ID and Other Call Management Services

A variety of "call management" services now permit phone companies to convey and sell call management information to users at either or both ends of a call. The most familiar is Caller ID. Caller ID displays the telephone number of an incoming call before the phone is answered or (if combined with other capabilities) before the phone even rings.[263] It is indeed quite straightforward to combine the service with customer premises capabilities that will allow almost any degree of advanced electronic screening thereafter, based entirely on the number from which the incoming call originated. Businesses are, of course, very interested in the service in that it can be used to direct calls rapidly to appropriate agents and to pull up associated electronic records instantly when a phone is answered.

Telcos have also added the display of the name of the caller to their Caller ID services. Other comparable services provide benefits somewhat similar to those of Caller ID, but have been far less controversial. Call Block allows customers to screen calls by preventing their phones from ringing in response to a list of numbers specified beforehand. Priority Call provides a distinctive ring for a small number of high-priority calls. Call Trace allows the customer to trace a call by sending a printout of the called and calling numbers, and the date and time of the call traced, to the local telephone company.[264] Call Waiting briefly

---

[262] T. Bridis, Government Confronts Internet Privacy, and Lack of It, Associated Press, June 23, 1998. *See generally* Online Privacy Alliance, Welcome <http://www.privacyalliance.org>.

[263] *See generally* Newton's Telecom Dictionary 106 (11th ed. 1996).

[264] Smith, We've Got Your Number! (Is It Constitutional to Give It Out?): Caller Identification and the Right to Informational Privacy, 37 UCLA L. Rev. 145, 149 (1989).

interrupts an ongoing call to alert either party that some other caller is trying to reach them on their (now busy) line.

Proposals to offer Caller ID have provoked vigorous debate. Domestic violence agencies, which sometimes make confidential calls to the homes of victims, have expressed concern that their calls would be revealed to abusers and that even the threat of such revelation would discourage victims from seeking help. Telephone marketing companies, of course, attacked a technology that would permit phone owners to evade their solicitations. State public advocate offices and state chapters of the American Civil Liberties Union have opposed the service as a violation of the caller's right to keep his or her telephone number private.

On the other hand, Caller ID received support from a number of groups, including law enforcement agencies.[265] Caller ID allows pizzerias to cut down on prank orders, permits banks and credit card companies to ascertain caller bona fides, and so forth. Caller ID can reduce false alarms, fake bomb threats, and other harassing and life-threatening prank telephone calls. In emergency situations, Caller ID is so essential that enhanced 911 (E911) services permit an attendant to identify the calling party's address through the use of an external automatic location identification database.[266]

The Commission has required LECs to provide access to 911 services to competing carriers that purchase local switching on an unbundled basis.[267] The Commission's universal service order also provided that access to the "network components necessary" for E911 services be supported by universal service

---

[265] *See, e.g., id.* at 146–147.

[266] *See* Letter from Chief, Common Carrier Bureau, to Alfred E. Green (Dec. 24, 1982) (granting a waiver to AT&T (and then to the Bell Operating Companies) to provide E911 services and associated terminal equipment without structural separation). This directly promoted the statutory objective of "promoting safety of life and property through the use of wire and radio communication." 47 U.S.C. §151. A fully enhanced 911 system may also provide the name of the subscriber, city, zip code, telephone number, date, time of day, and class of telephone service (business, residential, etc.).

[267] Implementation of the Local Competition Provisions in the Telecommunications Act of 1996, First Report and Order, 11 F.C.C. Rec. 15,499, 15,706 ¶412 (1996); 47 U.S.C. §251.

mechanisms.[268] RBOCs must also establish that they are offering "nondiscriminatory access to 911 and E911 services" prior to receiving permission to offer long-distance services.[269]

Initially state criminal statutes prohibiting wiretapping presented an obstacle to Caller ID services. In 1992, the Pennsylvania Supreme Court ruled that Caller ID services violated the state's Wiretapping and Electronic Surveillance Control Act and could not be offered to subscribers.[270] The Texas Public Utilities Commission reached a similar conclusion.[271] Washington State lawmakers, reacting to the Pennsylvania decision, amended their wiretap statute to *exclude* "any common carrier automatic number, caller, or location identification service" approved by the state utilities commission.[272] Many states balanced the demand for the service and the demand for privacy by allowing callers to turn off the Caller ID function before dialing, that is, to allow callers to stop their number from being passed to the called party.[273]

---

[268] Federal-State Joint Board on Universal Service, Report and Order, 12 F.C.C. Rec. 8776, 8816 ¶73 (1997) ("For universal service purposes, we define access to E911 as the capability of providing both" number identification and location information.).

[269] 47 U.S.C. §271(c)(2)(B)(vii)(I).

[270] Barasch v. Public Util. Commn., 605 A.2d 1198 (Pa. 1992) (finding that Caller ID falls within the general prohibition of section 5771(a) of trap-and-trace devices and cannot be used by anyone without first obtaining a court order). In 1993, Pennsylvania enacted Caller ID legislation for the "dissemination of telephone numbers and other identifying information." *See* 66 Pa. Cons. Stat. §2906. *Cf.* Southern Bell v. Hamm, 409 S.E.2d 775 (S.C. 1991) (ruling that Caller ID does not violate either constitutionally protected privacy rights or the state wiretap act). *See generally* Laurie Thomas Lee, U.S. Telecommunications Privacy Policy and Caller ID, 30 Cal. W. L. Rev. 1 (1993).

[271] Application of Southwestern Bell Telephone Co. to Introduce Caller Identification Services, Order, Docket No. 11362, 1993 Tex. PUC LEXIS 19 (Feb. 8, 1993) (finding Southwestern Bell's Caller ID units violated Texas penal law against unauthorized wiretaps). Following this decision, in June 1993 the Texas legislature passed a law clarifying the existing trap-and-trace statute to allow for Caller ID. Southwestern Bell refiled with the Commission, which approved the service in November 1993. Texas became the 40th state to allow Caller ID.

[272] H. 1489, 52d Leg. Sess. of Wash. (1991).

[273] Delaware, Florida, Maryland, Maine, and Vermont were among the first states to require a free per-call or per-line blocking option.

As with telco censorship of dial-a-porn (discussed in section 14.6 below), the one thing that seems fairly clear here is that a telco's decision in favor of Caller ID is *not* "state action" and so does not implicate any serious federal constitutional issues.[274] In establishing uniform rules for interstate Caller ID, the Commission concluded that carriers offering Caller ID services are not engaged in "state action"; there is therefore no possible violation of any constitutional right of privacy.[275] The Commission also noted that federal courts "have not, to date, recognized an individual privacy right in telephone numbers."[276]

The single most cogent argument against arming recipients of telephone calls with Caller ID is that it is somehow more important to be fair to people who make calls than to those who receive them, that the called parties already have sufficient protection in their power to hang up. But as the Supreme Court itself has recognized, the power to hang up is hardly as effective as the power

---

[274] The Supreme Court in recent years has become more stringent in enforcing the state action requirement. *See, e.g.,* NCAA v. Tarkanian, 488 U.S. 179 (1988); Blum v. Yaretzky, 457 U.S. 991 (1982); Rendell-Baker v. Kohn, 457 U.S. 830 (1982); Jackson v. Metropolitan Edison Co., 419 U.S. 345 (1974); Moose Lodge No. 107 v. Irvis, 407 U.S. 163 (1972).

Indeed, the Supreme Court ruled in Smith v. Maryland, 442 U.S. 735 (1979), that the Fourth Amendment does not even apply to the installation of a pen register, a device that records the numbers dialed on a telephone. The Court said that, even vis-à-vis the government, a calling party has no reasonable expectation of privacy because he voluntarily "assume[s] the risk" that the numbers he exposes to the telephone company will in turn be disclosed to others. Smith v. Maryland, 442 U.S. 735, 744–745 (1979). On the other hand, at least one court has apparently found state action. See Barasch v. Public Utility Commission, 576 A.2d 79, 87 (Pa. Commw. 1989). And there is an older Supreme Court precedent, never overruled, that could offer support for a finding of state action in certain circumstances. *See also* Public Utils. Commn. v. Pollak, 343 U.S. 451, 462 (1952) (state action found where commission reviewed and endorsed company's practice of piping in music on streetcars and buses); *cf.* Smith, We've Got Your Number! at 163–167 (arguing that close involvement between regulators and regulated party should constitute state action because of the "subtle and symbiotic regulatory relationship").

[275] Rules and Policies Regarding Calling Number Identification Service, Report and Order and Further Notice of Proposed Rulemaking, 9 F.C.C. Rec. 1764, 1769 ¶29 (1994) (hereinafter *Caller ID Order*).

[276] *Id.* at 1769 ¶30.

not to answer at all.[277] The opposition to Caller ID services comes down ultimately to a self-contradiction: listeners must tolerate unwelcome calls to protect callers from unwelcome calls on the rebound. But it seems likely that first-round unwelcome calls are a much greater problem than second.

§14.5.3.1 Interstate Caller ID

Caller ID service is now permitted in all states on a tariffed basis.[278] Interstate delivery of Caller ID requires interconnection

---

[277] "One may hang up on an indecent phone call, but that option does not give the caller a constitutional immunity or avoid a harm that has already taken place." FCC v. Pacifica Found., 438 U.S. 726, 749 (1978). The Court further noted that Congress had dealt appropriately with harassing telephone calls, in part, by requiring the caller to identify himself:
The problem of harassing phone calls is hardly hypothetical. Congress has recently found it necessary to prohibit debt collectors from "plac[ing] telephone calls without meaningful disclosure of the caller's identity"; from "engaging any person in telephone conversation repeatedly or continuously with intent to annoy, abuse, or harass any person at the called number"; and from "us[ing] obscene or profane language or language the natural consequence of which is to abuse the hearer or reader." Id. at 749 n.27 (quoting Consumer Credit Protection Act Amendments, 91 Stat. 877, 15 U.S.C. §1692d (1976 ed., Supp. II)).

[278] See generally Telcomp, Inc., State-by-State Coverage Chart (First Quarter 1996) <http://www.telcomp.com/coverage.html>, and FCC, Welcome to the Caller ID Page <http://www.fcc.gov/ccb/CID/welcome. html>. On December 1, 1995, FCC rules governing interstate calls opened the way for interstate Caller ID services. Reversing an earlier ruling that required separate systems for intrastate and interstate calls, the new rules also permitted carriers to extend per-line blocking options selected by consumers for intrastate calls to interstate calls. See Rules and Policies Regarding Calling Number Identification Services, Second Report and Order and Third Notice of Proposed Rulemaking, 10 F.C.C. Rec. 11,700 (1995).
Although Caller ID had been deployed in 49 states, implementation of this service was delayed in California, which had adopted a default rule that emergency service organizations and subscribers with nonpublished numbers would have their numbers blocked unless the calling party expressly chooses to unblock a particular call. In its 1995 order, the FCC concluded that a per-line blocking default was incompatible with federal goals for interstate Caller ID services, and it preempted the California rule. The Ninth Circuit denied the petition to review the FCC order in California v. FCC, 75 F.3d 1350 (9th Cir. 1996) (California), concluding that the FCC's preemption order was narrowly tailored to fit federal policies.

of the local and long-distance signaling networks. In March 1994, the Commission directed interexchange carriers to pass Caller ID information through to local carriers when "technically feasible,"[279] so that local carriers can pass interstate Caller ID information on to customers that subscribe to Caller ID services.[280] Inconsistent state regulation was preempted.[281] The Commission rejected a demand for compensation by interexchange carriers.[282] Carriers had to be in compliance by December 1, 1995. Pay phone providers were given until January 1, 1997, to upgrade their systems, but this requirement was eventually abandoned by the Commission.[283] In 1997, the Commission responded to several petitions for reconsideration by requiring only carriers with signaling system 7 (SS7) capabilities and with custom local area signaling services (CLASS) software to pass the calling party's number.[284]

§14.5.3.2 Caller ID Blocking: FCC Preemption of State per-Line Blocking Rules

Most phone companies also offer, and most states have approved, Caller ID blocking services. By dialing a three-digit code (e.g., *67), a caller can block downstream transmission of his or her number. Telcos have offered a countermeasure, too:

---

[279] Because the "transmission of the calling party number requires SS7 technology, technical feasibility exists wherever SS7 technology is used." *Caller ID Order,* 9 F.C.C. Rec. at 1767 ¶17. The Commission emphasized, however, that "carriers are not required to invest in SS7 technology in order to facilitate delivery of the calling party number." *Id.*

[280] *Id.* at 1768 ¶23; 47 C.F.R. §64.1601.

[281] *Caller ID Order,* 9 F.C.C. Rec. at 1776 ¶69. The Commission stated it would examine the need for further preemption of state regulations case by case and "endeavor to accommodate state regulations whenever possible." *Id.* at 1776 ¶70.

[282] *Id.* at 1768 ¶23 ("In most cases, SS7 signaling replaces older signaling methods used in an IXC network and provides benefits to the carrier such as more efficient call routing and reduced exposure to fraud. We thus conclude . . . that the costs of transmitting CPN are de minimis").

[283] *See* 47 C.F.R. §64.1601(d)(1); Rules and Policies Regarding Calling Number Identification Service, Third Report and Order, 12 F.C.C. Rec. 3867, 3878 ¶30 (1997).

[284] *Id.* at 3868 ¶2.

anonymous call rejection (ACR) or, more commonly "block the blocker."[285] The service allows a called person to automatically reject calls from any caller that uses call blocking. The called telephone does not ring; instead, the caller is informed by a recording that the called person will not take calls from a caller using call blocking.

Some states have required phone companies to offer (free) per-call blocking, per-line blocking, or other variations on the same.[286] Others have considered requiring a caller to *unblock* the Caller ID transmission before dialing if he wants his number transmitted.[287]

Much debate centered on what the default condition should be, since the chances are that few callers or called parties will bother to activate either blocking or blockers. Caller ID opponents insisted that customers should have the general power to turn off Caller ID on all calls initiated on their line. Per-call blocking, by contrast, supplies the extra measure of privacy only when the caller takes the initiative, thus preserving more of the value of the Caller ID service that blocking effectively thwarts.[288]

The FCC took up the issue in 1991, concerned that a conflicting patchwork of state rules might undermine Caller ID service and the privacy interests it serves at the called-party end of the line.[289] The Commission's 1994 order on interstate Caller ID

[285] This service is available in Florida, for example. 92 F.P.S.C. 9:398 (1992).

[286] Cal. Pub. Util. Code §2893 (1991). In 1992, California required local telephone companies to provide subscribers with a choice of free per-call blocking, free per-line blocking, or free per-line blocking with per-call enabling. Application of Pacific Bell, a Corporation, for Approval of COMM-STAR Features, Interim Opinion, 1992 Cal. PUC LEXIS 688 (June 19, 1992).

[287] 16 TAC 23.57, Texas PUC (Proj. No. 8547) (1991). H. 333, 87th Gen. Assembly of IL (1991). The Texas and Illinois Public Utility Commissions (PUCs) ultimately adopted the opposite approach, allowing for per-call anonymous blocking. *See* 16 TAC 23.57, Texas PUC (1997); 126 P.U.R.4th 313 (1991).

[288] Often lost in the debate is that a simple and inexpensive piece of CPE can readily be installed to dial the per-call blocking code (*67) automatically every time the handset is lifted from the phone.

[289] Rules and Policies Regarding Calling Number Identification Service, Notice of Proposed Rulemaking, 6 F.C.C. Rec. 6752 (1991). Some calling parties

initially required originating LECs to offer per-call blocking on all interstate calls.[290] Callers were not to be charged for per-call blocking.[291] For all practical purposes, this requirement permeated intrastate Caller ID services as well because most switches were incapable of distinguishing intrastate and interstate Caller ID calls.

Initially the Commission preempted state mandates that required LECs to offer per-line Caller ID blocking. But on reconsideration, the Commission modified its order to permit per-line blocking for interstate calls in states that permit it for intrastate calls.[292] As mentioned above, the Commission required in 1995 per-call blocking for interstate calls and per-line blocking where states allowed it. The Commission was forced to stay this requirement, however, upon learning that special CLASS software was needed to block and unblock passage of the calling party

---

for whom identification could have an undesirable effect are law enforcement investigators—particularly those involving illegal drugs—counseling and medical professionals and information services, and residents of domestic violence shelters. *Id.* at 6756 ¶18.

Though the Commission does not propose to preempt any state regulations regarding Caller ID services, it does express a concern that conflicting policies may circumvent the development of interstate Caller ID and suggests that therefore a model federal regulatory structure should be implemented to ensure the introduction of interstate Caller ID into the marketplace. *Id.* at 6752 ¶2.

[290] Report and Order and Further Notice of Proposed Rulemaking, 9 F.C.C. Rec. 1764 (1994). A caller can block his number by first dialing *67. Rules and Policies Regarding Calling Number Identification Service, Memorandum Opinion and Order on Reconsideration, 10 F.C.C. Rec. 11,700, 11,703 ¶5 (1995). The requirement applied only to carriers that used SS7 signaling for call setup of interstate calls.

[291] *Caller ID Order,* 9 F.C.C. Rec. at 1772 ¶49.

[292] For states that allow per-line blocking, the customer must have the option of dialing *82 to unblock a call. Rules and Policies Regarding Calling Number Identification Service, Memorandum Opinion and Order on Reconsideration, 10 F.C.C. Rec. 11,700, 11,728–11,729 ¶¶81–83 (1995). In a November 30, 1995, order, the Common Carrier Bureau stayed the application of the *82 requirement for all carriers, for calls originating on lines served by DCO switches, until January 1, 1997. Rules and Policies Regarding Calling Number Identification Service, Order and Fourth Notice of Proposed Rulemaking, 10 F.C.C. Rec. 13,796 (1995).

number. In 1997, the Commission exempted LECs that were not equipped with CLASS software from blocking mandates.[293]

Separately the Commission addressed the use of interstate automatic number identification (ANI), which is generally used by local and interexchange carriers for billing purposes,[294] but which has also been made available to businesses that receive inbound 800- and 900-number calls on dedicated lines. For technical reasons, ANI cannot be blocked on a per-call basis in the same way as ordinary Caller ID. The Commission decided not to restrict continued delivery to business subscribers, in part because they are the ones who pay for transmission of the call. The better approach to protect competing privacy interests, the Commission decided, was to require education by the carriers and to restrict how 800- and 900-type services subscribers may use "ANI data."[295] The Commission prohibited the reuse or sale of ANI information by 800, 900, and other service subscribers absent affirmative subscriber consent.[296]

§14.5.4 Content and Site IDs

The increasing graphic depictions of violence and sex on television and other media have led to demands for technology

---

[293] Rules and Policies Regarding Calling Number Identification Service, Third Report and Order, 12 F.C.C. Rec. 3867, 3868 ¶2 (1997).

[294] As the Commission explains, "[ANI] based services were developed in the pre-SS7 (multifrequency) signaling environment as the billing telephone number of the calling party, and are transmitted primarily on toll/access calls on the trunk side connection of the LEC switch." *Caller ID Order,* 9 F.C.C. Rec. at 1765 n.6.

[295] *Id.* at 1773 ¶57.

[296] *Id.*; 47 C.F.R. §64.1602(a). In a similar vein, the Commission established rules regarding solicitation by ANI services subscribers. The Commission permitted ANI services subscribers to offer products or services to an established customer that are directly related to products or services previously provided by the ANI services subscriber to that customer. *Caller ID Order,* 9 F.C.C. Rec. at 1773–1774 ¶58; 47 C.F.R. §64.1602(b). The rules also permit the disclosure of ANI information in aggregate form "if it is compiled in a manner which precludes identification of individual telephone subscribers." *Caller ID Order,* 9 F.C.C. Rec. at 1774 ¶58; 47 C.F.R. §64.1602(a)(3).

analogous to the service Caller ID performs for call recipients: the ability to screen unwanted broadcasts. The "V-chip" is one such device that will detect a rating signal imbedded in a broadcast and block any broadcast that exceeds a certain violence rating, for example. Parents will be able to block programming they do not want their children to see. As part of the Telecommunications Act of 1996, Congress required televisions to be equipped with a feature that "enables viewers to block display of all programs with a common rating."[297] In an effort to limit indecent computer-mediated communications, the Commission prescribed reverse blocking, whereby Internet providers had to restrict access to indecent material until affirmatively requested by the user through the establishment of an account or method of payment.[298]

§14.5.5   Credit Bureaus, Cable Companies, and Video Stores

These issues of informational privacy are by no means unique to telephony; indeed, they crystallized much earlier in other contexts. The law in these other areas is generally relevant to its interpretation in the telecom context, and we survey it very briefly here.

The Fair Credit Reporting Act of 1970 (FCRA),[299] the first information privacy legislation, attempted to address the concerns of the public about credit bureaus' misuse of personal information. It required that credit reporting agencies use "reasonable measures" to protect the confidentiality of consumer information and ensure proper utilization of such data. The law also conferred

---

[297] 47 U.S.C. 303(x). While there is no requirement that broadcasters rate their programs, the V-chip may also allow viewers to block access to all unrated programs, similar to the way a person can refuse to accept calls from callers who block passage of their number.

[298] *See* 47 U.S.C. §223(b)–(c). The Ninth Circuit affirmed the Commission's rules in Information Service Providers Coalition v. FCC, 928 F.2d 866 (9th Cir. 1991).

[299] 15 U.S.C. §§1681 et seq.

civil liability to any credit agency that is negligent or willful in its noncompliance with the FRCA.

The Cable Communications Policy Act of 1984 forbids cable operators and third parties from monitoring the viewing habits of subscribers.[300] The Act places elaborate restrictions on the collection and disclosure of personally identifiable information.[301]

At least once a year cable operators must notify their customers of what kind of personally identifiable information is being collected, how long it will be stored, and how it is being used. Customers may access these records and be afforded the opportunity to correct them.[302] Cable operators must destroy records that are no longer necessary for the purpose for which they were collected.[303]

Finally, the Video Privacy Protection Act of 1988[304]—enacted in outraged reaction to unauthorized disclosures about the video-rental tastes of Supreme Court nominee Judge Robert Bork[305]—forbids retailers from disclosing video-rental records or other personally identifiable information about any customer.[306]

---

[300] 47 U.S.C. §551 (1988). For a general discussion of the privacy protections of the Cable Act, see Scofield v. Telecable of Overland Park, Inc., 973 F.2d 874 (10th Cir. 1992). In *Scofield,* the court observed that the privacy requirements were included in the Act in response to Congress's observation that "cable systems, particularly those with a "two-way" capability, have an enormous capacity to collect and store personally identifiable information about each cable subscriber." H.R. Rep. No. 934, 98th Cong., 2d Sess. 29 (1984). "Subscriber records from interactive systems," Congress noted, "can reveal details about bank transactions, shopping habits, political contributions, viewing habits and other significant personal decisions." *Scofield,* 973 F.2d at 876.

[301] 47 U.S.C. §551(b), (c). Sale of mailing lists is permitted when a subscriber has been given the opportunity to limit disclosure and such disclosure does not reveal the subscriber's viewing habits.

[302] *Id.* §551(d).

[303] *Id.* §551(e).

[304] 18 U.S.C. §2710.

[305] The City Paper, a weekly newspaper in Washington, printed a list of 146 video cassettes rented by Bork and his family over an 18-month period. The list revealed Bork's fondness for Cary Grant and Alfred Hitchcock. G. Henderson, Bill Introduced to Ban Dispersal of Video Lists, United Press Intl., Oct. 21, 1987.

[306] 18 U.S.C. §2710(b). Disclosure for marketing and direct marketing purposes is still permitted (18 U.S.C. §2710(b)(2)(D)(ii)) and mailing lists may be distributed. *Id.* §2710 (1988).

§14.5.6   The European Directive[307]

The 1998 European Directive on the Protection of Individuals with Regard to the Processing of Personal Data and on the Free Movement of Such Data[308] requires European countries to block the export of personal data to countries lacking "adequate" data protection.[309] The Directive is extraordinarily comprehensive. It requires each of the 15 European Union Member States to enact laws governing the "processing of personal data." National laws enacted in compliance with the Directive must guarantee that "processing of personal data" is accurate, up to date, relevant, and not excessive. The Directive guarantees confidentiality of telephone calls.[310]

The Directive, with its broad extraterritorial provisions,[311] took effect in October 1998. The use of Caller ID to identify a

[307] See generally Fred H. Cate, Business Law Symposium: Entering a New Era in Telecommunications Law: Article: Privacy and Telecommunications, 33 Wake Forest L. Rev. 1 (1998); Peter P. Swire & Robert E. Litan, None of Your Business: World Data Flows, Electronic Commerce, and the European Privacy Directive, Interim Report Issued for a Conference of the Brookings Institution (Oct. 21, 1997).

[308] European Parliament and Council Directive 95/46 on the Protection of Individuals with Regard to the Processing of Personal Data and on the Free Movement of Such Data, 1995 O.J. (L 281) 31 (hereinafter Directive on the Protection of Individuals).

[309] See id. art. 25(1).

[310] The Directive makes it unlawful to listen in to calls, to intercept them, or to record them except "when the data subject has given his consent unambiguously; processing is necessary for the performance of a contract to which the data subject is party or in order to take steps at the request of the data subject entering into a contract; processing is necessary for compliance with a legal obligation to which the controller is subject; processing is necessary in order to protect the vital interests of the data subject; processing is necessary for the performance of a task carried out in the public interest or in the exercise of official authority vested in the controller or in a third party to whom the data are disclosed; processing is necessary for the purposes of the legitimate interests pursued by the controller or by the third party or parties to whom the data are disclosed, except where such interests are overridden by the interests or fundamental rights and freedoms of the data subject." See id. art. 7.

[311] S. Lloyd, Media and the Law: Pros and Cons of Bills, Guardian (London), Feb. 7, 1998, at 13.

caller from Europe invokes the fair information requirements of the Directive.[312] Cellular roaming, which is now available between Europe and the United States, implicates the requirements of the Directive when one considers the amount of personal information that must be transmitted across borders to enable the cellular provider to bill the subscriber.

In response to the Directive, the U.S. Department of Commerce recently announced that there have been ongoing negotiations with the European Commission to create a "safe harbor" for U.S. companies that would allow them to continue to transfer or receive personal information from the European Community.[313] In order to receive this voluntary protection, these organizations would agree to self-certify that they will follow the "safe harbor" principles by providing "'adequate' privacy protection for European citizens," all the while reflecting "U.S. views on privacy" by allowing "for relevant U.S. legislation, regulation, and other public interest requirements."[314]

§14.6 Free Speech

In 1883, a court in Ohio upheld a local phone company's decision to terminate service to a subscriber who had uttered a naughty word on the line.[315] The subscriber had said to an operator: "If you can not get the party I want, you can shut up your damned old telephone."[316] The company's contract stipulated that its lines weren't to be used for any "profane, indecent or rude language."[317] One judge dissented from the court's ruling.

[312] Directive on the Protection of Individuals art. 26.

[313] Letter from David L. Aaron, Undersecretary for International Trade, Department of Commerce, to U.S. industry representatives (Nov. 4, 1998).

[314] *Id.* (insisting on "a cost-effective framework for the private sector").

[315] Pugh v. City and Suburban Telephone Assn., 9 Ohio Dec. Reprint 644 (1883). The judgment in this case was affirmed by the Supreme Court Commission, without report, February 17, 1885.

[316] *Id.* at 645.

[317] *Id.* The telephone company was at the time regulated as a telegraph company; the court ruled that the company's termination of service pursuant to the contract was reasonable under the laws applicable to the telegraph. *Id.* at 649.

"Damn" was not profane, he felt. And in any event, the subscriber was entitled to a hearing before termination.[318]

When they arrived some decades later, common carrier regulators should, of course, have sided with profanity. The core principle of common carriage, the most ancient and important of all, is nondiscrimination. Business, gossip, seduction, and pillow talk should all travel on precisely equal terms down all lines.

Instead, Congress drew the line at pillows. The 1934 Communications Act prohibited knowingly "permitting a telephone under [one's] control" to be used to make "any comment, request, suggestion or proposal which is obscene, lewd, lascivious, filthy, or indecent."[319] This echoed laws written in the 1860s, in which Congress had banned immoral, indecent, fraudulent, and obscene materials from the mails.[320]

No one took much notice until the 1980s. Then phone companies began offering a new category of high-toll "dial-it" lines, prefaced by the digits 976 or 900. Porno-logues rushed in. One early dial-a-porn service in New York City received six million calls a month.[321] When the Reagan FCC decided that no law barred dial-a-porn,[322] Congress immediately passed one that did.[323] When a federal appellate court struck down the "indecent" part of that law as unconstitutional,[324] Congress passed another.[325]

---

[318] *Id.* at 651–653.

[319] 47 U.S.C. §223; Denver Area Educ. Telecomms. Consortium, Inc. v. FCC, 518 U.S. 727 (1996).

[320] *See* Public Clearing House v. Coyne, 194 U.S. 497, 507 (1904); Enterprise Sav. Assn. v. Zurnstein, 67 F. 1000, 1004 (6th Cir. 1895); United States v. Wilson, 58 F. 768 (N.D. Cal. 1893); United States v. Gaylord, 17 F. 438 (S.D. Ill. 1803); United States v. Loftis, 12 F. 671 (D. Or. 1802).

[321] *See* Sable Communications of Cal., Inc. v. FCC, 492 U.S. 115, 120 n.3. (1989) (*Sable*).

[322] Application for Review of Complaint Filed by Peter F. Cohalan, FCC File No. E-83-14 (May 13, 1983).

[323] Pub. L. No. 98-214, §8(a)(3), 97 Stat. 1467 (1983) (amending 47 U.S.C. §223 to include a new subsection (b)).

[324] Carlin Communications, Inc. v. FCC, 837 F.2d 546 (1988).

[325] Pub. L. No. 100-690, §7524 (1988) (amending 47 U.S.C. §223(b)).

By 1996, dirty pictures from the Internet had replaced dirty talk as the main center of concern. One section of the 1996 Telecommunications Act made it a federal crime to convey dirty pictures to minors.[326] It didn't matter who initiated the call. Bulletin board operators were directed to demand credit card payment or interpose some other adults-only filter.

Section 14.6.1 below provides a brief background to the different First Amendment protections enjoyed by publishers, broadcasters, and carriers. Section 14.6.2 discusses forbidden carriage: regulation by which the state bars the carrier from delivering its own content. Sections 14.6.3 and 14.6.4 discuss various efforts to regulate the content carried on telephone lines. Section 14.6.5 surveys federal immunities (both statutory and constitutional) from liability for speech-related civil or criminal actions (like defamation). Section 14.6.6 discusses a carrier's right to censor the content of its own customers, and section 14.6.7 addresses federal immunities for such private censorship. Section 14.6.8 discusses mandatory carriage: regulation that requires a telco to provide facilities to serve customers who generate content the carrier would rather not transmit or deliver that content to customers the carrier would rather not convey it to. Finally, section 14.6.9 discusses the implications of an exclusive franchise.

§14.6.1 First Amendment Background: Gutenberg, Marconi, and Bell[327]

Gutenberg, Marconi, and Bell—publisher, broadcaster, and carrier—invented what have been until recently three quite distinct communications media. The framers of the Constitution

---

[326] 47 U.S.C. §223(d)–(h). The Communications Decency Act was struck down as unconstitutional in American Civil Liberties Union v. Reno, 117 S. Ct. 2329 (1997).

[327] *See* Laurence H. Tribe, American Constitutional Law §12-25 (2d ed. 1988). *See generally* Angela J. Campbell, Publish or Carriage: Approaches to Analyzing the First Amendment Rights of Telephone Companies, 70 N.C. L. Rev. 1071 (1992).

were familiar with only one of them, or (arguably) two. Congress "shall make no law abridging the freedom of speech or of the press," the First Amendment declares.[328] The Post Office (tele-communications carrier of an earlier day) is addressed in a different context.[329] There is no mention of asymmetrical digital subscriber lines or integrated broadband service.

Judges have responded with three distinct bodies of First Amendment jurisprudence.[330] "The moving picture screen, the radio, the newspaper, the handbill, the sound truck and the street corner orator have differing natures, values, abuses and dangers," Justice Robert H. Jackson wrote in a 1949 case dealing with a sound truck. "Each, in my view, is a law unto itself. . . ."[331] In a 1969 ruling on the "fairness doctrine," the Court said it again: "differences in the characteristics of new media justify differences in the first amendment standards applied to them."[332]

Different has meant unequal. In rulings from the 1800s to the 1920s, the Court had upheld the government's right to ban lottery promotions and socialist magazines from the mails[333] and to condition use of the mails however else it pleased.[334] It wasn't until 1945 that the Court struck down the Postmaster's attempt to deny second-class mailing privileges to the depraved pages of *Esquire*.[335]

Two years earlier, however, in a seminal opinion by Justice Felix Frankfurter, the Court had upheld broad FCC oversight of the airwaves.[336] A federal licensing commission is needed to

---

[328] U.S. Const. amend. I.

[329] "The Congress shall have power . . . [t]o establish post offices and post roads." U.S. Const. art. I, §8, cl. 7.

[330] Ithiel de Sola Pool, Technologies of Freedom 26–27 (1983). *See also* Office of Technology Assessment, U.S. Congress, Critical Connections 50 (1990).

[331] Kovacs v. Cooper, 336 U.S. 77, 97 (1949) (Jackson, J., concurring); *see generally* Jonathan W. Emord, Freedom, Technology and the First Amendment 278 (1991).

[332] Red Lion Broad. Co. v. FCC, 395 U.S. 367, 386 (1969) (*Red Lion*).

[333] Ex parte Jackson, 96 U.S. 727 (1877).

[334] Public Clearing House v. Coyne, 194 U.S. 497, 506 (1904).

[335] Hannegan v. Esquire, 327 U.S. 146 (1945).

[336] National Broad. Co. v. United States, 319 U.S. 190 (1943).

ration the shortage of spectrum, Frankfurter reasoned. Once rationing-by-Commission is accepted, it's reasonable to supervise content, fairness, and advancement of the public interest as well. From the 1930s on, courts had upheld general content prescriptions for broadcasters on similar grounds.[337] This same scarcity logic persuaded the Supreme Court to uphold the fairness doctrine, unanimously, in 1969.[338]

What gradually emerged was a First Amendment triad. Print publishers clearly get the most protection. Broadcasters come next, though they remain less protected than the print press because (the Supreme Court continues to assert) the broadcast medium is scarce or because its reach is so "uniquely pervasive."[339] Wires get more First Amendment protection in some respects because they are (apparently) not scarce, but carriers — until recently, at least — have not been thought of as deserving much First Amendment protection at all. The Supreme Court has never expressly so ruled, but it has made noises to that effect.[340]

§14.6.2 Forbidden Carriage

Regulators' attempts to forbid or limit carriage over telco lines fall into two categories: (1) limits on a telco's transmission of

---

[337] *See* KFKB Broad. Assn. v. FRC, 47 F.2d 670 (D.C. Cir. 1931); *see also* FCC v. Pacifica Found., 438 U.S. 726 (1978) (*Pacifica*); National Assn. for Better Broad. v. FCC, 591 F.2d 812 (D.C. Cir. 1978).

[338] *Red Lion*, 395 U.S. 367.

[339] *Pacifica*, 438 U.S. at 748.

[340] *See* FCC v. Midwest Video Corp., 440 U.S. 689 (1979) (*Midwest Video II*); Columbia Broadcasting Sys., Inc. v. Democratic Natl. Comm., 412 U.S. 94 (1973); *see also* League of Women Voters Educ. Fund v. FCC, 731 F.2d 995 (D.C. Cir.), *aff'd*, 468 U.S. 364, 378 (1984); Miami Herald Publishing Co. v. Tornillo, 418 U.S. 241, 259 (1974) (White, J., concurring) (*Tornillo*). Turner Broadcasting System, Inc. v. FCC, however, suggests that at least four Justices view telephone companies as on a par with cable. *See* Turner Broad. Sys., Inc. v. FCC, 512 U.S. 622, 684 (1994) (O'Connor, J., dissenting, joined by Scalia, Ginsburg, and Thomas, JJ.) ("Setting aside any possible Takings Clause issues . . . if Congress may demand that telephone companies operate as common carriers, it can ask the same of cable companies; such an approach would not suffer from the defect of preferring one speaker to another.").

content created by the telco itself and (2) limits on transmission of content created by its customers. Limits of the first kind have generally been justified on economic and antitrust grounds—they are said to be necessary to protect unaffiliated electronic publishers, video programmers, and such from having to compete in the content end of the business against the carrier on whom they depend for the transport end of things. Limits of the second kind have generally been naked exercises in censorship of undesirable content, indecency in particular.

§14.6.2.1 A Carrier's Transmission of Its Own Content

Other sections describe in detail the various limits that have been placed on a telco's carriage of content the telco creates or controls itself. See sections 12.7.11.1 (information services in general), 12.7.11.2 (electronic publishing, 12.7.11.3 (alarm services), and 13.7.2 (video services). For a time, the need for such restraints was considered so self evident that Congress and the Commission hardly bothered justifying them at all. When justification was presented, it was invariably that a monopoly provider of transport would be able to extend its monopoly into the content end of the business if it were permitted to provide content, too.[341] There was rarely much of a factual record for indulging that presumption. For the most part, lawmakers and regulators did not even bother much with the basic economic essentials that underlie such ideas—things like market definition,

---

[341] *See generally* Telephone Company-Cable Television Cross-Ownership Rules, Fourth Further Notice of Proposed Rulemaking, 10 F.C.C. Rec. 4617, 4622 ¶6 (1995) (describing "video dialtone rules" allowing telephone companies to provide a basic common carrier video delivery platform capable of accommodating multiple video programmers, while prohibiting them from "providing video programming directly to subscribers in their telephone service areas, either though the telephone operating company or through an affiliate"); Richard Klingler, The New Information Industry: Regulatory Challenges and the First Amendment 160–161 (1996) ("many of the categorical cross-ownership and related restrictions rest on antiquated market analysis and crude conceptions of the necessity for separation between markets").

for example, or the extent to which other transport media (print, cable, airwaves, etc.) may substitute for telco lines.

Regulators have placed some analogous limits on vertical integration between broadcast networks and local stations and between distributors of video programming and cable networks. We review these in more detail in another treatise.[342]

§14.6.2.2 Constitutional Limits on Restricting a Carrier's Transmission of Its Own Content

Are vertical restraints on communications companies constitutional under the First Amendment? They stop network operators from speaking and speakers from networking. One could not constitutionally separate Rupert Murdoch from his printing press, Madonna from her mike, or any plain old rabble-rouser from his megaphone. In other contexts, the Supreme Court has consistently struck down laws that deny speakers access to channels of communication.[343] Moreover, the vertical rules are all "broad prior restraints," of the kind that normally get particularly close scrutiny.[344]

---

[342] *See* J. Thorne, P. Huber & M. Kellogg, *Federal Broadband Law* ch. 8, for a discussion of vertical integration.

[343] For example, the Supreme Court has applied heightened First Amendment scrutiny to laws regulating a publisher's ability to distribute newspapers. City of Cincinnati v. Discovery Network, Inc., 507 U.S. 410, 410 (1993) (holding unconstitutional city's decision to remove newsracks distributing commercial handbills on the grounds that "city has not met its burden of establishing a 'reasonable fit' between its legitimate interests in safety and esthetics and the means it chose to serve those interests"); City of Lakewood v. Plain Dealer Publishing Co., 486 U.S. 750, 750 (1988) (striking down ordinance giving mayor unfettered control of newsrack permits on grounds that "such a statue constitutes prior restraint, and may result in censorship, engendering risks to free expression"). It has also applied it to laws prohibiting the use of loudspeakers. Saia v. New York, 334 U.S. 558 (1948). And laws regulating the distribution of handbills also merit heightened review. Schneider v. New Jersey, 308 U.S. 147 (1939); Martin v. Struthers, 319 U.S. 141 (1943).

[344] Prior restraints share one characteristic in common: "they [give] public officials the power to deny use of a forum in advance of actual expression." Southeastern Promotions, Ltd. v. Conrad, 420 U.S. 546, 553 (1975). Prior restraints are said to be "the most serious and the least tolerable infringement

Associated Press v. United States[345] is often cited for the proposition that antitrust limits on vertical integration readily survive constitutional scrutiny.[346] In that case, the Supreme Court did emphasize that the First Amendment "affords not the slightest support for the contention that a combination to restrain trade in news and views has any constitutional immunity."[347] What it approved, however, was a consent decree that required Associated Press (AP) to stop discriminating anticompetitively in granting access to its wire service.[348] The agreement did not bar AP from any news-gathering activities, nor did it limit AP's right to combine a wire service with newspaper publishing. More important still, as the Supreme Court emphasized in its 1994 ruling in *Turner Broadcasting System, Inc. v. FCC,*[349] *Associated Press* "involved actions against members of the press brought under the Sherman Antitrust Act, a law of general application."[350] While "the enforcement of a generally applicable law may or may not be subject to heightened scrutiny under the First Amendment," such enforcement is less inherently suspect than "laws that single out the press, or certain elements thereof, for special treatment."[351]

Under *Associated Press,* as read in *Turner Broadcasting System,* antitrust prosecutions against exclusive deals that curtail competition probably survive First Amendment attack. Specific laws aimed at particular segments of the telecommunications industry may survive, too, but will be subject to closer scrutiny. Broadcast networks can perhaps be required to make programming available to independent broadcasters, but there will have to

---

on First Amendment rights." Nebraska Press Assn. v. Stuart, 427 U.S. 539, 559 (1976). While a threat of criminal or civil liability after publication "chills" speech, a prior restraint "freezes" it; *see also* Heller v. New York, 413 U.S. 483, 491 (1973); New York Times Co. v. United States, 403 U.S. 713, 714 (1971); Organization for a Better Austin v. Keefe, 402 U.S. 415, 418–420 (1971).

[345] 326 U.S. 1 (1945).

[346] Associated Press argued that its restrictive bylaws were constitutionally immune from antitrust scrutiny. *Id.* at 19.

[347] *Id.* at 20.

[348] *Id.* at 21.

[349] *Turner Broad. Sys.,* 512 U.S. 622 (1994).

[350] *Id.* at 640.

[351] *Id.*

be a solid base of legislative findings that the requirement is essential to protect competition. Cablecasters may perhaps be required to make their programming fare available to unaffiliated cable, satellite, and other multichannel distributors, but again, only if a solid economic foundation for doing so has been laid. Many vertical restraints go much further, however, to bar certain kinds of speech rather than to promote access. *Associated Press* does not establish their validity, nor does *Turner Broadcasting System.*

Can strict limits on vertical integration be justified instead on the ground that regulatees consent to them at the outset, when they get into the business? That telephone companies, for example, have received certain "benefits" (such as franchises) from state governments does not justify comprehensive federal curtailment of their First Amendment rights. Franchises are given out by states and municipalities, not by Congress, without suggestion that they are conditioned on a telephone company's waiver of First Amendment video rights.[352] The constitutionally harmonious solution to problems that arise from government franchises is to get rid of franchises, not free speech. The Supreme Court has flatly rejected the analogous argument that restrictions on corporate speech could be justified as a "choice" that an organization makes in return for a charter and limited liability when it assumes the corporate form.[353]

Similarly, actual or incipient monopolists may be regulated in all sorts of ways, but they may not be silenced without limit. Government may prevent an electric utility from acquiring a competing gas utility, but it may not specifically prevent an electric

[352] *See* Chesapeake and Potomac Tel. Co. v. United States, 830 F. Supp. 909, 920 (E.D. Va. 1993) ("the sovereign which purportedly provided the benefit to the [telcos] is not the same sovereign that placed the condition on the benefit"), *aff'd*, 42 F.3d 181 (4th Cir. 1994), *dismissed as moot*, 516 U.S. 415 (1996). *Cf.* First Natl. Bank of Boston v. Bellotti, 435 U.S. 765, 778–779, 779 n.14 (1978) (noting that restriction imposed by one sovereign cannot be justified by grant of benefit by different sovereign).

[353] *See* First Natl. Bank of Boston v. Bellotti, 435 U.S. at 778–786.

utility from including inserts on political issues in its monthly billing envelopes.[354]

Up to a point, government may guarantee equality of access to private premises that are dedicated to public use,[355] but such regulation cannot ordinarily be pushed to the point where it seriously impedes or extinguishes the owner's freedom to go about his own expressive business there, too.[356] A property owner usually has a constitutional right to exclude others from using his property for expressive purposes; that surely implies a complementary right to use the property himself, for his own expressive purposes.[357]

---

[354] *See, e.g.,* Pacific Gas & Elec. v. Public Utils. Commn. of Cal., 475 U.S. 1, 8 (1986) (plurality opinion) (*Pacific Gas*); *see also* Consolidated Edison Co. v. Public Service Commission of New York, 447 U.S. 530 (1980), expressly distinguishing cases such as Greer v. Spock, 424 U.S. 828 (1976), and Lehman v. Shaker Heights, 418 U.S. 298 (1974) (plurality opinion), where "a private party asserted a right of access to public facilities," *Consolidated Edison,* 447 U.S. at 539. The Court emphasized that "Consolidated Edison has not asked to use the offices of the Commission as a forum from which to promulgate its views. Rather, it seeks merely to utilize its own billing envelopes to promulgate its views on controversial issues of public policy." *Id.* at 539–540.

[355] *See, e.g.,* PruneYard Shopping Ctr. v. Robins, 447 U.S. 74, 81 (1980) (state may require shopping center owner to admit pamphleteers).

[356] *See Pacific Gas,* 475 U.S. at 12 ("Notably absent from *PruneYard* was any concern that [the state law] might affect the shopping center owner's exercise of his own right to speak. . . . "). Justice Marshall, concurring in the judgment, stated that "[w]hile the shopping center owner in *PruneYard* wished to be free of unwanted expression, [the owner] nowhere alleged that his own expression was hindered in the slightest." *Id.* at 24.

[357] *See Pacific Gas,* 475 U.S. at 22 n.1 (Marshall, J., concurring) (a utility has the "right to use [its] property for expressive purposes"); Los Angeles v. Preferred Communications, Inc., 476 U.S. 488 (1986) (striking down an exclusive franchise that barred additional speakers) (*Preferred Communications*). *Cf.* United States v. Eichman, 496 U.S. 310, 316 & n.5 (1990) (suggesting government can protect publicly owned, but not privately owned, flags from incineration); Spence v. Washington, 418 U.S. 405, 408–409, 415 (1974) (per curiam) (overturning conviction for displaying flag with peace symbol attached, in part because "this was a privately owned flag . . . displayed . . . on private property"); Lloyd Corp. v. Tanner, 407 U.S. 551, 567–570 (1972) (owner of private shopping center may exclude distribution of handbills on his property); Media Gen. Cable of Fairfax, Inc. v. Sequoyah Condominium Council of Co-Owners, 991 F.2d 1169 (4th Cir. 1993) (recognizing that private property is entitled to special solicitude, even in communicative context).

Nor can constitutional protections be easily suspended by way of "conditions" attached to the government's issuance of a franchise or other formal benefit of that kind.[358] The government may confer benefits with strings attached to prevent their misuse; some governmentally conferred privileges (it is argued) create such a risk of abuse that they must be simultaneously qualified with limits on how they may be used, by whom, and in what context. A government franchisor, for example, might insist on protecting all other markets by excluding a sole franchisee from engaging in any other business at all; the federal government might likewise claim it had to protect competition against misuse of benefits conferred by local franchisors. Such rationales for structural restraints cannot be dismissed out of hand, at least not when the restraints have been expressly linked to benefits concretely created by the government itself.

Common carrier status does not suspend a business's First Amendment rights either. Common carriers may be required to carry freight for others, but that does not mean they may constitutionally be barred from carrying expressive freight for themselves. The obligation to carry does not always deprive the carrier of the right to publish: there is no either/or choice. Many quasi-carrier activities enjoy First Amendment protection in any event. The cable business, for example, clearly ranks as "press" for First Amendment purposes.[359] Even if cable companies merely

---

[358] *See, e.g.,* Rutan v. Republican Party, 497 U.S. 62, 71–76 (1990); Nollan v. California Coastal Commn., 483 U.S. 825, 837 (1987). Government may indeed subsidize some speakers and not others. Regan v. Taxation with Representation, 461 U.S. 540, 544 (1983). It may also restrict the provision of public funds to political candidates who agree to observe expenditure limits. Buckley v. Valeo, 424 U.S. 1, 57 n.65 (1976) (per curiam). But the logic of these cases lends little support to the argument that the federal government may regulate the speech of any telephone or cable company that has been issued a local franchise. Neither case involved federal burdens and local benefits. And in both cases, the would-be speaker could continue doing what he was doing (campaigning, for example) and simply turn down the government largesse. The analogous issue here is not whether government may silence the speech of a franchisee, but whether it may deny a franchise to a would-be new entrant. Exclusive franchises do indeed raise serious constitutional issues.

[359] *See* Leathers v. Medlock, 499 U.S. 439, 444 (1991) ("Cable television provides to its subscribers news, information, and entertainment. It is engaged

retransmit the programming of others, they pick, choose, and edit, just like *Reader's Digest*.[360] Nor does use of public facilities suspend First Amendment rights. Newspapers place their boxes on public sidewalks;[361] demonstrators parade on public streets; cable operators and telephone companies run their wires overhead along the same routes.[362] No rationale based on real estate justifies any suspension of First Amendment protections.[363] And the mere fact of monopoly doesn't permit a government to muzzle the monopolist itself.[364]

---

in 'speech' under the First Amendment, and is, in much of its operation, part of the 'press.'"); *Preferred Communications*, 476 U.S. at 494; Quincy Cable TV, Inc. v. FCC, 768 F.2d 1434, 1444 (D.C. Cir. 1985) ("It is now clearly established . . . that cable operators engage in conduct protected by the First Amendment.").

[360] *Turner Broad. Sys.*, 512 U.S. at 636 ("There can be no disagreement on an initial premise: Cable programmers and cable operators engage in and transmit speech, and they are entitled to the protection of the speech and press provisions of the First Amendment. . . . Through 'original programming or by exercising editorial discretion over which stations or programs to include in its repertoire,' cable programmers and operators 'seek to communicate messages on a wide variety of topics and in a wide variety of formats.'") (quoting *Preferred Communications*, 476 U.S. at 494).

[361] *Cf.* City of Cincinnati v. Discovery Network, Inc., 507 U.S. 410 (1993). Cincinnati, faced with a proliferation of cumbersome newsracks on its sidewalks and street corners, revoked the permission it had given to two companies to distribute their commercial handbills in newsracks on public spaces. It based its ban on the grounds that it was concerned with the "safety and attractive appearance of its streets" and that commercial speech had been established as being of lower value than noncommercial speech. *Id.* at 412. The Supreme Court struck down the municipal ban on the grounds that the restriction was content-based and had the effect of barring "from its sidewalks a whole class of constitutionally protected speech." *Id.* at 430.

[362] In asserting the First Amendment rights of cablecos, the National Cable Television Association (NCTA) has argued that the use of public rights-of-way does not lower the appropriate First Amendment level of scrutiny. *See* Reply Memorandum in Support of Motions of NCTA for Summary Judgment and Preliminary Injunction at 30–31, NCTA v. United States, No. 92-2495 et seq. (D.D.C. Feb. 25, 1993).

[363] Multimedia Publishing Co. v. Greenville-Spartanburg Airport Dist., 21 Media L. Rep. (BNA) 1369, 1371 (4th Cir. 1993).

[364] *See Tornillo*, 418 U.S. at 249–250 & n.13 (striking down a right-of-reply statute despite the assumption that "'one-newspaper towns have become the rule, with effective competition operating in only 4 percent of our large cities'"); *see also* Consolidated Edison Co. v. Public Service Commn. of New

In 1992, the Bell Atlantic companies successfully challenged the constitutionality of section 533(b), enacted as part of the 1984 Cable Act, which barred telcos from providing video programming.[365] Their First Amendment claims were consistently vindicated in federal district and appellate courts. The Supreme Court granted certiorari, the issue was fully briefed, and the Court heard oral argument. The case was then mooted by passage of the 1996 Act, which repealed the video ban.[366]

York, 447 U.S. 530, 534 n.1 (1980); Pacific Gas & Electric Co. v. Public Utils. Commn. of Cal., 475 U.S. 1 (1986); Chesapeake & Potomac Tel. Co. of Va. v. United States, 830 F. Supp. 909, 919 (E.D. Va. 1993), *aff'd,* 42 F.3d 181 (4th Cir. 1994), *dismissed as moot,* 516 U.S. 415 (1996). *But see Turner Broad. Sys.,* 512 U.S. 622 (government has a valid interest in restricting cable's monopoly power).

[365] Chesapeake & Potomac Tel. Co. v. United States, 830 F. Supp. 909 (E.D. Va. 1993) *aff'd,* 42 F.3d 181 (4th Cir. 1994), *dismissed as moot,* 516 U.S. 415 (1996). This was the first time the issue had been squarely presented. The claim that §533(b) violated the First Amendment had been raised only once before, but the D.C. Circuit did not reach the issue. Northwestern Ind. Tel. Co. v. FCC, 872 F.2d 465, 470 (D.C. Cir. 1989), *cert. denied,* 493 U.S. 1035 (1990). The FCC's 1970 ban on CATV service by telephone companies was upheld against a due process challenge in a case where no First Amendment claim was raised. General Tel. Co. of Southwest v. United States, 449 F.2d 846 (5th Cir. 1971). In the AT&T Decree litigation, Judge Harold Greene refused to entertain First Amendment objections relating to the information services restriction because, inter alia, the Decree prohibition had been entered with the parties' consent and thus represented a voluntary decision by the telephone companies not to speak. United States v. Western Elec. Co., 673 F. Supp. 525, 586 n.273 (D.D.C. 1987). Judge Greene was reversed on other grounds, and the court of appeals did not find it necessary to reach the First Amendment question. United States v. Western Elec. Co., 900 F.2d 283 (D.C. Cir.), *cert. denied,* 498 U.S. 911 (1990). Somewhat surprisingly the Department of Justice largely *endorsed* the First Amendment argument in the Decree litigation. "The United States agrees [with Bell Atlantic] that a ban on electronic publishing by the [Bell Companies]—especially a *nonconsensual* ban not based on competitive concerns—would raise serious First Amendment issues." Response of the United States at 94 n.175, United States v. Western Elec. Co., No. 82-0192 (D.D.C. Apr. 27, 1987) (emphasis added). Continuing the "ban on electronic publishing by the [Bell Companies] would be contrary to the diversity goals underlying the First Amendment." Report and Recommendations of the United States at 137 n.273, United States v. Western Elec. Co., No. 82-0192 (D.D.C. Feb. 2, 1987).

[366] Telecommunications Act of 1996, §302(b)(1); 516 U.S. 415 (1996). *See* §13.7.2.6.

Section 274 of the 1996 Act, however, establishes a new prohibition on "electronic publishing" by BOCs. As discussed in section 12.7.11.2, a 1998 challenge to that provision based on First Amendment and bill of attainder grounds was rejected by the D.C. Circuit.[367]

§14.6.3   Mandatory Blocking of the Content of Others

In 1983, Congress added section 223(b) to the Communications Act to prohibit commercial dissemination of either obscene or indecent telephone messages to anyone under the age of 18.[368] The amendment provided an affirmative defense if the service restricted child access in compliance with FCC regulations.

The FCC's first set of regulations created a safe harbor for services that either operated only between the hours of 9:00 P.M. and 8:00 A.M. Eastern Time ("time channeling") or required payment by credit card ("screening").[369] The Second Circuit, however, set aside the time channeling regulations and remanded to the FCC to examine less restrictive alternatives, including blocking or screening schemes and access codes.[370]

The Commission's next round of regulations, promulgated in October 1985, approved defenses of credit card screening or access codes issued upon written application to persons who established they were over 18.[371] These, too, were set aside; this time the Second Circuit chided the FCC's failure to consider adequately the less restrictive alternative of "customer-premises

---

[367] BellSouth Corp., v. FCC, 144 F.3d 58 (D.C. Cir. 1998), *cert. denied,* 119 S. Ct. 1495 (1999).

[368] 47 U.S.C. §223(b) (1983).

[369] Restrictions on Indecent Telephone Message Services, 47 C.F.R. §64.201 (1984).

[370] Carlin Communications, Inc. v. FCC, 749 F.2d 113, 121 (2d Cir. 1984). The court concluded that the operating hours requirement was "both over-inclusive and underinclusive" because it denied "access to adults between certain hours, but not to youths who can easily pick up a private or public telephone and call dial-a-porn during the remaining hours." *Id.* at 121.

[371] 47 C.F.R. §64.201 (1985).

blocking," which would block or screen telephone numbers at the customer's premises or at the telephone company offices.[372]

The third time around, the FCC (after considering, but again rejecting customer premises blocking) retained the access code and credit card defenses, but added a third defense: message scrambling, which makes the message unintelligible unless adult customers purchase and utilize a descrambling device.[373] The Second Circuit upheld the validity of these regulations, finding that inexpensive portable and nonportable scrambling devices could be purchased from the service without undue burden to patrons.[374] However, the court directed the FCC to reopen proceedings if an even less restrictive technology, such as a beep-tone device, became available.[375]

Having concluded that the regulations themselves were valid, the court for the first time addressed the constitutionality of the underlying legislation under the First Amendment. The court found that the "indecency" standard, though approved by the Supreme Court for regulating broadcast messages in *FCC v. Pacifica Foundation*,[376] did not justify the regulation of indecent telephone messages. Therefore, the court invalidated section 223(b) as applied to nonobscene speech.[377]

§14.6.3.1 Congress's Absolute Ban and the *Sable* Decision

Congress was not deterred by the Second Circuit's ruling that indecent dial-a-porn messages cannot be regulated. In April 1988 (an election year, naturally), Congress passed the Telephone Decency Act, amending section 223(b) to prohibit indecent as well as obscene interstate telephone communications directed to any person, regardless of age.[378] The amended statute also elim-

---

[372] Carlin Communications, Inc. v. FCC, 787 F. 2d 846, 848 (2d Cir. 1986).
[373] 47 C.F.R. §64.201(a)(4) (1987).
[374] Carlin Communications, Inc. v. FCC, 837 F.2d 546, 556 (2d Cir.), *cert. denied,* 488 U.S. 924 (1988).
[375] *Id.* at 556.
[376] 438 U.S. 726 (1978).
[377] *Carlin Communications,* 837 F.2d at 561.
[378] 47 U.S.C. §223(b) (1988).

inated the requirement that the FCC promulgate regulations for restricting access to minors: a total ban was imposed on dial-a-porn, making it illegal for adults, as well as children, to have access to sexually explicit messages. Within a year, the new statute came before the Supreme Court in *Sable Communications of California, Inc. v. FCC.*[379]

The Supreme Court upheld the prohibition against obscene interstate commercial telephone messages, but struck down the ban insofar as it extended to indecent speech. The legislation, in the eyes of the Court, was not reasonably restricted to the evil with which it was said to deal. Quoting Justice Frankfurter, the Court noted that "'[s]urely this is to burn the house to roast the pig.'"[380] The Court rejected the government's argument that nothing less than a total ban could prevent children from gaining access to dial-a-porn messages and dismissed as unpersuasive the notion that it should defer to Congress's conclusions and factual findings to that effect.

The Court had upheld the FCC's earlier proscription of vulgar radio broadcasts, but the Court asserted that broadcast radio is a fundamentally different medium from telephony.[381] Broadcasting is "uniquely pervasive, can intrude on the privacy of the home without prior warning as to program content, and is uniquely accessible to children, even those too young to read."[382] In sharp contrast to "public displays, unsolicited mailings and other means of expression which the recipient has no meaningful opportunity to avoid, the dial-it medium requires the listener to take affirmative steps to receive the communication."[383]

---

[379] 492 U.S. 115 (1989).

[380] *Id.* at 127 (quoting Butler v. Michigan, 352 U.S. 380 (1957)).

[381] *Id.* at 127–128 (discussing *Pacifica*). Moreover, the regulations at issue in *Pacifica* simply sought to channel indecent communication to times of day when children most likely would not be exposed to it. Congress in 1988, however, extended the *Pacifica* broadcasting ban to apply 24 hours a day, but that measure was struck down by the courts. *See* Action for Children's Television v. FCC, 932 F.2d 1504 (D.C. Cir. 1991), *cert. denied,* Children's Legal Found. v. Action for Children's Television, 503 U.S. 913 (1992).

[382] *Pacifica,* 438 U.S. at 748–749.

[383] *Sable,* at 127–128. *See generally* Dunn, Regulation of Dial-a-Porn Is a Tough Call, 16 Ohio N.U. L. Rev. 719 (1989).

§14.6.3.2   Post-*Sable:* Return to Regulating Access

Sable returned the legal terrain to its previous state: the transmission of obscene telecommunications was banned, and the transmission of indecent material to minors was regulated by the FCC. In response to *Sable,* however, Congress passed a new statute in 1989, the "Helms Amendment,"[384] to prohibit providers of indecent telephone communications from making their services available to persons under 18 years of age. The Act established a "safe harbor" defense for providers that restrict access to persons 18 years of age or older either by establishing a presubscription requirement on telcos that collect charges from subscribers or by implementing other protections in accordance with current FCC regulations.

In August 1990, a United States district court in New York issued a preliminary injunction against the enforcement or implementation of the Helms Amendment.[385] The Second Circuit promptly reversed.[386] The FCC's goal was to prevent access to indecent messages by children. The means chosen had to be effective. Voluntary blocking might be a less restrictive option, but it clearly was not as effective.[387] The statute was not unconstitutionally vague and did not impose a "prior restraint" on protected speech.[388] "A requirement that one desiring access make an advance request . . . simply does not constitute a prior restraint."[389] The Supreme Court declined to review the Second Circuit's decision.[390]

---

[384] Pub. L. No. 101-166, 103 Stat. 1159 (1989) (as codified at 47 U.S.C. §223).

[385] American Info. Enters. v. Thornburgh, 742 F. Supp. 1255, 1275 (S.D.N.Y. 1990). The court held that a voluntary blocking provision for dial-a-porn messages was "adequately protective of children and . . . less restrictive than either a presubscription requirement or an independent billing mechanism." *Id.* at 1264.

[386] Dial Info. Servs. Corp. v. Thornburgh, 938 F.2d 1535 (2d Cir. 1991).

[387] *Id.* at 1541–1542.

[388] *American Info. Enters.,* 742 F. Supp. at 1275.

[389] Dial Info. Servs. Corp. v. Thornburgh, 938 F.2d at 1543.

[390] Dial Info. Servs. Corp. v. Barr, 502 U.S. 1072 (1992).

The Commission acted quickly to promulgate regulations to implement the amendment. The Commission's rules prescribed reverse blocking, whereby telephone companies had to restrict access to indecent material such as sexually oriented messages until affirmatively requested by the user through the establishment of an account or method of payment.[391] A challenge to the Commission's regulations implementing the legislation was also rebuffed.[392] The Commission later clarified that its regulations require interexchange carriers and other carriers that contract with adult message providers to notify the local telephone company providing billing services that "such calls should be separately labeled as calls to adult message services on the bill."[393]

§14.6.3.3 Regulation of Providers of Content

In the Telephone Disclosure and Dispute Resolution Act of 1992 (TDDRA),[394] Congress extended its regulatory reach beyond dial-a-porn to dial-it services generally. The TDDRA mandated new rules, promulgated by both the FTC and the FCC,[395] for all pay-per-call (900 and 976) services.[396] Purchasing

[391] 47 C.F.R. §64.201 (1990). Service is available to adults who subscribe to the service in writing, have been assigned an access code, have received credit card authorization, or possess a descrambling device.

[392] Information Providers' Coalition v. FCC, 928 F.2d 866 (9th Cir. 1991). Petitioners, a collection of information service providers, argued that the Commission should have required central office or "voluntary" blocking, whereby access is available to all unless the subscriber requests access by blocked.

[393] Regulations Concerning Indecent Communications by Telephone, Order on Partial Reconsideration, 10 F.C.C. Rec. 665, 666–667 ¶10 (1995).

[394] Pub. L. No. 102-556, 106 Stat. 4181 (codified at 15 U.S.C. §5701, 15 U.S.C. §5714, 47 U.S.C. §227, 47 U.S.C. §228, 47 U.S.C. §302a, 15 U.S.C. §§5711–5712, 15 U.S.C. §§5721–5724).

[395] Title I of the TDDRA added a new section to the Communications Act providing an explicit statutory framework for the FCC's regulation of the provision of pay-per-call services through common carriers. 47 U.S.C. §228. Title II requires the Federal Trade Commission (FTC) to regulate advertising and service standards applicable to pay-per-call programs, and Title III requires the FTC to regulate telephone-billed purchases with rules substantially similar to the provisions of the Truth in Lending and Fair Credit Billing Acts. 15 U.S.C. §§1601 et seq.

[396] Trade Regulation Rule Pursuant to the Telephone Disclosure and Dispute Resolution Act of 1992, 16 C.F.R. §308 (adopted July 27, 1993).

a pay-per-call telephone service was to resemble purchasing Twinkies or Preparation H. Advertising, labeling, and payment disputes will be strictly regulated.

Under the new rules, companies that offer pay-per-call services are required to disclose the costs of these services in their advertising[397] and are required to begin calls costing more than $2 with a preamble stating, among other things, the cost of the call and informing the caller that he or she may hang up immediately and avoid the charges.[398] The rules ban pay-per-call services advertised or directed to children under 12 years old.[399]

---

[397] Pay-per-call providers must disclose the following information in any print, radio, or television advertisement: for flat-fee services, the total cost of each call; for time-sensitive services, the cost per minute and any minimum charges, as well as the maximum charge if it can be determined in advance; for services billed at varying rates depending on which options callers select, the cost of the initial portion of the call, any minimum charges, and the range of rates that may be charged; and for all other fees: the cost of any other pay-per-call services to which the callers may be transferred. 16 C.F.R. §308.3(b).

Other required advertising disclosures include the following: for pay-per-call sweepstakes services, a statement about the odds of winning and the fact that consumers do not have to call to enter the sweepstakes (as well as a description of the free alternative method of entering the sweepstakes); for services that provide information about federal programs, but that are not affiliated with the federal government, a statement that the service is not affiliated, endorsed, or approved by the federal government; and for services directed to consumers under the age of 18, a statement that parental permission is required before calling the service. 16 C.F.R. §308.5(a).

[398] The preamble must identify the company providing the service, state the cost of the call, and inform the caller that charges will begin three seconds after the tone following the preamble and that the caller must hang up before that time to avoid charges. *Id.* The preamble must also inform callers that anyone under the age of 18 must have a parent's or guardian's permission to make the call. 16 C.F.R. §308.5(a)(4). No preamble is required for calls to data services. 16 C.F.R. §308.5(d). In addition, pay-per-call providers are permitted to offer frequent callers or regular subscribers the option of activating a bypass mechanism to avoid listening to the preamble, provided that the bypass mechanism is disabled for a period of at least 30 days after any price increase. 16 C.F.R. §308.5(e); *see also* 15 U.S.C. §5711.

[399] The FTC adopted a two-part test to determine whether a service is impermissibly advertised. The first test is whether the ad appears during programming or in publications for which 50 percent of the audience or readership is under 12. 16 C.F.R. §308.3(e)(2). The second test, which applies if reliable audience data are not available, requires the FTC to consider the placement of the ad, subject matter, visual content, language, age of any models, and any characters used in the ad. 16 C.F.R. §308.3(e)(3). Pay-per-call advertisements could thus appear during *Roger Rabbit,* but not *Bugs Bunny;*

The rules also ban companies from running ads that emit touch-tone signals that dial pay-per-call numbers automatically.[400] Further, 800 numbers can no longer be used for pay-per-call services.[401] The rules also contain provisions to avoid and resolve billing disputes.[402]

The ban on automated telemarketing calls was challenged on First Amendment grounds and upheld. The court found the ban was not an attempt to favor a particular viewpoint and left open other alternatives to communications with consumers.[403]

The TDDRA requires local telcos to offer blocking of all pay-per-call services and prohibited both local telcos and long-distance carriers from discontinuing service for nonpayment of charges incurred in connection with these services.[404]

Jurassic Park, but not *The Land Before Time.* The FTC has recognized that there are possible First Amendment difficulties in making such content-based distinctions (*cf.* Cincinnati v. Discovery Network, Inc., 507 U.S. 410 (1993); Moser v. FCC, 826 F. Supp. 360 (D. Ore. 1993)), but the FTC believes that the rules are nonetheless "reasonable" and narrowly tailored. Statement of Basis and Purpose at 57–58 n.149, Trade Regulation Rule Pursuant to the Telephone Disclosure and Dispute Resolution Act of 1992 (F.T.C. July 27, 1993).

[400] 16 C.F.R. §308.3(g). One of the incidents that led to the enactment of the TDDRA was a Christmas television program that instructed young children to hold the phone up to the TV set in order to call Santa. The television program then emitted touch tones that automatically dialed the pay-per-call service.

[401] 16 C.F.R. §308.5(i); *see also* 47 U.S.C. §228(c)(7).

[402] The rules require that carriers providing billing services notify consumers of their right to dispute any charges for these services and explaining the procedures for doing so. 16 C.F.R. §308.7(n). A customer may notify the billing entity of an error within 60 days after the statement is sent. *Id.* §308.7(b). The billing entity must acknowledge the customer's notice in writing and either correct the bill or explain to the customer the reason for not doing so. *Id.* §308.7(d). A billing entity that fails to comply with the prescribed procedures forfeits the right to collect the disputed amount at all (up to $50 per transaction). *Id.* §308.7(j).

[403] Moser v. FCC, 46 F.3d 970 (9th Cir.), *cert. denied,* 515 U.S. 1161 (1995).

[404] Policies and Rules Implementing the Telephone Disclosure and Dispute Resolution Act, Notice of Proposed Rulemaking and Notice of Inquiry, 8 F.C.C. Rec. 2331 (1993). Additional FCC rules concerning the content and specific application of its preamble requirements can be found in Policies and Rules Concerning Interstate 900 Telecommunications Services, Order on Reconsideration, 8 F.C.C. Rec. 2343 (1993). The FCC has proposed to follow the requirements of the Act very closely. It has solicited comments, however,

The 1996 Act's V-chip is an analogous feature, requiring television manufacturers to equip new sets with technology that would permit viewers to block the display of any program carrying a particular rating.[405] For their part, broadcasters, cable companies, and moviemakers have worked out a system for rating content and transmitting ratings in a format detectable by the chip.[406] TV owners would then have the power to block all programming that did not meet their own tastes, or their children's.[407]

---

on whether to expand the statute to include such things as specially designated office codes for audiotext services and whether to extend the prohibition against disconnection for nonpayment to collect calls that offer access to audiotext services. The rules promulgated by the FTC expand and clarify the Commission's statutory requirements in several ways. The FTC has required that the preamble identify the provider of the service, a requirement not specifically mentioned in the statute. The Act allows the FTC to exempt from the preamble requirement pay-per-call services provided at "nominal" cost by providers who would otherwise suffer economic hardship from imposition of the rule. *See* 16 C.F.R. §308.5(c). The FTC has defined several terms used in the Act and expanded their applicability. The term "preexisting agreement" is equated with the term "presubscription or comparable arrangement" defined in section 308.2(e), and the term "billing entity" is applied to any person—whether a common carrier, vendor, third-party biller, or other person—who sends a billing statement to a customer for a telephone-billed purchase. The definition of "customer" is broadened to cover any person who is billed for a telephone-billed purchase, whether or not that person placed the call or received the goods or services in question. *See* 16 C.F.R. §308.7(a)(3).

[405] 47 U.S.C. §303(x). Congress called for the establishment of guidelines and recommended procedures for rating certain television programming and for the transmission of rating information for programs that are rated. 47 U.S.C. §§303(w), 330.

[406] Technical Requirements to Enable Blocking of Video Programming Based on Program Ratings, Report and Order, 13 F.C.C. Rec. 11,248 (1998). "We are requiring that covered television receivers respond to ratings based on a system of voluntary parental guidelines ('TV Parental Guidelines') developed jointly by the National Association of Broadcasters, the National Cable Television Association, and the Motion Picture Association ('the Industry')." *Id.* at 11,248 ¶1.

[407] Implementation of Section 551 of the Telecommunications Act of 1996, Report and Order, 13 F.C.C. Rec. 8232 (1998).

§14.6.4   The Communications Decency Act of 1996

One of the most controversial titles of the 1996 Telecommunications Act targeted sleaze in the three main segments of the telecosm. Title V, known as the Communications Decency Act of 1996 (CDA),[408] criminalized or regulated various forms of obscenity, indecency, violence, harassment,[409] and the enticement of minors[410] on telephone networks, cable, and television. Section 507 amended current obscenity statutes to include the prohibition on using a computer to import and distribute "obscene" material.[411]

The most hotly disputed provision in the new law addressed sleaze in cyberspace. Introduced by Senator James Exon, the "Exon amendment" was a sweeping new law for online smut.

The Exon amendment clarified existing federal proscriptions against interstate trafficking in "obscenity."[412] Those laws already prohibited interstate transport of obscenity, by any means, whether for commercial or noncommercial purposes. The 1996 Act underlines that computer networks are covered, too.[413] The CDA prohibited the use of communications devices to transmit any communication that was "obscene or indecent, knowing that the recipient is under 18 years of age, regardless of whether the

---

[408] Telecommunications Act of 1996, Pub. L. No. 104-104, tit. v, §§501 et seq., 110 Stat. 56 (Communications Decency Act of 1996).

[409] The Act modifies existing telephone harassment laws to cover not only speech, but data, too. *See* §14.7.1. "Telephone" in the existing law becomes "telecommunications device," and "conversation" is supplemented with "communications." 47 U.S.C. §223(a)(1). The content proscribed by this section is broadly defined to include anything "obscene, lewd, lascivious, filthy, or indecent." *Id.* §223(a)(1)(A)(ii). But as before, the proscription extends only to communications made "with intent to annoy, abuse, threaten, or harass any person." *Id.* §223(a)(1)(C).

[410] The Act also criminalizes the use of interstate telecommunications for luring, enticing, or coercing a minor into prostitution or a sexual crime. 18 U.S.C. §2422(b).

[411] Telecommunications Act of 1996, §507 (codified at 18 U.S.C. §§1462, 1467, 1469). These sections of Title 18 prohibit the interstate transport of obscenity for sale or distribution.

[412] 18 U.S.C. §§1462, 1467, 1469.

[413] *Id.* §§1462, 1465.

maker of such communications placed the call or initiated the communication."[414] The CDA also prohibited the use of interactive computer services to send or to display to a minor "any communication that in context depicts or describes, in terms patently offensive as measured by contemporary community standards, sexual or excretory activities or organs."[415]

The critical limitations on speech were the proscriptions on "indecent" and "patently offensive" communications. Congress considered, but rejected, the "harmful to minors" alternative.[416] The conference statement insisted that these terms were neither overly broad nor unconstitutionally vague.[417] According to the Conference Statement, "patent offensiveness" required both the intention to give and the effect of giving patent offense.[418] "Material with serious redeeming value was quite obviously intended to edify and educate, not to offend"[419] and is not therefore proscribed. The indecency standard "poses no significant risk to the free-wheeling and vibrant nature of discourse or to serious, literary, and artistic works that currently can be found on the Internet, and which is expected to continue and grow."[420]

Significantly, Congress decided on a national standard for online indecency. Obscenity, the Supreme Court has ruled, is defined by the norms of each local community.[421] But the 1996 Act

---

[414] 47 U.S.C. §223(a)(1). A violation of the section carried fines as prescribed by Title 18 or up to two years' imprisonment.

[415] 47 U.S.C. §223(d)(1).

[416] Conference Report at 189 (citing Ginsberg v. New York, 390 U.S. 629, 641–643 (1968)).

[417] *Id.* at 188 (1996) (citing Alliance for Community Media v. FCC, 56 F.3d 105, 124–125 (D.C. Cir. 1995), *cert. granted sub. nom.* Denver Area Education Telecommunications Consortium v. FCC, 518 U.S. 727 (1996)); Action for Children's Television v. FCC, 932 F.2d 1504, 1508 (D.C. Cir. 1991) (size of safe harbor required by First Amendment)). The Conference Report also states that "indecency" is defined in line with the laws tested in FCC v. Pacifica Foundation, 438 U.S. 726 (1978), and Sable Communications of California, Inc. v. FCC, 492 U.S. 115 (1989). Conference Report at 188.

[418] Conference Report at 189 (citing Sagittarius Broadcasting Corp. et al., 7 F.C.C. Rec. 6873, 6875 (1992); Audio Enterprises, Inc., 3 F.C.C. Rec. 930, 932 (1987)).

[419] H.R. Rep. 458 at 70.

[420] *Id.*

[421] *See* Bolger v. Youngs Drug Prods. Corp., 463 U.S. 60 (1983); Pinkus v. United States, 436 U.S. 293 (1978); Miller v. California, 413 U.S. 15, 24 (1973);

barred state and local governments from imposing any inde-
cency-related liability that is inconsistent with the new federal
laws. They were permitted to enact and enforce "complementary" liability and regulatory schemes, but only to govern strictly
intrastate services, and only to the extent that they did not impose "inconsistent rights, duties or obligations" on interstate services.[422] This section was "intended to establish a uniform
national standard of content regulation for a national, and
indeed a global medium."[423]

The Act also provided a good-faith defense for "reasonable,
effective, and appropriate" measures to restrict access to prohibited communications,[424] such as "requiring use of a verified
credit card, debit account, adult access code, or adult personal
identification number."[425] The FCC was authorized to "describe"
other "appropriate measures" that are "feasible under available
technology."[426] The Commission's views on this score are admis-
sible as evidence in any prosecution.[427]

In a gesture to the disappearing past, this section of the Act
also insists that it does not apply to "broadcasting station licensees" or "cable operations."[428] But cable companies are already beginning to provide access to the Web, phone companies

---

Butler v. Michigan, 352 U.S. 380, 383 (1957). Pornography is judged by local
standards even if obtained on the Internet. *See, e.g.,* Sable Communications
of Cal., Inc. v. FCC, 492 U.S. 115, 125 (1989); United States v. Thomas, 78
F.3d 701 (1997).

[422] 47 U.S.C. §223(f)(2).

[423] Conference Report at 191.

[424] The Conference Report states that "the word 'effective' is given its common meaning and does not require an absolute 100 percent restriction of
access to be judged 'effective.'" *Id.* at 188.

[425] 47 U.S.C. §223(e)(5)(B).

[426] *Id.* §223(e)(5)(A), (e)(6). The Commission, however, has no authority to
"enforce," "approve, sanction, or permit" use of any such measure. Nor does
the Commission have any enforcement authority over the "failure" to use
them. *Id.* §223(e)(6).

[427] *Id.* §223(e)(6). But the Commission is granted no further authority, and
according to the Conference Report, this section "should be narrowly construed." Conference Report at 191.

[428] 47 U.S.C. §223(h)(1)(A).

are performing as "broadcasters," and broadcasters are supplying carriage. As data networks speed up, every connection to the Web will become all of the above—telephone, television, and cable. Existing lines between "telecommunications," "cable," and "broadcast" will fade away, and eventually disappear.

§14.6.4.1 *Reno v. ACLU:* The CDA's Indecency Provisions Overturned

Not long after the CDA took affect, 20 plaintiffs challenged the act on the grounds that "indecent" was too vague to provide a basis for criminal prosecution.[429] A three-judge panel enjoined the enforcement of section 223(a)(1)(B) insofar as it related to "indecent" communications.[430] The Supreme Court took the case directly.[431] In an opinion authored by Justice Stevens, the Supreme Court invalidated two key provisions of the CDA: the "indecent" half of section 223(a)(1)(B), which prohibited sending "obscene or indecent" communications to minors, and section 223(d) in its entirety, which prohibited displaying patently offensive material to minors.

The Court rejected the government's argument that these provisions merely zoned the Internet. The provisions constituted a "content based blanket restriction on speech" and not "a form of time, place and manner regulation."[432] Dissenting in part, Justice O'Connor gave more credence to the CDA's attempt to segregate "indecent material on the Internet into certain areas that minors cannot access" and thereby create adult zones.[433] But Justice O'Connor acknowledged that the Internet "as it exists today" was not technologically capable of creating with any

---

[429] Judge Buckwalter issued a temporary restraining order against enforcement of §223(a)(1)(B)(ii). This case was consolidated with another suit filed by a second set of plaintiffs.

[430] ACLU v. Reno, 929 F. Supp. 824 (E.D. Pa 1996).

[431] Reno v. ACLU, 117 S. Ct. 2329 (1997). The Telecommunications Act provided for direct appeal to the Supreme Court from any judgment or decree holding any provision of the CDA unconstitutional. Pub. L. No. 104-104, §561(b), *reprinted at* 47 U.S.C. §223 note.

[432] Reno v. ACLU, 117 S. Ct. at 2342.

[433] *Id.* at 2352.

type of assurance the same adult zones that exist in the physical world.[434]

The Court recognized that the special circumstances associated with restrictions on broadcast services were not present with the Internet. Unlike the long history of government supervision and regulation of the broadcast industry, the Internet had evolved free from any type of regulation.[435] While broadcast communications "invade" an individual's home, sexually explicit images on the Internet are usually preceded by warnings and require the individual to take some affirmative steps to view them.[436] Further, the Internet is not a "scarce" resource the way the broadcast spectrum was at one time. Consequently, the Court was unwilling to "qualify the level of First Amendment scrutiny" that it would apply to the Internet.[437]

The Court was especially disturbed by Congress's failure either to define "indecent" or to delimit material that is "patently offensive as measured by contemporary community standards." As required by *Miller v. California*,[438] Congress failed to "specifically define" the proscribed material "by applicable state law."[439] The Court explained that, absent a "societal value" component to circumscribe the statute's application, there was no way for "appellate courts to impose some limitations and regularity on the definition by setting, as a matter of law, a national floor for socially redeeming value." The Court rejected the argument that the "knowledge" requirement saved the statute from being overbroad. Because the Internet is open to all comers and contains no method to verify a user's age, the speaker "must be charged with knowing that one or more minors will likely view it." Nor did the credit card or adult verification defenses sufficiently nar-

---

[434] *Id.* at 2354. Justice O'Connor therefore concurred in finding that the display provision was unconstitutional because it was too uncertain for the speaker to know who would be viewing the displayed communication and if it would reach only adults.

[435] *Id.* at 2344.

[436] This makes them similar to dial-a-porn services. *See* §14.6.3.1.

[437] Reno v. ACLU, 117 S. Ct. at 2344.

[438] Miller v. California, 413 U.S. 15, 15 (1973).

[439] Reno v. ACLU, 117 S. Ct. at 2345.

row the CDA's application because noncommercial speakers cannot economically employ such techniques.[440]

Reno v. ACLU invalidated only the "indecency" clause of section 223(a); federal criminal prosecutions remain possible for use of a "telecommunications device" to send an "obscene" communication knowing the recipient is a minor or with the intent to threaten or harass another person.[441]

§14.6.4.2   The Child Online Protection Act and *ACLU v. Reno II*

As part of the Omnibus Appropriations Bill that was signed into law on October 21, 1998, Congress crafted new legislation to replace the invalidated CDA—the Child Online Protection Act (COPA).[442] The law makes it a crime punishable by a fine of no more than $50,000 and imprisonment for no more than six months for anyone "knowingly and with knowledge of the character of the material, in interstate or foreign commerce by means of the World Wide Web, [to] make[] any communication for commercial purposes that is available to any minor and that includes any material that is harmful to minors."[443] The Act defines material that is "harmful to minors" as "any communication, picture, image, graphic image file, article, recording, writing, or other matter of any kind that is obscene or that—(A) the average person, applying contemporary community standards, would find, taking the material as a whole and with respect to minors, is designed to appeal to, or is designed to pander to, the prurient interest; (B) depicts, describes, or represents, in a manner patently offensive with respect to minors, an actual or simulated sexual act or sexual contact, an actual or simulated normal or perverted sexual act, or a lewd exhibition of the genitals or post-pubescent female breast; and (C) taken as a whole, lacks serious literary, artistic, political, or scientific value for minors."[444]

---

[440] *Id.* at 2349.
[441] *Id.* at 2350.
[442] 47 U.S.C. §231.
[443] *Id.* §231(a)(1).
[444] *Id.* §231(e)(6).

COPA provides for the same affirmative defenses as originally contemplated under the CDA: it is a defense to prosecution where the defendant, in good faith, has restricted access by minors to material that is harmful to minors by requiring use of a credit card, debit account, adult access code, or adult personal identification number; by accepting a digital certificate that verifies age; or "by any other reasonable measures that are feasible under available technology."[445]

The law was to go into effect on November 20, 1998, but the District Court for the Eastern District of Pennsylvania issued a temporary restraining order, prohibiting the Attorney General from "enforcing or prosecuting matters premised upon [COPA] at any time for any conduct that occurs while this Order is in effect."[446] Relying on testimony from Norman Laurila, founder and owner of *A Different Light,* and David Talbot, CEO and editor of *Salon Magazine,* Judge Lowell A. Reed, Jr., was satisfied "that plaintiffs raised serious and substantial questions as to the technological and economic feasibility of [the] affirmative defenses," without which "COPA on its face would prohibit speech which is protected as to adults."[447] Plaintiffs demonstrated "a likelihood of success on the merits on their claim that COPA violates the First Amendment rights of adults."[448] After five days of testimony and one day of argument, the court granted plaintiffs' motion for a preliminary injunction on February 1, 1999.[449] The Attorney General has appealed the decision to the Third Circuit.

---

[445] *Id.* §231(c)(1).

[446] ACLU v. Reno, Memorandum and Temporary Restraining Order, Civ. Act. No. 98-5591, U.S. Dist. LEXIS 18546 (E.D. Pa. Nov. 20, 1998).

[447] ACLU v. Reno, Memorandum and Temporary Restraining Order, Civ. Act. No. 98-5591 (E.D. Pa. Nov. 20, 1998).

[448] *Id.* Indeed, in their complaint, plaintiffs alleged that under COPA any speech that some community might consider to be "harmful to minors"—including Ken Starr's report on the Clinton-Lewinsky scandal or a Mapplethorpe photograph—is potentially criminal if displayed for free on the World Wide Web and accessible by minors. Complaint for Declaratory and Injunctive Relief ¶1, ACLU v. Reno, Civ. Act. No. 98-5591 (E.D. Pa. Oct. 22, 1998).

[449] ACLU v. Reno, Memorandum, Civ. Act. No. 98-5591 (E.D. Pa. Feb. 1, 1999).

§14.6.5 Federal Defenses to and Immunities from Federal Criminal Liability Under Section 223

As noted, the CDA imposes criminal liability in section 223 (a)–(d); in section 223(e), it establishes immunities and limits on that federal liability. (None of these provisions limits liability under state or other federal obscenity laws, however.)

Section 223(e)(1) exempts from liability passive software writers, transmitters, and carriers who only provide "access or connection," "transmission," "intermediate storage," "access software," and so forth, but do not "creat[e] . . . the content of the [forbidden] communication."[450] This defense, according to the Conference Statement, is to be "construed broadly to avoid impairing the growth of on-line communications through a regime of vicarious liability."[451] This "access provider" defense is expressly intended to protect "commercial and non-profit Internet operators who provide access to the Internet and other interactive computer services."[452]

Section 223(e)(5) states that it is a defense to criminal prosecution under sections 223(a)(1)(B) and 223(d) if a person has taken certain steps to restrict minors from accessing such communications. "[R]easonable, effective, and appropriate" measures to restrict a minor's access to communications prohibited by section 223 are a defense.[453] It is also a sufficient defense to

---

[450] 47 U.S.C. §223(e)(1).

[451] Conference Report at 190. Employers are exempt from vicarious liability for the unauthorized, outside-the-scope cyberfrolics of employees, but only insofar as they are not in "reckless disregard" of supervising employees. 47 U.S.C. §223(e)(4).

[452] Conference Report at 190. Section 223(e)(1) reads, "No person shall be held to have violated subsection (a) or (d) of this section solely for providing access. . . ."

[453] 47 U.S.C. §223(e)(5). §223(e)(5)(A). The Conference Report states that "the word 'effective' is given its common meaning and does not require an absolute 100 percent restriction of access to be judged 'effective.'" Conference Report at 188. The CDA gives the Commission authority to "describe" measures that are reasonable, effective, and appropriate, but does not permit the Commission to enforce such measures. 47 U.S.C. §223(e)(6). However, in

restrict access by requiring the use of a credit card or adult access code.[454]

§14.6.6   A Carrier's Right to Censor the Content of Its Customers

Only "state action" implicates the First Amendment. A private publisher may censor all it likes.[455] This is why there should be no First Amendment question (as distinct from common carrier question) when a telephone company cuts off service for the utterance of a profanity on its lines, as the Ohio phone company did when civility still reigned in 1883.[456]

The filing of a tariff by a telephone company does not transform the tariff itself into "state action," so it does not usually implicate the same constitutional issues at stake when government takes the initiative.[457] Telco tariffs may therefore declare that

---

Reno v. ACLU, the Supreme Court suggested that this is not much of defense, in actual practice. "It is the requirement that the good faith must be 'effective' that makes this defense illusory. The proposed screening software does not exist. Even if it did, there is no way to know whether a potential recipient will actually block the encoded material." 117 S. Ct. at 2349. The government had argued that transmitters could tag their communication with an encoded message that indicated its content. Unless everyone had the ability to screen unwanted tagged material, there is no way such "tagging" would be effective as required by §223(e)(5)(A)'s good-faith defense. *Id.* But better screening software will surely be developed; in any event, the Act and legislative history require only "reasonable" efficacy, not perfection.

[454] 47 U.S.C. §223(e)(5)(B).

[455] *See, e.g.,* Information Providers' Coalition for Defense of First Amendment v . FCC, 928 F.2d 866, 877 (9th Cir. 1991) ("a carrier is free under the Constitution to terminate service to dial-a-porn operators altogether"); Carlin Communications, Inc. v. Mountain States Tel. & Tel. Co., 827 F.2d 1291, 1297 (9th Cir. 1987) (same); *see also* Sable Communications of Cal., Inc. v. FCC, 492 U.S. 115, 133 (1989) (Scalia, J., concurring) ("I note that while we hold the Constitution prevents Congress from banning indecent speech in this fashion, we do not hold that the Constitution requires public utilities to carry it.").

[456] Pugh v. City and Suburban Tel. Assn., 9 Ohio Dec. Reprint 644 (1883).

[457] State action may, however, be found "when the state exercises coercive power or such significant encouragement, either overt or covert, that the private

---

there will be no carriage of dial-a-porn or, more modestly but no less effectively, that the telco declines to do billing for dial-a-porn services unless they limit subscribers to those who affirmatively agree to pay.[458] As soon as telcos insert such clauses in their tariffs, however, they may run afoul of their traditional obligations as "common" carriers and their more recently developed duties to provide "equal access" under the 1996 Act or FCC regulations. But the line between private and public action remains muddy.[459] The government may not escape the First Amendment simply through pseudo-privatization of what really remains a government operation or order a private operator to do what government itself could not do directly. Thus, even with the ostensible acquiescence of the carrier, the government may not order a carrier to censor particular kinds of otherwise lawful communication over its wires.

---

action must be deemed that of the state." *See* Morgan, The Scoop on Dial-A-Porn, 21 Ariz. St. L.J. 543, 547 (1989). The requisite state coercion and direction were established when the local prosecutor actually threatened the telephone company with criminal charges if it did not drop a dial-a-porn service. Carlin Communications, Inc. v. Mountain States Tel. & Tel. Co., 827 F.2d 1291, 1295 (1987). Coercive conduct, however, will not typically be found in the state's allowing private entities to make their own decisions. Nor do constitutional provisions generally impose affirmative duties on government to protect the interests of "its citizens against invasion by private actors." *See, e.g.,* De Shaney v. Winnebago County Dept. of Social Servs., 489 U.S. 189, 195 (1989) (construing Fourteenth Amendment's due process clause).

[458] Before 1996, Judge Greene had to review these issues separately in connection with the Divestiture Decree's independent equal access obligations. The issue raised in his courtroom concerned billing services offered by regional telephone companies to dial-it providers. United States v. Western Elec. Co., 1989 Trade Cas. (CCH) ¶68,710, at 61,735–61,738 (D.D.C. June 26, 1989). Judge Greene ruled that it was not discriminatory for a regional phone company to refuse to provide billing services to dial-a-porn providers unless they first affirmatively agreed to pay the charges for calls to their programs. *Id.*

[459] *See, e.g.,* NCAA v. Tarkanian, 488 U.S. 179 (1988); Blum v. Yaretzky, 457 U.S. 991 (1982); Rendell-Baker v. Kohn, 457 U.S. 830 (1982); Jackson v. Metropolitan Edison Co., 419 U.S. 345 (1974); Moose Lodge No. 107 v. Irvis, 407 U.S. 163 (1972). One respected commentator has labeled the Court's decisions on the subject "a conceptual disaster area." Charles L. Black, Jr., The Supreme Court, 1966 Term Foreword: "State Action", Equal Protection and California's Proposition 14, 81 Harv. L. Rev. 69, 95 (1967).

A telco's right to discriminate against dial-a-porn providers has been the subject of a few federal cases. In 1987, the Ninth Circuit held that a regional telephone company's decision to exclude dial-a-porn from its network did not violate its duty, under an Arizona statute, to offer service without discrimination.[460] The company had the right, the court ruled, to exercise its own business judgment about what messages it would carry, at least insofar as it was serving more as a broadcast medium than a common carrier. Moreover, the principle of nondiscrimination under Arizona law was held not to preclude distinctions based on reasonable business classifications.[461] The Eleventh Circuit had reached a similar conclusion in rejecting a dial-a-porn provider's claim that the First Amendment guaranteed access to the network.[462]

The picture grows more complicated, however, when publishers edge into the carriage business from the other side of the First Amendment aisle. Viewed as traditional "publishers," cablecasters can refuse to carry anything at all. Federal statutes permit franchisors to demand channel set-asides for carrierlike operations—which would ordinarily imply a complete surrender of content control on those channels. The government chooses instead to leave a bit of control with the cablecaster so far as indecency is concerned.[463] It is the access channels themselves that undermine a cableco's editorial discretion,[464] not the give-back embodied in the indecency clauses of the 1992 Cable Act. How the give-back can be unconstitutional when the original take-away (apparently) is not[465] is hard to fathom.

---

[460] Carlin Communications, Inc. v. Mountain States Tel. & Tel. Co., 827 F.2d 1291 (9th Cir. 1987).

[461] *Id.* at 1292.

[462] Carlin Communications, Inc. v. Southern Bell Tel., 802 F.2d 1352 (11th Cir. 1986). *See also* Morgan, The Scoop on Dial-A-Porn at 552.

[463] 47 U.S.C. §531.

[464] William E. Lee, Cable Leased Access and the Conflict Among First Amendment Rights and First Amendment Values, 35 Emory L.J. 563 (1986).

[465] Daniels Cablevision, Inc. v. United States, 835 F. Supp. 1, 6–7 (D.D.C. 1993) (public, educational, or governmental (PEG) programming and leased access provisions of 1992 Cable Act do not violate First Amendment). *See* §14.6.8.1.

§14.6.7   Federal Immunities for Private
Censorship

A carrier that attempts to censor the content of its customers runs the risk of violating common carrier mandates, some of which we revisit below. A separate risk is that by engaging in such censorship, the carrier will forfeit its status as "passive carrier," and the broad defenses that such carriers have as "contributory" players in defamation, copyright infringement, and other content-related torts.

"General republishers" (authors, printers, newspapers, publishers, and, today, broadcasters) of a defamatory statement are fully liable for it, alongside the original author.[466] But "deliverers and restransmitters" (news vendors, libraries, bookstores, printers, and others who do not ordinarily control content) have traditionally been held liable only upon a showing of some additional fault.[467] Broadcasters have been ranked as authors when working from scripts and as vendors (in some states) with regard to spontaneous defamatory remarks made by performers, advertisers, or call-in commentators.[468] The 1984 Cable Act expressly

---

[466] Restatement (Second) of Torts §578. *See also id.* §581 comment g (bringing radio and television broadcasters under §578).

[467] Prosser and Keeton on the Law of Torts §115.

[468] Harper et al., Law of Torts §5.18. Some early courts analogized the broadcaster to a library or a news vendor and allowed the broadcaster to escape liability if the original script did not contain the defamatory statement, the broadcaster had no reason to expect such a statement, and it was not technically possible for the broadcaster to prevent the words from being transmitted to the audience. Other courts insisted that the broadcaster was, like a newspaper, strictly liable. *See* Coffey v. Midland Broad. Co., 8 F. Supp. 889, 890 (W.D. Mo. 1934). Some states sponsored legislation immunizing broadcasters except where they failed to take due care. Later the Supreme Court's constitutional decisions precluded strict liability, at least where the defamatory statement concerned a public figure or a public issue. But in some states, the broadcaster could still be liable as a republisher for negligent defamation of a private person on a call-in program if it failed to use technological devices at its disposal to screen out defamatory remarks. *See* Harper et al., Law of Torts §5.18. Broadcasters perform as pure distributors, too—they are required to provide uncensored air time to candidates for public office, for example. The Supreme Court has ruled that broadcasters are not liable for defamation that occurs in this context. Farmers Educ. & Coop. Union v. WDAY, Inc., 360 U.S. 525 (1959).

preserved cable operators' liability for defamation, incitement, invasion of privacy, and so on, at least when cable performs like a broadcaster.[469] But it also required cable to carry and offered concomitant immunities.[470]

As noted in section 14.4.1 above, common carriers are generally immune from liability when their networks are used to enable or facilitate the violation of copyrights.[471] Much the same holds for other content-related torts, like defamation. Telegraph and telephone common carriers have traditionally enjoyed broad immunity from defamation suits.[472] Common carriers must take on all comers. They are therefore much more like libraries or bookstores than publishers.[473] Telegraph companies

---

[469] 47 U.S.C. §558.

[470] Immunity from liability applies to channels designated for public, educational, or governmental (PEG) use and any other channels obtained under §532 or under "similar arrangements." *Id.* §558.

[471] Carriers also benefit, of course, from the same constitutional limits and immunities for speech-related torts that extend to speakers themselves. New York Times v. Sullivan, 376 U.S. 254 (1964); Gertz v. Robert Welch, Inc., 418 U.S. 323 (1974).

[472] Andrew B. Sims, Symposium: Current Issues in Media and Telecommunications Law: Food Lion and the Media's Liability for News-Gathering Torts, 7 Fordham I.P., Media & Ent. L.J. 389 (1997); Jonathan Wallace & Michael Green, Symposium: Bridging the Analogy Gap: The Internet, the Printing Press and Freedom of Speech, 20 Seattle U. L. Rev. 711 (1997); Douglas B. Luftman, Defamation Liability for On-Line Services: The Sky Is Not Falling, 65 Geo. Wash. L. Rev. 1071 (1997); David P. Miranda, Defamation in Cyberspace: Stratton Oakmont, Inc. v. Prodigy Services Co., 5 Alb. L.J. Sci. & Tech. 229 (1996); Bruce W. Sanford & Michael J. Lorenger, Teaching an Old Dog New Tricks: The First Amendment in an Online World, 28 Conn. L. Rev. 1137 (1996); David R. Johnson & Kevin A. Marks, Mapping Electronic Data Communications onto Existing Legal Metaphors: Should We Let Our Conscience (and Our Contracts) Be Our Guide?, 38 Vill. L. Rev. 487 (1993); Henry H. Perritt, Jr., Tort Liability, the First Amendment, and Equal Access to Electronic Networks, 5 Harv. J.L. & Tech. 65, 67 (1992); Note, Cyberspace, 81 Geo. L.J. 409 (1992); Note, Computer Bulletin Boards and Defamation: Who Should Be Liable? Under What Standard, 2 Harv. J.L. & Tech. 121 (1987); Comment, An Electronic Soapbox: Computer Bulletin Boards and the First Amendment, 39 Fed. Comm. L.J. 217 (1987); Joseph P. Thornton, Gary G. Gerlach, & Richard L. Gibson, Symposium, Legal Issues in Electronic Publishing, 36 Fed. Comm. L.J. 178 (1984).

[473] *See* Perritt, Tort Liability at 103 & n.195; Restatement (Second) of Torts §581 comment f.

remained liable for transmitting messages that were defamatory on their face,[474] but perhaps only because telegraph operators were necessary human intermediaries.[475] They had no affirmative duty to inquire whether communications were privileged.[476] Telephone companies are even harder to sue; they typically have no occasion at all to know what is being transmitted.

In *Cubby Inc. v. CompuServe Inc.*,[477] the operator of one of the largest electronic information services argued that it should be treated as a print distributor rather than as a publisher. A federal district court agreed. Like a book distributor, the court reasoned, "CompuServe may decline to carry a given publication altogether, [but] in reality, once it does decide to carry a publication, it will have [as a practical matter] little or no control over the publication's content."[478] Because of the vast number of publications placed in its servers, and made available online, CompuServe could not have known or have had reason to know of the defamatory statement published on its system by a user, the publisher of a newsletter.[479]

---

[474] Western Union Tel. Co. v. Lesesne, 198 F.2d 154 (4th Cir. 1952). *See* Harper et al., Law of Torts §5.18. If the message was apparently innocent, however, the telegraph company would not be liable. Nye v. Western Union Tel. Co., 104 F. 628 (D. Minn. 1900).

[475] The telegraph company is insulated from liability if it is under a duty as a public utility to transmit all messages so long as it does so with a reasonable belief in the privilege of the one who provides it with the message. Restatement (Second) of Torts §612 comment g; *see* Harper et al., Law of Torts §5.18; Western Union Tel. Co. v. Lesesne, 182 F.2d 135; O'Brien v. Western Union Tel. Co., 113 F.2d 539, 541 (4th Cir. 1940). *See also* Perritt, Tort Liability at 102.

[476] Restatement (Second) of Torts §612 comment g; Perritt, Tort Liability at 103 & n.195.

[477] 776 F. Supp. 135 (S.D.N.Y. 1991).

[478] *Id.* at 140.

[479] *Id.* at 140–141. *See generally* David J. Lundy, E-Law: Computer Information Systems Law and System Operator, 21 Seattle U. L. Rev. 1075 (1998); Kean J. DeCarlo, Tilting at Windmills: Defamation and the Private Person in Cyberspace, 13 Ga. St. U. L. Rev. 547 (1997); Douglas B. Luftman, Defamation Liability for On-Line Services: The Sky Is Not Falling, 65 Geo. Wash. L. Rev. 1071 (1997); Note, Cubby, Inc. v. CompuServe, Inc.: Comparing Apples to Oranges: The Need for a New Media Classification, 5 Software L.J. 821 (1992); Note, Computer Bulletin Boards and Defamation at 139–140; Note,

What one finds in the new media is not a sharp line, but a continuum from the publisher's "editorial control," to carrier "censorship," to pure carriage. The *Cubby* court emphasized CompuServe's First Amendment right to distribute a lot of material without checking every byte for possible defamation. Other commentators labor to characterize services like CompuServe as quasi-carriers and insist that users of such services have the right not to have their utterances checked out and censored.[480] They see the CompuServes as modern-day post offices, telephone companies, or public parks, there to carry and serve, not to censor or discriminate.[481] If judges buy this model of things, CompuServe and its rivals, like traditional carriers, will have little to worry about from defamation law.

Section 230, which was added by the 1996 Act, extended these civil immunities to Internet users and providers.[482] The stated purpose was to "protect[] from liability those providers and users of interactive computer services who seek to clean up the Internet."[483] The provisions in question cover initiatives by both providers and users[484] "to restrict . . . access to objectionable online material."[485] No one is to be treated as a "publisher or speaker of any information provided by another information content provider."[486] And no provider of an on-line service may be held civilly liable on account of "any action voluntarily taken

---

Computer Bulletin Board Operator Liability for User Misuse, 54 Fordham L. Rev. 439 n.2 (1985).

[480] *See, e.g.,* Comment, Dueling Forums: The Public Forum Doctrine's Failure to Protect the Electronic Forum, 60 U. Cin. L. Rev. 757 (1992).

[481] Thus, the Electronic Communications Privacy Act (ECPA) imposes a duty on network operators not to intercept e-mail messages or to alter their contents. 18 U.S.C. §§2701–2702. *See* §2.4 (discussing the ECPA).

[482] 47 U.S.C. §230.

[483] Conference Report at 194.

[484] By making this provision applicable to both "provider and user of an interactive computer service," the Act clearly contemplates including individual computer users, Internet access providers (e.g., UUNET or PSI), online service providers (e.g., CompuServe, America Online), and libraries and universities that offer Internet access. Conference Report at 194.

[485] *Id.*

[486] 47 U.S.C. §230(c)(1).

in good faith to restrict access to or availability of material that the provider or user considers to be obscene, lewd, lascivious, filthy, excessively violent, harassing, or otherwise objectionable, whether or not such material is constitutionally protected."[487] Legal immunity is also extended to anyone who provides technical means to restrict access to such material.[488]

The purpose of these provisions was to extend the civil immunities of "carriers" and secondary distributors (like electronic bookstores) to those who might otherwise be categorized as "publishers." According to the Conference Statement, one express purpose was to overrule *Stratton Oakmont v. Prodigy Servs. Co.*[489] and similar decisions.[490] In that 1995 case, a New York state judge ruled that Prodigy could be held liable for defamatory material posted on its system. Prodigy was a "publisher," and therefore responsible for the content of messages on its system because it exercised a certain degree of active control over those postings.[491] The "Good Samaritan" provisions help well-intentioned, private censors of dirty pictures and such to avoid increasing their risk of liability for failing to expunge copyright infringements,[492] libel, intrusions on privacy and so forth. All of those

---

[487] *Id.* §230(c)(2)(A).

[488] *Id.* §230(c)(2)(B).

[489] 1995 WL 323710, No. 94-031063 (N.Y. Sup. Ct. 1995).

[490] Conference Report at 194.

[491] The suit was eventually settled, although the judge declined to vacate his controversial decision. *See generally* David P. Miranda, Defamation in Cyberspace: Stratton Oakmont, Inc. v. Prodigy Services Co., 5 Alb. L.J. Sci. & Tech. 229 (1996). Prodigy immediately moved to reargue on the grounds that the record initially presented to the court was inadequate and that Stratton Oakmont had misrepresented facts. Prior to the court's ruling on the motion to reargue, Stratton Oakmont surprisingly agreed no longer to oppose Prodigy's motion if Prodigy offered a public apology for the statements. Jared Sandberg, Securities Company That Had Sued Prodigy Services for Libel Drops Suit, Wall St. J., Oct. 25, 1995, at B7. Prodigy expressed regret that Stratton Oakmont may have been hurt by the anonymous message, but refused to accept legal responsibility for any offense. *Id.*

[492] *See, e.g.*, Religious Technology Center v. Netcom On-Line Communication Services, Inc., 907 F. Supp. 1361 (N.D. Cal. 1995) (holding that access provider is not liable for copies made and stored on its computer because it did not receive any direct financial benefit from infringing activity).

liabilities typically turn on similar dichotomies between "active publisher" and "passive carrier." At the same time, however, the "Good Samaritan" immunity purports not to change any aspect of intellectual property law or privacy law.[493] Nor does it limit the enforcement of the criminal provisions in section 223.[494]

The civil immunity provisions have already been invoked to block a suit by an Internet user that accused America Online of unreasonable delay in removing a defamatory message by an unidentified third party.[495] The unidentified party had inserted the plaintiff's phone number in a fictitious advertisement offering "naughty Oklahoma T-Shirts." A court of appeals refused to adopt a distinction between publishers and distributors whereby the latter were not immune under section 230 for defamatory statements.[496] Another district court has held that interactive service providers, like America Online, cannot be held liable for making available content prepared by others that contains

[493] 47 U.S.C. §230(d)(2), (4). The statute explicitly refers to "the Electronic Communications Privacy Act of 1986 or any of the amendments made by such Act, or any similar State law." *Id.* §230(d)(4). The Conference Statement also declares that the immunity does not extend to so-called "'cancelbotting,' in which recipients of a message respond by deleting the message from the computer systems of others without the consent of the originator or without having the right to do so." Conference Report at 194.

[494] 47 U.S.C. §230(d)(1). There is a certain superficial logic for Congress to have included both "Bad Actor" (47 U.S.C. §223) and "Good Samaritan" (47 U.S.C. §230) provisions in the 1996 Act. Yet these two sections were not coordinated at all. The former originated in the criminal provisions of the Senate bill and the latter in the civil provisions of the House bill, and no attempt was made to harmonize them. Including both provisions in the final act was a political compromise that did not resolve fundamental disagreements. The "Good Samaritan" provisions view online operators as largely "passive carriers," who should not be held liable as "publishers" if they voluntarily remove objectionable material from their systems. The criminal "Bad Actor" provisions from the Senate bill treat online service providers as presumptive "publishers," with concomitant responsibility to minors, unless they meet the bill's standards of ignorance or passivity.

[495] Zeran v. America Online, Inc., 129 F.3d 327 (4th Cir. 1997) ("§230 creates a federal immunity to any cause of action that would make service providers liable for information originating with a third party user of the service").

[496] *Id.* at 332, 333 (also rejecting the contention that notice of the defamatory statement was a basis to hold AOL liable).

defamatory statements even where the provider is contracting with the third party for rights to allow subscribers to access the material.[497]

The Senate's expansion of criminal liability through the CDA has been almost completely nullified by the Supreme Court. By contrast, the broad ranging civil immunities written by the House remain fully in effect.

§14.6.8 Mandatory Carriage

Carriers are often required to offer universal service. That means extending wires, transmitters, and the accompanying speech itself to people that the franchisee might, for economic or other reasons, prefer not to serve. Is this constitutional? The *New York Times* cannot be ordered to sell papers to all comers. Until recently an exclusive franchise was often so valuable that universal service obligations were accepted without a murmur. With media multiplying on all sides, however, exclusivity isn't what it used to be.

An obligation to transmit the speech of others raises First Amendment concerns. The right to paste a "Live Free or Die" bumper sticker on the back of your car is meaningless without the right *not* to.[498] Is a telephone company yoked to the plow of universal service, like a New Hampshire driver who prefers slavery to death?[499]

---

[497] Blumenthal v. Drudge, 992 F. Supp. 44, 52 (D.D.C. 1998) ("Congress had made a different policy choice by providing immunity even where the interactive service provider has an active, even aggressive role in making available content prepared by others.").

[498] Wooley v. Maynard, 430 U.S. 705 (1977).

[499] *Id.* at 713–714 ("The right of freedom of thought protected by the First Amendment against state action includes both the right to speak freely and the right to refrain from speaking at all.").

The First Amendment implies what have been called "negative rights,"[500] too—rights not to salute, not to pledge,[501] not to
embrace government propaganda,[502] not to publish replies,[503]
not to insert proclamations in bills,[504] not to disclose membership lists,[505] and not to pay unwillingly for the political speech

---

[500] *See generally* Tribe, American Constitutional Law §12.4, at 804. For fur-
ther discussion of the rights not to speak and associate, the so-called negative
First Amendment rights, see Glen O. Robinson, The Electronic First Amend-
ment: An Essay for the New Age, 47 Duke, L.J. 899 (1998); David R. Papke,
Understanding "Rights" in Contemporary American Discourse, 2 Mich. J.
Race & L. 521 (1997); Victor Brudney, Association, Advocacy, and the First
Amendment, 4 Wm. & Mary Bill of Rts. J. 1 (1995); Leora Harpaz, Justice
Jackson's Flag Salute Legacy: The Supreme Court Struggles to Protect Intel-
lectual Individualism, 64 Tex. L. Rev. 817 (1986); Melvin B. Nimmer, Nimmer
on Freedom Of Speech: A Treatise on the Theory of the First Amendment
§4.10, at 4-140 to 4-146 (1984); David B. Gaebler, First Amendment Protection Against Government Compelled Expression and Association, 23 B.C. L.
Rev. 995, 996 (1982); *see also, e.g.,* Hurley v. Irish-American Gay, Lesbian and
Bi-sexual Group of Boston, 515 U.S. 557 (1995) (holding that a Massachusetts
Supreme Court decision, which mandated that parade organizers include a
group that imparted a message that the organizers did not wish to convey, violated the First Amendment); Ilbanez v. Florida Bd. of Accountancy, 512 U.S.
136 (1994) (holding that the board's decision to censure the plaintiff for misleading advertising was incompatible with First Amendment restraints on official action); Zauderer v. Office of Disciplinary Counsel of the Supreme Court
of Ohio, 471 U.S. 626 (1985) (nonexpressive nature of advertising allows state
to compel disclosure designed to ensure the flow of accurate information to
the public); Branzburg v. Hayes, 408 U.S. 665, 667–671 (1972) (rejecting
reporter's claim of a privilege not to testify before a grand jury when
reporter did not want to reveal identity of news sources for fear of discouraging future revelations).

[501] West Virginia Bd. of Educ. v. Barnette, 319 U.S. 624 (1943) (a state may
not force public school students to salute or pledge allegiance to the flag).

[502] Wooley v. Maynard, 430 U.S. at 713.

[503] Miami Herald Publishing Co. v. Tornillo, 418 U.S. 241 (1974).

[504] Pacific Gas & Elec. Co. v. Public Utils. Commn. of Cal., 475 U.S. 1
(1986) (a public utility may not be required to allow a consumer group to
insert a newsletter into "extra space" in the utility's billing envelopes). "[F]or
corporations, as for individuals, the choice to speak includes within it the
choice of what not to say. And we have held that speech does not lose its protection because of the corporate identity of the speaker." *Id.* at 16.

[505] NAACP v. State of Alabama, 357 U.S. 449, 460 (1958) (state could
not constitutionally compel NAACP to reveal membership lists); Bates v. City
of Little Rock, 361 U.S. 516, 527–528 (1960) (Black, J., and Douglas J., concurring) ("freedom of association" is a First Amendment right "entitled to no
less protection than any other First Amendment right").

of others.[506] Freedom of association is tied directly to "the purpose of engaging in those activities protected by the First Amendment—speech, assembly, petition for the redress of grievances, and the exercise of religion."[507]

But the freedom not to speak has its limits. The owners of a private shopping mall required by a state constitution to permit high school students to distribute pamphlets and solicit signatures on its premises have no recourse under the federal constitution, at least when there is little risk that the owner will be mistakenly associated with the unwanted speech.[508] Lawyers may be required to join bar associations.[509] Gender discrimination

[506] Abood v. Detroit Bd. of Educ., 431 U.S. 209, 219–223, 232–237 (1977) (compulsory payment by state employees to union for bargaining services does not violate right of freedom of association, but nonunion members may refuse to fund union's political activities); *see also* In re Chapman, 509 A.2d 753 (N.H. 1986) (New Hampshire's bar association violates members' First Amendment rights when its activities before the state legislature go beyond matters within the mandate of the association's constitution). *See generally* Mark S. Pulliam, Union Security Clauses in Public Sector Labor Contracts and Abood v. Detroit Board of Education: A Dissent, 31 Lab. L.J. 539, 544–545 (1980) (compelled financial support of a union interferes with the right of free association, even where nonpolitical activities are involved); Thomas R. Haggard, Compulsory Unionism, the NLRB, And the Courts: A Legal Analysis of Union Security Agreements 38 (1977) (freedom of association protects one's right not to join a union); David B. Gaebler, First Amendment Protection Against Government Compelled Expression and Association, 23 B.C. L. Rev. 995, 1017–1023 (1982). Thomas Jefferson stated that "to compel a man to furnish contributions of money for the propagation of opinions which he disbelieves, is sinful and tyrannical." I. Brant, James Madison: The Nationalist 354 (1948).

[507] Roberts v. United States Jaycees, 468 U.S. 609, 618 (1984).

[508] PruneYard Shopping Center v. Robins, 447 U.S. 74, 87–88 (1980). The California Supreme Court held that the students had a right to enter the shopping center under the state constitution and further held that this did not infringe the federal constitutional rights of the shopping center owner. Robins v. PruneYard Shopping Center, 592 P.2d 341, 347 (Cal. 1979). The United States Supreme Court affirmed, ruling that the enforcement of the students' rights under the California Constitution did not violate the shopping center's rights under the federal Constitution. The Court did not rule, however, that the mall was a public forum. PruneYard Shopping Center v. Robins, 447 U.S. 74.

[509] Lathrop v. Donohue, 367 U.S. 820 (1961) (compulsory dues to bar association or union do not violate rights of speech or association if dues are used in conjunction with the principal function of the organization); Levine v. Heffernan, 864 F.2d 457 (7th Cir. 1988).

laws may be enforced against an association that exists mainly for commercial, not expressive, purposes.[510]

The provider's objection to a universal service mandate is that it requires connecting up to listeners and/or speakers that the provider would rather avoid. The provider's objection is usually based on commercial reasons; the speech-chilling effects at issue in the right of reply and billing insert cases are not directly present.[511] The economic factors, however, can be very chilling indeed. Universal service requirements can easily be pushed to the point where they overwhelmingly favor an established incumbent over new entrants, and monopoly over competition.[512] Being forced to build more network than is economically attractive can be quite as chilling as being limited to less.

Subsidies can depress free speech equally sharply. The decade-long attempts to suppress cable in favor of free television simply prevented programmers from selling to the highest bidder. When cable was unleashed, demand for programming soared, and supply followed.[513] Price-averaging can depress output, too. The free speech of the *New York Times* costs 60 cents a copy in the city, more out of town. Those market-established prices generate

---

[510] Roberts v. United States Jaycees, 468 U.S. 609 (1994).

[511] In *Pacific Gas*, the Court found an affirmative speech violation because the Commission allowed only those parties who disagreed with Pacific Gas & Electric's views access to the envelopes. Thus, there was a danger that the utility would "avoid controversy" by not sending out any of its own messages, thereby reducing the free flow of ideas. Pacific Gas & Elec. v. Public Utils. Commn. of Cal., 475 U.S. 1, 14 (1986). *See generally* Elizabeth A. Cowles, Must-Carry and the Continuing Search for a First Amendment Standard of Review for Cable Regulation, 57 Geo. Wash. L. Rev. 1248 (May 1989) (application of *Pacific Gas* to cable carriage).

[512] For that reason, a 1990 FCC report recommended that to encourage competition, new entrants should initially be exempt from any "universal service" obligations imposed by franchisers. Competition, Rate Deregulation and the Commission's Policies Relating to the Provision of Cable Television Service, Report to Congress, 5 F.C.C. Rec. 4962 (1990). The 1992 Cable Act did not adopt the recommendations in the FCC's report. Cable Television Consumer Protection and Competition Act of 1992, Pub. L. No. 102–385.

[513] *See* Evaluation of the Syndication and Financial Interest Rules, Report and Order, 6 F.C.C. Rec. 3094 (1991) (reviewing the network financial interest and syndication rules, describing declining market power of networks, and describing the migration of talent from broadcast to cable).

more newsprint, not less, than forcing the paper to sell nation-wide at a uniform price.

Economics aside, the more freely a speaker is allowed to limit its audience, the more freely it will be allowed to speak. The right to limit one's audience promotes free speech because free speech ultimately depends on mutual consent. Narrower audiences will accept more shocking, idiosyncratic, unorthodox—in sum, unaverage—messages than broader ones. The soap-box orator can say things from his box in the sun that Peter Jennings cannot say from his desk under the lights. Forcing a larger audience on a speaker can silence him quite as effectively as forcing a smaller one. We accept regulation of children's television and dial-a-porn telephone precisely because the instruments that deliver the dirt are so very universal. Place the same instruments behind market-driven doors and unsubsidized cash-registers, and there will be far less demand for the Thought Police.

Courts have only just begun to grapple seriously with arguments like these. In its 1969 *National Association of Theatre Owners v. FCC* ruling, the D.C. Circuit had no difficulty rejecting the argument that the FCC's licensing of pay television somehow subverted First Amendment rights of would-be viewers who couldn't afford it.[514] In *Home Box Office, Inc. v. FCC,* the D.C. Circuit went a step further and affirmed cable's own First Amendment right to "siphon" programming away from free broadcast television.[515] These cases, however, addressed only the universal service policies that have been pushed to the extreme of excluding all but one favored, incumbent monopolist.[516]

---

[514] 420 F.2d 194 (D.C. Cir. 1969).

[515] Home Box Office, Inc. v. FCC, 567 F.2d 9, 22 (D.C. Cir. 1977).

[516] On remand from the Supreme Court in the endless *Preferred* litigation, the district court upheld the universal service requirement on the ground that the city asserted a substantial and important governmental interest in assuring cable service to all regardless of income. Preferred Communications, Inc. v. City of Los Angeles, 1989 U.S. Dist. LEXIS 18383 at *11 (C.D. Cal. 1989). The City appealed, and the Ninth Circuit agreed that exclusivity was unconstitutional. Preferred Communications, Inc. v. City of Los Angeles, 13 F.3d 1327, 1332 (9th Cir.), *cert. denied,* 512 U.S. 1235 (1994). A lawyer for the association that represents incumbent operators has argued that the first cable company to serve an area should have greater First Amendment rights than

A few other courts have weighed the constitutionality of requiring providers to offer a standard package of service, at a standard price, throughout a defined territory. In the 1991 challenge to the universal service requirement mandate in Florida's Riviera Beach,[517] the cable operator raised First Amendment objections along with preemption.[518] A federal district court rejected the argument that the ordinance was content specific[519] and so reviewed — and upheld — it under *United States v. O'Brien.*[520] The ordinance might diminish the cable operator's profits, but was not unconstitutional "in the absence of a showing of economic harm bordering on censorship."[521] The court noted that Singer Island, the only area served by Telesat, is "a middle to high income, predominately white area of the City."[522] The court admitted that an operator's decision not to serve low-income areas might result from "logical business decisions," but noted that it would subject the city to chronic complaints from residents not yet served.[523] The court also accepted the argument that a "cream-skimming" overbuilder, not subject to universal service requirements, could give an operator serving a wider area the incentive to improve its service only in those areas in which it is subject to competition.[524] The court rejected Telesat's

---

the second. Daniel Brenner, Cable Television and the Freedom of Expression, 1988 Duke L.J. 329, 336–341.

[517] Telesat Cablevision, Inc. v. City of Riviera Beach, 773 F. Supp. 383 (S.D. Fla. 1991).

[518] The plaintiff argued that the universal service requirement was a content-based restriction on its right not to speak insofar as it "interferes with its editorial discretion to decide to whom, when, and where to distribute its cable programming." *Id.* at 404 (citing Century Fed., Inc. v. Palo Alto, 710 F. Supp. 1552, 1555–1556 (N.D. Cal. 1987), and Group W Cable, Inc. v. City of Santa Cruz, 669 F. Supp. 954, 970–971 (N.D. Cal. 1987)).

[519] *Id.*

[520] 391 U.S. 367, 377 (1968).

[521] *Telesat Cablevision,* 773 F. Supp. at 405 (quoting Home Box Office, Inc. v. FCC, 567 F.2d 49 n.97 (D.C. Cir. 1977) (*HBO*)).

[522] *Id.* at 401.

[523] *Id.*

[524] *Id.* at 401–402.

argument that the universal service requirement amounted to race-based income redistribution.[525]

Other courts have reached different conclusions. In 1987, a federal district court struck down a Palo Alto ordinance that required the cable franchisee to wire the entire service area except where access was infeasible.[526] This was an impermissible, content-based interference with the cable operator's right not to speak, the court concluded. The city could not have required a newspaper, movie house, or bookstore to deliver to or be located in a particular geographic area of the community. Cable was no different.[527] Another California district judge struck down a universal service requirement in Santa Cruz.[528] The city had required the operator to provide service to every home in the community. This, the court reasoned, was equivalent to requiring a newspaper to "offer home delivery to any subscriber residing anywhere in the community at a price fixed by the government."[529] While the city did have an interest in minimizing disruption on the public streets, a universal service requirement was likely to cause more, not less, disruption.[530]

---

[525] *Id.* at 405–406. The court upheld the requirement as a valid exercise of the city's interest in providing broad access to information and in preventing discrimination on the basis of income or race. *Id.* at 404–406 (citing Associated Press v. United States, 326 U.S. 1, 20 (1945), and Red Lion Broad. Co. v. FCC, 395 U.S. 367, 390, 392 (1969)). The court also noted the city's interest in controlling disruption to rights-of-way. *Id.* at 404. The court did not explain what this interest had to do with a universal service mandate, which would seem to increase such disruption rather than limit it.

[526] Century Federal, Inc. v. City of Palo Alto, 710 F. Supp. 1552 (N.D. Cal. 1987) (city's access channel, universal service, and state-of-the-art requirements violated the First Amendment); *see also* Century Federal, Inc. v. City of Palo Alto, 648 F. Supp. 1465, 1476 (N.D. Cal. 1986) (rejecting municipality's argument that to prevent cream-skimming, cable franchises had to be exclusive).

[527] *Century Federal,* 710 F. Supp. at 1556. In 1989, after five years of losing legal battles in the district court, the city paid the would-be cable operator $1.8 million to go away. *See* Senate Passes Cable TV Bill, United Press Intl., Sept. 1, 1989.

[528] *Group W Cable,* 669 F. Supp. at 970–971 (universal service requirement unlawfully burdened cable operator's editorial discretion and was content-based).

[529] *Id.* at 970.

[530] *Id.* at 970–971.

The "right of association" precedents suggest some lines of argument that have yet to be seriously explored in the telecom arena. In 1990, the New York Court of Appeals agreed that ratepayers could not be required to shoulder any part of a utility's charitable contributions, even though approved by the state commission.[531] If the ratepayer may not constitutionally be required to subsidize the utility's speech, why are other subsidies—ratepayer-to-ratepayer or utility-to-ratepayer—any more tolerable? Courts may hesitate to drag the delicate fabric of the Constitution through this economic briar patch, but the issues are both real and serious. Any requirement of price-averaged universal service puts the telecom utility and all its customers in a single economic pot. Under anything but strictly cost-based pricing, phone bills will subsidize (or be subsidized by) escort services, handgun dealers, and dial-a-porn operators. The telephone company must put up with the whole lot. Neither association nor speech seems altogether free in such circumstances.

§14.6.8.1 Mandatory Carriage on Cable Channels

The 1984 Cable Act affords cable operators no general power to control the content of programming transmitted over public access channels;[532] the Act also bars operators from exercising "any editorial control" over programming over leased channels.[533] A franchise contract may, however, specify that no "obscene or otherwise unprotected" programming will be shown on public access channels.[534]

---

[531] "[R]atepayers are entitled to protection against forced financial support for causes and messages personally distasteful to them, because that would render those individuals faithless to their own beliefs." Cahill v. Public Serv. Commn., 556 N.E.2d 133, 136 (N.Y. 1990). Indeed, "the constitutional canopy" of the First Amendment is especially needed by objecting ratepayers because they "are powerless against governmentally regulated monopolies and have no place else to seek indispensable public utilities services." Id.

[532] 47 U.S.C. §531(e).

[533] Id. §532(c)(2).

[534] Id. §544(d)(1).

The 1992 Cable Act permits franchisors or cable operators to bar programming from leased access channels that they deem to be obscene, "lewd, lascivious, filthy, or indecent" or "otherwise unprotected" by the First Amendment.[535] Both before and after the 1992 Cable Act, operators have applied a relatively heavy hand in screening leased access materials, often requiring as a condition of carriage that they be permitted to preview the material.

In 1993, a group of cable programmers and viewer organizations challenged the FCC's implementing regulations of indecent programming on public access and leased access channels. In *Alliance for Community Media v. FCC*,[536] a three-judge panel of the D.C. Circuit held that the First Amendment prohibits the government itself from banning all indecent speech from access channels, and so likewise bars the government from "deputizing" cablecos to effect such a ban. The government leaves the cablecaster with some modest discretion to censor, if it chooses, "patently offensive" programming on the set-aside channels.[537]

---

[535] *Id.* §532(h). This provision also permits cable operators to bar leased access programming "the cable operator reasonably believes describes or depicts sexual or excretory activities in a patently offensive manner as measured by contemporary community standards." The cable operator may exercise this right only under a "written and published policy." *Id.* §532(h). In case the operator does not issue such a policy, the FCC is directed to require indecent leased access programming to be contained on a single channel and to require cable operators to block the channel at the subscriber's request. *Id.* §532(j). Under this provision, it is the responsibility of leased access programmers to determine whether their programs are indecent. *Id.* §532(j) (1)(C). *See* Implementation of Section 10 of the Cable Consumer Protection and Competition Act of 1992, Notice of Proposed Rulemaking, 7 F.C.C. Rec. 7709 (1992); First Report and Order, 8 F.C.C. Rec. 998 (1993) (leased access channels, 47 C.F.R. §76.701); Second Report and Order, 8 F.C.C. Rec. 2638 (1993) (PEG access, 47 C.F.R. §76.702).

[536] Alliance for Community Media v. FCC, 10 F.3d 812 (D.C. Cir. 1993), *vacated and rev'd en banc,* 56 F.3d 105 (D.C. Cir. 1995), *aff'd in part and rev'd in part sub nom.* Denver Area Educational Telecommunications Consortium, Inc. v. FCC, 518 U.S. 727 (1996); *see also* Missouri Knights of the Ku Klux Klan v. Kansas City, 723 F. Supp 1347 (W.D. Mo. 1989) (*Missouri KKK*) (public access channels are public forum for purposes of denying motion to dismiss). *See generally* Symposium: Censorship of Cable Television's Leased and Public Access Channels: Current Status of Alliance for Community Media v. FCC, 6 Fordham I.P., Media & Ent. L.J. 465 (1996).

[537] 47 U.S.C. §531.

The full D.C. Circuit reversed the panel decision, concluding that it was permissible under the First Amendment for cable operators either to allow or to forbid the transmission of "patently offensive sex-related materials" over both leased and public access channels and for cable operators to segregate and to block transmission of those materials until receiving a subscriber's written request for access.

In a highly fractured opinion, the Supreme Court reversed in part and affirmed in part. Although they could not agree on a single opinion, seven members of the Court concluded that a cable operator could prohibit "patently offensive" sex-related materials on leased access channels;[538] six members agreed that the "segregate and block" requirements were neither were the "least restrictive alternative" to an outright ban nor "narrowly tailored" to meet the government's legitimate objective of protecting children from exposure to "patently offensive sex-related material";[539] and five members agreed that it was unconstitutional for Congress and the FCC to permit a cable operator to prevent transmission of "patently offensive" programming on public access channels.[540]

The Court failed to understand that access channels themselves—which are mandatory creations of government—infringe on a cablecaster's editorial discretion, too.[541] The majority never directly explains why returning to the private sector some

[538] Denver Area Educ. Telecomms. Consortium, Inc. v. FCC, 518 U.S. 727, 737–753 (1996) (opinion of Breyer, J., joined by Stevens, O'Connor, and Souter, JJ.); *id.* at 812–838 (opinion of Thomas, J., joined by Rehnquist, C.J., and Scalia, J.).

[539] *Id.* at 753–761 (opinion of Breyer, J., joined by Stevens, O'Connor, Kennedy, Souter, and Ginsburg, JJ.).

[540] *Id.* at 761–766 (opinion of Breyer, J., joined by Stevens and Souter, JJ.); *id.* at 787–812 (opinion of Kennedy, J., joined by Ginsburg, J.).

[541] *Id.* at 820 (Thomas, J., dissenting in part) ("There is no getting around the fact that leased and public access are a type of forced speech."). *But see id.* at 796 (Kennedy, J., concurring in part) ("Laws requiring cable operators to provide leased access are the practical equivalent of making them common carriers, analogous in this respect to telephone companies: They are obliged to provide a conduit for the speech of others.").

of what government first took away infringes on First Amendment principles.[542]

§14.6.8.2 Mandatory Carriage and the Audience's Veto

Mandatory carriage or universal service requirements have a second, albeit indirect, impact on the carrier's free speech rights. The audience's likely reaction often figures in whether or not speech can constitutionally be regulated or banned. Under current First Amendment doctrine, the careful choice of a phlegmatic audience can clear the way for speech that is that much more inflammatory. Deliberately or otherwise, the government regulator that mandates service to a larger community strengthens its power to require less controversial speech.

Many of the most important limits to free speech—on fighting words, obscenity, and time-place-and-manner regulation—turn on audience reaction.[543] Obscenity, a category of speech that falls outside of First Amendment protection,[544] is defined specifically by reference to "contemporary community standards."[545] Free speech rights, in short, depend on who is being addressed, and where. Some people are more easily shocked, incited, harassed, or intimidated than others. Speech to a self-selected, consenting audience can be much freer than speech to unwilling listeners. Indecency inside a movie theater is not the same as indecency on the sidewalk outside.

---

[542] *Id.* at 822 (Thomas, J., dissenting in part) ("It is one thing to compel an operator to carry leased and public access speech, in apparent violation of *Tornillo,* but it is another thing altogether to say that the First Amendment forbids Congress to give back part of the operators' editorial discretion, which all recognize as fundamentally protected, in favor of a broader access right.").

[543] Chaplinsky v. New Hampshire, 315 U.S. 568, 571–573 (1942). *See generally* Tribe, American Constitutional Law §12–10.

[544] *See generally* Kalven, The Metaphysics of the Law of Obscenity, 1960 Sup. Ct. Rev. 1 (1960).

[545] Miller v. California, 413 U.S. 15, 24 (1973); *see also* Laurence H. Winer, The Signal Cable Sends, Part II—Interference from the Indecency Cases, 55 Fordham L. Rev. 459 (1987).

Until recently the accessibility and ubiquity of telephone net-works (and broadcast networks) have provided the excuse for regulating these media the most strictly. Indecency that could not be censored out of magazines could readily be barred from the radio or television. In the broadcast context, the FCC crafted a definition of indecency that attempted to track the Supreme Court's definition of obscenity, referring to communi-cation that is "patently offensive under contemporary commu-nity standards applicable to the broadcast medium."[546]

§14.6.9   Implications of an Exclusive Franchise

As discussed in section 1.9, the exclusive telecom franchise is for the most part a thing of the past. But its vestiges still linger in the marketplace. And the First Amendment implications of exclusive franchises still merit review, if only to clarify why the logic of much of yesterday's jurisprudence in the area is no longer valid.

One body of law suggests that if the government grants an exclusive carrier franchise *to itself,* it may not then limit what the government itself carries. The Post Office has long been an exclusive franchise, though the precise scope of the exclusivity has varied over the years.[547] Beginning in the 1860s, Congress passed a series of laws banning immoral, indecent, fraudulent, and obscene materials from the mails.[548] In 1877, the Supreme

---

[546] Pacifica Foundation, Memorandum Opinion and Order, 2 F.C.C. Rec. 2698, 2699 ¶13 (1987). This definition was upheld in Action for Children's Television v. FCC, 852 F.2d 1332 (D.C. Cir. 1988).

[547] United States Postal Serv. v. Greenburgh Civic Assn., 453 U.S. 114, 128–129 (1981). To this day, the nineteenth-century Private Express Statutes that give the Postal Service a monopoly on mail service forbid the use of pri-vate express carriers to send mail that is not "urgent." 18 U.S.C. §1694. *See also* 39 U.S.C. §601(a)(1)–(6) (Private Express Statutes); 39 C.F.R. §320.6 (sus-pends operation of the Private Express Statutes for "extremely urgent let-ters"). The Post Office defends the law as necessary to support universal service. *See* D. Bauman, Franks Unveils Legislation Aimed at "Postal Police," Gannett News Service, Feb. 3, 1994. Technological advances, such as e-mail and fax, however, have rendered the law exceedingly silly.

[548] *See generally* de Sola Pool, Technologies of Freedom at 75–78. In 1836, President Andrew Jackson sought to ban antislavery propaganda from the mails.

Court upheld the government's right to ban from the mail material relating to lotteries.[549] In an elegant twist, however, Justice Field noted the danger of censorship and stated that whatever the Post Office refused to carry, private citizens were free to distribute by other means.[550] The suggestion was that government could have its monopoly, or it could censor what it carried, but not both.

In 1904, however, the Court backed away. It now accepted the argument that the Post Office was operated by the government to raise revenue; it was simply a "popular and efficient method of taxation."[551] Congress could therefore condition its use however it pleased. The postmaster's refusal to carry mail used for purposes of fraud was upheld accordingly. In 1908, an anarchist journal was banned from the mails as indecent.[552] In 1921, the Supreme Court upheld the denial of second-class mailing rights to a socialist paper.[553] This was not inconsistent with the First Amendment, the Supreme Court reasoned, so long as the first class mails remained open as an alternative. Justice Holmes dissented.[554]

The Court came around to Holmes's view in 1945. (Ironically, this was almost the same time that the Court upheld sweeping regulation of broadcasters.) *Hannegan v. Esquire* addressed the Postmaster's denial of second-class mailing status to *Esquire*.[555]

Senator Calhoun, a defender of both slavery and the First Amendment and the chair of the Senate Committee considering the request, insisted that so long as the government maintained a monopoly on the mails, it had no discretion to ban content. *Id.* at 83–87.

[549] Ex Parte Jackson, 96 U.S. 727 (1877).

[550] *Id.* at 733.

[551] Public Clearing House v. Coyne, 194 U.S. 497, 506 (1904).

[552] *See* de Sola Pool, Technologies of Freedom at 86.

[553] Milwaukee Social Democratic Publishing Co. v. Burleson, 255 U.S. 407 (1921); *see also* Lewis Publishing Co. v. Morgan, 229 U.S. 288 (1913).

[554] *Burleson*, 255 U.S. at 436. *See also* Leach v. Carlile, 258 U.S. 138 (1922).

[555] 327 U.S. 146 (1945). *Cf.* National Broad. Co. v. United States, 319 U.S. 190, 226–227 (1943). In Lamont v. Postmaster General, 381 U.S. 301 (1965), the Supreme Court unanimously declared unconstitutional a law requiring the Post Office to hold delivery of "communist political propaganda" mailed from abroad and ask the addressee whether he or she wished to receive it. *See*

Esquire's contribution to the public interest, the Court now declared, was not something that should be weighed on the Postmaster General's scales. Since then, the Post Office has been expected to carry any communication that in itself is protected by the First Amendment. In determining what is not protected (such as obscenity), the Post Office must use suitably careful procedures.[556]

But most U.S. phone companies are not owned or operated by the government, and their once-exclusive franchises are exclusive no more. Phone companies still make extensive use of public property, but that alone cannot justify governmental censorship.[557] Digging up a public street might justify regulations to prevent noise, disruption of traffic, and the like. Placing newsracks on sidewalks might justify regulations to allow free flow of pedestrian traffic. But a city could not constitutionally mandate, as a condition of a newspaper's operation on city sidewalks, that the newspaper turn over a portion of its front page for use by the city officials or that the newspaper deliver each week self-serving bulletins from the city's mayor to the newspaper's readers.[558] In general, land use regulations must bear an "essential nexus" to the rationale for the regulation.[559]

---

generally William E. Lee, The Supreme Court and the Right to Receive Expression, 19XX Sup. Ct. Rev. 303.

[556] 39 U.S.C. §§3001–3011. *See* Blount v. Rizzi, 400 U.S. 410 (1971); Bolger v. Youngs Drug Prods. Corp., 463 U.S. 60 (1983).

[557] The public property argument proves too much: cable companies string their cable over public rights-of-way, newspapers place newsracks on public sidewalks, broadcasters use public spectrum, and demonstrators parade on public streets.

[558] *See Tornillo,* 418 U.S. at 256; City of Lakewood v. Plain Dealer Publishing Co., 486 U.S. 750 (1988); City of Cincinnati v. Discovery Network, Inc., 507 U.S. 410 (1993).

[559] Nollan v. California Coastal Commn., 483 U.S. 825, 837–838 (1987) ("When that essential nexus is eliminated, the situation becomes the same as if California law forbade shouting fire in a crowded theater, but granted dispensations to those willing to contribute $100 to the state treasury."); Dolan v. City of Tigard, 512 U.S. 374 (1994). Nevertheless, cable companies are routinely required, as a condition of their franchises, to finance construction of municipally controlled television studios, to deliver free production equipment to city officials and institutions, and to give city officials absolute programming control over certain channels. *See, e.g.,* David J. Saylor, Municipal

Any remaining doubt about the First Amendment status of landline phone companies should have been dissipated by the passage of the 1996 Act. The old rationales for curtailing First Amendment rights of carriers were entirely circular. Regulation of a carrier's speech was justified by the fact that the target had a franchise, operated as a common carrier, or provided universal service that was readily accessible to children. But the franchise, the duty of common carriage, and the universal service obligations were themselves creations of government. If granting an exclusive franchise was what permitted government to limit speech, then franchise, not free speech, was what should have been eliminated.[560] The First Amendment should simply have been engaged earlier, when government established the monopoly, rather than later, when government set out to regulate the monopolist into silence.

If the government itself has promoted or protected the monopoly of a privately owned carrier, the solution most consistent with the First Amendment is for government to stop doing so. This was the approach suggested by Justice Field almost a century ago, in connection with censorship by the Post Office, and that is precisely what Congress and the President finally did in 1996.

§14.7 Telephone Harassment

Nearly every state has a criminal statute forbidding telephone harassment in the form of obscene, anonymous, repeated, or nonconsensual calls.[561] Such calls may also give rise to a tort

---

Ripoff: The Unconstitutionality of Cable Television Franchise Fees and Access Support Payments, 35 Cath. U. L. Rev. 671, 672 (1986).

[560] Moreover, franchises are often granted by one authority (a municipality, say), while burdens on speech are imposed by another quite separate one—the federal government, say. *Cf.* First Natl. Bank of Boston v. Bellotti, 435 U.S. 765, 778–779 n.14 (1978) (noting that restriction imposed by one sovereign cannot be justified by grant of benefit by different sovereign). This eviscerates the argument that burdens on speech go hand in hand with government-issue privileges.

[561] *See* Annotation, 95 A.L.R.3d 411 (discussing each of the state statutes).

action for invasion of privacy.[562] Many states have yet to pass legislation to prohibit the use of the Internet for harassment or the harming of children. Existing laws probably cover such crimes already,[563] but there have been calls for additional, Internet-specific state legislation.[564] Several states have considered amending stalking and harassment laws already on the books to include electronic communications expressly.[565]

This section surveys the much smaller body of federal law that bears on the same issues—insofar as it either bars unwelcome or harmful speech or immunizes the same from liability. Much of the indecency legislation and First Amendment jurisprudence discussed in section 14.6 above concerns similar issues, but in the context of content made available to the public generally rather than directed to a specific, known recipient.

---

[562] *See, e.g.,* B-W Acceptance Corp. v. Callaway, 162 S.E.2d 430 (Ga. 1968) (use of vile, vicious, abusive, or profane language); Summit Loans, Inc., v. Pecola, 228 A.2d 114 (Md. 1972) (late hour of phone calls); Carey v. Statewide Finance Co., 223 A.2d 405 (Conn. Cir. Ct. 1966) (harassment of debtor's spouse).

[563] For example, an Illinois man was convicted in Will County for harassing a minor set to testify against the man. Officials charged the man under a statute prohibiting witness harassment. Stanley Ziembcha, Will County Focusing on Internet Criminals, Chi. Trib., May 26, 1998, at 1. In Massachusetts, the state Supreme Judicial Court upheld a decision dismissing a harassment complaint against a man who had sent a series of faxes on the grounds that existing law applies only to telephone communications. Bill Would Include E-Mail, Faxes as Harassment, Telegram & Gazette (Worcester, Mass.), Feb. 20, 1998, at B6.

[564] In all, approximately 20 states now have laws against online stalking, up from fewer than a half-dozen in mid-1997. B. Masters, When E-Mail Is a Weapon, Victims Struggle for Protection, Wash. Post, Nov. 1, 1998, at B01.

[565] In 1998, the Pennsylvania State House passed an amendment making it a first-degree misdemeanor to threaten someone "electronically, including . . . electronic mail and communications via the Internet." *See also* Ala. Code §13A-11-8(b)(1)(a) (1994) (including "electronic communication" within its proscribed forms of harassing communications); Wyo. Stat. tit. VI, art. 5, §6-2-506(b)(i).

§14.7.1 Federal Telephone Harassment Laws[566]

Section 14.6.4 above discusses the federal statutory provisions that criminalize obscene and indecent communications. Those same provisions include clauses that cover harassing communications, too. Some calls can, of course, be both.[567]

The Federal Telephone Harassment Statute initially enacted in 1968 imposed criminal liability for the interstate use of the telephone to make anonymous calls "with intent to annoy, threaten, or harass," or to "repeatedly or continuously to ring, with intent to harass," or indeed to make calls with the sole intent to harass.[568] A person who "knowingly permits any telephone facility under his control to be used for" any such purpose is also liable.[569] The 1996 Act amended the federal statute to cover harassment via any "telecommunications devices," not just telephones,[570] and in any form of "communication," not just "conversation." A new section 223(a)(1)(A) prohibits any communication that is "obscene, lewd, lascivious, or filthy with intent to abuse, threaten or harass."[571] Despite the mention of obscenity in this section, the core of the

---

[566] See generally Gene Barton, Taking a Byte out of Crime: E-Mail Harassment and the Inefficacy of Existing Law, 70 Wash. L. Rev. 465 (1995).

[567] The law of obscenity punishes people for the very content of their offensive expressions, whereas telephone harassment statutes punish intentional invasions of individual privacy. In telephone harassment, the use of obscene language is merely a factor aggravating an independently proscribable offense. Comment, Constitutionally Regulating Telephone Harassment: An Exercise in Statutory Precision, 56 U. Chi. L. Rev. 1403, 1413–1414 (1989).

[568] 47 U.S.C. §223(a)(1) (1988). See United States v. Darsey, 342 F. Supp. 311, 312–313 (E.D. Pa. 1972).

[569] 47 U.S.C. §223(a)(2). The statute provides for a fine and/or a prison sentence of not more than two years. Id. §223(a). Section 223(a) was originally the entire statute. A new section 223(b) was added in 1983 to reach dial-a-porn services, which play sexually explicit messages to callers, but which do not initiate the call and therefore were not previously covered. After the Supreme Court partially invalidated the "dial-a-porn" law in 1989, Sable Communications of California, Inc. v. FCC, 492 U.S. 115 (1989); see §14.6.3.1, Congress added section 223(c) to prevent common carriers from granting access to such services from a telephone unless the subscriber at that telephone had previously requested such access in writing.

[570] See 47 U.S.C. §223.

[571] Id. §223(a)(1)(A).

offense is not obscenity, indecency, or some variation on the term, but harassment.[572] Federal online harassment laws were further bolstered when, on October 30, 1998, the President signed the Child Protection and Sexual Predator Punishment Act of 1998.[573] Among other measures aimed at protecting children, this bill amends Title 18 of the United States Code to set penalties for sexual predators who target minors, particularly over the Internet.[574] In addition, in a section likely to provoke controversy, the Act establishes penalties against electronic communication services that knowingly fail to report knowledge of facts or circumstances regarding child pornography.[575]

Most issues in the interpretation of section 223 have arisen because of the concern that the statute swept within its reach legitimate, if unpleasant, communications or at the very least that the provision may "chill" legitimate communication by the fear of criminal liability. In *United States v. Darsey*,[576] for example, Judge Newcomer construed the "sole intent to harass" requirement of section 223(a)(1)(D) narrowly, recognizing that "[i]n many situations, and most especially in romantic and family conflicts," conversations "may become more or less unsatisfactory, unpleasant, heated, or vulgar." He concluded that Congress had not intended to extend the criminal law to such "normal risks of human intercourse," nor had it intended "the flooding of the Federal courts with complaints from persons who feel annoyed with some dealing they have had with another which happened to be by way of an interstate telephone call."[577]

The *Darsey* court held that only when "some completely unjustifiable motive, such as revenge or cruelty, motivates such repeated contacts . . . can such calls be properly labeled 'solely to harass.'"[578] Thus, the court acquitted the defendant, who had

[572] Numerous courts have upheld obscene call statutes. *See, e.g.,* Baker v. State, 494 P.2d 68, 70–71 (Az. App. 1972); State v. Jaeger, 249 N.W.2d 688, 691 (Iowa 1977); State v. Crelly, 313 N.W.2d 455, 456 (S.D. 1981).
[573] *See* Pub. L. 105-314, 112 Stat. 2975 (1998).
[574] *Id.* §101.
[575] *Id.* §227.
[576] 342 F. Supp. at 313–314.
[577] *Id.* at 313, 314.
[578] *Id.* at 314.

repeatedly called his mother-in-law, using abusive language, in an effort to speak with his young son who was in the custody of his estranged wife. Employing a similar rationale, a Missouri state court held that repeated calls made to collect a legitimate debt were not made solely to harass the debtor within the meaning of subpart (D).[579]

Another question raised by subpart (D) is what constitutes a pattern of "repeated" calls. Concerned, once again, to avoid flooding the courts and chilling citizens' efforts to achieve legitimate goals through telephone communications, the *Darsey* court ruled that calls to an answering service, which never reached the called party personally, did not qualify as repeated calls.[580] In addition, the court held that calls would be deemed "repeated" only if they "came in close enough proximity to one another to rightly be called a single episode, and [were] not separated by periods of months or years."[581]

The same defenses that the 1996 Act extended to violations of the obscenity clauses of section 223 also cover the harassment clauses.[582] It is hard to imagine that many harassers will preface their verbal assaults with a demand for a credit card number or an adult access code. But two other defenses are important in the context of harassment as well: the defense for those who "solely provide access to a facility or network not under that person's control"[583] and the defense for employers whose employees make harassing calls without the employer's knowledge.[584]

§14.7.2 *Federal Constitutional Immunities*

"[I]n the privacy of the home," the Supreme Court has written (in reference to a vulgar radio broadcast), "the individual's right

---

[579] R.H. Macy & Co. v. Bell, 531 S.W.2d 58, 62–63 (Mo. App. 1975).
[580] *Darsey*, 342 F. Supp. at 314.
[581] *Id.* at 313.
[582] 47 U.S.C. §223(e). See §14.6.5 for application of these defenses to the obscenity provisions.
[583] 47 U.S.C. §223(e)(1).
[584] *Id.* §223(e)(4).

to be left alone plainly outweighs the first amendment rights of an intruder."[585] Governments unquestionably have an interest in protecting citizens from the sort of "intolerable" intrusions typified by the obscene, threatening, or anonymous phone call.[586] There is no doubt, moreover, that communications of that character are what most harassment statutes are aimed at.

But drafting commensurately narrow statutory language has proved difficult.[587] Pragmatically speaking, this doesn't much matter: legitimate though annoying forms of telephone conversation are rarely prosecuted and, if prosecuted, are usually quickly dismissed.[588] But under the First Amendment doctrine of overbreadth, even a caller whose conduct is entirely lacking in any legitimate justification, and who is making a call that would not in itself be entitled to First Amendment protection, may escape

[585] FCC v. Pacifica Found., 438 U.S. 726, 749–750 (1978) (upholding FCC ban on "indecent" or offensive material broadcast into home during hours while children were awake). *Cf.* Frisby v. Schultz, 487 U.S. 474 (1988); Rowan v. United States Post Office Dept., 397 U.S. 728, 736–737 (1970); Kovacs v. Cooper, 336 U.S. 77, 86–87 (1949) (upholding a conviction for emitting "loud and raucous" noises over a vehicle loudspeaker; recognizing that an unwilling listener "[i]n his home or on the street . . . is practically helpless to escape the interference with his privacy by loudspeakers except through the protection of the municipality"). *See generally* Comment, Constitutionally Regulating Telephone Harassment at 1414–1417 (1989).

[586] Cohen v. California, 403 U.S. 15, 21 (1971). Cohen indicates that government may "shut off discourse solely to prevent others from hearing it" *if* "substantial privacy interests are being invaded in an essentially intolerable manner." *Id.*

[587] As one federal judge has argued, "Telephone calls by irate citizens to their Congressmen, by collectors seeking payment of legitimate bills overdue, [or] by customers voicing to a seller dissatisfaction with goods or services purchased . . . are likely to be annoying, even harassing, to the recipients. [Yet] [n]o one could seriously question the caller's free speech right under the First Amendment to engage in such telephone conversations." Gormley v. Director, Conn. State Dept. of Probations, 632 F.2d 938, 944 (2d Cir.) (Mansfield, J., concurring), *cert. denied*, 449 U.S. 1023 (1980). *See also, e.g.*, City of Everett v. Moore, 683 P.2d 617 (Wash. App. 1984) ("A discussion of any political, social, economic, philosophic or religious topic might well vex, irritate or bother the listener. . . . The people of Everett must not live in the continual fear that something they say to another might bother the listener to the point of invoking the ordinance.").

[588] *See Darsey*, 342 F. Supp. at 313–314 (refusing to extend 47 U.S.C. §223 to many "romantic and family conflicts" that are "the normal risks of human intercourse, and are and should be below the cognizance of the law").

conviction because the criminal statute sweeps too far into *other* conduct that *would* be protected.[589] The related doctrine of vagueness demands that criminal laws regulating speech be drawn with "narrow specificity."[590]

The overbreadth and vagueness doctrines have proved fatal to a number of state statutes prohibiting telephone harassment.[591] The decisions, however, have not been uniform,[592] and

---

[589] As the Supreme Court has stated, a statute "may be invalid conduct [as 'overbroad'] if it prohibits privileged exercises of First Amendment rights *whether or not* the record discloses that the petitioner has engaged in privileged conduct." NAACP v. Button, 371 U.S. 415, 432 (1963) (emphasis added). The overbreadth doctrine therefore is "strong medicine," forbidding the state to enforce laws against harmful conduct because the laws might have some other unconstitutional application. Broadrick v. Oklahoma, 413 U.S. 601, 613 (1973). For this reason, the Court in *Broadrick* and subsequent cases has permitted the application of the doctrine only when the overbreadth is a "substantial concern in the content of the statute as a whole." *Id.* at 616; *see also* Village of Schaumburg v. Citizens for a Better Environment, 444 U.S. 620, 636–638 (1980). "[T]here must be a realistic danger that the statute itself will significantly compromise recognized First Amendment protections of parties not before the Court for it to be facially challenged on overbreadth grounds." City Council of Los Angeles v. Taxpayers for Vincent, 466 U.S. 789, 801 (1984).

[590] *Button*, 371 U.S. at 433. The doctrine is aimed at similar vices addressed by the overbreadth doctrine. "A vague law [raises] dangers of arbitrary and discriminatory application"; moreover, "[u]ncertain meanings inevitably lead citizens to 'steer far wider of the unlawful zone.'" Grayned v. City of Rockford, 408 U.S. 104, 108–109 (1972) (citations omitted). *See* Kolender v. Lawson, 461 U.S. 352, 357–358 (1983). On several occasions, the Court has declared statutes "void for vagueness" and therefore unconstitutional. *See* City of Houston v. Hill, 482 U.S. 451 (1987); Smith v. Goguen, 415 U.S. 566 (1974); Erznoznik v. City of Jacksonville, 422 U.S. 205 (1975); Hynes v. Mayor & Council of Oradell, 425 U.S. 610 (1976).

A number of other constitutional challenges have been brought to aspects of laws regulating telephone harassment. Various classifications in such laws have been challenged on the ground that they lack sufficient justification to satisfy the due process and equal protection clauses. Courts generally have not been hospitable to such claims. *See, e.g.*, Alobaidi v. State, 433 S.W.2d 440 (Tex. Crim. App. 1968), *cert. denied*, 393 U.S. 943 (1969) (finding rational basis for exempting calls made "for a lawful business purpose").

[591] *See* People v. Klick, 362 N.E.2d 329 (Ill. 1977) (holding that §26(1)(a)(2) of the Illinois Criminal Code deprived the defendants of First Amendment freedoms and made otherwise protected conduct criminal); State v. Dronso, 279 N.W.2d 710 (Wis. App. 1979) (holding that §947.01(2) of the Wisconsin Statutes was unconstitutionally overbroad and in violation of both the U.S. and Wisconsin Constitutions).

[592] *See* State v. Hagen, 558 P.2d 750, 753 (Ariz. App. 1976) (rejecting challenge to state's telephone harassment law, stating that "[b]y specifying the

the Supreme Court has so far declined to provide authoritative guidance.[593]

It appears that the most significant factors in determining whether a telephone harassment statute is consistent with the First Amendment are whether it contains a requirement of a specific, or even a "sole," intent "to harass" and whether its language narrows the scope of such broad words as "annoy" or "harass." Thus, courts have struck down statutes that do not contain a specific intent to harass,[594] while upholding statutes that do have such a requirement.[595] Nevertheless, as one commentator has pointed out, "[a] statute requiring 'intent to annoy'. . . is arguably no more definite than a statute with no intent requirement, because the term 'annoy' lacks clarity."[596] To be certain that a statute is constitutional, it appears, the broad terms "annoy" and "harass" must also be limited by tying them to particular aggravating circumstances that remove the speech from First Amendment protection.

As with obscene calls, a relatively small number of anonymous calls are likely to be constitutionally protected, and therefore, the addition of a scienter requirement of "intent to harass" in section 223(a)(1)(C) has been sufficient to overcome constitutional objections.[597] Certainly some anonymous calls have high First

---

intent with which the call must be made and the nature of the language prohibited, the statute clearly demonstrates that the prohibited activities find no protection under the First Amendment"); People v. Taravella, 350 N.W.2d 780 (Mich. App. 1984).

[593] See Gormley v. Director, Conn. State Dept. of Probations, 449 U.S. 1023, 1025 (White, J., dissenting from denial of certiorari), denying cert. to 632 F.2d 938 (2d Cir. 1980); Thorne v. Bailey, 488 U.S. 984, denying cert. to 846 F.2d 241 (4th Cir. 1988).

[594] See, e.g., Walker v. Dillard, 523 F.2d 3, 5–6 (4th Cir.), cert. denied, 423 U.S. 906 (1975); Radford v. Webb, 446 F. Supp. 608, 610–611 (W.D.N.C. 1978), aff'd, 596 F.2d 1205 (1979).

[595] See, e.g., State v. Hagen, 558 P.2d 750 (Ariz. App. 1976); Kinney v. State, 404 N.E.2d 49, 51 (Ind. App. 1980); Bachowski v. Salamone, 407 N.W.2d 533, 537–538 (1980); Thorne, 846 F.2d at 243–244; Gormley, 632 F.2d at 942.

[596] See Comment, Constitutionally Regulating Telephone Harassment at 1408. See also Gormley, 632 F.2d at 944.

[597] See Comment, Constitutionally Regulating Telephone Harassment at 1410 & nn.31, 33; id. at 1426 n.85.

Amendment value—including anonymous "tips" to the police and anonymous "whistle-blower" calls. But there is little risk that such calls will be deterred by a statute that encompasses only calls made "with intent to harass."[598]

Section 223(a)(1)(E) of the telephone harassment statute, which encompasses "repeated telephone calls during which conversation ensues," could potentially reach a large number of legitimate activities—for example, concerted efforts to collect a debt or to reach an estranged relative who refuses to talk—without a stringent intent requirement. Thus, the statute provides that such calls are not prohibited unless they are made "*solely to harass.*" Federal courts, as noted, have construed this term narrowly to include only "completely unjustifiable motive[s], such as revenge or cruelty."[599] In *United States v. Lampley,*[600] the Third Circuit found that this "narrow intent requirement precludes the proscription of mere communication" and upheld the provision against a First Amendment challenge. State courts have likewise limited their harassment statutes to constitutional applications by requiring "sole" intent to harass.[601] The section of the telephone harassment statute that prohibits causing the telephone to ring repeatedly for purposes of harassment involves very little speech at all, though the activity is still communicative in that it conveys (anonymous) hatred or some similar sentiment.[602]

---

[598] *Id.* at 1426 n.85.

[599] *See Darsey,* 342 F. Supp. at 314.

[600] 573 F.2d 783, 787 (3d Cir. 1978).

[601] *See* State v. Brown, 266 S.E.2d 64, 65 (S.C. 1980); Jones v. Municipality of Anchorage, 754 P.2d 275, 279 (Alaska App. 1988).

[602] Some courts have labeled the other varieties of prohibited telephone harassment as "conduct" as well and therefore have determined that they are entitled to little or no First Amendment protection. *See, e.g.,* Thorne v. Bailey, 846 F.2d at 243–244 ("Prohibiting harassment is not prohibiting speech, because harassment . . . is not communication, [even though] it may take the form of speech."); Gormley v. Director, Conn. State Dept. of Probations, 632 F.2d at 941–942; *Baker,* 494 P.2d at 70; State v. Elder, 382 So. 2d 687, 690 (Fla. 1980). But attempting to decide such cases on the "speech/conduct" distinction is an exercise in verbal legerdemain. An obscene phone call is unquestionably speech; what is missing is not speech, but the listener's consent. *See Gormley,* 632 F.2d at 944 (Mansfield, J., concurring); State v. Thorne, 333 S.E.2d 817, 824 (W. Va.) (Miller, C.J., dissenting), *cert. denied,* 477 U.S. 996

A final factor raised by several state statutes and decisions, though not by the federal statute, is whether the called party has indicated a lack of consent to receive such calls. For example, the Florida Supreme Court, reacting to constitutional concerns, has construed its state's statute to reach only unwarranted, unsolicited, or nonconsensual calls.[603] It seems likely, however, that the caller must be given notice of the lack of consent before his next call is constitutionally unprotected.

§14.7.3 Telephone Solicitation

While not in the same league as threats of violence or sexual predation, telephone solicitations can be most unwelcome, too. The development of the automatic dialing and recorded message player (ADRMP) has enabled solicitors of any description to make thousands of calls per day at very low cost.[604] A similar problem has arisen with regard to the mass mailing of unsolicited e-mails, a practice known as "spamming."

(1985). A possible answer has been suggested: "speech" in the First Amendment implies something more than "communication." *See* Barnes v. Glen Theatre, Inc., 501 U.S. 560 (1991) (nude dancing).

[603] *Elder,* 382 So. 2d at 691–693.

[604] *See* Joshua A. Marcus, Commercial Speech on the Internet: Spam and the First Amendment, 16 Cardozo Arts & Ent. L.J. 245 (1998); Fabian D. Gonell, Statutory Interpretation of Federal Jurisdictional Statutes: Jurisdiction of the Private Right of Action Under the TCPA, 66 Fordham L. Rev. 1895 (1998); David E. Sorkin, Unsolicited Commercial E-Mail and the Telephone Consumer Protection Act of 1991, 45 Buffalo L. Rev. 1001 (1997); Nadel, Rings of Privacy: Unsolicited Telephone Calls and the Right of Privacy, 4 Yale J. Reg. 99, 99 & n.5 (1986); Luten, Give Me a Home Where No Salesmen Phone: Telephone Solicitation and the First Amendment, 7 Hastings Const. L.Q. 129, 129–131 (1979). *See also* Telemarketing Fraud Prevention Act of 1997, H.R. Rep. No. 158, 105th Cong., 2d Sess. (1997); Protecting Consumers Against Cramming and Spamming: Oversight Hearing Before the Subcomm. on Telecommunications Trade and Consumer Protection, 105th Cong., 2d Sess. (Sept. 28, 1998); The Scourge of Telemarketing Fraud: What Can Be Done Against It?, Fifteenth Report by the House Comm. on Govt. Affairs, H.R. Rep. No. 421, 102d Cong., 1st Sess. (1991).

States have passed various laws banning automatic dialing, or at least limiting the hours it could be used.[605] State and federal laws against Internet spamming now seem inevitable.[606] And at least one company successfully sued a spammer for trespass.[607]

The Telephone Consumer Protection Act of 1991 (TCPA) addresses these issues at the federal level.[608] The law bars automatically dialed or prerecorded telephone calls and faxes.[609]

The FCC is directed to grant exemptions from this prohibition for types of calls that will not "adversely affect" consumer privacy rights.[610] The Senate Committee Report explained that the exemptions are to be crafted business by business, product by product, service by service on the basis of a predictive heckler's veto — so that consumers may continue receiving calls of a type "the consumer would not ordinarily object to receiving."[611] For example, the Senate Committee noted that survey research should be exempted (unless combined with a sales pitch),[612] that "local" solicitations by small businesses and holders of second-class mail permits (that is, newspapers) should be exempted depending on the "extent and effectiveness" of local "better

---

[605] *See, e.g.,* Wash. Rev. Code §80.36.400(2) ("No person may use an automatic dialing and announcing device for purposes of commercial solicitation. This section applies to all commercial solicitation intended to be received by telephone customers within the state."); Ky. Rev. Stat. Ann. §367.461 (1992); Neb. Rev. Stat. §86-1212 (1993); N.C. Gen. Stat. §75-30 (1993); Ohio Rev. Code Ann. §2917.21 (1996); Vt. Stat. Ann. tit. 9, §2511 (1992); Cal. Bus. & Prof. Code §17563.5(b) (Deering 1987); N.Y. Gen. Bus. Law §399-p(2) (McKinney 1988).

[606] A bill has been introduced in Congress to ban the use of e-mails to send unsolicited advertisements. H.R. 1748, Netizens Protection Act of 1997.

[607] CompuServe Inc. v. Cyber Promotions, Inc., 962 F. Supp. 1015 (1997) (holding that plaintiff had a viable claim for trespass and to injunctive relief where defendants repeatedly transmitted a substantial volume of electronic data in the form of unsolicited e-mail to the plaintiff's proprietary computer equipment, after repeated demands to stop).

[608] Pub. L. No. 102-243, 105 Stat. 2395 (1991) (codified at 47 U.S.C. §227).

[609] 47 U.S.C. §227.

[610] *Id.* §227(b)(2)(B)(ii)(I).

[611] S. Rep. No. 178, 102d Cong. at 5 (1991).

[612] *Id.* The Senate Committee noted that the need for legislation had been based on a "survey [that] found that about 75 percent of persons contacted favored some form of regulation of these calls, and one-half of these favored a prohibition against all unsolicited calls." *Id.* at 3.

business" community standards,[613] and that the FCC may also
want to exempt some (but probably not all) calls from companies
the consumer has previously done business with.[614] In making all
these minute adjustments of speech and privacy rights, the FCC
is implored to remain "consistent with the free speech protections embodied in the First Amendment of the Constitution."[615]

The TCPA directed the FCC to study the feasibility of a national database of persons who do not want to be disturbed
by either live voice solicitations or autodialed or prerecorded

---

[613] *Id.* at 6.

[614] *Id.* at 5. The further directions provided by the Senate Committee to
the Commission are worth quoting at length to show the scope of the inquiry:

> The FCC may find that consumers generally do not object to receiv-
> ing calls from an entity concerning a specific product or service that
> they have already purchased from that entity. For instance, if a con-
> sumer purchases a product from a particular company, the FCC may
> find that that consumer generally would not object to a follow-up call
> concerning additions or updates for that product offered by that com-
> pany or its affiliate. Such may not be the case, however, with respect to
> calls made by that same company concerning different products or ser-
> vices unrelated to the initial transaction, or to calls concerning the ini-
> tial transaction made by another company. At the same time, the FCC
> also should keep in mind the need to establish terms for fair competi-
> tion—the FCC should recognize that it may be anticompetitive to allow
> certain companies to call consumers to offer a product or service related
> to the initial transaction and not to allow competitors to make such
> calls.
>
> The FCC also should consider the case of group contracts with affin-
> ity groups. For instance, if the governing board of an organization signs
> an agreement with a life insurance company to offer discounted life
> insurance policies to the members of the organization, the members of
> that organization may be considered to have given their "implied" con-
> sent to be called by this life insurance company. Such consent need not
> necessarily be implied simply because of the consumer's membership in
> an organization. Whether such implied consent exists or not may
> depend upon whether the representative of the group who signs the
> agreement is accountable (in the form of direct elections or otherwise)
> to its members.

Id. at 5.

[615] Telephone Consumer Protection Act, §2(13), *reprinted at* 47 U.S.C. §227
note.

solicitations.[616] Congress instructed the Commission, when adopting rules to implement the TCPA, that "[i]ndividuals' privacy rights, public safety interests, and commercial freedoms of speech must be balanced in a way that protects the privacy of individuals and permits legitimate telemarketing practices."[617]

The Commission adopted restrictions on telephone solicitation in 1992.[618] The Commission rejected grand proposals for a national database, for upgrades in existing network technologies, or for special directory markings as too expensive, burdensome, and ineffective for all parties involved.[619] Instead, the Commission prohibited any person from initiating a "telephone call" using an automatic telephone dialing system or an artificial or prerecorded voice to any emergency telephone line, to any patient room in a hospital, to any service for which the called party is charged for the call (e.g., cellular service), or to any residential telephone line.[620] For purposes of this prohibition, the Commission defined "telephone call" to *exclude* a call (1) not made for a commercial purpose, or (2) made for a commercial purpose that does not include the transmission of any unsolicited advertisement, or (3) made to a person with whom the caller has an established business relationship at the time the call is made, or (4) made by or on behalf of a caller that is a tax-exempt nonprofit organization.[621]

Furthermore, the Commission placed significant restrictions on the ability of telephone marketers to solicit residential telephone subscribers. For example, telemarketers cannot telephone residential telephone subscribers before 8 A.M. or after

---

[616] 47 U.S.C. §227(c) (directing Commission to study "electronic databases, telephone network technologies, special directory markings, industry-based or company-specific 'do not call' systems, and any other alternatives").

[617] Telephone Consumer Protection Act, §2(9), *reprinted at* 47 U.S.C. §227 note.

[618] *See* Rules and Regulations Implementing the Telephone Consumer Protection Act of 1991, Report and Order, 7 F.C.C. Rec. 8752 (1992).

[619] *Id.* at 8758–8763, ¶¶11–19.

[620] 47 C.F.R. §64.1200(a).

[621] *Id.* §64.1200(c).

9 P.M.,[622] and they must identify themselves to called parties.[623] Under the Commission's rules, commercial telemarketers are required to maintain lists of consumers who do not wish to be called.[624] Telemarketing companies are required to develop written policies for maintaining their do-not-call lists,[625] and they must inform their employees of the list's existence and train them to use the lists.[626] But the most powerful protections of all are likely to be electronic—taking the form of call screening and Caller ID.

The TCPA has so far withstood constitutional scrutiny. *Destination Ventures, Ltd. v. Federal Communication Commission* upheld the constitutionality of the restrictions on unsolicited fax advertising.[627] The restriction on auto dialing was upheld in *Moser v. FCC*,[628] which overturned a lower court ruling that found the Act unconstitutional because the ban on using an artificial or prerecorded voice to deliver some kinds of commercial messages to residential phone lines could not be justified as a content-neutral, time, place, or manner restriction.[629] In reversing the

---

[622] *Id.* §64.1200(e)(1).

[623] *Id.* §64.1200(e)(2)(iv).

[624] *Id.* §64.1200(e)(2). The Commission originally ruled that these lists must be maintained on a permanent basis by the companies. In a subsequent order, however, the Commission required companies to maintain these lists for ten years. *See* Rules and Regulations Implementing the Telephone Consumer Protection Act of 1991, Memorandum Opinion and Order, 10 F.C.C. Rec. 12,391, 12,398 ¶15; 47 C.F.R. §64.1200(e)(2)(vi).

[625] 47 C.F.R. §64.1200(e)(2)(i).

[626] *Id.* §64.1200(e)(2)(ii).

[627] 46 F.3d 54 (9th Cir. 1995) (holding that the ban on unsolicited fax advertising did not violate advertiser's First Amendment rights because the ban reasonably fit the government's interest in preventing shifting of advertising costs to consumers—in the form of paper, ink, and telephone line time—and the ban was evenhanded as it applied to any organization).

[628] 46 F.3d 970, 975 (9th Cir. 1994) (concluding that automated telemarketing calls are a threat to privacy that can be regulated, though not curtailed entirely, under the statute without violating the First Amendment), *cert. denied,* 515 U.S. 1161 (1995).

[629] Moser v. FCC, 826 F. Supp. 360 (D. Ore. 1993) (finding the statute was content-based not only because it draws distinctions between the manner in which some speech is delivered (recorded versus live), but also because it distinguishes between messages on the basis of content (commercial versus noncommercial)).

lower court, the court of appeals recognized that Congress had sufficient evidence to conclude that automated telemarketing calls were a threat to privacy.[630] The ban also left open other means of communication for telemarketers.[631]

In an effort further to punish telemarketing swindlers, Congress passed the Telemarketing Fraud Prevention Act of 1998,[632] which the President signed into law on June 23, 1998. It includes provisions requiring criminal asset forfeiture[633] and mandatory victim restitution.[634]

§14.7.4 Federal Constitutional Immunities

Solicitations, whether charitable or commercial, nearly always fall within the realm of speech covered by the First Amendment—as opposed to entirely unprotected communications, such as obscenities or threats.[635] Almost by definition, solicitation is motivated by something other than the "intent to harass." Moreover, studies show that while many are irritated by "junk" calls, many others are not.[636]

A number of Supreme Court decisions have addressed by-mail and door-to-door solicitations.[637] The Court has generally struck

[630] *Id.* at 974.

[631] *Id.* at 975. Telemarketers were still free to use taped messages introduced first by live speakers or use taped messages to which consumers had consented.

[632] Pub. L. No. 105-184, 112 Stat. 520 (1998) (codified at 18 U.S.C. §2325).

[633] 18 U.S.C. §982.

[634] *Id.* §2327.

[635] Commercial speech (primarily advertising and solicitation) has received First Amendment protection since Bigelow v. Virginia, 421 U.S. 809 (1975), and Virginia Board of Pharmacy v. Virginia Consumer Council, 425 U.S. 748 (1976). Charitable solicitation has been recognized as high-value First Amendment speech in, among other cases, Schaumburg v. Citizens for a Better Environment, 444 U.S. 620, 631–632 (1980).

[636] Nadel, Rings of Privacy, at 99–100 & nn.6–7.

[637] For example, the U.S. Supreme Court has held that the right of a person to solicit by mail could be "circumscribed" by—but "only by"—"an affirmative act of the addressee giving notice that he wishes no further mailings from that mailer." Rowan v. United States Post Office Dept., 397 U.S. 728, 737

down absolute bans on such solicitations, but has approved narrower remedies, such as prohibiting intrusions at certain hours or allowing the resident to give notice that he does not wish to be disturbed with solicitations. The states probably have even greater authority to regulate telephone solicitation. Like the radio broadcast involved in *FCC v. Pacifica Foundation,* incoming telephone calls are "a uniquely pervasive presence in the lives of all Americans."[638] While those who receive "junk mail" can fend it off by a "short, though regular, journey from mailbox to trashcan,"[639] a ringing telephone permits avoidance less easily: it "gives no indication of the nature or source of the call and requires answering if only to restore peace to the home."[640]

States have adopted a number of approaches in their attempts to keep their laws constitutional.[641] Many just rely on their telephone harassment statutes to nab those few solicitations that go far beyond the pale. Other states specifically prohibit calls made at "inconvenient" or late hours or that significantly prevent the recipient from using his or her own phone. Local telephone company tariffs also generally forbid calls that "'interfere unreasonably with the use of the service by one or more other [c]ustomers.'"[642]

(1970). But in striking down a broad ban on unsolicited mailings of contraceptive advertisements in Bolger v. Youngs Drug Products Corp., 463 U.S. 60 (1983), the Court held that government may not "shut off the flow of mailings to protect those recipients who *might potentially* be offended." *Id.* at 72 (emphasis added). In another case, the Court struck down an absolute ban on door-to-door solicitation, but indicated that it could be made unlawful "to ring the bell of a householder who has appropriately indicated that he is unwilling to be disturbed." Martin v. Struthers, 319 U.S. 141, 148 (1943). On the other hand, the Court upheld a ban on door-to-door *commercial* solicitation in Breard v. Alexandria, 341 U.S. 622 (1951).

[638] *Pacifica,* 438 U.S. at 748.

[639] *Bolger,* 463 U.S. at 72 (quoting Lamont v. Commissioner of Motor Vehicles, 269 F. Supp. 880, 883 (S.D.N.Y.), *aff'd,* 386 F.2d 449 (2d. Cir. 1967), *cert. denied,* 391 U.S. 915 (1968)).

[640] Luten, Give Me a Home Where No Salesmen Phone at 150.

[641] See the listings of categories provided in Nadel, Rings of Privacy at 106–108 & nn.42–55.

[642] *See Unsolicited Telephone Calls,* Memorandum Opinion and Order, 77 F.C.C.2d 1023, 1037 (1980).

A law allowing individuals to give notice that they do not want certain kinds of calls—analogous to the law regarding mail solicitation upheld in *Rowan v. United States Post Office Department*—seems best to balance the First Amendment rights of solicitors and the privacy rights of recipients.[643] Such a system has the advantage of leaving the decision as to what calls are too intrusive "where it belongs—with the homeowner himself."[644]

§14.8 Privacy, Property, and Free Speech: A Synthesis Based on Consent

The linchpin of every issue discussed in this chapter is consent.[645] For there truly to be free speech, a speaker must wish to speak and to have information conveyed or disclosed to one or another recipient. Wiretapping, signal piracy, informational privacy, and intellectual property are concerned with the unwilling speaker. The excesses of free speech—harassment, solicitation, and such—are mainly concerned with the unwilling listener. "Free speech" is free only when it is completely consensual at both ends of the line.

The line from telephone harassment, through telephone solicitation, to agreeable telephone depravity is one drawn against a scale of varying consent. Almost no one wants to be harassed by telephone; opinion is more equally divided on telephone solicitation, and, children aside, dial-a-porn is clearly consensual. Roughly speaking, First Amendment considerations favor-

[643] This is the method that the FCC has now adopted. *See* 47 C.F.R. §64.1200(e)(2)(iii) ("If a person or entity making a telephone solicitation . . . receives a request from a residential telephone subscriber not to receive calls from that person or entity, the person or entity must record the request and place the subscriber's name and telephone number on the do-not-call list at the time the request is made"; *id.* §64.1200(e)(2)(vi) ("[a] do not call request must be honored for 10 years from the time the request is made").

[644] Martin v. Struthers, 319 U.S. at 148.

[645] The dial-a-porn cases typically emphasize the protection of children, but the underlying logic is, of course, that children cannot make certain choices for themselves and parents must therefore be able to maintain control over what they hear.

ing the right to make a phone call rise, and all interests opposing that right decline, as the likelihood of there being *mutual*
consent between caller and calling party increases.

Indeed, consent is in the end the only real difference between
nudity in the bedroom and nudity in a public park, between dial-
a-porn and dirty language on the public radio, between a boom
box and a pair of earphones, between courtship and sexual harassment. A marketplace of ideas—a truly free market—depends
on mutual consent. The important freedom is not privacy, intellectual property, or free speech. It is freedom to choose among
them.

Thus, free speech is not a right that can be intelligently
defined by exclusive reference to speakers, or in exclusively positive terms. The privacy right is a quintessentially negative right,
a right *not* to have one's utterances, performances, or preferences shared or observed by others. Intellectual property, like all
other forms of property, is in large part a negative right, too—
a right to exclude others. Inevitably the freedom at stake here is
as much one of silence as of speech. The various labels—privacy,
property, and speech—all protect the same fundamental interests. A right of speech cannot be meaningfully distinguished
from a right to listen,[646] or from a right not to speak,[647] or from

---

[646] First Natl. Bank v. Bellotti, 435 U.S. 765 (1978); Tribe, American Constitutional Law §12-3, at 796.

[647] The First Amendment protects speakers from being required to convey
messages with which they disagree. Wooley v. Maynard, 430 U.S. 705 (1977)
(striking down requirement that motor vehicles bear license plate carrying
state motto, "Live Free or Die"). It also protects companies whose business
involves editorial discretion of what to say and not to say. Miami Herald Co.
v. Tornillo, 418 U.S. 241 (1974) (invalidating a statute that required newspapers to publish letters to the editor); Los Angeles v. Preferred Communications, Inc., 476 U.S. 488 (1986) (the selection and organization of programs
on cable television involve some degree of protected editorial discretion); *cf.*
FCC v. Midwest Video Corp., 440 U.S. 689, 707 (1979) (cable operators exercise "a significant amount of editorial discretion regarding what their programming will include").

Similarly, although a union and an employer may require that all bargaining unit employees become union members, the union may not compel
those members to support financially "union activities beyond those germane
to collective bargaining, contract administration, and grievance adjustment."

a right not to be heard against one's will, or from a right not to listen.[648]

The negative dimensions of free speech rights are growing increasingly important. New technologies are making information extremely easy to deliver, across space, across time, and across the walls that traditionally established a man's home as his castle. Unless the owner of content is empowered to prevent its dissemination, unless a listener is empowered *not* to listen to most of the voices in the torrent, useful content will be suppressed, and willing listeners will be deafened by a torrent of useless noise. Too much information will lead to a "cacophony of competing voices, none of which could be clearly and predictably heard."[649]

The trouble is that half a loaf of consent is often much easier to find than a whole. This is especially true of telephone solicitation, the middle ground. Many people who are called do not purchase the cut-rate magazine subscription or donate to their patrolmen's association, but many do—which proves (after the fact) that although many of these calls are not particularly welcome, a good many are. The problem is endemic. My handbill

---

Communications Workers of Am. v. Beck, 487 U.S. 735, 745, 761 (1988) (a "serious constitutional question" would "be raised by a construction permitting unions to expend governmentally compelled fees on political causes that nonmembers find objectionable"); *see also* Abood v. Detroit Bd. of Educ., 431 U.S. 209 (1977) (compelling nonmember employees to contribute to union political activities infringes First Amendment rights).

[648] Courts must and, of course, often do make pragmatic judgments about which way to tilt when these various rights appear to collide. Public forum doctrine, for example, often affirms the right of the identified and certifiably willing speaker over the rights of the unidentified and hypothetically unwilling listener; as a general rule, a real person who wants to speak counts more than a government official claiming to represent some broad public right not to listen. Up to a point at least, governments and unions are likewise allowed to spend public money for communicative purposes: this promotes the rights of some citizens or members who approve of what is said over the rights of those who disapprove. What these qualifications demonstrate, however, is that speech remains a messy business, and the rights that go with it therefore continue to be defined with one eye on principle, the other on pragmatism.

[649] Red Lion Broad. Co. v. FCC, 395 U.S. 367, 376 (1969) (footnote omitted).

may be your litter, my political soundtruck your interrupted rest, my radio broadcast your static, my street art your ugly graffiti, my cross burning your intimidation, my inept wooing your sexual harassment, my privacy your inability to pry,[650] my pillow talk your vulgarity, my flashing your indecent exposure. In public places, the speech I direct to willing listeners may reach unwilling ones as well.

The seemingly unresolvable problem is that even a private invitation to converse—the exploratory preliminaries to conversation itself—may be offensive or annoying. Every right to speak may collide with some reciprocal right not to listen; not to speak; not to watch; not to give away your own words, thoughts, privacy, or solitude. Mutual consent is the ideal, but locating it is often difficult, and the very search—the solicitation to speech—may itself be inimical to an equally important interest in privacy.

There are two generic solutions to the cacophony problem. One is to protect the speaker's and listener's respective abilities to discriminate among who may listen, or who must be listened to. The other is to affirm government's power to control which voices are heard, where.

For a time, the government control solution was adopted by Congress and ratified by the Supreme Court for broadcast.[651] Three decades ago it was believed "that broadcast frequencies constituted a scarce resource whose use could be regulated and rationalized only by the Government."[652] This view has been

---

[650] Though not usually viewed in this light, invasion of privacy is, of course, a form of communication—a transfer of information from an unwilling "speaker" to ears lurking behind the eaves or eyes concealed behind the keyhole. Invasion of privacy is, quite simply, telecommunication without consent.

[651] The problem of government regulation of broadcast speech is well described in chapter 15, Broadcast Press Licensing: Governmental Determinations of Who May Speak and What May Be Said, in Jonathan W. Emord, Freedom, Technology, and the First Amendment 205–215 (1991). *See also* M. Spitzer, The Constitutionality of Licensing Broadcasters, 64 N.Y.U. L. Rev. 990 (1989).

[652] Red Lion Broad. Co. v. FCC, 395 U.S. at 376 (1969).

severely questioned on technological and economic grounds,[653] although not quite yet abandoned by the courts.[654]

Most of the debate today is to what extent similar government-centered solutions are needed for telephony. With autodialers, dial-it services, and spammers, after all, the telephone network and the Internet can readily be used to the same effect as a broadcast medium.[655] Should government then prohibit

---

[653] *See* de Sola Pool, Technologies of Freedom at 138–148; M. Spitzer, The Constitutionality of Licensing Broadcasters at 1013–1018 (1989); M. Spitzer, Seven Dirty Words and Six Other Stories 9–18 (1986); Charles L. Jackson, Technology for Spectrum Markets(1976) (Ph.D. thesis, MIT).

Ten years before *Red Lion*, Ronald Coase argued that spectrum should be allocated through a market. R. H. Coase, The Federal Communications Commission, 2 J.L. & Econ. 1 (1959).

> [I]t is a commonplace of economics that almost all resources used in the economic system (and not simply radio and television frequencies) are limited in amount and scarce, in that people would like to use more than exists. Land, labor, and capital are all scarce, but this, of itself, does not call for governmental regulation. It is true that some mechanism has to be employed to decide who, out of the many claimants, should be allowed to use the scarce resource. But the way this is usually done in the American economic system is to employ the price mechanism, and this allocates resources to users without the need for government regulation.

Id. at 14.

[654] In Telecommunications Research & Action Center v. FCC, 801 F.2d 501 (D.C. Cir. 1986), then-Judge Bork (joined by then-Judge Scalia and Senior Judge MacKinnon) wrote for the D.C. Circuit Court of Appeals that spectrum scarcity is an illegitimate basis for government controls on broadcast speech. "[S]carcity" is a "universal fact" that applies to all media. *Id.* at 509. *But see* FCC v. League of Women Voters, 468 U.S. 364, 376–377 n.11 (1984) (refusing to reconsider scarcity rationale "without some signal from Congress or the FCC").

[655] The court of appeals in Carlin Communications, Inc. v. Mountain States Telephone & Telegraph Co., 827 F.2d 1291, 1294 (9th Cir. 1987), *cert. denied*, 485 U.S. 1029 (1988), pointed out that a 976 network is comparable to a broadcast medium in which "[the] phone company resembles less a common carrier than it does a small radio station."

Autodialers have the same broadcast effect. "Consumers are especially frustrated because there appears to be no way to prevent these calls. The telephone companies usually do not know when their lines are being used for telemarketing purposes. . . . Having an unlisted number does not prevent those telemarketers that call numbers randomly or sequentially." S. Rep. No. 178, 102d Cong. at 1–2 (1991). The result is that other speech is crowded out

---

entire categories of voice or data calls that seem likely to give offense? Should government engage in a continuous and infinitely delicate weighing of competing interests—the right to speech, the right of privacy, the right to talk, the right not to listen—in an attempt to strike just the right wholesale balance between the rights that sometimes collide? Yesterday, with the crude, indiscriminate media of over-the-air broadcast—electronic soundtrucks, so to speak—such balancing was perhaps inevitable and necessary. Today, with the precise media of narrowcast—electronic packages in brown-paper wrapping—no such balancing is required. By arming individuals, technology makes it possible to disarm government. The key to truly free speech—mutual consent—can now be vindicated, at least in telephony, without government interference or assistance.

In matters of speech, how is mutual consent established? Honest identification and truth in packaging are plainly necessary, if not always sufficient. The *New York Times* puts its banner on the top of the first page, and the government may not bar it from doing so. From the speaker's perspective, identification is part of the speech itself.[656] So, too, from the listener's perspective: the identity of the speaker is ordinarily a part of the speech because it is critical to the listener's decision whether or not to listen.[657] Any government attempt to prevent a willing speaker and willing listener from exchanging information as to each other's

---

by unwanted messages. "[A]utomated calls are placed to lines reserved for emergency purposes, such as hospitals and fire and police stations"; "the automated calls fill the entire tape of an answering machine, preventing other callers from leaving messages"; "the automated calls will not disconnect the line for a long time after the called party hangs up the phone, thereby preventing the called party from placing his or her own calls"; "automated calls do not respond to human voice commands to disconnect the phone, especially in times of emergency"; "some automatic dialers will dial numbers in sequence, thereby tying up all the lines of a business and preventing any outgoing calls." *Id.* at 2.

[656] *See generally* Tribe, American Constitutional Law §12-14, at 887–890, §15-15, at 1386–1389.

[657] Respecting autodialer calls, for example, consumers complain that "the entity placing the automated call does not identify itself." S. Rep. No. 178, 102d Cong. at 2.

identities would clearly run afoul of the First Amendment. It seems equally clear that the government could not require identification if both sides to a communication preferred to maintain anonymity. As always, the difficult cases are those in which anonymity is desired by one communicator over the objection of the other.[658]

With telephone calls, there are, of course, many familiar screening methods already in place, all designed to enhance free speech (and its twin, free listening) through private censorship. Executives have private secretaries. Anyone else who answers a call can simply ask who's calling and hang up if no answer is forthcoming.[659] Essentially all transmissions of electronic data begin with an ID protocol[660] and often additional "logon" requirements to make sure that only authorized users are using the service.[661] Automatic number identification accomplishes much the same for voice calls, only much more quickly and reliably than, say, a human intermediary. Comparable—and much more detailed—instruments of labeling and identification are readily included with communications conveyed over the Internet.

None of this runs afoul of any cosmic principle of privacy or right of anonymity. Freedom of speech, unlike freedom of conscience, is necessarily "public" in some measure—it takes at least two to have a dialog, and ideally one side should have no greater

---

[658] *Cf.* Talley v. California, 362 U.S. 60 (1960); NAACP v. Alabama, 357 U.S. 449 (1957).

[659] Some telemarketers apparently use prison inmates to place their calls and instruct them not to discuss their own status at any length. Miller, That Sales Pitch Interrupting Dinner Is by a Real Con Man, Wall St. J., Jan. 2, 1992, at 1.

[660] The International Telegraph and Telephone Consultative Committee under the International Telecommunications Union (CCITT) defines data protocols to include provisions for automatic identification of communicating entities. Data protocols may involve "identification of intended communications partners (e.g., by name, by address, by generic description)" and "authentication of intended communications partners." CCITT Recommendation X.200, in CCITT, Data Communication Networks, vol. VIII, fascicle VIII.5, at 29 (1985).

[661] All calling cards and all credit card billing of phone calls likewise require identification so that the carrier itself may ascertain that the bills for the service will be paid.

rights than the other. Thus, speakers often have no right to conceal their identities from other listeners. The Supreme Court has upheld laws requiring disclosure of the membership lists of subversive organizations.[662] State laws may ban Ku Klux Klan (KKK) members from wearing hoods.[663] Radio and TV broadcast stations must identify themselves every hour.[664] Sponsors of radio and TV broadcasts must be identified for every program.[665] Sponsors of paid political advertising in any medium must be identified.[666] Fax machines must identify themselves on every transmission.[667] Debt collectors must identify themselves when

---

[662] "Where the mask of anonymity which an organization's members wear serves the double purpose of protecting them from popular prejudice and of enabling them to . . . enlist the support of persons who would not, if the truth were revealed, lend their support, it would be a distortion of the First Amendment to hold that it prohibits Congress from removing the mask." Communist Party v. Subversive Activities Control Bd., 367 U.S. 1, 102–103 (1961). *But see* Talley v. California, 362 U.S. 60 (1960) (reversing conviction for violation of city ordinance prohibiting distribution of anonymous handbills on grounds that prohibition violated defendant's freedom of speech and press); NAACP v. Alabama, 357 U.S. 449 (1957) (ruling that state could not constitutionally compel NAACP to provide list of its membership).

[663] *See, e.g.,* State v. Miller, 398 S.E.2d 547 (Ga. 1990). *See generally* Allen, Klan, Cloth and Constitution: Anti-mask Laws and the First Amendment, 25 Ga. L. Rev. 819 (1991). *See also* Bryant v. Zimmerman, 278 U.S. 63, 75 (1928) (endorsing the use of compulsory membership disclosure as a deterrent against the KKK, which "functions largely at night, its members disguised by hoods and gowns and doing things calculated to strike terror into the minds of people").

[664] 47 C.F.R. §73.1201(a) (1990) ("Broadcast station identification announcements shall be made: (1) At the beginning and ending of each time of operation, and (2) hourly, as close to the hour as feasible, at a natural break in program offerings.").

[665] 47 U.S.C. §317; 47 C.F.R. §73.1212 (1990).

[666] *See* McIntyre v. Ohio Election Commn., 514 U.S. 334 (1995) (holding that Ohio statute that prohibited distribution of anonymous campaign literature violated First Amendment).

[667] "It shall be unlawful for any person within the United States . . . (B) to use a computer or other electronic device to send any message via a telephone facsimile machine unless such person clearly marks, in a margin at the top or bottom of each transmitted page of the message or on the first page of each transmission, the date and time it is sent and an identification of the business sending the message and the telephone number of the sending machine or of such business." 47 U.S.C. §227(d)(1)(B).

they call.[668] It is a federal criminal offense to make an intentionally harassing telephone call "without disclosing identity."[669] A provider of operator services must "identify itself, audibly and distinctly, to the consumer at the beginning of each telephone call. . . ."[670] Packaging for hazardous materials sent through the U.S. mail must identify the name and address of the sender.[671] On the other hand, the Supreme Court has repeatedly upheld the right to speak anonymously against state laws that attempted to strip it away.[672] Overall, the principle of identification is fairly well accepted, though not by any means absolute. Caller ID in telephony is controversial principally because it is novel.

§14.8.1   A Search for Consistent Legal Principle

The law of privacy, intellectual property, and free speech — and particularly First Amendment jurisprudence — has traditionally drawn sharp distinctions between carriers and broadcasters. Those distinctions cannot endure.

Online information services,[673] like America Online or EarthLink, are electronic publishers in their own right, but also provide, maintain, or lease space to "forums" that operate as

---

[668] Consumer Credit Protection Act Amendments, Pub. L. No. 95-109, 91 Stat. 877 (codified at 15 U.S.C. §1692).

[669] 47 U.S.C. §223(a)(1)(B).

[670] Telephone Operator Consumer Services Improvement Act of 1990, Pub. L. No. 101-435, 104 Stat. 987, *amended by* Pub. L. No. 101-555, 104 Stat. 2760 (codified at 47 U.S.C. §226(b)(1)(C)).

[671] 39 C.F.R. §111.1 (incorporating by reference 41 Domestic Mail Manual §124.11, at 142 (Dec. 1991)).

[672] McIntyre v. Ohio Election Commn., 514 U.S. 334 (1995); Talley v. California, 362 U.S. 60 (1960); NAACP v. Alabama, 357 U.S. 449 (1957).

[673] There were over 4,800 Internet service providers (ISPs) operating in 1998. B. McCarthy, Introduction, Boardwatch Magazine's Directory of Internet Service Providers 4 (Winter 1998/Spring 1999). America Online is the largest commercial ISP, with over 14 million subscribers, followed by Microsoft Network, with 2.3 million users. Other large commercial ISPs include AT&T WorldNet (1 million subscribers) and EarthLink (500,000).

interactive bulletin boards.[674] Many forums are innocuous. Some are bizarre, outrageous, or viciously offensive. There have been inevitable calls for censorship, answered by claims that the operator of an online service, like a carrier, has no right to exclude.[675] For the most part, operators like CompuServe insist they do have the right to censor and then generally choose not to exercise it.[676] Prodigy, for example, insisted it would not carry messages "grossly repugnant to community standards."[677] But it also declined to censor many controversial forums, including one debating whether the Holocaust was a hoax. As yet, government involvement with these services has not reached the level of "state action." Nor could these services be fairly categorized as public forums.

It seems likely that the law will have to abandon the long obsolete notion that an entire *medium* is either a "publisher" or a "carrier" and focus instead on specific services. *New York Times v. Sullivan* itself might have more seriously questioned the traditional view that a publisher is responsible for everything in its pages, even advertising, which is obviously "carried" more than

---

[674] *See generally* Finley P. Maxson, A Pothole on the Information Superhighway: BBS Operator Liability for Defamatory Statements, 75 Wash. U. L.Q. 673 (1997); David G. Post, Pooling Intellectual Capital: Thoughts on Anonymity, Pseudonymity, and Limited Liability in Cyberspace, 1996 U. Chi. Legal F. 139 (1996); Jeffrey M. Taylor, Liability for Usenet Operators for Defamation Published by Others: Flinging the Law of Defamation into Cyberspace, 47 Fla. L. Rev. 247 (1995); David J. Loundy, Revising the Copyright Law for Electronic Publishing, 14 J. Marshall J. Computer & Info. L. 1 (1995); Note, Is Cyberspace a Public Forum? Computer Bulletin Boards, Free Speech, and State Action, 81 Geo. L.J. 409 (1992) (hereinafter Note, Cyberspace); Note, The TRAC to Fairness: Teletext and the Political Broadcasting Regulations, 39 Hastings L.J. 165 (1987); Note, The Future of Teletext: Legal Implications of the FCC Deregulation of Electronic Publishing, 70 Iowa L. Rev. 709 (1985).

[675] *See, e.g.,* Note, Cyberspace, 81 Geo. L.J. 409; Note, New Technology, Old Problem: Determining the First Amendment Status of Electronic Information Services, 61 Fordham L. Rev. 1147 (1993).

[676] *See* Note, Cyberspace, 81 Geo. L.J. 409.

[677] *See* S. Sugawara, Computer Network to Ban "Repugnant" Comments, Wash. Post, Oct. 24, 1991, at A4; *see also* J. Sandberg, America Online Ends Some of Its Accounts over Pornography, Wall St. J., Jan. 9, 1995, at B5 (child pornography).

it is "published."[678] Services like CompuServe provide every possible function, from Post Office (e-mail) to distributor to direct publisher. Confusing and muddled though this is, defamation law really has no choice but to address problems service by service. Hammering an eclectic, category-defying service like CompuServe into a single, traditional legal pigeonhole only makes nonsense of the law and inhibits the bundling of services that the market clearly desires.

In short, the triad of First Amendment law discussed at the beginning of this chapter is under great and growing strain.[679] The Supreme Court's fractured 1994 analysis of the status of cable television in *Turner Broadcasting System*—with voting among the Justices broken down into no fewer than four camps—richly illustrates the problem. No one can even decide whether something as simple as cable, still quite a primitive broadband technology, is more like a newspaper, a television, or a telephone line for constitutional purposes.

From an engineering perspective, the whole "more-like" inquiry is silly. Broadband technology is capacious and powerful enough to swallow them all, just as the personal computer will inevitably swallow not only the mainframe computer, but also the calculator, telephone, fax, cable decoder, mail box, VCR, and Nintendo. Broadband networks cannot be shoehorned into any one of the old legal molds. The technologies of print, broadcast, and carriage are converging. Somehow or other constitutional jurisprudence will have to converge, too.

---

[678] Some courts have insisted (and the Supreme Court has hinted) that "commercial speech" is not entitled to constitutional protection against defamation actions. *See* Comment, First Amendment Crossroads—Extending Constitutional Defamation Protection to Commercial Speech: A Critique of U.S. Healthcare, Inc. v. Blue Cross of Greater Philadelphia and Some Suggestions, 39 UCLA L. Rev. 633 (1992).

[679] Glen O. Robinson, The Electronic First Amendment: An Essay for the New Age, 47 Duke L.J. 899 (1998); Michael H. Spencer, Anonymous Internet Communication and the First Amendment: A Crack in the Dam of National Sovereignty, 3 Va. J.L. & Tech. 1 (1998); Christopher M. Kelly, "The Spectre of a 'Wired' Nation": Denver Area Educational Telecommunications Consortium v. FCC and First Amendment Analysis in Cyberspace, 10 Harv. J.L. & Tech. 559 (1997); Henry H. Perritt, Jr., The Congress, the Courts and Computer Based Communications Networks: Answering Questions About Access

Even the narrowband online networks in operation today cut across all the traditional lines. A CompuServe or a Prodigy distributes text like a newspaper or bookstore. It also carries two-way e-mail like the telcos or the Post Office. Its "bulletin boards" are quasi-public forums like comparable boards in shopping malls.[680] So who has what First Amendment rights?

Some commentators have suggested that the old legal models can be dusted off and applied according to which particular function an online service is performing. When Prodigy (say) performs as a carrier, it can be regulated like Bell Atlantic; when it performs as a publisher, it can be regulated like the *New York Times,* and so on.

Yet it seems unlikely that this quacks-like-a-duck approach to discovering First Amendment rights can be sustained. If a bulletin board is a newspaper, whose newspaper is it? The *New York Times* belongs to those who write it, not to those who supply the newsprint. The difference between a bulletin board and e-mail turns simply on the number of recipients and how tightly each is controlled by the sender. But mailing lists can be as open-ended as one pleases, while bulletin boards can be privatized to any degree. In an electronic medium, this flexible and powerful difference among a letter, a newspaper, and a broadcast can be split indefinitely. The lines between them don't just blur a bit. They disappear completely. The law of electronic networks cannot be derived inductively by analogy and metaphor.

The prospect of having to reinvent First Amendment law from scratch is a daunting one. Happily, however, most of the reinventing can be in the direction of simpler, clearer constitutional

---

and Content Control Introduction, 38 Vill. L. Rev. 319 (1993); Michael I. Meyerson, Impending Legal Issues for Integrated Broadband Networks, 3 U. Fla. J.L. & Pub. Poly. 49 (1990); Henry H. Perritt, Jr., Tort Liability, the First Amendment, Equal Access, and Commercialization of Electronic Networks, 2 Electronic Networking 29 (1992); Perritt, Tort Liability, 5 Harv. J.L. & Tech. 65; Note, Cyberspace, 81 Geo. L.J. 409.

[680] *See* PruneYard Shopping Center v. Robins, 447 U.S. 74 (1980) (state constitution prohibited a shopping center from excluding pamphleteers); Allen S. Hammond IV, Regulating Broadband Communication Networks, 9 Yale J. on Reg. 181 (1992).

principles that tolerate less government intrusion than used to be considered acceptable.

Free speech that is welcome, or at least tolerated by most listeners, may provoke crime, sexual assault, or deep offense on the fringe. Courts have thus searched endlessly for a fit (or lack of it) among what the speaker is saying, what listeners collectively want (or don't want) to hear, and how well regulation accommodates interests all around.

At first blush, broadband networks might seem to make the problems worse. With broadband, one can transmit to any number of people, anywhere. The new networks penetrate every wall. Running across someone who will react badly to whatever may be shown or said seems inevitable. But in fact the technology itself also erects walls and creates shelters of quiet and solitude. Cataracts of information are useless without powerful switches, tuners, scramblers, and lock boxes to determine precisely what goes where. Those tools can be lodged at every level of the network. The censor may be in a central office, like the headquarters of CompuServe or Dow Jones. Or it may be on end users' premises, as it will be with the V-chip. Broadband technology need not be broadcast. To the contrary, the higher the bandwidth, the narrower the "cast." Senders and receivers alike have more power than ever to narrow the range of broadband connections established.

The upshot can be more speech, including more commercials, indecency, and so on, with less need for regulation. Communities of speakers and listeners can become completely voluntary on both sides. Indeed, "obscenity" (as defined by the Supreme Court) cannot really exist at all in well-ordered cyberspace: "community standards" within any group of speakers and listeners can be completely uniform and harmonious, even if uniformly depraved or violent by standards outside that network community.[681] "Deviance" loses its meaning when communities of the like-minded are formed entirely by consent. Freedom of

---

[681] Decisions such as Paris Adult Theatre I v. Slaton, 413 U.S. 49 (1973) (holding that community standards, not audience standards, define obscenity) will have to be revisited.

association is so complete in cyberspace that traditional limits on freedom of *speech* are no longer needed.

There remains, of course, speech that provokes antisocial conduct in response. Technology like the V-chip partly solves the problem so far as children are concerned, but only partly. With broadband networks ubiquitous, psychotics and sociopaths will be able to hear and see more carnage than they safely can, and far more than they could through traditional media. There is no obvious solution to this problem, if indeed it is a problem. Broadband technology does connect more willing speakers to more willing listeners, whatever their tastes and however they may react to what they hear. By making speech freer than ever, broadband technology amplifies the costs of freedom along with the benefits. One can only hope—this is ultimately a matter of sociological faith—that the overall ledger will remain in the black.

Similar evolution, toward simpler, more basic First Amendment principles, can be expected in the rules governing political speech. The old broadcast media clearly conferred enormous political power. Goebbels loved the radio. His political successors have always adored television. There's nothing a man like Fidel Castro, Slobodan Milosevic, or Kim Jong Il appreciates more than a broadcast studio and a couch potato. Many of our rules that attempt to limit media spending by politicians and large corporations were conceived out of concern for the traditional, perhaps too powerful synergies among incumbency, money, and the technology of broadcast.

The media are getting more powerful, but the problems are nonetheless abating. So far as the law is concerned, what exactly is a man like telegenic Pat Robertson? A political candidate, subject to strict spending limits? A broadcaster, subject to FCC regulation? A corporation that supplies its chief executive and principal stakeholders with an affluent lifestyle? And how about the countless fund-raisers, interest groups, and coalitions that can coalesce around a Robertson or a Jim Bakker, created and maintained through the fast-converging media of television, telephone, e-mail, bulletin boards, credit cards, and financial networks?

In the broadband society, the individual candidate for a specific public office may remain well defined, but the communities and the funds that back her, elect her, and lobby her endlessly thereafter will not. Here again, legal attempts to regulate are at war with electronic reality. Traditional lines among politics, art, religion, and finance all dissolve and disappear in boundless spaces of broadband networks. Any attempt to regulate "campaigns" or "political action committees" will either fail miserably or end up regulating religion, association, and free speech itself.

§14.8.2 The Electronic Theater

The traditional First Amendment choice in matters of objectionable speech has been framed as one between government-enforced silence and "more speech."[682] With the electronic media available today, however, there is a third option—private censorship by individuals, empowered to designate well in advance what or whom they prefer *not* to hear. The more power individuals have to protect themselves, the less justification there is for government to proscribe speech on their behalf.

Across the board, the prospects for privacy, property, and free speech are therefore bright. We are moving rapidly toward the day when speech in public spaces will no longer need to be regulated because the public spaces—or at least the ones of greatest importance—will be infinitely vast. On tomorrow's network, any soap-box orator will have not just a soap box in Speaker's Corner, but a personal Hyde Park. There will be room enough for any number of willing listeners. Bulletin boards, auditoriums, theaters, schools, stadia, squares, subway walls—replacements for all the traditional public fora—will be created electronically on the network at little cost, upon demand. There will be a new frontier—cyberspace, it has been called—with boundless room for every word, every expression, every thought that any human

---

[682]Whitney v. California, 274 U.S. 357, 377 (1927) (Brandeis, J., concurring).

mind may wish to communicate.[683] When space is infinite, there will be no more problem of pollution. People will be able to assemble in any numbers, at any distance, in groups that are infinitely variable.

Must scarcity then give way to excess? Must tomorrow's network place everyone at the mercy of the loud, vulgar, and intrusive; the hecklers, the pranksters, and the noisy; the infringers of copyrights and the pirates of signals? No. The new network will be boundlessly public, but also as private as a citadel. You will designate who may hear you. You will designate whom you wish to hear. You will broadcast to the world from your own bedroom or reserve your great novel for the exclusive enjoyment of a few friends. You will effortlessly screen out all racists, sexists, pornographers, drug peddlers, or anyone else whose message you find hateful. Distance used to be privacy but also isolation, peace but also loneliness. The network of tomorrow will erase distance, but only for those who choose proximity. The network will be the master of distance — it will maintain distance as easily as it will bridge it. Communication will be by consent. In such a world, people will be permitted to cry fire whenever they wish. The theater will no longer be crowded.

[683] L. Tribe, The Constitution in Cyberspace: Law and Liberty Beyond the Electronic Frontier, Keynote Address at the First Conference on Computers, Freedom, & Privacy (Mar. 26, 1991). *See also* Hammond, Regulating Broadband Communication Networks, 9 Yale J. on Reg. 181 (Winter 1992).

Glossary

1+access: *See* Dialing parity.

Access charges: Charges that long-distance carriers must pay to local exchange carriers (LECs) for their use of the local exchange in completing long-distance calls. Interstate access charges are regulated by the FCC; intrastate access charges are regulated by the states.

Access line: A communications facility extending from a customer's premises to a serving central office.

Access service: Also exchange-access service. Service that local-exchange carriers (LECs) provide to interexchange carriers (IXCs): the termination and origination of long-distance calls over a LEC's local facilities. The term is often used in contradistinction to local-exchange service, which involves purely local calls.

ADRMP: *See* Automatic dialing and recorded message player.

ADSL: *See* Asymmetric digital subscriber line.

Advanced services: High speed services, such as ADSL and cable modem, which enable users to originate and receive high-quality voice, data, graphics, and video communications.

Alternative access providers: *See* Competitive access provider.

Alternative operator service (AOS): AOS companies offer calling and billing services comparable to those offered by AT&T and local telco operators, including credit card calls, collect calls, and bill-to-third-number calls. Their services are primarily targeted at travelers, the pay phone industry, and traffic aggregators such as hotels, hospitals, and universities.

Analog transmission: A transmission system for voice, video, or data in which the transmitted signal has a continuous range of values as a function of time.

AOS: *See* Alternative operator service.

Asymmetric digital subscriber line (ADSL): A high-speed Internet access technology that uses the customer's telephone copper loop. It provides a dedicated circuit from the customer premises to the local exchange carrier's central office and can transmit data at speeds from 384 kbps to 1.5 Mbps. It is asymmetric because it transmits data along the upstream and downstream channels at different speeds.

Asynchronous communications: Communications in which the time interval between characters is variable. By contrast, in synchronous data transmission the transmitting and receiving devices can have character synchronization for a significant period of time. During the time that the devices are synchronized it is possible to transfer data without marking the extremes of each character. This makes it possible to omit stop and start bits and increase transmission efficiency and speed.

Asynchronous transfer mode (ATM): A packet-like switching and multiplexing technique with very high bandwidth.

Audiotex: Voice information services delivered over an ordinary voice telephone line or by other means—typically prerecorded messages covering such things as sports scores, jokes, and lewd messages. Local pay-per-listen audiotex services generally use a 976 number; national services use a 900 number.

ATM: *See* Asynchronous transfer mode.

Glossary

Automatic dialing and recorded message player (ADRMP): Device that enables solicitors to make thousands of calls per day at very low cost.

Automatic call delivery: A call-forwarding service for wireless telephones that automatically locates a traveling customer and forwards the call to the customer.

Automatic number identification (ANI): Similar to caller ID but cannot be blocked on a per-call basis in the same way as caller ID. Generally used by local and interexchange carriers for billing purposes, but has also been made available to businesses that receive inbound 800 and 900 number calls or dedicated lines.

Back channel: A return link in a two-way data circuit, used typically for communication in the upstream direction.

Bandwidth: Transmission capacity. A line with a relatively large bandwidth is a line capable of carrying relatively large quantities of voice, video, or data.

Basic interconnection charge: A charge paid by enhanced service providers (BOC affiliates included) for interconnection to the local exchange.

Basic services: Unadorned switching and transmission service; as defined by the FCC, service that does not store or change the content of what is transmitted (as opposed to "enhanced services"). Also referred to as plain old telephone service (POTS) and dialtone.

Basic service elements (BSEs): Signaling, switching, billing, network management, and other unbundled "building blocks" offered to providers of enhanced services by local telcos as part of the "open network architecture."

Basic serving arrangement (BSA): Fundamental tariffed switching and transport services that allow enhanced service providers to obtain access to BSEs. Examples of BSAs include line-side and trunk-side circuit-switched service, line-side and trunk-side packet-switched service, and various grades of local private line service.

BBS: *See* Bulletin Board Service.

Bell Operating Company (BOC): One of the 22 local Bell Operating Companies (e.g. Ohio Bell, Pacific Bell) that were split off from AT&T at the 1984 divestiture. The BOCs were organized into seven "Regional Holding Companies" (RHCs) or "Regional Bell Operating Companies" (RBOCs). Since 1984, some of the RBOCs have reorganized or renamed the 22 original BOCs: for example, Bell Atlantic has renamed each of its BOCs into "Bell Atlantic—[State], Inc." The term BOC is now often used interchangeably with RBOC.

Bill-and-keep: An arrangement in which neither of two interconnecting networks charges the other network for terminating traffic that originated on the other network.

Billed party preference: A service where the person paying for a long-distance pay phone call determines which long-distance carrier to use.

Binary code: A code in which every element can take only one of two forms, such as the presence or absence of a pulse. The code can be used to transmit voice, video, or data.

Bit: The smallest unit of data processed by a computer. A bit is limited to the values zero or one; the term bit is a contraction of the term binary digit.

Bits per second (bps): The number of bits transmitted per second; a unit for measuring transmission speed through a digital channel.

BOC: *See* Bell Operating Company.

Bps: *See* Bits per second.

Broadband communications: High-capacity transmission systems—typically coaxial and fiber.

BSA: *See* Basic serving arrangement.

BSE: *See* Basic service elements.

Bulletin board service (BBS): An electronic bulletin board that callers can access by computer to post messages or download the postings of others.

Bypass: Usually used to describe direct connections between customers and long-distance carriers that avoid either services (e.g., switching services) or facilities traditionally furnished by local-exchange carriers (LECs).

Byte: One byte is equivalent to eight bits of data composed of zeros and/or ones; one byte of data is used to represent one character of information such as a letter or a number.

C-band: The part of the electromagnetic spectrum at 4-8 GHz range used for satellite transmissions.

Cable modem: A high-speed Internet access technology that uses a customer's cable wire.

CALEA: *See* Communications Assistance for Law Enforcement Act.

Call blocking: A service that permits customers to block either incoming or outgoing calls from or to certain designated numbers or categories of service (e.g., 976 services).

Caller ID: A service that displays the telephone number (and sometimes also the name) of an incoming caller.

Caller ID blocking: Allows a caller to block transmission of his or her number.

CAP: *See* Competitive access provider.

Carrier access codes: Also called carrier identification codes. An access code (e.g., 10-10-321) dialed by a customer to use the services of an interexchange carrier other than the interexchange carrier with whom the customer presubscribes.

Carrier common line charge (CCLC): A traffic sensitive charge that, under the FCC's access charge rules, LECs are required to charge IXCs. The charge recovers traffic-sensitive and non-traffic-sensitive costs. The amount of the charge will decrease as non-traffic-sensitive costs are increasingly recovered through the presubscribed interexchange carrier charge (PICC).

CARS: *See* Community antenna relay service.

CATV: Community antenna television or cable TV.

CCLC: *See* Carrier common line charge.

CCS: *See* Common channel signaling.

CCSA: *See* Common control switching arrangement.

CDA: *See* Communications Decency Act of 1996.

CEI: *See* Comparably efficient interconnection.

Cellular geographic service area (CGSA): Licensee-defined area covered by an FCC cellular license; the area that the licensee's transmitters may reach. The FCC originally planned to permit license applicants to define their own CGSAs. The FCC concluded, however, that this approach would be too cumbersome to administer, so it adopted the Standard Metropolitan Statistical Area (SMSA) instead to define the area in which first round licensees could operate their systems.

Cellular service: Wireless telephone service where the service area is divided into "cells" that often cover no more than a few city blocks. Each cell is covered by a transceiver. As the customer enters a new cell, the call is handed off to the transceiver covering that cell; sometimes distinguished from personal communications services (PCS), which came later.

Central office: Also class 5 office or end office. A telephone company's premises that contains the basic local telephone switch and ancillary equipment.

Central office equipment: Equipment, such as the basic local switch, that a LEC keeps in its central office.

Centrex: Provides remote switching service for business and institutional customers, providing custom-tailored capabilities such as four-digit dialing.

CGSA: *See* Cellular geographic service area.

Cherry picking: *See* Cream skimming.

CLASS: *See* Custom local area switching service.

Class 5 office: *See* Central office.

Class 4 office: Basic long-distance switch.

CLEC: *See* Competitive local-exchange carrier.

CMRS: *See* Commercial mobile radio service.

CNS: *See* Complementary network service.

Coaxial cable: A copper sheath with a wire running down its center typically used by cable TV operators; capable of carrying very large amounts of information with low attenuation.

Collocation (also co-location): The placement of CLEC equipment on ILEC premises. Virtual collocation is its functional equivalent without the CLEC's property actually being on the ILEC's premises.

Commercial mobile radio service: Wireless service such as cellular, PCS, SMR, and paging service. All mobile services that are not commercial are deemed "private mobile radio services" (PMRSs).

Common carrier: A firm "affected with a public interest" that voluntarily holds itself open to the general public and serves all comers.

Common channel signaling (CCS): *See* Signaling System 7.

Common control switching arrangement (CCSA): A private line system used to link the various offices of a company through large switches on a local or long-distance telephone company's premises instead of through private branch exchange (PBX) switches on the customer's premises.

Common costs: Costs that need to be incurred only once to produce two services; similar in concept to joint costs.

Communications Assistance for Law Enforcement Act (CALEA): Requires telecommunications carriers to ensure that their equipment, facilities, or services used to originate, terminate, or direct communications, are capable of enabling the government—pursuant to court order—to intercept, to the exclusion of any other communications, all wires and electronic communications carried by the carrier within a service area in real time.

Communications Decency Act of 1996 (CDA): Criminalizes or regulates various forms of obscenity, indecency, violence, harassment, and the enticement of minors on telephone networks, cable, and television.

Communications Satellite Corporation (COMSAT): A quasi-governmental satellite operating company created by the U.S. government in 1962 to provide international satellite communications to carriers.

Community antenna relay service (CARS): Licensed non-common-carrier microwave facility; typically used by cable operators.

Comparably efficient interconnection (CEI): Competing enhanced service providers have the right to obtain those components of a basic local-exchange network that are needed to provide enhanced services to local telephone subscribers. Under current FCC rules, access to the components needed by competing enhanced service providers must be comparable in quality to the access used by the BOCs and AT&T in supplying their own enhanced services.

Competitive access provider (CAP): Also alternative access provider. Carrier that competes with an incumbent local-exchange carrier (ILEC) in providing a connection between end users' premises and long-distance companies' points of presence. Initially, CAPs limited themselves to providing dedicated, nonswitched facilities, but many have become competitive local-exchange carriers (CLECs) and provide a bundle of full local and long-distance services.

Competitive Impact Statement: An explanation submitted by the Department of Justice of a proposed antitrust consent decree.

Competitive local exchange carrier (CLEC): Carrier providing local-exchange service in competition with an incumbent local-exchange carrier (ILEC).

Complementary network service (CNS): Optional, unbundled basic service elements, associated with end users' access arrangements. Such services give end users access to the network for a variety of applications, not merely enhanced service applications.

Compulsory license: Allows others to use copyrighted work without the owner's consent, provided the user complies with certain formalities and pays a legislatively prescribed fee to the owner.

COMSAT: *See* Communications Satellite Corporation.

Consent Decree: A procedural mechanism frequently used by DOJ to settle an antitrust case. *See also* Divestiture Decree and GTE Decree.

Cost-plus regulation: *See* Rate-of-return regulation.

CPE: *See* Customer premises equipment.

CPNI: *See* Customer proprietary network information.

Cream skimming: Also cherry picking. A business strategy, adopted by MCI in the early days of long-distance competition and by most competitive local-exchange carriers (CLECs) today, that focuses competitive efforts on the lowest cost, highest value priced customers (usually businesses) and forgoing other customers (usually residences); targeting services where profit margins are high (e.g., voice mail).

Cross-polarization: The use of two transmitters, both operating on the same frequency; one transmitter-receiver pair is vertically polarized, the other horizontally polarized.

Cross subsidy: A variety of pricing or costing practices; *e.g.,* when one service or product is priced above cost so that another service or product can be priced below cost, or when costs from one product are shifted to another product.

Custom local area switching service (CLASS): A cluster of advanced switching services providing enhanced call management—services include caller ID, call waiting, call forwarding, variable ringing patterns, call blocking, call tracing.

Customer premises equipment (CPE): Products (including ordinary telephones, modems, fax machines, computers, etc.) that interconnect with the network on the customer's premises, or (if collocated on telco premises) that are owned by someone other than the telco itself.

Customer-programmers: Customers of DBS carriers that lease channels to distribute programming directly to individual viewers.

Customer proprietary network information (CPNI): Information about a customer's use of network services that an LEC may acquire in providing those services.

Cyberspace: The virtual space where messages and information reside in transit between telephones, televisions, and computers.

Dark fiber: An unlit fiber-optic line (i.e., a line with no associated electronics needed to provide a communications transmission); the physical facility itself, rather than a certain amount of bandwidth or transport capacity.

DBS: *See* Direct broadcast satellite.

Dedicated line: Unswitched line providing user-defined, point-to-point connection.

Dialing parity: The ability to route a call to a CLEC without dialing an access code. Section 251(b)(3) of the 1996 Act

requires LECs to provide dialing parity to competing providers of telephone exchange and toll service.

Digital: Use of a binary code to represent voice, video, or data.

Digital subscriber line access multiplexer (DSLAM): A network
device located in the local exchange customer's serving wire
center that is used to provide ADSL service.

Digital television (DTV): Uses digital rather than analog for
transmitting and receiving broadcast signals. Digital signals
are superior to analog signals because they do not generate noise and are more resistant to signal interference.

Direct broadcast satellite (DBS): A satellite transmitting television programming to small and relatively inexpensive dish
antennas.

Directory services: Electronic and printed name, telephone
number, and address listings.

Divestiture Decree: The 1982 decree that broke up the Bell System into AT&T and the seven RBOCs and imposed line-of-
business restrictions on local Bell Companies. Also referred
to as the Modification of Final Judgement or MFJ because
it "modified" the consent decree entered against AT&T's
Western Electric in 1956.

DOJ: Department of Justice (Antitrust Division); the "prime
mover" in most government antitrust litigation involving
telecommunications.

Dominant carriers: Carriers believed to have market power.
Dominant carriers are regulated by the FCC to a greater
extent than carriers that are nondominant.

Downlink: The portion of a satellite transmission link traveling
from the satellite to the ground.

DSLAM: *See* Digital subscriber line access multiplexer.

DTV: *See* Digital television.

Dumb terminal: Voice or video terminal that relies on remote
switches or computers for most of its electronic storage or
processing.

EAS: *See* Non-optional extended area service.

ECPA: *See* Electronic Communications Privacy Act of 1986.

Electronic Communications Privacy Act of 1986 (ECPA): Updates and clarifies privacy protections in light of new computer and telecommunications technologies.

Electronic publishing: The provision of an electronic database, generally accessed remotely with a computer and modem, or through a radio-receiving device, or by way of a compact optical disk and personal computer.

Encryption: The process by which data are transformed into an unintelligible series of bits—"cipher text"—that can only be read by the use of a deciphering key.

End office: *See* Central office.

End user: A customer (i.e., at the "end" of the telephone line).

Enhanced services: A telephone service that is not "basic" (i.e., that acts on the format, content, code, protocol, or similar aspects of the subscriber's transmitted information or provides the subscriber with additional, different, or restructured information).

Enhanced service providers (ESP): Providers that offer enhanced services. *See also* Information services.

Enhanced specialized mobile radio (ESMR): Two-way dispatch service with the ability also to provide wireless telephone service.

Equal access: The provision of "exchange-access" and "exchange services for such access" to all long-distance carriers on equal terms. Equal access was a cornerstone of the divestiture decree and was intended to place AT&T and competing providers of long distance and information services on functionally equal terms. *See also* Dialing parity.

ESP: *See* Enhanced service providers.

Exchange: A geographic area where all customers face the same pricing and service options; an exchange can have one or more central offices and any customer within the exchange can obtain service from any of those offices; in the Divestiture Decree it was used (incorrectly) as a synonym for LATA; an exchange can also refer to the central office switch.

Exchange-access: *See* Access service.

Facilities-based carrier: Local or long-distance company that carries traffic largely over its own transmission and switching facilities; distinguished from "resellers" that simply buy service wholesale from facilities-based carriers for resale to end users.

Facilities bypass: Switching and transmission facilities that compete head-to-head with local telco facilities and services. Usually used to refer to the use of such facilities for the provision of non-ILEC local access for long-distance calls.

Fair Credit Reporting Act (FCRA): First information privacy legislation attempting to address the concerns of the public about the credit bureau's misuse of personal information.

FCC: Federal Communications Commission.

FCRA: *See* Fair Credit Reporting Act.

FDC: *See* Fully distributed costing.

Fiber optics: Thin, lightweight cables made of glass or plastic capable of transmitting very large quantities of information.

FISA: *See* Foreign Intelligence Surveillance Act.

Fixed satellite service (FSS): Communications between fixed earth stations via one or more satellites. FSS operates principally in the C-band and is regulated by the FCC's Common Carrier Bureau.

Footprint: The geographic reach of a particular communications service; the portion of the earth's surface where the signals from a satellite can be received.

Foreign attachment (obsolete term): Non-Bell System provided product interconnected with Bell's network. The old Bell System, with the support of federal and state regulators, long forbade foreign attachments in its tariffs.

Foreign exchange (FX): A private line service connecting customer premises in one exchange area directly to the local phone exchange in another.

Foreign Intelligence Surveillance Act (FISA): Authorizes the President, through the Attorney General, to conduct electronic surveillance in the United States after obtaining authorization from a judicial panel.

Glossary

Frame relay: A high-speed packet transport technology that includes such features as low error-rate and software-based switching.

FSS: *See* Fixed satellite service.

Fully distributed costing (FDC): Method of allocating common costs such that the costs are allocated based on each service's contributing share of those costs.

FX: *See* Foreign exchange.

Gateways: Host computers that enable a caller to access additional information service providers.

GTE Decree: The 1984 Consent Decree that settled the government's antitrust suit against GTE.

HDTV: *See* High definition television.

Hertz (Hz): A unit for measuring frequency in cycles per second; one hertz equals one cycle per second.

High definition television (HDTV): Television that offers picture quality comparable to 35 mm photographic film. Also referred to as Advanced Television (ATV).

HTTP: *See* Hypertext transfer protocol.

Hypertext transfer protocol (HTTP): The language that Web clients and servers use to communicate.

Hz: *See* Hertz.

Incumbent local-exchange carriers (ILECs): Term used to refer to the traditional local telephone companies, usually in contrast to CLECs.

IMTS: *See* International message toll service.

IN: *See* Intelligent network.

Incremental cost: The additional cost of providing a service.

Incentive regulation: *See* Price-cap regulation.

Independent telephone company: Non-Bell incumbent local telephone company (e.g., GTE, United Telecommunications, Inc. (Sprint), etc.).

Industry standard architecture (ISA): The bus architecture on the motherboard of MS-DOS computers.

Information services: The offering of a capability for generating, acquiring, storing, transforming, processing, retrieving, utilizing, or making available information via telecommunications. All enhanced services are information services but not all information services are enhanced services.

Inside wiring: Telephone wiring on a customer premises.

Integrated services digital network (ISDN): Standardized all-digital network that integrates voice and data communications through existing copper wires. Provides access to the Internet at 128 kbps.

Intelligent network (IN): Also advanced intelligent network or AIN; service independent platforms that give local-exchange carriers the ability to provide new services without reprogramming individual central office switches. IN allows LECs to become less dependent on vendors and gives them more flexibility to provide customized services.

INTELSAT: *See* International Telecommunications Satellite Consortium.

Interexchange carrier (IXC): Long-distance company, like AT&T, MCI WorldCom, or Sprint. An IXC carries communications traffic across LATA boundaries. BOCs provide intraLATA "long-distance" (toll) services that did not fall within the divestiture decree's definition of "interexchange." BOCs are also permitted to provide intraLATA "long-distance" service under the Telecommunications Act of 1996.

Interexchange service: The carriage of voice or data traffic across LATA boundaries.

International message telephone service (IMTS): International voice calls over the public switched network.

International record carrier (IRC): A carrier of international telegraph, telex, and data services.

International settlements policy (ISP): A series of rules promulgated by the FCC to reform the process by which U.S. and foreign carriers settle their accounts. ISP rules have become more flexible as competition in international markets has increased.

Glossary

International Telecommunications Satellite Consortium (INTELSAT): A multinational organization whose original mission was to deploy a worldwide commercial telecommunications satellite system.

International Telecommunications Union (ITU): Agency of the United Nations with general jurisdiction over the international aspects of telecommunications.

Internet service provider (ISP): Firm that provides access to the Internet.

Interoffice transmission facilities (IOF): Transmission facilities between end offices and a tandem switch, between LEC end offices or between LEC offices and those of competing carriers.

Intersystem handoff: Usually used in reference to connections between mobile switching offices; handoff enables the user of a cellular phone to remain connected continuously even when driving or flying from one service territory to another.

Internet Backbone: A long-haul network used to connect Internet service providers.

Internet Protocol (IP): A standard protocol designed for use in interconnected systems of packet-switched computer communication networks. The Internet Protocol allows packets of data to be transmitted from their source to destinations. Sources and destinations are computers identified by a numerical IP address (e.g., 255.122.155.255). *See also* Transmission Control Protocol.

IRC: *See* International record carrier.

ISA: *See* Industry standard architecture.

ISP (1): *See* International settlements policy.

ISP (2): *See* Internet service provider.

ISDN: *See* Integrated services digital network.

ITU: *See* International Telecommunications Union.

IVDS: *See* Interactive video data service.

IXC: *See* Interexchange carrier.

Joint Cost Order: The FCC's principle regulatory vehicle to prevent cost shifting between regulated and unregulated telco businesses.

Joint costs: *See* Common costs.

Kingsbury Commitment: The Bell System's 1914 agreement with the Department of Justice to refrain from acquiring and denying interconnection to competing independent telephone companies. Seen by many as the beginning of the "regulated monopoly" era in which the Bell System agreed to rate regulation in exchange for the grant of an "exclusive franchise" to provide phone service.

Ku-band: Spectrum used for satellite communications in the 12- to 18-GHz range.

LAN: *See* Local area network.

Landing fees: Prices carriers pay to foreign PTTs to have their calls terminated.

Last mile: The first and final leg of a phone call—the twisted pair of copper wires that connect to the end user's premises.

LATA: *See* Local access and transport area.

Leaky PBX: A private exchange that switches calls from distant users into the local public network. This "leakage" is of regulatory interest because incoming calls handled through public local exchanges are assessed access charges that private exchanges avoid.

LEC: *See* Local-exchange carrier.

Line-of-business restrictions: Imposed upon the Bell companies by the divestiture decree, the line-of-business restrictions originally forbade them to provide interexchange or information services, to manufacture telecommunications equipment or CPE, or to engage in other nontelephone businesses.

Line side: Connects the telephone switch to end users.

LMDS: *See* Local multipoint distribution service.

Local access and transport area (LATA): Geographically based service islands created by the divestiture decree, marking the boundaries beyond which a Bell company may not carry telephone calls. LATAs generally center upon a metropolitan area (a Standard Metropolitan Statistical Area) or a community of interest. There are 164 LATAs.

Local area network (LAN): Dedicated data communications facilities that provide high-speed addressable connections, typically for intraoffice communications.

Local-exchange: *See* Exchange.

Local-exchange carrier (LEC): Provider of local telephone service. Includes the Bell companies, all independent telcos, and now their competitors.

Local multipoint distribution service (LMDS): A service providing multiple channels of video programming through high-frequency microwave channels.

Low-power television (LPTV): Provision of scrambled television channels via VHF or UHF spectra as a subscription television service.

LPTV: *See* Low-power television.

MAN: *See* Metropolitan area networks.

MDS: *See* Multipoint distribution service.

Message toll service (MTS): Ordinary, switched, long-distance service charged on a usage-sensitive basis.

Metropolitan area networks (MANs): Networks offered by telco competitors, which typically provide business with alternative connections among their offices and to long-distance carriers, usually in the form of high-capacity, digital, fiber-optic links.

MFJ: *See* Modification of Final Judgement.

Microprocessor: An electronic circuit that serves as the computer's brain. Microprocessors perform mathematical, logical, and control functions.

Microwave communications: High-capacity, point-to-point, radio services. These services have long been used for local and long-distance telephone traffic ("MCI" originally stood for Microwave Communications Inc.). Though long seen as incapable of providing high-quality voice connections, and largely replaced by fiber in long-distance networks, microwave communications have seen a recent resurgence, particularly in local markets, because of the growth in data traffic with their enhanced error correction capabilities.

Miscellaneous common carriers: Relayers of video and audio signals via terrestrial microwave. *See* Radio common carriers.

MMDS: *See* Multipoint multichannel distribution service.

Mobile satellite service (MSS): Satellite service that serves ships, aircraft, and land vehicles in the 1610–1626.5/2483.5–2500 MHz (1.6/2.4 GHz) frequency bands.

Mobile telephone switching office (MTSO): The local exchange office of a cellular system.

Modification of Final Judgment (MFJ): *See* Divestiture Decree.

Motion picture experts group (MPEG): Devises standards for compression of video programming. The first two MPEG compression standards were MPEG1 (which offers VCR-quality video in 1.5 Mbps) and MPEG2 (which offers higher quality video at 3 to 15 Mbps).

MPEG: *See* Motion picture experts group.

MSA: Metropolitan statistical area. *See* Standard metropolitan statistical area.

MSO: *See* Multiple system operator.

MSS: *See* Mobile satellite service.

MTS: *See* Message toll service.

MTSO: *See* Mobile telephone switching office.

Multiple system operator (MSO): Cable conglomerate; an operator of more than one cable television franchise. For example, AT&T's TCI is an MSO operating cable television systems in Washington, D.C., Chicago, IL, and elsewhere.

Multiplexer: A device that interleaves multiple signals and transmits them down a single, high-capacity communication channel.

Multipoint distribution service (MDS): Also multipoint multichannel distribution service (MMDS); a wireless cable service; microwave radio channels are used to transmit video programming.

Narrowband: Subvoice grade channels capable of carrying 100 to 200 bits per second; sometimes refers to ordinary telephone service or any transmission that is not "broadband."

National Exchange Carrier Association (NECA): An organization established by the FCC to oversee the "pooling" and disbursement of local telco revenues to promote universal service.

National research and educational network (NREN): A fiber-optic network capable of transmitting data among the nation's leading research centers several times faster than previous Internet speeds.

National Television Systems Committee (NTSC): This industry consortium of major electronics manufacturers set the standard for the generation, transmission, and reception of television communications at 525 lines per frame with 30 frames per second.

NCTE: *See* Network channel terminating equipment.

NECA: *See* National Exchange Carrier Association.

Network channel terminating equipment (NCTE): Equipment through which phones, modems, or computers connect to a digital network.

Network control signaling: Electronic signaling used to set up and supervise calls by controlling switches and circuits in a network.

Network interface device (NID): A device located between a telephone protector and inside wiring to separate the customer's equipment from the network; one of the unbundled network elements.

Network utilization rate element: A charge paid by carrier-affiliated, enhanced service providers to account for the distortion or degradation of basic services caused by the affiliate's use of the network.

NID: *See* Network interface device.

Nondominant carrier: Carriers (as defined by the FCC) that are unable to raise price, curtail overall output, or engage in predatory or discriminatory pricing because they lack market power.

Nonoptional extended area service (EAS): Nontoll (i.e., "free") calling to nearby local exchanges, even across LATA boundaries.

Non-traffic-sensitive costs (NTS costs): Costs that do not vary with usage. The local loop is an example of an NTS cost

because its cost is not a function of the number of calls that
it transports.

NREN: *See* National research and educational network.

NTSC: *See* National Television Systems Committee.

NTS costs: *See* Non-traffic-sensitive costs.

Number portability: The capability of allowing a subscriber to
continue using the same telephone number even when
changing carriers.

Number translation: The process of converting a number (such
as an 800 number) into an ordinary telephone number for
routing through the network.

NXX codes: The first three digits in a telephone number after
the area code. Every telephone switch is assigned at least
one NXX code. In telephone convention, "N" is any number from 2 to 9; "X" is any number from 0 to 9.

OCC: *See* Other common carriers.

Official services: Administrative or business-related communications by a BOC within its own offices or with its customers.

ONA: *See* Open network architecture.

Open network architecture (ONA): FCC Regime designed to
unbundle basic network features in order to facilitate interconnection with enhanced/information services that outside vendors provide.

Open video system (OVS): Video dialtone's less restrictive successor.

Operation support systems (OSS): The computerized pre-
ordering, ordering, provisioning, maintenance and repair,
and billing systems that incumbents employ—as well as
information these systems contain.

Operator service: Service provided to process and bill "dial 0"
calls, including calling card and credit card calls, collect
calls, and third number billing calls.

Other common carriers (OCC): Outdated term used to refer to
long-distance carriers other than AT&T.

OVS: *See* Open video system.

Ozark Plan: The 1970 separations agreement allocating common costs of non-traffic-sensitive subscriber plant between interstate and intrastate accounts.

Packet (also Packet Switch): A device that receives unstructured data signals and electronically wraps and addresses them in "packets" suitable for efficient transmission through the network.

Pay-per-view (PPV): Cable television service in which a particular broadcast (e.g., *Wrestlemania*) is sold directly to viewers.

PBX: *See* Private branch exchange.

PCA: *See* Protective connecting arrangement.

PCS: *See* Personal communications service.

Personal communications service (PCS): Wireless service similar to cellular. In the early 1980s, the FCC licensed two cellular providers for each franchise area. In the 1990s, the FCC licensed a set of additional (up to five) PCS providers per area. PCS is transmitted over a higher frequency than cellular.

PIC: *See* Presubscribed interexchange carrier.

PICC: *See* Presubscribed interexchange carrier charge.

Pixel: Short for "picture element"; the smallest unit of a video picture that may be modified in intensity or turned on and off. The greater the number of pixels, the higher the resolution on a screen, or facsimile.

Plain old telephone service (POTS): Basic, no-frills telephone service; sometimes referred to as dialtone.

Plan of reorganization (POR): A plan drafted by AT&T, then reviewed and modified by the Department of Justice and Judge Greene, for implementing the breakup of the old Bell System.

Platform: The sum of the various constituent network elements. FCC rules allow a CLEC to provide local service by leasing the incumbent's entire preassembled network (i.e., platform). This makes the 1996 Act's resale provision redundant, except that platform prices usually are substantially lower than the wholesale prices available for resale.

Point-to-point connections: A continuous, nonswitched connection between equipment at different points.

Point of presence (POP): IXC facility at which the IXC's network connects with a LEC's network. The large IXCs have at least one POP in almost every LATA. Many have numerous POPs in particular LATAs, primarily to facilitate local bypass.

Pole attachments: The attachment of wires belonging to a cable operator on a telephone or electric company's poles.

POP: *See* Point of presence.

POR: *See* Plan of reorganization.

POTS: *See* Plain old telephone service.

PPV: *See* Pay-per-view.

Presubscribed interexchange carrier (PIC): The carrier designated by a subscriber to carry his or her long-distance traffic.

Presubscribed interexchange carrier charge (PICC): A flat charge paid by IXCs to LECs that, together with the subscriber line charge (SLC), recovers the non-traffic-sensitive costs of interstate access.

Presubscription: A subscriber's ability to designate in advance which long-distance carrier will carry ordinary long-distance calls placed on his or her line.

Price-averaging: *See* Rate averaging.

Price-cap regulation: Regulation that places a ceiling (and in some instances also a floor) on prices rather than attempting to assess costs and rates of return. Generally seen as more successful than rate-of-return regulation in providing carriers with an incentive to become more efficient.

Primary instrument concept (obsolete): The primary instrument concept was an attempt by the pre-divestiture Bell System to require every regular subscriber to lease at least one set from the telephone company. The proposal was summarily rejected by the FCC.

Priority call: Service that provides a distinctive ring for high priority calls.

Private branch exchange (PBX): An on-premises switch that operates as a private "local-exchange," typically providing reduced-digit dialing for internal calls.

Private line charge: A flat $25-a-month "special access" surcharge on private lines supplied by local telcos to originate or terminate interstate connections.

Private line service: Also, leased-line or non-switched service. Term used in contradistinction to switched service. A subscriber to private line service buys exclusive access to a particular circuit, which is at her disposal at all times. Private line service is usually priced on a flat-rated basis. Traditional private line service is being replaced increasingly by "virtual private line service," and "software defined networks." These newer services mimic private lines: switches are programmed to guarantee the desired amount of bandwidth on demand except that they use switched circuits.

Protective connecting arrangement (PCA) (obsolete): Telco-supplied device proposed during the transition to competition in the provision of CPE. PCAs were ostensibly required to protect the public network from the possibility of damage caused by privately supplied equipment.

Protocol conversion: Electronic translation between machines that use different formats. Protocol conversion is invisible to end users.

PSTN: *See* Public switched telephone network.

Public switched telephone network: Usually refers to an ILEC's network.

Radio common carrier: A more common name for miscellaneous common carrier; a radio service provider not engaged in the business of providing either a public landline message telephone service or public message telegraph service.

Ramsey pricing: A pricing method that maximizes economic efficiency by recovering a disproportionate amount of fixed costs from consumers whose demand is the least elastic (i.e., whose quantity demanded is least sensitive to changes in price).

RARCs: *See* Regional Administrative Radio Conferences.

Rate-averaging: A pricing strategy where customers on different routes are charged uniform prices despite the cost difference associated with servicing those customers.

Rate-of-return regulation: A form of regulation under which firms can set prices to recover allowable operating expenses and earn enough of a return to cover the cost of capital acquired in debt and equity markets. Formerly, the primary means of regulating the price of telephone service. The FCC and many states have since adopted price-cap regulation.

Rate base: A telephone company's undepreciated investment.

RBOC: Regional Bell Operating Company. Also sometimes called regional holding company (RHC). *See also* Bell Operating Company.

Record carriage: Originally telegraph services, which have since been eclipsed by facsimile, electronic mail, and other data services.

Reciprocal compensation: Compensation paid by one LEC to another LEC for the recovery of the marginal cost of terminating a call on the terminating carrier's network.

Remote call processing: Processing of a call outside the LATA in which it originates.

RHC: Regional holding company. *See* Bell Operating Company.

Routers: Specialized computers that perform functions for data networks that are roughly analogous to the role of a switch in the switched telephone network.

RSA: *See* Rural service area.

Rural service area (RSA): Service area defined by the FCC for allotting cellular licenses in rural areas.

Satellite master antenna television (SMATV): A private cable service; a satellite dish connected to a coaxial wire, usually operated by a landlord on behalf of tenants in a multitenant building.

SCSA: *See* Standard consolidated statistical area.

SDN: *See* Software-defined network.

Send-a-call service: A telco service that permits a caller to record a message to be dispatched later.

Separations: The regulatory division of telco assets between interstate and intrastate jurisdictions.

Separations Manual: Published by the National Association of Regulatory Utility Commissioners (NARUC) and approved by the FCC (incorporated under 47 C.F.R. §67.1), the Separations Manual provides a standardized procedure for allocating costs to intra- and interstate jurisdictions.

Service bypass: Generally refers to the use of dedicated private lines rather than switched service for connecting between a customer and a long-distance carrier. The customer still buys transport from the local telco but "bypasses" the telco switch.

Set-top box: Small computer that sits on top of a television set and connects the coaxial cable and television.

Shared tenant services: Services provided to multiple dwelling units (MDUs) and large business locations. Though MDUs are part of the residential market (which is generally less attractive to CLECs than the business market), MDUs tend to be the first places where residential competition occurs. This is so because the cost of serving an MDU tends to be much lower than the cost of serving individual homes: a single trunk to the MDU gives the CLEC access to many customers. A CLEC can provide service simply by installing multiplexing equipment in the MDU and connecting it to the already existing inside wiring.

Signaling: Electronic information about calls, transferred between switches and computers.

Signaling System 7 (SS7): Out-of-band signaling network overlaid on the public telephone network to provide network management. An SS7 signal is a request to any number of other facilities and switches down the line to open up circuits, engage billing systems, and otherwise prepare to carry, process, bill, answer, block, screen, record, or respond to a call.

Slamming: Changing a customer's presubscribed interexchange carriers without the customer's permission.

SLC: *See* Subscriber line charge.

SMDS: *See* Switched multimegabit data service.

SMSA: *See* Standard metropolitan statistical area.

Software-defined network (SDN): A virtual private network service for large customers.

SONET: *See* Synchronous optical network.

Spamming: Mass mailing of unsolicited e-mails.

Special access line: A dedicated (unswitched) line between a long-distance carrier and a customer.

Specialized common carrier: *See* Other common carrier (OCC).

Spectrum unbundling: Unbundling channels of a single wire. Allows a single wire to transport both voice services provided by a LEC, and data services provided by an unaffiliated data carrier.

SS7: *See* Signaling system 7.

Standard consolidated statistical area (SCSA): Combinations of SMSAs adjacent to one another.

Standard metropolitan statistical area (SMSA): U.S. Department of Commerce designation of a region, including a core city and its suburbs, with a population of at least 50,000.

STV: *See* Subscription television.

Subscriber Line Charge (SLC): Flat-rated charge that, under the FCC's access-charge rules, LECs are required to charge their subscribers. The FCC instituted the SLC in 1983 as part of a new access-charge regime in anticipation of the Bell System's divestiture. The FCC had originally intended to recover all non-traffic-sensitive access costs from end users through the SLC, but this proved politically unpalatable. Instead, the FCC capped the SLC at $3.50 (for residential lines) and required LECs to recover any costs above that amount from IXCs in the form of a usage-sensitive carrier common line charge (CCL).

Subscription television (STV): Pay TV service on scrambled UHF or VHF signals.

Superstation: A television broadcast station, other than a network station, whose signal is retransmitted by satellite. Prime examples are TBS in Atlanta and WGN in Chicago.

Switched line: A regular phone line routed through a LEC end-office switch.

Switched multimegabit data service (SMDS): A high-capacity, switched transport service that offers seamless interconnection with ethernet, token-ring, FDDI, and ATM networks, as well as with frame relay and dedicated private lines.

Switched service: The opposite of private line service in that an end user's transmission path varies with each call. *See also* Private line service.

Switched video: An addressable video network capable of originating, routing, and delivering video signals in the same way as telephone calls ("video dial tone").

Synchronous optical network (SONET): A protocol for high-capacity transmission of information using fiber optics.

T-1 service (also DS1): A 1.5 megabit/sec digital channel, the equivalent of 24 simultaneous telephone calls.

Tandem switch: Also access tandem. A LEC or IXC switch that has only trunks (no lines) connected to it. Tandem switches are no different from long-distance switches, and the same machine (e.g., Lucent's 4ESS) is often used for both purposes. The equal access obligations imposed on BOCs in the wake of divestiture increased the proliferation of tandem switches. BOCs must give equal access to IXCs, even if an IXC has only a single POP in a LATA where a LEC has multiple end offices. IXCs connect to the LEC's tandem, which then routes traffic to the appropriate end office.

TCP: *See* Transmission Control Protocol.

TCPA: *See* Telephone Consumer Protection Act of 1991.

TDD: *See* Telecommunications devices for the deaf.

TDDRA: *See* Telephone Disclosure and Dispute Resolution Act of 1992.

Telecommunications devices for the deaf (TDD): Typewriter-like devices that connect to a telephone for use by speech- and hearing-impaired customers.

Telco: Telephone company; used in the industry as a synonym for LEC (i.e., ILEC).

Telemessaging service: Voice mail and other services used to record, transcribe or relay messages.

Telephone Consumer Protection Act of 1991 (TCPA): Law that bans automatically dialed or prerecorded telephone calls and faxes.

Telephone Disclosure and Dispute Resolution Act of 1992 (TDDRA): Directs the FCC to promulgate rules making it unlawful to manufacture or import any radio scanner capable of intercepting cellular radio transmissions.

Teleport: A cluster of satellite earth stations, both uplinks and downlinks, connected to a community by way of microwave, fiber-optic or coax cable, and engineered to carry traffic in both directions.

Television receive-only antenna (TVRO): Satellite dish six to ten feet in diameter, typically used by bars, hotels, and individuals to receive video programming directly from geostationary satellites.

TELRIC: *See* Total element long-run incremental cost.

Terminal equipment: *See* Customer premises equipment.

Time channeling: Restricting dial-a-porn and similar services to evening hours of operation.

Total element long-run incremental cost (TELRIC): Measure for determining the price at which an ILEC must sell unbundled elements to CLECs. This measure is a so-called forward-looking one. It does not allow the ILEC to charge a CLEC its actual costs, but only costs that it would incur if it would construct the element today. The FCC adopted this measure in its August 8, 1996, Interconnection Order.

Total service long-run incremental cost (TSLRIC): Same as TELRIC, except that TSLRIC is a measure for pricing whole services (say, for resale), not mere network elements.

Transmission Control Protocol (TCP): A protocol that controls the division of information into packets as well as packet identification and addressing. This is distinguished from Internet Protocol (IP), which transfers the packets from host to host.

Transponder: A radio device (typically in a satellite) that receives and then rebroadcasts signals.

Trunk side: A telephone switch's connections to other switches, as distinguished from its connection to customers. *See also* Line side.

Trunks: Facilities (usually high-capacity copper or fiber-optic cables) that carry communications between switching equipment, as distinguished from facilities that extend between switching equipment and customer premises equipment.

TVRO: *See* Television receive-only antenna.

UHF: Ultra high frequency spectrum between 300 MHz and 3 GHz assigned to TV channels 14 to 69.

Unbundled network element (UNE): One of the network elements (e.g., loop or switch) that, under the Telecommunications Act of 1996, ILECs must lease to CLECs at cost-based rates.

UNE: *See* Unbundled network element.

Uniform resource locator (URL): A Web page's unique address.

Uniform system of accounts (USOA): The FCC-mandated accounting system.

Uplink: The portion of a satellite transmission traveling from the ground to the satellite.

URL: *See* Uniform resource locator.

USOA: *See* Uniform system of accounts.

Value added network (VAN): In general, networks that provide anything more than "plain old telephone service." The term usually refers to data networks that provide packetizing and protocol conversion.

Value added resellers: Companies that lease circuits from common carriers to provided packet-switching, protocol, and speed conversion, and security, administrative, and billing features.

VAN: *See* Value added network.

VBI: *See* Vertical blanking interval.

V-chip: Device in a television screen that screens unwanted broadcasts. It detects a rating signal imbedded in a broadcast and blocks any broadcast that exceeds a certain violence rating.

VDT: *See* Video dialtone.

Vertical blanking interval (VBI): The interval between television frames; it is possible to provide nonbroadcast service within this interval.

Very small aperture terminal (VSAT): A small satellite ground station antenna for one- or two-way communications.

VHF: Very high frequency spectrum between 30 MHz and 300 MHz assigned to TV channels 2 to 13.

Video dialtone (VDT): Now defunct FCC regulatory regime for ILEC-operated addressable video network capable of originating, routing, and delivering video signals in the same way as telephone calls ("switched video").

Videotex: Also videotext; Information services providing text and/or graphics.

Virtual private network: A private network (typically including such features as reduced-digit dialing) implemented by means of specialized carrier software; the facilities used are not dedicated to the customer.

Voice-messaging (voice mail): Services similar to those of an answering machine, implemented in the public network, typically including additional capabilities and convenience such as the ability to leave messages when a line is busy.

VSAT: *See* Very small aperture terminal.

WAN: *See* Wide area networks.

WARCs: *See* World Administrative Conferences.

WATS: *See* Wide area telecommunications services.

Waveguide: Another name for fiber-optic transmission media.

Western Electric Company: The part of the Bell System that manufactured equipment before divestiture. After divestiture, AT&T renamed it AT&T Network Systems (AT&T-NS). At AT&T's 1995 trivestiture, AT&T-NS was spun off and renamed Lucent.

Wide area networks (WAN): Private or virtual private data networks that link together offices and machines not clustered in a single building or campus.

Wide area telecommunications services (WATS): AT&T's long-distance discount service for volume users.

World Administrative Conferences (WARCs): A part of the ITU, responsible for assigning international frequencies.

X.25: Internationally agreed-upon packet-switching protocol that defines the standards for communication between the data terminating equipment (customer's premises equipment) and the data communications equipment (the packet switch).

Table of Cases

Table of Cases

Table of Cases

Table of Cases

Table of Cases

Table of Cases

Table of Cases

Table of Cases

Table of Cases

Table of Cases

Table of Cases

Table of Cases

Table of
Secondary
Authorities

[References are to section numbers.]

A

Allen, Klan, Cloth and Constitution: Anti-Mask Laws and the First Amendment, 25 Ga. L. Rev. 819 (1991), 14.8

Allocating Copyright Liability to Telecommunications Common Carriers Supplying Cable Systems, 67 Minn. L. Rev. 963 (1983), 14.4.2

American Bar Ass'n, Antitrust Section, Antitrust Law Developments, (3d ed. 1992), 7.3.2, 7.4.1, 7.4.2

Anderson, Modifications of Antitrust Consent Decrees: Over a Double Barrel, 84 Mich. L. Rev. 134 (1985), 4.5

Anthony, R.A., Towards Simplicity and Rationality in Comparative Broadcast Licensing Proceedings, 24 Stan. L. Rev. (1971), 10.3

Areeda, P. & Hovenkamp, H., Antitrust Law (1998), 7.6

Areeda, P. & Hovenkamp, H., Antitrust Law (1997 Supp.), 4.2.5

Areeda, P. & Hovenkamp, H., Antitrust Law (1978), 4.5

Areeda, P., Hovenkamp, H., & Solow, J., Antitrust Law (1996), 7.4.2

Areeda, P. & Kaplow, L., Antitrust Analysis (4th ed. 1988), 7.6

Areeda, P. & Turner, D., Antitrust Law (1980), 7.1, 7.4.1, 7.4.2, 9.4.3

Areeda, P. & Turner, D., Predatory Pricing and Related Practices Under Section 2 of the Sherman Act, 88 Harv. L. Rev. 697 (1975), 4.2.4

Averch, H. & Johnson, L., Behavior of the Firm Under Regulatory Constraint, 52 Am. Econ. Rev. 1052 (1962), 2.2.3

Ayres & Miller, "I'll Sell It To You At Cost": Legal Methods to Promote Retail Markup Disclosure, 84 Nw. U.L. Rev. 1047 (1990), 4.2.5

B

Table of Secondary Authorities

Table of Secondary Authorities

Table of Secondary Authorities

Table of Secondary Authorities

N

Table of Secondary Authorities

Note, Who Owns the Air? Unscrambling the Satellite Viewing Rights Dilemma, 20 Loy. L.A. L. Rev. 145 (1986), 14.3.2

O

O'Connor, B., Universal Service and NREN, 6 Edge 75 (1991), 6.1.2

P

Paglin, A Legislative History of the Communications Act of 1934 (1989), 6.1.1

Palmer, Rate-of-Return versus Price Caps: The Long-distance Regulation Battle, 14 Columbia-VLA J. of L. and Arts 571 (1990), 2.2.3, 3.12.3

Panzar, J. & Willig, R., Free Entry and the Sustainability of Natural Monopoly, 8 Bell J. Econ. 1 (1977), 2.2.1

Paper, L.J., Getting Personal: The Politics of the Wireless Revolution, Institute for Information Studies (1996), 10.3.5, 11.8.3

Papke, D.R., Understanding "Rights" in Contemporary American Discourse, 2 Mich. J. Race & L. 521 (1997), 14.6.8

Pay Television Piracy: Does Section 605 of the Federal Communications Act of 1934 Prohibit Signal Piracy–and Should It?, 10 Wm. Mitchell L. Rev. 531 (1984), 14.3.2

Perritt, H.H., Jr., The Congress, The Courts and Computer Based Communications Networks: Answering Questions About Access and Content Control Introduction, 38 Vill. L. Rev. 319 (1993), 14.6.7

Perritt, H.H., Jr., Tort Liability, the First Amendment, and Equal Access to Electronic Networks, 5 Harv. J.L. & Tech. 65 (1992), 14.4.1, 14.6.7, 14.8.1

Perritt, H.H., Jr., Tort Liability, the First Amendment, Equal Access and Commercialization of Electronic Networks, 2 Electronic Networking 29 (1992), 14.8.1

Phillips, A., The Impossibility of Competition in Telecommunications: Public Policy Gone Awry, in Regulation Reform and Public Utilities 7 (Crew ed. 1982), 2.1.2

Pierce, Reconsidering the Roles of Regulation and Competition in the Natural Gas Industry, 97 Harv. L. Rev. 345 (1983), 4.2.5

Pool, I., Technologies of Freedom (1983), 1.2.4, 1.3.3, 1.8, 14.6.1, 14.6.9, 14.8

Poole, R., Unnatural Monopolies: The Case for Deregulating Public Utilities (1985), 2.1.2

Posner, R., A Statistical Study of Antitrust Enforcement, 13 J.L. & Econ. 365 (1970), 4.5

Posner, R., Natural Monopoly and Its Regulation, 21 Stan. L. Rev. 548 (1969), 2.1.2, 3.11.3

Posner, R., Taxation by Regulation, 2 Bell J. Econ. & Mgmt. Sci. 22 (1971), 2.2.1

Post, D.G., Pooling Intellectual Capital: Thoughts on Anonymity, Pseudonymity, and Limited Liability in Cyberspace, 1996 U. Chi. Legal F. 139 (1996), 14.8.1

Pressler, L. & Schieffer, K.V., A Proposal for Universal Telecommunications Service, 40 Fed. Comm. L.J. 351 (1988), 3.2.1, 3.2.5, 6.1.3

Table of Secondary Authorities

Index

Index

Index

Index

Index

Index

local competitors, 1.12
long distance service, 2.3.3.2. *See also* Long distance service
mergers, effect. *See* Mergers and acquisitions
promotion of, 2.1.1
wireless and wireline services, 10.8.3
Competitive access providers (CAPs), 2.1.3, 2.1.4, 2.3.3.3(viii), 2.4.2, 2.4.2.1, 9.4.5
interconnection, 5.3.2
Competitive local exchange carriers (CLECs)
access charges, 2.3.3.3(ix)
duties, interconnection, 5.5.3.1
rate structure modifications, 2.3.3.3(ix)
rebundlers, 2.4.4.3
unbundling, 2.4.4.2
UNE platform, 2.4.4.3
Complimentary Network Services (CNSs), 5.4.1
Computer I, 5.4.1, 12.1, 12.4.1
maximum separation policy, 12.7.3
Computer II, 5.4.2, 5.4.3, 5.4.3.1, 11.3.1, 12.3, 12.4.2, 12.5.1
collapse of, 12.7.6
maximum separation policy, 12.7.3
Computer III, 3.7, 5.4.4, 5.4.5, 12.4.3, 12.5.1, 12.5.3, 12.7.7–12.7.10, 14.5.2
Further Notice (1998), 12.7.11.5
Ninth Circuit
first decision, vacation, 12.7.8
FCC response on remand, 12.7.9
second decision and FCC response, 12.7.10
Remand Proceeding, 12.5.2
COMSAT (Communications Satellite Corp.), 9.3.3
nondominant carrier classification, 9.5.2.1
Confidentiality. *See* Privacy
Consent and free speech issues, 14.8

Consolidations. *See* Mergers and acquisitions
Constitutional law. *See also specific amendments*
Bell Operating Companies, interLATA restrictions, 9.6.2.3
due process and taking clause, 2.6.2, 5.1, 5.3.2
common carrier rate regulation, 3.11.3
interconnection, 4.6
regulation, limits on, 2.6
wireless services, spectrum allocation, 10.3.8
Consumer information. *See* Privacy
Consumer Productivity Dividend (CPD), 2.2.3.2, 2.2.3.3
Contestable market theory, 2.1.2
Contracts
long distance service, shift from public tariffs to private contracts, 9.5.3
mutual recognition agreements, foreign equipment, 8.4.2
Contract Service Arrangements (CSAs), 5.5.3.6(iii)
Convergence of technology industry, 1.8
COPA (Child Online Protection Act), 14.6.4.2
Copyright, 14.4
common carriers, 14.4.1, 14.6.7
ISPs, 14.4.6
No Electronic Theft (NET) Act, 14.4.6
passive carrier exemption, 14.4.2, 14.6.7
private carriers, 14.4.5
signal interception as copyright violation, 14.3.2
telephone companies, 14.4.1
telephone directories, 12.7.2
Cordless telephones, wiretaps of, 14.2.3, 14.2.6
Cost allocation, 2.2.2.5, 2.2.2.6, 2.3.3.1, 2.3.3.2
fair, 2.2.2.10
manuals, 2.2.2.10
Cost categories, separation, 2.2.2.4

Definitions (*continued*)
telecommunications services, 12.2.2
universal service, 6.1, 6.1.1, 6.3.1
DeForest, L., 1.2.4
DEM weighing. *See* Digital equipment minute (DEM) weighing
Department of Justice. *See* Justice Department
Depreciation, 2.2.1, 3.13.3
competitive environment, 2.2.3.1
"equal life," 2.2.3.1, 2.2.3.2
FCC regulation, 2.2.3.1, 2.2.3.2, 3.3.3, 3.15
inside wiring costs, 2.2.3.1
intrastate ratemaking, 2.2.3.1
Louisiana Public Service Commission v. FCC (Louisiana PSC), 3.6
monopoly environment, 2.2.3.1
NARUC, 2.2.3.1
preemption of inconsistent state rates, 2.2.3.1
rate base, 2.2.3
"remaining life," 2.2.3.1, 2.2.3.2
"vintage year," 2.2.3.1
"whole life," 2.2.3.1
Descramblers, 14.3.1, 14.3.4
Detariffing, 2.1.4
competitive access providers (CAP), 2.4.2.1
customer premises equipment (CPE), 5.2.1.3, 5.2.4
inside wiring, 2.3.1.1
Internet, 2.3.4.1
long-distance services, 2.3.3.3(x)
permissive, 3.11.2
wireless carriers, 2.4.3.1
"Dial-it" services, 14.6, 14.6.3
consent, 14.8
telephone companies refusing to bill unless services restrict access, 14.6.6
Telephone Disclosure and Dispute Resolution Act, 14.6.3.3
Digital audio radio service (DARS), 10.4.6, 10.4.6.3

Digital equipment minute (DEM) weighing, 6.2.2.2
Digital Millennium Copyright Act, 14.4.6
Digital Subscriber Line (DSL) technologies, 2.3.4.1, 11.2.2.2
Digital technology, 1.10
bandwidth, 2.3.4.3
telephone companies using, 1.10, 13.1
Digital television, 1.10, 11.2.2.3, 11.8.2
DirecDuo service, Internet local access, 11.2.2.3
Direct broadcast satellite (DBS) service, 9.3.4
data transmission, deregulation, 11.8.2
future availability, 1.10
Internet access through, 11.2.2.3
jurisdiction of FCC, 13.2
licenses, 10.4.6.4
dezoning, 10.3.4
renewal expectancy, 10.3.1
piracy, 14.3.2
spectrum allocation, 10.4.6, 10.4.6.4
flexibility, 10.3.4
spectrum unbundling, 11.4.2.2
Direct inward dialing, 5.5.2.2
Directive on the Protection of Individuals with Regard to the Processing of Personal Data and on the Free Movement of Such Data, 14.5.6
Directories
antitrust, 12.7.2
on-line directories, 12.7.11.7(ii)
Yellow Pages, 4.4.3.3
Directory assistance, 5.5.3.5(v)
BOCs permitted to provide, 9.6.1.2
Disabled persons
duties of telecommunication carriers, 5.5.1.2
telecommunications equipment, accessibility, 8.4.2
Disclosure. *See* Privacy
Discontinuation of service, 3.12

Index

Index

Index

Index

Index

Index

Index

Index

Index

Index

Index

Index

Index

Index

Index

universal service, 10.7
  build-out requirements, 10.7.2
  competing directly with
    wireline service, state
    regulation, 10.2
  contribution to, 10.7.2
  wireless "local loop" technology,
    10.8.3
  zoning, 10.3.3
  dezoning, 10.3.4
Wiretap Act of 1968, 14.2.3, 14.2.5
Wiretapping, 14.2. *See also* Antisnooping
  Anti-Terrorism Act of 1996,
    applicability, 14.2.8
  Communications Act of 1934,
    applicability, 14.2.2
  ECPA, applicability, 14.2.4,
    14.5.2
  Foreign Intellectual Service Act?,
    applicability, 14.2.9
  Fourth Amendment rights, 14.2.1
  government wiretaps, 14.2.1
  signal piracy, 14.3. *See also* Piracy
  telephone companies, 14.5.2
  violations and penalties, 14.2.3

Wiring. *See* Inside wiring
**World Trade Organization's Basic
  Telecommunications
  Agreement (WTO),** 7.1, 7.5.4.1,
    7.5.4.5
World Wide Web. *See generally*
  Internet
WTBS, 14.4.3

X

xDSL services
  availability, 1.10
  classification unclear, 11.4.1
  Part 68, applicability, 8.4.2

Y

Yellow pages. *See* Directories

Z

Zoning
  media, since 1934 Act, 1.3.5
  wireless licenses, 10.3.3
  dezoning, 10.3.4